THE
ENDURING
QUESTIONS

THIRD EDITION

THE ENDURING QUESTIONS

MAIN PROBLEMS OF PHILOSOPHY

Melvin Rader

UNIVERSITY OF WASHINGTON

HOLT, RINEHART AND WINSTON
NEW YORK CHICAGO SAN FRANCISCO ATLANTA
DALLAS MONTREAL TORONTO LONDON SYDNEY

Library of Congress Cataloging in Publication Data
Rader, Melvin Miller, 1903-
    The enduring questions.
    Bibliography p. 819
    Includes index.
    1. Philosophy. I. Title.
BD31.R32 1976   108   75-42007
ISBN: 0-03-089804-8

Preface

Socrates was asked where he was from. He replied, not "Athens," but "the World." He whose imagination was fuller and more extensive, embraced the universe as his city, and distributed his knowledge, his company, and his affections to all mankind, unlike us who look only at what is underfoot.

The spirit of philosophy—its enlargement and liberation of the mind through the greatness of the objects it contemplates—is captured in these words of Montaigne. The major philosophers, whether Plato or Spinoza or Whitehead, have been "citizens of the universe, not only of one walled city at war with the rest."

The Enduring Questions has grown out of the conviction that the great philosophers have grappled with questions that are enduring because they are of deep concern to every thoughtful individual. Substantial progress has been made in clarifying and answering these questions, but they are not ephemeral and not easily dismissed. In stressing the universal and permanent values of the Western philosophical tradition, the book draws mainly upon acknowledged classics, including the best of recent philosophy. And by emphasizing such issues as free will versus determinism the book has acquired a sharply interrogative character. The editorial comments stress the questions to which the readings naturally give rise.

The reader is presented with many angles of vision; he may suit himself, keeping here and rejecting there; or he may gather ideas for a synthesis of his own. The teacher, drawing upon this abundance, may vary his assignments as he sees fit.

The chapters have been arranged in logical order, but this it not necessarily the order in which they should be read. The parts are designed to be relatively independent and can be studied in whatever order is preferred. Background information has been supplied to help the reader understand difficult material and to interrelate the selections, but commentary that reflects the editor's philosophical preferences has been minimized. Students and teachers are left free to grapple with questions in their own way without contending with an editorially imposed viewpoint.

The greatest change from previous editions is the movement toward longer selections. The authors represented by more ample readings are Aristotle, Spinoza, Pascal, Kant, Marx, and Mill. Readings from authors not represented in the second edition—Marcus Aurelius, Hegel, Lovejoy, Wittgenstein, Blake, Kolakowski, and Cohen and Nagel—have been added. Bergson, Whitehead, Dewey, James, Santayana, and Russell are represented by different readings. To make room for longer selections and new authors I have omitted Ryle, Broad, Royce, Feuerbach, Stace, Bates. Smart, Stevenson, Buber, and Thoreau. Ryle's discussion of Wittgenstein and philosophical analysis has been eliminated but this is compensated by a lecture from Wittgenstein himself. Altogether these revisions represent more extensive readings from the great philosophers and deeper probing of philosophical questions. Translations have been chosen for their clearness and readability. Trotter's translation of Pascal's *Thoughts* and Freidrich's translation of Kant's *Metaphysical Foundation of Morals* are better than the translations of these classics in the second edition.

I am indebted to Holt, Rinehart and Winston for permission to incorporate passages from my *Ethics and the Human Community*, and to other publishers or individuals who have kindly granted permission to reprint copyrighted materials; and I am grateful to my students and colleagues who helped to lay the groundwork of this book during years of teaching and discussion.

January 1976   Melvin Rader

Contents

Preface   v

Introduction: THE NATURE OF PHILOSOPHY   1

Part One. KNOWLEDGE AND REALITY   7

1. THE SOCRATIC QUEST   9

    PLATO
      Apology   12
      Crito   32
      Phaedo (Death Scene)   42

2. TELEOLOGY   45

    ARISTOTLE   45
      The Physics   46

3. MATERIALISM   65

    LUCRETIUS   65
      On the Nature of the Universe   65

4. DUALISM AND THE QUEST FOR CERTAINTY   93

    RENÉ DESCARTES   93
      Rules for the Direction of the Mind   95
      Meditations   104
    ARTHUR O. LOVEJOY   122
      The Revolt against Dualism   122

5. MONISM   139

    BARUCH SPINOZA   139
      Ethics   140
      Correspondence   145
    WILLIAM JAMES   152
      The One and the Many (from *Pragmatism*)   153

6.   EMPIRICISM   168

JOHN LOCKE   168
An Essay Concerning Human Understanding   169
CHARLES PEIRCE   190
The Fixation of Belief   191
How To Make Our Ideas Clear
   (from *Popular Science Monthly*, 1877-1878)   204
MORRIS R. COHEN and ERNST NAGEL   216
Scientific Method (from *An Introduction to Logic and Scientific Method*)   217

7.   IDEALISM   238

GEORGE BERKELEY   238
Three Dialogues between Hylas and Philonous   239

8.   CAUSATION, FREE WILL, AND THE LIMITS OF KNOWLEDGE   278

DAVID HUME   278
A Treatise of Human Nature
An Enquiry Concerning Human Understanding   279
IMMANUEL KANT   300
Critique of Pure Reason and Other Works   302

9.   INDIVIDUALITY AND CREATIVE PROCESS   325

SÖREN KIERKEGAARD   325
Individuality and Subjective Truth (from *The Point of View* and
   Concluding Unscientific Postscript)   327
HENRI BERGSON   338
The Individual and the Type (from *Laughter*)   338
ALFRED NORTH WHITEHEAD   346
Requisites for Social Progress (from *Science and the Modern World*)   346

Part Two.   RELIGION   **367**

10.   THE BASIS OF RELIGIOUS BELIEF   368

BLAISE PASCAL   368
Thoughts   369
WILLIAM JAMES   389
The Will To Believe   389
Mysticism (from *The Varieties of Religious Experience*)   389
GEORGE SANTAYANA
Religion and Poetry (from *Interpretations of Poetry and Religion*)   412

11. GOD AND MAN   430

     SAINT ANSELM   430
       Proslogium   431
     SAINT THOMAS AQUINAS   432
       Summa Theologica and *Summa Contra Gentiles*   432
     DAVID HUME   436
       Dialogues Concerning Natural Religion   436
     WILLIAM P. MONTAGUE   453
       The Problem of Good and Evil (from *Belief Unbound*)   453
     BERTRAND RUSSELL   456
       A Free Man's Worship (from *Why I Am Not a Christian*)   458

Part Three. THE BASIS OF MORALITY   **473**

12. REASON   475

     ARISTOTLE
       The Nicomachean Ethics   476

13. NATURE   499

     CICERO   499
       The Laws   500
       The Republic   504
     MARCUS AURELIUS   505
       Meditations   505
     RALPH MASON BLAKE   516
       On Natural Rights (from *Ethics*, 1925)   517

14. DUTY   528

     IMMANUEL KANT   528
       The Metaphysical Foundations of Morals   529

15. UTILITY   566

     JEREMY BENTHAM   566
       Introduction to the Principles of Morals and Legislation   567
     JOHN STUART MILL   573
       Utilitarianism   574

16. POWER   598

     FRIEDRICH NIETZSCHE   598
       Beyond Good and Evil   599

17. EXPERIMENT   613

    JOHN DEWEY   613
      Ethics   614

18. LANGUAGE AND MORALS   639

    LUDWIG WITTGENSTEIN   639
      A Lecture on Ethics (from *The Philosophical Review*, 1965)   640

Part Four. SOCIAL PHILOSOPHY   **653**

19. ARISTOCRACY   655

    PLATO   655
      The Republic   656

20. HISTORY AND FREEDOM   696

    GEORG WILHELM FRIEDRICH HEGEL   696
      Logic and *The Philosophy of History*   697

21. COMMUNISM   719

    KARL MARX   719
      Communism and History (from *A Contribution to the Critique of*
        Political Economy and Other Works)   720
    LESZEK KOLAKOWSKI   747
      What Is Socialism? (from *The New Leader*, 1957)   747

22. LIBERAL DEMOCRACY   754

    JOHN STUART MILL   754
      On Liberty   754
      Of the Stationary State (from *Principles of Political Economy*)   788

23. THE CONTROL OF HUMAN BEHAVIOR   797

    B. F. SKINNER and CARL ROGERS   797
      Some Issues Concerning the Control of Human Behavior
        (from *Science*, 1956)   798

Selected Bibliography   819

Index   835

THE
ENDURING
QUESTIONS

Introduction:
THE NATURE
OF PHILOSOPHY

THE GENERAL INTERPRETATION
OF EXPERIENCE

If the philosopher can be called a "specialist," he is a specialist in the general. Socrates (in Plato's *Republic*) defines the philosopher as "the spectator of all time and all existence"; and William James declares that philosophy deals "with the principles of explanation that underlie all things without exception, the elements common to gods and men and animals and stones, the first *whence* and the last *whither* of the whole cosmic procession, the conditions of all knowing, and the most general rules of human conduct."[1]

C. D. Broad similarly characterizes philosophy. He distinguishes between *critical* and *speculative* philosophy, both of which deal with what is general. The task of critical philosophy is to analyze and define our most fundamental and general concepts, such as "goodness," "truth," "reality," and "causation." The object of speculative philosophy is "to take over the results of the various sciences, to add to them the results of the religious and ethical experiences of mankind, and then to reflect upon the whole" in an attempt "to reach some general conclusions as to the nature of the Universe, and as to our position and prospects in it."[2]

These characterizations seem to fit the problems that philosophers most often discuss: What is a good life? What is the relation between mind and body? Do we have free will? Is there a God? Is the world fundamentally material or spiri-

---

[1] *Some Problems of Philosophy* (New York: Longmans, Green, 1911), p. 5.
[2] *Scientific Thought* (New York: Harcourt, Brace & World, 1923). Partially reprinted herein, pp. 146–153. See p. 152.

1

tual? Can we know the ultimate nature of reality? These are basic questions involved in a general interpretation of the world. Accordingly, Herbert Spencer defines philosophy as "knowledge of the highest degree of generality."[3]

There are certain difficulties in this view. First, science also is sometimes *very* general. Newton's theory of gravitation, for example, characterizes the nearest and the most remote, the least and the greatest of objects—the pin in one's bedroom as well as the most distant galaxy. Similarly, modern atomic physics is applicable to every material entity in the universe; and the theory of evolution, summarizing the whole history of life from the first germs in the primordial sea to the highest stages of human life, is also exceedingly wide in scope. Secondly, the synthesis of all the sciences, or the interpretation of the whole of reality, is a pretty big order. A person would need to be a kind of god, or at least a universal genius, to succeed at so prodigious an undertaking. But philosophy is not the peculiar business of the gods or of rare geniuses; it is everyman's business.

THE PURSUIT OF MEANING

Such considerations have led many philosophers to define their field in a more restricted way. One of the most widely accepted definitions is that philosophy is the analysis, or systematic study, of meanings. This definition would in effect limit the field to what C. D. Broad calls critical philosophy.

Those who adopt this interpretation sometimes cite Socrates as an example of a philosopher. In employing his favorite conversational method of giving and receiving questions and answers, he is usually trying to analyse the meaning of some basic concept, such as "knowledge," "justice," "courage," "friendship," or "beauty."

One of the most influential philosophers of modern times, Moritz Schlick (1882–1936), has said:

> . . . Socrates' philosophy consists of what we may call "The Pursuit of Meaning."
> He tried to clarify thought by analyzing the meaning of our expressions and
> the real sense of our propositions. Here then we find a definite contrast between
> this philosophic method, which has for its object the discovery of meaning, and
> the method of the sciences, which have for their object the discovery of truth. . . .
> Science should be defined as the "pursuit of truth" and philosophy as the "pursuit of meaning." Socrates has set the example of the true philosophic method
> for all times.[4]

I do not believe that this is an adequate characterization of the method of Socrates or the nature of philosophy. Socrates was engaged not only in the pursuit of meaning but also in the pursuit of truth, and the former was largely instrumental

[3] *First Principles* (New York: Burt, 1880), p. 111.
[4] "The Future of Philosophy," in D. J. Bronstein, Y. H. Krikorian, and P. P. Wiener, *Basic Problems of Philosophy* (Englewood Cliffs, N.J.: Prentice Hall, 1947), p. 739.

to the latter. His definitions were intended not as arbitrary or merely verbal: they were what philosophers call "real" definitions—that is, they sought to characterize actually existent things. When Socrates asserted that justice or friendship or beauty was this or that, he implied that justice or friendship or beauty really existed and actually bore the character marked off and fixed in the definition. Consequently, he kept referring to the facts of experience so as to make his definitions truthful. Also, he was interested in fitting together the various insights thus gained into a critical interpretation of man's nature, his destiny, and his values.

To define philosophy as the pursuit of meaning is at once too broad and too narrow. It is too broad because scientists as well as philosophers seek to clarify meanings. As C. J. Ducasse has said:

> To mention but a few, such concepts as salt, acid, gas, liquid, solid, water, air, iron, etc. are concepts the exact meaning of which is investigated and discovered not by metaphysicians, logicians, or mathematicians, but by chemists and physicists; and the same is true of such even more basic physical concepts as light, electricity, matter, mass, etc. Moreover, although physicists do give us precise accounts of the meaning of these and numerous other concepts, they do so in their capacity as natural scientists, *i.e.,* on the basis, ultimately, of observations and experiments. . . .[5]

In another sense, Schlick's definition of philosophy is too narrow. If Plato, Aristotle, Aquinas, Descartes, Spinoza, and Kant, for example, are to be considered philosophers—and no one has a better claim—it would appear that their field includes what Broad calls "speculative philosophy." Schlick seeks to dismiss the problems of speculative philosophy as either nonsensical or nonphilosophical. "Some of them will disappear by being shown to be mistakes and misunderstandings of our language," he declares, "and the others will be found to be ordinary scientific questions in disguise."[6] But it is unlikely that all the problems of speculative philosophy will either vanish when they are stated clearly or will turn out to be nonphilosophical problems, more appropriately treated by science. Moreover, the sharp distinction between the pursuit of meaning and the pursuit of truth is artificial, for the clarification of meaning and the discovery of truth go hand in hand. Broad rightly includes under "critical philosophy" not only the clarification of concepts but the resolute criticism of our fundamental beliefs.

THE CULTIVATION OF WISDOM

Philosophy, we conclude, involves both the analysis of meanings and the search for generic truths. To complete our definition, we need to distinguish the kinds

[5] *Philosophy as a Science* (New York: Oskar Piest, 1941), pp. 77–78.
[6] *Philosophy as a Science*, p. 745.

of meanings and generic truths that are essentially philosophical from the kinds that are scientific.

It will help us to consider the original meaning of "philosophy." Etymologically, philosophy means "the love of wisdom" (from the Greek *"philein,"* to love, and *"sophia,"* wisdom). The word has ordinarily been used to designate an activity rather than an emotion—the activity of pursuing wisdom rather than the emotion motivating that pursuit. The essential question that we need to consider is what, exactly, is the wisdom that the philosopher seeks.

"Wisdom" has been used in two senses. First, it is contrasted with ignorance. The wise man is he who knows and therefore is not ignorant. This meaning, however, does not help us to distinguish philosophy from science, since the scientist also, of course, is trying to replace ignorance by knowledge. In the second sense, wisdom is contrasted with foolishness. The wise man is he who has good judgment and therefore is not foolish. The fool may have a great deal of knowledge about ordinary matters of fact, but he lacks the balance and maturity and ripe insight that make it possible not only to live but to live well.

If philosophy is the pursuit of wisdom as contrasted with foolishness, it *is* marked off from ordinary science. The subject matter of science is facts, and science attempts to discover verifiable laws—regularities—among these facts. These laws give a *description* of the facts. It is obvious that the physicist does not talk about wicked atoms or beneficent motions, and even the sociologist, in his purely scientific role, tries to *describe* rather than to *evaluate* the behavior of social groups. If philosophy, on the other hand, seeks wisdom as the opposite of foolishness, it must be a kind of critical activity concerned with appraisals. Matthew Arnold has defined poetry as "the criticism of life," but this definition fits philosophy better than poetry. It is similar to the definition of Ducasse, who maintains that "philosophy is the general theory of criticism,"[7] and the definition of Dewey, who declares that "philosophy is inherently criticism, having its distinctive position among various modes of criticism in its generality: a criticism of criticisms, as it were."[8]

It is characteristic of criticism that it is yea-saying or nay-saying—a favoring or a disfavoring. The ways of saying "yea" or "nay" are quite various, and they correspond to different pairs of adjectives. In logic, for example, we speak of *valid* or *fallacious;* in epistemology, of *true* or *false;* in metaphysics, of *real* or *unreal;* in theology, of *holy* or *unholy;* in esthetics, of *beautiful* or *ugly;* in ethics, of *right* or *wrong.* In using these adjectives, we are making judgments. The function of philosophy is to provide the intellectual bases of sound judgments about the great issues of life.

Even when philosophy wears the garb of science, it is distinctive. For example, Lucretius was not primarily concerned with the hypotheses of atoms and evolution as scientific descriptions of the nature of things: he was concerned with the

---

[7] *The Philosophy of Art* (New York: Dial, 1929), p. 3.
[8] *Experience and Nature* (Chicago: Open Court, 1925), p. 398.

right way to think and live in the sort of universe that he regarded as real. Metaphysics should not be interpreted—as it often is—as potential or generalized natural science; rather, it should be regarded as the attempt to achieve a true understanding of man and his place in the cosmos so that we can distinguish the deep and permanent from the superficial and temporary, the important from the unimportant. Thus to distinguish is to *judge,* and metaphysics, like other branches of philosophy, provides a basis for judgment.

Philosophy resembles science not so much in its aim as in its method. Both employ reason and evidence as means to the discovery of truth and the clarification of meaning. Both are forms of inquiry—science being an inquiry into the laws of nature; philosophy, into the norms of criticism. The faith of the philosopher, like that of the scientist, is that inquiry is worth while. In the *Apology,* Socrates expresses the fundamental conviction of all true philosophers: "The unexamined life," he declares, "is not worth living." Likewise, in the *Meno,* his faith rings out sharp and clear:

> Some things I have said of which I am not altogether confident. But that we shall be better and braver and less helpless if we think that we ought to inquire, than we should have been if we indulged in the idle fancy that there was no knowing and no use in seeking to know what we do not know;—that is a theme upon which I am ready to fight, in word and deed, to the utmost of my power.[9]

We can fully appreciate the brave words of Socrates only if we too engage in the quest for wisdom. The proof of the pudding is in the eating—we can best judge the value of philosophy after we have philosophized. Each person must himself taste of the pudding; no one can do it for him. Of course, it is immensely helpful to study the great thinkers, such as Plato, Aristotle, Hume, and Kant, or nearer to us, William James, Santayana, and Russell. As Descartes declares in the opening chapter of his *Discourse on Method,* "The reading of good books is, as it were, to engage in talk with their authors, the finest minds of past ages, artfully contrived talk in which they give us none but the best and most select of their thoughts."[10] But like all the very good things of life, wisdom is something that cannot be given and that each must attain for himself.

In thumbing through some old lecture notes, I have found a definition of philosophy that sums up much that I have said: "Philosophy is an effort to give unity to human arts and sciences by a critical examination of the grounds of our meanings, values, and beliefs."

[9] *The Dialogues of Plato,* trans. by Benjamin Jowett (London: Oxford, 1924), II, p. 47.
[10] *Discourse on Method,* in *Descartes' Philosophical Writings* (London: Macmillan, 1952), p. 119.

Part One

KNOWLEDGE
AND
REALITY

One of the main divisions of philosophy is epistemology, or the theory of knowledge. Epistemology asks such fundamental questions as these: How much do we know? How much *can* we know? *How* do we know? How can we distinquish between appearance and reality? What is the nature of truth, and how can we separate it from falsehood? We shall be dealing with such questions in Part One.

It is difficult, if not impossible, to separate epistemology, the theory of knowledge, from metaphysics, the theory of reality. In this part, we shall examine the philosophies of Descartes, Locke, Berkeley, Hume, and Kant, all of whom have contributed greatly to both metaphysics and epistemology. Hence Part One is entitled "Knowledge and Reality."

We shall consider the question "What is the fundamental nature of man and the surrounding universe?" This question directs attention to "the metaphysics of the microcosm"—of the "I" or self as a small part of the whole scheme of things— and "to the metaphysics of the macrocosm"—of the great, all-enveloping system of reality. We shall not attempt to separate these two inquiries, and, indeed, any sharp separation would be artificial. Each of the theories that we shall consider will throw light upon the nature of the human person and the nature of his total environment.

We shall scrutinize the career of Socrates, who personifies, as well as anyone, the commitment to philosophy as a way of life. Plato's stirring portrayal of his teacher, Socrates, will be followed by selections from Aristotle, Lucretius, Descartes, Spinoza, Locke, Berkeley, Hume, Kant, Kierkegaard, and Peirce. The philosophy of the twentieth century will be represented by Lovejoy, James, Bergson, Whitehead, and Cohen and Nagel. These readings from eminent philosophers are an exciting introduction to the great problems of epistemology and metaphysics.

7

1

The Socratic Quest

SOCRATES (470?–399 B.C.)

We have been considering the meaning of philosophy and its relation to the sciences. But to understand the nature of philosophy we must have in mind more than a set of definitions and abstract distinctions. "Philosophy," as we have said, means literally the love of wisdom, and this is what philosophy at its best has always meant. As Thoreau put it, to be a philosopher means so to love wisdom as to live according to its dictates.

There is no better way in which to grasp the personal import of philosophy than to study the life and character of Socrates. More than anyone else in the history of thought, he represents the very type and ideal of the philosopher. His portrait, drawn by the genius of Plato, has for more than two thousand years been the standard by which all philosophy and philosophers have been measured. No one has loved wisdom more fervently than Socrates, and no one has lived more truly according to its dictates. In him, philosophy is not merely a way of thinking but a way of living.

Born about 470 B.C., Socrates grew up during the time of Athens' greatest power and achievement—the half century following the victories over the Persians—and he lived through the supreme crisis of Athenian history—the bitter, protracted, and catastrophic war with Sparta. He was a contemporary of many of the greatest figures in the history of culture, among them Sophocles, Herodotus, Phidias, and Pericles. Thus he knew the city both in the height of her glory and in the depths of her crisis and defeat.

His father was a sculptor or stone-mason and his mother a midwife. The family was apparently of good standing and aristocratic connections. Socrates, perhaps in jest, declared that the family pedigree could be traced back to Daedalus, a legendary maker of wooden images. Whatever his background, he moved with ease in the best and most select circles of Athenian society.

It was inevitable that a man of Socrates' bent should display a penchant for philosophy. He is said to have studied under Archelaus, the first native Athenian philosopher, and he was also familiar with the teachings of the Sophists—humanistic philosophers and paid educators who traveled from city to city. But, preferring intellectual leisure to lucrative employment, he was too poor to take formal instruction from the Sophists, whose "wisdom," moreover, he regarded as somewhat hollow. He also studied science, becoming familiar with the doctrines of the Sicilian Empedocles about biological evolution, the theories of the Italian Alcmaeon about the brain as the organ of mental life, the mathematical doctrines of Pythagoras and Zeno, and the theory of Diogenes of Apollonia that everything consists of "air." But he soon became disillusioned by the flat contradictions of such rival tenets; and when one day he read in the book of Anaxagoras (the first important philosopher to live in Athens) that "mind" is the cause of the natural order, the concept struck him with the force of revelation. Reading on, he discovered that Anaxagoras introduced a cosmic mind to explain only the initial impetus given to matter and then employed mechanical principles to explain the general structure of reality. Socrates, in contrast, vowed that he would try really to understand mind and its place in the cosmos. Thenceforth his main endeavor was to search his own mind and the minds of his fellow citizens in an attempt to discover the essence of man and of goodness.

In pursuing his "mission," Socrates was trying to explore the human mind and to reach the truth by dint of question and answer, dialogue, and debate. This give-and-take method of investigation by discussion is called "dialectic" or "the Socratic method"—and it is still the essential method of the philosopher. It may be carried on between two or more persons or within the mind of a single inquirer, as he puts questions to himself and wrestles with his answers. Usually its objective is to establish a definition, to fix in mind the essential reality of some basic value or property. Each proposed definition is tested by a process of critical examination. Is it internally consistent? Does it fit the facts? Does it agree with what we already know? In formulating and testing the definition, the philosopher continually refers to the particular data of experience; but he examines the particulars as instances of a type, and he defines the type—the "idea," "form," or "universal"—by establishing its significance in the particulars.

The years of Socrates' mission and the last thirty years of his life fell mainly in the period of the war with Sparta, when Athens was fighting for her existence. As we gather from the pages of the great historian Thucydides, it was a period of intense crisis and civil strife. Toward the close of this difficult time, it became apparent that Athens was losing the war, and revolutions were taking place within the city. Socrates, by his independence, his critical spirit, and his refusal to adopt unjust methods, offended both the democratic and aristocratic parties.

In 404 B.C. the city was finally compelled to surrender. After a short and bloody interval of oligarchical dictatorship, the old democratic form of government was restored. But the political situation remained tense, and the ruling democrats were fearful of counter-revolution. It was Socrates' misfortune that a number of his former close associates had proved themselves traitors or vicious enemies of the democratic cause. Alcibiades, Socrates' young friend, had been a brilliant general of the Athenian army, but when he was accused of religious sacrilege and ordered to stand trial, he deserted to Sparta and became a most formidable enemy of the Athenian state. Similarly, Critias and Charmides, two associates of Socrates, had been leaders of the violent oligarchical dictatorship which was established at the conclusion of the war. Inevitably, Socrates, who had long been known as a vigorous critic of democratic follies, was suspected of subversive activities. Political motives, combined with their intense dislike of Socrates' unconventional teachings, prompted Anytus, a prominent democratic politician, and two lesser associates, Meletus and Lycon, to bring charges against Socrates in 399 B.C., about four years after the war's end. The indictment, as recorded by the later historian Diogenes Laertius, read:

> Socrates is guilty of not worshipping the gods whom the State worships, but introducing new and unfamiliar religious practices; and, further, of corrupting the young. The prosecutor demands the death penalty.

The main "offense," not specified in the indictment or at the trial, was that Socrates had fostered the anti-democratic spirit that had inspired the oligarchical revolutions. According to an amnesty that had been officially declared in the year 404–403, no one could be prosecuted for political offences committed before that date. Hence the accusations in the formal indictment were, to some extent, trumpery charges, designed to bring Socrates to trial for an offense that, perforce, remained unspecified. Yet the charges were not merely manufactured: there was widespread hostility against Socrates for his critical spirit and his unremitting search for a new rationale and norm for life. In the eyes of conservatives, he *had* blasphemed and corrupted youth. Indeed, he had questioned the very foundation of the social order, and the guardians of the *status quo,* hurt to the quick, retaliated by seeking to impose the ultimate penalty—death.

Tried before five hundred jurors selected by lot, Socrates spoke with such uncompromising independence that he angered the jury and provoked the death penalty. Some of his friends made a last-minute attempt to effect his escape, but he would brook no such disgraceful tactics. After a serene philosophical conversation with a group of intimates in his prison cell, he drank the fatal hemlock.

Such, in brief outline, is the story of Socrates. Now let us fill in some of the details by examining a number of Plato's dialogues.

The Apology

CHARACTERS

Socrates

Meletus

Scene.—The Court of Justice.

Socrates. I cannot tell what impression my accusers have made upon you, Athenians: for my own part, I know that they nearly made me forget who I was, so plausible were they; and yet they have scarcely uttered one single word of truth. But of all their many falsehoods, the one which astonished me most, was when they said that I was a clever speaker, and that you must be careful not to let me mislead you. I thought that it was most impudent of them not to be ashamed to talk in that way; for as soon as I open my mouth the lie will be exposed, and I shall prove that I am not a clever speaker in any way at all: unless, indeed, by a clever speaker they mean a man who speaks the truth. If that is their meaning, I agree with them that I am a much greater orator than they. My accusers, then I repeat, have said little or nothing that is true; but from me you shall hear the whole truth. Certainly you will not hear an elaborate speech, Athenians, drest up, like theirs, with

The following dialogues of Plato are from the translation of F. J. Church, first published by Macmillan and Company, London, 1880.

words and phrases. I will say to you what I have to say, without preparation, and in the words which come first, for I believe that my cause is just; so let none of you expect anything else. Indeed, my friends, It would hardly be seemly for me, at my age, to come before you like a young man with his specious falsehoods. But there is one thing, Athenians, which I do most earnestly beg and entreat of you. Do not be surprised and do not interrupt, if in my defence I speak in the same way that I am accustomed to speak in the market-place, at the tables of the money-changers, where many of you have heard me, and elsewhere. The truth is this. I am more than seventy years old, and this is the first time that I have ever come before a Court of Law; so your manner of speech here is quite strange to me. If I had been really a stranger, you would have forgiven me for speaking in the language and the fashion of my native country: and so now I ask you to grant me what I think I have a right to claim. Never mind the style of my speech—it may be better or it may be worse—give your whole attention to the question, Is what I say just, or is it not? That is what makes a good judge, as speaking the truth makes a good advocate.

I have to defend myself, Athenians, first against the old false charges of my old accusers, and then against the later ones of my present accusers. For many men have been accusing me to you, and for very many years, who have not uttered a word of truth: and I fear them more than I fear Anytus and his companions, formidable as they are. But, my friends, those others are still more formidable; for they got hold of most of you when you were children, and they have been more persistent in accusing me with lies, and in trying to persuade you that there is one Socrates, a wise man, who speculates about the heavens, and who examines into all things that are beneath the earth, and who can "make the worse appear the better reason." These men, Athenians, who spread abroad this report, are the accusers whom I fear; for their hearers think that persons who pursue such inquiries never believe in the gods. And then they are many, and their attacks have been going on for a long time: and they spoke to you when you were at the age most readily to believe them: for you were all young, and many of you were children: and there was no one to answer them when they attacked me. And the most unreasonable thing of all is that commonly I do not even know their names: I cannot tell you who they are, except in the case of the comic poets. But all the rest who have been trying to prejudice you against me, from motives of spite and jealousy, and sometimes, it may be, from conviction, are the enemies whom it is hardest to meet. For I cannot call any one of them forward in Court, to cross-examine him: I have, as it were, simply to fight with shadows in my defence, and to put questions which there is no one to answer. I ask you, therefore, to believe that, as I say, I have been attacked by two classes of accusers—first by Meletus and his friends, and then by those older ones of whom I have spoken. And, with your leave, I will defend myself first against my old enemies; for you heard their accusations first, and they were much more persistent than my present accusers are.

Well, I must make my defence, Athenians, and try in the short time allowed me to remove the prejudice which you have had against me for a long time. I hope that I may manage to do this, if it be good for you and for me, and that my defence may be successful; but I am quite aware of the nature of my task, and I know that it is a difficult one. Be the issue, however, as God wills, I must obey the law, and make my defence.

Let us begin again, then, and see what is the charge which has given rise to the prejudice against me, which was what Meletus relied on when he drew his indictment. What is the calumny which my enemies have been spreading about me? I must assume that they are formally accusing me, and read their indictment. It would run somewhat in this fashion: "Socrates is an evil-doer, who meddles with inquiries into things beneath the earth, and in heaven, and who 'makes the worse appear the better reason,' and who teaches others these same things." That is what they say; and in the Comedy of Aristophanes [*The Clouds*] you yourselves saw a man called Socrates swinging round in a basket, and saying that he walked the air, and talking a great deal of nonsense about matters of which I understand nothing, either more or less. I do not mean to disparage that kind of knowledge, if there is any man who possesses it. I trust Meletus may never be able to prosecute me for that. But, the truth is, Athenians, I have nothing to do with these matters, and almost all of you are yourselves my witnesses of this. I beg all of you who have ever heard me converse, and they are many, to inform your neighbors and tell them if any of you have ever heard me conversing about such matters, either more or less. That will show you that the other common stories about me are as false as this one.

But, the fact is, that not one of these stories is true; and if you have heard that I undertake to educate men, and exact money from them for so doing, that is not true either; though I think that it would be a fine thing to be able to educate men, as Gorgias of Leontini, and Prodicus of Ceos, and Hippias of Elis do. For each of them, my friends, can go into any city, and persuade the young men to leave the society of their fellow-citizens, with any of whom they might associate for nothing, and to be only too glad to be allowed to pay money for the privilege of associating with themselves. And I believe that there is another wise man from Paros residing in Athens at this moment. I happened to meet Callias, the son of Hipponicus, a man who has spent more money on the Sophists than every one else put together. So I said to him—he has two sons—Callias, if your two sons had been foals or calves, we could have hired a trainer for them who would have made them perfect in the excellence which belongs to their nature. He would have been either a groom or a farmer. But whom do you intend to take to train them, seeing that they are men? Who understands the excellence which belongs to men and to citizens? I suppose that you must have thought of this, because of your sons. Is there such a person, said I, or not? Certainly there is, he replied. Who is he, said I, and where does he come from, and what is his fee? His name is Evenus, Socrates, he replied: he comes from Paros, and his fee is five minæ. Then I thought that Evenus was a fortunate person if he really understood this art and could teach so cleverly. If I had possessed knowledge of that kind, I should have given myself airs and prided myself on it. But, Athenians, the truth is that I do not possess it.

Perhaps some of you may reply: But, Socrates, what is this pursuit of yours? Whence come these calumnies against you? You must have been engaged in some pursuit out of the common. All these stories and reports of you would never have gone about, if you had not been in some way different from other men. So tell us what your pursuits are, that we may not give our verdict in the dark. I think that that is a fair question, and I will try to explain to you what it is that has raised these calumnies against me, and given me this name. Listen, then: some of you perhaps will think that I am jesting; but I assure you that I will tell you the whole truth. I have gained this name, Athenians, simply by reason of a certain wisdom. But by what kind of wisdom? It is by just that wisdom which is, I believe, possible to men. In that, it may be, I am really wise. But the men of whom I was speaking just now must be wise in a wisdom which is greater than human wisdom, or in some way which I cannot describe, for certainly I know nothing of it myself, and if any man says that I do, he lies and wants to slander me. Do not interrupt me, Athenians, even if you think that I am speaking arrogantly. What I am going to say is not my own: I will tell you who says it, and he is worthy of your credit. I will bring the god of Delphi to be the witness of the fact of my wisdom and of its nature. You remember Chærephon. From youth upwards he was my comrade; and he went into exile with the people,[1] and with the people he returned. And you remember, too, Chærephon's character; how vehement he was in carrying through whatever he took in hand. Once he went to Delphi and ventured to put this question to the oracle—I entreat you again, my friends, not to cry out—he asked if there was any man who was wiser than I: and the priestess answered that there was no man. Chærephon himself is dead, but his brother here will confirm what I say.

Now see why I tell you this. I am going to explain to you the origin of my unpopularity. When I heard of the oracle I began to reflect: What can God mean by this dark saying? I know very well that I am not wise, even in the smallest degree. Then what can he mean by saying that I am the wisest of men? It cannot be that he is speaking falsely, for he is a god and cannot lie. And for a long time I was at a loss to understand his meaning: then, very reluctantly, I turned to seek for it in

[1] Chærephon was forced into exile during the anti-democratic dictatorship of the Thirty in 404 B.C.

this manner. I went to a man who was reputed to be wise, thinking that there, if anywhere, I should prove the answer wrong, and meaning to point out to the oracle its mistake, and to say, "You said that I was the wisest of men, but this man is wiser than I am." So I examined the man—I need not tell you his name, he was a politician—but this was the result, Athenians. When I conversed with him I came to see that, though a great many persons, and most of all he himself, thought that he was wise, yet he was not wise. And then I tried to prove to him that he was not wise, though he fancied that he was: and by so doing I made him, and many of the bystanders, my enemies. So when I went away, I thought to myself, "I am wiser than this man: neither of us probably knows anything that is really good, but he thinks that he has knowledge, when he has not, while I, having no knowledge, do not think that I have. I seem, at any rate, to be a little wiser than he is on this point: I do not think that I know what I do not know." Next I went to another man who was reputed to be still wiser than the last, with exactly the same result. And there again I made him, and many other men, my enemies.

Then I went on to one man after another, seeing that I was making enemies every day, which caused me much unhappiness and anxiety: still I thought that I must set God's command above everything. So I had to go to every man who seemed to possess any knowledge, and search for the meaning of the oracle: and, Athenians, I must tell you the truth; verily, by the dog of Egypt, this was the result of the search which I made at God's bidding. I found that the men, whose reputation for wisdom stood highest, were nearly the most lacking in it; while others, who were looked down on as common people, were much better fitted to learn. Now, I must describe to you the wanderings which I undertook, like a series of Heraclean labors, to make full proof of the oracle. After the politicians, I went to the poets, tragic, dithyrambic, and others, thinking that there I should find myself manifestly more ignorant than they. So I took up the poems on which I thought that they had spent most pains, and asked them what they meant, hoping at the same time to learn something from them. I am ashamed to tell you the truth, my friends, but I must say it. Almost any one of the bystanders could have talked about the works of these poets better than the poets themselves. So I soon found that it is not by wisdom that the poets create their works, but by a certain natural power and by inspiration, like soothsayers and prophets, who say many fine things, but who understand nothing of what they say. The poets seemed to me to be in a similar case. And at the same time I perceived that, because of their poetry, they thought that they were the wisest of men in other matters too, which they were not. So I went away again, thinking that I had the same advantage over the poets that I had over the politicians.

Finally, I went to the artisans, for I knew very well that I possessed no knowledge at all, worth speaking of, and I was sure that I should find that they knew many fine things. And in that I was not mistaken. They knew what I did not know, and so far they were wiser than I. But, Athenians, it seemed to me that the skilled artisans made the same mistake as the poets. Each of them believed himself to be extremely wise in matters of the greatest importance, because he was skillful in his own art: and this mistake of theirs threw their real wisdom into the shade. So I asked myself, on behalf of the oracle, whether I would choose to remain as I was, without either wisdom or their ignorance, or to possess both, as they did. And I made answer to myself and to the oracle that it was better for me to remain as I was.

By reason of this examination, Athenians, I have made many enemies of a very fierce and bitter kind, who have spread abroad a great number of calumnies about me, and people say that I am "a wise man." For the bystanders always think that I am wise myself in any matter wherein I convict another man of ignorance. But, my friends, I believe that only God is really wise: and that by this oracle he meant that men's wisdom is worth little or nothing. I do not think that he meant that Socrates was wise. He only made use of my name, and took me as an example, as though he would say to men, "He among you is the wisest, who, like Socrates, knows that in very truth his wisdom is worth nothing at all." And therefore I still go about testing and examining every man whom I think wise, whether he be a citizen or a stranger, as God has commanded me; and whenever I find that he is not wise, I point out to him on the part of God that he is not wise. And I am so busy in this pursuit that I have never had leisure to take any part worth mentioning in public matters, or to look after my private affairs. I am in very great poverty by reason of my service to God.

And besides this, the young men who follow me about, who are the sons of wealthy persons and have a great deal of spare time, take a natural pleasure in hearing men cross-examined: and they often imitate me among themselves: then they try their hands at cross-examining other people. And, I imagine, they find a great abundance of men who think that they know a great deal, when in fact they know little or nothing. And then the persons who are cross-examined, get angry with me instead of with themselves, and say that Socrates is an abominable fellow who corrupts young men. And when they are asked, "Why, what does he do? what does he teach?" they do not know what to say; but, not to seem at a loss, they repeat the stock charges against all philosophers, and allege that he investigates things in the air and under the earth, and that he teaches people to disbelieve in the gods, and "to make the worse appear the better reason." For, I fancy, they would not like to confess the truth, which is that they are shown up as ignorant pretenders to knowledge that they do not possess. And so they have been filling your ears with their bitter calumnies for a long time, for they are zealous and numerous and bitter against me; and they are well disciplined and plausible in speech. On these grounds Meletus and Anytus and Lycon have attacked me. Meletus is indignant with me on the part of the poets, and Any-

tus on the part of the artisans and politicians, and Lycon on the part of the orators. And so, as I said at the beginning, I shall be surprised if I am able, in the short time allowed me for my defence, to remove from your minds this prejudice which has grown so strong. What I have told you, Athenians, is the truth: I neither conceal, nor do I suppress anything, small or great. And yet I know that it is just this plainness of speech which makes me enemies. But that is only a proof that my words are true, and that the prejudice against me, and the causes of it, are what I have said. And whether you look for them now or hereafter, you will find that they are so.

What I have said must suffice as my defence against the charges of my first accusers. I will try next to defend myself against that "good patriot" Meletus, as he calls himself, and my later accusers. Let us assume that they are a new set of accusers, and read their indictment, as we did in the case of the others. It runs thus. He says that Socrates is an evil-doer who corrupts the youth, and who does not believe in the gods whom the city believes in, but in other new divinities. Such is the charge. Let us examine each point in it separately. Meletus says that I do wrong by corrupting the youth: but I say, Athenians, that he is doing wrong; for he is playing off a solemn jest by bringing men lightly to trial, and pretending to have a great zeal and interest in matters to which he has never given a moment's thought. And now I will try to prove to you that it is so.

Come here, Meletus. Is it not a fact that you think it very important that the younger men should be as excellent as possible?

Meletus. It is.

Socr. Come then: tell the judges, who is it who improves them? You take so much interest in the matter that of course you know that. You are accusing me, and bringing me to trial, because, as you say, you have discovered that I am the corrupter of the youth. Come now, reveal to the judges who improves them. You see, Meletus, you have nothing to say; you are silent. But don't you think that this is a scandalous thing? Is not your silence a conclusive proof of what I say, that you have never given a moment's thought to the matter? Come, tell us, my good sir, who makes the young men better citizens?

Mel. The laws.

Socr. My excellent sir, that is not my question. What man improves the young, who starts with a knowledge of the laws?

Mel. The judges here, Socrates.

Socr. What do you mean, Meletus? Can they educate the young and improve them?

Mel. Certainly.

Socr. All of them? or only some of them?

Mel. All of them.

Socr. By Hêrê that is good news! There is a great abundance of benefactors. And do the listeners here improve them, or not?

Mel. They do.

Socr. And do the senators?

Mel. Yes.

Socr. Well then, Meletus; do the members of the Assembly corrupt the younger men? or do they again all improve them?

Mel. They too improve them.

Socr. Then all the Athenians, apparently, make the young into fine fellows except me, and I alone corrupt them. Is that your meaning?

Mel. Most certainly; that is my meaning.

Socr. You have discovered me to be a most unfortunate man. Now tell me: do you think that the same holds good in the case of horses? Does one man do them harm and every one else improve them? On the contrary, is it not one man only, or a very few—namely, those who are skilled in horses—who can improve them; while the majority of men harm them, if they use them, and have to do with them? Is it not so, Meletus, both with horses and with every other animal? Of course it is, whether you and Anytus say yes or no. And young men would certainly be very fortunate persons if only one man corrupted them, and every one else did them good. The truth is, Meletus, you prove conclusively that you have never thought about the youth in your life. It is quite clear, on your own showing, that you take no interest at all in the matters about which you are prosecuting me.

Now, be so good as to tell us, Meletus, is it better to live among good citizens or bad ones? Answer, my friend: I am not asking you at all a difficult question. Do not bad citizens do harm to their neighbors and good citizens good.

Mel. Yes.

Socr. Is there any man who would rather be injured than benefited by his companions? Answer, my good sir:

you are obliged by the law to answer. Does any one like to be injured?

Mel. Certainly not.

Socr. Well then; are you prosecuting me for corrupting the young, and making them worse men, intentionally or unintentionally?

Mel. For doing it intentionally.

Socr. What, Meletus? Do you mean to say that you, who are so much younger than I, are yet so much wiser than I, that you know that bad citizens always do evil, and that good citizens always do good, to those with whom they come in contact, while I am so extraordinarily stupid as not to know that if I make any of my companions a rogue, he will probably injure me in some way, and as to commit this great crime, as you allege, intentionally? You will not make me believe that, nor any one else either, I should think. Either I do not corrupt the young at all; or if I do, I do so unintentionally: so that you are a liar in either case. And if I corrupt them unintentionally, the law does not call upon you to prosecute me for a fault like that, which is an involuntary one: you should take me aside and admonish and instruct me: for of course I shall cease from doing wrong involuntarily, as soon as I know that I have been doing wrong. But you declined to instruct me: you would have nothing to do with me: instead of that, you bring me up before the Court, where the law sends persons, not for instruction, but for punishment.

The truth is, Athenians, as I said, it is quite clear that Meletus has never paid the slightest attention to these matters. However, now tell us, Meletus, how do you say that I corrupt the younger men? Clearly, according to your indictment, by teaching them not to believe in the gods of the city, but in other new divinities instead. You mean that I corrupt young men by that teaching, do you not?

Mel. Yes: most certainly; I mean that.

Socr. Then in the name of these gods of whom we are speaking, explain yourself a little more clearly to me and to the judges here. I cannot understand what you mean. Do you mean that I teach young men to believe in some gods, but not in the gods of the city? Do you accuse me of teaching them to believe in strange gods? If that is your meaning, I myself believe in some gods, and my crime is not that of absolute atheism. Or do you mean that I do not believe in the gods at all myself, and that I teach other people not to believe in them either?

Mel. I mean that you do not believe in the gods in any way whatever.

Socr. Wonderful, Meletus! Why do you say that? Do you mean that I believe neither the sun nor the moon to be gods, like other men?

Mel. I swear he does not, judges: he says that the sun is a stone, and the moon earth.

Socr. My dear Meletus, do you think that you are prosecuting Anaxagoras? You must have a very poor opinion of the judges, and think them very unlettered men, if you imagine that they do not know that the works of Anaxagoras of Clazomenæ are full of these doctrines. And so young men learn these things from me, when they can often buy places in the theater[2] for a

[2] Socrates here alludes to the references to

drachma at most, and laugh Socrates to scorn, were he to pretend that these doctrines, which are very peculiar doctrines, too, were his. But please tell me, do you really think that I do not believe in the gods at all?

Mel. Most certainly I do. You are a complete atheist.

Socr. No one believes that, Meletus, and I think that you know it to be a lie yourself. It seems to me, Athenians, that Meletus is a very insolent and wanton man, and that he is prosecuting me simply in the insolence and wantonness of youth. He is like a man trying an experiment on me, by asking me a riddle that has no answer. "Will this wise Socrates," he says to himself, "see that I am jesting and contradicting myself? or shall I outwit him and every one else who hears me?" Meletus seems to me to contradict himself in his indictment: it is as if he were to say, "Socrates is a wicked man who does not believe in the gods, but who believes in the gods." But that is mere trifling.

Now, my friends, let us see why I think that this is his meaning. Do you answer me, Meletus: and do you, Athenians, remember the request which I made to you at starting, and do not interrupt me if I talk in my usual way.

Is there any man, Meletus, who believes in the existence of things pertaining to men and not in the existence of men? Make him answer the question, my friends, without these absurd interruptions. Is there any man who

Anaxagoras by Aristophanes, Euripedes, and other Greek dramatists. Anaxagoras' doctrine that the sun is a stone is mentioned in the *Orestes* of Euripedes.

believes in the existence of horsemanship and not in the existence of horses? or in flute-playing and not in flute-players? There is not, my excellent sir. If you will not answer, I will tell both you and the judges that. But you must answer my next question. Is there any man who believes in the existence of divine things and not in the existence of divinities?

Mel. There is not.

Socr. I am very glad that the judges have managed to extract an answer from you. Well then, you say that I believe in divine beings, whether they be old or new ones, and that I teach others to believe in them; at any rate, according to your statement, I believe in divine beings. That you have sworn in your deposition. But if I believe in divine beings, I suppose it follows necessarily that I believe in divinities. Is it not so? It is. I assume that you grant that, as you do not answer. But do we not believe that divinities are either gods themselves or the children of the gods? Do you admit that?

Mel. I do.

Socr. Then you admit that I believe in divinities: now, if these divinities are gods, then, as I say, you are jesting and asking a riddle, and asserting that I do not believe in the gods, and at the same time that I do, since I believe in divinities. But if these divinities are the illegitimate children of the gods, either by the nymphs or by other mothers, as they are said to be, then, I ask, what man could believe in the existence of the children of the gods, and not in the existence of the gods? That would be as strange as believing in the existence of the offspring of horses and asses, and not in the existence of horses and asses. You must have indicted me in this manner, Meletus, either to test my skill, or because you could not find any crime that you could accuse me of with truth. But you will never contrive to persuade any man, even of the smallest understanding, that a belief in divine things and things of the gods does not necessarily involve a belief in divinities, and in the gods, and in heroes.

But in truth, Athenians, I do not think that I need say very much to prove that I have not committed the crime for which Meletus is prosecuting me. What I have said is enough to prove that. But, I repeat, it is certainly true, as I have already told you, that I have incurred much unpopularity and made many enemies. And that is what will cause my condemnation, if I am condemned; not Meletus, nor Anytus either, but the prejudice and suspicion of the multitude. They have been the destruction of many good men before me, and I think that they will be so again. There is no fear that I shall be their last victim.

Perhaps some one will say: "Are you not ashamed, Socrates, of following pursuits which are very likely now to cause your death?" I should answer him with justice, and say: My friend, if you think that a man of any worth at all ought to reckon the chances of life and death when he acts, or that he ought to think of anything but whether he is acting rightly or wrongly, and as a good or a bad man would act, you are grievously mistaken. According to you, the demi-gods who died at Troy would be men of no great worth, and among them the son of Thetis, who thought nothing of

danger when the alternative was disgrace. For when his mother, a goddess, addressed him, as he was burning to slay Hector, I suppose in this fashion, "My son, if thou avengest the death of thy comrade Patroclus, and slayest Hector, thou wilt die thyself, for 'fate awaits thee straightway after Hector's death,'" he heard what she said, but he scorned danger and death; he feared much more to live a coward, and not to avenge his friend. "Let me punish the evil-doer and straightway die," he said, "that I may not remain here by the beaked ships, a scorn of men, encumbering the earth." Do you suppose that he thought of danger or of death? For this, Athenians, I believe to be the truth. Wherever a man's post is, whether he has chosen it of his own will, or whether he has been placed at it by his commander, there it is his duty to remain and face the danger, without thinking of death, or of any other thing, except dishonor.

When the generals whom you chose to command me, Athenians, placed me at my post at Potidæa, and at Amphipolis, and at Delium, I remained where they placed me, and ran the risk of death, like other men: and it would be very strange conduct on my part if I were to desert my post now from fear of death or of any other thing, when God has commanded me, as I am persuaded that he has done, to spend my life in searching for wisdom, and in examining myself and others. That would indeed be a very strange thing: and then certainly I might with justice be brought to trial for not believing in the gods: for I should be disobeying the oracle, and fearing death, and thinking myself wise, when I was not wise. For to fear death, my friends, is only to think ourselves wise, without being wise: for it is to think that we know what we do not know. For anything that men can tell, death may be the greatest good that can happen to them: but they fear it as if they knew quite well that it was the greatest of evils. And what is this but that shameful ignorance of thinking that we know what we do not know? In this matter too, my friends, perhaps I am different from the mass of mankind: and if I were to claim to be at all wiser than others, it would be because I do not think that I have any clear knowledge about the other world, when, in fact, I have none. But I do know very well that it is evil and base to do wrong, and to disobey my superior, whether he be man or god. And I will never do what I know to be evil, and shrink in fear from what, for all that I can tell, may be a good. And so, even if you acquit me now, and do not listen to Anytus' argument that, if I am to be acquitted, I ought never to have been brought to trial at all; and that, as it is, you are bound to put me to death, because, as he said, if I escape, all your children will forthwith be utterly corrupted by practising what Socrates teaches; if you were therefore to say to me, "Socrates, this time we will not listen to Anytus: we will let you go; but on this condition, that you cease from carrying on this search of yours, and from philosophy; if you are found following those pursuits again, you shall die": I say, if you offered to let me go on these terms, I should reply: —Athenians, I hold you in the highest regard and love; but I will obey God rather than you: and as long as I have breath and strength I will not cease from philosophy, and from exhorting you, and declaring the truth to every one of you whom I meet, saying, as I am wont: "My excellent friend, you are a citizen of Athens, a city which is very great and very famous for wisdom and power of mind; are you not ashamed of caring so much for the making of money, and for reputation, and for honor? Will you not think or care about wisdom and truth, and the perfection of your soul?" And if he disputes my words, and says that he does care about these things, I shall not forthwith release him and go away: I shall question him and cross-examine him and test him: and if I think that he has not virtue, though he says that he has, I shall reproach him for setting the lower value on the most important things, and a higher value on those that are of less account. This I shall do to every one whom I meet, young or old, citizen or stranger: but more especially to the citizens, for they are more nearly akin to me. For, know well, God has commanded me to do so. And I think that no better piece of fortune has ever befallen you in Athens than my service to God. For I spend my whole life in going about and persuading you all to give your first and chiefest care to the perfection of your souls, and not till you have done that to think of your bodies, or your wealth; and telling you that virtue does not come from wealth, but that wealth, and every other good thing which men have, whether in public, or in private, comes from virtue. If then I corrupt the youth by this teaching, the mischief is great: but if any man says that I teach anything else, he speaks falsely. And therefore, Athenians, I say, either listen to Anytus, or do not listen to him: either acquit me, or do not acquit me: but be sure that I shall not alter my way of life; no, not if I have to die for it many times.

Do not interrupt me, Athenians. Remember the request which I made to you, and listen to my words. I think that it will profit you to hear them. I am going to say something more to you, at which you may be inclined to cry out: but do not do that. Be sure that if you put me to death, who am what I have told you that I am, you will do yourselves more harm than me. Meletus and Anytus can do me no harm: that is impossible: for I am sure that God will not allow a good man to be injured by a bad one. They may indeed kill me, or drive me into exile, or deprive me of my civil rights; and perhaps Meletus and others think those things great evils. But I do not think so: I think that it is a much greater evil to do what he is doing now, and to try to put a man to death unjustly. And now, Athenians, I am not arguing in my own defence at all, as you might expect me to do: I am trying to persuade you not to sin against God, by condemning me, and rejecting his gift to you. For if you put me to death, you will not easily find another man to fill my place. God has sent me to attack the city, as if it were a great and noble horse, to use a quaint simile, which was rather sluggish from its size, and which needed to be aroused by a gadfly: and I think that I am the gadfly that God has sent to the city to attack it; for I never cease from settling upon you, as it were, at every point, and rousing, and exhorting, and reproaching each man of you all day long. You will not easily find any one else, my friends, to fill my place: and if you take my advice, you will spare my life. You are vexed, as drowsy persons are, when they are awakened, and of course, if you listened to Anytus, you could easily kill me with a single blow, and then sleep on undisturbed for the rest of your lives, unless God were to care for you enough to send another man to arouse you. And you may easily see that it is God who has given me to your city: a mere human impulse would never have led me to neglect all my own interests, or to endure seeing my private affairs neglected now for so many years, while it made me busy myself unceasingly in your interests, and go to each man of you by himself, like a father, or an elder brother, trying to persuade him to care for virtue. There would have been a reason for it, if I had gained any advantage by this conduct, or if I had been paid for my exhortations; but you see yourselves that my accusers, though they accuse me of everything else without blushing, have not had the effrontery to say that I ever either exacted or demanded payment. They could bring no evidence of that. And I think that I have sufficient evidence of the truth of what I say in my poverty.

Perhaps it may seem strange to you that, though I am so busy in going about in private with my counsel, yet I do not venture to come forward in the assembly, and take part in the public councils. You have often heard me speak of my reason for this, and in many places: it is that I have a certain divine sign from God, which is the divinity that Meletus has caricatured in his indictment. I have had it from childhood: it is a kind of voice, which whenever I hear it, always turns me back from something which I was going to do, but never urges me to act. It is this which forbids me to take part in politics. And I think that it does well to forbid me. For, Athenians, it is quite certain that if I had attempted to take part in politics, I should have perished at once and long ago, without doing any good either to you or to myself. And do not be vexed with me for telling the truth. There is no man who will preserve his life for long, either in Athens or elsewhere, if he firmly opposes the wishes of the people, and tries to prevent the commission of much injustice and illegality in the State. He who would really fight for injustice, must do so as a private man, not in public, if he means to preserve his life, even for a short time.

I will prove to you that this is so by very strong evidence, not by mere words, but by what you value highly, actions. Listen then to what has happened to me, that you may know that there is no man who could make me consent to do wrong from the fear of death; but that I would perish at once rather than give way. What I am going to tell you may be a commonplace in the Courts of Law; nevertheless it is true. The only office that I ever held in the State, Athenians, was that of Senator. When you wished to try the ten generals, who did not rescue their men after the battle of Arginusæ, in a body, which was illegal, as you all came to think afterwards, the tribe Antiochis, to which I belong, held

the presidency. On that occasion I alone of all the presidents opposed your illegal action, and gave my vote against you. The speakers were ready to suspend me and arrest me; and you were clamoring against me, and crying out to me to submit. But I thought that I ought to face the danger out in the cause of law and justice, rather than join with you in your unjust proposal, from fear of imprisonment or death. That was before the destruction of the democracy. When the oligarchy came, the Thirty sent for me, with four others, to the Council-Chamber, and ordered us to bring over Leon the Salaminian from Salamis, that they might put him to death. They were in the habit of frequently giving similar orders to many others, wishing to implicate as many men as possible in their crimes. But then I again proved, not by mere words, but by my actions, that, if I may use a vulgar expression, I do not care a straw for death; but that I do care very much indeed about not doing anything against the laws of God or man. That government with all its power did not terrify me into doing anything wrong; but when we left the Council-Chamber, the other four went over to Salamis, and brought Leon across to Athens; and I went away home: and if the rule of the Thirty had not been destroyed soon afterwards, I should very likely have been put to death for what I did then. Many of you will be my witnesses in this matter.

Now do you think that I should have remained alive all these years, if I had taken part in public affairs, and had always maintained the cause of justice like an honest man, and had held it a paramount duty, as it is, to do so? Certainly not, Athenians, nor any other man either. But throughout my whole life, both in private, and in public, whenever I have had to take part in public affairs, you will find that I have never yielded a single point in a question of right and wrong to any man; no, not to those whom my enemies falsely assert to have been my pupils.[3] But I was never any man's teacher. I have never withheld myself from any one, young or old, who was anxious to hear me converse while I was about my mission; neither do I converse for payment, and refuse to converse without payment: I am ready to ask questions of rich and poor alike, and if any man wishes to answer me, and then listen to what I have to say, he may. And I cannot justly be charged with causing these men to turn out good or bad citizens: for I never either taught, or professed to teach any of them any knowledge whatever. And if any man asserts that he ever learnt or heard any thing from me in private, which every one else did not hear as well as he, be sure that he does not speak the truth.

Why is it, then, that people delight in spending so much time in my company? You have heard why, Athenians. I told you the whole truth when I said that they delight in hearing me examine persons who think that they are wise when they are not wise. It is certainly very amusing to listen to that. And, I say, God has commanded me to examine men in oracles, and in dreams, and in every way in which the divine will was ever declared to man. This is the truth, Athenians, and if it were not the truth,

it would be easily refuted. For if it were really the case that I have already corrupted some of the young men, and am now corrupting others, surely some of them, finding as they grew older that I had given them evil counsel in their youth, would have come forward today to accuse me and take their revenge. Or if they were unwilling to do so themselves, surely their kinsmen, their fathers, or brothers, or other relatives, would, if I had done them any harm, have remembered it, and taken their revenge. Certainly I see many of them in Court. Here is Crito, of my own deme and of my own age, the father of Critobulus; here is Lysanias of Sphettus, the father of Æschinus: here is also Antiphon of Cephisus, the father of Epigenes. Then here are others, whose brothers have spent their time in my company; Nicostratus, the son of Theozotides, and brother of Theodotus—and Theodotus is dead, so he at least cannot entreat his brother to be silent: here is Paralus, the son of Demodocus, and the brother of Theages: here is Adeimantus, the son of Ariston, whose brother is Plato here: and Æantodorus, whose brother is Aristodorus. And I can name many others to you, some of whom Meletus ought to have called as witnesses in the course of his own speech: but if he forgot to call them then, let him call them now—I will stand aside while he does so—and tell us if he has any such evidence. No, on the contrary, my friends, you will find all these men ready to support me, the corrupter, the injurer of their kindred, as Meletus and Anytus call me. Those of them who have been already corrupted might perhaps have some reason for supporting

---

[3] For example, Critias and Alcibiades.

me: but what reason can their relatives, who are grown up, and who are uncorrupted, have, except the reason of truth and justice, that they know very well that Meletus is a liar, and that I am speaking the truth?

Well, my friends, this, together it may be with other things of the same nature, is pretty much what I have to say in my defence. There may be some one among you who will be vexed when he remembers how, even in a less important trial than this, he prayed and entreated the judges to acquit him with many tears, and brought forward his children and many of his friends and relatives in Court, in order to appeal to your feelings; and then finds that I shall do none of these things, though I am in what he would think the supreme danger. Perhaps he will harden himself against me when he notices this: it may make him angry, and he may give his vote in anger. If it is so with any of you—I do not suppose that it is, but in case it should be so—I think that I should answer him reasonably if I said: "My friend, I have kinsmen too, for, in the words of Homer, 'I am not born of stocks and stones,' but of woman"; and so, Athenians, I have kinsmen, and I have three sons, one of them a lad, and the other two still children. Yet I will not bring any of them forward before you, and implore you to acquit me. And why will I do none of these things? It is not from arrogance, Athenians, nor because I hold you cheap: whether or no I can face death bravely is another question: but for my own credit, and for your credit, and for the credit of our city, I do not think it well, at my age, and with my name, to do anything of that kind.

Rightly or wrongly, men have made up their minds that in some way Socrates is different from the mass of mankind. And it will be a shameful thing if those of you who are thought to excel in wisdom, or in bravery, or in any other virtue, are going to act in this fashion. I have often seen men with a reputation behaving in a strange way at their trial, as if they thought it a terrible fate to be killed, and as though they expected to live for ever, if you did not put them to death. Such men seem to me to bring discredit on the city: for any stranger would suppose that the best and most eminent Athenians, who are selected by their fellow-citizens to hold office, and for other honors, are no better than women. Those of you, Athenians, who have any reputation at all, ought not to do these things: and you ought not to allow us to do them: you should show that you will be much more merciless to men who make the city ridiculous by these pitiful pieces of acting, than to men who remain quiet.

But apart from the question of credit, my friends, I do not think that it is right to entreat the judge to acquit us, or to escape condemnation in that way. It is our duty to convince his mind by reason. He does not sit to give away justice to his friends, but to pronounce judgment: and he has sworn not to favor any man whom he would like to favor, but to decide questions according to law. And therefore we ought not to teach you to forswear yourselves; and you ought not to allow yourselves to be taught, for then neither you nor we would be acting righteously. Therefore, Athenians, do not require me to do these things, for I believe them to be neither good nor just nor holy; and, more especially do not ask me to do them today, when Meletus is prosecuting me for impiety. For were I to be successful, and to prevail on you by my prayers to break your oaths, I should be clearly teaching you to believe that there are no gods; and I should be simply accusing myself by my defence of not believing in them. But, Athenians, that is very far from the truth. I do believe in the gods as no one of my accusers believes in them: and to you and to God I commit my cause to be decided as is best for you and for me.

[*He is found guilty by 281 votes to 220.*]

I am not vexed at the verdict which you have given, Athenians, for many reasons. I expected that you would find me guilty; and I am not so much surprised at that, as at the numbers of the votes. I, certainly, never thought that the majority against me would have been so narrow. But now it seems that if only thirty votes had changed sides, I should have escaped. So I think that I have escaped Meletus, as it is: and not only have I escaped him; for it is perfectly clear that if Anytus and Lycon had not come forward to accuse me too, he would not have obtained the fifth part of the votes, and would have had to pay a fine of a thousand drachmæ.

So he proposes death as the penalty. Be it so. And what counter-penalty shall I propose to you, Athenians? What I deserve, of course, must I not? What then do I deserve to pay or to suffer for having determined not to spend my life in ease? I neglected the things which most men value, such as wealth, and family interests, and military commands, and popular oratory, and all the political appointments, and clubs, and factions, that there are in Athens; for I thought that I was really too conscientious a man to preserve my life if I engage in these matters. So I did not go where I should have done no good either to you or to myself. I went instead to each one of you by himself, to do him, as I say, the greatest of services, and strove to persuade him not to think of his affairs, until he had thought of himself, and tried to make himself as perfect and wise as possible; nor to think of the affairs of Athens, until he had thought of Athens herself; and in all cases to bestow his thoughts on things in the same manner. Then what do I deserve for such a life? Something good, Athenians, if I am really to propose what I deserve; and something good which it would be suitable to me to receive. Then what is a suitable reward to be given to a poor benefactor, who requires leisure to exhort you? There is no reward, Athenians, so suitable for him as a public maintenance in the Prytaneum. It is a much more suitable reward for him than for any of you who has won a victory at the Olympic games with his horse or his chariots. Such a man only makes you seem happy, but I make you really happy: and he is not in want, and I am. So if I am to propose the penalty which I really deserve, I propose this, a public maintenance in the Prytaneum.

Perhaps you think me stubborn and arrogant in what I am saying now, as in what I said about the entreaties and tears. It is not so, Athenians; it is rather that I am convinced that I never wronged any man intentionally, though

I cannot persuade you of that, for we have conversed together only a little time. If there were a law at Athens, as there is elsewhere, not to finish a trial of life and death in a single day, I think that I could have convinced you of it: but now it is not easy in so short a time to clear myself of the gross calumnies of my enemies. But when I am convinced that I have never wronged any man, I shall certainly not wrong myself, or admit that I deserve to suffer any evil, or propose any evil for myself as a penalty. Why should I? Lest I should suffer the penalty which Meletus proposes, when I say that I do not know whether it is a good or an evil? Shall I choose instead of it something which I know to be an evil, and propose that as a penalty? Shall I propose imprisonment? And why should I pass the rest of my days in prison, the slave of successive officials? Or shall I propose a fine, with imprisonment until it is paid? I have told you why I will not do that. I should have to remain in prison for I have no money to pay a fine with. Shall I then propose exile? Perhaps you would agree to that. Life would indeed be very dear to me, if I were unreasonable enough to expect that strangers would cheerfully tolerate my discussions and reasonings, when you who are my fellow-citizens cannot endure them, and have found them so burdensome and odious to you, that you are seeking now to be released from them. No, indeed, Athenians, that is not likely. A fine life I should lead for an old man, if I were to withdraw from Athens, and pass the rest of my days in wandering from city to city, and continually being expelled. For I know very well that the young men will listen to me, wherever I go, as they do here; and if I drive them away, they will persuade their elders to expel me: and if I do not drive them away, their fathers and kinsmen will expel me for their sakes.

Perhaps some one will say, "Why cannot you withdraw from Athens, Socrates, and hold your peace?" It is the most difficult thing in the world to make you understand why I cannot do that. If I say that I cannot hold my peace, because that would be to disobey God, you will think that I am not in earnest and will not believe me. And if I tell you that no better thing can happen to a man than to converse every day about virtue and the other matters about which you have heard me conversing and examining myself and others, and that an unexamined life is not worth living, then you will believe me still less. But that is the truth, my friends, though it is not easy to convince you of it. And, what is more, I am not accustomed to think that I deserve any punishment. If I had been rich, I would have proposed as large a fine as I could pay: that would have done me no harm. But I am not rich enough to pay a fine, unless you are willing to fix it at a sum within my means. Perhaps I could pay you a mina: so I propose that. Plato here, Athenians, and Crito, and Critobulus, and Apollodorus bid me propose thirty minæ, and they will be sureties for me. So I propose thirty minæ. They will be sufficient sureties to you for the money.

[He is condemned to death.]

You have not gained very much time, Athenians, and, as the price of it, you will have an evil name from all who wish to revile the city, and they will cast in your teeth that you put Socrates, a wise man, to death. For they will certainly call me wise, whether I am wise or not, when they want to reproach you. If you would have waited for a little while, your wishes would have been fulfilled in the course of nature; for you see that I am an old man, far advanced in years, and near to death. I am speaking not to all of you, only to those who have voted for my death. And now I am speaking to them still. Perhaps, my friends, you think that I have been defeated because I was wanting in the arguments by which I could have persuaded you to acquit me, if, that is, I had thought it right to do or to say anything to escape punishment. It is not so. I have been defeated because I was wanting, not in arguments, but in overboldness and effrontery: because I would not plead before you as you would have liked to hear me plead, or appeal to you with weeping and wailing, or say and do many other things, which I maintain are unworthy of me, but which you have been accustomed to from other men. But when I was defending myself, I thought that I ought not to do anything unmanly because of the danger which I ran, and I have not changed my mind now. I would very much rather defend myself as I did, and die, than as you would have had me do, and live. Both in a law suit, and in war, there are some things which neither I nor any other man may do in order to escape from death. In battle a man often sees that he may at least escape from death by throwing down his arms and falling on his knees before the pursuer to beg for his life. And there are many other ways of avoiding death in every danger, if a man will not scruple to say and to do anything. But, my friends, I think that it is a much harder thing to escape from wickedness than from death; for wickedness is swifter than death. And now I, who am old and slow, have been overtaken by the slower pursuer: and my accusers, who are clever and swift, have been overtaken by the swifter pursuer, which is wickedness. And now I shall go hence, sentenced by you to death; and they will go hence, sentenced by truth to receive the penalty of wickedness and evil. And I abide by this award as well as they. Perhaps it was right for these things to be so: and I think that they are fairly measured.

And now I wish to prophesy to you, Athenians who have condemned me. For I am going to die, and that is the time when men have most prophetic power. And I prophesy to you who have sentenced me to death, that a far severer punishment than you have inflicted on me, will surely overtake you as soon as I am dead. You have done this thing, thinking that you will be relieved from having to give an account of your lives. But I say that the result will be very different from that. There will be more men who will call you to account, whom I have held back, and whom you did not see. And they will be harder masters to you than I have been, for they will be younger, and you will be more angry with them. For if you think that you will restrain men from reproaching you for your evil lives by putting them to death, you are very much mistaken. That way of escape is hardly possible, and it is not a good one. It is much better, and much easier, not to silence reproaches, but to make yourselves as perfect as you can. This is my parting prophecy to you who have condemned me.

With you who have acquitted me I should like to converse touching this thing that has come to pass, while the authorities are busy, and before I go to the place where I have to die. So, I pray you, remain with me until I go hence: there is no reason why we should not converse with each other while it is possible. I wish to explain to you, as my friends, the meaning of what has befallen me. A wonderful thing has happened to me, judges—for you I am right in calling judges. The prophetic sign, which I am wont to receive from the divine voice, has been constantly with me all through my life till now, opposing me in quite small matters if I were not going to act rightly. And now you yourselves see what has happened to me; a thing which might be thought, and which is sometimes actually reckoned, the supreme evil. But the sign of God did not withstand me when I was leaving my house in the morning, nor when I was coming up hither to the Court, nor at any point in my speech, when I was going to say anything: though at other times it has often stopped me in the very act of speaking. But now, in this matter, it has never once withstood me, either in my words or my actions. I will tell you what I believe to be the reason of that. This thing that has come upon me must be a good: and those of us who think that death is an evil must needs be mistaken. I have a clear proof that that is so; for my accustomed sign would certainly have opposed me, if I had not been going to fare well.

And if we reflect in another way we shall see that we may well hope that death is a good. For the state of death is one of two things: either the dead man wholly ceases to be, and loses all sensation; or, according to the common belief, it is a change and a migration of the soul unto another place. And if death is the absence of all sensation, and like the sleep of one whose slumbers are unbroken by any dreams, it will be a wonderful gain. For if a man had to select that night in which he slept so soundly that he did not even see any dreams, and had to compare with it all the other nights and days of his life, and then had to say how many days and nights in his life he had spent better and more pleasantly than this night, I think that a private person, nay, even the great King [of Persia] himself, would find them easy to count, compared with the others. If that is the nature of death, I for one count it a gain. For then it appears that eternity is nothing more than a single night. But if death is a journey to another place, and the common belief be true, that there are all who have died, what good could be greater than this, my judges? Would a journey not be worth taking, at the end of which, in the other world, we should be released from the self-styled judges who are here, and should find the true judges, who are said to sit in judgment below, such as Minos, and Rhadamanthus, and Æacus, and Triptolemus, and the other demi-gods who were just in their lives? Or what would you not give to converse with Orpheus and Musæus and Hesiod and Homer?

I am willing to die many times, if this be true. And for my own part I should have a wonderful interest in meeting there Palamedes, and Ajax the son of Telamon, and the other men of old who have died through an unjust judgment, and in comparing my experiences with theirs. That I think would be no small pleasure. And, above all, I could spend my time in examining those who are there, as I examine men here, and in finding out which of them is wise, and which of them thinks himself wise, when he is not wise. What would we not give, my judges, to be able to examine the leader of the great expedition against Troy, or Odysseus, or Sisyphus, or countless other men and women whom we could name? It would be an infinite happiness to converse with them, and to live with them, and to examine them. Assuredly there they do not put men to death for doing that. For besides the other ways in which they are happier than we are, they are immortal, at least if the common belief be true.

And you too, judges, must face death with a good courage, and believe this as a truth, that no evil can happen to a good man, either in life, or after death. His fortunes are not neglected by the gods; and what has come to me today has not come by chance. I am persuaded that it was better for me to die now, and to be released from trouble: and that was the reason why the sign never turned me back. And so I am hardly angry with my accusers, or with those who have condemned me to die. Yet it was not with this mind that they accused me and condemned me, but meaning to do me an injury. So far I may find fault with them.

Yet I have one request to make of them. When my sons grow up, visit them with punishment, my friends, and vex them in the same way that I have vexed you, if they seem to you to care for riches, or for any other thing, before virtue: and if they think that they are something, when they are nothing at all, reproach them, as I have reproached you, for not caring for what they should, and for thinking that they are great men when in fact they are worthless. And if you will do this, I myself and my sons will have received our deserts at your hands.

But now the time has come, and we must go hence; I to die, and you to live. Whether life or death is better is known to God, and to God only.

Crito

SCENE.—The prison of Socrates.

Socrates. Why have you come at this hour, Crito? Is it not still early?

Crito. Yes, very early.

Socr. About what time is it?

Crito. It is just day-break.

Socr. I wonder that the jailor was willing to let you in.

Crito. He knows me now, Socrates, I come here so often; and besides, I have done him a service.

Socr. Have you been here long?

Crito. Yes, some time.

Socr. Then why did you sit down without speaking? why did you not wake me at once?

Crito. Indeed, Socrates, I wish that I myself were not so sleepless and sorrowful. But I have been wondering to see how sweetly you sleep. And I purposely did not wake you, for I was anxious not to disturb your repose. Often before, all through your life, I have thought that your temper was a happy one; and I think so more than ever now, when I see how easily and calmly you bear the calamity that has come to you.

Socr. Nay, Crito, it would be absurd if at my age I were angry at having to die.

Crito. Other men as old are overtaken by similar calamities, Socrates; but their age does not save them from being angry with their fate.

Socr. That is so: but tell me, why are you here so early?

Crito. I am the bearer of bitter news, Socrates: not bitter, it seems, to you; but to me, and to all your friends, both bitter and grievous: and to none of them, I think, is it more grievous than to me.

Socr. What is it? Has the ship come from Delos, at the arrival of which I am to die?

Crito. No, it has not actually arrived: but I think that it will be here today, from the news which certain persons have brought from Sunium, who left it there. It is clear from their news that it will be here today; and then, Socrates, tomorrow your life will have to end.

Socr. Well, Crito, may it end fortunately. Be it so, if so the gods will. But I do not think that the ship will be here today.

Crito. Why do you suppose not?

Socr. I will tell you. I am to die on the day after the ship arrives, am I not?

Crito. That is what the authorities say.

Socr. Then I do not think that it will come today, but tomorrow. I judge from a certain dream which I saw a little while ago in the night: so it seems to be fortunate that you did not wake me.

Crito. And what was this dream?

Socr. A fair and comely woman, clad in white garments, seemed to come to me, and call me and say, "O Socrates—

The third day hence shalt thou fair Phthia reach."[1]

Crito. What a strange dream, Socrates!

Socr. But its meaning is clear; at least to me, Crito.

Crito. Yes, too clear, it seems. But, O my good Socrates, I beseech you for the last time to listen to me and save yourself. For to me your death will be more than a single disaster: not only shall I lose a friend the like of whom I shall never find again, but many persons, who do not know you and me well, will think that I might have saved you if I had been willing to spend money, but that I neglected to do so. And what character could be more disgraceful than the character of caring more for money than for one's friends? The world will never believe that we were anxious to save you, but that you yourself refused to escape.

Socr. But, my excellent Crito, why should we care so much about the opinion of the world? The best men, of whose opinion it is worth our while to think, will believe that we acted as we really did.

Crito. But you see, Socrates, that it is necessary to care about the opinion of the world too. This very thing that has happened to you proves that the multitude can do a man not the least, but almost the greatest harm, if he be falsely accused to them.

Socr. I wish that the multitude were able to do a man the greatest harm,

[1] Homer, *Iliad,* ix, 363.

Crito, for then they would be able to do him the greatest good too. That would have been well. But, as it is, they can do neither. They cannot make a man either wise or foolish: they act wholly at random.

Crito. Well, be it so. But tell me this, Socrates. You surely are not anxious about me and your other friends, and afraid lest, if you escape, the informers should say that we stole you away, and get us into trouble, and involve us in a great deal of expense, or perhaps in the loss of all our property, and, it may be, bring some other punishment upon us besides? If you have any fear of that kind, dismiss it. For of course we are bound to run those risks, and still greater risks than those if necessary, in saving you. So do not, I beseech you, refuse to listen to me.

Socr. I am anxious about that, Crito, and about much besides.

Crito. Then have no fear on that score. There are men who, for no very large sum, are ready to bring you out of prison into safety. And then, you know, these informers are cheaply bought, and there would be no need to spend much upon them. My fortune is at your service, and I think that it is sufficient: and if you have any feeling about making use of my money, there are strangers in Athens, whom you know, ready to use theirs; and one of them, Simmias of Thebes, has actually brought enough for this very purpose. And Cebes and many others are ready too. And therefore, I repeat, do not shrink from saving yourself on that ground. And do not let what you said in the Court, that if you went into exile you would not know what to do with yourself, stand in your way; for there are many places for you to go to, where you will be welcomed. If you choose to go to Thessaly, I have friends there who will make much of you, and shelter you from any annoyance from the people of Thessaly.

And besides, Socrates, I think that you will be doing what is wrong, if you abandon your life when you might preserve it. You are simply playing the game of your enemies; it is exactly the game of those who wanted to destroy you. And what is more, to me you seem to be abandoning your children too: you will leave them to take their chance in life, as far as you are concerned, when you might bring them up and educate them. Most likely their fate will be the usual fate of children who are left orphans. But you ought not to beget children unless you mean to take the trouble of bringing them up and educating them. It seems to me that you are choosing the easy way, and not the way of a good and brave man, as you ought, when you have been talking all your life long of the value that you set upon virtue. For my part, I feel ashamed both for you, and for us who are your friends. Men will think that the whole of this thing which has happened to you —your appearance in court to take your trial, when you need not have appeared at all; the very way in which the trial was conducted; and then lastly this, for the crowning absurdity of the whole affair, is due to our cowardice. It will look as if we had shirked the danger out of miserable cowardice; for we did not save you, and you did not save yourself, when it was quite possible to do so, if we had been good for anything at all.

Take care, Socrates, lest these things be not evil only, but also dishonorable to you and to us. Consider then; or rather the time for consideration is past; we must resolve; and there is only one plan possible. Everything must be done tonight. If we delay any longer, we are lost. O Socrates, I implore you not to refuse to listen to me.

Socr. My dear Crito, if your anxiety to save me be right, it is most valuable: but if it be not right, its greatness makes it all the more dangerous. We must consider then whether we are to do as you say, or not; for I am still what I always have been, a man who will listen to no voice but the voice of the reasoning which on consideration I find to be truest. I cannot cast aside my former arguments because this misfortune has come to me. They seem to me to be as true as ever they were, and I hold exactly the same ones in honor and esteem as I used to: and if we have no better reasoning to substitute for them, I certainly shall not agree to your proposal, not even though the power of the multitude should scare us with fresh terrors, as children are scared with hobgoblins, and inflict upon us new fines, and imprisonments, and deaths. How then shall we most fitly examine the question? Shall we go back first to what you say about the opinions of men, and ask if we used to be right in thinking that we ought to pay attention to some opinions, and not to others? Used we to be right in saying so before I was condemned to die, and has it now become apparent that we were talking at random, and arguing for the sake of argument, and that it was really nothing but play and nonsense? I am anxious, Crito, to examine our former reasoning with your help, and to see whether my present position will appear to me to have affected its truth in any way, or not; and whether we are to set it aside, or to yield assent to it. Those of us who thought at all seriously, used always to say, I think, exactly what I said just now, namely, that we ought to esteem some of the opinions which men form highly, and not others. Tell me, Crito, if you please, do you not think that they were right? For you, humanly speaking, will not have to die tomorrow, and your judgment will not be biassed by that circumstance. Consider then: do you not think it reasonable to say that we should not esteem all the opinions of men, but only some, nor the opinions of all men, but only of some men? What do you think? Is not this true?

Crito. It is.

Socr. And we should esteem the good opinions, and not the worthles ones?

Crito. Yes.

Socr. But the good opinions are those of the wise, and the worthless ones those of the foolish?

Crito. Of course.

Socr. And what used we to say about this? Does a man who is in training, and who is in earnest about it, attend to the praise and blame and opinion of all men, or of the one man only who is a doctor or a trainer

Crito. He attends only to the opinion of the one man.

Socr. Then he ought to fear the blame and welcome the praise of this one man, not of the many?

Crito. Clearly.

Socr. Then he must act and exercise, and eat and drink in whatever way the one man who is his master, and who understands the matter, bids him; not as others bid him?

Crito. That is so.

Socr. Good. But if he disobeys this one man, and disregards his opinion and his praise, and esteems instead what the many, who understand nothing of the matter, say, will he not suffer for it?

Crito. Of course he will.

Socr. And how will he suffer? In what direction, and in what part of himself?

Crito. Of course in his body. That is disabled.

Socr. You are right. And, Crito, to be brief, is it not the same, in everything? And, therefore, in questions of right and wrong, and of the base and the honorable, and of good and evil, which we are now considering, ought we to follow the opinion of the many and fear that, or the opinion of the one man who understands these matters (if we can find him), and feel more shame and fear before him than before all other men? For if we do not follow him, we shall cripple and maim that part of us which, we used to say, is improved by right and disabled by wrong. Or is this not so?

Crito. No, Socrates, I agree with you.

Socr. Now, if, by listening to the opinions of those who do not understand, we disable that part of us which is improved by health and crippled by disease, is our life worth living, when it is crippled? It is the body, is it not?

Crito. Yes.

Socr. Is life worth living with the body crippled and in a bad state?

Crito. No, certainly not.

Socr. Then is life worth living when that part of us which is maimed by wrong and benefited by right is crippled? Or do we consider that part of us, whatever it is, which has to do with right and wrong to be of less consequence than our body?

Crito. No, certainly not.

Socr. But more valuable?

Crito. Yes, much more so.

Socr. Then, my excellent friend, we must not think so much of what the many will say of us; we must think of what the one man, who understands right and wrong, and of what Truth herself will say of us. And so you are mistaken to begin with, when you invite us to regard the opinion of the multitude concerning the right and the honorable and the good, and their opposites. But, it may be said, the multitude can put us to death?

Crito. Yes, that is evident. That may be said, Socrates.

Socr. True. But, my excellent friend, to me it appears that the conclusion which we have just reached, is the same as our conclusion of former times. Now consider whether we still hold to the belief, that we should set the highest value, not on living, but on living well?

Crito. Yes, we do.

Socr. And living well and honorably and rightly mean the same thing: do we hold to that or not?

Crito. We do.

Socr. Then, starting from these premises, we have to consider whether it is right or not right for me to try to escape from prison, without the consent of the Athenians. If we find that is right, we will try: if not, we will let

it alone. I am afraid that considerations of expense, and of reputation, and of bringing up my children, of which you talk, Crito, are only the reflections of our friends, the many, who lightly put men to death, and who would, if they could, as lightly bring them to life again, without a thought. But reason, which is our guide, shows us that we can have nothing to consider but the question which I asked just now: namely, shall we be doing right if we give money and thanks to the men who are to aid me in escaping, and if we ourselves take our respective parts in my escape? Or shall we in truth be doing wrong, if we do all this? And if we find that we should be doing wrong, then we must not take any account either of death, or of any other evil that may be the consequence of remaining quietly here, but only of doing wrong.

Crito. I think that you are right, Socrates. But what are we to do?

Socr. Let us consider that together, my good sir, and if you can contradict anything that I say, do so, and I will be convinced: but if you cannot, do not go on repeating to me any longer, my dear friend, that I should escape without the consent of the Athenians. I am very anxious to act with your approval: I do not want you to think me mistaken. But now tell me if you agree with the doctrine from which I start, and try to answer my questions as you think best.

Crito. I will try.

Socr. Ought we never to do wrong intentionally at all; or may we do wrong in some ways, and not in others? Or, as we have often agreed in former times, is it never either good or honorable to do wrong? Have all our former conclusions been forgotten in these few days? Old men as we were, Crito, did we not see, in days gone by, when we were gravely conversing with each other, that we were no better than children? Or is not what we used to say most assuredly the truth, whether the world agrees with us or not? Is not wrong-doing an evil and a shame to the wrong-doer in every case, whether we incur a heavier or a lighter punishment than death as the consequence of doing right? Do we believe that?

Crito. We do.

Socr. Then we ought never to do wrong at all?

Crito. Certainly not.

Socr. Neither, if we ought never to do wrong at all, ought we to repay wrong with wrong, as the world thinks we may?

Crito. Clearly not.

Socr. Well then, Crito, ought we to do evil to any one?

Crito. Certainly I think not, Socrates.

Socr. And is it right to repay evil with evil, as the world thinks, or not right?

Crito. Certainly it is not right.

Socr. For there is no difference, is there, between doing evil to a man, and wronging him?

Crito. True.

Socr. Then we ought not to repay wrong with wrong or do harm to any man, no matter what we may have suffered from him. And in conceding this, Crito, be careful that you do not concede more than you mean. For I know that only a few men hold, or ever will hold this opinion. And so those who hold it, and those who do not, have no common ground of argument; they can of necessity only look with contempt on each other's belief. Do you therefore consider very carefully whether you agree with me and share my opinion. Are we to start in our inquiry from the doctrine that it is never right either to do wrong, or to repay wrong with wrong, or to avenge ourselves on any man who harms us, by harming him in return? Or do you disagree with me and dissent from my principle? I myself have believed in it for a long time, and I believe in it still. But if you differ in any way, explain to me how. If you still hold to our former opinion, listen to my next point.

Crito. Yes, I hold to it, and I agree with you. Go on.

Socr. Then, my next point, or rather my next question, is this: Ought a man to perform his just agreements, or may he shuffle out of them?

Crito. He ought to perform them.

Socr. Then consider. If I escape without the state's consent, shall I be injuring those whom I ought least to injure, or not? Shall I be abiding by my just agreements or not?

Crito. I cannot answer your question, Socrates. I do not understand it.

Socr. Consider it in this way. Suppose the law and the commonwealth were to come and appear to me as I was preparing to run away (if that is the right phrase to describe my escape) and were to ask, "Tell us, Socrates, what have you in your mind to do? What do you mean by trying to escape, but to destroy us the laws, and the whole city, so far as in you lies? Do you think that a state can exist and not be overthrown, in which the decisions of law are of no force, and are disregarded and set at nought by private individuals?" How shall we answer questions like that, Crito? Much might be said, especially by an orator, in defence of the law which makes judicial decisions supreme. Shall I reply, "But the state has injured me: it has decided my cause wrongly." Shall we say that?

Crito. Certainly we will, Socrates.

Socr. And suppose the laws were to reply, "Was that our agreement? or was it that you would submit to whatever judgments the state should pronounce?" And if we were to wonder at their words, perhaps they would say, "Socrates, wonder not at our words, but answer us; you yourself are accustomed to ask questions and to answer them. What complaint have you against us and the city, that you are trying to destroy us? Are we not, first, your parents? Through us your father took your mother and begat you. Tell us, have you any fault to find with those of us that are the laws of marriage?" "I have none," I should reply. "Or have you any fault to find with those of us that regulate the nurture and education of the child, which you, like others, received? Did not we do well in bidding your father educate you in music and gymnastic?" "You did," I should say. "Well then, since you were brought into the world and nurtured and educated by us, how, in the first place, can you deny that you are our child and our slave, as your fathers were before you? And if this be so, do you think that your rights are on a level with ours? Do you think that you have a

right to retaliate upon us if we should try to do anything to you. You had not the same rights that your father had, or that your master would have had, if you had been a slave. You had no right to retaliate upon them if they ill-treated you, or to answer them if they reviled you, or to strike them back if they struck you, or to repay them evil with evil in any way. And do you think that you may retaliate on your country and its laws? If we try to destroy you, because we think it right, will you in return do all that you can to destroy us, the laws, and your country, and say that in so doing you are doing right, you, the man, who in truth thinks so much of virtue? Or are you too wise to see that your country is worthier, and more august, and more sacred, and holier, and held in higher honor both by the gods and by all men of understanding, than your father and your mother and all your other ancestors; and that it is your bounden duty to reverence it, and to submit to it, and to approach it more humbly than you would approach your father, when it is angry with you; and either to do whatever it bids you to do or to persuade it to excuse you; and to obey in silence if it orders you to endure stripes or imprisonment, or if it send you to battle to be wounded or to die? That is what is your duty. You must not give way, nor retreat, nor desert your post. In war, and in the court of justice, and everywhere, you must do whatever your city and your country bid you do, or you must convince them that their commands are unjust. But it is against the law of God to use violence to your father or to your mother; and much more so is it against the law of God to use violence to your country." What answer shall we make, Crito? Shall we say that the laws speak truly, or not?

Crito. I think that they do.

Socr. "Then consider, Socrates," perhaps they would say, "if we are right in saying that by attempting to escape you are attempting to injure us. We brought you into the world, we nurtured you, we educated you, we gave you and every other citizen a share of all the good things we could. Yet we proclaim that if any man of the Athenians is dissatisfied with us, he may take his goods and go away whithersoever he pleases: we give that permission to every man who chooses to avail himself of it, so soon as he has reached man's estate, and sees us, the laws, and the administration of our city. No one of us stands in his way or forbids him to take his gods and go wherever he likes, whether it be to an Athenian colony, or to any foreign country, if he is dissatisfied with us and with the city. But we say that every man of you who remains here, seeing how we administer justice, and how we govern the city in other matters, has agreed, by the very fact of remaining here, to do whatsoever we bid him. And, we say, he who disobeys us, does a threefold wrong: he disobeys us who are his parents, and he disobeys us who fostered him, and he disobeys us after he has agreed to obey us, without persuading us that we are wrong. Yet we did not bid him sternly to do whatever we told him. We offered him an alternative; we gave him his choice, either to obey us, or to convince us that we were wrong: but he does neither.

"These are the charges, Socrates, to which we say that you will expose yourself, if you do what you intend; and that not less, but more than other Athenians." And if I were to ask, "And why?" they might retort with justice that I have bound myself by the agreement with them more than other Athenians. They would say, "Socrates, we have very strong evidence that you were satisfied with us and with the city. You would not have been content to stay at home in it more than other Athenians, unless you had been satisfied with it more than they. You never went away from Athens to the festivals, save once to the Isthmian games, nor elsewhere except on military service; you never made other journeys like other men; you had no desire to see other cities or other laws; you were contented with us and our city. So strongly did you prefer us, and agree to be governed by us: and what is more, you begat children in this city, you found it so pleasant. And besides, if you had wished, you might at your trial have offered to go into exile. At that time you could have done with the state's consent, what you are trying now to do without it. But then you gloried in being willing to die. You said that you preferred death to exile. And now you are not ashamed of those words: you do not respect us the laws, for you are trying to destroy us: and you are acting just as a miserable slave would act, trying to run away, and breaking the covenant and agreement which you made to submit to our government. First, therefore, answer this question.

Are we right, or are we wrong, in saying that you have agreed not in mere words, but in reality, to live under our government?" What are we to say, Crito? Must we not admit that it is true?

Crito. We must, Socrates.

Socr. Then they would say, "Are you not breaking your covenants and agreements with us? And you were not led to make them by force or by fraud: you had not to make up your mind in a hurry. You had seventy years in which you might have gone away, if you had been dissatisfied with us, or if the agreement had seemed to you unjust. But you preferred neither Lacedæmon nor Crete, though you are fond of saying that they are well governed, nor any other state, either of the Hellenes, or the Barbarians. You went away from Athens less than the lame and the blind and the cripple. Clearly you, far more than other Athenians, were satisfied with the city, and also with us who are its laws: for who would be satisfied with a city which had no laws? And now will you not abide by your agreement? If you take our advice, you will, Socrates: then you will not make yourself ridiculous by going away from Athens.

"For consider: what good will you do yourself or your friends by thus transgressing, and breaking your agreement? It is tolerably certain that they, on their part, will at least run the risk of exile, and of losing their civil rights, or of forfeiting their property. For yourself, you might go to one of the neighboring cities, to Thebes or to Megara for instance—for both of them are well governed—but, Socrates, you will come as an enemy to these commonwealths; and all who care for their city will look askance at you, and think that you are a subverter of law. And you will confirm the judges in their opinion, and make it seem that their verdict was a just one. For a man who is a subverter of the law, may well be supposed to be a corrupter of the young and thoughtless. Then will you avoid well-governed states and civilized men? Will life be worth having, if you do? Or will you consort with such men, and converse without shame— about what, Socrates? About the things which you talk of here? Will you tell them that virtue, and justice, and institutions, and law are the most precious things that men can have? And do you not think that that will be a shameful thing in Socrates? You ought to think so. But you will leave these places; you will go to the friends of Crito in Thessaly: for there there is most disorder and licence: and very likely they will be delighted to hear of the ludicrous way in which you escaped from prison, dressed up in peasant's clothes, or in some other disguise which people put on when they are running away, and with your appearance altered. But will no one say how you, an old man, with probably only a few more years to live, clung so greedily to life that you dared to transgress the highest laws? Perhaps not, if you do not displease them. But if you do, Socrates, you will hear much that will make you blush. You will pass your life as the flatterer and the slave of all men; and what will you be doing but feasting in Thessaly? It will be as if you had made a journey to Thessaly for an entertainment. And where will be all our old sayings about justice and virtue then? But you wish to live for the sake of your children? You want to bring them up and educate them? What? will you take them with you to Thessaly, and bring them up and educate them there? Will you make them strangers to their own country, that you may bestow this benefit on them too? Or supposing that you leave them in Athens, will they be brought up and educated better if you are alive, though you are not with them? Yes; your friends will take care of them. Will your friends take care of them if you make a journey to Thessaly, and not if you make a journey to Hades? You ought not to think that, at least if those who call themselves your friends are good for anything at all.

"No, Socrates, be advised by us who have fostered you. Think neither of children, nor of life, nor of any other thing before justice, that when you come to the other world you may be able to make your defence before the rulers who sit in judgment there. It is clear that neither you nor any of your friends will be happier, or juster, or holier in this life, if you do this thing, nor will you be happier after you are dead. Now you will go away wronged, not by us, the laws, but by men. But if you repay evil with evil, and wrong with wrong in this shameful way, and break your agreements and covenants with us, and injure those whom you should least injure, yourself, and your friends, and your country, and us, and so escape, then we shall be angry with you while you live, and when you die our brethren, the laws in Hades, will not receive you kindly; for they will know that on earth you did all that you could to destroy us. Listen then to us, and let not Crito persuade you to do as he says."

Know well, my dear friend Crito, that this is what I seem to hear, as the worshipers of Cybele seem, in their frenzy, to hear the music of flutes: and the sound of these words rings loudly in my ears, and drowns all other words. And I feel sure that if you try to change my mind you will speak in vain; nevertheless, if you think that you will succeed, say on.

Crito. I can say no more, Socrates.

Socr. Then let it be, Crito: and let us do as I say, seeing that God so directs us.

Phaedo
(Death Scene)

CHARACTERS OF THE
DIALOGUE

SOCRATES
CRITO
A GROUP OF INTIMATE FRIENDS

SCENE.—The prison of Socrates at the close of a long conversation.

When Socrates had finished speaking Crito said, Be it so, Socrates. But have you any commands for your friends or for me about your children, or about other things? How shall we serve you best?

Simply by doing what I always tell you, Crito. Take care of your own selves, and you will serve me and mine and yourselves in all that you do, even though you make no promises now. But if you are careless of your own selves, and will not follow the path of life which we have pointed out in our discussions both today and at other times, all your promises now, however profuse and earnest they are, will be of no avail.

We will do our best, said Crito. But how shall we bury you?

As you please, he answered; only you must catch me first, and not let me escape you. And then he looked at us with a smile and said, My friends, I cannot convince Crito that I am the Socrates who has been conversing with you, and arranging his arguments in order. He thinks that I am the body which he will presently see a corpse, and he asks how he is to bury me. All the arguments which I have used to prove that I shall not remain with you after I have drunk the poison, but that I shall go away to the happiness of the blessed, with which I tried to comfort you and myself, have been thrown away on him. Do you therefore be my sureties to him, as he was my surety at the trial, but in a different way. He was surety for me then that I would remain; but you must be my sureties to him that I shall go away when I am dead, and not remain with you: then he will feel my death less; and when he sees my body being burnt or buried, he will not be grieved because he thinks that I am suffering dreadful things: and at my funeral he will not say that it is Socrates whom he is laying out, or bearing to the grave, or burying. For, dear Crito, he continued, you must know that to use words wrongly is not only a fault in itself; it also creates evil in the soul. You must be of good cheer, and say that you are burying my body: and you must bury it as you please, and as you think right.

With these words he rose and went into another room to bathe himself: Crito went with him and told us to wait. So we waited, talking of the argument, and discussing it, and then again dwelling on the greatness of the calamity which had fallen upon us: it seemed as if we were going to lose a father, and to be orphans for the rest of our life. When he had bathed, and his children had been brought to him —he had two sons quite little, and one grown up—and the women of his family were come, he spoke with them in Crito's presence, and gave them his last commands; then he sent the women and children away, and returned to us. By that time it was near the hour of sunset, for he had been a long while within. When he came back to us from the bath he sat down, but not much was said after that. Presently the servant of the Eleven came and stood before him and said, "I know that I shall not find you unreasonable like other men, Socrates. They are angry with me and curse me when I bid them drink the poison because the authorities make me do it. But I have found you all along the noblest and gentlest and best man that has ever come here; and now I am sure that you will not be angry with me, but with those who you know are to blame. And so farewell, and try to bear what must be as lightly as you can; you know why I have come." With that he turned away weeping, and went out.

Socrates looked up at him, and replied, Farewell: I will do as you say. Then he turned to us and said, How courteous the man is! And the whole time that I have been here, he has constantly come in to see me, and sometimes he has talked to me, and has been the best of men; and now, how

generously he weeps for me! Come, Crito, let us obey him: let the poison be brought if it is ready; and if it is not ready, let it be prepared.

Crito replied: Nay, Socrates, I think that the sun is still upon the hill; it has not set. Besides, I know that other men take the poison quite late, and eat and drink heartily, and even enjoy the company of their chosen friends, after the announcement has been made. So do not hurry; there is still time.

Socrates replied: And those whom you speak of, Crito, naturally do so; for they think that they will be gainers by so doing. And I naturally shall not do so; for I think that I should gain nothing by drinking the poison a little later, but my own contempt for so greedily saving up a life which is already spent. So do not refuse to do as I say.

Then Crito made a sign to his slave who was standing by; and the slave went out, and after some delay returned with the man who was to give the poison, carrying it prepared in a cup. When Socrates saw him, he asked, You understand these things, my good sir, what have I to do?

You have only to drink this, he replied, and to walk about until your legs feel heavy, and then lie down; and it will act of itself. With that he handed the cup to Socrates, who took it quite cheerfully, Echecrates, without trembling, and without any change of color or of feature, and looked up at the man with that fixed glance of his, and asked, What say you to making a libation from this draught? May I, or not? We only prepare so much as we think sufficient, Socrates, he answered. I understand, said Socrates. But I suppose that I may, and must, pray to the gods that my journey hence may be prosperous: that is my prayer; be it so. With these words he put the cup to his lips and drank the poison quite calmly and cheerfully. Till then most of us had been able to control our grief fairly well; but when we saw him drinking, and then the poison finished, we could do so no longer: my tears came fast in spite of myself, and I covered my face and wept for myself: it was not for him, but at my own misfortune in losing such a friend. Even before that Crito had been unable to restrain his tears, and had gone away; and Apollodorus, who had never once ceased weeping the whole time, burst into a loud cry, and made us one and all break down by his sobbing and grief, except only Socrates himself. What are you doing, my friends? he exclaimed. I sent away the women chiefly in order that they might not offend in this way; for I have heard that a man should die in silence. So calm yourselves and bear up. When we heard that we were ashamed, and we ceased from weeping. But he walked about, until he said that

his legs were getting heavy, and then he lay down on his back, as he was told. And the man who gave the poison began to examine his feet and legs, from time to time: then he pressed his foot hard, and asked if there was any feeling in it; and Socrates said, No: and then his legs, and so higher and higher, and showed us that he was cold and stiff. And Socrates felt himself, and said that when it came to his heart, he should be gone. He was already growing cold about the groin, when he uncovered his face, which had been covered, and spoke for the last time. Crito, he said, I owe a cock to Asclepius; do not forget to pay it. It shall be done, replied Crito. Is there anything else that you wish? He made no answer to this question; but after a short interval there was a movement, and the man uncovered him, and his eyes were fixed. Then Crito closed his mouth and his eyes.

Such was the end, Echecrates, of our friend, a man, I think, who was the wisest and justest, and the best man that I have ever known.

2

Teleology

ARISTOTLE (384 B.C.–322 B.C.)

The greatest proponent of a teleological interpretation of existence is Aristotle. He was born in Stagira, a town in Macedonia colonized by Greeks. At the time of his birth, Socrates had been dead for fifteen years and Plato was thirty-three. Aristotle's father Nichomachus, having achieved some renown, became court physician to King Amyntas II of Macedonia. Refusing to follow his father's profession, Aristotle at the age of eighteen migrated to Athens, where he lived for twenty years as a member of Plato's school, the Academy. When the master died, Aristotle left Athens to spend four years on the coast of Asia Minor, engaged mainly in biological research. During this period he married, and his wife eventually bore him a daughter. Subsequently he married a second time and had two sons, although one of them was adopted.

Meanwhile Philip, the son of Amyntas, having become King of Macedonia, invited Aristotle to take charge of the education of his son Alexander, then thirteen years old. In consequence of accepting this invitation, Aristotle must have acquired intimate knowledge of court affairs, but he makes no mention of the great Macedonian empire built up by Philip and Alexander the Great. Perhaps he was too close to kings to be greatly impressed by courtly glitter.

He stayed with Philip for seven years, until the monarch's death, and lingered at the court for about a year after Alexander's accession to the throne. Then he returned to Athens to resume his philosophical career. At this time the Academy was being reorganized, and Xenocrates, a second-rate philosopher, was made head. Evidently disappointed at the choice, Aristotle withdrew and founded a school of his own, the Lyceum, which he directed for twelve years. It was during this period that he was his most productive.

Aristotle's reputation and the prosperity of his school suffered from the anti-Macedonian reaction which took place after Alexander's death in 323 B.C. Accused of impiety, Aristotle, unlike Socrates, fled to the island of Euboea, vowing that he would not "give the Athenians a second chance of sinning against philosophy." A year later, in 322 B.C., he died of a stomach disease, at the age of sixty-three.

His writings, as they have come down to us, lack the beauty of Plato's dialogues and are without wit, personal charm, or poetry. He also wrote popular works, including dialogues, which were praised by Cicero for "the incredible flow and sweetness of their diction"; but like many other ancient compositions, these dialogues have been lost. The works that remain touch upon almost every phase of human knowledge, and they establish Aristotle's reputation not only as an extremely versatile philosopher but as an accomplished biologist.

The Physics

1. [Explanation of Change]

Our first step must be to recognize that one thing does not act upon nor become affected by nor turn into any other thing at random, except "in an incidental sense." We could not describe a man's "pallid whiteness" as arising from his "being cultured" unless this had been incidentally connected with a quality opposed to whiteness—*i.e.,* "swarthy blackness." White can arise

Parts 1, 3, 4, and 5 are from *Aristotle: Containing Selections from Seven of the Most Important Books of Aristotle,* translated by Philip Wheelwright, copyright by the Odyssey Press, 1935, 1951. Part 2 is a translation by Henry M. Magid in *Landmarks for Beginners in Philosophy,* copyright by the editors, Irwin Edman and Herbert W. Schneider: Reynal and Hitchcock; Henry Holt and Company, 1941. Reprinted by permission.

only from "not-white"; and by not-white I do not mean just any quality at random that happens to be other than white, but black or some intermediate color. "Being cultured," in turn, does not arise from anything at random, but from the "*un*cultured"—unless, of course, we postulate some quality intermediate between the two.

Qualities are restricted similarly in their disappearance. White does not pass into the quality of being cultured, except in an incidental sense; strictly speaking, it can pass only into the opposite of white—*i.e.,* not into anything at all that happens to be other than white, but into black or some intermediate color. So too, "being cultured" will not pass into anything at random, but only into the state of being uncultured, or else into some state intermediate between the two.

It is the same with everything else. Even composite structures, as distinguished from simple qualities, follow the same law; we overlook this aspect, however, because the corresponding lack of structure has received no name. Nevertheless, a particular harmony or arrangement of parts can only have arisen from a state in which that particular arrangement was lacking; and when it is destroyed it will pass not into anything at random, but into that state which is its specific opposite. Whether such an arrangement of parts is called a harmony or an order or a combination is immaterial: the rule holds good in any case. In fact, it holds good even of a house or a statue or any other such product. A house comes into existence out of materials previously unjoined; a statue, or anything else that has been molded into shape, out of a material previously unwrought; all such constructions involving either a combination or an ordering of parts.

This being so, we may conclude that whenever anything is created or destroyed it necessarily passes out of or into either its opposite or some intermediate state. And since each group of intermediates is derived from some pair of opposites (colors, for instance, from white and black), it follows that whatever comes into existence by a natural process is either itself one of a pair of opposites or a product of such a pair. . . .

"Coming into existence" takes place in several ways: (1) by change of shape, as a bronze statue; (2) by accretion, as things that grow; (3) by subduction, as a Hermes chiseled from a block of marble; (4) by combination, as a house; and (5) by "qualitative alteration," where the material itself assumes different properties. In all of these cases it is evident that the process of coming into existence presupposes a substratum which is already existing.

Hence it appears that whatever "becomes" is always composite: there is something [a new element of form] that comes into existence, and something else that becomes it. This "something else" may be conceived in a double sense: as the enduring substratum, or as the original qualification which in the process is replaced by its opposite. In the example previously employed, "uncultured" is the original qualification, "man" is the subject; in the making of a statue the lack of form, shape, and order is the original qualification, while the bronze or stone or gold is the subject. If we grant, then, that all things are determined by causes and basic principles, of which they are the essential, not the accidental, result, it plainly follows that everything comes into existence at one and the same time from the subject and from a certain form. For "cultured man" consists, so to speak, of both "man" and "cultured"; and the meaning of the composite term can be analyzed into these two component meanings. Elements like these, then, are the conditions of any becoming.

The subject of any change is numerically one, but with a duality of form. A man, or gold, or any other "material susceptible of form," can be regarded as a unit, and is the essential basis of the process that transpires; but the "lack of form" and its opposite are related to the process only incidentally. At the same time it is also possible to regard the acquired form—the order, or the state of culture attained—as something unitary. Thus we must recognize a sense in which the principles are two, añd another sense in which they are three. From one point of view it seems enough to take as principles some pair of opposites such as cultured vs. uncultured, hot vs. cold, or joined vs. unjoined; but there is another point of view from which this interpretation is inadequate, inasmuch as opposites cannot be acted on by each other. We therefore solve the difficulty by postulating a substratum distinct from either of the opposites which successively inhere in it, and not itself the opposite of anything. . . .

What the underlying substratum is, can be understood by analogy. As bronze is to a completed statue, wood to a bed, and still unformed materials to the objects fashioned from them, so the underlying substratum is to anything substantial, particular, and existent. . . .

2. [The Four Causes]

In the first place, one calls cause that which composes a thing, and that from which it arises. Thus one can say in this sense that bronze is the cause of the statue, and silver is the cause of the phial; and one applies this way of speaking to all things of the same kind. (Material cause.) In a second sense, the cause is the form and the model of things; it is the essential character of the thing and its kind. Thus in music, the cause of the octave is the ratio 2:1, and, in a more general way, it is number; and with number, it is the part which enters into its definition. (Formal cause.) In a third sense, the cause is the source from which movement or rest comes. Thus he who, in a certain case, has given advice to act is the cause of the acts which are accomplished; the father is the cause of the child; and generally speaking that which acts is the cause of that which is done; that which produces a change is the cause of the change produced. (Efficient cause.) Fourthly, cause signifies the end and the goal of a thing. Thus health is the cause of walking. If we ask, "Why is he walking?" the answer is, "In order to be well," and when we say this, we believe that we have the cause of the walking. This meaning applies to all the intermediaries who contribute to the attainment of the final end, after the first mover has started the movement. For example, dieting and purgation, or drugs and the instruments of the surgeon can be regarded as means to health; and the only difference is that some are acts and others are instruments. (Final cause.)

These are briefly the meanings of the word cause. In accordance with this diversity of senses, a single thing can have several causes at the same time, and not simply. Thus, for the statue, one can assign to it as causes both the art of the sculptor who has made it and the bronze of which it is made and not in any other sense than as a statue. The two causes are not to be understood in the same sense; they differ in that one is the material and the other is the source of the movement. It is also because of this that there can be said to be things that are reciprocally the causes of each other. Thus exercise is the cause of health, and health is the cause of exercise; but not in the same sense, for, in the first case, health is the end, while in the second health is the source of the movement. Moreover, a single thing is at times the cause of opposite results; for, the same thing which is the cause of a given effect when it is present, can be the cause of an opposite effect when it is absent. For example, the absence of the pilot can be considered the cause of the loss of the ship, because the presence of the same pilot could have guaranteed its safety.

All the causes mentioned can be reduced to these four very obvious kinds. The letters of the alphabet are the cause of the syllables; the material is the cause of the things which art produces; fire and the other elements are the causes of the bodies which they compose; the parts are the cause of the whole, and the propositions are the causes of the conclusions which are drawn from them. Each of these is a cause since it is that out of which the other thing comes. Of these, the causes are either the subject of the thing, as parts relative to the whole; or the essential character of the thing, as the whole and the synthesis and the form; or the source of change or rest, as the germ, the physician, the giver of advice, and in general that which has effects; and finally, in the fourth place, the end and the good of other things; the attainment of the best is that for the sake of which the thing exists, and it would make no difference whether one said the real or the apparent good.

3. [Luck and Chance]

"Luck" and "pure spontaneous chance" are sometimes included in the list of explanatory factors, and many things are said to come about "as luck would have it" or "by chance." In what sense may luck and chance be included among the types of determining factor just enumerated? Further, is luck the same thing as pure chance or something different? And exactly what is each of them?

Some people question even their existence. Nothing, they declare, happens fortuitously; whatever we ascribe to luck or pure chance has been somehow determined. Take, for instance, the case of a man who goes to market and "as luck would have it" meets someone whom he wanted but did not expect to meet: his going to market, they say, was responsible for this. So they argue that of any other occurrence ascribed to luck there is always some more positive explanation to be found. Luck [they say] cannot have been the reason, for it would be paradoxical to regard luck as something real. Further, they consider it noteworthy that none of the ancient philosophers mentioned luck when discussing the reasons of becoming and perishing—an indication, apparently, that they disbelieved in the possibility of fortuitous occurrences.

Yet it is odd that while people theoretically accept the venerable argument which assumes that every chance happening and stroke of luck can be attributed to some reason or other, they nevertheless continue to speak of some things as matters of luck, others not. The earlier philosophers ought to have taken some account of this popular distinction, but among their various principles—love and strife, mind, fire, etc.—luck finds no place. The omission is equally surprising whether we suppose them to have disbelieved in luck or to have believed in but disregarded it; for at any rate they were not above employing the idea in their explanations. Empedocles, for example, remarks that air is sifted up into the sky not uniformly but "as it may chance"; or, in the words of his *Cosmogony*, "Now it 'happened' to run this way, now that." And the parts of animals, he declares, came to be what they are purely by chance.

Some go so far as to attribute the heavens and all the worlds to "chance happenings," declaring that the vortex— *i.e.,* the motion which separated and arranged the entire universe in its present order—arose "of itself." We may well be surprised at this assertion that while the existence and generation of animals and plants must be attributed not to chance but to nature or mind or something of the sort (what issues from a particular sperm or seed is obviously not a matter of chance, since from one kind of seed there comes forth an olive, from another a man), yet the heavens and the divinest of visible things have come into existence spontaneously and have no determining factors such as animals and plants have. Even if this were true, it would be something to give us pause, and ought to have elicited some comment. For apart from the generally paradoxical nature of such a theory it is rather odd that people should accept it when they can find no evidence of spontaneous

occurrences among celestial phenomena but plenty of such evidence among the things in which they deny the presence of chance. The evidence is just the opposite of what should have been expected if their theory were true.

There are other people who, while accepting luck as a determining factor of things, regard it as something divinely mysterious, inscrutable to human intelligence.

Accordingly we must investigate the nature of luck and chance, and see whether they are the same as each other or different, and how they fit into our classification of determining factors.

To begin with, when we see certain things occurring in a certain way either uniformly or "as a general rule," we obviously would not ascribe them to mere luck. A stroke of luck is not something that comes to pass either by uniform necessity or as a general rule. But as there is also a third sort of event which is found to occur, which everyone speaks of as being a matter of luck, and which we all know is meant when the word "lucky" is used, it is plain that such a thing as luck and "pure spontaneous chance" must exist.

Some events "serve a purpose," others do not. Of the former class, some are in accordance with the intention of the purposer, others not; but both are in the class of things that serve a purpose. Evidently, then, even among occurrences that are not the predictable (*i.e.,* neither the constant nor normal) results of anyone's actual intention, there are some which may be spoken of as serving a purpose. What serves a purpose may have originated either in thought or in nature: in either case when its occurrence is accidental[1] we call it a matter of luck. Just as everything has both an essential nature and a number of incidental attributes, so when anything is considered as a determining factor it may have similarly a twofold aspect. When a man builds a house, for instance, his faculty of house-building is the essential determinant of the house, while the fact that he is blond or cultured is only incidental to that result. The essential determinant can be calculated, but the incidentally related factors are incalculable, for any number of them may inhere in one subject.

As already explained, then, we attribute to chance or luck whatever happens [accidentally] in such a way as to serve a purpose. (The specific difference between chance and luck will be explained later; for the present it is enough to emphasize that both of them refer to actions that happen to serve a purpose.) As an illustration, suppose that we wish to solicit a man for a contribution of money. Had we known where he was we should have gone there and accosted him. But if with some other end in view we go to a place which it is not our invariable nor even our usual practice to visit, then, since the end effected (getting the money) is not a spontaneous process of nature, but is the type of thing that results from conscious choice and reflection, we describe the meeting as a stroke of luck. It would not be a matter of luck, however, if we were to visit the place for the express purpose of seeking our man, or if we regularly went there when taking up subscriptions. Luck, then, is evidently an incidental aspect of the real reason of something in the sphere of actions that involve purposive choice and reflection. Hence, since choice implies "intelligent reflection," we may conclude that luck and intelligent reflection both refer to the same sphere of things and activities. . . .

According as the result of a fortuitous action is good or bad we speak of good and bad luck. In more serious matters we use the terms "good fortune" and "misfortune"; and when we escape by a hair's breadth some great evil or just miss some great good we consider ourselves fortunate or unfortunate accordingly—the margin having been so slight that we can reflect upon the good or ill in question as if it were actually present. Moreover, as all luck is unstable (for nothing invariable or normal could be attributed to luck), we are right in regarding good fortune as also unstable.

Both luck and spontaneous chance, then as has been said, are determining factors in a purely incidental sense and are attributed to the type of occurrence which is neither constant nor normal and which might have been aimed at for its own sake.

The difference between luck and chance is that "chance" is the more inclusive term. Every case of luck is a case of chance, but not all cases of chance are cases of luck.

Luck, together with lucky or unlucky occurrences, is spoken of only in connection with agents that are capable of enjoying good [or ill] fortune and of

---

[1] *I.e.,* when in the case of deliberate actions the result is unforeseen, and when in the case of natural occurrences the result is neither certain nor usual.

performing moral actions. It follows, then, that luck always has some reference to conduct—a conclusion which is further enforced by the popular belief that "good fortune" is the same, or practically the same, as "happiness"; and that happiness, as it involves "well-doing," is a kind of "moral action." Hence only what is capable of moral conduct can perform actions that are lucky or the reverse. Luck does not pertain to the activities of a lifeless thing, a beast, or a child, for these exercise no "deliberate choice." If we call them lucky or unlucky we are speaking figuratively—as when Protarchus speaks of altar stones as fortunate because they are treated with reverence while their fellows are trampled underfoot. All such objects are affected by luck only in so far as a moral agent may deal with them in a manner that is lucky or unlucky [to himself].

"Pure spontaneous chance," on the other hand, is found both among the lower animals and in many lifeless things. We say of a horse, for example, that it went "by chance" to a place of safety, meaning that it was not for the sake of safety that it went there. Again, we say of a tripod that it fell onto its feet "by chance," because although it could then be used to sit on, it did not fall for sake of that.

[The distinction, then, may be summarized as follows.] We attribute to "pure chance" all those events which are such as ordinarily admit of a telic explanation, but which happen on this occasion to have been produced without any reference to the actual result. The word "luck," on the other hand, is restricted to that special type of chance events which (1) are possible objects of choice, and (2) affect persons capable of exercising choice. . . . The difference between chance and luck becomes clearest when applied to the productions of nature: when she produces a monster we attribute it to chance but we do not call nature unlucky. Even this, however, is not quite the same type of situation as that of the horse who chances to escape; for the horse's escape was due to factors independent of the horse, while the reasons for nature's miscarriages are private to herself.

Thus we have explained the meaning of, and distinction between, chance and luck. Both, it may be added, belong to the order of "propelling factors" or "sources of movement"; for the determining factors to which they are incidental are either natural forces or intelligent agents—the particular kinds of which are too numerous to mention.

Inasmuch as the results of chance and luck, while of a sort that nature or a conscious intelligence might well have intended, have in fact emerged as a purely incidental result of some determinative process, and as there can be nothing incidental without something prior for it to be incidental to, it is clear that an incidental connection presupposes a determinative relation that is authentic and direct. Chance and luck, then, presuppose intelligence and nature as determinative agents. Hence, however true it may be that the heavens are due to spontaneous chance, intelligence and nature must be the prior reasons, not only of many other things, but of this universe itself.

4. [The Meaning of Nature]

Some things exist by nature, some from other causes. Animals and their bodily organs, plants, and the physical elements—earth, fire, air, and water—such things as these we say exist "by nature." There is one particular in which all the objects just named are observed to differ from things that are not constituted by nature: each of them has within itself a principle of movement and rest—whether this movement be locomotion, or growth and decrease, or qualitative change. In such objects as beds and coats, on the other hand—provided we are speaking [not of their materials but] of the beds and coats themselves as products of craftwork—there is no inherent tendency to change. Of course, in respect of the stone or earth or composite matter of which such things are made, they do to that extent have such a tendency.[2] This, however, is a purely incidental aspect; [although it offers, to be sure, additional evidence that] what causes a thing to change or be at rest is its "nature"—*i.e.,* the nature that belongs to it primarily, not as an incidental attribute. As an illustration of what is meant by this last qualification, consider the case of a physician who cures himself. It would not be *quâ* patient that he possessed the art of healing; it would merely happen that in this exceptional case the same man was doctor and patient. So it is with all artificial products: none of them has within itself the principle of its own production. But while in some

[2] It is *quâ* wood or other heavy material that a bed tends to fall, not *quâ* bed.

cases (*e.g.,* a house or any other such product of manual labor) the moving principle resides in some external agent, there are also cases where the principle is found as an incidental attribute within the thing produced.

Since this is what is meant by "nature," anything may be said to "have a nature" so far as it possesses within itself a principle of the sort just described. Whatever possesses such a principle is "something substantial, a concrete thing"; for it is *subject* [to change], and subjects are what have inherent natures. We may note also the phrase "according to nature," which is applied not only to the things themselves but also their esential attributes. When, for example, fire is borne upwards, that phenomenon *is* not nature, nor does it *have* a nature, but it takes place *in accordance with nature.* This, then, is the distinction between nature, [existing] by nature, and [being or occurring] in accordance with nature.

5. [Teleology and Necessity in Nature]

We must now explain in what sense nature belongs to the class of telic determinants. Then we shall consider what is meant by necessity when spoken of with reference to natural phenomena; for people are constantly appealing to necessity as the cause of things, arguing that since the hot and the cold and all the other qualities are each of a certain definitive nature, the objects which they characterize must exist and be created by necessity. Even those who admit some further determining principle of things, such as Love and Strife, or Mind, do not consistently adhere to their explanations [but fall back upon the idea of necessity].

[With reference to our first question] it may be objected that nature does not act with reference to a goal nor by reason of the fact that one thing is better than another, but for the same reason that it rains—not to make the corn grow, but of necessity. When rain falls, so the argument runs, it is simply because the rising vapor has become cooled, and being cooled turns to water, which descends, causing the corn to grow; on the same basis as, when rain spoils the crops on the threshing-floor, we do not suppose that it fell for the sake of spoiling them but that it merely happened to do so. Why, then, should it not be the same with the organic parts of nature? Take the case of our teeth, for example—the front teeth sharp and suitable for tearing the food, the back ones broad and flat, suitable for grinding it—may they not have grown up thus by simple necessity,[3] and their adaptation to their respective functions be purely a coincidence? The same argument can be offered about any organic structure to which purpose is commonly ascribed; and it is further explained that where the organic structures happen to have been formed *as if* they had been arranged on purpose, the creatures which thus happen to be suitably organized have survived, while the others have perished—as Empedocles relates of his "man-faced ox-creatures."

[3] *I.e.,* by virtue of material and efficient determinants [causes] only, and without reference to any telic determinant [final cause].

While these and similar arguments may cause difficulties, they certainly do not represent the truth. For in the first place, (1) teeth and all other natural phenomena come about in a certain way if not invariably at least normally, and this is inconsistent with the meaning of luck or chance. We do not appeal to luck or coincidence in explaining the frequency of rain in winter nor of heat in mid-summer; we would, however, if the situation were to be reversed. As every occurrence must be ascribed either to coincidence or to purpose, if such cases as the foregoing cannot be ascribed to coincidence or chance, they must be ascribed to purpose. But since even our opponents will admit that all such occurrences are natural events, it follows that there is such a thing as purpose in nature and its processes.

(2) Furthermore, [in any human art or technique] where there is an end to be achieved, the first and each succeeding step of the operation are performed for the sake of that end. As in human operations, so in the processes of nature; and as in nature, so in each human undertaking—unless there is something to interfere. Human operations, however, are for the sake of an end; hence natural processes must be so too. If a house, for example, had been a natural product it would have been made by the same successive stages as it passed through when made by human technique; and if natural objects could be duplicated artificially it would be by the same series of steps as now produce them in nature. In art and in nature alike each stage is for the sake of the one that follows; for generally speaking, human technique either gives the

finishing touches to what nature has had to leave incomplete, or else imitates her. Hence, if the operations that constitute a human technique are for the sake of an end, it is clear that this must be no less true of natural processes. The relation of earlier to later terms of the series is the same for both.

(3) This is most clearly true in the case of the lower animals, whose behavior is admittedly independent of any conscious technique or experimentation or deliberation—so much so, in fact, that it is debated whether the work of spiders, ants, and the like is due to intelligence or to some other faculty. Passing gradually down the scale we find that plants too produce organs subservient to their "natural end": leaves, for instance, are put forth to provide shade for the fruit. Hence, if it is both "by nature" and also "for a purpose" that the swallow builds its nest and the spider its web, and that plants put forth leaves for the sake of the fruit and push down rather than up with their roots for the sake of nourishment, it is evident that the type of determining factor which we have called telic is operative in the objects and processes of nature.

[What, then, is a telic determinant?] Consider first that nature exists under a twofold aspect—as "composed of materials" and "as consisting in the ways in which things are shaping up"; that by the second of these aspects is meant "the perfected results at which processes tend to arrive," and that all the earlier stages in any process are for the sake of such perfected results [*i.e.,* are telically determined by them]: it follows that the telic determinant of a thing is nothing other than the "way in which it tends to shape up" [*i.e.,* its "form"].

No human technique is free from error: the man of letters makes mistakes in grammar, and the physician may administer a wrong dose. Hence it is not surprising that there should be errors in the processes of nature too. Just as in the arts and other human techniques there are certain procedures which correctly serve their specific ends, while to aim at such ends and miss them is to fail; so it presumably is with nature, and what we call freaks are simply failures or errors in respect of nature's proper ends. . . .

[A consequence of Empedocles' theory[4]] is that it would be entirely a matter of chance what might spring up from a given seed. But such an assertion would be a denial of nature and of the whole natural order. For we call anything "natural" when by virtue of an "initiating principle" inherent in itself it progresses continuously toward some goal. Such principles do not all make for the same goal, nor, on the other hand, is the goal picked at random; but each inner principle makes always for the same goal of its own, if nothing interferes. There are other cases, to be sure, where a certain end, as well as the means of attaining it, may come about entirely by luck. Thus we call it a stroke of luck that a stranger should come and before departing pay the ransom; for the ransom is paid just as if payment of it had been the stranger's

---

[4] That "man headed ox-creatures" and countless other such combinations originally arose at random, but being ill-adapted did not survive.

purpose in coming, although actually it was not. In this case the result achieved is incidental [to the stranger's real purpose in coming]; since luck, as we have already explained, is incidental causation. But when a certain result is achieved either invariably or normally, it is no incidental or merely lucky occurrence; and in the processes of nature each result is achieved if not invariably at least normally, provided nothing hinders.

There are some who deny the existence of purpose in nature on the ground that they can never detect the physical force in the act of deliberating. Such an argument is illogical, for human techniques also may be carried on without deliberation. Yet if the shipbuilding art were inherent in the timber the construction of the ship would then proceed naturally in the same way as it now proceeds by human skill—showing that if purpose is inherent in human techniques it must inhere in nature too.

The processes of nature are best illustrated by the case of a doctor who doctors himself. Nature similarly is agent and patient at once.

In conclusion, it is clear that nature is a "determining principle," whose manner of determination is telic.

As for necessity, does it exist conditionally or unconditionally? People tend to think of necessity as something inherent in the process of production; which is pretty much as if they should suppose that a wall might be built by [an accidental conjunction of] necessary forces—*i.e.,* that as heavy things are naturally borne downward and light things toward the top, so the stones and

foundations would necessarily fall to the lowest place, the earth more lightly rising above, and the wood, because it was lightest of all, forming the roof. But while it is true that the wall cannot be built unless these materials [with their respective properties] are present; still, being only its material conditions, they will not suffice to account for the completed wall, which is brought into existence for the sake of sheltering us and protecting our goods. And so with all other cases of working toward an end: although the end cannot be attained without certain materials possessing definitive properties, these are only the material precondition of its attainment; properly speaking, what brings it into existence is a certain purpose. Suppose, for example, we were to ask why a saw is what it is. In order that it may perform a certain work and thereby serve a certain end, we should reply. But [let us suppose] this work cannot be performed unless the saw is made of iron. We may then declare that if it is to be truly a saw and perform its function it "must necessarily" be made of iron. Necessity, then, is conditional. It is not of the same order as the end; for while necessity resides only in the "material preconditions," the "end or purpose" is found in the definition. . . .

From the foregoing analogy it is plain that when we speak of necessity we are referring to the "material aspect" of nature and the changes proper to that aspect. While the natural scientist must deal with the material aspect too, his primary concern is with the "purposive aspect"; for the goal may determine the material changes, but these do not determine the goal. The principle that determines the goal, or inherent purpose, of a thing is to be found in its meaning and definition. In the case of human techniques, when we have determined what kind of a house we want, certain materials must then "of necessity" be either had or got in order to build it; and when we have determined what we mean by health, certain things become necessary in order to secure it. [So it is with nature]: if man has a certain meaning, certain antecedent conditions are requisite to his existence, and these conditions will in turn presuppose others.

From another point of view we may refer necessity to the definition of a thing. For if we define sawing as a particular kind of scission, it will follow that this cannot be accomplished unless the saw possesses teeth of a particular character, and to have such a character the teeth must be made of iron. The definition, no less than the physical object, contains parts which are, so to speak, its matter.

COMMENT

Aristotle's Basic Concepts

Aristotle employs certain key concepts that must be understood if we are to grasp his argument. Perhaps the most important of these concepts are *substance* and *attributes, matter* and *form, potentiality* and *actuality,* the *four causes,* and *motion.* His interpretation of these concepts in itself constitutes a very penetrating analysis of the nature of reality.

1. SUBSTANCE AND ATTRIBUTES. Aristotle distinguishes a "primary" and a "secondary" meaning of substance. In the primary sense, a substance is an absolutely individual thing: *this* man, *this* dog, *this* apple, *this* rock. In the secondary sense, a substance is a *class* of things, such as "man," "dog," "apple," "rock"—one of the kinds of things that we find in nature and that we note in describing and classifying objects. In both senses, a substance is distinguished from the changeable qualities that attach to things.

The changing characteristics of the substance are called its attributes. They are *universals* in the sense that they can apply to an indefinite number of particular things. For example, the attribute of being musical can apply to many human beings. Aristotle did not suppose, as Plato apparently did, that universals have an existence or being apart from particular things. The universal is simply the characteristic common to all members of the group—as, for example, redness is to be found in all red things. The theory that universals are *in* things gives an empirical tone to Aristotle's thought. Science, he believed, has no need for pure disembodied forms, unrealized in the actual world. It should be observational in method, finding those attributes or universals that are actually in things.

2. MATTER AND FORM. Primary substances can be analyzed into two constituent factors, matter and form. Matter is the stuff of which the thing consists, and this stuff may be the same in kind as the stuff of which quite different things consist. Thus gold is the stuff out of which rings, bracelets, watch casings, and many other things are made. This conception of matter is extended beyond any merely physical stuff. For example, psychological dispositions are the matter out of which a man's character is formed, and various propositions are the matter out of which an argument is made.

The form is the determination or organization given to the matter. Wherever there is matter there is form, and wherever there is form there is matter. The concepts of matter and form are relative—what is form from one standpoint is matter from another standpoint. A piece of lumber, for example, has a certain form—namely, a shape or structure. But the lumber, in turn, is the matter used, for example, in making a table, and the table, with its form, is matter used in furnishing a home. One can even think of homes as matter out of which a city is made, and of cities as matter that enters into the larger form of a nation.

In a primary substance, the matter and form are thought of as combined to make an individual thing. The substance is *this* matter combined with *this* form to make this particular entity. But matter and form can also be conceived generically. For example, flesh and bones, in general, are the matter out of which human bodies, in general, are made.

3. POTENTIALITY AND ACTUALITY. Thus far we have been looking at substances statically. If we now look at them dynamically—as moving, changing things—we also have a twofold division: *potentiality,* what *may* be, and *actuality,* what *is.* Of a given acorn we can say, this is not *actually* an oak, but it is *potentially* an oak. When once the development is complete, we can say that the oak tree is an actuality.

Potentiality is related to matter and actuality is related to form. Matter has the potentiality of being shaped into a certain form. Lumber, for example, has the potentiality of becoming a table, a door, a fence, etc. But when the lumber takes on the form of the completed thing, we can say that a certain potentiality has been actualized. This conception of development from the potential to the actual imparts a certain characteristic flavor to Aristotle's metaphysics. Whereas Plato was primarily interested in *being,* the static and enduring, Aristotle was more interested in *becoming,* the change and development everywhere going on in nature.

Since potentiality involves what *may* be, and since matter usually has many potentialities, matter is more indeterminate than form; but it is not utterly amorphous and indeterminate. A male baby, for example, is potentially a man but not an elephant, umbrella, volcano, or a woman. The potentiality of a thing is limited by its real characteristics and tendencies.

4. THE FOUR CAUSES. The conception of reality involved in these antitheses of matter and form and actuality and potentiality finds more detailed expression in the doctrine of the four causes. Aristotle used the word "cause" in a broad sense to include any "why or wherefore"—any factor that makes a thing what it is. A complete explanation requires a statement of all four causes: (*a*) the *material* cause, or the elements out of which the thing is made; (*b*) the *formal* cause, or the mold into which the material is put; (*c*) the *efficient* cause, or the means by which the change is wrought; and (*d*) the *final* cause, or the end for which the process occurs.

There is a tendency for the formal, efficient, and final causes to coalesce. In the building of a house, the *plan* of the house is the formal cause, this plan as it exists in the mind of the architect or builder is part of the efficient cause, and the plan as the end to be achieved in the completed house is the final cause. Similarly, in the growth of a tree, the form of the fully developed tree is the final and formal cause, and the parent tree, which exhibits the form, is the efficient cause. The material cause, on the other hand, is the relatively independent and passive factor, having a potentiality without power to actualize itself until it is acted upon by the final-formal-efficient cause.

5. MOTION. The effect of the propelling causes upon the matter is to set up a "motion" which forces the matter to assume a specific form. Motion is thus the actualization of potentiality. This is a broader meaning than we give to the term "motion" at the present time: it includes not only change of place (motion in our modern sense) but change in quality and quantity.

Since motion is matter taking on form, the form must be lacking in the matter before the motion takes place. This lack is called *privation*. For example, if a person *becomes* wise, he is unwise in the beginning, and thus lack of wisdom is the privation presupposed by the motion. Whenever a potentiality is actualized, it can be taken for granted that the actuality was lacking at the start.

Motion may be either artificial or natural. The motion is artificial if the form is imposed upon the matter by some external force or agency. A piece of gold, for example, will not spontaneously form itself into a bracelet but must be wrought into this shape by a craftsman. On the other hand, a motion is natural if it results from an inherent tendency in the matter. An acorn, for example, naturally tends to grow into a tree, and a gaseous body naturally tends to expand into a larger and more diffuse shape.

The Teleological Interpretation of Reality

Having defined the key concepts in Aristotle's philosophy, we are in a position to formulate his theory of teleology. A teleological interpretation of reality emphasizes the role of final causes. It thus differs from mechanism—the doctrine that all phenomena are totally explicable in terms of physically efficient causes. In the next chapter, we shall consider the theory that the world can be explained in terms of moving atoms and the void. Aristotle was thoroughly opposed to this type of mechanistic theory, maintaining that motions can be fully explained only in terms of ends or purposes.

He begins by distinguishing between "nature" and "art," a distinction corresponding to natural and artificial motions. *Nature,* in one sense of the term, is an *inherent* tendency to bring about change. Thus the tendency of a seed to germinate and grow is part of its nature, and the tendency of smoke to rise and spread is part of *its* nature. *Art,* on the other hand, is the activity of an *external* agent in imposing form upon matter. When a doctor, by the use of medicines, makes his patients well, he is practicing the art of medicine, and when a tailor, by cutting and sewing cloth, makes a suit of clothes, he is practicing the art of tailoring. Aristotle remarks that we also give the name of nature to the products of nature, and the name of art to the products of art.

It is fairly obvious that human art must be explained, in part, teleologically. The doctor treats his patients for the sake of health, and the painter creates his pictures for the sake of beauty. Most human activities are goal-seeking and hence can be fully explained only in terms of final causes. But Aristotle believes that even the "art" of animals—such as that of the bee in making its honeycomb or the beaver in building its dam—is instinctively goal-directed; and that nature—the inherent tendency of a thing to actualize its potentialities—is likewise teleological. This does not mean that *every* characteristic of an animal can be explained teleologically. Whereas an eye, as a functional organ, must be explained by reference to its end or function, the particular color of the eye is the result of non-teleological causes (since blue and brown eyes can see equally well).

Although Aristotle believed that we should not always look for a final cause, his approach to the problems of organic life was primarily teleological. He maintained that final causes, for the biologist, are generally more important than merely material or efficient causes. The earlier phases of a natural process must be explained by the later, by the climax or culmination; the organ must be explained by its function, the body by the life that it sustains, and the life of each species must be understood by reference to the highest level it ever attains. Thus the end, or final cause, of each species is to realize the fully developed characteristics of that form, that kind of being. The basic structure of an animal is not due to the purpose of the *individual* animal but to a kind of vital force that impels it to realize the development characteristic of its *type.* Although described as acting for a purpose, nature is not a conscious agent but a kind of unconscious inner drive or propulsion.

The principal mistake of earlier Greek scientists and philosophers, Aristotle declared, is that they sought material and efficient causes to the neglect of formal and final causes. In one sphere, however, Aristotle himself recognized that final causes are inoperative. This is the realm of coincidence. For example, when a flower seed that has begun to germinate is swept away by a flooding stream, we should not try to explain this event teleologically but should rather attribute it to coincidence, the accidental meeting of two or more chains of causation. In the example cited, one set of causes led to the germination of the seed by the brink of the stream; another set of causes brought the spring rains and the consequent flooding; and the two chains fortuitously merged in the sweeping away of the seed, thus frustrating a normal natural result, namely, the growth of a flower.

When a coincidence serves or defeats a purpose, it is called by Aristotle a case of *luck* or *chance*. The word "chance" is the more inclusive term: "Every case of luck is a case of chance, but not all cases of chance are cases of luck." If a person, while shopping, accidentally meets a long-sought friend, this is good luck—because the meeting happens to serve a purpose. But if he accidentally meets someone he wishes to avoid, this is bad luck, since it frustrates a purpose. Without *conscious* motives, which are accidentally served or impeded, there can be no good or bad luck. But "chance," a wider term, applies not only to cases of luck but also to coincidences that abet or hinder *unconscious* teleological tendencies. When an animal, incapable of conscious purposiveness, accidentally moves out of the way of an advancing avalanche, we should call this a fortunate chance rather than "good luck." Both chance and luck are not *actually* teleological but *seemingly* so: they do not happen as a result of teleological tendencies but aid or hinder these tendencies.

The climax of Aristotle's teleological theory of reality is to be found in his conception of God as "the Unmoved Mover." As the highest and best of beings, God is the unchanging source of all changes—"an eternal Thinker eternally thinking the selfsame eternal thoughts." Hence He does not act as a providential God, answering prayers and intervening in particular circumstances. Instead, He acts as a final cause—"the object of the world's desire." His function is to impart motion to the whole order by serving as a kind of supreme goal. Nature has a tendency to move toward God, who acts, so to speak, as a kind of magnet. In addition to the Unmoved Mover, there are subordinate intelligences (like the angels of Christian theology) which aspire toward God and move the heavenly spheres.

Some Critical Questions

One of the "enduring questions" of philosophy is whether and to what extent events should be explained teleologically. No one today would defend all the details of Aristotle's teleological interpretation of reality. Nevertheless, most psychologists, social scientists, and philosophers maintain that we must refer to goals and purposes in explaining much of human behavior. Purposiveness is so characteristic of human beings that the person who seems to lack a goal is denounced as a "drifter" or "ne'er do well." To deny that purposes ever operate in human life verges on the absurd or contradictory. Whitehead somewhere remarks that scientists animated by the *purpose* of proving that they are purposeless constitute an interesting subject for study.

Moreover, there certainly appears to be teleological activity at the subhuman level; for example:

> . . . when a dog hides an unfinished bone in a very unusual place; . . . when rooks take fresh-water mussels to a great height and let them fall on the single shingle beneath so that they are broken; when a mother weasel, accompanied by one of her offspring, about to be overtaken on the links, seizes the youngster in her mouth, dashes on ahead, and lays it in a sandy hole; when beavers cut a canal right through a large island in a river; when mares, some past foaling, unite to lift up between them a number of foals on the occasion of a great flood.[1]

Such illustrations can be multiplied indefinitely, and they certainly suggest that human purposes have their instinctive counterparts in animals.

On the other hand, Aristotle's conception of unconscious teleology, especially at the level of plants and lower animals, is paradoxical. One can certainly question the notion of purpose that is not the purpose of any mind. Of course, in a purely temporal sense, there is an end to every process. In this sense, the full development of the oak is the end toward which the acorn moves. But it is hazardous to interpret this temporal finis as a goal or end in a teleological sense. Whereas a conscious purpose acts as a cause and helps to realize itself, there appears to be no reason to suppose that a temporal end, such as the culminating phase of a tree's growth, is actually operating as a cause to bring about its own realization.

The functional adaptation of organisms to their environments is not necessarily a sign of the operation of final causes. Darwin advanced an alternative explanation. All plants and animals, he maintained, multiply more rapidly than the means of subsistence, and therefore many perish. Most of those that survive are in some way better fitted to cope with their environments than the perishing. Their greater life span is the result of fortunate chance variations which are transmitted, through heredity, to their offspring. The accumulation of such variations, generation after generation, gradually produces a change in type, perhaps the evolution of a new species. Consequently, there is adaptation without design, an appearance of purposiveness without purpose, a seeming teleology in which there is no more ultimate explanation than the sifting out of the functional from the unfunctional by a mechanical process of selection. Whether natural selection without teleology is sufficient to account for evolution is one of the great questions of science.

[1] J. Arthur Thompson, *The System of Animate Nature* (New York: Holt, 1920), I, pp. 335–336.

Finally, Aristotle's belief that God is "the object of the world's desire" seems to require elucidation. How literally are we to understand his language? Does fire as it darts upward aspire toward divinity? Do the stars in their courses yearn toward God, and is this the reason for their motion? Obviously there are difficulties in any such interpretation. One of the classic arguments for God—that nature exhibits a design which implies God as a designer—is somewhat akin to Aristotle's view of the Unmoved Mover; but it leads to the conception of God as an artificer and not merely as a final cause. In Chapter 15, we shall review this question of the relation to God to design and purpose in nature.

Most twentieth-century philosophers are wary of the Design Argument. In addition, they would not accept teleological explanations of inorganic things. "There are no failures among the stars," as Susanne Langer observes. "Rocks have no interests. The oceans roar for nothing."[2] Some philosophers have tended to interpret animals and even human beings as exceedingly complicated machines, akin to electronic computers.[3] Whether and to what extent life should be interpreted teleogically remains a live issue.

[2] *Mind: An Essay on Human Feeling* (Baltimore: Johns Hopkins Press, 1967), I, p. 220.
[3] See also A. R. Anderson (editor), *Minds and Machines* (Englewood Cliffs, N.J.: Prentice-Hall, 1964).

3

Materialism

TITUS LUCRETIUS CARUS (95?–52? B.C.)

We know nothing certain about the life of Lucretius. St. Jerome, a hostile critic, declared that he had fits of madness, composed his poem during intervals of sanity, and killed himself in his forty-fourth year. This report, as George Santayana has remarked, must be taken with a large grain of salt. From his book we discover that he revered Epicurus, detested religious superstition, and delighted in the bounty of nature.

On the Nature
of the Universe

1. [*Prayer to the creative force of Nature (personified as Venus) to inspire the poet, to bless his patron Memmius, and to bring peace to the world.*]

Translated by Robert Latham. Penguin Books, 1951. Reprinted by permission of Penguin Books, Ltd., Harmondsworth, Middlesex.

Mother of Aeneas and his race, delight of men and gods, life-giving

Venus, it is your doing that under the wheeling constellations of the sky all nature teems with life, both the sea that buoys up our ships and the earth that yields our food. Through you all living creatures are conceived and come forth to look upon the sunlight. Before you the winds flee, and at your coming the clouds forsake the sky. For you the inventive earth flings up sweet flowers. For you the ocean levels laugh, the sky is calmed and glows with diffused radiance. When first the day puts on the aspect of spring, when in all its force the fertilizing breath of Zephyr is unleashed, then, great goddess, the birds of air give the first intimation of your entry; for yours is the power that has pierced them to the heart. Next the cattle run wild, frisk through the lush pastures and swim the swift-flowing streams. Spell-bound by your charm, they follow your lead with fierce desire. So throughout seas and uplands, rushing torrents, verdurous meadows and the leafy shelters of the birds, into the breasts of one and all you instil alluring love, so that with passionate longing they reproduce their several breeds.

Since you alone are the guiding power of the universe and without you nothing emerges into the shining sunlit world to grow in joy and loveliness, yours is the partnership I seek in striving to compose these lines *On the Nature of the Universe* for my noble Memmius. For him, great goddess, you have willed outstanding excellence in every field and everlasting fame. For his sake, therefore, endow my verse with everlasting charm.

Meanwhile, grant that this brutal business of war by sea and land may everywhere be lulled to rest. For you alone have power to bestow on mortals the blessing of quiet peace. In your bosom Mars himself, supreme commander in this brutal business, flings himself down at times, laid low by the irremediable wound of love. Gazing upward, his neck a prostrate column, he fixes hungry eyes on you, great goddess, and gluts them with love. As he lies outstretched, his breath hangs upon your lips. Stoop, then, goddess most glorious, and enfold him at rest in your hallowed bosom and whisper with those lips sweet words of prayer, beseeching for the people of Rome untroubled peace. In this evil hour of my country's history, I cannot pursue my task with a mind at ease, as an illustrious scion of the house of Memmius cannot at such a crisis withhold his service from the common weal.

2. [*Exhortation to Memmius to listen to an exhortation of "true reason."*]

For what is to follow, my Memmius, lay aside your cares and lend undistracted ears and an attentive mind to true reason. Do not scornfully reject, before you have understood them, the gifts I have marshalled for you with zealous devotion. I will set out to discourse to you on the ultimate realities of heaven and the gods. I will reveal those *atoms* from which nature creates all things and increases and feeds them and into which, when they perish, nature again resolves them. To these in my discourse I commonly give such names as the 'raw material', or 'generative bodies' or 'seeds' of things. Or I may call them 'primary particles', because they come first and everything else is composed of them.

3. [*Praise of Epicurus for delivering mankind from superstition.*]

When human life lay groveling in all men's sight, crushed to the earth under the dead weight of superstition whose grim features loured menacingly upon mortals from the four quarters of the sky, a man of Greece was first to raise mortal eyes in defiance, first to stand erect and brave the challenge. Fables of the gods did not crush him, nor the lightning flash and the growling menace of the sky. Rather, they quickened his manhood, so that he, first of all men, longed to smash the constraining locks of nature's doors. The vital vigour of his mind prevailed. He ventured far out beyond the flaming ramparts of the world and voyaged in mind throughout infinity. Returning victorious, he proclaimed to us what can be and what cannot: how a limit is fixed to the power of everything and an immovable frontier post. Therefore superstition in its turn lies crushed beneath his feet, and we by his triumph are lifted level with the skies.

4. [*Superstition, its cause and cure.*]

One thing that worries me is the fear that you may fancy yourself embarking on an impious course, setting your feet on the path of sin. Far from it. More often it is this very superstition that is the mother of sinful and impious deeds.

Remember how at Aulis the altar of the Virgin Goddess was foully stained with the blood of Iphigeneia by the leaders of the Greeks, the patterns of chivalry. The headband was bound about her virgin tresses and hung down evenly over both her cheeks. Suddenly she caught sight of her father standing sadly in front of the altar, the attendants beside him hiding the knife and her people bursting into tears when they saw her. Struck dumb with terror, she sank on her knees to the ground. Poor girl, at such a moment it did not help her that she had been first to give the name of father to a king. Raised by the hands of men, she was led trembling to the altar. Not for her the sacrament of marriage and the loud chant of Hymen. It was her fate in the very hour of marriage to fall a sinless victim to a sinful rite, slaughtered to her greater grief by a father's hand, so that a fleet might sail under happy auspices. Such are the heights of wickedness to which men are driven by superstition.

You yourself, if you surrender your judgement at any time to the blood-curdling declamations of the prophets, will want to desert our ranks. Only think what phantoms they can conjure up to overturn the tenor of your life and wreck your happiness with fear. And not without cause. For, if men saw that a term was set to their troubles, they would find strength in some way to withstand the hocus-pocus and intimidations of the prophets. As it is, they have no power of resistance, because they are haunted by the fear of eternal punishment after death. They know nothing of the nature of the spirit. Is it born, or is it implanted in us at birth? Does it perish with us, dissolved by death, or does it visit the murky depths and dreary sloughs of Hades? Or is it transplanted by divine power into other creatures, as described in the poems of our own Ennius, who first gathered on the delectable slopes of Helicon an evergreen garland destined to win renown among the nations of Italy? Ennius indeed in his immortal verses proclaims that there is also a Hell, which is peopled not by our actual spirits or bodies but only by shadowy images, ghastly pale. It is from this realm that he pictures the ghost of Homer, of unfading memory, as appearing to him, shedding salt tears and revealing the nature of the universe.

I must therefore give an account of celestial phenomena, explaining the movements of sun and moon and also the forces that determine events on earth. Next, and no less important, we must look with keen insight into the make-up of spirit and mind: we must consider those alarming phantasms that strike upon our minds when they are awake but disordered by sickness, or when they are buried in slumber, so that we seem to see and hear before us men whose dead bones lie in the embraces of earth.

I am well aware that it is not easy to elucidate in Latin verse the obscure discoveries of the Greeks. The poverty of our language and the novelty of the theme compel me often to coin new words for the purpose. But your merit and the joy I hope to derive from our delightful friendship encourage me to face any task however hard. This it is that leads me to stay awake through the quiet of the night, studying how by choice of words and the poet's art I can display before your mind a clear light by which you can gaze into the heart of hidden things.

5. [*Nothing is ever created out of nothing.*]

This dread and darkness of the mind cannot be dispelled by the sunbeams, the shining shafts of day, but only by an understanding of the outward form and inner workings of nature. In tackling this theme, our starting-point will be this principle: *Nothing can ever be created by divine power out of nothing.* The reason why all mortals are so gripped by fear is that they see all sorts of things happening on the earth and in the sky with no discernible cause, and these they attribute to the will of a god. Accordingly, when we have seen that nothing can be created out of nothing, we shall then have a clearer picture of the path ahead, the problem of how things are created and occasioned without the aid of the gods.

First then, if things were made out of nothing, any species could spring from any source and nothing would require seed. Men could arise from the sea and scaly fish from the earth, and birds could be hatched out of the sky. Cattle and other domestic animals and every kind of wild beast, multiplying indiscriminately, would occupy cultivated and waste lands alike. The same fruits would not grow constantly on the same trees, but they would keep changing: any tree might bear any fruit. If each species were not composed of its own generative bodies, why should each be born always of the same kind of mother? Actually, since each is formed out of specific seeds, it is born and emerges into the sunlit world only from a place where there exists the right material, the right kind of atoms. This is why everything cannot be born of everything, but a specific power of generation inheres in specific objects.

Again, why do we see roses appear in spring, grain in summer's heat, grapes under the spell of autumn? Surely, because it is only after specific seeds have drifted together at their own proper time that every created thing stands revealed, when the season is favourable and the life-giving earth can safely deliver delicate growths into the sunlit world. If they were made out of nothing, they would spring up suddenly after varying lapses of time and at abnormal seasons, since there would of course be no primary bodies which could be prevented by the harshness of the season from entering into generative unions. Similarly, in order that things might grow, there would be no need of any lapse of time for the accumulation of seed. Tiny tots would turn suddenly into grown men, and trees would shoot up spontaneously out of the earth. But it is obvious that none of these things happens, since everything grows gradually, as is natural, from a specific seed and retains its specific character. It is a fair inference that each is increased and nourished by its own raw material.

Here is a further point. Without seasonable showers the earth cannot send up gladdening growths. Lacking food, animals cannot reproduce their kind or sustain life. This points to the conclusion that many elements are common to many things, as letters are to words, rather than to the theory that anything can come into existence without atoms.

Or again, why has not nature been able to produce men on such a scale that they could ford the ocean on foot or demolish high mountains with their hands or prolong their lives over many generations? Surely, because each thing requires for its birth a particular material which determines what can be produced. It must therefore be admitted that nothing can be made out of nothing, because everything must be generated from a seed before it can emerge into the unresisting air.

Lastly, we see that tilled plots are superior to untilled, and their fruits are improved by cultivation. This is because the earth contains certain atoms which we rouse to productivity by turning the fruitful clods with the ploughshare and stirring up the soil. But for these, you would see great improvements arising spontaneously without any aid from our labours.

6. [*Nothing is ever annihilated.*]

The second great principle is this: *nature resolves everything into its component atoms and never reduces anything to nothing.* If anything were perishable in all its parts, anything might perish all of a sudden and vanish from sight. There would be no need of any force to separate its parts and loosen their links. In actual fact, since everything is composed of indestructible seeds, nature obviously does not allow anything to perish till it has encountered a force that shatters it with a blow or creeps into chinks and unknits it.

If the things that are banished from the scene by age are annihilated through the exhaustion of their material, from what source does Venus bring back the several races of animals into the light of life? And, when they are brought back, where does the inventive earth find for each the special food required for its sustenance and growth? From what fount is the sea replenished by its native springs and the streams that flow into it from afar? Whence does the ether draw nutriment for the stars? For everything consisting of a mortal body must have been exhausted by the long day of time, the illimitable past. If throughout this bygone eternity there have persisted bodies from which the universe has been perpetually renewed, they must certainly be possessed of immortality. Therefore things cannot be reduced to nothing.

Again, all objects would regularly be destroyed by the same force and the same cause, were it not that they are sustained by imperishable matter more or less tightly fastened together. Why, a mere touch would be enough to bring about destruction supposing there were no imperishable bodies whose union could be dissolved only by the appropriate force. Actually, because the fastenings of the atoms are of various kinds while their matter is imperishable, compound objects remain intact until one of them encounters a force that proves strong enough to break up its particular constitution. Therefore nothing returns to nothing, but everything is resolved into its constituent bodies.

Lastly, showers perish when father ether has flung them down into the lap of mother earth. But the crops spring up fresh and gay; the branches on the trees burst into leaf; the trees themselves grow and are weighed down with fruit. Hence in turn man and brute draw nourishment. Hence we see flourishing cities blest with children and every leafy thicket loud with new broods of songsters. Hence in lush pastures cattle wearied by their bulk fling down their bodies, and the white milky juice oozes from their swollen udders. Hence a new generation frolic friskily on wobbly legs through the fresh grass, their young minds tipsy with undiluted milk. Visible objects therefore do not perish utterly, since nature repairs one thing from another and allows nothing to be born without the aid of another's death.

7. [*Matter exists in the form of invisible particles (atoms).*]

Well, Memmius, I have taught you that things cannot be created out of nothing nor, once born be summoned back to nothing. Perhaps, however, you are becoming mistrustful of my words, because these atoms of mine are not visible to the eye. Consider, therefore, this further evidence of *bodies whose existence you must acknowledge though they cannot be seen.* First, wind, when its force is roused, whips up waves, founders tall ships and scatters cloud-rack. Sometimes scouring plains with hurricane force it strews them with huge trees and batters mountain peaks with blasts that hew down forests. Such is wind in its fury, when it whoops aloud with a mad menace in its shouting. Without question, therefore, there must be invisible particles of wind which sweep sea and land and the clouds in the sky, swooping upon them and whirling them along in a headlong hurricane. In the way they flow and the havoc they spread they are no different from a torrential flood of water when it rushes down in a sudden spate from the mountain heights, swollen by heavy rains, and heaps together wreckage from the forest and entire trees. Soft though it is by nature, the sudden shock of oncoming water is more than even stout bridges can withstand, so furious is the force with which the turbid, storm-flushed torrent surges against their piers. With a mighty roar it lays them low, rolling huge rocks under its waves and brushing aside every obstacle from its course. Such, therefore, must be the movement of blasts of wind also. When they have come surging along some course like a rushing river, they push obstacles before them and buffet them with repeated blows; and sometimes, eddying round and round, they snatch them up and carry them along in a swiftly circling vortex. Here then is proof upon proof that winds have invisible bodies, since in their actions and behaviour they are found to rival great rivers, whose bodies are plain to see.

Then again, we smell the various scents of things though we never see them approaching our nostrils. Similarly, heat and cold cannot be detected by our eyes, and we do not see sounds. Yet all these must be composed of bodies, since they are able to impinge upon our senses. For nothing can touch or be touched except body.

Again, clothes hung out on a surf-beaten shore grow moist. Spread in the sun they grow dry. But we do not see how the moisture has soaked into them, nor again how it has been dispelled by the heat. It follows that the moisture is split up into minute parts which the eye cannot possibly see.

Again, in the course of many annual revolutions of the sun a ring is worn thin next to the finger with continual rubbing. Dripping water hollows a stone. A curved ploughshare, iron though it is, dwindles imperceptibly in the furrow. We see the cobble-stones of the highway worn by the feet of many wayfarers. The bronze statues by the city gates show their right hands worn thin by the touch of travellers who have greeted them in passing. We see that all these are being diminished, since they are worn away. But to perceive what particles drop off at any particular time is a power grudged to us by our ungenerous sense of sight.

To sum up, whatever is added to things gradually by nature and the passage of days, causing a cumulative increase, eludes the most attentive scrutiny of our eyes. Conversely, you cannot see what objects lose by the wastage of age—sheer sea-cliffs, for instance, exposed to prolonged erosion by the mordant brine—or at what time the loss occurs. It follows that nature works through the agency of invisible bodies.

8. [*Besides matter, the universe contains empty space (vacuity).*]

On the other hand, things are not hemmed in by the pressure of solid bodies in a tight mass. This is because *there is vacuity in things.* A grasp of this fact will be helpful to you in many respects and will save you from much bewildered doubting and questioning about the universe and from mistrust of my teaching. Well then, by vacuity I mean intangible and empty space. If it did not exist, things could not move at all. For the distinctive action of matter, which is counteraction and obstruction, would be in force always and everywhere. Nothing could proceed, because nothing would give it a starting-point by receding. As it is, we see with our own eyes at sea and on land and high up in the sky that all sorts of things in all sorts of ways are on the move. If there were no empty space, these things would be denied the power of restless movement—or rather, they could not possibly have come into existence, embedded as they would have been in motionless matter.

Besides, there are clear indications that things that pass for solid are in fact porous. Even in rocks a trickle of water seeps through into caves, and copious drops ooze from every surface. Food percolates to every part of an animal's body. Trees grow and bring forth their fruit in season, because their food is distributed throughout their length from the tips of the roots through the trunk and along every branch. Noises pass through walls and fly into closed buildings. Freezing cold penetrates to the bones. If there were no vacancies through which the various bodies could make their way, none of these phenomena would be possible.

Again, why do we find some things outweigh others of equal volume? If there is as much matter in a ball of wool as in one of lead, it is natural that it should weigh as heavily, since it is the function of matter to press everything downwards, while it is the function of space on the other hand to remain weightless. Accordingly, when one thing is not less bulky than another but obviously lighter, it plainly declares that there is more vacuum in it, while the heavier object proclaims that there is more matter in it and much less empty space. We have therefore reached the goal of our diligent inquiry: there is in things an admixture of what we call vacuity.

In case you should be misled on this question by the idle imagining of certain theorists, I must anticipate their argument. They maintain that water yields and opens a penetrable path to scaly bodies of fish that push against it, because they leave spaces behind them into which the yielding water can flow together. In the same way, they suppose, other things can move by mutually changing places, although every place remains filled. This theory has been adopted utterly without warrant. For how can the fish advance till the water has given way? And how can the water retire when the fish cannot move? There are thus only two alternatives: either all bodies are devoid of movement, or you must admit that things contain an admixture of vacuity whereby each is enabled to make the first move.

Lastly, if two bodies suddenly spring apart from contact on a broad surface, all the intervening space must be void until it is occupied by air. However quickly the air rushes in all round, the entire space cannot be filled instantaneously. The air must occupy one spot after another until it has taken possession of the whole space. If anyone supposes that this consequence of such springing apart is made possible by the condensation of air, he is mistaken. For condensation implies that something that was full becomes empty, or *vice versâ*. And I contend that air could not condense so as to produce this effect; or at any rate, if there were no vacuum, it could not thus shrink into itself and draw its parts together.

However many pleas you may advance to prolong the argument, you must end by admitting that there is vacuity in things. There are many other proofs I could add to the pile in order to strengthen conviction; but for an acute intelligence these small clues should suffice to enable you to discover the rest for yourself. As hounds that range the hills often smell out the lairs of wild beasts screened in thickets, when once they have got on to the right trail, so in such questions one thing will lead on to another, till you can succeed by yourself in tracking down the truth to its lurking-places and dragging it forth. If you grow weary and relax from the chase, there is one thing, Memmius, that I can safely promise you: my honeyed tongue will pour from the treasury of my breast such generous draughts, drawn from inexhaustible springs, that I am afraid slow-plodding age may creep through my limbs and unbolt the bars of my life before the full flood of my arguments on any single point has flowed in verse through your ears.

9. [*The universe consists of matter (with its properties and accidents) and of vacuity and nothing else.*]

To pick up the thread of my discourse, all nature as it is in itself consists of two things—bodies and the vacant space in which the bodies are situated and through which they move in different directions. The existence of bodies is vouched for by the agreement of the senses. If a belief resting directly on this foundation is not valid, there will be no standard to which we can refer any doubt on obscure questions for rational confirmation. If there were no place and space, which we call vacuity, these bodies could not be situated anywhere or move in any direction whatever. This I have just demonstrated. It remains to show that *nothing exists that is distinct both from body and from vacuity* and could be ranked with the others as a third substance. For whatever *is* must also be something. If it offers resistance to touch, however light and slight, it will increase the mass of body by such amount, great or small, as it may amount to, and will rank with it. If, on the other hand, it is intangible, so that it offers no resistance whatever to anything passing through it, then it will be that empty space which we call vacuity. Besides, whatever it may be in itself, either it will act in some way, or react to other things acting upon it, or else it will be such that things can be and happen in it. But without body nothing can act or react; and nothing can afford a place except emptiness and vacancy. Therefore, besides matter and vacuity, we cannot include in the number of things any third substance that can either affect our senses at any time or be grasped by the reasoning of our minds.

You will find that anything that can be named is either a property or an accident of these two. A *property* is something that cannot be detached or separated from a thing without destroying it, as weight is a property of rocks, heat of fire, fluidity of water, tangibility of all bodies, intangibility of vacuum. On the other hand, servitude and liberty, poverty and riches, war and peace, and all other things whose advent or departure leaves the essence of a thing intact, all these it is our practice to call by their appropriate name, *accidents*.

Similarly, time by itself does not exist; but from things themselves there results a sense of what has already taken place, what is now going on and what is to ensue. It must not be claimed that anyone can sense time by itself apart from the movement of things or their restful immobility.

Again, when men say it *is* a fact that Helen was ravished or the Trojans were conquered, do not let anyone drive you to the admission that any such event *is* independently of any object, on the ground that the generations of men of whom these events were accidents have been swept away by the irrevocable lapse of time. For we could put it that whatever has taken place is an accident of a particular tract of earth or of the space it occupied. If there had been no matter and no space or place in which things could happen, no spark of love kindled by the beauty of Tyndareus' daughter would ever have stolen into the breast of Phrygian Paris to light that dazzling blaze of pitiless war; no Wooden Horse, unmarked by the sons of Troy, would have set the towers of Ilium aflame through the midnight issue of Greeks from its womb. So you may see that events cannot be said to *be* by themselves like matter or in the same sense as space. Rather, you should describe them as accidents of matter, or of the place in which things happen.

10. [*The atoms are indestructible.*]

Material objects are of two kinds, atoms and compounds of atoms. The atoms themselves cannot be swamped by any force, for they are preserved indefinitely by their absolute solidity. Admittedly, it is hard to believe that anything can exist that is absolutely solid. The lightning stroke from the sky penetrates closed buildings, as do shouts and other noises. Iron glows molten in the fire, and hot rocks are cracked by untempered scorching. Hard gold is softened and melted by heat; and bronze, ice-like, is liquefied by flame. Both heat and piercing cold seep through silver, since we feel both alike when a cooling shower of water is poured into a goblet that we hold ceremonially in our hands. All these facts point to the conclusion that nothing is really solid. But sound reasoning and nature itself drive us to the opposite conclusion. Pay attention, therefore, while I demonstrate in a few lines that there exist certain bodies that are absolutely solid and indestructible, namely those atoms which according to our teaching are the seeds or prime units of things from which the whole universe is built up.

In the first place, we have found that nature is twofold, consisting of two totally different things, matter and the space in which things happen. Hence each of these must exist by itself without admixture of the other. For, where there is empty space (what we call vacuity), there matter is not; where matter exists, there cannot be a vacuum. Therefore the prime units of matter are solid and free from vacuity.

Again, since composite things contain some vacuum, the surrounding matter must be solid. For you cannot reasonably maintain that anything can hide vacuity and hold it within its body unless you allow that the container itself is solid. And what contains the vacuum in things can only be an accumulation of matter. Hence matter, which possesses absolute solidity, can be everlasting when other things are decomposed.

Again, if there were no empty space, everything would be one solid mass; if there were no material objects with the property of filling the space they occupy, all existing space would be utterly void. It is clear, then, that there is an alternation of matter and vacuity, mutually distinct, since the whole is neither completely full nor completely empty. There are therefore solid bodies, causing the distinction between empty space and full. And these, as I have just shown, can be neither decomposed by blows from without nor invaded and unknit from within nor destroyed by any other form of assault. For it seems that a thing without vacuum can be neither knocked to bits nor snapped nor chopped in two by cutting; nor can

it let in moisture or seeping cold or piercing fire, the universal agents of destruction. The more vacuum a thing contains within it, the more readily it yields to these assailants. Hence, if the units of matter are solid and without vacuity, as I have shown, they must be everlasting.

Yet again, if the matter in things had not been everlasting, everything by now would have gone back to nothing, and the things we see would be the product of rebirth out of nothing. But, since I have already shown that nothing can be created out of nothing nor any existing thing be summoned back to nothing, the atoms must be made of imperishable stuff into which everything can be resolved in the end, so that there may be a stock of matter for building the world anew. The atoms, therefore, are absolutely solid and unalloyed. In no other way could they have survived throughout infinite time to keep the world in being.

Furthermore, if nature had set no limit to the breaking of things, the particles of matter in the course of ages would have been ground so small that nothing could be generated from them so as to attain in the fullness of time to the summit of its growth. For we see that anything can be more speedily disintegrated than put together again. Hence, what the long day of time, the bygone eternity, has already shaken and loosened to fragments could never in the residue of time be reconstructed. As it is, there is evidently a limit set to breaking, since we see that everything is renewed and each according to its kind has a fixed period in which to grow to its prime.

Here is a further argument. Granted that the particles of matter are absolutely solid, we can still explain the composition and behaviour of soft things—air, water, earth, fire—by their intermixture with empty space. On the other hand, supposing the atoms to be soft, we cannot account for the origin of hard flint and iron. For there would be no foundation for nature to build on. Therefore there must be bodies strong in their unalloyed solidity by whose closer clustering things can be knit together and display unyielding toughness.

If we suppose that there is no limit set to the breaking of matter, we must still admit that material objects consist of particles which throughout eternity have resisted the forces of destruction. To say that these are breakable does not square with the fact that they have survived throughout eternity under a perpetual bombardment of innumerable blows.

Again, there is laid down for each thing a specific limit to its growth and its tenure of life, and the laws of nature ordain what each can do and what it cannot. No species is ever changed, but each remains so much itself that every kind of bird displays on its body its own specific markings. This is a further proof that their bodies are composed of changeless matter. For, if the atoms could yield in any way to change, there would be no certainty as to what could arise and what could not, at what point the power of everything was limited by an immovable frontier-post; nor could successive generations so regularly repeat the nature, behaviour, habits and movements of their parents.

To proceed with our argument, there is an ultimate point in visible objects which represents the smallest thing that can be seen. So also there must be an ultimate point in objects that lie below the limit of perception by our senses. This point is without parts and is the smallest thing that can exist. It never has been and never will be able to exist by itself, but only as one primary part of something else. It is with a mass of such parts, solidly jammed together in order, that matter is filled up. Since they cannot exist by themselves, they must needs stick together in a mass from which they cannot by any means be pried loose. The atoms therefore are absolutely solid and unalloyed, consisting of a mass of least parts tightly packed together. They are not compounds formed by the coalescence of their parts, but bodies of absolute and everlasting solidity. To these nature allows no loss or diminution, but guards them as seeds for things. If there are no such least parts, even the smallest bodies will consist of an infinite number of parts, since they can always be halved and their halves halved again without limit. On this showing, what difference will there be between the whole universe and the very least of things? None at all. For, however endlessly infinite the universe may be, yet the smallest things will equally consist of an infinite number of parts. Since true reason cries out against this and denies that the mind can believe it, you must needs give in and admit that there are least parts which themselves are partless. Granted that these parts exist, you must needs admit that the atoms they compose are also solid and everlasting. But, if all things were compelled by all-creating nature to be broken up into these least parts, nature would lack the power to rebuild anything out of them. For partless objects cannot have the essential properties of generative matter—those varieties of attachment, weight, impetus, impact and movement on which everything depends. . . .

11. [*Occasionally they swerve slightly from the vertical.*]

. . . There is another fact that I want you to grasp. *When the atoms are travelling straight down through empty space by their own weight, at quite indeterminate times and places they swerve ever so little from their course,* just so much that you can call it a change of direction. If it were not for this swerve, everything would fall downwards like rain-drops through the abyss of space. No collision would take place and no impact of atom on atom would be created. Thus nature would never have created anything.

If anyone supposes that heavier atoms on a straight course through empty space could outstrip lighter ones and fall on them from above, thus causing impacts that might give rise to generative motions, he is going far astray from the path of truth. The reason why objects falling through water or thin air vary in speed according to their weight is simply that the matter composing water or air cannot obstruct all objects equally, but is forced to give way more speedily to heavier ones. But empty space can offer no resistance to any object in any quarter at any time, so as

not to yield free passage as its own nature demands. Therefore, through undisturbed vacuum all bodies must travel at equal speed though impelled by unequal weights. The heavier will never be able to fall on the lighter from above or generate of themselves impacts leading to that variety of motions out of which nature can produce things. We are thus forced back to the conclusion that the atoms swerve a little— but only a very little, or we shall be caught imagining slantwise movements, and the facts will prove us wrong. For we see plainly and palpably that weights, when they come tumbling down, have no power of their own to move aslant, so far as meets the eye. But who can possibly perceive that they do not diverge in the very least from a vertical course?

Again, if all movement is always interconnected, the new arising from the old in a determinate order—if the atoms never swerve so as to originate some new movement that will snap the bonds of fate, the everlasting sequence of cause and effect—what is the source of the free will possessed by living things throughout the earth? What, I repeat, is the source of that will-power snatched from the fates, whereby we follow the path along which we are severally led by pleasure, swerving from our course at no set time or place but at the bidding of our own hearts? There is no doubt that on these occasions the will of the individual originates the movements that trickle through his limbs. Observe, when the starting barriers are flung back, how the race-horses in the eagerness of their strength cannot break away as suddenly as their hearts desire. For the whole supply of matter must first be mobilized throughout every member of the body: only then, when it is mustered in a continuous array, can it respond to the prompting of the heart. So you may see that the beginning of movement is generated by the heart; starting from the voluntary action of the mind, it is then transmitted throughout the body and the limbs. Quite different is our experience when we are shoved along by a blow inflicted with compulsive force by someone else. In that case it is obvious that all the matter of our body is set going and pushed along involuntarily, till a check is imposed through the limbs by the will. Do you see the difference? Although many men are driven by an external force and often constrained involuntarily to advance or to rush headlong, yet there is within the human breast something that can fight against this force and resist it. At its command the supply of matter is forced to take a new course through our limbs and joints or is checked in its course and brought once more to a halt. So also in the atoms you must recognize the same possibility: besides weight and impact there must be a third cause of movement, the source of this inborn power of ours, since we see that nothing can come out of nothing. For the weight of an atom prevents its movements from being completely determined by the impact of other atoms. But the fact that the mind itself has no internal necessity to determine its every act and compel it to suffer in helpless passivity—this is due to the slight swerve of the atoms at no determinate time or place.

12. [*The atoms themselves are devoid of colour.*]

Give ear now to arguments that I have searched out with an effort that was also a delight. Do not imagine that white objects derive the snowy aspect they present to your eyes from white atoms, or that black objects are composed of a black element. And in general do not believe that anything owes the colour it displays to the fact that its atoms are tinted correspondingly. *The primary particles of matter have no colour whatsoever,* neither the same colour as the objects they compose nor a different one. If you think the mind cannot lay hold of such bodies, you are quite wrong. Men who are blind from birth and have never looked on the sunlight have knowledge by touch of bodies that have never from the beginning been associated with any colour. It follows that on our minds also an image can impinge of bodies not marked by any tint. Indeed the things that we ourselves touch in pitch darkness are not felt by us as possessing any colour.

Having proved that colourless bodies are not unthinkable, I will proceed to demonstrate that the atoms must be such bodies.

First, then, any colour may change completely to any other. But the atoms cannot possibly change colour. For something must remain changeless, or everything would be absolutely annihilated. For, if ever anything is so transformed as to overstep its own limits, this means the immediate death of what was before. So do not stain the atoms with colour, or you will find everything slipping back into nothing.

Let us suppose, then, that the atoms are naturally colourless and that it is through the variety of their shapes that they produce the whole range of colours, a great deal depending on their combinations and positions and their reciprocal motions. You will now find it easy to explain without more ado why things that were dark-coloured a moment since can suddenly become as white as marble—as the sea, for instance, when its surface is ruffled by a fresh breeze, is turned into white wavecrests of marble lustre. You could say that something we often see as dark is promptly transformed through the churning up of its matter and a reshuffling of atoms, with some additions and subtractions, so that it is seen as bleached and white. If, on the other hand, the waters of the sea were composed of blue atoms, they could not possibly be whitened; for, however you may stir up blue matter, it can never change its colour to the pallor of marble.

It might be supposed that the uniform lustre of the sea is made up of particles of different colours, as for instance a single object of a square shape is often made up of other objects of various shapes. But in the square we discern the different shapes. So in the surface of the sea or in any other uniform lustre we ought, on this hypothesis, to discern a variety of widely different colours. Besides, differences in the shapes of the parts are no hindrance to the whole being square in outline. But differences in colour completely prevent it from displaying an unvariegated lustre.

The seductive argument that sometimes tempts us to attribute colours to the atoms is demolished by the fact that white objects are not created from white material nor black from black, but both from various colours. Obviously, white could much more readily spring from no colour at all than from black, or from any other colour that interferes and conflicts with it.

Again, since there can be no colours without light and the atoms do not emerge into the light, it can be inferred that they are not clothed in any colour. For what colour can there be in blank darkness? Indeed, colour is itself changed by a change of light, according as the beams strike it vertically or aslant. Observe the appearance in sunlight of the plumage that rings the neck of a dove and crowns its nape: sometimes it is tinted with the brilliant red of a ruby; at others it is seen from a certain point of view to mingle emerald greens with the blue of the sky. In the same way a peacock's tail, profusely illumined, changes colour as it is turned this way or that. These colours, then, are created by a particular incidence of light. Hence, no light, no colour.

When the pupil of the eye is said to perceive the colour white, it experiences in fact a particular kind of impact. When it perceives black, or some other colour, the impact is different. But, when you touch things, it makes no odds what colour they may be, but only what is their shape. The inference is that the atoms have no need of colour, but cause various sensations of touch according to their various shapes.

Since there is no natural connexion

between particular colours and particular shapes, atoms (if they were not colourless) might equally well be of any colour irrespective of their form. Why then are not their compounds tinted with every shade of colour irrespective of their kind? We should expect on this hypothesis that ravens in flight would often emit a snowy sheen from snowy wings; and that some swans would be black, being composed of black atoms, or would display some other uniform or variegated colour.

Again, the more anything is divided into tiny parts, the more you can see its colour gradually dimming and fading out. When red cloth, for instance, is pulled to pieces thread by thread, its crimson or scarlet colour, than which there is none brighter, is all dissipated. From this you may gather that, before its particles are reduced right down to atoms, they would shed all their colour.

Finally, since you acknowledge that not all objects emit noise or smell, you accept that as a reason for not attributing sounds and scents to everything. On the same principle, since we cannot perceive everything by eye, we may infer that some things are colourless, just as some things are scentless and soundless, and that these can be apprehended by the percipient mind as readily as things that are lacking in some other quality.

13. [*The atoms are also devoid of heat, sound, taste, and smell.*]

Do not imagine that colour is the only quality that is denied to the atoms. *They are also wholly devoid of warmth and cold and scorching heat; they are barren of sound and starved of savour,* *and emit no inherent odour from their bodies.* When you are setting out to prepare a pleasant perfume of marjoram or myrrh or flower of spikenard, breathing nectar into our nostrils, your first task is to select so far as possible an oil that is naturally odourless and sends out no exhalation to our nostrils. This will be least liable to corrupt the scents blended and concocted with its substance by contamination with its own taint. For the same reason the atoms must not impart to things at their birth a scent or sound that is their own property, since they can send nothing out of themselves; nor must they contribute any flavour or cold or heat, whether scorching or mild, or anything else of the kind.

These qualities, again, are perishable things, made pliable by the softness of their substance, breakable by its crumbliness and penetrable by its looseness of texture. They must be kept far apart from the atoms, if we wish to provide the universe with imperishable foundations on which it may rest secure; or else you will find everything slipping back into nothing.

14. [*And of sentience.*]

At this stage you must admit that *whatever is seen to be sentient is nevertheless composed of atoms that are insentient.* The phenomena open to our observation do not contradict this conclusion or conflict with it. Rather, they lead us by the hand and compel us to believe that the animate is born, as I maintain, of the insentient.

As a particular instance, we can point to living worms, emerging from foul dung when the earth is soaked and rotted by intemperate showers. Besides, we see every sort of substance transformed in the same way. Rivers, foliage and lush pastures are transformed into cattle; the substance of cattle is transformed into our bodies; and often enough our bodies go to build up the strength of predatory beasts or the bodies of the lords of the air. So nature transforms all foods into living bodies and generates from them all the senses of animate creatures, just as it makes dry wood blossom out in flame and transfigures it wholly into fire. So now do you see that it makes a great difference in what order the various atoms are arranged and with what others they are combined so as to impart and take over motions?

What is it, then, that jogs the mind itself and moves and compels it to express certain sentiments, so that you do not believe that the sentient is generated by the insentient? Obviously it is the fact that a mixture of water and wood and earth cannot of itself bring about vital sensibility. There is one relevant point you should bear in mind: I am not maintaining that sensations are generated automatically from all the elements out of which sentient things are created. Everything depends on the size and shape of the sense-producing atoms and on their appropriate motions, arrangements and positions. None of these is found in wood or clods. And yet these substances, when they are fairly well rotted by showers, give birth to little worms, because the particles of matter are jolted out of their old arrangements by a new factor and combined in such a way that animate objects must result.

Again, those who would have it that sensation can be produced only be sensitive bodies, which originate in their turn from others similarly sentient—these theorists are making the foundations of our senses perishable, because they are making them soft. For sensitivity is always associated with flesh, sinews, veins—all things that we see to be soft and composed of perishable stuff.

Let us suppose, for argument's sake, that particles of these substances could endure everlastingly. The sensation with which they are credited must be either that of a part or else similar to that of an animate being as a whole. But it is impossible for parts by themselves to experience sensation: all the sensations felt in our limbs are felt by us as a whole; a hand or any other member severed from the whole body is quite powerless to retain sensation on its own. There remains the alternative that such particles have senses like those of an animate being as a whole. They must then feel precisely what we feel, so as to share in all our vital sensations. How then can they pass for elements and escape the path of death, since they are animate beings, and animate and mortal are one and the same thing? Even supposing they could escape death, yet they will make nothing by their combination and conjunction but a mob or horde of living things, just as men and cattle and wild beasts obviously could not combine so as to give birth to a single thing. If we suppose that they shed their own sentience from their bodies and acquire another one, what is the point of giving them the one that is taken away? Besides, as we saw before, from the fact that we perceive eggs turning into live fledgelings and worms swarming out when the earth has been rotted by intemperate showers, we may infer that sense can be generated from the insentient.

Suppose someone asserts that sense can indeed emerge from the insentient, but only by some transformation or some creative process comparable to birth. He will be adequately answered by a clear demonstration that birth and transformation occur only as the result of union or combination. Admittedly sensation cannot arise in any body until an animate creature has been born. This of course is because the requisite matter is dispersed through air and streams and earth and the products of earth: it has not come together in the appropriate manner, so as to set in mutual operation those vitalizing motions that kindle the all-watchful senses which keep watch over every animate creature.

When any animate creature is suddenly assailed by a more powerful blow than its nature can withstand, all the senses of body and mind are promptly thrown into confusion. For the juxtapositions of the atoms are unknit, and the vitalizing motions are inwardly obstructed, until the matter, jarred and jolted throughout every limb, loosens the vital knots of the spirit from the body and expels the spirit in scattered particles through every pore. What other effect can we attribute to the infliction of a blow than this of shaking and shattering everything to bits? Besides, it often happens, when the blow is less

violently inflicted, that such vitalizing motions as survive emerge victorious; they assuage the immense upheavals resulting from the shock, recall every particle to its own proper courses, break up the lethal motion when it is all but master of the body and rekindle the well-nigh extinguished senses. How else could living creatures on the very threshold of death rally their consciousness and return to life rather than make good their departure by a route on which they have already travelled most of the way?

Again, pain occurs when particles of matter have been unsettled by some force within the living flesh of the limbs and stagger in their inmost stations. When they slip back into place, that is blissful pleasure. It follows that the atoms cannot be afflicted by any pain or experience any pleasure in themselves, since they are not composed of any primal particles, by some reversal of whose movements they might suffer anguish or reap some fruition of vitalizing bliss. They cannot therefore be endowed with any power of sensation.

Again, if we are to account for the power of sensation possessed by animate creatures in general by attributing sentience to their atoms, what of those atoms that specifically compose the human race? Presumably they are not merely sentient, but also shake their sides with uproarious guffaws and besprinkle their cheeks with dewy teardrops and even discourse profoundly and at length about the composition of the universe and proceed to ask of what elements they are themselves composed. If they are to be likened to entire mortals, they must certainly consist of other elemental particles, and these again of others. There is no point at which you may call a halt, but I will follow you there with your argument that whatever speaks or laughs or thinks is composed of particles that do the same. Let us acknowledge that this is stark madness and lunacy: one can laugh without being composed of laughing particles, can think and proffer learned arguments though sprung from seeds neither thoughtful nor eloquent. Why then cannot the things that we see gifted with sensation be compounded of seeds that are wholly senseless?

Lastly, we are all sprung from heavenly seed. All alike have the same father, from whom all-nourishing mother earth receives the showering drops of moisture. Thus fertilized, she gives birth to smiling crops and lusty trees, to mankind and all the breeds of beasts. She it is that yields the food on which they all feed their bodies, lead their joyous lives and renew their race. So she has well earned the name of mother. In like manner this matter returns: what came from earth goes back into the earth; what was sent down from the ethereal vault is readmitted to the precincts of heaven. Death does not put an end to things by annihilating the component particles but by breaking up their conjunction. Then it links them in new combinations, making everything change in shape and colour and give up in an instant its acquired gift of sensation. So you may realize what a difference it makes in what combinations and positions the same elements occur, and what motions they mutually pass on and take over. You

will thus avoid the mistake of conceiving as permanent properties of the atoms the qualities that are seen floating on the surface of things, coming into being from time to time and as suddenly perishing. Obviously it makes a great difference in these verses of mine in what context and order the letters are arranged. If not all, at least the greater part is alike. But differences in their position distinguish word from word. Just so with actual objects: when there is a change in the combination, motion, order, position or shapes of the component matter, there must be a corresponding change in the object composed. . . .

15. [*Mind and spirit were born and will die.*]

A tree cannot exist high in air, or clouds in the depths of the sea, as fish cannot live in the fields, or blood flow in wood or sap in stones. There is a determined and allotted place for the growth and presence of everything. So mind cannot arise alone without body or apart from sinews and blood. If it could do this, then surely it could much more readily function in head or shoulders or the tips of the heels and be born in any other part, so long as it was held in the same container, that is to say in the same man. Since, however, even in the human body we see a determined and allotted place set aside for the growth and presence of spirit and mind, we have even stronger grounds for denying that they could survive or come to birth outside the body altogether. You must admit, therefore, that when the body has perished there is an end also of the spirit diffused through it. It is surely crazy to couple a mortal object with an eternal and suppose that they can work in harmony and mutually interact. What can be imagined more incongruous, what more repugnant and discordant, than that a mortal object and one that is immortal and everlasting should unite to form a compound and jointly weather the storms that rage about them?

Again, there can be only three kinds of everlasting objects. The first, owing to the absolute solidity of their substance, can repel blows and let nothing penetrate them so as to unknit their close texture from within. Such are the atoms of matter, whose nature I have already demonstrated. The second kind can last for ever because it is immune from blows. Such is empty space, which remains untouched and unaffected by any impact. Last is that which has no available place surrounding it into which its matter can disperse and disintegrate. It is for this reason that the sum total of the universe is everlasting, having no space outside it into which the matter can escape and no matter that can enter and disintegrate it by the force of impact.

Equally vain is the suggestion that the spirit is immortal because it is shielded by life-preserving powers; or because it is unassailed by forces hostile to its survival; or because such forces, if they threaten, are somehow arrested before we are conscious of the threat. Apart from the spirit's participation in the ailments of the body, it has maladies enough of its own. The prospect of the future torments it with fear and wearies it with worry, and past misdeeds leave

the sting of remorse. Lastly, it may fall a prey to the mind's own specific afflictions, madness and amnesia, and plunge into the black waters of oblivion.

From all this it follows that *death is nothing to us* and no concern of ours, since our tenure of the mind is mortal. In days of old, we felt no disquiet when the hosts of Carthage poured in to battle on every side—when the whole earth, dizzied by the convulsive shock of war, reeled sickeningly under the high ethereal vault, and between realm and realm the empire of mankind by land and sea trembled in the balance. So, when we shall be no more—when the union of body and spirit that engenders us has been disrupted—to us, who shall then be nothing, nothing by any hazard will happen any more at all. Nothing will have power to stir our senses, not though earth be fused with sea and sea with sky. . . .

16. [*Happiness lies in cheerful acceptance of the universal lot.*]

Here is something that you might well say to yourself from time to time: 'Even good king Ancus looked his last on the daylight—a better man than you, my presumptuous friend, by a long reckoning. Death has come to many another monarch and potentate, who lorded it over mighty nations. Even that King of Kings who once built a highway across the deep—who gave his legions a path to tread among the waves and taught them to march on foot over the briny gulfs and with his charger trampled scornfully upon the ocean's roar—even he was robbed of the light and poured out the spirit from a dying frame. Scipio, that thunderbolt of war, the terror of Carthage, gave his bones to the earth as if he had been the meanest of serfs. Add to this company the discoverers of truth and beauty. Add the attendants of the Muses, among them Homer who in solitary glory bore the sceptre but has sunk into the same slumber as the rest. Democritus, when ripe age warned him that the mindful motions of his intellect were running down, made his unbowed head a willing sacrifice to death. And the Master himself, when his daylit race was run, Epicurus himself died, whose genius outshone the race of men and dimmed them all, as the stars are dimmed by the rising of the fiery sun. And will *you* kick and protest against your sentence? You, whose life is next-door to death while you are still alive and looking on the light. You, who waste the major part of your time in sleep and, when you are awake, are snoring still and dreaming. You, who bear a mind hagridden by baseless fear and cannot find the commonest cause of your distress, hounded as you are, poor creature, by a pack of troubles and drifting in a drunken stupor upon a wavering tide of fantasy.'

Men feel plainly enough within their minds, a heavy burden, whose weight depresses them. If only they perceived with equal clearness the causes of this depression, the origin of this lump of evil within their breasts, they would not lead such a life as we now see all too commonly—no one knowing what he really wants and everyone for ever trying to get away from where he is, as though mere locomotion could throw off the load. Often the owner of some

stately mansion, bored stiff by staying at home, takes his departure, only to return as speedily when he feels himself no better off out of doors. Off he goes to his country seat, driving his carriage and pair hot-foot, as though in haste to save a house on fire. No sooner has he crossed its doorstep than he starts yawning or retires moodily to sleep and courts oblivion, or else rushes back to revisit the city. In so doing the individual is really running away from himself. Since he remains reluctantly wedded to the self whom he cannot of course escape, he grows to hate him, because he is a sick man ignorant of the cause of his malady. If he did but see this, he would cast other thoughts aside and devote himself first to studying the nature of the universe. It is not the fortune of an hour that is in question, but of all time—the lot in store for mortals throughout the eternity that awaits them after death.

What is this deplorable lust of life that holds us trembling in bondage to such uncertainties and dangers? A fixed term is set to the life of mortals, and there is no way of dodging death. In any case the setting of our lives remains the same throughout, and by going on living we do not mint any new coin of pleasure. So long as the object of our craving is unattained, it seems more precious than anything besides. Once it is ours, we crave for something else. So an unquenchable thirst for life keeps us always on the gasp. There is no telling what fortune the future may bring—what chance may throw in our way, or what upshot lies in waiting. By prolonging life, we cannot subtract or whittle away one jot from the duration of our death. The time after our taking off remains constant. However many generations you may add to your store by living, there waits for you none the less the same eternal death. The time of not-being will be no less for him who made an end of life with yesterday's daylight than for him who perished many a moon and many a year before.

COMMENT

Ancient and Modern Materialism

Although Lucretius wrote his poem over two thousand years ago, his vision of a materialistic universe remains as fresh and vivid as ever it was. This may seem strange to a reader familiar with the history of ideas. Have not science and the naturalistic philosophy based upon it undergone an immense revolution since the time of Lucretius? Even the more modern materialism of Hobbes and La Mettrie appears quaint and archaic in the light of recent science and philosophy. We can no longer conceive of matter in the form of tiny indivisible particles, like the motes of dust that we see dancing about in a shaft of sunlight. The atomic theory has been transplanted from metaphysical speculation to experimental research, and the resulting discoveries have radically transformed it.

Few people would now question the existence of atoms, but the atoms are no longer conceived as inert, eternal, and indivisible particles moving in a featureless void. Instead of being inert, they are made up of electrical charges which behave like waves. Instead of being eternal, they emit radiations and are subject to splittings and fusions. Instead of being indivisible, they can be analyzed into electrons, protons, neutrons, mesons, positrons, and so on. Instead of moving in a void, they are enmeshed in "electromagnetic fields" within "curved" space-time. These modern concepts of radiation, fission, quanta, waves, fields, and relativity are a far cry from Lucretius.

Yet the naturalistic temper of his philosophy as distinguished from the archaic details of his science remains as up-to-date as ever. Nothing in modern physics contradicts his vision of all things arising from and returning to a material base. W. H. Mallock, in a free poetic translation of a passage from Lucretius, has expressed the essence of this naturalism:

> No single thing abides; but all things flow.
> Fragment to fragment clings—the things thus grow
> Until we know and name them. By degrees
> They melt, and are no more the things we know.
>
> Globed from the atoms falling slow or swift
> I see the suns, I see the systems lift
> Their forms; and even the systems and the suns
> Shall go back slowly to the eternal drift.
>
> Thou too, oh earth—thine empires, lands, and seas—
> Least, with thy stars, of all the galaxies,
> Globed from the drift like these, like these thou too
> Shalt go. Thou art going, hour by hour, like these.[1]

Can Materialism Explain Secondary Qualities?

Extreme materialism tries to explain every process in terms of matter and motion quantitatively described. "Primary qualities," which are abstract and measurable, are conceived to be more ultimate or objective, whereas "secondary qualities," which are concrete and unmeasureable, are regarded as more derivative or subjective. This distinction was first clearly stated by Democritus:

> There are two kinds of knowledge: real knowledge and obscure knowledge. To obscure knowledge belong all things of sight, sound, odor, taste, and touch; real knowledge is distinct from this . . . Sweet and bitter, heat and cold, and color, are only opinions; there is nothing true but atoms and the void.[2]

For Democritus, the only objective properties of things are size, shape, weight, and motion. All other qualities, such as sound, color, odor, taste, and touch, are sensations in us caused by the motions and arrangements of the atoms.

[1] William Hurrell Mallock, *Lucretius on Life and Death, in the Metre of Omar Khayyam* (London: A. C. Black, 1900).
[2] Translated by Philip Wheelwright, *The Way of Philosophy* (Odyssey Press, 1954), p. 162.

This theory was revived by Galileo and was reformulated by Hobbes, Locke, Newton, and other influential modern thinkers. It has figured very prominently in modern theories of perception. Warmth, for example, is explained as the reaction of our sense organs and nervous systems to molecular motions; sound, as our reaction to air waves; color, as our reaction to electromagnetic vibrations. Thus the "secondary qualities"—colors, sounds, odors, and so on—exist, as such, only for our minds. In the absence of our mental reactions, the universe is a pretty dull and abstract affair—a collection of soundless, colorless, and odorless particles, in various arrangements, drifting through space and time.

Lucretius, departing from the views of Democritus, had a different theory. He agreed that the atoms individually are without any of the secondary qualities, but maintained that these qualities spring into existence when the atoms are combined in certain ways. "The first-bodies," he tells us, are not only "bereft . . . of color, they are also sundered altogether from warmth and cold, and fiery heat, and are carried along barren of sound and devoid of taste, nor do they give off any scent of their own from their body." But these qualities *are* properties of compounds, formed by combinations of atoms. The compounds, being new and different entities, have color, sound, odor, taste, and heat, none of which can belong to the atoms as individual particles. When we perceive these secondary qualities we are grasping real objective properties, for the complex body perceived by our senses is as real as the atoms.

There are difficulties in both the Lucretian and the Democritean theory. Some critics have objected that if the atoms of Lucretius are devoid of secondary qualities, it is difficult to understand how by mere juxtaposition or arrangement they can produce things which possess these qualities. This difficulty is increased by the contention that the atoms are utterly unchangeable, possessing the secondary qualities neither before nor after they combine. It would seem that elementary particles that are themselves unmodifiable could not by their combination give rise to entities having radically new qualities. Perhaps more serious is the fact that Lucretius rests his theory upon a rather naïve trust in perception. He insists that we see objects as they really are, that our senses rarely deceive us. Perhaps! We naturally attribute the sounds, colors, odors, tastes, and tactile qualities which we perceive to supposedly real external objects. But there is evidence to show that these qualities depend at least in part upon physiological and psychological reactions in the perceiving organisms. To suppose that our senses perfectly reveal the nature of the external world is, therefore, a very big assumption.

The theory of Democritus, with its modern counterparts, can also be challenged. The primary qualities may be no less subjective than the secondary. If the sounds and colors that I perceive do not exist in the external world but come into being when my mind is acted upon in certain ways, why may not the same be true of the shapes and motions which I seem to perceive in things? As we shall see when we study Berkeley, it can be argued that the considerations that drive us to conclude that the secondary qualities are subjective apply also to the primary qualities.

On the other hand, some philosophers maintain that *both* primary and secondary qualities are objective. They would agree with Lucretius that compounds, if not more elementary bodies, possess secondary qualities. The real world, they believe, has the vivid colors, odors, sounds, tastes, and tactile qualities that it appears to have. The problem, to which we shall return in the next chapter, is difficult, and no solution is obviously the right one.

Can Materialism Explain Life?

Can a materialist account for the difference between animate and inanimate things?

An extreme materialist will not admit any such fundamental cleavage. Plant and animal activity, he will maintain, is reducible simply to physical and chemical forces exactly like those found in inorganic bodies. Living things are composed exclusively of substances that may also be found in nonliving things, and there are no teleological or vitalistic forces that explain life. In opposition to this point of view, "vitalists" such as Henri Bergson maintain that life is distinct and fundamentally different from nonlife.

There certainly *appears* to be a gap between living organisms and mere physical mechanisms. No machine grows by what it feeds on. No machine has the capacity to produce a germ which will develop into another thing like itself—Ford cars do not produce little Ford cars. No machine can grow new tissue and thus repair its own injuries. No machine has memories. No machine has purposes or expectations. No machine, not even a computer, sets problems for itself to solve—it can solve only those problems fed into it. A man can invent a machine or, like Luther Burbank, breed a new species of organism, but a machine cannot invent another machine or breed even the lowliest organism. No machine is conscious of itself or of other things. Computers can perform computations far beyond the power of a human mind and machines can simulate the behavior of animate creatures, but there still remains a great chasm between the most adroit machines and real organisms. To say that machines can reason, remember, criticize, plan, love, or imagine is to speak in a purely metaphorical sense.

A considerable number of philosophers and biologists, moreover, have argued that no purely materialistic theory can explain the facts of organic evolution. The usual explanation is in terms of Darwin's theory of random variations, struggle for existence, and survival of the fittest—and there are interesting anticipations of Darwinism in Lucretius' poem. But if mere survival is the sole requirement, it is difficult to account for the upward drive of life to high and unstable evolutionary levels. Some of the very simplest species are today what they were at the remotest times of the paleozoic era, a half billion years ago. They are as perfectly adapted as any organisms, judged by their capacity to survive. Why did not life stop at this very stable level? Why has it gone on, complicating itself more and more dangerously? "The truth is that adaptation explains the sinuosities of the movement of evolution," declared Henri Bergson, "but not its general directions, still less the movement itself."[3] Throughout organic nature, he argued there is a persistent vital impetus which explains the vast ascending movement of evolution. Life is in no sense a product of matter. It is an opposite current that builds up organisms out of matter. Matter is governed by the Law of Entropy—the tendency of purely material systems to run down through the loss of radiant energy. But life moves in the opposite direction from matter and stores up and concentrates energy and evolves ever higher and more complex beings. This philosophy of "creative evolution," as Bergson dubbed it, makes a clean break with materialism.

If scientists should eventually succeed in producing life—not something that merely simulates life but something indubitably alive—by synthesis of certain chemicals, this feat would refute Bergson's contention that life is underivable from "matter." But even so, materialism would not be proved—what we take to be inorganic matter might be organic. This is the view that has been elaborately formulated by Alfred North Whitehead, who interprets evolution as the development of complex organisms from antecedent states of simpler organisms. Just as disease viruses are very elementary organisms, so are atoms—though they are organisms of a different type. Hence evolution does not involve a leap from the inorganic to the organic, as in the theory of Lucretius, but merely a greater and greater complication of organisms. The philosophy of Whitehead, like that of Bergson, thus represents an alternative to materialism.

Can Materialism Explain Mind?

Can a materialist account for mental characteristics?

The most extreme kind of materialism, exemplified by some radical mechanists and behaviorists, is the virtual denial that we have minds at all. Since we are all aware that there are mental processes, such as reasoning, willing, feeling, perceiving, remembering, and imagining, we need not argue the point.

Lucretius was not a materialist of this extreme reductive type. He was a believer in the theory that new qualities, including mental functions, spring into existence as a result of the complex combinations of material elements. He pointed out that men can speak and laugh and think whereas it would be absurd to attribute these capacities to atoms. A human organism, made up of innumerable atoms, has vital characteristics which the atoms taken singly do not possess. Just as the meaning of a sentence results from the combinations of meaningless letters, so life and mind result from the meetings and configurations of lifeless and mindless atoms. Applied to evolution, this theory means the recognition of diverse levels of complexity and organization, each with its emergent qualities, and the interpretation of these levels as successive stages in an evolutionary process. We associate this type of theory with such modern philosophers as Samuel Alexander (1859–1938), but it was maintained by Lucretius two thousand years ago.

[3] *Creative Evolution* (Henry Holt, 1911), p. 102.

Its implications are, in the wide sense of the word, "materialistic." Mind, it declares, arises out of matter and is a function of complex material bodies. "Out of dust man arises and to dust will he return." Vital processes, including thought, cannot survive the dissolution of the body any more than a football game can continue after the disbanding of the opposing teams.

The adequacy of this type of theory to explain mental life is a subject of much dispute. Some philosophers maintain that the phenomena of life are so essentially disparate from and discontinuous with merely material happenings that they cannot possibly "emerge" from a previous state of lifeless matter. To maintain the doctrine of emergence, it is said, is to assert the miracle of creation out of nothing. "Wherever mind is taken to begin" in this way, declares G. F. Stout, "it bursts into being like a shot out of a pistol that is not previously in the pistol."[4]

The type of materialism called "epiphenomenalism" admits that there are mental processes but regards them as mere ineffectual byproducts of physical processes. The only causal relations are between physical events and other physical events, or between physical antecedents and mental consequents. Our thoughts and feelings are caused by molecular changes in the brain or other physical processes and have no causal efficacy of their own. The mind has as little to do with the movement of the body as the shadow cast by a locomotive has to do with the racing of the locomotive.

Lucretius is not consistent enough to be called an epiphenomenalist, but for the most part he clings to a materialistic interpretation of the *causes* of mental events. He maintains, for example, that all knowledge is derived from sensations caused by the impact on the mind-atoms of surface-films emanating from external physical objects. But he departs from epiphenomenalism with its extreme mechanistic implications in his theory of "swerving" atoms and concomitant free will.

This theory, although unsubstantiated and somewhat naïvely stated, is similar to the famous "principle of indeterminacy" formulated in 1927 by Werner Heisenberg, a German physicist. Heisenberg found that it is impossible to determine the position and the velocity of an electron simultaneously—*i.e.,* to state that the electron is at a precise spot while moving at a specific speed. This uncertainty, he maintained, is caused not by the inadequacy of scientific measurement and observation but by the capriciousness of the external physical order. Nature itself is "throwing dice" in a somewhat unpredictable way.

A number of distinguished scientists, such as Arthur Eddington and James Jeans, have interpreted Heisenberg's principle of indeterminacy as supporting the doctrine of free will. If physical events, they reason, are somewhat indeterminate and unpredictable, the human mind may be exempt from rigid determinism. Eddington suggests that the indeterminacy may exist in living matter and more particularly in the human brain, and that free choice may

[4] *Mind and Matter* (Cambridge University Press, 1931), p. 110.

influence the movements of the brain-atoms in one direction rather than another. There has been much dispute as to whether this application of Heisenberg's principle is justifiable; but it is a modern analogue of Lucretius' theory of swerving atoms and free will.

4

Dualism
and the Quest
for Certainty

RENÉ DESCARTES (1596–1650)

Descartes' father was Councillor of the Parliament of Brittany and owner of a fair amount of landed property. His mother, apparently consumptive, died during his infancy and left him with enfeebled health. Anxious to surround the delicate boy with every care, his father entrusted Descartes' education to the Jesuits. It was at the newly established Jesuit college at La Flèche that the young Descartes fell in love with geometry.

Leaving school at seventeen, Descartes spent the next four years in Paris studying law. Thereafter for several years, he lived as a traveler and a soldier, serving as a volunteer in three European armies, in the Netherlands, Bavaria, and Hungary. During this period, when he had a good deal of time to reflect, he came to doubt the value of everything he had learned with the single exception of mathematics.

On November 10, 1619, he had the remarkable experience to which he refers at the beginning of Part II of the *Discourse on Method*. He spent this cold November day in a stove-heated room, meditating about the mathematical and scientific ideas that had been tumbling through his mind for several days. Nervously exhausted, he finally fell asleep and had three strange dreams, which he interpreted as pointing to a life of philosophical reflection. As a result of these dreams, which he thought were inspired by God, and the intense intellectual activity that preceded them, he saw himself at the parting of the ways, and he resolved thenceforth to follow the path of philosophy and scientific research.

Although Descartes has not given us a detailed account of "the foundations of a wonderful science" which he discovered at this time, we know he had the conviction that the method of mathematics could be generalized to apply to all the sciences and that thereby certainty could be gained. Moreover, he conceived the method of applying algebraic symbolism to geometry and of using coordinates to describe geometrical figures; in other words, he founded analytical geometry. Finally, he was convinced that science and philosophy should form one whole, subject to a single method.

He vowed that no ties of marriage or society should deter him from a life of intellectual research devoted to the development of these insights. Although he continued to travel and to study "the great book of the world" for the next nine years (1619–1628), he still found time to work on various problems of mathematics and science. Growing tired of his wanderings at last, in 1628 he sold his inherited estates in France and settled in a quiet country house in Holland. With abundant leisure and a few servants to take care of his material needs, he formed the habit of staying in bed until about noon, reading, writing, or meditating. He soon acquired a wide reputation and was visited by, or corresponded with, many notable scientists and philosophers of the age. During this sojourn in Holland, he had what was apparently his only love affair. The daughter who was the product of this alliance died at the age of five, much to her father's sorrow.

In the autumn of 1649, Descartes accepted an invitation from Queen Christina of Sweden to spend a winter at her court. An imperious though learned monarch, Christina thought that she had the right to command his services at any hour she chose. Daily at five in the morning throughout the bitterly cold winter, Descartes was ushered into the presence of the Queen, where he discoursed to her about philosophy while he stood shivering on the marble floor. Unused to the biting climate and the rigors of such early rising, he caught pneumonia and died in March 1650, a few days before his fifty-fifth birthday.

Rules
for the Direction
of the Mind

Rule I

The end of study should be to direct the mind towards the enunciation of sound and correct judgments on all matters that come before it.

Whenever men notice some similarity between two things, they are wont to ascribe to each, even in those respects in which the two differ, what they have found to be true of the other. Thus they erroneously compare the sciences, which entirely consist in the cognitive exercise of the mind, with the arts, which depend upon an exercise and disposition of the body. They see that not all the arts can be acquired by the same man, but that he who restricts himself to one, most readily becomes the best executant, since it is not so easy for the same hand to adapt itself both to agricultural operations and to harp-playing, or to the performance of several such tasks as to one alone. Hence they have held the same to be true of the sciences also, and distin-

The following excerpts from the *Rules* are from *The Philosophical Works of Descartes,* translated by Elizabeth S. Haldane and G. R. T. Ross. Copyright 1911 by the Cambridge University Press. Reprinted by permission.

guishing them from one another according to their subject matter, they have imagined that they ought to be studied separately, each in isolation from all the rest. But this is certainly wrong. For since the sciences taken all together are identical with human wisdom, which always remains one and the same, however applied to different subjects, and suffers no more differentiation proceeding from them than the light of the sun experiences from the variety of the things which it illumines, there is no need for minds to be confined at all within limits; for neither does the knowing of one truth have an effect like that of the acquisition of one art and prevent us from finding out another, it rather aids us to do so . . . . Hence we must believe that. all the sciences are so inter-connected, that it is much easier to study them all together than to isolate one from all the others . . . .

Rule II

Only those objects should engage our attention, to the sure and indubitable knowledge of which our mental powers seem to be adequate.

Science in its entirety is true and evident cognition. He is no more learned who has doubts on many matters than the man who has never thought of them; nay he appears to be less learned if he has formed wrong opinions on any particulars. Hence it were better not to study at all than to occupy one's self with objects of such difficulty, that, owing to our inability to distinguish true from false, we are forced to regard the doubtful as certain; for in those matters any hope of augmenting our knowledge is exceeded by the risk of diminishing it. Thus in accordance with the above maxim we reject all such merely probable knowledge and make it a rule to trust only what is completely known and incapable of being doubted. . . .

But if we adhere closely to this rule we shall find left but few objects of legitimate study. For there is scarce any question occurring in the sciences about which talented men have not disagreed. But whenever two men come to opposite decisions about the same matter one of them at least must certainly be in the wrong, and apparently there is not even one of them in the right; for if the reasoning of the second was sound and clear he would be able so to lay it before the other as finally to succeed in convincing *his* understanding also. Hence apparently we cannot attain to a perfect knowledge in any such case of probable opinion, for it would be rashness to hope for more than others have attained to. Consequently if we reckon correctly, of the sciences already discovered, Arithmetic and Geometry alone are left, to which the observance of this rule reduces us . . . .

Now let us proceed to explain more

carefully our reasons for saying that of all the sciences known as yet, Arithmetic and Geometry alone are free from any taint of falsity or uncertainty. We must note then that there are two ways by which we arrive at the knowledge of facts, viz., by experience and by deduction. We must further observe that while our inferences from experience are frequently fallacious, deduction, or the pure illation of one thing from another, though it may be passed over, if it is not seen through, cannot be erroneous when performed by an understanding that is in the least degree rational. . . . My reason for saying so is that none of the mistakes which men can make (men, I say, not beasts) are due to faulty inference; they are caused merely by the fact that we base inferences upon poorly comprehended experiences, or that propositions are posited which are hasty and groundless.

This furnishes us with an evident explanation of the great superiority in certitude of Arithmetic and Geometry to other sciences. The former alone deal with an object so pure and uncomplicated, that they need make no assumptions at all which experience renders uncertain, but wholly consist in the rational deduction of consequences. They are on that account much the easiest and clearest of all, and possess an object such as we require, for in them it is scarce humanly possible for anyone to err except by inadvertence. And yet we should not be surprised to find that plenty of people of their own accord prefer to apply their intelligence to other studies. The reason for this is that every person permits himself the liberty of making guesses in the matter of an obscure subject with more confidence than in one which is clear, and that it is much easier to have some vague notion about any subject, no matter what, than to arrive at the real truth about a single question however simple that may be.

But one conclusion now emerges out of these considerations, viz. not, indeed, that Arithmetic and Geometry are the sole sciences to be studied, but only that in our search for the direct road towards truth we should busy ourselves with no object about which we cannot attain a certitude equal to that of the demonstrations of Arithmetic and Geometry.

Rule III

In the subjects we propose to investigate, our inquiries should be directed, not to what others have thought, nor to what we ourselves conjecture, but to what we can clearly and perspicuously behold and with certainty deduce; for knowledge is not won in any other way.

To study the writings of the ancients is right, because it is a great boon for us to be able to make use of the labours of so many men; and we should do so, both in order to discover what they have correctly made out in previous ages, and also that we may inform ourselves as to what in the various sciences is still left for investigation. But yet there is a great danger lest in a too absorbed study of these works we should

become infected with their errors, guard against them as we may. For it is the way of writers, whenever they have allowed themselves rashly and credulously to take up a position in any controverted matter, to try with the subtlest of arguments to compel us to go along with them. But when, on the contrary, they have happily come upon something certain and evident, in displaying it they never fail to surround it with ambiguities, fearing, it would seem, lest the simplicity of their explanation should make us respect their discovery less, or because they grudge us an open vision of the truth.

Further, supposing now that all were wholly open and candid, and never thrust upon us doubtful opinions as true, but expounded every matter in good faith, yet since scarce anything has been asserted by any one man the contrary of which has not been alleged by another, we should be eternally uncertain which of the two to believe. It would be no use to total up the testimonies in favour of each, meaning to follow that opinion which was supported by the greater number of authors; for if it is a question of difficulty that is in dispute, it is more likely that the truth would have been discovered by few than by many. But even though all these men agreed among themselves, what they teach us would not suffice for us. For we shall not, e.g., all turn out to be mathematicians though we know by heart all the proofs that others have elaborated, unless we have an intellectual talent that fits us to resolve difficulties of any kind. Neither, though we have mastered all the arguments of Plato and Aristotle, if yet we have not the capacity for passing a solid judgment on these matters, shall we become Philosophers; we should have acquired the knowledge not of a science, but of history.

I lay down the rule also, that we must wholly refrain from ever mixing up conjectures with our pronouncements on the truth of things. This warning is of no little importance. There is no stronger reason for our finding nothing in the current Philosophy which is so evident and certain as not to be capable of being controverted, than the fact that the learned, not content with the recognition of what is clear and certain, in the first instance hazard the assertion of obscure and ill-comprehended theories, at which they have arrived merely by probable conjecture. Then afterwards they gradually attach complete credence to them, and mingling them promiscuously with what is true and evident, they finish by being unable to deduce any conclusion which does not appear to depend upon come proposition of the doubtful sort, and hence is not uncertain.

But lest we in turn should slip into the same error, we shall here take note of all those mental operations by which we are able, wholly without fear of illusion, to arrive at the knowledge of things. Now I admit only two, viz., intuition and deduction.

By *intuition* I understand, not the fluctuating testimony of the senses, nor the misleading judgment that proceeds from the blundering constructions of imagination, but the conception which an unclouded and attentive mind gives us so readily and distinctly that we are wholly freed from doubt about that which we understand. Or, what comes to the same thing, *intuition* is the undoubting conception of an unclouded and attentive mind, and springs from the light of reason alone; it is more certain than deduction itself, in that it is simpler, though deduction, as we have noted above, cannot by us be erroneously conducted. Thus each individual can mentally have intuition of the fact that he exists, and that he thinks; that the triangle is bounded by three lines only, the sphere by a single superficies, and so on. Facts of such a kind are for more numerous than many people think, disdaining as they do . . . to direct their attention upon such simple matters. . . .

This evidence and certitude, however, which belongs to intuition, is required not only in the enunciation of propositions, but also in discursive reasoning of whatever sort. For example consider this consequence: 2 and 2 amount to the same as 3 and 1. Now we need to see intuitively not only that 2 and 2 make 4, and likewise 3 and 1 make 4, but further that the third of the above statements is a necessary conclusion from these two.

Hence now we are in a position to raise the question as to why we have, besides intuition, given this supplementary method of knowing, viz., knowing by *deduction,* by which we understand all necessary inference from other facts that are known with certainty. This, however, we could not avoid, because many things are known with certainty, though not by themselves evident, but only deduced from true and known principles by the continuous and uninterrupted action of a mind that has a clear vision of each step in the process. It is in a similar way that we know that the last link in a long chain is connected with the first, even though we do not take in by means of one and the same act of vision all the intermediate links on which that connection depends, but only remember that we have taken them successively under review and that each single one is united to its neighbour, from the first even to the last. Hence we distinguish this mental intuition from deduction by the fact that into the conception of the latter there enters a certain movement or succession, into that of the former there does not. Further deduction does not require an immediately presented evidence such as intuition possesses; its certitude is rather conferred upon it in some way by memory. The upshot of the matter is that it is possible to say that those propositions indeed which are immediately deduced from first principles are known now by intuition, now by deduction, i.e., in a way that differs according to our point of view. But the first principles themselves are given by intuition alone, while, on the contrary, the remote conclusions are furnished only by deduction.

These two methods are the most certain routes to knowledge, and the mind should admit no others. All the rest should be rejected as suspect of error and dangerous. . . .

Rule IV

There is need of a method for finding out the truth.

So blind is the curiosity by which mortals are possessed, that they often conduct their minds along unexplored routes, having no reason to hope for success, but merely being willing to risk the experiment of finding whether the truth they seek lies there. As well might a man burning with an unintelligent desire to find treasure, continuously roam the streets, seeking to find something that a passerby might have chanced to drop. This is the way in which most Chemists, many Geometricians, and Philosophers not a few prosecute their studies. I do not deny that sometimes in these wanderings they are lucky enough to find something true. But I do not allow that this argues greater industry on their part, but only better luck. But, however that may be, it were far better never to think of investigating truth at all, than to do so without a method. For it is very certain that unregulated inquiries and confused reflections of this kind only confound the natural light and blind our mental powers. Those who so become accustomed to walk in darkness weaken their eye-sight so much that afterwards they cannot bear the light of day. This is confirmed by experience; for how often do we not see that those who have never taken to letters, give a sounder and clearer decision about obvious matters than those who have spent all their time in the schools? Moreover by a method I mean certain and simple rules, such that, if a man observe them accurately, he shall never assume what is false as true, and will never spend his mental efforts to no purpose, but will always gradually increase his knowledge and so arrive at a true understanding of all that does not surpass his powers. . . .

Rule V

Method consists entirely in the order and disposition of the objects towards which our mental vision must be directed if we would find out any truth. We shall comply with it exactly if we reduce involved and obscure propositions step by step to those that are simpler, and then starting with the intuitive apprehension of all those that are absolutely simple, attempt to ascend to the knowledge of all others by precisely similar steps.

In this alone lies the sum of all human endeavour, and he who would approach the investigation of truth must hold to this rule as closely as he who enters the labyrinth must follow the thread which guided Theseus. But many people either do not reflect on the precept at all, or ignore it altogether, or presume not to need it. Consequently they often investigate the most difficult questions with so little regard to order, that, to my mind, they act like a man who should attempt to leap with one bound from the base to the summit of a house, either making no account of the ladders provided for his ascent or not noticing them. It is thus that all Astrologers behave, who, though in ignorance of the nature of the heavens, and even without having made proper observations of the movements of the heavenly bodies, expect to be able to indicate their effects. This is also what

many do who study Mechanics apart from Physics, and readily set about devising new instruments for producing motion. Along with them go also those Philosophers who, neglecting experience, imagine that truth will spring from their brain like Pallas from the head of Zeus.

Now it is obvious that all such people violate the present rule. But since the order here required is often so obscure and intricate that not everyone can make it out, they can scarcely avoid error unless they diligently observe what is laid down in the following proposition.

Rule VI

In order to separate out what is quite simple from what is complex, and to arrange these matters methodically, we ought, in the case of every series in which we have deduced certain facts the one from the other, to notice which fact is simple, and to mark the interval, greater, less or equal, which separates all the others from this.

Although this proposition seems to teach nothing very new, it contains, nevertheless, the chief secret of method, and none in the whole of this treatise is of greater utility. For it tells us that all facts can be arranged in certain series, not indeed in the sense of being referred to some ontological genus such as the categories employed by Philosophers in their classification, but in so far as certain truths can be known from others; and thus, whenever a difficulty occurs we are able at once to perceive whether it will be profitable to examine certain others first, and which, and in what order.

Further, in order to do that correctly, we must note first that for the purpose of our procedure, which does not regard things as isolated realities, but compares them with one another in order to discover the dependence in knowledge of one upon the other, all things can be said to be either absolute or relative.

I call that absolute which contains within itself the pure and simple essence of which we are in quest. Thus the term will be applicable to whatever is considered as being independent, or a cause, or simple, universal, one, equal, like, straight, and so forth; and the absolute I call the simplest and the easiest of all, so that we can make use of it in the solution of questions.

But the relative is that which, while participating in the same nature, or at least sharing in it to some degree which enables us to relate it to the absolute and to deduce it from that by a chain of operations, involves in addition something else in its concept which I call relativity. Examples of this are found in whatever is said to be dependent, or an effect, composite, particular, many, unequal, unlike, oblique, etc. These relatives are the further removed from the absolute, in proportion as they contain more elements of relativity subordinate the one to the other. We state in this rule that these should all be distinguished and their correlative connection and natural order so observed, that we may be able by

traversing all the intermediate steps to proceed from the most remote to that which is in the highest degree absolute. . . .

Finally we must note that our inquiry ought not to start with the investigation of difficult matters. Rather, before setting out to attack any definite problem, it behooves us first, without making any selection, to assemble those truths that are obvious as they present themselves to us, and afterwards, proceeding step by step, to inquire whether any others can be deduced from these, and again any others from these conclusions and so on, in order. This done, we should attentively think over the truths we have discovered and mark with diligence the reasons why we have been able to detect some more easily than others, and which these are. Thus, when we come to attack some definite problem we shall be able to judge what previous questions it were best to settle first. For example, if it comes into my thought that the number 6 is twice 3, I may then ask what is twice 6, viz., 12; again, perhaps I seek for the double of this, viz., 24, and again of this, viz., 48. Thus I may deduce that there is the same proportion between 3 and 6, as between 6 and 12, and likewise 12 and 24, and so on, and hence that the numbers 3, 6, 12, 24, 48, etc., are in continued proportion. But though these facts are all so clear as to seem almost childish, I am now able by attentive reflection to understand what is the form involved by all questions that can be propounded about the proportions or relations of things, and the order in which they should be investigated; and this discovery embraces the sum of the entire science of Pure Mathematics.

Rule VII

If we wish our science to be complete, those matters which promote the end we have in view must one and all be scrutinized by a movement of thought which is continuous and nowhere interrupted; they must also be included in an enumeration which is both adequate and methodical.

It is necessary to obey the injunctions of this rule if we hope to gain admission among the certain truths for those which, we have declared above, are not immediate deductions from primary and self-evident principles. For this deduction frequently involves such a long series of transitions from ground to consequent that when we come to the conclusion we have difficulty in recalling the whole of the route by which we have arrived at it. This is why I say that there must be a continuous movement of thought to make good this weakness of the memory. Thus, e.g., if I have first found out by separate mental operations what the relation is between the magnitudes A and B, then what between B and C, between C and D, and finally between D and E, that does not entail my seeing what the relation is between A and E, nor can the truths previously learnt give me a precise knowledge of it unless I recall them all. To remedy this I would run them over from time to time, keeping the imagination moving continuously

in such a way that while it is intuitively perceiving each fact it simultaneously passes on to the next; and this I would do until I had learned to pass from the first to the last so quickly, that no stage in the process was left to the care of the memory, but I seemed to have the whole in intuition before me at the same time. This method will both relieve the memory, diminish the sluggishness of our thinking, and definitely enlarge our mental capacity.

But we must add that this movement should nowhere be interrupted. Often people who attempt to deduce a conclusion too quickly and from remote principles do not trace the whole chain of intermediate conclusions with sufficient accuracy to prevent them from passing over many steps without due consideration. But it is certain that wherever the smallest link is left out the chain is broken and the whole of the certainty of the conclusion falls to the ground. . . .

Rule VIII

If in the matters to be examined we come to a step in the series of which our understanding is not sufficiently well able to have an intuitive cognition, we must stop short there. We must make no attempt to examine what follows; thus we shall spare ourselves superfluous labour.

. . . If a man proposes to himself the problem of examining all the truths for the knowledge of which human reason suffices—and I think that this is a task which should be undertaken once at least in his life by every person who seriously endeavors to attain equilibrium of thought—he will, by the rules given above, certainly discover that nothing can be known prior to the understanding, since the knowledge of all things else depends upon this and not conversely. Then, when he has clearly grasped all those things which follow proximately on the knowledge of the naked understanding, he will enumerate among other things whatever instruments of thought we have other than the understanding; and these are only two, viz., imagination and sense. He will therefore devote all his energies to the distinguishing and examining of these three modes of cognition, and seeing that in the strict sense truth and falsity can be a matter of the understanding alone, though often it derives its origin from the other two faculties, he will attend carefully to every source of deception in order that he may be on his guard. He will also enumerate exactly all the ways leading to truth which lie open to us, in order that he may follow the right way. They are not so many that they cannot all be easily discovered and embraced in an adequate enumeration. And though this will seem marvellous and incredible to the inexpert, as soon as in each matter he has distinguished those cognitions which only fill and embellish the memory, from those which cause one to be deemed really more instructed, which it will be easy for him to do, he will feel assured that any absence of further knowledge is not due to lack of intelligence or of skill, and that nothing at all can be known by anyone else which he is not capable of knowing, provided only that he gives to it his utmost mental application.

Meditations on the First Philosophy in Which the Existence of God and the Distinction between Mind and Body are Demonstrated

Meditation I

Of the things which may be brought within the sphere of the doubtful.

It is now some years since I detected how many were the false beliefs that I had from my earliest youth admitted as true, and how doubtful was everything I had since constructed on this basis; and from that time I was convinced that I must once for all seriously undertake to rid myself of all the opinions which I had formerly accepted, and commence to build anew from the foundation, if I wanted to establish any firm and permanent structure in the sciences. But as this enter-

The following excerpts from the *Meditations* are from *The Philosophical Works of Descartes,* translated from the Latin by Elizabeth S. Haldane and G. R. T. Ross, and published by Cambridge at the University Press, 1931. Where it seems desirable an alternative reading from the French is given in brackets. Reprinted by permission.

prise appeared to be a very great one, I waited until I had attained an age so mature that I could not hope that at any later date I should be better fitted to execute my design. This reason caused me to delay so long that I should feel that I was doing wrong were I to occupy in deliberation the time that yet remains to me for action. Today, then, since very opportunely for the plan I have in view I have delivered my mind from every care [and am happily agitated by no passions] and since I have procured for myself an assured leisure in a peaceable retirement, I shall at last seriously and freely address myself to the general upheaval of all my former opinions.

Now for this object it is not necessary that I should show that all of these are false—I shall perhaps never arrive at this end. But inasmuch as reason already persuades me that I ought no less carefully to withhold my assent from matters which are not entirely certain and indubitable than from those which appear to me manifestly to be false, if I am able to find in each one some reason to doubt, this will suffice to justify my rejecting the whole. And for that end it will not be requisite that I should examine each in particular, which would be an endless undertaking; for owing to the fact that the destruction of the foundations of necessity brings with it the downfall of the rest of the edifice, I shall only in the first place attack those principles upon which all my former opinions rested.

All that up to the present time I have accepted as most true and certain I have learned either from the senses or through the senses; but it is sometimes proved to me that these senses are deceptive, and it is wiser not to trust entirely to any thing by which we have once been deceived.

But it may be that although the senses sometimes deceive us concerning things which are hardly perceptible, or very far away, there are yet many others to be met with as to which we cannot reasonably have any doubt, although we recognize them by their means. For example, there is the fact that I am here, seated by the fire, attired in a dressing gown, having this paper in my hands and other similar matters. And how could I deny that these hands and this body are mine, were it not perhaps that I compare myself to certain persons, devoid of sense, whose cerebella are so troubled and clouded by the violent vapors of black bile, that they constantly assure us that they think they are kings when they are really quite poor, or that they are clothed in purple when they are really without covering, or who imagine that they have an earthenware head or are nothing but pumpkins or are made of glass. But they are mad, and I should not be any the less insane were I to follow examples so extravagant.

At the same time I must remember that I am a man, and that consequently I am in the habit of sleeping, and in my dreams representing to myself the same things or sometimes even less probable things, than do those who are insane in their waking moments. How often has it happened to me that in the night I dreamt that I found myself in this particular place, that I was dressed and seated near the fire, whilst in reality I was lying undressed in bed! At this moment it does indeed seem to me that it is with eyes awake that I am looking at this paper; that this head which I move is not asleep, that it is deliberately and of set purpose that I extend my hand and perceive it; what happens in sleep does not appear so clear nor so distinct as does all this. But in thinking over this I remind myself that on many occasions I have in sleep been deceived by similar illusions, and in dwelling carefully on this reflection I see so manifestly that there are no certain indications by which we may clearly distinguish wakefulness from sleep that I am lost in astonishment. And my astonishment is such that it is almost incapable of persuading me that I now dream.

Now let us assume that we are asleep and that all these particulars, *e.g.* that we open our eyes, shake our head, extend our hands, and so on, are but false delusions; and let us reflect that possibly neither our hands nor our whole body are such as they appear to us to be. At the same time we must at least confess that the things which are represented to us in sleep are like painted representations which can only have been formed as the counterparts of something real and true, and that in this way those general things at least, *i.e.* eyes, a head, hands, and a whole body, are not imaginary things, but things really existent. For, as a matter of fact, painters, even when they study with the greatest skill to represent sirens and satyrs by forms the most strange and extraordinary, cannot give them natures which are entirely new, but merely make a certain medley of the members of different animals; or if their imagination is extravagant enough to invent something so novel that nothing similar has ever before been seen, and that then their work represents a thing purely fictitious and absolutely false, it is certain all the same that the colors of which this is composed are necessarily real. And for the same reason, although these general things, to wit, [a body], eyes, a head, and such like, may be imaginary, we are bound at the same time to confess that there are at least some other objects yet more simple and more universal, which are real and true; and of these just in the same way as with certain real colors, all these images of things which dwell in our thoughts, whether true and real or false and fantastic, are formed.

To such a class of things pertains corporeal nature in general, and its extension, the figure of extended things, their quantity or magnitude and number, as also the place in which they are,

the time which measures their duration, and so on.

That is possibly why our reasoning is not unjust when we conclude from this that Physics, Astronomy, Medicine and all other sciences which have as their end the consideration of composite things, are very dubious and uncertain; but that Arithmetic, Geometry and other sciences of that kind which only treat of things that are very simple and very general, without taking great trouble to ascertain whether they are actually existent or not, contain some measure of certainty and an element of the indubitable. For whether I am awake or asleep, two and three together always form five, and the square can never have more than four sides, and it does not seem possible that truths so clear and apparent can be suspected of any falsity [or uncertainty].

Nevertheless I have long had fixed in my mind the belief that an all-powerful God existed by whom I have been created such as I am. But how do I know that He has not brought it to pass that there is no earth, no heaven, no extended body, no magnitude, no place, and that nevertheless [I possess the perceptions of all these things and that] they seem to me to exist just exactly as I now see them? And, besides, as I sometimes imagine that others deceive themselves in the things which they think they know best, how do I know that I am not deceived every time that I add two and three, or count the sides of a square, or judge of things yet simpler, if anything simpler can be imagined? But possibly God has not desired that I should be thus deceived, for He is said to be supremely good. If, however, it is contrary to His goodness to have made me such that I constantly deceive myself, it would also appear to be contrary to His goodness to permit me to be sometimes deceived, and nevertheless I cannot doubt that He does permit this.

There may indeed be those who would prefer to deny the existence of a God so powerful, rather than believe that all other things are uncertain. But let us not oppose them for the present, and grant that all that is said of a God is a fable; nevertheless in whatever way they suppose that I have arrived at the state of being that I have reached—whether they attribute it to fate or to accident, or make out that it is by a continual succession of antecedents, or by some other method—since to err and deceive oneself is a defect, it is clear that the greater will be the probability of my being so imperfect as to deceive myself ever, as is the Author to whom they assign my origin the less powerful. To these reasons I have certainly nothing to reply, but at the end I feel constrained to confess that there is nothing in all that I formerly believed to be true, of which I cannot in some measure doubt, and that not merely through want of thought or through levity, but for reasons which are very powerful and maturely considered; so that henceforth I ought not the less carefully to refrain from giving credence to these opinions than to that which is manifestly false, if I desire to arrive at any certainty [in the sciences].

But it is not sufficient to have made these remarks, we must also be careful to keep them in mind. For these ancient and commonly held opinions still revert frequently to my mind, long and familiar custom having given them the right to occupy my mind against my inclination and rendered them almost masters of my belief; nor will I ever lose the habit of deferring to them or of placing my confidence in them, so long as I consider them as they really are, *i.e.* opinions in some measure doubtful, as I have just shown, and at the same time highly probable, so that there is much more reason to believe than to deny them. That is why I consider that I shall not be acting amiss, if, taking of set purpose a contrary belief, I allow myself to be deceived, and for a certain time pretend that all these opinions are entirely false and imaginary, until at last, having thus balanced my former prejudices with my latter [so that they cannot divert my opinions more to one side than to the other], my judgment will no longer be dominated by bad usage or turned away from the right knowledge of the truth. For I am assured that there can be neither peril nor error in this course, and that I cannot at present yield too much to distrust, since I am not considering the question of action, but only of knowledge.

I shall then suppose, not that God who is supremely good and the fountain of truth, but some evil genius not less powerful than deceitful, has employed his whole energies in deceiving me; I shall consider that the heavens, the earth, colors, figures, sound, and all other external things are nought but the illusions and dreams of which this genius has availed himself in order to lay traps for my credulity; I shall consider myself as having no hands, no eyes, no flesh, no blood, nor any senses, yet falsely believing myself to possess all these things; I shall remain obstinately attached to this idea, and if by this means it is not in my power to arrive at the knowledge of any truth, I may at least do what is in my power [*i.e.* suspend my judgment], and with firm purpose avoid giving credence to any false thing, or being imposed upon by this arch deceiver, however powerful and deceptive he may be. But this task is a laborious one, and insensibly a certain lassitude leads me into the course of my ordinary life. And just as a captive who in sleep enjoys imaginary liberty, when he begins to suspect that his liberty is but a dream, fears to awaken, and conspires with these agreeable illusions that the deception may be prolonged, so insensibly of my own accord I fall back into my former opinions, and I dread awakening from this slumber, lest the laborious wakefulness which would follow the tranquillity of this repose should have to be spent not in daylight, but in the excessive darkness of the difficulties which have just been discussed.

Meditation II

Of the Nature of the Human Mind; and that it is more easily known than the Body.

The Meditation of yesterday filled my mind with so many doubts that it is no longer in my power to forget them. And yet I do not see in what manner I can resolve them; and, just as if I had all of a sudden fallen into very deep water, I am so disconcerted that I can neither make certain of setting my feet on the bottom, nor can I swim and so support myself on the surface. I shall nevertheless make an effort and follow anew the same path as that on which I yesterday entered, *i.e.* I shall proceed by setting aside all that in which the least doubt could be supposed to exist, just as if I had discovered that it was absolutely false; and I shall ever follow in this road until I have met with something which is certain, or at least, if I can do nothing else, until I have learned for certain that there is nothing in the world that is certain. Archimedes, in order that he might draw the terrestrial globe out of its place, and transport it elsewhere, demanded only that one point should be fixed and immovable; in the same way I shall have the right to conceive high hopes if I am happy enough to discover one thing only which is certain and indubitable.

I suppose, then, that all the things that I see are false; I persuade myself that nothing has ever existed of all that my fallacious memory represents to me. I consider that I possess no senses; I imagine that body, figure, extension, movement and place are but the fictions of my mind. What, then, can be esteemed as true? Perhaps nothing at all, unless that there is nothing in the world that is certain.

But how can I know there is not something different from those things that I have just considered, of which one cannot have the slightest doubt? Is there not some God, or some other being by whatever name we call it, who puts these reflections into my mind? That is not necessary, for is it not possible that I am capable of producing them myself? I myself, am I not at least something? But I have already denied that I had senses and body. Yet I hesitate, for what follows from that? Am I so dependent on body and senses that I cannot exist without these? But I was persuaded that there was nothing in all the world, that there was no heaven, no earth, that there were no minds, nor any bodies: was I not then likewise persuaded that I did not exist? Not at all; of a surety I myself did exist since I persuaded myself of something [or merely because I thought of something]. But there is some deceiver or other, very powerful and very cunning, who ever employs his ingenuity in deceiving me. Then without doubt I exist also if he deceives me, and let him deceive me as much as he will, he can never cause me to be nothing so long as I think that I am something. So that after having reflected well and carefully examined all things, we must come to the definite conclusion that this proposition: I am, I exist, is necessarily true each time that I pronounce it, or that I mentally conceive it.

But I do not yet know clearly enough what I am, I who am certain that I am; and hence I must be careful to see that I do not imprudently take some other object in place of myself, and thus that I do not go astray in respect of this knowledge that I hold to be the most certain and most evident of all that I have formerly learned. That is why I shall now consider anew what I believed myself to be before I embarked upon these last reflections; and of my former opinions I shall withdraw all that might even in a small degree be invalidated by the reasons which I have just brought forward, in order that there may be nothing at all left beyond what is absolutely certain and indubitable.

What then did I formerly believe myself to be? Undoubtedly I believed myself to be a man. But what is a man? Shall I say a reasonable animal? Certainly not; for then I should have to inquire what an animal is, and what is reasonable; and thus from a single question I should insensibly fall into an infinitude of others more difficult; and I should not wish to waste the little time and leisure remaining to me in trying to unravel subtleties like these. But I shall rather stop here to consider the thoughts which of themselves spring up in my mind, and which were not inspired by anything beyond my own nature alone when I applied myself to the consideration of my being. In the first place, then, I considered myself as having a face, hands, arms, and all that system of members composed of bones and flesh as seen in a corpse which I designated by the name of body. In addition to this I considered that I was nourished, that I walked, that I felt, and that I thought, and I referred all these actions to the soul: but I did not stop to consider what the soul was, or if I did stop, I imagined that it was something extremely rare and subtle like a wind, a flame, or an ether, which was spread throughout my grosser parts. As to body I had no manner of doubt about its nature, but thought I had a very clear knowledge of it; and if I had desired to explain it according to the notions that I had then formed of it, I should have described it thus: By the body I understand all that which can be defined by a certain figure: something which can be confined in a certain place, and which can fill a given space in such a way that every other body will be excluded from it; which can be perceived either by touch, or by sight, or by hearing, or by taste, or by smell: which can be moved in many ways not, in truth, by itself, but by something which is foreign to it, by which it is touched [and from which it receives impressions]: for to have the power of self-movement, as also of feeling or of thinking, I did not consider to appertain to the nature of body: on the contrary, I was rather astonished to find that faculties similar to them existed in some bodies.

But what am I, now that I suppose that there is a certain genius which is extremely powerful, and, if I may say so, malicious, who employs all his powers in deceiving me? Can I affirm that I possess the least of all those things which I have just said pertain to the nature of body? I pause to consider, I resolve all these things in my mind, and find none of which I can say that it pertains to me. It would be tedious to stop to enumerate them. Let us pass to the attributes of soul and see if there is any one which is in me? What of nutrition or walking [the first mentioned]? But if it is so that I have no body, it is also true that I can neither walk nor take nourishment. Another attribute is sensation. But one cannot feel without body, and besides I have thought I perceived many things during sleep that I recognized in my waking moments as not having been experienced at all. What of thinking? I find here that thought is an attribute that belongs to me; it alone cannot be

separated from me. I am, I exist, that is certain. But how often? Just when I think; for it might possibly be the case if I ceased entirely to think, that I should likewise cease altogether to exist. I do not now admit anything which is not necessarily true: to speak accurately I am not more than a thing which thinks, that is to say a mind or a soul, or an understanding, or a reason, which are terms whose significance was formerly unknown to me. I am, however, a real thing and really exist; but what thing? I have answered: a thing which thinks.

And what more? I shall exercise my imagination [in order to see if I am not something more]. I am not a collection of members which we call the human body: I am not a subtle air distributed through these members, I am not a wind, a fire, a vapor, a breath, nor anything at all which I can imagine or conceive; because I have assumed that all these were nothing. Without changing that supposition I find that I only leave myself certain of the fact that I am somewhat. But perhaps it is true that these same things which I supposed were non-existent because they are unknown to me, are really not different from the self which I know. I am not sure about this, I shall not dispute about it now; I can only give judgment on things that are known to me. I know that I exist, and I inquire what I am, I whom I know to exist. But it is very certain that the knowledge of my existence taken in its precise significance does not depend on things whose existence is not yet known to me; consequently it does not depend on those which I can feign in imagination. And indeed the very term *feign* in imagination proves to me my error, for I really do this if I image myself a something, since to imagine is nothing else than to contemplate the figure or image of a corporeal thing. But I already know for certain that I am, and that it may be that all these images, and, speaking generally, all things that relate to the nature of body are nothing but dreams [and chimeras]. For this reason I see clearly that I have as little reason to say, "I shall stimulate my imagination in order to know more distinctly what I am," than if I were to say, "I am now awake," and I perceive somewhat that is real and true: but because I do not yet perceive it distinctly enough, I shall go to sleep of express purpose, so that my dreams may represent the perception with greatest truth and evidence." And, thus, I know for certain that nothing of all that I can understand by means of my imagination belongs to this knowledge which I have of myself, and that it is necessary to recall the mind from this mode of thought with the utmost diligence in order that it may be able to know its own nature with perfect distinctness.

But what then am I? A thing which thinks. What is a thing which thinks? It is a thing which doubts, understands, [conceives], affirms, denies, wills, refuses, which also imagines and feels.

Certainly it is no small matter if all these things pertain to my nature. But why should they not so pertain? Am I not that being who now doubts nearly everything, who nevertheless understands certain things, who affirms that one only is true, who denies all the others, who desires to know more, is averse from being deceived, who imagines many things, sometimes indeed despite his will, and who perceives many likewise, as by the intervention of the bodily organs? Is there nothing in all this which is as true as it is certain that I exist, even though I should always sleep and though he who has given me being employed all his ingenuity in deceiving me? Is there likewise any one of these attributes which can be distinguished from my thought, or which might be said to be separated from myself? For it is so evident of itself that it is I who doubts, who understands, and who desires, that there is no reason here to add anything to explain it. And I have certainly the power of imagining likewise; for although it may happen (as I formerly supposed) that none of the things which I imagine are true, nevertheless this power of imagining does not cease to be really in use, and it forms part of my thought. Finally, I am the same who feels, that is to say, who perceives certain things, as by the organs of sense, since in truth I see light, I hear noise, I feel heat. But it will be said that these phenomena are false and that I am dreaming. Let it be so; still it is at least quite certain that it seems to me that I see light, that I hear noise and that I feel heat. That cannot be false; properly speaking it is what is in me called feeling; and used in this precise sense that is no other thing than thinking.

From this time I begin to know what I am with a little more clearness and distinction than before; but nevertheless it still seems to me, and I cannot prevent myself from thinking, that corporeal things, whose images are framed by thought, which are tested by the senses, are much more distinctly known than that obscure part of me which does not come under the imagination. Although really it is very strange to say that I know and understand more distinctly these things whose existence seems to me dubious, which are unknown to me, and which do not belong to me, than others of the truth of which I am convinced, which are known to me and which pertain to my real nature, in a word, than myself. But I see clearly how the case stands: my mind loves to wander, and cannot yet suffer itself to be retained within the just limits of truth. Very good, let us once more give it the freest rein, so that, when afterwards we seize the proper occasion for pulling up, it may the more easily be regulated and controlled.

Let us begin by considering the commonest matters, those which we believe to be the most distinctly comprehended, to wit, the bodies which we touch and see; not indeed bodies in general, for these general ideas are usually a little more confused, but let us consider one body in particular. Let us take for example, this piece of wax: it has been taken quite freshly from the hive, and it has not yet lost the sweetness of the honey which it contains; it still retains somewhat of the odor of the flowers from which it has been culled; its color, its figure, its size are apparent; it is hard, cold, easily handled, and if you strike it with the finger, it will emit a sound. Finally all the things which are requisite to cause us distinctly to recognize a body, are met within it. But notice that while I speak and approach the fire what remained of the taste is exhaled, the smell evaporates, the color alters, the figure is destroyed, the size increases, it becomes liquid, it heats, scarcely can one handle it, and when one strikes it, no sound is emitted. Does the same wax remain after this change? We must confess that it remains; none would judge otherwise. What then did I know so distinctly in this piece of wax? It could certainly be nothing of all that the senses brought to my notice, since all these things which fall under taste, smell, sight, touch, and hearing, are found to be changed, and yet the same wax remains.

Perhaps it was what I now think, viz. that this wax was not that sweetness of honey, nor that agreeable scent of flowers, nor that particular whiteness, nor that figure, nor that sound, but simply a body which a little before appeared to me as perceptible under these forms, and which is now perceptible under others. But what, precisely, is that I imagine when I form such conceptions? Let us attentively consider this, and, abstracting from all that does not belong to the wax, let us see what remains. Certainly nothing remains excepting a certain extended thing which is flexible and movable. But what is the meaning of flexible and movable? Is it not that I imagine that this piece of wax being round is capable of becoming square and of passing from a square to a triangular figure? No, certainly it is not that, since I imagine it admits of an infinitude of similar changes, and I nevertheless do not know how to compass the infinitude by my imagination, and consequently this conception which I have of the wax is not brought about by the faculty of imagination. What now is this extension? Is it not also unknown? For it becomes greater when the wax is melted, greater when it is boiled, and greater still when the heat increases; and I should not conceive [clearly] according to truth what wax is, if I did not think that even this piece that we are considering is capable of receiving more variations in extension than I have ever imagined. We must then grant that I could not even understand through the imagination what this piece of wax is, and that it is my mind alone which perceives it. I say this piece of wax in particular, for as to wax in general it is yet clearer. But what is this piece of wax which cannot be understood excepting by the [understanding or] mind? It is certainly the same that I see, touch, imagine, and finally it is the same which I have always believed it to be from the beginning. But what must particularly be observed is that its perception is neither an act of vision, nor of touch, nor of imagination, and has never been such although it may have appeared formerly to be so, but only an intuition of the mind, which may be imperfect and confused as it was formerly, or clear and distinct as it is at present, according as my attention is more or less directed to the elements which are found in it, and of which it is composed.

Yet in the meantime I am greatly astonished when I consider [the great feebleness of mind] and its proneness to fall [insensibly] into error; for although without giving expression to my thoughts I consider all this in my own mind, words often impede me and I am almost deceived by the terms of ordinary language. For we say that we see the same wax, if it is present, and not that we simply judge that it is the same from its having the same color and figure. From this I should conclude that I knew the wax by means of vision and not simply by the intuition of the mind; unless by chance I remember that, when looking from a window and saying I see men who pass in the street, I really do not see them, but infer that what I see is men, just as I say that I see wax. And yet what do I see from the window but hats and coats which may cover automatic machines? Yet I judge these to be men. And similarly solely by the faculty of judgment which rests in my mind, I comprehend that which I believed I saw with my eyes.

A man who makes it his aim to raise his knowledge above the common should be ashamed to derive the occasion for doubting from the forms of speech invented by the vulgar; I prefer to pass on and consider whether I had a more evident and perfect conception of what the wax was when I first perceived it, and when I believed I knew it by means of the external senses or at least by the common sense as it is called, that is to say by the imaginative faculty, or whether my present conception is clearer now that I have most carefully examined what it is, and in what way it can be known. It would certainly be absurd to doubt as to this. For what was there in this first perception which was distinct? What was there which might not as well have been perceived by any of the animals? But when I distinguish the wax from its external forms, and when, just as if I had taken from it its vestments, I consider it quite naked, it is certain that although some error may still be found in my judgment, I can nevertheless not perceive it thus without a human mind.

But finally what shall I say of this mind, that is, of myself, for up to this point I do not admit in myself anything but mind? What then, I who seem to perceive this piece of wax distinctly, do I not know myself, not only with much more truth and certainty, but also with much more distinctness and clearness? For if I judge that the wax is or exists from the fact that I see it, it certainly follows much more clearly that I am or that I exist myself from the fact that I see it. For it may be that what I see is not really wax, it may also be that I do not possess eyes with which to see anything; but it cannot be that when I see, or (for I no longer take account of the distinction) when I think I see, that I myself who think am nought. So if I judge that the wax exists from the fact that I touch it, the same thing will follow, to wit, that I am; and if I judge that my imagination, or some other cause, whatever it is, persuades me that the wax exists, I shall still conclude the same. And what I have here remarked of wax may be applied to all other things which are external to me [and which are met with outside of me]. And further, if the [notion or] perception of wax has seemed to me

clearer and more distinct, not only after the sight or the touch, but also after many other causes have rendered it quite manifest to me, with how much more [evidence] and distinctness must it be said that I now know myself, since all the reasons which contribute to the knowledge of wax, or any other body whatever, are yet better proofs of the nature of my mind! And there are so many other things in the mind itself which may contribute to the elucidation of its nature, that those which depend on body such as these just mentioned, hardly merit being taken into account.

But finally here I am, having insensibly reverted to the point I desired, for, since it is now manifest to me that even bodies are not properly speaking known by the senses or by the faculty of imagination, but by the understanding only, and since they are not known from the fact that they are seen or touched, but only because they are understood, I see clearly that there is nothing which is easier for me to know than my mind. But because it is difficult to rid oneself so promptly of an opinion to which one was accustomed for so long, it will be well that I should halt a little at this point, so that by the length of my meditation I may more deeply imprint on my memory this new knowledge.

Meditation III

Of God: that He exists.

I shall now close my eyes, I shall stop my ears, I shall call away all my senses, I shall efface even from my thoughts all the images of corporeal things, or at least (for that is hardly possible). I shall esteem them as vain and false; and thus holding converse only with myself and considering my own nature, I shall try little by little to reach a better knowledge of and a more familiar acquaintanceship with myself. I am a thing that thinks, that is to say, that doubts, affirms, denies, that knows a few things, that is ignorant of many, [that loves, that hates], that wills, that desires, that also imagines and perceives; for as I remarked before, although the things which I perceive and imagine are perhaps nothing at all apart from me and in themselves, I am nevertheless assured that these modes of thought that I call perceptions and imaginations, inasmuch only as they are modes of thought, certainly reside [and are met with] in me.

And in the little that I have just said, I think I have summed up all that I really know, or at least all that hitherto I was aware that I knew. In order to try to extend my knowledge further, I shall now look around more carefully and see whether I cannot still discover in myself some other things which I have not hitherto perceived. I am certain that I am a thing which thinks; but do I not then likewise know what is requisite to render me certain of a truth? Certainly in this first knowledge there is nothing that assures me of its truth, excepting the clear and distinct perception of that which I state, which would not indeed suffice to assure me that what I say is true, if it could ever happen that a thing which I conceived so clearly and distinctly could be false; and accord-

ingly it seems to me that already I can establish as a general rule that all things which I perceive very clearly and very distinctly are true.

At the same time I have before received and admitted many things to be very certain and manifest, which yet I afterwards recognized as being dubious. What then were these things? They were the earth, sky, stars and all other objects which I apprehended by means of the senses. But what did I clearly [and distinctly] perceive in them? Nothing more than that the ideas or thoughts of these things were presented to my mind. And not even now do I deny that these ideas are met with in me. But there was yet another thing which I affirmed, and which, owing to the habit which I had formed of believing it, I thought I perceived very clearly, although in truth I did not perceive it at all, to wit, that there were objects outside of me from which these ideas proceeded, and to which they were entirely similar. And it was in this that I erred, or, if perchance my judgment was correct, this was not due to any knowledge arising from my perception.

But when I took anything very simple and easy in the sphere of arithmetic or geometry into consideration, *e.g.* that two and three together made five, and other things of the sort, were not these present to my mind so clearly as to enable me to affirm that they were true? Certainly if I judged that since such matters could be doubted, this would not have been so for any other reason than that it came into my mind that perhaps a God might have endowed me with such a nature that I may have been deceived even concerning things which seemed to me most manifest. But every time that this preconceived opinion of the sovereign power of a God presents itself to my thought, I am constrained to confess that it is easy to Him, if He wishes it, to cause me to err, even in matters in which I believe myself to have the best evidence. And, on the other hand, always when I direct my attention to things which I believe myself to perceive very clearly, I am so persuaded of their truth that I let myself break out into words such as these: Let who will deceive me, He can never cause me to be nothing while I think that I am, or some day cause it to be true to say that I have never been, it being true now to say that I am, or that two and three make more or less than five, or any such thing in which I see a manifest contradiction. And certainly, since I have no reason to believe that there is a God who is a deceiver, and as I have not yet satisfied myself that there is a God at all, the reason for doubt which depends on this opinion alone is very slight, and so to speak metaphysical. But in order to be able altogether to remove it, I must inquire whether there is a God as soon as the occasion presents itself; and if I find that there is a God, I must also inquire whether He may be a deceiver; for without a knowledge of these two truths I do not see that I can ever be certain of anything.

[*To answer this lingering doubt, Descartes "proves" that there is a God who, as perfect, would not deceive me. Since arguments for the existence of God will be considered in detail in Chapter 14, a brief summary of Descartes' arguments will here be sufficient.*

His first argument for the existence of God consists of four steps: (1) I have an idea of God. (2) Everything, including my idea, has a cause. (3) Since the greater cannot proceed from the less, nothing less than God is adequate to explain my idea of God. This step involves the notion that the idea of a Perfect Being is, in conception, perfect; that no imperfect being is capable of producing such an idea; and that hence it requires a perfect Cause to produce it. (4) Therefore God exists.

Descartes advances a second argument for God, once again starting with "I think, therefore I am." He argues (still using the first person pronoun) that God is the cause, not only of my idea of God, but of me. This is an argument by elimination: (1) I am not the cause of myself, for if I were, I would not be the highly imperfect and fallible being that I know myself to be. (2) No other finite being could be the sufficient cause of my existence, for if such a being existed, it in turn would have to be explained, as would any prior finite cause as well. I would thus have to trace the causal process back from stage to stage to the ultimate cause, an eternal and necessary being who requires no explanation beyond himself. Only such an infinite cause could be conceived as existing, not merely through my life, but through all the lives involved in the total succession of finite beings—and only such a cause would be adequate to maintain as well as to originate the entire succession.

(3) *The ultimate cause could not be multiple, because I conceive of God as absolutely one, and the cause of this idea must be no less perfect than its effect, not falling short of the idea in its unity or in any other respect.* (4) *The only possibility that remains is that an infinite and monotheistic God is the cause. Therefore God exists.*

In Meditation V which has been omitted in the present book, Descartes presents a third argument for God's existence—a restatement of the so-called Ontological Argument of Saint Anselm, an early medieval philosopher. Since this argument is dealt with in Chapter 14, we shall not consider it here.

The importance of God in Descartes' system is that He is used to guarantee not a system of dogma but science and philosophy. Science and philosophy are based upon reason and memory, and God is needed to guarantee their reliability. God, being perfect, would not deceive me—he would not, like a malignant demon, so mislead me as to invalidate my most vivid memory and careful reasoning. Descartes' constructive argument starts with "I think, therefore I am." But, almost surreptitiously, he admits three other "self-evident truths":

1. *Whatever is clearly and distinctly perceived is true.*

2. *Nothing can be without a cause.*

3. *The cause must be at least as great as the effect.*

From these premises he deduces two additional "truths":

4. *God exists.*

5. *God, being perfect, cannot deceive me.*

The rest of his argument follows rather quickly. He argues for the existence of other minds and material objects alike on the grounds of God's veracity. This means not that all my ideas are true but simply that the faculties God has given me are reliable when used correctly—without prejudice, hastiness, or naïveté. I can trust only "firm conceptions born in a sound and attentive mind from the light of reason alone" and rigorous deductions from these conceptions.

The remainder of Meditation III and Meditations IV and V are omitted.]

Meditation VI

Of the existence of Material Things, and of the real distinction between the Soul and Body of Man.

. . . First of all I shall recall to my memory those matters which I hitherto held to be true, as having perceived them through the senses, and the foundations on which my belief has rested; in the next place I shall examine the reasons which have since obliged me to place them in doubt; in the last place I shall consider which of them I must now believe.

First of all, then, I perceived that I had a head, hands, feet, and all other members of which this body—which I considered as a part, or possibly even as the whole, of myself—is composed. Further I was sensible that this body was placed amidst many others, from which it was capable of being affected in many different ways, beneficial and hurtful, and I remarked that a certain feeling of pleasure accompanied those that were beneficial, and pain those which were harmful. And in addition to this pleasure and pain, I also experienced hunger, thirst, and other similar appetites, as also certain corporeal inclinations towards joy, sadness, anger, and other similar passions. And outside myself, in addition to extension, figure, and motions of bodies, I remarked in them hardness, heat, and all other tactile qualities, and, further, light and color, and scents and sounds, the variety of which gave me the means of distinguishing the sky, the earth, the sea, and generally all the other bodies, one from the other. And certainly, considering the ideas of all these qualities which presented themselves to my mind, and which alone I perceived properly or immediately, it was not without reason that I believed myself to perceive objects quite different from my thought, to wit, bodies from which those ideas proceeded; for I found by experience that these ideas presented themselves to me without my consent being requisite, so that I could not perceive any object, however desirous I might be, unless it were present to the organs of sense; and it was not in my power not to perceive it, when it was present. And because the ideas which I perceived through the senses were much more lively, more clear, and even, in their own way, more distinct than any of those which I could of myself frame in meditation, or than those I found impressed on my memory, it appeared as though they could not have proceeded from my mind, so that they must necessarily have been produced in me by some other things.

And having no knowledge of those objects excepting the knowledge which the ideas themselves gave me, nothing was more likely to occur to my mind than that the objects were similar to the ideas which were caused. And because I likewise remembered that I had formerly made use of my senses rather than my reason, and recognized that the ideas which I formed of myself were not so distinct as those which I perceived through the senses, and that they were most frequently even composed of portions of these last, I persuaded myself easily that I had no idea in my mind which had not formerly come to me through the senses. Nor was it without some reason that I believed that this body (which by a certain special right I call my own) belonged to me more properly and more strictly than any other; for in fact I could never be separated from it as from other bodies; I experienced in it and on account of it all my appetites and affections, and finally I was touched by the feeling of pain and the titillation of pleasure in its parts, and not in the parts of other bodies which were separated from it. But when I inquired, why, from some, I know not what, painful sensation, there follows sadness of mind, and from the pleasurable sensation there arises joy, or why this mysterious emotion of the stomach which I call hunger causes me to desire to eat, and dryness of throat causes a desire to drink, and so on, I could give no reason excepting that nature taught me so; for there is certainly no affinity (that I at least can understand) between the craving of the stomach and the desire to eat, any more than between the perception of whatever causes pain and the thought of sadness which arises from this perception. And in the same way it appeared to me that I had learned from nature all the other judgments which I formed regarding the objects of my senses, since I remarked that these judgments were formed in me before I had the leisure to weigh and consider any reasons which might oblige me to make them.

But afterwards many experiences little by little destroyed all the faith which I had rested in my senses; for I from time to time observed that those towers which from afar appeared to me to be round, more closely observed seemed square, and that colossal statues raised on the summit of these towers, appeared as quite tiny statues when viewed from the bottom; and so in an infinitude of other cases I found error in judgments founded on the external senses. And not only in those founded on the external senses, but even in those founded on the internal as well; for is there anything more intimate or more internal than pain? And yet I have learned from some persons whose arms or legs have been cut off, that they sometimes seemed to feel pain in the part which had been amputated, which made me think that I could not be quite certain that it was a certain member which pained me, even although I felt pain in it. And to those grounds of doubt I have lately added two others, which are very general; the first is that I never have believed myself to feel anything in waking moments which I cannot also sometimes believe myself to feel when I sleep, and as I do not think that these things

which I seem to find in sleep, proceed from objects outside of me, I do not see any reason why I should have this belief regarding objects which I seem to perceive while awake. The other was that being still ignorant, or rather supposing myself to be ignorant, of the author of my being, I saw nothing to prevent me from having been so constituted by nature that I might be deceived even in matters which seemed to me to be most certain. And as to the grounds on which I was formerly persuaded of the truth of sensible objects, I had not much trouble in replying to them. For since nature seemed to cause me to lean towards many things from which reason repelled me, I did not believe that I should trust much to the teachings of nature. And although the ideas which I receive by the senses do not depend on my will, I did not think that one should for that reason conclude that they proceeded from things different from myself, since possibly some faculty might be discovered in me—though hitherto unknown to me—which produced them.

But now that I begin to know myself better, and to discover more clearly the author of my being, I do not in truth think that I should rashly admit all the matters which the senses seem to teach us, but, on the other hand, I do not think that I should doubt them all universally.

And first of all, because I know that all things which I apprehend clearly and distinctly can be created by God as I apprehend them, it suffices that I am able to apprehend one thing apart from another clearly and distinctly in order to be certain that the one is different from the other, since they may be made to exist in separation at least by the omnipotence of God; and it does not signify by what power this separation is made in order to compel me to judge them to be different: and, therefore, just because I know certainly that I exist, and that meanwhile I do not remark that any other thing necessarily pertains to my nature or essence, excepting that I am a thinking thing, I rightly conclude that my essence consists solely in the fact that I am a thinking thing [or a substance whose whole essence or nature is to think]. And although possibly (or rather certainly, as I shall say in a moment) I possess a body with which I am very intimately conjoined, yet because, on the one side, I have a clear and distinct idea of myself inasmuch as I am only a thinking and unextended thing, and as, on the other, I possess a distinct idea of body, inasmuch as it is only an extended and unthinking thing, it is certain that this I [that is to say, my soul by which I am what I am], is entirely and absolutely distinct from my body, and can exist without it. . . .

. . . There is a great difference between mind and body, inasmuch as body is by nature always divisible, and the mind is entirely indivisible. For, as a matter of fact, when I consider the mind, that is to say, myself inasmuch as I am only a thinking thing, I cannot distinguish in myself any parts, but apprehend myself to be clearly one and entire; and although the whole mind seems to be united to the whole body, yet if a foot, or an arm, or some other part, is separated from my body, I am aware that nothing has been taken away

from my mind. And the faculties of willing, feeling, conceiving, etc., cannot be properly speaking said to be its parts, for it is one and the same mind which employs itself in willing and in feeling and understanding. But it is quite otherwise with corporeal or extended objects, for there is not one of these imaginable by me which my mind cannot easily divide into parts, and which consequently I do not recognize as being divisible; this would be sufficient to teach me that the mind or soul of man is entirely different from the body, if I have not already learned it from other sources. . . .

From this it is quite clear that, notwithstanding the supreme goodness of God, the nature of man, inasmuch as it is composed of mind and body, cannot be otherwise than sometimes a source of deception. For if there is any cause which excites, not in the foot but in some parts of the nerves which are extended between the foot and the brain, or even the brain itself, the same movement which usually is produced when the foot is detrimentally affected, pain will be experienced as though it were in the foot, and the sense will thus naturally be deceived; for since the same movement in the brain is capable of causing but one sensation in the mind, and this sensation is much more frequently excited by a cause which hurts the foot than by another existing in some other quarter, it is reasonable that it should convey to the mind pain in the foot rather than in any other part of the body. And although the parchedness of the throat does not always proceed, as it usually does, from the fact that drinking is essential for the health of the body, but sometimes comes from quite a different cause, as is the case with dropsical patients, it is yet much better that it should mislead on this occasion than if, on the other hand, it were always to deceive us when the body is in good health; and so on in similar cases.

And certainly this consideration is of great service to me, not only in enabling me to recognize all the errors to which my nature is subject, but also in enabling me to avoid them or to correct them more easily. For knowing that all my senses more frequently indicate to me truth than falsehood respecting the things which concern that which is beneficial to the body, and being able almost always to avail myself of many of them in order to examine one particular thing, and, besides that, being able to make use of my memory in order to connect the present with the past, and of my understanding which already has discovered all the causes of my errors, I ought no longer to fear that falsity may be found in matters every day presented to me by my senses. And I ought to set aside all the doubts of these past days as hyperbolical and ridiculous, particularly that very common uncertainty respecting sleep, which I could not distinguish from the waking state; for at present I find a very notable difference between the two, inasmuch as our memory can never connect our dreams one with the other, or with the whole course of our lives, as it unites events which happen to us while we are awake. And, as a matter of fact, if someone, while I was awake, quite suddenly appeared to me and disappeared as fast as do the images which I see in sleep, so that I could not know from whence the form came nor whither it went, it would not be without reason that I should deem it a specter or a phantom formed by my brain [and similar to those which I form in sleep], rather than a real man. But when I perceive things as to which I know distinctly both the place from which they proceed, and that in which they are, and the time at which they appeared to me; and when, without any interruption, I can connect the perceptions which I have of them with the whole course of my life, I am perfectly assured that these perceptions occur while I am waking and not during sleep. And I ought in no wise to doubt the truth of such matters, if, after having called up all my senses, my memory, and my understanding, to examine them, nothing is brought to evidence by any one of them which is repugnant to what is set forth by the others. For because God is in no wise a deceiver, it follows that I am not deceived in this. But because the exigencies of action often oblige us to make up our minds before having leisure to examine matters carefully, we must confess that the life of man is very frequently subject to error in respect to individual objects, and we must in the end acknowledge the infirmity of our nature.

ARTHUR O. LOVEJOY (1873–1962)

Lovejoy was born in Berlin, the son of the Reverend W. W. Lovejoy and Sara Oncken of Hamburg. He was educated at the University of California (Berkeley) and Harvard, and taught at a number of universities, including Stanford and Columbia. In 1910 he was appointed to the staff of Johns Hopkins University, where he remained until his retirement in 1938. Defending the dualism derived from Descartes and Locke, he was widely admired as an epistemologist and metaphysician. He was the first editor of the *Journal of the History of Ideas*, and was an acknowledged authority on Primitivism, Romanticism, and other movements in the history of thought. As a man of action, he helped to organize the American Association of University Professors and was an inveterate defender of academic freedom.

The Revolt
Against Dualism

The revolt . . . against dualism, both psychophysical and epistemological, has failed. The content of our actual experience does not consist wholly, and it is unprovable and improbable that any part of it consists, of entities which, upon *any* plausible theory of the constitution of the physical world, can be supposed to be members of that world; it consists of particulars which arise

through the functioning of percipient organisms, are present only within the private fields of awareness of such organisms, are destitute of certain of the essential properties and relations implied either by the historic concept of the "physical" or by the contemporary physicist's concept of it, and possess properties which physical things lack. They *are*, in short, essentially of the nature of "ideas," as Descartes and Locke (for the most part) used that term. And it is through these entities that any knowledge which we may attain of the concrete characters of the physical world, and of any other realities extraneous to our several private fields of awareness, must be mediated; so that we are brought back to Locke's conclusion, despite the heroic efforts of so many philosophers of our age to escape from it: "it is evident that the mind knows not things immediately, but by the intervention of the ideas it has of them." If the word "nature" is used—though I think it is unhappily so used—to mean exclusively the world as it is, or may conceivably be, apart from all experience, *i.e.*, apart from the processes of conscious perception and thought and phantasy and feeling, then between "nature" and experience there is a radical discontinuity; for the occurrence of those processes adds to the sum of reality not only particular existents, but kinds of existents, which "nature"—if so defined—though it engenders them, cannot plausibly be supposed to contain.

It may, however, seem that the triumph of dualism has been all too complete, that these arguments explode the foundations of all realism. Especially may the developments in recent physics to which I have referred appear to some to have this effect. The question that now presses for consideration, it may be said, is no longer whether (as the pan-objectivist happily and innocently supposed) everything we perceptually experience is "objective" and "physical," but whether *anything* we experience is (even in the epistemological sense) objective and revelatory of the nature of the physical world. The theory of relativity is generally conceived to have rendered dubious and equivocal, if not to have disproved, the spatiality of physical objects in their macroscopic aspect; and the latest hypotheses concerning the minute components of "matter" and their relation to energy-quanta to have, so to say, disembodied matter itself. And what is left is a set of mathematical formulas useful for predicting the sequences of perceptions, but which many physicists find it impossible to construe as descriptions of physical reality. Thus Jeans, speaking of intra-atomic processes and of radiation, writes: "It is difficult to form even the remotest conception of the realities underlying all these phenomena. . . . Indeed, it it may be doubted whether we shall ever properly understand the realities involved; they may well be so fundamental as to be beyond the grasp of the human mind." [1] Similarly Eddington concludes his recent summary of the philosophical implications—and non-implications—of contemporary science by assuring us that all that physics has to report about external nature is that "something unknown is doing we don't know what"; that when, for example, we see an elephant sliding down a hill, the impression of the "bulkiness" of the elephant which we experience "presumably has some direct counterpart in the external world," but that this "counterpart must be of a nature beyond our apprehension," and that "science can make nothing of it." Or, as Eddington alternatively suggests, it is possible that "our final conclusion as to the world of physics will resemble Kronecker's view of pure mathematics: 'God made the integers; all else is the work of man.'"

This new agnosticism among the physicists, then, manifestly verges upon

---

[1] *The Universe Around Us*, p. 128.

phenomenalism, and it thus seems to threaten the position of the psychophysical dualist from another side. So little seems to be left of the physical world of the older realism that the residuum may appear hardly worth salvaging. Thus the result, not merely of the present discussion, but of recent reflection in general, will doubtless be regarded by idealists as tending to vindicate *their* type of monism. It will appear to them that if it can be shown from realistic premises that the only internally possible kind of realism is a dualistic realism, then it is by so much the more evident that no kind of realism is tenable. What has been exhibited in the foregoing lectures, they will be likely to say, is the pleasing and instructive spectacle of the armies of realistic philosophy marching up the hill and then marching down again, to pretty much the position which had been reached at the beginning of the eighteenth century—a position which at that time had already been shown to be incapable of defense against the idealist's attack. If it is admitted that, as Locke declared, "the mind, in all its thoughts and reasonings, hath no immediate object but its own ideas," then the consequences which Locke's successors drew from this proposition must, we shall be told, again be drawn. And if the new physics—also setting out from realistic preconceptions—reduces the so-called physical universe to a bare *x*, of which we can say, at most, only that there must be in it *some* difference corresponding to every difference in our perceptual content, then the term "physical," as applied to it, ceases to have any distinct meaning. . . .

The belief in the continuance of things or processes between perceptions is not a blank act of faith, as would be the postulation of an external causal object for a single momentary percept; it may be said to be—not, indeed, rigorously verified—but strengthened by one of the most familiar of empirical facts —namely, that the same uniform causal sequences of natural events which may be observed within experience appear to go on in the same manner when not experienced. You build a fire in your grate of a certain quantity of coal, of a certain chemical composition. Whenever you remain in the room there occurs a typical succession of sensible phenomena according to an approximately regular schedule of clock-time; in, say, a half-hour the coal is half consumed; at the end of the hour the grate contains only ashes. If you build a fire of the same quantity of the same material under the same conditions, leave the room, and return after any given time has elapsed, you get approximately the same sense-experiences as you would have had at the corresponding moment if you had remained in the room. You infer, therefore, that the fire has been burning as usual during your absence, and that being perceived is not a condition necessary for the occurrence of the process. But a consistent idealist or phenomenalist cannot say this. He is committed to the proposition either that the fire has not been or, at all events, cannot legitimately be assumed to have been, burning when no one was perceiving it; his doctrine amounts to a gratuitous assumption of the universal jumpiness or temporal discontinuity of causal sequences. The most that he can admit— and he cannot admit less—is that fires and other natural processes behave as *if* they went on when unobserved; if he desires to make this seem more intelligible, he may invoke some pre-established harmony, or resort to a species of occasionalism—assuming that when you return to the room after an hour God (as Descartes would have said) deceives you by putting into your mind a percept of a grate full of ashes, though *these* ashes are not the effects of any fire. But such "explanations" of the facts are plainly arbitrary and far-fetched; they multiply types of causal agency beyond necessity. And to be content with a mere *Philosophie des Als-Ob* in such a case—to say that, although nothing at all that was like a fire or would have caused you to perceive a fire, if you had remained in the room, was really happening while you were absent, nevertheless all goes on as though the fire had been burning during that interval —this, surely, is a singularly strained and artificial notion, wholly foreign to the normal propensities of our intelligence.

Naïve realism, however, infers more from this type of fact than is warranted; it supposes that while you were not in the room *exactly the same* phenomena were going on as you would have experienced had you been there—the play of color in the flames, the qualities experienced by you in thermal sensation, and so on. To suppose this is to assume that certain of the factors in the case— namely, your presence in the room and your psychophysical constitution—make no difference in the content of your experience. This positive assumption of the complete irrelevance of certain actual antecedents or concomitants of a given effect is not only gratuitous and improbable, but is in conflict with familiar empirical evidences of the concomitant variation of sense-data with differences in the perceptible natures or states of percipients. What is reasonably inferrible is that some process capable of causing an organism, constituted as you are to have the perceptual experience of a burning fire, has been continuously going on while you were not in such relations to it as actually to perceive any fire. The causal theory of perception is thus derivative from, not logically prior to, the postulate of the continuance of the orderly sequences of nature during interperceptual intervals. The world of external causal entities or events is the world that you are obliged to assume when you accept the evidence for such continuance, while recognizing the probability that your own makeup, as a body or a mind or both, plays some part in determining the qualitative character of your percepts. The specific qualities characteristic of the potentially unperceived, that is, interperceptual, process, remain, so far as these considerations go, undetermined; you cannot, thus far, tell how much of what you experience is due to external events, how much to the nature of "that which is acted upon" by these events. But this does not weaken the reasons for believing that there *are* such temporally persistent and therefore independent events. Matter, or the physical order, still remains, not only as, in Mill's phrase, "a permanent possibility of sensation," but as a continuing existent capable of causing sensations under certain circumstances. . . .

It is perhaps worth remarking . . .

that men of science . . . are radically agnostic about the physical world only intermittently, or when the wind is in a certain quarter. Thus physicists and astronomers are accustomed to debate, from the standpoint of the relativity theory, whether the universe is finite or infinite in extent, and, if it can be shown to be finite, of just what shape it is, and how many million years would be required for a ray of light to complete "the journey round the whole of space" and return to its starting-point. . . . The habitual fashion of speech of our astronomers and physicists plainly betrays the fact that they conceive themselves to be concerned with the problem of ascertaining the probable nature of relatively persistent physical realities behind, and causally related to, the diversities of our transitory perceptual data.

But it will, no doubt, be said that this is merely a careless or syncopated way of expressing themselves which men of science have fallen into—or, if seriously meant by them, that it is at all events of no philosophical moment. None of these hypotheses and discussions really relate to a "background"—to the characters of realities either actually or potentially outside sense-experience. . . . All such terms express merely a conceptual frame-work devised for theoretical purposes, a series of scientific fictions. Our perceptual experience takes place as if such entities existed and such events occurred; it is therefore useful to employ the notions of them; but the only factual elements in the scheme consist of private sense-data of individual physicists, *plus*, perhaps, certain unknown quantities of which merely the number may be supposed to be correspondent with the number of differences in the percepts.

From this conception of the character of the business in which the physicist is engaged one consequence not always noted seems to follow. If all specific hypotheses relating to things other than perceptual data are to be regarded as fictions, certain classes of hypotheses frequently advanced and discussed must be illegitimate. For though it may be useful to interpolate in thought fictitious processes *between* actual perceptions, it can hardly be useful to extrapolate them beyond the region of any possible perception. Yet astronomers are accustomed to advance hypotheses concerning, for example, the sources of solar energy, from which they draw inferences as to the past and future duration of organic life upon the earth, and the state of this planet and of the solar system long before man's appearance and long after his disappearance. They describe for us the birth of the earth through the tidal action of some other celestial body which (fortunately for us) approached near to the sun probably some 2000 million years ago. They usually affirm the almost certain truth of the second law of thermodynamics, and therefore predict the eventual, though unimaginably remote, "heat-death" of the physical world. Now the events described by these propositions in astronomy and physics are presumably neither actual nor possible experiences of any mortal; nor can the propositions be considered fictions which somehow enable us to infer past or predict future actual experiences. If, then, the sole legitimate subject-matter of science consists of percepts and their inter-connections, together with the number of correlated differences in an otherwise entirely undefined background, no propositions concerning the origin and early history of our system, or the ultimate distribution of energy, would be admissible in science. The temporal range of the discourse of the astronomer would be limited to the history of our species, or at most of percipient organisms. All else would be gratuitous, if not meaningless, fairy-tales—neither true nor useful. If, on the other hand, cosmogonies, histories of the solar system, accounts of what took place in early geological time, and the like, are to be regarded as legitimate and significant parts of the province of science, it can only be upon the condition that these hypotheses are propounded as descriptions of events that actually happened without observation. The descriptions must in any case, of course, be admitted to be highly incomplete and abstract; but they do not, if of any scientific consequence, reduce to the vague proposition that "something, we don't know what," happened before, and will happen after, the presence of human or other percipients upon the cosmic scene.

But even these considerations are less than conclusive with respect to the question with which we are now concerned: whether any intelligible and consistent theory, in terms of particular existences or events, which would accord with, coördinate, and account for the uniformities and differences of our sense-experiences, can be formulated. For the dualist may (I should maintain) legitimately adopt the rule of procedure . . . that *if* a theory, and only one theory, of this kind appears attainable, the fact

constitutes a positive reason for regarding that theory as a probable (though doubtless exceedingly inadequate) account of the constitution of the independent causal background of experience. If everything in perception—when we "study it carefully and in detail"—takes place as if certain extra-perceptual events were occurring, in accordance with certain laws, as the common determinants of the otherwise inexplicable similarities and diversities of the data of different percipients, and if through such a theory we are led to the discovery of perceptible facts previously unknown, it is simpler and more in harmony with the normal assumptions of our reason to suppose that those events do occur, rather than that they do not. Though the universe *may* be a systematic and elaborate deception, in which everything in our experience intricately conspires with everything else to suggest to us beliefs which are not true, it does not seem necessary or rational to start with the supposition that this is the case. . . .

Contemporary physics, then, does not seem as yet to have given the death-blow to man's natural belief that he lives in a physical world which is, in its general structure and the modes of relatedness of its components, somewhat like the world which he perceptually experiences. That it conclusively vindicates this belief I am not maintaining, though I think it still lends some support to it. But the belief in question is at worst a natural and almost universal prejudice of mankind; and I can not but think that the burden of proof rests upon those who demand that we abandon a prejudice of this sort. What is certain is that, unless or until full and clear evidence of its falsity is offered, the prejudice will not disappear from men's minds—just as it manifestly has not really disappeared from the minds of physicists.

I speak of this belief as a prejudice; yet it is at least not a blind nor wholly inexplicable prejudice. It is born of, or at all events is nourished by, certain specific experiences at the macroscopic level and of perceptual objects. Let us, then, return to the world of perception to note what those particular aspects of it are which chiefly sustain such a belief, and to ask whether these are not such as to suggest its legitimacy. And in doing so, let us hold fast to the results reached in our inquiry before we entered upon the consideration of the bearing upon this belief of modern physical theories. We shall, that is to say, take three conclusions as already established: (a) there is an order of existences or events which persists when unperceived; (b) this is causally related to our sensa; (c) the particulars belonging to it cannot be identical with our sensa. Our problem, then, is whether, given these premises and the common facts of every-day experience, we can reach any further probable propositions concerning the extra-perceptual, neutral, causal order. One such proposition, manifestly, is that we have power to act upon this order. Processes which apparently go on unperceived can be initiated by percipient beings. And the unobserved interperceptual causal processes will vary (as their subsequently observed effects will show) with variations in the specific characters of our sense-data while we are initiating those

processes; *e.g.*, if I build my fire of wood instead of coal, the time required for it to burn out will be shorter and the ashes which I find on returning to the room will be of a different quality. It is equally a fact of every-day experience that certain percepts or images do not initiate (or are not correlated with) processes capable of continuing during interperceptual intervals and producing observable terminal effects identical with those observable when the entire sequence of intermediate stages has been attended to. If I merely imagine or dream of a fire in the grate, I do not—after ceasing so to dream or imagine—experience the visual and tactual content called ashes. Purely visual content is not found by us to be sufficient to start fires (or to give sensible evidence of the physical equivalent of a fire having started in the extra-perceptual world), or to be correlated with the initiation by us of any sterility process. The same fact is illustrated by the comparative sterility of pink rats. If I am able to initiate a physical process, my action (if experienced at all by myself) is experienced in the form of tactual and kinaesthetic as well as (in some cases) visual sense-data; it is, in short, one of the primary discoveries of experience that tactual and kinaesthetic sensations have a different and more constant relation to the physical causal order than do visual percepts or images. The former are the phases of our experience in which we as percipients appear to have causal contact with that order. And it is reasonable to suppose that this fact throws some light upon the nature of the external causal world.

Furthermore, if, like everyone else,

we assume that there are many percipients, and that they can through language convey some information to one another about the characteristics of their respective sense-data, we find that each of them is able to act upon the other percipients, that is, to determine in some degree what experiences they shall have; and that this action upon them is usually, and probably always, conditioned upon initiating (in the sense and in the manner already indicated) physical processes. If I light a fire, other men as well as myself will feel the heat; they may, in consequence of my action, observe a sensible fire continuously while I do not; while if I imagine or dream of a fire, their experience remains unaffected. One of the two principal reasons why we do not regard dream-fires as indications of the occurrence of events (at least the kind of events ordinarily connected with sensible fires) in the persistent and therefore independent world is that they do not cause others to have sensations of warmth or to find perceptible ashes in their perceptible grates. Purely private percepts are called illusory, not merely because they happen to be private, but because they do not causally interact directly, or in the manner in which other qualitatively similar percepts do, with the world which is the medium of communication and interaction between us.

Now what observably happens when I thus act upon the external world and through it affect other men's experiences and my own subsequent experiences, is usually that with my perceptible body I push and pull other perceptible objects about in my perceptual space. And with the movements which I thus determine

as data of my own perception there may be—under conditions empirically definable—correlated perceptions of movement in the experience of others. They report to me that they see what they call my body moving, and other objects moving in ways uniformly connected with my bodily movements. That their percepts of what they call my body are not my body itself is true—if the arguments on this matter previously set forth are correct; and it is also true that the perceptual objects which they see moving in consequence of my bodily movements are not existentially nor qualitatively identical with those which I see, nor yet any entity in the neutral causal order. The question may nevertheless be asked: Are the causal processes in the external world which are initiated by motions (*i.e.*, by those which I perceive) and which terminate in motions (*i.e.*, those which other men perceive) also of the nature of motions? The idealist answers definitely in the negative; the phenomenalist and the all-but agnostic physicist answer that we have, at any rate, no reason whatever for thinking so. But there are, I think, certain considerations which, though not demonstrative, make an affirmative answer to the question the more plausible.

(a) In the first place, it is at least not *impossible* that the processes which cause and link together the percepts of different times and different persons are of the same general sort as the causal sequences which empirically occur within our perceptual experience. No fact of experience, obviously, can prove the contrary.

(b) It is a simpler assumption about the unperceived causal processes that they are of the same sort as those perceived, rather than of some wholly different sort. In making such an assumption we still follow the rule of continuity in our conjectures about that which we cannot directly experience. We do not postulate differences in the nature of things beyond necessity. If I suppose that, when I have the experience of moving my body and pushing and pulling something about, thereby producing effects in the neutral causal order, I *am* pushing or pulling something about, and that this *is* a way in which effects in that order are produced, I am enabled to conceive of the external world with which I am in relation in action as fundamentally homogeneous with the perceptual world; and though it may not be so, it appears to me more sensible to proceed upon the hypothesis that it is, so long as there is no good evidence to the contrary.

(c) The spaces in which our perceptible effective bodily movements take place, whether or not they are literally parts of a single Space, are at all events congruent; they fit together in a remarkable way. For example, a hundred men from as many different places are summoned to attend an international conference in Geneva. They thereupon consult maps, time-tables, Baedekers, to find the routes to take in order to reach that city. These usful works were prepared by yet other men. They do not, however, purport to be descriptions of the arrangement of things in private perceptual spaces of their authors; they profess to represent a set of spatial relations which will hold good in the perceptual experience of any inhabitant of the earth. The routes which they describe are not routes to a hundred private Genevas, but to a single Geneva conceived to have a determinate position in some common or public spatial order. And by a series of movements of their own legs, assisted by motions of trains and steamships, which follow spatial directions symbolized in the maps and guidebooks, the delegates to the conference presently find themselves having similar (though not identical) visual and tactual percepts, for example, percepts of the Quai Mont Blanc, and in a position in which they can sit down in the same room and talk to one another. The result may be that the construction of battleships in certain other places will be discontinued. The idealistic or phenomenalistic account of this affair is that there is no common space such as is represented by the maps, and that no motion of what could strictly be called the body of any delegate took place. What happened was merely that their minds—which were throughout in no place at all—after first having private percepts of maps and then having visual and other sensations of motion, resulting, perhaps, in sensations of seasickness, subsequently experienced certain resemblant sense-percepts which they mistakenly called by the single name "Geneva," and others which they called the bodies and voices of their fellow delegates. In reality, therefore, the delegates never met. Their private sequences of sense-data, for no known or conjecturable reason, happened eventually to coincide in part; at approximately the time when one of them had the kinaestheic sensations of opening his mouth and using his vocal organs, the others had correspondent visual sensations and also certain sound-sensations of (more or less) intelligible words; but they were no nearer one another when this occurred than at the beginning. Now this is, no doubt, conceivable, in the sense that it is not formally self-contradictory; but it seems to me incredibly far-fetched, and I cannot avoid the suspicion that the human species (including physicists and even idealistic philosophers) is constitutionally incapable of really believing it—of thinking in this fashion of this type of experience. Men have always believed, and will, doubtless, continue to believe, that the way to arrive at a place is to go there; and they will always be recalcitrant to a view which requires them to hold, or to regard it as probable, that (for example) the ill-fated passengers of the *Titanic* were not really in the same ship or even in the same space. So long as the experienced bodily movements of a number of separate percipients thus fit into a single spatial pattern; so long as, in consequence of motions in convergent directions in that pattern (and not otherwise), the percipients find themselves face to face; so long as (to vary the illustration) through such bodily movements (and not otherwise) they are enabled not only to destroy the bodies of other men but also to bring all *their* perceiving to an end, by firing bullets in the direction in which the other men's bodies are perceived—so long men will naturally conceive of the processes in the common world through which their respective sense-data are caused as occurring in a single common spatial or spatio-temporal order and as consisting of motions therein. That this conceived common space is literally identical with their perceived spaces they may find reason to doubt; that the bodies which effectively move in it have all the properties of the bodies sensibly perceived, or are particulars existentially identical with them, they will find good reasons for denying. But the fact that their apprehension of bodies must be recognized by them to be mediate or representational and to contain "psychic additions" and distortions need not, and pretty certainly will not, prevent them from thinking that they have bodies—unique bodies, that is, each of which belongs to one percipient, and is not merely the multitudious aggregate of the percepts of it—bodies which are therefore assignable to the public spatial system, which have positions relative to other bodies, which can change these positions, and in doing so cause changes in other bodies and modify thereby the sense-content, or even bring to an end the existence, of other percipient beings.

In all this, it may be said, I am forgetting the theory of relativity, which shows that there is no general frame of nature, no common space or time for different percipients. But I have never observed relativistic physicists hesitating to assume that the imaginary voyagers whom they describe as roving about the heavens at enormous speeds can send light-signals to one another, whatever their relative velocities or the length of their journeys; and I find such physicists always assuming that these signals will take time in passing from one "system" to another, and that their course will be deflected if they happen to pass through the gravitational fields to be found in the neighborhood of material bodies. That relativity physics dispenses, and shows the plain man how to dispense, with the notions of a general spatial order (whatever its novel geometrical properties) or of moving entities therein, consequently still seems to me difficult to make out; and I surmise, therefore, that the plain man's prejudice in favor of the belief that he has a body which moves in a public space, and that, in general, the causal processes in the persistent neutral world consist (at least in part) of the motions of bodies, will not by this doctrine be corrected, but rather confirmed.

COMMENT

Descartes' Method

In this chapter we have quoted from both Descartes' *Rules for the Direction of the Mind* and *Meditations*. The former is concerned with method, the latter with both epistemological and metaphysical questions. We shall first comment on the method.

The question of method became a matter of keen and widespread interest with the great flowering of science in the seventeenth and eighteenth centuries. The discoveries of such great scientists as Kepler, Galileo, Newton, Gilbert, and Harvey and the rapid development of mathematics and natural science forced men to reflect upon the nature of scientific knowledge and the means to its attainment.

The principal cleavage among the philosophers was between the *rationalists* and the *empiricists*. The rationalists, among them Descartes, Spinoza, and Leibniz, relied chiefly upon reason as the source of genuine knowledge, taking the methods of mathematics, especially geometry, as their model. The empiricists, among them Locke, Berkeley, and Hume, depended mainly upon experience, regarding the methods of hypothesis, observation, and experiment as the principal foundations of knowledge. Actually, the differences between the two groups were not so sharp as they are often represented. Both groups recognized the necessity of a combination of experience and reason, but they veered toward opposite sides in their emphasis.

Of primary significance in considering Descartes' philosophy as an example of rationalism is his intense desire for certainty: "I always had an excessive desire to learn to distinguish the true from the false, in order to see clearly in my actions and to walk with confidence in this life."[1] He believed that the key to certainty, the way in which to dispel his innumerable doubts, lay in a sound and logical method of reasoning. The proper employment of reason, he believed, would make vast provinces accessible to human knowledge.

Descartes asserted that all certain knowledge is based upon two mental opera-

---

[1] *Discourse on Method,* in *The Philosophical Works of Descartes,* translated by Elizabeth S. Haldane and G. R. T. Ross (Cambridge University Press, 1931), I, p. 87.

tions: *intuition*—which he also called "the natural light of reason"—and *deduction*. His definition of these terms are contained in his *Rules for the Direction of the Mind*. (See page 95.)

In formulating these definitions, Descartes was thinking specifically of the method of mathematics, particularly geometry. The certainty of rigorous mathematical reasoning, he believed, consists in starting with meanings and insights so clear and distinct that they cannot be doubted, and then accepting nothing as true unless it follows no less evidently from these foundations, An intuited truth is such that reason has only to understand its meaning fully to see that it *must* be true. Examples of intuitions are the insights that five is more than four, that a triangle is bounded by only three lines, and that things equal to the same thing are equal to each other. Given such manifest and self-evident premises, our conclusion will be certain provided that it is *necessarily* implied by what precedes and that nothing is admitted in the steps of reasoning that does not thus necessarily follow. Thus, in a chain of reasoning symbolized by letters, if p implies q, and q implies r, and r implies s, then s is certain provided that p is certain and that each subsequent step leading to s is also certain. Descartes believed that thinkers have succeeded in the past and will succeed in the future to the extent that they have rigorously employed, or will employ, intuition and deduction.

Even when Descartes turned to natural science, his ideal of attaining certainty remained the same. All of natural science appears to be subject to rational deduction from self-evident premises. "As for physics," he declared, "I should believe myself to know nothing of it if I were able to say only how things may be without demonstrating that they cannot be otherwise; for having reduced physics to the laws of mathematics, it is possible to do this, and I believe that I can do it in all that little I believe myself to know."[2]

In practice, however, he was forced to qualify or abandon such extreme claims. The deduction of physics from mathematics and metaphysics, it appears, applies only to *general* principles. In more specialized research, he discovered that brute fact eludes determination by pure deductive reasoning. He was guided to this conclusion by his own experience as a keen observer of nature, dissecting the bodies of various animals and investigating experimentally the weight of air, the laws of light and sound, the characteristics of various oils, waters, spirits, and salts, and other natural phenomena. Not only did he discover that he must himself fall back upon empirical methods, but he strongly recommended to others that such observations and experiments be conducted.

Although, as we have said, Descartes thought that the quite general principles of natural science could be demonstrated *a priori*, he believed that experience serves a valuable function as an additional check and confirmation. Such empirical checking-up should be carried out to make doubly certain of the principles. In

[2] Letter to Mersenne, March 11, 1649, in *Discourse on Method,* trans. by Haldane and Ross, III, p. 39.

Book VI of the *Discourse on Method*, he confessed that it is necessary to combine experience with *a priori* principles in order to derive the special hypotheses of science and to devise crucial experiments to decide between the alternative hypotheses that are thus derived.

Thus his conception of method was not so extreme and one-sided as is often supposed. He recognized that there are two ways of reaching knowledge—by pure reason and by experience—and that in natural science both are indispensable.[3]

The success of the Cartesian method depends upon having a sure foundation upon which to build and thereafter upon successfully applying the rule to admit nothing that is uncertain. To do this Descartes resolved to doubt everything that he could possibly doubt, provisionally retaining only those ordinary maxims of conduct that are necessary in order to live decently. To doubt in this methodical way is not to consider something false or improbable but to recognize that it is not *absolutely* certain. The function of systematic doubt is to find a solid foundation for science and philosophy and thus to dispel scepticism.

The kind of indubitable foundation for which Descartes was searching is not any formal principle of logic or mathematics, such as the principle that one and the same proposition cannot be both true and false. Such a principle, although a necessary foundation of reasoning, tells us nothing about *what exists* and hence cannot provide the necessary basis for a philosophy or science of *reality*. The kind of premise that he sought, therefore, must be such that its truth cannot be doubted; it must be self-evident and not deduced from something else; and it must refer to something actually existing.

In resolutely admitting nothing except what is certain, Descartes was forced to doubt almost everything that he had ever believed. I shall not analyze the steps by which he reached this conclusion, since his argument is reasonably lucid and he himself summarized the steps at the beginning of Meditation VI.

It would seem that nothing at all is left to believe; but something remains even when doubt has done its worst. "I suppose myself to be deceived," Descartes exclaimed; "doubtless, then, I exist, since I am deceived." My very act of doubting proves something that I cannot doubt. "I think, therefore I am."

Here is the first principle—the absolute and indubitable certainty—for which Descartes was searching, and here also is the main point of departure of modern epistemology. The certainty of self-consciousness had been proclaimed earlier by St. Augustine (354–430) and St. Thomas Aquinas (1225?–1274). But Descartes gave the idea wide currency, backing it up with systematic doubt, and without admitting the element of faith essential to Augustine and Aquinas. No one before him had so deliberately adopted doubt as a method of procedure or employed it so boldly and sweepingly. Most later philosophers have agreed that the existence

---

[3] See Ralph M. Blake, "The Role of Experience in Descartes' Theory of Method," in Ralph M. Blake, Curt J. Ducasse, and Edward H. Madden, *Theories of Scientific Method: The Renaissance through the Nineteenth Century* (Seattle: University of Washington Press, 1960).

of mind is more certain than the existence of matter, and that the existence of *my* mind—for *me*—is more certain than the existence of other minds. Modern philosophy has largely radiated out from this focal point.

When I say "I think, therefore I am," what do I mean by "I"? Clearly I mean a *thinking being*—hence thought enters into the very essence of the self. Thought is to be understood in a broad sense; perception, memory, imagination, desire, will, reason—all are forms of thought, and, through introspection, we are immediately aware of all these mental operations. At this stage, Descartes was prepared to say only that there is thought, which consists of conscious mental operations, and that there is a thinker. By a "thinker," however, he meant a "substance"—that is to say, an enduring *thing* that has changing states or characteristics (which he calls "accidents"). "It is certain," he declared, "that no thought can exist apart from a thing that thinks; no activity, no accident can be without a substance in which to exist."[4] What is certain, then, is that there is an "I"—a thinking thing—with its various forms of thought.

Minds and Bodies

Descartes thus had a starting point—the certainty of his own existence. He noted that the truth of this premise—"I think, therefore I am"—was *clearly* and *distinctly* perceived. Since it is this clear and distinct perception that guarantees the truth of the premise, it seemed to him that he could take as a general rule that all that is thus clearly and distinctly perceived is true.

But what else can I know? It is doubtful whether anything else can be certain so long as there is the possibility of a deceiving demon. This difficulty must somehow be removed. (The "deceiving demon" should not be understood too literally. It is a device to indicate the possibility that thinking may be utterly treacherous and that whatever exists may be so irrational that our reasoning cannot be trusted.) Descartes must show that reality is not irrational. He can do this by proving that a rational and beneficient God, rather than a malicious and deceitful demon, is the foundation of what is real, for if God is indeed the basis of reality, surely our most careful reasoning is trustworthy—God would not be a deceiver. I have already summarized Descartes' arguments for the existence of God in the italicized paragraphs on pages 116–117.

God has given me such a strong and unavoidable inclination to believe in a physical world that He would be deceitful if no such world existed. But I can be sure only of my very clear and distinct ideas of external reality. Impressions of color, odor, sound, touch, and taste, not being susceptible of precise mathematical formulation, are too unclear to be regarded as trustworthy reports of the real properties of material bodies. But *extension* can be measured; and we cannot

---

[4] *Reply to Third Objections,* in *The Philosophical Works of Descartes,* trans. by Eilzabeth S. Haldane and G. R. T. Ross (Cambridge University Press, 1931), II, p. 64.

even conceive of a material body apart from extension, since an unextended body is a contradiction in terms. Therefore the very essence of body is to be extended.

A further argument, using *permanence* as the criterion of what is real, is introduced in Meditation II. Descartes pointed out that a piece of wax, if heated, will change its color, odor, taste, and tactile qualities. Nothing remains constant except extension, flexibility, and mobility. But flexibility is not a property of all bodies, and mobility is relational (*i.e.*, a thing can be said to move only by reference to another thing). Hence extension is the only known *intrinsic* quality of all matter.

Just as I have a very strong inclination to believe in a physical world, so I have an equally strong inclination to believe that other people are not mere dream phantoms or physical automata but real persons like myself. In this regard also, God would not deceive me.

Descartes recognized two distinct realms of being. One is the world described by physics, a world which does not depend upon our thoughts. It would continue to exist and operate if there were no human beings at all. Its essence is to be extended. The other is the world whose essence is thought—perception, willing, feeling, reasoning, imagining, and the corresponding ideas or mental representations.

A human being, as a compound of mind and body, belongs to both realms. How a person can thus be both two and one poses a difficult problem. Despite the apparent paradox, Descartes believed that mind and body, although radically different, are harmoniously combined in the human organism, and that the unextended mind somehow interacts with the extended body.

The Mind-Body Problem

The distinction between mind and body is closely related to the method of doubt. Descartes notes that he can be certain that he exists as a thinking being even when he is still in doubt whether he has a body—hence he concludes that the mind and body must be distinct and that his real essence is to think. The argument fails to prove all that it is intended to prove. It leaves us with the puzzle what happens to the "I" when it is not thinking, as for example in a dreamless sleep. Descartes leaps from the premise that when one thinks one must exist, to the much stronger claim that thought is *the* essential property of the self. The latter claim entails, among other things, that a person cannot exist without thinking. Now this appears to be going too far. At the moment of thinking, I know that I am thinking, and if I reflect, I know that my thinking implies my existence. But I am not inclined to say that my existence ceases whenever I stop thinking. In some sense the "I" continues even when one is unconscious.

Descartes, believing that his very essence is to think, regarded his mind as the thinker and his body as merely the support. At present we would be more inclined to say that a man is a psychophysical organism with body and "subconscious" mind and conscious mind so intimately connected as to constitute a single being.

Just as the physical hormones, for example, have a decisive influence upon man's temperament, so psychic conflict may profoundly disturb physical functions. More and more, both health and disease appear to be psychosomatic, having both a bodily and a mental aspect.

The facts are susceptible of a number of interpretations. Included in the present volume are the following: (1) the theory of mind as bodily function, represented by Lucretius, (2) the theory of body as mental representation, held by Berkeley, (3) the double-aspect theory, illustrated by Spinoza's doctrine that mind and body are complementary aspects of an underlying substance, and (4) dualistic inter-actionism, advocated by Descartes. Interactionism is still a plausible theory if we soften the extreme dualism of Descartes' theory. The third and fourth interpretations, in their more moderate formulations, are not mutually exclusive. Even if we should adopt the double-aspect theory, it does not logically follow that physical and mental events cannot causally interact. So long as we clearly distinguish between the physical and mental sides of the mind-body organism, there would seem to be no reason why a physical event cannot cause a mental event, or a mental cause a physical.

Whatever be our final conclusion, we cannot sensibly deny that there is a qualitative difference between mental and physical processes. Without talking nonsense, we cannot say that knowing is an inch across, or that love is rectangular, or that sincerity is orange. Thoughts are not at all like vibrations in the brain, nor feelings like the movements of atoms. Different predicates apply to thoughts than apply to physical objects.

The mind-body problem is a fascinating subject for research and debate. I could explore it at greater length, but I shall leave the exploration to the initiative of my readers.

Lovejoy's Defense of Epistemological Dualism

Granted mind and matter, there are difficult problems about their relation, whether we are thinking about the human body and mind, or about matter and mind in general. One of the most important questions is whether and how the the human mind knows physical objects. This is the question that Arthur O. Lovejoy considers in his modern sophisticated defense of the dualistic hypothesis.

One sort of "revolt against dualism" that he rejects is direct realism. This is the theory that the mind is directly aware of physical objects. Lovejoy believes that the untenability of this theory is shown by both the familiar facts of ordinary experience and the scientific account of perception. When we look up at the sky and "see the moon," the bright yellow disk that looks about a foot across is different from the real moon. In the case of distant stars, the time lag is so great between the emission of light rays from the star and their arrival at the retina of the eye that the two are light-years apart. The star that we "see" may even have become extinct light-years ago. Not so great is the time-interval between an explosion and the sound we hear, but the interval is enough to establish the duality between object and sensum. If we add to such evidence all the facts about the unreliability of appearances, the relativities of perspective, and the physiology of perception, we cannot hold that our senses give us faithful and direct information. We must conclude that the vivid sensory qualities of normal perception, such as colors, sounds, smells, and touches, are generated in part by the brain reactions and other responses of the percipient, and are unlike the states of physical objects.

Nevertheless Lovejoy denies that we are condemned to know nothing whatsoever of the external world. Qualities such as color, sound, odor, and tactile impressions are subjective, but the primary qualities of extension, shape, position, number, motion, and temporal succession are more revealing. While their exact correspondence with physical objects cannot be assumed, they tell us too much about the continuities of experience, the causal processes which continue in the absence of observers, and the events in far distant times and places, for us to dismiss them as nonindicative of the nature of things. If we believe that these primary qualities characterize both the phenomena of our experience and the real objective world, we shall be able to frame coherent, unifying, and serviceable explanations of the laws of nature and the genesis of our experience. No other hypothesis, Lovejoy believes, is so explanatory.

This kind of defense of dualism will be challenged by Spinoza the monist, Berkeley the idealist, Hume the sceptic, Kant the agnostic, Bergson the vitalist, and Whitehead the organicist, in the chapters that lie ahead.

5

Monism

BARUCH SPINOZA (1632–1677)

Born into the Jewish community of Amsterdam, Spinoza was educated in the Rabbinical tradition but studied such non-Jewish philosphers as Bruno and Descartes. By the time he was twenty-three he rebelled against orthodox Judaism, even refusing a bribe to conceal his views. In consequence, he was cursed in the name of God and his Holy Angels by the Jewish authorities and excommunicated from the Synagogue. Changing his Jewish name, Baruch, to its Latin equivalent, Benedictus, he dwelt for many years in a nearby village earning a modest living by polishing optical lenses. Later he moved to The Hague. As an excommunicated Jew, he had few ties with either his Dutch or his Jewish neighbors, but he was loved and respected by the few who knew him.

He devoted much of his time studying philosophy and corresponding with the great scientists, mathematicians, and philosophers of the period. In 1663 he published an expository account of Descartes' philosophy and in 1670 published his *Tractatus Theologico-Politicus*. The latter, a work of biblical criticism and political theory, although prohibited by both Catholics and Protestants, achieved fame in learned and emancipated circles. As result, Spinoza was offered a professorship at the University of Heidelberg if he would promise not to disturb the established religion. He refused the offer because the proviso would restrict his freedom of speech and the academic duties would cut into his studies.

The grinding of lenses may have brought on or aggravated the tuberculosis of which he died at the age of forty-three. At the time of his death, he left behind a few personal belongings and some unpublished manuscripts, including the *Ethics*. It was one of the richest estates ever left by any man.

Ethics

I have now explained the nature of God and its properties. I have shown that He necessarily exists; that He is one God; that from the necessity alone of His own nature He is and acts; that He is, and in what way He is, the free cause of all things; that all things are in Him, and so depend upon Him that without Him they can neither be nor can be conceived; and, finally, that all things have been predetermined by Him, not indeed from freedom of will or from absolute good pleasure, but from His absolute nature or infinite power.

Moreover, wherever an opportunity was afforded, I have endeavoured to remove prejudices which might hinder the perception of the truth of what I have demonstrated; but because not a few still remain which have been and are now sufficient to prove a very great hindrance to the comprehension of the connection of things in the manner in which I have explained it, I have thought it worth while to call them up to be examined by reason. But all these prejudices which I here undertake to point out depend upon this solely: that it is commonly supposed that all things in nature, like men, work to some end;

From Benedict Spinoza, *Ethics*, Appendix to Part I. Translated from the Latin by William Hale White. London: Trübner and Company, 1883.

and indeed it is thought to be certain that God himself directs all things to some sure end, for it is said that God has made all things for man, and man that he may worship God. This, therefore, I will first investigate by inquiring, firstly, why so many rest in this prejudice, and why all are so naturally inclined to embrace it? I shall then show its falsity, and, finally, the manner in which there have arisen from it prejudices concerning *good* and *evil, merit* and *sin, praise* and *blame, order* and *disorder, beauty* and *deformity,* and so forth. This, however, is not the place to deduce these things from the nature of the human mind. It will be sufficient if I here take as an axiom that which no one ought to dispute, namely that man is born ignorant of the causes of things, and that he has a desire, of which he is conscious, to seek that which is profitable to him. From this it follows, firstly, that he thinks himself free because he is conscious of his wishes and appetites, whilst at the same time he is ignorant of the causes by which he is led to wish and desire, not dreaming what they are; and, secondly, it follows that man does everything for an end, namely, for that which is profitable to him, which is what he seeks. Hence it happens that he attempts to discover merely the final causes of that which has happened; and when he has heard them he is satisfied, because there is no longer any cause for further uncertainty. But if he cannot hear from another what these final causes are, nothing remains but to turn to himself and reflect upon the ends which usually determine him to the like actions, and thus by his own mind he necessarily judges that of another. Moreover, since he discovers, both within and without himself, a multitude of means which contribute not a little to the attainment of what is profitable to himself—for example, the eyes, which are useful for seeing, the teeth for mastication, plants and animals for nourishment, the sun for giving light, the sea for feeding fish, &c. —it comes to pass that all natural objects are considered as means for obtaining what is profitable. These too being evidently discovered and not created by man, hence he has a cause for believing that some other person exists, who has prepared them for man's use. For having considered them as means it was impossible to believe that they had created themselves, and so he was obliged to infer from the means which he was in the habit of providing for himself that some ruler or rulers of nature exist, endowed with human liberty, who have taken care of all things for him, and have made all things for his use. Since he never heard anything about the mind of these rulers, he was compelled to judge of it from his own, and hence he affirmed that the gods direct everything for his advantage, in order that he may be bound to them and hold them in the highest honour. This is the reason why each man has devised for himself, out of his own brain, a different mode of worshipping God, so that God might love him above others, and direct all nature to the service of his blind cupidity and insatiable avarice.

Thus has this prejudice been turned into a superstition and has driven deep roots into the mind—a prejudice which was the reason why every one has so eagerly tried to discover and explain the final causes of things. The attempt, however, to show that nature does nothing in vain (that is to say, nothing which is not profitable to man), seems to end in showing that nature, the gods, and man are alike mad.

Do but see, I pray, to what all this has led. Amidst so much in nature that is beneficial, not a few things must have been observed which are injurious, such as storms, earthquakes, diseases, and it was affirmed that these things happened either because the gods were angry because of wrongs which had been inflicted on them by man, or because of sins committed in the method of worshipping them; and although experience daily contradicted this, and showed by an infinity of examples that both the beneficial and the injurious were indiscriminately bestowed on the pious and the impious, the inveterate prejudices on this point have not therefore been abandoned. For it was much easier for a man to place these things aside with others of the use of which he was ignorant, and thus retain his present and inborn state of ignorance, than to destroy the whole superstructure and think out a new one. Hence it was looked upon as indisputable that the judgments of the gods far surpass our comprehension; and this opinion alone would have been sufficient to keep the human race in darkness to all eternity, if mathematics, which does not deal with ends, but with the essences and properties of forms, had not placed before us another rule of truth. In addition to mathematics, other causes also might be assigned, which it is superfluous here to enumerate, tending to make men reflect upon these universal prejudices, and leading them to a true knowledge of things.

I have thus sufficiently explained what I promised in the first place to explain. There will now be no need of many words to show that nature has set no end before herself, and that all final causes are nothing but human fictions. For I believe that this is sufficiently evident both from the foundations and causes of this prejudice, and from Prop. 16 and Corol. Prop. 32, as well as from all those propositions in which I have shown that all things are begotten by a certain eternal necessity of nature and in absolute perfection. Thus much, nevertheless, I will add, that this doctrine concerning an end altogether overturns nature. For that which is in truth the cause it considers as the effect, and *vice versa*. Again, that which is first in nature it puts last; and, finally, that which is supreme and most perfect it makes the most imperfect. For (passing by the first two assertions as self-evident) it is plain from Props. 21, 22, and 23, that that effect is the most perfect which is immediately produced by God, and in proportion as intermediate causes are necessary for the production of a thing is it imperfect. But if things which are immediately produced by God were made in order that He might obtain the end He

had in view, then the last things for the sake of which the first exist, must be the most perfect of all. Again, this doctrine does away with God's perfection. For if God works to obtain an end, He necessarily seeks something of which he stands in need. And although theologians and metaphysicians distinguish between the end of want and the end of assimilation (*finem indegentiæ et finem assimilationis*), they confess that God has done all things for His own sake, and not for the sake of the things to be created, because before the creation they can assign nothing excepting God for the sake of which God could do anything; and therefore they are necessarily compelled to admit that God stood in need of and desired those things for which He determined to prepare means. This is self-evident. Nor is it here to be overlooked that the adherents of this doctrine, who have found a pleasure in displaying their ingenuity in assigning the ends of things, have introduced a new species of argument, not the *reductio ad impossible,* but the *reductio ad ignorantiam,* to prove their position, which shows that it had no other method of defence left. For, by way of example, if a stone has fallen from some roof on somebody's head and killed him, they will demonstrate in this manner that the stone has fallen in order to kill the man. For if it did not fall for that purpose by the will of God, how could so many circumstances concur through chance (and a number often simultaneously do concur)? You will answer, perhaps, that the event happened because the wind blew and the man was passing that way. But, they will urge, why did the wind blow at that time, and why did the man pass that way precisely at the same moment? If you again reply that the wind rose then because the sea on the preceding day began to be stormy, the weather hitherto having been calm, and that the man had been invited by a friend, they will urge again—because there is no end of questioning—But why was the sea agitated? why was the man invited at that time? And so they will not cease from asking the causes of causes, until at last you fly to the will of God, the refuge for ignorance.

So, also, when they behold the structure of the human body, they are amazed; and because they are ignorant of the causes of such art, they conclude that the body was made not by mechanical but by a supernatural or divine art, and has been formed in such a way so that the one part may not injure the other. Hence it happens that the man who endeavours to find out the true causes of miracles, and who desires as a wise man to understand nature, and not to gape at it like a fool, is generally considered and proclaimed to be a heretic and impious by those whom the vulgar worship as the interpreters both of nature and the gods. For these know that if ignorance be removed, amazed stupidity, the sole ground on which they rely in arguing or in defending their authority, is taken away also. But these things I leave and pass on to that which I determined to do in the third place.

After man has persuaded himself that all things which exist are made for him, he must in everything adjudge that to be of the greatest importance which is most useful to him, and he must esteem that to be of surpassing worth by which he is most beneficially affected. In this way he is compelled to form those notions by which he explains nature; such, for instance, as *good, evil, order, confusion, heat, cold, beauty,* and *deformity,* &c.; and because he supposes himself to be free, notions like those of *praise* and *blame, sin* and *merit,* have arisen. These latter I shall hereafter explain when I have treated of human nature; the former I will here briefly unfold.

It is to be observed that man has given the name *good* to every thing which leads to health and the worship of God; on the contrary, everything which does not lead thereto he calls *evil.* But because those who do not understand nature affirm nothing about things themselves, but only imagine them, and take the imagination to be understanding, they therefore, ignorant of things and their nature, firmly believe an *order* to be in things; for when things are so placed that, if they are represented to us through the senses, we can easily imagine them, and consequently easily remember them, we call them well arranged; but if they are not placed so that we can imagine and remember them, we call them badly arranged or *confused.* Moreover, since those things are more especially pleasing to us which we can easily imagine, men therefore prefer order to confusion, as if order were something in nature apart from our own imagination; and they say that God has created everything in order, and in this manner they ignorantly attribute imagination to God, unless they mean perhaps that God, out of consideration for the human imagination, has disposed things in the manner in which they can most easily be imagined. No hesitation either seems to be caused by the fact that an infinite number of things are discovered which far surpass our imagination, and very many which confound it through its weakness. But enough of this. The other notions which I have mentioned are nothing but modes in which the imagination is affected in different ways, and nevertheless they are regarded by the ignorant as being specially attributes of things, because, as we have remarked, men consider all things as made for themselves, and call the nature of a thing good, evil, sound, putrid, or corrupt, just as they are affected by it. For example if the motion by which the nerves are affected by means of objects represented to the eye conduces to well-being, the objects by which it is caused are called *beautiful;* while those exciting a contrary motion are called *deformed.* Those things, too, which stimulate the senses through the nostrils are called sweet-smelling or stinking; those which act through the taste are called sweet or bitter, full-flavoured or insipid; those which act through the touch, hard or soft, heavy or light; those, lastly, which act through the ears are said to make a noise, sound, or harmony, the last having caused men to lose their senses to such a degree that they have believed that God even is delighted with it. Indeed, philosophers may be found who have persuaded themselves that the celestial motions beget a harmony. All these things sufficiently show that every one judges things by the constitution of his brain, or rather accepts the affections of his imagination in the place of things. It is not, therefore, to be wondered at, as we may observe in passing, that all those controversies which we see have arisen amongst men, so that at last scepticism has been the result. For although human bodies agree in many things, they differ in more, and therefore that which to one person is good will appear to another evil, that which to one is well arranged to another is confused, that which pleases one will displease another, and so on in other cases which I pass by both because we cannot notice them at length here, and because they are within the experience of every one. For every one has heard the expressions: So many heads, so many ways of thinking; Every one is satisfied with his own way of thinking; Differences of brains are not less common than differences of taste;—all which maxims show that men decide upon matters according to the constitution of their brains, and imagine rather than understand things. If men understood things, they would, as mathematics prove, at least be all alike convinced if they were not all alike attracted. We see, therefore, that all those methods by which the common people are in the habit of explaining nature are only different sorts of imaginations, and do not reveal the nature of anything in itself, but only the constitution of the imagination; and because they have names as if they were entities existing apart from the imagination, I call them entities not of the reason but of the imagination. All argument, therefore, urged against us based upon such notions can be easily refuted. Many people, for instance, are accustomed to argue thus:—If all things have followed from the necessity of the most perfect nature of God, how is it that so many imperfections have arisen in nature—corruption, for instance, of things till they stink; deformity, exciting disgust; confusion, evil, crime, &c.? But, as I have just observed, all this is easily answered. For the perfection of things is to be judged by their nature and power alone; nor are they more or less perfect because they delight or offend the human senses, or because they are beneficial or prejudicial to human nature. But to those who ask why God has not created all men in such a manner that they might be controlled by the dictates of reason alone, I give but this answer: Because to Him material was not wanting for the creation of everything, from the highest down to the very lowest grade of perfection; or, to speak more properly, because the laws of His nature were so ample that they suffered for the production of everything which can be conceived by an infinite intellect, as I have demonstrated in Prop. 16.

These are the prejudices which I undertook to notice here. If any others of a similar character remain, they can easily be rectified with a little thought by any one.

Correspondence

Letter XXXII

TO THE VERY NOBLE AND LEARNED MR. HENRY OLDENBURG.

Most noble Sir,

I thank you and the very Noble Mr. Boyle very much for kindly encouraging me to go on with my Philosophy. I do indeed proceed with it, as far as my slender powers allow, not doubting meanwhile of your help and goodwill.

When you ask me what I think about the question which turns on *the Knowl-*

From *The Correspondence of Spinoza*, translated and edited by Abraham Wolf, 1928, new impression, 1966. By permission of George Allen & Unwin, London, and Russell & Russell, New York.

edge how each part of Nature accords with the whole of it, and in what way it is connected with the other parts, I think you mean to ask for the reasons on the strength of which we believe that each part of Nature accords with the whole of it, and is connected with the other parts. For I said in my preceding letter that I do not know how the parts are really interconnected, and how each part accords with the whole; for to know this it would be necessary to know the whole of Nature and all its Parts.

I shall therefore try to show the reason which compels me to make this assertion; but I should like first to warn you that I do not attribute to Nature beauty or ugliness, order or confusion. For things cannot, except with respect to our imagination, be called beautiful, or ugly, ordered or confused.

By connection of the parts, then, I mean nothing else than that the laws, or nature, of one part adapt themselves to the laws, or nature, of another part in such a way as to produce the least possible opposition. With regard to whole and parts, I consider things as parts of some whole, in so far as their natures are mutually adapted so that they are in accord among themselves, as far as possible; but in so far as things differ among themselves, each produces an idea in our mind, which is distinct from the others, and is therefore considered to be a whole, not a part. For instance, since the motions of the particles of lymph, chyle, etc., are so mutually adapted in respect of magnitude and figure that they clearly agree among themselves, and all together constitute one fluid, to that extent only, chyle, lymph, etc., are considered to be parts of the blood: but in so far as we conceive the lymph particles as differing in respect of figure and motion from the particles of chyle, to that extent we consider them to be a whole, not a part.

Let us now, if you please, imagine that a small worm lives in the blood, whose sight is keen enough to distinguish the particles of blood, lymph, etc., and his reason to observe how each part on collision with another either rebounds, or communicates a part of its own motion, etc. That worm would live in this blood as we live in this part of the universe, and he would consider each particle of blood to be a whole, and not a part. And he could not know

how all the parts are controlled by the universal nature of blood, and are forced, as the universal nature of blood demands, to adapt themselves to one another, so as to harmonize with one another in a certain way. For if we imagine that there are no causes outside the blood to communicate new motions to the blood, and that outside the blood there is no space, and no other bodies, to which the particles of blood could transfer their motion, it is certain that the blood would remain always in its state, and its particles would suffer no changes other than those which can be conceived from the given relation of the motion of the blood to the lymph and chyle, etc., and so blood would have to be considered always to be a whole and not a part. But, since there are very many other causes which in a certain way control the laws of the nature of blood, and are in turn controlled by the blood, hence it comes about that other motions and other changes take place in the blood, which result not only from the mere relation of the motion of its parts to one another, but from the relation of the motion of the blood and also the external causes to one another: in this way the blood has the character of a part and not of a whole. I have only spoken of whole and part.

Now, all the bodies of nature can and should be conceived in the same way as we have here conceived the blood: for all bodies are surrounded by others, and are mutually determined to exist and to act in a definte and determined manner, while there is preserved in all together, that is, in the whole universe, the same proportion of motion and rest. Hence it follows that every body, in so far as it exists modified in a certain way, must be considered to be a part of the whole universe, to be in accord with the whole of it, and to be connected with the other parts. And since the nature of the universe is not limited, like the nature of the blood, but absolutely infinite, its parts are controlled by the nature of this infinite power in infinite ways, and are compelled to suffer infinite changes. But I conceive that with regard to substance each part has a closer union with its whole. For as I endeavoured to show in my first letter, which I wrote to you when I was still living at Rhynsburg, since it is of the nature of substance to be infinite, it follows that each part belongs to the nature of corporeal substance, and can neither exist nor be conceived without it.

You see, then, in what way and why I think that the human Body is a part of Nature. As regards the human Mind I think it too is a part of Nature: since I state that there exists in Nature an infinite power of thought, which in so far as it is infinite, contains in itself subjectively the whole of Nature, and its thoughts proceed in the same way as Nature, which, to be sure, is its ideatum.

Then I declare that the human mind is this same power, not in so far as it is infinite, and perceives the whole of Nature, but in so far as it is finite and perceives only the human Body, and in this way I declare that the human Mind is a part of a certain infinite intellect. . . .

In all affection yours

B. de SPINOZA

[Voorburg, 20 November 1665]

Letter LVI

To the Very Honourable and Prudent Mr. HUGO BOXEL.

Most honourable Sir,

I hasten to answer your letter, which I received yesterday, because if I go on delaying longer I shall be compelled to postpone my reply longer than I should wish. Your health would cause me anxiety if I had not heard that you are better, and I hope you are now entirely recovered.

How difficult it is for two persons who follow different principles to meet one another and agree on a subject which depends on many others, would be clear from this question alone, even if no argument demonstarted it. Tell me, I pray, whether you have seen or read any Philosophers who hold the opinion that the world was made by chance, that is, in the sense in which you understand it, namely, that God, when creating the world had set Himself a definite aim, and yet transgressed His own decree. I do not know that such a thing even occurred to any man's thought. Similarly, I am in the dark about the arguments by which you endeavour to persuade me to believe that *Fortuitious* and *Necessary* are not contraries. As soon as I realize that the three angles of a triangle are necessarily equal to two right angles, I also deny that this is the result of chance. Similarly as soon as I realize that heat is the necessary effect of fire, I also deny that it occurs by chance. It seems no less absurd and opposed to reason to suppose that *Necessary* and *Free* are contraries. For no one can deny that God knows

Himself and everything else freely, and yet all are agreed in admitting that God knows Himself necessarily. Thus you seem to me to make no distinction between coercion or force, and Necessity. That man desires to live, to love, etc., is not a compulsory activity, but it is none the less necessary, and much more so is God's will to be, and to know, and to act. If, apart from these remarks, you turn over in your mind the fact that indifference is nothing but ignorance or doubt, and that a will ever constant and determined in all things is a virtue, and a necessary property of the intellect, then you will see that my words are thoroughly in accord with the truth. If we assert that God had it in His power not to will a thing, and did not have it in His power not to understand it, then we attribute to God two different kinds of freedom, one being that of necessity, the other that of indifference, and consequently we shall conceive the will of God as differing from His essence and His intellect, and in that case we shall fall into one absurdity after another. . . .

Further, when you say that if I deny to God the acts of seeing, of hearing, of attending and of willing, etc., and their occurrence in Him in an eminent degree, then you do not know what kind of God I have, I suspect therefrom that you believe that there is no perfection greater than that which is unfolded in the said attributes. I do not wonder at this, since I believe that a triangle, if only it had the power of speech, would say in like manner that God is eminently triangular, and a circle would say that the Divine Nature is eminently circular, and in this way each thing would ascribe its own attributes to God, and make itself like unto God, while all else would appear to it deformed.

The small compass of a letter, and limitation of time, do not permit me to explain in detail my opinion about the Divine Nature, or the other Questions which you put forward, to say nothing of the fact that to raise difficulties is not the same as to advance reasons. It is true that in the world we often act on conjecture; but it is false that our reflections are based on conjecture. In ordinary life we must follow what is most probable, but in philosophical speculations, the truth. Man would perish of thirst and hunger if he would not eat or drink until he had obtained a perfect proof that food and drink would do him good. But in contemplation this has no place. On the contrary, we must be cautious not to admit as true something which is merely probable. For when we admit one falsity, countless others follow.

Further, from the fact that divine and human sciences are full of disputes and controversies it cannot be inferred that all the things which are treated therein are uncertain: for there have been very many people who were so possessed by the love of contradiction that they laughed even at Geometrical proofs. Sextus Empiricus and other Sceptics whom you cite say that it is not true that the whole is greater than its part, and they have the same view of the other axioms.

But, putting aside and admitting the fact that in default of proofs we must be satisfied with probabilities, I say that a probable Proof ought to be such that, although we can doubt it, yet we cannot contradict it; because that which can be contradicted is not likely to be true, but likely to be false. If, for instance, I say that Peter is alive, because I saw him in good health yesterday, this is indeed likely to be true so long as no one can contradict me; but if someone else says that yesterday he saw Peter suffering from loss of consciousness, and that he believes that Peter died from it, he makes my words seem false. That your conjecture about spectres and ghosts seems false and not even probable, I have so clearly shown that I find nothing worthy of consideration in your answer.

To your question whether I have as clear an idea of God as I have of a triangle, I answer in the affirmative. But if you ask me whether I have as clear a mental image of God as I have of a triangle, I shall answer No. For we cannot imagine God, but we can, indeed, conceive Him. Here also it should be noted that I do not say that I know God entirely, but only that I understand some of His attributes, though not all, nor even the greater part of them, and it is certain that our ignorance of the majority of them does not hinder our having a knowledge of some of them. When I learnt Euclid's elements I first understood that the three angles of a triangle are equal to two right angles, and I clearly perceived this property of a triangle although I was ignorant of many others.

As regards spectres, or ghosts, I have never yet heard of an intelligible property of theirs, but only of Phantasies which no-one can grasp. When you say that spectres, or ghosts, here in this lower region (I follow your form of expression, although I do not know that the matter here in this lower region is

less valuable than that above) consist of the finest, thinnest, and most subtle substance, you seem to be speaking of spiders' webs, of air, or of vapours. To say that they are invisible means for me as much as if you said what they are not, but not what they are; unless perhaps you want to indicate that, according as they please, they make themselves now visible, now invisible, and that in these as in other impossibilities, the imagination will find no difficulty.

The authority of Plato, Aristotle, and Socrates has not much weight with me. I should have been surprised had you mentioned Epicurus, Democritus, Lucretius or any one of the Atomists, or defenders of the atoms. It is not surprising that those who invented occult Qualities, intentional Species, substantial Forms, and a thousand other trifles, should have devised spectres and ghosts, and put their faith in old women, in order to weaken the authority of Democritus, of whose good repute they were so envious that they burnt all his books, which he had published amidst so much praise. If you have a mind to put faith in them, what reasons have you for denying the miracles of the Holy Virgin, and of all the Saints, which have been described by so many very famous Philosophers, Theologians, and Historians that I can produce an hundred of them to scarcely one of the others?

Lastly, most honoured Sir, I have gone further than I intended. I do not wish to annoy you further with things which (I know) you will not admit, since you follow other principles which differ widely from my own, etc.

[The Hague, October 1674]

Letter LVIII

To the Very Learned and Expert
Mr. G. H. SCHULLER.

Most Expert Sir,

. . . I say that that thing is free which exists and acts solely from the necessity of its own nature; but that that thing is under compulsion which is determined by something else to exist, and to act in a definite and determined manner. For example, God, although He exists necessarily, nevertheless exists freely, since He exists solely from the necessity of His own nature. So also God freely understands Himself and absolutely all things, since it follows solely from the necessity of His own nature that He should understand everything. You see, therefore, that I do not place Freedom in free decision, but in free necessity.

Let us, however, descend to created things, which are all determined by external causes to exist, and to act in a definite and determined manner. In order that this may be clearly understood, let us think of a very simple thing. For instance, a stone receives from an external cause, which impels it, a certain quantity of motion, with which it will afterwards necessarily continue to move when the impact of the external cause has ceased. This continuance of the stone in its motion is compelled, not because it is necessary, but because it must be defined by the impact of an external cause. What is here said of the stone must be understood of each individual thing, however composite and however adapted to various ends it may be thought to be: that is, that each thing is necessarily determined by an external cause to exist and to act in a definite and determinate manner.

Next, conceive, if you please, that the stone while it continues in motion thinks, and knows that it is striving as much as possible to continue in motion. Surely this stone, inasmuch as it is conscious only of its own effort, and is far from indifferent, will believe that it is completely free, and that it continues in motion for no other reason than because it wants to. And such is the human freedom which all men boast that they possess, and which consists solely in this, that men are conscious of their desire, and ignorant of the causes by which they are determined. So the infant believes that it freely wants milk; the boy when he is angry that he freely wants revenge; the timid that he wants to escape. Then too the drunkard believes that, by the free decision of his mind, he says those things which afterwards when sober he would prefer to have left unsaid. So the delirious, the garrulous and many others of the same sort, believe that they are acting in accordance with the free decision of their mind, and not that they are carried away by impulse. Since this preconception is innate in all men, they are not so easily freed from it. For, although experience teaches sufficiently and more than sufficiently that the last thing that men can do is to moderate their appetites, and that often, when they are tormented by conflicting feelings, they see the better and follow the worse, yet they believe themselves to be free, because they desire some things slightly, and their appetites for these can easily be repressed by the memory of some other thing, which we frequently call to mind.

With these remarks, unless I am mistaken, I have sufficiently explained what my view is about free and compelled necessity, and about imaginary human freedom: and from this it will be easy to answer the objections of your friend. For, when he says with Descartes, that he is free who is compelled by no external cause, if by a man who is compelled he means one who acts against his will, I admit that in certain matters we are in no way compelled, and that in this respect we have a free will. But if by compelled he means one who, although he does not act against his will, yet acts necessarily (as I explained above), then I deny that we are free in anything.

Your friend, on the contrary, asserts that *we can exercise our reason with complete freedom, that is, absolutely.* He persists in this opinion with sufficient, not to say too much, confidence. *For who,* he says, *without contradicting his own consciousness, would deny that in my thoughts I can think that I want to write, and that I do not want to do so.* I should very much like to know of what consciousness he speaks, other than that which I explained above in my example of the stone. Indeed, in order not to contradict my consciousness, that is, my reason and experience, and in order not to foster preconceived ideas and ignorance, I deny that I can, by any absolute power of thought, think that I want, and that I do not want to write. But I appeal to his own consciousness, for he has doubtless experienced the fact that in dreams he has not the power of thinking that he

wants, and does not want to write; and that when he dreams that he wants to write he has not the power of not dreaming that he wants to write. I believe he has had no less experience of the fact that the mind is not always equally capable of thinking about the same subject; but that according as the body is more fit for the excitation of the image of this or that object, so the mind is more capable of contemplating this or that object.

When he adds, further, that the causes of his applying himself to writing have stimulated him to write, but have not compelled him, he means nothing else (if you will examine the matter fully) than that his mind was at that time so constituted that the causes which on other occasions, that is, when they were in conflict with some powerful feeling, could not influence him, could now influence him easily, that is, that causes which on other occasions could not compel him, have now compelled him, not to write against his will, but necessarily to desire to write.

Again, as to his statement that *if we were compelled by external causes then no one would be able to acquire the habit of virtue*, I do not know who has told him that we cannot be of a firm and constant disposition as a result of fatalistic necessity, but only from the free decision of the Mind.

As to his last addition, that *if this were granted all wickedness would be excusable*; what then? For wicked men are no less to be feared, and no less pernicious, when they are necessarily wicked. But on these things, look up, if you please, Part II, Chapter VIII, of my *Appendix to Descartes' Principles,*

Books I and II, geometrically demon-strated.

Lastly, I should like your friend, who makes these objections to my theory, to tell me how he conceives human virtue, which he says arises from the free decision of the mind, together with the preordination of God. For if, with Descartes, he admits that he does not know how to reconcile them, then he is endeavouring to hurl against me the weapon by which he has already been pierced. But in vain. For if you will attentively examine my view, you will see that it is entirely consistent, etc.

[The Hague, October 1674]

WILLIAM JAMES (1842-1910)

Born in New York City in 1842, William James grew up in a family remarkable for its high spirits, intelligence, and congeniality. His father, Henry James, Senior, a man of intense religious and philosophical disposition, used his considerable inherited fortune to surround his five children with an atmosphere of culture. The family traveled a great deal, and William, like his sister and three brothers, was educated in various schools in the United States, England, France, Germany, and Switzerland. Thus he acquired the cosmopolitanism and *savoir faire* which distinguished him throughout his life. Uncertain of the choice of a career, he dabbled in painting, then studied chemistry, physiology, and medicine at Harvard. Still unable to reach a decision, he accompanied Louis Agassiz, the great naturalist, on a field trip up the Amazon, and spent the next two years studying in Europe, mainly Germany. During this period and the subsequent three years spent in America, he suffered from a profound mental depression, at times even considering suicide.

Although he completed the work for his Doctor's degree at the Harvard Medical School in 1869, it was not until 1872, when he was appointed to the post of Instructor in Physiology at Harvard, that he found regular employment. This appointment, which he called "a perfect God-send to me," contributed to a happier outlook. The last traces of his morbid mental state had apparently disappeared by 1878, when he married Alice Gibbens.

By this time, aged 36, he was an established teacher of physiology and psychology at Harvard. In 1880, he became Assistant Professor of Philosophy and before long Professor. During his tenure, the Department of Philosophy attained a high point of distinction, including among its faculty Josiah Royce, Hugo Münsterberg, and George Santayana. James' own importance as an original thinker was established with the publication, in 1890 of his master work, *Principles of Psychology*, the product of eleven years of labor. Although he finally won great acclaim as a philosopher, he never succeeded in writing a philosophical work as substantial and comprehensive as this great treatise in psychology.

Among his favorite recreations was mountain climbing. In June 1899, while climbing alone in the Adirondacks, he lost his way and overstrained his heart in a desperate thirteen-hour scramble. The result was an irreparable lesion, which forced him to curtail his intellectual activities. Finally, in 1910, his heart trouble became very serious, and he died in his New Hampshire home in August of that year.

Witty, kindly, urbane, but restless and neurasthenic, James was a remarkably complex and attractive character—"a being," to quote his sister, "who would bring life and charm to a treadmill." This charm he communicated in his writing, which often lends a rollicking sprightliness to the most abstruse subjects. Despite his artistic flair, he had the scientist's keen sense of fact and the moralist's high seriousness. But his seriousness was never stuffy—he was always opposed to the snobs, the dogmatists, the dry-as-dusts, and the goody-goodies that would fence in the human spirit.

The One and the Many

. . . Philosophy has often been defined as the quest or the vision of the world's unity. Few persons ever challenge this definition, which is true as far as it goes, for philosophy has indeed manifested above all things its interest in unity. But how about the *variety* in things? Is that such an irrelevant matter? If instead of using the term philosophy, we talk in general of our intellect and its needs, we quickly see that unity is only one of them. Acquaintance with the details of fact is always reckoned, along with their reduction to system, as an indispensable mark of mental greatness. Your 'scholarly' mind, of encyclopedic, philo-

From *Pragmatism: A New Name for Some Old Ways of Thinking.* New York: Longmans, Green & Co., Inc., 1907.

logical type, your man essentially of *learning*, has never lacked for praise along with your philosopher. What our intellect really aims at is neither variety nor unity taken singly, but *totality*. In this, acquaintance with reality's diversities is as important as understanding their connexion. Curiosity goes *pari passu* with the systematizing passion.

In spite of this obvious fact the unity of things has always been considered more *illustrious*, as it were, than their variety. When a young man first conceives the notion that the whole world forms one great fact, with all its parts moving abreast, as it were, and interlocked, he feels as if he were enjoying a great insight, and looks superciliously on all who still fall short of this sublime conception. Taken thus abstractly as it first comes to one, the monistic insight is so vague as hardly to seem worth defending intellectually. Yet probably every one in this audience in some way cherishes it. A certain abstract monism, a certain emotional response to the character of oneness, as if it were a feature of the world not co-ordinate with its manyness, but vastly more excellent and eminent, is so prevalent in educated circles that we might almost call it a part of philosophic common sense. Of *course* the world is One, we say. How else could it be a world at all? Empiricists as a rule, are as stout monists of this abstract kind as rationalists are.

The difference is that the empiricists are less dazzled. Unity doesn't blind them to everything else, doesn't quench their curiosity for special facts, whereas there is a kind of rationalist who is sure to interpret abstract unity mystically and to forget everything else, to treat it as a principle; to admire and worship it; and thereupon to come to a full stop intellectually.

'The world is One!'—the formula may become a sort of number-worship. 'Three' and "seven" have, it is true, been reckoned sacred numbers; but, abstractly taken, why is 'one' more excellent than 'forty-three,' or than 'two million and ten'? In this first vague conviction of the world's unity, there is so little to take hold of that we hardly know what we mean by it.

The only way to get forward with our notion is to treat it pragmatically. Granting the oneness to exist, what facts will be different in consequence? What will the unity be known as? The world is One—yes, but *how* one. What is the practical value of the oneness for *us*.

Asking such questions, we pass from the vague to the definite, from the abstract to the concrete. Many distinct ways in which a oneness predicated of the universe might make a difference, come to view. I will note successively the more obvious of these ways.

1. First, the world is at least *one subject of discourse*. If its manyness were so irremediable as to permit *no* union whatever of its parts, not even our minds could 'mean' the whole of it at once: they would be like eyes trying to look in opposite directions. But in point of fact we mean to cover the whole of it by our abstract term 'world' or 'universe,' which expressly intends that no part shall be left out. Such unity of discourse carries obviously no farther monistic specifications. A 'chaos,' once so named, has as much unity of discourse as a cosmos. It is an odd fact that many monists consider a great victory scored for their side when pluralists say 'the universe is many.' " 'The Universe'!" they chuckle—"his speech betrayeth him. He stands confessed of monism out of his own mouth." Well, let things be one in so far forth! You can then fling such a word as universe at the whole collection of them, but what matters it? It still remains to be ascertained whether they are one in any further or more valuable sense.

2. Are they, for example, *continuous?* Can you pass from one to another, keeping always in your one universe without any danger of falling out? In other words, do the parts of our universe *hang together,* instead of being like detached grains of sand?

Even grains of sand hang together through the space in which they are embedded, and if you can in any way move through such space, you can pass continuously from number one of them to number two. Space and time are thus vehicles of continuity by which the world's parts hang together. The practical difference to us, resultant from these forms of union, is immense. Our whole motor life is based upon them.

3. There are innumerable other paths of practical continuity among things. Lines of *influence* can be traced by which they hang together. Following any such line you pass from one thing to another till you may have covered a good part of the universe's extent. Gravity and heat-conduction are such all-uniting influences, so far as the physical world goes. Electric, luminous and chemical influences follow similar lines of influence. But opaque and inert bodies interrupt the continuity here, so that you have to step round them, or change your mode of progress if you wish to get farther on that day. Practically, you have then lost your universe's unity, *so far as it was constituted by those first lines of influence.*

There are innumerable kinds of connexion that special things have with other special things; and the *ensemble* of any one of these connexions forms one sort of *system* by which things are conjoined. Thus men are conjoined in a vast network of *acquaintanceship.* Brown knows Jones, Jones knows Robinson, etc.; and *by choosing your farther intermediaries rightly* you may carry a message from Jones to the Empress of China, or the Chief of the African Pigmies, or to any one else in the inhabited world. But you are stopped short, as by a non-conductor, when you choose one man wrong in this experiment. What may be called love-systems are grafted on the acquaintance-system. A loves (or hates) B; B loves (or hates) C, etc. But these systems are smaller than the great acquaintance-system that they presuppose.

Human efforts are daily unifying the world more and more in definite systematic ways. We found colonial, postal, consular, commercial systems, all the parts of which obey definite influences that propagate themselves within the system but not to facts outside of it. The result is innumerable little hangings-together of the world's parts within the larger hangings-together, little worlds, not only of discourse but of operation, within the wider universe. Each system exemplifies one type or grade of union, its parts being strung on that peculiar kind of relation, and the same part may figure in many different systems, as a man may hold various offices and belong to several clubs. From this 'systematic' point of view, therefore, the pragmatic value of the world's unity is that all these definite networks actually and practically exist. Some are more enveloping and extensive, some less so; they are superposed upon each other; and between them all they let no individual elementary part of the universe escape. Enormous as is the amount of disconnexion among things (for these systematic influences and conjunctions follow rigidly exclusive paths), everything that exists is influenced in *some* way by something else, if you can only pick the way out rightly. Loosely speaking, and in general, it may be said that all things cohere and adhere to each other *somehow*, and that the universe exists practically in reticulated or concatenated forms which make of it a continuous or 'integrated' affair. Any kind of influence whatever helps to make the world one, so far as you can follow it from next to next. You may then say that 'the world *is* One,'—meaning in these respects, namely, and just so far as they obtain. But just as definitely is it *not* One, so far as they do not obtain; and there is no species of connexion which will not fail, if, instead of choosing conductors for it you choose non-conductors. You are then arrested at your very first step and have to write the world down as a pure *many* from that particular point of view. If our intellect had been as much interested in disjunctive as it is in conjunctive relations, philosophy would have equally successfully celebrated the world's *disunion*.

The great point is to notice that the oneness and the manyness are absolutely co-ordinate here. Neither is primordial or more essential or excellent than the other. Just as with space, whose separating of things seems exactly on a par with its uniting of them, but sometimes one function and sometimes the other is what comes home to us most, so, in our general dealings with the world of influences, we now need conductors and now need non-conductors, and wisdom lies in knowing which is which at the appropriate moment.

4. All these systems of influence or non-influence may be listed under the general problem of the world's *causal unity*. If the minor causal influences among things should converge towards one common causal origin of them in the past, one great first cause for all that is, one might then speak of the absolute causal unity of the world. God's *fiat* on creation's day has figured in traditional philosophy as such an absolute cause and origin. Transcendental Idealism, translating 'creation' into 'thinking' (or 'willing to think') calls the divine act 'eternal' rather than 'first'; but the union of the many here is absolute, just the same—the many would not *be*, save for the One. Against this notion of the unity of origin of all things there has always stood the pluralistic notion of an eternal self-existing many in the shape of atoms or even of spiritual units of some sort. The alternative has doubtless a pragmatic meaning, but perhaps, as far as these lectures go, we had better leave the question of unity of origin unsettled.

5. The most important sort of union that obtains among things, pragmatically speaking, is their *generic unity*. Things exist in kinds, there are many specimens in each kind, and what the 'kind' implies for one specimen, it implies also for every other specimen of that kind. We can easily conceive that every fact in the world might be singular, that is, unlike any other fact and sole of its kind. In such a world of singulars our logic would be useless, for logic works by predicating of the single instance what is true of all its kind. With no two things alike in the world, we should be unable to reason from our past experiences to our future ones. The existence of so much generic unity in things is thus perhaps the most

momentous pragmatic specification of what it may mean to say 'the world is One.' *Absolute* generic unity would obtain if there were one *summum genus* under which all things without exception could be eventually subsumed. 'Beings,' 'thinkables,' 'experiences,' would be candidates for this position. Whether the alternatives expressed by such words have any pragmatic significance or not, is another question which I prefer to leave unsettled just now.

6. Another specification of what the phrase 'the world is one' may mean is *unity of purpose.* An enormous number of things in the world subserve a common purpose. All the man-made systems, administrative, industrial, military, or what not, exist each for its controlling purpose. Every living being pursues its own peculiar purposes. They co-operate, according to the degree of their development, in collective or tribal purposes, larger ends thus enveloping lesser ones, until an absolutely single, final and climacteric purpose subserved by all things without exception might conceivably be reached. It is needless to say that the appearances conflict with such a view. Any resultant, as I said in my third lecture, *may* have been purposed in advance, but none of the results we actually know in this world have in point of fact been purposed in advance in all their details. Men and nations start with a vague notion of being rich, or great, or good. Each step they make brings unforeseen chances into sight, and shuts out older vistas, and the specifications of the general purpose have to be daily changed. What is reached in the end may be better or worse than what was proposed, but it is always more complex and different.

Our different purposes also are at war with each other. Where one can't crush the other out, they compromise; and the result is again different from what any one distinctly proposed beforehand. Vaguely and generally, much of what was purposed may be gained; but everything makes strongly for the view that our world is incompletely unified teleologically and is still trying to get its unification better organized.

Whoever claims *absolute* teleological unity, saying that there is one purpose that every detail of the universe subserves, dogmatizes at his own risk. Theologians who dogmatize thus find it more and more impossible, as our acquaintance with the warring interests of the world's parts grows more concrete, to imagine what the one climacteric purpose may possibly be like. We see indeed that certain evils minister to ulterior goods, that the bitter makes the cocktail better, and that a bit of danger or hardship puts us agreeably to our trumps. We can vaguely generalize this into the doctrine that all the evil in the universe is but instrumental to its greater perfection. But the scale of the evil actually in sight defies all human tolerance; and transcendental idealism, in the pages of a Bradley or a Royce, brings us no farther than the book of Job did—God's ways are not our ways, so let us put our hands upon our mouth. A God who can relish such superfluities of horror is no God for human beings to appeal to. His animal spirits are too high. In other words the 'Absolute' with his one purpose, is not the man-like God of common people.

7. *Aesthetic union* among things also obtains, and is very analogous to teleological union. Things tell a story. Their parts hang together so as to work out a climax. They play into each other's hands expressively. Retrospectively, we can see that altho no definite purpose presided over a chain of events, yet the events fell into a dramatic form, with a start, a middle, and a finish. In point of fact all stories end; and here again the point of view of a many is the more natural one to take. The world is full of partial stories that run parallel to one another, beginning and ending at odd times. They mutually interlace and interfere at points, but we can not unify them completely in our minds. In following your life-history, I must temporarily turn my attention from my own. Even a biographer of twins would have to press them alternately upon his reader's attention.

It follows that whoever says that the whole world tells one story utters another of those monistic dogmas that a man believes at his risk. It is easy to see the world's history pluralistically, as a rope of which each fibre tells a separate tale; but to conceive of each cross-section of the rope as an absolutely single fact, and to sum the whole longitudinal series into one being living an undivided life, is harder. We have indeed the analogy of embryology to help us. The microscopist makes a hundred flat cross-sections of a given embryo, and mentally unites them into one solid whole. But the great world's ingredients, so far as they are beings, seem, like the rope's fibres, to be discontinuous, cross-wise, and to cohere only in the longitudinal direction. Followed in

that direction they are many. Even the embryologist, when he follows the *development* of his object, has to treat the history of each single organ in turn. *Absolute* aesthetic union is thus another barely abstract ideal. The world appears as something more epic than dramatic.

So far, then, we see how the world is unified by its many systems, kinds, purposes, and dramas. That there is more union in all these ways than openly appears is certainly true. That there *may* be one sovereign purpose, system, kind, and story, is a legitimate hypothesis. All I say here is that it is rash to affirm this dogmatically without better evidence than we possess at present.

8. The *great* monistic *denkmittel* for a hundred years past has been the notion of *the one Knower*. The many exist only as objects for his thought— exist in his dream, as it were; and *as he knows* them, they have one purpose, form one system, tell one tale for him. This notion of an *all enveloping noetic unity* in things is the sublimest achievement of intellectualist philosophy. Those who believe in the Absolute, as the all-knower is termed, usually say that they do so for coercive reasons, which clear thinkers can not evade. The Absolute has far-reaching practical consequences, to some of which I drew attention in my second lecture. Many kinds of difference important to us would surely follow from its being true. I can not here enter into all the logical proofs of such a Being's existence, farther than to say that none of them seem to me sound. I must therefore treat the notion of an All-Knower simply as an hypothesis, exactly on a par logically with the pluralist notion that there is no

point of view, no focus of information extant, from which the entire content of the universe is visible at once. "God's conscience," says Professor Royce,[1] "forms in its wholeness one luminously transparent conscious moment"—this is the type of noetic unity on which rationalism insists. Empiricism on the other hand is satisfied with the type of noetic unity that is humanly familiar. Everything gets known by *some* knower along with something else; but the knowers may in the end be irreducibly many, and the greatest knower of them all may yet not know the whole of everything, or even know what he does know at one single stroke:—he may be liable to forget. Whichever type obtained, the world would still be a universe noetically. Its parts would be cojoined by knowledge, but in the one case the knowledge would be absolutely unified, in the other it would be strung along and overlapped.

The notion of one instantaneous or eternal Knower—either adjective here means the same thing—is, as I said, the great intellectualist achievement of our time. It has practically driven out that conception of 'Substance' which earlier philosophers set such store by, and by which so much unifying work used to be done—universal substance which alone has being in and from itself, and of which all the particulars of experience are but forms to which it gives support. Substance has succumbed to the pragmatic criticisms of the English school. It appears now only as another name for the fact that phenomena as

[1] *The Conception of God,* New York, 1897, p. 292.

they come are actually grouped and given in coherent forms, the very forms in which we finite knowers experience or think them together. These forms of conjunction are as much parts of the tissue of experience as are the terms which they connect; and it is a great pragmatic achievement for recent idealism to have made the world hang together in these directly representable ways instead of drawing its unity from the "inherence" of its parts—whatever that may mean—in an unimaginable principle behind the scenes.

'The world is One,' therefore, just so far as we experience it to be concatenated, One by as many definite conjunctions as appear. But then also *not* One by just as many definite *dis*junctions as we find. The oneness and the manyness of it thus obtain in respects which can be separately named. It is neither a universe pure and simple nor a multiverse pure and simple. And its various manners of being One suggest, for their accurate ascertainment, so many distinct programs of scientific work. Thus the pragmatic question 'What is the oneness known as? What practical difference will it make?' saves us from all feverish excitement over it as a principle of sublimity and carries us forward into the stream of experience with a cool head. The stream may indeed reveal far more connexion and union than we now suspect, but we are not entitled on pragmatic principles to claim absolute oneness in any respect in advance.

It is so difficult to see definitely what absolute oneness can mean, that probably the majority of you are satisfied with the sober attitude which we have reached. Nevertheless there are possibly some radically monistic souls among you who are not content to leave the one and the many on a par. Union of various grades, union of diverse types, union that stops at non-conductors, union that merely goes from next to next, and means in many cases outer nextness only, and not a more internal bond, union of concatenation, in short; all that sort of thing seems to you a halfway stage of thought. The oneness of things, superior to their manyness, you think must also be more deeply true, must be the more real aspect of the world. The pragmatic view, you are sure, gives us a universe imperfectly rational. The real universe must form an unconditional unit of being, something consolidated, with its parts co-implicated through and through. Only then could we consider our estate completely rational.

There is no doubt whatever that this ultramonistic way of thinking means a great deal to many minds. "One Life, One Truth, one Love, one Principle, One Good, One God"—I quote from a Christian Science leaflet which the day's mail brings into my hands—beyond doubt such a confession of faith has pragmatically an emotional value, and beyond doubt the word 'one' contributes to the value quite as much as the other words. But if we try to realize *intellectually* what we can possibly *mean* by such a glut of oneness we are thrown right back upon our pragmatistic determinations again. It means either the mere name One, the universe of discourse; or it means the sum total of all the ascertainable particular conjunctions and concatenations; or, finally, it means some one vehicle of conjunction treated as all-inclusive, like one origin, one purpose, or one knower. In point of fact it always means one *knower* to those who take it intellectually to-day. The one knower involves, they think, the other forms of conjunction. His world must have all its parts co-implicated in the one logical-aesthetical-teleological unit-picture which is his eternal dream.

The character of the absolute knower's picture is however so impossible for us to represent clearly, that we may fairly suppose that the authority which absolute monism undoubtedly possesses, and probably always will possess over some persons, draws its strength far less from intellectual than from mystical grounds. To interpret absolute monism worthily, be a mystic. Mystical states of mind in every degree are shown by history, usually tho not always, to make for the monistic view. This is no proper occasion to enter upon the general subject of mysticism, but I will quote one mystical pronouncement to show just what I mean. The paragon of all monistic systems is the Vedânta philosophy of Hindostan, and the paragon of Vedântist missionaries was the late Swami Vivekananda who visited our land some years ago. The method of Vedântism is the mystical method. You do not reason, but after going through a certain discipline *you see*, and having seen, you can report the truth. Vivekananda thus reports the truth in one of his lectures here:

"Where is there any more misery for him who sees this Oneness in the universe, this Oneness of life, Oneness of everything? . . . This separation between man and man, man and woman, man and child, nation from nation, earth from moon, moon from sun, this separation between atom and atom is the cause really of all the misery, and the Vedânta says this separation does not exist, it is not real. It is merely apparent, on the surface. In the heart of things there is unity still. If you go inside you find that unity between man and man, women and children, races and races, high and low, rich and poor, the gods and men: all are One, and animals too, if you go deep enough, and he who has attained to that has no more delusion. . . . Where is there any more delusion for him? What can delude him? He knows the reality of everything, the secret of everything. Where is there any more misery for him? What does he desire? He has traced the reality of everything unto the Lord, that centre, that Unity of everything, and that is Eternal Bliss, Eternal Knowledge, Eternal Existence. Neither death nor disease nor sorrow nor misery nor discontent is There . . . In the Centre, the reality, there is no one to be mourned for, no one to be sorry for. He has penetrated everything, the Pure One, the Formless, the Bodiless, the Stainless, He the Knower, He the great Poet, the Self-Existent, He who is giving to every one what he deserves."

Observe how radical the character of the monism here is. Separation is not simply overcome by the One, it is denied to exist. There is no many. We are not parts of the One; It has no parts; and since in a sense we undeniably *are*, it must be that each of us *is* the One, indivisibly and totally. *An Absolute One, and I that One,*—surely we have here a religion which, emotionally considered, has a high pragmatic value; it imparts a perfect sumptuosity of security. As our Swami says in another place:

"When man has seen himself as One with the infinite Being of the universe, when all separateness has ceased, when all men, all women, all angels, all gods, all animals, all plants, the whole universe has been melted into that oneness, then all fear disappears. Whom to fear? Can I hurt myself? Can I kill myself? Can I injure myself? Do you fear yourself? Then will all sorrow disappear. What can cause me sorrow? I am the One Existence of the universe. Then all jealousies will disappear; of whom to be jealous? Of myself? Then all bad feelings disappear. Against whom shall I have this bad feeling? Against myself? There is none in the universe but me . . . kill out this differentiation, kill out this superstition that there are many. 'He who, in this world of many, sees that One; he who, in this mass of insentiency, sees that One Sentient Being; he who in this world of shadow, catches that Reality, unto him belongs eternal peace, unto none else, unto none else.'"

We all have some ear for this monistic music: it elevates and reassures. We all have at least the germ of mysticism in us. And when our idealists recite their arguments for the Absolute, saying that the slightest union admitted anywhere carries logically absolute Oneness with it, and that the slightest separation admitted anywhere logically carries disunion remediless and complete, I cannot help suspecting that the palpable weak places in the intellectual reasonings they use are protected from their own criticism by a mystical feeling that, logic or no logic, absolute Oneness must somehow at any cost be true. Oneness overcomes *moral* separateness at any rate. In the passion of love we have the mystic germ of what might mean a total union of all sentient life. This mystical germ wakes up in us on hearing the monistic utterances, acknowledges their authority, and assigns to intellectual considerations a secondary place. . . .

Leave . . . out of consideration for the moment the authority which mystical insights may be conjectured eventually to possess; treat the problem of the One and the Many in a purely intellectual way; and we see clearly enough where pragmatism stands. With her criterion of the practical differences that theories make, we see that she must equally abjure absolute monism and absolute pluralism. The world is One just so far as its parts hang together by any definite connexion. It is many just so far as any definite connexion fails to obtain. And finally it is growing more and more unified by those systems of connexion at least which human energy keeps framing as time goes on.

It is possible to imagine alternative universes to the one we know, in which the most various grades and types of union should be embodied. Thus the lowest grade of universe would be a world of mere *withness*, of which the parts were only strung together by the conjunction 'and.' Such a universe is even now the collection of our several inner lives. The spaces and times of your imagination, the objects and events of your day-dreams are not only more or less incoherent *inter se*, but are wholly out of definite relation with the similar contents of any one else's mind. Our various reveries now as we sit here compenetrate each other idly without influencing or interfering. They coexist, but in no order and in no receptacle, being the nearest approach to an absolute 'many' that we can conceive. We can not even imagine any reason why they *should* be known all together, and we can imagine even less, if they were known together, how they could be known as one systematic whole.

But add our sensations and bodily actions, and the union mounts to a much higher grade. Our *audita et visa* and our acts fall into those receptacles of time and space in which each event finds its date and place. They form 'things' and are of 'kinds' too, and can be classed. Yet we can imagine a world of things and of kinds in which the causal interactions with which we are so familiar should not exist. Everything there might be inert towards everything else, and refuse to propagate its influence. Or gross mechanical influences might pass, but no chemical action. Such worlds would be far less unified than ours. Again there might be complete physio-chemical interaction, but no minds; or minds, but altogether private ones, with no social life; or social life limited to acquaintance, but no love; or love, but no customs or institutions that should systematize it. No one of these grades of universe would be absolutely irrational or disintegrated, inferior tho it might appear when looked at from the higher grades. For instance, if our minds should ever become 'telepathically' connected, so that we knew immediately, or could under certain conditions know immediately, each what the other was thinking, the world we now live in would appear to the thinkers in that world to have been of an inferior grade.

With the whole of past eternity open for our conjectures to range in, it may be lawful to wonder whether the various kinds of union now realized in the universe that we inhabit may not possibly have been successively evolved after the fashion in which we now see human systems evolving in consequence of human needs. If such an hypothesis were legitimate, total oneness would appear at the end of things rather than at their origin. In other words the notion of the 'Absolute' would have to be replaced by that of the 'Ultimate.' The two notions would have the same content—the maximally unified content of fact, namely—but their time-relations would be positively reversed.[2]

After discussing the unity of the universe in this pragmatic way, you ought to see why I said in my second lecture, borrowing the word from my friend G. Papini, that pragmatism tends to *unstiffen* all our theories. The world's oneness has generally been affirmed abstractly only, and as if any one who questioned it must be an idiot. The temper of monists has been so vehement, as almost at times to be convulsive; and this way of holding a doctrine does not easily go with reasonable discussion and the drawing of distinctions. The theory of the Absolute, in particular, has had to be an article of faith, affirmed dogmatically and exclusively.

[2] Compare on the Ultimate, Mr. Schiller's essay "Activity and Substance," in his book entitled *Humanism*, p. 204.

The One and All, first in the order of being and of knowing, logically necessary itself, and uniting all lesser things in the bonds of mutual necessity, how could it allow of any mitigation of its inner rigidity? The slightest suspicion of pluralism, the minutest wiggle of independence of any one of its parts from the control of the totality would ruin it. Absolute unity brooks no degrees,— as well might you claim absolute purity for a glass of water because it contains but a single little cholera-germ. The independence, however infinitesimal, of a part, however small, would be to the Absolute as fatal as a cholera-germ.

Pluralism on the other hand has no need of this dogmatic rigoristic temper. Provided you grant *some* separation among things, some tremor of independence, some free play of parts on one another, some real novelty or chance, however minute, she is amply satisfied, and will allow you any amount, however great, of real union. How much of union there may be is a question that she thinks can only be decided empirically. The amount may be enormous, colossal; but absolute monism is shattered if, along with all the union, there has to be granted the slightest modicum, the most incipient nascency, or the most residual trace, of a separation that is not 'overcome.'

Pragmatism, pending the final empirical ascertainment of just what the balance of union and disunion among things may be, must obviously range herself upon the pluralistic side. Some day, she admits, even total union, with one knower, one origin, and a universe consolidated in every conceivable way, may turn out to be the most acceptable of all hypotheses. Meanwhile the opposite hypothesis, of a world imperfectly unified still, and perhaps always to remain so, must be sincerely entertained. This latter hypothesis is pluralism's doctrine. Since absolute monism forbids its being even considered seriously, branding it as irrational from the start, it is clear that pragmatism must turn its back on absolute monism, and follow pluralism's more empirical path.

This leaves us with the common-sense world, in which we find things partly joined and partly disjoined. . . .

COMMENT

Spinoza's Monism

"Monism" is the name commonly given to theories that stress the oneness of reality. "Dualism" is the doctrine that there are at least two distinct kinds of things—mind and matter. "Pluralism" is the doctrine that there is not one (Monism), not two (Dualism), but a larger number of ultimate kinds or things.

How many things are there in the world? Quantitative monism is the doctrine that there is only one thing. Spinoza is a quantitative monist. How many *kinds* are there in the world? Qualitative monism answers "Only one kind." Spinoza distinguishes between mind and matter as qualitatively different aspects ("attributes") of the one cosmic being. Hence he is not a qualitative monist in the sense of maintaining that all reality is mental (Idealism) or that all reality is material (Materialism). But in another sense he is a monist. He believes that mind and matter pervade the entire universe and are attributes of the same ultimate substance. In the human being, as well as in the universe at large, mind is not reducible to matter nor matter to mind, but both are aspects of a single reality. This view is sometimes called "the double-aspect theory." Finally Spinoza believes that the one cosmic being is infinite in an infinite number of others ways, each of which is as ultimate and unique as mind and matter. In addition to the one substance and its infinite attributes, there are so-called individual things—a rock, a horse, a man, a planet—which Spinoza calls "modes." To call them modes is to emphasize their adjectival nature—they are merely modifications of the single substance.

Spinoza seizes upon the Cartesian notion (derived from Aristotle) that substance is an enduring thing independent of other things, but he rejects utterly the notion of a finite substance or a plurality of substances. "By substance," he says, "I understand that which is in itself and is conceived through itself; in other words, that the conception of which does not need the conception of another thing from which it must be formed."[1] Substance is thus, by definition absolutely independent and self-sustaining. Spinoza then proceeds to prove that there can be only one

[1] *Ethics,* First Part, Def. III.

substance, and that this substance is infinite and all-inclusive. Finally he "proves" that this single substance, which he calls God or Nature, must exist. The argument, which we shall not trace, is modeled after geometry, being based upon definitions and axioms from which various propositions are deduced.

In the Appendix reproduced above, Spinoza sums up his argument briefly and combats misconceptions of Nature or God. These all arise from the idea that the God-Universe works toward some goal or "final cause." Human beings interpret themselves as goal-seeking and God as like themselves. They think that He has created every natural object and guided every event for an end or purpose. According to Spinoza, this whole approach is false, because God, who is absolutely infinite and self-complete, is made to appear in need of, and dependent upon, an end not yet attained. Those who accept this anthropomorphic belief make the will of God a "refuge of ignorance" by referring every event of which they do not know the cause to God.

Pitted against these "superstitions" is Spinoza's own interpretation of the nature of things. God's causality, far from being teleological, must be conceived on the analogy of logical ground and consequent. ". . . From the supreme power of God, or from His infinite nature, infinite things in infinite ways, that is to say, all things, have necessarily flowed, or continually follow by the same necessity, in the same way as it follows from the nature of a triangle, from eternity to eternity, that its three angles are equal to two right angles."[2] This kind of causality precludes all chance anywhere and anytime. "Necessary" alone expresses what is, and "impossible" what is not. Hence there is no divine purpose and no indeterminism. Man, in distinction from God, thinks he acts freely and purposively, but ultimately his action is determined by forces over which he has no exclusive control, since the only completely adequate ground, and the only real and ultimate agent, is God, from whom everything follows by logical necessity.

According to Spinoza, happiness depends upon the quality of the object of one's love, and love toward the greatest of objects, God or Nature, feeds the mind with a profound joy. This joy, accompanied with a clear understanding of its cause, is called by Spinoza "intellectual love." He who has comprehensive knowledge of himself and the natural world loves God: his intellectual love, in effect, is that very love of God whereby God loves himself. The finite human being is then virtually at one with the eternal nature of things. His life is a communion with that sublime and marvellous order of nature in which God is manifest. He who loves God in this "intellectual" way is a free man; he is caught up into the impersonal infinitude of being, and knows the deepest happiness of which a human being is capable. Because his account of the nature of things culminates in this ecstatic vision, Spinoza regarded metaphysics as a prelude to ethics and gave to his great metaphysical treatise the name of "Ethics."

Even highly trained philosophers find the *Ethics* a very difficult book to under-

[2] *Ethics,* Prop. XVII, Scholium.

stand. But in the Appendix and the Correspondence that we have quoted the doctrine is easier to grasp. With the help that we have provided in this Comment, the student should find no insuperable difficulty.

No one today would altogether accept Spinoza's rationalism and extreme monism. To set up cosmic monism and determinism as necessary truths, and to demonstrate them in the style of Euclid's geometry, with definitions, axioms, and theorems, is no longer plausible. Nevertheless, his vision of an integrated, deterministic, and nonpurposive universe retains a kind of impersonal grandeur, and his conception of freedom as the understanding of necessity has a deep and enduring appeal. There is more than a touch of Spinoza's spirit in Bertrand Russell's essay, "A Free Man's Worship," in Chapter 11.

James' Concatenism

When we turn from the austere monism of Spinoza to the genial pragmatism of James, we seem to have entered another world. Spinoza would have been profoundly shocked by James' question, "What is the practical value of oneness for *us*?" and the suggestion that this value may serve as a criterion for the truth or falsity of monism. James comes close to characterizing the God-Universe of Spinoza when he refers to "the One and All, first in the order of being and of knowing, logically necessary itself, and uniting all lesser things in the bonds of mutual necessity." His dislike for this concept of absolute unity and his feeling that it does not truly serve the needs of mankind are implicit in his statement: "The slightest suspicion of pluralism, the minutest wiggle of any one of its parts from the control of the totality would ruin it."

It is characteristic of his concrete, empirical approach to metaphysical problems that he is not content with the idea of unity in its abstract generality. He distinguishes between various forms of oneness: one in discourse, one cause, one kind, one purpose, one story, one knower, one in mystical trance. Each of these he examines in terms of its meaningfulness for human thought and action. Although he concedes that oneness in each of these modes is alluring, he finds that manyness is a stubborn fact of experience and an ineradicable human need.

Note that James is presenting an alternative to both extreme monism and extreme pluralism. He is indicating that things may be related in some ways without being related in others; that these relations may be of various degrees of intensity; that the world is a mixture of conductors and nonconductors; and that in a long concatenation, the connections become nonexistent when interrupted by nonconductors, or increasingly tenuous as the links are farther and farther apart. His metaphor of a chain conveys the notion that things may be connected next to next without being connected in any significant way across great distances of time and space or across great disparities in kind. Your present thought may have no real connection, or the very slightest, with a particular grain of sand in the Sahara desert. The coughing of someone near you in a theater is annoying, but the coughing of someone in an ancient Greek theater, very far removed in time and space, has no discernible effect upon you. Every movement of your eyelash may influence every star in the universe, but the influence is so slight as to be negligible. Such homely considerations as these lead James to adopt an intermediate theory, which may be called "concatenism" in distinction from either monism or pluralism pure and simple.

So vivid is James' literary style, and so keen and clear is his analysis, that no further comment is needed to aid understanding or awaken interest. He makes such old problems as the One and the Many come alive. The oversimplification that may exist in his pragmatism is outweighed by his ability to rescue philosophical questions from the fog of abstraction and to make them relevant to our practical and personal concerns.

6

Empiricism

JOHN LOCKE (1632–1704)

Reared in a liberal Puritan family, Locke received his higher education at Oxford, where he remained after he received his Master's degree as a teacher of Greek and Latin. Even as a student he turned against a narrow scholastic education and leaned toward the new experimental sciences. After receiving a small inheritance from his father, he studied medicine and practiced as an assistant to a distinguished Oxford physician. In 1667 he moved to London to become the personal physician, friend, and advisor to the Earl of Shaftesbury, a leading opponent of the Stuart dynasty. Shaftesbury introduced him to "the wisest men and the greatest wits" in England, and during a prolonged vacation in France, Locke came in contact with the foremost philosophers and scientists of the continent.

When he returned to England, the King was suspicious of him because of his connection with Shaftesbury, and in 1683 Locke fled to Holland. He remained in exile until the revolution of 1688, when James II was deposed and William, the Prince of Orange, was elevated to the English throne. Locke championed this "bloodless revolution" in his *Two Treatises on Civil Government,* a main source of democratic political theory. Soon thereafter he published his *Essay Concerning Human Understanding,* which he had been writing for many years. Although he continued to be active in political and intellectual circles, his health steadily declined, and he died on October 28, 1704.

An Essay Concerning Human Understanding

Introduction

1. *An inquiry into the understanding, pleasant and useful.*—Since it is the *understanding* that sets man above the rest of sensible beings, and gives him all the advantage and dominion which he has over them, it is certainly a subject, even for its nobleness, worth our labor to inquire into. The understanding, like the eye, whilst it makes us see and perceive all other things, takes no notice of itself; and it requires art and pains to set it at a distance, and make it its own object. But whatever be the difficulties that lie in the way of this inquiry, whatever it be that keeps us so much in the dark to ourselves, sure I am that all the light we can let in upon our own minds, all the acquaintance we can make with our own understandings, will not only be very pleasant, but bring us great advantage in directing our thoughts in the search of other things.

2. *Design.*—This, therefore, being my purpose, to inquire into the original, certainty, and extent of *human knowledge,* together with the grounds and degrees of *belief, opinion,* and *assent,* I shall not at present meddle with the physical consideration of the mind, or trouble myself to examine wherein its essence consists or by what motions

An Essay Concerning Human Understanding was published in London in 1690.

of our spirits, or alterations of our bodies, we come to have any *sensation* by our organs, or any *ideas* in our understandings; and whether those ideas do, in their formation, any or all of them, depend on matter or not. These are speculations which, however curious and entertaining, I shall decline, as lying out of my way in the design I am now upon. It shall suffice to my present purpose, to consider the discerning faculties of a man, as they are employed about the objects which they have to do with. And I shall imagine I have not wholly misemployed myself in the thoughts I shall have on this occasion, if, in this historical, plain method, I can give any account of the ways whereby our understandings come to attain those notions of things we have, and can set down any measures of the certainty of our knowledge, or the grounds of those persuasions which are to be found amongst men, so various, different, and wholly contradictory; and yet asserted somewhere or other with such assurance and confidence, that he that shall take a view of the opinions of mankind, observe their opposition, and at the same time consider the fondness and devotion wherewith they are embraced, the resolution and eagerness wherewith they are maintained, may perhaps have reason to suspect that either there is no such thing as truth at all, or that mankind hath no sufficient means to attain a certain knowledge of it. . . .

4. *Useful to know the extent of our comprehension.*—If by this inquiry into the nature of the understanding, I can discover the powers thereof, how far they reach, to what things they are in any degree proportionate, and where they fail us, I suppose it may be of use to prevail with the busy mind of man to be more cautious in meddling with things exceeding its comprehension, to stop when it is at the utmost extent of its tether, and to sit down in a quiet ignorance of those things which, upon examination, are found to be beyond the reach of our capacities. We should not then, perhaps, be so forward, out of an affectation of an universal knowledge, to raise questions, and perplex ourselves and others with disputes, about things to which our understandings are not suited, and of which we cannot frame in our minds any clear or distinct perceptions, or whereof (as it has, perhaps, too often happened) we have not any notions at all. If we can find out how far the understanding can extend its view, how far it has faculties to attain certainty, and in what cases it can only judge and guess, we may learn to content ourselves with what is attainable by us in this state. . . .

7. *Occasion of this Essay.*—This was that which gave the first rise to this Essay concerning the Understanding. For I thought that the first step towards satisfying several inquiries the mind of man was very apt to run into, was, to take a survey of our own understandings, examine our own powers, and see to what things they were adapted. Till that was done, I suspected we began at the wrong end, and in vain sought for satisfaction in a quiet and sure possession of truths that most concerned us, whilst we let loose our thoughts into the vast ocean of being; as if all that boundless extent were the natural and undoubted possession of our understandings, wherein there was nothing exempt from its decisions, or that escaped its comprehension. Thus men, extending their inquiries beyond their capacities, and letting their thoughts wander into those depths where they can find no sure footing, it is no wonder that they raise questions and multiply disputes, which, never coming to any clear resolution, are proper only to continue and increase their doubts, and to confirm them at last in perfect scepticism. Whereas, were the capacities of our understandings well considered, the extent of our knowledge once discovered, and the horizon found which sets the bounds between the enlightened and dark parts of things—between what is and what is not comprehensible by us—men would, perhaps with less scruple, acquiesce in the avowed ignorance of the one, and employ their thoughts and discourse with more advantage and satisfaction in the other.

8. *What 'idea' stands for.*—Thus much I thought necessary to say concerning the occasion of this inquiry into human understanding. But, before I proceed on to what I have thought on this subject, I must here, in the entrance, beg pardon of my reader for the frequent use of the word 'idea' which he will find in the following treatise. It being that term which, I

think, serves best to stand for whatsoever is the *object* of the understanding when a man thinks, I have used it to express whatever is meant by phantasm, notion, species, or whatever it is which the mind can be employed about in thinking; and I could not avoid frequently using it.

I presume it will be easily granted me, that there are such *ideas* in men's minds. Everyone is conscious of them in himself; and men's words and actions will satisfy him that they are in others.

Our first inquiry, then, shall be, how they come into the mind. . . .

Of Ideas in General, and Their Original

1. *Idea is the object of thinking.*—Every man being conscious to himself that he thinks, and that which his mind is applied about whilst thinking being the ideas that are there, it is past doubt that men have in their mind several ideas, such as are those expressed by the words whiteness, hardness, sweetness, thinking, motion, man, elephant, army, drunkenness, and others: it is in the first place then to be inquired, How he comes by them? I know it is a received doctrine, that men have native ideas and original characters stamped upon their minds in their very first being. This opinion I have at large examined already; and, I suppose, what I have said in the foregoing book will be much more easily admitted, when I have shown whence the understanding may get all the ideas it has, and by what ways and degrees they may come into the mind; for which I shall

appeal to everyone's own observation and experience.

2. *All ideas come from sensation or reflection.*—Let us then suppose the mind to be, as we say, white paper, void of all characters, without any ideas; how comes it to be furnished? Whence comes it by that vast store, which the busy and boundless fancy of man has painted on it with an almost endless variety? Whence has it all the materials of reason and knowledge? To this I answer, in one word, from experience. In that all our knowledge is founded, and from that it ultimately derives itself. Our observation, employed either about external sensible objects, or about the internal operations of our minds, perceived and reflected on by ourselves, is that which supplies our understandings with all the materials of thinking. These two are the fountains of knowledge, from whence all the ideas we have, or can naturally have, do spring.

3. *The object of sensation one source of ideas.*—First, our senses, conversant about particular sensible objects, do convey into the mind several distinct perceptions of things, according to those various ways wherein those objects do affect them; and thus we come by those ideas we have of yellow, white, heat, cold, soft, hard, bitter, sweet, and all those which we call sensible qualities; which when I say the senses convey into the mind, I mean, they from external objects convey into the mind what produces there those perceptions. This great source of most of the ideas we have, depending wholly upon our senses, and derived by them to the understanding, I call *sensation.*

4. *The operations of our minds the other source of them.*—Secondly, the other fountain, which from experience furnisheth the understanding with ideas, is the perception of the operations of our own minds within us, as it is employed about the ideas it has got; which operations when the soul comes to reflect on and consider, do furnish the understanding with another set of ideas which could not be had from things without; and such are perception, thinking, doubting, believing, reasoning, knowing, willing, and all the different actings of our own minds; which we, being conscious of, and observing in ourselves, do from these receive into our understandings as distinct ideas, as we do from bodies affecting our senses. This source of ideas every man has wholly in himself; and though it be not sense as having nothing to do with external objects, yet it is very like it, and might properly enough be called *internal sense*. But as I call the other sensation, so I call this *reflection,* the ideas it affords being such only as the mind gets by reflecting on its own operations within itself. By reflection, then, in the following part of this discourse, I would be understood to mean that notice which the mind takes of its own operations, and the manner of them, by reason whereof there come to be ideas of these operations in the understanding. These two, I say, viz., external material things as the objects of sensation, and the operations of our own minds within as the objects of reflection, are, to me, the only originals from whence all our ideas take their beginnings. The term *operations* here,

I use in a large sense, as comprehending not barely the actions of the mind about its ideas, but some sort of passions arising sometimes from them, such as is the satisfaction or uneasiness arising from any thought.

5. *All our ideas are of the one or the other of these.*—The understanding seems to me not to have the least glimmering of any ideas which it doth not receive from one of these two. *External objects* furnish the mind with the ideas of sensible qualities, which are all those different perceptions they produce in us; and *the mind* furnishes the understanding with ideas of its own operations.

These, when we have taken a full survey of them, and their several modes, combinations, and relations, we shall find to contain all our whole stock of ideas; and that we have nothing in our minds which did not come in one of these two ways. Let anyone examine his own thoughts, and thoroughly search into his understanding, and then let him tell me, whether all the original ideas he has there, are any other than of the objects of his senses, or of the operations of his mind considered as objects of his reflection; and how great a mass of knowledge soever he imagines to be lodged there, he will, upon taking a strict view, see that he has not any idea in his mind but what one of these two have imprinted, though perhaps with infinite variety compounded and enlarged by the understanding, as we shall see hereafter. . . .

7. *Men are differently furnished with these according to the different objects they converse with.*—Men then

come to be furnished with fewer or more simple ideas from without, according as the objects they converse with afford greater or less variety; and from the operations of their minds within, according as they more or less reflect on them. For, though he that contemplates the operations of his mind cannot but have plain and clear ideas of them; yet, unless he turn his thoughts that way, and considers them attentively, he will no more have clear and distinct ideas of all the operations of his mind, and all that may be observed therein, than he will have all the particular ideas of any landscape, or of the parts and motions of a clock, who will not turn his eyes to it, and with attention heed all the parts of it. The picture or clock may be so placed, that they may come in his way every day; but yet he will have but a confused idea of all the parts they are made of, till he applies himself with attention to consider them each in particular.

8. *Ideas of reflection later, because they need attention.*—And hence we see the reason why it is pretty late before most children get ideas of the operations of their own minds; and some have not any very clear or perfect ideas of the greatest part of them all their lives: because, though they pass there continually, yet like floating visions, they make not deep impressions enough to leave in the mind, clear, distinct, lasting ideas, till the understanding turns inwards upon itself, reflects on its own operations, and makes them the objects of its own contemplation. Children, when they come first into it, are surrounded with a world of new things, which, by a constant solicitation of their senses, draw the mind constantly to them, forward to take notice of new, and apt to be delighted with the variety of changing objects. Thus the first years are usually employed and diverted in looking abroad. Men's business in them is to acquaint themselves with what is to be found without; and so, growing up in a constant attention to outward sensations, seldom make any considerable reflection on what passes within them till they come to be of riper years; and some scarce ever at all. . . .

Of Simple Ideas

1. *Uncompounded appearances.*—The better to understand the nature, manner, and extent of our knowledge, one thing is carefully to be observed concerning the ideas we have; and that is, that some of them are *simple,* and some *complex.*

Though the qualities that affect our senses are, in the things themselves, so united and blended that there is no separation, no distance between them; yet it is plain the ideas they produce in the mind enter by the senses simple and unmixed. For though the sight and touch often take in from the same object, at the same time, different ideas —as a man sees at once motion and color, the hand feels softness and warmth in the same piece of wax—yet the simple ideas thus united in the same subject are as perfectly distinct as those that come in by different senses; the coldness and hardness which a man feels in a piece of ice being as distinct ideas in the mind as the smell and whiteness of a lily, or as the taste of sugar and smell of a rose: and there is nothing can be plainer to a man than the clear and distinct perception he has of those simple ideas; which, being each in itself uncompounded, contains in it nothing but *one uniform appearance or conception in the mind,* and is not distinguishable into different ideas.

2. *The mind can neither make nor destroy them.*—These simple ideas, the materials of all our knowledge, are suggested and furnished to the mind only by those two ways above mentioned, viz., sensation and reflection. When the understanding is once stored with these simple ideas, it has the power to repeat, compare, and unite them, even to an almost infinite variety, and so can make at pleasure new complex ideas. But it is not in the power of the most exalted wit or enlarged understanding, by any quickness or variety of thought, to *invent* or *frame* one new simple idea in the mind, not taken in by the ways before mentioned; nor can any force of the understanding *destroy* those that are there: the dominion of man in this little world of his own understanding, being muchwhat the same as it is in the great world of visible things; wherein his power, however managed by art and skill, reaches no farther than to compound and divide the materials that are made to his hand but can do nothing towards the making the least particle of new matter, or destroying one atom of what is already in being. The same inability will everyone find in himself, who shall go about to fashion in his understanding any simple idea not received in by his senses from external objects, or by reflection from the operations of his own mind about them. I would have anyone try to fancy any taste which had never affected his palate, or frame the idea of a scent he had never smelt; and when he can do this, I will also conclude that a blind man hath *ideas* of colors, and a deaf man true, distinct notions of sounds.

3. *Only the qualities that affect the senses are imaginable.*—This is the reason why, though we cannot believe it impossible to God to make a creature with other organs, and more ways to convey into the understanding the notice of corporeal things than those five as they are usually counted, which He has given to man; yet I think it is not possible for anyone to imagine any other qualities in bodies, howsoever constituted, whereby they can be taken notice of, besides sounds, tastes, smells, visible and tangible qualities. And had mankind been made with but four senses, the qualities then which are the objects of the fifth sense had been as far from our notice, imagination, and conception, as now any belonging to sixth, seventh, or eighth sense can possibly be; which, whether yet some other creatures, in some other parts of this vast and stupendous universe, may not have, will be a great presumption to deny. He that will not set himself proudly at the top of all things, but will consider the immensity of this fabric, and the great variety that is to be found in this little and inconsiderable part of it which he has to do with, may be apt to think, that in other mansions of it there may be other and different intelligible beings, of whose

faculties he has as little knowledge or apprehension, as a worm shut up in one drawer of a cabinet hath of the senses or understanding of a man; such variety and excellency being suitable to the wisdom and power of the Maker. I have here followed the common opinion of man's having but five senses, though perhaps there may be justly counted more; but either supposition serves equally to my present purpose.

Of Simple Ideas of Sense

1. *Division of simple ideas.*—The better to conceive the ideas we receive from sensation, it may not be amiss for us to consider them in reference to the different ways whereby they make their approaches to our minds, and make themselves perceivable by us.

First, then, there are some which come into our minds *by one sense only*.

Secondly, there are others that convey themselves into the mind *by more senses than one*.

Thirdly, others that are had *from reflection only*.

Fourthly, there are some that make themselves way, and are suggested to the mind, *by all the ways of sensation and reflection*.

We shall consider them apart under these several heads.

There are some ideas which have admittance only through one sense, which is peculiarly adapted to receive them. Thus light and colors, as white, red, yellow, blue, with their several degrees or shades and mixtures, as green, scarlet, purple, sea-green, and the rest, come in only by the eyes; all kinds of noises, sounds, and tones, only by the ears; the several tastes and smells, by the nose and palate. And if these organs, or the nerves which are the conduits to convey them from without to their audience in the brain—the mind's presence-room (as I may so call it)—are, any of them, so disordered as not to perform their functions, they have no postern to be admitted by, no other way to bring themselves into view, and be received by the understanding.

The most considerable of those belonging to the touch are heat, and cold, and solidity; all the rest—consisting almost wholly in the sensible configuration, as smooth and rough; or else more or less firm adhesion of the parts, as hard and soft, tough and brittle—are obvious enough. . . .

Of Simple Ideas of Divers Senses

Ideas received both by seeing and touching.—The ideas we get by more than one sense are of *space* or *extension, figure, rest* and *motion*. For these make perceivable impressions both on the eyes and touch; and we can receive and convey into our minds the ideas of the extension, figure, motion, and rest of bodies, both by seeing and feeling. . . .

Of Simple Ideas of Reflection

1. *Simple ideas of reflection are the operations of the mind about its other ideas.*—The mind, receiving the ideas mentioned in the foregoing chapters from without, when it turns its view inward upon itself, and observes its

own actions about those ideas it has, takes from thence other ideas, which are as capable to be the objects of its contemplation as any of those it received from foreign things.

2. *The idea of perception, and idea of willing, we have from reflection.*— The two great and principal actions of the mind, which are most frequently considered, and which are so frequent that every one that pleases may take notice of them in himself, are these two: *perception* or *thinking,* and *volition* or *willing.* The power of thinking is called the *understanding,* and the power of volition is called the *will;* and these two powers or abilities in the mind are denominated *faculties.* Of some of the models of these simple ideas of reflection, such as are remembrance, discerning, reasoning, judging, knowledge, faith, etc., I shall have occasion to speak hereafter.

Of Simple Ideas of Both Sensation and Reflection

1. *Ideas of pleasure and pain.*—There be other simple ideas which convey themselves into the mind by all the ways of sensation and reflection: viz., pleasure or delight, and its opposite, pain or uneasiness, power, existence, unity.

2. Delight or uneasiness, one or other of them, join themselves to almost all our ideas both of sensation and reflection; and there is scarce any affection of our senses from without, any retired thought of our mind within, which is not able to produce in us pleasure or pain. By pleasure and pain,

I would be understood to signify whatsoever delights or molests us; whether it arises from the thoughts of our minds, or any thing operating on our bodies. For whether we call it satisfaction, delight, pleasure, happiness, etc., on the one side; or uneasiness, trouble, pain, torment, anguish, misery, etc., on the other; they are still but different degrees of the same thing, and belong to the ideas of pleasure and pain, delight or uneasiness; which are the names I shall most commonly use for those two sorts of ideas. . . .

7. *Ideas of existence and unity.*—Existence and unity are two other ideas that are suggested to the understanding by every object without, and every idea within. When ideas are in our minds, we consider them as being actually there, as well as we consider things to be actually without us: which is, that they exist, or have existence: and whatever we can consider as one thing, whether a real being or idea, suggests to the understanding the idea of unity.

8. *Idea of power.*—Power also is another of those simple ideas which we receive from sensation and reflection. For, observing in ourselves that we do and can think, and that we can at pleasure move several parts of our bodies which were at rest; the effects also that natural bodies are able to produce in one another occurring every moment to our senses, we both these ways get the idea of power.

9. *Idea of succession.*—Besides these there is another idea, which though suggested by our senses, yet is more constantly offered us by what passes in our minds; and that is the idea of suc-

cession. For if we look immediately into ourselves, and reflect on what is observable there, we shall find our ideas always, whilst we are awake or have any thought, passing in train, one going and another coming without intermission.

10. *Simple ideas the materials of all our knowledge.*—These, if they are not all, are at least (as I think) the most considerable of those simple ideas which the mind has, and out of which is made all its other knowledge: all of which it receives only by the two forementioned ways of sensation and reflection. . . .

Some Farther Considerations Concerning Our Simple Ideas of Sensation

7. . . . *Ideas in the mind, qualities in bodies.*—To discover the nature of our ideas the better, and to discourse of them intelligibly, it will be convenient to distinguish them, as they are *ideas or perceptions in our minds,* and as they are *modifications of matter in the bodies that cause such perceptions in us;* that so we may not think (as perhaps usually is done) that they are exactly the images and resemblances of something inherent in the subject; most of those of sensation being in the mind no more the likeness of something existing without us than the names that stand for them are the likeness of our ideas, which yet upon hearing they are apt to excite in us.

8. Whatsoever the mind perceives in itself, or is the immediate object of perception, thought, or understanding, that I call *idea;* and the power to produce any idea in our mind, I call *quality* of the subject wherein that power is. Thus a snowball having the power to produce in us the ideas of white, cold, and round, the powers to produce those ideas in us as they are in the snowball, I call qualities; and as they are sensations or perceptions in our understandings, I call them ideas; which ideas, if I speak of them sometimes as in the things themselves, I would be understood to mean those qualities in the objects which produce them in us.

9. *Primary Qualities.*—Qualities thus considered in bodies are, first, such as are utterly inseparable from the body, in what state soever it be; such as, in all the alterations and changes it suffers, all the force can be used upon it, it constantly keeps; and such as sense constantly finds in every particle of matter which has bulk enough to be perceived, and the mind finds inseparable from every particle of matter, though less than to make itself singly be perceived by our senses; v.g., take a grain of wheat, divide it into two parts, each part has still solidity, extension, figure, and mobility; divide it again, and it retains still the same qualities; and so divide it on till the parts become insensible, they must retain still each of them all those qualities. For, division (which is all that a mill or pestle or any other body does upon another, in reducing it to insensible parts) can never take away either solidity, extension, figure, or mobility from any body, but only makes two or more distinct separate masses of matter of that which was but one before; all which distinct masses, reck-

oned as so many distinct bodies, after division, make a certain number. These I call *original* or *primary* qualities of body, which I think we may observe to produce simple ideas in us, viz., solidity, extension, figure, motion or rest, and number.

10. *Secondary Qualities.*—Secondly, such qualities, which in truth are nothing in the objects themselves but powers to produce various sensations in us by their primary qualities, i.e., by the bulk, figure, texture, and motion of their insensible parts, as colours, sounds, tastes, etc., these I call *secondary* qualities. To these might be added a third sort, which are allowed to be barely powers, though they are as much real qualities in the subject as those which I, to comply with the common way of speaking, call qualities, but, for distinction, *secondary* qualities. For the power in fire to produce a new colour or consistency in wax or clay by its primary qualities is as much a quality in fire as the power it has to produce in me a new idea or sensation of warmth or burning, which I felt not before, by the same primary qualities, viz., the bulk, texture, and motion of its insensible parts.

11. *How primary qualities produce ideas in us.*—The next thing to be considered is, how bodies produce ideas in us; and that is manifestly by impulse, the only way which we can conceive bodies to operate in.

12. If, then, external objects be not united to our minds when they produce ideas therein, and yet we perceive these original qualities in such of them as singly fall under our senses, it is evident that some motion must be thence continued by our nerves, or animal spirits, by some parts of our bodies, to the brains or the seat of sensation, there to produce in our minds the particular ideas we have of them. And since the extension, figure, number, and motion of bodies of an observable bigness, may be perceived at a distance by the sight, it is evident some singly imperceptible bodies must come from them to the eyes, and thereby convey to the brain some motion which produces these ideas which we have of them in us.

13. *How secondary.*—After the same manner that the ideas of these original qualities are produced in us, we may conceive that the ideas of secondary qualities are also produced, viz., by the operation of insensible particles on our senses. For it being manifest that there are bodies, and good store of bodies, each whereof are so small that we cannot by any of our senses discover either their bulk, figure, or motion (as is evident in the particles of the air and water, and others extremely smaller than those, perhaps as much smaller than the particles of air or water as the particles of air or water are smaller than peas or hailstones): let us suppose at present that the different motions and figures, bulk and number, of such particles, effecting the several organs of our senses, produce in us those different sensations which we have from the colors and smells of bodies, v.g., that a violet, by the impulse of such insensible particles of matter of peculiar figures and bulks, and in different degrees and modifications of their motions, causes the ideas of the blue colour and sweet scent of that

flower to be produced in our minds; it being no more impossible to conceive that God should annex such ideas to such motions, with which they have no similitude, than that He should annex the idea of pain to the motion of a piece of steel dividing our flesh, with which the idea hath no resemblance.

14. What I have said concerning colors and smells may be understood also of tastes and sounds, and other the like sensible qualities; which, whatever reality we by mistake attribute to them, are in truth nothing in the objects themselves, but powers to produce various sensations in us, and depend on those primary qualities, viz., bulk, figure, texture, and motion of parts as I have said.

15. *Ideas of primary qualities are resemblances; of secondary, not.*—From whence I think it is easy to draw this observation, that the ideas of primary qualities of bodies are resemblances of them, and their patterns do really exist in the bodies themselves; but the ideas produced in us by these secondary qualities have no resemblance of them at all. There is nothing like our ideas existing in the bodies themselves. They are, in the bodies we denominate from them, only a power to produce those sensations in us; and what is sweet, blue, or warm in idea, is but the certain bulk, figure, and motion of the insensible parts in the bodies themselves, which we call so. . . .

17. The particular bulk, number, figure, and motion of the parts of fire or snow are really in them, whether anyone's senses perceive them or no; and therefore they may be called *real*

qualities, because they really exist in those bodies. But light, heat, whiteness, or coldness, are no more really in them than sickness or pain is in manna. Take away the sensation of them; let not the eyes see light or colours, nor the ears hear sounds; let the palate not taste, nor the nose smell; and all colours, tastes, odors, and sounds, as they are such particular ideas, vanish and cease, and are reduced to their causes, i.e., bulk, figure, and motion of parts. . . .

21. Ideas being thus distinguished and understood, we may be able to give an account how the same water, at the same time, may produce the idea of cold by one hand, and of heat by the other; whereas it is impossible that the same water, if those ideas were really in it, should at the same time be both hot and cold. For if we imagine warmth as it is in our hands, to be nothing but a certain sort and degree of motion in the minute particles of our nerves or animal spirits, we may understand how it is possible that the same water may at the same time produce the sensation of heat in one hand, and cold in the other; which yet figure never does, that never producing the idea of a square by one hand which has produced the idea of a globe by another. But if the sensation of heat and cold be nothing but the increase or diminution of the motion of the minute parts of our bodies, caused by the corpuscles of any other body, it is easy to be understood that if that motion be greater in one hand than in the other, if a body be applied to the two hands, which has in its minute particles a greater motion than in those of one of the hands, and a less than in those of the other, it will

increase the motion of the one hand, and lessen it in the other, and so cause the different sensations of heat and cold that depend thereon. . . .

Of Complex Ideas

1. *Made by the mind out of simple ones.*—We have hitherto considered those ideas, in the reception whereof the mind is only passive, which are those simple ones received from sensation and reflection before mentioned, whereof the mind cannot make one to itself, nor have any ideas which does not wholly consist of them. But as the mind is wholly passive in the reception of all its simple ideas, so it exerts several acts of its own, whereby out of its simple ideas, as the materials and foundations of the rest, the others are framed. The acts of the mind wherein it exerts its power over its simple ideas are chiefly these three: (1) Combining several simple ideas into one compound one; and thus all *complex ideas* are made. (2) The second is bringing two ideas, whether simple or complex, together, and setting them by one another, so as to take a view of them at once, without uniting them into one; by which way it gets all its *ideas of relations*. (3) The third is separating them from all other ideas that accompany them in their real existence; this is called abstraction: and thus all its *general ideas* are made. This shows man's power and its way of operation to be much the same in the material and intellectual world. For, the materials in both being such as he has no power over, either to make or destroy, all that man can do is either to unite them together, or to set

them by one another, or wholly separate them. I shall here begin with the first of these in the consideration of complex ideas, and come to the other two in their due places. As simple ideas are observed to exist in several combinations united together, so the mind has a power to consider several of them united together as one idea; and that not only as they are united in external objects, but as itself has joined them. Ideas thus made up of several simple ones put together I call *complex;* such as are beauty, gratitude, a man, an army, the universe; which, though complicated of various simple ideas or complex ideas made up of simple ones, yet are, when the mind pleases, considered each by itself as one entire thing, and signified by one name.

2. *Made voluntarily.*—In this faculty of repeating and joining together its ideas, the mind has great power in varying and multiplying the objects of its thoughts infinitely beyond what sensation or reflection furnished it with; but all this still confined to those simple ideas which it received from those two sources, and which are the ultimate materials of all its compositions. For, simple ideas are all from things themselves; and of these the mind can have no more nor other than what are suggested to it. It can have no other ideas of sensible qualities than what come from without by the senses, nor any ideas of other kind of operations of a thinking substance than what it finds in itself. But when it has once got these simple ideas, it is not confined barely to observation, and what offers itself from without; it can, by its own power, put together those ideas it has, and make new

complex ones which it never received so united.

3. *Complex ideas are either of modes, substances, or relations.*—Complex ideas, however compounded and decompounded, though their number be infinite, and the variety endless wherewith they fill and entertain the thoughts of men, yet I think they may be all reduced under these three heads: (1) Modes. (2) Substances. (3) Relations.

4. *Ideas of modes.*—First, *modes* I call such complex ideas which, however compounded, contain not in them the supposition of subsisting by themselves, but are considered as dependences on, or affections of, substances; such are the ideas signified by the words, triangle, gratitude, murder, etc. And if in this I use the word mode in somewhat a different sense from its ordinary signification, I beg pardon; it being unavoidable in discourses differing from the ordinary received notions, either to make new words or to use old words in somewhat a new signification: the latter whereof, in our present case, is perhaps the more tolerable of the two.

5. *Simple and mixed modes.*—Of these modes there are two sorts which deserve distinct consideration. First, there are some which are only variations or different combinations of the same simple idea, without the mixture of any other, as a dozen, or score; which are nothing but the ideas of so many distinct units added together: and these I call *simple modes,* as being contained within the bounds of one simple idea. Secondly, there are others compounded of simple ideas, of several kinds, put together to make one complex one; v.g., beauty, consisting of a certain composi-

tion of colour and figure, causing delight in the beholder; theft, which, being the concealed change of the possession of any thing, without the consent of the proprietor, contains, as is visible, a combination of several ideas of several kinds; and these I call *mixed modes.*

6. *Ideas of substances, single or collective.*—Secondly, the ideas of *substances* are such combinations of simple ideas as are taken to represent distinct *particular* things subsisting by themselves, in which the supposed or confused idea of substance, such as it is, is always the first and chief. Thus, if to substance be joined the simple idea of a certain dull, whitish colour, with certain degrees of weight, hardness, ductility, and fusibility, we have the idea of lead; and a combination of the ideas of a certain sort of figure, with the powers of motion, thought, and reasoning, joined to substance, make the ordinary idea of a man. Now of substances also there are two sorts of ideas, one of single substances, as they exist separately, as of a man or a sheep; the other of several of those put together, as an army of men or flock of sheep; which collective ideas of several substances thus put together, are as much each of them one single idea as that of a man or an unit.

7. *Relation.*—Thirdly, the last sort of complex ideas is that we call *relation,* which consists in the consideration and comparing one idea with another. Of these several kinds we shall treat in their order.

8. *The abstrusest ideas are from the two sources.*—If we trace the progress of our minds, and with attention observe how it repeats, adds together, unites its simple ideas received from

sensation or reflection, it will lead us farther than at first perhaps we should have imagined. And I believe we shall find, if we warily observe the originals of our notions, that even the most abtruse ideas, how remote soever they may seem from sense, or from any operation of our own minds, are yet only such as the understanding frames to itself, by repeating and joining together ideas that it had either from objects of sense, or from its own operations about them: so that those even large and abstract ideas are derived from sensation or reflection, being no other than what the mind, by the ordinary use of its own faculties, employed about ideas received from objects of sense, or from the operations it observes in itself about them, may and does attain unto. This I shall endeavor to show in the ideas we have of space, time, and infinity, and some few others, that seem the most remote from those originals. . . .

Of Our Complex Ideas of Substances

1. *Ideas of particular substances, how made.*—The mind being, as I have declared, furnished with a great number of the simple ideas conveyed in by the senses, as they are found in exterior things, or by reflection on its own operations, takes notice, also, that a certain number of these simple ideas go constantly together; which being presumed to belong to one thing, and words being suited to common apprehensions, and made use of for quick despatch, are called, so united in one subject, by one name; which, by inadvertency, we are apt afterward to talk of and consider as

one simple idea, which indeed is a complication of many ideas together: because, as I have said, not imagining how these simple ideas can subsist by themselves, we accustom ourselves to suppose some *substratum* wherein they do subsist, and from which they do result; which therefore we call *substance*.

2. *Our obscure idea of substance in general.*—So that if anyone will examine himself concerning his notion of pure substance in general, he will find he has no other idea of it at all, but only a supposition of he knows not what support of such qualities which are capable of producing simple ideas in us; which qualities are commonly called accidents. If anyone should be asked, what is the subject wherein color or weight inheres, he would have nothing to say but, the solid extended parts. And if he were demanded, what is it that solidity and extension inhere in, he would not be in a much better case than the Indian before mentioned, who, saying that the world was supported by a great elephant, was asked, what the elephant rested on; to which his answer was, a great tortoise; but being again pressed to know what gave support to the broad-backed tortoise, replied—something, he knew not what. And thus here, as in all other cases where we use words without having clear and distinct ideas, we talk like children: who, being questioned what such a thing is which they know not, readily give this satisfactory answer, that it is *something;* which in truth signifies no more, when so used, either by children or men, but that they know not what; and that the thing they pretend to know and talk of, is what they have no

distinct idea of at all, and so are perfectly ignorant of it, and in the dark. The idea, then, we have, to which we give the *general* name substance, being nothing but the supposed, but unknown, support of those qualities we find existing, which we imagine cannot subsist *sine re substante,* "without something to support them," we call that support *substantia;* which, according to the true import of the word, is, in plain English, standing under, or upholding.

3. *Of the sorts of substances.*—An obscure and relative idea of substance in general being thus made, we come to have the ideas of particular sorts of substances, by collecting such combinations of simple ideas as are by experience and observation of men's senses taken notice of to exist together, and are therefore supposed to flow from the particular internal constitution or unknown essence of that substance. Thus we come to have the ideas of a man, horse, gold, water, etc., of which substances, whether anyone has any other clear idea, farther than of certain simple ideas coexistent together, I appeal to every one's own experience. It is the ordinary qualities observable in iron or a diamond, put together, that make the true complex idea of those substances, which a smith or a jeweller commonly knows better than a philosopher; who, whatever substantial forms he may talk of, has no other idea of those substances than what is framed by a collection of those simple ideas which are to be found in them. Only we must take notice that our complex ideas of substances, besides all these simple ideas they are made up of, have always the confused idea of something

to which they belong, and in which they subsist: and therefore when we speak of any sort of substance, we say it is a thing having such or such qualities; as, body is a thing that is extended, figured, and capable of motion; spirit, a thing capable of thinking; and so hardness, friability, and power to draw iron, we say, are qualities to be found in a loadstone. These and the like fashions of speaking, intimate that the substance is supposed always something, besides the extension, figure, solidity, motion, thinking, or other observable ideas, though we know not what it is.

4. *No clear or distinct idea of substance in general.*—Hence, when we talk or think of any particular sort of corporeal substances, as horse, stone, etc., though the idea we have of either of them be but the complication or collection of those several simple ideas of sensible qualities which we used to find united in the thing called horse or stone; yet because we cannot conceive how they should subsist alone, nor one in another, we suppose them existing in, and supported by, some common subject; which support we denote by the name substance, though it be certain we have no clear or distinct idea of that thing we suppose a support.

5. *As clear an idea of spirit as body.* —The same happens concerning the operations of the mind; viz., thinking, reasoning, fearing, etc., which we, concluding not to subsist of themselves, nor apprehending how they can belong to body, or be produced by it, we are apt to think these the actions of some other substance, which we call *spirit;* whereby yet it is evident, that having no other idea or notion of matter but something

wherein those many sensible qualities which affect our senses do subsist; by supposing a substance wherein thinking, knowing, doubting, and a power of moving, etc., do subsist, we have as clear a notion of the substance of spirit as we have of body: the one being supposed to be (without knowing what it is) the *substratum* to those simple ideas we have from without; and the other supposed (with a like ignorance of what it is) to be the *substratum* to those operations which we experiment in ourselves within. It is plain, then, that the idea of *corporeal substance* in matter is as remote from our conceptions and apprehensions as that of *spiritual substance,* or spirit; and therefore, from our not having any notion of the substance of spirit, we can no more conclude its non-existence than we can, for the same reason, deny the existence of body: it being as rational to affirm there is no body, because we have no clear and distinct idea of the substance of matter, as to say there is no spirit, because we have no clear and distinct idea of the substance of a spirit.

Of Knowledge in General

1. *Our knowledge conversant about our ideas only.*—Since the mind, in all its thoughts and reasonings, hath no other immediate object but its own ideas, which it alone does or can contemplate, it is evident that our knowledge is only conversant about them.

2. *Knowledge is the perception of the agreement or disagreement of two ideas.*—Knowledge then seems to me to be nothing but the perception of the connection of and agreement, or dis-

agreement and repugnancy, of any of our ideas. In this alone it consists. Where this perception is, there is knowledge; and where it is not, there, though we may fancy, guess, or believe, yet we always come short of knowledge. For, when we know that white is not black, what do we else but perceive that these two ideas do not agree? When we possess ourselves with the utmost security of the demonstration that the three angles of a triangle are equal to two right ones, what do we more but perceive that equality to two right ones does necessarily agree to, and is inseparable from, the three angles of a triangle?

3. *This agreement fourfold.*—But, to understand a little more distinctly, wherein this agreement or disagreement consists, I think we may reduce it all to these four sorts: (i) Identity, or diversity. (ii) Relation. (iii) Coexistence, or necessary connection. (iv) Real existence.

4. (i) *Of identity or diversity.*—First, as to the first sort of agreement or disagreement, viz., *identity,* or *diversity.* It is the first act of the mind, when it has any sentiments or ideas at all, to perceive its ideas, and, so far as it perceives them, to know each what it is, and thereby also to perceive their difference, and that one is not another. This is so absolutely necessary, that without it there could be no knowledge, no reasoning, no imagination, no distinct thoughts at all. By this the mind clearly and infallibly perceives each idea to agree with itself, and to be what it is; and all distinct ideas to disagree, i.e., the one not to be the other: and this it does without pains, labor, or deduction, but at first view, by its natural power

of perception and distinction. And though men of art have reduced this into those general rules, "What is, is," and, "It is impossible for the same thing to be and not to be," for ready application in all cases where in there may be occasion to reflect on it; yet it is certain that the first exercise of this faculty is about particular ideas. A man infallibly knows, as soon as ever he has them in his mind, that the ideas he calls 'white' and 'round' are the very ideas they are, and that they are not other ideas which he calls 'red' or 'square.' Nor can any maxim or proposition in the world make him know it clearer or surer than he did before and without any such general rule. This, then, is the first agreement or disagreement which the mind perceives in its ideas, which it always perceives at first sight; and if there ever happen any doubt about it, it will always be found to be about the names, and not the ideas themselves, whose identity and diversity will always be perceived as soon and as clearly as the ideas themselves are, nor can it possibly be otherwise.

5. (ii) *Of relations.*—Secondly, the next sort of agreement or disagreement the mind perceives in any of its ideas may, I think, be called *relative,* and is nothing but the perception of the relation between any two ideas, of what kind soever, whether substances, modes, or any other. For, since all distinct ideas must eternally be known not to be the same, and so be universally and constantly denied one of another; there could be no room for any positive knowledge at all, if we could not perceive any relation between our ideas, and find out the agreement or disagree-

ment they have one with another, in several ways the mind takes of comparing them.

6. (iii) *Of coexistence.*—Thirdly, the third sort of agreement or disagreement to be found in our ideas, which the perception of the mind is employed about, is *coexistence, or non-coexistence in the same subject;* and this belongs particularly to substances. Thus when we pronounce concerning gold that it is fixed, our knowledge of this truth amounts to no more but this, that fixedness, or a power to remain in the fire unconsumed, is an idea that always accompanies and is joined with that particular sort of yellowness, weight, fusibility, malleableness and solubility in *aqua regia,* which make our complex idea, signified by the word gold.

7. (iv) *Of real existence.*—Fourthly, the fourth and last sort is that of *actual real existence agreeing to any idea.* Within these four sorts of agreement or disagreement is, I suppose, contained all the knowledge we have or are capable of; for, all the inquiries that we can make concerning any of our ideas, all that we know or can affirm concerning any of them, is, that it is or is not the same with some other; that it does or does not always coexist with some other in the same subject; that it has this or that relation to some other idea; or that it has a real existence without the mind. Thus, "Blue is not yellow," is of identity. "Two triangles upon equal bases between two parallels are equal," is of relation. "Iron is susceptible of magnetical impressions," is of coexistence. "God is," is of real existence. Though identity and coexistence are truly nothing but relations, yet they are

such peculiar ways of agreement or disagreement of our ideas, that they deserve well to be considered as distinct heads, and not under relation in general; since they are so different grounds of affirmation and negation, as will easily appear to any one who will but reflect on what is said in several places of this *Essay*. I should now proceed to examine the several degrees of our knowledge, but that it is necessary first to consider the different acceptations of the word knowledge. . . .

Of the Degrees of Our Knowledge

1. *Intuitive*.—All our knowledge consisting, as I have said, in the view the mind has of its own ideas, which is the utmost light and greatest certainty we, with our faculties and in our way of knowledge, are capable of, it may not be amiss to consider a little the degrees of its evidence. The different clearness of our knowledge seems to me to lie in the different way of perception the mind has of the agreement or disagreement of any of its ideas. For if we will reflect on our own ways of thinking, we will find that sometimes the mind perceives the agreement or disagreement of two ideas immediately by themselves, without the intervention of any other; and this, I think, we may call *intuitive knowledge*. For in this the mind is at no pains of proving or examining, but perceives the truth, as the eye doth light, only by being directed towards it. Thus the mind perceives that white is not black, that a circle is not a triangle, that three are more than two, and equal to one and two. Such kind of truths the mind perceives at the first sight of the ideas together, by bare intuition, without the intervention of any other idea; and this kind of knowledge is the clearest and most certain that human frailty is capable of. This part of knowledge is irresistible, and, like bright sunshine, forces itself immediately to be perceived as soon as ever the mind turns its view that way; and leaves no room for hesitation, doubt or examination, but the mind is presently filled with the clear light of it. It is on this intuition that depends all the certainty and evidence of all our knowledge, which certainty everyone finds to be so great, that he cannot imagine, and therefore not require, a greater: for a man cannot conceive himself capable of a greater certainty, than to know that any idea in his mind is such as he perceives it to be; and that two ideas, wherein he perceives a difference, are different and not precisely the same. He that demands a greater certainty than this demands he knows not what, and shows only that he has a mind to be a sceptic without being able to be so. Certainty depends so wholly on this intuition, that in the next degree of knowledge, which I call demonstrative, this intuition is necessary in all the connections of the intermediate ideas, without which we cannot attain knowledge and certainty.

2. *Demonstrative*.—The next degree of knowledge is, where the mind perceives the agreement or disagreement of any ideas, but not immediately. Though wherever the mind perceives the agreement or disagreement of any of its ideas, there be certain knowledge; yet it does not always happen that the mind sees that agreement or disagree-

ment which there is between them, even where it is discoverable; and in that case remains in ignorance, and at most gets no farther than a probable conjecture. The reason why the mind cannot always perceive presently the agreement or disagreement of two ideas, is, because those ideas concerning whose agreement or disagreement the inquiry is made, cannot by the mind be so put together as to show it. In this case then, when the mind cannot so bring its ideas together as, by their immediate comparison and, as it were, juxtaposition or application one to another, to perceive their agreement or disagreement, it is fain, *by the intervention of other ideas* (one or more, as it happens), to discover the agreement or disagreement which it searches; and this is that which we call *reasoning.* Thus the mind, being willing to know the agreement or disagreement in bigness between the three angles of a triangle and two right ones, cannot, by an immediate view and comparing them, do it: because the three angles of a triangle cannot be brought at once, and be compared with any one or two angles; and so of this the mind has no immediate, no intuitive knowledge. In this case the mind is fain to find out some other angles, to which the three angles of a triangle have an equality; and finding those equal to two right ones, comes to know their equality to two right ones.

3. *Depends on proofs.*—Those intervening ideas which serve to show the agreement of any two others, are called *proofs;* and where the agreement or disagreement is by this means plainly and clearly perceived, it is called *demonstration,* it being *shown* to the understand-

ing, and the mind made to see that it is so. . . .

7. *Each step must have intuitive evidence.*—Now, in every step reason makes in demonstrative knowledge, there is an intuitive knowledge of that agreement or disagreement it seeks with the next intermediate idea, which it uses as a proof: for if it were not so, that yet would need a proof; since without the perception of such agreement or disagreement there is no knowledge produced. If it be perceived by itself, it is intuitive knowledge; if it cannot be perceived by itself, there is need of some intervening idea, as a common measure, to show their agreement or disagreement.

14. *Sensitive knowledge of particular existence.*—These two, viz. intuition and demonstration, are the degrees of our knowledge; whatever comes short of one of these, with what assurance soever embraced, is but faith or opinion, but not knowledge, at least in all general truths. There is, indeed, another perception of the mind employed about the particular existence of finite beings without us; which, going beyond bare probability, and yet not reaching perfectly to either of the foregoing degrees of certainty, passes under the name of knowledge. There can be nothing more certain than that the idea we receive from an external object is in our minds: this is intuitive knowledge. But whether there be anything more than barely that idea in our minds, whether we can thence certainly infer the existence of anything without us which corresponds to that idea, is that whereof some men think there may be a question made; because men may have such ideas in

their minds when no such thing exists, no such object affects their senses. But yet here, I think, we are provided with an evidence that puts us past doubting; for I ask anyone whether he be not invincibly conscious to himself of a different perception when he looks on the sun by day, and thinks on it by night; when he actually tastes wormwood, or smells a rose, or only thinks on that savor or odor? We as plainly find the difference there is between any idea revived in our minds by our own memory, and actually coming into our minds by our senses, as we do between any two distinct ideas. If anyone say, "A dream may do the same thing, and all these ideas may be produced in us without any external objects"; he may please to dream that I make him this answer: (i) That it is no great matter whether I remove his scruple or no; where all is but dream, reasoning and arguments are of no use, truth and knowledge nothing. (ii) That I believe he will allow a very manifest difference between dreaming of being in the fire, and being actually in it. But yet if he be resolved to appear so sceptical as to maintain that what I call 'being actually in the fire' is nothing but a dream, and that we cannot thereby certainly know that any such thing as fire actually exists without us; I answer that we certainly finding that pleasure or pain follows upon the application of certain objects to us, whose existence we perceive, or dream that we perceive, by our senses; this certainty is as great as our happiness or misery, beyond which we have no concernment to know or to be. So that, I think, we may add to the two former sorts of knowledge this also, of the existence of particular external objects by that perception and consciousness we have of the actual entrance of ideas from them, and allow these three degrees of knowledge, viz., intuitive, demonstrative, and sensitive; in each of which there are different degrees and ways of evidence and certainty.

Of the Extent of Human Knowledge

1. KNOWLEDGE, as has been said, lying in the perception of the agreement or disagreement of any of our ideas, it follows from hence that,

(i) *No farther than we have ideas.*— First, we can have knowledge no farther than we have ideas.

2. (ii) *No farther than we can perceive their agreement or disagreement.* —Secondly, that we can have no knowledge farther than we can have perception of that agreement or disagreement: which perception being, (1) either by intuition, or the immediate comparing any two ideas, or (2) by reason, examining the agreement or disagreement of two ideas by the intervention of some others, or, (3) by sensation, perceiving the existence of particular things; hence it also follows,

3. (iii) *Intuitive knowledge extends itself not to all the relations of all our ideas.*—Thirdly, that we cannot have an intuitive knowledge that shall extend itself to all our ideas, and all that we would know about them; because we cannot examine and perceive all the relations they have one to another by juxtaposition, or an immediate comparison one with another. Thus having the ideas of an obtuse and an acute-angled

triangle, both drawn from equal bases and between parallels, I can by intuitive knowledge perceive the one not to be the other, but cannot that way know whether they be equal or no: because their agreement or disagreement in equality can never be perceived by an immediate comparing them; the difference of figure makes their parts incapable of an exact immediate application; therefore there is need of some intervening qualities to measure them by, which is demonstration or rational knowledge.

4. (iv) *Nor demonstrative knowledge.*—Fourthly, it follows also, from what is above observed, that our rational knowledge cannot reach to the whole extent of our ideas: because between two different ideas we would examine, we cannot always find such mediums as we can connect one to another with an intuitive knowledge, in all parts of the deduction; and wherever that fails, we come short of knowledge and demonstration.

5. (v) *Sensitive knowledge narrower than either.*—Fifthly, sensitive knowledge, reaching no farther than the existence of things actually present to our senses, is yet much narrower than either of the former.

6. (vi) *Our knowledge therefore narrower than our ideas.*—From all which it is evident that the extent of our knowledge comes not only short of the reality of things, but even of the extent of our own ideas. Though our knowledge be limited to our ideas, and cannot exceed them either in extent or perfection; and though these be very narrow bounds in respect of the extent of all Being, and far short of what we may justly imagine to be in some even created understandings not tied down to the dull and narrow information that is to be received from some few and not very acute ways of perception, such as are our senses; yet it would be well with us if our knowledge were but as large as our ideas, and there were not many doubts and inquiries concerning the ideas we have, whereof we are not, nor I believe ever shall be in this world, resolved. Nevertheless, I do not question but that human knowledge, under the present circumstances of our beings and constitutions, may be carried much farther than it hitherto has been, if men would sincerely, and with freedom of mind, employ all that industry and labor of thought in improving the means of discovering truth which they do for the colouring or support of falsehood, to maintain a system, interest, or party they are once engaged in.

CHARLES SANDERS PEIRCE (1839-1914)

Peirce was born in Cambridge, Massachusetts, the second son of Benjamin Peirce, a professor at Harvard and one of America's foremost mathematicians. At the time of Peirce's birth, Cambridge was one of the main centers of American culture, and the Peirce home was a principal gathering place of celebrities. Such famous scientists as Louis Agassiz and Asa Gray and such great literary figures as Longfellow, Emerson, and Oliver Wendell Holmes were frequent guests. Peirce's father, himself remarkable, gave his son Charles an impressive education in logic, mathematics, philosophy, and experimental science. At the age of twelve, Charles set up a chemical laboratory in which he undertook some rather advanced experiments. At Harvard, which he attended from the age of sixteen until he was twenty, he did not buckle down to a strict routine of study but roamed over a vast philosophical and scientific literature. After being graduated, he continued his studies at Harvard, receiving a Master's degree in mathematics and an additional degree in chemistry.

This wide reading and scientific training was supplemented by a great deal of practical experience in scientific research. He was an assistant for three years in the Harvard astronomical observatory, where he carried out the investigations published in *Photometric Researches* (1878), the only one of his books to appear during his lifetime. He also conducted extensive scientific research for the United States Coastal and Geodetic Survey, with which he was associated from 1861 to 1891. His researches led to important original contributions in chemistry, astronomy, optics, the theory of gravity and pendulum movement, and the determination of weights and measures.

During the 1860's he found time to give a number of lecture courses at Harvard on logic and the history of science, and from 1879 to 1884, he was a lecturer in logic at the Johns Hopkins University. But he never received a permanent university appointment, largely because his ideas were too bold and original and his personality was too eccentric. Publishers showed themselves indifferent to an author who had no official university backing; and consequently a great deal of his writing was never presented to the public during his own lifetime. His reputation at Harvard also suffered as a result of his divorce from his first wife, who belonged to a very respectable family and was popular in Cambridge. Although he contracted a happy second marriage to a French woman, he never quite regained his status in the eyes of the community.

In his younger days, Peirce was a member, along with William James and Oliver Wendell Holmes, Jr., of an intimate circle of brilliant thinkers in Cambridge; but as he grew older he became more isolated. In 1881, at the age of forty-eight, he retired to Milford, Pennsylvania, where he lived in seclusion with his French wife. Here he waged a gradually losing battle against poverty, eking out a small income by writing articles for popular scientific magazines. Dogged by his creditors and seeking intellectual refuge, he would retire to his attic, pulling up a rope ladder after him so that no one could follow. To make matters worse, in the last years of his life, he suffered from slow cancer. When he finally became too ill to do any sustained work, he was supported mainly by the charity of William James and a few other friends.

During these final years of illness and poverty, he heroically persevered in his philosophical labors, often writing the whole night through. Nothing daunted him— not physical pain, the lack of a publisher, the isolation from friends, the failure to achieve public recognition. He continued to write even when he trembled so much that he was compelled to steady one hand against the other. Only death, at the age of seventy-five, could quell his spirit.

The Fixation
of Belief

I

Few persons care to study logic, because everybody conceives himself to be proficient enough in the art of reasoning already. But I observe that this satisfaction is limited to one's own ratiocination, and does not extend to that of other men.

We come to the full possession of our

Reprinted from *Popular Science Monthly,* 1877, with a few slight omissions.

power of drawing inferences the last of all our faculties, for it is not so much a natural gift as a long and difficult art. The history of its practice would make a grand subject for a book. The medieval schoolman, following the Romans, made logic the earliest of a boy's studies after grammar, as being very easy. So it was as they undertood it. Its fundamental principle, according to them, was, that all knowledge rests on either authority or reason; but that whatever is deduced by reason depends ultimately on a premise derived from authority. Accordingly, as soon as a boy was perfect in the syllogistic procedure, his intellectual kit of tools was held to be complete.

To Roger Bacon, that remarkable mind who in the middle of the thirteenth century was almost a scientific man, the schoolmen's conception of reasoning appeared only an obstacle to truth. He saw that experience alone teaches anything—a proposition which to us seems easy to understand, because a distinct conception of experience has been handed down to us from former generations; which to him also seemed perfectly clear, because its difficulties had not yet unfolded themselves. Of all kinds of experience, the best, he thought, was interior illumination, which teaches many things about Nature which the external senses could never discover, such as the transubstantiation of bread.

Four centuries later, the more celebrated Bacon, in the first book of his "Novum Organum," gave his clear account of experience as something which must be opened to verification and reëxamination. But, superior as Lord Bacon's conception is to earlier notions, a modern reader who is not in awe of his grandiloquence is chiefly struck by the inadequacy of his view of scientific procedure. That we have only to make some crude experiments, to draw up briefs of the results in certain blank forms, to go through these by rule, checking off everything disproved and setting down the alternatives, and that thus in a few years physical science would be finished up— what an idea! "He wrote on science like a Lord Chancellor," indeed.

The early scientists, Copernicus, Tycho Brahe, Kepler, Galileo and Gilbert, had methods more like those of their modern brethren. Kepler undertook to draw a curve through the places of Mars; and his greatest service to science was in impressing on men's minds that this was the thing to be done if they wished to improve astronomy; that they were not to content themselves with inquiring whether one system of epicycles was better than another but that they were to sit down by the figures and find out what the curve, in truth, was. He accomplished this by his incomparable energy and courage, blundering along in the most inconceivable way (to us), from one irrational hypothesis to another, until, after trying twenty-two of these, he fell, by the mere exhaustion of his invention, upon the orbit which a mind well furnished with the weapons of modern logic would have tried almost at the outset.[1]

In the same way, every work of sci-

[1] Twenty-one years later (in 1893), Peirce retracted this criticism of Kepler, saying that it was a "foolish remark" made because he had not as yet read the original work of Kepler, which was "a marvellous piece of inductive reasoning." [Editor]

ence great enough to be remembered for a few generations affords some exemplification of the defective state of the art of reasoning of the time when it was written; and each chief step in science has been a lesson in logic. It was so when Lavoisier and his contemporaries took up the study of Chemistry. The old chemist's maxim had been, "Lege, lege, lege, labora, ora, et relege."[2] Lavoisier's method was not to read and pray, not to dream that some long and complicated chemical process would have a certain effect, to put it into practice with dull patience, after its inevitable failure, to dream that with some modification it would have another result, and to end by pushing the last dream as a fact: his way was to carry his mind into his laboratory, and to make of his alembics and cucurbits instruments of thought, giving a new conception of reasoning as something which was to be done with one's eyes open, by manipulating real things instead of words and fancies. . . .

II

The object of reasoning is to find out, from the consideration of what we already know, something else which we do not know. Consequently, reasoning is good if it be such as to give a true conclusion from true premises, and not otherwise. Thus, the question of validity is purely one of fact and not of thinking. A being the premises and B being the conclusion, the question is, whether these facts are really so related that if A is B is. If so, the inference is valid;

[2] "Read, read, read, work, pray, and read again."

if not, not. It is not in the least the question whether, when the premises are accepted by the mind, we feel an impulse to accept the conclusion also. It is true that we do generally reason correctly by nature. But that is an accident; the true conclusion would remain true if we had no impulse to accept it; and the false one would remain false, though we could not resist the tendency to believe in it.

We are, doubtless, in the main logical animals, but we are not perfectly so. Most of us, for example, are naturally more sanguine and hopeful than logic would justify. We seem to be so constituted that in the absence of any facts to go upon we are happy and self-satisfied; so that the effect of experience is continually to counteract our hopes and aspirations. Yet a lifetime of the application of this corrective does not usually eradicate our sanguine disposition. Where hope is unchecked by any experience, it is likely that our optimism is extravagant. Logicality in regard to practical matters is the most useful quality an animal can possess, and might, therefore, result from the action of natural selection; but outside of these it is probably of more advantage to the animal to have his mind filled with pleasing and encouraging visions, independently of their truth; and thus, upon unpractical subjects, natural selection might occasion a fallacious tendency of thought.

That which determines us, from given premises, to draw one inference rather than another, is some habit of mind, whether it be constitutional or acquired. The habit is good or otherwise, according as it produces true conclusions from true premises or not; and an inference is regarded as valid or not, without reference to the truth or falsity of its conclusion specially, but according as the habit which determines it is such as to produce true conclusions in general or not. The particular habit of mind which governs this or that inference may be formulated in a proposition whose truth depends on the validity of the inferences which the habit determines; and such a formula is called a *guiding principle* of inference. Suppose, for example, that we observe that a rotating disk of copper quickly comes to rest when placed between the poles of a magnet, and we infer that this will happen with every disk of copper. The guiding principle is, that what is true of one piece of copper is true of another. Such a guiding principle with regard to copper would be much safer than with regard to many other substances—brass, for example.

A book might be written to signalize all the most important of these guiding principles of reasoning. It would probably be, we must confess, of no service to a person whose thought is directed wholly to practical subjects, and whose activity moves along thoroughly beaten paths. The problems which present themselves to such a mind are matters of routine which he has learned once for all to handle in learning his business. But let a man venture into an unfamiliar field, or where his results are not continually checked by experience, and all history shows that the most masculine intellect will ofttimes lose his orientation and waste his efforts in directions which bring him no nearer to his goal, or even carry him entirely astray. He is like a ship on the open sea, with no one on board who understands the rules of navigation. And in such a case some general study of the guiding principles of reasoning would be sure to be found useful.

The subject could hardly be treated, however, without being first limited; since almost any fact may serve as a guiding principle. But it so happens that there exists a division among facts, such that in one class are all those which are absolutely essential as guiding principles, while in the other are all those which have any other interest as objects of research. This division is between those which are necessarily taken for granted in asking whether a certain conclusion follows from certain premises, and those which are not implied in that question. A moment's thought will show that a variety of facts are already assumed when the logical question is first asked. It is implied, for instance, that there are such states of mind as doubt and belief —that a passage from one to the other is possible, the object of thought remaining the same, and that this transition is subject to some rules which all minds are alike bound by. As these are facts which we must already know before we can have any clear conception of reasoning at all, it cannot be supposed to be any longer of much interest to inquire into their truth or falsity. On the other hand, it is easy to believe that those rules of reasoning which are deduced from the very idea of the process are the ones which are the most essential; and, indeed, that so long as it conforms to these it will, at least, not lead to false conclusions from true premises. In point of fact, the importance of what may be deduced from the assumptions involved in the logical questions turns out to be greater than might be supposed, and this for reasons which it is difficult to exhibit at the outset. The only one which I shall here mention is, that conceptions which are really products of logical reflections, without being readily seen to be so, mingle with our ordinary thoughts, and are frequently the causes of great confusion. This is the case, for example, with the conception of quality. A quality as such is never an object of observation. We can see that a thing is blue or green, but the quality of being blue and the quality of being green are not things which we see; they are products of logical reflections. The truth is, that common-sense, or thought as it first emerges above the level of the narrowly practical, is deeply imbued with that bad logical quality to which the epithet *metaphysical* is commonly applied; and nothing can clear it up but a severe course of logic.

III

We generally know when we wish to ask a question and when we wish to pronounce a judgment, for there is a dissimilarity between the sensation of doubting and that of believing.

But this is not all which distinguishes doubt from belief. There is a practical difference. Our beliefs guide our desires and shape our actions. The Assassins, or followers of the Old Man of the Mountain, used to rush into death at his least command, because they believed that obedience to him would insure everlasting felicity. Had they doubted this, they would not have acted as they did. So it is with every belief, according to its degree. The feeling of believing is a more or less sure indication of there being established in our nature some habit which will determine our actions. Doubt never has such an effect.

Nor must we overlook a third point of difference. Doubt is an uneasy and dissatisfied state from which we struggle to free ourselves and pass into the state of belief; while the latter is a calm and satisfactory state which we do not wish to avoid, or to change to a belief in anything else. On the contrary, we cling tenaciously, not merely to believing, but to believing just what we do believe.

Thus, both doubt and belief have positive effects upon us, though very different ones. Belief does not make us act at once, but puts us into such a condition that we shall behave in a certain way, when the occasion arises. Doubt has not the least effect of this sort, but stimulates us to action until it is destroyed. This reminds us of the irritation of a nerve and the reflex action produced thereby; while for the analogue of belief, in the nervous system, we must look to what are called nervous associations—for example, to that habit of the nerves in consequence of which the smell of a peach will make the mouth water.

IV

The irritation of doubt causes a struggle to attain a state of belief. I shall term this struggle *inquiry,* though it must be admitted that this is sometimes not a very apt designation.

The irritation of doubt is the only immediate motive for the struggle to attain belief. It is certainly best for us that our beliefs should be such as may truly guide our actions so as to satisfy our desires; and this reflection will make us reject any belief which does not seem to have been so formed as to insure this result. But it will only do so by creating a doubt in the place of that belief. With the doubt, therefore, the struggle begins, and with the cessation of doubt it ends. Hence, the sole object of inquiry is the settlement of opinion. We may fancy that this is not enough for us, and that we seek not merely an opinion, but a true opinion. But put this fancy to the test, and it proves groundless; for as soon as a firm belief is reached we are entirely satisfied, whether the belief be false or true. And· it is clear that nothing out of the sphere of our knowledge can be our object, for nothing which does not affect the mind can be a motive for a mental effort. The most that can be maintained is, that we seek for a belief that we shall *think* to be true. But we think each one of our beliefs to be true, and, indeed, it is mere tautology to say so.

That the settlement of opinion is the sole end of inquiry is a very important proposition. It sweeps away, at once, various vague and erroneous conceptions of proof. A few of these may be noticed here.

1. Some philosophers have imagined that to start an inquiry it was only necessary to utter a question or set it down on paper, and have even recommended us to begin our studies with questioning everything! But the mere putting of a proposition into the interrogative form does not stimulate the mind to any struggle after belief. There must be a real and living doubt, and without this all discussion is idle.

2. It is a very common idea that a demonstration must rest on some ultimate and absolutely indubitable propositions. These, according to one school, are first principles of a general nature; according to another, are first sensations. But, in point of fact, an inquiry, to have that completely satisfactory result called demonstration, has only to start with propositions perfectly free from all actual doubt. If the premises are not in fact doubted at all, they cannot be more satisfactory than they are.

3. Some people seem to love to argue a point after all the world is fully convinced of it. But no further advance can be made. When doubt ceases, mental action on the subject comes to an end; and, if it did go on, it would be without a purpose.

V

If the settlement of opinion is the sole object of inquiry, and if belief is of the nature of a habit, why should we not attain the desired end, by taking any answer to a question, which we may fancy, and constantly reiterating to ourselves, dwelling on all which may conduce to that belief, and learning to turn with contempt and hatred from anything which might disturb it? This simple and direct method is really pursued by many men. I remember once being entreated not to read a certain newspaper lest it might change my opinion upon free-trade. "Lest I might be entrapped by its fallacies and misstatements," was the form of expression. "You are not," my friend said, "a special student of political economy. You might, therefore, easily be deceived by fallacious arguments upon the subject. You might, then, if you read this paper, be led to believe in protection. But you admit that free-trade is the true doctrine; and you do not wish to believe what is not true." I have often known this system to be deliberately adopted. Still oftener, the instinctive dislike of an undecided state of mind, exaggerated into a vague dread of doubt, makes men cling spasmodically to the views they already take. The man feels that, if he only holds to his belief without wavering, it will be entirely satisfactory. Nor can it be denied that a steady and immovable faith yields great peace of mind. It may, indeed, give rise to inconveniences, as if a man should resolutely continue to believe that fire would not burn him, or that he would be eternally damned if he received his *ingesta* otherwise than through a stomach-pump. But then the man who adopts this method will not allow that its inconveniences are greater than its advantages. He will say, "I hold steadfastly to the truth and the truth is always wholesome." And in many cases it may very well be that the pleasure he derives from his calm faith overbalances any inconveniences resulting from its deceptive character. Thus, if it be true that death is annihilation, then the man who believes that he will certainly go straight to heaven when he dies, provided he has fulfilled certain simple observances in this life, has a cheap pleasure which will not be followed by the least disappointment. A similar consideration seems to have weight with many persons in religious topics, for we frequently hear it said, "Oh, I could not believe so-and-so, because I should be wretched if I did." When an ostrich buries its head in the sand as danger approaches, it very likely takes the happiest course. It hides the danger, and then calmly says there is no danger; and, if it feels perfectly sure there is none, why should it raise its head to see? A man may go through life, systematically keeping out of view all that might cause a change in his opinions, and if he only succeeds—basing his method, as he does, on two fundamental psychological laws—I do not see what can be said against his doing so. It would be an egotistical impertinence to object that his procedure is irrational, for that only amounts to saying that his method of settling belief is not ours. He does not propose to himself to be rational, and indeed, will often talk with scorn of man's weak and illusive reason. So let him think as he pleases.

But this method of fixing belief, which may be called the method of tenacity, will be unable to hold its ground in practice. The social impulse is against it. The man who adopts it will find that other men think differently from him, and it will be apt to occur to him in some saner moment that their opinions are quite as good as his own, and this will shake his confidence in his belief. This conception, that another man's thought or sentiment may be equivalent to one's own, is a distinctly new step, and a highly important one. It arises from an impulse too strong in man to be suppressed, without danger of destroying the human species. Unless we make ourselves hermits, we shall necessarily influence each other's opinions; so that the problem becomes how to fix belief, not in the individual merely, but in the community.

Let the will of the state act, then, instead of that of the individual. Let an institution be created which shall have for its object to keep correct doctrines before the attention of the people, to reiterate them perpetually, and to teach them to the young; having at the same time power to prevent contrary doctrines from being taught, advocated, or expressed. Let all possible causes of a change of mind be removed from men's apprehensions. Let them be kept ignorant, lest they should learn of some reason to think otherwise than they do. Let their passions be enlisted, so that they may regard private and unusual opinions with hatred and horror. Then, let all men who reject the established belief be terrified into silence. Let the people turn out and tar-and-feather such men, or let inquisitions be made into the manner of thinking of suspected persons, and, when they are found guilty of forbidden beliefs, let them be subjected to some signal punishment. When complete agreement could not otherwise be reached, a general massacre of all who have not thought in a certain way has proved a very effective means of settling opinion in a country. If the power to do this be wanting, let a list of opinions be drawn up, to which no man of the least independence of thought can assent, and let the faithful be required to accept all these propositions, in order to segregate them as radically as possible

from the influence of the rest of the world.

This method has, from the earliest times, been one of the chief means of upholding correct theological and political doctrines, and of preserving their universal or catholic character. In Rome, especially, it has been practiced from the days of Numa Pompilius to those of Pius Nonus. This is the most perfect example in history; but wherever there is a priesthood—and no religion has been without one—this method has been more or less made use of. Wherever there is an aristocracy, or a guild, or any association of a class of men whose interests depend, or are supposed to depend, on certain propositions, there will be inevitably found some traces of this natural product of social feeling. Cruelties always accompany this system; and when it is consistently carried out, they become atrocities of the most horrible kind in the eyes of any rational man. Nor should this occasion surprise, for the officer of a society does not feel justified in surrendering the interests of that society for the sake of mercy, as he might his own private interests. It is natural, therefore, that sympathy and fellowship should thus produce a most ruthless power.

In judging this method of fixing belief, which may be called the method of authority, we must, in the first place, allow its immeasurable mental and moral superiority to the method of tenacity. Its success is proportionately greater; and, in fact, it has over and over again worked the most majestic results. The mere structures of stone which it has caused to be put together —in Siam, for example, in Egypt, and in Europe—have many of them a sub-limity hardly more than rivaled by the greatest works of Nature. And, except the geological epochs, there are no periods of time so vast as those which are measured by some of these orga-nized faiths. If we scrutinize the matter closely, we shall find that there has not been one of their creeds which has re-mained always the same; yet the change is so slow as to be imperceptible during one person's life, so that individual belief remains sensibly fixed. For the mass of mankind, then, there is per-haps no better method than this. If it is their highest impulse to be intellectual slaves, then slaves they ought to remain.

But no institution can undertake to regulate opinions upon every subject. Only the most important ones can be attended to, and on the rest men's minds must be left to the action of natural causes. This imperfection will be no source of weakness so long as men are in such a state of culture that one opinion does not influence another —that is, so long as they cannot put two and two together. But in the most priest-ridden states some individuals will be found who are raised above that condition. These men possess a wider sort of social feeling; they see that men in other countries and in other ages have held to very different doctrines from those which they themselves have been brought up to believe; and they cannot help seeing that it is the mere accident of their having been taught as they have, and of their having been surrounded with the manners and asso-ciations they have, that has caused them to believe as they do and not far differ-ently. Nor can their candor resist the

reflection that there is no reason to rate their own views at a higher value than those of other nations and other cen-turies; thus giving rise to doubts in their minds.

They will further perceive that such doubts as these must exist in their minds with reference to every belief which seems to be determined by the caprice either of themselves or of those who originated the popular opinions. The willful adherence to a belief, and the arbitrary forcing of it upon others, must, therefore, both be given up. A different new method of settling opin-ions must be adopted, that shall not only produce an impulse to believe, but shall also decide what proposition it is which is to be believed. Let the action of natural preferences be unim-peded, then and under their influence let men, conversing together and re-garding matters in different lights, grad-ually develop beliefs in harmony with natural causes. This method resembles that by which conceptions of art have been brought to maturity. The most perfect example of it is to be found in the history of metaphysical philosophy. Systems of this sort have not usually rested upon any observed facts, at least not in any great degree. They have been chiefly adopted because their funda-mental propositions seemed "agreeable to reason." This is an apt expression; it does not mean that which agrees with experience, but that which we find our-selves inclined to believe. Plato, for ex-ample, finds it agreeable to reason that the distances of the celestial spheres from one another should be proportional to the different lengths of strings which produce harmonious chords. Many philosophers have been led to their main conclusions by considerations like this; but this is the lowest and least developed form which the method takes, for it is clear that another man might find Kepler's theory, that the celestial spheres are proportional to the inscribed and circumscribed spheres of the different regular solids, more agreeable to *his* reason. But the shock of opinions will soon lead men to rest on preferences of a far more universal nature. Take, for example, the doctrine that man only acts selfishly—that is, from the consideration that acting in one way will afford him more pleasure than acting in another. This rests on no fact in the world, but it has had a wide acceptance as being the only reasonable theory.

This method is far more intellectual and respectable from the point of view of reason than either of the others which we have noticed. But its failure has been the most manifest. It makes of inquiry something similar to the development of taste; but taste, unfortunately, is always more or less a matter of fashion, and accordingly metaphysicians have never come to any fixed agreement, but the pendulum has swung backward and forward between a more material and a more spiritual philosophy, from the earliest times to the latest. And so from this, which has been called the *a priori* method, we are driven, in Lord Bacon's phrase, to a true induction. We have examined into this *a priori* method as something which promised to deliver our opinions from their accidental and capricious element. But development, while it is a process which eliminates the effect of some casual circumstances, only magnifies that of others. This method, therefore, does not differ in a very essential way from that of authority. The government may not have lifted its finger to influence my convictions; I may have been left outwardly quite free to choose, we will say, between monogamy and polygamy, and, appealing to my conscience only, I may have concluded that the latter practice is in itself licentious. But when I come to see that the chief obstacle to the spread of Christianity among a people of as high culture as the Hindoos has been a conviction of the immorality of our way of treating women, I cannot help seeing that, though governments do not interfere, sentiments in their development will be very greatly determined by accidental causes. Now, there are some people, among whom I must suppose that my reader is to be found, who, when they see that any belief of theirs is determined by any circumstance extraneous to the facts, will from that moment not merely admit in words that that belief is doubtful, but will experience a real doubt of it, so that it ceases in some degree to be a belief.

To satisfy our doubts, therefore, it is necessary that a method should be found by which our beliefs may be caused by nothing human, but by some external permanency—by something upon which our thinking has no effect. Some mystics imagine that they have such a method in a private inspiration from on high. But that is only a form of the method of tenacity, in which the conception of truth as something public is not yet developed. Our external permanency would not be external, in our sense, if it was restricted in its influence to one individual. It must be something which affects, or might affect, every man. And, though these affections are necessarily as various as are individual conditions, yet the method must be such that the ultimate conclusion of every man shall be the same. Such is the method of science. Its fundamental hypothesis, restated in more familiar language, is this: There are Real things, whose characters are entirely independent of our opinions about them; those realities affect our senses according to regular laws, and, though our sensations are as different as are our relations to the objects, yet, by taking advantage of the laws of perception, we can ascertain by reasoning how things really are; and any man, if he have sufficient experience and he reason enough about it, will be led to the one True conclusion. The new conception here involved is that of Reality. It may be asked how I know that there are any realities. If this hypothesis is the sole support of my method of inquiry, my method of inquiry must not be used to support my hypothesis. The reply is this: 1. If investigation cannot be regarded as proving that there are Real things, it at least does not lead to a contrary conclusion; but the method and the conception on which it is based remain ever in harmony. No doubts of the method, therefore, necessarily arise from its practice, as is the case with all the others. 2. The feeling which gives rise to any method of fixing belief is a dissatisfaction at two repugnant propositions. But here already is a vague concession that there is some *one* thing to which a proposition should conform. Nobody, therefore, can really doubt that there are realities, for, if he did, doubt would not be a source of dissatisfaction.

The hypothesis, therefore, is one which every mind admits. So that the social impulse does not cause men to doubt it. 3. Everybody uses the scientific method about a great many things, and only ceases to use it when he does not know how to apply it. 4. Experience of the method has not led us to doubt it, but, on the contrary, scientific investigation has had the most wonderful triumphs in the way of settling opinion. These afford the explanation of my not doubting the method or the hypothesis which it supposes; and not having any doubt, nor believing that anybody else whom I could influence has, it would be the merest babble for me to say more about it. If there be anybody with a living doubt upon the subject, let him consider it. . . .

This is the only one of the four methods which presents any distinction of a right and a wrong way. If I adopt the method of tenacity, and shut myself out from all influences, whatever I think necessary to doing this, is necessary according to that method. So with the method of authority: the state may try to put down heresy by means which, from a scientific point of view, seem very ill-calculated to accomplish its purposes; but the only test *on that method* is what the state thinks; so that it cannot pursue the method wrongly. So with the *a priori* method. The very essence of it is to think as one is inclined to think. All metaphysicians will be sure to do that, however they may be inclined to judge each other to be perversely wrong. The Hegelian system recognizes every natural tendency of thought as logical, although it is certain to be abolished by counter-tendencies.

Hegel thinks there is a regular system in the succession of these tendencies, in consequence of which, after drifting one way and the other for a long time, opinion will at last go right. And it is true that metaphysicians get the right ideas at last; Hegel's system of Nature represents tolerably the science of that day; and one may be sure that whatever scientific investigation has put out of doubt will presently receive *a priori* demonstration on the part of the metaphysicians. But with the scientific method the case is different. I may start with known and observed facts to proceed to the unknown; and yet the rules which I follow in doing so may not be such as investigation would approve. The test of whether I am truly following the method is not an immediate appeal to my feelings and purposes, but, on the contrary, itself involves the application of the method. Hence it is that bad reasoning as well as good reasoning is possible; and this fact is the foundation of the practical side of logic.

It is not to be supposed that the first three methods of settling opinion present no advantage whatever over the scientific method. On the contrary, each has some peculiar convenience of its own. The *a priori* method is distinguished for its comfortable conclusions. It is the nature of the process to adopt whatever belief we are inclined to, and there are certain flatteries to the vanity of man which we all believe by nature, until we are awakened from our pleasing dream by rough facts. The method of authority will always govern the mass of mankind; and those who wield the various forms of organized force in the state will never be convinced that dangerous reasoning ought not to be suppressed in some way. If liberty of speech is to be untrammeled from the grosser forms of constraint, then uniformity of opinion will be secured by a moral terrorism to which the respectability of society will give its thorough approval. Following the method of authority is the path of peace. Certain non-conformities are permitted; certain others (considered unsafe) are forbidden. These are different in different countries and in different ages; but, wherever you are, let it be known that you seriously hold a tabooed belief, and you may be perfectly sure of being treated with a cruelty less brutal but more refined than hunting you like a wolf. Thus, the greatest intellectual benefactors of mankind have never dared, and dare not now, to utter the whole of their thought; and thus a shade of *prima facie* doubt is cast upon every proposition which is considered essential to the security of society. Singularly enough, the persecution does not all come from without; but a man torments himself and is oftentimes most distressed at finding himself believing propositions which he has been brought up to regard with aversion. The peaceful and sympathetic man will, therefore, find it hard to resist the temptation to submit his opinions to authority. But most of all I admire the method of tenacity for its strength, simplicity, and directness. Men who pursue it are distinguished for their decision of character, which becomes very easy with such a mental rule. They do not waste time in trying to make up their minds what they want, but, fastening like lightning upon whatever alternative comes first, they hold it to the end, whatever happens, without an instant's irresolution. This is one of the splendid qualities which generally accompany brilliant, unlasting success. It is impossible not to envy the man who can dismiss reason, although we know how it must turn out at last.

Such are the advantages which the other methods of settling opinion have over scientific investigation. A man should consider well of them; and then he should consider that, after all, he wishes his opinions to coincide with the fact, and that there is no reason why the results of those three methods should do so. To bring about this effect is the prerogative of the method of science. Upon such considerations he has to make his choice—a choice which is far more than the adoption of any intellectual opinion, which is one of the ruling decisions of his life, to which, when once made, he is bound to adhere. The force of habit will sometimes cause a man to hold on to old beliefs, after he is in a condition to see that they have no sound basis. But reflection upon the state of the case will overcome these habits, and he ought to allow reflection its full weight. People sometimes shrink from doing this, having an idea that beliefs are wholesome which they cannot help feeling rest on nothing. But let such persons suppose an analogous though different case from their own. Let them ask themselves what they would say to a reformed Mussulman who should hesitate to give up his old notions in regard to the relations of the sexes; or to a reformed Catholic who should still shrink from reading the Bible. Would they not say that these persons ought to consider the matter fully, and clearly understand the new doctrine, and then ought to embrace it, in its entirety? But, above all, let it be considered that what is more wholesome than any particular belief is integrity of belief, and that to avoid looking into the support of any belief from a fear that it may turn out rotten is quite as immoral as it is disadvantageous. The person who confesses that there is such a thing as truth, which is distinguished from falsehood simply by this, that if acted on it will carry us to the point we aim at and not astray, and then, though convinced of this, dares not know the truth and seeks to avoid it, is in a sorry state of mind indeed.

Yes, the other methods do have their merits: a clear logical conscience does cost something—just as any virtue, just as all that we cherish, costs us dear. But we should not desire it to be otherwise. The genius of a man's logical method should be loved and reverenced as his bride, whom he has chosen from all the world. He need not contemn the others; on the contrary, he may honor them deeply, and in doing so he only honors her the more. But she is the one that he has chosen, and he knows that he was right in making that choice. And having made it, he will work and fight for her, and will not complain that there are blows to take, hoping that there may be as many and as hard to give, and will strive to be the worthy knight and champion of her from the blaze of whose splendors he draws his inspiration and his courage.

How to Make
Our Ideas Clear

I

Whoever has looked into a modern treatise on logic of the common sort, will doubtless remember the two distinctions between *clear* and *obscure* conceptions, and between *distinct* and *confused* conceptions. They have lain in the books now for nigh two centuries, unimproved and unmodified, and are generally reckoned by logicians as among the gems of their doctrine.

A clear idea is defined as one which is so apprehended that it will be recognized wherever it is met with, and so that no other will be mistaken for it. If it fails of this clearness, it is said to be obscure.

This is rather a neat bit of philosophical terminology; yet, since it is clearness that they were defining, I wish the logicians had made their definition a little more plain. Never to fail to recognize an idea, and under no circumstances to mistake another for it, let it come in how recondite a form it may, would indeed imply such prodigious force and clearness of intellect as is seldom met with in this world. On the other hand, merely to have such an acquaintance with the idea as to have become familiar with it, and to have lost all hesitancy in recognizing it in ordinary cases, hardly

This essay is a sequel to "The Fixation of Belief." Reprinted from *Popular Science Monthly*, 1878, with some omissions.

seems to deserve the name of clearness of apprehension, since after all it only amounts to a subjective feeling of mastery which may be entirely mistaken. I take it, however, that when the logicians speak of "clearness," they mean nothing more than such a familiarity with an idea, since they regard the quality as but a small merit, which needs to be supplemented by another, which they call *distinctness*.

A distinct idea is defined as one which contains nothing which is not clear. This is technical language; by the *contents* of an idea logicians understand whatever is contained in its definition. So that an idea is *distinctly* apprehended, according to them, when we can give a precise definition of it, in abstract terms. Here the professional logicians leave the subject; and I would not have troubled the reader with what they have to say, if it were not such a striking example of how they have been slumbering through ages of intellectual activity, listlessly disregarding the enginery of modern thought, and never dreaming of applying its lessons to the improvement of logic. It is easy to show that the doctrine that familiar use and abstract distinctness make the perfection of apprehension has its only true place in philosophies which have long been extinct; and it is now time to formulate the method of attaining to a more perfect clearness of thought, such as we see and admire in the thinkers of our own time.

When Descartes set about the reconstruction of philosophy, his first step was to (theoretically) permit scepticism and to discard the practice of the schoolmen of looking to authority as the ultimate source of truth. That done, he sought a more natural fountain of true principles, and professed to find it in the human mind; thus passing, in the directest way, from the method of authority to that of a priority, as described in my first paper. Self-consciousness was to furnish us with our fundamental truths, and to decide what was agreeable to reason. But since, evidently, not all ideas are true, he was led to note, as the first condition of infallibility, that they must be clear. The distinction between an idea *seeming* clear and really being so, never occurred to him. Trusting to introspection, as he did, even for a knowledge of external things, why should he question its testimony in respect to the contents of our own minds? But then, I suppose, seeing men, who seemed to be quite clear and positive, holding opposite opinions upon fundamental principles, he was further led to say that clearness of ideas is not sufficient, but that they need also to be distinct, *i.e.,* to have nothing unclear about them. What he probably meant by this (for he did not explain himself with precision) was, that they must sustain the test of dialectical examination; that they must not only seem clear at the outset, but that discussion must never be able to bring to light points of obscurity connected with them.

Such was the distinction of Descartes, and one sees that it was precisely on the level of his philosophy. It was somewhat developed by Leibnitz. This great and singular genius was as remarkable for what he failed to see as for what he saw. That a piece of mechanism could not do work perpetually without being fed with power in some form, was a thing perfectly apparent to him; yet he did not understand that the machinery of the mind can only transform knowledge, but never originate it, unless it be fed with facts of observation. He thus missed the most essential point of the Cartesian philosophy, which is, that to accept propositions which seem perfectly evident to us is a thing which, whether it be logical or illogical, we cannot help doing. Instead of regarding the matter in this way, he sought to reduce the first principles of science to formulas which cannot be denied without self-contradiction, and was apparently unaware of the great difference between his position and that of Descartes. So he reverted to the old formalities of logic, and, above all, abstract definitions played a great part in his philosophy. It was quite natural, therefore, that on observing that the method of Descartes labored under the difficulty that we may seem to ourselves to have clear apprehensions of ideas which in truth are very hazy, no better remedy occurred to him than to require an abstract definition of every important term. Accordingly, in adopting the distinction of *clear* and *distinct* notions, he described the latter quality as the clear apprehension of everything contained in the definition; and the books have ever since copied his words. There is no danger that his chimerical scheme will ever again be overvalued. Nothing new can ever be learned by analyzing definitions. Nevertheless, our existing beliefs can be set in order by this process, and order is an essential element of intellectual economy, as of every other. It may be acknowledged, therefore, that the books are right in making familiarity with a notion the first step toward clearness of apprehension, and the defining of it the second. But in omitting all mention of any higher perspicuity of thought, they simply mirror a philosophy which was exploded a hundred years ago. That much-admired "ornament of logic"—the doctrine of clearness and distinctness—may be pretty enough, but it is high time to relegate to our cabinet of curiosities the antique *bijou,* and to wear about us something better adapted to modern uses.

The very first lesson that we have a right to demand that logic shall teach us is, how to make our ideas clear; and a most important one it is, depreciated only by minds who stand in need of it. To know what we think, to be masters of our own meaning, will make a solid foundation for great and weighty thought. It is most easily learned by those whose ideas are meager and restricted; and far happier they than such as wallow helplessly in a rich mud of conceptions. A nation, it is true, may, in the course of generations, overcome the disadvantage of an excessive wealth of language and its natural concomitant, a vast, unfathomable deep of ideas. We may see it in history, slowly perfecting its literary forms, sloughing at length its metaphysics, and, by virtue of the untirable patience which is often a compensation, attaining great excellence in every branch of mental acquirement.

The page of history is not yet unrolled which is to tell us whether such a people will or will not in the long run prevail over one whose ideas (like the words of their language) are few, but which possesses a wonderful mastery over those which it has. For an individual, however, there can be no question that a few clear ideas are worth more than many confused ones. A young man would hardly be persuaded to sacrifice the greater part of his thoughts to save the rest; and the muddled head is the least apt to see the necessity of such a sacrifice. Him we can usually only commiserate, as a person with a congenital defect. Time will help him, but intellectual maturity with regard to clearness comes rather late, an unfortunate arrangement of Nature, inasmuch as clearness is of less use to a man settled in life, whose errors have in great measure had their effect, than it would be to one whose path lies before him. It is terrible to see how a single unclear idea, a single formula without meaning, lurking in a young man's head, will sometimes act like an obstruction of inert matter in an artery, hindering the nutrition of the brain, and condemning its victim to pine away in the fullness of his intellectual vigor and in the midst of intellectual plenty. Many a man has cherished for years as his hobby some vague shadow of an idea, too meaningless to be positively false; he has, nevertheless, passionately loved it, has made it his companion by day and by night, and has given to it his strength and his life, leaving all other occupations for its sake, and in short has lived with it and for it, until it has become, as it were, flesh of his flesh and bone of his bone; and then he has waked up some bright morning to find it gone, clean vanished away like the beautiful Melusina of the fable, and the essence of his life gone with it. I have myself known such a man; and who can tell how many histories of circle-squarers, metaphysicians, astrologers, and what not, may not be told in the old German story?

II

The principles set forth in the first of these papers lead, at once, to a method of reaching a clearness of thought of a far higher grade than the "distinctness" of the logicians. We have there found that the action of thought is excited by the irritation of doubt, and ceases when belief is attained; so that the production of belief is the sole function of thought. All these words, however, are too strong for my purpose. It is as if I had described the phenomena as they appear under a mental microscope. Doubt and Belief, as the words are commonly employed, relate to religious or other grave discussions. But here I use them to designate the starting of any question, no matter how small or how great, and the resolution of it. If, for instance, in a horse-car, I pull out my purse and find a five-cent nickel and five coppers, I decide, while my hand is going to the purse, in which way I will pay my fare. To call such a question Doubt, and my decision Belief, is certainly to use words very disproportionate to the occasion. To speak of such a doubt as causing an irritation which needs to be appeased, suggests a temper which is uncomfortable to the verge of insanity. Yet, looking at the matter minutely, it must be

admitted that, if there is the least hesitation as to whether I shall pay the five coppers or the nickel (as there will be sure to be, unless I act from some previously contracted habit in the matter), though irritation is too strong a word, yet I am excited to such small mental activity as may be necessary to deciding how I shall act. Most frequently doubts arise from some indecision, however momentary, in our action. Sometimes it is not so. I have, for example, to wait in a railway-station, and to pass the time I read the advertisements on the walls, I compare the advantages of different trains and different routes which I never expect to take, merely fancying myself to be in a state of hesitancy, because I am bored with having nothing to trouble me. Feigned hesitancy, whether feigned for mere amusement or with a lofty purpose, plays a great part in the production of scientific inquiry. However the doubt may originate, it stimulates the mind to an activity which may be slight or energetic, calm or turbulent. Images pass rapidly through consciousness, one incessantly melting into another, until at last, when all is over—it may be in a fraction of a second, in an hour, or after long years—we find ourselves decided as to how we should act under such circumstances as those which occasioned our hesitation. In other words, we have attained belief.

In this process we observe two sorts of elements of consciousness, the distinction between which may best be made clear by means of an illustration. In a piece of music there are the separate notes, and there is the air. A single tone may be prolonged for an hour or a day, and it exists as perfectly in each second of that time as in the whole taken to-gether; so that, as long as it is sounding, it might be present to a sense from which everything in the past was as completely absent as the future itself. But it is different with the air, the performance of which occupies a certain time, during the portions of which only portions of it are played. It consists in an orderliness in the succession of sounds which strike the ear at different times; and to perceive it there must be some continuity of consciousness which makes the events of a lapse of time present to us. We certainly only perceive the air by hearing the separate notes; yet we cannot be said to directly hear it, for we hear only what is present at the instant, and an orderliness of succession cannot exist in an instant. These two sorts of objects, what we are *immediately* conscious of and what we are *mediately* conscious of, are found in all consciousness. Some elements (the sensations) are completely present at every instant so long as they last, while others (like thought) are actions having the beginning, middle, and end, and consist in a congruence in the succession of sensations which flow through the mind. They cannot be immediately present to us, but must cover some portion of the past or future. Thought is a thread of melody running through the succession of our sensations.

We may add that just as a piece of music may be written in parts, each part having its own air, so various systems of relationship of succession subsist together between the same sensations. These different systems are distinguished by having different motives, ideas, or functions. Thought is only one such sys-tem, for its sole motive, idea, and function, is to produce belief, and whatever does not concern that purpose belongs to some other system of relations. The action of thinking may incidentally have other results; it may serve to amuse us, for example, and among *dillettanti* it is not rare to find those who have so perverted thought to the purposes of pleasure that it seems to vex them to think that the questions upon which they delight to exercise it may ever get finally settled; and a positive discovery which takes a favorite subject out of the arena of literary debate is met with ill-concealed dislike. This disposition is the very debauchery of thought. But the soul and meaning of thought, abstracted from the other elements which accompany it, though it may be voluntarily thwarted, can never be made to direct itself toward anything but the production of belief. Thought in action has for its only possible motive the attainment of thought at rest; and whatever does not refer to belief is no part of the thought itself.

And what, then, is belief? It is the demicadence which closes a musical phrase in the symphony of our intellectual life. We have seen that it has just three properties: First, it is something that we are aware of; second, it appeases the irritation of doubt; and, third, it involves the establishment in our nature of a rule of action, or, say, for short, a *habit*. As it appeases the irritation of doubt, which is the motives for thinking, thought relaxes, and comes to rest for a moment when belief is reached. But, since belief is a rule for action, the application of which involves further doubt and further thought, at the same time that it is a stopping-place, it is also a new starting-place for thought. That is why I have permitted myself to call it thought at rest, although thought is essentially an action. The *final* upshot of thinking is the exercise of volition, and of this thought no longer forms a part; but belief is only a stadium of mental action, an effect upon our nature due to thought, which will influence future thinking.

The essence of belief is the establishment of a habit, and different beliefs are distinguished by the different modes of action to which they give rise. If be-

Fig. 1

liefs do not differ in this respect, if they appease the same doubt by producing the same rule of action, then no mere differences in the manner of consciousness of them can make them different beliefs, any more than playing a tune in different keys is playing different tunes. Imaginary distinctions are often drawn between beliefs which differ only in their mode of expression;—the wrangling which ensues is real enough, however. To believe that any objects are arranged as in Fig. 1, and to believe that they are arranged [as] in Fig. 2, are one

and the same belief; yet it is conceivable that a man should assert one proposition and deny the other. Such false distinctions do as much harm as the confusion of beliefs really different, and are among the pitfalls of which we ought constantly to beware, especially when we are upon metaphysical ground. One singular deception of this sort, which often occurs, is to mistake the sensation produced by our own unclearness of thought for a character of the object we are thinking. Instead of perceiving that the obscurity is purely subjective, we fancy that we contem-

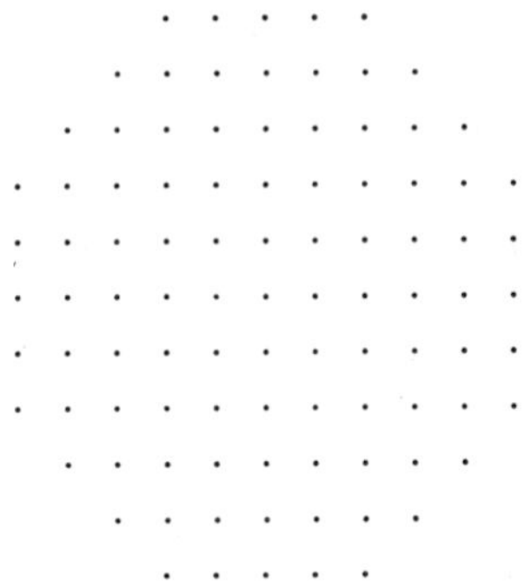

Fig. 2

plate a quality of the object which is essentially mysterious; and if our conception be afterward presented to us in a clear form we do not recognize it as the same, owing to the absence of the feeling of unintelligibility. So long as this deception lasts, it obviously puts an impassable barrier in the way of perspicuous thinking; so that it equally interests the opponent of rational thought to perpetuate it, and its adherents to guard against it.

Another such deception is to mistake a mere difference in the grammatical construction of two words for a distinction between the ideas they express. In this pedantic age, when the general mob of writers attend so much more to words than to things, this error is common enough. When I just said that thought is an *action,* and that it consists in a relation, although a person performs an action but not a relation, which can only be the result of an action, yet there was no inconsistency in what I said, but only a grammatical vagueness.

From all these sophisms we shall be perfectly safe so long as we reflect that the whole function of thought is to produce habits of action; and that whatever there is connected with a thought, but irrelevant to its purpose, is an accretion to it, but no part of it. If there be a unity among our sensations which has no reference to how we shall act on a given occasion, as when we listen to a piece of music, why, we do not call that thinking. To develop its meaning, we have, therefore, simply to determine what habits it produces, for what a thing means is simply what habits it involves. Now, the identity of a habit depends on how it might lead us to act, not merely under such circumstances as are likely to arise, but under such as might possibly occur, no matter how improbable they may be. What the habit is depends on *when* and *how* it causes us to act. As for the *when,* every stimulus to action is derived from perception; as for the how, every purpose of action is to produce some sensible result. Thus, we come down to what is tangible and conceivably practical, as the root of every real distinction of thought, no

matter how subtle it may be; and there is no distinction of meaning so fine as to consist in anything but a possible difference of practice.

To see what this principle leads to, consider in the light of it such a doctrine as that of transubstantiation. The Protestant churches generally hold that the elements of the sacrament are flesh and blood only in a tropical sense; they nourish our souls as meat and the juice of it would our bodies. But the Catholics maintain that they are literally just that; although they possess all the sensible qualities of wafer-cakes and diluted wine. But we can have no conception of wine except what may enter into a belief, either—

1. That this, that, or the other, is wine; or,

2. That wine possesses certain properties.

Such beliefs are nothing but self-notification that we should, upon occasion, act in regard to such things as we believe to be wine according to the qualities which we believe wine to possess. The occasion of such an action would be some sensible perception, the motive of it to produce some sensible result. Thus our action has exclusive reference to what affects the senses, our habit has the same bearing as our action, our belief the same as our habit, our conception the same as our belief; and we can consequently mean nothing by wine but what has certain effects, direct or indirect, upon our senses; and to talk of something as having all the sensible characters of wine, yet being in reality blood, is senseless jargon. Now, it is not my object to pursue the theological question; and having used it as a logical example I drop it, without caring to anticipate the theologian's reply. I only desire to point out how impossible it is that we should have an idea in our minds which relates to anything but conceived sensible effects of things. Our idea of anything *is* our idea of its sensible effects; and if we fancy that we have any other we deceive ourselves, and mistake a mere sensation accompanying the thought for a part of the thought itself. It is absurd to say that thought has any meaning unrelated to its only function. It is foolish for Catholics and Protestants to fancy themselves in disagreement about the elements of the sacrament, if they agree in regard to all their sensible effects, here or hereafter.

It appears, then, that the rule for attaining the third grade of clearness of apprehension is as follows: Consider what effects, which might conceivably have practical bearings, we conceive the object of our conception to have. Then, our conception of these effects is the whole of our conception of the object.

III

Let us illustrate this rule by some examples; and, to begin with the simplest one possible, let us ask what we mean by calling a thing *hard*. Evidently that it will not be scratched by many other substances. The whole conception of this quality, as of every other, lies in its conceived effects. There is absolutely no difference between a hard thing and a soft thing so long as they are not brought to the test. Suppose, then, that a diamond could be crystallized in the midst of a cushion of soft cotton, and should remain there until it was finally burned up. Would it be false to say that that diamond was soft? This seems a foolish question, and would be so, in fact, except in the realm of logic. There such questions are often of the greatest utility as serving to bring logical principles into sharper relief than real discussions ever could. In studying logic we must not put them aside with hasty answers, but must consider them with attentive care, in order to make out the principles involved. We may, in the present case, modify our question, and ask what prevents us from saying that all hard bodies remain perfectly soft until they are touched, when their hardness increases with the pressure until they are scratched. Reflection will show that the reply is this: there would be no *falsity* in such modes of speech. They would involve a modification of our present usage of speech with regard to the words hard and soft, but not of their meanings. For they represent no fact to be different from what it is; only they involve arrangements of facts which would be exceedingly maladroit. This leads us to remark that the question of what would occur under circumstances which do not actually arise is not a question of fact, but only of the most perspicuous arrangement of them. For example, the question of free-will and fate in its simplest form, stripped of verbiage, is something like this: I have done something of which I am ashamed; could I, by an effort of the will, have resisted the temptation, and done otherwise? The philosophical reply is, that this is not a question of fact, but only of the arrangement of facts.

Arranging them so as to exhibit what is particularly pertinent to my question —namely, that I ought to blame myself for having done wrong—it is perfectly true to say that, if I had willed to do otherwise than I did, I should have done otherwise. On the other hand, arranging the facts so as to exhibit another important consideration, it is equally true that, when a temptation has once been allowed to work, it will, if it has a certain force, produce its effect, let me struggle how I may. There is no objection to a contradiction in what would result from a false supposition. The *reductio ad absurdum* consists in showing that contradictory results would follow from a hypothesis which is consequently judged to be false. Many questions are involved in the free-will discussion, and I am far from desiring to say that both sides are equally right. On the contrary, I am of opinion that one side denies important facts, and that the other does not. But what I do say is, that the above single question was the origin of the whole doubt; that, had it not been for this question, the controversy would never have arisen; and that this question is perfectly solved in the manner which I have indicated.

Let us next seek a clear idea of weight. This is another very easy case. To say that a body is heavy means simply that, in the absence of opposing force, it will fall. This (neglecting certain specifications of how it will fall, etc., which exist in the mind of the physicist who uses the word) is evidently the whole conception of weight. It is a fair question whether some particular facts may not *account* for grav-

ity; but what we mean by the force itself is completely involved in its effects. . . .

IV

Let us now approach the subject of logic, and consider a conception which particularly concerns it, that of *reality*. Taking clearness in the sense of familiarity, no idea could be clearer than this. Every child uses it with perfect confidence, never dreaming that he does not understand it. As for clearness in its second grade, however, it would probably puzzle most men, even among those of a reflective turn of mind, to give an abstract definition of the real. Yet such a definition may perhaps be reached by considering the points of difference between reality and its opposite, fiction. A figment is a product of somebody's imagination; it has such characters as his thought impresses upon it. That whose characters are independent of how you or I think is an external reality. There are, however, phenomena within our own minds, dependent upon our thought, which are at the same time real in the sense that we really think them. But though their characters depend on how we think, they do not depend on what we think those characters to be. Thus, a dream has a real existence as a mental phenomenon, if somebody has really dreamt it; that he dreamt so and so, does not depend on what anybody thinks was dreamt, but is completely independent of all opinion on the subject. On the other hand, considering, not the fact of dreaming but the thing dreamt, it retains its peculiarities by virtue of no other fact than that it was dreamt to possess them. Thus we may define the real as that whose characters are independent of what anybody may think them to be.

But, however satisfactory such a definition may be found, it would be a great mistake to suppose that it makes the idea of reality perfectly clear. Here, then, let us apply our rules. According to them, reality, like every other quality, consists in the peculiar sensible effects which things partaking of it produce. The only effect which real things have is to cause belief, for all the sensations which they excite emerge into consciousness in the form of beliefs. The question therefore is, how is true belief (or belief in the real) distinguished from false belief (or belief in fiction). Now, as we have seen in the former paper, the ideas of truth and falsehood, in their full development, appertain exclusively to the scientific method of settling opinion. A person who arbitrarily chooses the propositions which he will adopt can use the word truth only to emphasize the expression of his determination to hold on to his choice. Of course, the method of tenacity never prevailed exclusively; reason is too natural to men for that. But in the literature of the dark ages we find some fine examples of it. When Scotus Erigena is commenting upon a poetical passage in which hellebore is spoken of as having caused the death of Socrates, he does not hesitate to inform the inquiring reader that Helleborus and Socrates were two eminent Greek philosophers, and that the latter having been overcome in argument by the former took the matter to heart and died of it! What sort of an idea of

truth could a man have who could adopt and teach, without the qualification of a perhaps, an opinion taken so entirely at random? The real spirit of Socrates, who I hope would have been delighted to have been "overcome in argument," because he would have learned something by it, is in curious contrast with the naïve idea of the glossist, for whom discussion would seem to have been simply a struggle. When philosophy began to awake from its long slumber, and before theology completely dominated it, the practice seems to have been for each professor to seize upon any philosophical position he found unoccupied and which seemed a strong one, to intrench himself in it, and to sally forth from time to time to give battle to the others. Thus, even the scanty records we possess of those disputes enable us to make out a dozen or more opinions held by different teachers at one time concerning the question of nominalism and realism. Read the opening part of the "Historia Calamitatum" of Abelard, who was certainly as philosophical as any of his contemporaries, and see the spirit of combat which it breathes. For him, the truth is simply his particular stronghold. When the method of authority prevailed, the truth meant little more than the Catholic faith. All the efforts of the scholastic doctors are directed toward harmonizing their faith in Aristotle and their faith in the Church, and one may search their ponderous folios through without finding an argument which goes any further. It is noticeable that where different faiths flourish side by side, renegades are looked upon with contempt even by the party whose belief they adopt; so completely has the idea of loyalty replaced that of truth-seeking. Since the time of Descartes, the defect in the conception of truth has been less apparent. Still, it will sometimes strike a scientific man that the philosophers have been less intent on finding out what the facts are, than on inquiring what belief is most in harmony with their system. It is hard to convince a follower of the *a priori* method by adducing facts; but show him that an opinion he is defending is inconsistent with what he has laid down elsewhere, and he will be very apt to retract it. These minds do not seem to believe that disputation is ever to cease; they seem to think that the opinion which is natural for one man is not so for another, and that belief will, consequently, never be settled. In contenting themselves with fixing their own opinions by a method which would lead another man to a different result, they betray their feeble hold of the conception of what truth is.

On the other hand, all the followers of science are fully persuaded that the processes of investigation, if only pushed far enough, will give one certain solution to every question to which they can be applied. One man may investigate the velocity of light by studying the transits of Venus and the aberration of the stars; another by the oppositions of Mars and the eclipses of Jupiter's satellites; a third by the method of Fizeau; a fourth by that of Foucault; a fifth by the motions of the curves of Lissajous; a sixth, a seventh, an eighth, and a ninth, may follow the different methods of comparing the measures of statical and dynamical elec-

tricity. They may at first obtain different results, but, as each perfects his method and his processes, the results will move steadily together toward a destined center. So with all scientific research. Different minds may set out with the most antagonistic views, but the progress of investigation carries them by a force outside of themselves to one and the same conclusion. This activity of thought by which we are carried, not where we wish, but to a foreordained goal, is like the operation of destiny. No modification of the point of view taken, no selection of other facts for study, no natural bent of mind even, can enable a man to escape the predestinate opinion. This great law is embodied in the conception of truth and reality. The opinion which is fated[1] to be ultimately agreed to by all who investigate, is what we mean by the truth, and the object represented in this opinion is the real. That is the way I would explain reality.

But it may be said that this view is directly opposed to the abstract definition which we have given of reality, inasmuch as it makes the characters of the real to depend on what is ultimately thought about them. But the answer to this is that, on the one hand, reality is independent, not necessarily of thought in general, but only of what you or I or any finite number of men may think about it; and that, on the other hand,

---

[1] Fate means merely that which is sure to come true, and can nohow be avoided. It is a superstition to suppose that a certain sort of events are ever fated, and it is another to suppose that the word fate can never be freed from its superstitious taint. We are all fated to die. [Footnote added in later reprinting.]

though the object of the final opinion depends on what that opinion is, yet what that opinion is does not depend on what you or I or any man thinks. Our perversity and that of others may indefinitely postpone the settlement of opinion; it might even conceivably cause an arbitrary proposition to be universally accepted as long as the human race should last. Yet even that would not change the nature of the belief, which alone could be the result of investigation carried sufficiently far; and if, after the extinction of our race, another should arise with faculties and disposition for investigation, that true opinion must be the one which they would ultimately come to. "Truth crushed to earth shall rise again," and the opinion which would finally result from investigation does not depend on how anybody may actually think. But the reality of that which is real does depend on the real fact that investigation is destined to lead, at last, if continued long enough, to a belief in it.

But I may be asked what I have to say to all the minute facts of history, forgotten never to be recovered, to the lost books of the ancients, to the buried secrets.

Full many a gem of purest ray serene
   The dark, unfathomed caves of ocean bear;
Full many a flower is born to blush unseen,
   And waste its sweetness on the desert air.

Do these things not really exist because they are hopelessly beyond the reach of our knowledge? And then, after the universe is dead (according to the prediction of some scientists), and all life has ceased forever, will not the shock of atoms continue though there will be no mind to know it? To this I reply that, though in no possible state of knowledge can any number be great enough to express the relation between the amount of what rests unknown and the amount of the known, yet it is unphilosophical to suppose that, with regard to any given question (which has any clear meaning), investigation would not bring forth a solution of it, if it were carried far enough. Who would have said, a few years ago, that we could ever know of what substances stars are made whose light may have been longer in reaching us than the human race has existed? Who can be sure of what we shall not know in a few hundred years? Who can guess what would be the result of continuing the pursuit of science for ten thousand years, with the activity of the last hundred? And if it were to go on for a million, or a billion, or any number of years you please, how is it possible to say that there is any question which might not ultimately be solved?

But it may be objected, "Why make so much of these remote considerations, especially when it is your principle that only practical distinctions have a meaning?" Well, I must confess that it makes very little difference whether we say that a stone on the bottom of the ocean, in complete darkness, is brilliant or not—that is to say, that it *probably* makes no difference, remembering always that that stone *may* be fished up tomorrow. But that there are gems at the bottom of the sea, flowers in the untraveled desert, etc., are propositions which, like that about a diamond being hard when it is not pressed, concern much more the arrangement of our language than they do the meaning of our ideas.

We have, hitherto, not crossed the threshold of scientific logic. It is certainly important to know how to make our ideas clear, but they may be ever so clear without being true. . . . How to give birth to those vital and procreative ideas which multiply into a thousand forms and diffuse themselves everywhere, advancing civilization and making the dignity of man, is an art not yet reduced to rules, but of the secret of which the history of science affords some hints.

MORRIS R. COHEN (1880–1947)
and
ERNEST NAGEL (1901–   )

Morris Raphael Cohen was born in Minsk, Russia. When he was twelve years old, his Jewish parents migrated to New York City in search of freedom and opportunity. Growing up in the metropolis, Cohen attended the College of the City of New York (City College), from which he was graduated in 1900. He then studied philosophy at Harvard as a student of Josiah Royce and William James, receiving his doctor's degree in 1906. Famous as a great teacher, he served on the faculty at City College from 1912 to 1938 and at the University of Chicago from 1938 through 1941. He was also a lecturer or visiting professor at Columbia, Yale, Harvard, Cornell, the New School for Social Research, and other institutions. His works include *Reason and Nature: An Essay on the Meaning of the Scientific Method* (1931), *Law and the Social Order* (1933), *The Meaning of Human History* (1947), and his autobiography, *A Dreamer's Journey* (1949).

Ernest Nagel was born at Nove Mesto, Czechoslovakia. His family migrated to the United States when he was ten years old and he was naturalized in 1919. He studied under Morris Cohen at City College, and received an M.A. degree in mathematics and a Ph.D. degree in philosophy at Columbia University, where he was deeply influenced by John Dewey. As professor of philosophy at Columbia and author of important books and articles, he is noted for his defence of naturalism and his contributions to the philosophy of science. Among his publications are *Sovereign Reason* (1954) and *The Structure of Science* (1961). He and Morris Cohen collaborated in writing *An Introduction to Logic and Scientific Method* (1934).

Scientific Method

Facts and Scientific Method

The method of science does not seek to impose the desires and hopes of men upon the flux of things in a capricious manner. It may indeed be employed to satisfy the desires of men. But its successful use depends upon seeking, in a deliberate manner, and irrespective of what men's desires are, to recognize, as well as to take advantage of, the structure which the flux possesses.

1. Consequently, scientific method aims to discover what the facts truly are, and the use of the method must be guided by the discovered facts. But, as we have repeatedly pointed out, what the facts are cannot be discovered without reflection. Knowledge of the facts cannot be equated to the brute immediacy of our sensations. When our skin comes into contact with objects having high temperatures or with liquid air, the immediate experiences may be similar. We cannot, however, conclude without error that the temperatures of the substances touched are the same.

From *An Introduction to Logic and Scientific Method* by Morris R. Cohen and Ernest Nagel, copyright, 1934, by Harcourt Brace Jovanovich, Inc.; renewed, 1962, by Ernest Nagel and Leonora Cohen Rosenfeld. Reprinted by permission of the publishers.

Sensory experience sets the *problem* for knowledge, and just because such experience is immediate and final it must become informed by reflective analysis before knowledge can be said to take place.

2. Every inquiry arises from some felt problem, so that no inquiry can even get under way unless some selection or sifting of the subject matter has taken place. Such selection requires, we have been urging all along, some hypothesis, preconception, prejudice, which guides the research as well as delimits the subject matter of inquiry. Every inquiry is specific in the sense that it has a definite problem to solve, and such solution terminates the inquiry. It is idle to collect "facts" unless there is a problem upon which they are supposed to bear.

3. The ability to formulate problems whose solution may also help solve other problems is a rare gift, requiring extraordinary genius. The problems which meet us in daily life can be solved, if they can be solved at all, by the application of scientific method. But such problems do not, as a rule, raise far-reaching issues. The most striking applications of scientific method are to be found in the various natural and social sciences.

4. The "facts" for which every in-

quiry reaches out are propositions for whose truth there is considerable evidence. Consequently what the "facts" are must be determined by inquiry, and cannot be determined antecedently to inquiry. Moreover, what we believe to be the facts clearly depends upon the stage of our inquiry. There is therefore no sharp line dividing facts from guesses or hypotheses. During any inquiry the status of a proposition may change from that of hypothesis to that of fact, or from that of fact to that of hypothesis. Every so-called fact, therefore, *may* be challenged for the evidence upon which it is asserted to be a fact, even though no such challenge is actually made.

Hypotheses and Scientific Method

The method of science would be impossible if the hypotheses which are suggested as solutions could not be elaborated to reveal what they imply. The full meaning of a hypothesis is to be discovered in its implications.

1. Hypotheses are suggested to an inquirer by something in the subject matter under investigation, and by his previous knowledge of other subject matters. No rules can be offered for obtaining fruitful hypotheses, any more than rules can be given for discovering significant problems.

2. Hypotheses are required at every stage of an inquiry. It must not be forgotten that what are called general principles or laws (which may have been confirmed in a previous inquiry) can be applied to a present, still unterminated inquiry only with some risk. For they may not in fact be applicable. The general laws of any science func-

tion as hypotheses, which guide the inquiry in all its phases.

3. Hypotheses can be regarded as suggestions of possible connections between actual facts or imagined ones. The question of the truth of hypotheses need not, therefore, always be raised. The necessary feature of a hypothesis, from this point of view, is that it should be statable in a determinate form, so that its implications can be discovered by logical means.

4. The number of hypotheses which may occur to an inquirer is without limit, and is a function of the character of his imagination. There is a need, therefore, for a technique to choose between the alternative suggestions, and to make sure that the alternatives are in fact, and not only in appearance, *different* theories. Perhaps the most important and best explored part of such a technique is the technique of formal inference. For this reason, the structure of formal logic has been examined at some length. The object of that examination has been to give the reader an adequate sense of what formal validity means, as well as to provide him with a synoptic view of the power and range of formal logic.

5. It is convenient to have on hand—in storage, so to speak—different hypotheses whose consequences have been carefully explored. It is the task of mathematics to provide and explore alternative hypotheses. Mathematics receives hints concerning what hypotheses to study from the natural sciences; and the natural sciences are indebted to mathematics for suggestions concerning the type of order which their subject matter embodies.

6. The deductive elaboration of hypotheses is not the sole task of scientific method. Since there is a plurality of possible hypotheses, it is the risk of inquiry to determine which of the possible explanations or solutions of the problem is in best agreement with the facts. Formal considerations are therefore never sufficient to establish the material truth of any theory.

7. No hypothesis which states a general proposition can be demonstrated as absolutely true. We have seen that all inquiry which deals with matters of fact employs probable inference. The task of such investigations is to select that hypothesis which is the most probable on the factual evidence; and it is the task of further inquiry to find other factual evidence which will increase or decrease the probability of such a theory.

Evidence and Scientific Method

Scientific method pursues the road of systematic doubt. It does not doubt *all* things, for this is clearly impossible. But it does question whatever lacks adequate evidence in its support.

1. Science is not satisfied with psychological certitude, for the mere intensity with which a belief is held is no guarantee of its truth. Science demands and looks for logically adequate grounds for the propositions it advances.

2. No single proposition dealing with matters of fact is beyond every significant doubt. No proposition is so well supported by evidence that other evidence may not increase or decrease its probability. However, while no single

proposition is indubitable, the body of knowledge which supports it, and of which it is itself a part, is better grounded than any alternative body of knowledge.

3. Science is thus always ready to abandon a theory when the facts so demand. But the facts must really demand it. It is not unusual for a theory to be modified so that it may be retained in substance even though "facts" contradicted an earlier formulation of it. Scientific procedure is therefore a mixture of a willingness to change, and an obstinacy in holding on to, theories apparently incompatible with facts.

4. The verification of theories is only approximate. Verification simply shows that, within the margin of experimental error, the experiment is *compatible* with the verified hypothesis.

System in the Ideal of Science

The ideal of science is to achieve a systematic interconnection of facts. Isolated propositions do not constitute a science. Such propositions serve merely as an opportunity to find the logical connection between them and other propositions.

1. "Common sense" is content with a miscellaneous collection of information. As a consequence, the propositions it asserts are frequently vague, the range of their application is unknown, and their mutual compatibility is generally very questionable. The advantages of discovering a system among facts is therefore obvious. A condition for achieving a system is the introduction of accuracy in the assertions made. The

limit within which propositions are true is then clearly defined. Moreover, inconsistencies between propositions asserted become eliminated gradually because propositions which are part of a system must support and correct one another. The extent and accuracy of our information is thus increased. In fact, scientific method differs from other methods in the accuracy and number of facts it studies.

2. When, as frequently happens, a science abandons one theory for another, it is a mistake to suppose that science has become "bankrupt" and that it is incapable of discovering the structure of the subject matter it studies. Such changes indicate rather that the science is progressively realizing its ideal. For such changes arise from correcting previous observations or reasoning, and such correction means that we are in possession of more reliable facts.

3. The ideal of system requires that the propositions asserted to be true should be connected without the introduction of further propositions for which the evidence is small or nonexistent. In a system the number of unconnected propositions and the number of propositions for which there is no evidence are at a minimum. Consequently, in a system the requirements of simplicity, as expressed in the principle of Occam's razor, are satisfied in a high degree. For that principle declares that entities should not be multiplied beyond necessity. This may be interpreted as a demand that whatever is capable of proof should be proved. But the ideal of system requires just that.

4. The evidence for propositions which are elements in a system accumulates more rapidly than that for isolated propositions. The evidence for a proposition may come from its own verifying instances, or from the verifying instances of *other* propositions which are connected with the first in a system. It is this systematic character of scientific theories which gives such high probabilities to the various individual propositions of a science.

The Self-Corrective Nature of Scientific Method

Science does not desire to obtain conviction for its propositions in *any* manner and at *any* price. Propostions must be supported by logically acceptable evidence, which must be weighed carefully and tested by the well-known canons of necessary and probable inference. It follows that the *method* of science is more stable, and more important to men of science, than any particular result achieved by its means.

1. In virtue of its method, the enterprise of science is a self-corrective process. It appeals to no special revelation or authority whose deliverances are indubitable and final. It claims no infallibility, but relies upon the methods of developing and testing hypotheses for assured conclusions. The canons of inquiry are themselves discovered in the process of reflection, and may themselves become modified in the course of study. The method makes possible the noting and correction of errors by continued application of itself.

2. General propositions can be established only by the method of repeated

sampling. Consequently, the propositions which a science puts forward for study are either confirmed in all possible experiments or modified in accordance with the evidence. It is this self-corrective nature of the method which allows us to challenge any proposition, but which also assures us that the theories which science accepts are more probable than any alternative theories. By not claiming more certainty than the evidence warrants, scientific method succeeds in obtaining more logical certainty than any other method yet devised.

3. In the process of gathering and weighing evidence, there is a continuous appeal from facts to theories or principles, and from principles to facts. For there is nothing intrinsically indubitable, there are no absolutely first principles, in the sense of principles which are self-evident or which must be known prior to everything else.

4. The method of science is thus essentially circular. We obtain evidence for principles by appealing to empirical material, to what is alleged to be "fact"; and we select, analyze, and interpret empirical material on the basis of principles. In virtue of such give and take between facts and principles, everything that is dubitable falls under careful scrutiny at one time or another.

The Abstract Nature of Scientific Theories

No theory asserts *everything* that can possibly be asserted about a subject matter. Every theory selects certain aspects of it and excludes others. Unless it were

possible to do this—either because such other aspects are irrelevant or because their influence on those selected is very minute—science as we know it would be impossible.

1. All theories involve abstraction from concrete subject matter. No rule can be given as to which aspects of a subject matter should be abstracted and so studied independently of other aspects. But in virtue of the goal of science—the achievement of a systematic interconnection of phenomena—in general those aspects will be abstracted which make a realization of this goal possible. Certain common elements in the phenomenon studied must be found, so that the endless variety of phenomena may be viewed as a system in which their structure is exhibited.

2. Because of the abstractness of theories, science often seems in patent contradiction with "common sense." In "common sense" the unique character and the pervasive character of things are not distinguished, so that the attempt by science to disclose the invariant features often gives the appearance of artificiality. Theories are then frequently regarded as "convenient fictions" or as "unreal." However, such criticisms overlook the fact that it is just certain *selected invariant relations* of things in which science is interested, so that many familiar properties of things are necessarily neglected by the sciences. Moreover, they forget that "common sense" itself operates in terms of abstractions, which are familiar and often confused, and which are inadequate to express the complex structure of the flux of things.

Types of Scientific Theories

Scientific explanation consists in subsuming under some rule or law which expresses an invariant character of a group of events, the particular events it is said to explain. Laws themselves may be explained, and in the same manner, by showing that they are consequences of more comprehensive theories. The effect of such progressive explanation of events by laws, laws by wider laws or theories, is to reveal the interconnection of many apparently isolated propositions.

1. It is clear, however, that the process of explanation must come to a halt at some point. Theories which cannot be shown to be special consequences from a wider connection of facts must be left unexplained, and accepted as a part of the brute fact of existence. Material considerations, in the form of contingent matters of fact, must be recognized in at least two places. There is contingency at the level of sense: just *this* and not *that* is given in sense experience. And there is contingency at the level of explanation: a definite system, although not the only possible one from the point of view of formal logic, is found to be exemplified in the flux of things.

2. In a previous chapter we have enumerated several kinds of "laws" which frequently serve as explanations of phenomena. There is, however, another interesting distinction between theories. Some theories appeal to an easily imagined *hidden mechanism* which will explain the observable phenomena; other theories eschew all reference to such hidden mechanisms, and make use of *relations* abstracted from the phenomena actually observable. The former are called *physical* theories; the latter are called *mathematical* or *abstractive* theories.

It is important to be aware of the difference between these two kinds of theories, and to understand that some minds are especially attracted to one kind, while others are comfortable only with the other kind. But it is also essential not to suppose that either kind of theory is more fundamental or more valid than the other. In the history of science there is a constant oscillation between theories of these two types; sometimes both types of theories are used successfully on the same subject matter. Let us, however, make clear the difference between them.

The English physicist Rankine explained the distinction as follows: There are two methods of framing a theory. In a mathematical or abstractive theory, "a class of objects or phenomena is defined . . . by describing . . . that assemblage of properties which is common to all the objects or phenomena composing the class, as perceived by the senses, without introducing anything hypothetical." In a physical theory "a class of objects is defined . . . as being constituted, in a manner not apparent to the senses, by a modification of some other class of objects or phenomena whose laws are already known."[1]

In the second kind of theory, some visualizable model is made the pattern for a mechanism hidden from the sense. Some physicists, like Kelvin, cannot be satisfied with anything less than a me-

[1] W. J. M. Rankine, *Miscellaneous Scientific Papers,* 1881, p. 210.

chanical explanation of observable phenomena, no matter how complex such a mechanism may be. Examples of this kind of theory are the atomic theory of chemistry, the kinetic theory of matter as developed in thermodynamics and the behavior of gases, the theory of the gene in studies on heredity, the theory of lines of force in electrostatics, and the recent Bohr model of the atom in spectroscopy.

In the mathematical type of theory, the appeal to hidden mechanisms is eliminated, or at any rate is at a minimum. How this may be done is graphically described by Henri Poincaré: "Suppose we have before us any machine; the initial wheel work and the final wheel work alone are visible, but the transmission, the intermediary machinery by which the movement is communicated from one to the other, is hidden in the interior and escapes our view; we do not know whether the communication is made by gearing or by belts, by connecting-rods or by other contrivances. Do we say that it is impossible for us to understand anything about this machine so long as we are not permitted to take it to pieces? You know well we do not, and that the principle of the conservation of energy suffices to determine for us the most interesting point. We easily ascertain that the final wheel turns ten times less quickly than the initial wheel, since these two wheels are visible; we are able thence to conclude that a couple applied to the one will be balanced by a couple ten times greater applied to the other. For that there is no need to penetrate the mechanism of this equilibrium and to know how the forces compensate

each other in the interior of the machine."[2] Examples of such theories are the theory of gravitation, Galileo's laws of falling bodies, the theory of the flow of heat, the theory of organic evolution, and the theory of relativity.

As we suggested, it is useless to quarrel as to which type of theory is the more fundamental and which type should be universally adopted. Both kinds of theories have been successful in coördinating vast domains of phenomena, and fertile in making discoveries of the most important kind. At some periods in the history of a science, there is a tendency to mechanical models and atomicity; at others, to general principles connecting characteristics abstracted from directly observable phenomena; at still others, to a fusion or synthesis of these two points of view. Some scientists, like Kelvin, Faraday, Lodge, Maxwell, show an exclusive preference for "model" theories; other scientists, like Rankine, Ostwald, Duhem, can work best with the abstractive theories; and still others, like Einstein, have the unusual gift of being equally at home with both kinds.

§ 2. The Limits and the Value of Scientific Method

The desire for knowledge for its own sake is more widespread than is generally recognized by anti-intellectualists. It has its roots in the animal curiosity which shows itself in the cosmological questions of children and in the gossip of adults. No ulterior utilitarian motive makes people want to know about the

[2] *Op. cit.,* p. 290–291.

private lives of their neighbors, the great, or the notorious. There is also a certain zest which makes people engage in various intellectual games or exercises in which one is required to find out something. But while the desire to know is wide, it is seldom strong enough to overcome the more powerful organic desires, and few indeed have both the inclination and the ability to face the arduous difficulties of scientific method in more than one special field. The desire to know is not often strong enough to sustain critical inquiry. Men generally are interested in the results, in the story or romance of science, not in the technical methods whereby these results are obtained and their truth continually is tested and qualified. Our first impulse is to accept the plausible as true and to reject the uncongenial as false. We have not the time, inclination, or energy to investigate everything. Indeed, the call to do so is often felt as irksome and joy-killing. And when we are asked to treat our cherished beliefs as mere hypotheses, we rebel as violently as when those dear to us are insulted. This provides the ground for various movements that are hostile to rational scientific procedure (though their promoters do not often admit that it is science to which they are hostile).

Mystics, intuitionists, authoritarians, voluntarists, and fictionalists are all trying to undermine respect for the rational methods of science. These attacks have always met with wide acclaim and are bound to continue to do so, for they strike a responsive note in human nature. Unfortunately they do not offer any reliable alternative method for obtaining verifiable knowledge. The great

French writer Pascal opposed to logic the spirit of subtlety or finesse (*esprit géometrique* and *esprit de finesse*) and urged that the heart has its reasons as well as the mind, reasons that cannot be accurately formulated but which subtle spirits apprehend none the less. Men as diverse as James Russell Lowell and George Santayana are agreed that:

"The soul is oracular still,"

and

"It is wisdom to trust the heart . . .
To trust the soul's invincible surmise."

Now it is true that in the absence of omniscience we must trust our soul's surmise; and great men are those whose surmises or intuitions are deep or penetrating. It is only by acting on our surmise that we can procure the evidence in its favor. But only havoc can result from confusing a surmise with a proposition for which there is already evidence. Are all the reasons of the heart sound? Do all oracles tell the truth? The sad history of human experience is distinctly discouraging to any such claim. Mystic intuition may give men absolute subjective certainty, but can give no proof that contrary intuitions are erroneous. It is obvious that when authorities conflict we must weigh the evidence in their favor logically if we are to make a rational choice. Certainly, when a truth is questioned it is no answer to say, "I am convinced," or, "I prefer to rely on this rather than on another authority." The view that physical science is no guide to proof, but is a mere fiction, fails to explain why it has enabled us to anticipate phenomena of nature and to control them. These attacks on scientific method receive a certain color of plausibility because of some indefensible claims made by uncritical enthusiasts. But it is of the essence of scientific method to limit its own pretension. Recognizing that we do not know everything, it does not claim the ability to solve all of our practical problems. It is an error to suppose, as is often done, that science denies the truth of all unverified propositions. For that which is unverified today may be verified tomorrow. We may get at truth by guessing or in other ways. Scientific method, however, is concerned with verification. Admittedly the wisdom of those engaged in this process has not been popularly ranked as high as that of the sage, the prophet, or the poet. Admittedly, also, we know of no way of supplying creative intelligence to those who lack it. Scientists, like all other human beings, may get into ruts and apply their techniques regardless of varying circumstances. There will always be formal procedures which are fruitless. Definitions and formal distinctions may be a sharpening of tools without the wit to use them properly, and statistical information may conform to the highest technical standards and yet be irrelevant and inconclusive. Nevertheless, scientific method is the only way to increase the general body of tested and verified truth and to eliminate arbitrary opinion. It is well to clarify our ideas by asking for the precise meaning of our words, and to try to check our favorite ideas by applying them to accurately formulated propositions.

In raising the question as to the social need for scientific method, it is well to recognize that the suspension of judgment which is essential to that method is difficult or impossible when we are pressed by the demands of immediate action When my house is on fire, I must act quickly and promptly— I cannot stop to consider the possible causes, nor even to estimate the exact probabilities involved in the various alternative ways of reacting. For this reason, those who are bent upon some specific course of action often despise those devoted to reflection; and certain ultramodernists seem to argue as if the need for action guaranteed the truth of our decision. But the fact that I must either vote for candidate X or refrain from doing so does not of itself give me adequate knowledge. The frequency of our regrets makes this obvious. Wisely ordered society is therefore provided with means for deliberation and reflection *before* the pressure of action becomes irresistible. In order to assure the most thorough investigation, all possible views must be canvassed, and this means toleration of views that are *prima facie* most repugnant to us.

In general the chief social condition of scientific method is a widespread desire for truth that is strong enough to withstand the powerful forces which make us cling tenaciously to old views or else embrace every novelty because it is a change. Those who are engaged in scientific work need not only leisure for reflection and material for their experiment, but also a community that respects the pursuit of truth and allows freedom for the expression of intellectual doubt as to its most sacred or established institutions. Fear of offending established dogmas has been an obstacle to the growth of astronomy and geology and other physical sciences; and the fear of offending patriotic or respected sentiment is perhaps one of the strongest hindrances to scholarly history and social science. On the other hand, when a community indiscriminately acclaims every new doctrine the love of truth becomes subordinated to the desire for novel formulations.

On the whole it may be said that the safety of science depends on there being men who care more for the justice of their methods than for any results obtained by their use. For this reason it is unfortunate when scientific research in the social field is largely in the hands of those not in a favorable position to oppose established or popular opinion.

We may put it the other way by saying that the physical sciences can be more liberal because we are sure that foolish opinions will be readily eliminated by the shock of facts. In the social field, however, no one can tell what harm may come of foolish ideas before the foolishness is finally, if ever, demonstrated. None of the precautions of scientific method can prevent human life from being an adventure, and no scientific investigator knows whether he will reach his goal. But scientific method does enable large numbers to walk with surer steps. By analyzing the possibilities of any step or plan, it becomes possible to anticipate the future and adjust ourselves to it in advance. Scientific method thus minimizes the shock of novelty and the uncertainty of life. It enables us to frame policies of actions and of moral judgment fit for a wider outlook than those of immediate physical stimulus or organic response.

Scientific method is the only effective way of strengthening the love of truth. It develops the intellectual courage to face difficulties and to overcome illusions that are pleasant temporarily but destructive ultimately. It settles differences without any external force by appealing to our common rational nature. The way of science, even if it is up a steep mountain, is open to all. Hence, while sectarian and partisan faiths are based on personal choice or temperament and divide men, scientific procedure unites men in something nobly devoid of all pettiness. Because it requires detachment, disinterestedness, it is the finest flower and test of a liberal civilization.

COMMENT

The Empirical Tradition

Even before Descartes outlined his rationalistic theory of knowledge, Francis Bacon (1561–1626), a prominent figure in the Court of Queen Elizabeth and James I of England, had set forth the basic tenets of empiricism in his two great books *The Advancement of Learning* and *Novum Organum*. With the intensity and earnestness of a prophet, Bacon proclaimed that induction is the true road to knowledge and that none before him had tried this method. The statement is itself, however, a faulty induction, since even a superficial survey of the history of science reveals that a number of Bacon's predecessors—Roger Bacon, Leonardo da Vinci, Telesio, and Campanella, to name but a few—were also heralds of empirical science. Even Aristotle, whom Bacon denounced, knew very well how to handle the inductive method. After the time of Bacon, there was a great succession of English philosophers—Locke, Berkeley, Hume and Mill—whose emphasis was empirical. On the Continent, the method of empiricism has been notably represented by the "positivists" Mach, Comte, and Poincaré.

No one has been more identified with empiricism, especially in its epistemological aspects, than John Locke. Although modern epistemologists have been greatly influenced by Descartes, he was not nearly so epistemological in his orientation as Locke. In his *Rules for the Direction of the Mind*, Descartes spoke of the great importance "of determining the nature of human knowledge and how far it extends," but he referred to it as "a question one must face once in one's life." The question which is thus recommended to each man for consideration once in his life became for Locke the subject of lifelong study. No one before him, not even Descartes, realized so clearly the importance of this inquiry and pursued it with so much persistence.

The nature of Locke's contribution to epistemology has often been inaccurately described. He spoke of the mind as a blank of paper that experience writes on. This metaphor is misleading to the extent that it suggests that the mind is merely a passive entity. Locke denied that there were innate ideas but never that there were innate powers. The mind, he declared, has "inherent faculties" which it brings into the world with it, and knowledge is to be won only through the active employment of these faculties. By selective acts of attention, the mind acquires an original stock of sensory and introspective data; it then compounds, abstracts, and relates, and in so doing, creates new complex ideas. Although Locke avoided the cruder sort of sensationism, he was still an empiricist in contending that all complex ideas are generated out of the original stuff of experience, whether sensory or introspective. His great achievement was the development of an empirical epistemology and metaphysics upon this basis, pursuing the "historical plain method" of tracing our ideas back to their origins.

Implicit Assumptions

In *Science and the Modern World*, Alfred North Whitehad speaks of the "fundamental assumptions" which the exponents of the philosophy of an epoch "unconsciously presuppose." An example of such a cosmological idea is Locke's assumption that wholes are the mere additive sum of their parts. The "composition theory," as this notion has been called, was implicitly held by most scientists and philosophers in the seventeenth, the eighteenth, and, to some extent, the nineteenth century. These thinkers supposed that a physical body is the sum of discrete atoms, that a complex mental state is the sum of discrete "ideas," and that a social organization is the sum of discrete persons. Synthesis adds nothing substantially new; the way to understand any whole is by analysis. Relations are regarded as extrinsic and inessential, the reality being the aggregated individuals.[1]

In accordance with this implicit assumption, Locke took it for granted that the components in a complex whole did not undergo any intrinsic modification as a result of their combination. The mind, he thought, can produce nothing genuinely new in fusing or relating mental content. "The mind," he says, "can neither make nor destroy" any simple idea. Holding this view, Locke supposed that a complex idea is resolvable without remainder into the simple ideas that enter into its constitution. But in the account that he gave of abstractions, universals, and relations, he was forced to recognize tacitly that syntheses are created within the mind. At times he also recognized organic relations and configurational unities in nature. Yet he nowhere explicitly repudiated the composition theory.

According to Whitehead, another implicit assumption of philosophy in the age of Locke is "the fallacy of misplaced concreteness." This is the error of mistaking the abstract for the concrete. Whatever exists is a concrete thing, not a bare abstraction, and to mistake the latter for the former is a fallacy. As an example Whitehead cites "the concept of simple location"—the idea that each bit of matter is self-contained, indifferent to and unaffected by the space and time within which it moves. Another example is Locke's concept of substance and quality—substance as "a something-I-know-not-what" and qualities distinguished into "primary" and "secondary." I have discussed this distinction briefly in my comment on materialism (pages 87–89). Berkeley sharply criticized this Lockian doctrine in his argument for idealism.

I will not add to these discussions except to call attention to the precise manner in which Locke phrases his distinction. Some ideas, he says, correspond to qualities in the object, but others do not. When the qualities are correctly represented by our ideas they are called *primary*. These primary qualities are solidity, extension, figure, motion or rest, and number. When the qualities do *not* correspond to our ideas they are called *secondary*. The secondary qualities are simply powers to produce in us the "ideas" (sensa) of colors, sounds, tastes, odors, heat, cold, warmth, and so on. The physical world, despite appearances, has none of these vivid sensory characteristics. It is odorless, colorless, silent, a world of abstract measurable properties and mathematically computable motions.

Representative Perception and the Problem of Knowledge

According to Locke, the mind can know directly only what is mental; hence all knowledge of nonmental things must be indirect: by the intervention of the ideas the mind has of them. This is the theory of representative perception, com-

---

[1] For an excellent discussion of the composition theory and its implications, see James Gibson, *Locke's Theory of Knowledge and Its Historical Relations* (Cambridge at the University Press, 1931), especially pages 47–50, 63–64, 74, 77–78, 87–89, 91, 119.

mon to both Descartes and Locke, and based upon a metaphysical dualism of mind and matter. The mind, through introspection, knows itself, and it alone, of "the things the mind contemplates," is "present to the understanding," and does not need to be represented by a sign.

The question arises, how do we know that an idea is a reliable sign? Since material things never present themselves directly, how can we determine the agreement of "ideas" with these concealed objects? In Locke's own words, "How shall the mind, when it perceives nothing but its ideas, know that they agree with things themselves?" His answer is that ideas of actual things are coercive and independent of the will, and this coerciveness guarantees their reliability. In practice he accepted Newtonian physics as revealing the character of the real world.

The careful reader will note certain inconsistencies in his argument. He defines knowledge as "the perception of the connection and agreement, or disagreement and repugnancy of any of our ideas." Knowledge so defined is confined to the sphere of ideas and does not apply to real things beyond this sphere. The definition fits well enough some types of knowledge but not others. It fits "intuitive" and "demonstrative" knowledge but not "sensitive." It fits knowledge of "identity," "relation," and "coexistence" but not "real existence." Here is a weakness in Locke's theory that Berkeley and Hume were quick to exploit. They argued that there is no way to verify the supposed correspondence between *idea* and *quality* or between *idea* and *substance*, and that consequently Locke's metaphysical dualism is without sound foundations. These arguments, plausible though they were, did not dispose of Locke's theories. Lovejoy's defence of dualism in Chapter 4 is as applicable to the philosophy of Locke as to the philosophy of Descartes.

Peirce's Revolt against Cartesianism

No one is better suited to represent the tenets of empiricism than Charles Sanders Peirce (pronounced "purse"), the most versatile and original of American philosophers, and one of the greatest figures in the history of modern thought. Peirce is often considered a pragmatist, but his thought far transcends the limits of the pragmatic approach. As Morris R. Cohen has remarked, "Peirce's analysis of the method of science . . . is one of the best introductions to a theory of liberal or Hellenic civilization, as opposed to those of despotic societies."[2] His philosophy, in addition, constitutes an antithesis to Descartes' thesis, since it was in part conceived as an answer to Cartesianism. Perhaps no one else has criticized the rationalistic method of Descartes so profoundly, and no one has more suggestively outlined the alternative method of empiricism. Hence a consideration of Peirce will serve admirably as a contrast to the chapter devoted to Descartes.

Since "contrast is the soul of clearness," we shall begin with Peirce's very penetrating criticism of Cartesianism. It may be summarized as follows:

[2] *Chance, Love and Logic* (Harcourt, Brace and Company, 1932), p. xxix.

1. Against the Method of Doubt. Peirce sharply rejected Descartes' method of universal doubt:

> We cannot begin with complete doubt. We must begin with all the prejudices which we actually have when we enter into the study of philosophy. These prejudices are not to be dispelled by a maxim, for they are things which it does not occur to us *can be questioned*. . . . A person may, it is true, in the course of his studies, find reason to doubt what he began by believing; but in that case he doubts because he has a positive reason for it, and not on account of the Cartesian maxim. Let us not pretend to doubt in philosophy what we do not doubt in our hearts.[3]

Peirce's criticism is partly psychological and partly logical. The crux of the psychological criticism is that *real* doubt arises from the conflict of beliefs and hence involves nondoubt. It is an error to suppose that one can doubt at will. "For belief, while it lasts, is a strong habit, and as such, forces the man to believe until surprise breaks up the habit."[4] The surprise occurs when a belief comes into conflict with either some other belief or some novel experience, and a mind empty of belief cannot be surprised. If you try to doubt without such positive occasion for doubting, you are merely feigning doubt. "Do you call it *doubting* to write it down on a piece of paper that you doubt? If so, doubt has nothing to do with any serious business."[5] Underneath all the "paper doubts" will remain a solid core of beliefs, many of which will be implicit and more or less subconscious. The Cartesian method is naïve in assuming, first, that a man can be thoroughly aware of his beliefs and presuppositions and, second, that he can shed his beliefs at will.

Logically as well as psychologically, inquiry does not begin with an empty mind but involves beliefs as the presuppositions of inquiry. Just what these presuppositions are must be discovered through inquiry; but an investigator who doubted his memory, the principles of logic, the reliability of reason, and all the evidence of his senses would be completely hamstrung. The moment one advances beyond the first "self-evident" premise ("I think, therefore I am"), one must employ some of the very beliefs that one has pretended to doubt. "Descartes and others have endeavored to bolster up the light of reason by make-believe arguments from the 'veracity of God' and the like. They had better not have pretended

---

[3] *Collected Papers of Charles Sanders Peirce,* ed. by Charles Hartshorne and Paul Weiss (Harvard University Press, 1931), V, para. 265. Following the practice of Peirce's editors, we shall hereafter give first the number of the volume, then a decimal point, then the number of the paragraph. Thus the notation of this first quotation would be 5.265. Since "The Fixation of Belief" and "How to Make Our Ideas Clear" are reprinted in the present volume, quotations from these essays have not been footnoted.

[4] 5.524.

[5] 5.416.

to call that in question which they intended to prove, since the proofs, themselves, call for the same light to make them evident."[6]

2. AGAINST AN INDIVIDUALISTIC CRITERION OF TRUTH. Peirce rejected individual intuition, or "clear and distinct perception," as the test of truth, substituting a *social* criterion. The Cartesian view, it will be remembered, emphasizes intuition, defined as the individual mind's immediate insight into self-evident truth, as the ultimate source of knowledge. It thus involves a simple two-term relation between the knowing mind and the known truth—a relation that takes no account of other minds or other truths. For if the grasp of truth were dependent upon the agreement of other minds, or upon connections with other truths, it would lose its immediate and intuitive character. What guarantees the reliability of intuition is not only its immediacy but its clarity and distinctness.

According to Peirce, this Cartesian interpretation of inquiry is radically false. Descartes failed to distinguish between an idea that seemed clear and one that really was so, or a proposition that seemed self-evident and one that really was so. Philosophers have notoriously disagreed about what really is clear or self-evident. Hence the appeal to intuition simply results in assertion and counter-assertion. Peirce wittily remarked that metaphysicians who adopt the Cartesian method "will all agree that metaphysics has reached a pitch of certainty far beyond that of the physical sciences;—only they can agree on nothing else."[7] To assert, as Descartes did, that whatever is clearly and distinctly perceived is true is to abandon all tests of truth beyond individual opinion. "Ideas," moreover, "may be ever so clear without being true"[8]—a fact that Descartes apparently did not grasp.

Peirce proposed a quite different approach to truth and clarity. First, he maintained that the way in which to clarify the meaning of an idea or proposition is to envisage its practical consequences. We establish clear meaning by *testing* an idea in *use*—by tracing out its concrete applications and consequences rather than by intuitive inspection or abstract definition. Secondly, Peirce contended that truth is established by public agreement rather than private insight—and not just the agreement of ignorant minds but the agreement of qualified investigators converging toward an ideal limit of accuracy and objectivity. The ultimate test of truth is that it is verified by facts open to inspection and admitted to be such by all qualified observers. So long as an "intuition" remains the object of a single individual's perspective and is not submitted to the test of *social* verification, there is nothing to guarantee its reliability. "Truth is public."[9] Thirdly, Peirce denied that we ever grasp ideas or statements in isolation and immediately discern their truth or clarity. Thinking is fundamentally contextualistic—we understand things

[6] 2.28.
[7] 5.265.
[8] 5.410.
[9] Letter to William James quoted in Ralph Barton Perry, *The Thought and Character of William James* (Harvard University Press, 1935), II, p. 437.

when we relate them to other things; we connect the immediately given with the nongiven. Even a very simple perception, such as your awareness of "this moment," involves such contextualistic interpretation. You are aware that it is *a* moment, a particular instance of a universal—and you are aware that it is *this* moment only because it stands in contrast to a moment ago, which you now remember, and the next moment, which you anticipate. Peirce never tired of pointing out such connections. In his theory of inquiry, he argued that we can establish the truth of statements only by fitting them into the context of our beliefs and of socially verified perceptions and judgments. It would be difficult to find a sharper contrast than that between Peirce's experimental, social, and contextualistic approach to truth and Descartes' intuitive, individual, and isolationist approach.

3. AGAINST THE PRIMACY OF SELF-CONSCIOUSNESS. Descartes maintained that the awareness each one of us has of himself and his own mental states is the most immediate and indubitable form of knowledge. In the main, modern epistemology has accepted this point of view. Now, Peirce did not deny that in some way and to some degree each person is aware of himself and his own mental states; but he did strenuously deny that this self-knowledge is wholly immediate and private.[10] He believed that a child becomes self-conscious by comparing and contrasting himself with others, and that this process of interpreting oneself through relations with others continues throughout adulthood. Consequently, self-knowledge is inseparably connected with knowledge of other people. We cannot know ourselves and our own mental states, moreover, unless our thoughts are expressed in words or other signs. Whereas Descartes had maintained that self-knowledge involves a direct two-term relation between a knowing mind and a known object ("myself"), Peirce maintained that all knowledge, including knowledge about oneself, involves at least *three* terms—sign, object signified, and interpreter. A person does not know what he is thinking, even when he is thinking about himself, unless he can put his thoughts into words or other symbols. "One's thoughts," declared Peirce, "are what he is 'saying to himself'; that is, is saying to that other self that is just coming into life in the flow of time. When one reasons, it is that critical self that one is trying to persuade; and all thought whatsoever is a sign, and is mostly in the nature of language."[11] Now, language is a means to social communication, and all words and other symbols are normally expressed in some overt, physical way, such as speaking, writing, or gesturing. Hence self-knowledge, since it is mediated through signs, involves outward, physical facts, and is social. It is therefore not prior to other forms of knowledge and has no unique, privileged status.

[10] For a fuller statement of this criticism, see "Concerning Certain Faculties Claimed for Man," in *Collected Papers*, V.
[11] 5.421.

4. AGAINST THE METHOD OF LINEAR INFERENCE. For Descartes, the attainment of knowledge involves a step-by-step process of reasoning from the simplest and clearest intuitions to the more and more complex deductions, following the one and only right order. He found the model of such reasoning in mathematics, especially Euclidean geometry. Peirce denied that it is necessary or desirable to follow such a single thread of reasoning. Even in mathematics, he pointed out, there are usually several ways of proving a theorem, and in empirical science a conclusion may be reached by many routes. "There may . . . be," he declared, "a hundred ways of thinking in passing from a premise to a conclusion."[12] And, again: "Philosophy ought to imitate the successful sciences in its method, . . . and to trust rather to the multitude and variety of its arguments than to the conclusiveness of any one. Its reasoning should not form a chain which is no stronger than its weakest link, but a cable whose fibres may be ever so slender, provided they are sufficiently numerous and intimately connected."[13]

5. AGAINST THE QUEST FOR CERTAINTY. Peirce believed that is it a mistake to seek, as Descartes did, for indubitable first premises and necessary deductions to certain conclusions. The notion that there are such premises and conclusions smacks of dogmatism and "blocks the road of inquiry." In opposition to Descartes, Peirce urged a doctrine that he called "critical common-sensism." This doctrine may be said to consist of three main contentions:

First, the starting point of philosophy is common sense rather than indubitable intuitions. By common sense Peirce meant those fundamental beliefs that we share with almost all human beings and that our human situation forces upon us. Examples of common-sense beliefs are our conviction that fire burns, that some things are red and others blue, that we can usually trust our memories, and that there is a certain amount of order in the universe. Peirce maintained that the human mind has been conditioned by a long course of evolution to have such fundamental beliefs, and that they must be useful and generally sound to have arisen in this natural way.

Second, all opinions about matters of fact, including our common-sense beliefs, are fallible and hence subject to criticism. Peirce did not deny "that people can usually count with accuracy"; he did not question formal reasoning in which the sole objective is logical consistency; and he did not doubt the common-sense position that we should trust our reasoning faculties. What he said is "that people cannot obtain absolute certainty concerning matters of fact."[14] Both the factual premises and the conclusions of philosophy are never more than probable—though perhaps very highly probable.

Third, the correct method of inquiry, in philosophy as well as in science, is not

[12] 2.54.
[13] 5.265.
[14] 1.149.

Descartes' rationalistic method of intuition and deduction but an observational and experimental method. By this method we can uncover and criticize our common-sense beliefs and advance to new probable conclusions.

The Origin and Development of Pragmatism

The word "pragmatism" was introduced into modern philosophy by Charles Peirce to designate the "method of ascertaining the meaning of hard words and abstract conceptions" which he had advocated in "How to Make Our Ideas Clear" (1878). Even before he wrote this essay, Peirce had expressed the basic principle of his pragmatism in a review (1871) of Fraser's edition of Berkeley's *Works*, in which he offered the following "rule for avoiding the deceits of language": "Do things fulfill the same function practically? Then let them be signified by the same word. Do they not? Then let them be distinguished." In neither of these early statements did Peirce use the word "pragmatism." But in 1898, at the University of California, William James delivered a lecture entitled "Philosophical Conceptions and Practical Results," in which he hailed Peirce not only as the founder of pragmatism but as the originator of the term. It appears that Peirce used the word orally for some time before he first committed it to print in 1902, when he contributed an article on the subject to Baldwin's *Philosophical Dictionary*.

The terms "pragmatic" and "pragmatism" were suggested to Peirce by his study of Kant. In *The Metaphysic of Morals*, Kant distinguished between "pragmatic" and "practical." The former term, deriving from the Greek *pragma* (things done), applies to the rules of art or technique based upon experience; the latter term applies to moral rules which Kant regarded as *a priori*. Hence Peirce, wishing to emphasize an experimental and non-*a priori* type of reasoning, chose the word "pragmatic" to designate his way of clarifying meanings.

The pragmatic movement first sprang to life in the early eighteen-seventies in the "Metaphysical Club," a philosophical discussion group founded by Peirce, which included among its members William James and Oliver Wendell Holmes, Jr. Two of the brilliant young members of the club, Chauncey Wright and Nicholas St. John Green, emphasized the practical bearing and function of ideas. They thus suggested to Peirce the criterion of clarity which he expressed in "How to Make Our Ideas Clear." But this essay lay unnoticed for twenty years until James, in his address of 1898, pointed to Peirce as the founder of an important new philosophical movement.

As Peirce initially used the term, pragmatism referred to a maxim for the clarification of ideas and hypotheses, not for their verification; it was a theory of meaning, not of truth. Later he also used the term to designate the rule that only hypotheses that are *clear* should be admitted in scientific or philosophical inquiry. As interpreted and amplified by James, "pragmatism" became a theory of truth and so changed into something alien to Peirce's way of thinking. "The modern movement known as pragmatism," Ralph Barton Perry has remarked, "is largely the result of James' misunderstanding of Peirce."[15]

While James was developing his own version of pragmatism, John Dewey was working along similar lines at the University of Michigan and later at the University of Chicago. As early as 1886, he and James began to exchange letters, and in 1903, in the Preface to *Studies in Logical Theory*, Dewey acknowledged "a preëminent obligation" to James. In certain ways, however, Dewey shows a closer affinity to Peirce—for example, in his close study of the experimental methods of natural science, in his rejection of James' criterion of emotional satisfaction as a test of truth, in his emphasis on the *social* bearing of ideas, and in his opposition to all "intuitionist" theories of knowledge.

However much he differed in some respects from James, Dewey fully agreed with the forward-looking and empirical temper of James' pragmatism—"the attitude of looking away from first things, principles, 'categories,' supposed necessities; and of looking toward last things, fruits, consequences, facts." He also agreed that thinking is essentially instrumental to the attainment of human purposes, although the purposes of the scientist are to be distinguished from the purposes of the practical man of affairs. Like James, moreover, he vehemently rejected a dualism of experience and nature: the stuff of the world is natural events such as we directly experience. His interpretation of inquiry, however, was more akin to Peirce's experimentalism than to James' ethical pragmatism.[16]

Conceiving philosophical and scientific method in this way, Dewey regards fruitful inquiry as essentially active and prospective rather than passive and retrospective:

> Intelligence develops within the sphere of action for the sake of possibilities not yet given. . . . Intelligence *as* intelligence is inherently forward-looking. . . . A pragmatic intelligence is a creative intelligence, not a routine mechanic. . . . Intelligence is . . . instrumental *through* action to the determination of the qualities of future experience.[17]

Accordingly, Dewey proposes to determine meanings and test beliefs by examining the *consequences* that flow from them. What can the idea or belief promise for the future? How can it help us in resolving our perplexities? What predictions are implied by the hypothesis and how can they be verified?

Such questions apply even to propositions about the past, and even these propositions must be verified in terms of future consequences: "The past event has

---

[15] *The Thought and Character of William James,* Briefer Version (Harvard University Press, 1935), p. 281.

[16] For readings from James that illustrate his pragmatic mode of reasoning, see "The One and the Many" in Chapter 8 and "The Will to Believe" in Chapter 12.

[17] *Creative Intelligence* (Henry Holt, 1917), p. 65.

left effects, consequences, that are present and that will continue in the future. Our belief about it, if genuine, must also modify action in *some* way and so have objective effects. If these two sets of effects interlock harmoniously, then the judgment is true."[18] For example, the assassination of Lincoln *had* consequences, such as records of the event. My belief about it *has* consequences, such as expectations that the records will be so-and-so. If the two sets of consequences harmoniously coincide so that my expectations are fulfilled, the statement is true.

Dewey regarded this emphasis on consequences as the essential characteristic of pragmatism. "The term 'pragmatic,'" he declared, "means only the rule of referring all thinking, all reflective considerations, to *consequences* for final meaning and test."[19] This insistence upon consequent rather than antecedent phenomena is, as we have noted, like the pragmatism of James except that it does not define truth in terms of emotional satisfactions and the play of desires, as James did in his more extreme statements.

There were other important contributors to pragmatism, such as George Herbert Mead (1863–1931) in America and F. C. S. Schiller (1864–1937) in England; but Peirce, James, and Dewey are the towering figures. For reasons of space, I have not included readings from James and Dewey in this chapter. James' pragmatic mode of reasoning is sufficiently illustrated in his essays on "The One and the Many" in Chapter 5 and "The Will to Believe" in Chapter 10. Similarly Dewey's pragmatic orientation emerges clearly in his advocacy of the experimental approach to ethics in Chapter 17. Pragmatism, in its enduring significance, is an offshoot of empiricism, and this empirical character is exemplified by the writings of Peirce.

Cohen and Nagel on Scientific Method

Morris R. Cohen was a student of James and Ernest Nagel was a student of Dewey, but it is the more scientific side of the pragmatism of Dewey and James that has influenced their writing. Cohen described his view as realistic rationalism, a view that emphasizes the importance of scientific reasoning as applied to the actual world. Nagel similarly described his philosophy as naturalism, which he carefully distinguished from the kind of materialism that seeks to reduce ideas and values to physical terms such as 'molecules.' Both Cohen and Nagel shared with Dewey certain fundamental convictions: the need for an empirical and naturalistic approach to human problems, the necessity of extending the scientific method into the sphere of social affairs, and the insistence of the factual basis of sound normative judgments. Although they differed from Dewey in certain respects, their attainment to the scientific method marks them as well as Dewey as empiricists.

[18] *The Influence of Darwin on Philosophy and Other Essays* (Henry Holt, 1910), p. 160.
[19] *Essays in Experimental Logic* (University of Chicago Press, 1916), p. 330.

Despite the difference between the work of the physicist and the biologist, the astronomer and the sociologist, certain methodological patterns are common to all. This common method of science Cohen and Nagel describe and defend. Since their discussion is a model of clarity, it needs no explication. The reader who seeks an understanding of scientific method would be well advised to study their book.

7

Idealism

GEORGE BERKELEY (1685–1753)

Berkeley was born in Kilkenny County, Ireland. His parents, having a comfortable income, gave him a good education at Kilkenny School and Trinity College, Dublin. While scarcely more than a boy, he began to fill notebooks with original philosophical reflections. His first major publication, *An Essay Toward a New Theory of Vision,* appeared when he was twenty-four, and *Principles of Human Knowledge,* which set forth his whole idealistic philosophy, was published only a year later. Finding that his ideas were ridiculed, if not neglected, he reformulated his argument in *Three Dialogues Between Hylas and Philonous,* which appeared in 1713. Thus, by the time he was twenty-eight, he had published his three major works, remarkable both for the felicity of their style and for the daring and profundity of their thought.

During this period of his greatest literary activity, Berkeley was a fellow and tutor at Trinity College, but he spent the next years after publishing his *Dialogues* in London, France, and Italy. In London, he became the friend of Pope, Steele, Addison, and Swift. Subsequently he traveled in Europe as secretary and chaplain to an earl and tutor to a bishop's son. While in Sicily, he lost the manuscript of the second part of *The Principles of Human Knowledge* and never had the heart to rewrite it.

Returning to Ireland, he was appointed Lecturer in Greek and Theology at Trinity College and eventually an ecclesiastical Dean (1724). Shortly thereafter, to his immense surprise, he inherited three thousand pounds from Hester Van Homrigh (Swift's former friend "Vanessa"), a lady whom he had met once and then only casually.

At about the same time, he conceived the project of founding a college in the Bermudas for training missionaries to the Indians and clergymen for the American colonists. By his eloquence and personal charm, he was able to obtain a considerable sum to finance his project from private donors and the promise of twenty thousand pounds from the House of Commons. With a new wife, he set sail for America in 1728. But Walpole, the Prime Minister, refused to fulfill the promise of Parliament, and Berkeley remained for three years at Newport, Rhode Island, his hopes gradually diminishing. Finally, in 1731, despairing of further aid and saddened by the death of an infant daughter, he sailed with his wife and tiny son back to England.

His later life was spent as Bishop of Cloyne and head of a growing family. He divided his time between ecclesiastical duties, philosophical studies, agitation for social reform, and family affairs. His main publication in these years was *Siris* (1744), a rather odd work in which he extolled the medicinal virtues of tar-water and expounded an idealistic interpretation of the Universe. In the final year of his life, Berkeley and his family moved to Oxford, where, "suddenly and without the least previous notice or pain," he died in 1753.

Three Dialogues between Hylas and Philonous, in Opposition to Sceptics and Atheists

The First Dialogue

Philonous. Good morning, *Hylas:* I did not expect to find you abroad so early.

Hyl. It is indeed something unusual;

London, 1713. Second unchanged edition, 1725. Third edition, 1734. The present text is that of A. Campbell Fraser, *The Works of George Berkeley.* Oxford: Clarendon Press, 1871. (With omissions.)

but my thoughts were so taken up with a subject I was discoursing of last night, that finding I could not sleep, I resolved to rise and take a turn in the garden.

Phil. It happened well, to let you see what innocent and agreeable pleasures you lose every morning. Can there be a pleasanter time of the day, or a more delightful season of the year? That purple sky, those wild but sweet notes of birds, the fragrant bloom upon the trees and flowers, the gentle influence of the rising sun, these and a thousand nameless beauties of nature inspire the soul with secret transports; its faculties too being at this time fresh and lively, are fit for these meditations, which the solitude of a garden and tranquillity of the morning naturally dispose us to. But I am afraid I interrupt your thoughts: for you seemed very intent on something.

Hyl. It is true, I was, and shall be obliged to you if you will permit me to go on in the same vein; not that I would by any means deprive myself of your company, for my thoughts always flow more easily in conversation with a friend, than when I am alone: but my request is, that you would suffer me to impart my reflections to you.

Phil. With all my heart, it is what I should have requested myself if you had not prevented me.

Hyl. I was considering the odd fate of those men who have in all ages, through an affectation of being distinguished from the vulgar, or some unaccountable turn of thought, pretended either to believe nothing at all, or to believe the most extravagant things in the world. This however might be borne, if their paradoxes and scepticism did not draw after them some consequences of general disadvantage to mankind. But the mischief lieth here; that when men of less leisure see them who are supposed to have spent their whole time in the pursuits of knowledge professing an entire ignorance of all things, or advancing such notions as are repugnant to plain and commonly received principles, they will be tempted to entertain suspicions concerning the most important truths, which they had hitherto held sacred and unquestionable.

Phil. I entirely agree with you, as to the ill tendency of the affected doubts of some philosophers, and fantastical conceits of others. I am even so far gone of late in this way of thinking, that I have quitted several of the sublime notions I had got in their schools for vulgar opinions. And I give it you on my word, since this revolt from metaphysical notions, to the plain dictates of nature and common sense, I find my understanding strangely enlightened, so that I can now easily comprehend a great many things which before were all mystery and riddle.

Hyl. I am glad to find there was nothing in the accounts I heard of you.

Phil. Pray, what were those?

Hyl. You were represented in last night's conversation, as one who maintained the most extravagant opinion that ever entered into the mind of man, to wit, that there is no such thing as *material substance* in the world.

Phil. That there is no such thing as what Philosophers call *material substance*, I am seriously persuaded: but, if I were made to see anything absurd or sceptical in this, I should then have the same reason to renounce this that I imagine I have now to reject the contrary opinion.

Hyl. What! can anything be more fantastical, more repugnant to common sense, or a more manifest piece of Scepticism, than to believe there is no such thing as *matter*?

Phil. Softly, good *Hylas*. What if it should prove, that you, who hold there is, are, by virtue of that opinion, a greater sceptic, and maintain more paradoxes and repugnances to common sense, than I who believe no such thing?

Hyl. You may as soon persuade me, the part is greater than the whole, as that, in order to avoid absurdity and Scepticism, I should ever be obliged to give up my opinion in this point.

Phil. Well then, are you content to admit that opinion for true, which, upon examination, shall appear most agreeable to common sense, and remote from Scepticism?

Hyl. With all my heart. Since you are for raising disputes about the plainest things in nature, I am content for once to hear what you have to say.

Phil. Pray, *Hylas,* what do you mean by a *sceptic?*

Hyl. I mean what all men mean, one that doubts of everything.

Phil. He then who entertains no doubt concerning some particular point, with regard to that point cannot be thought a sceptic.

Hyl. I agree with you.

Phil. Whether doth doubting consist in embracing the affirmative or negative side of a question?

Hyl. In neither; for whoever understands English cannot but know that *doubting* signifies a suspense between both.

Phil. He then that denieth any point, can no more be said to doubt of it, than he who affirmeth it with the same degree of assurance.

Hyl. True.

Phil. And, consequently, for such his denial is no more to be esteemed a sceptic than the other.

Hyl. I acknowledge it.

Phil. How cometh it to pass then, *Hylas,* that you pronounce me a *sceptic,* because I deny what you affirm, to wit, the existence of Matter? Since, for aught you can tell, I am as peremptory in my denial, as you in your affirmation.

Hyl. Hold, *Philonous,* I have been a little out in my definition; but every false step a man makes in discourse is not to be insisted on. I said indeed that a *sceptic* was one who doubted of everything; but I should have added, or who denies the reality and truth of things.

Phil. What things? Do you mean the principles and theorems of sciences? But these you know are universal intellectual notions, and consequently independent of Matter; the denial therefore of this doth not imply the denying them.

Hyl. I grant it. But are there no other things? What think you of distrusting the senses, of denying the real existence of sensible things, or pretending to know nothing to them. Is not this sufficient to denominate a man a *sceptic?*

Phil. Shall we therefore examine which of us it is that denies the reality of sensible things, or professes the greatest ignorance of them; since, if I take you rightly, he is to be esteemed the greatest *sceptic?*

Hyl. That is what I desire.

Phil. What mean you by Sensible Things?

Hyl. Those things which are perceived by the senses. Can you imagine that I mean anything else?

Phil. Pardon me, *Hylas,* if I am desirous clearly to apprehend your notions, since this may much shorten our inquiry. Suffer me then to ask you this further question. Are those things only perceived by the senses which are perceived immediately? Or, may those things properly be said to be *sensible* which are perceived mediately, or not without the intervention of others?

Hyl. I do not sufficiently understand you.

Phil. In reading a book, what I immediately perceive are the letters, but mediately, or by means of these, are suggested to my mind the notions of God, virtue, truth, &c. Now, that the letters are truly sensible things, or perceived by sense, there is no doubt: but I would know whether you take the things suggested by them to be so too.

Hyl. No, certainly; it were absurd to think *God* or *virtue* sensible things, though they may be signified and suggested to the mind by sensible marks, with which they have an arbitrary connection.

Phil. It seems then, that by *sensible things* you mean those only which can be perceived *immediately* by sense?

Hyl. Right.

Phil. Doth it not follow from this, that though I see one part of the sky red, and another blue, and that my reason doth thence evidently conclude there must be some cause of that diversity of colors, yet that cause cannot be said to be a sensible thing, or perceived by the sense of seeing?

Hyl. It doth.

Phil. In like manner, though I hear variety of sounds, yet I cannot be said to hear the causes of those sounds?

Hyl. You cannot.

Phil. And when by my touch I perceive a thing to be hot and heavy, I cannot say, with any truth or propriety,

that I feel the cause of its heat or weight?

Hyl. To prevent any more questions of this kind, I tell you once for all, that by *sensible things* I mean those only which are perceived by sense, and that in truth the senses perceive nothing which they do not perceive immediately: for they make no inferences. The deducing therefore of causes or occasions from effects and appearances, which alone are perceived by sense, entirely relates to reason.

Phil. This point then is agreed between us—that *sensible things are those only which are immediately perceived by sense.* You will further inform me, whether we immediately perceive by sight anything beside light, and colors, and figures; or by hearing, anything but sounds; by the palate, anything beside tastes; by the smell, beside odors; or by the touch, more than tangible qualities.

Hyl. We do not.

Phil. It seems, therefore, that if you take away all sensible qualities, there remains nothing sensible?

Hyl. I grant it.

Phil. Sensible things therefore are nothing else but so many sensible qualities, or combinations of sensible qualities?

Hyl. Nothing else.

Phil. Heat is then a sensible thing?

Hyl. Certainly.

Phil. Doth the reality of sensible things consist in being perceived? or, is it something distinct from their being perceived, and that bears no relation to the mind?

Hyl. To *exist* is one thing, and to be *perceived* is another.

Phil. I speak with regard to sensible things only: and of these I ask, whether by their real existence you mean a subsistence exterior to the mind, and distinct from their being perceived?

Hyl. I mean a real absolute being, distinct from, and without any relation to their being perceived.

Phil. Heat therefore, if it be allowed a real being, must exist without the mind?

Hyl. It must.

Phil. Tell me, *Hylas,* is this real existence equally compatible to all degrees of heat, which we perceive; or is there any reason why we should attribute it to some, and deny it to others? and if there be, pray let me know that reason.

Hyl. Whatever degree of heat we perceive by sense, we may be sure the same exists in the object that occasions it.

Phil. What! the greatest as well as the least?

Hyl. I tell you, the reason is plainly the same in respect of both: they are both perceived by sense; nay, the greater degree of heat is more sensibly perceived; and consequently, if there is any difference, we are more certain of its real existence than we can be of the reality of a lesser degree.

Phil. But is not the most vehement and intense degree of heat a very great pain?

Hyl. No one can deny it.

Phil. And is any unperceiving thing capable of pain or pleasure?

Hyl. No certainly.

Phil. Is your material substance a senseless being, or a being endowed with sense and perception?

Hyl. It is senseless without doubt.

Phil. It cannot therefore be the subject of pain?

Hyl. By no means.

Phil. Nor consequently of the greatest heat perceived by sense, since you acknowledge this to be no small pain?

Hyl. I grant it.

Phil. What shall we say then of your external object; is it a material Substance, or no?

Hyl. It is a material substance with the sensible qualities inhering in it.

Phil. How then can a great heat exist in it, since you own it cannot in a material substance? I desire you would clear this point.

Hyl. Hold, *Philonous,* I fear I was out in yielding intense heat to be a pain. It should seem rather, that pain is something distinct from heat, and the consequence or effect of it.

Phil. Upon putting your hand near the fire, do you perceive one simple uniform sensation, or two distinct sensations?

Hyl. But one simple sensation.

Phil. Is not the heat immediately perceived?

Hyl. It is.

Phil. And the pain?

Hyl. True.

Phil. Seeing therefore they are both immediately perceived at the same time, and the fire affects you only with one simple, or uncompounded idea, it follows that this same simple idea is both the intense heat immediately perceived, and the pain; and, consequently, that the intense heat immediately perceived, is nothing distinct from a particular sort of pain.

Hyl. It seems so.

Phil. Again, try in your thoughts,

Hylas, if you can conceive a vehement sensation to be without pain or pleasure.

Hyl. I cannot.

Phil. Or can you frame to yourself an idea of sensible pain or pleasure, in general, abstracted from every particular idea of heat, cold, tastes, smells? &c.

Hyl. I do not find that I can.

Phil. Doth it not therefore follow, that sensible pain is nothing distinct from those sensations or ideas—in an intense degree?

Hyl. It is undeniable; and, to speak the truth, I begin to suspect a very great heat cannot exist but in a mind perceiving it.

Phil. What! are you then in that *sceptical* state of suspense, between affirming and denying?

Hyl. I think I may be positive in the point. A very violent and painful heat cannot exist without the mind.

Phil. It hath not therefore, according to you, any real being?

Hyl. I own it.

Phil. Is it therefore certain, that there is no body in nature really hot?

Hyl. I have not denied there is any real heat in bodies. I only say, there is no such thing as an intense real heat.

Phil. But, did you not say before that all degrees of heat were equally real; or, if there was any difference, that the greater were more undoubtedly real than the lesser?

Hyl. True: but it was because I did not then consider the ground there is for distinguishing between them, which I now plainly see. And it is this:—because intense heat is nothing else but a particular kind of painful sensation; and pain cannot exist but in a perceiving being; it follows that no intense heat can really exist in an unperceiving corporeal substance. But this is no reason why we should deny heat in an inferior degree to exist in such a substance.

Phil. But how shall we be able to discern those degrees of heat which exist only in the mind from those which exist without it?

Hyl. That is no difficult matter. You know the least pain cannot exist unperceived; whatever, therefore, degree of heat is a pain exists only in the mind. But, as for all other degrees of heat, nothing obliges us to think the same of them.

Phil. I think you granted before that no unperceiving being was capable of pleasure, any more than of pain.

Hyl. I did.

Phil. And is not warmth, or a more gentle degree of heat than what causes uneasiness, a pleasure?

Hyl. What then?

Phil. Consequently, it cannot exist without the mind in an unperceiving substance, or body.

Hyl. So it seems.

Phil. Since, therefore, as well those degrees of heat that are not painful, as those that are, can exist only in a thinking substance; may we not conclude that external bodies are absolutely incapable of any degree of heat whatsoever?

Hyl. On second thoughts, I do not think it is so evident that warmth is a pleasure, as that a great degree of heat is a pain.

Phil. I do not pretend that warmth is as great a pleasure as heat is a pain. But, if you grant it to be even a small pleasure, it serves to make good my conclusion.

Hyl. I could rather call it an *indolence*. It seems to be nothing more than a privation of both pain and pleasure. And that such a quality or state as this may agree to an unthinking substance, I hope you will not deny.

Phil. If you are resolved to maintain that warmth, or a gentle degree of heat, is no pleasure, I know not how to convince you otherwise, than by appealing to your own sense. But what think you of cold?

Hyl. The same that I do of heat. An intense degree of cold is a pain; for to feel a very great cold, is to perceive a great uneasiness: it cannot therefore exist without the mind; but a lesser degree of cold may, as well as a lesser degree of heat.

Phil. Those bodies, therefore, upon whose application to our own, we perceive a moderate degree of heat, must be concluded to have a moderate degree of heat or warmth in them; and those, upon whose application we feel a like degree of cold, must be thought to have cold in them.

Hyl. They must.

Phil. Can any doctrine be true that necessarily leads a man into an absurdity?

Hyl. Without doubt it cannot.

Phil. Is it not an absurdity to think that the same thing should be at the same time both cold and warm?

Hyl. It is.

Phil. Suppose now one of your hands hot, and the other cold, and that they are both at once put into the same vessel of water, in an intermediate state;

will not the water seem cold to one hand, and warm to the other?

Hyl. It will.

Phil. Ought we not therefore, by our principles, to conclude it is really both cold and warm at the same time, that is, according to your own concession, to believe an absurdity?

Hyl. I confess it seems so.

Phil. Consequently, the principles themselves are false, since you have granted that no true principle leads to an absurdity.

Hyl. But, after all, can anything be more absurd than to say, *there is no heat in the fire?*

Phil. To make the point still clearer; tell me whether, in two cases exactly alike, we ought not to make the same judgment?

Hyl. We ought.

Phil. When a pin pricks your finger, doth it not rend and divide the fibers of your flesh?

Hyl. It doth.

Phil. And when a coal burns your finger, doth it any more?

Hyl. It doth not.

Phil. Since, therefore, you neither judge the sensation itself occasioned by the pin, nor anything like it to be in the pin; you should not, conformably to what you have now granted, judge the sensation occasioned by the fire, or anything like it, to be in the fire.

Hyl. Well, since it must be so, I am content to yield this point, and acknowledge that heat and cold are only sensations existing in our minds. But there still remain qualities enough to secure the reality of external things.

Phil. But what will you say, *Hylas,* if it shall appear that the case is the same with regard to all other sensible qualities, and that they can no more be supposed to exist without the mind, than heat and cold?

Hyl. Then indeed you will have done something to the purpose; but that is what I despair of seeing proved.

Phil. Let us examine them in order. What think you of *tastes*—do they exist without the mind, or no?

Hyl. Can any man in his senses doubt whether sugar is sweet, or wormwood bitter?

Phil. Inform me, *Hylas*. Is a sweet taste a particular kind of pleasure or pleasant sensation, or is it not?

Hyl. It is.

Phil. And is not bitterness some kind of uneasiness or pain?

Hyl. I grant it.

Phil. If therefore sugar and wormwood are unthinking corporeal substances existing without the mind, how can sweetness and bitterness, that is, pleasure and pain, agree to them?

Hyl. Hold, *Philonous,* I now see what it was deluded me all this time. You asked whether heat and cold, sweetness and bitterness, were not particular sorts of pleasure and pain; to which I answered simply, that they were. Whereas I should have thus distinguished:—those qualities, as perceived by us, are pleasures or pains; but not as existing in the external objects. We must not therefore conclude absolutely, that there is no heat in the fire, or sweetness in the sugar, but only that heat or sweetness, as perceived by us, are not in the fire or sugar. What say you to this?

Phil. I say it is nothing to the purpose. Our discourse proceeded altogether concerning sensible things, which you defined to be, *the things we immediately perceive by our senses.* Whatever other qualities, therefore, you speak of, as distinct from these, I know nothing of them, neither do they at all belong to the point in dispute. You may, indeed, pretend to have discovered certain qualities which you do not perceive, and assert those insensible qualities exist in fire and sugar. But what use can be made of this to your present purpose, I am at a loss to conceive. Tell me then once more, do you acknowledge that heat and cold, sweetness and bitterness (meaning those qualities which are perceived by the senses), do not exist without the mind?

Hyl. I see it is to no purpose to hold out, so I give up the cause as to those mentioned qualities. Though I profess it sounds oddly, to say that sugar is not sweet.

Phil. But, for your further satisfaction, take this along with you: that which at other times seems sweet, shall, to a distempered palate, appear bitter. And, nothing can be plainer than that divers persons perceive different tastes in the same food; since that which one man delights in, another abhors. And how could this be, if the taste was something really inherent in the food?

Hyl. I acknowledge I know not how.

Phil. In the next place, *odors* are to be considered. And, with regard to these, I would fain know whether what has been said of tastes doth not exactly agree to them? Are they not so many pleasing or displeasing sensations?

Hyl. They are.

Phil. Can you then conceive it possible that they should exist in an unperceiving thing?

Hyl. I cannot.

Phil. Or, can you imagine that filth and ordure affect those brute animals that feed on them out of choice, with the same smells which we perceive in them?

Hyl. By no means.

Phil. May we not therefore conclude of smells, as of the other forementioned qualities, that they cannot exist in any but a perceiving substance or mind.

Hyl. I think so.

Phil. Then as to *sounds,* what must we think of them: are they accidents really inherent in external bodies, or not?

Hyl. That they inhere not in the sonorous bodies is plain from hence; because a bell struck in the exhausted receiver of an air-pump sends forth no sound. The air, therefore, must be thought the subject of sound.

Phil. What reason is there for that, *Hylas?*

Hyl. Because, when any motion is raised in the air, we perceive a sound greater or lesser, according to the air's motion; but without some motion in the air, we never hear any sound at all.

Phil. And granting that we never hear a sound but when some motion is produced in the air, yet I do not see how you can infer from thence, that the sound itself is in the air.

Hyl. It is this very motion in the external air that produces in the mind the sensation of *sound.* For, striking on the drum of the ear, it causeth a vibration, which by the auditory nerves being communicated to the brain, the soul is thereupon affected with the sensation called *sound.*

Phil. What! is sound then a sensation?

Hyl. I tell you, as perceived by us, it is a particular sensation in the mind.

Phil. And can any sensation exist without the mind?

Hyl. No, certainly.

Phil. How then can sound, being a sensation, exist in the air, if by the *air* you mean a senseless substance existing without the mind?

Hyl. You must distinguish, *Philonous,* between sound as it is perceived by us, and as it is in itself; or (which is the same thing) between the sound we immediately perceive, and that which exists without us. The former, indeed, is a particular kind of sensation, but the latter is merely a vibrative or undulatory motion in the air.

Phil. I thought I had already obviated that distinction, by the answer I gave when you were applying it in a like case before. But, to say no more of that, are you sure then that sound is really nothing but motion?

Hyl. I am.

Phil. Whatever therefore agrees to real sound, may with truth be attributed to motion?

Hyl. It may.

Phil. It is then good sense to speak of *motion* as of a thing that is *loud, sweet, acute, or grave.*

Hyl. I see you are resolved not to understand me. Is it not evident those accidents or modes belong only to sensible sound, or *sound* in the common acceptation of the word, but not to *sound* in the real and philosophic sense; which, as I just now told you, is nothing but a certain motion of the air?

Phil. It seems then there are two sorts

of sound—the one vulgar, or that which is heard, the other philosophical and real?

Hyl. Even so.

Phil. And the latter consists in motion?

Hyl. I told you so before.

Phil. Tell me, *Hylas,* to which of the senses, think you, the idea of motion belongs? to the hearing?

Hyl. No, certainly; but to the sight and touch.

Phil. It should follow then, that, according to you, real sounds may possibly be *seen* or *felt,* but never *heard.*

Hyl. Look you, *Philonous,* you may, if you please, make a jest of my opinion, but that will not alter the truth of things. I own, indeed, the inferences you draw me into, sound something oddly; but common language, you know, is framed by, and for the use of the vulgar: we must not therefore wonder, if expressions adapted to exact philosophic notions seem uncouth and out of the way.

Phil. Is it come to that? I assure you, I imagine myself to have gained no small point, since you make so light of departing from common phrases and opinions; it being a main part of our inquiry, to examine whose notions are widest of the common road, and most repugnant to the general sense of the world. But, can you think it no more than a philosophical paradox, to say that *real sounds are never heard,* and that the idea of them is obtained by some other sense? And is there nothing in this contrary to nature and the truth of things?

Hyl. To deal ingeniously, I do not like it. And, after the concessions already made, I had as well grant that sounds too have no real being without the mind.

Phil. And I hope you will make no difficulty to acknowledge the same of *colors.*

Hyl. Pardon me: the case of colors is very different. Can anything be plainer than that we see them on the objects?

Phil. The objects you speak of are, I suppose, corporeal Substances existing without the mind?

Hyl. They are.

Phil. And have true and real colors inhering in them?

Hyl. Each visible object hath that color which we see in it.

Phil. How! is there anything visible but what we perceive by sight?

Hyl. There is not.

Phil. And, do we perceive anything by sense which we do not perceive immediately?

Hyl. How often must I be obliged to repeat the same thing? I tell you, we do not.

Phil. Have patience, good *Hylas;* and tell me once more, whether there is anything immediately perceived by the senses, except sensible qualities. I know you asserted there was not; but I would now be informed, whether you still persist in the same opinion.

Hyl. I do.

Phil. Pray, is your corporeal substance either a sensible quality, or made up of sensible qualities?

Hyl. What a question that is! who ever thought it was?

Phil. My reason for asking was, because in saying, *each visible object hath that color which we see in it,* you make visible objects to be corporeal substances; which implies either that corporeal substances are sensible qualities, or else that there is something beside sensible qualities perceived by sight: but, as this point was formerly agreed between us, and is still maintained by you, it is a clear consequence, that your corporeal substance is nothing distinct from sensible qualities.

Hyl. You may draw as many absurd consequences as you please, and endeavor to perplex the plainest things; but you shall never persuade me out of my senses. I clearly understand my own meaning.

Phil. I wish you would make me understand it too. But, since you are unwilling to have your notion of corporeal substance examined, I shall urge that point no further. Only be pleased to let me know, whether the same colors which we see exist in external bodies, or some other.

Hyl. The very same.

Phil. What! are then the beautiful red and purple we see on yonder clouds really in them? Or do you imagine they have in themselves any other form than that of a dark mist or vapor?

Hyl. I must own, *Philonous,* those colors are not really in the clouds as they seem to be at this distance. They are only apparent colors.

Phil. Apparent call you them? how shall we distinguish these apparent colors from real?

Hyl. Very easily. Those are to be thought apparent which, appearing only at a distance, vanish upon a nearer approach.

Phil. And those, I suppose, are to be thought real which are discovered by the most near and exact survey.

Hyl. Right.

Phil. Is the nearest and exactest survey made by the help of a microscope, or by the naked eye?

Hyl. By a microscope, doubtless.

Phil. But a microscope often discovers colors in an object different from those perceived by the unassisted sight. And, in case we had microscopes magnifying to any assigned degree, it is certain that no object whatsoever, viewed through them, would appear in the same color which it exhibits to the naked eye.

Hyl. And what will you conclude from all this? You cannot argue that there are really and naturally no colors on objects: because by artificial managements they may be altered, or made to vanish.

Phil. I think it may evidently be concluded from your own concessions, that all the colors we see with our naked eyes are only apparent as those on the clouds, since they vanish upon a more close and accurate inspection which is afforded us by a microscope. Then, as to what you say by way of prevention: I ask you whether the real and natural state of an object is better discovered by a very sharp and piercing sight, or by one which is less sharp?

Hyl. By the former without doubt.

Phil. Is it not plain from *Dioptrics* that microscopes make the sight more penetrating, and represent objects as they would appear to the eye in case it were naturally endowed with a most exquisite sharpness?

Hyl. It is.

Phil. Consequently the microscopical representation is to be thought that which best sets forth the real nature of the thing, or what it is in itself. The colors, therefore, by it perceived are more genuine and real than those perceived otherwise.

Hyl. I confess there is something in what you say.

Phil. Besides, it is not only possible but manifest, that there actually are animals whose eyes are by nature framed to perceive those things which by reason of their minuteness escape our sight. What think you of those inconceivably small animals perceived by glasses? must we suppose they are all stark blind? Or, in case they see, can it be imagined their sight hath not the same use in preserving their bodies from injuries, which appears in that of all other animals? And if it hath, is it not evident they must see particles less than their own bodies, which will present them with a far different view in each object from that which strikes our senses? Even our own eyes do not always represent objects to us after the same manner. In the *jaundice* every one knows that all things seem yellow. Is it not therefore highly probable those animals in whose eyes we discern a very different texture from that of ours, and whose bodies abound with different humors, do not see the same colors in every object that we do? From all which, should it not seem to follow that all colors are equally apparent, and that none of those which we perceive are really inherent in any outward object?

Hyl. It should.

Phil. The point will be past all doubt, if you consider that, in case colors were real properties or affections inherent in external bodies, they could admit of no alteration without some change

wrought in the very bodies themselves; but, is it not evident from what hath been said that, upon the use of microscopes, upon a change happening in the humors of the eye, or a variation of distance, without any manner of real alteration in the thing itself, the colors of any object are either changed, or totally disappear? Nay, all other circumstances remaining the same, change but the situation of some objects, and they shall present different colors to the eye. The same thing happens upon viewing an object in various degrees of light. And what is more known than that the same bodies appear differently colored by candlelight from what they do in the open day? Add to these the experiment of a prism which, separating the heterogeneous rays of light, alters the color of any object, and will cause the whitest to appear of a deep blue or red to the naked eye. And now tell me whether you are still of opinion that every body hath its true real color inhering in it; and, if you think it hath, I would fain know farther from you, what certain distance and position of the object, what peculiar texture and formation of the eye, what degree or kind of light is necessary for ascertaining that true color, and distinguishing it from apparent ones.

Hyl. I own myself entirely satisfied, that they are all equally apparent, and that there is no such thing as color really inhering in external bodies, but that it is altogether in the light. And what confirms me in this opinion is that in proportion to the light, colors are still more or less vivid; and if there be no light, then are there no colors perceived. Besides, allowing there are colors on external objects, yet, how is it possible for us to perceive them? For no external body affects the mind, unless it acts first on our organs of sense. But the only action of bodies is motion; and motion cannot be communicated otherwise than by impulse. A distant object therefore cannot act on the eye, nor consequently make itself or its properties perceivable to the soul. Whence it plainly follows that it is immediately some contiguous substance, which, operating on the eye, occasions a perception of colors: and such is light.

Phil. How! is light then a substance?

Hyl. I tell you, *Philonous,* external light is nothing but a thin fluid substance, whose minute particles being agitated with a brisk motion, and in various manners reflected from the different surfaces of outward objects to the eyes, communicate different motions to the optic nerves; which, being propagated to the brain, cause therein various impressions; and these are attended with the sensations of red, blue, yellow, &c.

Phil. It seems then the light doth no more than shake the optic nerves.

Hyl. Nothing else.

Phil. And, consequent to each particular motion of the nerves, the mind is affected with a sensation, which is some particular color.

Hyl. Right.

Phil. And these sensations have no existence without the mind.

Hyl. They have not.

Phil. How then do you affirm that colors are in the light; since by *light* you understand a corporeal substance external to the mind?

Hyl. Light and colors, as immedi- ately perceived by us, I grant cannot exist without the mind. But, in themselves they are only the motions and configurations of certain insensible particles of matter.

Phil. Colors, then, in the vulgar sense, or taken for the immediate objects of sight, cannot agree to any but a perceiving substance.

Hyl. That is what I say.

Phil. Well then, since you give up the point as to those sensible qualities which are alone thought colors by all mankind beside, you may hold what you please with regard to those invisible ones of the philosophers. It is not my business to dispute about them; only I would advise you to bethink yourself, whether, considering the inquiry we are upon, it be prudent for you to affirm—*the red and blue which we see are not real colors, but certain unknown motions and figures, which no man ever did or can see, are truly so.* Are not these shocking notions, and are not they subject to as many ridiculous inferences, as those you were obliged to renounce before in the case of sounds?

Hyl. I frankly own, *Philonous,* that it is in vain to stand out any longer. Colors, sounds, tastes, in a word all those termed *secondary qualities,* have certainly no existence without the mind. But, by this acknowledgment I must not be supposed to derogate anything from the reality of Matter or external objects; seeing it is no more than several philosophers maintain, who nevertheless are the farthest imaginable from denying Matter. For the clearer understanding of this, you must know sensible qualities are by philosophers divided into *primary* and *secondary*. The former are Extension, Figure, Solidity, Gravity, Motion, and Rest. And these they hold exist really in bodies. The latter are those above enumerated; or, briefly, all sensible qualities beside the Primary, which they assert are only so many sensations or ideas existing nowhere but in the mind. But all this, I doubt not, you are apprised of. For my part, I have been a long time sensible there was such an opinion current among philosophers, but was never thoroughly convinced of its truth until now.

Phil. You are still then of opinion that *extension* and *figures* are inherent in external unthinking substances?

Hyl. I am.

Phil. But what if the same arguments which are brought against Secondary Qualities will hold good against these also?

Hyl. Why then I shall be obliged to think, they too exist only in the mind.

Phil. Is it your opinion the very figure and extension which you perceive by sense exist in the outward object or material substance?

Hyl. It is.

Phil. Have all other animals as good grounds to think the same of the figure and extension which they see and feel?

Hyl. Without doubt, if they have any thought at all.

Phil. Answer me, *Hylas.* Think you the senses were bestowed upon all animals for their preservation and wellbeing in life? or were they given to men alone for this end?

Hyl. I make no question but they have the same use in all other animals.

Phil. If so, is it not necessary they should be enabled by them to perceive their own limbs, and those bodies which are capable of harming them?

Hyl. Certainly.

Phil. A mite therefore must be supposed to see his own foot, and things equal or even less than it, as bodies of some considerable dimension; though at the same time they appear to you scarce discernible, or at best as so many visible points?

Hyl. I cannot deny it.

Phil. And to creatures less than the mite they will seem yet larger?

Hyl. They will.

Phil. Insomuch that what you can hardly discern will to another extremely minute animal appear as some huge mountain?

Hyl. All this I grant.

Phil. Can one and the same thing be at the same time in itself of different dimensions?

Hyl. That were absurd to imagine.

Phil. But, from what you have laid down it follows that both the extension by you perceived, and that perceived by the mite itself, as likewise all those perceived by lesser animals, are each of them the true extension of the mite's foot; that is to say, by your own principles you are led into an absurdity.

Hyl. There seems to be some difficulty in the point.

Phil. Again, have you not acknowledged that no real inherent property of any object can be changed without some change in the thing itself?

Hyl. I have.

Phil. But, as we approach to or recede from an object, the visible extension varies, being at one distance ten or a hundred times greater than at another. Doth it not therefore follow from hence likewise that it is not really inherent in the object?

Hyl. I own I am at a loss what to think.

Phil. Your judgment will soon be determined, if you will venture to think as freely concerning this quality as you have done concerning the rest. Was it not admitted as a good argument, that neither heat nor cold was in the water, because it seemed warm to one hand and cold to the other?

Hyl. It was.

Phil. Is it not the very same reasoning to conclude there is no extension or figure in an object, because to one eye it shall seem little, smooth, and round, when at the same time it appears to the other, great, uneven, and angular?

Hyl. The very same. But does this latter fact ever happen?

Phil. You may at any time make the experiment, by looking with one eye bare, and with the other through a microscope.

Hyl. I know not how to maintain it, and yet I am loath to give up *extension,* I see so many odd consequences following upon such a concession.

Phil. Odd, say you? After the concessions already made, I hope you will stick at nothing for its oddness.[1] But, on the other hand, should it not seem very odd, if the general reasoning which includes all other sensible qualities did not also include extension? If it be allowed that no idea nor anything like an idea can exist in an unperceiving substance, then surely it follows that no figure or mode of extension,

[1] The remainder of the present paragraph was not contained in the first and second editions.

which we can either perceive or imagine, or have any idea of, can be really inherent in Matter; not to mention the peculiar difficulty there must be in conceiving a material substance, prior to and distinct from extension, to be the *substratum* of extension. Be the sensible quality what it will—figure, or sound, or color; it seems alike impossible it should subsist in that which doth not perceive it.

Hyl. I give up the point for the present, reserving still a right to retract my opinion, in case I shall hereafter discover any false step in my progress to it.

Phil. That is a right you cannot be denied. Figures and extensions being dispatched, we proceed next to *motion.* Can a real motion in any external body be at the same time both very swift and very slow?

Hyl. It cannot.

Phil. Is not the motion of a body swift in a reciprocal proportion to the time it takes up in describing any given space? Thus a body that describes a mile in an hour moves three times faster than it would in case it described only a mile in three hours.

Hyl. I agree with you.

Phil. And is not time measured by the succession of ideas in our minds?

Hyl. It is.

Phil. And is it not possible ideas should succeed one another twice as fast in your mind as they do in mine, or in that of some spirit of another kind?

Hyl. I own it.

Phil. Consequently, the same body may to another seem to perform its motion over any space in half the time that it doth to you. And the same reasoning will hold as to any other proportion:

that is to say, according to your principles (since the motions perceived are both really in the object) it is possible one and the same body shall be really moved the same way at once, both very swift and very slow. How is this consistent either with common sense, or with what you just now granted?

Hyl. I have nothing to say to it.

Phil. Then as for *solidity;* either you do not mean any sensible quality by that word, and so it is beside our inquiry: or if you do, it must be either hardness or resistance. But both the one and the other are plainly relative to our senses: it being evident that what seems hard to one animal may appear soft to another, who hath greater force and firmness of limbs. Nor is it less plain that the resistance I feel is not in the body.

Hyl. I own the very sensation of resistance, which is all you immediately perceive, is not in the *body,* but the cause of that sensation is.

Phil. But the causes of our sensations are not things immediately perceived, and therefore not sensible. This point I thought had been already determined.

Hyl. I own it was; but you will pardon me if I seem a little embarrassed: I know not how to quit my old notions.

Phil. To help you out, do but consider that if *extension* be once acknowledged to have no existence without the mind, the same must necessarily be granted of motion, solidity, and gravity —since they all evidently suppose extension. It is therefore superfluous to inquire particularly concerning each of them. In denying extension, you have denied them all to have any real existence.

Hyl. I wonder, *Philonous,* if what you say be true, why those philosophers who deny the Secondary Qualities any real existence, should yet attribute it to the Primary. If there is no difference between them, how can this be accounted for?

Phil. It is not my business to account for every opinion of the philosophers. But, among other reasons which may be assigned for this, it seems probable that pleasure and pain being rather annexed to the former than the latter may be one. Heat and cold, tastes and smells, have something more vividly pleasing or disagreeable than the ideas of extension, figure, and motion affect us with. And, it being too visibly absurd to hold that pain or pleasure can be in an unperceiving Substance, men are more easily weaned from believing the external existence of the Secondary than the Primary Qualities. You will be satisfied there is something in this, if you recollect the difference you made between an intense and more moderate degree of heat; allowing the one a real existence, while you denied it to the other. But, after all, there is no rational ground for that distinction; for, surely an indifferent sensation is as truly *a sensation* as one more pleasing or painful; and consequently should not any more than they be supposed to exist in an unthinking subject.

Hyl. It is just come into my head, *Philonous,* that I have somewhere heard of a distinction between absolute and sensible extension. Now, though it be acknowledged that *great* and *small,* consisting merely in the relation which other extended beings have to the parts of our own bodies, do not really inhere in the Substances themselves; yet nothing obliges us to hold the same with regard to *absolute extension,* which is something abstracted from *great* and *small,* from this or that particular magnitude or figure. So likewise as to motion; *swift* and *slow* are altogether relative to the succession of ideas in our own minds. But, it doth not follow, because those modifications of motion exist not without the mind, that therefore absolute motion abstracted from them doth not.

Phil. Pray what is it that distinguishes one motion, or one part of extension, from another? Is it not something sensible, as some degree of swiftness or slowness, some certain magnitude or figure peculiar to each?

Hyl. I think so.

Phil. These qualities, therefore, stripped of all sensible properties, are without all specific and numerical differences, as the schools call them.

Hyl. They are.

Phil. That is to say, they are extension in general, and motion in general.

Hyl. Let it be so.

Phil. But it is a universally received maxim that *Everything which exists is particular.* How then can motion in general, or extension in general, exist in any corporeal Substance?

Hyl. I will take time to solve your difficulty.

Phil. But I think the point may be speedily decided. Without doubt you can tell whether you are able to frame this or that idea. Now I am content to put our dispute on this issue. If you can frame in your thoughts a distinct abstract idea of motion or extension; divested of all those sensible modes, as

swift and slow, great and small, round and square, and the like, which are acknowledged to exist only in the mind, I will then yield the point you contend for. But, if you cannot, it will be unreasonable on your side to insist any longer upon what you have no notion of.

Hyl. To confess ingenuously, I cannot.

Phil. Can you even separate the ideas of extension and motion from the ideas of all those qualities which they who make the distinction term *secondary?*

Hyl. What! is it not an easy matter to consider extension and motion by themselves, abstracted from all other sensible qualities? Pray how do the mathematicians treat of them?

Phil. I acknowledge, *Hylas,* it is not difficult to form general propositions and reasonings about those qualities, without mentioning any other; and, in this sense, to consider or treat of them abstractedly. But, how doth it follow that, because I can pronounce the word *motion* by itself, I can form the idea of it in my mind exclusive of body? Or, because theorems may be made of extension and figures, without any mention of *great* or *small,* or any other sensible mode or quality, that therefore it is possible such an abstract idea of extension, without any particular size or figure, or sensible quality, should be distinctly formed, and apprehended by the mind? Mathematicians treat of quantity, without regarding what other sensible qualities it is attended with, as being altogether indifferent to their demonstrations. But, when laying aside the words, they contemplate the bare ideas, I believe you will find, they are not the pure abstracted ideas of extension.

Hyl. But what say you to *pure intellect?* May not abstracted ideas be framed by that faculty?

Phil. Since I cannot frame abstract ideas at all, it is plain I cannot frame them by the help of *pure intellect;* whatsoever faculty you understand by those words. Besides, not to inquire into the nature of pure intellect and its spiritual objects, as *virtue, reason, God,* or the like, thus much seems manifest, that sensible things are only to be perceived by sense, or represented by the imagination. Figures, therefore, and extension, being originally perceived by sense, do not belong to pure intellect: but, for your further satisfaction, try if you can frame the idea of any figure, abstracted from all particularities of size, or even from other sensible qualities.

Hyl. Let me think a little. . . . I do not find that I can.

Phil. And can you think it possible that should really exist in nature which implies a repugnancy in its conception?

Hyl. By no means.

Phil. Since therefore it is impossible even for the mind to disunite the ideas of extension and motion from all other sensible qualities, doth it not follow, that where the one exist there necessarily the other exist likewise?

Hyl. It should seem so.

Phil. Consequently, the very same arguments which you admitted as conclusive against the Secondary Qualities are, without any further application of force, against the Primary too. Besides, if you will trust your senses, is it not plain all sensible qualities coexist, or to them appear as being in the same place? Do they ever represent a motion, or figure, as being divested of all other visible and tangible qualities?

Hyl. You need say no more on this head. I am free to own, if there be no secret error or oversight in our proceedings hitherto, that all sensible qualities are alike to be denied existence without the mind. But, my fear is that I have been too liberal in my former concessions, or overlooked some fallacy or other. In short, I did not take time to think.

Phil. For that matter, *Hylas,* you may take what time you please in reviewing the progress of our inquiry. You are at liberty to recover any slips you might have made, or offer whatever you have omitted which makes for your first opinion.

Hyl. One great oversight I take to be this—that I did not sufficiently distinguish the *object* from the *sensation.* Now, though this latter may not exist without the mind, yet it will not thence follow that the former cannot.

Phil. What object do you mean? The object of the senses?

Hyl. The same.

Phil. It is then immediately perceived?

Hyl. Right.

Phil. Make me to understand the difference between what is immediately perceived, and a sensation.

Hyl. The sensation I take to be an act of the mind perceiving; besides which, there is something perceived; and this I call the *object.* For example, there is red and yellow on that tulip. But then the act of perceiving those colors is in me only, and not in the tulip.

Phil. What tulip do you speak of? Is it that which you see?

Hyl. The same.

Phil. And what do you see beside color, figure, and extension?

Hyl. Nothing.

Phil. What you would say then is that the red and yellow are coexistent with the extension; is it not?

Hyl. That is not all; I would say they have a real existence without the mind, in some unthinking substance.

Phil. That the colors are really in the tulip which I see is manifest. Neither can it be denied that this tulip may exist independent of your mind or mine; but, that any immediate object of the senses—that is, any idea, or combination of ideas—should exist in an unthinking substance, or exterior to all minds, is in itself an evident contradiction. Nor can I imagine how this follows from what you said just now, to wit, that the red and yellow were on the tulip *you saw,* since you do not pretend to *see* that unthinking substance.

Hyl. You have an artful way, *Philonous,* of diverting our inquiry from the subject.

Phil. I see you have no mind to be pressed that way. To return then to your distinction between *sensation* and *object;* if I take you right, you distinguish in every perception two things, the one an action of the mind, the other not.

Hyl. True.

Phil. And this action cannot exist in, or belong to, any unthinking thing; but, whatever beside is implied in a perception may?

Hyl. That is my meaning.

Phil. So that if there was a perception without any act of the mind, it were possible such a perception should exist in an unthinking substance?

Hyl. I grant it. But it is impossible there should be such a perception.

Phil. When is the mind said to be active?

Hyl. When it produces, puts an end to, or changes, anything.

Phil. Can the mind produce, discontinue, or change anything, but by an act of the will?

Hyl. It cannot.

Phil. The mind therefore is to be accounted *active* in its perceptions so far forth as *volition* is included in them?

Hyl. It is.

Phil. In plucking this flower I am active; because I do it by the motion of my hand, which was consequent upon my volition; so likewise in applying it to my nose. But is either of these smelling?

Hyl. No.

Phil. I act too in drawing the air through my nose; because my breathing so rather than otherwise is the effect of my volition. But neither can this be called *smelling:* for, if it were, I should smell every time I breathed in that manner?

Hyl. True.

Phil. Smelling then is somewhat consequent to all this?

Hyl. It is.

Phil. But I do not find my will concerned any further. Whatever more there is—as that I perceive such a particular smell, or any smell at all—this is independent of my will, and therein I am altogether passive. Do you find it otherwise with you, *Hylas?*

Hyl. No, the very same.

Phil. Then, as to seeing, is it not in your power to open your eyes, or keep them shut; to turn them this or that way?

Hyl. Without doubt.

Phil. But, doth it in like manner depend on your will that in looking on this flower you perceive *white* rather than any other color? Or, directing your open eyes towards yonder part of the heaven, can you avoid seeing the sun? Or is light or darkness the effect of your volition?

Hyl. No certainly.

Phil. You are then in these respects altogether passive?

Hyl. I am.

Phil. Tell me now, whether *seeing* consists in perceiving light and colors, or in opening and turning the eyes?

Hyl. Without doubt, in the former.

Phil. Since therefore you are in the very perception of light and colors altogether passive, what is become of that action you were speaking of as an ingredient in every sensation? And, doth it not follow from your own concessions, that the perception of light and colors, including no action in it, may exist in an unperceiving substance? And is not this a plain contradiction?

Hyl. I know not what to think of it.

Phil. Besides, since you distinguish the *active* and *passive* in every perception, you must do it in that of pain. But how is it possible that pain, be it as little active as you please, should exist in an unperceiving substance? In short, do but consider the point, and then confess ingenuously, whether light and colors, tastes, sounds, &c., are not all equally passions or sensations in the soul. You may indeed call them *external objects,* and give them in words what subsistence you please. But, examine your own thoughts, and then tell me whether it be not as I say?

Hyl. I acknowledge, *Philonous,* that, upon a fair observation of what passes in my mind, I can discover nothing else but that I am a thinking being, affected with variety of sensations; neither is it possible to conceive how a sensation should exist in an unperceiving substance. But then, on the other hand, when I look on sensible things in a different view, considering them as so many modes and qualities, I find it necessary to suppose a material *substratum,* without which they cannot be conceived to exist.

Phil. Material substratum call you it? Pray, by which of your senses came you acquainted with that being?

Hyl. It is not itself sensible; its modes and qualities only being perceived by the senses.

Phil. I presume then it was by reflection and reason you obtained the idea of it?

Hyl. I do not pretend to any proper positive idea of it. However, I conclude it exists, because qualities cannot be conceived to exist without a support.

Phil. It seems then you have only a relative notion of it, or that you conceive it not otherwise than by conceiving the relation it bears to sensible qualities?

Hyl. Right.

Phil. Be pleased therefore to let me know wherein that relation consists.

Hyl. Is it not sufficiently expressed in the term *substratum* or *substance?*

Phil. If so, the word *substratum* should import that it is spread under the sensible qualities or accidents?

Hyl. True.

Phil. And consequently under extension?

Hyl. I own it.

Phil. It is therefore somewhat in its own nature entirely distinct from extension?

Hyl. I tell you, extension is only a mode, and Matter is something that supports modes. And is it not evident the thing supported is different from the thing supporting?

Phil. So that something distinct from, and exclusive of, extension is supposed to be the *substratum* of extension?

Hyl. Just so.

Phil. Answer me, *Hylas.* Can a thing be spread without extension? or is not the idea of extension necessarily included in *spreading?*

Hyl. It is.

Phil. Whatsoever therefore you suppose spread under anything must have in itself an extension distinct from the extension of that thing under which it is spread?

Hyl. It must.

Phil. Consequently, every corporeal substance being the *substratum* of extension must have in itself another extension, by which it is qualified to be a *substratum* and so on to infinity? And I ask whether this be not absurd in itself, and repugnant to what you granted just now, to wit, that the *substratum* was something distinct from and exclusive of extension?

Hyl. Aye, but, *Philonous,* you take me wrong. I do not mean that Matter is *spread* in a gross literal sense under extension. The word *substratum* is used only to express in general the same thing with *substance.*

Phil. Well then, let us examine the relation implied in the term *substance.* Is it not that it stands under accidents?

Hyl. The very same.

Phil. But, that one thing may stand under or support another, must it not be extended?

Hyl. It must.

Phil. Is not therefore this supposition liable to the same absurdity with the former?

Hyl. You still take things in a strict literal sense; that is not fair, *Philonous.*

Phil. I am not for imposing any sense on your words: you are at liberty to explain them as you please. Only, I beseech you, make me understand something by them. You tell me Matter supports or stands under accidents. How! is it as your legs support your body?

Hyl. No; that is the literal sense.

Phil. Pray let me know any sense, literal or not literal, that you understand it in. . . . How long must I wait for an answer, *Hylas?*

Hyl. I declare I know not what to say. I once thought I understood well enough what was meant by Matter's supporting accidents. But now, the more I think on it the less can I comprehend it; in short I find that I know nothing of it.

Phil. It seems then you have no idea at all, neither relative nor positive, of Matter; you know neither what it is in itself, nor what relation it bears to accidents?

Hyl. I acknowledge it.

Phil. And yet you asserted that you could not conceive how qualities or accidents should really exist, without conceiving at the same time a material support of them?

Hyl. I did.

Phil. That is to say, when you conceive the real existence of qualities, you do withal conceive something which you cannot conceive?

Hyl. It was wrong I own. But still I fear there is some fallacy or other. Pray what think you of this? It is just come into my head that the ground of all our mistake lies in your treating of each quality by itself. Now, I grant that each quality cannot singly subsist without the mind. Color cannot without extension, neither can figure without some other sensible quality. But, as the several qualities united or blended together form entire sensible things, nothing hinders why such things may not be supposed to exist without the mind.

Phil. Either, *Hylas,* you are jesting, or have a very bad memory. Though indeed we went through all the qualities by name one after another, yet my arguments, or rather your concessions, nowhere tended to prove that the Secondary Qualities did not subsist each alone by itself; but, that they were not *at all* without the mind. Indeed, in treating of figure and motion we concluded they could not exist without the mind, because it was impossible even in thought to separate them from all secondary qualities, so as to conceive them existing by themselves. But then this was not the only argument made use of upon that occasion. But (to pass by all that hath been hitherto said, and

reckon it for nothing, if you will have it so) I am content to put the whole upon this issue. If you can conceive it possible for any mixture or combination of qualities, or any sensible object whatever, to exist without the mind, then I will grant it actually to be so.

Hyl. If it comes to that the point will soon be decided. What more easy than to conceive a tree or house existing by itself, independent of, and unperceived by, any mind whatsoever? I do at this present time conceive them existing after that manner.

Phil. How say you, *Hylas,* can you see a thing which is at the same time unseen?

Hyl. No, that were a contradiction.

Phil. Is it not as great a contradiction to talk of *conceiving* a thing which is *unconceived?*

Hyl. It is.

Phil. The tree or house therefore which you think of is conceived by you?

Hyl. How should it be otherwise?

Phil. And what is conceived is surely in the mind?

Hyl. Without question, that which is conceived is in the mind.

Phil. How then came you to say, you conceived a house or tree existing independent and out of all minds whatsoever?

Hyl. That was I own an oversight; but stay, let me consider what led me into it.—It is a pleasant mistake enough. As I was thinking of a tree in a solitary place where no one was present to see it, methought that was to conceive a tree as existing unperceived or unthought of—not considering that I myself conceived it all the while. But now

I plainly see that all I can do is to frame ideas in my own mind. I may indeed conceive in my own thoughts the idea of a tree, or a house, or a mountain, but that is all. And this is far from proving that I can conceive them *existing out of the minds of all Spirits*.

Phil. You acknowledge then that you cannot possibly conceive how any one corporeal sensible thing should exist otherwise than in a mind?

Hyl. I do.

Phil. And yet you will earnestly contend for the truth of that which you cannot so much as conceive?

Hyl. I profess I know not what to think; but still there are some scruples remain with me. Is it not certain I *see* things at a distance? Do we not perceive the stars and moon, for example, to be a great way off? Is not this, I say, manifest to the senses?

Phil. Do you not in a dream too perceive those or the like objects?

Hyl. I do.

Phil. And have they not then the same appearance of being distant?

Hyl. They have.

Phil. But you do not thence conclude the apparitions in a dream to be without the mind?

Hyl. By no means.

Phil. You ought not therefore to conclude that sensible objects are without the mind, from their appearance or manner wherein they are perceived.

Hyl. I acknowledge it. But doth not my sense deceive me in those cases?

Phil. By no means. The idea or thing which you immediately perceive, neither sense nor reason informs you that it actually exists without the mind. By sense you only know that you are affected with such certain sensations of light and colors, &c. And these you will not say are without the mind.

Hyl. True: but, beside all that, do you not think the sight suggests something of *outness* or *distance*?

Phil. Upon approaching a distant object, do the visible size and figure change perpetually, or do they appear the same at all distances?

Hyl. They are in a continual change.

Phil. Sight therefore doth not suggest or any way inform you that the visible object you immediately perceive exists at a distance,[2] or will be perceived when you advance farther onward; there being a continued series of visible objects succeeding each other during the whole time of your approach.

Hyl. It doth not; but still I know, upon seeing an object, what object I shall perceive after having passed over a certain distance: no matter whether it be exactly the same or no: there is still something of distance suggested in the case.

Phil. Good *Hylas*, do but reflect a little on the point, and then tell me whether there be any more in it than this:—From the ideas you actually perceive by sight, you have by experience learned to collect what other ideas you will (according to the standing order of nature) be affected with, after such a certain succession of time and motion.

Hyl. Upon the whole, I take it to be nothing else.

Phil. Now, is it not plain that if we suppose a man born blind was on a sudden made to see, he could at first

2 See the "Essay towards a New Theory of Vision," and its "Vindication."—AUTHOR, 1734.

have no experience of what may be suggested by sight?

Hyl. It is.

Phil. He would not then, according to you, have any notion of distance annexed to the things he saw; but would take them for a new set of sensations existing only in his mind?

Hyl. It is undeniable.

Phil. But, to make it still more plain: is not *distance* a line turned endwise to the eye?

Hyl. It is.

Phil. And can a line so situated be perceived by sight?

Hyl. It cannot.

Phil. Doth it not therefore follow that distance is not properly and immediately perceived by sight?

Hyl. It should seem so.

Phil. Again, is it your opinion that colors are at a distance?

Hyl. It must be acknowledged they are only in the mind.

Phil. But do not colors appear to the eye as coexisting in the same place with extension and figures?

Hyl. They do.

Phil. How can you then conclude from sight that figures exist without, when you acknowledge colors do not; the sensible appearance being the very same with regard to both?

Hyl. I know not what to answer.

Phil. But, allowing that distance was truly and immediately perceived by the mind, yet it would not thence follow it existed out of the mind. For, whatever is immediately perceived is an idea: and can any *idea* exist out of the mind?

Hyl. To suppose that were absurd: but, inform me, *Philonous,* can we perceive or know nothing beside our ideas?

Phil. As for the rational deducing of causes from effects, that is beside our inquiry. And, by the senses you can best tell whether you perceive anything which is not immediately perceived. And I ask you, whether the things immediately perceived are other than your own sensations or ideas? You have indeed more than once, in the course of this conversation, declared yourself on those points; but you seem, by this last question, to have departed from what you then thought.

Hyl. To speak the truth, *Philonous,* I think there are two kinds of objects:— the one perceived immediately, which are likewise called *ideas;* the other are real things or external objects, perceived by the mediation of ideas, which are their images and representations. Now, I own ideas do not exist without the mind; but the latter sort of objects do. I am sorry I did not think of this distinction sooner; it would probably have cut short your discourse.

Phil. Are those external objects perceived by sense, or by some other faculty?

Hyl. They are perceived by sense.

Phil. How! is there anything perceived by sense which is not immediately perceived?

Hyl. Yes, *Philonous,* in some sort there is. For example, when I look on a picture or statue of Julius Cæsar, I may be said after a manner to perceive him (though not immediately) by my senses.

Phil. It seems then you will have our ideas, which alone are immediately perceived, to be pictures of external things: and that these also are perceived by sense, inasmuch as they have a conformity or resemblance to our ideas?

Hyl. That is my meaning.

Phil. And, in the same way that Julius Cæsar, in himself invisible, is nevertheless perceived by sight; real things, in themselves imperceptible, are perceived by sense.

Hyl. In the very same.

Phil. Tell me, *Hylas,* when you behold the picture of Julius Cæsar, do you see with your eyes any more than some colors and figures, with a certain symmetry and composition of the whole?

Hyl. Nothing else.

Phil. And would not a man who had never known anything of Julius Cæsar see as much?

Hyl. He would.

Phil. Consequently he hath his sight, and the use of it, in as perfect a degree as you?

Hyl. I agree with you.

Phil. Whence comes it then that your thoughts are directed to the Roman emperor, and his are not? This cannot proceed from the sensations or ideas of sense by you then perceived; since you acknowledge you have no advantage over him in that respect. It should seem therefore to proceed from reason and memory: should it not?

Hyl. It should.

Phil. Consequently, it will not follow from that instance that anything is perceived by sense which is not immediately perceived. Though I grant we may, in one acceptation, be said to perceive sensible things mediately by sense—that is, when, from a frequently perceived connection, the immediate perception of ideas by one sense sug-

gest to the mind others, perhaps belonging to another sense, which are wont to be connected with them. For instance, when I hear a coach drive along the streets, immediately I perceive only the sound; but, from the experience I have had that such a sound is connected with a coach, I am said to hear the coach. It is nevertheless evident that, in truth and strictness, nothing can be *heard* but *sound;* and the coach is not then properly perceived by sense, but suggested from experience. So likewise when we are said to see a red-hot bar of iron; the solidity and heat of the iron are not the objects of sight, but suggested to the imagaination by the color and figure which are properly perceived by that sense. In short, those things alone are actually and strictly perceived by any sense, which would have been perceived in case that same sense had then been first conferred on us. As for other things, it is plain they are only suggested to the mind by experience, grounded on former perceptions. But, to return to your comparison of Cæsar's picture, it is plain, if you keep to that, you must hold the real things or archetypes of our ideas are not perceived by sense, but by some internal faculty of the soul, as reason or memory. I would therefore fain know what arguments you can draw from reason for the existence of what you call *real things* or *material objects.* Or, whether you remember to have seen them formerly as they are in themselves; or, if you have heard or read of any one that did.

Hyl. I see, *Philonous,* you are disposed to raillery; but that will never convince me.

Phil. My aim is only to learn from you the way to come at the knowledge of *material beings.* Whatever we perceive is perceived immediately or mediately: by sense; or by reason and reflection. But, as you have excluded sense, pray show me what reason you have to believe their existence; or what *medium* you can possibly make use of to prove it, either to mine or your own understanding.

Hyl. To deal ingenuously, *Philonous,* now I consider the point, I do not find I can give you any good reason for it. But, thus much seems pretty plain, that it is at least possible such things may really exist. And, as long as there is no absurdity in supposing them, I am resolved to believe as I did, till you bring good reasons to the contrary.

Phil. What! is it come to this, that you only believe the existence of material objects, and that your belief is founded barely on the possibility of its being true? Then you will have me bring reasons against it: though another would think it reasonable the proof should lie on him who holds the affirmative. And, after all, this very point which you are now resolved to maintain, without any reason, is in effect what you have more than once during this discourse seen good reason to give up. But, to pass over all this; if I understand you rightly, you say our ideas do not exist without the mind; but that they are copies, images, or representations, of certain originals that do?

Hyl. You take me right.

Phil. They are then like external things?

Hyl. They are.

Phil. Have those things a stable and permanent nature, independent of our senses; or are they in a perpetual change, upon our producing any motions in our bodies, suspending, exerting, or altering, our faculties or organs of sense?

Hyl. Real things, it is plain, have a fixed and real nature, which remains the same notwithstanding any change in our senses, or in the posture and motion of our bodies; which indeed may affect the ideas in our minds, but it were absurd to think they had the same effect on things existing without the mind.

Phil. How then is it possible that things perpetually fleeting and variable as our ideas should be copies or images of anything fixed and constant? Or, in other words, since all sensible qualities, as size, figure, color, &c., that is, our ideas, are continually changing upon every alteration in the distance, medium, or instruments of sensation; how can any determinate material objects be properly represented or painted forth by several distinct things, each of which is so different from and unlike the rest? Or, if you say it resembles some one only of our ideas, how shall we be able to distinguish the true copy from all the false ones?

Hyl. I profess, *Philonous,* I am at a loss. I know not what to say to this.

Phil. But neither is this all. Which are material objects in themselves—perceptible or imperceptible?

Hyl. Properly and immediately nothing can be perceived but ideas. All material things, therefore, are in themselves insensible, and to be perceived only by our ideas.

Phil. Ideas then are sensible, and their archetypes or originals insensible?

Hyl. Right.

Phil. But how can that which is sensible be like that which is insensible? Can a real thing, in itself *invisible,* be like a *color;* or a real thing, which is not *audible,* be like a *sound?* In a word, can anything be like a sensation or idea, but another sensation or idea?

Hyl. I must own, I think not.

Phil. Is it possible there should be any doubt on the point? Do you not perfectly know your own ideas?

Hyl. I know them perfectly; since what I do not perceive or know can be no part of my idea.

Phil. Consider, therefore, and examine them, and then tell me if there be anything in them which can exist without the mind? or if you can conceive anything like them existing without the mind?

Hyl. Upon inquiry, I find it is impossible for me to conceive or understand how anything but an idea can be like an idea. And it is most evident that *no idea can exist without the mind.*

Phil. You are therefore, by our principles, forced to deny the reality of sensible things; since you made it to consist in an absolute existence exterior to the mind. That is to say, you are a downright sceptic. So I have gained my point, which was to show your principles led to Scepticism.

Hyl. For the present I am, if not entirely convinced, at least silenced.

Phil. I would fain know what more you would require in order to a perfect conviction. Have you not had the liberty of explaining yourself all manner of ways? Were any little slips in discourse laid hold and insisted on? Or were you not allowed to retract or reinforce anything you had offered, as best served your purpose? Hath not everything you could say been heard and examined with all the fairness imaginable? In a word, have you not in every point been convinced out of your own mouth? and, if you can at present discover any flaw in any of your former concessions, or think of any remaining subterfuge, any new distinction, color, or comment whatsoever, why do you not produce it?

Hyl. A little patience, *Philonous.* I am at present so amazed to see myself ensnared, and as it were imprisoned in the labyrinths you have drawn me into, that on the sudden it cannot be expected I should find my way out. You must give me time to look about me and recollect myself?

Phil. Hark; is not this the college bell?

Hyl. It rings for prayers.

Phil. We will go in then, if you please, and meet here again tomorrow morning. In the meantime, you may employ your thoughts on this morning's discourse, and try if you can find any fallacy in it, or invent any new means to extricate yourself.

Hyl. Agreed.

The Second Dialogue

Hylas. I beg your pardon, *Philonous,* for not meeting you sooner. All this morning my head was so filled with our late conversation that I had not leisure to think of the time of the day, or indeed of anything else.

Philonous. I am glad you were so

intent upon it, in hopes if there were any mistakes in your concessions, or fallacies in my reasonings from them, you will now discover them to me.

Hyl. I assure you I have done nothing ever since I saw you but search after mistakes and fallacies, and, with that view, have minutely examined the whole series of yesterday's discourse: but all in vain, for the notions it led me into, upon review, appear still more clear and evident; and, the more I consider them, the more irresistibly do they force my assent.

Phil. And is not this, think you, a sign that they are genuine, that they proceed from nature, and are conformable to right reason? Truth and beauty are in this alike, that the strictest survey sets them both off to advantage; while the false luster of error and disguise cannot endure being reviewed, or too nearly inspected.

Hyl. I own there is a great deal in what you say. Nor can any one be more entirely satisfied of the truth of those odd consequences, so long as I have in view the reasonings that lead to them. But, when these are out of my thoughts, there seems, on the other hand, something so satisfactory, so natural and intelligible, in the modern way of explaining things that, I profess, I know not how to reject it.

Phil. I know not what way you mean.

Hyl. I mean the way of accounting for our sensations or ideas.

Phil. How is that?

Hyl. It is supposed the soul makes her residence in some part of the brain, from which the nerves take their rise, and are thence extended to all parts of the body; and that outward objects, by the different impressions they make on the organs of sense, communicate certain vibrative motions to the nerves; and these being filled with spirits propagate them to the brain or seat of the soul, which, according to the various impressions or traces thereby made in the brain, is variously affected with ideas.

Phil. And call you this an explication of the manner whereby we are effected with ideas?

Hyl. Why not, *Philonous;* have you anything to object against it?

Phil. I would first know whether I rightly understand your hypothesis. You make certain traces in the brain to be the causes or occasions of our ideas. Pray tell me whether by the *brain* you mean any sensible thing.

Hyl. What else think you I could mean?

Phil. Sensible things are all immediately perceivable; and those things which are immediately perceivable are ideas; and these exist only in the mind. Thus much you have, if I mistake not, long since agreed to.

Hyl. I do not deny it.

Phil. The brain therefore you speak of, being a sensible thing, exists only in the mind. Now, I would fain know whether you think it reasonable to suppose that one idea or thing existing in the mind occasions all other ideas. And, if you think so, pray how do you account for the origin of that primary idea or brain itself?

Hyl. I do not explain the origin of our ideas by that brain which is perceivable to sense, this being itself only a combination of sensible ideas, but by another which I imagine.

Phil. But are not things imagined as truly *in the mind* as things perceived?

Hyl. I must confess they are.

Phil. It comes, therefore, to the same thing; and you have been all this while accounting for ideas by certain motions or impressions of the brain, that is, by some alterations in an idea, whether sensible or imaginable it matters not.

Hyl. I begin to suspect my hypothesis.

Phil. Besides spirits, all that we know or conceive are our own ideas. When, therefore, you say all ideas are occasioned by impressions in the brain, do you conceive this brain or no? If you do, then you talk of ideas imprinted in an idea causing that same idea, which is absurd. If you do not conceive it, you talk unintelligibly, instead of forming a reasonable hypothesis.

Hyl. I now clearly see it was a mere dream. There is nothing in it.

Phil. You need not be much concerned at it; for after all, this way of explaining things, as you called it, could never have satisfied any reasonable man. What connection is there between a motion in the nerves, and the sensations of sound or color in the mind? Or how is it possible these should be the effect of that?

Hyl. But I could never think it had so little in it as now it seems to have.

Phil. Well then, are you at length satisfied that no sensible things have a real existence; and that you are in truth an arrant *sceptic?*

Hyl. It is too plain to be denied.

Phil. Look! are not the fields covered with a delightful verdure? Is there not something in the woods and groves, in the rivers and clear springs, that soothes, that delights, that transports the soul? At the prospect of the wide and deep ocean, or some huge mountain whose top is lost in the clouds, or of an old gloomy forest, are not our minds filled with a pleasing horror? Even in rocks and deserts is there not an agreeable wildness? How sincere a pleasure is it to behold the natural beauties of the earth! To preserve and renew our relish for them, is not the veil of night alternately drawn over her face, and doth she not change her dress with the seasons? How aptly are the elements disposed! What variety and use in the meanest productions of nature! What delicacy, what beauty, what contrivance, in animal and vegetable bodies! How exquisitely are all things suited, as well to their particular ends, as to constitute opposite parts of the whole! And, while they mutually aid and support, do they not also set off and illustrate each other? Raise now your thoughts from this ball of earth to all those glorious luminaries that adorn the high arch of heaven. The motion and situation of the planets, are they not admirable for use and order? Were those (miscalled *erratic*) globes ever known to stray, in their repeated journeys through the pathless void? Do they not measure areas round the sun ever proportioned to the times? So fixed, so immutable are the laws by which the unseen Author of nature actuates the universe. How vivid and radiant is the luster of the fixed stars! How magnificent and rich that negligent profusion with which they appear to be scattered throughout the whole azure vault! Yet, if you take the telescope, it brings into your sight a new host of stars that escape the naked eye. Here they seem contiguous and minute, but to a nearer view immense orbs of light at various distances, far sunk in the abyss of space. Now you must call imagination to your aid. The feeble narrow sense cannot descry innumerable worlds revolving round the central fires; and in those worlds the energy of an all-perfect Mind displayed in endless forms. But, neither sense nor imagination are big enough to comprehend the boundless extent, with all its glittering furniture. Though the laboring mind exert and strain each power to its utmost reach, there still stands out ungrasped a surplusage immeasurable. Yet all the vast bodies that compose this mighty frame, how distant and remote soever, are by some secret mechanism, some divine art and force, linked in a mutual dependence and intercourse with each other, even with this earth, which was almost slipped from my thoughts and lost in the crowd of worlds. Is not the whole system immense, beautiful, glorious beyond expression and beyond thought! What treatment, then, do those philosophers deserve, who would deprive these noble and delightful scenes of all reality? How should those Principles be entertained that lead us to think all the visible beauty of the creation a false imaginary glare? To be plain, can you expect this Scepticism of yours will not be thought extravagantly absurd by all men of sense?

Hyl. Other men may think as they please; but for your part you have nothing to reproach me with. My comfort is, you are as much a sceptic as I am.

Phil. There, *Hylas,* I must beg leave to differ from you.

Hyl. What! have you all along agreed to the premises, and do you now deny the conclusion, and leave me to maintain those paradoxes by myself which you led me into? This surely is not fair.

Phil. I deny that I agreed with you in those notions that led to Scepticism. You indeed said the *reality* of sensible things consisted in an *absolute existence* out of the minds of spirits, or distinct from their being perceived. And, pursuant to this notion of reality, you are obliged to deny sensible things any real existence: that is, according to your own definition, you profess yourself a sceptic. But I neither said nor thought the reality of sensible things was to be defined after that manner. To me it is evident, for the reasons you allow of, that sensible things cannot exist otherwise than in a mind or spirit. Whence I conclude, not that they have no real existence, but that, seeing they depend not on my thought, and have an existence distinct from being perceived by me, *there must be some other mind wherein they exist.* As sure, therefore, as the sensible world really exists, so sure is there an infinite omnipresent Spirit, who contains and supports it.

Hyl. What! this is no more than I and all Christians hold; nay, and all others too who believe there is a God, and that He knows and comprehends all things.

Phil. Aye, but here lies the difference. Men commonly believe that all things are known or perceived by God, because they believe the being of a God; whereas I, on the other side, immediately and necessarily conclude the being of a God, because all sensible things must be perceived by him. . . . It is evident that the things I perceive are my own ideas, and that no idea can exist unless it be in a mind. Nor is it less plain that these ideas or things by me perceived, either themselves or their archetypes, exist independently of my mind; since I know myself not to be their author, it being out of my power to determine at pleasure what particular ideas I shall be affected with upon opening my eyes or ears. They must therefore exist in some other mind, whose will it is they should be exhibited to me. The things, I say, immediately perceived are ideas or sensations, call them which you will. But how can any idea or sensation exist in, or be produced by, anything but a mind or spirit? This indeed is inconceivable; and to assert that which is inconceivable is to talk nonsense: is it not?

Hyl. Without doubt.

Phil. But, on the other hand, it is very conceivable that they should exist in and be produced by a Spirit; since this is no more than I daily experience in myself, inasmuch as I perceive numberless ideas; and, by an act of my will, can form a great variety of them; and raise them up in my imagination: though, it must be confessed, these creatures of the fancy are not altogether so distinct, so strong, vivid, and permanent, as those perceived by my senses, which latter are called *real things.* From all which I conclude, *there is a Mind which affects me every moment with all the sensible impressions I perceive.* And, from the variety, order, and manner of these, I conclude the Author of them to be *wise, powerful, and good, and beyond comprehension.* . . .

[*The Third Dialogue is omitted.*]

COMMENT

Berkeley and Locke

The speakers in Berkeley's *Dialogues* are Hylas, a "materialist," and Philonous, who represents the point of view of the author. Physical objects, according to Philonous, have no existence independent of thought. The whole universe is made up of minds and the immaterial objects of minds, and nothing more. This doctrine, which is called "idealism" (idea-ism, with the "l" inserted for the sake of euphony), may strike beginning students as exceedingly odd; but it is quite possible that the Universe *is* very odd, and the arguments for idealism are strong. Since Berkeley's presentation of these arguments is lucid, I shall not summarize them except to point out their connection with Locke, whom Berkeley regarded as his philosophical opponent. This relation can be summarized under the following headings:

1. THE INFERENCE TO OBJECTS HAVING ONLY PRIMARY QUALITIES. Both Locke and Berkeley rejected the naïve view that our ideas literally picture material things as they are. They agree that our impressions ("ideas") are too variable and rela-

tive to be faithful copies of independently existing objects. Colored objects change their hue as we approach them; the "same" food will taste different to different people or to the same person at different times; the temperature of a room will seem more or less warm depending upon the condition of the perceiver. By such examples, which we need not multiply, Berkeley shows that things appear to have extremely variable and even incompatible qualities. But a physical thing cannot at one and the same time have opposite qualities, such as heat and cold, or be so changeable. Hence, we must conclude that our ideas are not exact copies of external things.

Locke and Descartes conceded that "secondary qualities"—colors, odors, sounds, tastes, and tactile qualities—are not actually inherent in physical objects. Were I in the dark, for example, a peach would have no color; if I did not bite into it, the taste would not exist; if I did not feel it, it would not be soft, etc. All such qualities are like the tickle of a feather, which is not *in* the feather but in one's reaction to it. So, likewise, colors, odors, sounds, tastes, and touch impressions are not in the external things but in our mental reactions to these things. Physical objects emit "particles" which, by impact upon the nervous system, *cause* the ideas of secondary qualities to arise in the mind. But, according to the same philosophers, there also are "primary qualities"—extension, figure, motion, rest, solidity, and number—which physical science requires to describe the external world. These qualities exist in the physical things, whether we perceive them or not.

This distinction between primary and secondary qualities was made for two main reasons. First, the secondary qualities are so variable and fluctuating that they cannot be considered objective, whereas the primary qualities are relatively stable and fixed. Secondly, the laws of the physical science of the day were framed in terms of primary but not secondary qualities and therefore seemed to imply the objectivity of the former but not of the latter. This impression was reinforced by scientific explanation of perception, which described color, sound, odor, etc., as psychological reactions to external motions.

Berkeley offers a three-pronged rebuttal to this separation of primary and secondary qualities. First, he contends that primary qualities are quite as relative and mind-dependent as secondary qualities. A tower looks tiny when seen from a distance but large at close quarters; the shape of a table top appears to change as perspectives change; a nut that seems solid to a child seems relatively fragile to a blacksmith; a tree that appears to be in motion as we sail by in a boat seems stationary when we drop anchor. Thus primary qualities, as directly perceived, are also relative to the perceiver.

Secondly, the supposition that our *ideas* of the primary qualities resemble the physical things can never be put to the test. According to Locke's own theory, nothing is available in experience except our ideas; matter is never experienced. Hence there is no way of comparing our ideas with material objects in order to judge whether the latter in any way correspond to the former. If all we ever perceive are the effects produced in our minds, then the supposed cause is imperceptible and unknowable. To assume that it has a certain sort of nature—that it possesses primary qualities, for example, but not secondary—is mere guesswork.

Thirdly, the primary qualities cannot exist all by themselves. There can be no motion without something to be moved, no extension without something to be extended, no shape without something to be shaped, no number without something to be numbered, no solidity without something to be solid. Actually, the primary qualities are known only in inextricable relation to secondary qualities. The sensation of extension, for example, comes to us only by way of our sight and touch. When it comes by sight, it is invariably conjoined with sense data of color; when it comes by touch, it is invariably conjoined with tactile sense data. Bare extension, disengaged from all secondary qualities, is never experienced, and we cannot even imagine what it would be like to experience it. We cannot make a physical world out of such mere abstractions.

2. THE INFERENCE TO SUBSTANCE. Locke distinguished between the qualities of an object and the underlying substance in which the qualities supposedly inhere. After we have taken note of all the colors, shapes, motions, textures, odors, or other qualities, whether primary or secondary, that might conceivably characterize an object, there remains something more—an unexperienced substratum which "supports" whatever qualities are finally deemed to be objective. This substance is an indefinite, indefinable something of which we can form no positive idea. Unlike Aristotle's "substance," which is conceived to be the more permanent core of *experienceable* qualities, Locke's substance turns out to be no more than an unknown *x*, a deeper and hidden nature, which underlies all assignable properties of the object. Nevertheless, Locke believed that this mysterious substratum must exist to hold the qualities together and give them necessary support.

Berkeley emphatically rejects this conception. Since Locke's substance is indefinable and inexperienceable, there is no way of verifying its existence. Obviously there can be no evidence for something that, by its very definition, is absolutely unknown and unknowable.

Berkeley also finds that the notion of *support*, which the substance supposedly gives to the qualities, is very unclear: "It is evident *support* cannot be taken in its usual or literal sense, as when we say that pillars support a building. In what sense therefore must it be taken? For my part, I am not able to discover any sense at all that can be applicable to it." Such ill-defined concepts can win no credence from a critical thinker.

Berkeley also objects to the concept of "substance" because of its abstractness. In the Introduction to *Principles of Human Knowledge*, he launches a determined attack against abstract ideas, charging that they are mere dust clouds raised by philosophers who then foolishly complain that they cannot see. Universals, such as "triangle," do not exist; there are only particular triangles of a definite character. Everyone who responds fully to the word *triangle* thinks of a concrete triangular shape. The image thus formed in the mind may become a representative sign of other triangles, but any actually existing thing or quality is always concrete and particular. Berkeley, holding this nominalistic view of universals, rejects the notion of "substance" as too abtsract to have genuine meaning.

A "thing" for Berkeley is not a mysterious "something" possessing certain qualities. It is nothing but a collection of ideas of sense. A beefsteak, for example, is just a complex of sense data—the brown color, the irregular shape, the appetizing aroma, the meaty taste, the texture that we feel with our tongue. There is no need to speak of a physical substance somehow distinct from these concrete qualities. Certain "ideas" are observed repeatedly to go together and are accounted one distinct thing, signified by the word "beefsteak." But the *thing* is just the collection of ideas—nothing more. Unlike Hume, whom we shall discuss in the next chapter, Berkeley retained the concept of spiritual substance, in the sense of an enduring self. He agreed with Descartes that thought requires a thinker. But sense qualities, he was convinced, do not require a physical substance in which to inhere.

3. The Inference to an External World. Like everyone else including Locke, Berkeley distinguished between dreams and waking perceptions, between illusions and realities. Real objects are usually more vivid and distinct than illusory objects; they are not, like the figments of imagination, of our own making; they exhibit a superior order and coherence; they change or recur in predictable ways, permitting us to formulate "laws of nature"; they seem to continue to exist in the intervals between our experiences. For example, a candle burns down even when we are not present; a dog gets hungry when we are absent and do not feed it; a hill gradually erodes, whether we observe it or not. Such things, we have ample reason to suppose, exist and go on changing even when we do not perceive them.

The materialist concludes from these marks of objectivity that there must be physical objects independent of perceptions. But opposed to this hypothesis are all of the foregoing arguments against materialism. Is there any other alternative?

Berkeley believes that there is. He points out that all the marks of objectivity are features of experience, not of any thing or substance *beyond* experience. They simply mean that experience has a certain regularity and dependable character—that we can make verifiable predictions as to what we shall experience. We can predict, for example, that when we again perceive a candle after an hour's interval it will be of diminished size.

In accounting for such facts, it is sound empirical method to stick close to actual experience. What sorts of things do I actually know? I know ideas because I actually experience them. I know myself, my own mind and mental operations, because I have an immediate introspective awareness of myself and my own mental states. Suppose I try to interpret reality in terms of immediate experience, recognizing that others have similar minds and experiences.

First, there is my mind and other finite minds. Second, there are my ideas and the ideas of other finite minds. Third, there is a far greater Mind, or God, which I can conceive as analogous to my own mind although immeasurably greater.

Fourth, there are His ideas, which, in their regular order, constitute nature. Being omnipotent, God can communicate ideas to us by a kind of divine mental telepathy. The "real objects" which we perceive, not being of our own imagining, have their cause, but that cause is not matter; it is God. He coordinates my experiences and the experiences of all other finite spirits so that we live in a dependable and common "world."

The natural universe has a kind of double existence. On the one hand, it is a steady, interconnected, and comprehensive set of ideas in the Divine Mind; and, on the other hand, it is a regular and somewhat repetitious set of ideas in finite minds, communicated to them by God. Berkeley's account does not indicate whether we somehow share in God's ideas, or whether He gives us a corresponding but independent set of ideas. Of course, God has an infinitely larger stock of ideas than all finite minds put together. He conserves objects in the intervals when no finite mind is perceiving them. The burning candle which continues to exist when no finite mind sees it depends upon perception (its *esse est percipi*), but the perception involved in this instance is God's, not man's.

This idealistic hypothesis is supported by Berkeley's interpretation of causation. Like David Hume (whom we shall study in the next chapter), he maintained that no inspection of our sense data discloses any causal force or power. We say, for example, that cold makes water freeze. But the closest inspection fails to disclose any *power* in cold that *makes* water become solid. All we actually observe is that cold is followed by the solidification of water; we discover a sequence, nothing more. Unlike Hume, however, Berkeley maintained that we do have insight into causal connection through knowledge of our mental operations. We have introspective awareness of ourselves as active, volitional, creative beings, with the power to produce imaginary ideas. It is a natural inference that the power to produce perceived ideas is similarly mental, the difference being that imaginary ideas are created by finite minds whereas perceived ideas are created and communicated to us by an Infinite Mind.

To a religious person such as Berkeley, this idealistic interpretation has an immense appeal. He sees the Universe as through and through spiritual—a system of spirits with God the supreme author and creator. But his idealism also has great logical advantages, since it bears so close a relation to the immediate facts of experience and relieves us of such unempirical abstractions as Locke's substances and primary qualities. It adheres to the logical principle of parsimony—the principle that we should suppose no more entities than necessary to explain the given facts. Materialists believe in substances and material entities; but they never find them in experience—they find only ideas. The world would look the same and behave in the same way if these unexperienced things were omitted. Berkeley proposes to omit them. Thus he achieves an immense housecleaning, getting rid of a tremendous amount of metaphysical rubbish.

At the same time, he preserves science intact. Science does not need substances or invisible matter: it needs only laws. If the external causes of our minds and their experiences have a constant nature, the ideas of sense which are their effects will exhibit lawful regularities and permit scientific predictions. God, as a non-material cause, can have a nature as constant as that of any material cause. When God is substituted for matter in Berkeley's metaphysics, all the laws of science still hold good, but their metaphysical basis has been reinterpreted. Atheism and other heresies creep in when scientists forget the empirical foundations of their science and engage in metaphysical speculation about imperceivable entities. They thus turn legitimate science into illegitimate metaphysics. Genuine science rests upon *perceptions* and will not err so long as it remains true to its concrete, empirical basis. Berkeley believes that he is recalling science to its true foundations and that he has provided a sound alternative to Locke's inference to a physical external world.

Some Critical Questions

Idealism seems to the present writer, if not true, at least irrefutable. But certain critical questions will occur to a reflective reader:

1. Is the Essence of an Object To Be Perceived? Over and over again, Berkeley insisted that "things" are mere collections of "ideas" and that ideas cannot exist unless they are perceived. The plausibility of his contention depends upon his constant use of the word *idea*. We think of "idea" as something in the mind and therefore as incapable of existing apart from the mind. Hence, if we are told that an apple consists entirely of "ideas," it is natural for us to suppose that the apple can exist only in some mind. But "idea," as Berkeley used it, really means "immediate object of thought or experience" (including both imaginative and perceptual experience). If we understand idea in this sense, there is a possibility—not lightly to be dismissed—that an object known as a set of ideas may continue to exist when the thought of it ceases.

The point can be illustrated by an amusing passage from Lewis Carroll's *Through the Looking Glass*. Alice is warned by Tweedledum and Tweedledee not to awaken the Red King:

> "He's dreaming now," said Tweedledee: "and what do you think he's dreaming about?"
>
> Alice said, "Nobody can guess that."
>
> "Why about *you!*" Tweedledee exclaimed, clapping his hands triumphantly. "And if he left off dreaming about you, where do you suppose you'd be?"
>
> "Where I am now, of course," said Alice.
>
> "Not you!" Tweedledee retorted contemptuously. "You'd be nowhere. Why, you're only a sort of thing in his dream!"
>
> "If that there King was to wake," added Tweedledum, "you'd go out—bang! —just like a candle!"

The delicious absurdity of this passage depends upon the supposition of Tweedledum and Tweedledee that to *exist* is to be *borne in mind*, and that when Alice is not borne in mind by the Red King she cannot exist. But no real person is merely a thought or idea in anybody's mind.

This point would be admitted by Berkeley. His formula for summing up the nature of reality is *"esse est percipi aut percipere,"* not just *"esse est percipi."* But if a person can exist independently of someone's idea of him, why cannot a *thing* exist independently? To argue that an apple must be in our minds because we are thinking of it is like arguing that a person must be in our minds because we are thinking of him. If we distinguish clearly between the act of thinking and the object of thought, the act of perceiving and the object perceived, there is no absurdity in supposing that things may exist even when they are unperceived or unthought.

2. Is the "Egocentric Predicament" a Reason for Believing in Idealism? Berkeley pointed out that everyone's knowledge is incurably egocentric. Even when I think of the unobserved interior of the earth, I am *thinking* about it, and, in that sense, it is an object before my mind. Every object we ever perceive or think about in any way stands *ipso facto* in relation to our minds. Does this "egocentric predicament"[1] provide a valid argument for idealism?

Ralph Barton Perry answers in the negative. The fact that no one can eliminate himself as the subject of his own experiences proves nothing at all about the nature of the external world. We may have good reason to suppose that there are unknown stars, unexperienced atoms, unsighted grains of sand in the Sahara Desert, and unobserved physical processes beneath the earth's crust. Our reasons for believing in them should be judged on the basis of logic and evidence and should not be rejected merely because no one can think about these matters without using his mind.

3. Does the Relativity of Perception Prove Idealism? The fact that sense data are relative to the perceiver can scarcely be denied; but does it prove idealism? So long as we can explain *why* things appear differently to different observers, we can still maintain that there are real objective qualities.

Let us consider one of Berkeley's own examples. He pointed out that if one hand has been chilled and the other warmed, and both hands are put simultaneously into the same pan of water, the water will seem warm to one hand and cool to the other. But this is just what we should expect if the water is *really tepid*. What the person who puts his hands in the water feels is not the temperature of the water but the temperature in his hands—and the preheated hand naturally has a different temperature than the prechilled hand. If the two hands

---

[1] See also Ralph Barton Perry, *Present Philosophical Tendencies* (Longmans, Green, 1929), pp. 129–132.

remain in the water long enough, the temperature of the water will finally pervade them, and then the water will feel tepid to *both* hands. Similarly, if light and color are truly objective, an object will naturally appear to have a different color in a different light. Or if a microscope enables us to see features of an object that were before invisible, it is not surprising that we see colors and shapes that we did not see before. However variously things may *appear*, we can often distinguish between "appearances" and "realities." Whether we can do this in a sufficient number of cases to invalidate Berkeley's argument is a question worth debating.

4. DOES THE INSEPARABILITY OF PRIMARY AND SECONDARY QUALITIES COMMIT US TO IDEALISM? Suppose we grant Berkeley's contention that primary and secondary qualities are inseparable. We might therefore conclude that both are objective (*not* mind-dependent) rather than that both are subjective (mind-dependent). Some critics maintain that Berkeley's arguments fail to show that even secondary qualities are "in the mind." They believe that colors, sounds, odors, and textures (though perhaps not tastes) are no less objective than the primary qualities.

Another alternative would be the agnostic position that things-in-themselves are unknowable, and that consequently we can no more assert idealism than we can assert materialism. This is the position favored by Kant, Hume, and the positivists—all of whom admit the inseparability of primary and secondary qualities.

But it is also possible to reject Berkeley's thesis that primary and secondary qualities are inseparable. Actually, there is a very significant difference between the two sets of qualities. The secondary qualities are *sensory* properties, whereas the primary qualities are *formal* characteristics—the structures, relations, and quantities of things. This difference may justify the supposition that the primary qualities have a different epistemological status than the secondary qualities.

According to modern scientific theories of perception, the secondary qualities seem to depend upon physiological and mental factors and thus appear to be qualitative events in the perceiving organisms. Sounds seem to depend upon organic reactions to air-waves; colors upon organic reactions to electro-magnetic vibrations; and so on. Our *impressions* of primary qualities are similarly dependent upon our minds, but there is a significant difference: the laws of physics are framed in terms of abstract orders and quantitative relations—primary qualities— rather than in terms of concrete secondary qualities. We therefore have scientific warrant for believing that our impressions of primary but not of secondary qualities have objective counterparts—*if* science is dealing with a real objective world.

Relational properties cannot exist all by themselves; they must attach to the things related. On this point Berkeley is perfectly right. Yet it is conceivable that physical science reveals the relational structure of the real world without revealing its contents. Atoms may exist and conform to Einstein's equations even though their ultimate qualitative nature remains a mystery.

5. Can We Test the Correspondence Between Ideas and Things? Once we distinguish between objects as we apprehend them and objects as they really are, how can we ever know that the former agree with the latter? Not only Berkeley, but Kant and Hegel as well, maintain that the correspondence test of truth is unworkable.

The impossibility of directly comparing ideas (or sense data) with things outside experience must be admitted. But we can *infer* things that we do not experience. No one, for example, *directly* observes another person's toothache, but he can be reasonably certain that the other person *is* suffering toothache. Such indirect knowledge involves the interpretation of signs, and we can often infer from signs what we cannot observe.

It is a striking fact that the signs of minds differ very markedly from the signs of external things. When we hear a person talk, see him gesture, or read what he has written, we are interpreting signs of a very different sort than when we are looking at a rock. The first set of signs are clearly indicative of a thinking person and his thoughts, whereas the second set of signs, to all appearances, indicates something nonconscious and nonintelligent. It seems a bit fantastic and gratuitous to attribute a *mind* to the rock, or even to the system of nature of which the rock is a minute part. The sensible aspects of human behavior from which we infer a human mind have little resemblance to the sensible characteristics of nature from which Berkeley would have us infer God. Perhaps Kant and the positivists are right—perhaps we can never know the rock as a thing-in-itself—but such clues as we have for judging the nature of inorganic things are quite different from the clues whereby we infer the minds of our friends and acquaintances. Reality *appears* to be dualistic, made up of both mental and physical qualities, and it involves a sharp break with common sense to suppose that this appearance is quite illusory.

Berkeley has raised issues of profound and lasting importance. Perhaps his greatest service is to stimulate us to think rather than give us final answers.

8

Causation,
Free Will,
and the Limits
of Knowledge

DAVID HUME (1711–1776)

Born in Edinburgh, Hume was the youngest son of a gentleman landowner. His father died when he was an infant, and he was reared by his mother, who, somewhat critical of his bookish tendencies, is said to have remarked that "oor Davie's a fine good-natured crater but uncommon wake-minded." Hume's studies at the University of Edinburgh instilled in him a love of literature and philosophy which kept him from settling down to a legal or business career. He decided to devote his life to scholarly pursuits, and at the age of twenty-three crossed the Channel to live in France, studying at La Flèche, where Descartes had gone to school.

There he completed, before he reached the age of twenty-five, his greatest philosophical work, the *Treatise of Human Nature.* In his brief autobiography he remarked that the book "fell dead-born from the press." Although this remark is an exaggeration, it suggests Hume's great disappointment that his ideas did not find a wider public. His *An Enquiry Concerning Human Understanding* (1748) and *An Enquiry Concerning the Principles of Morals* (1751), which restated principal parts of the *Treatise,* were somewhat more popular, but his literary reputation was based mainly upon his *Political Discourses* (1752) and his *History of England,* published in 1755 and following years. He also wrote *Dialogues Concerning Natural Religion,* which he regarded as a bit too shocking to publish during his own lifetime.

Although the income from his books gradually increased and he remained a frugal bachelor, he had to find other means of livelihood. Early in his career, he applied first to the University of Edinburgh and then to the University of Glasgow for a teaching position, but both universities rejected him because of the heterodoxy of his views. For a short time he was tutor to a lunatic, the Marquis of Annandale, and then secretary to a general, St. Clair. Thereafter he secured a six-year post as Keeper of Advocates' Library in Edinburgh, and from 1763 to 1765 served as secretary to the British Embassy in Paris. His French acquaintances included the most famous intellectuals of the period—D'Alembert, Diderot, Holbach, and Rousseau. After his sojourn in France, he spent two years in London (1767–1769) as Under Secretary of State for Scotland. In Great Britain as in France, he was a friend of distinguished wits, such as Burke, Gibbon, and Adam Smith. Having received a moderate pension, he finally retired to Edinburgh, where he lived quietly with his sister until his death in 1776.

In a self-obituary, he describes himself as follows:

> I was a man of mild disposition, of command of temper, of an open, social and cheerful humor, capable of attachment but little susceptible of enmity, and of great moderation in all my passions. Even my love of literary fame, my ruling passion, never soured my temper, notwithstanding my frequent disappointments.

This characterization appears to be entirely accurate. Hume was a canny Scot, with a kindly, humorous, equable disposition.

A Treatise
of Human Nature
and
An Enquiry Concerning
Human Understanding

1. [Impressions and Ideas]

Everyone will readily allow, that there is a considerable difference between the perceptions of the mind, when a man feels the pain of excessive heat, or the pleasure of moderate

---

Section 1 combines excerpts from the *Treatise* and the *Enquiry;* sections 2, 4, 5, 6, and 8 are from the *Enquiry;* sections 3 and 7 are from the *Treatise.* The *Treatise* was published in 1739; the *Enquiry* in 1748.

warmth, and when he afterwards recalls to his memory this sensation, or anticipates it by his imagination. These faculties may mimic or copy the perceptions of the senses; but they never can entirely reach the force and vivacity of the original sentiment. The utmost we say of them, even when they operate with greatest vigor, is, that they represent their object in so lively a manner, that we could *almost* say we feel or see it: But, except the mind be disordered by disease or madness, they never can arrive at such a pitch of vivacity, as to render these perceptions altogether undistinguishable. All the colors of poetry, however splendid, can never paint natural objects in such a manner as to make the description be taken for a real landskip. The most lively thought is still inferior to the dullest sensation.

We may observe a like distinction to run through all the other perceptions of the mind. A man in a fit of anger, is actuated in a very different manner from one who only thinks of that emotion. If you tell me, that any person is in love, I easily understand your meaning, and form a just conception of his situation; but never can mistake that conception for the real disorders and agitations of the passion. When we reflect on our past sentiments and affections, our thought is a faithful mirror, and copies its objects truly; but the colors which it employs are faint and dull, in comparison of those in which our original perceptions were clothed. It requires no nice discernment or metaphysical head to mark the distinction between them.

Here therefore we may divide all the perceptions of the mind into two classes or species, which are distinguished by their different degrees of force and vivacity. The less forcible and lively are commonly denominated *Thoughts* or *Ideas.* The other species want a name in our language, and in most others; I suppose, because it was not requisite for any, but philosophical purposes, to rank them under a general term or appellation. Let us, therefore, use a little freedom, and call them *Impressions;* employing that word in a sense somewhat different from the usual. By the term *impression,* then, I mean all our more lively perceptions, when we hear, or see, or feel, or love, or hate, or desire, or will. And impressions are distinguished from ideas, which are the less lively perceptions, of which we are conscious, when we reflect on any of those sensations or movements above mentioned. . . .

Impressions may be divided into two kinds, those of *sensation,* and those of *reflection.* The first kind arises in the soul originally, from unknown causes. The second is derived, in a great measure, from our ideas, and that in the following order. An impression first strikes upon the senses, and makes us perceive heat or cold, thirst or hunger, pleasure or pain, of some kind or other. Of this impression there is a copy taken by the mind, which remains after the impression ceases; and this we call an idea. This idea of pleasure or pain, when it returns upon the soul, produces the new impressions of desire and aversion, hope and fear, which may properly be called impressions of reflection, because derived from it. These again are copied by the memory and imagination, and become ideas: which, perhaps, in their turn, give rise to other impressions and ideas; so that the impressions of reflection, are not only antecedent to their correspondent ideas, but posterior to those of sensation, and derived from them. . . .

We find, by experience, that when any impression has been present with the mind, it again makes its appearance there as an idea; and this it may do after two different ways: either when, in its new appearance, it retains a considerable degree of its first vivacity, and is somewhat intermediate betwixt an impression and an idea; or when it entirely loses that vivacity, and is a perfect idea. The faculty by which we repeat our impressions in the first manner, is called the *memory,* and the other the *imagination.* It is evident, at first sight, that the ideas of the memory are much more lively and strong than those of the imagination, and that the former faculty paints its objects in more distinct colors than any which are employed by the latter. When we remember any past event, the idea of it flows in upon the mind in a forcible manner; whereas, in the imagination, the perception is faint and languid, and cannot, without difficulty, be preserved by the mind steady and uniform for any considerable time. Here, then, is a sensible difference betwixt one species of ideas and another.

There is another difference betwixt these two kinds of ideas, which is no less evident, namely, that though neither the ideas of the memory nor imagination, neither the lively nor faint ideas, can make their appearance in the mind, unless their correspondent impressions have gone before to prepare the way for them, yet the imagination is not restrained to the same order and form with the original impressions; while the memory is in a manner tied down in that respect, without any power of variation.

Nothing, at first view, may seem more unbounded than the thought of man, which not only escapes all human power and authority, but is not even restrained within the limits of nature and reality. To form monsters, and join incongruous shapes and appearances, costs the imagination no more trouble than to conceive the most natural and familiar objects. And while the body is confined to one planet, along which it creeps with pain and difficulty; the thought can in an instant transport us into the most distant regions of the universe; or even beyond the universe, into the unbounded chaos, where nature is supposed to lie in total confusion. What never was seen, or heard of, may yet be conceived; nor is anything beyond the power of thought, except what implies an absolute contradiction.

But though our thought seems to possess this unbounded liberty, we shall find, upon a nearer examination, that it is really confined within very narrow limits, and that all this creative power of the mind amounts to no more than the faculty of compounding, transposing, augmenting, or diminishing the materials afforded us by the senses and experience. When we think of a golden mountain, we only join two consistent ideas, *gold,* and *mountain,* with which we were formerly acquainted. A virtuous horse we can conceive; because, from our own feeling, we can conceive virtue; and this we may unite to the figure and shape of a horse, which is an animal familiar to us. In short, all the materials of thinking are derived either from our outward or inward sentiment: the mixture and composition of these belongs alone to the mind and will. Or, to express myself in philosophical language, all our ideas or more feeble perceptions are copies of our impressions or more lively ones. . . .

Here, therefore, is a proposition, which not only seems, in itself, simple and intelligible; but, if a proper use were made of it, might render every dispute equally intelligible, and banish all that jargon, which has so long taken possession of metaphysical reasonings, and drawn disgrace upon them. All ideas, especially abstract ones, are naturally faint and obscure: the mind has but a slender hold of them: they are apt to be confounded with other resembling ideas; and when we have often employed any term, though without a distinct meaning, we are apt to imagine it has a determinate idea annexed to it. On the contrary, all impressions, that is, all sensations, either outward or inward, are strong and vivid: the limits between them are more exactly determined: nor is it easy to fall into any error or mistake with regard to them. When we entertain, therefore, any suspicion that a philosophical term is employed without any meaning or idea (as is but too frequent), we need but enquire, *from what impression is that supposed idea derived?* And if it be impossible to assign any, this will serve to confirm our suspicion. By bringing ideas into so clear a light we may reasonably hope to remove all dispute, which may arise, concerning their nature and reality.

2. [The Forms of Reasoning]

All the objects of human reason or enquiry may naturally be divided into two kinds, to wit, *Relations of Ideas,* and *Matters of Fact.* Of the first kind are the sciences of Geometry, Algebra, and Arithmetic; and in short, every affirmation which is either intuitively or demonstratively certain. *That the square of the hypothenuse is equal to the square of the two sides,* is a proposition which expresses a relation between these figures. *That three times five is equal to the half of thirty,* expresses a relation between these numbers. Propositions of this kind are discoverable by the mere operation of thought, without dependence on what is anywhere existent in the universe. Though there never were a circle or triangle in nature, the truths demonstrated by Euclid would for ever retain their certainty and evidence.

Matters of fact, which are the second objects of human reason, are not ascertained in the same manner; nor is our evidence of their truth, however great, of a like nature with the foregoing. The contrary of every matter of fact is still possible; because it can never imply a contradiction, and is conceived by the mind with the same facility and distinctness, as if ever so comformable to reality. *That the sun will not rise tomorrow* is no less intelligible a proposition, and implies no more contradiction than the affirmation, *that it will rise*. We should in vain, therefore, attempt to demonstrate its falsehood. Were it demonstratively false, it would imply a contradiction, and could never be distinctly conceived by the mind.

It may, therefore, be a subject worthy of curiosity, to enquire what is the nature of that evidence which assures us of any real existence and matter of fact, beyond the present testimony of our senses, or the records of our memory. This part of philosophy, it is observable, has been little cultivated, either by the ancients or moderns; and therefore our doubts and errors, in the prosecution of so important an enquiry, may be the more excusable; while we march through such difficult paths without any guide or direction. They may even prove useful, by exciting curiosity, and destroying that implicit faith and security, which is the bane of all reasoning and free enquiry. The discovery of defects in the common philosophy, if any such there be, will not, I presume, be a discouragement, but rather an incitement, as is usual, to attempt something more full and satisfactory than has yet been proposed to the public.

All reasonings concerning matter of fact seem to be founded on the relation of *Cause and Effect*. By means of that relation alone we can go beyond the evidence of our memory and senses. If you were to ask a man, why he believes any matter of fact, which is absent; for instance, that his friend is in the country, or in France; he would give you a reason; and this reason would be some other fact; as a letter received from him, or the knowledge

of his former resolutions and promises. A man finding a watch or any other machine in a desert island, would conclude that there had once been men in that island. All our reasonings concerning fact are of the same nature. And here it is constantly supposed that there is a connection between the present fact and that which is inferred from it. Were there nothing to bind them together, the inference would be entirely precarious. The hearing of an articulate voice and rational discourse in the dark assures us of the presence of some person: Why? because these are the effects of the human make and fabric, and closely connected with it. If we anatomize all the other reasonings of this nature, we shall find that they are founded on the relation of cause and effect, and that this relation is either near or remote, direct or collateral. Heat and light are collateral effects of fire, and the one effect may justly be inferred from the other.

If we would satisfy ourselves, therefore, concerning the nature of that evidence, which assures us of matters of fact, we must enquire how we arrive at the knowledge of cause and effect.

I shall venture to affirm, as a general proposition, which admits of no exception, that the knowledge of this relation is not, in any instance, attained by reasonings *a priori;* but arises entirely from experience, when we find that any particular objects are constantly conjoined with each other. Let an object be presented to a man of ever so strong natural reason and abilities; if that object be entirely new to him, he will not be able, by the most accurate examination of its sensible qualities, to discover any of its causes or effects. Adam, though his rational faculties be supposed, at the very first, entirely perfect, could not have inferred from the fluidity and transparency of water that it would suffocate him, or from the light and warmth of fire that it would consume him. No object ever discovers, by the qualities which appear to the senses, either the causes which produced it, or the effects which will arise from it; nor can our reason, unassisted by experience, ever draw any inference concerning real existence and matter of fact.

This proposition, *that causes and effects are discoverable, not by reason but by experience,* will readily be admitted with regard to such objects, as we remember to have once been altogether unknown to us; since we must be conscious of the utter inability, which we then lay under, of foretelling what would arise from them. Present two smooth pieces of marble to a man who has no tincture of natural philosophy; he will never discover that they will adhere together in such a manner as to require great force to separate them in a direct line, while they make so small a resistance to a lateral pressure. Such events, as bear little analogy to the common course of nature, are also readily confessed to be known only by experience; nor does any man imagine that the explosion of gunpowder, or the attraction of a loadstone, could ever be discovered by arguments *a priori*. In like manner, when an effect is supposed to depend upon an intricate machinery or secret structure of parts, we make no difficulty in attributing all our knowledge of it to

experience. Who will assert that he can give the ultimate reason, why milk or bread is proper nourishment for a man, not for a lion or a tiger? . . .

3. [The Idea of Causation]

We must consider the idea of *causation,* and see from what origin it is derived. It is impossible to reason justly, without understanding perfectly the idea concerning which we reason; and it is impossible perfectly to understand any idea, without tracing it up to its origin, and examining that primary impression, from which it arises. The examination of the impression bestows a clearness on the idea; and the examination of the idea bestows a like clearness on all our reasoning.

Let us therefore cast our eye on any two objects, which we call cause and effect, and turn them on all sides, in order to find that impression, which produces an idea of such prodigious consequence. At first sight I perceive, that I must not search for it in any of the particular *qualities* of the objects; since, whichever of these qualities I pitch on, I find some object that is not possessed of it, and yet falls under the denomination of cause or effect. And indeed there is nothing existent, either externally or internally, which is not to be considered either as a cause or an effect; though it is plain there is no one quality which universally belongs to all beings, and gives them a title to that denomination.

The idea then of causation must be derived from some *relation* among objects; and that relation we must now endeavor to discover. I find in the first place, that whatever objects are considered as causes or effects, are *contiguous;* and that nothing can operate in a time or place, which is ever so little removed from those of its existence. Though distant objects may sometimes seem productive of each other, they are commonly found upon examination to be linked by a chain of causes, which are contiguous among themselves, and to the distant objects; and when in any particular instance we cannot discover this connection, we still presume it to exist. We may therefore consider the relation of *contiguity* as essential to that of causation. . . .

The second relation I shall observe as essential to causes and effects, is . . . that of *priority* of time in the cause before the effect. . . .

[A third] relation betwixt cause and effect . . . is their *constant conjunction.* Contiguity and succession are not sufficient to make us pronounce any two objects to be cause and effect, unless we perceive that these two relations are preserved in several instances. . . . Thus we remember to have seen that species of object we call *flame,* and to have felt that species of sensation we call *heat.* We likewise call to mind their constant conjunction in all past instances. Without any farther ceremony, we call the one *cause* and the other *effect,* and infer the existence of the one from that of the other. . . .

There is [also] a *necessary connection* to be taken into consideration; and that relation is of much greater importance. . . .

What is our idea of necessity, when we say that two objects are necessarily connected together? Upon this head I repeat, what I have often had occasion to observe, that as we have no idea that is not derived from an impression, we must find some impression that gives rise to this idea of necessity, if we assert we have really such an idea. In order to this, I consider in what objects necessity is commonly supposed to lie; and, finding that it is always ascribed to causes and effects, I turn my eye to two objects supposed to be placed in that relation, and examine them in all the situations of which they are susceptible. I immediately perceive that they are *contiguous* in time and place, and that the object we call cause *precedes* the other we call effect. In no one instance can I go any further, nor is it possible for me to discover any third relation betwixt these objects. I therefore enlarge my view to comprehend several instances, where I find like objects always existing in like relations of contiguity and succession. At first sight this seems to serve but little to my purpose. The reflection on several instances only repeats the same objects; and therefore can never give rise to a new idea. But upon further enquiry I find, that the repetition is not in every particular the same, but produces a new impression, and by that means the idea which I at present examine. For after a frequent repetition I find, that upon the appearance of one of the objects, the mind is *determined* by custom to consider its usual attendant, and to consider it in a stronger light upon account of its relation to the first object. It is this impression, then, or *determination,* which affords me the idea of necessity. . . .

Suppose two objects to be presented to us, of which the one is the cause and the other the effect; it is plain that, from the simple consideration of one, or both these objects, we never shall perceive the tie by which they are united, or be able certainly to pronounce, that there is a connection betwixt them. It is not, therefore, from any one instance, that we arrive at the idea of cause and effect, of a necessary connection of power, of force, of energy, and of efficacy. Did we never see any but particular conjunctions of objects, entirely different from each other, we should never be able to form any such ideas [as cause and effect].

But, again, suppose we observe several instances in which the same objects are always conjoined together, we immediately conceive a connection betwixt them, and begin to draw an inference from one to another. This multiplicity of resembling instances, therefore, constitutes the very essence of power or connection, and is the source from which the idea of it arises. . . .

Though the several resembling instances, which give rise to the idea of power, have no influence on each other, and can never produce any new quality *in the object,* which can be the model of that idea, yet the *observation* of this resemblance produces a new impression *in the mind,* which is its real model. For after we have observed the resemblance in a sufficient number of instances, we immediately feel a determination of the mind to pass from one object to its usual attendant, and to conceive it in a stronger light upon account of that relation. This determination is the only effect of the resemblance; and,

therefore, must be the same with power or efficacy, whose idea is derived from the resemblance. The several instances of resembling conjunctions lead us into the notion of power and necessity. These instances are in themselves totally distinct from each other, and have no union but in the mind, which observes them, and collects their ideas. Necessity, then, is the effect of this observation, and is nothing but an internal impression of the mind, or a determination to carry our thoughts from one object to another. Without considering it in this view, we can never arrive at the most distant notion of it, or be able to attribute it either to external or internal objects, to spirit or body, to causes or effects. . . .

The idea of necessity arises from some impression. There is no impression conveyed by our senses, which can give rise to that idea. It must, therefore, be derived from some internal impression, or impression of reflection. There is no internal impression which has any relation to the present business, but that propensity, which custom produces, to pass from an object to the idea of its usual attendant. This, therefore, is the essence of necessity. Upon the whole, necessity is something that exists in the mind, not in objects; nor is it possible for us ever to form the most distant idea of it, considered as a quality in bodies. Either we have no idea of necessity, or necessity is nothing but that determination of the thought to pass from causes to effects, and from effects to causes, according to their experienced union.

Thus, as the necessity, which makes two times two equal to four, or three angles of a triangle equal to two right ones, lies only in the act of the understanding, by which we consider and compare these ideas; in like manner, the necessity of power, which unites causes and effects, lies in the determination of the mind to pass from the one to the other. The efficacy or energy of causes is neither placed in the causes themselves, nor in the Deity, nor in the concurrence of these two principles; but belongs entirely to the soul, which considers the union of two or more objects in all past instances. It is here that the real power of causes is placed, along with their connection and necessity. . . .

4. [Of Liberty and Necessity]

I hope . . . to make it appear that all men have ever agreed in the doctrine both of necessity and of liberty, according to any reasonable sense, which can be put on these terms; and that the whole controversy has hitherto turned merely upon words. We shall begin with examining the doctrine of necessity.

It is universally allowed that matter, in all its operations, is actuated by a necessary force, and that every natural effect is so precisely determined by the energy of its cause that no other effect, in such particular circumstances, could possibly have resulted from it. The degree and direction of every motion is, by the laws of nature, prescribed with such exactness that a living creature may as soon arise from the shock of two bodies as motion in any other degree or direction than what is actually produced by it. Would we, therefore, form a just and precise idea of *necessity,* we must con-

sider whence that idea arises when we apply it to the operation of bodies.

It seems evident that, if all the scenes of nature were continually shifted in such a manner that no two events bore any resemblance to each other, but every object was entirely new, without any similitude to whatever had been seen before, we should never, in that case, have attained the least idea of necessity, or of a connexion among these objects. We might say, upon such a supposition, that one object or event has followed another; not that one was produced by the other. The relation of cause and effect must be utterly unknown to mankind. Inference and reasoning concerning the operations of nature would, from that moment, be at an end; and the memory and senses remain the only canals, by which the knowledge of any real existence could possibly have access to the mind. Our idea, therefore, of necessity and causation arises entirely from the uniformity observable in the operations of nature, where similar objects are constantly conjoined together, and the mind is determined by custom to infer the one from the appearance of the other. These two circumstances form the whole of that necessity, which we ascribe to matter. Beyond the constant *conjunction* of similar objects, and the consequent *inference* from one to the other, we have no notion of any necessity or connexion.

If it appear, therefore, that all mankind have ever allowed, without any doubt or hesitation, that these two circumstances take place in the voluntary actions of men, and in the operations of mind; it must follow, that all mankind have ever agreed in the doctrine of necessity, and that they have hitherto disputed, merely for not understanding each other.

As to the first circumstance, the constant and regular conjunction of similar events, we may possibly satisfy ourselves by the following considerations. It is universally acknowledged that there is a great uniformity among the actions of men, in all nations and ages, and that human nature remains still the same, in its principles and operations. The same motives always produce the same actions: The same events follow from the same causes. Ambition, avarice, self-love, vanity, friendship, generosity, public spirit: these passions, mixed in various degrees, and distributed through society, have been, from the beginning of the world, and still are, the source of all the actions and enterprises, which have ever been observed among mankind. . . .

We must not, however, expect that this uniformity of human actions should be carried to such a length as that all men, in the same circumstances, will always act precisely in the same manner, without making any allowance for the diversity of characters, prejudices, and opinions. Such a uniformity in every particular, is found in no part of nature. On the contrary, from observing the variety of conduct in different men, we are enabled to form a greater variety of maxims, which still suppose a degree of uniformity and regularity.

Are the manners of men different in differen ages and countries? We learn thence the great force of custom and education, which mould the human mind from its infancy and form it into a fixed and established character. Is the behaviour and conduct of the one sex very unlike that of the other? Is it thence we become acquainted with the different characters which nature has impressed upon the sexes, and which she preserves with constancy and regularity? Are the actions of the same person much diversified in the different periods of his life, from infancy to old age? This affords room for many general observations concerning the gradual change of our sentiments and inclinations, and the different maxims which prevail in the different ages of human creatures. Even the characters, which are peculiar to each individual, have a uniformity in their influence; otherwise our acquaintance with the persons and our observation of their conduct could never teach us their dispositions, or serve to direct our behaviour with regard to them.

I grant it possible to find some actions, which seem to have no regular connexion with any known motives, and are exceptions to all the measures of conduct which have ever been established for the government of men. But if we would willingly know what judgment should be formed of such irregular and extraordinary actions, we may consider the sentiments commonly entertained with regard to those irregular events which appear in the course of nature, and the operations of external objects. All causes are not conjoined to their usual effects with like uniformity. An artificer, who handles only dead matter, may be disappointed of his aim, as well as the politician, who directs the conduct of sensible and intelligent agents.

The vulgar, who take things according

to their first appearance, attribute the uncertainty of events to such an uncertainty in the causes as makes the latter often fail of their usual influence; though they meet with no impediment in their operation. But philosophers, observing that, almost in every part of nature, there is contained a vast variety of springs and principles, which are hid, by reason of their minuteness or remoteness, find, that it is at least possible the contrariety of events may not proceed from any contingency in the cause, but from the secret operation of contrary causes. This possibility is converted into certainty by farther observation, when they remark that, upon an exact scrutiny, a contrariety of effects always betrays a contrariety of causes, and proceeds from their mutual opposition. A peasant can give no better reason for the stopping of any clock or watch than to say that it does not commonly go right: But an artist easily perceives that the same force in the spring or pendulum has always the same influence on the wheels; but fails of its usual effect, perhaps by reason of a grain of dust, which puts a stop to the whole movement. From the observation of several parallel instances, philosophers form a maxim that the connexion between all causes and effects is equally necessary, and that its seeming uncertainty in some instances proceeds from the secret opposition of contrary causes.

Thus, for instance, in the human body, when the usual symptoms of health or sickness disappoint our expectation; when medicines operate not with their wonted powers; when irregular events follow from any particular cause; the philosopher and physician are not surprised at the matter, nor are ever tempted to deny, in general, the necessity and uniformity of those principles by which the animal economy is conducted. They know that a human body is a mighty complicated machine: That many secret powers lurk in it, which are altogether beyond our comprehension: That to us it must often appear very uncertain in its operations: And that therefore the irregular events, which outwardly discover themselves, can be no proof that the laws of nature are not observed with the greatest regularity in its internal operations and government.

The philosopher, if he be consistent, must apply the same reasoning to the actions and volitions of intelligent agents. The most irregular and unexpected resolutions of men may frequently be accounted for by those who know every particular circumstance of their character and situation. A person of an obliging disposition gives a peevish answer: But he has the toothache, or has not dined. A stupid fellow discovers an uncommon alacrity in his carriage: But he has met with a sudden piece of good fortune. Or even when an action, as sometimes happens, cannot be particularly accounted for, either by the person himself or by others; we know, in general, that the characters of men are, to a certain degree, inconstant and irregular. This is, in a manner, the constant character of human nature; though it be applicable, in a more particular manner, to some persons who have no fixed rule for their conduct, but proceed in a continued course of caprice and inconstancy. The internal principles and motives may operate in a uniform manner, notwithstanding these seeming irregularities; in the same manner as the winds, rain, clouds, and other variations of the weather are supposed to be governed by steady principles; though not easily discoverable by human sagacity and enquiry.

Thus it appears, not only that the conjunction between motives and voluntary actions is as regular and uniform as that between the cause and effect in any part of nature; but also that this regular conjunction has been universally acknowledged among mankind, and has never been the subject of dispute, either in philosophy or common life. Now, as it is from past experience that we draw all inferences concerning the future, and as we conclude that objects will always be conjoined together which we find to have always been conjoined; it may seem superfluous to prove that this experienced uniformity in human actions is a source whence we draw *inferences* concerning them. But in order to throw the argument into a greater variety of lights we shall also insist, though briefly, on this latter topic.

The mutual dependence of men is so great in all societies that scarce any human action is entirely complete in itself, or is performed without some reference to the actions of others, which are requisite to make it answer fully the intention of the agent. The poorest artificer, who labours alone, expects at least the protection of the magistrate, to ensure him the enjoyment of the fruits of his labour. He also expects that, when he carries his goods to market, and offers them at a reasonable price, he shall find purchasers, and shall be able, by the money he acquires, to engage others to supply him with those commodities which are requisite for his subsistence. In proportion as men extend their dealings, and render their intercourse with others more complicated, they always comprehend, in their schemes of life, a greater variety of voluntary actions, which they expect, from the proper motives, to co-operate with their own. In all these conclusions they take their measures from past experience, in the same manner as in their reasonings concerning external objects; and firmly believe that men, as well as all the elements, are to continue, in their operations, the same that they have ever found them. A manufacturer reckons upon the labour of his servants for the execution of any work as much as upon the tools which he employs, and would be equally surprised were his expectations disappointed. In short, this experimental inference and reasoning concerning the actions of others enters so much into human life that no man, while awake, is ever a moment without employing it. Have we not reason, therefore, to affirm that all mankind have always agreed in the doctrine of necessity according to the foregoing definition and explication of it? . . .

I have frequently considered, what could possibly be the reason why all mankind, though they have ever, without hesitation, acknowledged the doctrine of necessity in their whole practice and reasoning, have yet discovered such a reluctance to acknowledge it in words, and have rather shown a propensity, in all ages, to profess the contrary opinion. The matter, I think, may be accounted for after the following manner. If we examine the operations of body, and the production of effects from their causes, we shall find that all our faculties can never carry us farther in our knowledge of this relation than barely to observe that particular objects are *constantly conjoined* together, and that the mind is carried, by a *customary transition,* from the appearance of one to the belief of the other. But though this conclusion concerning human ignorance be the result of the strictest scrutiny of this subject, men still entertain a strong propensity to believe that they penetrate farther into the powers of nature, and perceive something like a necessary connexion between the cause and the effect. When again they turn their reflections towards the operations of their own minds, and *feel* no such connexion of the motive and the action; they are thence apt to suppose, that there is a difference between the effects which result from material force, and those which arise from thought and intelligence. But being once convinced that we know nothing farther of causation of any kind than merely the *constant conjunction* of objects, and the consequent *inference* of the mind from one to another, and finding that these two circumstances are universally allowed to have place in voluntary actions; we may be more easily led to own the same necessity common to all causes. . . .

It would seem, indeed, that men begin at the wrong end of this question concerning liberty and necessity, when they enter upon it by examining the faculties of the soul, the influence of the understanding, and the operations of the will. Let them first discuss a more simple question, namely, the operations of body and of brute unintelligent matter; and try whether they can there form any idea of causation and necessity, except that of a constant conjunction of objects, and subsequent inference of the mind from one to another. If these circumstances form, in reality, the whole of that necessity, which we conceive in matter, and if these circumstances be also universally acknowledged to take place in the operations of the mind, the dispute is at an end; at least, must be owned to be thenceforth merely verbal. But as long as we will rashly suppose, that we have some farther idea of necessity and causation in the operations of external objects; at the same time, that we can find nothing farther in the voluntary actions of the mind; there is no possibility of bringing the question to any determinate issue, while we proceed upon so erroneous a supposition. The only method of undeceiving us is to mount up higher; to examine the narrow extent of science when applied to material causes; and to convince ourselves that all we know of them is the constant conjunction and inference above mentioned. We may, perhaps, find that it is with difficulty we are induced to fix such narrow limits to human understanding: But we can afterwards find no difficulty when we come to apply this doctrine to the actions of the will. For as it is evident that these have a regular conjunction with motives and circumstances and characters, and as we always draw inferences from one to the other, we must be obliged to acknowledge in words that necessity, which we have already avowed, in every deliberation of our lives, and in every step of our conduct and behaviour. . . .

But to proceed in this reconciling project with regard to the question of liberty and necessity; the most contentious question of metaphysics, the most contentious science; it will not require many words to prove, that all mankind have ever agreed in the doctrine of liberty as well as in that of necessity, and that the whole dispute, in this respect also, has been hitherto merely verbal. For what is meant by liberty, when applied to voluntary actions? We cannot surely mean that actions have so little connexion with motives, inclinations, and circumstances, that one does not follow with a certain degree of uniformity from the other, and that one affords no inference by which we can conclude the existence of the other. For these are plain and acknowledged matters of fact. By liberty, then, we can only mean *a power of acting or not acting, according to the determinations of the will;* that is, if we choose to remain at rest, we may; if we choose to move, we also may. Now this hypothetical liberty is universally allowed to belong to every one who is not a prisoner and in chains. Here, then, is no subject of dispute.

Whatever definition we may give of liberty, we should be careful to observe two requisite circumstances; *first,* that it be consistent with plain matter of fact; *secondly,* that it be consistent with itself. If we observe these circumstances, and render our definition intelligible, I am persuaded that all mankind will be found of one opinion with regard to it.

It is universally allowed that nothing exists without a cause of its existence, and that chance, when strictly examined, is a mere negative word, and means not any real power which has anywhere a being in nature. But it is pretended that some causes are necessary, some not necessary. Here then is the advantage of definitions. Let any one *define* a cause, without comprehending, as a part of the definition, a *necessary connexion* with its effect; and let him show distinctly the origin of the idea, expressed by the definition; and I shall readily give up the whole controversy. But if the foregoing explication of the matter be received, this must be absolutely impracticable. Had not objects a regular conjunction with each other, we should never have entertained any notion of cause and effect; and this regular conjunction produces that inference of the understanding, which is the only connexion, that we can have any comprehension of. Whoever attempts a definition of cause, exclusive of these circumstances, will be obliged either to employ unintelligible terms or such as are synonymous to the term which he endeavours to define. And if the definition above mentioned be admitted; liberty, when opposed to necessity, not to constraint, is the same thing with chance; which is universally allowed to have no existence.

5. [Will the Future Resemble the Past?]

It must certainly be allowed, that nature has kept us at a great distance from all her secrets, and has afforded us only the knowledge of a few superficial qualities of objects; while she conceals from us those powers and principles on which the influence of those objects entirely depends. Our senses inform us of the color, weight, and consistence of bread; but neither sense nor reason can ever inform us of those qualities which fit it for the nourishment and support of a human body. Sight or feeling conveys an idea of the actual motion of bodies; but as to that wonderful force or power, which would carry on a moving body for ever in a continued change of place, and which bodies never lose but by communicating it to others; of this we cannot form the most distant conception. But notwithstanding this ignorance of natural powers and principles, we always presume, when we see like sensible qualities, that they have like secret powers, and expect that effects, similar to those which we have experienced, will follow from them. If a body of like color and consistence with that bread, which we have formerly eat, be presented to us, we make no scruple of repeating the experiment, and foresee, with certainty, like nourishment and support. Now this is a process of the mind or thought, of which I would willingly know the foundation. It is allowed on all hands that there is no known connexion between the sensible qualities and the secret powers; and consequently, that the mind is not led to form such a conclusion concerning their constant and regular conjunction, by anything which it knows of their nature. As to past *Experience,* it can be allowed to give *direct* and *certain* information of those precise objects only, and that precise period of time, which fell under its cognizance: but why this experience should be extended to future times, and to other objects, which for

aught we know, may be only in appearance similar; this is the main question on which I would insist. The bread, which I formerly eat, nourished me; that is, a body of such sensible qualities was, at that time, endued with such secret powers: but does it follow, that other bread must also nourish me at another time, and that like sensible qualities must always be attended with like secret powers? The consequence seems nowise necessary. At least, it must be acknowledged that there is here a consequence drawn by the mind; that there is a certain step taken; a process of thought, and an inference, which wants to be explained. These two propositions are far from being the same, *I have found that such an object has always been attended with such an effect,* and *I foresee, that other objects, which are, in appearance, similar, will be attended with similar effects.* I shall allow, if you please, that the one proposition may justly be inferred from the other: I know, in fact, that it always is inferred. But if you insist that the inference is made by a chain of reasoning, I desire you to produce that reasoning. . . .

All reasonings may be divided into two kinds, namely, demonstrative reasoning, or that concerning relations of ideas, and moral reasoning, or that concerning matter of fact and existence. That there are no demonstrative arguments in the case seems evident; since it implies no contradiction that the cause of nature may change, and that an object, seemingly like those which we have experienced, may be attended with different or contrary effects. May I not clearly and distinctly conceive that a body, falling from the clouds, and which, in all other respects, resembles snow, has yet the taste of salt or feeling of fire? Is there any more intelligible proposition than to affirm, that all the trees will flourish in December and January, and decay in May and June? Now whatever is intelligible, and can be distinctly conceived, implies no contradiction, and can never be proved false by any demonstrative argument or abstract reasoning *a priori*.

If we be, therefore, engaged by arguments to put trust in past experience, and make it the standard of our future judgment, these arguments must be probable only, or such as regard matter of fact and real existence, according to the division above mentioned. But that there is no argument of this kind, must appear, if our explication of that species of reasoning be admitted as solid and satisfactory. We have said that all arguments concerning existence are founded on the relation of cause and effect; that our knowledge of that relation is derived entirely from experience; and that all our experimental conclusions proceed upon the supposition that the future will be conformable to the past. To endeavor, therefore, the proof of this last supposition by probable arguments, or arguments regarding existence, must be evidently going in a circle, and taking that for granted, which is the very point in question. . . .

Should it be said that, from a number of uniform experiments, we *infer* a connexion between the sensible qualities and the secret powers; this, I must confess, seems the same difficulty, couched in different terms. The question still recurs, on what process of argument this *inference* is founded?

Where is the medium, the interposing ideas, which join propositions so very wide of each other? It is confessed that the color, consistence, and other sensible qualities of bread appear not, of themselves, to have any connection with the secret powers of nourishment and support. For otherwise we could infer these secret powers from the first appearance of these sensible qualities, without the aid of experience; contrary to the sentiment of all philosophers, and contrary to plain matter of fact. Here, then, is our natural state of ignorance with regard to the powers and influence of all objects. How is this remedied by experience? It only shows us a number of uniform effects, resulting from certain objects, and teaches us that those particular objects, at that particular time, were endowed with such powers and forces. When a new object, endowed with similar sensible qualities, is produced, we expect similar powers and forces, and look for a like effect. From a body of like color and consistence with bread we expect like nourishment and support. But this surely is a step or progress of the mind, which wants to be explained. When a man says, *I have found in all past instances, such sensible qualities conjoined with such secret powers:* And when he says, *Similar sensible qualities will always be conjoined with similar secret powers,* he is not guilty of a tautology, nor are these propositions in any respect the same. You say that the one proposition is an inference from the other. But you must confess that the inference is not intuitive; neither is it demonstrative: Of what nature is it, then? To say it is experimental, is begging the question. For all inferences from experience suppose, as their foundation, that the future will resemble the past, and that similar powers will be conjoined with similar sensible qualities. If there be any suspicion that the course of nature may change, and that the past may be no rule for the future, all experience becomes useless, and can give rise to no inference or conclusion. It is impossible, therefore, that any arguments from experience can prove this resemblance of the past to the future; since all these arguments are founded on the supposition of that resemblance. Let the course of things be allowed hitherto ever so regular; that alone, without some new argument or inference, proves not that, for the future, it will continue so. In vain do you pretend to have learned the nature of bodies from your past experience. Their secret nature, and consequently all their effects and influence, may change, without any change in their sensible qualities. This happens sometimes, and with regards to some objects: Why may it not happen always, and with regard to all objects? What logic, what process of argument secures you against this supposition? My practice, you say, refutes my doubts. But you mistake the purport of my question. As an agent, I am quite satisfied in the point; but as a philosopher, who has some share of curiosity, I will not say scepticism, I want to learn the foundation of this inference. No reading, no enquiry has yet been able to remove my difficulty, or give me satisfaction in a matter of such importance. Can I do better than propose the difficulty to the public, even though, perhaps, I have small hopes of obtaining a solution? We shall at least, by this means, be sensible of our ignorance, if we do not augment our knowledge.

6. [Can We Know External Objects?]

It seems evident, that men are carried, by a natural instinct or prepossession, to repose faith in their senses; and that, without any reasoning, or even almost before the use of reason, we always suppose an external universe, which depends not on our perception, but would exist, though we and every sensible creature were absent or annihilated. Even the animal creation are governed by a like opinion, and preserve this belief of external objects, in all their thoughts, designs, and actions.

It seems also evident, that, when men follow this blind and powerful instinct of nature, they always suppose the very images, presented by the senses, to be the external objects, and never entertain any suspicion, that the one are nothing but representations of the other. This very table, which we see white, and which we feel hard, is believed to exist, independent of our perception, and to be something external to our mind, which perceives it. Our presence bestows not being on it: our absence does not annihilate it. It preserves its existence uniform and entire, independent of the situation of intelligent beings, who perceive or contemplate it.

But this universal and primary opinion of all men is soon destroyed by the slightest philosophy, which teaches us, that nothing can ever be present to the mind but an image or perception, and that the senses are only the inlets, through which these images are conveyed, without being able to produce any immediate intercourse between the mind and the object. The table, which we see, seems to diminish, as we remove farther from it: but the real table, which exists independent of us, suffers no alteration: it was, therefore, nothing but its image, which was present to the mind. These are the obvious dictates of reason; and no man, who reflects, ever doubted, that the existences, which we consider, when we say, *this house* and *that tree,* are nothing but perceptions in the mind, and fleeting copies or representations of other existences, which remain uniform and independent.

So far, then, we are necessitated by reasoning to contradict or depart from the primary instincts of nature, and to embrace a new system with regard to the evidence of our senses. But here philosophy finds herself extremely embarrassed, when she would justify this new system, and obviate the cavils and objections of the sceptics. She can no longer plead the infallible and irresistible instinct of nature: for that led us to a quite different system, which is acknowledged fallible and even erroneous. And to justify this pretended philosophical system, by a chain of clear and convincing argument, or even any appearance of argument, exceeds the power of all human capacity.

By what argument can it be proved, that the perceptions of the mind must be caused by external objects, entirely different from them, though resembling them (if that be possible) and could not arise either from the energy of the mind itself, or from the suggestion of some invisible and unknown spirit, or from some other cause still more unknown to us? It is acknowledged, that, in fact, many of these perceptions arise not from anything external, as in dreams, madness, and other diseases. And nothing can be more inexplicable than the manner, in which body should so operate upon mind as ever to convey an image of itself to a substance, supposed of so different, and even contrary a nature.

It is a question of fact, whether the perceptions of the senses be produced by external objects, resembling them: how shall this question be determined? By experience surely; as all other questions of a like nature. But here experience is, and must be entirely silent. The mind has never anything present to it but the perceptions, and cannot possibly reach any experience of their connection with objects. The supposition of such a connexion is, therefore, without any foundation in reasoning.

To have recourse to the veracity of the Supreme Being, in order to prove the veracity of our senses, is surely making a very unexpected circuit. If his veracity were at all concerned in this matter, our senses would be entirely infallible; because it is not possible that he can ever deceive. Not to mention, that, if the external world be once called in question, we shall be at a loss to find arguments, by which we may prove the existence of that Being or any of his attributes.

This is a topic, therefore, in which the profounder and more philosophical sceptics will always triumph, when they endeavor to introduce an universal doubt into all subjects of human knowledge and enquiry. Do you follow the instincts and propensities of nature, may they say, in assenting to the veracity of sense? But these lead you to believe that the very perception or sensible image is the external object. Do you disclaim this principle, in order to embrace a more rational opinion, that the perceptions are only representations of something external? You here depart from your natural propensities and more obvious sentiments; and yet are not able to satisfy your reason, which can never find any convincing argument from experience to prove, that the perceptions are connected with any external objects. . . .

It is universally allowed by modern enquirers, that all the sensible qualities of objects, such as hard, soft, hot, cold, white, black, &c. are merely secondary, and exist not in the objects themselves, but are perceptions of the mind, without any external archetype or model, which they represent. If this be allowed, with regard to secondary qualities, it must also follow, with regard to the supposed primary qualities of extension and solidity; nor can the latter be any more entitled to that denomination than the former. The idea of extension is entirely acquired from the senses of sight and feeling; and if all the qualities, perceived by the senses, be in the mind, not in the object, the same conclusion must reach the idea of extension, which is wholly dependent on the sensible ideas or the ideas of secondary qualities. . . .

Thus the first philosophical objection to the evidence of sense or to the opinion of external existence consists in this, that such an opinion, if rested on natural instinct, is contrary to reason, and if referred to reason, is contrary to natural instinct, and at the same time carries no rational evidence with it, to convince an impartial enquirer. The second objection goes farther, and represents this opinion as contrary to reason: at least, if it be a principle of reason, that all sensible qualities are in the mind, not in the object. Bereave matter of all its intelligible qualities, both primary and secondary, you in a manner annihilate it, and leave only a certain unknown, inexplicable *something,* as the cause of our perceptions; a notion so imperfect, that no sceptic will think it worth while to contend against it.

7. [The Idea of Self]

There are some philosophers, who imagine we are every moment intimately conscious of what we call our *self;* that we feel its existence and its continuance in existence; and are certain, beyond the evidence of a demonstration, both of its perfect identity and simplicity. The strongest sensation, the most violent passion, say they, instead of distracting us from this view, only fix it the more intensely, and make us consider their influence on *self* either by their pain or pleasure. To attempt a further proof of this were to weaken its evidence; since no proof can be derived from any fact of which we are so intimately conscious; nor is there any thing, of which we can be certain, if we doubt of this.

Unluckily all these positive assertions are contrary to that very experience which is pleaded for them; nor have we any idea of *self,* after the manner it is here explained. For, from what impression could this idea be derived? This question it is impossible to answer without a manifest contradiction and absurdity; and yet it is a question which must necessarily be answered, if we would have the idea of self pass for clear and intelligible. It must be some one impression that gives rise to every real idea. But self or person is not any one impression, but that to which our several impressions and ideas are supposed to have a reference. If any impression gives rise to the idea of self, that impression must continue invariably the same, through the whole course of our lives; since self is supposed to exist after that manner. But there is no impression constant and invariable. Pain and pleasure, grief and joy, passions and sensations succeed each other, and never all exist at the same time. It cannot therefore be from any of these impressions, or from any other, that the idea of self is derived; and consequently there is no such idea.

But further, what must become of all our particular perceptions upon this hypothesis? All these are different, and distinguishable, and separable from each other, and may be separately considered, and may exist separately, and have no need of any thing to support their existence. After what manner therefore do they belong to self, and how are they connected with it? For my part, when I enter most intimately into what I call *myself,* I always stumble on some particular perception or other, of heat or cold, light or shade, love or hatred, pain or pleasure. I never can catch *myself* at any time without a perception, and never can observe any thing but the per-

ception. When my perceptions are removed for any time, as by sound sleep, so long am I insensible of *myself,* and may truly be said not to exist. And were all my perceptions removed by death, and could I neither think, nor feel, nor see, nor love, nor hate, after the dissolution of my body, I should be entirely annihilated, nor do I conceive what is further requisite to make me a perfect nonentity. If any one, upon serious and unprejudiced reflection, thinks he has a different notion of *himself,* I must confess I can reason no longer with him. All I can allow him is, that he may be in the right as well as I, and that we are essentially different in this particular. He may, perhaps, perceive something simple and continued, which he calls *himself;* though I am certain there is no such principle in me.

But setting aside some metaphysicians of this kind, I may venture to affirm of the rest of mankind, that they are nothing but a bundle or collection of different perceptions, which succeed each other with an inconceivable rapidity, and are in a perpetual flux and movement. Our eyes cannot turn in their sockets without varying our perceptions. Our thought is still more variable than our sight; and all our other senses and faculties contribute to this change; nor is there any single power of the soul, which remains unalterably the same, perhaps for one moment. The mind is a kind of theater, where several perceptions successively make their appearance; pass, repass, glide away, and mingle in an infinite variety of postures and situations. There is properly no *simplicity* in it at one time, nor identity in different, whatever natural propension we may have to imagine that simplicity and identity. The comparison of the theater must not mislead us. They are the successive perceptions only, that constitute the mind; nor have we the most distant notion of the place where these scenes are represented, or of the materials of which it is composed.

8. [On the Proper Limits of Enquiry]

The *imagination* of man is naturally sublime, delighted with whatever is remote and extraordinary, and running, without control, into the most distant parts of space and time in order to avoid the objects, which custom has rendered too familiar to it. A correct *Judgment* observes a contrary method, and avoiding all distant and high enquiries, confines itself to common life and to such subjects as fall under daily practice and experience; leaving the more sublime topics to the embellishment of poets and orators, or to the arts of priests and politicians. . . . Those who have a propensity to philosophy, will still continue their researches; because they reflect, that, besides the immediate pleasure, attending such an occupation, philosophical decisions are nothing but the reflections of common life, methodized and corrected. But they will never be tempted to go beyond common life, so long as they consider the imperfection of those faculties which they employ, their narrow reach, and their inaccurate operations. While we cannot give a satisfactory reason, why we believe, after a thousand experiments, that a stone will fall, or fire burn; can we ever satisfy ourselves concerning any determination, which we may form, with regard to the origin of worlds, and the situation of nature, from, and to eternity?

This narrow limitation, indeed, of our enquiries, is, in every respect, so reasonable that it suffices to make the slightest examination into the natural powers of the human mind and to compare them with their objects, in order to recommend it to us. We shall then find what are the proper subjects of science and enquiry.

It seems to me, that the only objects of the abstract science or of demonstration are quantity and number, and that all attempts to extend this more perfect species of knowledge beyond these bounds are mere sophistry and illusion. As the component parts of quantity and number are entirely similar, their relations become intricate and involved; and nothing can be more curious, as well as useful, than to trace, by a variety of mediums, their equality or inequality, through their different appearances. But as all other ideas are clearly distinct and different from each other, we can never advance farther, by our utmost scrutiny, than to observe this diversity, and, by an obvious reflection, pronounce one thing not to be another. Or if there be any difficulty in these decisions, it proceeds entirely from the undeterminate meaning of words, which is corrected by juster definitions. That *the square of the hypothenuse is equal to the squares of the other two sides,* cannot be known, let the terms be ever so exactly defined, without a train of reasoning and enquiry. But to convince us of this proposition, *that where there is no property, there can be no injustice,* it is only necessary to define the terms, and explain injustice, to be a violation of property. This proposition is, indeed, nothing but a more imperfect definition. It is the same case with all those pretended syllogistical reasonings, which may be found in every other branch of learning, except the sciences of quantity and number; and these may safely, I think, be pronounced the only proper objects of knowledge and demonstration.

All other enquiries of men regard only matter of fact and existence; and these are evidently incapable of demonstration. Whatever *is* may *not be.* No negation of a fact can involve a contradiction. The nonexistence of any being, without exception, is as clear and distinct an idea as its existence. The proposition, which affirms it not to be, however false, is no less conceivable and intelligible, than that which affirms it to be. The case is different with the sciences, properly so called. Every proposition, which is not true, is there confused and unintelligible. That the cube root of 64 is equal to the half of 10, is a false proposition, and can never be distinctly conceived. But that Cæsar, or the angel Gabriel, or any being never existed, may be a false proposition, but still is perfectly conceivable, and implies no contradiction.

The existence, therefore, of any being can only be proved by arguments from its cause or its effect; and these arguments are founded entirely on experience. If we reason *a priori,* anything may appear able to produce anything. The falling of a pebble may, for aught we know, extinguish the sun; or the wish of a man control the planets in their orbits. It is only experience, which teaches us the nature and bounds of cause and effect, and enables us to infer the existence of one object from that of another. . . .

When we run over libraries, persuaded of these principles, what havoc must we make? If we take in our hand any volume; of divinity or school metaphysics, for instance; let us ask, *Does it contain any abstract reasoning concerning quantity or number?* No. *Does it contain any experimental reasoning concerning matter of fact and existence?* No. Commit it then to the flames: for it can contain nothing but sophistry and illusion.

IMMANUEL KANT (1724–1804)

The fourth child of an humble saddle-maker, Kant was born in Königsberg, East Prussia. His parents belonged to the Pietists, a revivalist sect within the Lutheran Church, and the family life was characterized by simple religious devotion. Kant detested the mechanical discipline and narrow range of ideas of the Pietist school to which he was sent. At sixteen, he enrolled in the University of Königsberg, supporting himself mainly by tutoring well-to-do students. There his intellectual interests turned to physics and astronomy. After six years at the University, Kant became a private tutor in several homes in East Prussia, a profession which he followed for some nine years. Returning to the University in 1755, he obtained a higher degree and a subordinate post on the faculty. For the next fifteen years he lived in academic poverty, until, in 1770, he was finally appointed a full Professor. In his lectures, he enthralled his student audiences with his knowledge, eloquence, and wit. The popular form of his teaching was in marked contrast to the difficult and technical style of his writing.

He never married, and the clocklike regularity of his bachelor ways became proverbial. His servant awakened him at four forty-five every morning; he spent the next hour drinking tea, smoking his pipe, and planning the day's work; from six to seven he prepared his lectures; from seven to nine or ten he taught; then he wrote until half-past eleven; at twelve he ate a hearty dinner; in the afternoon, rain or shine, he took a regular walk; after that, he read or wrote until, at ten, he went to bed. The rigidity of his routine did not prevent him from enjoying the society of ladies and enlivening many social gatherings with his dry wit. He had many friends in the town and, until he was old, he always dined with friends. His gallantry never deserted him; even when he was so old and feeble that he lost his footing and fell in the street, he courteously presented one of the two unknown ladies who helped him to his feet with the rose that he happened to be carrying.

Although he never traveled far from Königsberg, he was fond of travel books and sympathetic with intellectual and political emancipation the world over. "Have the courage to use your own intelligence!" he advised. He applauded the American and French revolutions, but not the Reign of Terror. "It was a time in Königsberg," wrote one of his colleagues, "when anyone who judged the Revolution even mildly, let alone favorably, was put on a black list as a Jacobin. Kant did not allow himself by that fact to be deterred from speaking up for the Revolution even at the table of noblemen."

Except for a remarkable astronomical treatise (1755), in which he anticipated Laplace's nebular hypothesis, all of his more important works were published late in his life, after he was awakened by Hume from his "dogmatic slumber." In an amazing decade, from 1780 to 1790, there appeared a series of epoch-making books, *The Critique of Pure Reason* (1781), *The Prolegomena to All Future Metaphysics* (1783), *The Foundations of the Metaphysic of Morals* (1785), *The Critique of Practical Reason* (1788), and *The Critique of Judgment* (1790). He subsequently published works on politics and religion, but his main task was done. After 1796, his health gradually declined, and he died in 1804, aged nearly eighty.

The Critique
of Pure Reason
and Other Works

1. [Kant's Indebtedness to Hume]

Since the essays of Locke and Leibniz were written, or better, since the beginning of metaphysics, as history records it, no event has been more decisive for this science than the attack of David Hume. He shed no light but he did strike a spark from which a light might be kindled in receptive tinder, if its glow were carefully tended.

Hume began with one important metaphysical idea. It was the supposed connection of cause and effect. He challenged the claim that this connection was conceived in the mind itself. He wanted to know how anyone could think anything so constituted that its mere existence necessarily called for the existence of something else; for this is what the notion of cause means. He proved conclusively that it is quite impossible to conceive the connection of cause and effect abstractly, solely by means of thought, because it involves

The following excerpts are from *An Immanuel Kant Reader,* edited and translated by Raymond B. Blakney (New York: Harper & Row, 1960). Reprinted by permission of the publishers. The first section is from *The Prolegomena to All Future Metaphysics* and the final section is from *The Critique of Judgment.* All else is from *The Critique of Pure Reason.*

the idea of necessity. We do not see that if one thing exists, another has to exist in consequence, and we do not know how an abstract idea of this relation could occur to anyone.

Hume concluded that the idea of cause constitutes a delusion which seems to be a human brain child but is just the bastard of imagination sired by experience. Thus, certain perceptions are joined together as the law of association provides. Then habit, which is a psychological necessity, is passed off as objective and as being discovered through insight. He then inferred that we cannot conceive a causal connection between events, even in general; for if we did, our ideas would be fictional, and knowledge, which is supposed to be abstract and necessary, would be nothing but common experience under a false label. This, plainly, means that there is not and cannot be such a thing as metaphysics.

However hasty and mistaken Hume's conclusion may be, it was at least based on investigation. This made it worthwhile for the bright people of the day to co-operate in finding a happier solution to the problem as he explained it. The outcome might well have been a complete reform of the science, but the unhappy genius of metaphysicians caused him not to be understood.

I frankly confess that many years ago it was the memory of David Hume that first interrupted my dogmatic slumber and gave new direction to my studies in the field of speculative philosophy.

I tried first to see if Hume's objection could be put in a general form. I soon found that the idea of a connection between cause and effect was by no means the only idea we conceive abstractly of relations between things. Metaphysics consists first and last of such ideas. I tried to count them and when I had succeeded as I wished, taking first one and then another, I went on to explain them. I was now certain that they are not derived from experience, as Hume has asserted, but that they spring from the mind alone. These explanations had seemed impossible to my smart predecessor and had not even occurred to anyone else, although everyone used such ideas without asking what the security behind them might be. This, I say, was the most difficult work ever undertaken on behalf of metaphysics. The worst of it was that no help at all could be had from metaphysics itself because the very possibility of metaphysics depends on this kind of explanation.

Having now succeeded in the solution of Hume's problem, not only in special cases but with a view to the whole reasoning function of mind, I could proceed safely, if slowly, to survey the field of pure reasoning, its boundaries as well as its contents, and I could do this working from general principles. This is exactly what meta-physics needs to build a system which is securely planned.

2. [A New Way of Thinking]

In metaphysics, thought is continually coming to a dead end, even when laws which common experience supports are under examination, purely as laws. Times without number it is necessary to go back to the fork because the road does not take us where we want to go. As for unanimity among the practitioners of metaphysics, there is so little of it that the discipline seems more like an arena, a ring constructed for those who like to exercise their skills in mock combat. At any rate, no contestant has yet succeeded in getting and holding a spot of his own. It appears, then, that to date, the procedure in metaphysics has just been to grope and worse than that, to grope among ideas.

How can it be explained that in this field, scientific certainty has not yet been found? Can it be impossible? If it is, why has nature visited our minds with a restless drive for certainty, as if this were the most important business of all? Not only that but there would be little reason ever to trust the powers of thought, if they fail in one of the most important projects of human curiosity, proffering illusions and giving at last betrayal. Perhaps it is only that up to now we have failed to read the road signs correctly. If we renew the search, may we hope to have better luck than has been the lot of those who preceded us?

It seems to me that the examples of mathematics and physics, having become what they are by sudden revolution, are remarkable enough to warrant attention to the essential element of their change, the change that proved so beneficial. It may be worth our while also to make the experiment of imitating them, to the degree the analogy between these two rational disciplines and metaphysics permits.

Hitherto it has been assumed that knowledge must conform to the things known; but on this basis all attempts to find out about the world of things by abstract thought, and thus to permit an extension of human knowledge, have come to nothing. Let us then experiment to see whether or not we do better with the problems of metaphysics if we assume that things to be known must conform in advance to our knowing process. This would appear to lead to what we want, namely, knowledge that tells us something about an object of thought before it becomes a part of our experience.

If my perception of an object has to conform to the object, I do not see how there could be any abstract knowledge of it; but if the objects of my perceptions conform to the laws by which I know them, it is easy to conceive of abstract knowledge, for all experience is a kind of knowledge involving the mind, the laws of which I must suppose were a part of me before I ever saw anything. Those laws get expressed in abstract terms but all my experience must agree with them.

This experiment succeeds as well as could be desired. It promises scientific certainty for the part of metaphysics that deals in abstract ideas, the corresponding objects of which may be checked off in experience. It involves a new way of thinking which enables us to explain perfectly how abstract knowledge, knowledge prior to experience, is possible. It also furnishes satisfactory proofs of the laws which form the mental framework of the natural world. Both of these achievements had been impossible heretofore.

3. [Empirical and A Priori Knowledge]

There is no doubt that knowledge begins with experience. How else could mental powers be awakened to action, if not by the objects that excite our senses, in part arousing images and in part stimulating the mental activity by which the images are compared? Images must then be combined or separated and the raw material of sense impressions worked over into the knowledge of things called experience. In the order of time, life begins with experience; there is no knowledge before that.

But if knowledge begins with experience, it does not follow that all of it is derived from experience. It may well be that whatever knowledge we do get from experience is already a combination of impressions and mental activity, the sense impressions being merely the occasion. It may be that the mental additive cannot be distinguished from the basic stuff until long practice makes one alert to it and skilled to pick it out.

This then is a question that needs close study and for which no offhand answer will do: Is there knowledge apart from both experience and sense impressions? This kind of knowledge is called abstract and prior (*a priori*) in contrast to knowledge derived from experience, which is empirical (*a posteriori*).

The word "*a priori*" is not yet definite enough to indicate the full meaning of the question at hand. It is often said of knowledge derived from experience that it is abstract because it does not come immediately from experience, but from some general rule borrowed from experience. Of a man who undermines the foundations of his house, we might say that he might have known *a priori,* that is, abstractly and beforehand, that the house would fall. He need not have waited for the actual experience of seeing it go down. He could not, however, have known about the house falling, from abstract principles only. He needs first to learn that bodies are heavy and that they fall when supports are removed; this would have to be learned from experience.

In what follows, by *abstract* knowledge we do not mean knowledge independent of this or that experience but knowledge *utterly independent of all experience.* In contrast, there is empirical, or *a posteriori* knowledge which we get only through experience. Abstract knowledge is called *pure* when it contains no trace of experience. So, for example, the proposition, "Every change has its cause," is abstract but not pure because *change* is an idea drawn only from experience.

We need now a criterion by which to distinguish pure from empirical knowledge. Experience teaches one that an object is what it is, but not

that it could not be otherwise. So, first, if a proposition cannot be conceived without thinking it *necessary,* it is *abstract.* Secondly, a judgment based on experience is never truly or strictly universal but only relatively so. But if a judgment is strictly *universal* and there is no possible exception to this, then it is not derived from experience and is valid, absolutely *abstract, pure.*

We need also to distinguish between two kinds of judgments, or statements: *analytic,* in which the predicate merely analyzes the subject; and *synthetic,* or *amplifying* in which the predicate adds something to the subject. If A is the subject of a statement and B is the predicate, there are two choices. If B is contained in A, the statement is analytic; if B is not contained in A but is related to it otherwise, the statement is synthetic, or amplifying.

For example, if I say, "All bodies are extended," this is an analytic statement of judgment. I need not go beyond the very idea of "body" to find the idea of "extension." On the other hand when I say, "All bodies are heavy," the predicate is quite different from what I think in the idea of "body" as such, and the addition of this kind of predicate to the subject makes the statement synthetic. Statements of experience always amplify the subject.

In abstract, amplifying judgments, no help can be had from experience. If I go beyond idea A and find idea B related to it, on what could such an amplification be based? Take, for example, the proposition: Everything that happens has a cause. In the idea of "something that happens," I can think of a time before the event and from it derive analytic judgments. But the idea of "cause" is something else; it does not fall within the idea of "something that happens." How then can I say something about this subject that is entirely unrelated to it? How do I know that cause belongs necessarily to that "something that happens," even when that something does not contain any notion of it? What is the unknown X on which one depends when he discovers a predicate B, foreign to A, which is, nevertheless, connected with it?

The unknown X cannot be experience because the principle just discussed adds a second conception (cause) to the first (existence), not only with wider generalization than experience can proffer but with an assertion of necessity. It is therefore wholly abstract and unrelated to experience. The whole aim of our speculative, abstract knowledge depends on synthetic, or amplifying propositions of this kind. Analytic judgments are of the highest importance and necessary, but only to clarify conception. This, in turn, is required for the secure and broader amplification by which something really new may be added to the matter of knowledge.

Examples from science. Mathematical judgments always amplify. One might think at first that $7 + 5 = 12$ is a straight analytic proposition. On closer inspection, it appears that the sum $7 + 5$ contains nothing more than the combination of these two numbers. There is nothing to indicate what number embraces both. Arithmetical propositions always amplify.

Nor are geometric propositions analytic. That a straight line is the shortest distance between two points is an amplifying conception. Straightness has nothing to do with quantity, but only with quality. The idea of shortness is thus additive, and intuition is necessary at this point. Without it, amplification would be impossible.

The science of physics also contains principles which are abstract and amplifying. For example, there is the proposition that in all the changes of the physical world, the total quantity of matter remains unchanged. But in the idea of matter, I do not imagine its permanency. I think only of its presence in the space it fills. So I really have to go beyond the idea of matter itself and attribute something to it abstractly, something I never thought it involved. The proposition is thus not analytic but synthetic, or amplifying and yet it is abstractly conceived.

There must be amplifying and abstract knowledge in metaphysics too, even if metaphysics is regarded only as a pseudo science, necessary to human nature. It is not the duty of metaphysicians merely to dissect subjects and so, analytically, to illustrate abstract ideas. It is their duty to extend abstract knowledge and for this purpose they use principles which add to their ideas matter not originally contained in them. By means of abstract, amplifying judgments they may even go where experience cannot follow, as, for example, in the statement that "the world must have a beginning," and the like. So, metaphysics, at least by aim, consists of pure, amplifying propositions.

The characteristic problem then of pure reason is: How are abstract, amplifying judgments possible? That metaphysics has so far remained in the state of vacillating uncertainty and contradiction, is due to the fact that this problem was not recognized sooner, nor, perhaps, was the difference between analytic and amplifying judgment made clear.

4. [The Matter and Form of Intuition]

Of the varied processes by which things become known, there is one from which all thought stems. It is awareness (intuition), and it alone is direct or immediate. Ultimately all food for thought comes from the outside world through our awareness of it, but among humans this occurs only when mind is involved.

The property of mind by which external things are recognized may be called sensitivity. Objects appear to mind because of its sensitivity, and this is the only way awareness can occur. In functioning mind, then, awareness gives rise to thoughts and finally to concepts. Directly or indirectly, all thought goes back to awareness and so to sensitivity, because there is no other way to know external things. Sensation is the effect an object has on the sensitive mind. If awareness comes through sensation, it is said to be empirical; and the object so revealed, whatever it may be, is called "phenomenon," or simply "thing."

By matter, I mean the substance of a thing, to which sensations are traceable; by form, I refer to my awareness

that the substance of something is arranged in a given order.

It is clear that sensations are not put in form by other sensations. The matter of which things are composed may be known through sensation but their form is provided by the mind, and form is therefore separate from sensation.

I call awareness (intuition) which does not participate in sensation, *pure* (that is, belonging only to mind). The pure form which sense impressions take on, the form or order in which the many elements of things are arranged by the mind, must be in mind beforehand. The pure form of sensitivity may be called pure awareness.

If, from your awareness of a body, you subtract the contribution of thought processes such as substance, forces, divisibility, etc., and then take away all that pertains to sensation, such as impenetrability, color, etc., there will still remain extension and form. These belong to pure awareness and exist only in mind, as forms for sense impressions, even if there were present no external objects or sensations from them.

5. [The Pure Forms of Intuition —Space and Time]

There is a sense or sensitivity of mind, by which we reach out to things and see them located in external space. Within this space their form, size, and relative positions are or can be fixed.

There is an internal sense by which the mind is aware of itself or its internal states. This sense does not present the soul as an object to be observed. It is, however, a fixed function without which an awareness of internal states of mind would be impossible. Its operations pertain to the relationships of time. Time cannot appear as an external matter any more than space can appear to be something within.

What then are space and time? Are they real entities? Or if not, are they the delimitations of things or relations between things which exist whether anyone observes them or not? Or are they delimitations and relations which are inherent in one's awareness of the world and thus in the subjective character of the mind? If so, then without these properties of mind, predicates like space and time would never appear anywhere.

To understand this matter more clearly, let us first consider space.

1. Space is not an idea derived from experience of the external world. If my sensations are to be referred to things outside me, i.e., to things located at some point of space other than where I am, or if I am to be able to refer my sensations to differing objects located at several points, the idea of space must be present in advance. My conception of space therefore cannot be the product of experience or borrowed from the relations of things to each other. On the contrary, it is only by means of the idea of space that external experience becomes possible at all.

2. Space is the visualization which is necessary to the mind, and the basis of all external perceptions. One might imagine space with no objects to fill it, but it is impossible to imagine that there should be no space. Space is therefore a condition of the possibility of phenomena and not a form required by them. It is subjective, a vizualization which precedes all external experience.

3. The demonstrable certainty of geometric propositions depends on the necessity of this mental visualization of space. If space were a conception gained empirically or borrowed from general external experience, the first principles of mathematical definition would be merely perceptions. They would be subject to all the accidents of perception and there would be no necessity that there should be only one straight line between two points. A theorem would be something to be learned in each case by experience. Whatever is derived from experience possesses only relative generality, based on reasoning from observations. We should accordingly be able to say only that so far as anyone can see, there is no space having more than three dimensions.

4. Space is not a discursive or general idea of the relations between things. It is pure awareness or mental visualization. First of all, only one space is imaginable, and if many spaces are mentioned, they are all parts of the one space. They are not to be considered as leading up to the one all-embracing space, or the component parts from which an aggregate of space is formed.

Space is essentially one. The general idea of a mutiplicity of spaces is the result of imposing limitations on space. Hence, it follows that the foundation of all ideas of space is a mental awareness, and it is thus not derived from experience. So geometrical principles, such as "The sum of two sides of a triangle is greater than the third," may never be derived from the general conception of sides and triangles but from an awareness or visualization which is purely mental and which is derived thence with demonstrable certainty.

5. Space is visualized as an infinite quantity. The general idea of space, which is to be found in a foot as well as a yard, would furnish no information about the quantity of the space involved if there were not infinity in the reach of awareness. Without this, no conception of relations in space could ever contain the principle of infinity.

Space is not in any sense a property of things or the relation between them. It is nothing but the form the appearances of things take to man's outer senses. It is the mental basis of sensitivity and makes possible one's awareness of the external world.

One may speak of space, extension, etc., only from the human point of view. Apart from one's awareness of the outer world, the idea of space means nothing at all. The space predicate is attributed to things only as they are sensed.

The rule that "things are juxtaposed in space" is valid within the limitation that "things" are taken only as objects of awareness. Add one condition and say that "things as they appear externally are juxtaposed in space," and the rule is universally valid.

This exposition therefore teaches the *reality* (objective validity) of space. Space is as real as anything else in the world. At the same time, it teaches the *ideality* of space, when things are viewed as only the mind can view them, as they are by themselves, apart from the activity of human sense. We also assert the reality of space as veri-fiable fact in human experience of the external world.

The *formal* idea of phenomena in space is a critical reminder that there is nothing of which one is aware that is a thing-itself (that is, something apart from man's perception of it). Space is not the form of things-themselves. The phenomena of which we are aware tell us nothing about things as they are apart from us, and in experience nobody ever asks about them as such.

[*Kant's treatment of time parallels that of space, and need not be quoted. Time, like space, is a form of perception, not a thing perceived. Just as phenomena are spread out in space, above or below, near or far, to the right or the left, so likewise are they ordered in time, before, after, or simultaneous with other events. Anything experienced as spatial is thought of as belonging to the outer world, but temporal order applies to one's psychological acts of apprehension. Hence time is "the form of inner sense, that is, of our awareness of ourselves and our own inner states." But both space and time are necessary forms of human perception, and cannot be ascribed to objects in themselves apart from experience.*]

6. [How the Categories of the Understanding Unify and Organize Our Experience]

Among the many strands from which the complicated web of human knowledge is woven there are some which are destined from the start to be used abstractly and to continue independent of experience. The claims made for these ideas generally require special demonstration (deduction). Their legitimacy is not established by a deduction based on experience, even though we do want to know how these ideas can refer to objects within one's experience, and yet be derived apart from it. The explanation of the way abstract and prior ideas refer to objects is to be called *formal deduction*. This is distinguished from *empirical deduction,* which shows how an idea is derived by reflection from experience. *Empirical deduction* applies not to the legitimacy of the use of the ideas but to the facts from which they arise.

Without doubt an investigation of the functioning of man's power to know, beginning with single perceptions and climbing to general ideas, is useful. We have to thank the celebrated John Locke for opening up this avenue. The deduction of pure ideas is not, however, to be achieved along these lines; it is to be worked out in another direction. Their future use, independent of experience, requires for them a very particular birth certificate, in which descent from experience is denied. Locke's attempted psychological derivation is not deduction at all, because it depends on matters of fact. It is rather an explanation of the possession of pure knowledge. It is clear, therefore, that only a formal deduction of pure ideas is usable and that empirical deductions will not do.

Our entire investigation of the formal deduction of pure ideas should be based on this principle: Pure ideas are the abstract and prior conditions of experience. They supply the objective ground of experience and are, accordingly, necessary. To know how they occur, the abstract and prior conditions necessary to experience must be discovered and kept separate from knowledge derived from experience. The categories are pure ideas which express the formal and objective conditions of experience with sufficient generality and which contain the pure thought involved in every experience. It is really a sufficient deduction of the categories and a justification of their objective validity to prove that no object is conceivable without them.

The famous John Locke, lacking these considerations and having come across pure ideas in the course of experience, proceeded to derive them from experience itself. Then, inconsistently, he went far beyond the bounds of experience in studies of knowledge. David Hume saw that to do this, ideas from pure origins are needed. He could not explain, however, how it was that ideas, disconnected in one's mind, came together in some object of thought. It never occurred to him that mind itself might be the author of the experience of its object.

So he, too, was led to derive pure ideas from experience, or habit, i.e., from a subjective necessity begotten of frequent associations of experiences. This finally came to be accepted as objective, but falsely so. Subsequently Hume explained, and quite consistently this time, that with ideas so derived and with their attendant principles, it is not possible to get beyond personal experience. The deduction of pure ideas from experience, as practiced by Locke and Hume, cannot be reconciled with the abstract and prior knowledge encountered in pure mathematics and natural science. It is therefore refuted by the facts.

The first of these men left the door wide open to fantasy. It is hard to keep reasoning within due bounds once it has had unlimited prestige. The second gave in entirely to skepticism because he believed he had found in the knowing process an illusion which generally passed as reasonable. We now turn to study whether or not reasoning can be steered between these two cliffs, its limits indicated, and still keep its proper field of function open.

If every perception or idea were isolated from every other, there could be no knowledge as we know it, because knowledge consists of perceptions and ideas conjoined and compared to each other. Since the senses cover a whole field of awareness, they need a synopsis corresponding to the organization that makes knowledge possible when mind spontaneously comprehends sense data. Spontaneity is the beginning of a threefold organization which is necessary to every kind of knowledge. It consists of (1) *comprehension,* in which awareness is made into perceptions by ideas; (2) imagination in the *recollection* of the various elements necessary to knowledge; (3) *recognition* of the resultant ideas. Thus we have three inner sources of knowledge which make understanding and its empirical product, experience, possible.

However ideas or images arise, whether from the influence of external things or inner causes, or abstractly, or empirically as phenomena, they belong to man's inner sense because they are simply modifications of mind. All knowledge is, accordingly, subject to the formal condition of inner sense, namely, time. Everything is arranged, connected, and related by time. This general remark is fundamental to all subsequent discussion.

Generally speaking, awareness means being aware of many things at once, and this could not be imagined if time were not marked in the mind by a succession of impressions. In any given instant each impression is an absolute unity by itself; so, in order to get unity in awareness (as the idea of space requires), it is first necessary to let the various elements of awareness run in succession through the mind and then pull them together. This is the act which I call the organization of apprehension, or understanding. It is applied directly to awareness, which actually is multiple and so requires organization if it is to be unified or comprehended by means of a single idea.

The synthesis, or organization of understanding must be carried out abstractly and in advance, since ideas which are not empirical are involved. The ideas of space and time would be impossible without it; the many elements of sense data must be organized before they appear. This is how the pure organization of understanding is accomplished.

Again, it is apparent that if I draw an imaginary line, or consider the time lapse from one noon to the next, or even think of a certain number, I must begin by getting a general idea of the aggregates or sets of perceptions involved. If I were to lose from thought the antecedent part of either of them, say the first part of the line, the first hours of the day, or the digits preceding my number, and if I were unable to reproduce the lost parts as I went on, then no general idea of either of these sets would be possible to me. Neither could I, in that case, have the foregoing thoughts of even the first and purest ideas of space and time.

The organization of understanding is inseparably connected with recollection. Since the former is the formal basis of all knowledge, both empirical and pure, the organization of recollection by imagination belongs to the formal activity of mind and is here to be called *formal imagination*.

Again, if I were not aware that what I now think is the same as what I was thinking a moment ago, recollection of a lost step in a series of perceptions would be useless. Each perception in its place would be new, and not part of the action that made the series. A series of experiences could never be complete because it would lack the unity which only consciousness can give it. When I count, if I forget how the series of numbers now in my thought has been added up, one by one, I can never understand how the final sum is produced. The sum is a concept which depends on my consciousness of the organized unity of the number series.

The very word "idea" could have been the occasion of these remarks; consciousness gathers up the items in a series or a field, one by one, then recollection pulls them all together in a single idea. The consciousness involved may be so weak that it is felt, not in the act or process of production but only in the final idea. Nevertheless, even though it is not very clear, consciousness must always be there. Without it, ideas and all knowledge of objects would be impossible. . . .

If it is desired to follow up the inward connections among perceptions to their point of convergence, where they are unified as experience requires, we must begin with pure self-consciousness. Awareness amounts to nothing until it merges into consciousness, directly or indirectly. If this did not happen there would be no knowledge. Among all the perceptions of a given moment, we are conscious, abstractly and in advance, of our own identity. This is how any perception becomes possible, and it is a firm principle which may be called the formal principle of unity in one's perception of a field of sense data.

This unity, however, presupposes or involves an organization which is as necessary to knowledge and as prior and abstract as the unity itself. Unification depends on pure imagination to organize a field of perceptions into knowledge. Such an organization is said to be formal if, ignoring differences of awareness, it effects only the necessary unification of the field. The unity involved is also formal when it refers only to the original unity of self and thus becomes prior and necessary. Formal and organizing imagination is thus the pure form of knowledge by means of which, abstractly and in advance, objects of experience become known.

Understanding is the self at work in imagination, unifying and organizing experience; pure understanding is the self at work when imagination effects a formal organization. Understanding, therefore, involves pure, abstract forms for knowledge, which carry the unity the imagination uses to organize the data or experience into phenomena. These forms are the categories; that is, they are the mind's pure conceptions, or ideas. This then is how man learns from experience: Mind focuses on objects of sense by its own necessity, via awareness and by means of an organizing imagination; then phenomena, the data of experience, conform to mind; by means of the categories, pure mind constitutes a formal and organizing principle of experience, and this shows how, necessarily, phenomena are related to mind. . . .

Imagination, therefore, is man's prior and necessary capacity to organize things, and this makes us call it *productive imagination*. If imagination effects only necessary unity in the organization of phenomena, it can be called formal. The foregoing may appear strange, but it must be clear by now that the affinity, the association of phenomena and their recollection according to law, which is to say the whole of human experience, is made possible by formal imagination. Without this, ideas of objects could never foregather in a single experience.

It is the permanent and unchanging "I" (pure apperception) that correlates perceptions when we become conscious of them. All consciousness belongs to one all-embracing pure apperception, "I," as sense awareness belongs to one pure inner awareness, namely, time. So that this "I" may function mentally, imagination is added and the organiza-

tion effected by imagination, though of itself prior and necessary, is carried out in the senses. Phenomena are connected in a field of impressions only as they appear in awareness: for example, a triangle. When the field is once related to the "I," ideas of it fit into the mind, and imagination relates them to sense awareness.

Pure imagination is therefore a fundamental operation of the soul, and abstractly, in advance, all knowledge depends on it. It connects all that one is aware of with the unitary "I." It brings the two extremes of sense and mind together. Without it, the senses might report phenomena but not empirical knowledge, and so experience would be impossible. Real experience comes of apprehension, association, and recognition of phenomena and contains the ultimate and highest ideas, the ideas that formally unify experience and validate empirical knowledge objectively. These ideas constitute the basis on which a field of sense data is recognized. If they concern only the form of experience, they are, accordingly, categories. The whole formal unity of recognition by means of imagination depends on the categories, and in turn the whole empirical use of the categories (in recognition, recollection, association, and apprehension), even down to phenomena, depends on imagination. These four elements of knowing make it possible for a phenomenon to belong to our consciousness and so to ourselves.

It is we who bring order and regularity to phenomena and call the result "nature." These properties would not be discovered in nature if our own minds had not first put them there; for unity in nature means a prior, necessary, and certain connection of phenomena. How indeed could organized unity in nature be conceived in advance, if the original source of knowledge, the inner core of our minds, did not first contain it? What would there be to see if this mental condition of ours were not objectively valid, valid because it is the condition by which objects become part of experience?

7. [Phenomena and Noumena]

We have now explored the land of pure reasoning and carefully surveyed every part of it. We have measured its extent and put everything in its right place. It is an island, by nature enclosed within unchangeable limits. It is the land of truth (enchanting name!), surrounded by a wide and stormy ocean, the native home of illusion, where cloud banks and icebergs falsely prophesy new lands and incessantly deceive adventurous seafarers with empty hopes, engaging them in romantic pursuits which they can neither abandon nor fulfill. Before we venture on this sea, we ought to glance at the map of the island and consider whether or not to be satisfied with it, lest there be no other territory on which to settle. We should know what title we have to it, by which we may be secure against opposing claims.

We have seen that the produce of mind is not borrowed from experience but is for use only in experience. The mind's principles may be either abstract and constitutive, like mathematical principles, or merely regulative, like dynamic principles. In either case they contain nothing but the pure schema of possible experience. Unity comes into experience from the organizing unity of mind, which the mind confers on self-consciousness via imagination; and phenomena, as the data of possible experience, must fit into that unity abstractly and in advance. These rules of mind not only are true but also are the source of all truth, the reason for the agreement of our knowledge with objects. They contain the basis on which experience is possible, that is, experience viewed as the sum of one's knowledge of objects. We are not, however, satisfied with an exposition merely of what is true; we want also to know what mankind otherwise wants to know. This long, critical inquiry would hardly seem worthwhile if at the end of it, we have learned only what would have gone on anyway in everyday mental operations.

Even if our minds do work satisfactorily without such an inquiry as this, the inquiry has one advantage. The mind that is in us is unable to determine for itself the limits of its own uses. That is why the deep inquiry we have set up is required. If we cannot decide whether certain questions lie within our mental horizon, we must be prepared for getting lost among the delusions that result from overstepping our limitations.

If we can know certainly whether the mind can use its principles only within experience and never purely formally, this knowledge will have important consequences. The formal use of an idea is its application to things in general and to entities for which we have no sense data; the empirical use of an idea is its application to phenomena, or to objects of possible experience. It is evident that only the latter application is practicable. For example, consider the ideas of mathematics, first as pure awareness: space has three dimensions; there can be but one straight line between two points; etc. Although these principles are generated abstractly in the mind, they would mean nothing if their meaning could not be demonstrated in phenomena. It is therefore required that a pure idea be made sensible, that is, that one should or can be aware of an object corresponding to it. Otherwise, the idea, we say, would make no sense, i.e., it would be meaningless.

The mathematician meets this need by the construction of a figure which is, to the senses, a phenomenon, even though abstractly produced. In the same science, the idea of size finds its meaning and support in number, whether by fingers, or abacus beads, or in strokes and points on the printed page. The idea is always abstractly conceived, as are the amplifying principles and formulas derived from them; but finally, their use and their relation to their indicated objects appear only in experience, even though they contain the formal conditions of the possibility of that experience.

That this is the case with all the categories and the principles spun out of them, appears as follows. We cannot really define the categories, or make the possibility of their objects intelligible, without descending at once to the conditions of sense and the forms of phenomena, to which, as their only

objects, the categories must be limited. If this condition is removed, all meaning, all relation to an object disappears, and no example will make the meaning of such an idea comprehensible....

If *noumenon* means something which is not an object of sense and so is abstracted from awareness, this is the negative sense of the term. If, however, it means an object of nonsensible awareness, we presuppose a special kind of awareness, which is purely mental, not part of our equipment, and of which we cannot imagine even the possibility. That would be *noumenon* in the positive sense of the word. . . .

The division of objects into phenomena and noumena, and the world into a world of the senses and a world of mind, is not admissible in the positive sense, even though the division of ideas as sensible and mental is legitimate. For we cannot conceive a mind which knows objects, not discursively or through categories, but by a nonsensible awareness. What mind acquires through the idea of noumenon is a negative extension. It is not then limited by sense but rather, it limits sense by applying the term "noumena" to things-themselves, which are not phenomena. It also limits itself, since noumena are not to be known by means of categories. They can be thought of only as unknown somethings.

8. [God, Freedom, and Immortality]

God, freedom, and the immortality of the soul are the problems to the solution of which all the labors of metaphysics are directed. It used to be believed that the doctrine of freedom was necessary only as a negative condition of practical philosophy, and that the ideas of God and the soul belonged to theoretical philosophy; they had to be demonstrated separately. Religion was achieved subsequently by adding morality to these ideas.

It soon appears, however, that such an attempt must miscarry. It is absolutely impossible to conceive an original Being whose characteristics make him experienceable, and therefore knowable, if one starts with only simple, abstract, ontological ideas. Neither would an idea based on the experience of physical appropriateness in nature adequately demonstrate morality or acquaintance with God. Just as little would knowledge of the soul, acquired from experience in this life, provide an idea of the soul's spiritual, immortal nature, adequate to morality. Neither theology nor spiritualism can be established by empirical data. They deal with matters that transcend human knowledge. Ideas of God and the immortal soul can be defined only by predicates drawn from supersensible sources, predicates whose reality is demonstrated by experience. This is the only way a supersensible Being can be known.

The freedom of man under moral law conjoined with the final end which freedom prescribes by means of the moral law compose the only predicate of this kind. This combination of ideas contains the conditions necessary to the possibility of both God and man.

An inference can then be made to the actuality and the nature of God and the soul, both of which would otherwise be entirely hidden from us.

Theoretical proofs of God and immortality fail because natural ideas tell us nothing about supersensible matters. Proofs via morality and freedom do succeed because there is causality in these ideas and their roots are supersensible. The causal law of freedom here establishes its own actuality by the way men behave. It also provides means of knowing other supersensible objects, such as the final moral end and its practicability. The conception of freedom's causality is, of course, based on practical considerations, but that happens to be all religion needs.

It is remarkable that of the three pure, rational ideas—God, freedom, and immortality—whose objects are supersensible, freedom alone proves its objective reality in the world of nature by what it can effect there. Freedom, therefore, makes possible the connection of the other two ideas with nature and of all three with religion. We may thus conceive the supersensible realm within man and around him, so that it becomes practical knowledge. Speculative philosophy, which offers only a negative idea even of freedom itself, can never accomplish anything like this. The idea of freedom, fundamental to unconditioned practical law, reaches beyond the limits within which natural, theoretical ideas remain hopelessly restricted.

COMMENT

Impressions and Ideas

The supreme advocate of the sceptical spirit is David Hume. He is a member of the sequence of classic British empiricists, which includes such great figures as Bacon, Hobbes, Locke, Berkeley, and Mill. More consistent in his empiricism than his predecessors, Hume pushed the sceptical implications of this approach to its logical extreme. Many philosophers have tried to refute his arguments, but his influence continues to be immense.

A thorough empiricist, Hume traced all knowledge back to some original basis in experience. The stream of experience, he pointed out, is made up of *perceptions*, a term he employed to designate any mental content whatever. He divided perceptions into *impressions*, the original sensations or feelings, and *ideas*, the images, copies, or representations of these originals. It is important to note that Hume, unlike Locke and Berkeley, reserved the word "idea" for mental copies or representations of original data.

Impressions are (1) more forcible or vivid than ideas, and (2) prior in occurrence to ideas, being their necessary cause or source. There are two types of impressions—those of *sensation* and those of *reflection*. Impressions of sensation are the data that come from the external senses—sight, hearing, touch, taste, and smell. Impressions of reflection, such as emotions and desires, are internal to the mind and are frequently occasioned by ideas. The *idea* of death, for example, may arouse the impression of fear. The impressions of reflection are, in this sense, less original than impressions of sensation. But both types of impressions may be copied by the memory and imagination; and simple ideas, which are exact copies of impressions, may be combined in many different ways to form complex ideas. Unlike simple ideas, our complex ideas need not exactly resemble impressions. We can imagine a mermaid without ever having seen one, but the *constituents* of the complex idea—in this instance, the idea of a fish and the idea of a woman—must ultimately go back to original impressions.

Hume's practice of tracing ideas back to their original impressions becomes a *logical test* of the soundness of concepts. If a concept, such as that of substance, cannot be traced back to some reliable basis in impressions, it immediately becomes suspect. A fertile source of confusion in our thinking is the tendency to impute to outer things the qualities that belong to internal impressions. Thus an internal feeling of necessity may be falsely imputed to some outer chain of events. The human mind, if it does not carefully analyze the sources of its ideas, is prone to fall into such errors. Hume's philosophy consists largely in exposing these pitfalls in our thinking.

317

Criticism of the Idea of Causation

The most famous example of this critical method is Hume's analysis of the idea of causation. He began by pointing out that this idea is extremely crucial in our thinking. "The only connection or relation of objects," he declared, "which can lead us beyond the immediate impressions of our memory and senses, is that of cause and effect; and that because it is the only one on which we can found a just inference from one object to another."[1] We infer external objects only because we suppose them to be the causes of the immediate data of experience. The idea of causation is thus the basis of empirical science and the ultimate ground for belief in an external world. For Hume, scientific knowledge as a whole stands or falls according to whether causation can be validated as a principle of reasoning.

Upon analysis, the idea of causation breaks up into four notions: (1) *succession*, (2) *contiguity*, (3) *constant conjunction*, and (4) *necessary connection*. Hume maintained that the first three notions can be defended—we can verify them by recalling the original sensory impressions from which they are derived. But *necessity* cannot thus be verified—try as we may, we cannot trace it back to any sensory impressions. It turns out, therefore, to be a confused and illegitimate notion. I shall not analyze the details of his argument, since this exercise in analysis is excellent practice for students.

Sceptical Implications

Hume was quick to draw the consequences from his theory of causation. One implication is that our common-sense idea that the future will resemble the past is merely an assumption, an expectation begotten by habit, not a rational conviction. Since we never discover an objective necessity binding effect to cause, we have no reason to assume that this cause-and-effect relation must continue to hold. The sun has risen many times, but this does not mean that it will rise tomorrow. There is no "law" that the sun must rise: there is only inexplicable repetition.

Indeed, we cannot even say that it is *probable* that the sun will rise tomorrow. Probability is based upon regularity, and this is just what we have no right to assume. Every event is, so far as we can see, "loose and separate" from every other; and hence every moment we start from scratch with no logical basis for prediction. The previous regularity of nature may be just a run of luck; for all we know to the contrary, something may happen in the very next moment to upset nature's apple cart.

It may be said in reply that we *count* on the ordinary course of events. But we do not *rationally* count on it: we *bet* on it, so to speak, and we are so used to the betting that we overlook the irrational nature of the bet. Practically speaking,

---

[1] *An Enquiry Concerning Human Understanding,* edited by L. A. Selby-Bigge (Oxford: Clarendon Press, 1902), p. 89.

we have to bet on the future if we are to survive, but we must not mistake this practical necessity for a logical insight. Nature repeats the same tales again and again, but *why* she repeats them, and whether she will continue to repeat them, we cannot tell. The scientist, in this regard, has no better insight than the rest of us.

One of the most significant applications of Hume's analysis of causation is his attack upon the arguments for an external world. Both Locke and Berkeley, whose arguments Hume had primarily in mind, inferred the existence of an external world on the basis of a theory of causation. They reasoned that the regular character of experience, which is largely determined for us independently of our wills, must have some external cause. Locke found the cause in material substances and primary qualities; Berkeley in God and the ideas which He imprints upon our minds. Now Hume, in attack, went to the nerve of the argument and maintained that we are not justified in employing the idea of cause in this way.

Up to a point, he agreed with Locke and Berkeley. He fully accepted their destructive arguments: the argument of Locke that secondary qualities are subjective, and the argument of Berkeley that primary qualities and material substances are not extramentally real He agreed that external physical objects cannot be known directly—that the objects with which we are directly acquainted are merely sense-data:

> It is universally allowed by modern enquirers that all the sensible qualities of objects, such as hard, soft, hot, cold, white, black, etc., are merely secondary, and exist not in the objects themselves, but are perceptions of the mind, without any external archetype or model which they represent. If this be allowed with regard to secondary qualities, it must also follow with regard to the supposed primary qualities of extension and solidity. . . . Nothing can ever be present to the mind but an image or perception . . . ; and no man who reflects ever doubted that the existences which we consider when we say *this house* and *that tree* are nothing but perceptions in the mind. . . .[2]

We know directly only perceptions; all else is inference. But at this point Hume parted company with Locke and Berkeley. Locke and Berkeley supposed that the regular character of experience implies an external world as its cause, but Hume maintained that cause is only a kind of associational connection between items *within* experience. We often observe a relation of cause and effect between *perceptions*, but we can never observe it between perceptions and *external objects*:

> The only conclusion we can draw from the existence of one thing to that of another is by means of the relation of cause and effort, which shows that there is a connection betwixt them, and that the existence of one is dependent on that

[2] *Enquiry,* pp. 152, 154.

of the other. . . . But as no beings are ever present to the mind but perceptions, it follows that we may observe a conjunction or a relation of cause and effort between different perceptions, but can never observe it between perceptions and objects. 'Tis impossible, therefore, that from the existence of any of the qualities of the former, we can ever form any conclusion concerning the existence of the latter. . . .[3]

What emerges from this devastating criticism? If we are resolved thus to stay within the closed circle of experience, we can either accept our perceptions as the ultimate character of existence or say that there may be something more—*some* kind of external world—but that we cannot know what that something more is. There is little basis here for positive belief.

A final twist to Hume's scepticism is his denial of a substantial self. Just as Berkeley rejected Locke's doctrine of material substance, so Hume for similar reasons rejected Berkeley's doctrine of a mental substance. He denied that we ever have an *impression* of a self, and in the absence of any such impression, he saw no way of proving that a self exists. All the content of experience is fleeting, evanescent, whereas the self is supposed to be identical through succeeding states. Impressions, being variable and evanescent, are incapable of revealing a permanent self; and to *infer* an unexperienced self as the necessary cause of our mental states is to project illegitimately the relation of cause and effect, which is through and through experiential, beyond the circle of experience.

Hume thus reduced reality, so far as it can be verified, to a stream of "perceptions" neither caused nor sustained by any mental or material substance. Existence is made up of mental facts, perceptions, with no selves to which the perceptions belong and no material world in which they reside.

Whence comes, then, our idea of an identical self—a spiritual substance—or an identical thing—a material substance? Why do we suppose that there are enduring entities behind the flux of experience? The answer, Hume believed, is that we notice relatively permanent or recurrent qualities in experience, and we try to account for them by supposing self-identical objects that persist underneath all changes and between the gaps of experience. Hence we speak of the "same" table and the "same" person, although actually there is constant change, if we would but notice it.

The preceding discussion has emphasized the sceptical aspects of Hume's philosophy. This scepticism, if accepted as a basis for living, would have an extremely paralyzing effect. Hume avoided this paralysis by falling back upon what he termed "natural instinct." We instinctively tend to believe many doctrines that we cannot *logically* justify; and, indeed, we must do so for the purposes of living. Hence common sense and science are justified in assuming that the future *will* resemble the past, and every man is justified in adopting the working faith that

[3] *A Treatise of Human Nature,* edited by L. A. Selby-Bigge (Oxford: Clarendon Press, 1896), p. 212.

is necessary to live a sensible life. "Be a philosopher," Hume admonished, "but amidst all your philosophy, be still a man."[4] We must act and reason and believe, even though we cannot, by the most diligent intellectual inquiry, satisfy ourselves concerning the intellectual foundations of belief.

How Kant Differed from Hume

Kant was struck, as Hume himself had been struck, by the largely negative results of Hume's inquiry. "I am . . . affrighted and confounded with the forlorn solitude in which I am placed by my philosophy," Hume confessed, "and fancy myself some strange uncouth monster, utterly abandoned and disconsolate." The effect of Hume's scepticism upon Kant was different—not to fill his mind with fright and confusion, but to awaken him from his "dogmatic slumbers." Hume convinced Kant that traditional metaphysics was bankrupt and that a new start was necessary. But Kant was also convinced that there must be something fundamentally wrong with an empiricism that led to such devastating conclusions. He was not content to fall back upon "natural instinct" but sought some kind of rationale for his trust in science and his moral and religious convictions. The task that he set himself, in the words of one of his contemporaries, was "to limit Hume's scepticism on the one hand, and the old dogmatism on the other, and to refute and destroy materialism, fatalism, atheism, as well as sentimentalism and superstition."

In the *Critique of Pure Reason*, Kant undertook to prove that all genuine scientific knowledge, whether in mathematics or in the natural sciences, is universally valid, but that speculative metaphysics, which seeks to go beyond experience to determine the ultimate and absolute nature of things, cannot be established upon any sound and dependable basis. Science is reliable because it deals with *phenomena*—things as they *appear* in human experiences; but metaphysics is unreliable because it tries to interpret *noumena*—things as they are in themselves apart from experience. The world of ultimate reality, in contrast to the world of appearance, can never be known to reason. The noumenal realities must be interpreted, if at all, by moral conviction and religious faith—not by science or pure theoretical philosophy.

The phenomena, Kant insisted, exhibit spatial and temporal forms and rational connections, such as cause and effect. In grasping these forms and connections, consciousness is an awareness of meanings—not passive contemplation but active judgment, not mere perception but synthetic interpretation. We can never know things as they are apart from these synthetic modes of apprehension and judgment, which are the necessary conditions, of all human experience. To interpret *ultimate* reality as either finite or infinite, one or many, mechanistic or teleological, mental or material, is to attempt to probe the supersensible nature of existence— and this human reason can never do. But if the positive claims of transcendent

[4] *Enquiry*, p. 9.

metaphysics are thus overthrown, so are its negative claims. The metaphysician is as powerless to *disprove* the existence of God as to prove His existence, or to *disprove* an idealistic account of reality as to prove it. When the overweening claims of "pure reason" are thus refuted, our "practical reason" is no longer inhibited by atheism, materialism, or mechanistic determinism.

Reason, according to Kant, is not limited to its theoretical uses. There are two basic and irreducible ways in which the mind conducts itself, cognitively and morally, and correspondingly there are two forms of reason, "pure" and "practical." Matching these forms of reason, there are two kinds of reality, each with its own kind of impressiveness. "Two things strike me with the deepest awe," Kant remarked, "the starry heavens overhead and the moral law within." The stars belong to the world of phenomena, and to this world man as a phenomenal being also belongs. In this dimension man is as much the effect of natural causes as the rocks underfoot or the stars overhead. There is another dimension to man's being, the realm of moral decisions, and in this sphere he transcends the phenomenal order and reaches into the noumenal. "Duty," the validity of which Kant did not question, is possible only on the supposition that the will is free—since I *ought* implies I *can*. Kant was convinced that not only belief in free will but faith in God and an after life are justified because essential to a robust morality.

Let me sum up his answer to Hume's scepticism. He tries to make secure the foundations of natural science by demonstrating that the order and regularity necessary to science—the sensory forms of space and time and the intelligible order of substance, causation, and the other "categories"—inhere necessarily in phenomena because they are contributed by the mind in the very act of knowing (knowledge being a joint-product of mind and things-in-themselves). To Hume's reduction of the mind to a succession of awarenesses, Kant opposes the mind's awareness of succession, which he says is unaccountable without more synthesis and continuity than Hume recognized. While he agrees with Hume that the doctrines of speculative metaphysics cannot be demonstrated, he tries to justify the ideas of God, freedom, and immortality on moral grounds.

I shall not trace the arguments by which Kant reached these conclusions. Since Blakney's translation is remarkably lucid, the reader who studies the text carefully should find no insuperable difficulty in understanding its meaning.

The Question of Free Will

Since the question of free will is fascinating, I shall consider it at greater length. The question has been touched upon in previous chapters. Lucretius, as we have seen, correlated free will in the human being with the indeterministic swerving of the atoms. Far different was Spinoza's monistic cosmic determinism. Even Spinoza, however, contended that God is free because he is the totality, and His nature is not limited by anything external to it. So far as man shares in God's nature, he also is free—not in the sense of being undetermined, but in the sense of participating in God's free and infinite being. Freedom is here opposed to constraint.

Hume rejected Spinoza's metaphysical system but retained the idea that freedom is the absence of constraint. It is a mere confusion of thought to identify freedom and indeterminism, since nothing is more fatal than an accident, and nothing is more accidental than an undetermined event. Necessity, he argued, applies to human life as much as to nature, but in no way destroys man's liberty. So long as the necessity springs from the man's nature and does not involve constraint, he is free. The free man is unhindered in the realization of his desires; the unfree man is chained, locked up, or otherwise constrained.

Kant rejected this analysis. He believed in a freedom exempt from necessity, and attributed this kind of free action to the transcendental self—the "I" existing outside of the phenomenal order in the realm of things-in-themselves. He thought, paradoxically, that a self could be at once under necessity *qua* phenomenon and free *qua* noumenon. Just how freedom and necessity can thus be joined remains a mystery, since we lack all knowledge of the noumenal world.

Although most philosophers would reject this attempt to reconcile phenomenal necessity with noumenal freedom, many would accept Kant's argument that "I ought" implies "I can." One of the better known defenders of free will, C. A. Campbell of Glasgow University, has written:

> Let us put the argument implicit in the common view a little more sharply. The moral 'ought' implies 'can'. If we say that A morally ought to have done X, we imply that in our opinion, he could have done X. But we assign moral blame to a man only for failing to do what we think he morally ought to have done. Hence if we morally blame A for not having done X, we imply that he could have done X even though in fact he did not. In other words, we imply that A could have acted otherwise than he did. And that means that we imply, as a necessary condition of a man's being morally blameworthy, that he enjoyed a freedom of a kind not compatible with unbroken causal continuity.[5]

Campbell also agrees with Kant in ascribing to human beings a contra-causal type of freedom that is distinguished sharply from ordinary deterministic causality. At the moment of choice, everyone feels that there are genuinely open possibilities, and Campbell is not prone to dismiss this feeling as illusion. He believes that it is possible, by an effort of will, to "rise to duty" even though we may be strongly inclined to yield to temptation. Similarly William James, in his famous essay "The Dilemma of Determinism," contends that the *modus operandi* of free choice is the resolute effort of attention and will that we direct to one alternative rather than another. There is no way, he thinks, to show that this effort does not occur or that it is inefficacious.

[5] C. A. Campbell, "Is 'Freewill' a Pseudo-Problem?" *Mind*, Vol. 60 (October 1951).

To sum up, Lucretius believed in a modicum of indeterminacy that exempts human beings from a rigid determinism and permits free choice; Spinoza, while rejecting all indeterminism, maintained that freedom consists in knowing the causes that determine one's action, thus making the causes internal and to this extent independent of external constraint; Hume contended that freedom is determination in accordance with the motives and ideals of the agent even though these in turn are determined; Kant, while respectful toward science, appealed to our moral consciousness of free choice. In this clash of opinion, there is abundant material for reflection and controversy.

9

Individuality
and
Creative Process

SÖREN KIERKEGAARD (1813–1855)

The youngest son of rather elderly parents, Kierkegaard was born in Copenhagen and reared in a pious Lutheran family. His father was a wealthy and retired merchant with a strong sense of sin which he impressed upon his children. As a young University student, Sören lived a Bohemian life in revolt against his father and religious pietism. After a moral conversion, he returned to his studies and passed his theological examinations at the University of Copenhagen in 1840. The next year he went to Berlin to attend Schelling's lectures, which confirmed his dislike of Hegel's philosophy. The abstractions of Hegelianism did not supply what he demanded—"a truth which is true *for me*, to find the *idea for which I can live and die* (*Journal*, Aug. 1, 1935)."

Thenceforth the driving force of his life was to "become a Christian," a task that, in his opinion, would not be easy. Although he was in love with 17-year-old Regine Olsen, he broke the engagement because it seemed incompatible with his religious commitment. This break not only hurt his fiancee's pride but had a profoundly traumatic effect upon him. He thereafter searched his tormented soul for self-knowledge in book after book.

During his later years he was involved in intense controversy with the Danish State Church, which he accused of being pseudo-Christian. On the point of death he refused the sacrament. "Pastors are royal officials," he explained. "Royal officials have nothing to do with Christianity." The epitaph that he composed for himself was simply, "That individual."

Individuality
and Subjective Truth

The Single Individual
and the Crowd[1]

This that follows is in part the expression of a way of thinking and feeling characteristic of my nature, which possibly is in need of revision (which I myself would welcome), and as it does not claim to be more than that, it is at the farthest remove from claiming the reader's adherence and is rather inclined to concessions. In part, however, it is a well-thought-out view of 'the Life', of 'the Truth', of 'the Way'.[2]

There is a view of life which conceives that where the crowd is, there also is the truth, and that in truth itself there is need of having the crowd on its side. There is another view of life which conceives that wherever there is a crowd there is untruth, so that (to consider for a moment the extreme case), even if every individual, each for himself in private, were to be in possession of the truth, yet in case they were all to get together in a crowd—a crowd to which any sort of *decisive* significance is attributed, a voting, noisy, audible crowd—untruth would at once be in evidence.[3]

For a 'crowd' is the untruth. In a godly sense it is true, eternally, Christianly, as St. Paul says, that 'only one attains the goal'—which is not meant in a comparative sense, for comparison takes others into account. It means that every man can be that one, God helping him therein—but only one attains the goal. And again this means that every man should be chary about having to do with 'the others', and essentially should talk only with God and with himself—for only one attains the goal. And again this means that man, or to

[1] From *The Point of View* by Sören Kierkegaard, translated and edited by Dr. Walter Lowrie. London, New York, and Toronto: Oxford University Press, 1939. Reprinted by permission. Footnotes followed by (K) are by Kierkegaard.

[2] Perhaps it may be well to note here once and for all a thing that goes without saying and which I never have denied, that in relation to all temporal, earthly, worldly matters the crowd may have competency, and even decisive competency as a court of last resort. But it is not of such matters I am speaking, nor have I ever concerned myself with such things. I am speaking about the ethical, about the ethico-religious, about 'the truth', and I am affirming the untruth of the crowd, ethico-religiously regarded, when it is treated as a criterion for what 'truth' is. (K)

[3] Perhaps it may be well to note here, although it seems to me almost superfluous, that it naturally could not occur to me to object to the fact, for example, that preaching is done or that the truth is proclaimed, even though it were to an assemblage of hundreds of thousands. Not at all; but if there were an assemblage even of only ten—and if they should put the truth to the ballot, that is to say, if the assemblage should be regarded as the authority, if it is the crowd which turns the scale—then there *is* untruth. (K)

be a man, is akin to deity.—In a worldly and temporal sense, it will be said by the man of bustle, sociability, and amicableness, 'How unreasonable that only one attains the goal; for it is far more likely that many, by the strength of united effort, should attain the goal; and when we are many success is more certain and it is easier for each man severally.' True enough, it is far more *likely*; and it is true also with respect to all earthly and material goods. If it is allowed to have its way, this becomes the only true point of view, for it does away with God and eternity and with man's kinship with deity. It does away with it or transforms it into a fable, and puts in its place the modern (or, we might rather say, the old pagan) notion that to be a man is to belong to a race endowed with reason, to belong to it as a specimen, so that the race or species is higher than the individual, which is to say that there are no more individuals but only specimens. But eternity which arches over and high above the temporal, tranquil as the starry vault at night, and God in heaven who in the bliss of that sublime tranquillity holds in survey, without the least sense of dizziness at such a height, these countless multitudes of men and knows each single individual by name—He, the great Examiner, says that only one attains the goal. That means, every one can and every one should be this *one*— but only one attains the goal. Hence where there is a multitude, a crowd, or where decisive significance is attached to the fact that there is a multitude, *there* it is sure that no one is working, living, striving for the highest aim, but only for one or another earthly aim;

since to work for the eternal decisive aim is possible only where there is one, and to be this one which all can be is to let God be the helper—the 'crowd' is the untruth.

A crowd—not this crowd or that, the crowd now living or the crowd long deceased, a crowd of humble people or of superior people, of rich or of poor, &c.—a crowd in its very concept[4] is the untruth, by reason of the fact that it renders the individual completely impenitent and irresponsible, or at least weakens his sense of responsibility by reducing it to a fraction. Observe that there was not one single soldier that dared lay hands upon Caius Marius— this was an instance of truth. But given merely three or four women with the consciousness or the impression that they were a crowd, and with hope of a sort in the possibility that no one could say definitely who was doing it or who began it—then they had courage for it. What a falsehood! The falsehood first of all is the notion that the crowd does what in fact only the *individual* in the crowd does, though it be every *individual*. For 'crowd' is an abstraction and has no hands: but each individual has ordinarily two hands, and so when

[4] The reader will also remember that here the word 'crowd' is understood in a purely formal sense, not in the sense one commonly attaches to 'the crowd' when it is meant as an invidious qualification, the distinction which human selfishness irreligiously erects between 'the crowd' and superior persons, &c. Good God! How could a religious man hit upon such an inhuman equality! No, 'crowd' stands for number, the numerical, a number of noblemen, millionaires, high dignitaries, &c.—as soon as the numerical is involved it is 'crowd', 'the crowd'. (K)

an individual lays his two hands upon Caius Marius they are the two hands of the individual, certainly not those of his neighbour, and still less those of the . . . crowd which has no hands. In the next place, the falsehood is that the crowd had the 'courage' for it, for no one of the individuals was ever so cowardly as the crowd always is. For every individual who flees for refuge into the crowd, and so flees in coward-ice from being an individual (who had not the courage to lay his hands upon Caius Marius, nor even to admit that he had it not), such a man contributes his share of cowardliness to the coward-liness which we know as the 'crowd'.— Take the highest example, think of Christ—and the whole human race, all the men that ever were born or are to be born. But let the situation be one that challenges the individual, requir-ing each one for himself to be alone with Him in a solitary place and as an individual to step up to Him and spit upon Him—the man never was born and never will be born with courage or insolence enough to do such a thing. This is untruth.

The crowd is untruth. Hence none has more contempt for what it is to be a man than they who make it their pro-fession to lead the crowd. Let some one approach a person of this sort, some in-dividual—that is an affair far too small for his attention, and he proudly repels him. There must be hundreds at the least. And when there are thousands, he defers to the crowd, bowing and scrap-ing to them. What untruth! No, when it is a question of a single individual man, then is the time to give expression to the truth by showing one's respect for what it is to be a man; and if per-haps it was, as it is cruelly said, a poor wretch of a man, then the thing to do is to invite him into the best room, and one who possesses several voices should use the kindest and most friendly. That is truth. If on the other hand there were an assemblage of thousands or more and the truth was to be decided by ballot, then this is what one should do (unless one were to prefer to utter silently the petition of the Lord's Prayer, 'Deliver us from evil') : one should in godly fear give expression to the fact that the crowd, regarded as a judge over ethical and religious matters, is untruth, whereas it is eternally true that every man can be the *one*. This is truth.

The crowd is untruth. Therefore was Christ crucified, because, although He addressed himself to all, He would have no dealings with the crowd, because He would not permit the crowd to aid him in any way, because in this regard He repelled people absolutely, would not found a party, did not permit balloting, but would be what He is, the Truth, which relates itself to the individual.— And hence every one who truly would serve the truth is *eo ipso*, in one way or another, a martyr. If it were possible for a person in his mother's womb to make the decision to will to serve the truth truly, then, whatever his martyrdom turns out to be, he is *eo ipso* from his mother's womb a martyr. For it is not so great a trick to win the crowd. All that is needed is some talent, a certain dose of falsehood, and a little acquaint-ance with human passions. But no witness for the truth (ah! and that is what every man should be, including you and me)—no witness for the truth dare become engaged with the crowd. The witness for the truth—who naturally has nothing to do with politics and must above everything else be most vigilantly on the watch not to be confounded with the politician—the God-fearing work of the witness to the truth is to engage himself if possible with all, but always individually, talking to every one severally on the streets and lanes . . . in order to disintegrate the crowd, or to talk even to the crowd, though not with the intent of educating the crowd as such, but rather with the hope that one or another individual might return from this assemblage and become a single individual. On the other hand the 'crowd', when it is treated as an authority and its judgement regarded as the final judgement, is detested by the witness for the truth more heartily than a maiden of good morals detests the public dance-floor; and he who addresses the crowd as the supreme authority is regarded by him as the tool of the untruth. For (to repeat what I have said) that which in politics or in similar fields may be justifiable, wholly or in part, becomes untruth when it is transferred to the intellectual, the spiritual, the religious fields. And one thing more I would say, perhaps with a cautiousness which is exaggerated. By 'truth' I mean always 'eternal truth'. But politics, &c., have nothing to do with 'eternal truth'. A policy which in the proper sense of 'eternal truth' were to make serious work of introducing 'eternal truth' into real life would show itself in that very same second to be in the most eminent degree the most 'impolitic' thing that can be imagined.

A crowd is untruth. And I could weep, or at least I could learn to long for eternity, at thinking of the misery of our age, in comparison even with the greatest misery of bygone ages, owing to the fact that the daily press with its anonymity makes the situation madder still with the help of the public, this abstraction which claims to be the judge in matters of 'truth'. For in reality assemblies which make this claim do not now take place. The fact that an anonymous author by the help of the press can day by day find occasion to say (even about intellectual, moral, and religious matters) whatever he pleases to say, and what perhaps he would be very far from having the courage to say as an individual; that every time he opens his mouth (or shall we say his abysmal gullet?) he at once is addressing thousands of thousands; that he can get ten thousand times ten thousand to repeat after him what he has said—and with all this nobody has any responsibility, so that it is not as in ancient times the relatively unrepentant crowd which possesses omnipotence, but the absolutely unrepentant thing, a nobody, an anonymity, who is the producer (*auctor*), and another anonymity, the public, sometimes even anonymous subscribers, and with all this, nobody, nobody! Good God! And yet our states call themselves Christian states! Let no one say that in this case it is possible for 'truth' in its turn by the help of the press to get the better of lies and errors. O thou who speakest thus, dost thou venture to maintain that men regarded as a crowd are just as quick to seize upon truth which is not always palatable as upon falsehood which always is prepared delicately to give delight?— not to mention the fact that acceptance of the truth is made the more difficult by the necessity of admitting that one has been deceived! Or dost thou venture even to maintain that 'truth' can just as quickly be understood as falsehood, which requires no preliminary knowledge, no schooling, no discipline, no abstinence, no self-denial, no honest concern about oneself, no patient labour?

Nay, truth—which abhors also this untruth of aspiring after broad dissemination as the one aim—is not nimble on its feet. In the first place it cannot work by means of the fantastical means of the press, which is the untruth; the communicator of the truth can only be a single individual. And again the communication of it can only be addressed to the individual; for the truth consists precisely in that conception of life which is expressed by the individual. The truth can neither be communicated nor be received except as it were under God's eyes, not without God's help, not without God's being involved as the middle term, He himself being the Truth. It can therefore only be communicated by and received by 'the individual', which as a matter of fact can be every living man. The mark which distinguishes such a man is merely that of the truth, in contrast to the abstract, the fantastical, the impersonal, the crowd—the public which excludes God as the middle term (for the *personal* God cannot be a middle term in an *impersonal* relationship), and thereby excludes also the truth, for God is at once the Truth and the middle term which renders it intelligible.

And to honour every man, absolutely every man, is the truth, and this is what it is to fear God and love one's 'neighbour'. But from an ethico-religious point of view, to recognize the 'crowd' as the court of last resort is to deny God, and it cannot exactly mean to love the 'neighbour'. And the 'neighbour' is the absolutely true expression for human equality. In case every one were in truth to love his neighbour as himself, complete human equality would be attained. Every one who loves his neighbour in truth, expresses unconditionally human equality. Every one who, like me, admits that his effort is weak and imperfect, yet is aware that the task is to love one's neighbour, is also aware of what human equality is. But never have I read in Holy Scripture the commandment, Thou shalt love the crowd—and still less, Thou shalt recognize, ethico-religiously, in the crowd the supreme authority in matters of 'truth'. But the thing is simple enough: this thing of loving one's neighbour is self-denial; that of loving the crowd, or of pretending to love it, of making it the authority in matters of truth, is the way to material power, the way to temporal and earthly advantages of all sorts—at the same time it is the untruth, for a crowd is the untruth.

But he who acknowledges the truth of this view, which is seldom presented (for it often happens that a man thinks that the crowd is the untruth, but when it—the crowd—accepts his opinion *en masse,* everything is all right again), admits for himself that he is weak and impotent; for how could it be possible for an individual to make a stand against the crowd which possesses the power! And he could not wish to get the crowd on his side for the sake of ensuring that his view would prevail, the crowd, ethico-religiously regarded, being the untruth—that would be mocking himself. But although from the first this view involves an admission of weakness and impotence, and seems therefore far from inviting, and for this reason perhaps is so seldom heard, yet it has the good feature that it is even-handed, that it offends no one, not a single person, that it makes no invidious distinctions, not the least in the world. The crowd, in fact, is composed of individuals; it must therefore be in every man's power to become what he is, an individual. From becoming an individual no one, no one at all, is excluded, except he who excludes himself by becoming a crowd. To become a crowd, to collect a crowd about one, is on the contrary to affirm the distinctions of human life. The most well-meaning person who talks about these distinctions can easily offend an individual. But then it is not the crowd which possesses power, influence, repute, and mastery over men, but it is the invidious distinctions of human life which despotically ignore the single individual as the weak and impotent, which in a temporal and worldly interest ignore the eternal truth—the single individual.

How Johannes Climacus Became an Author[5]

It is now about four years since I got the notion of wanting to try my hand

as an author. I remember it quite clearly; it was on a Sunday, yes, that's it, a Sunday afternoon. As usual I was sitting out-of-doors at the café in the Frederiksberg Garden, that wonderful garden which for the child was fairy-land, where the King dwelt with his Queen, that delightful garden which afforded the youth happy diversion in the merriment of the populace, that friendly garden where now for the man of riper years there is such a homely feeling of sad exaltation above the world and all that is of the world, where even the invidious glory of royal dignity is what it is now out there—a queen's remembrance of her deceased lord.[6] There I sat as usual and smoked my cigar. . . .

I had been a student for ten years. Although never lazy, all my activity nevertheless was like a glittering in-activity, a kind of occupation for which I still have a strong predilection, and perhaps even a little talent. I read much, spent the rest of the day idling and thinking, or thinking and idling, but that was all it came to; the earliest sproutings of my productivity barely sufficed for my daily use and were consumed in their first greening. An inexplicable and overwhelming might constantly held me back, by strength as well as by artifice. This might was my indolence. It is not like the vehement

[5] This and the following excerpt on "The Subjective Truth: Inwardness" are from *Concluding Unscientific Postscript* translated by David F. Swenson, Lillian Marvin Swenson, and Walter Lowrie, in *A Kierkegaard Anthology,* edited by Robert Bretall. Copyright 1946 by Princeton University Press. Reprinted by permission.

[6] Referring to the widow of Frederick VI, who continued to reside there a great part of the year. (Note by Lowrie. The remaining notes are by Kierkegaard.)

aspiration of love, nor like the strong incentive of enthusiasm, it is rather like a housekeeper who holds one back, and with whom one is very well off, so well off that it never occurs to one to get married. This much is sure: though with the comforts of life I am not on the whole unacquainted, of all, indolence is the most comfortable.

So there I sat and smoked my cigar until I lapsed into reverie. Among other thoughts I remember this: "You are now," I said to myself, "on the way to becoming an old man, without being anything, and without really undertaking to do anything. On the other hand, wherever you look about you, in literature and in life, you see the celebrated names and figures, the precious and much heralded men who are coming into prominence and are much talked about, the many benefactors of the age who know how to benefit mankind by making life easier and easier, some by railways, others by omnibuses and steamboats, others by telegraph, others by easily apprehended compendiums and short recitals of everything worth knowing, and finally the true benefactors of the age who by virtue of thought make spiritual existence systematically easier and easier, and yet more and more significant. And what are you doing?"

Here my self-communion was interrupted, for my cigar was burned out and a new one had to be lit. So I smoked again, and then suddenly there flashed through my mind this thought: "You must do something, but inasmuch as with your limited capacities it will be impossible to make anything easier than it has become, you must, with the

same humanitarian enthusiasm as the others, undertake to make something harder." This notion pleased me immensely, and at the same time it flattered me to think that I, like the rest of them, would be loved and esteemed by the whole community. For when all combine in every way to make everything easier and easier, there remains only one possible danger, namely, that the easiness might become so great that it would be too great; then only one want is left, though not yet a felt want —that people will want difficulty. Out of love for mankind, and out of despair at my embarrassing situation, seeing that I had accomplished nothing and was unable to make anything easier than it had already been made, and moved by a genuine interest in those who make everything easy, I conceived it my task to create difficulties everywhere. I was struck also by the strange reflection that, after all, I might have to thank my indolence for the fact that this task became mine. For far from having found it, as Aladdin did the lamp, I must rather suppose that my indolence, by hindering me from intervening at an opportune time to make things easy, had forced upon me the only task that was left. . . .

The Subjective Truth: Inwardness Truth is Subjectivity

WHEN *the question of truth is raised in an objective manner, reflection is directed objectively to the truth, as an object to which the knower is related. Reflection is not focused upon the relationship, however, but upon the question of whether it is the truth to which the knower is related. If only the object to which he is related is the truth, the subject is accounted to be in the truth. When the question of the truth is raised subjectively, reflection is directed subjectively to the nature of the individual's relationship: if only the mode of this relationship is in the truth, the individual is in the truth, even if he should happen to be thus related to what is not true.*[7] Let us take as an example the knowledge of God. Objectively, reflection is directed to the problem of whether this object is the true God; subjectively, reflection is directed to the question whether the individual is related to a something *in such a manner* that his relationship is in truth a God-relationship. On which side is the truth now to be found? Ah, may we not here resort to a mediation, and say: It is on neither side, but in the mediation of both? Excellently well said, provided we might have it explained how an existing individual manages to be in a state of mediation. For to be in a state of mediation is to be finished, while to exist is to become. Nor can an existing individual be in two places at the same time—he cannot be an identity of subject and object. When he is nearest to being in two places at the same time he is in passion; but passion is merely momentary, and passion is also the highest expression of subjectivity.

The existing individual who chooses

to pursue the objective way enters upon the entire approximation-process by which it is proposed to bring God to light objectively. But this is in all eternity impossible, because God is a subject, and therefore exists only for subjectivity in inwardness. The existing individual who chooses the subjective way apprehends instantly the entire dialectical difficulty involved in having to use some time, perhaps a long time, in finding God objectively; and he feels this dialectical difficulty in all its painfulness, because he must use God at that very moment, since every moment is wasted in which he does not have God.[8] That very instant he has God, not by virtue of any objective deliberation but by virtue of the infinite passion of inwardness. The objective inquirer, on the other hand, is not embarrassed by such dialectical difficulties as are involved in devoting an entire period of investigation to finding God—since it is possible that the inquirer may die tomorrow; and if he lives he can scarcely regard God as something to be taken along if convenient, since God is precisely that which one takes *a tout prix,* which in the understanding of

[7] The reader will observe that the question here is about essential truth, or about the truth which is essentially related to existence, and that it is precisely for the sake of clarifying it as inwardness or as subjectivity that this contrast is drawn. (K)

[8] In this manner God certainly becomes a postulate, but not in the otiose manner in which this word is commonly understood. It becomes clear rather that the only way in which an existing individual comes into relation with God is when the dialectical contradiction brings his passion to the point of despair, and helps him to embrace God with the "category of despair" (faith). Then the postulate is so far from being arbitrary that it is precisely a life-necessity. It is then not so much that God is a postulate as that the existing individual's postulation of God is a necessity. (K)

passion constitutes the true inward relationship to God.

It is at this point, so difficult dialectically, that the way swings off for everyone who knows what it means to think, and to think existentially; which is something very different from sitting at a desk like a fantastical being and writing about what one has never done, something very different from writing *de omnibus dubitandum,* and at the same time being as existentially credulous as the most sensuous of men. Here is where the way swings off, and the change is marked by the fact that, while objective knowledge rambles comfortably on by way of the long road of approximation without being impelled by the urge of passion, subjective knowledge counts every delay a deadly peril, and the decision so infinitely important and so instantly pressing that it is as if the opportunity had already passed unutilized.

Now when the problem is to reckon up on which side there is most truth, whether on the side of one who seeks the true God objectively, and pursues the approximate truth of the God-idea; or on the side of one who, driven by the infinite passion of his need of God, feels an infinite concern for his own relationship to God in truth (and to be at one and the same time on both sides equally is, as we have noted, not possible for an existing individual, but is merely the happy delusion of an imaginary I-am-I): the answer cannot be in doubt for anyone who has not been demoralized with the aid of science. If one who lives in the midst of Christianity goes up to the house of God, the house of the true God, with the true conception of God in his knowledge, and prays, but prays in a false spirit; and one who lives in an idolatrous community prays with the entire passion of the infinite, although his eyes rest upon the image of an idol: where is there most truth? The one prays in truth to God though he worships an idol; the other prays falsely to the true God, and hence worships in fact an idol.

When one man investigates objectively the problem of immortality, and another embraces an uncertainty with the passion of the infinite: where is there most truth, and who has the greater certainty? The one has entered upon a never-ending approximation, for the certainty of immortality lies precisely in the subjectivity of the individual; the other is immortal, and fights for his immortality by struggling with the uncertainty. Let us consider Socrates. Nowadays everyone dabbles in a few proofs; some have several such proofs, others fewer. But Socrates! He puts the question objectively in a problematic manner: *if* there is an immortality. Must he therefore be accounted a doubter in comparison with one of our modern thinkers with the three proofs? By no means. On this "if" he risks his entire life, he has the courage to meet death, and he has with the passion of the infinite so determined the pattern of his life that it must be found acceptable—*if* there is an immortality. Can any better proof be given for the immortality of the soul? But those who have the three proofs do not at all determine their lives in conformity therewith; if there is an immortality, it must feel disgust over their manner of life:

can any better refutation be given of the three proofs? The "bit" of uncertainty that Socrates had helped him, because he himself contributed the passion of the infinite; the three proofs that the others have do not profit them at all, because they are and remain dead to spirit and enthusiasm, and their three proofs, in lieu of proving anything else, prove just this. A young girl may enjoy all the sweetness of love on the basis of what is merely a weak hope; but she is beloved, because she rests everything on this weak hope; but many a wedded matron more than once subjected to the strongest expressions of love has in so far indeed had proofs, but strangely enough has not enjoyed *quod erat demonstrandum*. The Socratic ignorance, which Socrates held fast with the entire passion of his inwardness, was thus an expression for the principle that the eternal truth is related to an existing individual, and that this truth must therefore be a paradox for him as long as he exists; and yet it is possible that there was more truth in the Socratic ignorance as it was in him, than in the entire objective truth of the System, which flirts with what the times demand and accommodates itself to *Privatdocents*.

The objective accent falls on WHAT is said, the subjective accent on HOW it is said. This distinction holds even in the aesthetic realm, and receives definite expression in the principle that what is in itself true may in the mouth of such and such a person become untrue. In these times this distinction is particularly worthy of notice for, if we wish to express in a single sentence the difference between ancient times and our own, we should doubtless have to say: "In ancient times only an individual here and there knew the truth; now all know it, but the inwardness of its appropriation stands in an inverse relationship to the extent of its dissemination. Aesthetically the contradiction that truth becomes untruth in this or that person's mouth is best construed comically. In the ethico-religious sphere, the accent is again on the "how." But this is not to be understood as referring to demeanor, expression, delivery, or the like; rather it refers to the relationship sustained by the existing individual, in his own existence, to the content of his utterance. Objectively the interest is focused merely on the thought-content, subjectively on the inwardness. At its maximum this inward "how" is the passion of the infinite, and the passion of the infinite is the truth. But the passion of the infinite is precisely subjectivity, and thus subjectivity becomes the truth. Objectively there is no infinite decision, and hence it is objectively in order to annul the difference between good and evil, together with the principle of contradiction, and therewith also the infinite difference between the true and the false. Only in subjectivity is there decision, to seek objectivity is to be in error. It is the passion of the infinite that is the decisive factor and not its content, for its content is precisely itself. In this manner subjectivity and the subjective "how" constitute the truth.

But the "how" which is thus subjectively accentuated, precisely because the subject is an existing individual, is also subject to a dialectic with respect to time. In the passionate moment of decision, where the road swings away from objective knowledge, it seems as if the infinite decision were thereby realized. But in the same moment the existing individual finds himself in the temporal order, and the subjective "how" is transformed into a striving, a striving which receives indeed its impulse and a repeated renewal from the decisive passion of the infinite, but is nevertheless a striving.

When subjectivity is the truth, the conceptual determination of the truth must include an expression for the antithesis to objectivity, a memento of the fork in the road where the way swings off; this expression will also indicate the tension of the subjective inwardness. Here is such a definition of truth: *An objective uncertainty held fast in an appropriation-process of the most passionate inwardness is the truth,* the highest truth attainable for an *existing individual.* At the point where the way swings off (and where this is cannot be specified objectively, since it is a matter of subjectivity), there objective knowledge is placed in abeyance. Thus the subject merely has, objectively, the uncertainty; but it is this which precisely increases the tension of that infinite passion which constitutes his

inwardness. The truth is precisely the venture which chooses an objective uncertainty with the passion of the infinite. I contemplate nature in the hope of finding God, and I see omnipotence and wisdom; but I also see much else that disturbs my mind and excites anxiety. The sum of all this is an objective uncertainty. But it is for this very reason that the inwardness becomes as intense as it is, for it embraces this objective uncertainty with the entire passion of the infinite. In the case of a mathematical proposition the objectivity is given, but for this reason the truth of such a proposition is also an indifferent truth.

But the above definition of truth is an equivalent expression for faith. Without risk there is no faith. Faith is precisely the contradiction between the infinite passion of the individual's inwardness and the objective uncertainty. If I am capable of grasping God objectively, I do not believe, but precisely because I cannot do this I must believe. If I wish to preserve myself in faith I must constantly be intent upon holding fast the objective uncertainty, so that in the objective uncertainty I am out "upon the seventy thousand fathoms of water," and yet believe. . . .

HENRI BERGSON (1859–1941)

Bergson was born in Paris of an English mother and a Polish father. From his father, an accomplished musician, he may have inherited the artistic temperament that is reflected throughout his work. Although interested in literature and science, he devoted himself to philosophy, which he taught in various lycées and, from 1900 to 1921, at the Collège de France.

In 1888 he published his first major work, *Time and Free Will*, but it was not until 1908, with the appearance of his *Creative Evolution*, that he suddenly became the most popular figure in the philosophic world. The audience gathered in the lecture hall an hour in advance to secure seats and people from many countries flocked to his lectures. Among his honors were election to the Council of the Legion of Honor, the French Academy, and the Academy of Sciences, and the award of the Nobel Prize in literature.

After World War I, he devoted himself to the cause of peace, presiding over the International Commission for Intellectual Cooperation of the League of Nations. When the Vichy government introduced anti-Semitic measures during the Nazi occupation, it proposed to exempt Bergson despite his Jewish extraction. As a protest against the infamy of the regime, he refused exemption and renounced his various honors. Finally, at the age of eighty-one, he rose from his sickbed and waited in line to register as a Jew. He died a few days later.

The Individual
and the Type

What is the object of art? Could reality come into direct contact with sense

From Henri Bergson's *Laughter* from COMEDY, copyright © 1956 by Wylie Sypher. Reprinted by permission of Doubleday & Company, Inc. *Laughter* was published in France in 1909. The present translation by Cloudesley Brereton and Fred Rothwell was first published by The Macmillan Company in 1913.

and consciousness, could we enter into immediate communion with things and with ourselves, probably art would be useless, or rather we should all be artists, for then our soul would continually vibrate in perfect accord with nature. Our eyes, aided by memory, would carve out in space and fix in time the most inimitable of pictures. Hewn in the living marble of the human form, fragments of statues, beautiful as the relics of antique statuary, would strike the passing glance. Deep in our souls we should hear the strains of our inner life's unbroken melody—a music that is ofttimes gay, but more frequently plaintive and always original. All this is around and within us, and yet no whit of it do we distinctly perceive. Between nature and ourselves, nay, between ourselves and our own consciousness a veil is interposed: a veil that is dense and opaque for the common herd—thin, almost transparent, for the artist and the poet. What fairy wove that veil? Was it done in malice or in friendliness? We had to live, and life demands that we grasp things in their relations to our own needs. Life is action. Life implies the acceptance only of the *utilitarian* side of things in order to respond to them by appropriate reactions: all other impressions must be dimmed or else reach us vague and blurred. I look and I think I see, I listen and I think I hear, I examine myself and I think I am reading the very depths of my heart. But what I see and hear of the outer world is purely and simply a selection made by my senses to serve as a light to my conduct; what I know of myself is what comes to the surface, what participates in my actions. My senses and my consciousness, therefore, give me no more than a practical simplification of reality. In the version they furnish me of myself and of things, the differences that are useless to man are obliterated, the resemblances that are useful to him are emphasized; ways are traced out for me in advance, along which my activity is to travel. These ways are the ways which all mankind has trod before me.

Things have been classified with a view to the use I can derive from them. And it is this classification I perceive, far more clearly than the color and the shape of things. Doubtless man is vastly superior to the lower animals in this respect. It is not very likely that the eye of a wolf makes any distinction between a kid and a lamb; both appear to the wolf as the same identical quarry, alike easy to pounce upon, alike good to devour. We, for our part, make a distinction between a goat and a sheep; but can we tell one goat from another, one sheep from another? The *individuality* of things or of beings escapes us, unless it is materially to our advantage to perceive it. Even when we do take note of it—as when we distinguish one man from another—it is not the individuality itself that the eye grasps, *i.e.*, an entirely original harmony of forms and colors, but only one or two features that will make practical recognition easier.

In short, we do not see the actual things themselves; in most cases we confine ourselves to reading the labels affixed to them. This tendency, the result of need, has become even more pronounced under the influence of speech; for words—with the exception of proper nouns—all denote genera. The word, which only takes note of the most ordinary function and commonplace aspect of the thing, intervenes between it and ourselves, and would conceal its form from our eyes, were that form not already masked beneath the necessities that brought the word into existence. Not only external objects, but even our own mental states, are screened from us in their inmost, their personal aspect, in the original life they possess. When we feel love or hatred, when we are gay or sad, is it really the feeling itself that reaches our consciousness with those innumerable fleeting shades of meaning and deep resounding echoes that make it something altogether our own? We should all, were it so, be novelists or poets or musicians. Mostly, however, we perceive nothing but the outward display of our mental state. We catch only the impersonal aspect of our feelings, that aspect which speech has set down once for all because it is almost the same, in the same conditions, for all men. Thus, even in our own individual, individuality escapes our ken. We move amidst generalities and symbols, as within a tilt-yard in which our force is effectively pitted against other forces; and fascinated by action, tempted by it, for our own good, on to the field it has selected, we live in a zone midway between things and ourselves, externally to things, externally also to ourselves. From time to time, however, in a fit of absentmindedness, nature raises up souls that are more detached from life. Not with that intentional, logical, systematical detachment—the result of reflection and philosophy—but rather with a natural detachment, one innate in the structure of sense or consciousness, which at once reveals itself by a virginal manner, so to speak, of seeing, hearing or thinking. Were this detachment complete, did the soul no longer cleave to action by any of its perceptions, it would be the soul of an artist such as the world has never yet seen. It would excel alike in every art at the same time; or rather, it would fuse them all into one. It would perceive all

things in their native purity: the forms, colors, sounds of the physical world as well as the subtlest movement of the inner life. But this is asking too much of nature. Even for such of us as she has made artists, it is by accident, and on one side only, that she has lifted the veil. In one direction only has she forgotten to rivet the perception to the need. And since each direction corresponds to what we call a *sense*—through one of his senses, and through that sense alone, is the artist usually wedded to art. Hence, originally, the diversity of arts. Hence also the speciality of predispositions. This one applies himself to colors and forms, and since he loves color for color and form for form, since he perceives them for their sake and not for his own, it is the inner life of things that he sees appearing through their forms and colors. Little by little he insinuates it into our own perception, baffled though we may be at the outset. For a few moments at least, he diverts us from the prejudices of form and color that come between ourselves and reality. And thus he realizes the loftiest ambition of art, which here consists in revealing to us nature. Others, again, retire within themselves. Beneath the thousand rudimentary actions which are the outward and visible signs of an emotion, behind the commonplace, conventional expression that both reveals and conceals an individual mental state, it is the emotion, the original mood, to which they attain in its undefiled essence. And then, to induce us to make the same effort ourselves, they contrive to make us see something of what they have seen: by rhythmical arrangement of words, which thus become organized and animated with a life of their own, they tell us—or rather suggest—things that speech was not calculated to express. Others delve yet deeper still. Beneath these joys and sorrows which can, at a pinch, be translated into language, they grasp something that has nothing in common with language, certain rhythms of life and breath that are closer to man than his inmost feelings, being the living law—varying with each individual—of his enthusiasm and despair, his hopes and regrets. By setting free and emphasizing this music, they force it upon our attention; they compel us, willy-nilly, to fall in with it, like passers-by who join in a dance. And thus they impel us to set in motion, in the depths of our being, some secret chord which was only waiting to thrill. So art, whether it be painting or sculpture, poetry or music, has no other object than to brush aside the utilitarian symbols, the conventional and socially accepted generalities, in short, everything that veils reality from us, in order to bring us face to face with reality itself. It is from a misunderstanding on this point that the dispute between realism and idealism in art has arisen. Art is certainly only a more direct vision of reality. But this purity of perception implies a break with utilitarian convention, an innate and specially localized disinterestedness of sense or consciousness, in short, a certain immateriality of life, which is what has always been called idealism. So that we might say, without in any way playing upon the meaning of the words, that realism is in the work when idealism is in the soul, and that it is only through ideality that we can resume contact with reality.

Dramatic art forms no exception to this law. What drama goes forth to discover and brings to light, is a deep-seated reality that is veiled from us, often in our own interests, by the necessities of life. What is this reality? What are these necessities? Poetry always expresses inward states. But amongst these states some arise mainly from contact with our fellow-men. They are the most intense as well as the most violent. As contrary electricities attract each other and accumulate between the two plates of the condenser from which the spark will presently flash, so, by simply bringing people together, strong attractions and repulsions take place, followed by an utter loss of balance, in a word, by that electrification of the soul known as passion. Were man to give way to the impulse of his natural feelings, were there neither social nor moral law, these outbursts of violent feeling would be the ordinary rule in life. But utility demands that these outbursts should be foreseen and averted. Man must live in society, and consequently submit to rules. And what interest advises, reason commands: duty calls, and we have to obey the summons. Under this dual influence has perforce been formed an outward layer of feelings and ideas which make for permanence, aim at becoming common to all men, and cover, when they are not strong enough to extinguish it, the inner fire of individual passions. The slow progress of mankind in the direction of an increasingly peaceful social life has gradually consolidated this layer, just as the life of our planet itself has been one long effort to cover over with a cool and solid crust the fiery mass of seething metals.

But volcanic eruptions occur. And if the earth were a living being, as mythology has feigned, most likely when in repose it would take delight in dreaming of these sudden explosions, whereby it suddenly resumes possession of its innermost nature. Such is just the kind of pleasure that is provided for us by drama. Beneath the quiet humdrum life that reason and society have fashioned for us, it stirs something within us which luckily does not explode, but which it makes us feel in its inner tension. It offers nature her revenge upon society. Sometimes it makes straight for the goal, summoning up to the surface, from the depths below, passions that produce a general upheaval. Sometimes it effects a flank movement, as is often the case in contemporary drama; with a skill that is frequently sophistical, it shows up the inconsistencies of society; it exaggerates the shams and shibboleths of the social law; and so indirectly, by merely dissolving or corroding the outer crust, it again brings us back to the inner core. But, in both cases, whether it weakens society or strengthens nature, it has the same end in view: that of laying bare a secret portion of ourselves—what might be called the tragic element in our character. This is indeed the impression we get after seeing a stirring drama. What has just interested us is not so much what we have been told about others as the glimpse we have caught of ourselves—a whole host of ghostly feelings, emotions and events that would fain have come into real existence, but, fortunately for us, did not. It also seems as if an appeal had been made within us to certain ancestral memories belonging to a far-away past

—memories so deep-seated and so foreign to our present life that this latter, for a moment, seems something unreal and conventional, for which we shall have to serve a fresh apprenticeship. So it is indeed a deeper reality that drama draws up from beneath our superficial and utilitarian attainments, and this art has the same end in view as all the others.

Hence it follows that art always aims at what is *individual*. What the artist fixes on his canvas is something he has seen at a certain spot, on a certain day, at a certain hour, with a coloring that will never be seen again. What the poet sings of is a certain mood which was his, and his alone, and which will never return. What the dramatist unfolds before us is the life-history of a soul, a living tissue of feelings and events—something, in short, which has once happened and can never be repeated. We may, indeed, give general names to these feelings, but they cannot be the same thing in another soul. They are *individualized*. Thereby, and thereby only, do they belong to art; for generalities, symbols or even types, form the current coin of our daily perception. How, then, does a misunderstanding on this point arise?

The reason lies in the fact that two very different things have been mistaken for each other: the generality of things and that of the opinions we come to regarding them. Because a feeling is generally recognized as true, it does not follow that it is a general feeling. Nothing could be more unique than the character of Hamlet. Though he may resemble other men in some respects, it is clearly not on that account that he interests us most. But he is universally accepted and regarded as a living character. In this sense only is he universally true. The same holds good of all the other products of art. Each of them is unique, and yet, if it bear the stamp of genius, it will come to be accepted by everybody. Why will it be accepted? And if it is unique of its kind, by what sign do we know it to be genuine? Evidently, by the very effort it forces us to make against our predispositions in order to see sincerely. Sincerity is contagious. What the artist has seen we shall probably never see again, or at least never see in exactly the same way; but if he has actually seen it, the attempt he has made to lift the veil compels our imitation. His work is an example which we take as a lesson. And the efficacy of the lesson is the exact standard of the genuineness of the work. Consequently, truth bears within itself a power of conviction, nay, of conversion, which is the sign that enables us to recognize it. The greater the work and the more profound the dimly apprehended truth, the longer may the effect be in coming, but, on the other hand, the more universal will that effect tend to become. So the universality here lies in the effect produced, and not in the cause.

Altogether different is the object of comedy. Here it is in the work itself that the generality lies. Comedy depicts characters we have already come across and shall meet with again. It takes note of similarities. It aims at placing types before our eyes. It even creates new types, if necessary. In this respect it forms a contrast to all the other arts.

The very titles of certain classical comedies are significant in themselves. Le Misanthrope, l'Avare, le Joueur, le Distrait, etc., are names of whole classes of people; and even when a character comedy has a proper noun as its title, this proper noun is speedily swept away, by the very weight of its contents, into the stream of common nouns. We say "a Tartuffe," but we should never say "a Phèdre" or "a Polyeucte."

Above all, a tragic poet will never think of grouping around the chief character in his play secondary characters to serve as simplified copies, so to speak, of the former. The hero of a tragedy represents an individuality unique of its kind. It may be possible to imitate him, but then we shall be passing, whether consciously or not, from the tragic to the comic. No one is like him, because he is like no one. But a remarkable instinct, on the contrary, impels the comic poet, once he has elaborated his central character, to cause other characters, displaying the same general traits, to revolve as satellites round him. Many comedies have either a plural noun or some collective term as their title. "*Les* Femmes savantes," "*Les* Précieuses ridicules," "*Le Monde* où l'on s'ennuie," etc., represent so many rallying points on the stage adopted by different groups of characters, all belonging to one identical type. It would be interesting to analyze this tendency in comedy. Maybe dramatists have caught a glimpse of a fact recently brought forward by mental pathology, viz., that cranks of the same kind are drawn, by a secret attraction, to seek each other's company. Without precisely coming within the province of medicine, the comic individual, as we have shown, is in some way absentminded, and the transition from absentmindedness to crankiness is continuous. But there is also another reason. If the comic poet's object is to offer us types, that is to say, characters capable of self-repetition, how can he set about it better than by showing us, in each instance, several different copies of the same model? That is just what the naturalist does in order to define a species. He enumerates and describes its main varieties.

This essential difference between tragedy and comedy, the former being concerned with individuals and the latter with classes, is revealed in yet another way. It appears in the first draft of the work. From the outset it is manifested by two radically different methods of observation.

Though the assertion may seem paradoxical, a study of other men is probably not necessary to the tragic poet. We find some of the great poets have lived a retiring, homely sort of life, without having a chance of witnessing around them an outburst of the passions they have so faithfully depicted. But, supposing even they had witnessed such a spectacle, it is doubtful whether they would have found it of much use. For what interests us in the work of the poet is the glimpse we get of certain profound moods or inner struggles. Now, this glimpse cannot be obtained from without. Our souls are impenetrable to one another. Certain signs of passion are all that we ever apperceive externally. These we interpret—though always, by the way, defectively—only by analogy with what we have ourselves experienced. So what we experi-

ence is the main point, and we cannot become thoroughly acquainted with anything but our own heart—supposing we ever get so far. Does this mean that the poet has experienced what he depicts, that he has gone through the various situations he makes his characters traverse, and lived the whole of their inner life? Here, too, the biographies of poets would contradict such a supposition. How, indeed, could the same man have been Macbeth, Hamlet, Othello, King Lear, and many others? But then a distinction should perhaps here be made between the personality *we have* and all those we might have had. Our character is the result of a choice that is continually being renewed. There are points—at all events there seem to be—all along the way, where we may branch off, and we perceive many possible directions though we are unable to take more than one. To retrace one's steps, and follow to the end the faintly distinguishable directions, appears to be the essential element in poetic imagination. Of course, Shakespeare was neither Macbeth, nor Hamlet, nor Othello; still, he *might have been* these several characters if the circumstances of the case on the one hand, and the consent of his will on the other, had caused to break out into explosive action what was nothing more than an inner prompting. We are strangely mistaken as to the part played by poetic imagination, if we think it pieces together its heroes out of fragments filched from right and left, as though it were patching together a harlequin's motley. Nothing living would result from that. Life cannot be recomposed; it can only be looked at and reproduced. Poetic imagination is but a fuller view of reality. If the characters created by a poet give us the impression of life, it is only because they are the poet himself—a multiplication or division of the poet—the poet plumbing the depths of his own nature in so powerful an effort of inner observation that he lays hold of the potential in the real, and takes up what nature has left as a mere outline or sketch in his soul in order to make of it a finished work of art.

Altogether different is the kind of observation from which comedy springs. It is directed outwards. However interested a dramatist may be in the comic features of human nature, he will hardly go, I imagine, to the extent of trying to discover his own. Besides, he would not find them, for we are never ridiculous except in some point that remains hidden from our own consciousness. It is on others, then, that such observation must perforce be practiced. But it will, for this very reason, assume a character of generality that it cannot have when we apply it to ourselves. Settling on the surface, it will not be more than skin-deep, dealing with persons at the point at which they come into contact and become capable of resembling one another. It will go no farther. Even if it could, it would not desire to do so, for it would have nothing to gain in the process. To penetrate too far into the personality, to couple the outer effect with causes that are too deep-seated, would mean to endanger and in the end to sacrifice all that was laughable in the effect. In order that we may be tempted to laugh at it, we must localize its cause in some intermediate region of the soul. Conse-

quently, the effect must appear to us as an average effect, as expressing an average of mankind. And, like all averages, this one is obtained by bringing together scattered data, by comparing analogous cases and extracting their essence, in short by a process of abstraction and generalization similar to that which the physicist brings to bear upon facts with the object of grouping them under laws. In a word, method and object are here of the same nature as in the inductive sciences, in that observation is always external and the result always general.

And so we come back, by a roundabout way, to the double conclusion we reached in the course of our investigations. On the one hand, a person is never ridiculous except through some mental attribute resembling absent-mindedness, through something that lives upon him without forming part of his organism, after the fashion of a parasite; that is the reason this state of mind is observable from without and capable of being corrected. But, on the other hand, just because laughter aims at correcting, it is expedient that the correction should reach as great a number of persons as possible. This is the reason comic observation instinctively proceeds to what is general. It chooses such peculiarities as admit of being reproduced and consequently are not indissolubly bound up with the individuality of a single person—a possibly common sort of uncommonness, so to say—peculiarities that are held in common. By transferring them to the stage, it creates works which doubtless belong to art in that their only visible aim is to please, but which will be found to contrast with other works of art by reason of their generality and also of their scarcely confessed or scarcely conscious intention to correct and instruct. So we were probably right in saying that comedy lies midway between art and life. It is not disinterested as genuine art is. By organizing laughter, comedy accepts social life as a natural environment, it even obeys an impulse of social life. And in this respect it turns its back upon art, which is a breaking away from society and a return to pure nature.

ALFRED NORTH WHITEHEAD (1861–1947)

The son of a vicar in the Anglican Church, Whitehead was born at Ramsgate, a village near Canterbury Cathedral. He was educated at Sherborne, one of England's oldest boarding schools, and at Trinity College, Cambridge. He remained in the college for a quarter of a century as a teacher of mathematics, and then taught for an additional thirteen years at the University of London.

Meanwhile he had married Evelyn Wade, who bore him a daughter and two sons. "Her vivid life," he wrote in an autobiographical sketch, "has taught me that beauty, moral and esthetic, is the aim of existence; and that kindness, and love, and artistic satisfaction are among its modes of attainment."[1]

In 1924, at the age of sixty-three, he joined the Philosophy Department at Harvard, where he taught until his retirement in 1937. Although he had collaborated with Bertrand Russell in writing the great *Principia Mathematica* (1910–1913), it was not until his later life that he turned whole-heartedly to speculative philosophy, writing a brilliant series of books, including *The Concept of Nature* (1920), *Science and the Modern World* (1925), *Process and Reality* (1929), and *Adventures of Ideas* (1933). These works established his reputation as one of the towering figures in modern thought. He died in his eighty-seventh year in his small apartment near Harvard Yard.

[1] Paul Arthur Schilpp, *The Philosophy of Alfred North Whitehead* (Evanston, Ill. Northwestern University Press, 1941), p. 8.

Requisites for Social Progress

It has been the purpose of these lectures to analyze the reactions of science in forming that background of instinctive ideas which control the activities of successive generations. Such a background takes the form of a certain vague philosophy as to the last word about things, when all is said. The three centuries, which form the epoch of modern science, have revolved round the ideas of *God*, *mind*, *matter*, and also of *space* and *time* in their characters of expressing *simple location* for matter. Philosophy has on the whole emphasized *mind*, and has thus been out of touch with science during the two latter centuries. But it is creeping back into its old importance owing to the rise of psychology and its alliance with physiology. Also, this rehabilitation of philosophy has been facilitated by the recent breakdown of the seventeenth century settlement of the principles of physical science. But, until that collapse, science seated itself securely upon the concepts of matter, space, time, and latterly, of energy. Also there were arbitrary laws of nature determining locomotion. They were empirically observed, but for some obscure reason were known to be universal. Anyone who in practice or theory disregarded them was denounced with unsparing vigour. This position on the part of scientists was pure bluff, if one may credit them with believing their own statements. For their current philosophy completely failed to justify the assumption that the immediate knowledge inherent in any present occasion throws any light either on its past, or its future.

I have also sketched an alternative philosophy of science in which *organism* takes the place of *matter*. For this purpose, the mind involved in the materialist theory dissolves into a function of organism. The psychological field then exhibits what an event is in itself. Our bodily event is an unusually complex type of organism and consequently includes cognition. Further, space and time, in their most concrete signification, become the locus of events. An organism is the realization of a definite shape of value. The emergence of some actual value depends on limitation which excludes neutralizing cross-lights. Thus an event is a matter of fact which by reason of its limitation is a value for itself; but by reason of its very nature it also requires the whole universe in order to be itself.

Importance depends on endurance. Endurance is the retention through time of an achievement of value. What endures is identity of pattern, self-inherited. Endurance requires the favourable environment. The whole of science revolves round this question of enduring organisms.

The general influence of science at the present moment can be analyzed under the headings: General Conceptions Respecting the Universe, Technological Applications, Professionalism in Knowledge, Influence of Biological Doctrines on the Motives of Conduct. I have endeavoured in the preceding lectures to give a glimpse of these points. It lies within the scope of this concluding lecture to consider the reaction of science upon some problems confronting civilized societies.

The general conceptions introduced by science into modern thought cannot be separated from the philosophical situation as expressed by Descartes. I mean the assumption of bodies and minds as independent individual substances, each existing in its own right apart from any necessary reference to each other. Such a conception was very concordant with the individualism which had issued from the moral discipline of the Middle Ages. But, though the easy reception of the idea is thus explained, the derivation in itself rests upon a confusion, very natural but none the less unfortunate. The moral discipline had emphasized the intrinsic value of the individual entity. This emphasis had put the notions of the individual and of its experiences into the foreground of thought. At this point the confusion commences. The emergent individual value of each entity is transformed into the independent substantial existence of each entity, which is a very different notion.

I do not mean to say that Descartes made this logical, or rather illogical transition, in the form of explicit reasoning. Far from it. What he did, was first to concentrate upon his own conscious experiences, as being facts within the independent world of his own mentality. He was led to speculate in this way by the current emphasis upon the individual value of his total self. He implicitly transformed this emergent individual value, inherent in the very fact of his own reality, into a private world of passions, or modes, of independent substance.

Also the independence ascribed to bodily substances carried them away from the realm of values altogether. They degenerated into a mechanism entirely valueless, except as suggestive of an external ingenuity. The heavens had lost the glory of God. This state of mind is illustrated in the recoil of Protestantism from aesthetic effects dependent upon a material medium. It was taken to lead to an ascription of value to what is in itself valueless. This recoil was already in full strength antecedently to Descartes. Accordingly, the Cartesian scientific doctrine of bits of matter, bare of intrinsic value, was merely a formulation, in explicit terms, of a doctrine which was current before its entrance into scientific thought or Cartesian philosophy. Probably this doctrine was latent in the scholastic philosophy, but it did not lead to its consequences till it met with the mentality of northern Europe in the sixteenth century. But science, as equipped by Descartes, gave stability and intellectual status to a point of view which has had very mixed effects upon the moral presuppositions of modern communities. Its good effects arose from its efficiency as a method for scientific researches within those limited regions which were then best suited for exploration. The result was a general clearing of the European mind away from the stains left upon it by the hysteria of remote barbaric ages. This was all to the good, and was most completely exemplified in the eighteenth century.

But in the nineteenth century, when society was undergoing transformation into the manufacturing system, the bad effects of these doctrines have been very fatal. The doctrine of minds, as independent substances, leads directly not merely to private worlds of experience, but also to private worlds of morals. The moral intuitions can be held to apply only to the strictly private world of psychological experience. Accordingly, self-respect, and the making the most of your own individual opportunities, together constituted the efficient morality of the leaders among the industrialists of that period. The western world is now suffering from the limited moral outlook of the three previous generations.

Also the assumption of the bare valuelessness of mere matter led to a lack of reverence in the treatment of natural or artistic beauty. Just when the urbanization of the western world was entering upon its state of rapid development, and when the most delicate, anxious consideration of the aesthetic qualities of the new material environment was requisite, the doctrine of the irrelevance of such ideas was at its height. In the most advanced industrial countries, art was treated as a frivolity. A striking example of this state of mind in the middle of the nineteenth century is to be seen in London where the marvellous beauty of the estuary of the Thames, as it curves through the city, is wantonly defaced by the Charing Cross railway bridge, constructed apart from any reference to aesthetic values.

The two evils are: one, the ignoration of the true relation of each organism to its environment; and the other, the habit of ignoring the intrinsic worth of the environment which must be allowed its weight in any consideration of final ends.

Another great fact confronting the modern world is the discovery of the method of training professionals, who specialize in particular regions of thought and thereby progressively add to the sum of knowledge within their respective limitations of subject. In consequence of the success of this professionalizing of knowledge, there are two points to be kept in mind, which differ-

entiate our present age from the past. In the first place, the rate of progress is such that an individual human being, of ordinary length of life, will be called upon to face novel situations which find no parallel in his past. The fixed person for the fixed duties, who in older societies was such a godsend, in the future will be a public danger. In the second place, the modern professionalism in knowledge works in the opposite direction so far as the intellectual sphere is concerned. The modern chemist is likely to be weak in zoology, weaker still in his general knowledge of the Elizabethan drama, and completely ignorant of the principles of rhythm in English versification. It is probably safe to ignore his knowledge of ancient history. Of course I am speaking of general tendencies; for chemists are no worse than engineers, or mathematicians, or classical scholars. Effective knowledge is professionalized knowledge, supported by a restricted acquaintance with useful subjects subservient to it.

This situation has its dangers. It produces minds in a groove. Each profession makes progress, but it is progress in its own groove. Now to be mentally in a groove is to live in contemplating a given set of abstractions. The groove prevents straying across country, and the abstraction abstracts from something to which no further attention is paid. But there is no groove of abstractions which is adequate for the comprehension of human life. Thus in the modern world, the celibacy of the medieval learned class has been replaced by a celibacy of the intellect which is divorced from the concrete contemplation of the complete facts. Of course, no one is merely a mathematician, or merely a lawyer. People have lives outside their professions or their businesses. But the point is the restraint of serious thought within a groove. The remainder of life is treated superficially, with the imperfect categories of thought derived from one profession.

The dangers arising from this aspect of professionalism are great, particularly in our democratic societies. The directive force of reason is weakened. The leading intellects lack balance. They see this set of circumstances, or that set; but not both sets together. The task of coördination is left to those who lack either the force or the character to succeed in some definite career. In short, the specialized functions of the community are performed better and more progressively, but the generalized direction lacks vision. The progressiveness in detail only adds to the danger produced by the feebleness of coördination.

This criticism of modern life applies throughout, in whatever sense you construe the meaning of a community. It holds if you apply it to a nation, a city, a district, an institution, a family, or even to an individual. There is a development of particular abstractions, and a contraction of concrete appreciation. The whole is lost in one of its aspects. It is not necessary for my point that I should maintain that our directive wisdom, either as individuals or as communities, is less now than in the past. Perhaps it has slightly improved. But the novel pace of progress requires a greater force of direction if disasters are to be avoided. The point is that the discoveries of the nineteenth century were

in the direction of professionalism, so that we are left with no expansion of wisdom and with greater need of it.

Wisdom is the fruit of a balanced development. It is this balanced growth of individuality which it should be the aim of education to secure. The most useful discoveries for the immediate future would concern the furtherance of this aim without detriment to the necessary intellectual professionalism.

My own criticism of our traditional educational methods is that they are far too much occupied with intellectual analysis, and with the acquirement of formularized information. What I mean is, that we neglect to strengthen habits of concrete appreciation of the individual facts in their full interplay of emergent values, and that we merely emphasize abstract formulations which ignore this aspect of the interplay of diverse values.

In every country the problem of the balance of the general and specialist education is under consideration. I cannot speak with first-hand knowledge of any country but my own. I know that there, among practical educationalists, there is considerable dissatisfaction with the existing practice. Also, the adaptation of the whole system to the needs of a democratic community is very far from being solved. I do not think that the secret of the solution lies in terms of the antithesis between thoroughness in special knowledge and general knowledge of a slighter character. The make-weight which balances the thoroughness of the specialist intellectual training should be of a radically different kind from purely intellectual analytical knowledge. At present our education combines a thorough study of a few abstractions, with a slighter study of a larger number of abstractions. We are too exclusively bookish in our scholastic routine. The general training should aim at eliciting our concrete apprehensions, and should satisfy the itch of youth to be doing something. There should be some analysis even here, but only just enough to illustrate the ways of thinking in diverse spheres. In the Garden of Eden Adam saw the animals before he named them: in the traditional system, children named the animals before they saw them.

There is no easy single solution of the practical difficulties of education. We can, however, guide ourselves by a certain simplicity in its general theory. The student should concentrate within a limited field. Such concentration should include all practical and intellectual acquirements requisite for that concentration. This is the ordinary procedure; and, in respect to it, I should be inclined even to increase the facilities for concentration rather than to diminish them. With the concentration there are associated certain subsidiary studies, such as languages for science. Such a scheme of professional training should be directed to a clear end congenial to the student. It is not necessary to elaborate the qualifications of these statements. Such a training must, of course, have the width requisite for its end. But its design should not be complicated by the consideration of other ends. This professional training can only touch one side of education. Its centre of gravity lies in the intellect, and its chief tool is the printed book. The centre of gravity of the other side of training should lie in intuition without an analytical divorce from the total environment. Its object is immediate apprehension with the minimum of eviscerating analysis. The type of generality, which above all is wanted, is the appreciation of variety of value. I mean an aesthetic growth. There is something between the gross specialized values of the mere practical man, and the thin specialized values of the mere scholar. Both types have missed something; and if you add together the two sets of values, you do not obtain the missing elements. What is wanted is an appreciation of the infinite variety of vivid values achieved by an organism in its proper environment. When you understand all about the sun and all about the atmosphere and all about the rotation of the earth, you may still miss the radiance of the sunset. There is no substitute for the direct perception of the concrete achievement of a thing in its actuality. We want concrete fact with a high light thrown on what is relevant to its preciousness.

What I mean is art and aesthetic education. It is, however, art in such a general sense of the term that I hardly like to call it by that name. Art is a special example. What we want is to draw out habits of aesthetic apprehension. According to the metaphysical doctrine which I have been developing, to do so is to increase the depth of individuality. The analysis of reality indicates the two factors, activity emerging into individualized aesthetic value. Also the emergent value is the measure of the individualization of the activity. We must foster the creative initiative towards the maintenance of objective values. You will not obtain the apprehension without the initiative, or the initiative without the apprehension. As soon as you get towards the concrete, you cannot exclude action. Sensitiveness without impulse spells decadence, and impulse without sensitiveness spells brutality. I am using the words "sensitiveness" in its most general signification, so as to include apprehension of what lies beyond oneself; that is to say, sensitiveness to all the facts of the case. Thus "art" in the general sense which I require is any selection by which the concrete facts are so arranged as to elicit attention to particular values which are realizable by them. For example, the mere disposing of the human body and the eyesight so as to get a good view of a sunset is a simple form of artistic selection. The habit of art is the habit of enjoying vivid values.

But, in this sense, art concerns more than sunsets. A factory, with its machinery, its community of operatives, its social service to the general population, its dependence upon organizing and designing genius, its potentialities as a source of wealth to the holders of its stock is an organism exhibiting a variety of vivid values. What we want to train is the habit of apprehending such an organism in its completeness. It is very arguable that the science of political economy, as studied in its first period after the death of Adam Smith (1790), did more harm than good. It destroyed many economic fallacies, and taught how to think about the economic revolution then in progress. But it riveted on men a certain set of abstractions which were disastrous in their influence on modern mentality. It de-humanized industry. This is only one example of a

general danger inherent in modern science. Its methodological procedure is exclusive and intolerant, and rightly so. It fixes attention on a definite group of abstractions, neglects everything else, and elicits every scrap of information and theory which is relevant to what it has retained. This method is triumphant, provided that the abstractions are judicious. But, however triumphant, the triumph is within limits. The neglect of these limits leads to disastrous oversights. The anti-rationalism of science is partly justified, as a preservation of its useful methodology; it is partly mere irrational prejudice. Modern professionalism is the training of minds to conform to the methodology. The historical revolt of the seventeenth century, and the earlier reaction towards naturalism, were examples of transcending the abstractions which fascinated educated society in the Middle Ages. These early ages had an ideal of rationalism, but they failed in its pursuit. For they neglected to note that the methodology of reasoning requires the limitations involved in the abstract. Accordingly, the true rationalism must always transcend itself by recurrence to the concrete in search of inspiration. A self-satisfied rationalism is in effect a form of anti-rationalism. It means an arbitrary halt at a particular set of abstractions. This was the case with science.

There are two principles inherent in the very nature of things, recurring in some particular embodiments whatever field we explore—the spirit of change, and the spirit of conservation. There can be nothing real without both. Mere change without conservation is a passage from nothing to nothing. Its final integration yields mere transient non-entity. Mere conservation without change cannot conserve. For after all, there is a flux of circumstance, and the freshness of being evaporates under mere repetition. The character of existent reality is composed of organisms enduring through the flux of things. The low type of organisms have achieved a self-identity dominating their whole physical life. Electrons, molecules, crystals, belong to this type. They exhibit a massive and complete sameness. In the higher types, where life appears, there is greater complexity. Thus, though there is a complex, enduring pattern, it has retreated into deeper recesses of the total fact. In a sense, the self-identity of a human being is more abstract than that of a crystal. It is the life of the spirit. It relates rather to the individualization of the creative activity; so that the changing circumstances received from the environment, are differentiated from the living personality, and are thought of as forming its perceived field. In truth, the field of perception and the perceiving mind are abstractions which, in the concrete, combine into the successive bodily events. The psychological field, as restricted to sense-objects and passing emotions, is the minor permanence, barely rescued from the nonentity of mere change; and the mind is the major permanence, permeating that complete field, whose endurance is the living soul. But the soul would wither without fertilization from its transient experiences. The secret of the higher organisms lies in their two grades of permanences. By this means the freshness of the environment is absorbed into the permanence of the soul. The changing environment is no longer, by reason of its variety, an enemy to the endurance of the organism. The pattern of the higher organism has retreated into the recesses of the individualized activity. It has become a uniform way of dealing with circumstances; and this way is only strengthened by having a proper variety of circumstances to deal with.

This fertilization of the soul is the reason for the necessity of art. A static value, however serious and important, becomes unendurable by its appalling monotony of endurance. The soul cries aloud for release into change. It suffers the agonies of claustrophobia. The transitions of humour, wit, irreverence, play, sleep, and—above all—of art are necessary for it. Great art is the arrangement of the environment so as to provide for the soul vivid, but transient, values. Human beings require something which absorbs them for a time, something out of the routine which they can stare at. But you cannot subdivide life, except in the abstract analysis of thought. Accordingly, the great art is more than a transient refreshment. It is something which adds to the permanent richness of the soul's self-attainment. It justifies itself both by its immediate enjoyment, and also by its discipline of the inmost being. Its discipline is not distinct from enjoyment, but by reason of it. It transforms the soul into the permanent realization of values extending beyond its former self. This element of transition in art is shown by the restlessness exhibited in its history. An epoch gets saturated by the masterpieces of any one style. Something new must be discovered. The human being wanders on. Yet there is a balance in things. Mere change before the attainment of adequacy of achievement, either in quality or output, is destructive of greatness. But the importance of a living art, which moves on and yet leaves its permanent mark, can hardly be exaggerated.

In regard to the aesthetic needs of civilized society the reactions of science have so far been unfortunate. Its materialistic basis has directed attention to *things* as opposed to *values*. The antithesis is a false one, if taken in a concrete sense. But it is valid at the abstract level of ordinary thought. This misplaced emphasis coalesced with the abstractions of political economy, which are in fact the abstractions in terms of which commercial affairs are carried on. Thus all thought concerned with social organization expressed itself in terms of material things and of capital. Ultimate values were excluded. They were politely bowed to, and then handed over to the clergy to be kept for Sundays. A creed of competitive business morality was evolved, in some respects curiously high; but entirely devoid of consideration for the value of human life. The workmen were conceived as mere hands, drawn from the pool of labour. To God's question, men gave the answer of Cain—"Am I my brother's keeper?"; and they incurred Cain's guilt. This was the atmosphere in which the industrial revolution was accomplished in England, and to a large extent elsewhere. The internal history of England during the last half century has been an endeavour slowly and painfully to undo the evils wrought in the first stage of the new epoch. It may be that civilization will never recover from

the bad climate which enveloped the introduction of machinery. This climate pervaded the whole commercial system of the progressive northern European races. It was partly the result of aesthetic errors of Protestantism and partly the result of scientific materialism, and partly the result of the natural greed of mankind, and partly the result of the abstractions of political economy. An illustration of my point is to be found in Macaulay's Essay criticizing Southey's *Colloquies on Society*. It was written in 1830. Now Macaulay was a very favourable example of men living at that date, or at any date. He had genius; he was kind-hearted, honourable, and a reformer. This is the extract:—"We are told, that our age has invented atrocities beyond the imagination of our fathers; that society has been brought into a state compared with which extermination would be a blessing; and all because the dwellings of cotton-spinners are naked and rectangular. Mr. Southey has found out a way he tells us, in which the effects of manufactures and agriculture may be compared. And what is this way? To stand on a hill, to look at a cottage and a factory, and to see which is the prettier."

Southey seems to have said many silly things in his book; but, so far as this extract is concerned, he could make a good case for himself if he returned to earth after a lapse of nearly a century. The evils of the early industrial system are now a commonplace of knowledge. The point which I am insisting on is the stone-blind eye with which even the best men of that time regarded the importance of aesthetics in a nation's life. I do not believe that we have as yet nearly achieved the right estimate. A contributory cause, of substantial efficacy to produce this disastrous error, was the scientific creed that matter in motion is the one concrete reality in nature; so that aesthetic values form an adventitious, irrelevant addition.

There is another side to this picture of the possibilities of decadence. At the present moment a discussion is raging as to the future of civilization in the novel circumstances of rapid scientific and technological advance. The evils of the future have been diagnosed in various ways, the loss of religious faith, the malignant use of material power, the degradation attending a differential birth rate favouring the lower types of humanity, the suppression of aesthetic creativeness. Without doubt, these are all evils, dangerous and threatening. But they are not new. From the dawn of history, mankind has always been losing its religious faith, has always suffered from the malignant use of material power, has always suffered from the infertility of its best intellectual types, has always witnessed the periodical decadence of art. In the reign of the Egyptian king, Tutankhamen, there was raging a desperate religious struggle between Modernists and Fundamentalists; the cave pictures exhibit a phase of delicate aesthetic achievement as superseded by a period of comparative vulgarity; the religious leaders, the great thinkers, the great poets and authors, the whole clerical caste in the Middle Ages, have been notably infertile; finally, if we attend to what actually happened in the past, and disregard romantic visions of democracies, aristocracies, kings, generals, armies, and merchants, material power has generally been wielded with blindness, obstinacy and selfishness, often with brutal malignancy. And yet, mankind has progressed. Even if you take a tiny oasis of peculiar excellence, the type of modern man who would have most chance of happiness in ancient Greece at its best period is probably (as now) an average professional heavy-weight boxer, and not an average Greek scholar from Oxford or Germany. Indeed, the main use of the Oxford scholar would have been his capability of writing an ode in glorification of the boxer. Nothing does more harm in unnerving men for their duties in the present, than the attention devoted to the points of excellence in the past as compared with the average failure of the present day.

But, after all, there have been real periods of decadence; and yet at the present time, as at other epochs, society is decaying, and there is need for preservative action. Professionals are not new to the world. But in the past, professionals have formed unprogressive castes. The point is that professionalism has now been mated with progress. The world is now faced with a self-evolving system, which it cannot stop. There are dangers and advantages in this situation. It is obvious that the gain in material power affords opportunity for social betterment. If mankind can rise to the occasion, there lies in front a golden age of beneficent creativeness. But material power in itself is ethically neutral. It can equally well work in the wrong direction. The problem is not how to produce great men, but how to produce great societies. The great society will put up the men for the occasions. The materialistic philosophy emphasized the given quantity of material, and thence derivatively the given nature of the environment. It thus operated most unfortunately upon the social conscience of mankind. For it directed almost exclusive attention to the aspect of struggle for existence in a fixed environment. To a large extent the environment is fixed, and to this extent there is a struggle for existence. It is folly to look at the universe through rose-tinted spectacles. We must admit the struggle. The question is, who is to be eliminated. In so far as we are educators, we have to have clear ideas upon that point; for it settles the type to be produced and the practical ethics to be inculcated.

But during the last three generations, the exclusive direction of attention to this aspect of things has been a disaster of the first magnitude. The watchwords of the nineteenth century have been, struggle for existence, competition, class warfare, commercial antagonism between nations, military warfare. The struggle for existence has been construed into the gospel of hate. The full conclusion to be drawn from a philosophy of evolution is fortunately of a more balanced character. Successful organisms modify their environment. Those organisms are successful which modify their environments so as to assist each other. This law is exemplified in nature on a vast scale. For example, the North American Indians accepted their environment, with the result that a scanty population barely succeeded in maintaining themselves over the whole continent. The European races when they arrived in the same continent pur-

sued an opposite policy. They at once coöperated in modifying their environment. The results is that a population more than twenty times that of the Indian population now occupies the same territory, and the continent is not yet full. Again, there are associations of different species which mutually coöperate. This differentiation of species is exhibited in the simplest physical entities, such as the association between electrons and positive nuclei, and in the whole realm of animate nature. The trees in a Brazilian forest depend upon the association of various species of organisms, each of which is mutually dependent on the other species. A single tree by itself is dependent upon all the adverse chances of shifting circumstances. The wind stunts it: the variations in temperature check its foliage: the rains denude its soil: its leaves are blown away and are lost for the purpose of fertilization. You may obtain individual specimens of fine trees either in exceptional circumstances, or where human cultivation has intervened. But in nature the normal way in which trees flourish is by their association in a forest. Each tree may lose something of its individual perfection of growth, but they mutually assist each other in preserving the conditions for survival. The soil is preserved and shaded; and the microbes necessary for its fertility are neither scorched, nor frozen, nor washed away. A forest is the triumph of the organization of mutually dependent species. Further a species of microbes which kills the forest, also exterminates itself. Again the two sexes exhibit the same advantage of differentiation. In the history of the world, the prize has not gone to those species which specialized in methods of violence, or even in defensive armour. In fact, nature began with producing animals encased in hard shells for defence against the ills of life. It also experimented in size. But smaller animals, without external armour, warm-blooded, sensitive, and alert, have cleared these monsters off the face of the earth. Also, the lions and tigers are not the successful species. There is something in the ready use of force which defeats its own object. Its main defect is that it bars coöperation. Every organism requires an environment of friends, partly to shield it from violent changes, and partly to supply it with its wants. The Gospel of Force is incompatible with a social life. By *force*, I mean *antagonism* in its most general sense.

Almost equally dangerous is the Gospel of Uniformity. The differences between the nations and races of mankind are required to preserve the conditions under which higher development is possible. One main factor in the upward trend of animal life has been the power of wandering. Perhaps this is why the armour-plated monsters fared badly. They could not wander. Animals wander into new conditions. They have to adapt themselves or die. Mankind has wandered from the trees to the plains, from the plains to the seacoast, from climate to climate, from continent to continent, and from habit of life to habit of life. When man ceases to wander, he will cease to ascend in the scale of being. Physical wandering is still important, but greater still is the power of man's spiritual adventures—adventures of thought, adventures of passionate feeling, adventures of aesthetic experience. A diversification among human communities is essential for the provision of the incentive and material for the Odyssey of the human spirit. Other nations of different habits are not enemies: they are godsends. Men require of their neighbours something sufficiently akin to be understood, something sufficiently different to provoke attention, and something great enough to command admiration. We must not expect, however, all the virtues. We should even be satisfied if there is something odd enough to be interesting.

Modern science has imposed on humanity the necessity for wandering. Its progressive thought and its progressive technology make the transition through time, from generation to generation, a true migration into unchartered seas of adventure. The very benefit of wandering is that it is dangerous and needs skill to avert evils. We must expect, therefore, that the future will disclose dangers. It is the business of the future to be dangerous; and it is among the merits of science that it equips the future for its duties. The prosperous middle classes, who ruled the nineteenth century, placed an excessive value upon placidity of existence. They refused to face the necessities for social reform imposed by the new industrial system, and they are now refusing to face the necessities for intellectual reform imposed by the new knowledge. The middle class pessimism over the future of the world comes from a confusion between civilization and security. In the immediate future there will be less security than in the immediate past, less stability.

It must be admitted that there is a degree of instability which is inconsistent with civilization. But, on the whole, the great ages have been unstable ages.

I have endeavoured in these lectures to give a record of a great adventure in the region of thought. It was shared in by all the races of western Europe. It developed with the slowness of a mass movement. Half a century is its unit of time. The tale is the epic of an episode in the manifestation of reason. It tells how a particular direction of reason emerges in a race by the long preparation of antecedent epochs, how after its birth its subject-matter gradually unfolds itself, how it attains its triumphs, how its influence moulds the very springs of action of mankind, and finally how at its moment of supreme success its limitations disclose themselves and call for a renewed exercise of the creative imagination. The moral of the tale is the power of reason, its decisive influence on the life of humanity. The great conquerors, from Alexander to Caesar, and from Caesar to Napoleon, influenced profoundly the lives of subsequent generations. But the total effect of this influence shrinks to insignificance, if compared to the entire transformation of human habits and human mentality produced by the long line of men of thought from Thales to the present day, men individually powerless, but ultimately the rulers of the world.

COMMENT

Kierkegaard and Existentialism

Different though they are in important respects, Kierkegaard, Bergson, and Whitehead are alike in reacting against static abstractions and in emphasizing individuality and process. There is an aesthetic tinge in the philosophies of all three. Kierkegaard and Bergson can be regarded as forerunners of existentialism. Because of these similarities, I have grouped these philosophers together.

The relevance of Kierkegaard to the extentialist movement can best be understood in the context of history. The present century has witnessed crises of unparalleled scope and intensity: two world wars, a very severe economic depression, revolutionary movements of tremendous magnitude and fury, the threat of nuclear holocaust. Philosophers have reacted with different degrees of intensity to these world-shaking events. Apart from the Marxists, the existentialists have been the philosophers most responsive. Existentialism, in fact, is a philosophy of crisis—its popularity can be explained largely in these terms. Although Sartre and Camus in France, Heidegger and Jaspers in Germany, and the other existentialist philosophers have been able to agree upon almost nothing else, they are alike in reflecting a time out of joint, when men have been hungry for meaning, for identity, for some roots in existence, for some structure of purpose in human experience, for some protection against anxieties and frustrations.

Certainly the "existentialists" are a strange assortment of figures. Jaspers, for example, is a Protestant, Marcel a Catholic, Heidegger an agnostic, Sartre an atheist. Their political convictions are no less diverse. As a result, "existentialism" has come to mean so many things that, by itself, it would seem to mean nothing. Nevertheless the existentialists exhibit, as Wittgenstein would say, a "family resemblance." We can best understand this resemblance if we trace the family tree back to its roots in such forerunners as Kierkegaard and Nietzsche. It is Sören Kierkegaard, above all, who is the fountainhead of our contemporary existentialism. His influence, which rapidly increased in the period between the two world wars, has spread beyond the boundaries of the Scandinavian countries, and has largely molded the philosophy of extentialism in Germany, France, Spain, Latin America, and to a lesser degree, the United States. A number of writers represented in this volume, Pascal, Nietzsche, Bergson, and to some degree even Marx, can be counted in the existentialist camp, but no one illustrates existentialism better than Kierkegaard.

In the foregoing readings from Kierkegaard there are several themes that are typical of the existentialist movement:

1. Emphasis upon Concrete Individual Existence. Kierkegaard was convinced that his religious and philosophical mission could be fulfilled only through his own personal experience and not through abstract mental processes. He is an existentialist in the sense that his stress is upon the sheer factual existence of the individual. As Master Eckhart, the German mystic, has said:

> That I am a man, this I share with other men. That I see and hear and that I eat and drink is what all animals do likewise. But that I am I is only mine and belongs to me and to nobody else; to no other man nor to an angel nor to God— except inasmuch as I am one with Him.[1]

Every man is an individual. He is "man" in the singular; he is not the abstraction "mankind." He shares many characteristics with other animals and with other men; but there is always a peculiar temperament, a unique blend of talents, a separate and distinctive consciousness. There is always something about me that is never common to you and me. Respect for a person is respect for this core of individuality. It is appreciation of the real man of flesh and blood—the unique *me*.

Individuality for Kierkegaard is opposed to both the stereotypes of mass society and the abstractness of philosophical systems. He detested the anonymity of "the crowd" and every kind of dehumanizing collectivism. "The crowd is untruth,"

---

[1] Master Eckhart, *Fragments,* as quoted by Erich Fromm, *Man for Himself* (New York: Holt, Rinehart and Winston, 1947), p. 38.

he said again and again. The kind of "truth" that Kierkegaard valued most is realized inwardly in the life of the individual. Hence he had a profound distaste for all *systems* of thought, such as Hegelianism. To exist as an individual is to suffer and to struggle, to develop, to be open to new possibilities, to be incomplete and inconsistent—while a system by its very nature is closed, static, dead, complete. "A logical system is possible," he said, but "an existential system is impossible."[2]

The very titles of Kierkegaard's major works—*Philosophical Fragments* and *Concluding Unscientific Postscript*—suggest the deliberately untidy and fragmentary character of his reflections. He issued a number of his books under pseudonyms, different from book to book, so that he was free to attack his own work under a different pseudonym. He thus avoided even the appearance of trying to construct a single, consistent, systematic body of thought.

2. THE NEED TO MAKE THINGS DIFFICULT. "With everyone engaged everywhere in making things easier," the pseudonymous author Johannes Climacus remarks, "someone was needed to make them difficult again." The passage from which this sentence is taken is a witty piece of fiction, but there is an underlying seriousness about it. The modern world, with its labor-saving devices and pain-killers, its mass stereotypes and oversimplified explanations, has made things too easy. One should face up to the tragic conflicts, paradoxes, and complexities of human existence. Where a rigid scientific rationalism has postulated only one kind of truth—objective scientific truth—and but one kind of good—the value of scientific and technological mastery—someone is needed to stress the truths and values of other modes of experience.

Wisdom, as Job and Prometheus discovered, comes not from the pleasantries of life but from profound suffering.

> What is the price of Experience? Do men buy it for a song,
> Or wisdom for a dance in the street? No, it is bought with the price
> Of all that a man hath, his house, his wife, his children.
> Wisdom is sold in the desolate market where none come to buy,
> And in the withered field where the farmer ploughs for bread in vain.[3]

Few men have explored more deeply than Kierkegaard the meaning of dread, anguish, alienation, and self-estrangement, "sickness unto death," and the kind of wisdom that can be gleaned from such experiences.

In the "pregnant moment" of crisis, existence and thought are fused into unity,

[2] *Concluding Unscientific Postscript,* in Robert Bretall, *A Kierkegaard Anthology* (Princeton, N.J.: Princeton University Press, 1946), p. 196.

[3] William Blake, "The Four Zoas."

and a man attains, if ever he does, authentic existence. The individual in a crisis situation may make dramatic and irrevocable choices for which he must assume sole responsibility. One of the persistent themes of existentialism, from Pascal to Sartre, is the need and reality of choice. Sartre speaks as if every action expresses an individual choice, whereas Kierkegaard speaks more often of the choice of a way of life, aesthetic or moral or religious. This transition from one way of life to another is conceived as a kind of conversion, dramatic and sometimes catastrophic. But both Kierkegaard and Sartre agree that men do not have fixed natures or pre-determined roles.

3. THE CLAIM THAT TRUTH IS SUBJECTIVITY. Kierkegaard's view of truth is based upon the distinction between what we believe and how we believe. Objectively the interest is focused upon the object of belief, subjectively upon the attitude of the believer. When it comes to matters of scientific truth, it is the object as verifiable that is of primary concern. But Kierkegaard is not much interested in objective truth in this sense. He is primarily concerned with an existential relationship of the individual with God. When it comes to this, what is most important is an intense spirituality. Through faith the individual appropriates in passionate inwardness the eternal truth of God's existence. What he seeks is not scientific verification or rational understanding, which in this instance is impossible, but something that passes understanding, namely, a faith so intense that it amounts to salvation. With this kind of "truth" in mind, Kierkegaard proclaims his thesis: truth is subjectivity.

The reader may feel that such a conception of truth is highly paradoxical if not downright contradictory. To call "true" the existential status of the individual in believing may seem to be an abuse of language. In a revealing passage Kierkegaard declares: "It is impossible to express with more intensive inwardness the principle that subjectivity is truth, than when subjectivity is in the first instance untruth, and yet subjectivity is the truth,"[4] In other words, a superstition believed in a certain manner is subjectively "true," regardless of its objective falsity.

Almost everything that Kierkegaard has written is highly controversial. Before committing himself *pro* or *con* the reader might ponder such questions as these: Is Kierkegaard's individualism too extreme? Is his emphasis upon will and feeling, rather than reason or the scientific method, exaggerated? In his preference for passionate participation and commitment, does he undervalue a disinterested analytical attitude? Does he argue inconsistently both that ultimate choice is criterionless and that the choice of a religious way of life is more correct than any other? Is he a one-sided romanticist, and in that sense a reductionist, despite his proposal to "make things difficult"? In his preference for "existence" over "essence," is he begging the question as to what is "really real"? Does he undervalue

[4] *Concluding Unscientific Postscript* (Princeton, N.J.: Princeton University Press, 1946), p. 191.

the ability to sense the essential and to formulate it in something like a definition? These questions can best be answered if the point of view of Kierkegaard is critically compared with the views of the philosophers studied in the preceding chapters.

Art, Intuition, and the Nature of Things

The readings in the present chapter dealing with such matters as art and education may seem to be concerned only peripherally with knowledge and reality. But the metaphysical and epistemological doctrines of Bergson and Whitehead are not only presupposed but stated with thumbnail brevity. It may be helpful to the reader if we make these doctrines more explicit.

Bergson, in reacting like Kierkegaard against abstractions, is a defender of intuition as contrasted with intellect. The word "intuition" is derived from the Latin *intuere*—to look at. The looking, or directness of the insight, is its fundamental mark. Intuition can be defined as the direct apprehension that a proposition is true, or that something is the case. Both Descartes and Bergson, to mention an illuminating contrast, regard intuition as basic to philosophic method, but each differs in his conception of intuitive insight. For Descartes it is the immediate grasp of truths, for example, that six is more than five. As the source of axiomatic truths, it provides the premises from which deduction draws forth, by a process of logical inference, the conclusions which necessarily follow. For Bergson, intuition is the direct apprehension by a knowing subject of himself, of his mental states, or of anything with which he is immediately acquainted. It is more akin to sympathetic imagination than to abstract reasoning, and valued more for its own sake than as a foundation for deductive inference.

Bergson distinguishes between intellect, the analytical faculty whose function is to facilitate action by dissecting and classifying, and intuition, the synthetic faculty whose function is to grasp the wholeness and concrete individuality of things. Upon the basis of these distinctions, he rejects the claims of mechanistic and materialistic philosophy and espouses a theory of free will and creative evolution. There is an irreducible life force, or *élan vital*, moving not toward any fixed or final goal but thrusting upward toward new and higher forms of existence. The downward movement of usable matter governed by the law of entropy is counter to this vital impetus.

According to Bergson, all men possess the ability to intuit but only genius exhibits it to a high degree. "Between nature and ourselves," he declares, "nay, between ourselves and our own consciousness a veil is interposed: a veil that is dense and opaque for the common herd—thin, almost transparent, for the artist and the poet." The ordinary man moves about amid "generalities and symbols," but the intuitive person, whether he be called an artist or not, brushes aside "the utilitarian symbols, the conventional and socially accepted generalities, in short everything that veils reality from us, in order to bring us face to face with reality itself." In its innermost character, this reality is duration—the ceaseless, undivided flow of time, not clock-time, with its mathematical abstractions, but living time, in its qualitative richness, fullness, and density.

To know reality truly, in its uniqueness and flux, we need to relax the tension of practical effort and teach our minds a new docility to nature. We will then penetrate, by a kind of sympathy, to the real nature of the object, thus discovering for the first time its individuality and multiplicity. Turning our gaze inward, we will discern the continuity and freshness of our inner life. Intuition is this sympathy or direct vision, and the artist is unusually gifted with it. Most works of art are the records of intuition. But one type of art is an exception. In the art of comedy the intellect predominates, because we laugh at a person only when we are intellectually detached. A living human being is absurd and hence laughable when he violates his vital nature, behaving in a fixed, rigid, machine-like way, and when the spectator regards him with critical and amused detachment.

Whitehead's Revolt against Dualism

Whitehead did not believe, as did Bergson, that intellect is intrinsically tied to erroneous fictions, but he agreed with Bergson in rejecting a static materialism and a narrow scientism. He revolted against the dualism of mind and matter and primary and secondary qualities because he regarded it as insufferably narrow in its empirical basis.

The theme of *Science and the Modern World*, from which our selection is taken, is the influence of the scientific mentality upon Western civilization during the past three centuries. Science has probed some of the deepest mysteries of the universe and invented the most fecund machines. These achievements, however, have not been matched by a comparable moral, religious, and aesthetic advance. We have not learned how to relate human beings happily and creatively to one another. In philosophy, the remedy is to recognize more fully the role of values in existence; in industry, to put more stress upon quality and human costs; in education, to foster wide humanistic sympathies and the appreciation of beauty and art.

Whereas the older materialists, with their assumption of the bare valuelessness of matter, conceived of goodness and beauty as accidental appearances, Whitehead has sketched a metaphysics which has different implications. The history of the universe, as he envisages it, is the evolution of organisms from the simple to the complex. Electrons, atoms, molecules, cells, plants, animals, men, and human communities form a series of mounting complexity and inclusiveness, the higher organisms embracing innumerable lower ones. Even matter at its lowest level is "organic," and every organism is essentially influenced by others; each higher level exhibits its own emergent qualities; and values, such as beauty, are as real and fundamental as any other aspect of nature. This is a far cry from the reductive materialism characteristic of so much thought in the modern age.

Believing as Bergson did that time is fundamental to the nature of things, Whitehead envisaged the world as composed of interlocking events.

> An event has contemporaries. This means that an event mirrors within itself the modes of its contemporaries as a display of immediate achievement. An event has a past. This means that an event mirrors within itself the modes of its predecessors, as memories which are fused into its own content. An event has a future. This means that an event mirrors within itself such aspects as the future throws back onto the present, or, in other words, as the present has determined concerning the future. Thus an event has anticipation.[5]

In taking account of each other, the organisms function and the events occur in a concrete world of qualities, where color, sound, beauty, and selectivity are objective factors throughout nature.

Whitehead concludes his argument with a discussion of the requisites of social betterment, maintaining that progress depends upon the restoration of balance in our civilization. We should cease to sacrifice wisdom to knowledge, well-rounded development to specialized skill, concrete appreciation to abstract understanding, synthesis to analysis, quality to quantity. If we are to obtain a proper balance, art and aesthetic education must become much more pervasive in our society.

By art Whitehead means not merely poems and paintings and statues and musical compositions, but fondly made tools and comely attire and attractive gardens and dwellings and the pleasing appearance of highways and towns and cultivated fields. Whenever we enjoy vivid qualities for their own sake, our experience is aesthetic, and art is the control and creation of these qualities so as to elicit an appreciation of values. In this sense, art and aesthetic experience are as necessary to civilization as are science and technology.

Final Questions

In these selections from Bergson and Whitehead there are many things to debate. There is the question whether both philosophers have correctly interpreted the nature of art, or the importance of aesthetic values in human development. There is also the question whether Bergson puts too much trust in artistic intuition and too little trust in the scientific interpretation of reality. Is he too much the romantic, and too little the hardheaded realist? Similarly we can ask whether Whitehead has reacted too strongly against the alleged materialism of the modern scientific outlook.

Both Bergson and Whitehead, each in his own way, is a rebel against Cartesian dualism. As we have already seen, "the revolt against dualism" has been challenged by such able philosophers as Arthur Lovejoy. Who is more nearly right?

---

[5] *Science and the Modern World* (New York: Macmillan, 1925), pp. 106–107.

Can we agree with Whitehead that there are not basically different kinds of entities in the world—organic and inorganic, and minds and bodies—but rather different grades and levels of organism and mentality? Is it fanciful to speak of the inner life of molecules, as if they had feelings, memories, and anticipations? How could anybody verify such an hypothesis? And is Bergson's hypothesis of an *élan vital* any more verifiable?

Apart from these difficult epistemological and metaphysical problems, there are questions about human values. Is Bergson correct in thinking that life, in its true nature, is ever fresh and creative, and that its essence is violated whenever it is closed and repetitive? Is Whitehead correct in maintaining that modern civilization is lopsided? Have we been too neglectful of aesthetic values, too intent upon material power, too insistent upon uniformity, too lacking in comprehensive vision, too addicted to professional grooves, too narrowly concerned with facts, too afraid of the adventures of ideas, too willing to sacrifice the individual for the type?

In raising questions of this sort, the writings of Bergson and Whitehead, like the similar writings of Kierkegaard, are transitional to the remaining parts of this book. So far we have been preoccupied with epistemological and metaphysical questions, but henceforth we shall be mainly concerned with problems of value—religious, ethical, and social.

Part Two

RELIGION

The philosophy of religion, with which we shall be concerned in Part Two, does not fall neatly into any of the main categories of philosophical inquiry. So far as it examines the logical grounds of religious belief, it belongs to epistemology, or theory of knowledge; so far as it interprets the nature of the universe, it belongs to metaphysics, or theory of reality; so far as it considers religious values, such as the sense of sacredness, it belongs to axiology, or theory of values.

Since we cannot explore all of these areas in this book, our main emphasis will be upon the grounds of religious belief. In Chapter 10, we shall examine faith, mystical experience, and religious imagination. In Chapter 11, we shall consider whether there are sound arguments, either *a priori* or empirical, for believing in the existence of God.

All of these topics have an important bearing upon the nature of religion. J. M. E. McTaggart has said that religion "may best be described as an emotion resting on a conviction of a harmony between ourselves and the universe at large." Whether *all* religion should be so defined shall not be discussed, but we can ask whether there really *is* such a harmony between man and his universe. The question is crucially important and the attempt to answer it is an exciting venture. The philosophers represented in Part Two—Pascal, James, Santayana, St. Anselm, St. Thomas, Hume, Montague, and Russell—all seek some solution to this question, although their answers are extremely varied.

10

The Basis
of
Religious Belief

BLAISE PASCAL (1623–1662)

Younger by 27 years than Descartes, Pascal was born at Claremont, in Auvergne, France. His mother died when he was only four, and he was educated by his father, who moved with his children to Paris when Pascal was seven. Amazingly precocious, Blaise composed a treatise on sound at the age of twelve, and at sixteen one on conic sections which astounded "the most learned and scientific men in Paris." He was noted, among other great accomplishments, for his contributions to the theory of probability and the invention of a calculating machine. His experiments with the help of a barometer proved the familiar facts now known to every beginner in physics regarding the pressure of the atmosphere and the nature of a vacuum.

On the night of November 23, 1654, Pascal had a profound mystical experience which utterly changed his life. He abandoned his previous routine of scientist and man-about-town, and spent his days in ascetic discipline and religious writing. Much of his effort he devoted to a defense of the Jansenists, a controversial religious order. He died in 1662 at the age of thirty-nine. After his death, a record of his ecstatic mystical experience, written on parchment, was found sewn in the lining of his doublet.

368

Thoughts

Misery of Man Without God

72

The Disproportion of Man to Nature

. . . Let man . . . contemplate the whole of nature in her full and grand majesty, and turn his vision from the low objects which surround him. Let him gaze on that brilliant light, set like an eternal lamp to illumine the universe; let the earth appear to him a point in comparison with the vast circle described by the sun; and let him wonder at the fact that this vast circle is itself but a very fine point in comparison with that described by the stars in their revolution round the firmament. But if our view be arrested there, let our imagination pass beyond; it will sooner exhaust the power of conception than

From *Thoughts*, translated by W. F. Trotter (1904) from the French edition of Leon Brunschvicg (1897). Consisting of 924 numbered items, the *Thoughts* are posthumous notes for a projected defense of Christianity. Passages effaced by Pascal and restored by his French editor are enclosed in square brackets. The numbering of items is in accordance with the Brunschvicg text, but I have departed somewhat from his order in arranging the items. For an explanation of the order I have adopted see my Comment at the end of the chapter. [Editor]

nature that of supplying material for conception. The whole visible world is only an imperceptible atom in the ample bosom of nature. No idea approaches it. We may enlarge our conceptions beyond all imaginable space; we only produce atoms in comparison with the reality of things. It is an infinite sphere, the centre of which is everywhere, the circumference nowhere. In short it is the greatest sensible mark of the almighty power of God, that imagination loses itself in that thought.

Returning to himself, let man consider what he is in comparison with all existence; let him regard himself as lost in this remote corner of nature; and from the little cell in which he finds himself lodged, I mean the universe, let him estimate at their true value the earth, kingdoms, cities, and himself. What is a man in the Infinite?

But to show him another prodigy equally astonishing, let him examine the most delicate things he knows. Let a mite be given him, with its minute body and parts incomparably more minute, limbs with their joints, veins in the limbs, blood in the veins, humours in the blood, drops in the humours, vapours in the drops. Dividing these last things again, let him exhaust his powers of conception, and let the last object at which he can arrive be now that of our discourse. Perhaps he will think that here is the smallest point in nature. I will let him see therein a new abyss. I will paint for him not only the visible universe, but all that he can conceive of nature's immensity in the womb of this abridged atom. Let him see therein an infinity of universes, each of which has its firmament, its planets, its earth, in the same proportion as in the visible world; in each earth animals, and in the last mites, in which he will find again all that the first had, finding still in these others the same thing without end and without cessation. Let him lose himself in wonders as amazing in their littleness as the others in their vastness. For who will not be astounded at the fact that our body, which a little ago was imperceptible in the universe, itself imperceptible in the bosom of the whole, is now a colossus, a world, or rather a whole, in respect of the nothingness which we cannot reach? He who regards himself in this light will be afraid of himself, and observing himself sustained in the body given him by nature between those two abysses of the Infinite and Nothing, will tremble at the sight of these marvels; and I think that, as his curiosity changes into admiration, he will be more disposed to contemplate them in silence than to examine them with presumption.

For in fact what is man in nature? A Nothing in comparison with the Infinite, an All in comparison with the Nothing, a mean between nothing and everything. Since he is infinitely removed from comprehending the extremes, the end of things and their beginning are hopelessly hidden from him in an impenetrable secret; he is equally incapable of seeing the Nothing from which he was made, and the Infinite in which he is swallowed up.

What will he do then, but perceive the appearance of the middle of things, in an eternal despair of knowing either their beginning or their end. All things proceed from the Nothing, and are borne towards the Infinite. Who will follow these marvellous processes? The Author of these wonders understands them. None other can do so.

Through failure to contemplate these Infinites, men have rashly rushed into the examination of nature, as though they bore some proportion to her. It is strange that they have wished to understand the beginnings of things, and thence to arrive at the knowledge of the whole, with a presumption as infinite as their object. For surely this design cannot be formed without presumption or without a capacity infinite like nature.

If we are well-informed, we understand that, as nature has graven her image and that of her Author on all things, they almost all partake of her double infinity. Thus we see that all the sciences are infinite in the extent of their researches. For who doubts that geometry, for instance, has an infinite infinity of problems to solve? They are also infinite in the multitude and fineness of their premises; for it is clear that those which are put forward as ultimate are not self-supporting, but are based on others which, again having others for their support, do not permit of finality. But we represent some as ultimate for reason, in the same way as in regard to material objects we call that an indivisible point beyond which our senses can no longer perceive anything, although by its nature it is infinitely divisible.

Of these two Infinites of science, that of greatness is the most palpable, and hence a few persons have pretended to know all things. "I will speak of the whole," said Democritus.

But the infinitely little is the least obvious. Philosophers have much oftener claimed to have reached it, and it is here they have all stumbled. This has given rise to such common titles as *First Principles, Principles of Philosophy*, and the like, as ostentatious in fact, though not in appearance, as that one which blinds us, *De omni scibili*.[1]

We naturally believe ourselves far more capable of reaching the centre of things than of embracing their circumference. The visible extent of the world visibly exceeds us, but as we exceed little things, we think ourselves more capable of knowing them. And yet we need no less capacity for attaining the Nothing than the All. Infinite capacity is required for both, and it seems to me that whoever shall have understood the ultimate principles of being might also attain to the knowledge of the Infinite. The one depends on the other, and one leads to the other. These extremes meet and reunite by force of distance, and find each other in God, and in God alone.

Let us then take our compass; we are something, and we are not everything. The nature of our existence hides from us the knowledge of first beginnings which are born of the Nothing; and

the littleness of our being conceals from us the sight of the Infinite.

Our intellect holds the same position in the world of thought as our body occupies in the expanse of nature.

Limited as we are in every way, this state which holds the mean between two extremes is present in all our impotence. Our senses perceive no extreme. Too much sound deafens us; too much light dazzles us; too great distance or proximity hinders our view. Too great length and too great brevity of discourse tend to obscurity; too much truth is paralysing; (I know some who cannot understand that to take four from nothing leaves nothing). First principles are too self-evident for us; too much pleasure disagrees with us. Too many concords are annoying in music; too many benefits irritate us; we wish to have the wherewithal to over-pay our debts. *Beneficia co usque læta sunt dum videntur exsolvi posse; ubi multum antevenere, pro gratia odium redditur.*[2] We feel neither extreme heat nor extreme cold. Excessive qualities are prejudicial to us and not perceptible by the senses; we do not feel but suffer them. Extreme youth and extreme age hinder the mind, as also too much and too little education. In short, extremes are for us as though they were not, and we are not within their notice. They escape us, or we them.

This is our true state; this is what makes us incapable of certain knowledge and of absolute ignorance. We sail within a vast sphere, ever drifting

---

[1] "Concerning everything knowable"—the title under which Pico della Mirandola announced the 900 propositions which he undertook to defend in 1486.

[2] "Benefits are pleasant while it seems possible to requite them; when they become much greater, they produce hatred rather than gratitude."—Tacitus.

in uncertainty, driven from end to end. When we think to attach ourselves to any point and to fasten to it, it wavers and leaves us; and if we follow it, it eludes our grasp, slips past us, and vanishes for ever. Nothing stays for us. This is our natural condition, and yet most contrary to our inclination; we burn with desire to find solid ground and an ultimate sure foundation whereon to build a tower reaching to the Infinite. But our whole groundwork cracks, and the earth opens to abysses.

Let us therefore not look for certainty and stability. Our reason is always deceived by fickle shadows; nothing can fix the finite between the two Infinites, which both enclose and fly from it.

If this be well understood, I think that we shall remain at rest, each in the state wherein nature has placed him. As this sphere which has fallen to us as our lot is always distant from either extreme, what matters it that man should have a little more knowledge of the universe? If he has it, he but gets a little higher. Is he not always infinitely removed from the end, and is not the duration of our life equally removed from eternity, even if it lasts ten years longer?

In comparison with these Infinites all finites are equal, and I see no reason for fixing our imagination on one more than on another. The only comparison which we make of ourselves to the finite is painful to us.

If man made himself the first object of study, he would see how incapable he is of going further. How can a part know the whole? But he may perhaps aspire to know at least the parts to which he bears some proportion. But the parts of the world are all so related and linked to one another, that I believe it impossible to know one without the other and without the whole.

Man, for instance, is related to all he knows. He needs a place wherein to abide, time through which to live, motion in order to live, elements to compose him, warmth and food to nourish him, air to breathe. He sees light; he feels bodies; in short, he is in a dependant alliance with everything. To know man, then, it is necessary to know how it happens that he needs air to live, and, to know the air, we must know how it is thus related to the life of man, etc. Flame cannot exist without air; therefore to understand the one, we must understand the other.

Since everything then is cause and effect, dependant and supporting, mediate and immediate, and all is held together by a natural though imperceptible chain, which binds together things most distant and most different, I hold it equally impossible to know the parts without knowing the whole, and to know the whole without knowing the parts in detail.

[The eternity of things in itself or in God must also astonish our brief duration. The fixed and constant immobility of nature, in comparison with the continual change which goes on within us, must have the same effect.]

And what completes our incapability of knowing things, is the fact that they are simple, and that we are composed of two opposite natures, different in kind, soul and body. For it is impossible that our rational part should be other than spiritual; and if any one maintain that we are simply corporeal, this would far more exclude us from the knowledge of things, there being nothing so inconceivable as to say that matter knows itself. It is impossible to imagine how it should know itself.

So if we are simply material, we can know nothing at all; and if we are composed of mind and matter, we cannot know perfectly things which are simple, whether spiritual or corporeal. Hence it comes that almost all philosophers have confused ideas of things, and speak of material things in spiritual terms, and of spiritual things in material terms. For they say boldly that bodies have a tendency to fall, that they seek after their centre, that they fly from destruction, that they fear the void, that they have inclinations, sympathies, antipathies, all of which attributes pertain only to mind. And in speaking of minds, they consider them as in a place, and attribute to them movement from one place to another; and these are qualities which belong only to bodies.

Instead of receiving the ideas of these things in their purity, we colour them with our own qualities, and stamp with our composite being all the simple things which we contemplate.

Who would not think, seeing us compose all things of mind and body, but that this mixture would be quite intelligible to us? Yet it is the very thing we least understand. Man is to himself the most wonderful object in nature; for he cannot conceive what the body is, still less what the mind is, and least of all how a body should be united to a mind. This is the consummation of his difficulties, and yet it is his very being. . . .

82

Imagination

It is that deceitful part in man, that mistress of error and falsity, the more deceptive that she is not always so; for she would be an infallible rule of truth, if she were an infallible rule of falsehood. But being most generally false, she gives no sign of her nature, impressing the same character on the true and the false.

I do not speak of fools, I speak of the wisest men; and it is among them that the imagination has the great gift of persuasion. Reason protests in vain; it cannot set a true value on things.

This arrogant power, the enemy of reason, who likes to rule and dominate it, has established in man a second nature to show how all-powerful she is. She makes men happy and sad, healthy and sick, rich and poor; she compels reason to believe, doubt, and deny; she blunts the senses, or quickens them; she has her fools and sages; and nothing vexes us more than to see that she fills her devotees with a satisfaction far more full and entire than does reason. Those who have a lively imagination are a great deal more pleased with themselves than the wise can reasonably be. They look down upon men with haughtiness; they argue with boldness and confidence, others with fear and diffidence; and this gaiety of countenance often gives them the advantage in the opinion of the hearers, such favour have the imaginary wise in the eyes of judges of like nature. Imagination cannot make fools wise; but she can make them happy, to the envy of reason which can only make its friends miserable; the one covers them with glory, the other with shame.

What but this faculty of imagination dispenses reputation, awards respect and veneration to persons, works, laws, and the great? How insufficient are all the riches of the earth without her consent!

Would you not say that this magistrate, whose venerable age commands the respect of a whole people, is governed by pure and lofty reason, and that he judges causes according to their true nature without considering those mere trifles which only affect the imagination of the weak? See him go to sermon, full of devout zeal, strengthening his reason with the ardour of his love. He is ready to listen with exemplary respect. Let the preacher appear, and let nature have given him a hoarse voice or a comical cast of countenance, or let his barber have given him a bad shave, or let by chance his dress be more dirtied than usual, then however great the truths he announces, I wager our senator lose his gravity.

If the greatest philosopher in the world find himself upon a plank wider than actually necessary, but hanging over a precipice, his imagination will prevail, though his reason convince him of his safety. Many cannot bear the thought without a cold sweat. I will not state all its effects.

Every one knows that the sight of cats or rats, the crushing of a coal, etc., may unhinge the reason. The tone of voice affects the wisest, and changes the force of a discourse or a poem.

Love or hate alters the aspect of justice. How much greater confidence has an advocate, retained with a large fee, in the justice of his cause! How much

better does his bold manner make his case appear to the judges, deceived as they are by appearances! How ludicrous is reason, blown with a breath in every direction!

I should have to enumerate almost every action of men who scarce waver save under her assaults. For reason has been obliged to yield, and the wisest reason takes as her own principles those which the imagination of man has everywhere rashly introduced. [He who would follow reason only would be deemed foolish by the generality of men. We must judge by the opinion of the majority of mankind. Because it has pleased them, we must work all day for pleasures seen to be imaginary; and after sleep has refreshed our tired reason, we must forthwith start up and rush after phantoms, and suffer the impressions of this mistress of the world. This is one of the sources of error, but it is not the only one.]

Our magistrates have known well this mystery. Their red robes, the ermine in which they wrap themselves like furry cats, the courts in which they administer justice, the *fleurs-de-lis*, and all such august apparel were necessary; if the physicians had not their cassocks and their mules, if the doctors had not their square caps and their robes four times too wide, they would never have duped the world, which cannot resist so original an appearance. If magistrates had true justice, and if physicians had the true art of healing, they would have no occasion for square caps; the majesty of these sciences would of itself be venerable enough. But having only imaginary knowledge, they must employ those silly tools that strike the imgination with which they have to deal; and thereby in fact they inspire respect. Soldiers alone are not disguised in this manner, because indeed their part is the most essential; they establish themselves by force, the others by show.

Therefore our kings seek out no disguises. They do not mask themselves in extraordinary costumes to appear such; but they are accompanied by guards and halberdiers. Those armed and red-faced puppets who have hands and power for them alone, those trumpets and drums which go before them, and those legions round about them, make the stoutest tremble. They have not dress only, they have might. A very refined reason is required to regard as an ordinary man the Grand Turk, in his superb seraglio, surrounded by forty thousand janissaries.

We cannot even see an advocate in his robe and with his cap on his head, without a favourable opinion of his ability. The imagination disposes of everything; it makes beauty, justice, and happiness, which is everything in the world. I should much like to see an Italian work, of which I only know the title, which alone is worth many books, *Della opinione regina del mondo.*[3] I approve of the book without knowing it, save the evil in it, if any. These are pretty much the effects of that deceptive faculty, which seems to have been expressly given us to lead us into necessary error. We have, however, many other sources of error.

Not only are old impressions capable of misleading us; the charms of novelty

have the same power. Hence arise all the disputes of men, who taunt each other either with following the false impressions of childhood, or with running rashly after the new. Who keeps the due mean? Let him appear and prove it. There is no principle, however natural to us from infancy, which may not be made to pass for a false impression either of education or of sense.

"Because," say some, "you have believed from childhood that a box was empty when you saw nothing in it, you have believed in the possibility of a vacuum. This is an illusion of your senses, strengthened by custom, which science must correct." "Because," say others, "you have been taught at school that there is no vacuum, you have perverted your common sense which clearly comprehended it, and you must correct this by returning to your first state." Which has deceived you, your senses or your education?

We have another source of error in diseases. They spoil the judgment and the senses; and if the more serious produce a sensible change, I do not doubt that slighter ills produce a proportionate impression.

Our own interest is again a marvellous instrument for nicely putting out our eyes. The justest man in the world is not allowed to be judge in his own cause; I know some who, in order not to fall into this self-love, have been perfectly unjust out of opposition. The sure way of losing a just cause has been to get it recommended to these men by their near relatives.

Justice and truth are two such subtle points, that our tools are too blunt to touch them accurately. If they reach the

---

[3] "On opinion, queen of the world." The book has not been certainly identified.

point, they either crush it, or lean all round, more on the false than on the true.

[. . . But the most powerful cause of error is the war existing between the senses and reason.]

83

We must thus begin the chapter on the deceptive powers. Man is only a subject full of error, natural and ineffaceable, without grace. Nothing shows him the truth. Everything deceives him. These two sources of truth, reason and the senses, besides being both wanting in sincerity, deceive each other in turn. The senses mislead the reason with false appearances, and receive from reason in their turn the same trickery which they apply to her; reason has her revenge. The passions of the soul trouble the senses, and make false impressions upon them. They rival each other in falsehood and deception. . . .

100

Self-love

The nature of self-love and of this human Ego is to love self only and consider self only. But what will man do? He cannot prevent this object that he loves from being full of faults and wants. He wants to be great, and he sees himself small. He wants to be happy, and he sees himself miserable. He wants to be perfect, and he sees himself full of imperfections. He wants to be the object of love and esteem among men, and he sees that his faults merit only their hatred and contempt. This embarrassment in which he finds

himself produces in him the most unrighteous and criminal passion that can be imagined; for he conceives a mortal enmity against that truth which reproves him, and which convinces him of his faults. He would annihilate it, but, unable to destroy it in its essence, he destroys it as far as possible in his own knowledge and in that of others; that is to say, he devotes all his attention to hiding his faults both from others and from himself, and he cannot endure either that others should point them out to him, or that they should see them.

Truly it is an evil to be full of faults; but it is a still greater evil to be full of them, and to be unwilling to recognise them, since that is to add the further fault of a voluntary illusion. We do not like others to deceive us; we do not think it fair that they should be held in higher esteem by us than they deserve; it is not then fair that we should deceive them, and should wish them to esteem us more highly than we deserve.

Thus, when they discover only the imperfections and vices which we really have, it is plain they do us no wrong, since it is not they who cause them; they rather do us good, since they help us to free ourselves from an evil, namely, the ignorance of these imperfections. We ought not to be angry at their knowing our faults and despising us; it is but right that they should know us for what we are, and should despise us, if we are contemptible.

Such are the feelings that would arise in a heart full of equity and justice. What must we say then of our own heart, when we see in it a wholly different disposition? For is it not true that we hate truth and those who tell it us, and that we like them to be deceived in our favour, and prefer to be esteemed by them as being other than what we are in fact? One proof of this makes me shudder. The Catholic religion does not bind us to confess our sins indiscriminately to everybody; it allows them to remain hidden from all other men save one, to whom she bids us reveal the innermost recesses of our heart, and show ourselves as we are. There is only this one man in the world whom she orders us to undeceive, and she binds him to an inviolable secrecy, which makes this knowledge to him as if it were not. Can we imagine anything more charitable and pleasant? And yet the corruption of man is such that he finds even this law harsh; and it is one of the main reasons which have caused a great part of Europe to rebel against the Church.

How unjust and unreasonable is the heart of man, which feels it disagreeable to be obliged to do in regard to one man what in some measure it were right to do to all men! For is it right that we should deceive men?

There are different degrees in this aversion to truth; but all may perhaps be said to have it in some degree, because it is inseparable from self-love. It is this false delicacy which makes those who are under the necessity of reproving others choose so many windings and middle courses to avoid offence. They must lessen our faults, appear to excuse them, intersperse praises and evidence of love and esteem. Despite all this, the medicine does not cease to be bitter to self-love. It takes as little as it can, always with disgust, and often with a

secret spite against those who administer it.

Hence it happens that if any have some interest in being loved by us, they are averse to render us a service which they know to be disagreeable. They treat us as we wish to be treated. We hate the truth, and they hide it from us. We desire flattery, and they flatter us. We like to be deceived, and they deceive us.

So each degree of good fortune which raises us in the world removes us further from truth, because we are most afraid of wounding those whose affection is most useful and whose dislike is most dangerous. A prince may be the byword of all Europe, and he alone will know nothing of it. I am not astonished; to tell the truth is useful to whom it is spoken, but disadvantageous to those who tell it, because it makes them disliked. Now those who live with princes love their own interests more than that of the prince whom they serve; and so they take care not to confer on him a benefit so as to injure themselves.

This evil is no doubt greater and more common among the higher classes; but the lower are not exempt from it, since there is always some advantage in making men love us. Human life is thus only a perpetual illusion; men deceive and flatter each other. No one speaks of us in our presence as he does of us in our absence. Human society is founded on mutual deceit; few friendships would endure if each knew what his friend said of him in his absence, although he then spoke in sincerity and without passion.

Man is then only disguise, falsehood, and hypocrisy, both in himself and in regard to others. He does not wish any one to tell him the truth; he avoids telling it to others, and all these dispositions, so removed from justice and reason, have a natural root in his heart.

161

Vanity

How wonderful it is that a thing so evident as the vanity of the world is so little known, that it is a strange and surprising thing to say that it is foolish to seek greatness!

162

He who will know fully the vanity of man has only to consider the causes and effects of love. The cause is *I know not what* (Corneille), and the effects are dreadful. This *I know not what*, so small an object that we cannot recognise it, agitates a whole country, princes, armies, the entire world.

Cleopatra's nose: had it been shorter, the whole aspect of the world would have been altered.

176

Cromwell was about to ravage all Christendom; the royal family was undone, and his own for ever established, save for a little grain of sand which formed in his ureter. Rome herself was trembling under him; but this small piece of gravel having formed there, he is dead, his family cast down, all is peaceful, and the king is restored.

294

. . . On what shall man found the order of the world which he would govern? Shall it be on the caprice of each individual? What confusion! Shall it be on justice? Man is ignorant of it.

Certainly had he known it, he would not have established this maxim, the most general of all that obtain among men, that each should follow the customs of his own country. The glory of true equity would have brought all nations under subjection, and legislators would not have taken as their model the fancies and caprice of Persians and Germans instead of this unchanging justice. We should have seen it set up in all States on earth and in all times; whereas we see neither justice nor injustice which does not change its nature with change in climate. Three degrees of latitude reverse all jurisprudence; a meridian decides the truth. Fundamental laws change after a few years of possession; right has its epochs; the entry of Saturn into the lion marks to us the origin of such and such a crime. A strange justice that is bounded by a river! Truth on this side of the Pyrenees, error on the other side.

Men admit that justice does not consist in these customs, but that it resides in natural laws, common to every country. They would certainly maintain it obstinately, if reckless chance which has distributed human laws had encountered even one which was universal; but the farce is that the caprice of men has so many vagaries that there is no such law.

Theft, incest, infanticide, patricide, have all had a place among virtuous actions. Can anything be more ridiculous than that a man should have the right to kill me because he lives on the other side of the water, and because his ruler has a quarrel with mine, though I have none with him? . . .

298

Justice, Might

It is right that what is just should be obeyed; it is necessary that what is strongest should be obeyed. Justice without might is helpless; might without justice is tyrannical. Justice without might is gainsaid, because there are always offenders; might without justice is condemned. We must then combine justice and might, and for this end make what is just strong, or what is strong just.

Justice is subject to dispute; might is easily recognized and is not disputed. So we cannot give might to justice, because might has gainsaid justice, and has declared that it is she herself who is just. And thus being unable to make what is just strong, we have made what is strong just.

The Greatness of Man

339

I can well conceive a man without hands, feet, head (for it is only experience which teaches us that the head is more necessary than feet). But I cannot conceive man without thought; he would be a stone or a brute.

340

The arithmetical machine produces effects which approach nearer to thought than all the actions of animals. But it does nothing which would enable us to attribute will to it, as to the animals.

346

Thought constitutes the greatness of man.

347

Man is but a reed, the most feeble thing in nature, but he is a thinking reed. The entire universe need not arm itself to crush him. A vapour, a drop of water suffices to kill him. But, if the universe were to crush him, man would still be more noble than that which killed him, because he knows that he dies and the advantage which the universe has over him; the universe knows nothing of this.

All our dignity consists then in thought. By it we must elevate ourselves, and not by space and time which we cannot fill. Let us endeavour then to think well; this is the principle of morality.

348

A Thinking Reed

It is not from space that I must seek my dignity, but from the government of my thought. I shall have no more if I possess worlds. By space the universe encompasses and swallows me up like an atom; by thought I comprehend the world.

349

Immateriality of the Soul

Philosophers who have mastered their passions. What matter could do that?

358

Man is neither angel nor brute, and the unfortunate thing is that he who would act the angel acts the brute.

416

. . . Greatness and Wretchedness

Wretchedness being deduced from greatness, and greatness from wretchedness, some have inferred man's wretchedness all the more because they have taken his greatness as a proof of it, and others have inferred his greatness with all the more force, because they have inferred it from his very wretchedness. All that the one party has been able to say in proof of his greatness has only served as an argument of his wretchedness to the others, because the greater our fall, the more wretched we are, and *vice versa*. The one party is brought back to the other in an endless circle, it being certain that in proportion as men possess light they discover both the greatness and the wretchedness of man. In a word, man knows that he is wretched. He is therefore wretched, because he is so; but he is really great because he knows it.

417

This twofold nature of man is so evident that some have thought that we had two souls. A single subject seemed to them incapable of such sudden variations from unmeasured presumption to a dreadful dejection of heart.

418

It is dangerous to make man see too clearly his equality with the brutes without showing him his greatness. It is also dangerous to make him see his greatness too clearly, apart from his vileness. It is still more dangerous to leave him in ignorance of both. But it is very advantageous to show him both. Man must not think that he is on a level either with the brutes or with the angels, nor must he be ignorant of both sides of his nature; but he must know both.

793

The infinite distance between body and mind is a symbol of the infinitely more infinite distance between mind and charity; for charity is supernatural.

All the glory of greatness has no lustre for people who are in search of understanding.

The greatness of clever men is invisible to kings, to the rich, to chiefs, and to all the worldly great.

The greatness of wisdom, which is nothing if not of God, is invisible to the carnal-minded and to the clever. These are three orders differing in kind.

Great geniuses have their power, their glory, their greatness, their victory, their lustre, and have no need of worldly greatness, with which they are not in keeping. They are seen, not by the eye, but by the mind; this is sufficient.

The saints have their power, their glory, their victory, their lustre, and need no worldly or intellectual greatness, with which they have no affinity; for these neither add anything to them, nor take away anything from them. They are seen of God and the angels, and not of the body, nor of the curious mind. God is enough for them.

Archimedes, apart from his rank, would have the same veneration. He fought no battles for the eyes to feast upon; but he has given his discoveries to all men. Oh! how brilliant he was to the mind!

Jesus Christ, without riches, and without any external exhibition of knowledge, is in His own order of holiness. He did not invent; He did not reign. But He was humble, patient, holy, holy to God, terrible to devils, without any sin. Oh! in what great pomp, and in what wonderful splendour, He is come to the eyes of the heart, which perceive wisdom!

It would have been useless for Archimedes to have acted the prince in his books on geometry, although he was a prince.

It would have been useless for our Lord Jesus Christ to come like a king, in order to shine forth in His kingdom of holiness. But He came there appropriately in the glory of His own order.

It is most absurd to take offence at the lowliness of Jesus Christ, as if His lowliness were in the same order as the greatness which He came to manifest. If we consider this greatness in His life, in His passion, in His obscurity, in His death, in the choice of His disciples, in their desertion, in His secret resurrection, and the rest, we shall see it to be so immense, that we shall have no reason for being offended at a lowliness which is not of that order.

But there are some who can only admire worldly greatness, as though there were no intellectual greatness; and others who only admire intellectual greatness, as though there were not infinitely higher things in wisdom.

All bodies, the firmament, the stars, the earth and its kingdoms, are not equal to the lowest mind; for mind knows all these and itself; and these bodies nothing.

All bodies together, and all minds together, and all their products, are not equal to the least feeling of charity. This is of an order infinitely more exalted.

From all bodies together, we cannot obtain one little thought; this is impossible, and of another order. From all bodies and minds, we cannot produce a feeling of true charity; this is impossible, and of another and supernatural order.

Of the Necessity of the Wager

205

When I consider the short duration of my life, swallowed up in the eternity before and after, the little space which I fill, and even can see, engulfed in the infinite immensity of spaces of which I am ignorant, and which know me not, I am frightened, and am astonished at being here rather than there; for there is no reason why here rather than there, why now rather than then. Who has put me here? By whose order and direction have this place and time been alloted to me? *Memoria hospitis unius diei prætereuntis.*[4]

206

The eternal silence of these infinite spaces frighten me.

---

[4] "The remembrance of a guest that tarrieth but a day."—Wisdom, v. 14.

434

The chief arguments of the sceptics—I pass over the lesser ones—are that we have no certainty of the truth of these principles apart from faith and revelation, except in so far as we naturally perceive them in ourselves. Now this natural intuition is not a convincing proof of their truth; since, having no certainty, apart from faith, whether man was created by a good God, or by a wicked demon, or by chance, it is doubtful whether these principles given to us are true, or false, or uncertain, according to our origin. Again, no person is certain, apart from faith, whether he is awake or sleeps, seeing that during sleep we believe as firmly as we do that we are awake; we believe that we see space, figure, and motion; we are aware of the passage of time, we measure it; and in fact we act as if we were awake. So that half of our life being passed in sleep, we have on our own admission no idea of truth, whatever we may imagine. As all our intuitions are then illusions, who knows whether the other half of our life, in which we think we are awake, is not another sleep a little different from the former, from which we awake when we suppose ourselves asleep?

[And who doubts that, if we dreamt in company, and the dreams chanced to agree, which is common enough, and if we were always alone when awake, we should believe that matters were reversed? In short, as we often dream that we dream, heaping dream upon dream, may it not be that this half of our life, wherein we think ourselves awake, is itself only a dream on which the others

are grafted, from which we wake at death, during which we have as few principles of truth and good as during natural sleep, these different thoughts which disturb us being perhaps only illusions like the flight of time and the vain fancies of our dreams?]

These are the chief arguments on one side and the other.

I omit minor ones, such as the sceptical talk against the impressions of custom, education, manners, country, and the like. Though these influence the majority of common folk, who dogmatise only on shallow foundations, they are upset by the least breath of the sceptics. We have only to see their books if we are not sufficiently convinced of this, and we shall very quickly become so, perhaps too much.

I notice the only strong point of the dogmatists, namely, that, speaking in good faith and sincerely, we cannot doubt natural principles. Against this the sceptics set up in one word the uncertainty of our origin, which includes that of our nature. The dogmatists have been trying to answer this objection ever since the world began.

So there is open war among men, in which each must take a part, and side either with dogmatism or scepticism. For he who thinks to remain neutral is above all a sceptic. This neutrality is the essence of the sect; he who is not against them is essentially for them. [In this appears their advantage.] They are not for themselves; they are neutral, indifferent, in suspense as to all things, even themselves being no exception.

What then shall man do in this state? Shall he doubt everything? Shall he doubt whether he is awake, whether he is being pinched, or whether he is being burned? Shall he doubt whether he doubts? Shall he doubt whether he exists? We cannot go so far as that; and I lay it down as a fact there never has been a real complete sceptic. Nature sustains our feeble reason, and prevents it raving to this extent.

Shall he then say, on the contrary, that he certainly possesses truth—he who, when pressed ever so little, can show no title to it, and is forced to let go his hold?

What a chimera then is man! What a novelty! What a monster, what a chaos, what a contradiction, what a prodigy! Judge of all things, imbecile worm of the earth; depositary of truth, a sink of uncertainty and error; the pride and refuse of the universe!

Who will unravel this tangle? Nature confutes the sceptics, and reason confutes the dogmatists. What then will you become, O men! who try to find out by your natural reason what is your true condition? You cannot avoid one of these sects, nor adhere to one of them.

Know then, proud man, what a paradox you are to yourself. Humble yourself, weak reason; be silent, foolish nature; learn that man infinitely transcends man, and learn from your Master your true condition, of which you are ignorant. Hear God.

For in fact, if man had never been corrupt, he would enjoy in his innocence both truth and happiness with assurance; and if man had always been corrupt, he would have no idea of truth or bliss. But, wretched as we are, and more so than if there were no greatness in our condition, we have an idea of happiness, and cannot reach it. We perceive an image of truth, and possess only a lie. Incapable of absolute ignorance and of certain knowledge, we have thus been manifestly in a degree of perfection from which we have unhappily fallen.

It is, however, an astonishing thing that the mystery furthest removed from our knowledge, namely, that of the transmission of sin, should be a fact without which we can have no knowledge of ourselves. For it is beyond doubt that there is nothing which more shocks our reason than to say that the sin of the first man has rendered guilty those, who, being so removed from this source, seem incapable of participation in it. This transmission does not only seem to us impossible, it seems also very unjust. For what is more contrary to the rules of our miserable justice than to damn eternally an infant incapable of will, for a sin wherein he seems to have so little a share, that it was committed six thousand years before he was in existence? Certainly nothing offends us more rudely than this doctrine; and yet, without this mystery, the most incomprehensible of all, we are incomprehensible to ourselves. The knot of our condition takes its twists and turns in this abyss, so that man is more inconceivable without this mystery than this mystery is inconceivable to man.

[Whence it seems that God, willing to render the difficulty of our existence unintelligible to ourselves, has concealed the knot so high, or, better speaking, so low, that we are quite incapable of reaching it; so that it is not by the proud exertions of our reason, but by the simple submission of reason, that we can truly know ourselves.

These foundations, solidly established on the inviolable authority of religion, make us know that there are two truths of faith equally certain: the one, that man, in the state of creation, or in that of grace, is raised above all nature, made like unto God and sharing in His divinity; the other, that in the state of corruption and sin, he is fallen from this state and made like unto the beasts. . . .]

229

This is what I see and what troubles me. I look on all sides, and I see only darkness everywhere. Nature presents to me nothing which is not matter of doubt and concern. If I saw nothing there which revealed a Divinity, I would come to a negative conclusion; if I saw everywhere the signs of a Creator, I would remain peacefully in faith. But, seeing too much to deny and too little to be sure, I am in a state to be pitied; wherefore I have a hundred times wished that if a God maintains nature, she should testify to Him unequivocally, and that, if the signs she gives are deceptive, she should suppress them altogether; that she should say everything or nothing, that I might see which cause I ought to follow. Whereas in my present state, ignorant of what I am or what I ought to do, I know neither my condition nor my duty. My heart inclines wholly to know, where is the true good, in order to follow it; nothing would be too dear to me for eternity.

I envy those whom I see living in the faith with such carelessness, and who make such a bad use of a gift of which it seems to me I would make such a different use.

230

It is incomprehensible that God should exist, and it is incomprehensible that He should not exist, that the soul should be joined to the body, and that we should have no soul; that the world should be created, and that it should not be created, &c.; that original sin should be, and that it should not be.

543

Preface

The metaphysical proofs of God are so remote from the reasoning of men, and so complicated, that they make little impression; and if they should be of service to some, it would be only during the moment that they see such demonstration; but an hour afterwards they fear they have been mistaken.

233

Infinite—Nothing

Our soul is cast into a body, where it finds number, time, dimension. Thereupon it reasons, and calls this nature, necessity, and can believe nothing else.

Unity joined to infinity adds nothing to it, no more than one foot to an infinite measure. The finite is annihilated in the presence of the infinite, and becomes a pure nothing. So our spirit before God, so our justice before divine justice. There is not so great a disproportion between our justice and that of God, as between unity and infinity. . . .

We know that there is an infinite, and are ignorant of its nature. As we know it to be false that numbers are finite, it is therefore true that there is an infinity in number. But we do not know what it is. It is false that it is even, it is false that it is odd; for the addition of a unit can make no change in its nature. Yet it is a number, and every number is odd or even (this is certainly true of every finite number). So we may well know that there is a God without knowing what He is. Is there not one substantial truth, seeing there are so many things which are not the truth itself?

We know then the existence and nature of the finite, because we also are finite and have extension. We know the existence of the infinite, and are ignorant of its nature, because it has extension like us, but not limits like us. But we know neither the existence nor the nature of God, because He has neither extension nor limits.

But by faith we know His existence; in glory we shall know His nature. Now, I have already shown that we may well know the existence of a thing, without knowing its nature.

Let us now speak according to natural lights.

If there is a God, He is infinitely incomprehensible, since, having neither parts nor limits, He has no affinity to us. We are then incapable of knowing either what He is or if He is. This being so, who will dare to undertake the decision of the question? Not we, who have no affinity to Him.

Who then will blame Christians for not being able to give a reason for their belief, since they profess a religion for which they cannot give a reason? They declare, in expounding it to the world, that it is a foolishness, *stultitiam*; and then you complain that they do not prove it! If they proved it, they would not keep their word; it is in lacking proofs, that they are not lacking in sense. "Yes, but although this excuses those who offer it as such, and takes away from them the blame of putting it forward without reason, it does not excuse those who receive it." Let us then examine this point, and say, "God is, or He is not." But to which side shall we incline? Reason can decide nothing here. There is an infinite chaos which separates us. A game is being played at the extremity of this infinite distance where heads or tails will turn up. What will you wager? According to reason, you can do neither the one thing nor the other; according to reason, you can defend neither of the propositions.

Do not then reprove for error those who have made a choice; for you know nothing about it. "No, but I blame them for having made, not this choice, but a choice; for again both he who chooses heads and he who chooses tails are equally at fault, they are both in the wrong. The true course is not to wager at all."

—Yes; but you must wager. It is not optional. You are embarked. Which will you choose then? Let us see. Since you must choose, let us see which interests you least. You have two things to lose, the true and the good; and two things to stake, your reason and your will, your knowledge and your happiness; and your nature has two things to shun, error and misery. Your reason is no more shocked in choosing one rather than the other, since you must of necessity choose. This is one point settled. But your happiness? Let us weigh the gain and the loss in wagering that God is. Let us estimate these two chances. If you gain, you gain all; if you lose, you lose nothing. Wager then without hesitation that He is.—"That is very fine. Yes, I must wager; but I may perhaps wager too much."—Let us see. Since there is an equal risk of gain and of loss, if you had only to gain two lives, instead of one, you might still wager. But if there were three lives to gain, you would have to play (since you are under the necessity of playing), and you would be imprudent, when you are forced to play, not to chance your life to gain three at a game where there is an equal risk of loss and gain. But there is an eternity of life and happiness. And this being so, if there were an infinity of chances, of which one only would be for you, you would still be right in wagering one to win two, and you would act stupidly, being obliged to play, by refusing to stake one life against three at a game in which out of an infinity of chances there is one for you, if there were an infinity of an infinitely happy life to gain. But there is here an infinity of an infinitely happy life to gain, a chance of gain against a finite number of chances of loss, and what you stake is finite. It is all divided; wherever the infinite is and there is not an infinity of chances of loss against that of gain, there is no time to hesitate, you must give all. And thus, when one is forced to play, he must renounce reason to preserve his life, rather than risk it for infinite gain, as likely to happen as the loss of nothingness.

For it is no use to say it is uncertain if we will gain, and it is certain that we risk, and that the infinite distance between the *certainty* of what is staked and the *uncertainty* of what will be gained, equals the finite good which is certainly staked against the uncertain infinite. It is not so, as every player stakes a certainty to gain an uncertainty, and yet he stakes a finite certainty to gain a finite uncertainty, without transgressing against reason. There is not an infinite distance between the certainty staked and the uncertainty of the gain; that is untrue. In truth, there is an infinity between the certainty of gain and the certainty of loss. But the uncertainty of the gain is proportioned to the certainty of the stake according to the proportion of the chances of gain and loss. Hence it comes that, if there are as many risks on one side as on the other, the course is to play even; and then the certainty of the stake is equal to the uncertainty of the gain, so far is it from fact that there is an infinite distance between them. And so our proposition is of infinite force, when there is the finite to stake in a game where there are equal risks of gain and of loss, and the infinite to gain. This is demonstrable; and if men are capable of any truths, this is one.

"I confess it, I admit it. But still is there no means of seeing the faces of the cards?"—Yes, Scripture and the rest, &c.—"Yes, but I have my hands tied and my mouth closed; I am forced to wager, and am not free. I am not released, and am so made that I cannot believe. What then would you have me do?"

True. But at least learn your inability

to believe, since reason brings you to this, and yet you cannot believe. Endeavour then to convince yourself, not by increase of proofs of God, but by the abatement of your passions. You would like to attain faith, and do not know the way; you would like to cure yourself of unbelief, and ask the remedy for it. Learn of those who have been bound like you, and who now stake all their possessions. These are people who know the way which you would follow, and who are cured of an ill of which you would be cured. Follow the way by which they began; by acting as if they believe, taking the holy water, having masses said, &c. Even this will naturally make you believe, and deaden your acuteness.—"But this is what I am afraid of."—And why? What have you to lose?

But to show you that this leads you there, it is this which will lessen the passions, which are your stumbling-blocks.

The End of This Discourse

Now what harm will befall you in taking this side? You will be faithful, honest, humble, grateful, generous, a sincere friend, truthful. Certainly you will not have those poisonous pleasures, glory and luxury; but will you not have others? I will tell you that you will thereby gain in this life, and that, at each step you take on this road, you will see so great certainty of gain, so much nothingness in what you risk, that you will at last recognize that you have wagered for something certain and infinite, for which you have given nothing.

"Ah! This discourse transports me, charms me," &c.

If this discourse pleases you and seems impressive, know that it is made by a man who has knelt, both before and after it, in prayer to that Being, infinite and without parts, before whom he lays all he has, for you also to lay before Him all you have for your own good and for His glory, that so strength may be given to lowliness.

236

According to the doctrine of chance, you ought to put yourself to the trouble of searching for the truth; for if you die without worshipping the True Cause, you are lost.—"But," say you, "if He had wished me to worship Him, He would have left me signs of His will."
—He has done so; but you neglect them. Seek them therefore; it is well worth it.

Of the Means of Belief

277

The heart has its reasons, which reason does not know. We feel it in a thousand things. I say that the heart naturally loves the Universal Being, and also itself naturally, according as it gives itself to them; and it hardens itself against one or the other at its will. You have rejected the one, and kept the other. Is it by reason that you love yourself?

278

Is it the heart which experiences God, and not the reason. This, then, is faith: God felt by the heart, not by the reason.

279

Faith is a gift of God; do not believe that we said it was a gift of reasoning. Other religions do not say this of their faith. They only gave reasoning in order to arrive at it, and yet it does not bring them to it.

280

The knowledge of God is very far from the love of Him.

282

We know truth, not only by the reason, but also by the heart, and it is in this last way that we know first principles; and reason, which has no part in it, tries in vain to impugn them. The sceptics, who have only this for their object, labour to no purpose. We know that we do not dream, and however impossible it is for us to prove it by reason, this inability demonstrates only the weakness of our reason, but not, as they affirm, the uncertainty of all our knowledge. For the knowledge of first principles, as space, time, motion, number, is as sure as any of those which we get from reasoning. And reason must trust these intuitions of the heart, and must base on them every argument. (We have intuitive knowledge of the tri-dimensional nature of space, and of the infinity of number, and reason then shows that there are no two square numbers one of which is double of the other. Principles are intuited, propositions are inferred, all with certainty, though in different ways.) And it is as useless and absurd for reason to demand from the heart proofs of her first principles, before admitting them, as it would be for the heart to demand from reason an intuition of all demonstrated propositions before accepting them.

This inability ought, then, to serve only to humble reason, which would judge all, but not to impugn our certainty, as if only reason were capable of instructing us. Would to God, on the contrary, that we had never need of it, and that we knew everything by instinct and intuition! But nature has refused us this boon. On the contrary, she has given us but very little knowledge of this kind; and all the rest can be acquired only by reasoning.

Therefore, those to whom God has imparted religion by intuition are very fortunate, and justly convinced. But to those who do not have it, we can give it only by reasoning, waiting for God to give them spiritual insight, without which faith is only human, and useless for salvation.

WILLIAM JAMES

(For biographical note see pages 153-154.)

The Will
to Believe

In the recently published Life by Leslie Stephen of his brother, Fitz-James, there is an account of a school to which the latter went when he was a boy. The teacher, a certain Mr. Guest, used to converse with his pupils in this wise: "Gurney, what is the difference between justification and sanctification?—Stephen, prove the omnipotence of God!" etc. In the midst of our Harvard freethinking and indifference we are prone to imagine that here at your good old orthodox College conversation continues to be somewhat upon this order; and to show you that we at Harvard have not lost all interest in these vital subjects, I have brought with me tonight something like a sermon on justification by faith to read to you—I mean an essay in justification *of* faith, a defense of our right to adopt a believing attitude in religious matters, in spite of the fact that our merely logical intellect may not have been coerced. "The Will to

An Address to the Philosophical Clubs of Yale and Brown Universities. Published in the *New World*, June 1896.

Believe," accordingly, is the title of my paper.

I have long defended to my own students the lawfulness of voluntarily adopted faith; but as soon as they have got well imbued with the logical spirit, they have as a rule refused to admit my contention to be lawful philosophically, even though in point of fact they were personally all the time chock-full of some faith or other themselves. I am all the while, however, so profoundly convinced that my own position is correct, that your invitation has seemed to me a good occasion to make my statements more clear. Perhaps your minds will be more open than those with which I have hitherto had to deal. I will be as little technical as I can, though I must begin by setting up some technical distinctions that will help us in the end.

I

Let us give the name of *hypothesis* to anything that may be proposed to our belief; and just as the electricians speak of live and dead wires, let us speak of any hypothesis as either *live* or *dead*. A live hypothesis is one which appeals as a real possibility to him to whom it is proposed. If I ask you to believe in the Mahdi, the notion makes no electric connection with your nature —it refuses to scintillate with any credibility at all. As an hypothesis it is completely dead. To an Arab, however (even if he be not one of the Mahdi's followers), the hypothesis is among the mind's possibilities: it is alive. This shows that deadness and liveness in an hypothesis are not intrinsic properties, but relations to the individual thinker. They are measured by his willingness to act. The maximum of liveness in an hypothesis means willingness to act irrevocably. Practically, that means belief; but there is some believing tendency wherever there is willingness to act at all.

Next, let us call the decision between two hypotheses an *option*. Options may be of several kinds. They may be —first, *living* or *dead;* secondly, *forced* or *avoidable;* thirdly, *momentous* or *trivial;* and for our purposes we may call an option a genuine option when it is of the forced, living, and momentous kind.

1. A living option is one in which both hypotheses are live ones. If I say to you: "Be a theosophist or be a Mohammedan," it is probably a dead option, because for you neither hypothesis is likely to be alive. But if I say: "Be an agnostic or be a Christian," it is otherwise: trained as you are, each hypothesis makes some appeal, however small, to your belief.

2. Next, if I say to you: "Choose between going out with your umbrella or without it," I do not offer you a genuine option, for it is not forced. You can easily avoid it by not going out at all. Similarly, if I say, "Either love me or hate me," "Either call my theory true or call it false," your option is avoidable. You may remain indifferent to me, neither loving nor hating, and you may decline to offer any judgment as to my theory. But if I say, "Either accept this truth or go without it," I put on you a forced option, for there is no standing place outside of the alternative. Every dilemma based on a complete logical disjunction, with no possibility of not choosing, is an option of this forced kind.

3. Finally, if I were Dr. Nansen and proposed to you to join my North Pole expedition, your option would be momentous; for this would probably be your only similar opportunity, and your choice now would either exclude you from the North Pole sort of immortality altogether or put at least the chance of it into your hands. He who refuses to embrace a unique opportunity loses the prize as surely as if he tried and failed. *Per contra,* the option is trivial when the opportunity is not unique, when the stake is insignificant, or when the decision is reversible if it later prove unwise. Such trivial options abound in the scientific life. A chemist finds an hypothesis live enough to spend a year in its verification: he believes in it to that extent. But if his experiments prove inconclusive either way, he is quit for his loss of time, no vital harm being done.

It will facilitate our discussion if we keep all these distinctions well in mind.

II

The next matter to consider is the actual psychology of human opinion. When we look at certain facts, it seems as if our passional and volitional nature lay at the root of all our convictions. When we look at others, it seems as if they could do nothing when the intellect had once said its say. Let us take the latter facts up first.

Does it not seem preposterous on the very face of it to talk of our opinions being modifiable at will? Can our will either help or hinder our intellect in its perceptions of truth? Can we, by just willing it, believe that Abraham Lincoln's existence is a myth, and that the portraits of him in *McClure's Magazine* are all of some one else? Can we, by an effort of our will, or by any strength of wish that it were true, believe ourselves well and about when we are roaring with rheumatism in bed, or feel certain that the sum of the two one-dollar bills in our pocket must be a hundred dollars? We can *say* any of these things, but we are absolutely impotent to believe them; and of just such things is the whole fabric of the truths that we do believe in made up —matters of fact, immediate or remote, as Hume said, and relations between ideas, which are either there or not there for us if we see them so, and which if not there cannot be put there by any action of our own.

In Pascal's *Thoughts* there is a celebrated passage known in literature as Pascal's wager. In it he tries to force us into Christianity by reasoning as if our concern with truth resembled our concern with the stakes in a game of chance. Translated freely his words are these: You must either believe or not believe that God is—which will you do? Your human reason cannot say. A game is going on between you and the nature of things which at the day of judgment will bring out either heads or tails. Weigh what your gains and your losses would be if you should stake all you have on heads, or God's existence: if you win in such case, you gain eternal beatitude; if you lose, you lose nothing at all. If there were an infinity of chances, and only one for God in this wager, still you ought to stake your all on God; for though you surely risk a finite loss by this procedure, any finite loss is reasonable, even a certain one is reasonable, if there is but the possibility of infinite gain. Go, then, and take holy water, and have masses said; belief will come and stupefy your scruples—*Cela vous fera croire et vous abêtira* [This will make you believe and stupefy you]. Why should you not? At bottom, what have you to lose?

You probably feel that when religious faith expresses itself thus, in the language of the gaming-table, it is put to its last trumps. Surely Pascal's own personal belief in masses and holy water had far other springs; and this celebrated page of his is but an argument for others, a last desperate snatch at a weapon against the hardness of the unbelieving heart. We feel that a faith in masses and holy water adopted wilfully after such a mechanical calculation would lack the inner soul of faith's reality; and if we were ourselves in the place of the Deity, we should probably take particular pleasure in cutting off believers of this pattern from their infinite reward. It is evident that unless there be some pre-existing tendency to believe in masses and holy water, the option offered to the will by Pascal is not a living option. Certainly no Turk ever took to masses and holy water on its account; and even to us Protestants these means of salvation seem such foregone impossibilities that Pascal's logic, invoked for them specifically, leaves us unmoved. As well might the Mahdi write to us, saying, "I am the Expected One whom God has created in his effulgence. You shall be infinitely happy if you confess me; otherwise you shall be cut off from the light of the sun. Weigh, then, your infinite gain if I am genuine against your finite sacrifice if I am not!" His logic would be that of Pascal; but he would vainly use it on us, for the hypothesis he offers us is dead. No tendency to act on it exists in us to any degree.

The talk of believing by our volition seems, then, from one point of view, simply silly. From another point of view it is worse than silly, it is vile. When one turns to the magnificent edifice of the physical sciences, and sees how it was reared; what thousands of disinterested moral lives of men lie buried in its mere foundations; what patience and postponement, what choking down of preference, what submission to the icy laws of outer fact are wrought into its very stones and mortar; how absolutely impersonal it stands in its vast augustness—then how besotted and contemptible seems every little sentimentalist who comes blowing his voluntary smoke-wreaths, and pretending to decide things from out of his private dream! Can we wonder if those bred in the rugged and manly school of science should feel like spewing such subjectivism out of their mouths? The whole system of loyalties which grow up in the schools of science go dead against its toleration; so that it is only natural that those who have caught the scientific fever should pass over to the opposite extreme, and write sometimes as if the incorruptibly truthful intellect ought positively to prefer bitterness and unacceptableness to the heart in its cup.

> It fortifies my soul to know
> That though I perish, Truth is so—

sings Clough, while Huxley exclaims: "My only consolation lies in the reflection that, however bad our posterity may become, so far as they hold by the plain rule of not pretending to believe what they have no reason to believe, because it may be to their advantage so to pretend [the word 'pretend' is surely here redundant], they will not have reached the lowest depth of immorality." And that delicious *enfant terrible* Clifford writes: "Belief is desecrated when given to unproved and unquestioned statements for the solace and private pleasure of the believer.... Whoso would deserve well of his fellows in this matter will guard the purity of his belief with a very fanaticism of jealous care, lest at any time it should rest on an unworthy object, and catch a stain which can never be wiped away. . . . If [a] belief has been accepted on insufficient evidence [even though the belief be true, as Clifford on the same page explains] the pleasure is a stolen one. . . . It is sinful because it is stolen in defiance of our duty to mankind. That duty is to guard ourselves from such beliefs as from a pestilence which may shortly master our own body and then spread to the rest of the town. . . . It is wrong always, everywhere, and for every one, to believe anything upon insufficient evidence."

III

All this strikes one as healthy, even when expressed, as by Clifford, with somewhat too much of robustious pathos in the voice. Free will and simple wishing do seem, in the matter of our credences, to be only fifth wheels to the coach. Yet if any one should thereupon assume that intellectual insight is what remains after wish and will and sentimental preference have taken wing, or that pure reason is what then settles our opinions, he would fly quite as directly in the teeth of the facts.

It is only our already dead hypotheses that our willing nature is unable to bring to life again. But what has made them dead for us is for the most part a previous action of our willing nature of an antagonistic kind. When I say "willing nature," I do not mean only such deliberate volitions as may have set up habits of belief that we cannot now escape from—I mean all such factors of belief as fear and hope, prejudice and passion, imitation and partisanship, the circumpressure of our caste and set. As a matter of fact we find ourselves believing, we hardly know how or why. Mr. Balfour gives the name of "authority" to all those influences, born of the intellectual climate, that make hypotheses possible or impossible for us, alive or dead. Here in this room, we all of us believe in molecules and the conservation of energy, in democracy and necessary progress, in Protestant Christianity and the duty of fighting for "the doctrine of the immortal Monroe," all for no reasons worthy of the name. We see into these matters with no more inner clearness, and probably with much less, than any disbeliever in them might possess. His unconventionality would probably have some grounds to show for its conclusions; but for us, not insight, but the *prestige* of the opinions, is what makes the spark shoot from them and light up our sleeping magazines of faith. Our reason is quite satisfied, in nine hundred and ninety-nine cases out of every thousand of us, if it can find a few arguments that will do to recite in case our credulity is criticized by some one else. Our faith is faith in some one else's faith, and in the greatest matters this is most the case. Our belief in truth itself, for instance, that there is a truth, and that our minds and it are made for each other—what is it but a passionate affirmation of desire, in which our social system backs us up? We want to have a truth; we want to believe that our experiments and studies and discussions must put us in a continually better and better position towards it; and on this line we agree to fight out our thinking lives. But if a Pyrrhonistic sceptic asks us *how we know* all this, can our logic find a reply? No! certainly it cannot. It is just one volition against another—we willing to go in for life upon a trust or assumption which he, for his part, does not care to make.

As a rule we disbelieve all facts and theories for which we have no use. Clifford's cosmic emotions find no use for Christian feelings. Huxley belabors the bishops because there is no use for sacerdotalism in his scheme of life. Newman, on the contrary, goes over to Romanism, and finds all sorts of reasons good for staying there, because a priestly system is for him an organic need and delight. Why do so few "scientists" even look at the evidence for telepathy, so called? Because they think, as a leading biologist, now dead, once said to me, that even if such a thing were true, scientists ought to band together to keep it suppressed and concealed. It would undo the uniformity of Nature and all sorts of other things without which scientists cannot carry on their pursuits. But if this very man had been shown something which as a scientist he might *do* with telepathy, he might not only have examined the evidence, but even have found it good enough. This very law which the logicians would impose upon us—if I may give the name of logicians to those who would rule out our willing nature here—is based on nothing but their own natural wish to exclude all elements for which they, in their professional quality of logicians, can find no use.

Evidently, then, our non-intellectual nature does influence our convictions. There are passional tendencies and volitions which run before and others which come after belief, and it is only the latter that are too late for the fair; and they are not too late when the pre-vious passional work has been already in their own direction. Pascal's argument, instead of being powerless, then seems a regular clincher, and is the last stroke needed to make our faith in masses and holy water complete. The state of things is evidently far from simple; and pure insight and logic, whatever they might do ideally, are not the only things that really do produce our creeds.

IV

Our next duty, having recognized this mixed-up state of affairs, is to ask whether it be simply reprehensible and pathological, or whether, on the contrary, we must treat it as a moral element in making up our minds. The thesis I defend is, briefly stated, this: *Our passional nature not only lawfully may, but must, decide an option between propositions, whenever it is a genuine option that cannot by its nature be decided on intellectual grounds; for to say, under such circumstances, "Do not decide, but leave the question open," is itself a passional decision— just like deciding yes or no—and is attended with the same risk of losing the truth.* The thesis thus abstractly expressed will, I trust, soon become quite clear. . . .

VII

One more point, small but important, and our preliminaries are done. There are two ways of looking at our duty in the matter of opinion—ways entirely different, and yet ways about whose difference the theory of knowledge seems hitherto to have shown very little concern. *We must know the truth;* and *we must avoid error*—these are our first and great commandments as would-be knowers; but they are not two ways of stating an identical commandment, they are two separable laws. Although it may indeed happen that when we believe the truth *A,* we escape as an incidental consequence from believing the falsehood *B,* it hardly ever happens that by merely disbelieving *B* we necessarily believe *A.* We may in escaping *B* fall into believing other falsehoods, *C* or *D,* just as bad as *B;* or we may escape *B* by not believing anything at all, not even *A.*

Believe truth! Shun error!—these, we see, are two materially different laws; and by choosing between them we may end by coloring differently our whole intellectual life. We may regard the chase for truth as paramount, and the avoidance of error as secondary; or we may, on the other hand, treat the avoidance of error as more imperative, and let truth take its chance. Clifford, in the instructive passage which I have quoted, exhorts us to the latter course. Believe nothing, he tells us, keep your mind in suspense for ever, rather than by closing it on insufficient evidence incur the awful risk of believing lies. You, on the other hand, may think that the risk of being in error is a very small matter when compared with the blessings of real knowledge, and be ready to be duped many times in your investigation rather than postpone indefinitely the chance of guessing true. I myself find it impossible to go with Clifford. We must remember that these feelings of our duty about either truth or error

are in any case only expressions of our passional life. Biologically considered, our minds are as ready to grind out falsehood as veracity, and he who says, "Better go without belief forever than believe a lie!" merely shows his own preponderant private horror of becoming a dupe. He may be critical of many of his desires and fears, but this fear he slavishly obeys. He cannot imagine any one questioning its binding force. For my own part, I have also a horror of being duped; but I can believe that worse things than being duped may happen to a man in this world: so Clifford's exhortation has to my ears a thoroughly fantastic sound. It is like a general informing his soldiers that it is better to keep out of battle forever than to risk a single wound. Not so are victories either over enemies or over nature gained. Our errors are surely not such awfully solemn things. In a world where we are so certain to incur them in spite of all our caution, a certain lightness of heart seems healthier than this excessive nervousness on their behalf. At any rate, it seems the fittest thing for the empiricist philosopher.

VIII

And now, after all this introduction, let us go straight at our question. I have said, and now repeat it, that not only as a matter of fact do we find our passional nature influencing us in our opinions, but that there are some options between opinions in which this influence must be regarded both as an inevitable and as a lawful determinant of our choice.

I fear here that some of you my hearers will begin to scent danger, and lend an inhospitable ear. Two first steps of passion you have indeed had to admit as necessary—we must think so as to avoid dupery, and we must think so as to gain truth; but the surest path to those ideal consummations, you will probably consider, is from now onwards to take no further passional step.

Well, of course, I agree as far as the facts will allow. Wherever the option between losing truth and gaining it is not momentous, we can throw the chance of *gaining truth* away, and at any rate save ourselves from any chance of *believing falsehood,* by not making up our minds at all till objective evidence has come. In scientific questions, this is almost always the case; and even in human affairs in general, the need of acting is seldom so urgent that a false belief to act on is better than no belief at all. Law courts, indeed, have to decide on the best evidence attainable for the moment, because a judge's duty is to make law as well as to ascertain it, and (as a learned judge once said to me) few cases are worth spending much time over: the great thing is to have them decided on *any* acceptable principle, and got out of the way. But in our dealings with objective nature we obviously are recorders, not makers, of the truth; and decisions for the mere sake of deciding promptly and getting on to the next business would be wholly out of place. Throughout the breadth of physical nature facts are what they are quite independently of us, and seldom is there any such hurry about them that the risks of being

duped by believing a premature theory need be faced. The questions here are always trivial options, the hypotheses are hardly living (at any rate not living for us spectators), the choice between believing truth or falsehood is seldom forced. The attitude of sceptical balance is therefore the absolutely wise one if we would escape mistakes. What difference, indeed, does it make to most of us whether we have or have not a theory of the Röentgen rays, whether we believe or not in mind-stuff, or have a conviction about the causality of conscious states? It makes no difference. Such options are not forced on us. On every account it is better not to make them, but still keep weighing reasons *pro et contra* with an indifferent hand.

I speak, of course, here of the purely judging mind. For purposes of discovery such indifference is to be less highly recommended, and science would be far less advanced than she is if the passionate desires of individuals to get their own faiths confirmed had been kept out of the game. See for example the sagacity which Spencer and Weismann now display. On the other hand, if you want an absolute duffer in an investigation, you must, after all, take the man who has no interest whatever in its results: he is the warranted incapable, the positive fool. The most useful investigator, because the most sensitive observer, is always he whose eager interest in one side of the question is balanced by an equally keen nervousness lest he become deceived. Science has organized this nervousness into a regular *technique,* her so-called method of verification; and she has fallen so deeply in love with the method that one may even say she has ceased to care for truth by itself at all. It is only truth as technically verified that interests her. The truth of truths might come in merely affirmative form, and she would decline to touch it. Such truth as that, she might repeat with Clifford, would be stolen in defiance of her duty to mankind. Human passions, however, are stronger than technical rules. *"Le cœur a ses raisons,"* as Pascal says, *"que la raison ne connaît pas"* [The heart has its reasons which the reason does not know]; and however indifferent to all but the bare rules of the game the umpire, the abstract intellect, may be, the concrete players who furnish him the materials to judge of are usually, each one of them, in love with some pet "live hypothesis" of his own. Let us agree, however, that wherever there is no forced option, the dispassionately judicial intellect with no pet hypothesis, saving us, as it does, from dupery at any rate, ought to be our ideal.

The question next arises: Are there not somewhere forced options in our speculative questions, and can we (as men who may be interested at least as much in positively gaining truth as in merely escaping dupery) always wait with impunity till the coercive evidence shall have arrived? It seems *a priori* improbable that the truth should be so nicely adjusted to our needs and powers as that. In the great boarding-house of nature, the cakes and the butter and the syrup seldom come out so even and leave the plates so clean. Indeed, we should view them with scientific suspicion if they did.

IX

Moral questions immediately present themselves as questions whose solution cannot wait for sensible proof. A moral question is a question not of what sensibly exists, but of what is good, or would be good if it did exist. Science can tell us what exists; but to compare the *worths,* both of what exists and of what does not exist, we must consult not science, but what Pascal calls our heart. Science herself consults her heart when she lays it down that the infinite ascertainment of fact and correction of false belief are the supreme goods for man. Challenge the statement, and science can only repeat it oracularly, or else prove it by showing that such ascertainment and correction bring man all sorts of other goods which man's heart in turn declares. The question of having moral beliefs at all or not having them is decided by our will. Are our moral preferences true or false, or are they only odd biological phenomena, making things good or bad for *us,* but in themselves indifferent? How can your pure intellect decide? If your heart does not *want* a world of moral reality, your head will assuredly never make you believe in one. Mephistophelian scepticism, indeed, will satisfy the head's play-instincts much better than any rigorous idealism can. Some men (even at the student age) are so naturally cool-hearted that the moralistic hypothesis never has for them any pungent life, and in their supercilious presence the hot young moralist always feels strangely ill at ease. The appearance of knowingness is on their side, of *naïveté* and gullibility on his.

Yet, in the inarticulate heart of him, he clings to it that he is not a dupe, and that there is a realm in which (as Emerson says) all their wit and intellectual superiority is no better than the cunning of a fox. Moral scepticism can no more be refuted or proved by logic than intellectual scepticism can. When we stick to it that there *is* truth (be it of either kind), we do so with our whole nature, and resolve to stand or fall by the results. The sceptic with his whole nature adopts the doubting attitude; but which of us is the wiser, Omniscience only knows.

Turn now from these wide questions of good to a certain class of questions of fact, questions concerning personal relations, states of mind between one man and another. *Do you like me or not?*—for example. Whether you do or not depends, in countless instances, on whether I meet you half-way, am willing to assume that you must like me, and show you trust and expectation. The previous faith on my part in your liking's existence is in such cases what makes your liking come. But if I stand aloof, and refuse to budge an inch until I have objective evidence, until you shall have done something apt, as the absolutists say, *ad extorquendum assensum meum* [to compel my assent], ten to one your liking never comes. How many women's hearts are vanquished by the mere sanguine insistence of some man that they *must* love him! he will not consent to the hypothesis that they cannot. The desire for a certain kind of truth here brings about that special truth's existence; and so it is in innumerable cases of other sorts. Who gains promotions, boons, appoint-ments, but the man in whose life they are seen to play the part of live hypotheses, who discounts them, sacrifices other things for their sake before they have come, and takes risks for them in advance? His faith acts on the powers above him as a claim, and creates its own verification.

A social organism of any sort whatever, large or small, is what it is because each member proceeds to his own duty with a trust that the other members will simultaneously do theirs. Wherever a desired result is achieved by the cooperation of many independent persons, its existence as a fact is a pure consequence of the precursive faith in one another of those immediately concerned. A government, an army, a commercial system, a ship, a college, an athletic team, all exist on this condition, without which not only is nothing achieved, but nothing is even attempted. A whole train of passengers (individually brave enough) will be looted by a few highwaymen, simply because the latter can count on one another, while each passenger fears that if he makes a movement of resistance, he will be shot before any one else backs him up. If we believed that the whole car-full would rise at once with us, we should each severally rise, and train-robbing would never even be attempted. There are, then, cases where a fact cannot come at all unless a preliminary faith exists in its coming. *And where faith in a fact can help create the fact,* that would be an insane logic which should say that faith running ahead of scientific evidence is the "lowest kind of immorality" into which a thinking being can fall. Yet such is the logic by which our scientific abso-lutists pretend to regulate our lives!

X

In truths dependent on our personal action, then, faith based on desire is certainly a lawful and possibly an in-dispensable thing.

But now, it will be said, these are all childish human cases, and have nothing to do with great cosmical mat-ters, like the question of religious faith. Let us then pass on to that. Religions differ so much in their accidents that in discussing the religious question we must make it very generic and broad. What then do we now mean by the religious hypothesis? Science says things are; morality says some things are better than other things; and reli-gion says essentially two things.

First, she says that the best things are the more eternal things, the over-lapping things, the things in the uni-verse that throw the last stone, so to speak, and say the final word. "Per-fection is eternal"—this phrase of Charles Secrétan seems a good way of putting this first affirmation of religion, an affirmation which obviously cannot yet be verified scientifically at all.

The second affirmation of religion is that we are better off even now if we believe her first affirmation to be true.

Now, let us consider what the logi-cal elements of this situation are *in case the religious hypothesis in both its branches be really true.* (Of course, we must admit that possibility at the out-set. If we are to discuss the question at all, it must involve a living option. If for any of you religion be a hypothe-sis that cannot, by any living possibil-ity, be true, then you need go no far-ther. I speak to the "saving remnant" alone.) So proceeding, we see, first, that religion offers itself as a *momen-tous* option. We are supposed to gain, even now, by our belief, and to lose by our non-belief, a certain vital good. Secondly, religion is a *forced* option, so far as that good goes. We cannot escape the issue by remaining sceptical and waiting for more light, because, al-though we do avoid error in that way *if religion be untrue,* we lose the good, *if it be true,* just as certainly as if we positively chose to disbelieve. It is as if a man should hesitate indefinitely to ask a certain woman to marry him be-cause he was not perfectly sure that she would prove an angel after he brought her home. Would he not cut himself off from that particular angel-possibility as decisively as if he went and married some one else? Scepticism, then, is not avoidance of option; it is option of a certain particular kind of risk. *Better risk loss of truth than chance of error*—that is your faith-vetoer's exact position. He is actively playing his stake as much as the be-liever is; he is backing the field against the religious hypothesis, just as the be-liever is backing the religious hypothe-sis against the field. To preach scepti-cism to us as a duty until "sufficient evidence" for religion be found, is tan-tamount therefore to telling us, when in presence of the religious hypothesis, that to yield to our fear of its being error is wiser and better than to yield to our hope that it may be true. It is not intellect against all passions, then; it is only intellect with one passion laying down its law. And by what, forsooth, is the supreme wisdom of this passion warranted? Dupery for dupery, what proof is there that dupery through hope is so much worse than dupery through fear? I, for one, can see no proof; and I simply refuse obedience to the scientist's command to imitate his kind of option, in a case where my own stake is important enough to give me the right to choose my own form of risk. If religion be true and the evidence for it be still insufficient, I do not wish, by putting your extinguisher upon my nature (which feels to me as if it had after all some business in this matter), to forfeit my sole chance in life of getting upon the winning side—that chance depending, of course, on my willingness to run the risk of acting as if my passional need of taking the world religiously might be prophetic and right.

All this is on the supposition that it really may be prophetic and right, and that, even to us who are discussing the matter, religion is a live hypothesis which may be true. Now, to most of us religion comes in a still further way that makes a veto on our active faith even more illogical. The more perfect and more eternal aspect of the universe is represented in our religions as having personal form. The universe is no longer a mere *It* to us, but a *Thou,* if we are religious; and any relation that may be possible from person to person might be possible here. For instance, although in one sense we are passive portions of the universe, in another we show a curious autonomy, as if we were small active centers on our own account. We feel, too, as if the appeal of religion to us were made to our own active good-will, as if evidence might be forever withheld from us unless we met the hypothesis half-way. To take a trivial illustration: just as a man who in a company of gentlemen made no advances, asked a warrant for every concession, and believed no one's word without proof, would cut himself off by such churlishness from all the social rewards that a more trusting spirit would earn—so here, one who should shut himself up in snarling logicality and try to make the gods extort his recognition willy-nilly, or not get it at all, might cut himself off forever from his only opportunity of making the gods' acquaintance. This feeling, forced on us we know not whence, that by obstinately believing that there are gods (although not to do so would be so easy both for our logic and our life) we are doing the universe the deepest service we can, seems part of the living essence of the religious hypothesis. If the hypothesis *were* true in all its parts, including this one, then pure intellectualism, with its veto on our making willing advances, would be an absurdity; and some participation of our sympathetic nature would be logically required. I, therefore, for one, cannot see my way to accepting the agnostic rules for truth-seeking, or wilfully agree to keep my willing nature out of the game. I cannot do so for this plain reason, that *a rule of thinking which would absolutely prevent me from acknowledging certain kinds of truth if those kinds of truth were really there, would be an irrational rule.* That for me is the long and short of the formal logic of the situation, no matter what the kinds of truth might materially be.

I confess I do not see how this logic can be escaped. But sad experience makes me fear that some of you may still shrink from radically saying with me, *in abstracto,* that we have the right to believe at our own risk any hypothesis that is live enough to tempt our will. I suspect, however, that if this is so, it is because you have got away from the abstract logical point of view altogether, and are thinking (perhaps without realizing it) of some particular religious hypothesis which for you is dead. The freedom to "believe what we will" you apply to the case of some patent superstition; and the faith you think of is the faith defined by the schoolboy when he said, "Faith is when you believe something that you know ain't true." I can only repeat that this is misapprehension. *In concreto,* the freedom to believe can only cover living options which the intellect of the individual cannot by itself resolve; and living options never seem absurdities to him who has them to consider. When I look at the religious question as it really puts itself to concrete men, and when I think of all the possibilities which both practically and theoretically it involves, then this command that we shall put a stopper on our heart, instincts, and courage, and *wait*—acting of course meanwhile more or less as if religion were *not* true[1]—till

doomsday, or till such time as our intellect and senses working together may have raked in evidence enough— this command, I say, seems to me the queerest idol ever manufactured in the philosophic cave. Were we scholastic absolutists, there might be more excuse. If we had an infallible intellect with its objective certitudes, we might feel ourselves disloyal to such a perfect organ of knowledge in not trusting to it exclusively, in not waiting for its releasing word. But if we are empiricists, if we believe that no bell in us tolls to let us know for certain when truth is in our grasp, then it seems a piece of idle fantasticality to preach so solemnly our duty of waiting for the bell. Indeed we *may* wait if we will—I hope you do not think that I am denying that—but if we do so, we do so at our peril as much as if we believed. In either case we *act,* taking our life in our hands. No one of us ought to issue vetoes to the other, nor should we bandy words of abuse. We ought, on the contrary, delicately and profoundly to respect one another's mental freedom: then only shall we bring about the intellectual republic; then only shall we have that spirit of inner tolerance without which all our outer tolerance is soulless, and which is empiricism's glory;

---

[1] Since belief is measured by action, he who forbids us to believe religion to be true, necessarily also forbids us to act as we should if we did believe it to be true. The whole defense of religious faith hinges upon action. If the action required or inspired by the religious hypothesis is in no way different from that dictated by the naturalistic hypothesis, then religious faith is a pure superfluity, better pruned away, and controversy about its legitimacy is a piece of idle trifling, unworthy of serious minds. I myself believe, of course, that the religious hypothesis gives to the world an expression which specifically determines our reactions, and makes them in a large part unlike what they might be on a purely naturalistic scheme of belief.

then only shall we live and let live, in speculative as well as in practical things.

I began by a reference to Fitz-James Stephen; let me end by a quotation from him. "What do you think of yourself? What do you think of the world? . . . These are questions with which all must deal as it seems good to them. They are riddles of the Sphinx, and in some way or other we must deal with them. . . . In all important transactions of life we have to take a leap in the dark. . . . If we decide to leave the riddles unanswered, that is a choice; if we waver in our answer, that, too, is a choice: but whatever choice we make, we make it at our peril. If a man chooses to turn his back altogether on God and the future, no one can prevent him; no one can show beyond reasonable doubt that he is mis-

taken. If a man thinks otherwise and acts as he thinks, I do not see that any one can prove that *he* is mistaken. Each must act as he thinks best; and if he is wrong, so much the worse for him. We stand on a mountain pass in the midst of whirling snow and blinding mist, through which we get glimpses now and then of paths which may be deceptive. If we stand still we shall be frozen to death. If we take the wrong road we shall be dashed to pieces. We do not certainly know whether there is any right one. What must we do? 'Be strong and of a good courage.' Act for the best, hope for the best, and take what comes. . . . If death ends all, we cannot meet death better."[2]

[2] *Liberty, Equality, Fraternity*, p. 353, 2d edition. London, 1874.

Mysticism

One may say truly, I think, that personal religious experience has its roots and centre in mystical states of consciousness; so for us, who in these lectures are treating personal experience as the exclusive subject of our study, such states of consciousness ought to form the vital chapter from which the other chapters get their light. Whether my treatment of mystical states will

From *The Varieties of Religious Experience*. Copyright, 1902, by William James. New York: Longmans, Green and Company. The numerous footnotes in the original have been omitted.

shed more light or darkness, I do not know, for my own constitution shuts me out from their enjoyment almost entirely, and I can speak of them only at second hand. But though forced to look upon the subject so externally, I will be as objective and receptive as I can; and I think I shall at least succeed in convincing you of the reality of the states in question, and of the paramount importance of their function.

First of all, then, I ask, What does the expression "mystical states of consciousness" mean? How do we part off mystical states from other states?

The words "mysticism" and "mystical" are often used as terms of mere reproach, to throw at any opinion which we regard as vague and vast and sentimental, and without a base in either facts or logic. For some writers a "mystic" is any person who believes in thought-transference, or spirit-return. Employed in this way the word has little value: there are too many less ambiguous synonyms. So, to keep it useful by restricting it, I will do what I did in the case of the word "religion," and simply propose to you four marks which, when an experience has them, may justify us in calling it mystical for the purpose of the present lectures. In this way we shall save verbal disputation, and the recriminations that generally go therewith.

1. *Ineffability*

The handiest of the marks by which I classify a state of mind as mystical is negative. The subject of it immediately says that it defies expression, that no adequate report of its contents can be given in words. It follows from this that its quality must be directly experienced; it cannot be imparted or transferred to others. In this peculiarity mystical states are more like states of feeling than like states of intellect. No one can make clear to another who has never had a certain feeling, in what the quality or worth of it consists. One must have musical ears to know the value of a symphony; one must have been in love one's self to understand a lover's state of mind. Lacking the heart or ear, we cannot interpret the musician or the lover justly, and are even likely

to consider him weak-minded or absurd. The mystic finds that most of us accord to his experiences an equally incompetent treatment.

2. *Noetic quality*

Although so similar to states of feeling, mystical states seem to those who experience them to be also states of knowledge. They are states of insight into depths of truth unplumbed by the discursive intellect. They are illuminations, revelations, full of significance and importance, all inarticulate though they remain; and as a rule they carry with them a curious sense of authority for aftertime.

These two characters will entitle any state to be called mystical, in the sense in which I use the word. Two other qualities are less sharply marked, but are usually found. These are:—

3. *Transiency*

Mystical states cannot be sustained for long. Except in rare instances, half an hour, or at most an hour or two, seems to be the limit beyond which they fade into the light of common day. Often, when faded, their quality can but imperfectly be reproduced in memory; but when they recur it is recognized; and from one recurrence to another it is susceptible of continuous development in what is felt as inner richness and importance.

4. *Passivity*

Although the oncoming of mystical states may be facilitated by preliminary voluntary operations, as by fixing the attention, or going through certain bodily performances, or in other ways which manuals of mysticism prescribe; yet when the characteristic sort of consciousness once has set in, the mystic feels as if his own will were in abeyance, and indeed sometimes as if he were grasped and held by a superior power. This latter peculiarity connects mystical states with certain definite phenomena of secondary or alternative personality, such as prophetic speech, automatic writing, or the mediumistic trance. When these latter conditions are well pronounced, however, there may be no recollection whatever of the phenomenon, and it may have no significance for the subject's usual inner life, to which, as it were, it makes a mere interruption. Mystical states, strictly so-called, are never merely interruptive. Some memory of their content always remains, and a profound sense of their importance. They modify the inner life of the subject between the times of their recurrence. Sharp divisions in this region are, however, difficult to make, and we find all sorts of gradations and mixtures.

These four characteristics are sufficient to mark out a group of states of consciousness peculiar enough to deserve a special name and to call for careful study. Let it then be called the mystical group.

Our next step should be to gain acquaintance with some typical examples. . . . I will begin . . . with phenomena which claim no special religious significance, and end with those of which the religious pretensions are extreme.

The simplest rudiment of mystical experience would seem to be that deepened sense of the significance of a maxim or formula which occasionally sweeps over one. "I've heard that said all my life," we exclaim, "but I never realized its full meaning until now." "When a fellow-monk," said Luther, "one day repeated the words of the Creed: 'I believe in the forgiveness of sins,' I saw the Scripture in an entirely new light; and straightway I felt as if I were born anew. It was as if I had found the door of paradise thrown wide open." This sense of deeper significance is not confined to rational propositions. Single words, and conjunctions of words, effects of light on land and sea, odors and musical sounds, all bring it when the mind is tuned aright. Most of us can remember the strangely moving power of passages in certain poems read when we were young, irrational doorways as they were through which the mystery of fact, the wildness and the pang of life, stole into our hearts and thrilled them. The words have now perhaps become mere polished surfaces for us; but lyric poetry and music are alive and significant only in proportion as they fetch these vague vistas of a life continuous with our own, beckoning and inviting, yet ever eluding our pursuit. We are alive or dead to the eternal inner message of the arts according as we have kept or lost this mystical susceptibility.

A more pronounced step forward on the mystical ladder is found in an extremely frequent phenomenon, that sudden feeling, namely, which sometimes sweeps over us, of having "been here before," as if at some indefinite past time, in just this place, with just these people, we were already saying just these things. . . . Sir James Crichton-Browne has given the technical name of "dreamy states" to these sudden invasions of vaguely reminiscent consciousness. They bring a sense of mystery and of the metaphysical duality of things, and the feeling of an enlargement of perception which seems imminent but which never completes itself. . . .

Somewhat deeper plunges into mystical consciousness are met with in yet other dreamy states. Such feelings as these which Charles Kingsley describes are surely far from being uncommon, especially in youth:—

> When I walk the fields, I am oppressed now and then with an innate feeling that everything I see has a meaning, if I could but understand it. And this feeling of being surrounded with truths which I cannot grasp amounts to indescribable awe sometimes. . . . Have you not felt that your real soul was imperceptible to your mental vision, except in a few hallowed moments?

The next step into mystical states carries us into a realm that public opinion and ethical philosophy have long since branded as pathological, though private practice and certain lyric strains of poetry seem still to bear witness to its ideality. I refer to the consciousness produced by intoxicants and anæsthetics, especially by alcohol. The sway of alcohol over mankind is unquestionably due to its power to stimulate the mystical faculties of human nature, usually crushed to earth by the cold facts and dry criticisms of the sober hour. Sobriety diminishes, discriminates, and says no; drunkenness expands, unites, and says yes. It is in fact the great exciter of the *Yes* function in man. It brings its votary from the chill periphery of things to the radiant core. It makes him for the moment one with truth. Not through mere perversity do men run after it. To the poor and the unlettered it stands in the place of symphony concerts and of literature; and it is part of the deeper mystery and tragedy of life that whiffs and gleams of something that we immediately recognize as excellent should be vouchsafed to so many of us only in the fleeting earlier phases of what in its totality is so degrading a poisoning. The drunken consciousness is one bit of the mystic consciousness, and our total opinion of it must find its place in our opinion of that larger whole.

Nitrous oxide and ether, especially nitrous oxide, when sufficiently diluted with air, stimulate the mystical consciousness in an extraordinary degree. Depth beyond depth of truth seems revealed to the inhaler. This truth fades out, however, or escapes, at the moment of coming to; and if any words remain over in which it seemed to clothe itself, they prove to be the veriest nonsense. Nevertheless, the sense of a profound meaning having been there persists; and I know more than one person who is persuaded that in the nitrous oxide trance we have a genuine metaphysical revelation.

Some years ago I myself made some observations on this aspect of nitrous oxide intoxication, and reported them in print. One conclusion was forced upon my mind at that time, and my impression of its truth has ever since remained unshaken. It is that our normal waking consciousness, rational consciousness as we call it, is but one special type of consciousness, whilst all about it, parted from it by the filmiest of screens, there lie potential forms of consciousness entirely different. We may go through life without suspecting their existence; but apply the requisite stimulus, and at a touch they are there in all their completeness, definite types of mentality which probably somewhere have their field of application and adaptation. No account of the universe in its totality can be final which leaves these other forms of consciousness quite disregarded. How to regard them is the question—for they are so discontinuous with ordinary consciousness. Yet they may determine attitudes though they cannot furnish formulas, and open a region though they fail to give a map. At any rate, they forbid a premature closing of our accounts with reality. Looking back on my own experiences, they all converge towards a kind of insight to which I cannot help ascribing some metaphysical significance. The keynote of it is invariably a reconciliation. It is as if the opposites of the world, whose contradictoriness and conflict make all our difficulties and troubles, were melted into unity. Not only do they, as contrasted species, belong to one and the same genus, but *one of the species,* the nobler and better one, *is itself the genus, and so soaks up and absorbs its opposite into itself.* This is a dark saying, I know, when thus expressed in terms of common logic, but I cannot wholly escape from its authority. I feel as if it must mean something, something like what the Hegelian philosophy means, if one could only lay hold of it more clearly. Those who have ears to hear, let them hear; to me the living sense of its reality only comes in the artificial mystic state of mind. . . .

Certain aspects of nature seem to have a peculiar power of awakening such mystical moods. Most of the striking cases which I have collected have occurred out of doors. Literature has commemorated this fact in many passages of great beauty—this extract, for example, from Amiel's Journal Intime:—

> Shall I ever again have any of those prodigious reveries which sometimes came to me in former days? One day, in youth, at sunrise, sitting in the ruins of the castle of Faucigny; and again in the mountains, under the noonday sun, above Lavey, lying at the foot of a tree and visited by three butterflies; once more at night upon the shingly shore of the Northern Ocean, my back upon the sand and my vision ranging through the milky way;—such grand and spacious, immortal, cosmogonic reveries, when one reaches to the stars, when one owns the infinite! Moments divine, ecstatic hours; in which our thought flies from world to world, pierces the great enigma, breathes with a respiration broad, tranquil, and deep as the respiration of the ocean, serene and limitless as the blue firmament; . . . instants of irresistible intuition in which one feels one's self great as the universe, and calm as a god. . . . What hours, what memories! The vestiges they leave behind are enough to fill us with belief and enthusiasm, as if they were visits of the Holy Ghost. . . .

We have now seen enough of this cosmic or mystic consciousness, as it comes sporadically. We must next pass to its methodical cultivation as an element of the religious life. Hindus, Buddhists, Mohammedans, and Christians all have cultivated it methodically.

In India, training in mystical insight has been known from time immemorial under the name of yoga. Yoga means the experimental union of the individual with the divine. It is based on persevering exercise; and the diet, posture, breathing, intellectual concentration, and moral discipline vary slightly in the different systems which teach it. The yogi, or disciple, who has by these means overcome the obscurations of his lower nature sufficiently, enters into the condition termed *samâdhi,* "and comes face to face with facts which no instinct or reason can ever know." He learns—

> That the mind itself has a higher state of existence, beyond reason, a superconscious state, and that when the mind gets to that higher state, then this knowledge beyond reasoning comes. . . . All the different steps in yoga are intended to bring us scientifically to the superconscious state or Samâdhi. . . . Just as unconscious work is beneath consciousness, so there is another work which is above consciousness, and which, also, is not accompanied with the feeling of egoism. . . . There is no feeling of *I,* and yet the mind works, desireless, free from restlessness, objectless, bodiless. Then the Truth shines in its full effulgence, and we know ourselves—for Samâdhi lies potential in us all—for what we truly are, free, immortal, omnipotent, loosed from

the finite, and its contrasts of good and evil altogether, and identical with the Atman or Universal Soul.

The Vedantists say that one may stumble into superconsciousness sporadically, without the previous discipline, but it is then impure. Their test of its purity, like our test of religion's value, is empirical: its fruits must be good for life. When a man comes out of Samâdhi, they assure us that he remains "enlightened, a sage, a prophet, a saint, his whole character changed, his life changed, illumined." . . .

In the Christian church there have always been mystics. Although many of them have been viewed with suspicion, some have gained favor in the eyes of the authorities. The experiences of these have been treated as precedents, and a codified system of mystical theology has been based upon them, in which everything legitimate finds its place. The basis of the system is "orison" or meditation, the methodical elevation of the soul towards God. Through the practice of orison the higher levels of mystical experience may be attained. It is odd that Protestantism, especially evangelical Protestantism, should seemingly have abandoned everything methodical in this line. Apart from what prayer may lead to, Protestant mystical experience appears to have been almost exclusively sporadic. It has been left to our mind-curers to reintroduce methodical meditation into our religious life. . . .

In spite of their repudiation of articulate self-description, mystical states in general assert a pretty distinct theoretic drift. It is possible to give the outcome of the majority of them in terms that point in definite philosophical directions. One of these directions is optimism, and the other is monism. We pass into mystical states from out of ordinary consciousness as from a less into a more, as from a smallness into a vastness, and at the same time as from an unrest to a rest. We feel them as reconciling, unifying states. They appeal to the yes-function more than to the no-function in us. In them the unlimited absorbs the limits and peacefully closes the account. Their very denial of every adjective you may propose as applicable to the ultimate truth—He, the Self, the Atman, is to be described by "No! no!" only, say the Upanishads—though it seems on the surface to be a no-function, is a denial made on behalf of a deeper yes. Whoso calls the Absolute anything in particular, or says that it is *this,* seems implicitly to shut it off from being *that*—it is as if he lessened it. So we deny the "this," negating the negation which it seems to us to imply, in the interests of the higher affirmative attitude by which we are possessed. The fountain-head of Christian mysticism is Dionysius the Areopagite. He describes the absolute truth by negatives exclusively.

> The cause of all things is neither soul nor intellect; nor has it imagination, opinion, or reason, or intelligence; nor is it reason or intelligence; nor is it spoken or thought. It is neither number, nor order, nor magnitude, nor littleness, nor equality, nor inequality, nor similarity, nor dissimilarity. It neither stands, nor moves, nor rests. . . . It is neither essence, nor eternity, nor time. Even intellectual contact does not belong

to it. It is neither science nor truth. It is not even royalty or wisdom; not one; not unity; not divinity or goodness; nor even spirit as we know it," etc., *ad libitum.*

But these qualifications are denied by Dionysius, not because the truth falls short of them, but because it so infinitely excels them. It is above them. It is *super*-lucent, *super*-splendent, *super*-essential, *super*-sublime, *super everything* that can be named. Like Hegel in his logic, mystics journey towards the positive pole of truth only by the "Methode der Absoluten Negativität." . . .

To this dialectical use, by the intellect, of negation as a mode of passage towards a higher kind of affirmation, there is correlated the subtlest of moral counterparts in the sphere of the personal will. Since denial of the finite self and its wants, since asceticism of some sort, is found in religious experience to be the only doorway to the larger and more blessed life, this moral mystery intertwines and combines with the intellectual mystery in all mystical writings. . . .

In Paul's language, I live, yet not I, but Christ liveth in me. Only when I become as nothing can God enter in and no difference between his life and mine remains outstanding.

This overcoming of all the usual barriers between the individual and the Absolute is the great mystic achievement. In mystic states we both become one with the Absolute and we become aware of our oneness. This is the everlasting and triumphant mystical tradition, hardly altered by differences of clime or creed. In Hinduism, in Neoplatonism, in Sufism, in Christian mysticism, in Whitmanism, we find the same recurring note, so that there is about mystical utterances an eternal unanimity which ought to make a critic stop and think, and which brings it about that the mystical classics have, as has been said, neither birthday nor native land. Perpetually telling of the unity of man with God, their speech antedates languages, and they do not grow old.

"That art Thou!" say the Upanishads, and the Vedantists add: "Not a part, not a mode of That, but identically That, that absolute Spirit of the World." "As pure water poured into pure water remains the same, thus, O Gautama, is the Self of a thinker who knows. Water in water, fire in fire, ether in ether, no one can distinguish them: likewise a man whose mind has entered into the Self." . . .

I have now sketched with extreme brevity and insufficiency, but as fairly as I am able in the time allowed, the general traits of the mystic range of consciousness. *It is on the whole pantheistic and optimistic, or at least the opposite of pessimistic. It is anti-naturalistic, and harmonizes best with twice-bornness and so-called other-worldly states of mind.*

My next task is to inquire whether we can invoke it as authoritative. Does it furnish any *warrant for the truth* of the twice-bornness and supernaturality and pantheism which it favors? I must give my answer to this question as concisely as I can.

In brief my answer is this—and I will divide it into three parts:—

(1) Mystical states, when well developed, usually are, and have the right to be, absolutely authoritative over the individuals to whom they come.

(2) No authority emanates from them which should make it a duty for those who stand outside of them to accept their revelations uncritically.

(3) They break down the authority of the non-mystical or rationalistic consciousness, based upon the understanding and the senses alone. They show it to be only one kind of consciousness. They open out the possibility of other orders of truth, in which, so far as anything in us vitally responds to them, we may freely continue to have faith.

I will take up these points one by one.

1.

As a matter of psychological fact, mystical states of a well-pronounced and emphatic sort *are* usually authoritative over those who have them. They have been "there," and know. It is vain for rationalism to grumble about this. If the mystical truth that comes to a man proves to be a force that he can live by, what mandate have we of the majority to order him to live in another way? We can throw him into a prison or a madhouse, but we cannot change his mind—we commonly attach it only the more stubbornly to its beliefs. It mocks our utmost efforts, as a matter of fact, and in point of logic it absolutely escapes our jurisdiction. Our own more "rational" beliefs are based on evidence exactly similar in nature to that which mystics quote for theirs. Our senses, namely, have assured us of certain states of fact; but mystical experiences are as direct perceptions of fact for those who have them as any sensations ever were for us. The records show that even though the five senses be in abeyance in them, they are absolutely sensational in their epistemological quality, if I may be pardoned the barbarous expression —that is, they are face to face presentations of what seems immediately to exist.

The mystic is, in short, *invulnerable,* and must be left whether we relish it or not, in undisturbed enjoyment of his creed. Faith, says Tolstoy, is that by which men live. And faith-state and mystic state are practically convertible terms.

2.

But I now proceed to add that mystics have no right to claim that we ought to accept the deliverance of their peculiar experiences, if we are ourselves outsiders and feel no private call thereto. The utmost they can ever ask of us in this life is to admit that they establish a presumption. They form a consensus and have an unequivocal outcome; and it would be odd, mystics might say, if such a unanimous type of experience should prove to be altogether wrong. At bottom, however, this would only be an appeal to numbers, like the appeal of rationalism the other way; and the appeal to numbers has no logical force. If we acknowledge it, it is for "suggestive," not for logical reasons: we follow the majority because to do so suits our life.

But even this presumption from the unanimity of mystics is far from being strong. In characterizing mystic states as pantheistic, optimistic, etc., I am afraid I over-simplified the truth. I did so for expository reasons, and to keep the closer to the classic mystical tradition. The classic religious mysticism, it now must be confessed, is only a "privileged case." It is an *extract,* kept true to type by the selection of the fittest specimens and their preservation in "schools." It is carved out from a much larger mass; and if we take the larger mass as seriously as religious mysticism has historically taken itself, we find that the supposed unanimity largely disappears. To begin with, even religious mysticism itself, the kind that accumulates traditions and makes schools, is much less unanimous than I have allowed. It has been both ascetic and antinomianly self-indulgent within the Christian church. It is dualistic in Sankhya, and monistic in Vedanta philosophy. I called it pantheistic; but the great Spanish mystics are anything but pantheists. They are with few exceptions non-metaphysical minds, for whom "the category of personality" is absolute. The "union" of man with God is for them much more like an occasional miracle than like an original identity. How different again, apart from the happiness common to all, is the mysticism of Walt Whitman, Edward Carpenter, Richard Jefferies, and other naturalistic pantheists, from the more distinctively Christian sort. The fact is that the mystical feeling of enlargement, union, and emancipation has no specific intellectual content whatever of its own. It is capable of forming matrimonial alliances with material furnished by the most diverse philosophies and theologies, provided only they can find a place in their framework for its peculiar emotional mood. We have no right, therefore, to invoke its prestige as distinctively in favor of any special belief, such as that in absolute idealism, or in the absolute monistic identity, or in the absolute goodness, of the world. It is only relatively in favor of all these things—it passes out of common human consciousness in the direction in which they lie.

So much for religious mysticism proper. But more remains to be told, for religious mysticism is only one half of mysticism. The other half has no accumulated traditions except those which the text-books on insanity supply. Open any one of these, and you will find abundant cases in which "mystical ideas" are cited as characteristic symptoms of enfeebled or deluded states of mind. In delusional insanity, paranoia, as they sometimes call it, we may have a *diabolical* mysticism, a sort of religious mysticism turned upside down. The same sense of ineffable importance in the smallest events, the same texts and words coming with new meanings, the same voices and visions and leadings and missions, the same controlling by extraneous powers; only this time the emotion is pessimistic: instead of consolations we have desolations; the meanings are dreadful; and the powers are enemies to life. It is evident that from the point of view of their psychological mechanism, the classic mysticism and these lower mysticisms spring from the same mental level, from that great subliminal or transmarginal region of which science is beginning to admit the existence, but of which so little is really known. That region contains every kind of matter: "seraph and snake" abide there side by side. To come from thence is no infallible credential. What comes must be sifted and tested, and run the gauntlet of confrontation with the total context of experience, just like what comes from the outer world of sense. Its value must be ascertained by empirical methods, so long as we are not mystics ourselves.

Once more, then, I repeat that non-mystics are under no obligation to acknowledge in mystical states a superior authority conferred on them by their intrinsic nature.

3.

Yet, I repeat once more, the existence of mystical states absolutely overthrows the pretension of non-mystical states to be the sole and ultimate dictators of what we may believe. As a rule, mystical states merely add a supersensuous meaning to the ordinary outward data of consciousness. They are excitements like the emotions of love or ambition, gifts to our spirit by means of which facts already objectively before us fall into a new expressiveness and make a new connection with our active life. They do not contradict these facts as such, or deny anything that our senses have immediately seized. It is the rationalistic critic rather who plays the part of denier in the controversy, and his denials have no strength, for there never can be a state of facts to which new meaning may not truthfully be added, provided the mind ascend to a more enveloping point of view. It must always remain an open question whether mystical states may not possibly be such superior points of view, windows through which the mind looks out upon a more extensive and inclusive world. The difference of the views seen from the different mystical windows need not prevent us from entertaining this supposition. The wider world would in that case prove to have a mixed constitution like that of this world, that is all. It would have its celestial and its infernal regions, its tempting and its saving moments, its valid experiences and its counterfeit ones, just as our world has them; but it would be a wider world all the same. We should have to use its experiences by selecting and subordinating and substituting just as is our custom in this ordinary naturalistic world; we should be liable to error just as we are now; yet the counting in of that wider world of meanings, and the serious dealing with it, might, in spite of all the perplexity, be indispensable stages in our approach to the final fullness of the truth.

GEORGE SANTAYANA (1863–1952)

Santayana was born in Madrid of Spanish parents but spent most of his life outside of Spain. His mother, through an earlier marriage, had American connections, and brought her young son to Boston when he was nine. He stayed to graduate from Boston Latin School and Harvard College, and, after further study in Germany and England, he returned to teach philosophy at Harvard alongside his old masters, Josiah Royce and William James. In 1912, upon receipt of a legacy from his mother's estate, he resigned his professorship to live abroad. He spent the period of World War I in England and the postwar period in Rome. During World War II he took up residence in a Catholic hospital in Rome and remained there, in serene detachment, until his death in 1952.

Throughout a literary career of more than sixty years, he wrote a remarkable variety of books, including poetry, fiction, autobiography, literary essays, and systematic philosophy. These works, exquisite in style and urbane in thought, are among the classics of literature.

Although Catholic by tradition, Santayana was materialist by conviction and drew his inspiration from diverse sources. "I recited my Lucretius with as much gusto as my Saint Augustine," he declared; "and gradually Lucretius sank deeper and became more satisfying." The result is a materialism strangely blended with Catholic and Platonic ideas, and expressed with gentle irony.

Religion
and Poetry

. . . Religion and poetry are identical in essence, and differ merely in the way in which they are attached to practical affairs. Poetry is called religion when it intervenes in life, and religion, when it merely supervenes upon life, is seen to be nothing but poetry.

It would naturally follow from this conception that religious doctrines would do well to withdraw their pretension to be dealing with matters of fact. That pretension is not only the source of the conflicts of religion with science and of the vain and bitter controversies of sects; it is also the cause of the impurity and incoherence of religion in the soul, when it seeks its sanctions in the sphere of reality, and forgets that its proper concern is to express the ideal. For the dignity of religion, like that of poetry and of every moral ideal, lies precisely in its ideal adequacy, in its fit rendering of the meanings and values of life, in its anticipation of perfection; so that the excellence of religion is due to an idealization of experience which, while making religion noble if treated

From George Santayana, *Interpretations of Poetry and Religion,* Charles Scribner's Sons, 1900. Reprinted by permission of Charles Scribner's Sons and Constable & Company Ltd.

as poetry, makes it necessarily false if treated as science. Its function is rather to draw from reality materials for an image of that ideal to which reality ought to conform, and to make us citizens, by anticipation, in the world we crave.

It also follows from our general conception that poetry has a universal and a moral function. Its rudimentary essays in the region of fancy and pleasant sound, as well as its idealization of episodes in human existence, are only partial exercises in an art that has all time and all experience for its natural subject-matter and all the possibilities of being for its ultimate theme. As religion is deflected from its course when it is confused with a record of facts or of natural laws, so poetry is arrested in its development if it remains an unmeaning play of fancy without relevance to the ideals and purposes of life. In that relevance lies its highest power. As its elementary pleasantness comes from its response to the demands of the ear, so its deepest beauty comes from its response to the ultimate demands of the soul.

This theory can hardly hope for much commendation either from the apologists of theology, or from its critics. The mass of mankind is divided into two classes, the Sancho Panzas who have a sense for reality, but no ideals, and the Don Quixotes with a sense for ideals, but mad. The expedient of recognizing facts as facts and accepting ideals as ideals,—and this is all we propose,— although apparently simple enough, seems to elude the normal human power of discrimination. If, therefore, the champion of any orthodoxy should be offended at our conception, which would reduce his artful cosmos to an allegory, all that could be said to mitigate his displeasure would be that our view is even less favourable to his opponents than to himself.

The liberal school that attempts to fortify religion by minimizing its expression, both theoretic and devotional, seems from this point of view to be merely impoverishing religious symbols and vulgarizing religious aims; it subtracts from faith that imagination by which faith becomes an interpretation and idealization of human life, and retains only a stark and superfluous principle of superstition. For meagre and abstract as may be the content of such a religion, it contains all the venom of absolute pretensions; it is no less cursed than the more developed systems with a controversial unrest and with a consequent undertone of constraint and suspicion. It tortures itself with the same circular proofs in its mistaken ambition to enter the plane of vulgar reality and escape its native element of ideas. It casts a greater blight than would a civilized orthodoxy on any joyous freedom of thought. For the respect exacted by an establishment is limited and external, and not greater than its traditional

forms probably deserve, as normal expressions of human feeling and apt symbols of moral truth. A reasonable deference once shown to authority, the mind remains, under such an establishment, inwardly and happily free; the conscience is not intimidated, the imagination is not tied up. But the preoccupations of a hungry and abstract fanaticism poison the liberty nominally allowed, bias all vision, and turn philosophy itself, which should be the purest of delights and conclusions, into an obsession and a burden to the soul. In such a spectral form religious illusion does not cease to be illusion. Mythology cannot become science by being reduced in bulk, but it may cease, as a mythology, to be worth having.

On the other hand, the positivistic school of criticism would seem, if our theory is right, to have overlooked in its programme the highest functions of human nature. The environing world can justify itself to the mind only by the free life which is fosters there. All observation is observation of brute fact, all discipline is mere repression, until these facts digested and this discipline embodied in humane impulses become the starting-point for a creative movement of the imagination, the firm basis for ideal constructions in society, religion, and art. Only as conditions of these human activities can the facts of nature and history become normally intelligible or practically important. In themselves they are trivial incidents, gossips of the Fates, cacklings of their inexhaustible garrulity. To regard the function of man as accomplished when these chance happenings have been recorded by him or contributed to by his impulsive action, is to ignore his reason, his privilege,—shared for the rest with every living creature,—of using Nature as food and substance for his own life. This human life is not merely animal and passionate. The best and keenest part of it consists in that very gift of creation and government which, together with all the transcendental functions of his own mind, man has significantly attributed to God as to his highest ideal. Not to see in this rational activity the purpose and standard of all life is to have left human nature half unread. It is to look to the removal of certain incidental obstacles in the work of reason as to the solution of its positive tasks. In comparison with such apathetic naturalism, all the errors and follies of religion are worthy of indulgent sympathy, since they represent an effort, however misguided, to interpret and to use the materials of experience for moral ends, and to measure the value of reality by its relation to the ideal. . . .

A prophet, unless he be the merely mechanical vehicle of truths he does not understand, cannot be conceived as anything but a man of imagination, whose visions miraculously mirror the truth. A metaphysician who transcends the intellect by his reason can be conceived only as using his imagination to such good purpose as to divine by it the ideal laws of reality or the ultimate goals of moral effort. His reason is an imagination that succeeds, an intuition that guesses the principle of experience. But if this intuition were of such a nature that experience could verify it, then that higher reason or imagination would be brought down to the level of the understanding; for understanding, as we have

defined it, is itself a kind of imagination, an imagination prophetic of experience, a spontaneity of thought by which the science of perception is turned into the art of life. The same absence of verification distinguishes revelation from science; for when the prophecies of faith are verified, the function of faith is gone. Faith and the higher reason of the metaphysicians are therefore forms of imagination believed to be avenues to truth, as dreams or oracles may sometimes be truthful, not because their necessary correspondence to truth can be demonstrated, for then they would be portions of science, but because a man dwelling on those intuitions is conscious of a certain moral transformation, of a certain warmth and energy of life. This emotion, heightening his ideas and giving them power over his will, he calls faith or high philosophy, and under its dominion he is able to face his destiny with enthusiasm, or at least with composure.

The imagination, even when its premonitions are not wholly justified by subsequent experience, has thus a noble rôle to play in the life of man. Without it his thoughts would be not only far too narrow to represent, although it were symbolically, the greatness of the universe, but far too narrow even to render the scope of his own life and the conditions of his practical welfare. Without poetry and religion the history of mankind would have been darker than it is. Not only would emotional life have been poorer, but the public conscience, the national and family spirit, so useful for moral organization and discipline, would hardly have become articulate. By what a complex and uninspired argumentation would the pure moralist have to insist upon those duties which the imagination enforces so powerfully in oaths sworn before the gods, in commandments written by the finger of God upon stone tablets, in visions of hell and heaven, in chivalrous love and loyalty, and in the sense of family dignity and honour? What intricate, what unavailing appeals to positive interests would have to be made before those quick reactions could be secured in large bodies of people which can be produced by the sight of a flag or the sound of a name? The imagination is the great unifier of humanity. Men's perceptions may be various, their powers of understanding very unequal; but the imagination is, as it were, the self-consciousness of instinct, the contribution which the inner capacity and demand of the mind makes to experience. To indulge the imagination is to express the universal self, the common and contagious element in all individuals, that rudimentary potency which they all share. To stimulate the imagination is to produce the deepest, the most pertinacious emotions. To repress it is to chill the soul, so that even the clearest perception of the truth remains without the joy and impetuosity of conviction. . . .

We of this generation look back upon a variety of religious conceptions and forms of worship, and a certain unsatisfied hunger in our own souls attaches our attention to the spectacle. We observe how literally fables and mysteries were once accepted which can have for us now only a thin and symbolic meaning. Judging other minds and other ages by our own, we are tempted to ask if there ever was any fundamental difference between religion and poetry. Both seem to consist in what the imagination adds to science, to history, and to morals. Men looked attentively on the face of Nature: their close stuggle with her compelled them to do so: but before making statistics of her movements they made dramatizations of her life. The imagination enveloped the material world, as yet imperfectly studied, and produced the cosmos of mythology.

Thus the religion of the Greeks was, we might say, nothing but poetry: nothing but what imagination added to the rudiments of science, to the first impressions of a mind that pored upon natural phenomena and responded to them with a quick sense of kinship and comprehension. The religion of the Hebrews might be called poetry with as good reason. Their "sense for conduct" and their vivid interest in their national destiny carried them past any prosaic record of events or cautious theory of moral and social laws. They rose at once into a bold dramatic conception of their race's covenant with Heaven: just such a conception as the playwright would seek out in order to portray with awful acceleration the ways of passion and fate. Finally, we have apparently a third kind of poetry in what has been the natural religion of the detached philosophers of all ages. In them the imagination touches the precepts of morals and the ideals of reason, attributing to them a larger scope and more perfect fulfillment than experience can show them to have. Philosophers ever tend to clothe the harmonies of their personal thought with universal validity and to assign to their ideals a latent omnipotence and an ultimate victory over the forces of unreason. This which is obviously a kind of poetry is at the same time the spontaneous religion of conscience and thought.

Yet religion in all these cases differs from a mere play of the imagination in one important respect; it reacts directly upon life; it is a factor in conduct. Our religion is the poetry in which we believe. Mere poetry is an ineffectual shadow of life; religion is, if you will, a phantom also, but a phantom guide. While it tends to its own expansion, like any growth in the imagination, it tends also to its application in practice. Such an aim is foreign to poetry. The inspirations of religion demand fidelity and courageous response on our part. Faith brings us not only peace, not only the contemplation of ideal harmonies, but labour and the sword. These two tendencies—to imaginative growth and to practical embodiment—coexist in every living religion, but they are not always equally conspicuous. In the formative ages of Christianity, for instance, while its legends were being gathered and its dogma fixed, the imaginative expansion absorbed men's interest; later, when the luxuriant branches of the Church began to shake off their foliage, and there came a time of year

> When yellow leaves, or none, or
>   few, do hang
> Upon those boughs which shake
>   against the cold,

the energy of religious thought, released from the enlargement of doctrine, spent itself upon a more rigid and watchful application of the residuum of faith.

In the Pagan religion the element of applicability might seem at first sight to be lacking, so that nothing would subsist but a poetic fable. An unbiassed study of antiquity, however, will soon dispel that idea. Besides the gods whom we may plausibly regard as impersonations of natural forces, there existed others; the spirits of ancestors, the gods of the hearth, and the ideal patrons of war and the arts. Even the gods of Nature inspired reverence and secured a cultus only as they influenced the well-being of man. The worship of them had a practical import. The conception of their nature and presence became a sanction and an inspiration in the conduct of life. When the figments of the fancy are wholly divorced from reality they can have no clearness or consistency; they can have no permanence when they are wholly devoid of utility. The vividness and persistence of the figures of many of the gods came from the fact that they were associated with institutions and practices which controlled the conception of them and kept it young. The fictions of a poet, whatever his genius, do not produce illusion because they do not attach themselves to realities in the world of action. They have character without power and names without local habitations. The gods in the beginning had both. Their image, their haunts, the reports of their apparitions and miracles, gave a nucleus of empirical reality to the accretions of legend. The poet who came to sing their praise, to enlarge upon their exploits, and to explain their cultus, gave less to the gods in honour than he received from them in inspiration. All his invention was guided by the genius of the deity, as represented by the traditions of his shrine. This poetry, then, even in its most playful mood, is not mere poetry, but religion. It is a poetry in which men believe; it is a poetry that beautifies and justifies to their minds the positive facts of their ancestral worship, their social unity, and their personal conscience. . . .

The distinction of a poet—the dignity and humanity of his thought—can be measured by nothing, perhaps, so well as by the diameter of the world in which he lives; if he is supreme, his vision, like Dante's, always stretches to the stars. And Virgil, a supreme poet sometimes unjustly belittled, shows us the same thing in another form; his landscape is the Roman universe, his theme the sacred springs of Roman greatness in piety, constancy, and law. He has not written a line in forgetfulness that he was a Roman; he loves country life and its labours because he sees in it the origin and bulwark of civic greatness; he honours tradition because it gives perspective and momentum to the history that ensues; he invokes the gods, because they are symbols of the physical and moral forces by which Rome struggled to dominion. . . .

The function of poetry, like that of science, can only be fulfilled by the conception of harmonies that become clearer as they grow richer. As the chance note that comes to be supported by a melody becomes in that melody determinate and necessary, and as the melody, when woven into a harmony, is explicated in that harmony and fixed beyond recall; so the single emotion, the fortuitous dream, launched by the poet into the world of recognizable and immortal forms, looks in that world for its ideal supports and affinities. It must find them or else be blown back among the ghosts. The highest ideality is the comprehension of the real. Poetry is not at its best when it depicts a further possible experience, but when it initiates us, by feigning something which as an experience is impossible, into the meaning of the experience which we have actually had.

The highest example of this kind of poetry is religion; and although disfigured and misunderstood by the simplicity of men who believe in it without being capable of that imaginative interpretation of life in which its truth consists, yet this religion is even then often beneficent, because it colours life harmoniously with the ideal. Religion may falsely represent the ideal as a reality, but we must remember that the ideal, if not so represented, would be despised by the majority of men, who cannot understand that the value of things is moral, and who therefore attribute to what is moral a natural existence, thinking thus to vindicate its importance and value. But value lies in meaning, not in substance; in the ideal which things approach, not in the energy which they embody.

The highest poetry, then, is not that of the versifiers, but that of the prophets, or of such poets as interpret verbally the visions which the prophets have rendered in action and sentiment rather than in adequate words. That the intuitions of religion are poetical, and that in such intuitions poetry has its ultimate function, are truths of which both religion and poetry become more conscious the more they advance in refinement and profundity. A crude and superficial theology may confuse God with the thunder, the mountains, the heavenly bodies, or the whole universe; but when we pass from these easy identifications to a religion that has taken root in history and in the hearts of men, and has come to flower, we find its objects and its dogmas purely ideal, transparent expressions of moral experience and perfect counterparts of human needs. The evidence of history or of the senses is left far behind and never thought of; the evidence of the heart, the value of the idea, are alone regarded.

Take, for instance, the doctrine of transubstantiation. A metaphor here is the basis of a dogma, because the dogma rises to the same subtle region as the metaphor, and gathers its sap from the same soil of emotion. Religion has here rediscovered its affinity with poetry, and in insisting on the truth of its mystery it unconsciously vindicates the ideality of its truth. Under the accidents of bread and wine lies, says the dogma, the substance of Christ's body, blood, and divinity. What is that but to treat facts as an appearance, and their ideal import as a reality? And to do this is the very essence of poetry, for which everything visible is a sacrament—an outward sign of that inward grace for which the soul is thirsting.

In this same manner, where poetry rises from its elementary and detached expressions in rhythm, euphuism, characterization, and storytelling, and comes to the consciousness of its highest function, that of portraying the ideals of experience and destiny, then the poet becomes aware that he is essentially a prophet, and either devotes himself, like Homer or Dante, to the loving expression of the religion that exists, or like Lucretius or Wordsworth, to the heralding of one which he believes to be possible. Such poets are aware of their highest mission; others, whatever the energy of their genius, have not conceived their ultimate function as poets. They have been willing to leave their world ugly as a whole, after stuffing it with a sufficient profusion of beauties. Their contemporaries, their fellow-countrymen for many generations, may not perceive this defect, because they are naturally even less able than the poet himself to understand the necessity of so large a harmony. If he is short-sighted, they are blind, and his poetic world may seem to them sublime in its significance, because it may suggest some partial lifting of their daily burdens and some partial idealization of their incoherent thoughts.

Such insensibility to the highest poetry is no more extraordinary than the corresponding indifference to the highest religion; nobility and excellence, however, are not dependent on the suffrage of half-baked men, but on the original disposition of the clay and the potter; I mean on the conditions of the art and the ideal capacities of human nature. Just as a note is better than a noise because, its beats being regular, the ear and brain can react with pleasure on that regularity, so all the stages of harmony are better than the confusion out of which they come, because the soul that perceives that harmony welcomes it as the fulfillment of her natural ends. The Pythagoreans were therefore right when they made number the essence of the knowable world, and Plato was right when he said harmony was the first condition of the highest good. The good man is a poet whose syllables are deeds and make a harmony in Nature. The poet is a rebuilder of the imagination, to make a harmony in that. And he is not a complete poet if his whole imagination is not attuned and his whole experience composed into a single symphony.

For his complete equipment, then, it is necessary, in the first place, that he sing; that his voice be pure and well pitched, and that his numbers flow; then, at a higher stage, his images must fit with one another; he must be euphuistic, colouring his thoughts with many reflected lights of memory and suggestion, so that their harmony may be rich and profound; again, at a higher stage, he must be sensuous and free, that is, he must build up his world with the primary elements of experience, not with the conventions of common sense or intelligence; he must draw the whole soul into his harmonies, even if in doing so he disintegrates· the partial systematizations of experience made by abstract science in the categories of prose. But finally, this disintegration must not leave the poet weltering in a chaos of sense and passion; it must be merely the ploughing of the ground before a new harvest, the kneading of the clay before the modelling of a more perfect form. The expression of emotion should be rationalized by derivation from character and by reference to the real objects that arouse it—to Nature, to history, and to the universe of truth; the experience imagined should be conceived as a destiny, governed by principles, and issuing in the discipline and enlightenment of

the will. In this way alone can poetry become an interpretation of life and not merely an irrelevant excursion into the realm of fancy, multiplying our images without purpose, and distracting us from our business without spiritual gain.

If we may then define poetry, not in the formal sense of giving the minimum of what may be called by that name, but in the ideal sense of determining the goal which it approaches and the achievement in which all its principles would be fulfilled, we may say that poetry is metrical and euphuistic discourse, expressing thought which is both sensuous and ideal.

Such is poetry as a literary form; but if we drop the limitation to verbal expression, and think of poetry as that subtle fire and inward light which seems at times to shine through the world and to touch the images in our minds with ineffable beauty, then poetry is a momentary harmony in the soul amid stagnation or conflict,—a glimpse of the divine and an incitation to a religious life.

Religion is poetry become the guide of life, poetry substituted for science or supervening upon it as an approach to the highest reality. Poetry is religion allowed to drift, left without points of application in conduct and without an expression in worship and dogma; it is religion without practical efficacy and without metaphysical illusion. The ground of this abstractness of poetry, however, is usually only its narrow scope; a poet who plays with an idea for half an hour, or constructs a character to which he gives no profound moral significance, forgets his own thought, or remembers it only as a fiction of his leisure, because he has not dug his well deep enough to tap the subterraneous springs of his own life. But when the poet enlarges his theatre and puts into his rhapsodies the true visions of his people and of his soul, his poetry is the consecration of his deepest convictions, and contains the whole truth of his religion. What the religion of the vulgar adds to the poet's is simply the inertia of their limited apprehension, which takes literally what he meant ideally, and degrades into a false extension of this world on its own level what in his mind was a true interpretation of it upon a moral plane.

This higher plane is the sphere of significant imagination, of relevant fiction, of idealism become the interpretation of the reality it leaves behind. Poetry raised to its highest power is then identical with religion grasped in its inmost truth; at their point of union both reach their utmost purity and beneficence, for then poetry loses its frivolity and ceases to demoralize, while religion surrenders its illusions and ceases to deceive.

COMMENT

Pascal on Scepticism and Faith

Pascal, who died before he reached the age of forty, never completed the Apology for Religion which was to be his major work. Instead he left nearly a thousand fragmentary notes on a very great number of separate sheets of paper of various shapes and sizes. These had been sorted into over twenty bundles and sewn together by one thread for each bundle. The two most important editions of the *Thoughts*, that of Brunschvicg and that of Lafuma, have gathered these fragments together in a plausible order. The latter edition, based on a copy by one of Pascal's relatives, is generally considered the more authoritative, but neither editor has claimed that the order in his edition is the plan that Pascal would have followed if he had lived to complete his book. We must regard the fragments as merely the notes for a work which he left far from completion.

Lucien Goldmann, in *The Hidden God*,[1] maintains that the fragmentary character of the "thoughts" suits their paradoxical subject-matter. The fragment, Goldmann contends, is the only valid form of the expression of Pascal's view that man himself is a bundle of contradictions, incapable alike of pure truth and perfect order. But Goldmann concedes that the reader's understanding is improved if the the fragments are read in the following order: First, man is portrayed as a paradoxical being, who is both great and small, strong and weak, half-angel and half-

[1] *The Hidden God: A Study of Tragic Vision in the Pensées of Pascal and the Tragedies of Racine* (London: Routledge & Kegan Paul and New York: The Humanities Press, 1964), pp. 201–202.

beast, the glory and the scum of the world. Second, the Wager is advanced as a way of solving these intolerable contradictions, vindicating faith rather than nihilistic doubt. Third, faith is further justified by the historical and theological reasons for believing in Christianity. I have followed this order except that I have omitted the more doctrinaire apology for Christianity and have ended with the practical "reasons of the heart."

The argument is best understood if we grasp it in its historical context. As both physicist and mystic, Pascal experienced the full impact of the seventeenth-century scientific revolution upon religious belief. The physics and astronomy of Galileo and Newton had destroyed the old confidence that the world is a friendly place governed by spiritual forces. The thought of a dead, mechanical universe, with all the silent emptiness of its infinite spaces, struck Pascal with terror. Suspended between the infinitely great and the infinitely small, human beings appeared powerless to grasp the meaning of either extreme. With passionate conviction, Pascal recoiled from his abyss of scepticism and reaffirmed the importance of personal confrontation and communion with God. His agonizing doubt, anti-rationalism, and leap of faith foreshadow the thinking of religious existentialists such as Kierkegaard.

The main structural underpinning of Pascal's argument is the concept of man's double nature—his wretchedness and his greatness. This contrast between the misery and fraility of man's lot and the strength and dignity of his thought is the theme of many of Pascal's greatest aphorisms. It reminds us of Alexander Pope's characterization of the human species:

> Chaos of Thought and Passion all confused:
> Still by himself abused or disabused:
> Created half to rise, and half to fall:
> Great lord of all things, yet a prey to all:
> Sole judge of Truth, in endless Error hurled
> The glory, jest, and riddle of the world![2]

But these lines of Pope are merely clever in comparison with the poignancy of Pascal's meditations.

Torn apart by contradictory tendencies, equally incapable of achieving ultimate values in this world and giving up the quest for them, the human being is impelled to resort to such desperate expedients as the Wager. There are two ways of interpreting this famous argument. One way is to interpret it as addressed to the free thinker and not applicable to Pascal himself. Asked to extricate his friend the Chevalier de Mère from his gambling losses, Pascal, who was an expert on probability, speculated about extending the theory of betting to more exalted concerns. Since human reason is manifestly incapable of either proving or disproving the

[2] *Essay on Man*, II, 13–18.

existence of God, the question whether God exists can be regarded as a great gamble. Why not, therefore, approach the choice between theism and atheism as a bettor might? Even if the probability of winning eternal happiness by leading a religious life is small, nevertheless, since the gain may be infinite and the possible loss no more than finite, it is a good gambling venture to lead such a life and to incline to whatever belief may be necessary for its basis. The argument is an attempt to appeal to the worldling and free thinker by a pragmatic appeal to self-interest. It was never designed to stand alone. The most it can do is to provide some provisional grounds for religious assent in the hope that it will be followed by spiritual conversion. According to this interpretation of the argument, Pascal himself was influenced more by "reasons of the heart" than by cold calculations.

The other way is to interpret the argument as an inner dialogue representing contradictory sides of Pascal's own nature. The metaphor of gambling is used to make clear the reality of risk, the possibility of failure, and the hope of success. It is a natural metaphor to symbolize the precariousness of the human predicament. Pascal felt this predicament with tragic intensity: it seemed to him that misery without God and hope of happiness with God are ineradicable elements in life. He himself had wrestled with the demon of doubt and had found no way to exorcise the demon by logical argument. He had also known the ecstasy of mystical experience. Finally he was convinced that human life, here in this world and possibly hereafter, will be crucially affected by what we believe, and that belief is deeply affected by the will to believe. By hope and faith, we may gain the greatest felicity of which a human being is capable. By despair, we shall infallibly lose what we may gain if we hope. In addressing his imaginary interlocutor, Pascal appears to be speaking out of the fullness of his own experience:

> Learn of those who have been bound like you, and who now stake all their possessions. These are people who know the way which you would follow, and who are cured of an ill of which you would be cured.

Pascal here is surely speaking for himself, and not simply concocting an argument to persuade a free thinker.

He concludes by reliance in religious matters on the "heart" rather than reason. It is the heart, an indefinable faculty of intuition, which grasps first principles, themselves not demonstrable, and it is through the heart that men feel the presence of God.

James' Defense of the Right To Believe

Pascal's Wager is not only interesting in itself but important for its influence upon James' essay "The Will to Believe." The intent of James, in adapting Pascal's argument to his own purposes, is to defend not any and all kinds of faith but only belief entertained under the conditions that he specifies. He states three conditions which must be present in order for faith to be justified:

1. We are confronted by a *genuine* option—living, forced, and momentous. I shall leave it to the reader to determine exactly what he means by a living rather than a dead option, a forced rather than an avoidable option, and a momentous rather than a trivial option.

2. We do not have enough reason or evidence to prove that one hypothesis (e.g., that God exists) is more probable than the alternative hypothesis (that God does not exist).

3. The result of believing one of the alternatives is to make life substantially better.

There is an additional twist to the argument. James points out that belief in a proposition sometimes helps to make that proposition come true. He cites the example of a man's faith that his sweetheart really loves him. This faith helps to create a relation of confidence and intimacy that ensures, or helps to ensure, the very love which is the object of belief. In such case, faith is doubly justified.

Some Critical Comments

James' argument is ingenious, and many people regard is as valid. It should not be used to justify credulity, however, and it should be hedged with qualifications. First, if we believe on the basis of faith, we should be clear-headed about what we are doing. We should recognize that it *is* faith and not reason. We should distinguish between *valuable* and *probable*, between *allurement* and *evidence*, between *wishful thinking* and *rational demonstration*. The mere fact that we desire a certain state to be the case is no evidence that it *is* the case. I may desire immortality, but my desire will not make me immortal. Believing in God may make me happier, but this has no bearing on the truth of my belief. "If wishes were horses, beggars would ride." James himself insists that the will to believe comes into play only when the option is live, forced, and momentous and reason is unable to provide an answer.

Second, both Pascal and James speak as if there were no intermediate shades of opinion between complete belief and complete disbelief. Actually there are many shades of belief and doubt. We rightly distinguish between probability and certainty, and we recognize that there are innumerable degrees of probability, depending upon the strength of the evidence. In a rational mind, the degree of credence is generally proportional to the degree of probability.

Third, Pascal and James are perhaps too much inclined to interpret nonbelief as practically equivalent to disbelief. In some situations, there is indeed no practical difference between them, but very often there is a difference. Moreover, the nonbelief of an agnostic is quite different from the nonbelief of an inquirist. There are five attitudes that we should distinguish:

Complete belief—"It is so."
Tentativity—"It may be so."
Complete disbelief—"It is not so."
Agnostic nonbelief—"We can never know."
Inquiristic nonbelief—"Let us try to find out."

Complete belief, complete disbelief, and agnostic nonbelief tend to cut off inquiry, whereas tentativity and inquiristic nonbelief tend to stimulate inquiry. Here is a practical difference of great importance—a difference which James seems to overlook.

Fourth, James' point that faith sometimes creates its own verification has limited validity. When the outcome of one's endeavors depends upon one's morale, faith in the venture may help to ensure success. A football team's faith that it will win may help to make it win; a man's faith that he will get well may help him to recover from a psychological or psychosomatic illness. No one will argue, however, that a man's faith in God will ensure, or even help to ensure, God's existence. The truth or falsity of most beliefs depends upon objective factors, independent of how one feels or thinks. Of course, *if* God exists and *if* he is a Being that enters into personal relations with individuals, the faith that one can commune with God may be very helpful in establishing the communion.

These considerations do not disprove the need for faith. Certain kinds of facts, such as the beauty and power of love, can be known only if we open ourselves to their influence; and if our attitude is negative to begin with, this is impossible. The data of life are often ambiguous, and we may interpret them in very different ways. In some instances, the only way to realize the higher possibilities may be to respond with hope and trust. It is up to the reader to consider how far such faith is justified, and to what extent it should be hedged about by qualifications and exceptions.

The Question of Mysticism

Among the "higher possibilities" are those envisaged by the mystic. His conviction that it is possible "to awaken the unborn body of life within the body of this half-death we call life" is expressed in a poem by Edmond Holmes:

> Hemmed in by petty thoughts and petty things,
>   Intent on toys and trifles all my years,
> Pleased by life's gaudes, pained by its pricks and stings,
>   Swayed by ignoble hopes, ignoble fears;
> Threading life's tangled maze without life's clue,
>   Busy with means, yet heedless of their ends,
> Lost to all sense of what is real and true,
>   Blind to the goal to which all Nature tends:—
> Such is my surface self: but deep beneath,

A mighty actor on a world-wide stage,
Crowned with all knowledge, lord of life and death,
　　Sure of my aim, sure of my heritage,—
I—the true self—live on, in self's despite,
　that "life profound" whose darkness is God's light.

This contrast between the "surface self" and the "true self," and the belief based upon trance-like experiences that the true self is "at one with the One," are the essence of mysticism.

Some mysticism may be called "negative" because its object appears undifferentiated. Carried to its limits, it produces the contention of Oriental pantheism that "the distinction of objects known, knowers, acts of knowledge, etc. . . . . is fictitiously created by Nescience."[3] Another kind of negativism occurs in the dualistic mysticism that denies all likeness between nature and God and turns away from natural objects to seek identification with a completely transcendent Deity. Its votaries teach the unreality of material things; they often regard the flesh and spirit as at war; they view the ordinary world as a prison or scene of exile; and they reject science as a basis of belief.

There is also a *positive* mysticism, which can be illustrated by Wordsworth's famous *Lines* composed near Tintern Abbey, in which he speaks of an intense and joyous mood in which "we . . . become a living soul" and "see into the life of things." In this passage describing a trance-like state, the unitary "life" does not negate "things" in the plural. There is no turning away from the copious variety of nature. Because of the mystic vision, nature is more precious rather than less. Consequently, Wordsworth is

A lover of the meadows and the woods,
And mountains, and of all that we behold
From this green earth. . . .

Whereas negative mysticism sacrifices community to other-worldliness or featureless unity, positive mysticism retains the love of individualities which is the distinguishing mark of community. It realizes that the unity of love is higher than the unity of inclusion. Love enjoys the difference between "you" and "me" and hence is the natural bond of community. A positive mystic such as Blake spontaneously employed the language of the intimate community:

I am not a God afar off, I am a brother and friend;
Within your bosoms I reside, and you reside in me.[4]

[3] Sankara Acharya, in F. Max Müller (ed.), *Sacred Book of the East* (London: Oxford University Press, 1890), vol. 34, pp. 14–15.

[4] William Blake, *Poetry and Prose of William Blake* (New York: Random House, 1927), p. 552.

The unity is very close, but it is a unity of distinguishable members, each retaining its peculiar identity:

> He who would see the Divinity must see him in his Children . . .
> . . . he who wishes to see a Vision, a perfect Whole,
> Must see it in its Minute Particulars.[5]

Likewise in the case of another positive mystic, Walt Whitman, the strong feeling of oneness is combined with an equally insistent "thought of identity—yours for you, whoever you are, as mine for me."[6] The *each* is not submerged in the *all*. James does not emphasize the difference between positive and negative mysticism, but he does distinguish between "ascetic" mysticism and the "naturalistic" mysticism of Whitman and others.

It may be that the difference between positive and negative mysticism is not as radical as it appears. Perhaps the appearance of a sharp contrast is the result of the ineffable character of the mystical vision. As James suggests, many mystics speak in negative terms because they feel that all positive characterizations are inadequate.

The mystics disagree most sharply when they try to give a metaphysical interpretation of their experiences. Then the doctrinal differences among Christians, Buddhists, Hindus, Mohammedans, and contrasting Christian denominations become explicit. Each mystic tends to interpret his mystical experience in the light of his cultural and religious background. As James remarked, mysticism "is capable of forming matrimonial alliances with material furnished by the most diverse philosophies and theologies, provided only they can find a place in their framework for its peculiar emotional mood." This is natural enough, but it should put us on guard against identifying the "truth" of myticism with any particular creed or philosophy.

In a passage too long to quote, James suggests an interesting hypothesis: that the conscious person is not only continuous with a wider, subconscious self but that this wider self is continuous with a mystic unseen world. Thus the deep subconscious abyss of the human psyche is a well connecting the conscious self with spiritual reality. The religious mind, like that of the artist, draws upon this deep well; but in mystical experiences, it draws upon an even wider and deeper well, a kind of cosmic pool of spirituality. This is a highly speculative hypothesis, and I do not know how to prove or disprove it.

Religion and Poetry

George Santayana was a student and later a colleague of William James. Al-

---

[5] *Poetry and Prose of William Blake*, Blake, p. 737.

[6] *Democratic Vistas*, in *Leaves of Grass and Selected Prose* (New York: Modern Library, 1950), p. 552.

though they were good friends, they differed fundamentally in their thinking. When Santayana's *Interpretations of Poetry and Religion* was published in 1900, James greeted it with both admiration and antipathy. He expressed his ambivalent attitude in a letter to his friend George Herbert Palmer:

> The great event in my life recently has been the reading of Santayana's book. Although I absolutely reject the Platonism of it, I have literally squealed with delight at the imperturbable perfection with which the position is laid down on page after page. . . . Nevertheless, how fantastic a philosophy!—as if the "world of values" *were* independent of existence. It is only as *being*, that one thing is better than another. The idea of darkness is as good as that of light, as ideas. There is more value in light's *being*.[7]

Santayana's thesis, that religion is poetry believed in, seemed to James the very "perfection of rottenness." He was too insistent that "the ideal and the real are dynamically continuous" to look with favor on the denial that religion has any literal validity.

Santayana recognized that James "would let fall golden words, fresh from the heart, full of the knowledge of good and evil,"[8] but he felt that James succumbed too easily to superstition. Attacking both Pascal's Wager and James' "Will to Believe," he declared:

> To be boosted by an illusion is not to live better than to live in harmony with the truth; it is not nearly so safe, not nearly so sweet, and not nearly so fruitful. These refusals to part with a decayed illusion are really an infection to the mind. Believe, certainly; we cannot help believing; but believe rationally, holding what seems certain for certain, what seems probable for probable, and what seems false for false.[9]

When no good evidence or argument for the truth of a proposition is available, belief should be withheld.

The mysticism delineated by James appeared to Santayana to be nothing but illusion:

> Who would wish to be a mystic? James himself, who by nature was a spirited rather than a spiritual man, had no liking for sanctimonious transcendentalists, visionaries, or ascetics; he hated minds that run thin. But he hastened to correct

---

[7] Letter of April 2, 1900, quoted by Ralph Barton Perry, *The Thought and Character of William James* (Cambridge, Mass.: Harvard University Press, 1948), p. 251.

[8] George Santayana, *Character and Opinion in the United States* (New York: Doubleday & Company, 1956), p. 59.

[9] *Ibid.*, pp. 53–54.

this manly impulse, lest it should be unjust, and forced himself to overcome his repugnance.[10]

Santayana's objection to mysticism is that it does "run thin." This characterization of mysticism, as an over-simplification and impoverishment of life, applies more to negative than to positive mysticism.

Although critical of pragmatic and mystical faith, Santayana was a strong defender of religion. It must not impose itself as a literal rendering of what exists, as it all too often attempts to do, but it should be cherished for what it really is—a poetic enrichment and transformation of the moral life. Santayana strongly opposes the tendency of some modern rationalists to "demythologize" and scale down religion to abstract conceptions. Shorn of its poetry, "religion" is no longer religion—it is turned into some sort of abstract metaphysics or moral homily. The better expedient is to treasure it as "an imaginative echo of things natural and moral." As a clue to valuational insights, it cannot be dismissed as nonsense.

Santayana's interpretation differs from Bertrand Russell's essay, "The Free Man's Worship," in the next chapter. Russell is convinced that the universe surrounding us is nothing but an immense spiritual emptiness indifferent to our values. Santayana may be no less disillusioned but he writes in a different mood:

> Why should we not look on the universe with piety? Is it not our substance? Are we made of other clay? All our possibilities lie from eternity hidden in its bosom. It is the dispenser of all our joys. We may address it without superstitious terrors; it is not wicked. It follows its own habits abstractedly; it can be trusted to be true to its word. Society is not impossible between it and us, and since it is the source of all our energies, the home of all our happiness, shall we not cling to it and praise it, seeing that it vegetates so grandly and so sadly, and that it is not for us to blame it for what, doubtless, it never knew that it did? Where there is such infinite and laborious potency there is room for every hope.[11]

Santayana's words, it might be said, have a more up-to-date ring than Russell's essay. Science has now disclosed that the chemical building-blocks of life are widely dispersed in the universe, and life may exist at many stations in the cosmos. No human being can know what exists in the infinitude of time and space, but "there is room for every hope."

In this chapter and the next the reader will find a fascinating array of religious views—mystical and nonmystical, sceptical and orthodox, optimistic and pessimistic, rationalistic and poetic. These differences should provide abundant material for debate and discussion.

[10] *Ibid.*, p. 52.

[11] George Santayana, *Reason in Religion* (New York: Charles Scribner's Sons, 1928). First published in 1905.

11

God
and
Man

SAINT ANSELM (1033?–1109)

Although Italian by birth, Saint Anselm ended his career as Archbishop of Canterbury. He is famous not only for his philosophical works but also for his interpretation of Christian theology. As Abbot of a monastery in Normandy and as Archbishop in England, he was a zealous defender of the Church against the expansion of secular power.

Proslogium

. . . I do not seek to understand that I may believe, but I believe in order to understand. For this also I believe,— that unless I believed, I should not understand.

And so, Lord, do thou, who dost give understanding to faith, give me,

Translated by Sidney Norton Deane, Open Court Publishing Co., 1903. Reprinted by permission.

so far as thou knowest it to be profitable, to understand that thou art as we believe; and that thou art that which we believe. And, indeed, we believe that thou art a being than which nothing greater can be conceived. Or is there no such nature, since the fool hath said in his heart, there is no God? (Psalms xiv. 1). But, at any rate, this very fool, when he hears of this being of which I speak—a being than which nothing greater can be conceived—understands what he hears, and what he understands is in his understanding; although he does not understand it to exist.

For, it is one thing for an object to be in the understanding, and another to understand that the object exists. When a painter first conceives of what he will afterwards perform, he has it in his understanding, but he does not yet understand it to be, because he has not yet performed it. But after he has made the painting, he both has it in his understanding, and he understands that it exists, because he has made it.

Hence, even the fool is convinced that something exists in the understanding, at least, than which nothing greater can be conceived. For, when he hears of this, he understands it. And whatever is understood, exists in the understanding. And assuredly that, than which nothing greater can be conceived, cannot exist in the understanding alone. For, suppose it exists in the understanding alone: then it can be conceived to exist in reality; which is greater.

Therefore, if that, than which nothing greater can be conceived, exists in the understanding alone, the very being, than which nothing greater can be conceived, is one, than which a greater can be conceived. But obviously this is impossible. Hence, there is no doubt that there exists a being, than which nothing greater can be conceived, and

it exists both in the understanding and in reality.

And it assuredly exists so truly, that it cannot be conceived not to exist. For, it is possible to conceive of a being which cannot be conceived not to exist; and this is greater than one which can be conceived not to exist. Hence, if that, than which nothing greater can be conceived, can be conceived not to exist, it is not that, than which nothing greater can be conceived. But this is an irreconcilable contradiction. There is, then, so truly a being than which nothing greater can be conceived to exist, that it cannot even be conceived not to exist; and this being thou art, O Lord, our God.

So truly, therefore, dost thou exist, O Lord, my God, that thou canst not be conceived not to exist; and rightly. For, if a mind could conceive of a being better than thee, the creature would rise above the Creator; and this is most absurd. And, indeed, whatever else there is, except thee alone, can be conceived not to exist. To thee alone, therefore, it belongs to exist more truly than all other beings, and hence in a higher degree than all others. For, whatever else exists does not exist so truly, and hence in a less degree it belongs to it to exist. Why, then, has the fool said in his heart, there is no God, since it is so evident, to a rational mind, that thou dost exist in the highest degree of all? Why, except that he is dull and a fool?

SAINT THOMAS AQUINAS (1225?–1274)

Thomas, the son of Count Landolfo, of Aquino, was born at the ancestral castle near Naples. At the age of five, he was sent to the Benedictine monastery of Monte Cassino to be educated. When ten years old, he entered the University of Naples, where he remained for six years. He then joined the Dominican Order, very much against the will of his parents and so much to the disgust of his brothers that they kidnaped and imprisoned him in the family stronghold for two years. At last he escaped and continued his education at Paris and Cologne. In 1256, he became a Master of Theology, and thereafter taught at the University of Paris and elsewhere. During his career, he succeeded in constructing the greatest of all systems of Catholic philosophy. He died at the age of forty-nine. Three years after his death he was censured by the Bishop of Paris for his alleged heterodoxy, but in 1323 he was canonized by Pope John XXII.

Summa Theologica
and
Summa Contra Gentiles

1. [The Argument From Change]

[*In his first argument, St. Thomas argues from the fact of change to an Unmoved Mover; in his second argument, from the fact of causation to an Uncaused Cause; in his third argument, from the fact of non-necessary being to a Necessary Being. In each case the reasoning is an inference from something dependent (change, causation, or*

From St. Thomas Aquinas, *Philosophical Texts,* trans. by Thomas Gilby, Oxford University Press, London, New York, Toronto, 1951. Reprinted by permission.

contingent being) to something independent and self-sufficient—namely, God. Motion, movement, change, as employed in the first argument, are synonymous. Note that the argument is not restricted to change of place (motion as we ordinarily use the term), but refers to all change whatsoever.]

The first and most open way is presented by change or motion. It is evident to our senses and certain that in the world some things are in motion.

Whatever is in motion is set in motion by another. For nothing is in motion unless it be potential to that to which it is in motion; whereas a thing sets in motion inasmuch as it is actual, because to set in motion is naught else than to bring a thing from potentiality to actuality, and from potentiality a subject cannot be brought except by a being that is actual; actually hot makes potentially hot become actually hot, as when fire changes and alters wood. Now for the same thing to be simultaneously and identically actual and potential is not possible, though it is possible under different respects; what is actually hot cannot simultaneously be potentially hot, though it may be potentially cold. It is impossible, therefore, for a thing both to exert and to suffer motion in the same respect and according to the same motion.

If that which sets in motion is itself in motion then it also must be set in motion by another, and that in its turn by another again. But here we cannot proceed to infinity, otherwise there would be no first mover, and consequently no other mover, seeing that subsequent movers do not initiate motion unless they be moved by a former mover, as stick by hand.

Therefore we are bound to arrive at the first mover set in motion by no other, and this everyone understands to be God.

Summa Theologica, Ia. ii. 3

Having indicated that the attempt to prove God's existence is not hopeless from the outset, we proceed now to fix on the arguments of philosophers and theologians alike, beginning with Aristotle who sets off from the concept of change. His argument takes two directions, of which the first is as follows.

Everything in a process of change is set in motion by another. Our senses tell us that things are in motion, the sun for instance. Therefore they are set in motion by another. Now this setter-in-motion is either itself in motion or it is not. If not, then we have our conclusion, namely the necessity of inferring a motionless mover which we term God. But if it is itself in motion then it must be set in motion by another. Either we have an infinite series or we arrive at a changeless mover. But we cannot go back infinitely. Therefore we must infer a first changeless mover.

There are two propositions to be proved; first, that everything in motion is set in motion by another; second, that an infinite series of things setting and set in motion is impossible.

Summa Contra Gentiles, I, 13

2. [The Argument from Efficient Causality]

The second approach starts from the nature of efficient causality. Among phenomena we discover an order of efficient causes. But we never come across, nor ever shall, anything that is an efficient cause of itself; such a thing would be prior to itself, which is impossible. It is also impossible to go on to infinity with efficient causes, for in an ordered series the first is the cause of the intermediate and the intermediate is the cause of the last. Whether or not the intermediate causes be one or many is irrelevant. Take away the cause and the effect also goes. Therefore if there were not a first among efficient causes—which would be the case in an infinite series—there would be no intermediate causes nor an ultimate effect. This plainly is not the case. A first cause, generally termed God, must therefore be inferred.

Summa Theologica, Ia. ii. 3

An infinite series of efficient causes in essential subordination is impossible. Causes essentially required for the production of a determinate effect cannot consequently be infinitely multiplied, as if a block could be shifted by a crowbar, which in turn is levered by a hand, and so on to infinity.

But an infinite series of causes in accidental subordination is not reputed impossible, so long as all the causes thus multiplied are grouped as one cause and their multiplication is incidental to the causality at work. For instance a blacksmith may work with many hammers because one after another breaks in his hand, but that one particular hammer is used after another particular one ·is incidental. Similarly that in begetting a child a man was himself begotten by another man; for he is father as man, not as son. In a genealogy of efficient causes all men have the same status of particular generator. Hence, for such a line to stretch back to infinity is not unthinkable.

Summa Theologica, Ia. xlvi. 2, ad 7

3. [The Argument from Contingent Being]

We observe in our environment how things are born and die away; they may or may not exist; to be or not to be—

they are open to either alternative. All things cannot be so contingent, for what is able not to be may be reckoned as once a non-being, and were everything like that once there would have been nothing at all. Now were this true, nothing would ever have begun, for what is does not begin to be except because of something which is, and so there would be nothing even now. This is clearly hollow. Therefore all things cannot be might-not-have-beens; among them must be being whose existence is necessary.

Summa Theologica, Ia. ii. 3

Everything that is a possible-to-be has a cause, since its essence as such is equally uncommitted to the alternatives of existing and not existing. If it be credited with existence, then this must be from some cause. Causality, however, is not an infinite process. Therefore a necessary being is the conclusion. The principle of its necessity is either from outside or not. If not, then the being is inwardly necessary. If necessity comes from without, we must still propose a first being necessary of itself, since we cannot have an endless series of derivatively necessary beings.

Summa Contra Gentiles, I, 15

4. [The Argument from Degrees of Excellence]

The fourth argument is taken from the degrees of reality we discover in things. Some are truer and better and nobler than others, so also with other perfections. But more or less are attributed to different things in proportion as they variously approach something which is the maximum.

Hence, there is something truest, and best, and noblest, and in consequence the superlative being, for the greatest truths are the greatest beings. Now the maximum in any order is the cause of all the other realities of that order. Therefore there is a real cause of being and goodness and all perfections whatsoever in everything; and this we term God.

Summa Theologica, Ia. ii. 3

The argument can be gathered from words let fall by Aristotle in the *Metaphysics*. He says that the truest things are also the most real; and again, that there is a superlative truth. One piece of architecture is more sham than another, one more genuine; throughout a comparison is implied with what is true without qualification and most of all. We can go farther and conclude that there is something most real, and this we call God.

Summa Contra Gentiles, I, 13

5. [The Argument from Purpose or Design]

Contrary and discordant elements . . . cannot always, or nearly always, work harmoniously together unless they be directed by something providing each and all with their tendencies to a definite end. Now in the universe we see things of diverse natures conspiring together in one scheme, not rarely or haphazardly, but approximately always or for the most part. There must be

something, therefore, whose providence directs the universe.

Summa Contra Gentiles, I, 13

We observe that things without consciousness, such as physical bodies, operate with a purpose, as appears from their co-operating invariably, or almost so, in the same way in order to obtain the best result. Clearly then they reach this end by intention and not by chance. Things lacking knowledge move towards an end only when directed by someone who knows and understands, as an arrow by an archer. There is consequently an intelligent being who directs all natural things to their ends; and this being we call God.

Summa Theologica, Ia. ii. 3

When diverse things are co-ordinated the scheme depends on their directed unification, as the order of battle of a whole army hangs on the plan of the commander-in-chief. The arrangement of diverse things cannot be dictated by their own private and divergent natures; of themselves they are diverse and exhibit no tendency to make a pattern. It follows that the order of many among themselves is either a matter of chance or it must be resolved into one first planner who has a purpose in mind. What comes about always, or in the great majority of cases, is not the result of accident. Therefore the whole of this world has but one planner or governor.

Summa Contra Gentiles, I, 42

DAVID HUME

(For biographical note see pages 278–279.)

Dialogues Concerning Natural Religion

1. [The Argument for a First Cause]

The argument, replied Demea, which I would insist on is the common one. Whatever exists must have a cause or reason of its existence, it being absolutely impossible for anything to produce itself or be the cause of its own existence. In mounting up, therefore, from effects to causes, we must either go on in tracing an infinite succession, without any ultimate cause at all, or must at last have recourse to some ultimate cause that is *necessarily* existent. Now that the first supposition is absurd may be thus proved. In the infinite chain or succession of causes and effects, each single effect is determined to exist by the power and efficacy of that cause which immediately preceded; but the whole eternal chain or succession, taken together, is not deter-

Published in London, 1779. Critical edition by Norman Kemp Smith, Oxford University Press, 1935.

mined or caused by anything, and yet it is evident that it requires a cause or reason, as much as any particular object which begins to exist in time. The question is still reasonable why this particular succession of causes existed from eternity, and not any other succession or no succession at all. If there be no necessarily existent being, any supposition which can be formed is equally possible; nor is there any more absurdity in *nothing's* having existed from eternity than there is in that succession of causes which constitutes the universe. What was it, then, which determined *something* to exist rather than *nothing,* and bestowed being on a particular possibility, exclusive of the rest? *External causes,* there are supposed to be none. *Chance* is a word without a meaning. Was it *nothing?* But that can never produce anything. We must, therefore, have recourse to a necessarily existent Being who carries the *reason* of his existence in himself, and who cannot be supposed not to exist, without an express contradiction. There is, consequently, such a Being—that is, there is a Deity.

I shall not leave it to Philo, said Cleanthes, though I know that the starting objections is his chief delight, to point out the weakness of this metaphysical reasoning. It seems to me so obviously ill-grounded, and at the same time of so little consequence to the cause of true piety and religion, that I shall myself venture to show the fallacy of it.

I shall begin with observing that there is an evident absurdity in pretending to demonstrate a matter of fact, or to prove it by any arguments *a priori*. Nothing is demonstrable unless the contrary implies a contradiction. Nothing that is distinctly conceivable implies a contradiction. Whatever we conceive as existent, we can also conceive as non-existent. There is no being, therefore, whose non-existence implies a contradiction. Consequently there is no being whose existence is demonstrable. I propose this argument as entirely decisive, and am willing to rest the whole controversy upon it.

It is pretended that the Deity is a necessarily existent being; and this necessity of his existence is attempted to be explained by asserting that, if we knew his whole essence or nature, we should perceive it to be as impossible for him not to exist, as for twice two not to be four. But it is evident that this can never happen, while our faculties remain the same as at present. It will still be possible for us, at any time, to conceive the non-existence of what we formerly conceived to exist; nor can the mind ever lie under a necessity of sup-

posing any object to remain always in being; in the same manner as we lie under a necessity of always conceiving twice two to be four. The words, therefore, *necessary existence* have no meaning or, which is the same thing, none that is consistent.

But further, why may not the material universe be the necessarily existent Being, according to this pretended explication of necessity? We dare not affirm that we know all the qualities of matter; and, for aught we can determine, it may contain some qualities which, were they known, would make its non-existence appear as great a contradiction as that twice two is five. I find only one argument employed to prove that the material world is not the necessarily existent Being; and this argument is derived from the contingency both of the matter and the form of the world. "Any particle of matter," it is said, "may be *conceived* to be annihilated, and any form may be *conceived* to be altered. Such an annihilation or alteration, therefore, is not impossible."[1] But it seems a great partiality not to perceive that the same argument extends equally to the Deity, so far as we have any conception of him, and that the mind can at least imagine him to be non-existent or his attributes to be altered. It must be some unknown, inconceivable qualities which can make his non-existence appear impossible or his attributes unalterable; and no reason can be assigned why these qualities may not belong to matter. As they are altogether unknown

[1] Dr. Clarke.

and inconceivable, they can never be proved incompatible with it.

Add to this that in tracing an eternal succession of objects it seems absurd to inquire for a general cause or first author. How can anything that exists from eternity have a cause, since that relation implies a priority in time and a beginning of existence?

In such a chain, too, or succession of objects, each part is caused by that which preceded it, and causes that which succeeds it. Where then is the difficulty? But the *whole,* you say, wants a cause. I answer that the uniting of these parts into a whole, like the uniting of several distinct countries into one kingdom, or several distinct members into one body, is performed merely by an arbitrary act of the mind, and has no influence on the nature of things. Did I show you the particular causes of each individual in a collection of twenty particles of matter, I should think it very unreasonable should you afterwards ask me what was the cause of the whole twenty. This is sufficiently explained in explaining the cause of the parts.

Though the reasonings which you have urged, Cleanthes, may well excuse me, said Philo, from starting any further difficulties, yet I cannot forbear insisting still upon another topic. It is observed by arithmeticians that the products of 9 compose always either 9 or some lesser product of 9 if you add together all the characters of which any of the former products is composed. Thus, of 18, 27, 36, which are products of 9, you make 9 by adding 1 to 8, 2 to 7, 3 to 6. Thus 369 is a product also of 9; and if you add 3, 6, and 9, you make

18, a lesser product of 9. To a superficial observer so wonderful a regularity may be admired as the effect either of chance or design; but a skilful algebraist immediately concludes it to be the work of necessity, and demonstrates that it must for ever result from the nature of these numbers. Is it not probable, I ask, that the whole economy of the universe is conducted by a like necessity, though no human algebra can furnish a key which solves the difficulty? And instead of admiring the order of natural beings, may it not happen that, could we penetrate into the intimate nature of bodies, we should clearly see why it was absolutely impossible they could ever admit of any other disposition? So dangerous is it to introduce this idea of necessity into the present question! and so naturally does it afford an inference directly opposite to the religious hypothesis!

2. [The Argument from Design]

Not to lose any time in circumlocutions, said Cleanthes, . . . I shall briefly explain how I conceive this matter. Look round the world, contemplate the whole and every part of it: you will find it to be nothing but one great machine, subdivided into an infinite number of lesser machines, which again admit of subdivisions to a degree beyond what human senses and faculties can trace and explain. All these various machines, and even their most minute parts, are adjusted to each other with an accuracy which ravishes into admiration all men who have ever contemplated them. The curious adapting of means to ends, throughout all nature, resembles exactly, though it much exceeds, the productions of human contrivance—of human design, thought, wisdom, and intelligence. Since therefore the effects resemble each other, we are led to infer, by all the rules of analogy, that the causes also resemble, and that the Author of nature is somewhat similar to the mind of man, though possessed of much larger faculties, proportioned to the grandeur of the work which he has executed. By this argument *a posteriori,* and by this argument alone, do we prove at once the existence of a Deity and his similarity to human mind and intelligence.

I shall be so free, Cleanthes, said Demea, as to tell you that from the beginning I could not approve of your conclusion concerning the similarity of the Deity to men, still less can I approve of the mediums by which you endeavor to establish it. What! No demonstration of the Being of God! No abstract arguments! No proofs *a priori!* Are these which have hitherto been so much insisted on by philosophers all fallacy, all sophism? Can we reach no farther in this subject than experience and probability? I will not say that this is betraying the cause of a Deity; but surely, by this affected candor, you give advantages to atheists which they never could obtain by the mere dint of argument and reasoning.

What I chiefly scruple in this subject, said Philo, is not so much that all religious arguments are by Cleanthes reduced to experience, as that they appear not to be even the most certain and irrefragable of that inferior kind. That a stone will fall, that fire will burn, that the earth has solidity, we

have observed a thousand and a thousand times; and when any new instance of this nature is presented, we draw without hesitation the accustomed inference. The exact similarity of the cases gives us a perfect assurance of a similar event, and a stronger evidence is never desired nor sought after. But wherever you depart, in the least, from the similarity of the cases, you diminish proportionably the evidence, and may at last bring it to a very weak *analogy,* which is confessedly liable to error and uncertainty. After having experienced the circulation of the blood in human creatures, we make no doubt that it takes place in Titius and Maevius; but from its circulation in frogs and fishes it is only a presumption, though a strong one, from analogy that it takes place in men and other animals. The analogical reasoning is much weaker when we infer the circulation of the sap in vegetables from our experience that the blood circulates in animals; and those who hastily followed that imperfect analogy are found, by more accurate experiments, to have been mistaken.

If we see a house, Cleanthes, we conclude, with the greatest certainty, that it had an architect or builder because this is precisely that species of effect which we have experienced to proceed from that species of cause. But surely you will not affirm that the universe bears such a resemblance to a house that we can with the same certainty infer a similar cause, or that the analogy is here entire and perfect. The dissimilitude is so striking that the utmost you can here pretend to is a guess, a conjecture, a presumption concerning a similar cause; and how that pretension will be received in the world, I leave you to consider. . . .

That all inferences, Cleanthes, concerning fact are founded on experience, and that all experimental reasonings are founded on the supposition that similar causes prove similar effects, and similar effects similar causes, I shall not at present much dispute with you. But observe, I entreat you, with what extreme caution all just reasoners proceed in the transferring of experiments to similar cases. Unless the cases be exactly similar, they repose no perfect confidence in applying their past observation to any particular phenomenon. Every alteration of circumstances occasions a doubt concerning the event; and it requires new experiments to prove certainly that the new circumstances are of no moment or importance. A change in bulk, situation, arrangement, age, disposition of the air, or surrounding bodies—any of these particulars may be attended with the most unexpected consequences. And unless the objects be quite familiar to us, it is the highest temerity to expect with assurance, after any of these changes, an event similar to that which before fell under our observation. The slow and deliberate steps of philosophers here, if anywhere, are distinguished from the precipitate march of the vulgar, who, hurried on by the smallest similitude, are incapable of all discernment or consideration.

But can you think, Cleanthes, that your usual phlegm and philosophy have been preserved in so wide a step as you have taken when you compared to the universe houses, ships, furniture, machines, and, from their similarity in some circumstances, inferred a similarity in their causes? Thought, design, intelligence, such as we discover in men and other animals, is no more than one of the springs and principles of the universe, as well as heat or cold, attraction or repulsion, and a hundred others which fall under daily observation. It is an active cause by which some particular parts of nature, we find, produce alterations on other parts. But can a conclusion, with any propriety, be transferred from parts to the whole? Does not the great disproportion bar all comparison and inference? From observing the growth of a hair, can we learn anything concerning the generation of a man? Would the manner of a leaf's blowing, even though perfectly known, afford us any instruction concerning the vegetation of a tree?

But allowing that we were to take the *operations* of one part of nature upon another for the foundation of our judgment concerning the *origin* of the whole (which never can be admitted), yet why select so minute, so weak, so bounded a principle as the reason and design of animals is found to be upon this planet? What peculiar privilege has this little agitation of the brain which we call *thought,* that we must thus make it the model of the whole universe? Our partiality in our own favor does indeed present it on all occasions, but sound philosophy ought carefully to guard against so natural an illusion.

So far from admitting, continued Philo, that the operations of a part can afford us any just conclusion concerning the origin of the whole, I will not allow any one part to form a rule for another part if the latter be very remote from the former. Is there any reasonable ground to conclude that the inhabitants of other planets possess thought, intelligence, reason, or anything similar to these faculties in men? When nature has so extremely diversified her manner of operation in this small globe, can we imagine that she incessantly copies herself throughout so immense a universe? And if thought, as we may well suppose, be confined merely to this narrow corner and has even there so limited a sphere of action, with what propriety can we assign it for the original cause of all things? The narrow views of a peasant who makes his domestic economy the rule for the government of kingdoms is in comparison a pardonable sophism.

But were we ever so much assured that a thought and reason resembling the human were to be found throughout the whole universe, and were its activity elsewhere vastly greater and more commanding than it appears in this globe, yet I cannot see why the operations of a world constituted, arranged, adjusted, can with any propriety be extended to a world which is in its embryo state, and is advancing towards that constitution and arrangement. By observation we know somewhat of the economy, action, and nourishment of a finished animal, but we must transfer with great caution that observation to the growth of a fœtus in the womb, and still more to the formation of an animalcule in the loins of its male parent. Nature, we find, even from our limited experience, possesses an infinite number of springs and principles which incessantly discover themselves on every change of her

position and situation. And what new and unknown principles would actuate her in so new and unknown a situation as that of the formation of a universe, we cannot, without the utmost temerity, pretend to determine.

A very small part of this great system, during a very short time, is very imperfectly discovered to us; and do we thence pronounce decisively concerning the origin of the whole?

Admirable conclusion! Stone, wood, brick, iron, brass, have not, at this time, in this minute globe of earth, an order or arrangement without human art and contrivance; therefore, the universe could not originally attain its order and arrangement without something similar to human art. But is a part of nature a rule for another part very wide of the former? Is it a rule for the whole? Is a very small part a rule for the universe? Is nature in one situation a certain rule for nature in another situation vastly different from the former?

And can you blame me, Cleanthes, if I here imitate the prudent reserve of Simonides, who, according to the noted story, being asked by Hiero, *What God was?* desired a day to think of it, and then two days more; and after that manner continually prolonged the term, without ever bringing in his definition or description? Could you even blame me if I had answered, at first, *that I did not know,* and was sensible that this subject lay vastly beyond the reach of my faculties? You might cry out sceptic and rallier, as much as you pleased; but, having found in so many other subjects much more familiar the imperfections and even contradictions of human reason, I never should expect any success from its feeble conjectures in a subject so sublime and so remote from the sphere of our observation. When two *species* of objects have always been observed to be conjoined together, I can *infer,* by custom, the existence of one wherever I *see* the existence of the other; and this I call an argument from experience. But how this argument can have place where the objects, as in the present case, are single, individual, without parallel or specific resemblance, may be difficult to explain. And will any man tell me with a serious countenance that an orderly universe must arise from some thought and art like the human because we have experience of it? To ascertain this reasoning it were requisite that we had experience of the origin of worlds; and it is not sufficient, surely, that we have seen ships and cities arise from human art and contrivance. . . .

. . . I shall endeavor to show you, a little more distinctly, the inconveniences of that anthropomorphism which you have embraced, and shall prove that there is no ground to suppose a plan of the world to be formed in the Divine mind, consisting of distinct ideas, differently arranged, in the same manner as an architect forms in his head the plan of a house which he intends to execute.

It is not easy, I own, to see what is gained by this supposition, whether we judge of the matter by *reason* or by *experience.* We are still obliged to mount higher in order to find the cause of this cause which you had assigned as satisfactory and conclusive.

If *reason* (I mean abstract reason derived from inquiries *a priori*) be not alike mute with regard to all questions concerning cause and effect, this sentence at least it will venture to pronounce: that a mental world or universe of ideas requires a cause as much as does a material world or universe of objects, and, if similar in its arrangement, must require a similar cause. For what is there in this subject which should occasion a different conclusion or inference? In an abstract view, they are entirely alike; and no difficulty attends the one supposition which is not common to both of them.

Again, when we will needs force *experience* to pronounce some sentence, even on these subjects which lie beyond her sphere, neither can she perceive any material difference in this particular between these two kinds of worlds, but finds them to be governed by similar principles, and to depend upon an equal variety of causes in their operations. We have specimens in miniature of both of them. Our own mind resembles the one; a vegetable or animal body the other. Let experience, therefore, judge from these samples. Nothing seems more delicate, with regard to its causes, than thought; and as these causes never operate in two persons after the same manner, so we never find two persons who think exactly alike. Nor indeed does the same person think exactly alike at any two different periods of time. A difference of age, of the disposition of his body, of weather, of food, of company, of books, of passions—any of these particulars, or others more minute, are sufficient to alter the curious machinery of thought and communicate to it very different movements and operations. As far as we can judge, vegetables and animal bodies are not more delicate in their motions, nor depend upon a greater variety or more curious adjustment of springs and principles.

How, therefore, shall we satisfy ourselves concerning the cause of that Being whom you suppose the Author of nature, or, according to your system of anthropomorphism, the ideal world into which you trace the material? Have we not the same reason to trace that ideal world into another ideal world or new intelligent principle? But if we stop and go no farther, why go so far? why not stop at the material world? How can we satisfy ourselves without going on *in infinitum?* And, after all, what satisfaction is there in that infinite progression? Let us remember the story of the Indian philosopher and his elephant. It was never more applicable than to the present subject. If the material world rests upon a similar ideal world, this ideal world must rest upon some other, and so on without end. It were better, therefore, never to look beyond the present material world. By supposing it to contain the principle of its order within itself, we really assert it to be God; and the sooner we arrive at that Divine Being, so much the better. When you go one step beyond the mundane system, you only excite an inquisitive humor which it is impossible ever to satisfy.

To say that the different ideas which compose the reason of the Supreme Being fall into order of themselves and by their own nature is really to talk without any precise meaning. If it has a meaning, I would fain know why it is not as good sense to say that the parts of the material world fall into order of themselves and by their own nature. Can the one opinion be intelligible, while the other is not so?

We have, indeed, experience of ideas which fall into order of themselves and without any *known* cause. But, I am sure, we have a much larger experience of matter which does the same, as in all instances of generation and vegetation where the accurate analysis of the cause exceeds all human comprehension. We have also experience of particular systems of thought and of matter which have no order; of the first in madness, of the second in corruption. Why, then, should we think that order is more essential to one than the other? And if it requires a cause in both, what do we gain by your system, in tracing the universe of objects into a similar universe of ideas? The first step which we make leads us on for ever. It were, therefore, wise in us to limit all our inquiries to the present world, without looking farther. No satisfaction can ever be attained by these speculations which so far exceed the narrow bounds of human understanding. . . .

But to show you still more inconveniences, continued Philo, in your anthropomorphism, please to take a new survey of your principles. *Like effects prove like causes.* This is the experimental argument; and this, you say too, is the sole theological argument. . . .

Now, Cleanthes, said Philo, with an air of alacrity and triumph, mark the consequences. *First,* by this method of reasoning you renounce all claim to infinity in any of the attributes of the Deity. For, as the cause ought only to be proportioned to the effect, and the effect, so far as it falls under our cognizance, is not infinite, what pretensions have we, upon your suppositions, to ascribe that attribute to the Divine Being? You will still insist that, by removing him so much from all similarity to human creatures, we give in to the most arbitrary hypothesis, and at the same time weaken all proofs of his existence.

Secondly, you have no reason, on your theory, for ascribing perfection to the Deity, even in his finite capacity, or for supposing him free from every error, mistake, or incoherence, in his undertakings. There are many inexplicable difficulties in the works of nature which, if we allow a perfect author to be proved *a priori,* are easily solved, and become only seeming difficulties from the narrow capacity of man, who cannot trace infinite relations. But according to your method of reasoning, these difficulties become all real, and, perhaps, will be insisted on as new instances of likeness to human art and contrivance. At least, you must acknowledge that it is impossible for us to tell, from our limited views, whether this system contains any great faults or deserves any considerable praise if compared to other possible and even real systems. Could a peasant, if the *Æneid* were read to him, pronounce that poem to be absolutely faultless, or even assign to it its proper rank among the productions of human wit, he who had never seen any other production?

But were this world ever so perfect a production, it must still remain uncertain whether all the excellences of the work can justly be ascribed to the workman. If we survey a ship, what an exalted idea must we form of the in-

genuity of the carpenter who framed so complicated, useful, and beautiful a machine? And what surprise must we feel when we find him a stupid mechanic who imitated others, and copied an art which, through a long succession of ages, after multiplied trials, mistakes, corrections, deliberations, and controversies, had been gradually improving? Many worlds might have been botched and bungled, throughout an eternity, ere this system was struck out; much labor lost, many fruitless trials made, and a slow but continued improvement carried on during infinite ages in the art of world-making. In such subjects, who can determine where the truth, nay, who can conjecture where the probability lies, amidst a great number of hypotheses which may be proposed, and a still greater which may be imagined?

And what shadow of an argument, continued Philo, can you produce from your hypothesis to prove the unity of the Deity? A great number of men join in building a house or ship, in rearing a city, in framing a commonwealth; why may not several deities combine in contriving and framing a world? This is only so much greater similarity to human affairs. By sharing the work among several, we may so much further limit the attributes of each, and get rid of that extensive power and knowledge which must be supposed in one deity, and which, according to you, can only serve to weaken the proof of his existence. And if such foolish, such vicious creatures as man can yet often unite in framing and executing one plan, how much more those deities or demons, whom we may suppose several degrees more perfect! . . . .

It must be a slight fabric, indeed, said Demea, which can be erected on so tottering a foundation. While we are uncertain whether there is one deity or many, whether the deity or deities, to whom we owe our existence, be perfect or imperfect, subordinate or supreme, dead or alive, what trust or confidence can we repose in them? What devotion or worship address to them? What veneration or obedience pay them? To all the purposes of life the theory of religion becomes altogether useless; and even with regard to speculative consequences its uncertainty, according to you, must render it totally precarious and unsatisfactory.

To render it still more unsatisfactory, said Philo, there occurs to me another hypothesis which must acquire an air of probability from the method of reasoning so much insisted on by Cleanthes. That like effects arise from like causes—this principle he supposes the foundation of all religion. But there is another principle of the same kind, no less certain and derived from the same source of experience, that, where several known circumstances are observed to be similar, the unknown will also be found similar. Thus, if we see the limbs of a human body, we conclude that it is also attended with a human head, though hid from us. Thus, if we see, through a chink in a wall, a small part of the sun, we conclude that were the wall removed we should see the whole body. In short, this method of reasoning is so obvious and familiar that no scruple can ever be made with regard to its solidity.

Now, if we survey the universe, so far as it falls under our knowledge, it bears a great resemblance to an animal or organized body, and seems actuated with a like principle of life and motion. A continual circulation of matter in it produces no disorder; a continual waste in every part is incessantly repaired; the closest sympathy is perceived throughout the entire system; and each part or member, in performing its proper offices, operates both to its own preservation and to that of the whole. The world, therefore, I infer, is an animal; and the Deity is the *soul* of the world, actuating it, and actuated by it.

You have too much learning, Cleanthes, to be at all surprised at this opinion which, you know, was maintained by almost all the theists of antiquity, and chiefly prevails in their discourses and reasonings. For though, sometimes, the ancient philosophers reason from final causes, as if they thought the world the workmanship of God, yet it appears rather their favorite notion to consider it as his body whose organization renders it subservient to him. And it must be confessed that, as the universe resembles more a human body than it does the works of human art and contrivance, if our limited analogy could ever, with any propriety, be extended to the whole of nature, the inference seems juster in favor of the ancient than the modern theory.

There are many other advantages, too, in the former theory which recommended it to the ancient theologians. Nothing more repugnant to all their notions, because nothing more repugnant to common experience, than mind without body, a mere spiritual substance which fell not under their senses nor comprehension, and of which they had not observed one single instance throughout all nature. Mind and body they knew because they felt both; an order, arrangement, organization, or internal machinery, in both they likewise knew, after the same manner; and it could not but seem reasonable to transfer this experience to the universe, and to suppose the divine mind and body to be also coeval and to have, both of them, order and arrangement naturally inherent in them and inseparable from them.

Here, therefore, is a new species of anthropomorphism, Cleanthes, on which you may deliberate, and a theory which seems not liable to any considerable difficulties. You are too much superior, surely, to systematical prejudices to find any more difficulty in supposing an animal body to be, originally, of itself or from unknown causes, possessed of order and organization, than in supposing a similar order to belong to mind. But the vulgar prejudice that body and mind ought always to accompany each other ought not, one should think, to be entirely neglected; since it is founded on vulgar experience, the only guide which you profess to follow in all these theological inquiries. And if you assert that our limited experience is an unequal standard by which to judge of the unlimited extent of nature, you entirely abandon your own hypothesis, and must thenceforward adopt our mysticism, as you call it, and admit of the absolute incomprehensibility of the Divine Nature.

This theory, I own, replied Cleanthes, has never before occurred to me, though a pretty natural one; and I cannot readily, upon so short an examination and reflection, deliver any opinion with regard to it. You are very scrupulous, indeed, said Philo; were I to examine any system of yours, I should not have acted with half that caution and reserve, in stating objections and difficulties to it. However, if anything occur to you, you will oblige us by proposing it.

Why then, replied Cleanthes, it seems to me that, though the world does, in many circumstances, resemble an animal body, yet is the analogy also defective in many circumstances the most material: no organs of sense; no seat of thought or reason; no one precise origin of motion and action. In short, it seems to bear a stronger resemblance to a vegetable than to an animal, and your inference would be so far inconclusive in favor of the soul of the world. . . .

But here, continued Philo, in examining the ancient system of the soul of the world there strikes me, all on a sudden, a new idea which, if just, must go near to subvert all your reasoning, and destroy even your first inferences on which you repose such confidence. If the universe bears a greater likeness to animal bodies and to vegetables than to the works of human art, it is more probable that its cause resembles the cause of the former than that of the latter, and its origin ought rather to be ascribed to generation or vegetation than to reason or design. Your conclusion, even according to your own principles, is therefore lame and defective.

Pray open up this argument a little further, said Demea, for I do not rightly apprehend it in that concise manner in which you have expressed it.

Our friend Cleanthes, replied Philo, as you have heard, asserts that, since no question of fact can be proved otherwise than by experience, the existence of a Deity admits not of proof from any other medium. The world, says he, resembles the works of human contrivance; therefore its cause must also resemble that of the other. Here we may remark that the operation of one very small part of nature, to wit, man, upon another very small part, to wit, that inanimate matter lying within his reach, is the rule by which Cleanthes judges of the origin of the whole; and he measures objects, so widely disproportioned, by the same individual standard. But to waive all objections drawn from this topic, I affirm that there are other parts of the universe (besides the machines of human invention) which bear still a greater resemblance to the fabric of the world, and which, therefore, afford a better conjecture concerning the universal origin of this system. These parts are animals and vegetables. The world plainly resembles more an animal or a vegetable than it does a watch or a knitting-loom. Its cause, therefore, it is more probable, resembles the cause of the former. The cause of the former is generation or vegetation. The cause, therefore, of the world we may infer to be something similar or analogous to generation or vegetation.

. . . In this little corner of the world alone, there are four principles, *reason, instinct, generation, vegetation,* which are similar to each other, and are the causes of similar effects. What a number of other principles may we naturally suppose in the immense extent and variety of the universe could we travel from planet to planet, and from system to system, in order to examine each part of this mighty fabric? Any one of these four principles above mentioned (and a hundred others which lie open to our conjecture) may afford us a theory by which to judge of the origin of the world; and it is a palpable and egregious partiality to confine our view entirely to that principle by which our own minds operate. Were this principle more intelligible on that account, such a partiality might be somewhat excusable; but reason, in its internal fabric and structure, is really as little known to us as instinct or vegetation; and perhaps, even that vague, undeterminate word *nature* to which the vulgar refer everything is not at the bottom more inexplicable. The effects of these principles are all known to us from experience; but the principles themselves and their manner of operation are totally unknown; nor is it less intelligible or less conformable to experience to say that the world arose by vegetation, from a seed shed by another world, than to say that it arose from a divine reason or contrivance, according to the sense in which Cleanthes understands it.

But methinks, said Demea, if the world had a vegetative quality and could sow the seeds of new worlds into the infinite chaos, this power would be still an additional argument for design in its author. For whence could arise so wonderful a faculty but from design? Or how can order spring from anything which perceives not that order which it bestows?

You need only look around you, replied Philo, to satisfy yourself with regard to this question. A tree bestows order and organization on that tree which springs from it, without knowing the order; an animal in the same manner on its offspring; a bird on its nest; and instances of this kind are even more frequent in the world than those of order which arise from reason and contrivance. To say that all this order in animals and vegetables proceeds ultimately from design is begging the question; nor can that great point be ascertained otherwise than by proving, *a priori,* both that order is, from its nature, inseparably attached to thought and that it can never of itself or from original unknown principles belong to matter. . . .

I must confess, Philo, replied Cleanthes, that, of all men living, the task which you have undertaken, of raising doubts and objections, suits you best and seems, in a manner, natural and unavoidable to you. So great is your fertility of invention that I am not ashamed to acknowledge myself unable, on a sudden, to solve regularly such out-of-the-way difficulties as you incessantly start upon me, though I clearly see, in general, their fallacy and error. And I question not, but you are yourself, at present, in the same case, and have not the solution so ready as the objection, while you must be sensible that common sense and reason are entirely against you, and that such whimsies as you have delivered may puzzle but never can convince us.

What you ascribe to the fertility of my invention, replied Philo, is entirely owing to the nature of the subject. In subjects adapted to the narrow compass of human reason there is commonly but one determination which carries probability or conviction with it; and to a man of sound judgment all other suppositions but that one appear entirely absurd and chimerical. But in such questions as the present, a hundred contradictory views may preserve a kind of imperfect analogy, and invention has here full scope to exert itself. Without any great effort of thought, I believe that I could, in an instant, propose other systems of cosmogony which would have some faint appearance of truth, though it is a thousand, a million to one if either yours or any one of mine be the true system.

For instance, what if I should revive the old Epicurean hypothesis? This is commonly, and I believe justly, esteemed the most absurd system that has yet been proposed; yet I know not whether, with a few alterations, it might not be brought to bear a faint appearance of probability. Instead of supposing matter infinite, as Epicurus did, let us suppose it finite. A finite number of particles is only susceptible of finite transpositions; and it must happen, in an eternal duration, that every possible order or position must be tried an infinite number of times. This world, therefore, with all its events, even the most minute, has before been produced and destroyed, and will again be produced and destroyed, without any bounds and limitations. No one who has a conception of the powers of infinite, in comparison of finite, will ever scruple this determination.

But this supposes, said Demea, that matter can acquire motion without any voluntary agent or first mover.

And where is the difficulty, replied Philo, of that supposition? Every event, before experience, is equally difficult and incomprehensible; and every event, after experience, is equally easy and intelligible. Motion, in many instances, from gravity, from elasticity, from electricity, begins in matter, without any known voluntary agent; and to suppose . always, in these cases, an unknown voluntary agent is mere hypothesis and hypothesis attended with no advantages. The beginning of motion in matter itself is as conceivable *a priori* as its communication from mind and intelligence.

Besides, why may not motion have been propagated by impulse through all eternity, and the same stock of it, or nearly the same, be still upheld in the universe? As much as is lost by the composition of motion, as much is gained by its resolution. And whatever the causes are, the fact is certain that matter is and always has been in continual agitation, as far as human experience or tradition reaches. There is not probably, at present, in the whole universe, one particle of matter at absolute rest.

And this very consideration, too, continued Philo, which we have stumbled on in the course of the argument suggests a new hypothesis of cosmogony that is not absolutely absurd and improbable. Is there a system, an order, an economy of things, by which matter can preserve that perpetual agitation which seems essential to it, and yet maintain a constancy in the forms which it produces? There certainly is such an economy, for this is actually the case with the present world. The continual motion of matter, therefore, in less than infinite transpositions, must produce this economy or order, and, by its very nature, that order, when once established, supports itself for many ages if not to eternity. But wherever matter is so poised, arranged, and adjusted, as to continue in perpetual motion, and yet preserve a constancy in the forms, its situation must, of necessity, have all the same appearance of art and contrivance which we observe at present. All the parts of each form must have a relation to each other and to the whole; and the whole itself must have a relation to the other parts of the universe, to the element in which the form subsists, to the materials with which it repairs its waste and decay, and to every other form which is hostile or friendly. A defect in any of these particulars destroys the form, and the matter of which it is composed is again set loose, and is thrown into irregular motions and fermentations till it unite itself to some other regular form. If no such form be prepared to receive it, and if there be a great quantity of this corrupted matter in the universe, the universe itself is entirely disordered, whether it be the feeble embryo of a world in its first beginnings that is thus destroyed or the rotten carcass of one languishing in old age and infirmity. In either case, a chaos ensues till finite though innumerable revolutions produce, at last, some forms whose parts and organs are so adjusted as to support the forms amidst a continued succession of matter.

Suppose (for we shall endeavor to vary the expression) that matter were thrown into any position by a blind, unguided force; it is evident that this first position must, in all probability, be the most confused and most disorderly imaginable, without any resemblance to those works of human contrivance which, along with a symmetry of parts, discover an adjustment of means to ends and a tendency to self-preservation. If the actuating force cease after this operation, matter must remain for ever in disorder and continue an immense chaos, without any proportion or activity. But suppose that the actuating force, whatever it be, still continues in matter, this first position will immediately give place to a second which will likewise, in all probability, be as disorderly as the first, and so on through many successions of changes and revolutions. No particular order or position ever continues a moment unaltered. The original force, still remaining in activity, gives a perpetual restlessness to matter. Every possible situation is produced, and instantly destroyed. If a glimpse or dawn of order appears for a moment, it is instantly hurried away and confounded by that never-ceasing force which actuates every part of matter.

Thus the universe goes on for many ages in a continued succession of chaos and disorder. But is it not possible that it may settle at last, so as not to lose its motion and active force (for that we have supposed inherent in it), yet so as to preserve an uniformity of appearance, amidst the continual motion and fluctuation of its parts? This we find to be the case with the universe at present. Every individual is perpetually changing, and every part of every individual; and yet the whole remains, in appearance, the same. May we not hope for such a position or rather be assured of it

from the eternal revolutions of unguided matter; and may not this account for all the appearing wisdom and contrivance which is in the universe? Let us contemplate the subject a little, and we shall find that this adjustment, if attained by matter, of a seeming stability in the forms, with a real and perpetual revolution or motion of parts, affords a plausible, if not a true, solution of the difficulty.

It is in vain, therefore, to insist upon the uses of the parts in animals or vegetables, and their curious adjustment to each other. I would fain know how an animal could subsist unless its parts were so adjusted? Do we not find that it immediately perishes whenever this adjustment ceases, and that its matter, corrupting, tries some new form? It happens indeed that the parts of the world are so well adjusted that some regular form immediately lays claim to this corrupted matter; and if it were not so, could the world subsist? Must it not dissolve, as well as the animal, and pass through new positions and situations till in great but finite succession it fall, at last, into the present or some such order?

It is well, replied Cleanthes, you told us that this hypothesis was suggested on a sudden, in the course of the argument. Had you had leisure to examine it, you would soon have perceived the insuperable objections to which it is exposed. No form, you say, can subsist unless it possess those powers and organs requisite for its subsistence; some new order or economy must be tried, and so on, without intermission, till at last some order which can support and maintain itself is fallen upon. But according to this hypothesis, whence arise the many conveniences and advantages which men and all animals possess? Two eyes, two ears are not absolutely necessary for the subsistence of the species. Human race might have been propagated and preserved without horses, dogs, cows, sheep, and those innumerable fruits and products which serve to our satisfaction and enjoyment. If no camels had been created for the use of man in the sandy deserts of Africa and Arabia, would the world have been dissolved? If no loadstone had been framed to give that wonderful and useful direction to the needle, would human society and the human kind have been immediately extinguished? Though the maxims of nature be in general very frugal, yet instances of this kind are far from being rare; and any one of them is a sufficient proof of design—and of a benevolent design—which gave rise to the order and arrangement of the universe.

At least, you may safely infer, said Philo, that the foregoing hypothesis is so far incomplete and imperfect, which I shall not scruple to allow. But can we ever reasonably expect greater success in any attempts of this nature? Or can we ever hope to erect a system of cosmogony that will be liable to no exceptions, and will contain no circumstance repugnant to our limited and imperfect experience of the analogy of nature? Your theory itself cannot surely pretend to any such advantage, even though you have run into *anthropomorphism,* the better to preserve a conformity to common experience. Let us once more put it to trial. In all instances which we have ever seen, ideas are copied from real objects, and are ectypal, not archetypal, to express myself in learned terms. You reverse this order and give thought the precedence. In all instances which we have ever seen, thought has no influence upon matter except where that matter is so conjoined with it as to have an equal reciprocal influence upon it. No animal can move immediately anything but the members of its own body; and, indeed, the equality of action and reaction seems to be an universal law of nature; but your theory implies a contradiction to this experience. These instances, with many more which it were easy to collect (particularly the supposition of a mind or system of thought that is eternal or, in other words, an animal ingenerable and immortal)—these instances, I say, may teach all of us sobriety in condemning each other, and let us see that as no system of this kind ought ever to be received from a slight analogy, so neither ought any to be rejected on account of a small incongruity. For that is an inconvenience from which we can justly pronounce no one to be exempted.

All religious systems, it is confessed, are subject to great and insuperable difficulties. Each disputant triumphs in his turn, while he carries on an offensive war, and exposes the absurdities, barbarities, and pernicious tenets of his antagonist. But all of them, on the whole, prepare a complete triumph for the *sceptic,* who tells them that no system ought ever to be embraced with regard to such subjects: for this plain reason than no absurdity ought ever to be assented to with regard to any subject. A total suspense of judgment is here our only reasonable resource. And if every attack, as is commonly observed, and no defense among theologians is successful, how complete must be *his* victory who remains always, with all mankind, on the offensive, and has himself no fixed station or abiding city which he is ever, on any occasion, obliged to defend?

WILLIAM PEPPERELL MONTAGUE (1873–1953)

Montague was educated at Harvard during the golden years of its philosophy department. After receiving his Ph.D. degree in 1898, he taught briefly at Radcliffe, Harvard, and the University of California, and from 1903 until his retirement in 1947, at Barnard College and Columbia University. He also lectured at various other American universities, as well as in Japan, Czechoslovakia, and Italy. The reader can glean something of the daring of his philosophical vision and the charm of his personality by reading his "Confessions of an Animistic Materialist" in *The Ways of Things*.

The Problem of Good and Evil

In our opening discussion we defined religion as the belief in a power greater than ourselves that makes for good. We defended this definition on the ground that it left religion free from the proven falsities, ethical and physical, embodied in traditional creeds, while at the same time it avoided the emptiness and platitude of those schools of ultra-modernism which cling to the word "religion," but use it to mean only the recognition of some sort of unity and mystery in the universe, plus a praiseworthy devotion to whatever is praiseworthy, as, for example, the perfecting of humanity. Taking religion as we took it, we see at once that it is neither certainly and obviously true nor certainly and obviously false, but possibly true, and, if true, tremendously exciting. The question of its truth or falsity is exciting and

From *Belief Unbound*. Copyright © 1931 by Yale University Press. Reprinted by permission.

momentous because it is a question, not of the validity of this or that theory as to the nature of the physical world or as to the origin and destiny of the human race, but because it is the question whether the things we care for most are at the mercy of the things we care for least. If God is not, then the existence of all that is beautiful and in any sense good, is but the accidental and ineffective by-product of blindly swirling atoms, or of the equally unpurposeful, though more conceptually complicated, mechanisms of present-day physics. A man may well believe that this dreadful thing is true. But only the fool will say in his heart that he is glad that it is true. For to wish there should be no God is to wish that the things which we love and strive to realize and make permanent, should be only temporary and doomed to frustration and destruction. If life and its fulfilments are good, why should one rejoice at the news that God is dead and that there is nothing in the whole world except our frail and perishable selves that is concerned with anything that matters? Not that such a prospect would diminish the duty to make the best of what we have while we have it. Goodness is not made less good by a lack of cosmic support for it. Morality is sanctionless, and an ideal can never derive its validity from what is external to itself and to the life whose fulfilment it is. Atheism leads not to badness but only to an incurable sadness and loneliness. For it is the nature of life everywhere to outgrow its present and its past, and, in the life of man, the spirit has outgrown the body on which it depends and seeks an expan-

sion which no finite fulfiment can satisfy. It is this yearning for the infinite and the sense of desolation attending the prospect of its frustration that constitutes the motive to seek religion and to make wistful and diligent inquiry as to the possibility of its truth. . . .

There are two great problems which, taken together, comprise the prolegomena to every possible theology or atheology. They are the Problem of Evil and the Problem of Good.

How can the amount of evil and purposelessness in the world be compatible with the existence of a God? And how can the amount of goodness and purposefulness in the world be compatible with nonexistence of a God?

1. *The Problem of Evil*

The first of these problems has already been touched upon, but its importance justifies us in considering it again. Of one thing we can be certain, since the existing world contains evil, God's alleged attributes of infinite power and perfect goodness can be reconciled only by altering the one or the other of those attributes. For surely it would seem that since God does not abolish evil it must be either because he can't or because he won't, which means that he is limited either in his power or in his goodness. The line more commonly adopted by theological apologetics is to preserve the infinite power of God at any cost and do what one can with the goodness. Since evil occurs, God must be willing that it should occur. Why? Well, perhaps evil is a mere negation or illusion; perhaps it is good in disguise, a necessary ingredient of divine satisfaction; or a desirable and natural punishment of human sin; or a lesson and opportunity for human good. Or God's ideal of goodness may be quite different from ours, etc. To each and all of these suggestions there are two answers, one theoretical, the other practical. In the theoretical retort we ask, if evil is only a negation or illusion or disguise, then why should we and all other creatures suffer the failure to realize this? The experience of what is alleged to be unreal evil becomes itself the real evil. As for the portion of the world's evil that serves as a wholesome punishment or wholesome lesson for anybody, it is but an infinitesimal fraction of the total of the world's misery. Finally, if God's purposes are other than what we call good, then his nature is other than what we mean by good, while to go further and assume, as some absolute idealists have assumed, that our sin and agony actually contribute to God's enjoyment, would be to make him not merely lacking in good, but a demon of evil. In short, the explanations do not explain. But if they did (and this is the practical retort that follows and clinches the theoretical), the case of the theologians would be still worse; for if evil is really nothing, it is nothing to avoid; while if it is some disguised or indirect form of good, it is a duty to abet it, not oppose it. If the Vessels of Wrath, like the Vessels of Grace, contribute to the divine happiness, why should we care which sort of Vessels our brothers and ourselves become? We should not only be *"willing* to be damned for the glory of God," we should strive for it. Surely

no such vicious nonsense as that perpetrated by these defenders of God's unlimited power would ever have blackened the history of religious apologetics had it not been for man's ignoble and masochistic craving to have at any price a monarch or master, no matter how evil in the light of his own conscience such a master might be.

If our analysis of the Problem of Evil is valid, there can exist no omnipotent God. Possibly an omnipotent It, conceivably an omnipotent Demon, but not an omnipotent Goodness.

2. *The Problem of Good*

The world that we know contains a quantity of good which, though limited, is still far in excess of what could be expected in a purely mechanistic system.

If the Universe were composed entirely of a vast number of elementary entities, particles of matter or electricity, or pulses of radiant energy, which preserved themselves and pushed and pulled one another about according to merely physical laws, we should expect that they would occasionally agglutinate into unified structures, which in turn, though far less frequently, might combine to form structures still more complex, and so on. But that any considerable number of these higher aggregates would come about by mere chance would itself be a chance almost infinitely small. Moreover, there would be a steady tendency for such aggregates, as soon as they were formed, to break down and dissipate the matter and energy that had been concentrated in them. This increase of leveling, scattering, and disorganization to which all differentiated, concentrated, and organized aggregates are subject in our world, and in any world in which there is random motion alone, or random motion supplemented by such reciprocal *ab extra* determinations as are formulated in the laws of physics, is named the Increase of Entropy. This principle is exemplified in many familiar ways. The intense and concentrated waves caused by the stone dropped in the pool spread out and become less intense as their extensity increases. The hot stove in the cool room dissipates its differentiated and concentrated heat until a uniform level of temperature is reached. Stars radiate their energy and their mass into space, heavy and complex atoms break down into their simpler and lighter atomic constituents. Even the electrons and protons themselves are supposed to amalgamate and by so doing dissipate into space as short pulses of energy the very stuff of which they were made. And living organisms, with their minds, their societies, and their cultures, grow old, degenerate, and die, which is not merely the way of all flesh, but the way of all things.

And yet within this world that is forever dying, there have been born or somehow come to be, protons and electrons, atoms of hydrogen and helium, and the whole series of increasingly complex chemical elements culminating in radium and uranium. And these atoms not only gather loosely into nebulae, but in the course of time combine tightly into molecules, which in turn combine into the various complicated crystals and colloids that our senses can perceive. And on the only planet we really know, certain of the compounds of carbon gain the power of building themselves up by assimilation, and so growing and reproducing. Life thus started "evolves," as we say, into higher and higher forms, such as fishes, reptiles, and birds, mammals, primates, men, and, among men, sages and heroes.

Now the serious atheist must take his world seriously and seriously ask: What is the chance that all this ascent is, in a universe of descent, the result of chance? And of course by chance, as here used, we mean not absence of any causality, but absence of any causality except that recognized in physics. Thus it would be "chance" if a bunch of little cards, each with a letter printed on it, when thrown up into the breeze, should fall so as to make a meaningful sentence like "See the cat." Each movement of each letter would be mechanically caused, but it would be a chance and a real chance, though a small one, that they would so fall. And if a sufficiently large bundle of letters were thrown into the air there would also be a chance that they would fall back so as to spell out the entire play of Hamlet. The chance of this happening would be real enough, but it would be so small that, if properly expressed as a fraction, $1/n$, the string of digits contained in the denominator would, I suspect, reach from here to one of the fixed stars. And as for the probability that the atoms composing the brain of the author of *Hamlet,* if left to the mercy of merely mechanistic breezes, would fall into the combinations which that brain embodied—well, that is a chance that is smaller still. Surely we need not pursue the game further. Let the atheist lay the wager and name the odds that he will demand of us. Given the number of corpuscles, waves, or what not, that compose the universe, he is to bet that with only the types of mechanistic causality (or, if you are modern and fussy about the word "cause" you can call them "functional correlations") that are recognized in physics, there would result, I will not say the cosmos that we actually have, but any cosmos with an equal quantity of significant structures and processes. He certainly will not bet with us on even terms, and I am afraid that the odds that he will feel bound to ask of us will be so heavy that they will make him sheepish, because it is, after all, the truth of his own theory on which he is betting.

But what is the alternative to all this? Nothing so very terrible; merely the hypothesis that the kind of causality that we know best, the kind that we find in the only part of matter that we can experience directly and from within, the causality, in short, that operates in our lives and minds, is not an alien accident but an essential ingredient of the world that spawns us. The alternative to mere mechanistic determination is not some unknown thing concocted *ad hoc* to help us out of a difficulty. Surely, mind is a *vera causa* if ever there was one, and we merely suggest that the kind of anabolic and anti-entropic factor of whose existence we are certain in ourselves, is present and operative in varying degree in all nature. If we are right, we escape the universe of perpetual miracle, on which the atheist sets his heart. The organized structures and currents of ascent and evolution, from the atoms themselves to the lives of men, cease to be outrageously improbable runs of luck and become the normal expression of something akin to us. Material nature makes altogether too many winning throws for us not to suspect that she is playing with dice that are loaded, loaded with life and mind and purpose. This is the solution that seems to me almost inevitable of the problem which, for want of a better name, I have called the Problem of Good.

And so we are confronted with a God, or something very like a God, that exists, not as an omnipotent monarch, a giver of laws and punishments, but as an ascending force, a nisus, a thrust toward concentration, organization, and life. This power appears to labor slowly and under difficulties. We can liken it to a yeast that, through the aeons, pervades the chaos of matter and slowly leavens it with spirit.

BERTRAND RUSSELL (1872–1970)

The second son of Viscount Amberly and grandson of Lord John Russell, a famous liberal Prime Minister, Bertrand Russell was born on May 18, 1872, in the lovely valley of the Wye (described in Wordsworth's *Tintern Abbey*). His mother died when he was two years old and his father when he was three, so the boy was brought up in the home of his grandfather. Until he went to Cambridge University, at the age of eighteen, he lived a solitary life, supervised by German and Swiss governesses and English tutors and seeing little of other children. But Cambridge opened to him "a new world of infinite delight." Here he found mathematics and philosophy extremely exciting and formed warm friendships with a number of brilliant young men, including the philosophers McTaggart, Moore, and Whitehead.

The next two decades were the most intellectually productive in his long career. During this period he wrote a series of important books, including *A Critical Exposition of the Philosophy of Leibniz* (1900), *The Principles of Mathematics* (1903), *Principia Mathematica* (with Whitehead, 1910–1913), and *Our Knowledge of the External World* (1914). These books, especially *Principia Mathematica* which was the result of twelve years of intense labor, firmly established Russell's reputation as one of the great figures in modern thought.

Always interested in politics, Russell was profoundly disturbed by the outbreak of World War I and was quite unsatisfied with the melodramatic pronouncements of the belligerent governments. His bold defense of conscientious objectors and his anti-war publications brought him fines and imprisonment, as well as loss of his position as Fellow at Trinity College, Cambridge. He emerged from the war a changed man, aware of great social perils and pathological evil in human nature that he had never suspected. Ever after, he devoted a large part of his time and energy to writing about human political, educational, and moral affairs.

In 1921, after seventeen years of married life, his first marriage was dissolved, and he then wed Dora Winifred Black, who bore him a daughter and son, and from whom he was later divorced. Upon the death of his elder brother in 1931, he succeeded to the family earldom; and in 1934 he remarried, thus making Helen Patricia Spence, a young and beautiful woman, the Countess Russell. In 1950 he received the Nobel prize for literature, the same honor that Bergson had been awarded. Despite his advanced age, he continued to live a busy and adventurous life, writing prolifically and espousing the cause of peace.

A Free Man's Worship

To Dr. Faustus in his study Mephistopheles told the history of the Creation, saying:

"The endless praises of the choirs of angels had begun to grow wearisome; for, after all, did he not deserve their praise? Had he not given them endless joy? Would it not be more amusing to obtain undeserved praise, to be worshipped by beings whom he tortured? He smiled inwardly, and resolved that the great drama should be performed.

"For countless ages the hot nebula whirled aimlessly through space. At length it began to take shape, the central mass threw off planets, the planets cooled, boiling seas and burning mountains heaved and tossed, from black masses of cloud hot sheets of rain deluged the barely solid crust. And now the first germ of life grew in the depths of the ocean, and developed rapidly in the fructifying warmth into vast forest trees, huge ferns springing from the damp mould, sea monsters breeding,

fighting, devouring and passing away. And from the monsters, as the play unfolded itself, Man was born, with the power of thought, the knowledge of good and evil, and the cruel thirst for worship. And Man saw that all is passing in this mad, monstrous world, that all is struggling to snatch, at any cost, a few brief moments of life before Death's inexorable decree. And Man said: 'There is a hidden purpose, could we but fathom it, and the purpose is good; for we must reverence something, and in the visible world there is nothing worthy of reverence.' And Man stood aside from the struggle, resolving that God intended harmony to come out of chaos by human efforts. And when he followed the instincts which God had transmitted to him from his ancestry of beasts of prey, he called it Sin, and asked God to forgive him. But he doubted whether he could be justly forgiven, until he invented a divine Plan by which God's wrath was to have been appeased. And seeing the present was bad, he made it yet worse, that thereby the future might be better. And he gave God thanks for the strength that enabled him to forgo even the joys that were possible. And God smiled; and when he saw that Man had become perfect in renunciation and worship, he

From Bertrand Russell, *Why I am not a Christian*. Copyright © 1957 by George Allen and Unwin Ltd. Reprinted by permission of Simon and Schuster Inc. and George Allen and Unwin Ltd. First published in *The Independent Review*, 1903, and reprinted in Bertrand Russell, *Mysticism and Logic*, George Allen and Unwin Ltd., 1917.

sent another sun through the sky, which crashed into Man's sun; and all returned again to nebula.

" 'Yes,' he murmured, 'it was a good play; I will have it performed again.' "

Such, in outline, but even more purposeless, more void of meaning, is the world which Science presents for our belief. Amid such a world, if anywhere, our ideals henceforward must find a home. That Man is the product of causes which had no prevision of the end they were achieving; that his origin, his growth, his hopes and fears, his loves and his beliefs, are but the outcome of accidental collocations of atoms; that no fire, no heroism, no intensity of thought and feeling, can preserve an individual life beyond the grave; that all the labours of the ages, all the devotion, all the inspiration, all the noonday brightness of human genius, are destined to extinction in the vast death of the solar system, and that the whole temple of Man's achievement must inevitably be buried beneath the débris of a universe in ruins—all these things, if not quite beyond dispute, are yet so nearly certain, that no philosophy which rejects them can hope to stand. Only within the scaffolding of these truths, only on the firm foundation of unyielding despair, can the soul's habitation henceforth be safely built.

How, in such an alien and inhuman world, can so powerless a creature as Man preserve his aspirations untarnished? A strange mystery it is that Nature, omnipotent but blind, in the revolutions of her secular hurryings through the abysses of space, has brought forth at last a child, subject still to her power, but gifted with sight, with knowledge of good and evil, with the capacity of judging all the works of his unthinking Mother. In spite of Death, the mark and seal of the parental control, Man is yet free, during his brief years, to examine, to criticise, to know, and in imagination to create. To him alone, in the world with which he is acquainted, this freedom belongs; and in this lies his superiority to the resistless forces that control his outward life.

The savage, like ourselves, feels the oppression of his impotence before the powers of Nature; but having in himself nothing that he respects more than Power, he is willing to prostrate himself before his gods, without inquiring whether they are worthy of his worship. Pathetic and very terrible is the long history of cruelty and torture, of degradation and human sacrifice, endured in the hope of placating the jealous gods: surely, the trembling believer thinks, when what is most precious has been freely given, their lust for blood must be appeased, and more will not be required. The religion of Moloch—as such creeds may be generically called—is in essence the cringing submission of the slave, who dare not, even in his heart, allow the thought that his master deserves no adulation. Since the independence of ideals is not yet acknowledged, Power may be freely worshipped, and receive an unlimited respect, despite its wantom infliction of pain.

But gradually, as morality grows bolder, the claim of the ideal world begins to be felt; and worship, if it is not to cease, must be given to gods of another kind than those created by the savage. Some, though they feel the demands of the ideal, will still consciously reject them, still urging that naked Power is worthy of worship. Such is the attitude inculcated in God's answer to Job out of the whirlwind: the divine power and knowledge are paraded, but of the divine goodness there is no hint. Such also is the attitude of those who, in our own day, base their morality upon the struggle for survival, maintaining that the survivors are necessarily the fittest. But others, not content with an answer so repugnant to the moral sense, will adopt the position which we have become accustomed to regard as specially religious, maintaining that, in some hidden manner, the world of fact is really harmonious with the world of ideals. Thus Man creates God, all-powerful and all-good, the mystic unity of what is and what should be.

But the world of fact, after all, is not good; and, in submitting our judgment to it, there is an element of slavishness from which our thoughts must be purged. For in all things it is well to exalt the dignity of Man, by freeing him as far as possible from the tyranny of nonhuman Power. When we have realised that Power is largely bad, that man, with his knowledge of good and evil, is but a helpless atom in a world which has no such knowledge, the choice is again presented to us: Shall we worship Force, or shall we worship Goodness? Shall our God exist and be evil, or shall he be recognised as the creation of our own conscience?

The answer to this question is very momentous, and affects profoundly our whole morality. The worship of Force, to which Carlyle and Nietzsche and the creed of Militarism have accustomed us, is the result of failure to maintain our own ideals against a hostile universe: it is itself a prostrate submission to evil, a sacrifice of our best to Moloch. If strength indeed is to be respected, let us respect rather the strength of those who refuse that false "recognition of facts" which fails to recognise that facts are often bad. Let us admit that, in the world we know, there are many things that would be better otherwise, and that the ideals to which we do and must adhere are not realised in the realm of matter. Let us preserve our respect for truth, for beauty, for the ideal of perfection which life does not permit us to attain, though none of these things meet with the approval of the unconscious universe. If Power is bad, as it seems to be, let us reject it from our hearts. In this lies Man's true freedom: in determination to worship only the God created by our own love of the good, to respect only the heaven which inspires the insight of our best moments. In action, in desire, we must submit perpetually to the tyranny of outside forces; but in thought, in aspiration, we are free, free from our fellow-men, free from the petty planet on which our bodies impotently crawl, free even, while we live, from the tyranny of death. Let us learn, then, that energy of faith which enables us to live constantly in the vision of the good; and let us descend, in action, into the world of fact, with that vision always before us.

When first the opposition of fact and ideal grows fully visible, a spirit of fiery revolt, of fierce hatred of the gods, seems necessary to the assertion of freedom. To defy with Promethean constancy a hostile universe, to keep its evil always in view, always actively hated, to refuse no pain that the malice of Power can invent, appears to be the duty of all who will not bow before the inevitable. But indignation is still a bondage, for it compels our thoughts to be occupied with an evil world; and in the fierceness of desire from which rebellion springs there is a kind of self-assertion which it is necessary for the wise to overcome. Indignation is a submission of our thoughts, but not of our desires; the Stoic freedom in which wisdom consists is found in the submission of our desires, but not of our thoughts. From the submission of our desires springs the virtue of resignation; from the freedom of our thoughts springs the whole world of art and philosophy, and the vision of beauty by which, at last, we half reconquer the reluctant world. But the vision of beauty is possible only to unfettered contemplation, to thoughts not weighted by the load of eager wishes; and thus Freedom comes only to those who no longer ask of life that it shall yield them any of those personal goods that are subject to the mutations of Time.

Although the necessity of renunciation is evidence of the existence of evil, yet Christianity, in preaching it, has shown a wisdom exceeding that of the Promethean philosophy of rebellion. It must be admitted that, of the things we desire, some, though they prove impossible, are yet real goods; others, however, as ardently longed for, do not form part of a fully purified ideal. The belief that what must be renounced is bad, though sometimes false, is far less often false than untamed passion supposes; and the creed of religion, by providing a reason for proving that it is never false, has been the means of purifying our hopes by the discovery of many austere truths.

But there is in resignation a further good element: even real goods, when they are unattainable, ought not to be fretfully desired. To every man comes, sooner or later, the great renunciation. For the young, there is nothing unattainable; a good thing desired with the whole force of a passionate will, and yet impossible, is to them not credible. Yet, by death, by illness, by poverty, or by the voice of duty, we must learn, each one of us, that the world was not made for us, and that, however beautiful may be the things we crave, Fate may nevertheless forbid them. It is the part of courage, when misfortune comes, to bear without repining the ruin of our hopes, to turn away our thoughts from vain regrets. This degree of submission to Power is not only just and right: it is the very gate of wisdom.

But passive renunciation is not the whole of wisdom; for not by renunciation alone can we build a temple for the worship of our own ideals. Haunting forshadowings of the temple appear in the realm of imagination, in music, in architecture, in the untroubled kingdom of reason, and in the golden sunset magic of lyrics, where beauty shines and glows, remote from the touch of sorrow, remote from the fear of change, remote from the failures and disenchantments of the world of fact. In the contemplation of these things the vision of heaven will shape itself in our hearts, giving at once a touchstone to judge the world about us, and an inspiration by which to fashion to our needs whatever is not incapable of serving as a stone in the sacred temple.

Except for those rare spirits that are born without sin, there is a cavern of darkness to be traversed before that temple can be entered. The gate of the cavern is despair, and its floor is paved with the gravestones of abandoned hopes. There Self must die; there the eagerness, the greed of untamed desire must be slain, for only so can the soul be freed from the empire of Fate. But out of the cavern the Gate of Renunciation leads again to the daylight of wisdom, by whose radiance a new insight, a new joy, a new tenderness, shine forth to gladden the pilgrim's heart.

When, without the bitterness of impotent rebellion, we have learnt both to resign ourselves to the outward rule of Fate and to recognise that the nonhuman world is unworthy of our worship, it becomes possible at last so to transform and refashion the unconscious universe, so to transmute it in the crucible of imagination, that a new image of shining gold replaces the old idol of clay. In all the multiform facts of the world—in the visual shapes of trees and mountains and clouds, in the events of the life of man, even in the very omnipotence of Death—the insight of creative idealism can find the reflection of a beauty which its own thoughts first made. In this way mind asserts its subtle mastery over the thoughtless forces of Nature. The more evil the material with which it deals, the more thwarting to untrained desire, the greater is its achievement in inducing the reluctant rock to yield up its hidden treasures, the prouder its victory in compelling the opposing forces to swell the pageant of its triumph. Of all the arts, Tragedy is the proudest, the most triumphant; for it builds its shining citadel in the very centre of the enemy's country, on the very summit of his highest mountain; from its impregnable watchtowers, his camps and arsenals, his columns and forts, are all revealed; within its walls the free life continues, while the legions of Death and Pain and Despair, and all the servile captains of tyrant Fate, afford the burghers of that dauntless city new spectacles of beauty. Happy those sacred ramparts, thrice happy the dwellers on that all-seeing eminence. Honour to those brave warriors who, through countless ages of warfare, have preserved for us the priceless heritage of liberty, and have kept undefiled by sacrilegious invaders the home of the unsubdued.

But the beauty of Tragedy does but make visible a quality which, in more or less obvious shapes, is present always and everywhere in life. In the spectacle of Death, in the endurance of intolerable pain, and in the irrevocableness of a vanished past, there is a sacredness, an overpowering awe, a feeling of the vastness, the depth, the inexhaustible mystery of existence, in which, as by some strange marriage of pain, the sufferer is bound to the world by bonds of sorrow. In these moments of insight, we lose all eagerness of temporary desire, all struggling and striving for petty ends, all care for the little trivial things that, to a superficial view, make up the common life of day by day; we see, surrounding the narrow raft illumined by the flickering light of human comradeship, the dark ocean on whose rolling waves we toss for a brief hour; from the great night without, a chill blast breaks in upon our refuge; all the loneliness of humanity amid hostile forces is concentrated upon the individual soul, which must struggle alone, with what of courage it can command, against the whole weight of a universe that cares nothing for its hopes and fears. Victory, in this struggle with the powers of darkness, is the true baptism into the glorious company of heroes, the true initiation into the overmastering beauty of human existence. From that awful encounter of the soul with the outer world, renunciation, wisdom, and charity are born; and with their birth a new life begins. To take into the inmost shrine of the soul the irresistible forces whose puppets we seem to be—Death and change, the irrevocableness of the past, and the powerlessness of man before the blind hurry of the universe from vanity to vanity—to feel these things and know them is to conquer them.

This is the reason why the Past has such magical power. The beauty of its motionless and silent pictures is like the enchanted purity of late autumn, when the leaves, though one breath would make them fall, still glow against the sky in golden glory. The Past does not change or strive; like Duncan, after life's fitful fever it sleeps well; what was eager and grasping, what was petty and transitory, has faded away, the things that were beautiful and eternal shine out of it like stars in the night. Its beauty, to a soul not worthy of it, is unendurable; but to a soul which has conquered Fate it is the key of religion.

The life of Man, viewed outwardly, is but a small thing in comparison with the forces of Nature. The slave is doomed to worship Time and Fate and Death, because they are greater than anything he finds in himself, and because all his thoughts are of things which they devour. But, great as they are, to think of them greatly, to feel their passionless splendour, is greater still. And such thought makes us free men; we no longer bow before the inevitable in Oriental subjection, but we absorb it, and make it a part of ourselves. To abandon the struggle for private happiness, to expel all eagerness of temporary desire, to burn with passion for eternal things—this is emancipation, and this is the free man's worship. And this liberation is effected by a contemplation of Fate; for Fate itself is subdued by the mind which leaves nothing to be purged by the purifying fire of Time.

United with his fellow-men by the strongest of all ties, the tie of a common doom, the free man finds that a new vision is with him always, shedding over every daily task the light of love. The life of Man is a long march through the night, surrounded by invisible foes, tortured by weariness and pain, towards a goal that few can hope to reach, and where none may tarry long. One by one, as they march, our comrades vanish from our sight, seized by the silent orders of omnipotent Death. Very brief is the time in which we can help them, in which their happiness or misery is decided. Be it ours to shed sunshine on their path, to lighten their sorrows by the balm of sympathy, to give them the pure joy of a never-tiring affection, to strengthen failing courage, to instil faith in hours of despair. Let us not weigh in grudging scales their merits and demerits, but let us think only of their need—of the sorrows, the difficulties, perhaps the blindnesses, that make the misery of their lives; let us remember that they are fellow-sufferers in the same darkness, actors in the same tragedy with ourselves. And so, when their day is over, when their good and their evil have become eternal by the immortality of the past, be it ours to feel that, where they suffered, where they failed, no deed of ours was the cause; but wherever a spark of the divine fire kindled in their hearts, we were ready with encouragement, with sympathy, with brave words in which high courage glowed.

Brief and powerless is Man's life; on him and all his race the slow, sure doom falls pitiless and dark. Blind to good and evil, reckless of destruction, omnipotent matter rolls on its relentless way; for Man, condemned today to lose his dearest, tomorrow himself to pass through the gate of darkness, it remains only to cherish, ere yet the blow falls, the lofty thoughts that ennoble his little day; disdaining the coward terrors of the slave of Fate, to worship at the shrine that his own hands have built; undismayed by the empire of chance, to preserve a mind free from the wanton tyranny that rules his outward life; proudly defiant of the irresistible forces that tolerate, for a moment, his knowledge and his condemnation, to sustain alone, a weary but unyielding Atlas, the world that his own ideals have fashioned despite the trampling march of unconscious power.

COMMENT

The Meaning of Theism

For the theist, the key to reality lies in God and his design. This belief does not exclude several positions that we have already examined, since a theist can be a teleologist, a dualist, or an idealist; but he cannot be a complete materialist or an absolute sceptic.

God has been defined as "a being who is personal, supreme, and good." This definition is in accord with what most people mean when they use the word "God." They think of Him as personal—that is, as conscious mind or spirit. Of course, God's mind is conceived as much larger or greater than any human mind, but still somewhat like mind or spirit as we know it. God is also thought of as supreme—if not omnipotent, at least immensely great and powerful—so powerful, indeed, that He can profoundly affect the whole world. Finally, a personal and supreme being would not be called God if He were not also good—perhaps not perfect, but at least good in a measure that far surpasses our poor human capacities.

If it be granted that the concept of God should be so defined, the question arises whether the belief in God is mature and defensible—whether it is consistent with the life of reason, which Socrates declared is alone worth living. Is faith in God, as Freud maintained, a mere illusory compensation for fear, repression, and catastrophe? Or is it an inalienable possession of man's spiritual life, as rational as it is emotionally satisfying? Can this faith withstand the criticism of philosophy? What *reasons* are there for believing in the existence of God, and how valid are these reasons?

The main arguments *pro* and *con* are contained in this chapter. The ontological proof ("ontological" means "pertaining to the nature of being") as stated by St. Anselm is an *a priori* argument. From his definition of God as "that being than which no greater can be conceived," he reasons that we cannot, without contradiction, assert that God does not exist. St. Thomas rejected this form of proof, his five arguments all being *a posteriori*. They start with some fact given in experience—change, causality, nonnecessary being, degrees of excellence, or design—and they proceed to reason from this fact to the conclusion that God exists. The arguments of both St. Anselm and St. Thomas are intended to prove the existence of a perfect and omnipotent God. The argument of Montague resembles the fifth proof of St. Thomas but concludes that God must be limited in power.

Hume's *Dialogues Concerning Natural Religion* are conversations (sometimes long speeches) between three characters: Demea, a partisan of "the argument for a first cause," Cleanthes, a defender of "the argument from design," and Philo, who is sceptical of both arguments. Demea's argument resembles the first three proofs of St. Thomas, but Demea also falls back upon St. Anselm's contention that the nonexistence of God would be a logical contradiction. Cleanthes' argument is like the fifth proof of St. Thomas.

I shall not restate the arguments because the reader, perhaps with help from his instructor, should be able to understand them, but I will say something about the criticisms that have been brought to bear against these arguments.

Criticism of the Ontological Argument

The ontological argument has had a chequered history. It was immediately criticized by an aged monk, Gaunilo, and was rejected by the greatest medieval philosopher, St. Thomas Aquinas. Then it was revived by Descartes, restated by Spinoza and Leibniz, and sharply criticized by Locke, Hume, and Kant. Relatively few philosophers in more recent times have accepted it.

The import of the argument is clarified by Gaunilo's objection and Anselm's reply. As interpreted by Gaunilo, the argument can be restated as follows: God is thought of as perfect; existence is necessary to perfection; therefore, God exists. This argument, said Gaunilo, is fallacious because by the same kind of reasoning I could "prove" the existence of a perfect island, to wit: If the island did not exist it would lack one of the elements of perfection, namely, real existence, and hence it would not be a perfect island. But the conclusion that a perfect island must exist is obviously absurd, and hence this type of argument is fallacious.

Anselm promptly replied to this attempted *reductio ad absurdum* by pointing out that a "perfect island" is perfect only in a weak and limited sense. By its very nature, an island is finite, and hence can be "perfect" only in a relative or inaccurate manner of speaking—it cannot be *infinitely* perfect. God, and not the hypothetical island, is that being than which no greater can be conceived—a being perfect in the sense of being incomparably greatest. Such absolute and infinite perfection applies to God and to God alone, and only such perfection requires existence.

Another objection was advanced by St. Thomas Aquinas. Going to the root of the argument, he questioned whether we really have in mind the concept of an utterly infinite or perfect being. He pointed out that we finite human beings have only an inadequate and indirect knowledge of God. Because of the infirmity of our understanding, we cannot discern God as He is in Himself, but only by the effects that He produces. If we could know God's essence absolutely, we would surely see that His essence involves His existence. But since we know God only relatively, His existence is not self-evident to us. We cannot leap from our imperfect idea of God to the conclusion that an absolutely perfect being exists.

Perhaps the most profound criticism of the ontological argument was advanced by Kant, whose objection turns on the meaning of the word "exists." Suppose I say that God exists. Am I making the same sort of statement as when I say that God is omnipotent? Kant would say no. The first statement asserts nothing about the *characteristics* of God; it merely tells me that God, whatever He is, exists, just as a rabbit, a cabbage, a stone, or a planet exists. This statement can be denied in only one way—namely, by denying that God exists. This second statement, that God is omnipotent, does tell me something about the *character* of God, and this statement, unlike the first, can be denied in *two* ways—either by denying that there is a God, or by denying that God is omnipotent.

Since the question of a thing's existence is thus *additional* to the question of its characteristics, we can grasp its characteristics without knowing whether it exists. Take the following illustration. As I sit at my desk I wonder whether there is a dollar bill in my pocket. Before I reach into my pocket to find out, I have in mind what the dollar bill would be like. The characteristics of the dollar bill which I have in mind are the same whether or not there really is a dollar bill in my pocket. Hence, I can grasp the characteristics of a dollar bill without knowing that it exists. Can we likewise grasp God's characteristics without knowing whether He exists? Yes, declares Kant. It is logically possible to think of an infinite and perfect Being without knowing that there *is* such a Being. But suppose we *mean* by God a necessarily existent God. It would still not follow that there really is such a Being. It would merely follow that *if* there is a God, then He is a necessarily existent Being—because that is what we mean. At best, Anselm's argument shows only that the thought of God implies the *thought* of God's existence. The thought of perfection implies the thought of existence, and real perfection implies real existence. But the *thought* of perfection does imply *real* existence. This is the tenor of Kant's criticism.

But suppose, for the sake of argument, that Anselm's proof is sound. Just what would it prove? Would it prove the personal and transcendent God of Christian theology? Evidently not. As soon as we think of a being that is transcendent and hence does not include all things, we can immediately think of a greater being—namely, one that *does* include all things. Moreover, such a being would have to include all conceivable qualities that could be combined within a single being; otherwise we could conceive of a greater. On the basis of the ontological argument, Spinoza concluded that God must be all-inclusive and not only infinite but infinite in an infinite number of ways. And he also concluded that God could not be a person, because personality, in its very nature, involves limitation. It would appear that Spinoza's "God," rather than the God of orthodox theology, is in accord with Anselm's definition: "A Being than which no greater can be conceived." If we define God as *personal*, it seems that Anselm's argument, *even if valid*, would prove not the existence of God but the existence of another sort of Being.

Despite the usual "refutations" of the ontological proof, it still fascinates students and occasionally attracts support from philosophers. Two very able American philosophers, Norman Malcolm and Charles Hartshorne, have reformulated and defended the argument. Their reasoning is difficult, but if the reader wishes to pursue the matter, he will find references to their discussions in the biliography at the end of this volume.

Criticism of the Cosmological Proof

The term "cosmological proof" has been used in a blanket way to cover arguments like the first three of St. Thomas. These arguments are alike in maintaining that the insufficiency of nature requires the self-sufficiency of God to explain it. *Change* ("motion" in the sense of actualization of potentialities) cannot explain itself but requires an Unchanged Changer ("Unmoved Mover"—a fully actualized being) for its explanation. *Causation* (in the sense of bringing something into existence) cannot explain itself but requires an Uncaused Cause. *Contingent being* cannot explain itself but requires a Necessary Being for its explanation. Because these proofs are parallel they can be grouped together. It is the third that we shall take as the most instructive and consider in some detail.

Fundamental to the third argument is the contention that we cannot explain one dependent event merely by another or yet another dependent event, even if we push back the regress indefinitely. St. Thomas is prepared to admit, apart from Revelation, that contingent events may be causally linked to one another in a never-ending regress. What he denies is that we can have a *sufficient* explanation in terms of such an infinite regress of *dependent* causes.

So long as we have merely series of causes of causes, however infinitely extended, we are explaining one dependent event by another dependent event by still another dependent event, and so on and on. This is unsatisfactory for two reasons. First, each event is dependent upon its antecedents, and hence no event is more than *conditionally* necessary. If everything is dependent upon something else, the whole process hangs upon nothing. An explanation that thus never gives us an *ultimate* necessity is incomplete, and hence is not a full and satisfactory explanation. Secondly, even if there is an infinite regress of causes, we can always ask why this chain occurs rather than some other chain. Or even if we consider the sum total of nature, we can ask why we have *this* totality rather than some quite different totality. The only *sufficient* explanation is that natural events, and even the whole of nature, must ultimately depend upon a necessary Being. Such a Being cannot have had an external cause, because it is an infinite and eternal Being—namely, God—whose essence is to exist. The argument arrives at the same conclusion as the ontological proof but via a different route.

This argument can be criticized in a number of ways. First, we can ask what is meant by saying that God is a necessary Being. The word "necessity" applies to *propositions* whose denial would be contradictory. "Two plus two equals four" is a necessary proposition, since it would be contradictory to deny it. But does "necessity" apply to *things* as well as to propositions? The character Cleanthes, in Hume's dialogue, answers: "Nothing is demonstrable unless the contrary implies a contradiction. Nothing that is distinctly conceivable implies a contradiction. Whatever we conceive as existent, we can also conceive as nonexistent. There is no being, therefore, whose nonexistence implies a contradiction." If necessity thus applies to logically necessitated propositions and not to things, nothing, not even God, is a necessary Being.

Defenders of the cosmological argument might reply, in the words of Hume, that if we knew God's "whole essence or nature, we should perceive it to be as impossible for him not to exist as for twice two not to be four." But the point is, replies Cleanthes, that we do *not* know God's whole essence or nature, and hence it is not clear to us how a Being could necessitate himself. If, in some mysterious way, a Being can be necessary, why might not the natural universe be this necessarily existent Being? If you reply that every natural event is seen to be non-necessary (in the sense that its absence involves no contradiction), it does not follow that the whole of nature is non-necessary. A whole need not have the character of its parts. It does not follow from the fact that every note in a musical composition is short that the whole composition is short. Similarly, it does not follow from the fact that every natural thing or event is non-necessary that the whole of nature is non-necessary. If we are to insist upon a necessity that we do not understand, this necessity would seem as applicable to nature as to supernature.

But should we demand such an ultimate necessity? Why not simply suppose that the causal series of linked events stretches back infinitely and that there is no other explanation? If each part is determined by its antecedents, is not the whole sufficiently determined? It would seem to be absurd to demand an external cause for an infinite regress without beginning, since the causal relation implies priority in time and hence a beginning of existence. Our whole experience of causal connections, moreover, lies *within* nature, and we have no sufficient basis for projecting this relation *outside* of nature. Can we assume that what is true of particular things in the world—namely, that *they* are caused—is true of the universe in its totality? Must the universe have a cause outside its own nature? Or must it have any cause at all? To a consistent empiricist, such as Hume, the extension of the concept of causation beyond the field of all actual or possible experience offers special difficulties. On the other hand, if we understand the "necessity" of a necessary Being as logical rather than causal, we are faced by the difficulty already mentioned—that the necessity here involved is mysterious and seems applicable to the whole of nature no less than to supernature.

To these objections of Hume may be added one further objection. The cosmological argument, even if valid, throws no great light on the character of the absolutely necessary Being. We are simply left with the very abstract notion of a self-necessitated necessitator. There would seem to be nothing in this conclusion that compels us to suppose that the necessary Being is either personal or good, and hence the argument, even if valid, is not sufficient to prove the existence of God.

Is the argument, therefore, worthless? Many philosophers believe that it retains its cogency, and that the objections we have considered are invalid. It seems to such philosophers that the evident self-insufficiency of natural events requires an ultimate self-sufficient foundation. Nature as a composite whole, moreover, seems *not* self-sufficient, because any composite *could* be composed in a different way. Why should there be this total natural constellation rather than some other? Does not the existence of such dependent and conditioned being require the existence of independent and unconditioned Being? Only an infinite, eternal, completely actualized, and noncomposite Being—a pure spirit—could be thus independent and unconditioned, the guarantor of its own existence and all else besides. We may have to fall back upon other arguments to establish some of the attributes of God, but the cosmological argument at least proves that nature is dependent upon supernature, and this conclusion carries us a long way—or so the believer in the cosmological argument would continue to maintain.

Criticism of the Teleological Argument

The teleological argument, or argument from design, is very ancient but still popular. It was first expressly formulated by Plato, in the *Laws*, and has been restated by innumerable philosophers, among them St. Augustine, St. Thomas (in his Fifth Proof), Locke, and Rousseau. It was especially popular in the seventeenth and eighteenth centuries, when the astronomy and physics of Newton were interpreted as the disclosure of a wonderful natural order requiring God as its source.

The criticisms of Hume, as set forth by the character Philo in the *Dialogues*

Concerning Natural Religion, constitute a powerful attack upon the design argument. Are these criticisms conclusive? Evidently Hume did not think so. The criticisms are not presented as his but are put in the mouth of Philo, one of the three characters in the *Dialogues*. Hume abstains from indicating his own sympathies except at the very end of the book, where he suggests that "the opinions" of Cleanthes, the proponent of the design argument, are nearer to the truth than those of Philo. In a letter to a friend, George Elliot (dated March 10, 1751), Hume refers to Cleanthes as the "hero" of the dialogues, and asks for any suggestions which will strengthen that side of the dispute. Even Philo, in a final passage not quoted here, is made to remark that the apparent design in nature proves that its cause bears an analogy, though somewhat remote, to the human mind. Probably Hume felt that Philo's criticisms were weighty but by no means decisive.

One thing to note about most of these criticisms is that they do not tend to prove the *absence* of a designing agency or agencies. They indicate limitations rather than fatal defects in the design argument. They show that the finite order and goodness of nature are an insufficient basis for inferring an infinite, perfect, unitary, external, and conscious designer. Kant later pointed out an additional limitation—that the design argument can prove only a kind of architect, but it cannot prove a creator who makes the world out of nothing. Just as a watchmaker uses materials already in existence to make a watch, so the designer of a natural order may use pre-existing materials to compose his design. But these considerations are consistent with some kind of teleological explanation of the goodness and higher levels of order to be found in nature. It is true that Philo's final point, that the natural order may be the result of mere natural selection, is opposed to a teleological hypothesis, but the further course of the dialogue suggests that neither Cleanthes nor Philo regarded natural selection as sufficient, in itself, to explain the whole order of nature. It is also noteworthy that John Stuart Mill and William James could not bring themselves to the view that the Darwinian hypothesis of natural selection was alone sufficient to explain the higher levels of evolution. They preferred to believe in a finite God, struggling against evil but not wholly able to eliminate it. Moreover, this finite God need not be thought of as an external, transcendent Deity but can be construed as the total society of natural forces that are pushing on toward the good. Admittedly, this concept alters the usual meaning of "God," but some modern philosophers nevertheless prefer it.

Among arguments of this type none is more eloquent than the passage from W. P. Montague's *Belief Unbound* reproduced in this chapter. Montague refers to "the problem of evil" to refute the belief in a perfect and omnipotent God, and to "the problem of good" to refute an atheistic interpretation. He remarks, "Material nature makes altogether too many winning throws for us not to suspect that she is playing with dice that are loaded, loaded with life and mind and purpose." I will leave my readers to judge the strength of his argument.

I shall not discuss St. Thomas' Fourth Proof except to remark that it appears to me inconclusive. That there are degrees of excellence I do not doubt, but I see no reason to suppose that there must be Perfection at the top of the scale or that lower degrees of excellence must depend for their existence upon the highest degree.

"The Death of God"

In a famous passage in *The Joyful Wisdom*, Nietzsche tells the story of a "madman" who cries out in public places, "Where is God gone? I mean to tell you! *We have killed him,*—you and I!" The madman made his way into churches "and there intoned his *Requiem aeternam deo*. When led out and called to account, he always gave the reply: 'What are these churches now, if they are not the tombs and monuments of God?' "[1]

Among the philosophers of the twentieth century, no one has been more willing to recognize and accept the "death" of the old God than Bertrand Russell. He is an agnostic whose disbelief approaches atheism. "I do not pretend to be able to prove that there is no God," he says. "I equally cannot prove that Satan is a fiction. The Christian God may exist; so may the Gods of Olympus, or of ancient Egypt, or of Babylon." But the existence of any of these Gods seems to him so improbable that "there is no reason to consider any of them."[2]

Underlying this disbelief is Russell's intense conviction that the universe is indifferent, if not positively inimical, to human values. When the wife of his biographer, Alan Wood, remarked that it would be horribly unjust if the young men killed in war should have no second chance to achieve happiness in an after life, Russell heatedly replied:

> "But the universe *is* unjust. The secret of happiness is to face the fact that the world is horrible, horrible, *horrible* . . . you must feel it deeply and not brush it aside . . . you must feel it right here"—hitting his breast—"and then you can start being happy again."[3]

Whether we choose to call this attitude "religious" will depend upon our definition of religion. "At bottom the whole concern of . . . religion," wrote William James, "is with the manner of our acceptance of the universe." The manner of

---

[1] *The Joyful Wisdom*, translated by Thomas Common (New York: The Macmillan Company, 1910, 1924), pp. 167–168.

[2] Bertrand Russell, *Why I Am Not a Christian and Other Essays on Religion*, ed. by Paul Edwards (New York: Simon & Schuster, 1957), pp. 50–51.

[3] Alan Wood, *Bertrand Russell: The Passionate Sceptic* (London: Allen and Unwin, 1956), p. 237.

acceptance, he declared, may vary from "dull submission" to "enthusiastic assent."[4] Neither extreme characterizes Russell's attitude. He was far too keenly aware of evil to greet the world with "enthusiastic assent," and he was far too free a spirit to bow down in "dull submission." But if it is religious

> To defy Power, which seems omnipotent;
> To love, and bear;[5]

then Russell can truly be called religious.

In addition to this Promethean defiance there are two other attitudes of a quasi-religious sort. One of these is a kind of Spinozistic vision of "eternal things":

> The slave is doomed to worship Time and Fate and Death, because they are greater than anything he finds in himself, and because all his thoughts are of things which they devour. But, great as they are, to think of them greatly, to feel their passionless splendor, is greater still.

The other quasi-religious attitude is an idealistic humanism:

> Shall we worship force, or shall we worship goodness? Shall our God exist and be evil, or shall he be recognized as the creation of our own conscience?

Russell never abandoned the view, here so finely stated, that it is possible to live without fantasies, and that to maintain noble human ideals, disentangled from superstition, is the mature answer to the problem of life. There is an undercurrent of sadness in what he writes, but also of hope and courage.

The contrast between humanism and theism presents one of the great issues in the religious life of mankind. The humanist will contend that we have been recreant to natural love because we have been chasing a supernatural rainbow, and that love as a *human* bond must now come into its own. The theist will retort that the love of man for man and the love of man for God are interdependent—that human beings relate themselves most deeply to each other by relating themselves to an eternal Thou. But both sides, if they transcend their bitter opposition, can agree that fellowship should be the essential basis of human life, and that love becomes sacred when it is raised to its highest power and consecrated by the deepest feeling.

[4] William James, *The Varieties of Religious Experience* (New York: Longmans, Green & Co., 1928), pp. 41, 508.
[5] Shelley, *Prometheus Unbound*, concluding stanza.

Part Three

THE BASIS
OF MORALITY

In Part Three we shall deal with ethics. The fundamental concepts of ethics are *good* and *bad*, and *right* and *wrong*. Although such words as *good* and *right* can be used in a nonmoral sense, we shall be concerned with their moral usage. Both are closely related to *ought—good* is what ought to exist, and *right* is what ought to be done.

The readers of this book have already been introduced to ethics in Chapter 1. Socrates, in the *Apology* and *Crito*, was criticizing the ethics of custom and expediency and defending the ideal of wisdom. In Part Four, we shall again meet Socrates, this time as a character in Plato's *Republic*. In this dialogue, Socrates maintains that good is the harmonious development of all parts of the soul under the control of reason, and that the good of the state is the harmonious development of all classes under the control of wise men. Some readers of this book will prefer to consider the selections from the *Republic* in connection with the ethical problems of Part Three rather than the social problems of Part Four.

In Part Three, we have confined our survey to the following types of ethical theory:

1. *Rational development* (Aristotle). The good is the cultivation and fulfillment of man's faculties, especially reason.

2. *Natural law* (Cicero, Marcus Aurelius, and Ralph Blake). The good is life in harmony with the nature of man and his environment.

3. *Duty for duty's sake* (Kant). We have nonutilitarian duties based on *a priori* reason.

4. *Utilitarianism* (Bentham and Mill). Right acts are the most useful in achieving happiness.

5. *Will to power* (Nietzsche). Nobility is the triumph of power over weakness and mediocrity.

6. *Moral experiment* (Dewey). The good life is reflective and experimental rather than customary.

7. *Linguistic analysis* (Wittgenstein). The analysis of language is a key to escape from moral perplexities.

These seven types of theory exhibit a considerable range of doctrine and introduce the the most basic questions of ethics.

12

Reason

ARISTOTLE

(For biographical note see pages 45–46.)

The Nicomachean Ethics

1. [The Nature of Happiness]

[Aristotle begins, in a way character-
istic of his method, with a generaliza-
tion which, if accepted, will lead to a
more exact account of his subject. It is
a generalization which is fundamental
to his philosophy and in his own mind
there is no doubt about the truth of it.

The Ethics of Aristotle, translated by J. A.
K. Thomson, George Allen and Unwin, Lon-
don, and Barnes and Noble, New York, 1953.
Reprinted by permission. The sentences in
italics are explanatory comments by the trans-
lator except where initialed "M.R."

Yet he is not at this point asserting its
truth. He is content to state a position
which he has found reason to hold. It
may be defined in some such words as
these: The good is that at which all
things aim. *If we are to understand*
this, we must form to ourselves a clear
notion of what is meant by an aim or,
in more technical language, an "end."
The first chapter of the Ethics *is con-*
cerned with making the notion clear.]

It is thought that every activity, artistic or scientific, in fact every deliberate
action or pursuit, has for its object the

attainment of some good. We may therefore assent to the view which has been expressed that "the good" is "that at which all things aim." . . . Since modes of action involving the practiced hand and the instructed brain are numerous, the number of their ends is proportionately large. For instance, the end of medical science is health; of military science, victory; of economic science, wealth. All skills of that kind which come under a single "faculty"— a skill in making bridles or any other part of a horse's gear comes under the faculty or art of horsemanship, while horsemanship itself and every branch of military practice comes under the art of war, and in like manner other arts and techniques are subordinate to yet others—in all these the ends of the master arts are to be preferred to those of the subordinate skills, for it is the former that provide the motive for pursuing the latter. . . .

Now if there is an end which as moral agents we seek for its own sake, and which is the cause of our seeking all the other ends—if we are not to go on choosing one act for the sake of another, thus landing ourselves in an infinite progression with the result that desire will be frustrated and ineffectual —it is clear that this must be the good, that is the absolutely good. May we not then argue from this that a knowledge of the good is a great advantage to us in the conduct of our lives? Are we not more likely to hit the mark if we have a target? If this be true, we must do our best to get at least a rough idea of what the good really is, and which of the sciences, pure or applied, is concerned with the business of achieving it.

[*Ethics is a branch of politics. That is to say, it is the duty of the statesman to create for the citizen the best possible opportunity of living the good life. It will be seen that the effect of this injunction is not to degrade morality but to moralize politics. The modern view that "you cannot make men better by act of parliament" would have been repudiated by Aristotle as certainly as by Plato and indeed by ancient philosophers in general.*]

Now most people would regard the good as the end pursued by that study which has most authority and control over the rest. Need I say that this is the science of politics? It is political science that prescribes what subjects are to be taught in states, which of these the different sections of the population are to learn, and up to what point. We see also that the faculties which obtain most regard come under this science: for example, the art of war, the management of property, the ability to state a case. Since, therefore, politics makes use of the other practical sciences, and lays it down besides what we must do and what we must not do, its end must include theirs. And that end, in politics as well as in ethics, can only be the good for man. For even if the good of the community coincides with that of the individual, the good of the community is clearly a greater and more perfect good both to get and to keep. This is not to deny that the good of the individual is worth while. But what is good for a nation or a city has a higher, a diviner, quality.

Such being the matters we seek to investigate, the investigation may fairly be represented as the study of politics. . . .

[. . . *Let us consider what is the end of political science. For want of a better word we call it "Happiness." People are agreed on the word but not on its meaning.*]

. . . Since every activity involving some acquired skill or some moral decision aims at some good, what do we take to be the end of politics—what is the supreme good attainable in our actions? Well, so far as the name goes there is pretty general agreement. "It is happiness," say both intellectuals and the unsophisticated, meaning by "happiness" living well or faring well. But when it comes to saying in what happiness consists, opinions differ and the account given by the generality of mankind is not at all like that given by the philosophers. The masses take it to be something plain and tangible, like pleasure or money or social standing. Some maintain that it is one of these, some that it is another, and the same man will change his opinion about it more than once. When he has caught an illness he will say that it is health, and when he is hard up he will say that it is money. Conscious that they are out of their depths in such discussions, most people are impressed by anyone who pontificates and says something that is over their heads. Now it would no doubt be a waste of time to examine all these opinions; enough if we consider those which are most in evidence or have something to be said for them. Among these we shall have to discuss the view held by some that, over and above particular goods like those I have just mentioned, there is another which is good in itself and the cause of what-

ever goodness there is in all these others. . . .

[*A man's way of life may afford a clue to his genuine views upon the nature of happiness. It is therefore worth our while to glance at the different types of life.*]

. . . There is a general assumption that the manner of a man's life is a clue to what he on reflection regards as the good—in other words happiness. Persons of low tastes (always in the majority) hold that it is pleasure. Accordingly they ask for nothing better than the sort of life which consists in having a good time. (I have in mind the three well-known types of life—that just mentioned, that of the man of affairs, that of the philosophic student.) The utter vulgarity of the herd of men comes out in their preference for the sort of existence a cow leads. Their view would hardly get a respectful hearing, were it not that those who occupy great positions sympathize with a monster of sensuality like Sardanapalus. The gentleman, however, and the man of affairs identify the good with honor, which may fairly be described as the end which men pursue in political or public life. Yet honor is surely too superficial a thing to be the good we are seeking. Honor depends more on those who confer than on him who receives it, and we cannot but feel that the good is something personal and almost inseparable from its possessor. Again, why do men seek honor? Surely in order to confirm the favorable opinion they have formed of themselves. It is at all events by intelligent men who know them personally that they seek to be honored. And for what? For their moral qualities.

The inference is clear; public men prefer virtue to honor. It might therefore seem reasonable to suppose that virtue rather than honor is the end pursued in the life of the public servant. But clearly even virtue cannot be quite the end. It is possible, most people think, to possess virtue while you are asleep, to possess it without acting under its influence during any portion of one's life. Besides, the virtuous man may meet with the most atrocious luck or ill-treatment; and nobody, who was not arguing for argument's sake, would maintain that a man with an existence of that sort was "happy." . . . The third type of life is the "contemplative," and this we shall discuss later.

As for the life of the business man, it does not give him much freedom of action. Besides, wealth obviously is not the good we seek, for the sole purpose it serves is to provide the means of getting something else. So far as that goes, the ends we have already mentioned would have a better title to be considered the good, for they are desired on their own account. But in fact even their claim must be disallowed. We may say that they have furnished the ground for many arguments, and leave the matter at that. . . .

[*What then is the good? If it is what all men in the last resort aim at, it must be happiness. And that for two reasons: (1) happiness is everything it needs to be, (2) it has everything it needs to have.*]

. . . [The good] is one thing in medicine and another in strategy, and so in the other branches of human skill. We must inquire, then, what is the good which is the end common to all of them. Shall we say it is that for the sake of which everything else is done? In medicine this is health, in military science victory, in architecture a building, and so on—different ends in different arts; every consciously directed activity has an end for the sake of which everything that it does is done. This end may be described as its good. Consequently, if there be some one thing which is the end of all things consciously done, this will be the double good; or, if there be more than one end, then it will be all of these. . . .

In our actions we aim at more ends than one—that seems to be certain— but, since we choose some (wealth, for example, or flutes and tools or instruments generally) as means to something else, it is clear that not all of them are ends in the full sense of the word, whereas the good, that is the supreme good, is surely such an end. Assuming then that there is some one thing which alone is an end beyond which there are no further ends, we may call *that* the good of which we are in search. If there be more than one such final end, the good will be that end which has the highest degree of finality. An object pursued for its own sake possesses a higher degree of finality than one pursued with an eye to something else. A corollary to that is that a thing which is never chosen as a means to some remoter object has a higher degree of finality than things which are chosen both as ends in themselves and as means to such ends. We may conclude, then, that something which is always chosen for its own sake and never for the sake of something else is without qualification a final end.

Now happiness more than anything else appears to be just such an end, for we always choose it for its own sake and never for the sake of some other thing. It is different with honor, pleasure, intelligence and good qualities generally. We choose them indeed for their own sake in the sense that we should be glad to have them irrespective of any advantage which might accrue from them. But we also choose them for the sake of our happiness in the belief that they will be instrumental in promoting that. On the other hand nobody chooses happiness as a means of achieving them or anything else whatsoever than just happiness.

The same conclusion would seem to follow from another consideration. It is a generally accepted view that the final good is self-sufficient. By "self-sufficient" is meant not what is sufficient for oneself living the life of a solitary but includes parents, wife and children, friends and fellow-citizens in general. For man is a social animal. . . . A self-sufficient thing, then, we take to be one which on its own footing tends to make life desirable and lacking in nothing. And we regard happiness as such a thing. . . .

[*But we desire a clearer definition of happiness. The way to this may be prepared by a discussion of what is meant by the "function" of a man.*]

But no doubt people will say, "To call happiness the highest good is a truism. We want a more distinct account of what it is." We might arrive at this if we could grasp what is meant by the "function" of a human being. If we take a flutist or a sculptor or any craftsman—in fact any class of men at all who have some special job or profession —we find that his special talent and excellence comes out in that job, and this is his function. The same thing will be true of man simply as man—that is of course if "man" does have a function. But is it likely that joiners and shoemakers have certain functions or specialized activities, while man as such has none but has been left by Nature a functionless being? Seeing that eye and hand and foot and every one of our members has some obvious function, must we not believe that in like manner a human being has a function over and above these particular functions? Then what exactly is it? The mere act of living is not peculiar to man—we find it even in the vegetable kingdom—and what we are looking for is something peculiar to him. We must therefore exclude from our definition the life that manifests itself in mere nurture and growth. A step higher should come the life that is confined to experiencing sensations. But that we see is shared by horses, cows and the brute creation as a whole. We are left, then, with a life concerning which we can make two statements. First, it belongs to the rational part of man. Secondly, it finds expression in actions. The rational part may be either active or passive: passive in so far as it follows the dictates of reasoning. A similar distinction can be drawn within the rational life; that is to say, the reasonable element in it may be active or passive. Let us take it that what we are concerned with here is the reasoning power in action, for it will be generally allowed that when we speak of "reasoning" we really mean *exercising* our reasoning faculties. (This seems the more correct use of the word.)

Now let us assume for the moment the truth of the following propositions. (*a*) The function of a man is the exercise of his non-corporeal faculties or "soul" in accordance with, or at least not divorced from, a rational principle. (*b*) The function of an individual and of a *good* individual in the same class—a harp player, for example, and a good harp player, and so through the classes—is generically the same, except that we must add superiority in accomplishment to the function, the function of the harp player being merely to play on the harp, while the function of the good harp player is to play on it well. (*c*) The function of man is a certain form of life, namely an activity of the soul exercised in combination with a rational principle or reasonable ground of action. (*d*) The function of a good man is to exert such activity well. (*e*) A function is performed well when performed in accordance with the excellence proper to it.—If these assumptions are granted, we conclude that the good for man is "an activity of soul in accordance with goodness" or (on the supposition that there may be more than one form of goodness) "in accordance with the best and most complete form of goodness."

[*Happiness is more than momentary bliss.*]

There is another condition of happiness; it cannot be achieved in less than a complete lifetime. One swallow does not make a summer; neither does one fine day. And one day, or indeed any brief period of felicity, does not make a man entirely and perfectly happy. . . .

[. . . *Our first principle—our defini-*

tion of happiness—should be tested not only by the rules of logic but also by the application to it of current opinions on the subject.]

So we must examine our first principle not only logically, that is as a conclusion from premises, but also in the light of what is currently said about it. For if a thing be true, the evidence will be found in harmony with it; and, if it be false, the evidence is quickly shown to be discordant with it.

But first a note about "goods." They have been classified as (*a*) external, (*b*) of the soul, (*c*) of the body. Of these we may express our belief that goods of the soul are the best and are most properly designated as "good." Now according to our definition happiness is an expression of the soul in considered actions, and that definition seems to be confirmed by this belief, which is not only an old popular notion but is accepted by philosophers. We are justified, too, in saying that the end consists in certain acts or activities, for this enables us to count it among goods of the soul and not among external goods. We may also claim that our description of the happy man as the man who lives or fares well chimes in with our definition. For happiness has pretty much been stated to be a form of such living or faring well. Again, our definition seems to include the elements detected in the various analyses of happiness— virtue, practical wisdom, speculative wisdom, or a combination of these, or one of them in more or less intimate association with pleasure. All these definitions have their supporters, while still others are for adding material prosperity to the conditions of a happy life.

Some of these views are popular convictions of long standing; others are set forth by a distinguished minority. It is reasonable to think that neither the mass of men nor the sages are mistaken altogether, but that on this point or that, or indeed on most points, there is justice in what they say.

Now our definition of happiness as an activity in accordance with virtue is so far in agreement with that of those who say that it *is* virtue, that such an activity *involves* virtue. But of course it makes a great difference whether we think of the highest good as consisting in the *possession* or in the *exercise* of virtue. It is possible for a disposition to goodness to exist in a man without anything coming of it; he might be asleep or in some other way have ceased to exercise his function of a man. But that is not possible with the activity in our definition. For in "doing well" the happy man will of necessity *do*. Just as at the Olympic Games it is not the best-looking or the strongest men present who are crowned with victory but competitors—the successful competitors, so in the arena of human life the honors and rewards fall to those who show their good qualities in action.

Observe, moreover, that the life of the actively good is inherently pleasant. Pleasure is a psychological experience, and every man finds that pleasant for which he has a liking—"fond of" so and so is the expression people use. For example, a horse is a source of pleasure to a man who is fond of horses, a show to a man who is fond of sight-seeing. In the same way just actions are a source of pleasure to a man who likes to see justice done, and good actions in general to one who likes goodness. Now the mass of men do not follow any consistent plan in the pursuit of their pleasures, because their pleasures are not inherently pleasurable. But men of more elevated tastes and sentiments find pleasure in things which are in their own nature pleasant, for instance virtuous actions, which are pleasant in themselves and not merely to such men. So their life does not need to have pleasure fastened about it like a necklace, but possesses it as a part of itself. We may go further and assert that he is no good man who does not find pleasure in noble deeds. Nobody would admit that a man is just, unless he takes pleasure in just actions; or liberal, unless he takes pleasure in acts of liberality; and so with the other virtues. Grant this, and you must grant that virtuous actions are a source of pleasure in themselves. And surely they are also both good and noble, and that always in the highest degree, if we are to accept, as accept we must, the judgment of the good man about them, he judging in the way I have described. Thus, happiness is the best, the noblest, the most delightful thing in the world, and in it meet all those qualities which are separately enumerated in the inscription upon the temple at Delos:

Justice is loveliest, and health is best,
And sweetest to obtain is heart's desire.

All these good qualities inhere in the activities of the virtuous soul, and it is these, or the best of them, which we say constitute happiness.

For all that those are clearly right who, as I remarked, maintain the necessity to a happy life of an addition in the form of material goods. It is difficult, if not impossible, to engage in noble enterprises without money to spend on them; many can only be performed through friends, or wealth, or political influence. There are also certain advantages, such as the possession of honored ancestors or children, or personal beauty, the absence of which takes the bloom from our felicity. For you cannot quite regard a man as happy if he be very ugly to look at, or of humble origin, or alone in the world and childless, or—what is probably worse—with children or friends who have not a single good quality. . . .

[*Our definition of happiness compels us to consider the nature of virtue. But before we can do this we must have some conception of how the human soul is constituted. It will serve our purpose to take over (for what it is worth) the current psychology which divides the soul into "parts."*]

Happiness, then, being an activity of the soul in conformity with perfect goodness, it follows that we must examine the nature of goodness. . . . The goodness we have to consider is human goodness. This—I mean human goodness or (if you prefer to put it that way) human happiness—was what we set out to find. By human goodness is meant not fineness of physique but a right condition of the soul, and by happiness a condition of the soul. That being so, it is evident that the statesman ought to have some inkling of psychology, just as the doctor who is to specialize in diseases of the eye must have a general knowledge of physiology. Indeed, such a general background is even more necessary for the statesman in view of the fact that his science is of a higher order than the doctor's. Now the best kind of doctor takes a good deal of trouble to acquire a knowledge of the human body as a whole. Therefore the statesman should also be a psychologist and study the soul with an eye to his profession. Yet he will do so only as far as his own problems make it necessary; to go into greater detail on the subject would hardly be worth the labor spent on it.

Psychology has been studied elsewhere and some of the doctrines stated there may be accepted as adequate for our present purpose and used by us here. The soul is represented as consisting of two parts, a rational and an irrational. . . . As regards the irrational part there is one subdivision of it which appears to be common to all living things, and this we may designate as having a "vegetative" nature, by which I mean that it is the cause of nutrition and growth, since one must assume the existence of some such vital force in all things that assimilate food. . . . Now the excellence peculiar to this power is evidently common to the whole of animated nature and not confined to man. This view is supported by the admitted fact that the vegetative part of us is particularly active in sleep, when the good and the bad are hardest to distinguish. . . . Such a phenomenon would be only natural, for sleep is a cessation of that function on the operation of which depends the goodness or badness of the soul. . . . But enough of this, let us say no more about the nutritive part of the soul, since it forms no portion of goodness in the specifically *human* character.

But there would seem to be another constituent of the soul which, while irrational, contains an element of rationality. It may be observed in the types of men we call "continent" and "incontinent." They have a principle—a rational element in their souls—which we commend, because it encourages them to perform the best actions in the right way. But such natures appear at the same time to contain an irrational element in active opposition to the rational. In paralytic cases it often happens that when the patient wills to move his limbs to the right they swing instead to the left. Exactly the same thing may happen to the soul; the impulses of the incontinent man carry him in the opposite direction from that towards which he was aiming. The only difference is that, where the body is concerned, we see the uncontrolled limb, while the erratic impulse we do not see. Yet this should not prevent us from believing that besides the rational an irrational principle exists running opposite and counter to the other. . . . Yet, as I said, it is not altogether irrational; at all events it submits to direction in the continent man, and may be assumed to be still more amenable to reason in the "temperate" and in the brave man, in whose moral make-up there is nothing which is at variance with reason.

We have, then, this clear result. The irrational part of the soul, like the soul itself, consists of two parts. The first of these is the vegetative, which has nothing rational about it at all. The second is that from which spring the appetites and desire in general; and this does in a way participate in reason, seeing that it is submissive and obedient to it. . . .

That the irrational element in us need not be heedless of the rational is proved by the fact that we find admonition, indeed every form of censure and exhortation, not ineffective. It may be, however, that we ought to speak of the appetitive part of the soul as rational, too. In that event it will rather be the rational part that is divided in two, one division rational in the proper sense of the word and in its nature, the other in the derivative sense in which we speak of a child as "listening to reason" in the person of its father.

These distinctions within the soul supply us with a classification of the virtues. Some are called "intellectual," as wisdom, intelligence, prudence. Others are "moral," as liberality and temperance. When we are speaking of a man's *character* we do not describe him as wise or intelligent but as gentle or temperate. Yet we praise a wise man, too, on the ground of his "disposition" or settled habit of acting wisely. The dispositions so praised are what we mean by "virtues."

2. [Moral Goodness]

[. . . *We have to ask what moral virtue or goodness is. It is a confirmed disposition to act rightly, the disposition being itself formed by a continuous series of right actions.*]

Virtue, then, is of two kinds, intellectual and moral. Of these the intellectual is in the main indebted to teaching for its production and growth, and this calls for time and experience. Moral goodness, on the other hand, is the child of habit, from which it has got its very name, ethics being derived from *ethos,* "habit." . . . This is an indication that none of the moral virtues is implanted in us by nature, since nothing that nature creates can be taught by habit to change the direction of its development. For instance a stone, the natural tendency of which is to fall down, could never, however often you threw it up in the air, be trained to go in that direction. No more can you train fire to burn downwards. Nothing in fact, if the law of its being is to behave in one way, can be habituated to behave in another. The moral virtues, then, are produced in us neither *by* Nature nor *against* Nature. Nature, indeed, prepares in us the ground for their reception, but their complete formation is the product of habit.

Consider again these powers or faculties with which Nature endows us. We acquire the ability to use them before we do use them. The senses provide us with a good illustration of this truth. We have not acquired the sense of sight from repeated acts of seeing, or the sense of hearing from repeated acts of hearing. It is the other way round. We had these senses before we used them, we did not acquire them as a result of using them. But the moral virtues we do acquire by first exercising them. The same is true of the arts and crafts in general. The craftsman has to learn how to make things, but he learns in the process of making them. So men become builders by building, harp players by playing the harp. By a similar process we become just by performing just actions, temperate by performing temperate actions, brave by performing brave actions. Look at what happens in political societies—it confirms our view.

We find legislators seeking to make good men of their fellows by making good behavior habitual with them. . . .

We may sum it all up in the generalization, "Like activities produce like dispositions." This makes it our duty to see that our activities have the right character, since the differences of quality in them are repeated in the dispositions that follow in their train. So it is a matter of real importance whether our early education confirms us in one set of habits or another. It would be nearer the truth to say that it makes a very great difference indeed, in fact all the difference in the world. . . .

[*There is one way of discovering whether we are in full possession of a virtue or not. We possess it if we feel pleasure in its exercise; indeed, it is just with pleasures and pains that virtue is concerned.*]

We may use the pleasure (or pain) that accompanies the exercise of our dispositions as an index of how far they have established themselves. A man is temperate who abstaining from bodily pleasures finds this abstinence pleasant; if he finds it irksome, he is intemperate. Again, it is the man who encounters danger gladly, or at least without painful sensations, who is brave; the man who has these sensations is a coward. In a word, moral virtue has to do with pains and pleasures. There are a number of reasons for believing this. (1) Pleasure has a way of making us do what is disgraceful; pain deters us from doing what is right and fine. Hence the importance—I quote Plato—of having been brought up to find pleasure and pain in the right things. True education is just such a training. (2) The virtues operate with actions and emotions, each of which is accompanied by pleasure or pain. This is only another way of saying that virtue has to do with pleasures and pains. (3) Pain is used as an instrument of punishment. For in her remedies Nature works by opposites, and pain can be remedial. (4) When any disposition finds its complete expression it is, as we noted, in dealing with just those things by which it is its nature to be made better or worse, and which constitute the sphere of its operations. Now when men become bad it is under the influence of pleasures and pains when they seek the wrong ones among them, or seek them at the wrong time, or in the wrong manner, or in any of the wrong forms which such offenses may take; and in seeking the wrong pleasures and pains they shun the right. . . .

So far, then, we have got this result. Moral goodness is a quality disposing us to act in the best way when we are dealing with pleasures and pains, while vice is one which leads us to act in the worst way when we deal with them. . . .

[*We have now to state the "differentia" of virtue. Virtue is a disposition; but how are we to distinguish it from other dispositions? We may say that it is such a disposition as enables the good man to perform his function well. And he performs it well when he avoids the extremes and chooses the mean in actions and feelings.*]

. . . Excellence of whatever kind affects that of which it is the excellence in two ways. (1) It produces a good state in it. (2) It enables it to perform its function well. Take eyesight. The goodness of your eye is not only that which makes your eye good, it is also that which makes it function well. Or take the case of a horse. The goodness of a horse makes him a good horse, but it also makes him good at running, carrying a rider and facing the enemy. Our proposition, then, seems to be true, and it enables us to say that virtue in a man will be the disposition which (*a*) makes him a good man, (*b*) enables him to perform his function well. . . .

Every form . . . of applied knowledge, when it performs its function well, looks to the mean and works to the standard set by that. It is because people feel this that they apply the *cliché,* "You couldn't add anything to it or take anything from it" to an artistic masterpiece, the implication being that too much and too little alike destroy perfection, while the mean preserves it. Now if this be so, and if it be true, as we say, that good craftsmen work to the standard of the mean, then, since goodness like nature is more exact and of a higher character than any art, it follows that goodness is the quality that hits the mean. By "goodness" I mean goodness of moral character, since it is moral goodness that deals with feelings and actions, and it is in them that we find excess, deficiency and a mean. It is possible, for example, to experience fear, boldness, desire, anger, pity, and pleasures and pains generally, too much or too little or to the right amount. If we feel them too much or too little, we are wrong. But to have these feelings at the right times on the right occasions towards the right people for the right motive and in the right way is to have them in the right measure, that is somewhere between the extremes; and this is what characterizes goodness. The same may be said of the mean and extremes in actions. Now it is in the field of actions and feelings that goodness operates; in them we find excess, deficiency and, between them, the mean, the first two being wrong, the mean right and praised as such. . . . Goodness, then, is a mean condition in the sense that it aims at and hits the mean. Consider, too, that it is possible to go wrong in more ways than one. (In Pythagorean terminology evil is a form of the Unlimited, good of the Limited.) But there is only one way of being right. That is why going wrong is easy, and going right difficult; it is easy to miss the bull's eye and difficult to hit it. Here, then, is another explanation of why the too much and the too little are connected with evil and the mean with good. As the poet says,

Goodness is one, evil is multiform.

[*We are now in a position to state our definition of virtue with more precision. Observe that the kind of virtue meant here is moral, not intellectual, and that Aristotle must not be taken as saying that the kind of virtue which he regards as the highest and truest is any sort of mean.*]

We may now define virtue as a disposition of the soul in which, when it has to choose among actions and feelings, it observes the mean relative to us, this being determined by such a rule or principle as would take shape in the mind of a man of sense or practical wisdom. We call it a mean condition as lying between two forms of badness, one being excess and the other deficiency; and also for this reason, that, whereas badness either falls short of or exceeds the right measure in feelings and actions, virtue discovers the mean and deliberately chooses it. Thus, looked at from the point of view of its essence as embodied in its definition, virtue no doubt is a mean; judged by the standard of what is right and best, it is an extreme.

[*Aristotle enters a caution. Though we have said that virtue observes the mean in actions and passions, we do not say this of all acts and all feelings. Some are essentially evil and, when these are involved, our rule of applying the mean cannot be brought into operation.*]

But choice of a mean is not possible in every action or every feeling. The very names of some have an immediate connotation of evil. Such are malice, shamelessness, envy among feelings, and among actions adultery, theft, murder. All these and more like them have a bad name as being evil in themselves; it is not merely the excess or deficiency of them that we censure. In their case, then, it is impossible to act rightly; whatever we do is wrong. . . .

[*Aristotle now suggests some rules for our guidance.*]

. . . We shall find it useful when aiming at the mean to observe these rules. (1) *Keep away from that extreme which is the more opposed to the mean.* It is Calypso's advice:

Swing round the ship
    clear of this surf and surge.

For one of the extremes is always a more dangerous error than the other; and—since it is hard to hit the bull's-eye—we must take the next best course and choose the least of the evils. And it will be easiest for us to do this if we follow the rule I have suggested. (2) *Note the errors into which we personally are most liable to fall.* (Each of us has his natural bias in one direction or another.) We shall find out what ours are by noting what gives us pleasure and pain. After that we must drag ourselves in the opposite direction. For our best way of reaching the middle is by giving a wide berth to our darling sin. It is the method used by a carpenter when he is straightening a warped board. (3) *Always be particularly on your guard against pleasure and pleasant things.* When Pleasure is at the bar the jury is not impartial. So it will be best for us if we feel towards her as the Trojan elders felt towards Helen, and regularly apply their words to her. If we are for packing her off, as they were with Helen, we shall be the less likely to go wrong.

3. [Particular Virtues]

[*Aristotle now embarks upon a long analysis of the virtues and vices. These do not include the characteristically Christian virtues of piety, chastity and humility, which are not regarded by him as independent virtues at all. Yet however he may classify and name the moral feelings and habits which form the material for his analysis, that material is substantially the same for him as for us. The picture of the good man which emerges is perfectly recognizable and even familiar to us.*]

Let us begin with courage.

We have seen that it is a disposition which aims at the mean in situations inspiring fear and confidence. What we fear are of course things of a nature to inspire fear. Now these are, speaking generally, evil things, so that we get the definition of fear as 'an anticipation of evil.' Well, we do fear all evil things—ill-repute, poverty, sickness, friendlessness, death and so on—but in the opinion of most people courage is to be distinguished from the simple fear of all these. There are some evils which it is proper and honourable to fear and discreditable not to fear—disgrace, for example. The man who fears disgrace has a sense of what is due to himself as a man of character and to other people; the man who does not fear it has a forehead of brass. Such a man indeed is occasionally styled a brave fellow, but only by a transference of epithet made possible by the fact that there is one point of similarity between him and the truly brave man, namely their freedom from timidity. Then one ought not, of course, to fear poverty or illness or, indeed, anything at all that is not a consequence of vice or of one's own misconduct; still we do not call a man who is fearless in facing these things 'brave' except once more by analogy. For we find individuals who are cowardly on the field of battle and yet spend money lavishly and meet the loss of it with equanimity. And surely a man is not to be dubbed a coward because he dreads brutality to his wife and children, or the effects of envy towards himself, or anything of that nature. Nor is a man described as brave if he does not turn a hair at the prospect of a whipping.

What, then, are the objects of fear confronting which the brave man comes out in his true colours? Surely one would say the greatest, for it is just in facing fearful issues that the brave man excels. Now the most fearful thing is death; for death is an end, and to the dead man nothing seems good or evil any more for ever. Yet even death may be attended by circumstances which make it seem inappropriate to describe the man confronted by it as 'brave.' For instance, he might be drowned at sea or pass away in his bed. In what dangers, then, is courage most clearly displayed? Shall we not say, in the noblest? Well, the noblest death is the soldier's, for he meets it in the midst of the greatest and most glorious dangers. This is recognized in the honours conferred on the fallen by republics and monarchs alike. So in the strict meaning of the word the brave man will be one who fearlessly meets an honourable death or some instant threat to life; and it is war which presents most opportunities of that sort. Not but what the brave man will be fearless in plague, or in peril by sea, although it will be a different kind of fearlessness from that of the old salt. For in a shipwreck the brave man does not expect to be rescued, and he hates the thought of the inglorious end which threatens him, whereas the seaman who has weathered many a storm never gives up hope. Courage, too, may be shown on occasions when a man can put up a fight or meet a glorious death. But there is no opportunity for either when you are going down in a ship.

All men have not the same views about what is to be feared, although there are some terrors which are admitted to be more than human nature can face. Terrors of that order are experienced of course by every sane person. But there are great diversities in the extent and degree of the dangers that are humanly tolerable; and there is the same variety in the objects which instil courage. What characterizes the brave man is his unshaken courage wherever courage is humanly possible. No doubt even then he will not always be exempt from fear; but when he fears it will be in the right way, and he will meet the danger according to the rule or principle he has taken to guide his conduct, his object being to achieve moral dignity or beauty in what he does, for that is the end of virtue. Yet it is possible to feel such dangers too much, and possible to fear them too little, and possible also to fear things that are not fearful as much as if they were. One may fear what one ought not to fear, and that is one kind of error; one may fear it in the wrong way, and that is another. A third error is committed when one fears at the wrong time. And so on. We have the same possibilities of error when we deal with things that give us confidence. The brave man is the man who faces or fears the right thing for the right purpose in the right manner at the right moment, or who shows courage in the corresponding ways. . . .

The man who goes to the extreme in fear is a coward—one who fears the wrong things in the wrong way and all the rest of it. He also exhibits a deficiency in boldness. But what one particularly notices is the extremity of his fear in the face of pain. We may therefore describe the coward as a poor-spirited person scared of everything. This is the very opposite of the brave man, for a bold heart indicates a confident temper.

We may say, then, that the coward, the rash man, and the brave man work as it were with the same materials, but their attitudes to them are different. The coward has too much fear and too little courage, the rash man too much courage and too little fear. It is the brave man who has the right attitude, for he has the right disposition, enabling him to observe the mean. We may add that the rash man is foolhardy, ready for anything before the danger arrives; but, when it does, sheering off. On the other hand the brave man is gallant in action but undemonstrative beforehand.

Summing up, let us say that courage is the disposition which aims at the mean in conditions which inspire confidence or fear in the circumstances I have described; it feels confidence and faces danger because it is the fine thing to do so and because it is base to shrink from doing it. Yet to kill oneself as a means of escape from poverty or disappointed love or bodily or mental anguish is the deed of a coward rather than a brave man. To run away from trouble is a form of cowardice and, while it is true that the suicide braves death, he does it not for some noble object but to escape some ill.

[*The virtue of which Aristotle now gives an account is* Sophrosyne, *a word which cannot be rendered by any modern English equivalent. It is, however, what our moralists until quite recently called 'temperance,' and this, with its opposite 'intemperance,' will be used*

here. What Aristotle means by Sophrosyne *will gradually appear.*]

Let us next say something about temperance, which like courage is considered to be one of the virtues developed in the irrational parts of the soul.

We have already described it as aiming at the mean in pleasurable experiences. Intemperance is shown in the same field. So we must now say something definite about the quality of the pleasures which are the material on which temperance and its opposite work. Let us begin by drawing a distinction between (*a*) pleasures of the soul and (*b*) pleasures of the body.

(*a*) As an instance of pleasures of the soul consider the love of distinction in public life or in some branch of learning. The devotee in either case takes pleasure in what he loves without any physical sensations. What he feels is a spiritual or intellectual pleasure, and we do not speak of men who seek that kind of pleasure as 'temperate' or 'intemperate.' Nor do we apply these terms to any class of persons whose pleasures are not those of the flesh. For example, the kind of person who likes to swap stories and ancedotes, and wastes his time discussing trivialities, we call a 'gossip' or a 'chatterbox,' but not 'intemperate.' Neither should we so describe a man who makes a tragedy out of some loss he has met with of money or of friends.

(*b*) It is then the pleasures of sense that are the concern of temperance, though not all of these. The people who find pleasure in looking at things like colours and forms and pictures are not called temperate or intemperate. At the same time we must suppose that pleasure in these things can be felt too much or too little or in due measure. It is so with the pleasures of listening. A man may take inordinate delight in music or acting. But nobody is prepared to call him intemperate on that account; nor, if he takes neither too much nor too little, do we think of describing him as temperate. It is the same with the pleasures of smell, except when some association comes in. A man is not called intemperate if he happens to like the smell of apples or roses or incense. Yet he may be, if he inhales essences or the emanations of the cuisine, for these are odours which appeal to the voluptuary, because they remind him of the things that arouse his desires. And not only the voluptuary; everybody likes the smell of things to eat when he is hungry. Still the delight in such things is specially characteristic of the voluptuary or intemperate man, because it is on these that his heart is set. And if we extend our observation to the lower animals, we note that they, too, find nothing intrinsically pleasant in these sensations. A hunting-dog gets no pleasure from the scent of a hare. The pleasure is in eating it; all the scent did was to tell him the hare was there. It is not the lowing of an ox that gratifies a lion but the eating it, though the lowing tells him the ox is somewhere about, and that evidently gives him pleasure. Nor does he, as Homer thinks, rejoice when he has caught sight of 'stag or goat of the wild,' but because he is promising himself a meal.

Such are the pleasures with which temperance and intemperance deal, and they are pleasures in which the lower animals also share. On that account

they have the name of being illiberal and brutish, confined as they are to touch and taste. And even taste seems to count for little or nothing in the practice of temperance. It is the function of taste to discriminate between flavours, as connoisseurs do when they sample wines, and chefs when they prepare entrées; although it is not exactly the flavours that please (except, perhaps, with the intemperate), it is the enjoyment of the flavorous article, and that is wholly a tactile experience, whether in eating, drinking or what are called the pleasures of sex. This explains the anecdote of the epicure who prayed that his throat might be made longer than a crane's—the longer the contact, he thought, the more protracted the pleasure. So the sense in respect of which we give an intemperate man that name is the sense that comes nearest to being universal. This may seem to justify its ill-repute, for it belongs to us not as men but as animals. Therefore to delight in such sensations, and to prefer them to any other pleasure, is brutish.

[*Aristotle discusses other virtues, such as liberality, the golden mean between stinginess and prodigality; dignified self-respect, between humility and vanity; and friendliness, between quarrelsomeness and obsequiousness. He points out that acts like theft, adultery, and murder, and emotions like shamelessness, envy, and spite, are already excesses or defects, and therefore cannot exist in proper moderation. The virtue of justice, as a kind of fairness or impartiality, consists in treating equals equally and unequals unequally in proportion to their deserts. It is a mean, not as the other virtues are, but only* in the sense that it produces a state of affairs intermediate between giving too much or too little to one person compared with another.—*M.R.*]

4. [Self-love and Friendship]

[*How far, and with what justification, may a man love himself?*]

Another problem is whether one ought to love oneself or another most. The world blames those whose first thoughts are always for themselves and stigmatizes them as self-centred. It is also generally believed that a bad man does everything from a selfish motive, and does this the more, the worse he is.[1] On the other hand the good man is supposed never to act except on some lofty principle—the loftier the principle, the better the man—and to neglect his own interest in order to promote that of his friend. It is a view which is not borne out by the facts. Nor need this surprise us. It is common ground that a man should love his best friend most. But my best friend is the man who in wishing me well wishes it for my sake, whether this shall come to be known or not. Well, there is no one who fulfills this condition so well as I do in my behaviour towards myself; indeed it may be said of every quality which enters into the definition of a friend—I have it in a higher degree than any of my friends. For, as I have already observed, all the affectionate feelings of a man for others are an extension of his feelings for himself. You will find, too,

that all the popular bywords agree on this point. ('Two bodies and one soul,' 'Amity is parity,' 'The knee is nearer than the shin.') All the proverbs show how close are the ties of friendship, and they all apply best to oneself. For a man is his own best friend. From this it follows that he ought to love himself best. —Which then of these two opinions ought we to accept in practice? It is a reasonable question, since there is a degree of plausibility in both.

No doubt the proper method of dealing with divergent opinions of this sort is to distinguish between them, and so reach a definite conclusion on the point of how far and in what way each of them is true. So the present difficulty may be cleared up if we can discover what meaning each side attaches to the word 'self-love.' Those who make it a term of reproach give the epithet of 'self-loving' to those who assign to themselves more than they are entitled to in money, public distinctions and bodily pleasures, these being what most men crave for and earnestly pursue as the greatest blessings, so that they contend fiercely for the possession of them. Well, the man who grasps at more than his fair share of these things is given to the gratification of his desires and his passions generally and the irrational part of his soul. Now most men are like that, and we see from this that the censorious use of the epithet 'self-loving' results from the fact that the self-love of most men is a bad thing. Applied to them, the censorious epithet is therefore justified. And unquestionably it is people who arrogate too much of such things to themselves who are called 'self-loving' by the ordinary man. For if anybody

[1] A bad man is often accused of 'doing nothing until he has to.'

were to make it his constant business to take the lead himself over everyone else in the performance of just or temperate or any other kind whatever of virtuous actions, generally claiming the honourable rôle for himself, nobody would stigmatize *him* as a 'self-lover.' Yet the view might be taken that such a man was exceptionally self-loving. At any rate he arrogates to himself the things of greatest moral beauty and excellence, and what he gratifies and obeys throughout is the magistral part of himself, his higher intelligence. Now just as in a state or any other composite body it is the magistral or dominant part of it that is considered more particularly to *be* the state or body, so with a man; his intelligence, the governing part of him, *is* the man. Therefore he who loves and indulges this part is to the fullest extent a lover of himself. Further, we may note that the terms 'continent' and 'incontinent' imply that the intellect is or is not in control, which involves the assumption that the intellect is the man. Again, it is our reasoned acts that are held to be more especially those which we have performed ourselves and by our own volition. All which goes to show that a man is, or is chiefly the ruling part of himself, and that a good man loves it beyond any other part of his nature. It follows that such a man will be self-loving in a different sense from that attached to the word when it is used as a term of reproach. From the vulgar self-lover he differs as far as the life of reason from the life of passion, and as far as a noble purpose differs from mere grasping at whatever presents itself as an expedient. Hence those who are exceptionally devoted to the performance

of fine and noble actions receive the approval and commendation of all. And if everyone sought to outdo his neighbour in elevation of character, and laboured strenuously to perform the noblest actions, the common weal would find its complete actualization and the private citizen would realize for himself the greatest of goods, which is virtue.

Therefore it is right for the *good* man to be self-loving, because he will thereby himself be benefited by performing fine actions; and by the same process he will be helpful to others. The bad man on the other hand should not be a self-lover, because he will only be injuring himself and his neighbours by his subservience to base passions. As a result of this subservience what he does is in conflict with what he ought to do, whereas the good man does what he ought to do. For intelligence never fails to choose the course that is best for itself, and the good man obeys his intelligence.

But there is something else which we can truly say about the good man. Many of his actions are performed to serve his friends or his country, even if this should involve dying for them. For he is ready to sacrifice wealth, honours, all the prizes of life in his eagerness to play a noble part. He would prefer one crowded hour of glorious life to a protracted period of quiet existence and mild enjoyment spent as an ordinary man would spend it—one great and dazzling achievement to many small successes. And surely this may be said of those who lay down their lives for others; they choose for themselves a crown of glory. It is also a characteristic trait of the good man that he is prepared to lose money on condition that his friends get more. The friend gets the cash, and he gets the credit, so that he is assigning the greater good to himself. His conduct is not different when it comes to public honours and offices. All these he will freely give up to his friend, because that is the fine and praiseworthy thing for him to do. It is natural then that people should think him virtuous, when he prefers honour to everything else. He may even create opportunities for his friend to do a fine action which he might have done himself, and this may be the nobler course for him to take. Thus in the whole field of admirable conduct we see the good man taking the larger share of moral dignity. In this sense then it is, as I said before, right that he should be self-loving. But in the vulgar sense no one should be so.

[*It has been questioned whether the possession of friends is necessary to happiness. Aristotle has no doubt that it is so, and gives his reasons.*]

Another debatable point concerning the happy man is this. Will friends be necessary to his happiness or not? It is commonly said that the happy, being sufficient to themselves, have no need of friends. All the blessings of life are theirs already; so, having all resources within themselves, they are not in need of anything else, whereas a friend, being an *alter ego*, is only there to supply what one cannot supply for oneself. Hence that line in the *Orestes* of Euripides:

When Fortune smiles on us, what need of friends?

Yet it seems a strange thing that in the the process of attributing every blessing to the happy man we should not assign him friends, who are thought to be the greatest of all external advantages. Besides, if it is more like a friend to confer than to receive benefits, and doing good to others is an activity which especially belongs to virtue and the virtuous man, and if it is better to do a kindness to a friend than to a stranger, the good man will have need of friends as objects of his active benevolence. Hence a second question. Does one need friends more in prosperity than in adversity? There is a case for either of these alternatives. The unfortunate need people who will be kind to them; the prosperous need people to be kind to.

Surely also there is something strange in representing the man of perfect blessedness as a solitary or a recluse. Nobody would deliberately choose to have all the good things in the world, if there was a condition that he was to have them all by himself. Man is a social animal, and the need for company is in his blood. Therefore the happy man must have company, for he has everything that is naturally good, and it will not be denied that it is better to associate with friends than with strangers, with men of virtue than with the ordinary run of persons. We conclude then that the happy man needs friends. . . .

[*A little chapter on the value and influence of Friendship.*]

Well then, are we to say that, just as lovers find their chief delight in gazing upon the beloved and prefer sight to all the other senses—for this is the seat and source of love—so friends find the society of one another that which they prefer to all things else? For in the first place friendship is a communion or partnership. Secondly, a man stands in the same relation to his friend as to himself. Now the consciousness which he has of his own existence is something that would be chosen as a good. So the consciousness of his friend's existence must be a good. This consciousness becomes active in the intercourse of the friends, which accordingly they instinctively desire. Thirdly, every man wishes to share with his friends that occupation, whatever it may be, which forms for him the essence and aim of his existence. So we find friends who drink together, and others who dice together, while yet others go in together for physical training, hunting or philosophy. Each set spend their time in one another's company following the pursuit which makes the great pleasure of their lives. As their wish is to be always with their friends, they do what these do and take part with them in these pursuits to the best of their ability. But this means that the friendship of the unworthy is evil, for they associate in unworthy pursuits; and so becoming more and more like each other they turn out badly. But the friendship of the good is good and increases in goodness in consequence of their association. They seem to become positively better men by putting their friendship into operation and correcting each other's faults. For each seeks to transfer to himself the traits he admires in the other. Hence the famous saying:

From noble men you may learn noble deeds . . .

5. [Intellectual Goodness]

[. . . *Aristotle gives reasons for thinking that happiness in its highest and best manifestation is found in cultivating the "contemplative" life.*]

. . . If happiness is an activity in accordance with virtue, it is reasonable to assume that it will be in accordance with the highest virtue; and this can only be the virtue of the best part of us. Whether this be the intellect or something else—whatever it is that is held to have a natural right to govern and guide us, and to have an insight into what is noble and divine, either as being itself also divine or more divine than any other part of us—it is the activity of this part in accordance with the virtue proper to it that will be perfect happiness. Now we have seen already that this activity has a speculative or contemplative character. This is a conclusion which may be accepted as in harmony with our earlier arguments and with the truth. For "contemplation" is the highest form of activity, since the intellect is the highest thing in us and the objects which come within its range are the highest that can be known. But it is also the most continuous activity, for we can think about intellectual problems more continuously than we can keep up any sort of physical action. Again, we feel sure that a modicum of pleasure must be one of the ingredients of happiness. Now it is admitted that activity along the lines of "wisdom" is the pleasantest of all the good activities. At all events it is thought that philosophy ("the pursuit of wisdom") has pleasures marvelous in purity and duration, and it stands to reason that those who have knowledge pass their time more pleasantly than those who are engaged in its pursuit. Again, self-sufficiency will be found to belong in an exceptional degree to the exercise of the speculative intellect. The wise man, as much as the just man and everyone else, must have the necessaries of life. But, given an adequate supply of these, the just man also needs people with and towards whom he can put his justice into operation; and we can use similar language about the temperate man, the brave man, and so on. But the wise man can do more. He can speculate all by himself, and the wiser he is the better he can do it. Doubtless it helps to have fellow workers, but for all that he is the most self-sufficing of men. Finally it may well be thought that the activity of contemplation is the only one that is praised on its own account, because nothing comes of it beyond the act of contemplation, whereas from practical activities we count on gaining something more or less over and above the mere action. Again, it is commonly believed that, to have happiness, one must have leisure; we occupy ourselves in order that we may have leisure, just as we make war for the sake of peace. Now the practical virtues find opportunity for their exercise in politics and in war, but there are occupations which are supposed to leave no room for leisure. Certainly it is true of the trade of war, for no one deliberately chooses to make war for the sake of making it or tries to bring about a war. A man would be regarded as a bloodthirsty monster if he were to make war on a friendly state just to produce battles and slaughter. The business of the politician also makes leisure impossible. Besides the activity itself, politics aims at securing positions of power and honor or the happiness of the politician himself or his fellow citizens—a happiness obviously distinct from that which we are seeking.

We are now in a position to suggest the truth of the following statements. (*a*) Political and military activities, while preeminent among good activities in beauty and grandeur, are incompatible with leisure, and are not chosen for their own sake but with a view to some remoter end, whereas the activity of the intellect is felt to excel in the serious use of leisure, taking as it does the form of contemplation, and not to aim at any end beyond itself, and to own a pleasure peculiar to itself, thereby enhancing its activity. (*b*) In this activity we easily recognize self-sufficiency, the possibility of leisure and such freedom from fatigue as is humanly possible, together with all the other blessings of pure happiness. Now if these statements are received as true, it will follow that it is this intellectual activity which forms perfect happiness for a man—provided of course that it ensures a complete span of life, for nothing incomplete can be an element in happiness.

Yes, but such a life will be too high for *human* attainment. It will not be lived by us in our merely human capacity but in virtue of something divine within us, and so far as this divine particle is superior to man's composite nature, to that extent will its activity be superior to that of the other forms of excellence. If the intellect is divine compared with man, the life of the intellect must be divine compared with the life of a human creature. And we ought not to listen to those who counsel us *O man, think as man should* and *O mortal, remember your mortality.* Rather ought we, so far as in us lies, to put on immortality and to leave nothing unattempted in the effort to live in conformity with the highest thing within us. Small in bulk it may be, yet in power and preciousness it transcends all the rest. We may in fact believe that this is the true self of the individual, being the sovereign and better part of him. It would be strange, then, if a man should choose to live not his own life but another's. Moreover the rule, as I stated it a little before, will apply here —the rule that what is best and pleasantest for each creature is that which intimately belongs to it. Applying it, we shall conclude that the life of the intellect is the best and pleasantest for man, because the intellect more than anything else *is* the man. Thus it will be the happiest life as well.

COMMENT

In considering the merits of Aristotle's theory, we should keep certain key questions in mind:

1. *Can we deduce good from the nature of things?* The presupposition of Aristotle's ethics is that each kind of thing has certain characteristic tendencies and that the good is the fulfillment of these tendencies. Man's good, accordingly, can be deduced from human nature. It may be objected that this implies an optimistic and undemonstrated premise (that developed reality is fully good) and allows the tendencies of the actual world to dictate our standards of value. Some philosophers, such as Kant, deny that the *ought* (good and right) can be derived from the *is* (mattters of fact), and thus take fundamental issue with the basis of Aristotle's ethics. This issue is especially relevant to Cicero's theory of natural law, which we shall discuss in the next chapter, and hence we shall postpone its consideration.

2. *Is the wider definition of good correct?* We can distinguish, in Aristotle's theory, between a "wide" and a "narrow" definition of ultimate good. In its wide meaning, good is the actualization of potentialities. In its narrow meaning, it is the actualization of *human* potentialities, which are taken to be essentially rational.

Let us first consider the wider definition. It is very wide indeed, for it applies to animals, plants, and even inanimate things. Whether Aristotle would interpret it so broadly is not altogether clear. In his teleological metaphysics, he speaks of "end" or "final cause" in this very inclusive way, but he does not state explicitly that every end is good. If, however, the actualization of potentialities is taken to be the essence of good, there is no logical reason to stop short with conscious or even unconscious organisms.

This very wide definition, a critic might say, confuses an "end" in a temporal sense (the *finis* of a process) with an "end" in an ethical sense (good as an end rather than as a means). Another type of confusion may also be involved. We often say that something is a *good* example of its kind, and good in this sense, a biologist might claim, applies only to a fully developed animal, which clearly exhibits the powers and abilities of its species. But "good" in this sense does not imply positive value; a cancer specialist might speak of a perfectly good case of cancer, meaning a case so far developed that it clearly exhibits the generic characteristics of the malignancy. Has Aristotle confused good in this sense with good in its value import?

The attempt to extend the meaning of intrinsic goodness to include nonconscious things has often been challenged. If there were no feelings, no desires, no thoughts whatsoever—if all things in the universe were as unconscious as sticks and stones—would there be any value? Some philosophers maintain that a world without consciousness would be without value; if this were so, we should have to reject Aristotle's wider interpretation of good.

3. *Is the narrower definition of good correct?* Aristotle's interpretation of human goodness rests upon two premises: (*a*) the good is to be found in the life and work peculiar to man, and (*b*) rationality is the distinctive mark of the human creature. Both premises can be challenged.

(*a*) Why should we suppose that the human good is to be found in what is distinctive to man? That a certain factor is peculiar to a species does not necessarily imply any ethical superiority in that factor. If all human beings were just like other animals except that they alone had bowlegs, this would not prove that human good is bowleggedness. Perhaps Aristotle is taking it for granted that man *is* superior to other animals and that this superiority must lie in that which man alone possesses. But some philosophers would question this view. Hedonists, for example, would say that good is pleasure, and the fact that a dog can feel pleasure does not detract from human good. We may or may not believe that this view is mistaken and Aristotle's theory correct—but is there any way of supporting our conviction?

(*b*) Is reason the differentia of humankind? Certain psychologists, such as Wolfgang Köhler, have demonstrated that chimpanzees also have the capacity to reason. These clever animals can figure out ways of piling up and mounting boxes, for example, so as to reach a bunch of bananas hanging high from the top of their cage. Aristotle would no doubt reply that this is only *practical*, not *theoretical*, reason, but it may be that chimpanzees also have curiosity and enjoy satisfying it. At least it is not at all obvious that reason is *the* distinctive mark of human beings, or that any faculty is exclusively human. What fundamentally distinguishes man, it can be argued, is the whole development of his culture, including art and religion and social institutions in addition to philosophy and science. Does Aristotle's rather exclusive emphasis upon reason betray the natural bias of a philosopher?

4. *Does Aristotle, in stressing the generic nature of man, neglect the importance of individuality?* His emphasis is upon the reason that all men share, and

only in rare passages does he speak of self-realization in individualistic terms. He would probably have admitted, for example, that a person with very great musical talent should develop his special gift. But an existentialist such as Kierkegaard would charge that Aristotle shows too little respect for the matchless individuality that is the core of every human life. Who is right?

5. *Is moral virtue to be found in adherence to a mean between the extremes of excess and deficiency?* How adequate is Aristotle's theory of the golden mean? "Be cautious; avoid extremes; follow the mean," it can be argued, is a counsel of prudence and not necessarily of morality—even the wicked and crafty can find it useful. From the standpoint of attaining happiness, does it need to be counterbalanced by a relish for adventure and the careless rapture of intense moments of experience?

Still other questions can be posed. Is pleasure merely contributory to the happy life, as Aristotle supposed, or is it the very essence of happiness, as the hedonists contend? Is the ideal of intellectual contemplation unrealizable by all but the aristocratic few, and, if so, should we favor the development of an intellectual élite rather than the cultivation of the masses? Are ethics and politics inseparable in the way in which Aristotle supposed? Do you agree with his characterization of the nature and value of self-love? Of friendship? Other questions will probably occur to the reader.

13

Nature

MARCUS TULLIUS CICERO (106–43 B.C.)

Statesman, philosopher, and man of letters, Cicero was one of the greatest
intellectual figures during the last days of the Roman Republic. He won fame
as a young lawyer for his successful defense of Sextus Roscius, the victim of a
trumped-up murder charge and enemy of the powerful dictator, Sulla. In 75 B.C.,
Cicero was sent to Sicily as an administrator, and five years later acted as prosecutor of Verres, an unscrupulous governor whose cruel and corrupt rule had
excited the hostility of the Sicilians. So powerful was the indictment that Verres,
abandoning all hope of a defense, fled into exile.

In the year 66, Cicero, now a famous man, was elected a magistrate of Rome.
Two years later he became Roman consul, at a time when the Republic was in
a critical condition because of corruption and sedition. The courage and eloquence with which Cicero defeated the conspiracy of Catiline, whom he denounced before the Roman Senate in four famous orations, won him still greater
celebrity. One of his enemies, Publius Clodius, a tribune, thereupon charged him
with putting Catiline's fellow conspirators to death without public trial, and
he was forced into exile. But he soon returned to public office and brilliantly
defended the old forms of the Roman constitution against the encroachments
of autocracy. After Caesar's murder, he denounced Mark Antony in a series of
impassioned orations before the Senate. His death was then demanded by Antony,
and he was assassinated.

Despite his tumultuous public career, Cicero found time to write various philosophical and literary works. He developed the Stoic doctrine that the only just government is that based upon law and that the moral foundation of law is the natural kinship and equality of all men.

The Laws

PERSONS OF THE DIALOGUE: *Marcus Tullius Cicero* himself; *Quintus Tullius Cicero,* his brother; and *Titus Pomponius Atticus,* his friend.

Marcus. . . . Out of all the material of the philosophers' discussions, surely there comes nothing more valuable than the full realization that we are born for Justice, and that right is based, not upon men's opinions, but upon Nature. This fact will immediately be plain if you once get a clear conception of man's fellowship and union with his fellow-men. For no single thing is so like another, so exactly its counterpart, as all of us are to one another. Nay, if bad habits and false beliefs did not twist the weaker minds and turn them in whatever direction they are inclined, no one would be so like his own self as all men would be like all others. And so, however we may define man, a single definition will apply to all. This is a sufficient proof that there is no difference in kind between man and man; for if there were, one defi-

The following excerpts from Books I and II of *The Laws* and Book III of *The Republic* are taken from *De Re Publica, De Legibus,* with an English translation by Clinton Walker Keyes (Loeb Classical Library), Harvard University Press, Cambridge, Mass., 1943. Reprinted by permission.

nition could not be applicable to all men; and indeed reason, which alone raises us above the level of the beasts and enables us to draw inferences, to prove and disprove, to discuss and solve problems, and to come to conclusions, is certainly common to us all, and, though varying in what it learns, at least in the capacity to learn it is invariable. For the same things are invariably perceived by the senses, and those things which stimulate the senses, stimulate them in the same way in all men; and those rudimentary beginnings of intelligence to which I have referred, which are imprinted on our minds, are imprinted on all minds alike; and speech, the mind's interpreter, though differing in the choice of words, agrees in the sentiments expressed. In fact, there is no human being of any race who, if he finds a guide, cannot attain to virtue.

The similarity of the human race is clearly marked in its evil tendencies as well as in its goodness, for pleasure also attracts all men; and even though it is an enticement to vice, yet it has some likeness to what is naturally good. For it delights us by its lightness and agreeableness; and for this reason, by an error of thought, it is embraced as something wholesome. It is through a similar misconception that we shun death as though it were a dissolution of nature, and cling to life because it keeps us in the sphere in which we were born; and that we look upon pain as one of the greatest of evils, not only because of its cruelty, but also because it seems to lead to the destruction of nature. In the same way, on account of the similarity between moral worth and renown, those who are publicly honored are considered happy, while those who do not attain fame are thought miserable. Troubles, joys, desires, and fears haunt the minds of all men without distinction, and even if different men have different beliefs, that does not prove, for example, that it is not the same quality of superstition that besets those races which worship dogs and cats as gods, as that which torments other races. But what nation does not love courtesy, kindliness, gratitude, and remembrance of favors bestowed? What people does not hate and despise the haughty, the wicked, the cruel, and the ungrateful? Inasmuch as these considerations prove to us that the whole human race is bound together in unity, it follows, finally, that knowledge of the principles of right living is what makes men better.

If you approve of what has been said, I will go on to what follows. But if there is anything that you care to have explained, we will take that up first.

Atticus. We have no questions, if I may speak for both of us.

Marcus. The next point, then, is that we are so constituted by Nature as to share the sense of Justice with one another and to pass it on to all men. And in this whole discussion I want it understood that what I shall call Nature is [that which is implanted in us by Nature]; that, however, the corruption caused by bad habits is so great that the sparks of fire, so to speak, which Nature has kindled in us are extinguished by this corruption, and the vices which are their opposites spring up and are established. But, if the judgments of men were in agreement with Nature, so that, as the poet says, they considered "nothing alien to them which concerns mankind," then Justice would be equally observed by all. For those creatures who have received the gift of reason from Nature have also received right reason, and therefore they have also received the gift of Law, which is right reason applied to command and prohibition. And if they have received Law, they have received Justice also. Now, all men have received reason; therefore, all men have received Justice. Consequently, Socrates was right when he cursed, as he often did, the man who first separated utility from Justice; for this separation, he complained, is the source of all mischief. For what gave rise to Pythagoras' famous words about friendship? . . . From this it is clear that, when a wise man shows toward another endowed with equal virtue the kind of benevolence which is so widely diffused among men, that will then have come to pass which, unbelievable as it seems to some, is after all the inevitable result—namely, that he loves himself no whit more than he loves another. For what difference can there be among things which are all equal? But, if the least distinction should be made in friendship, then the very name of friendship would perish forthwith; for its essence is such that, as soon as either friend prefers anything for himself, friendship ceases to exist.

Now, all this is really a preface to what remains to be said in our discussion, and its purpose is to make it more easily understood that Justice is inherent in Nature. After I have said a few words more on this topic, I shall go on to the civil law, the subject which gives rise to all this discourse.

Quintus. You certainly need to say very little more on that head, for from what you have already said, Atticus is convinced, and certainly I am, that Nature is the source of Justice.

Atticus. How can I help being convinced, when it has just been proved to us, first, that we have been provided and equipped with what we may call the gifts of the gods; next, that there is only one principle by which men may live with one another, and that this is the same for all, and possessed equally by all; and, finally, that all men are bound together by a certain natural feeling of kindliness and good-will, and also by a partnership in Justice? Now that we have admitted the truth of these conclusions, and rightly, I think, how can we separate Law and Justice from Nature? . . .

Marcus. Once more, then, before we come to the individual laws, let us look at the character and nature of Law, for fear that, though it must be the standard to which we refer everything, we may now and then be led astray by an incorrect use of terms, and forget the rational principles on which our laws must be based.

Quintus. Quite so, that is the correct method of exposition.

Marcus. Well, then, I find that it has been the opinion of the wisest men that Law is not a product of human thought, nor is it any enactment of peoples, but something eternal which rules the whole universe by its wisdom in command and prohibition. Thus they have been accustomed to say that Law is the primal and ultimate mind of God, whose reason directs all things either by compulsion or restraint. Wherefore that Law which the gods have given to the human race has been justly praised; for it is the reason and mind of a wise lawgiver applied to command and prohibition.

Quintus. You have touched upon this subject several times before. But before you come to the laws of peoples, please make the character of this heavenly Law clear to us, so that the waves of habit may not carry us away and sweep us into the common mode of speech of such subjects.

Marcus. Ever since we were children, Quintus, we have learned to call, "If one summon another to court,"[1] and other rules of the same kind, laws. But we must come to the true understanding of the matter, which is as follows: this and other commands and prohibitions of nations have the power to summon to righteousness and away from wrongdoing; but this power is not merely older than the existence of nations and States, it is coeval with that God who guards and rules heaven and earth. For the divine mind cannot exist without reason, and divine reason cannot but have this power to establish

[1] A familiar quotation from the Laws of the Twelve Tables, the earliest written code of Roman law.

right and wrong. No written law commanded that a man should take his stand on a bridge alone, against the full force of the enemy, and order the bridge broken down behind him; yet we shall not for that reason suppose that the heroic Cocles[2] was not obeying the law of bravery and following its decrees in doing so noble a deed. Even if there was no written law against rape at Rome in the reign of Lucius Tarquinius, we cannot say on that account that Sextus Tarquinius did not break that eternal Law by violating Lucretia, the daughter of Tricipitinus. For reason did exist, derived from the Nature of the universe, urging men to right conduct and diverting them from wrongdoing, and this reason did not first become Law when it was written down, but when it first came into existence; and it came into existence simultaneously with the divine mind. Wherefore the true and primal Law, applied to command and prohibition, is the right reason of supreme Jupiter.

Quintus. I agree with you, brother, that what is right and true is also eternal, and does not begin or end with written statutes.

Marcus. Therefore, just as that divine mind is the supreme Law, so, when [reason] is perfected in man, [that also is Law; and this perfected reason exists] in the mind of the wise man; but those rules which, in varying forms and for the need of the moment, have been formulated for the guidance of nations, bear the title of laws rather by favor than because they are really such.

[2] Horatius Cocles, who, with two companions, held the bridge over the Tiber against the Etruscan army.

For every law which really deserves that name is truly praiseworthy, as they prove by approximately the following arguments. It is agreed, of course, that laws were invented for the safety of citizens, the preservation of States, and the tranquility and happiness of human life, and that those who first put statutes of this kind in force convinced their people that it was their intention to write down and put into effect such rules as, once accepted and adopted, would make possible for them an honorable and happy life; and when such rules were drawn up and put in force, it is clear that men called them "laws." From this point of view it can be readily understood that those who formulated wicked and unjust statutes for nations, thereby breaking their promises and agreements, put into effect anything but "laws." It may thus be clear that in the very definition of the term "law" there inheres the idea and principle of choosing what is just and true. I ask you then, Quintus, according to the custom of the philosophers: if there is a certain thing, the lack of which in a State compels us to consider it no State at all, must we consider this thing a good?

Quintus. One of the greatest goods, certainly.

Marcus. And if a State lacks Law, must it for that reason be considered no State at all?

Quintus. It cannot be denied.

Marcus. Then Law must necessarily be considered one of the greatest goods.

Quintus. I agree with you entirely.

Marcus. What of the many deadly, the many pestilential statutes which nations put in force? These no more deserve to be called laws than the rules a band of robbers might pass in their assembly. For if ignorant and unskilful men have prescribed deadly poisons instead of healing drugs, these cannot possibly be called physicians' prescriptions; neither in a nation can a statute of any sort be called a law, even though the nation, in spite of its being a ruinous regulation, has accepted it. Therefore Law is the distinction between things just and unjust, made in agreement with that primal and most ancient of all things, Nature; and in conformity to Nature's standard are framed those human laws which inflict punishment upon the wicked but defend and protect the good.

Quintus. I understand you completely, and believe that from now on we must not consider or even call anything else a law.

Marcus. Then you do not think the Titian or Apuleian Laws were really laws at all?

Quintus. No; nor the Livian Laws either.[3]

Marcus. And you are right, especially as the Senate repealed them in one sentence and in a single moment. But the Law whose nature I have explained can neither be repealed nor abrogated.

[3] Examples of laws passed in Rome. It is implied that these enacted laws are not laws in the profounder sense that applies to natural laws.

The Republic

. . . True law is right reason in agreement with nature; it is of universal application, unchanging and everlasting; it summons to duty by its commands, and averts from wrongdoing by its prohibitions. And it does not lay its commands or prohibitions upon good men in vain, though neither have any effect on the wicked. It is a sin to try to alter this law, nor is it allowable to attempt to repeal any part of it, and it is impossible to abolish it entirely. We cannot be freed from its obligations by senate or people, and we need not look outside ourselves for an expounder or interpreter of it. And there will not be different laws at Rome and at Athens, or different laws now and in the future, but one eternal and unchangeable law will be valid for all nations and all times, and there will be one master and ruler, that is, God, over us all, for he is the author of this law, its promulgator, and its enforcing judge. Whoever is disobedient is fleeing from himself and denying his human nature, and by reason of this very fact he will suffer the worst penalties, even if he escapes what is commonly considered punishment. . . .

MARCUS AURELIUS (121–180 A.D.)

Marcus Aurelius was the adopted son of his uncle, the Emperor Antoninus Pius. In early boyhood he was introduced to the doctrines of Stoicism, and he assumed the simple dress and practiced the austere way of life of the Stoics. After his marriage to the emperor's daughter Faustina, who bore him thirteen children, he was occupied with family affairs and learning the arts of government. At the death of Antoninus in 161 he became the ruler of the vast Roman Empire.

The remaining nineteen years of his life called for all the Stoic fortitude he could muster; for his reign was beset with calamities—floods, fires, earthquakes, pestilences, insurrections, wars, and barbarian invasions. He instituted many reforms and founded charitable institutions, but he violently persecuted the Christians whom he regarded as subversive. His *Meditations*, which apparently were private soliloquies intended for no eyes but his own, were written during military campaigns, the hardships of which eventually caused his death at his headquarters near present-day Vienna.

Meditations

Book II

Begin the morning by saying to thyself, I shall meet with the busybody, the ungrateful, arrogant, deceitful, envious, unsocial. All these things happen to them by reason of their ignorance of what is good and evil. But I who have seen the nature of the good that it is beautiful, and of the bad that it is ugly, and the nature of him who does wrong, that it is akin to me, not only of the same blood or seed, but that it participates in the same intelligence and the same portion of the divinity, I can neither be injured by any of them, for no one can fix on me what is ugly, nor

From *The Meditations of Marcus Aurelius Antoninus* translated by George Long (1862).

can I be angry with my kinsman, nor hate him. For we are made for co-operation, like feet, like hands, like eyelids, like the rows of the upper and lower teeth. To act against one another then is contrary to nature; and it is acting against one another to be vexed and to turn away.

9. This thou must always bear in mind, what is the nature of the whole, and what is my nature, and how this is related to that, and what kind of a part it is of what kind of a whole; and that there is no one who hinders thee from always doing and saying the things which are according to the nature of which thou are a part.

16. The soul of man does violence to itself, first of all, when it becomes an abscess and, as it were, a tumour on the

universe, so far as it can. For to be vexed at anything which happens is a separation of ourselves from nature, in some part of which the natures of all other things are contained. In the next place, the soul does violence to itself when it turns away from any man, or even moves towards him with the intention of injuring, such as are the souls of those who are angry. In the third place, the soul does violence to itself when it is overpowered by pleasure or by pain. Fourthly, when it plays a part, and does or says anything insincerely and untruly. Fifthly, when it allows any act of its own and any movement to be without an aim, and does anything thoughtlessly and without considering what it is, it being right that even the smallest things be done with reference to an end; and the end of rational animals is to follow the reason and the law of the most ancient city and polity.

17. Of human life the time is a point, and the substance is in a flux, and the perception dull, and the composition of the whole body subject to putrefaction, and the soul a whirl, and fortune hard to divine, and fame a thing devoid of judgement. And, to say all in a word, everything which belongs to the body is a stream, and what belongs to the soul is a dream and vapour, and life is a warfare and a stranger's sojourn, and after-fame is oblivion. What then is that which is able to conduct a man? One thing and only one, philosophy. But this consists in keeping the daemon within a man free from violence and unharmed, superior to pains and pleasures, doing nothing without a purpose, nor yet falsely and with hypocrisy, not

feeling the need of another man's doing or not doing anything; and besides, accepting all that happens, and all that it allotted, as coming from thence, wherever it is, from whence he himself came; and, finally, waiting for death with a cheerful mind, as being nothing else than a dissolution of the elements of which every living being is compounded. But if there is no harm to the elements themselves in each continually changing into another, why should a man have any apprehension about the change and dissolution of all the elements? For it is according to nature, and nothing is evil which is according to nature.

Book III

2. We ought to observe also that even the things which follow after the things which are produced according to nature contain something pleasing and attractive. For instance, when bread is baked some parts are split at the surface, and these parts which thus open, and have a certain fashion contrary to the purpose of the baker's art, are beautiful in a manner, and in a peculiar way excite a desire for eating. And again, figs, when they are quite ripe, gape open; and in the ripe olives the very circumstance of their being near to rottenness adds a peculiar beauty to the fruit. And the ears of corn bending down, and the lion's eyebrows, and the foam which flows from the mouth of wild boars, and many other things—though they are far from being beautiful, if a man should examine them severally—still, because they are consequent upon the things which are formed by nature, help

to adorn them, and they please the mind; so that if a man should have a feeling and deeper insight with respect to the things which are produced in the universe, there is hardly one of those which follow by way of consequence which will not seem to him to be in a manner disposed so as to give pleasure. And so he will see even the real gaping jaws of wild beasts with no less pleasure than those which painters and sculptors show by imitation; and in an old woman and an old man he will be able to see a certain maturity and comeliness; and the attractive loveliness of young persons he will be able to look on with chaste eyes; and many such things will present themselves, not pleasing to every man, but to him only who has become truly familiar with nature and her works.

11. To the aids which have been mentioned let this one still be added:— Make for thyself a definition or description of the thing which is presented to thee, so as to see distinctly what kind of a thing it is in its substance, in its nudity, in its complete entirety, and tell thyself its proper name, and the names of the things of which it has been compounded, and into which it will be resolved. For nothing is so productive of elevation of mind as to be able to examine methodically and truly every object which is presented to thee in life, and always to look at things so as to see at the same time what kind of universe this is, and what kind of use everything performs in it, and what value everything has with reference to the whole, and what with reference to man, who is a citizen of the highest city, of which all other cities are like families; what

each thing is, and of what it is composed, and how long it is the nature of this thing to endure which now makes an impression on me, and what virtue I have need of with respect to it, such as gentleness, manliness, truth, fidelity, simplicity, contentment, and the rest. Wherefore, on every occasion a man should say: this comes from God; and this is according to the apportionment and spinning of the thread of destiny, and such-like coincidence and chance; and this is from one of the same stock, and a kinsman and partner, one who knows not however what is according to his nature. But I know; for this reason I behave towards him according to the natural law of fellowship with benevolence and justice. At the same time however in things indifferent I attempt to ascertain the value of each.

Book IV

4. If our intellectual part is common, the reason also, in respect of which we are rational beings, is common: if this is so, common also is the reason which commands us what to do, and what not to do; if this is so, there is a common law also; if this is so, we are fellow-citizens; if this is so, we are members of some political community; if this is so, the world is in a manner a state. For of what other common political community will any one say that the whole human race are members? And from thence, from this common political community comes also our very intellectual faculty and reasoning faculty and our capacity for law; or whence do they come? For as my earthly part is a portion given to me from certain earth, and

that which is watery from another element, and that which is hot and fiery from some peculiar source (for nothing comes out of that which is nothing, as nothing also returns to non-existence), so also the intellectual part comes from some source.

23. Everything harmonizes with me, which is harmonious to thee, O Universe. Nothing for me is too early nor too late, which is in due time for thee. Everything is fruit to me which thy seasons bring, O Nature: from thee are all things, in thee are all things, to thee all things return. The poet says, Dear city of Cecrops; and wilt not thou say, Dear city of Zeus?

48. Think continually how many physicians are dead after often contracting their eyebrows over the sick; and how many astrologers after predicting with great pretensions the deaths of others; and how many philosophers after endless discourses on death or immortality; how many heroes after killing thousands; and how many tyrants who have used their power over men's lives with terrible insolence as if they were immortal; and how many cities are entirely dead, so to speak, Helice and Pompeii and Herculaneum, and others innumerable. Add to the reckoning all whom thou hast known, one after another. One man after burying another has been laid out dead, and another buries him: and all this in a short time. To conclude, always observe how ephemeral and worthless human things are, and what was yesterday a little mucus tomorrow will be a mummy or ashes. Pass then through this little space of time conformably to nature, and end thy journey in content, just as an olive falls off when it is ripe, blessing nature who produced it, and thanking the tree on which it grew.

49. Be like the promontory against which the waves continually break, but it stands firm and tames the fury of the water around it.

Unhappy am I, because this has happened to me.—Not so, but happy am I, though this has happened to me, because I continue free from pain, neither crushed by the present nor fearing the future. For such a thing as this might have happened to every man; but every man would not have continued free from pain on such an occasion. Why then is that rather a misfortune than this a good fortune? And dost thou in all cases call that a man's misfortune, which is not a deviation from man's nature? And does a thing seem to thee to be a deviation from man's nature, when it is not contrary to the will of man's nature? Well, thou knowest the will of nature. Will then this which has happened prevent thee from being just, magnanimous, temperate, prudent, secure against inconsiderate opinions and falsehood; will it prevent thee from having modesty, freedom, and everything else, by the presence of which man's nature obtains all that is its own? Remember too on every occasion which leads thee to vexation to apply this principle: not that this is a misfortune, but that to bear it nobly is good fortune.

Book V

In the morning when thou risest unwillingly, let this thought be present— I am rising to the work of a human being. Why then am I dissatisfied if I am going to do the things for which I exist and for which I was brought into the world? Or have I been made for this, to lie in the bed-clothes and keep myself warm?—But this is more pleasant.—Dost thou exist then to take thy pleasure, and not at all for action or exertion? Dost thou not see the little plants, the little birds, the ants, the spiders, the bees working together to put in order their several parts of the universe? And art thou willing to do the work of a human being, and dost thou not make haste to do that which is according to thy nature?—But it is necessary to take rest also.—It is necessary: however nature has fixed bounds to this too: she has fixed bounds both to eating and drinking, and yet thou goest beyond these bounds, beyond what is sufficient; yet in thy acts it is not so, but thou stoppest short of what thou canst do. So thou lovest not thyself, for if thou didst, thou wouldst love thy nature and her will. But those who love their several arts exhaust themselves in working at them unwashed and without food; but thou valuest thy own nature less than the turner values the turning art, or the dancer the dancing art, or the lover of money values his money, or the vainglorious man his little glory. And such men, when they have a violent affection to a thing, choose neither to eat nor to sleep rather than to perfect the things which they care for. But are the acts which concern society more vile in thy eyes and less worthy of thy labour?

2. How easy it is to repel and to wipe away every impression which is troublesome or unsuitable, and immediately to be in all tranquillity.

3. Judge every word and deed which are according to nature to be fit for thee; and be not diverted by the blame which follows from any people nor by their words, but if a thing is good to be done or said, do not consider it unworthy of thee. For those persons have their peculiar leading principle and follow their peculiar movement; which things do not thou regard, but go straight on, following thy own nature and the common nature; and the way of both is one.

16. Such as are thy habitual thoughts, such also will be the character of thy mind; for the soul is dyed by the thoughts. Dye it then with a continuous series of such thoughts as these: for instance, that where a man can live, there he can also live well. But he must live in a place;—well then, he can also live well in a palace. And again, consider that for whatever purpose each thing has been constituted, for this it has been constituted, and towards this it is carried; and its end is in that towards which it is carried; and where the end is, there also is the advantage and the good of each thing. Now the good for the reasonable animal is society; for that we are made for society has been shown above. Is it not plain that the inferior exist for the sake of the superior? But the things which have life are superior to those which have not life, and of those which have life the superior are those which have reason.

Book VI

15. Some things are hurrying into existence, and others are hurrying out of it; and of that which is coming into

existence part is already extinguished. Motions and changes are continually renewing the world, just as the uninterrupted course of time is always renewing the infinite duration of ages. In this flowing stream then, on which there is no abiding, what is there of the things which hurry by on which a man would set a high price? It would be just as if a man should fall in love with one of the sparrows which fly by, but it has already passed out of sight. Something of this kind is the very life of every man, like the exhalation of the blood and the respiration of the air. For such as it is to have once drawn in the air and to have given it back, which we do every moment, just the same is it with the whole respiratory power, which thou didst receive at thy birth yesterday and the day before, to give it back to the element from which thou didst first draw it.

16. Neither is transpiration, as in plants, a thing to be valued, nor respiration, as in domesticated animals and wild beasts, nor the receiving of impressions by the appearances of things, nor being moved by desires as puppets by strings, nor assembling in herds, nor being nourished by food; for this is just like the act of separating and parting with the useless part of our food. What then is worth being valued? To be received with clapping of hands? No. Neither must we value the clapping of tongues, for the praise which comes from the many is a clapping of tongues. Suppose then that thou hast given up this worthless thing called fame, what remains that is worth valuing? This is my opinion, to move thyself and to restrain thyself in conformity to thy proper constitution, to which end both all employments and arts lead. For every art aims at this, that the thing which has been made should be adapted to the work for which it has been made; and both the vine-planter who looks after the vine, and the horse-breaker, and he who trains the dog, seek this end. But the education and the teaching of youth aim at something. In this then is the value of the education and the teaching. And if this is well, thou wilt not seek anything else. Wilt thou not cease to value many other things too? Then thou wilt be neither free, nor sufficient for thy own happiness, nor without passion. For of necessity thou must be envious, jealous, and suspicious of those who can take away those things, and plot against those who have that which is valued by thee. Of necessity a man must be altogether in a state of perturbation who wants any of these things; and besides, he must often find fault with the gods. But to reverence and honour thy own mind will make thee content with thyself, and in harmony with society, and in agreement with the gods, that is, praising all that they give and have ordered.

Book VII

9. All things are implicated with one another, and the bond is holy; and there is hardly anything unconnected with any other thing. For things have been co-ordinated, and they combine to form the same universe (order). For there is one universe made up of all things, and one God who pervades all things, and one substance, and one law, one common reason in all intelligent animals, and one truth; if indeed there

is also one perfection for all animals which are of the same stock and participate in the same reason.

55. Do not look around thee to discover other men's ruling principles, but look straight to this, to what nature leads thee, both the universal nature through the things which happen to thee, and thy own nature through the acts which must be done by thee. But every being ought to do that which is according to its constitution; and all other things have been constituted for the sake of rational beings, just as among irrational things the inferior for the sake of the superior, but the rational for the sake of one another.

The prime principle then in man's constitution is the social. And the second is not to yield to the persuasions of the body, for it is the peculiar office of the rational and intelligent motion to circumscribe itself, and never to be overpowered either by the motion of the senses or of the appetites, for both are animal; but the intelligent motion claims superiority and does not permit itself to be overpowered by the others. And with good reason, for it is formed by nature to use all of them. The third thing in the rational constitution is freedom from error and from deception. Let then the ruling principle holding fast to these things go straight on, and it has what is its own.

Book VIII

7. Every nature is contented with itself when it goes on its way well; and a rational nature goes on its way well, when in its thoughts it assents to nothing false or uncertain, and when it directs its movements to social acts only, and when it confines its desires and aversions to the things which are in its power, and when it is satisfied with everything that is assigned to it by the common nature. For of this common nature every particular nature is a part, as the nature of the leaf is a part of the nature of the plant; except that in the plant the nature of the leaf is part of a nature which has not perception or reason, and is subject to be impeded; but the nature of man is part of a nature which is not subject to impediments, and is intelligent and just, since it gives to everything in equal portions and according to its worth, times, substance, cause (form), activity, and incident. But examine, not to discover that any one thing compared with any other single thing is equal in all respects, but by taking all the parts together of one thing comparing them with all the parts together of another.

34. If thou didst ever see a hand cut off, or a foot, or a head, lying anywhere apart from the rest of the body, such does a man make himself, as far as he can, who is not content with what happens, and separates himself from others, or does anything unsocial. Suppose that thou hast detached thyself from the natural unity—for thou wast made by nature a part, but now thou hast cut thyself off—yet here there is this beautiful provision, that it is in thy power again to unite thyself. God has allowed this to no other part, after it has been separated and cut asunder, to come together again. But consider the kindness by which he has distinguished man, for he has put it in his power not to be separated at all from the universal; and

when he has been separated, he has allowed him to return and to be united and to resume his place as a part.

47. If thou art pained by any external thing, it is not this thing that disturbs thee, but thy own judgement about it. And it is in thy power to wipe out this judgement now. But if anything in thy own disposition gives thee pain, who hinders thee from correcting thy opinion? And even if thou are pained because thou art not doing some particular thing which seems to thee to be right, why dost thou not rather act than complain?—But some insuperable obstacle is in the way?—Do not be grieved then, for the cause of its not being done depends not on thee.—But it is not worth while to live, if this cannot be done.—Take thy departure then from life contentedly, just as he dies who is in full activity, and well pleased too with things which are obstacles.

Book IX

3. Do not despise death, but be well content with it, since this too is one of those things which nature wills. For such as it is to be young and to grow old, and to increase and to reach maturity, and to have teeth and beard and grey hairs, and to beget, and to be pregnant and to bring forth, and all the other natural operations which the seasons of thy life bring, such also is dissolution. This, then, is consistent with the character of a reflecting man, to be neither careless nor impatient nor contemptuous with respect to death, but to wait for it as one of the operations of nature. As thou now waitest for the time when the child shall come out of thy wife's womb, so be ready for the time when thy soul shall fall out of this envelope. But if thou requirest also a vulgar kind of comfort which shall reach thy heart, thou wilt be made best reconciled to death by observing the objects from which thou art going to be removed, and the morals of those with whom thy soul will no longer be mingled. For it is no way right to be offended with men, but it is thy duty to care for them and to bear with them gently; and yet to remember that thy departure will be not from men who have the same principles as thyself. For this is the only thing, if there be any, which could draw us the contrary way and attach us to life, to be permitted to live with those who have the same principles as ourselves. But now thou seest how great is the trouble arising from the discordance of those who live together, so that thou mayest say, Come quick, O death, lest perchance I, too, should forget myself.

9. All things which participate in anything which is common to them all move towards that which is of the same kind with themselves. Everything which is earthy turns towards the earth, everything which is liquid flows together, and everything which is of an aërial kind does the same, so that they require something to keep them asunder, and the application of force. Fire indeed moves upwards on account of the elemental fire, but it is so ready to be kindled together with all the fire which is here, that even every substance which is somewhat dry, is easily ignited, because there is less mingled with it of that which is a hindrance to ignition. Accordingly then everything

also which participates in the common intelligent nature moves in like manner towards that which is of the same kind with itself, or moves even more. For so much as it is superior in comparison with all other things, in the same degree also is it more ready to mingle with and to be fused with that which is akin to it. Accordingly among animals devoid of reason we find swarms of bees, and herds of cattle, and the nurture of young birds, and in a manner, loves; for even in animals there are souls, and that power which brings them together is seen to exert itself in the superior degree, and in such a way as never has been observed in plants nor in stones nor in trees. But in rational animals there are political communities and friendships, and families and meetings of people; and in wars, treaties and armistices. But in the things which are still superior, even though they are separated from one another, unity in a manner exists, as in the stars. Thus the ascent to the higher degree is able to produce a sympathy even in things which are separated. See, then, what now takes place. For only intelligent animals have now forgotten this mutual desire and inclination, and in them alone the property of flowing together is not seen. But still though men strive to avoid this union, they are caught and held by it, for their nature is too strong for them; and thou wilt see what I say, if thou only observest. Sooner, then, will one find anything earthy which comes in contact with no earthy thing than a man altogether separated from other men.

42. When thou art offended with any man's shameless conduct, immediately ask thyself, Is it possible, then, that shameless men should not be in the world? It is not possible. Do not, then, require what is impossible. For this man also is one of those shameless men who must of necessity be in the world. Let the same considerations be present to thy mind in the case of the knave, and the faithless man, and of every man who does wrong in any way. For at the same time that thou dost remind thyself that it is impossible that such kind of men should not exist, thou wilt become more kindly disposed towards every one individually. It is useful to perceive this, too, immediately when the occasion arises, what virtue nature has given to man to oppose to every wrongful act. For she has given to man, as an antidote against the stupid man, mildness, and against another kind of man some other power. And in all cases it is possible for thee to correct by teaching the man who is gone astray; for every man who errs misses his object and is gone astray. Besides wherein hast thou been injured? For thou wilt find that no one among those against whom thou art irritated has done anything by which thy mind could be made worse; but that which is evil to thee and harmful has its foundation only in the mind. And what harm is done or what is there strange, if the man who has not been instructed does the acts of an uninstructed man? Consider whether thou shouldst not rather blame thyself, because thou didst not expect such a man to err in such a way. For thou hadst means given thee by the reason to suppose that it was likely that he would commit this error, and yet thou hast forgotten and art amazed that he has

erred. But most of all when thou blamest a man as faithless or ungrateful, turn to thyself. For the fault is manifestly thy own, whether thou didst trust that a man who had such a disposition would keep his promise, or when conferring thy kindness thou didst not confer it absolutely, nor yet in such way as to have received from thy very act all the profit. For what more dost thou want when thou hast done a man a service? Are thou not content that thou hast done something conformable to thy nature, and dost thou seek to be paid for it? Just as if the eye demanded a recompense for seeing, or the feet for walking. For as these members are formed for a particular purpose, and by working according to their several constitutions obtain what is their own; so also as man is formed by nature to acts of benevolence, when he has done anything benevolent or in any other way conducive to the common interest, he has acted conformably to his constitution, and he gets what is his own.

Book X

2. Observe what thy nature requires, so far as thou art governed by nature only: then do it and accept it, if thy nature, so far as thou art a living being, shall not be made worse by it. And next thou must observe what thy nature requires so far as thou art a living being. And all this thou mayest allow thyself, if thy nature, so far as thou art a rational animal, shall not be made worse by it. But the rational animal is consequently also a political (social) animal. Use these rules, then, and trouble thyself about nothing else.

6. Whether the universe is a concourse of atoms, or nature is a system, let this first be established, that I am a part of the whole which is governed by nature; next, I am in a manner intimately related to the parts which are of the same kind with myself. For remembering this, inasmuch as I am a part, I shall be discontented with none of the things which are assigned to me out of the whole; for nothing is injurious to the part, if it is for the advantage of the whole. For the whole contains nothing which is not for its advantage; and all natures indeed have this common principle, but the nature of the universe has this principle besides, that it cannot be compelled even by any external cause to generate anything harmful to itself. By remembering, then, that I am a part of such a whole, I shall be content with everything that happens. And inasmuch as I am in a manner intimately related to the parts which are of the same kind with myself, I shall do nothing unsocial, but I shall rather direct myself to the things which are of the same kind with myself, and I shall turn all my efforts to the common interest, and divert them from the contrary. Now, if these things are done so, life must flow on happily, just as thou mayest observe that the life of a citizen is happy, who continues a course of action which is advantageous to his fellow-citizens, and is content with whatever the state may assign to him.

Book XI

19. There are four principal aberrations of the superior faculty against which thou shouldst be constantly on

thy guard, and when thou hast detected them, thou shouldst wipe them out and say on each occasion thus: this thought is not necessary: this tends to destroy social union: this which thou art going to say comes not from the real thoughts; for thou shouldst consider it among the most absurd of things for a man not to speak from his real thoughts. But the fourth is when thou shalt reproach thyself for anything, for this is an evidence of the diviner part within thee being overpowered and yielding to the less honourable and to the perishable part, the body, and to its gross pleasures.

20. Thy aërial part and all the fiery parts which are mingled in thee, though by nature they have an upward tendency, still in obedience to the disposition of the universe they are overpowered here in the compound mass (the body). And also the whole of the earthy part in thee and the watery, though their tendency is downward, still are raised up and occupy a position which is not their natural one. In this manner then the elemental parts obey the universal, for when they have been fixed in any place perforce they remain there until again the universal shall sound the signal for dissolution. Is it not then strange that thy intelligent part only should be disobedient and discontented with its own place? And yet no force is imposed on it, but only those things which are conformable to its nature: still it does not submit, but is carried in the opposite direction. For the movement towards injustice and intemperance and to anger and grief and fear is nothing else than the act of one who deviates from nature. And also when the ruling faculty is discontented with

anything that happens, then too it deserts its post: for it is constituted for piety and reverence towards the gods no less than for justice. For these qualities also are comprehended under the generic term of contentment with the constitution of things, and indeed they are prior to acts of justice.

Book XII

26. When thou art troubled about anything, thou hast forgotten this, that all things happen according to the universal nature; and forgotten this, that a man's wrongful act is nothing to thee; and further thou hast forgotten this, that everything which happens, always happened so and will happen so, and now happens so everywhere; forgotten this too, how close is the kinship between a man and the whole human race, for it is a community, not of a little blood or seed, but of intelligence. And thou hast forgotten this too, that every man's intelligence is a god, and is an efflux of the deity; and forgotten this, that nothing is a man's own, but that his child and his body and his very soul came from the deity; forgotten this, that everything is opinion; and lastly thou hast forgotten that every man lives the present time only, and loses only this.

36. Man, thou hast been a citizen in this great state (the world): what difference does it make to thee whether for five years (or three)? For that which is conformable to the laws is just for all. Where is the hardship then, if no tyrant nor yet an unjust judge sends thee away from the state, but nature who brought thee into it? The same as if a

praetor who has employed an actor dismisses him from the stage.—'But I have not finished the five acts, but only three of them.'—Thou sayest well, but in life the three acts are the whole drama; for what shall be a complete drama is determined by him who was once the cause of its composition, and now of its dissolution: but thou art the cause of neither. Depart then satisfied, for he also who releases thee is satisfied.

RALPH MASON BLAKE (1889–1950)

Blake was born in Greenfield, Massachusetts, and graduated from Williams College. In 1912 he received his Master's degree and in 1915 his Doctor's degree from Harvard. He taught at Princeton University 1915–1917, the University of Washington 1919–1930, Brown University 1930–1950, and was a Visiting Professor at the University of Chicago 1927–1928 and Harvard 1928–1929. Remarkable for the clarity of his thinking, the range of his knowledge, and the cultivation of his taste, he could discourse with equal brilliance on the music of Palestrina or the method of Descartes. Blake was a lifelong bachelor and he enjoyed good food and good company.

On Natural Rights

At various times in the history of moral and political philosophy the concept of natural rights has played an important and prominent rôle in the thoughts of men. It has frequently, indeed, been the central and dominating idea of a whole system. At other periods, however—and it is through one of these that we seem at present to be passing—it has fallen out of favor. In many quarters it seems just now to be regarded as an outworn and exploded superstition of the past, and any appeal to the idea is looked upon as evidence of an antiquated and unenlight-

From Ralph Mason Blake, "On Natural Rights," *Ethics*, Volum 36 (October 1925). Reprinted by permission.

ened approach to the problems of the day. We may well ask ourselves, however, whether an idea of such vitality, appealed to at times, indeed, by the most diverse schools of thought as giving warrant to their views, and constantly reappearing in men's minds just when it seemed once more finally to have been got rid of, does not really embody some important notion which it would be useful to preserve and dangerous to lose sight of. It is this question which I propose here to examine.

It would be admitted, I suppose, that, speaking generally, "rights" are correlative with "duties" and are defined by laws. Thus, if we start with the positive law, whether constitutional or statutory, we find that there are many positive laws which define "rights" vested in certain individuals or groups of individuals (one of which groups may be society as a whole), and impose duties correlative with these rights upon other individuals or groups of individuals (or again upon society as a whole). The rights so defined seem usually to be of the nature of *claims* which their possessors may legitimately (i.e., in accordance with the law) make upon others, claims, therefore, which always imply some correlative duty on the part of these others. Thus if in accordance with the law a laborer, upon the performance of labor, has a right to the wages for which he contracted, this means that he may legitimately *claim* the sum agreed upon, and that it is the legal *duty* of the employer to satisfy this claim by paying the wage. Or again, if a man has a legal right to the exclusive enjoyment of a certain piece of property, this means that he may lawfully claim immunity from any interference on the part of others with such exclusive enjoyment, and that it is the legal duty of these others to refrain from such interference. It thus appears that positive laws may, on occasion, give rise to positive legal rights and duties; and such rights as thus arise seem to be of the nature of certain liberties or freedoms which their possessors may legitimately exercise.

The traditional conception of "natural" rights, whatever its other content, seems at least always to be that of a system of "rights" having a deeper and more fundamental character than any merely legal rights, of a system of rights possessing an ultimate and objective validity not derived from their relation to any system of positive law. Natural rights, as their name indicates, are supposed to be based instead upon a law of nature itself, independent of any positive enactments of men, and of a higher validity. It is therefore considered possible to contrast merely legal rights with natural rights, and in case of conflict to assert the superior claims of the latter. Just as positive rights are derived from positive laws and correlated with legal duties, so natural rights are conceived to be based upon the "natural law," prescribed by the very nature of things, and to be correlated with certain natural duties. And, like legal rights, natural rights appear usually in the form of *claims*, often to some freedom, immunity, or privileges, made legitimate by this "law of nature."

But now this conception of a "law of nature" is certainly not entirely clear. It merits further examination. Among what are commonly known as laws of nature are certain generalizations of physical, chemical, or biological phenomena. These in fact are what we nowadays have chiefly in mind when we speak of natural law, or of the laws of nature. But these laws, it is fairly clear, are precisely not what are in question when it is a matter of determining rights. Laws of nature, in this sense of the term, do not tell us in the least what is right or what ought to be; they merely describe for us, without reference to matters of value, how natural phenomena as a matter of fact actually do occur. They thus explicitly abstract from the whole question as to whether the natural occurrences which they describe embody any sort of right or justice.

The natural laws from which natural

rights could be supposed to arise must therefore be of quite another sort. They must *not* abstract from matters of value, but must instead deal primarily therewith. They must be statements of what claims various individuals or groups of individuals *ought* to be privileged to make. Not, then, from natural physical laws, but only from natural *moral* laws can natural rights be conceived to arise —from the principles of *natural morality*, if one may be permitted to employ so unfashionable a term.

And now it is necessary to point out a very significant difference between the conception of a "law" in the sense of a fundamental principle of natural morality, and a law in the sense of a positive law or legal precept. The latter is in essence a *command* or imperative issued by some competent authority and backed by the force of some sanction, some penalty or reward to accrue from the authority in question, whether this authority be state, church, public opinion, or the customs of society. Natural moral laws, on the other hand, are not necessarily to be thought of as commands or precepts issued by any authority whatever. If they chance to be backed by some authority, that is conceived to be a wholly accidental circumstance. Nor are they necessarily enforced by any sanctions whatever. A positive law issued by no authority is a contradiction in terms. Laws of nature, on the other hand, are conceived to be independent of any authority. They remain what they are and retain their entire validity whether any authority commands them and enforces them with penalties or not. A law of nature *may* be enacted into a positive law—indeed many have held

that in default of enactment by any human authority they must be conceived to form part of the positive law of God, and to be enforced by supernatural sanctions. But the very conception of a law of nature is that it does not derive its being or its validity from any enactment or positive command whatever, but would remain valid even if every positive law were to contravene it. It is not only independent of positive laws, it is also deeper and more fundamental than they, and possessed of a higher validity.

The conception of a "natural law" from which natural rights and natural duties are derived is, then, the conception of a principle stating that the claim to such and such liberties, freedoms, or privileges ought to be vested in such and such individuals or groups of individuals, a principle which is to remain true and valid no matter what the positive law of any authority may decree, and by which any positive law which contravenes it may be condemned as contrary to natural right and justice— as constituting a violation of natural rights. And by calling these principles "laws of nature" it is implied that they are prescribed and determined by the very nature of things and are therefore independent of any choice or arbitrary decree, human or divine.

Not only, however, are such natural laws conceived as prescribed by nature herself, and as therefore superior to any arbitrary decree or enforcing sanction; they are also thought of as constituting eternal and immutable principles, as possessed of no merely temporary validity, but as remaining permanently valid —so long at least as the present order of nature shall continue in its general features to remain substantially what it now is. It might perhaps be admitted that other principles may be "laws of nature" for beings other than human, placed in a different general scheme of things; but such laws of nature as affect us human beings are conceived to be permanently valid truths for this our world, lasting unchanged so long as it shall last. Moreover, such laws of nature are conceived as being not only permanent in time, but as being also universally applicable in place. Inasmuch as they are determined by the general nature of things, it is held that they must be valid for all men everywhere, whether as a matter of fact all men have always recognized or acted upon their validity or not. And finally these natural laws are held to be *rational* laws, that is to say, principles which right reason, reflecting upon the order of nature, must necessarily discover to be generally valid.

And now, if it be admitted that these are the features which form the core of the ideas of natural laws, and of natural rights and duties based upon such laws, as these ideas have commonly been conceived, we may well ask ourselves whether there actually is or even conceivably can be any such thing as a "law of nature" in this sense of the term. In what sense, namely, can "nature" or "the nature of things" determine laws as to what claims ought to be vested in certain individuals or groups of individuals, and as to what duties ought in turn to be imposed upon others? And at first sight we may well doubt whether anything of the sort is at all possible, for when we turn to

history we find the most diverse and incompatible opinions, not only as to what these "natural rights" and these "laws of nature" as a matter of fact *are*, but also as to the very way in which "nature" is supposed to supply these principles or standards. The conception of "living according to nature," according to natural right and justice, as opposed to and deeper than merely legal, customary, or conventional standards, has played a central part in many different philosophies; but the difficulty is that it has supplied so many and such diverse standards—many of them mutually incompatible. Thus Aristotle found the "natural" in the rational standard of the mean, and in all that distinguishes man as a rational animal from the brutes; the Epicureans, on the other hand, found the "natural" precisely in that which men share with the brutes—the tendency to seek pleasurable and to avoid painful experiences. Thus Hobbes found the natural man to be actuated only by the egoistic will to power, whilst to Rousseau he appeared as a model of innocent peaceableness and sympathetic affection. It seems impossible to bring any real order out of such a chaos, and the attempt to find any standard of "what ought to be" from a contemplation of "nature" may thus well appear to be wholly futile.

And in fact, as this attempt has usually been conceived, it really is futile. I do not believe it to be possible to derive any principles with regard to what ought to be, any principles of "natural morality" or "law of nature," from a contemplation, no matter how earnest, disinterested and thoroughgoing, of the facts of nature, as these are reported to us by the ordinary descriptive sciences of nature. There is no road to the derivation of such principles from the consideration, taken merely in themselves, of the truths of physics or astronomy, or even of those of biology, psychology, or history. The reason for this impossibility seems to be that from "nature" as it is studied in any of these sciences all matters of *value* have from the beginning been carefully excluded. The physicist, the astronomer, the biologist and the psychologist simply abstract from the value aspects of the phenomena which they study. They do not even ask the question—and *a fortiori* do not succeed in answering it—whether this or that phenomena with which they are dealing is good or bad, right or wrong, just or unjust—all such matters are left entirely to one side. And since a consideration of values is no part of the task of these sciences, no principles concerning values can possibly be derived from or determined by their results. The "nature" which they study is the natural order deliberately considered apart from any of the values which it may embody, and nature in this abstract sense can determine no standards. When we consider nature apart from value we have already deprived ourselves of any basis for rationally preferring one part of nature or one tendency manifested in nature to any other. We cannot deduce, solely from the fact that physical or psychological laws are what they are, any principles as to what ought to be.

But let us now note that if values are left out of the "nature" studied by these sciences, it by no means follows that values are not also themselves a part of the natural order, if that order be only

considered in a less partial and abstract fashion, nor that this value aspect of the natural order may not itself legitimately be made the object of a rational consideration. Reflexion upon human experience in the world discerns certain phases of it as "good" and certain others as "bad." We find thus as a matter of fact that the world of "nature" contains distinctions of value as an actual part of itself; and from an impartial consideration of these value aspects of the natural order it is not so entirely chimerical to hope or to expect that some principles or standards may be derived.

If we ask what are the primary or fundamental "values" of human experience, as discerned by such a consideration, I think that we can give a reply which will represent a very considerable measure of agreement on the part of contemporary students of the subject. It seems, namely, to be very widely held nowadays that intrinsic positive value attaches only to those conscious experiences which can be described as experiences of "happiness" or of "satisfaction," and that negative value, on the other hand, attaches only to conscious experiences of "unhappiness," "misery," or "dissatisfaction." The exact determination of the meaning of these phrases is of course still to a considerable extent a matter of dispute. There are, on the whole, two main schools of interpretation. According to the one, happiness and unhappiness consist respectively in the psychological states of feeling called pleasure and displeasure, whereas, according to the other they consist rather in what is called "fulfilment of interest or desire"—a matter which often goes under the name (implying also certain modifications of the view) of "self-realization." But in spite of the theoretical difference here indicated there appears to be such a very close connection in practical human experience between experiences of pleasure and experiences of fulfilment of interest, that the two theories seem bound in the end to come out practically at very much the same point.

In any case, if we admit that this widely accepted view, for instance, in one or the other of its divergent interpretations is correct, we are supplied at once with principles of value. And such principles, if they or anything like them be true, are not merely "ethical standards" imposed on the natural order from without. In fact they are genuinely *natural* standards. It seems to me, for example, that the proposition "misery is in itself an evil," or the proposition "happiness is in itself a good," is as much a truth about the natural order of things as is the proposition "fire burns," or "grass is green." Now from such principles of value we can derive principles of conduct. We can say, for instance, that what any person or group of persons "ought" to do is simply whatever will produce a greater balance of happiness over misery than any other alternative that is before him, and conversely, that what he "ought not" to do, or what it would be "wrong" for him to do, is just whatever would produce a lesser balance of positive over negative values—having in view, of course, the effects of his actions upon the experience of all conscious beings whatsoever. Doubtless all these conceptions lead to great difficulties when we try to apply them to the details of practical conduct; but I believe that we can and do guide ourselves more or less effectively by reference to such principles, and at any rate the principles themselves seem clear enough.

Now supposing principles of conduct to be determined in this way, it seems to me that they would rightly be called "natural principles," for they would be determined by "natural" standards—by standards, that is, which have a validity of their own, independent of the arbitrary command or prohibition of any authority whatever. They would be "natural laws" or the laws of "natural morality," and "natural rights" would be simply those "rights," those freedoms or privileges, which any individual "ought," in the sense defined, to be allowed to claim, i.e., in the sense that to allow these claims is a condition of the realization of the natural standard of, say, the increase of happiness and the decrease of misery or unhappiness. They would be claims which would be valid because they would rest upon the validity of a "natural law," because they would be prescribed by the very "nature of things."

In accordance with our previous discussion of the meaning of "natural rights" we must add, however, that "natural laws," so far as they are to define natural rights, must be principles of permanent, and not of merely transitory, validity, and furthermore that they must be such as are valid for all men everywhere. In other words, the truly natural rights must be those claims, liberties, and privileges the possession of which by the person or persons in question will continue, so long at least as human nature and the laws of the physical universe remain substantially what they now are, to constitute permanent and general conditions of human happiness.

But now, finally, *are* there any such natural rights, and, if so, what in particular are they? I believe that it is reasonable to hold that there are in this sense natural rights. We can scarcely doubt that there are certain general features of the physical order, of the psychological nature of man, and of the association of men in social and political aggregations, which have been, and will so far as we can see for a long time continue to be, permanent forces to be reckoned with in the human pursuit of happiness. And it seems reasonable to hold, these factors being what they are, and the values of human experience being also what they are, that so long as all these factors of the situation remain the same there will be certain permanent and general conditions for the attainment of values, and that some of these conditions will take the form of the allotment to certain individuals or groups of individuals of certain claims, privileges, and freedoms which all others shall be bound to respect. I shall not, however, attempt to say what in particular any such natural rights may be. In fact, I regard the determination of natural rights rather as a problem awaiting solution than as anything as yet at all fully or satisfactorily determined. But I do at least regard it as a legitimate problem, and as one which there is some fair hope of solving. Indeed, I suppose that sociologists and

political scientists, however unwilling they may be to state the problem in the terms which we have here employed, are already, at least in some measure, approximating to its solution.

What has brought the notion of natural rights into general, and as it seems to me undeserved, contempt has, I think, been the almost universal assumption on the part of those who have believed in them that the "natural rights of man" and the "laws of nature" on which they are based are readily discoverable either by a simple consideration of traditional commands and prohibitions, or by some short and easy method of insight or immediate intuition. Rather, their determination must be the result of long and careful investigation and experiment. And the defenders of natural rights have also made other serious errors. They have usually conceived of natural rights too abstractly, as if each stood quite on its own basis, independent of and indifferent to every other. On the contrary, natural rights must form a *system* of carefully interrelated and mutually adjusted rights and duties. And finally, natural rights have too often been thought of as vested in certain individuals apart from all reference to society and the interests of society. The very definition of a "right" should be sufficient to dispose of such a notion. A right is a claim which ought to be allowed to an individual in view of the general welfare. Allowed by whom? We can only answer, "By society." A claim upon what? Upon the forbearance and support of others. Society is implied at every turn.

COMMENT

The Ethics of Cicero

At the present time, Cicero is not generally considered to be one of the major figures in the history of philosophy. He is, however, very important in the history of thought, for he wielded an immense influence upon medieval and Renaissance culture. Because of the typicality of his ideas and the clarity and eloquence of his style, we have selected the philosophy of Cicero as representative of the "natural law" tradition. His ethical philosophy may be summarized under three interrelated headings: (1) the concept of a cosmic order as the ground of objective moral laws, (2) the idea of natural law, and (3) the doctrine of the natural kinship of all human beings. Let us glance at each of these tenets.

1. COSMIC ORDER AS THE BASIS OF OBJECTIVE MORAL LAW. The metaphysical background of Cicero's theory is the Stoic conception of nature as rational and divine. "Nature" is the divine reason infused through the cosmos—the inner essence and animating force of all things—and human reason is the divine element in man. By means of reason, man can discover the fundamental laws of the universe and can direct his conduct in conformity with these laws. To live according to nature is to develop one's essential faculties and, at the same time, to be in harmony with the divine order of the cosmos.

2. THE LAW OF NATURE. Cicero's theory of natural law is based on the conception of natural harmony. Grounded in the innermost nature of man, society, and the universe, natural law is independent of convention, legislation, and all other institutional devices. Far from being an arbitrary construction based on human wish or decree, it is both a law of nature and a moral law, universal, irrevocable, and inalienable. It provides the ultimate standard of right conduct, whether of individuals or of states.

As Blake points out, "natural law" should be clearly distinguished from what modern science means by *a* natural law. Physicists speak of the law of gravity, but this is a law in a purely descriptive and nonmoral sense. Everyone is subject to such a natural law and no one can disobey it, because it is imposed upon our bodies by physical necessity without the cooperation of our will or reason. It is just as binding upon a worm or a rock as it is upon a human being. But "natural law" in Cicero's sense is quite different. Man is obliged to obey it only by his reason and conscience: it is not automatically compulsory. The "natural law" that we should live in peace and friendship with our fellow men, for example, is frequently violated. It orders our conduct only to the extent that it is apprehended by our reason and imposed by our will.

Why, then, should such a thing be called a "law of nature"? Because the good for man depends upon the *nature* of man and his universe. Moral laws are not purely arbitrary. The "*ought*" is based upon what "*is*." Norms are founded on facts. Even when it is broken, the moral law remains a nonarbitrary standard, irrevocable in the sense that it is eternally valid. Those who violate it suffer evil and harm; those who live in harmony with it enjoy the highest blessedness. In this sense, it is enforced by natural sanctions.

This doctrine does not mean that there is a perfect identity between *what is* and *what ought to be*. Cicero does not deny that there are bad men and bad societies. But nature determines certain tendencies that require completion if good is to be achieved. Each individual entity possesses a nature which it shares with other members of the species. This essential nature determines its most fundamental tendencies. Good inheres in the fulfillment of these tendencies; evil, in their frustration.

3. THE NATURAL KINSHIP OF ALL HUMAN BEINGS. In Cicero's philosophy, the doctrine of natural law is combined with the doctrine of natural brotherhood and equality. All men by nature are kin. "No single thing is so like another . . . as all of us are to one another. . . . And so, however we may define man, a single definition will apply to all." This does not mean that all men are equal in learning or that they should be made equal in worldly goods, but, rather, that they all possess a similar psychological constitution and should be treated with the dignity and respect that befits a human being. In opposition to all forms of relativism and parochialism—the bias of race, nation, class, or creed—Cicero asserts the great doctrine of human brotherhood.

One of the momentous implications of this doctrine is that the highest allegiance is not to the local state but to the universal fellowship. All men, as children of nature, are bound in conscience by the same laws and belong, in this sense, to the same "commonwealth." "Those who share Law must also share Justice; and those who share these are to be regarded as members of the same commonwealth. . . . Hence we must now conceive of this whole universe as one commonwealth of which both gods and men are members." Cicero does not deny that we should be citizens of the particular state in which we find ourselves; he even emphasizes the importance of civic duties. Local allegiance, however, is ethically subordinate to the wider allegiance to nature and man. If the laws of the state do not conform to the laws of nature, they no more deserve to be called laws than do the dictates of a robber band. Here is the ultimate source of the revolutionary doctrine that men owe a higher allegiance to nature and to nature's God than to any temporal ruler and hence have the inalienable right to revolt against an unjust and tyrannical state.

Man's Harmony with His Natural Environment

In the writings of both Cicero and Marcus Aurelius, there is a strong overtone of pantheism in their doctrine that man should live in harmony with nature. Just as a soul or life force animates the human body, they maintained, so a spiritual force rolls through all things. This soul or life force can be called God,

Nature, Reason—synonyms for the inner essence and animating principle of the universe. It is the productive, formative power, the force that makes for movement and growth. It is divine reason, all pervasive and all-powerful. Hence Marcus Aurelius maintained that there is no sheer evil in the world, and nothing is left to chance. From this standpoint it is also fate—not a blind mechanical necessity but a purposive, providential force, the living activity of the whole expressing itself through every natural event.

The divine essence is in every man: reason is his governing principle, the core and center of his being. What corresponds to his reason and expresses his nature also corresponds to the world soul and expresses the universal nature. To "live according to nature" is to express our rational nature, and to be in harmony with the rational order of the world. The essence of morality is to make the "things in our power"—our inner attitudes—harmonize with the "things not in our power" —the rational outward course of events.

The need to live in harmony with nature is not just an ancient doctrine. It has been echoed and reechoed during our modern ecological crisis. We may choose to express this need more in scientific than in religious terms, but we too must recognize the necessity to live in symbiotic harmony wth nature. Willy-nilly, we have to dwell on this earth if we are to live at all. If the future is to be tolerable, we must bring human breeding under sensible control, we must conserve our dwindling natural resources, and we must bring to a halt the air and water pollution and the bulldozed devastation of the landscape.

The Stoic interpretation of nature, to a greater extent than Cicero's eclectic doctrine, tends to be inconsistent, with its paradoxical combinations of fate and free will, cosmopolitanism and self-sufficiency, tacit admission that certain things are preferable, and yet explicit teaching that all happens for the best. But there is much to admire in Marcus Aurelius' Stoicism: the courage, the tranquillity, the cosmopolitanism, the sense of universal fellowship, the attempt to see the rational connections and necessity of things, the poise and magnanimity of outlook that result from identifying oneself with the whole frame of nature.

Blake on Natural Law

Lest the theory of natural law be interpreted as an outmoded doctrine, I have included a restatement of the theory by a modern American philosopher, Ralph Mason Blake. He writes with such exceptional clarity that very little comment is needed. Blake has sheared away the dubious accompaniment of pantheism, and has linked the natural law doctrine with happiness conceived as a "genuinely *natural* standard." In this latter respect he is following the phrasing of Jefferson in the Declaration of Independence. In stating the fundamental natural rights, Jefferson changed Locke's phrase "life, liberty, and property" to "life, liberty, and the pursuit of happiness," implying that the right to pursue happiness takes precedence over the right to property.

Blake believes that there is no very fundamental difference between the hedonistic interpretation of happiness, illustrated in the present book by Bentham and Mill, and the interest-theory interpretation, illustrated in this book by Dewey. Both interpretations stand in contrast to the sharp distinction between the descriptive "is" and the moral "ought" in Kant's *a priori* ethics and Wittgenstein's linguistic analysis. Thus Blake's thesis will have to be considered in the light of later chapters.

Some Major Questions

The great question that is posed by the readings in this chapter is the relation between "facts" and "ideals," between "what is" and "what ought to be." This is a question to which the philosophers represented in Part Three will return again and again, and it is one of the most important and difficult questions in ethics. The serious student of philosophy will need to ponder its meaning and implications and to decide as best he can what is a reasonable answer.

It seems clear that *good*, in the sense of *what ought to be*, and *right*, in the sense of *what ought to be done*, are not natural characteristics, as are rectangularity or absent-mindedness. Many philosophers have concluded that these concepts have a distinctly *ethical* meaning—a meaning which must be grasped by intuition or *a priori* reason or a peculiar moral sense rather than by empirical science or a descriptive metaphysics. If so, does this invalidate the doctrine discussed in this chapter that morality is based on nature? Here is a question which the reader might ponder.

Another very fundamental question is whether the anti-relativistic implications of the theory of natural law are valid. Can we define man's legitimate aim as the unfolding of his basic powers according to the laws of his nature and in harmony with his natural environment? Or should we conclude that men are so variously moulded by patterns of culture that "human nature" is largely an empty word? Or that the natural environment counts less and less in comparison with the artificialities of urban civilization? If so, is this a disaster?

Other questions concern the relation between natural rights and democratic theory. The concept of natural rights has often been linked with the "social contract." This is the idea of an original convenant by which individuals, who possessed natural rights in an original nonpolitical "state of nature," joined together and through mutual consent formed a state and placed a fiduciary trust in the supreme power of government. The purpose of the covenant is to make these rights more secure, and if the government fails to do this, it forfeits the right to rule. Thus phrased the theory of the state of nature, natural rights, and the social contract formed the basis of democratic, sometimes revolutionary, tendencies. In Rousseau's formulation and even more clearly in Kant's the state of nature and the social contract were treated as useful fictions, meant to serve as a criterion for judging the legitimacy of acts of the state. Recently this constellation of ideas has been elaborated by John Rawl's much discussed book, *The Theory of Justice*

(Harvard University Press, 1971). The reader may wish to consider whether the tradition of natural law and natural rights is a satisfactory basis for a theory of democratic sovereignty and social justice. Is it an effective way to delineate the meaning of human rights? Or is it too abstract and nonhistorical? Must we seek some other basis for democratic theory, for example, the instrumentalist approach of John Dewey, or the socialist approach of Karl Marx? Or should we reject democracy altogether, as Plato and Nietzsche would have us do?

14

Duty

IMMANUEL KANT

(For biographical note see pages 300–301.)

The Metaphysical Foundations of Morals

First Section

Transition from the Common Rational Knowledge of Morality to the Philosophical

Nothing can possibly be conceived in the world, or even out of it, which can be called good without qualification, except a *good will*. Intelligence, wit, judgment, and the other *talents* of the mind, however they may be named, or courage, resolution, perseverance, as qualities of temperament, are undoubtedly good and desirable in many respects. But these gifts of nature may also become extremely bad and mischievous if the will which is to make use of these gifts, and which therefore constitutes what is called *character*, is not good. It

From *The Philosophy of Kant*, translated and edited by Carl J. Friedrich. Copyright 1949 by Random House, Inc. Reprinted by permission of the publisher.

is the same with the *gifts of fortune*. Power, riches, honor, even health, and the general well-being and contentment with one's condition which is called *happiness*, all inspire pride and often presumption if there is not a good will to correct the influence of these on the mind, and with this to rectify also the whole principle of acting and adapt it to its end. The sight of a being, not adorned with a single feature of a pure and good will, enjoying unbroken prosperity can never give pleasure to an impartial rational spectator. Thus a good will appears to constitute the indispensable condition for being even worthy of happiness.

Indeed, quite a few qualities are of service to this good will itself and may facilitate its action, yet have no intrinsic, unconditional value, but are always presupposing a good will; this qualifies the esteem that we justly have for these qualities and does not permit us to regard them as absolutely good. Moderation in the affections and passions, self-control and calm deliberation are not only good in many respects, but even seem to constitute part of the intrinsic worth of a person; but they are far from deserving to be called good without qualification, although they have been so unconditionally praised by the ancients. For without the principles of a good will, these qualities may become extremely bad. The coolness of a villain not only makes him far more dangerous, but also immediately makes him more abominable in our eyes than he would have been without it.

A good will is good not because of what it performs or effects, nor by its aptness for attaining some proposed end, but simply by virtue of the volition; that is, it is good in itself and when considered by itself is to be esteemed much higher than all that it can bring about in pursuing any inclination, nay even in pursuing the sum total of all inclinations. It might happen that, owing to special misfortune, or to the niggardly provision of a step-motherly nature, this will should wholly lack power to accomplish its purpose. If with its greatest efforts this will should yet achieve nothing and there should remain only good will (to be sure, not a mere wish but the summoning of all means in our power), then, like a jewel, good will would still shine by its own light as a thing having its whole value in itself. Its usefulness or fruitlessness can neither add to nor detract anything from this value. It would be, as it were, only the setting to enable us to handle it the more conveniently in common commerce and to attract to it the attention of those who are not yet experts, but not to recommend it to true experts or to determine its value.

However, there is something so strange in this idea of the absolute value of the mere will in which no account is taken of its utility, that notwithstanding the thorough assent of even common reason, a suspicion lingers that this idea may perhaps really be the product of mere high-flown fancy, and that we may have misunderstood the purpose of nature in assigning reason as the governor of the will. Therefore, we will examine this idea from this point of view:

We assume, as a fundamental principle, that no organ [designed] for any purpose will be found in the physical constitution of an organized being, except one which is also the fittest and best adapted for that purpose. Now if the proper object of nature for a being with reason and a will was its *preservation*, its *welfare*, in a word its happiness, then nature would have hit upon a very bad arrangement when it selected the reason of the creature to carry out this function. For all the actions which the creature has to perform with a view to this purpose, and the whole rule of its conduct would be far more surely prescribed by [its own] instinct, and that end [happiness] would have been attained by instinct far more certainly than it ever can be by reason. Should reason have been attributed to this favored creature over and above [such instinct], reason would only have served this creature for contemplating the happy constitution of its nature, for admiring it, and congratulating itself thereon, and for feeling thankful for it to the beneficent cause. But [certainly nature would not have arranged it so that] such a creature should subject its desires to that weak and deceptive guidance, and meddle with nature's intent. In a word, nature would have taken care that reason should not turn into *practical* exercise, nor have the presumption, with its feeble insight, to figure out for itself a plan of happiness and the means for attaining it. In fact, we find that the more a cultivated reason applies itself with deliberate purpose to enjoying life and happiness, so much more does the man lack true satisfaction. From this circumstance there arises in many men, if they are candid enough to confess it, a certain degree of *misology*; that is, hatred of reason, especially

in the case of those who are most experienced in the use of reason. For, after calculating all the advantages they derive, not only from the invention of all the arts of common luxury, but even from the sciences (which then seem to them only a luxury of the intellect after all) they find that they have actually only brought more trouble upon themselves, rather than gained in happiness. They end by envying, rather than despising, the common run of men who keep closer to the guidance of mere instinct and who do not allow their reason to have much influence on their conduct. We must admit this much; that the judgment of those, who would diminish very much the lofty eulogies on the advantages which reason gives us in regard to the happiness and satisfaction of life, or would even deny these advantages altogether, is by no means morose or ungrateful for the goodness with which the world is governed. At the root of these judgments lies the idea that the existence of world order has a different and far nobler end for which, rather than for happiness, reason is properly intended. Therefore this end must be regarded as the supreme condition to which the private ends of man must yield for the most part.

Thus reason is not competent enough to guide the will with certainty in regard to its objects and the satisfaction of all our wants which it even multiplies to some extent; this purpose is one to which an implanted instinct would have led with much greater certainty. Nevertheless, reason is imparted to us as a practical faculty; that is, as one which is to have influence on the *will*. Therefore, if we admit that nature generally in the distribution of natural propensities has adapted the means to the end, nature's true intention must be to produce a *will*, which is not merely good as a *means* to something else but *good in itself*. Reason is absolutely necessary for this sort of will. Then this will, though indeed not the sole and complete good, must be the supreme good and the condition of every other good, even of the desire for happiness. Under these circumstances, there is nothing inconsistent with the wisdom of nature in the fact that the cultivation of the reason which is requisite for the first and unconditional purpose, does in many ways interfere, at least in this life, with the attainment of the second purpose: happiness, which is always relative. Nay, it may even reduce happiness to nothing without nature failing thereby in her purpose. For reason recognizes the establishment of a good will as its highest practical destination, and is capable of only satisfying its own proper kind in attaining this purpose: the attainment of an end determined only by reason, even when such an attainment may involve many a disappointment over otherwise desirable purposes.

Therefore we must develop the notion of a will which deserves to be highly esteemed for itself and is good without a specific objective, a notion which is implied by sound natural common sense. This notion needs to be clarified rather than expounded. In evaluating our actions this notion always takes first place and constitutes the condition of all the rest. In order to do this we will take the notion of duty which includes that of a good will,

although implying certain subjective restrictions and hindrances. However, these hindrances, far from concealing it or rendering it unrecognizable, rather emphasize a good will by contrast and make it shine forth so much the brighter.

I omit here all actions which are already recognized as inconsistent with duty, although they may be useful for this or that purpose. The question whether these actions are done *from duty* cannot arise at all since they conflict with it. I also leave aside those actions which really conform to duty but to which men have *no* direct *inclination*, performing them because they are impelled to do so by some other inclination. For in this case we can readily distinguish whether the action which agrees with duty is done *out of duty* or from a selfish point of view. It is much harder to make this distinction when the action accords with duty and when besides the subject has a *direct* inclination toward it. For example, it is indeed a matter of duty that a dealer should not overcharge an inexperienced purchaser, and wherever there is much commerce the prudent tradesman does not overcharge, but keeps a fixed price for everyone, so that a child buys of him as well as any other. Men are thus *honestly* served; but this is not enough to make us believe that the tradesman has so acted from duty and from principles of honesty; his own advantage required it. It is out of the question in this case to suppose that he might have besides a direct inclination in favor of the buyers, so that out of love, as it were, he should give no advantage to one over another. Hence the action was done neither out of duty nor because of inclination but merely with a selfish view. On the other hand, it is a duty to maintain one's life; in addition everyone also has a direct inclination to do so. But on this account the often anxious care which most men take of their lives has no intrinsic worth and their maxim has no moral import. No doubt they preserve their life *as duty requires*, but not *because duty requires*. The case is different, when adversity and hopeless sorrow have completely taken away the relish for life; if the unfortunate one, strong in mind, indignant at his fate rather than despondent or dejected, longs for death and yet preserves his life without loving it. [If he does this] not from inclination or fear but from duty, then his maxim has a moral worth.

To be beneficent when we can is a duty; besides this, there are many minds so sympathetically constituted that without any other motive of vanity or self-interest, they find a pleasure in spreading joy [about them] and can take delight in the satisfaction of others so far as it is their own work. But I maintain that in such a case, however proper, however amiable an action of this kind may be, it nevertheless has no true moral worth, but is on a level with other inclinations; e.g. the inclination to honor which, if it is happily directed to that which is actually of public utility and accordant with duty and consequently honorable, deserves praise and encouragement but not respect. For the maxim lacks the moral ingredient that such actions be done *out of duty*, not from inclination. Put the case [another way and suppose] that the mind of that philanthropist were clouded by sorrow

of his own, extinguishing all sympathy with the lot of others, and that while he still has the power to benefit others in distress he is not touched by their trouble because he is absorbed with his own; suppose that he now tears himself out of this deadening insensibility, and performs the action without any inclination for it, but simply from duty; only then has his action genuine moral worth. Furthermore, if nature has put little sympathy into the heart of this or that man, if a supposedly upright man is by temperament cold and indifferent to the sufferings of others, perhaps because in respect of his own sufferings he is provided with the special gift of patience and fortitude so that he supposes or even requires that others should have the same; such a man would certainly not be the meanest product of nature. But if nature had not specially shaped him to be a philanthropist, would he not find cause in himself for attributing to himself a value far higher than the value of a good-natured temperament could be? Unquestionably. It is just in this that there is brought out the moral worth of the character which is incomparably the highest of all; namely, that he is beneficent, not from inclination, but from duty.

To secure one's own happiness is a duty, at least indirectly; for discontent with one's condition under pressure of many anxieties and amidst unsatisfied wants might easily become a great *temptation to transgression from duty*. But here again, without reference to duty, all men already have the strongest and most intense inclination to happiness, because it is just in this idea that all inclinations are combined in one total.

But the precept for happiness is often of such a sort that it greatly interferes with some inclinations. Yet a man cannot form any definite and certain conception of the sum of satisfying all of these inclinations, which is called happiness. It is not then to be wondered at that a single inclination, definite both as to what it promises and as to the time within which it can be gratified, is often able to overcome such a fluctuating idea [as the precept for happiness.] For instance, a gouty patient can choose to enjoy what he likes and to suffer what he may, since according to his calculation, at least on this occasion he has not sacrificed the enjoyment of the present moment for a possibly mistaken expectation of happiness supposedly found in health. But, if the general desire for happiness does not influence his will, and even supposing that in his particular case health was not a necessary element in his calculation, there yet remains a law even in this case, as in all other cases; that is, he should promote his happiness not from inclination but from duty. Only in following duty would his conduct acquire true moral worth.

Undoubtedly, it is in this manner that we are to understand those passages of the Scripture in which we are commanded to love our neighbor, even our enemy. For love, as an affection, cannot be commanded, but beneficence for duty's sake can be, even though we are not impelled to such kindness by any inclination, and may even be repelled by a natural and unconquerable aversion. This is *practical* love and not *psychological*. It is a love originating in the will and not in the inclination of senti-ment, in principles of action, not of sentimental sympathy.

The second proposition is: That an action done from duty derives its moral worth, *not from the purpose* which is to be attained by it, but from the maxim by which it is determined. Therefore the action does not depend on the realization of its objective, but merely on the *principle* of volition by which the action has taken place, without regard to any object of desire. It is clear from what proceeds that the purposes which we may have in view for our actions, or their effects as regarded as ends and impulsions of the will, cannot give to actions any unconditional or moral worth. Then in what can their worth consist if it does not consist in the will as it is related to its expected effect? It cannot consist in anything but the *principle of the will*, with no regard to the ends which can be attained by the action. For the will stands between its *a priori* principle which is formal, and its *a posteriori* impulse which is material, as between two roads. As it must be determined by something, it follows that the will must be determined by the formal principle of volition, as when an action is done from duty, in which case every material impulse has been withdrawn from it.

The third proposition, which is a consequence of the preceding two, I would express thus: *Duty is the necessity of an action, resulting from respect for the law.* I may have an *inclination* for an object as the effect of my proposed action, but I cannot have *respect* for an object just for this reason: that it is merely an effect and not an action of will. Similarly, I cannot have respect for an inclination, whether my own or another's; I can at most, if it is my own, approve it; if it is another's I can sometimes even cherish it; that is, look on it as favorable to my own interest. Only the law itself which is connected with my will by no means as an effect but as a principle which does not serve my inclination but outweighs it, or at least in case of choice excludes my inclination from its calculation; only such a law can be an object of respect and hence a command. Now an action done from duty must wholly exclude the influence of inclination, and with it every object of the will, so that nothing remains which can determine the will objectively except the *law*, and [determine the will] subjectively except *pure respect* for this practical law, and hence [pure respect] for the maxim[1] to follow this law even to the thwarting of all my inclinations.

Thus the moral worth of an action does not consist of the effect expected from it, nor from any principle of action which needs to borrow its motive from this expected effect. For, all these effects, agreeableness of one's condition and even the promotion of the happiness of others, all this could have also been brought about by other causes so that for this there would have been no need of the will of a rational being. However, in this will alone can the supreme and unconditional good be found. Therefore the pre-eminent good which we call moral can consist in nothing other than *the concept of law* in itself, which is certainly only possible *in a rational being*, in so far as this conception, and not the expected effect, determines the will. This is a good which is already present in the person acting according to it, and we do not have to wait for good to appear in the result.[2]

[1] A maxim is the subjective principle of volition. The objective principle, that is, what would also serve all rational beings subjectively as a practical principle if reason had full power over desire; this objective principle is the practical *law*.

[2] Here it might be objected that I take refuge in an obscure feeling behind the word *respect* instead of giving a distinct solution of the question by a concept of reason. But, although respect is a feeling, it is not a feeling *received* through outside influence, but is self-generated by a rational concept, and therefore is specifically distinct from all feelings of the former kind, which may be related either to inclination or fear. What I recognize immediately as a law, I recognize with respect. This merely signifies the consciousness that my will is *subordinate* to a law, without the intervention of other influences on my sense. The immediate determination of the will by the law and the consciousness of this may be called *respect*, so that this may then be regarded as an effect of the law on the subject and not as the *cause* of it. In a word, respect is the conceiving of a value which reduces my self-love. Accordingly, respect is considered neither an object of inclination nor of fear, though it has something analogous to both. The *object* of respect is the *law* only, a law that we impose on *ourselves* and yet recognize as necessary in itself. We are subjected to it as a law without consulting self-love; but as imposed by us on ourselves, it is a result of our will. In the former aspect it has analogy to fear, in the latter to inclination. Respect for a person is properly only respect for the law (of honesty, etc.) of which he gives us an example. Since we also look on the improvement of our talents as a duty we consider that we see in a person of talents the *example of a law*, as it were, to become like him in this by effort and this constitutes our respect. All so-called moral *interest* consists simply in *respect* for the law.

But what sort of law can it be the conception of which must determine the will, even without our paying any attention to the effect expected from it, in order that this will may be called good absolutely and without qualification? As I have stripped the will of every impulse which could arise for it from obedience to any law, there remains nothing but the general conformity of the will's actions to law in general. Only this conformity to law is to serve the will as a principle; that is, I am never to act in any way other than *so I could want my maxim also to become a general law*. It is the simple conformity to law in general, without assuming any particular law applicable to certain actions, that serves the will as its principle, and must so serve it, if duty is not to be a vain delusion and chimerical notion. The common reason of men in their practical judgments agrees perfectly with this and always has in view the principle suggested here. For example, let the question be: When in distress may I make a promise with the intention of not keeping it? I readily distinguish here between the two meanings which the question may have: Whether it is prudent, or whether it is in accordance with duty, to make a false promise. The former undoubtedly may often be the case. I [may] see clearly that it is not enough to extricate myself from a present difficulty by means of this subterfuge, but that it must be carefully considered whether there may not result from such a lie a much greater inconvenience than that from which I am now freeing myself. But, since in spite of all my supposed *cunning* the consequences cannot be foreseen easily; the loss of credit may be much more injurious to me than any mischief which I seek to avoid at present. That being the case, one might consider whether it would not be more *prudent* to act according to a general maxim, and make it a habit to give no promise except with the intention of keeping it. But, it is soon clear that such a maxim is still only based on the fear of consequences. It is a wholly different thing to be truthful from a sense of duty, than to be so from apprehension of injurious consequences. In the first case, the very conceiving of the action already implies a law for me; in the second case, I must first look about elsewhere to see what results may be associated with it which would affect me. For it is beyond all doubt wicked to deviate from the principle of duty; but to be unfaithful to my maxim of prudence may often be very advantageous to me, although it is certainly wiser to abide by it. However, the shortest way, and an unerring one, to discover the answer to this question of whether a lying promise is consistent with duty, is to ask myself, "Would I be content if this maxim of extricating myself from difficulty by a false promise held good as a general law for others as well as for myself?" Would I care to say to myself, "Everyone may make a deceitful promise when he finds himself in a difficulty from which he cannot extricate himself otherwise"? Then I would presently become aware that while I can decide in favor of the lie, I can by no means decide that lying should be a general law. For under such a law there would be no promises at all, since I would state my intentions in vain in regard to my future actions to those who would not believe my allegation, or, if they did so too hastily, they would pay me back in my own coin. Hence, as soon as such a maxim was made a universal law, it would necessarily destroy itself.

Therefore I do not need any sharp acumen to discern what I have to do in order that my will may be morally good. [As I am] inexperienced in the course of the world and incapable of being prepared for all its contingencies, I can only ask myself: "Can you will that your maxim should also be a general law?" If not, then my maxim must be rejected, not because of any disadvantage in it for myself or even for others, but because my maxim cannot fit as a principle into a possible universal legislation, and reason demands immediate respect from me for such legislation. Indeed, I do not *discern* as yet on what this respect is based; into this question the philosopher may inquire. But at least I understand this much: that this respect is an evaluation of the worth that far outweighs all that is recommended by inclination. The necessity of acting from *pure* respect for the practical law [of right action;] is what constitutes duty, to which every other motive must yield, because it is the condition of a will being good *in istelf*, and the value of such a will exceeds everything.

Thus we have arrived at the principle of moral knowledge of common human reason. Although common men no doubt do not conceive this principle in such an abstract and universal form, yet they really always have it before their eyes and use it as the standard for their decision. It would be easy to show here

how, with this compass in hand, men are well able to distinguish, in every case that occurs, what is good, bad, conformable to duty or inconsistent with it. Without teaching them anything at all new, we are only, like Socrates, directing their attention to the principle they employ themselves and [showing] that we therefore do not need science and philosophy to know what we should do to be honest and good and even wise and virtuous. Indeed, we might well have understood before that the knowledge of what every man ought to do, and hence also [what he ought] to know is within the reach of every man, even the commonest. We cannot help admiring what a great advantage practical judgment has over theoretical judgment in men's common sense. If, in theoretical judgments, common reason ventures to depart from the laws of experience and from the perceptions of the senses, it plunges into many inconceivabilities and self-contradictions, [or] at any rate into a chaos of uncertainty, obscurity and instability. But in the practical sphere [of just action] it is right that, when one excludes all sense impulses from [determining] practical laws, the power of judgment of common sense begins to show itself to special advantage. It then even becomes a subtle matter as to whether common sense provides tricky excuses for conscience in relation to other claims regarding what is to be called right, or whether, for its own guidance, common sense seeks to determine honestly the value of [particular] actions. In the latter case, common sense has as good a hope of hitting the mark as any philosopher can promise himself. A common man is almost more sure of doing so, because the philosopher cannot have any other [better] principle and may easily perplex his judgment by a multitude of considerations foreign to the matter in hand, and so he may turn from the right way. Therefore would it not be wiser in moral matters to acquiesce in the judgment of common reason, or at most to call in philosophy only for rendering the system of morals more complete and intelligible and its rules more convenient for use, especially for disputation, but not to deflect common sense from its happy simplicity, or to lead it through philosophy into a new path of inquiry and instruction?

Innocence is indeed a glorious thing, only it is a pity that it cannot maintain itself well and is easily seduced. On this account even wisdom, which otherwise consists more in conduct than in knowledge, yet has need of science, not in order to learn from it, but to secure for its own precepts acceptance and permanence. In opposition to all the commands of duty that reason represents to man as so greatly deserving respect, man feels within himself a powerful counterpoise in his wants and inclinations, the entire satisfaction of which he sums up under the name of happiness. Reason issues its commands unyieldingly, without promising anything to the inclinations and with disregard and contempt, as it were, for these demands which are so impetuous and at the same time so plausible and which will not allow themselves to be suppressed by any command. Hence there arises a natural *dialectic*; that is, a disposition to argue against these strict laws of duty and to question their validity, or at least

to question their purity and strictness. [There is also a disposition] to make them more accordant, if possible, with our wishes and inclinations; that is to say, to corrupt them at their very source and to destroy their value entirely, an act that even common practical reason cannot ultimately approve.

Thus the *common reason of man* is compelled to leave its proper sphere and to take a step into the field of a *practical philosophy*, but not for satisfying any desire to speculate, which never occurs to it as long as it is content to be mere sound reason. But the purpose is to secure on practical grounds information and clear instruction respecting the source of the principle [of common sense] and the correct definition of this principle as contrasted with the maxims which are based on wants and inclinations, so that common sense may escape from the perplexity of opposing claims, and not run the risk of losing all genuine moral principles through the equivocation into which it easily falls. Thus when practical, common reason cultivates itself, there arises insensibly in it a dialectic forcing it to seek aid in philosophy, just like what happens to practical reason in its theoretic use. Therefore in this case as well as in the other, [common sense] will find no rest but in a thorough critical examination of our reason.

Second Section

Transition from Popular Moral Philosophy to the Metaphysics of Morals

If hitherto we have drawn our concept of duty from the common use of our practical reason, it is by no means to be inferred that we have treated it as an empirical concept. On the contrary, if we attend to the experience of men's conduct, we meet frequent and, as we admit ourselves, just complaints that there is not to be found a single certain example of the disposition to act from pure duty. Although many things are done *in comformity* to what duty prescribes, it is nevertheless always doubtful whether they are done strictly *out of duty* [which would have to be the case if they are] to have a moral value. Hence, in all ages there have been philosophers who have denied altogether that this disposition actually exists in human actions at all, and who have ascribed everything to a more or less refined self-love. Not that they have on that account questioned the soundness of the conception of morality; on the contrary they have spoken with sincere regret of the frailty and corruption of human nature, which though noble enough to take as its law an idea so worthy of respect, is yet too weak to follow it, and employs reason, which ought to give it the law, only for the purpose of accommodating the inclinations, whether single or, at best, in the greatest possible harmony with one another. In fact it is absolutely impossible to ascertain by experience with complete certainty a single case in which the maxim of an action, however right in itself, rested simply on moral grounds and on the conception of duty. Sometimes it happens that with the sharpest self-examination we can find nothing, besides the moral principle of duty, powerful enough to move us to this or that action and to such a great sacrifice;

yet we cannot infer from this with certainty that it was not some really secret impulse of self-love, under the false appearance of that idea [of the moral principle of duty] that was the actual determining cause of the will. We then like to flatter ourselves by falsely taking credit for a more noble motive. In fact we can never, even by the strictest self-examination, penetrate completely [to the causes] behind the secret springs of action, since when we ask about moral worth, we are not concerned with actions but with their inward principles which we do not see.

Moreover, we cannot better serve the wishes of those people, who ridicule all morality as a mere chimera of human imagination overstepping itself through vanity, than by conceding to them that concepts of duty must be drawn only from experience, just as people are ready to think out of indolence that this is also the case with all other notions; doing this would prepare a certain triumph for them. Out of love for humanity, I am willing to admit that most of our actions accord with duty, but on examining them more closely we encounter everywhere the cherished self which is always dominant. It is this self that men have consideration for and not the strict command of duty which would often require self-denial. Without being an enemy to virtue, a cool observer who does not mistake an ardent wish for good for goodness itself, may sometimes doubt whether true virtue is actually found anywhere in the world, and do this especially as his years increase and his judgment is in part made wiser by experience and in part more acute by observation. This being so, nothing can save us from altogether abandoning our ideas of duty, nothing can maintain in our soul a well-grounded respect for the law; nothing but the clear conviction that, although there have never been actions really springing from such pure sources, yet . . . reason, by itself and independent of all experience, ordains what ought to be done. Accordingly actions, of which hitherto the world has perhaps never had an example and of which the feasibility might even be very much doubted by anyone basing everything on experience, are nevertheless inflexibly commanded by reason; e.g., even though a sincere friend might never have existed up till now, [just the same] pure sincerity in friendship is required of every man not a whit less, because above and beyond all experience this duty is obligatory in the idea of a reason that determines the will by *a priori* principles.

Unless we deny that the notion of morality has any truth or reference to any possible object, we must admit that its law must be valid not only for men, but for all *rational creatures generally*, not only under certain contingent conditions or with exceptions, but with *absolute necessity*. [When we admit this] then it is clear that no experience could enable us even to infer the possibility of such apodictic laws. What right have we to demand unbounded respect, as for a universal precept of every rational creature, for something that only holds true under the contingent conditions of humanity? Or, how could laws determining *our* will be regarded as laws determining the will of rational beings generally, if these laws were only empirical and did not originate wholly

a priori from pure and practical reason?

Nor could anything be more ill-advised for morality than our wishing to derive it from examples. Every example set before me must first be tested by principles of morality [to determine] whether it is worthy of serving as an original example; that is, as a model or pattern. An example can by no means furnish authoritatively the concept of morality. Even the Holy One of the Gospels must first be compared with our ideal of moral perfection before we can recognize Him as such; and so He says of himself, "Why call ye Me (whom ye see) good? None is good (the model of good) but God only (whom ye do not see)!" But whence do we acquire the concept of God as the supreme good? Simply from the *idea* of moral perfection which reason sketches *a priori* and connects inseparably with the concept of a free will. Imitation has no place at all in morality, and examples serve only for encouragement; that is, they make feasible beyond any doubt what the law commands and they make visible what the practical rule expresses more generally, but they can never authorize us to set aside the true original existing in reason and to guide ourselves by examples. Therefore, if there is no genuine supreme principle of morality, but only that which rests on pure reason independent of all experience, I think it is unnecessary even to put the question as to whether it is good to exhibit these concepts in their generality (*in abstracto*) as they are established *a priori* along with the principles belonging to them, if our knowledge is to be distinguished from the *vulgar* and called philosophical. Indeed, in our times this question might perhaps be necessary; for if we collected votes on whether pure rational knowledge, apart from everything empirical, that is to say, a metaphysic of morals, is to be preferred to a popular practical philosophy; it is easy to guess which side would carry more weight.

This descent to popular notions is certainly very commendable if the ascent to the principles of pure reason has taken place first and has been accomplished satisfactorily. This implies that first we should establish ethics on metaphysics and, when it is firmly founded, procure a hearing for ethics by giving it a popular character. But it is quite absurd to try to be popular in the first inquiry on which the soundness of the principles depends. Not only can this procedure never lay claim to having the very rare merit of a true *philosophical popularity* for there is no sense in being intelligible if one renounces all thoroughness of insight, but this procedure also produces a disgusting medley of compiled observations and half-reasoned principles. Shallow pates enjoy this because it can be used for everyday chat, but those with deeper understanding find only confusion in this method and, being unsatisfied and unable to assist themselves, turn away their eyes, while philosophers, seeing quite clearly through this confusion, are little heeded when they call men away for a time from this pretended popularity, so they may be rightfully popular after attaining a definite insight.

We only need to look at the attempts of moralists in [using] that favorite fashion and we shall find [a variety of things:] at one point the special destination of human nature including the idea of a rational nature generally, at another point perfection, at another happiness, here moral sense, there fear of God, a little of this and a little of that, all in a marvelous mixture. It does not occur to them to ask whether the principles of morality are to be sought at all in the knowledge of human nature which we can have only from experience. If this is not so, if these principles are completely *a priori* and are to be encountered free from everything empirical only in pure rational concepts and nowhere else, not even in the smallest degree, shall we then adopt the method of making this a separate inquiry as a pure practical philosophy? Or [shall we construct], if one may use a name so decried, a metaphysic of morals[3] and complete it by itself and ask the public wishing for popular treatment to await the outcome of this undertaking?

Such a metaphysic of morals, completely isolated and unmixed with any anthropology, theology, physics, or hyperphysics, and still less with occult qualities which we might call superphysical, is not only an indispensable condition for all sound theoretical

---

[3] Just as pure mathematics is differentiated from applied and pure logic from applied, so, if we choose, we may also differentiate pure philosophy of morals (metaphysics), from applied (viz., applied to human nature). Also, by this designation we are at once reminded that moral principles are not based on properties of human nature, but must exist *a priori* of themselves; practical rules for every rational nature must be capable of being deduced from such principles and accordingly deduced for the rational nature of man.

knowledge of duties, but at the same time it is a *desideratum* highly important to the actual fulfilment of the precepts of duties. For the pure concept of duty unmixed with any foreign element of experienced attractions, in a word, the pure concept of moral law in general, exercises an influence on the human heart through reason alone. . . . This influence is so much more powerful than all other impulses[4] which may be derived from the field of experience, that in the consciousness of its dignity it despises such impulses and by degrees can become their master. An eclectic ethics compounded partly of motives drawn from feelings and inclinations and partly from concepts of reason, will necessarily make the mind waver between motives which cannot be brought under any one principle, and will therefore lead to good only by mere accident, and may often lead to evil.

[4] I have a letter from the late excellent Sulzer, in which he asks me what might be the reason for moral instruction accomplishing so little although it contains much that is convincing to reason. My answer was postponed in order that I might make it complete. But it is simply this: teachers themselves do not have their own notions clear, and when they endeavor to make up for this by suggesting all kinds of motives for moral goodness and in trying to make their medicine strong they spoil it. For, the most ordinary observations show that this is an act of honesty done with steadfast mind and without regard for any advantage in this world or another, and when [persisted in] even under the greatest temptations of need or allurement it will . . . elevate the soul and inspire one with the wish to be able to act in a like manner. Even fairly young children feel this impression and one should never represent duties to them in any other light.

It is clear from what has been said that all moral concepts have their seat and origin completely *a priori* in the reason, and have it in the commonest reason just as truly as in what is speculative in the highest degree. Moral concepts cannot be obtained by abstraction from any empirical and hence merely contingent knowledge. It is exactly this purity in origin that makes them worthy of serving our supreme practical principle [for right action] and, as we add anything empirical, we detract in proportion from their genuine influence and from the absolute value of actions. It is not only very necessary from a purely speculative point of view, but it is also of the greatest practical importance to derive these notions and laws from pure reason, to present them pure and unmixed, and even to determine the compass of this practical or pure rational knowledge; that is, to determine the entire faculty of pure practical reason. In doing so we must not make the principles of pure practical reason dependent on the particular nature of human reason, though in speculative philosophy this may be permitted and even necessary at times. Since moral laws ought to hold true for every rational creature we must derive them from the general concept of a rational being. Although morality has need of anthropology for its application to man, yet in this way, as in the first step, we must treat morality independently as pure philosophy; that is, as metaphysics, complete in itself. . . . We must fully realize that unless we are in possession of this pure philosophy not only would it be vain to determine the moral element of duty in right actions for purposes of speculative criticism, but it would be impossible to base morals on their genuine principles. This is true even for common practical purposes, but more especially for moral instruction which is to produce pure moral dispositions and to engraft them on men's minds for promoting the greatest possible good in the world.

Our purpose in this study must be not only to advance by natural steps from common moral judgment, which is very worthy of respect, to the philosophical, as has been done already, but also to progress from a popular philosophy which only gets as far as it can by groping with the help of examples, to metaphysics, which does not allow itself to be held back by anything empirical and which goes as far as ideal concepts in measuring the whole extent of this kind of rational knowledge wherever examples fail us. [In order to accomplish this purpose] we must clearly describe and trace the practical faculty of reason, advancing from general rules to the point where the notion of duty springs from it.

Everything in nature works according to laws. Rational beings alone have the faculty for acting according *to the concept* of laws; that is, according to principles. [In other words, rational beings alone] have a will. Since deriving actions from principles requires *reason*, the will is nothing more than practical reason. If reason infallibly determines the will, then the actions of such a being that are recognized as objectively necessary are also subjectively necessary. The will is a faculty for choosing *only that* which reason, independently of inclination, recognizes as practically necessary; that is, as good. But if reason does not sufficiently determine the will by itself, if the latter is also subject to the subjective conditioning of particular impulses which do not always coincide with the objective conditions; in a word, if the will *in itself* does not completely accord with reason, as is actually the case with men, then the actions which are objectively recognized as necessary are subjectively contingent. Determining such a will according to objective laws is compulsory (*Nötigung*). This means that the relations of objective laws to a will not thoroughly good is conceived as the determination of the will of a rational being by principles of reason which the will, because of its nature, does not necessarily follow.

The concept of an objective principle, in so far as it is compulsory for a will, is called a command of reason and the formulation of such a command is called an IMPERATIVE.

All imperatives are expressed by the word *ought* (or *shall*) and are indicating thereby the relation of an objective law of reason to a will, which, because of its subjective constitution, is not necessarily determined by this [compulsion]. Such imperatives may state that something would be good to do or to forbear from doing, but they are addressing themselves to a will which does not always do a thing merely because that thing is represented as good to do. The practically *good* determines the will by means of the concepts of reason, and consequently from objective, not subjective causes; that is, [it determines them] on principles which are valid for every rational being as such. The practically good is distinguishable from the *pleasant* which influences the will only by means of sensations from subjective causes and which is valid only for the particular sense of this or that man and is not a principle of reason holding true for everyone.[5]

Therefore a perfectly good will would be equally subject to objective laws of good [action], but could not be conceived thereby as *compelled* to act lawfully by itself. Because of its subjective constitution it can only be determined by the concept of the good. Consequently no imperatives hold true for the Divine will, or in general for a *holy* will. *Ought* is out of place here because the act of willing is already necessarily in unison with the law. Therefore imperatives are only formulations for ex-

---

[5] The dependence of the desires on sensations is called inclination, and accordingly always indicates a *want*. The dependence of a contingently determinable will on principles of reason is called an *interest*. Therefore, this dependence is only found in the case of a dependent will, which of itself does not always conform to reason. We cannot conceive of the Divine will having any interest. But the human will can *take an interest* without necessarily acting *from interest*. The former signifies practical interest in the action, the latter *psychological* interest in the object of the action. The first merely indicates dependence of the will on principles of reason in themselves and the second merely indicates dependence on principles of reason for the sake of inclination, reason supplying only the practical rules of how the demands of inclination may be satisfied. In the first case the action interests me in the object of the action, inasmuch as it is pleasant for me. We have seen, in the first section, that in an action done from duty we must not look to the interest in the object but only to the interest in the action itself, and in its rational principle: the law.

pressing the relation of the objective laws of all volition to the subjective imperfections of the will of this or that rational being; that is, the human will.

All *imperatives* command either *hypothetically* or *categorically*. . . . Since every practical law represents a possible action as good, and on this account as necessary for a subject who can determine practically by reason, all imperatives are formulations determining an action which is necessary according to the principle of a will in some respects good. If the action is good only as a means to *something else*, then the imperative is *hypothetical*. If the action is conceived as good *in itself* and consequently as necessarily being the principle of a will which of itself conforms to reason then it is *categorical*.

Thus the imperative declares what, of my possible actions, would be good. It presents the practical rule in relation to a will which does not perform an action forthwith simply because it is good. For, either the subject does not always know that such action is good or, even should the subject know this, its maxims might be opposed to the objective principles of practical reason.

Consequently the hypothetical imperative only states that an action is good for some purpose, *potential* or *actual*. In the first case the principle is *problematical*, in the second is it *assertorial* [positively asserting a claim and may be called a] practical principle. The categorical imperative which declares an action to be objectively necessary in itself without reference to any purpose, i.e., without any other end, is valid as an *apodictic* (practical) principle.

Whatever is possible through the ability of some rational being may also be considered as a possible purpose of some will. Therefore the principles of action concerning the means needed to attain some possible purpose are really infinitely numerous. All sciences have a practical aspect consisting of problems expressing that some end is possible for us, and of imperatives directing how it may be attained. Therefore, these may, in general, be called imperatives of *skill*. There is no question as to whether the end is rational and good, but only as to what one must do in order to attain it. The precepts for the physician to make his patient thoroughly healthy, and for a poisoner to ensure certain death, are equivalent in that each serves to effect its purpose perfectly. Since in early youth it cannot be known what purposes are likely to occur to us in the course of life, parents seek to have their children taught a *great many things* and provide for their *skill* in using means for all sorts of purposes. They cannot be sure whether any particular purpose may perhaps hereafter be an objective for their pupil; it is possible that he might aim at any of them. This anxiety is so great that parents commonly neglect to form and correct their judgment on the value of the things which may be chosen as ends.

However there is *one* end which may actually be assumed to be an end for all rational beings, there is one purpose which they not only *may* have, but which we may assume with certainty that they all actually *do have* by natural necessity; that is *happiness*. The hypothetical imperative expressing the practical necessity of an action as a means for the advancement of happiness is as-

sertorial. We are not presenting it as necessary for an uncertain and merely possible purpose, but for a purpose which we may presuppose with certainty and *a priori* for every man, because it belongs to his being. Now a man's skill in choosing the means to his own greatest well-being may be called *prudence* in the most specific sense.[6] Thus the imperative which refers to the choice of means to one's own happiness, that is, the precept of prudence, is still hypothetical. The action is not commanded absolutely but only as a means to another purpose. Whereas, the categorical imperative directly commands a certain conduct without being conditioned by any other attainable purpose. . . . This imperative may be called the imperative of morality (*Sittlichkeit*).

There is also a marked distinction among the acts of willing according to these three kinds of principles resulting from the *dissimilarity* in the obligation of the will. In order to differentiate them more clearly, I think they would be most suitably classified as either *rules* of skill, *counsels* of prudence, or *commands* or laws of morality. For it is only *law* that involves the concept of

[6] The word prudence is taken in two senses: In one it may mean knowledge of the world, in the other, private prudence. The first is a man's ability to influence others so as to use them for his own purposes. The second is the insight to combine all these purposes for his own lasting benefit. This latter is properly that to which the value of even the former is reduced, and when a man is prudent in the former sense, but not in the latter, we might better say of him that he is clever and cunning, but on the whole, imprudent.

an *unconditional necessity* which is objective and hence universally valid. Commands are laws that must be obeyed; that is, must be adhered to even when inclination is opposed. Indeed, counsels involve [a certain kind of] necessity, but only one which can hold true under a contingent subjective condition. They depend on whether this or that man counts this or that [object] as essential to his happiness. By contrast, the categorical imperative is not limited by any condition. . . . We might also call the first kind of imperatives *technical* as belonging to art, the second *pragmatic*[7] as belonging to welfare, and the third *moral* as belonging to free conduct generally, that is, to morals.

The question now arises: How are all these imperatives possible? This question is to ascertain, not how the action commanded by the imperative can be carried out, but merely how the compulsion of will expressed by the imperative can be conceived. I should think that no special explanation is needed to show how an imperative related to skill is possible. Whoever wills the end, also wills, so far as reason decisively influences his conduct, the means in his power which are indispensable for achieving this end. This proposition is analytical in regard to the volition. For,

in willing an object as an effect, there is already implied therein that I myself am acting as a cause, that is, I make use of the means. From the concept of the willed end, the imperative derives the concept of the actions necessary for achieving this end. No doubt synthetic propositions will have to be employed in defining the means to a proposed end, but they do not concern the principle, the act of the will but only the object and its realization. To give an example: in order to bisect a line I must draw two intersecting arcs from its end points. Admittedly, this is taught by mathematics in synthetic propositions. But if I know that the intended operation can only be performed by this process, then it is an analytical proposition to say that in fully willing the operation, I also will the action required for it. For [assuming that I want a certain thing] it is just the same to conceive that thing as an effect which I can only produce in a certain way as to conceive of myself as acting in this way.

If it were equally easy to give a definite concept of happiness [as of simpler ends], the imperatives of prudence would correspond exactly with those of skill, and would likewise be analytical. It could then be said that whoever wills the end also wills the indispensable means thereto which are in his power. But unfortunately the notion of happiness is so indefinite that although every man wishes to attain it, he never can say definitely and consistently what it is that he really wishes and wills. The reason is that the elements belonging to the notion of happiness are altogether empirical; that is, they must be borrowed from experience. Nevertheless,

[7] It seems to me that the proper meaning of the word *pragmatic* may be most accurately defined in this way: *Sanctions* are called pragmatic when they flow properly not from the law of the states as necessary enactments, but from *precaution* for the general welfare. A history is composed pragmatically when it teaches *prudence*; i.e., instructs the world how it can better provide for its interests, or at least as well as did the men of former times.

the idea of happiness implies something absolute and whole; a maximum of well-being in my present and all future circumstances. Now, it is impossible for even the most clear-sighted and most powerful being, as long as it is supposedly finite, to frame for itself a definite concept of what it really wills [when it wants to be happy]. If he wills riches, how much anxiety, envy, and snares might not be drawn upon his shoulders thereby? If he wills knowledge and discernment, perhaps such knowledge might only prove to be so much sharper sight showing him much more fearfully the unavoidable evils now concealed from him, or suggesting more wants for his desires which already give him concern enough. If he should will a long life, who can guarantee him that it will not be a long misery? If he should at least have health, how often has infirmity of the body restrained a man from excesses into which perfect health would have allowed him to fall? And so on. In short, a human being is unable with certainty to determine by any principle what would make him truly happy, because to do so he would have to be omniscient. Therefore, we cannot act on any definite principles to secure happiness, but only on counsels derived from experience; e.g., the frugality, courtesy, reserve, etc., which experience teaches us will promote well-being, for the most part. Hence it follows that the imperatives of prudence do not command at all, strictly speaking; that is, they cannot present actions objectively as practically *necessary* so that they are to be regarded as *counsels* (*consilia*) of reason rather than precepts (*praecepta*).

The problem of determining certainly and generally which action would most promote the happiness of a rational being is completely insoluble. Consequently, no imperative respecting happiness is possible, for such a command should, in a strict sense, command men to do what makes them happy. Happiness is an ideal, not of reason, but of imagination resting solely on empirical grounds. It is vain to expect that these grounds should define an action for attaining the totality of a series of consequences that are really endless. However, this imperative of prudence could be an analytical proposition if we assume that the means to happiness could, with certainty, be assigned. For, this imperative is distinguished from the imperative of skill only by this; in the latter the end is merely possible [and available to be chosen]; in the former the end is given. However, both only prescribe the means to an end which we assume to have been willed. It follows that the imperative which calls for the willing of the means by him who wills the end is analytical in both cases. Thus there is no difficulty in regard to the possibility of this kind of imperative either.

On the other hand, the question of how the imperative of *morality* is possible is undoubtedly the only question demanding a solution as this imperative is not at all hypothetical, and the objective necessity it presents cannot rest on any hypothesis, as is the case with hypothetical imperatives. Only we must never leave out of consideration the fact that we *cannot* determine *by any example*, i.e., empirically, whether there is any such imperative at all. Rather is it to be feared that all those apparently categorical imperatives may actually be hypothetical. For instance, when you have a precept such as: thou shalt not promise deceitfully, and it is assumed that the [normative] necessity of this is not a mere counsel to avoid some other evil, [in which case] it might mean: you shall not make a lying promise lest it become known and your credit would be destroyed. On the contrary, an action of this kind should be regarded as evil in itself so that the imperative of the prohibition is categorical. Yet we cannot show with certainty in any instance that the will is determined merely by the law without any other source of action, although this may appear to be so. It is always possible that fear of disgrace, also perhaps obscure dread of other dangers, may have a secret influence on the will. Who can prove by experience the non-existence of a cause when all that experience tells us is that we do not perceive it? In such a case the so-called moral imperative, which appears to be categorical and unconditional, would really only be a pragmatic precept, drawing our attention to our own interests, and merely teaching us to take these interests into consideration.

Therefore we shall have to investigate *a priori* the possibility of a *categorical* imperative, since, in this case, we do not have the advantage that the imperative's reality is given in experience, so that the elucidation of its possibility would be needed only for explaining it, not for establishing it. It can be discerned that the categorical imperative has the purport of a practical law. All the rest may certainly be called *principles* of the will but not laws, since

whatever is merely necessary for attaining some casual purpose may be considered contingent in itself, and at any time we can be free from the precept if we give up the purpose. However, the unconditional command leaves the will no liberty to choose the opposite, and consequently only the will carries with it that necessity we require in a law.

Secondly, in the case of this categorical imperative or law of morality the difficulty [of discerning its possibility] is very profound. It is *a priori*, a synthetic, practical proposition[8] and as there is so much difficulty in discerning the possibility of speculative propositions of this kind, it may readily be supposed that the difficulty will be no less with the practical.

In [approaching] this problem we will first inquire whether the mere concept of a categorical imperative may not perhaps supply us with its formula also, which contains the proposition that alone can be a categorical imperative. Even if we know the tenor of such an absolute command, yet how it is possible will require further special and laborious study which we will postpone to the last section.

When I conceive of a hypothetical

---

[8] I connect the act with the will without presupposing a condition resulting from any inclination but *a priori*, and therefore necessarily (though only objectively; that is, assuming the idea of a reason possessing full power over all subjective motives). Therefore this is a practical proposition which does not analytically deduce the willing for an action from another already presupposed proposition (for we have not such a perfect will), but connects it immediately with the concept of the will of a rational being, as something not contained in it.

imperative at all, I do not know previously what it will contain until I am given the condition. But when I conceive of a categorical imperative I know at once what it contains. In addition to the law, the imperative contains only the necessity that the maxim[9] conform to this law. As the maxim contains no condition restricting the maxim, nothing remains but the general statement of the law to which the maxim of the action should conform, and it is only this conformity that the imperative properly represents as necessary.

Therefore there is only one categorical imperative, namely this: *Act only on a maxim by which you can will that it, at the same time, should become a general law*.

Now, if all imperatives of duty can be deduced from this one imperative as easily as from their principle, then we shall be able at least to show what we understand by it and what this concept means, although it would remain undecided whether what is called duty is not just a vain notion.

Since the universality of the law constitutes what is properly called *nature* in the most general sense [as to form]; that is, the existence of things as far as determined by general laws, the general imperative duty may be expressed thus:

[9] A maxim is a subjective principle of action and must be distinguished from an *objective principle*; namely, practical law. The former contains the practical rule set by reason according to the conditions of the subject (often its ignorance or its inclinations); hence it is the principle on which the subject *acts*; but the law is the objective principle valid for every rational being and is the principle on which the being *ought to act*; that is, an imperative.

Act as if the maxim of your action were to become by your will a general law of nature.

We will now enumerate a few duties, adopting the usual division of duties to ourselves and to others, and of perfect and imperfect duties.[10]

1. A man, while reduced to despair by a series of misfortunes and feeling wearied of life, is still so far in possession of his reason that he can ask himself whether it would not be contrary to his duty to himself to take his own life. Now he inquires whether the maxim of his action could become a general law of nature. His maxim is: Out of self-love I consider it a principle to shorten my life when continuing it is likely to bring more misfortune than satisfaction. The question then simply is whether this principle of self-love could become a general law of nature. Now we see at once that a system of nature, whose law would be to destroy life by the very feeling designed to compel the maintenance of life, would contradict itself, and therefore could not exist as a system of nature; hence that maxim cannot possibly be a general law of nature and consequently it would be wholly inconsistent with the supreme principle of all duty.

2. Another man finds himself forced by dire need to borrow money. He knows that he will not be able to repay it, but he also see that nothing will be lent him unless he promises firmly to repay it within a definite time. He would like to make this promise but he

[10] It must be noted here that I reserve the classification of duties for a future metaphysic of morals; so here I only give a few arbitrary duties as examples.

still has enough conscience to ask himself: Is it not unlawful and contrary to my duty to get out of a difficulty in this way? However, suppose that he does decide to do so; the maxim of his action would then be expressed thus: When I consider myself in want of money, I shall borrow money and promise to repay it although I know that I never can. Now this principle of self-love or of one's own advantage may perhaps be agreeable to my whole future well-being: but the question is now: Is it right? Here I change the suggestion of self-love into a general law and state the question thus: How would it be if my maxim were a general law? I then realize at once that it could never hold as a general law of nature but would necessarily contradict itself. For if it were a general law that anyone considering himself to be in difficulties would be able to promise whatever he pleases intending not to keep his promise, the promise itself and its object would become impossible since no one would believe that anything was promised him, but would ridicule all such statements as vain pretenses.

3. A third man finds in himself a talent which with the help of some education might make him a useful man in many respects. But he finds himself in comfortable circumstances, and prefers to indulge in pleasure rather than to take pains in developing and improving his fortunate natural capacities. He asks, however, whether his maxim of neglecting his natural gifts, besides agreeing with his inclination toward indulgence, agrees also with what is called duty. He sees then that nature could indeed subsist according to such

a general law, though men (like the South Sea Islanders) let their talents rust and devote their lives merely to idleness, amusement, and the propagation of their species, in a word, to enjoyment. But he cannot possibly *will* that this should be a general law of nature or be implanted in us as such by an instinct of nature. For, as a rational being, he necessarily wills that his faculties be developed, since they have been given to serve him for all sorts of possible purposes.

4. A fourth, prosperous man, while seeing others whom he could help having to struggle with great hardship thinks: What concern is it of mine? Let everyone be as happy as heaven pleases or as he can make himself. I will take nothing from him nor even envy him, but I do not wish either to contribute anything to his welfare or assist him in his distress. There is no doubt that if such a way of thinking were a general law, society might get along very well and doubtless even better than if everyone were to talk of sympathy and good will or even endeavor occasionally to put it into practice, but then [were to] cheat when one could and so betray the rights of man or otherwise violate them. But although it is possible that a general law of nature might exist in terms of that maxim, it is impossible to *will* that such a principle should have the general validity of a law of nature. For a will which resolved this would contradict itself, inasmuch as many a time one would need the love and sympathy of others and by such a law of nature, sprung from one's own will, one would deprive himself of all hope of the aid he desires.

These are a few of the many actual duties, or at least what we regard as such, which derive clearly from the one principle that we have established. We must be *able to will* that a maxim of our action should be a general law. This is the canon of any moral assessment at all of such action. Some actions are such that their maxims cannot even be *conceived* as a general law of nature without contradiction, let alone that one could *will* that these maxims *should* become such laws. Other actions reveal no such intrinsic impossibility, but still it is impossible to *will* that their maxim should be elevated to the universality of a law of nature, since such a will would contradict itself. It can be easily seen that the former would conflict with strict or more specific, inexorable duty, the latter merely with a broader (meritorious) duty. Therefore, all duties, in regard to their compulsory nature (not the object of their action), depend on the same principle as the above illustrations conclusively show.

If we now watch ourselves for any transgression of duty, we shall find that we actually do not will that our maxim should be a general law in such cases. On the contrary, we will that the opposite should remain a general law. We merely take the liberty of making an *exception* in our own favor or (just for this time) in favor of our inclination. Consequently, if we considered all cases from the point of view of reason, we should find a contradiction in our own will; namely, that a certain principle is objectively necessary as a general law and yet is subjectively not general but has exceptions. In regarding our action on the one hand from the point of view

of a will wholly conformed to reason, and on the other hand looking at the same action from the point of view of a will affected by inclination, there is really no contradiction but an antagonism on the part of inclination to the precept of reason which turns the universality of the principle into a mere generality, so that the principle of practical reason can meet the maxim half way.

Now although our own impartial judgment cannot justify this, it can prove that we do really acknowledge the validity of the categorical imperative and (with due respect) take just a few liberties with it, which we consider unimportant and at the same time forced upon us.

Thus we have at least established this much; that if duty is a concept which is to have any import and real controlling authority over our actions, it can only be expressed in a categorical and never in hypothetical imperatives. It is also of great importance that the content of the categorical imperative be presented clearly and definitely for every purpose; the categorical imperative must contain the principle of all duty if there is such a thing at all. However, we cannot yet prove *a priori* that such an imperative actually exists; that there is a practical law which commands absolutely by itself and without any other impulse and that compliance with this law is duty.

To be able to do that, it is extremely important to heed the warning that we cannot possibly think of deducing the reality of this principle from *particular attributes of human nature*. Duty is to be the practical, unconditional necessity for action; it must hold therefore for all rational beings (to whom an imperative can refer at all), and *for this reason only* it must also be a law for all human wills. On the other hand, whatever is deduced from the particular natural make-up of human beings, from certain feelings and propensities[11] and, if possible, even from any particular tendency of human reason proper which does not need to show in the will of every rational being. [Whatever is so deduced] may indeed furnish a maxim, but not a law. It may offer us a subjective principle on which we may act and may have propensities and inclinations, but [it does not give us] an objective principle by which we should be *constrained* to act, even though all our propensities, inclinations, and natural dispositions were opposed to it. In fact, the maxim evinces the sublime quality and intrinsic dignity of the command that the more clearly duty holds true, the less its subjective impulses favor it and the more they oppose such duty without being able in the slightest to weaken the binding character of the law, or to diminish its validity. . . .

Therefore, every empirical element is not only quite incapable of aiding the principle of morality, but is even highly prejudicial to the purity of morals. For the proper and inestimable value of a

genuine good will consists just in the principle of action being free from all contingent causes which experience alone can furnish. We cannot repeat our warning too often against this lax and even low habit of thought which searches empirical motives and laws for principles. Human reason when weary likes to rest on this cushion and in a dream of sweet illusions it substitutes for morality a bastard made up of limbs of quite different origin which appears as anything one chooses to see in it, save as virtue to one who has once beheld her in her true form.[12]

The question then is this: Is it a necessary law *for all rational beings* that they should always judge their actions by maxims which they can will themselves to serve as general laws? If this is so, then this must be related (altogether *a priori*) to the very concept of the will of a rational being. But in order to discover this relationship we must, however reluctantly, take a step into metaphysics, although into a domain of it distinct from speculative philosophy; namely into the metaphysics of morals. In practical philosophy, where one is not concerned with the reasons of what *happens* but with the laws of what *ought to happen* though it never may, that is, with objective practical laws, we need not inquire into the reasons why anything pleases or displeases,

---

[11] [Kant distinguishes *Hang* (propensity) from *Neigung* (inclination) as follows: *Hang* is a predisposition to the desire of some enjoyment; in other words, it is the subjective possibility of excitement of a certain desire preceding the concept of its object. When the enjoyment has been experienced it produces a *Neigung* (inclination) for it, which accordingly is defined "habitual, sensible desire."—Ed.]

[12] To behold virtue in her proper form is but to contemplate morality divested of all admixture of sensible things and of every spurious ornament of reward or self-love. To what extent she then eclipses everything else that charms the inclinations one may readily perceive with the least exertion of his reason, if it be not wholly spoiled for abstraction.

how the pleasure of mere sensation differs from taste, and whether the latter differs from a general rational enjoyment. [There we need not ask] for the grounds of pleasure or pain, how desires and inclinations arise from it, and how through the influence of reason from these in turn arise maxims. All this belongs to an empirical psychology which would constitute the second part of the natural sciences viewed as the *philosophy of nature* so far as it is based on *empirical laws*.

However, here we are concerned with objective practical laws and consequently with the relation of the will to itself so far as it is determined by reason alone, in which case whatever refers to the empirical is necessarily excluded. For, if *reason of itself* determines conduct (which possibility we are about to investigate), it must necessarily do so *a priori*.

The will is conceived as a faculty impelling a man to action *in accordance with the concept of certain laws*. Such a faculty can be found only in rational beings. Now, that which serves the will as the objective ground for its self-determination is the *end*, and if the end is given by reason alone, it must be so given for all rational beings. On the other hand, that which merely contains the ground of a possibility of action is called the *means*. The subjective ground of desire is the *main-spring*, the objective ground of volition is the *motive*; hence the distinction [arises] between subjective ends resting on main-springs, and objective ends depending on motives that hold for every rational being. Practical principles are *formal* when they abstract from all subjective ends,

they are *material* when they assume these and, therefore, particular main-springs of action. The ends which a rational being chooses to set himself as *effects* of his action (material ends) are altogether merely relative as only their relation to the specific capacity for desire of the subject gives them their value. Such value therefore cannot furnish general principles, i.e., practical laws valid and necessary for all rational beings and for every volition. Hence all these relative ends can only give rise to hypothetical imperatives. However, supposing that there were something *whose existence* was *in itself* of absolute value, something which, as an *end in itself*, could be a ground for definite laws, then this end and it alone, would be the ground for a possible categorical imperative, i.e., a practical law. Now I say that man, and generally every rational being, *exists* as an end in himself, *not merely as a means* for the arbitrary use of this or that will; he must always be regarded as an end in all his actions whether aimed at himself or at other rational beings. All objects of the inclinations have only a conditional value since, but for the inclinations and their respective wants, their object would be without value. But the inclinations themselves, being sources of want, are so far from having an absolute value that instead of relishing them it must rather be the general wish of every rational being to be wholly free from them. Hence the value of any object which *can be acquired* by our action is always conditional. Beings whose existence depends not on our will but on nature have, nevertheless, if they are irrational beings, only a relative value as means and are therefore called *things*; rational beings, on the other hand, are called *persons*. Their very nature constitutes them as ends in themselves; that is, as something which must not be used merely as means. To that extent, a person is limiting freedom of action and is an object of respect. Therefore persons are not merely subjective ends whose existence is an end for us as the result of our action, but they are objective ends; that is, things whose existence in itself is an end. No other end can be substituted (as a justification) for such an end, making it *merely* serve as a means, because otherwise nothing whatever could be found that would possess *absolute value*. If all value were conditional and therefore contingent, reason would have no supreme practical principle whatever.

Now, if a supreme practical principle ought to exist, or a categorical imperative with respect to the human will, it must be one which turns the concept of what is necessarily an end for everybody because it is *an end in itself* into an *objective* principle of the will which can serve as a general practical law. The basis of this principle is that *rational nature exists as an end in itself*. Man necessarily conceives his own existence as being this rational nature, to the extent that it is a *subjective* principle of human actions. But every other rational being regards its existence similarly for the same rational reason that holds true for me,[13] so at the same time it is an objective principle from which, as a

[13] This proposition is stated here as a postulate. Its grounds are to be found in the concluding section.

supreme practical ground, all laws of the will must needs be deductible. Accordingly, the practical imperative will be as follows: *Act so as to treat man, in your own person as well as in that of anyone else, always as an end, never merely as a means*. We shall now inquire whether this principle can be realized.

To use the previous examples:

First:

In regard to the concept of necessary duty to oneself, whoever contemplates suicide will ask himself whether his action is consistent with the idea of man as *an end in itself*. If he destroys himself to escape onerous conditions, he uses a person merely as a *means* to maintain a tolerable condition until life ends. But man is not a thing, that is to say, something which can be used *merely* as means, but in all his actions must always be considered as an end in itself. Therefore I cannot dispose in any way of man in my own person so as to mutilate, damage or kill him. (It is a matter of morals proper to define this principle more precisely to avoid all misunderstanding. Therefore I bypass such questions as that of the amputation of the limbs in order to preserve one's life, and of exposing one's life to danger with a view to preserving it, etc.)

Second:

As regards necessary or obligatory duties toward others, whoever is thinking of making a lying promise to others will see at once that he would be using another man *merely as a means*, without the latter being the end in itself at the same time. The person whom I propose to use by such a promise for my own purposes cannot possibly assent to my way of acting toward him. . . . This conflict with the principle of duty toward others becomes more obvious if we consider examples of attacks on the liberty and property of others. Here it is clear that whoever transgresses the rights of men intends to use the person of others merely as means without considering that as rational beings they shall always be regarded as ends also; that is, as beings who could possibly be the end of the very same action.[14]

Third:

As regards contingent (meritorious) duties to oneself, it is not enough that the action does not violate humanity in our own person as an end in itself; [such action] must also *be congruous to it.* Now, there are in mankind capacities for greater perfection which belong to the end of nature regarding humanity. . . . To neglect these capacities might at best be consistent with the *survival*

---

[14] This does not mean that the trite saying, *Quod tibi non vis fieri* etc., could serve here as the rule or principle. This saying is only a deduction from the above rule, though with several limitations: It cannot be a general law, for it does not contain the principle of duties to oneself, nor the duties of charity to others (for many a person would gladly consent that others need do no good deeds for him, provided only that he might be excused from doing good deeds for them), nor finally, that of obligatory duties to one another; by this reasoning the criminal might argue against judges, and so on.

of humanity as an end in itself, but [it is not consistent] with the *promotion* of nature's end regarding humanity.

Fourth:

As regards meritorious duties toward others, the natural end which all men have is their own happiness. Now, humanity might indeed subsist if no one contributed anything to the happiness of others as long as he did not deliberately diminish it; but this would be only negatively congruous to *humanity as an end in itself* if everyone does not also endeavor to promote the ends of others as far as he is able. For the ends of any subject which is an end in himself must be my ends too as far as possible, if that idea is to be *fully* effective in me.

This principle of man, and any rational creature, being *an end in itself,* which is the main limiting condition of every man's freedom of action, is not taken from experience for two reasons. First, its universal character, applying as it does to all rational beings whatever, is a fact which no experience can determine; second, because this principle does not present humanity as a subjective end of men; that is, as an object which actually we set ourselves as an end, but it [presents humanity as] an objective end which, whatever [subjective] ends we may have, is to constitute as a law the supreme limiting condition of all subjective ends. It must, therefore, derive from pure reason. In fact, according to the first principle, *the rule* and its universal character which enables [such legislation] to be some kind of law, for example, a law of nature, the *subjective* ground is the *end*. Since, according to the second principle the subject of all ends is some rational being, each being an end in itself, the third practical principle of the will follows as the ultimate prerequisite for the congruity [of will] with general practical reason; viz, the idea that *the will of every rational being is a will giving general laws*.

By virtue of this principle all maxims are rejected which cannot co-exist with the will as the general legislator. Thus the will is not being subjected simply to law, but is so subjected that it must be regarded *as giving itself the law*, and for this very reason is subject to the law of which it may consider itself the author. . . . Although a will *which is subject to laws* may be attached to such a law through interest, yet a will which is itself a supreme law-giver cannot possibly depend on any interest, since such a dependent will would still need another law which would restrict the interest of its self-love by the condition that it should be valid as general law.

Thus the principle that every human will *gives general laws through all its maxims*[15] if otherwise correct, could very well be *suited as* the categorical imperative because it is *not grounded in any interest* but rather in the idea of universal law-giving. Therefore, it alone among all possible imperatives can be *unconditional*. Or better still, to reverse the proposition: If there is a categorical imperative, i.e., a law for every [act of]

[15] I may be excused from offering examples to elucidate this principle, as those which have explained the categorical imperative and its formula would all serve the same purpose here.

willing by a rational being, it can only command that everything be done on account of maxims of a will which could at the same time consider itself the object of its general laws, because only then both the practical principle and the imperative which it obeys are unconditional, the latter not being based on any interest.

Looking back now on all previous efforts to discover the principle of morality, we need not wonder why they all failed. Man was seen to be bound to laws by duty, but no one realized that he is subject *only to his own general laws* and that he is only bound to act in conformity with his own will, a will designed by nature to make general laws. For, when man was conceived as being only subject to some kind of law, such a law had to be supplemented by some interest, by way either of attraction or of constraint, since it did not originate as a law from *his own* will. [In the absence of such autonomy of the will] the will was obliged by *something else* to act in some manner or other. Through this reasoning, as such entirely necessary, all labor spent in finding a supreme principle of *duty* was irrevocably lost. Its final conclusion was never that of duty, but only that of a necessity of acting from a certain interest, be it a personal or impersonal interest. The imperative had to turn out to be a conditional one and could not by any means serve as a moral command. I will therefore call this principle [of will based on no interest] the principle of *autonomy* of the will as contrasted with every other which I regard as *heteronomy*.

The idea of a rational being which must consider itself as giving general laws through all the maxims of its will in order to evaluate itself and its actions under it, this idea leads to another related and very fruitful idea, namely, that of a *realm of ends.*

By a realm I understand the linking of different rational beings by a system of common laws. Since laws determine the ends and their general validity, we are able to conceive all ends as constituting a sytematic whole of both rational beings as ends in themselves, and of the special ends of each being, if we disregard the personal differentiation of rational beings as well as the content of their private ends. In other words, we can conceive a realm of ends which is possible in accordance with principles stated previously. The reason is that all rational beings are governed by the *law* that each must treat itself and all other such beings, *never merely as means*, but also always *as ends in themselves.* This results in a systematic linking of rational beings through common objective laws, i.e., a realm which may be called a realm of ends. In such a realm (admittedly only an ideal) these laws are directed toward the relations of these beings to one another as ends and means.

A rational being belongs as a *member* to the realm of ends to the extent to which he is himself subject to these general laws, although giving them himself. He belongs to it *as ruler (Oberhaupt)* when, while giving laws, he is not subject to the will of any other.

A rational being must always regard himself as law-making in a realm of ends made possible by freedom of the will, be it as member or as ruler. He cannot, however, hold the latter position merely by the maxims of his will but only if he is completely independent, has no wants and possesses unrestricted power adequate for his will. . . . Reason then relates every maxim of the will, as general law-giving to every other will and also to every action toward oneself, not on account of any other practical motive or any future advantage, but because of the idea of the *dignity* of a rational being which obeys no law but that which he himself gives.

In the realm of ends everything has either a price or *dignity*. Whatever has a price can be replaced by something else which is *equivalent*; whatever is above all price, and therefore has no equivalent, has dignity.

Whatever is related to the general inclinations and needs of mankind has a *market price*; whatever answers, without presupposing a need, to a certain taste, that is, to pleasure in the mere purposeless play of our emotions (*Gemütskräfte*) has a *fancy price*. But that which constitutes the condition under which alone anything can be an end in itself has not merely a relative value or price, but has an intrinsic value; it has *dignity*.

Morality is the sole condition under which a rational being can be an end in himself, since only then can he possibly be a law-making member of the realm of ends. Thus, only good morals (*Sittlichkeit*) and mankind, so far as it is capable of it, have dignity. Skill and diligence in work have a market price; wit, lively imagination and whims have a fancy price; but faithfulness to promise, good will as a matter of principle, not as a matter of instinct, have an intrinsic value. Neither nature nor art has anything which, if dignity were lacking, they could put in its place. For, such intrinsic value consists neither in its effects, nor in the utility and advantage which it makes possible, but in convictions; that is, in the maxims of will which are ready to manifest themselves in actions, even when such action does not have the desired effect. These actions need no urging by any subjective taste or sentiment to be regarded with immediate favor and pleasure. They need no immediate propensity or feeling; they represent the will that performs them as an object of an immediate respect. Nothing but reason is required to oblige them. Reason need not *flatter* the will into doing them, which in the case of duties would be a contradiction anyhow. This respect therefore shows that the value of such an outlook is dignity and places it infinitely above all price. Such dignity cannot for a moment be evaluated in terms of price or compared with it without, as it were, violating its sanctity.

What entitles virtue or moral disposition to make such high claims? It is nothing less than the share in the making of general laws which affords the rational being, qualifying him thereby to be a member of a possible realm of ends, for which he was already destined by his own nature. . . . The laws setting all value must for that very reason possess dignity; that is, an unconditional incomparable value. The word *respect* alone offers a fitting expression of the esteem in which a rational being must hold it. *Autonomy* lies at the root of the dignity of human and of every other rational nature.

The aforementioned three modes of presenting the principle of morality are at bottom only so many formulae of the very same law, of which one comprises the other two. There is, however, a difference between them, but it is rather subjective than objective and practical. What is involved is bringing an idea of reason closer to what can be looked at and visualized (*Anschauung*) and thereby closer to feeling. All maxims, in fact, have three aspects.

First, there is *form,* consisting in being generalizations (*Allgemeinheit*). The formula of the moral imperative is stated thus: the maxims must be chosen as if they were as valid as general laws of nature.

Second, there is content or substance (*Materie*), in other words, an end. The formula states that the rational being, as an end by its own nature and therefore as an end in itself, must be for every maxim the condition limiting all merely relative and arbitrary ends.

Third, there is a *complete definition* of all maxims by this formula [of the categorical imperative], to wit: All maxims by virtue of their own law-making ought to harmonize so as to constitute together a possible realm of ends as a realm of nature.[16] This progression takes place through the categories of *unity* in the form of will (its generality), of *plurality* of the content or substance

---

[16] Teleology considers nature as a realm of ends; morals regards a possible realm of ends as a realm of nature. In the first case, the realm of ends is a theoretical idea explaining what actually is. In the latter it is a practical idea bringing about that which is not yet, but which can be realized in conforming to this idea in our conduct.

(the objects or ends), and of *totality* of their system. In forming a moral *judgment* about actions it is always better to proceed on the strict method and to start with the general formula of the categorical imperative: *Act according to a maxim which can become a general law*. If, however, we wish to introduce the moral law, it is very useful to evaluate the same action by the three specified concepts and thereby let it approach, as far as possible, something that is clearly envisaged (*Anschauung*).

We can conclude with what we started from, namely, with the concept of an absolutely good will. *That will is thoroughly good* which cannot be evil, or, whose maxim, if made a general law, could never contradict itself. This principle is also its supreme law: Act always on such a maxim as you can will to be a general law. This is the only condition under which a will can never contradict itself; and such an imperative is categorical. Since the validity of the will as a general law for possible actions is analogous to the general linking of the existence of things by general laws which is the formal aspect of nature in general, the categorical imperative can also be expressed as follows: *Act on maxims which can have themselves for their own object as general laws of nature*. Such then is the formula of a thoroughly good will.

Rational nature is distinguished from the rest of nature by setting itself an end. This end would be the content of every good will. But since the idea of an absolutely good will is not limited by any condition of attaining this or that end we must completely disregard every end *to be effected* which would make every will only relatively good. The end here must be understood to be not an end to be effected but an *independently existing* end, consequently only a negative one, i.e., one against which we must never act and therefore every act of williing must never be regarded merely as means, but as an end as well. This end can be nothing but the subject of all possible ends, since it is also the subject of a possible absolutely good will; because such a will cannot be related to any other object without contradiction. The principle: So act toward every rational being (yourself and others), that he may for you always be an end in himself, is therefore essentially identical with this other: Act upon a maxim which is generally valid for every rational being. . . .

In this way an intelligible world (*mundus intelligibilis*) is possible as a realm of ends, by virtue of the lawmaking of all persons as members. . . . Such a realm of ends would be actually realized if maxims conforming to the canon of the categorical imperative for all rational beings *were universally followed*. But a rational being, though punctiliously following this maxim himself, cannot count upon all others being equally faithful to it, nor [can he be certain] that the realm of nature and its purposive design so accord with him as a proper member as to form a realm made possible by himself; that is, favoring his expectation of happiness. Still the law remains in full force: Act according to the maxims of a member of a merely possible realm of ends in making general law since this law commands categorically. Therein lies the paradox; that merely the dignity of man as a rational creature, in other words, respect for a mere idea, should serve as an inflexible precept without any other end or advantage. The sublime character [of this dignity] consists precisely in this independence of maxims from all such springs of action. This makes every rational subject worthy to be a law-making member of the realm of ends. Otherwise he would have to be imagined as subject only to the natural law of his wants. Although we would suppose the realm of nature and the realm of ends to be united under one ruler, so that the realm of ends thereby would no longer be a mere idea but acquire true reality, [such reality] would no doubt gain an additional strong incentive, but never any increase of its intrinsic value. For, this sole unlimited law-giver must nonetheless always be conceived as evaluating the value of rational beings only by their disinterested behavior, as prescribed by the idea of the dignity of man alone. The essence of things is not altered by their external conditions and man must be judged by whatever constitutes his absolute value, irrespective of these [conditions], whoever be the judge, even it be the Supreme Being. Morality then is the relation of actions to the autonomy of the will, that is, to the possible general laws made by its maxims. An action that is consistent

with the autonomy of the will is *permissible*, one that is not congruous with it is *forbidden*. A will whose maxims necessarily are congruous with the laws of autonomy is a *sacred*, wholly good will. The dependence of a not absolutely good will on the principle of autonomy (moral compulsion) is [called] obligation. It cannot be applied to a holy being. The objective necessity of an action resulting from obligation is called *duty*.

It is easy to see, from what has been just said, why we ascribe a certain quality and sublime dignity to the person who fulfils all his duties, although we think of the concept of duty as implying subjection to the law. There is no sublime quality in him as far as he is *subject* to the moral law, but there is as far as he is at the same time a maker of that very law and on that account subject to it. Furthermore, we have shown above that neither fear nor inclination but simply respect for the law is the incentive which can give actions a moral value. Our own will, as far as it acts under the condition that its maxims may constitute possible general laws—and such a will is possible as an idea— is the real object of respect. The dignity of mankind consists just in this capacity of making general laws, always provided that it is itself subject to these laws.

COMMENT

Some Main Issues Presented by Kant's Ethics

The ethics of Kant is the most famous example of a "deontological" type of ethics. The adjective "deontological" is derived from the Greek words *deon* (duty) and *logos* (science, or theory). A deontological ethics is one based on the theory of duty. As the term is commonly used, it means an ethics of duty for duty's sake, expressed in its most uncompromising form in the motto, "Let me do right though the heavens fall." The opposite, or utilitarian, point of view, is that an act would be wrong, because disastrous, *if* the heavens fell. As indicated by the next chapter, utilitarians such as Bentham and Mill judge the morality of actions in terms of their consequences for weal or woe. Quite different is the point of view of Kant that the moral quality of acts depends upon conformity to laws, rules, or principles of action rather than upon goals or results.

Whatever our opinion of Kant's ethics—and there is much to admire as well as to criticize—we cannot deny that he presents issues of great importance. Some of these are as follows:

1. ARE ETHICAL PRINCIPLES EMPIRICAL OR A PRIORI? The motive of Kant's philosophy is the discovery and justification of *a priori* forms, concepts, and principles. In ethics, he draws a sharp distinction between "is" and "ought" and contends that the moral *ought* must be formulated in *a priori* principles. Is he correct?

If empirical science is a knowledge of *existence*, and if an "ideal" or "norm" is what ought to be but *is not*, the conception of a "normative empirical science" is contradictory. And if so, ethics is either merely subjective—as the advocates of the emotive theory contend—or it is *a priori*. Modern philosophers have been deeply disturbed by the problem thus posed.

The proponents of natural law, such as Cicero, try to solve the problem by denying the sharp antithesis between *what is* and *what ought to be*—and on this point they receive support from utilitarians such as Mill and pragmatists such as Dewey. What ought to be, it can be argued, is what satisfies genuine needs. A need arises when there is an uncompleted tendency in human nature—a frustrated, or at least unconsummated, impulse or desire. These needs can be determined scientifically, and plans to satisfy them can be elaborated with due regard to facts. The objective of securing the greatest possible fulfillment should determine which needs are to receive preferential treatment, and here, too, there are facts to guide us.

Kant would reply that such an empirical procedure is a mere begging of the question. It *assumes* that morality consists in the fulfillment of our needs—but this assumption he would sharply challenge. If *need* is interpreted in a nonmoral sense, it is not a moral concept and hence is irrelevant; but if it is interpreted in a moral sense, it must be connected with obligation—and obligation is not the sort of thing that empirical science can discover and justify. *Moral* objectivity is quite different from *scientific* objectivity, and an objective moral *ought* can never be determined scientifically. Rejecting the emotive view that morality is subjective, Kant concludes that moral objectivity must rest upon *a priori* foundations.

2. IS GOOD WILL, AND GOOD WILL ALONE, UNCONDITIONALLY GOOD? Let us consider Kant's contention that pleasure is good if combined with a good will

but evil if combined with a bad will. A hedonist would agree that pleasure gained from wanton torture is bad, but he would say that it is bad not *in* and *of itself* but in its evil consequences. Its bad effects greatly outweigh its intrinsic goodness—but *as pleasure*, it is intrinsically good. The hedonist would add that what makes good will "intrinsically good" is simply the pleasure that it involves, rather than the accompanying sense of duty.

This interpretation might seem to imply that if the pleasure gained from tormenting somebody were great enough to outweigh any pain that the act entails, such an act would therefore be legitimate—and of course Kant would deny this. A nonhedonist might admit that good will is intrinsically good, but maintain that there are other intrinsic goods, such as truth and beauty, that are no less ultimate and unconditional.

We can ask the question whether there is *any* unconditional good—pleasure or love or respect for duty or anything else. Pleasure can be sadistic, respect for duty can be chill and puritanical, and anything else can be degraded by its context.

3. Is Kant's Distinction between a Hypothetical and a Categorical Imperative Sound? If the criterion of right volition is neither inclination nor consequences, what is it? Kant answers that the rightness of the volition depends upon two factors: *right incentive* and *right maxim*.

The right incentive is respect and reverence for moral law. A moral act must be done for duty's sake (although other motivations may be involved). This requirement has already been discussed under the name, "good will."

The right maxim is the principle of "the categorical imperative." An imperative is an injunction or command; it says that a person ought to do so and so. A hypothetical imperative always takes a conditional form: "*If* you want to achieve *x*, then you ought to do *y*." Rules of skill and counsels of prudence are hypothetical imperatives: they tell us what we ought to do—"ought" in the sense of what we would be well advised to do—*if* we desire certain ends. They may be legitimate but they are not moral. A categorical imperative, on the other hand, asserts unconditionally, "You ought to act so and so." There is no "if" in front of the "ought." Obligation is not determined by inclination or expediency but by objective moral necessity, which can be stated in a universal rule.

The question is whether this distinction between a categorical and a hypothetical imperative is sound? Has Kant drawn the distinction too sharply? Is he, in pressing this distinction, too much the absolutist, not enough the relativist? Or is Kant right? Don't we believe that moral imperatives are, somehow or other, distinctive? And has he not correctly formulated the distinction? These are questions for the reader to ponder.

4. Does Kant's Ethics Provide a Sound Test of Right? An opponent might concede that there are categorical imperatives, and still find Kant's formulae for determining them unsatisfactory.

His first formula is: "Act only on that maxim which you can will as a universal law." One may object that this does not take account of individual differences which may be ethically decisive. Consider Kant's dispute with the French philosopher Benjamin Constant. The moral duty to tell the truth, Constant argued, is not unconditional. It would be ethically right to lie to a would-be murderer in order to save his intended victim, for a man bent on murder has forfeited all right to a truth which would abet his plot. To this contention Kant replied, "The duty of truthfulness makes no distinction between persons to whom one has this duty and to whom one can exempt himself from this duty; rather, it is an unconditional duty which holds in all circumstances."[1] Hence, we are duty-bound to tell even a truth that would result in murder. This is an extreme position that very few thinkers, whether philosophers or laymen, would endorse. In the case cited by Consant, there is a conflict between two duties: the duty to tell the truth and the duty to save a life. In such instances, how can we decide which duty is paramount without a consideration of consequences?

Kant would reply that there are "perfect duties," and that the duty to tell the truth is such a duty. We recognize a perfect obligation when we see that it is possible to universalize it and impossible to universalize its violation. For example, it is impossible to universalize lying (the violation of truth-telling) because if everybody lied, no one would believe you—lying is parasitic upon truth-telling. Hence telling the truth, which can be universalized with perfect consistency, is an absolute duty, and lying is an absolute violation of this duty. The duty to protect a life that is threatened is only an "imperfect duty"—derived from the fact that no one could consistently will that his own life be unprotected under such circumstances. The duties of perfect obligation, forbidding us to lie, break promises, steal, murder, and so forth, admit of no exceptions whatever in favor of duties of imperfect obligation.

Some writers have argued, in Kant's defense, that his universalization formula can be interpreted flexibly enough to meet common-sense objections. For example, we could universalize the principle that men should steal rather than starve to death. Or (to revert to the question that Constant raised) we could universalize the principle that one should lie in order to save an innocent man from the threat of murder. But can we reason in this way without a more empirical approach to ethics than Kant was prepared to admit? Can we do so without setting aside his concept of "perfect duties"?

We can agree with Kant up to a certain point: granted that an act is right for one person, it must be right *under the same conditions* for everybody. But when the conditions (physical or psychological or cultural) vary, philanthropic exception to the general rule may be warranted. If this is so, can morality be *a priori* and universal, as Kant supposed?

---

[1] "On a Supposed Right to Lie from Altruistic Motives," *Critique of Practical Reason and Other Writings in Moral Philosophy*, translated by L. W. Beck (University of Chicago Press, 1949), p. 349.

His second formula of the categorical imperative is: "Act so as to treat humanity, whether in your own person or in that of another, always as an end and never as a means only." This formula expresses our sense of the intrinsic value of the human spirit, and it has a profound moral appeal. Its deeper meaning is expressed in Martin Buber's little book, *I and Thou*. Basic to Buber's formulation of the Kantian principle is the distinction between two types of relation, a relation to human beings as ends-in-themselves and a relation to human beings as mere means. He states this distinction in enigmatic language:

> To man the world is twofold, in accordance with his twofold attitude. The attitude of man is twofold, in accordance with the twofold nature of the primary words which he speaks. The primary words are not isolated words, but combined words. The one primary word is the combination *I-Thou*. The other primary word is the combination *I-It*; wherein, without a change in the primary word, one of the words *He* and *She* can replace *It*. Hence the *I* of man is also twofold. For the *I* of the primary word *I-Thou* is a different *I* from that of the primary word *I-It*.[2]

Buber's meaning is this: Man adopts a twofold interpretation of his world, according to the "primary word" that he speaks. To speak the word is not to use one's vocal cords but to stand before existence and to comport oneself in a certain way. In the I-It relation, I regard the object, even if it be a He or a She, as if it were a mere thing. I stand apart from it in order coldly to scrutinize and exploit it: to observe, measure, categorize, and manipulate it—to bend it to my advantage. In this relation there is no reciprocity: the relation is that of master to instrument. If I treat someone as an *It*, I do not acknowledge *his* right to treat me as an *It* in return. In the I-Thou relation, on the other hand, one's essential being is in direct and sympathetic contact with another essential being. The Thou is cherished for what he is in his "singleness"—not as an *object* but as a *presence*, not as a *type* but as an *individual*, not as a *means* but as an *end*. The I-Thou relation is reciprocal: I-Thou implies Thou-I. I not only give but receive; I not only speak but listen; I not only respond but invite response. "My *Thou* affects me, as I affect it."[3] The *I* is constituted and remade in this act of meeting: "Through the *Thou* a man becomes I."[4]

Not only does the "Thou" differ from the "it," but the "I" in the first relation differs fundamentally from the "I" in the second. The first "I" is a real person in a world of persons; the second is a depersonalized individual in a world of things. A person is fully a person only in relation to other persons. He is not a real person so far as he regards others as things, as mere objects or implements. The real meeting between man and man comes about only when each regards the other

---

[2] *I and Thou* (New York: Charles Scribner's Sons, 1937), p. 3.
[3] *Ibid.*, p. 15.
[4] *Ibid.*, p. 28.

as an end. This is not always possible. To live, we need to use things, and what is more to the point, to use human beings. But in a real community, the means-relation between individuals, the "I-it" relation, is subordinated to the ends-relation between persons, the "I-Thou" relation. "Only men who are capable of truly saying *Thou* to one another can truly say *We* with one another."[5]

This way of restating Kant's second formula illuminates its profound moral implications. But is it possible to carry out the formula without a view to the effects of our actions? Must we not have some positive idea of the ends of man and how to achieve them? If so, is the second formula consistent with the first formula? The first formula, it could be argued, is a right for right's sake principle, and the second is a right for good's sake principle. Is Kant inconsistent?

The third formula is: "Act as a member of a kingdom of ends." Spelled out, this means that every man, as a rational agent, is ideally a member of a moral community, in which he is both sovereign (free) and subject (responsible), willing the universal laws of morality for himself and others. The moral law, according to this formula, must be the person's own free voice and is not a whit less a universal law for being freely chosen. But is genuine freedom consistent with Kant's interpretation of universality? Freedom does not consist merely in willing the dictates of universal abstract reason; it is warmer, more personal, and creative. In maintaining that morality is obedience to universal law, without regard to the individual and his peculiar circumstances, Kant dissolves the individual personality in an ocean of ethical abstraction, like an individual grain of sand dissolved in a vast sea. In so doing, he undermines his very demand for a moral community of free and responsible human beings. So at least might an existentialist, with his strong emphasis upon human individuality, argue.

In Kant's defense, it can be pointed out that *The Foundations of the Metaphysic of Morals*, from which our selection is taken, is the most abstract and formalistic of his ethical works. In the *Critique of Practical Reason*, Kant corrects the one-sidedness of the *Foundations* by discoursing at length on the concept of "good" as well as "duty," and in his *Lectures on Ethics* and *Metaphysics of Morals* (not to be confused with the *Foundations*) Kant discusses particular duties in a concrete way. The more teleological and less absolutistic elements in his theory emerge in these works.

[5] *Ibid.*, p. 176.

15

Utility

JEREMY BENTHAM (1748–1832)

The son of a well-to-do London barrister, Bentham studied law but never practiced it. He set himself to work out a new system of jurisprudence and to reform both the penal and the civil law. In pursuit of this aim he wrote thousands of pages, but was curiously indifferent about publishing them. Although his works were collected in eleven large volumes, the only major theoretical work that he published himself was the *Introduction to the Principles of Morals and Legislation* (1789), which contains an exposition of his hedonistic and utilitarian ethics.

Painfully shy, he could hardly endure the company of strangers, and yet he became a powerful political force. As a leader of the "Philosophical Radicals," he attracted such distinguished followers as James Mill and John Stuart Mill. He established the *Westminster Review,* at his own expense, as an organ of his movement, and he and his associates succeeded in founding University College, London. There his embalmed body, dressed in his customary clothes and topped with a wax model of his head, is still to be seen.

An Introduction to the Principles of Morals and Legislation

Chapter I

Of the Principle of Utility

I. Nature has placed mankind under the governance of two sovereign masters, *pain* and *pleasure*. It is for them alone to point out what we ought to do, as well as to determine what we shall do. On the one hand the standard of right and wrong, on the other the chain of causes and effects, are fastened to their throne. They govern us in all we do, in all we say, in all we think: every effort we can make to throw off our subjection, will serve but to demonstrate and confirm it. In words a man may pretend to abjure their empire: but in reality he will remain subject to it all the while. The *principle of utility*[1] recognizes this subjection, and

assumes it for the foundation of that system, the object of which is to rear the fabric of felicity by the hands of reason and of law. Systems which attempt to question it, deal in sounds instead of sense, in caprice instead of reason, in darkness instead of light.

But enough of metaphor and declamation: it is not by such means that moral science is to be improved.

New edition, Oxford, 1823. Some of [Bentham's] footnotes have been omitted. First published in 1789.

[1] Note by the Author, July 1822: To this denomination has of late been added, or substituted, the *greatest happiness or greatest felicity* principle: this for shortness, instead of saying at length *that principle* which states the greatest happiness of all those whose interest is in question, as being the right and proper, and only right and proper and universally desirable, end of human action: of human action in every situation, and in particular in that of a functionary or set of functionaries exercising the powers of Government. The word *utility* does not so clearly point to the ideas of *pleasure* and *pain* as the words *happiness* and *felicity* do: nor does it lead us to the consideration of the *number,* of the interests affected; to the *number,* as being the circumstance, which contributes, in the largest proportion, to the formation of the standard here in question; the *standard of right and wrong,* by which alone the propriety of human conduct, in every situation can with propriety be tried. This want of a sufficiently manifest connexion between the ideas of *happiness* and *pleasure* on the one hand, and the idea of *utility* on the other, I have every now and then found operating, and with but too much efficiency, as a bar to the acceptance, that might otherwise have been given, to this principle.

II. The principle of utility is the foundation of the present work: it will be proper therefore at the outset to give an explicit and determinate account of what is meant by it. By the principle of utility is meant that principle which approves or disapproves of every action whatsoever, according to the tendency which it appears to have to augment or diminish the happiness of the party whose interest is in question: or, what is the same thing in other words, to promote or to oppose that happiness. I say of every action whatsoever; and therefore not only of every action of a private individual, but of every measure of government.

III. By utility is meant that property in any object, whereby it tends to produce benefit, advantage, pleasure, good, or happiness, (all this in the present case comes to the same thing) or (what comes again to the same thing) to prevent the happening of mischief, pain, evil, or unhappiness to the party whose interest is considered: if that party be the community in general, then the happiness of the community: if a particular individual, then the happiness of that individual.

IV. The interest of the community is one of the most general expressions that can occur in the phraseology of morals: no wonder that the meaning of it is often lost. When it has a meaning, it is this. The community is a fictitious *body,* composed of the individual persons who are considered as constituting as it were its *members.* The interest of the community then is, what? —the sum of the interests of the several members who compose it.

V. It is in vain to talk of the interest of the community, without understanding what is the interest of the individual. A thing is said to promote the interest, or to be *for* the interest, of an individual, when it tends to add to the sum total of his pleasures: or, what comes to the same thing, to diminish the sum total of his pains.

VI. An action then may be said to be conformable to the principle of utility, or, for shortness sake, to utility, (meaning with respect to the community at large) when the tendency it has to augment the happiness of the community is greater than any it has to diminish it.

VII. A measure of government (which is but a particular kind of action, performed by a particular person or persons) may be said to be conformable to or dictated by the principle of utility, when in like manner the tendency which it has to augment the happiness of the community is greater than any which it has to diminish it.

VIII. When an action, or in particular a measure of government, is supposed by a man to be conformable to the principle of utility, it may be convenient, for the purposes of discourse, to imagine a kind of law or dictate, called a law or dictate of utility: and to speak of the action in question, as being conformable to such law or dictate.

IX. A man may be said to be a partizan of the principle of utility, when the approbation or disapprobation he annexes to any action, or to any measure, is determined by and proportioned to the tendency which he conceives it to have to augment or to diminish the happiness of the community: or in other words, to its conformity or unconformity to the laws or dictates of utility.

X. Of an action that is conformable to the principle of utility one may always say either that it is one that ought to be done, or at least that it is not one that ought not to be done. One may say also, that it is right it should be done; at least that it is not wrong it should be done: that it is a right action; at least that it is not a wrong action. When thus interpreted, the words *ought,* and *right* and *wrong,* and others of that stamp, have a meaning: when otherwise, they have none.

XI. Has the rectitude of this principle been ever formally contested? It should seem that it had, by those who have not known what they have been meaning. Is it susceptible of any direct proof? it should seem not: for that which is used to prove every thing else, cannot itself be proved: a chain of proofs must have their commencement somewhere. To give such proof is as impossible as it is needless.

XII. Not that there is or ever has been that human creature breathing, however stupid or perverse, who has not on many, perhaps on most occasions of his life, deferred to it. By the natural constitution of the human frame, on most occasions of their lives men in general embrace this principle, without thinking of it: if not for the ordering of their own actions, yet for the trying of their own actions, as well as those of other men. There have been, at the same time, not many, perhaps,

even of the most intelligent, who have been disposed to embrace it purely and without reserve. There are even few who have not taken some occasion or other to quarrel with it, either on account of their not understanding always how to apply it, or on account of some prejudice or other which they were afraid to examine into, or could not bear to part with. For such is the stuff that man is made of: in principle and in practice, in a right track and in a wrong one, the rarest of all human qualities is consistency.

XIII. When a man attempts to combat the principle of utility, it is with reasons drawn, without his being aware of it, from that very principle itself. His arguments, if they prove any thing, prove not that the principle is *wrong,* but that, according to the applications he supposes to be made of it, it is *misapplied.* Is it possible for a man to move the earth? Yes; but he must first find out another earth to stand upon.

XIV. To disprove the propriety of it by arguments is impossible; but, from the causes that have been mentioned, or from some confused or partial view of it, a man may happen to be disposed not to relish it. Where this is the case, if he thinks the settling of his opinions on such a subject worth the trouble, let him take the following steps, and at length, perhaps, he may come to reconcile himself to it.

1. Let him settle with himself, whether he would wish to discard this principle altogether; if so, let him consider what it is that all his reasonings (in matters of politics especially) can amount to?

2. If he would, let him settle with himself, whether he would judge and act without any principle, or whether there is any other he would judge and act by?

3. If there be, let him examine and satisfy himself whether the principle he thinks he has found is really any separate intelligible principle; or whether it be not a mere principle in words, a kind of phrase, which at bottom expresses neither more nor less than the mere averment of his own unfounded sentiments; that is, what in another person he might be apt to call caprice?

4. If he is inclined to think that his own approbation or disapprobation, annexed to the idea of an act, without any regard to its consequences, is a sufficient foundation for him to judge and act upon, let him ask himself whether his sentiment is to be a standard of right and wrong, with respect to every other man, or whether every man's sentiment has the same privilege of being a standard to itself?

5. In the first case, let him ask himself whether his principle is not despotical, and hostile to all the rest of the human race?

6. In the second case, whether it is not anarchical, and whether at this rate there are not as many different standards of right and wrong as there are men? and whether even to the same man, the same thing, which is right to-day, may not (without the least change in its nature) be wrong tomorrow? and whether the same thing is not right and wrong in the same place at the same time? and in either case,

whether all argument is not at an end? and whether, when two men have said, 'I like this,' and 'I don't like it,' they can (upon such a principle) have any thing more to say?

7. If he should have said to himself, No: for that sentiment which he proposes as a standard must be grounded on reflection, let him say on what particulars the reflection is to turn? if on particulars having relation to the utility of the act, then let him say whether this is not deserting his own principle, and borrowing assistance from that very one in opposition to which he sets it up: or if not on those particulars, on what other particulars?

8. If he should be for compounding the matter, and adopting his own principle in part, and the principle of utility in part, let him say how far he will adopt it?

9. When he has settled with himself where he will stop, then let him ask himself how he justifies to himself the adopting it so far? and why he will not adopt it any farther?

10. Admitting any other principle than the principle of utility to be a right principle, a principle that it is right for a man to pursue; admitting (what is not true) that the word *right* can have a meaning without reference to utility, let him say whether there is any such thing as a *motive* that a man can have to pursue the dictates of it: if there is, let him say what that motive is, and how it is to be distinguished from those which enforce the dictates of utility: if not, then lastly let him say what it is this other principle can be good for? . . .

Chapter IV

Value of a Lot of Pleasure or Pain, How To Be Measured

I. PLEASURES then, and the avoidance of pains, are the *ends* which the legislator has in view: it behoves him therefore to understand their *value*. Pleasures and pains are the *instruments* he has to work with: it behoves him therefore to understand their force, which is again, in other words, their value.

II. To a person considered *by himself*, the value of a pleasure or pain considered *by itself*, will be greater or less, according to the four following circumstances:[2]

1. Its *intensity*.
2. Its *duration*.
3. Its *certainty* or *uncertainty*.
4. Its *propinquity* or *remoteness*.

III. These are the circumstances which are to be considered in estimating a pleasure or a pain considered each of them by itself. But when the value of any pleasure or pain is considered for the purpose of estimating

[2] These circumstances have since been denominated *elements* or *dimensions* of *value* in a pleasure or a pain.

Not long after the publication of the first edition, the following memoriter verses were framed, in the view of lodging more effectually, in the memory, these points, on which the whole fabric of morals and legislation may be seen to rest.

Intense, long, certain, speedy, fruitful, pure—
Such marks in *pleasures* and in *pains* endure.
Such pleasures seek, if *private* be thy end:
If it be *public*, wide let them *extend*.
Such *pains* avoid, whichever be thy view:
If pains *must* come, let them *extend* to few.

the tendency of any *act* by which it is produced, there are two other circumstances to be taken into the account; these are,

5. Its *fecundity*, or the chance it has of being followed by sensations of the *same* kind: that is, pleasures, if it be a pleasure: pains, if it be a pain.

6. Its *purity*, or the chance it has of *not* being followed by sensations of the *opposite* kind: that is, pains, if it be a pleasure: pleasures, if it be a pain.

These two last, however, are in strictness scarcely to be deemed properties of the pleasure or the pain itself; they are not, therefore, in strictness to be taken into the account of the value of that pleasure or that pain. They are in strictness to be deemed properties only of the act, or other event, by which such pleasure or pain has been produced; and accordingly are only to be taken into the account of the tendency of such act or such event.

IV. To a *number* of persons, with reference to each of whom the value of a pleasure or a pain is considered, it will be greater or less, according to seven circumstances: to wit, the six preceding ones; viz.

1. Its *intensity*.
2. Its *duration*.
3. Its *certainty* or *uncertainty*.
4. Its *propinquity* or *remoteness*.
5. Its *fecundity*.
6. Its *purity*.

And one other; to wit:

7. Its *extent;* that is, the number of persons to whom it *extends;* or (in other words) who are affected by it.

V. To take an exact account then of the general tendency of any act, by which the interests of a community are affected, proceed as follows. Begin with any one person of those whose interests seem most immediately to be affected by it: and take an account,

1. Of the value of each distinguishable *pleasure* which appears to be produced by it in the *first* instance.

2. Of the value of each *pain* which appears to be produced by it in the *first* instance.

3. Of the value of each pleasure which appears to be produced by it *after* the first. This constitutes the *fecundity* of the first *pleasure* and the *impurity* of the first *pain*.

4. Of the value of each *pain* which appears to be produced by it after the first. This constitutes the *fecundity* of the first *pain*, and the *impurity* of the first *pleasure*.

5. Sum up all the values of all the *pleasures* on the one side, and those of all the *pains* on the other. The balance, if it be on the side of pleasure, will give the *good* tendency of the act upon the whole, with respect to the interests of that *individual* person; if on the side of pain, the *bad* tendency of it upon the whole.

6. Take an account of the *number* of persons whose interests appear to be concerned; and repeat the above process with respect to each. *Sum up* the numbers expressive of the degrees of *good* tendency which the act has, with respect to each individual, in regard to whom the tendency of it is *good* upon the whole: . . . do this again with respect to each individual, in regard to whom the tendency of it is *bad* upon the whole. Take the *balance;* which, if on the side of *pleasure*, will give the

general *good tendency* of the act, with respect to the total number or community of individuals concerned; if on the side of pain, the general *evil tendency*, with respect to the same community.

VI. It is not to be expected that this process should be strictly pursued previously to every moral judgment, or to every legislative or judicial operation. It may, however, be always kept in view: and as near as the process actually pursued on these occasions approaches to it, so near will such process approach to the character of an exact one.

VII. The same process is alike applicable to pleasure and pain, in whatever shape they appear: and by whatever denomination they are distinguished: to pleasure, whether it be called *good* (which is properly the cause or instrument of pleasure) or *profit* (which is distant pleasure, or the cause or instrument of distant pleasure,) or *convenience*, or *advantage, benefit, emolument, happiness*, and so forth: to pain, whether it be called *evil*, (which corresponds to *good*) or *mischief*, or *inconvenience*, or *disadvantage*, or *loss*, or *unhappiness*, and so forth.

VIII. Nor is this a novel and unwarranted, any more than it is a useless theory. In all this there is nothing but what the practice of mankind, wheresoever they have a clear view of their own interest, is perfectly conformable to. An article of property, an estate in land, for instance, is valuable, on what account? On account of the pleasures of all kinds which it enables a man to produce, and what comes to the same thing the pains of all kinds which it enables him to avert. But the value of such an article of property is universally understood to rise or fall according to the length or shortness of the time which a man has in it: the certainty or uncertainty of its coming into possession: and the nearness or remoteness of the time at which, if at all, it is to come into possession. As to the *intensity* of the pleasures which a man may derive from it, this is never thought of, because it depends upon the use which each particular person may come to make of it; which cannot be estimated till the particular pleasures he may come to derive from it, or the particular pains he may come to exclude by means of it, are brought to view. For the same reason, neither does he think of the *fecundity* or *purity* of those pleasures.

JOHN STUART MILL (1806–1873)

Mill was reared in London and was educated privately by his father, James Mill, a famous political philosopher. No child ever received a more prodigious education. Mill was reading Plato and Thucydides in the original Greek at an age when most children are reading nursery stories in their native language. His father set him to learn Greek at the age of three; Latin, algebra, and geometry at the age of eight; logic at twelve; and political economy at thirteen. Jeremy Bentham was an intimate friend of the family, and young John was thoroughly indoctrinated in his philosophy.

When Mill reached the age of seventeen, he was appointed a clerk in the East India Company, in whose service he remained for thirty-five years, rising steadily to the highest post in his department, that of examiner of correspondence and dispatches to India. This position afforded him considerable leisure for his intense intellectual pursuits.

In his twenty-first year, he fell into a deep mental depression, evidently the result of his unnatural childhood and years of intellectual cramming. He gradually emerged from this illness, but with a new sense of the insufficiency of his father's doctrinaire philosophy and a keener appreciation of the value of poetry, especially Wordsworth's. Thereafter he sought to broaden his outlook and succeeded in becoming a much better rounded (though less consistent) philosopher than either Bentham or his father. An important influence upon Mill was Harriet Taylor, the beautiful and talented wife of a London merchant, who finally married him (in 1851) after her husband died. They lived happily together for seven years, until they were separated by her untimely death. It was through her, Mill said, that he came to be more of a democrat and socialist, and *On Liberty* was their joint work.

After his long service in the India Office, he retired on a pension at the age of fifty-two. The remaining fifteen years of his life, although marred by ill health, were packed with intellectual and political activity. In 1865, he consented to run for Parliament as a representative of the working man for the constituency of Westminster; and during his single term of office (1866–1868), he made a considerable impression by his vigorous championing of reform. In 1869, he retired with his stepdaughter, Helen Taylor, to a small white stone cottage near Avignon, in France, where he continued to write. In May 1873 he died, the victim of a local fever.

Among his important books were *Logic* (1843), *The Principles of Political Economy* (1848), *On Liberty* (1859), *Utilitarianism* (1863), *Examination of Sir William Hamilton's Philosophy* (1865), and *Autobiography* (published after his death, in 1873).

Utilitarianism

Chapter II

What Utilitarianism Is

A passing remark is all that needs be given to the ignorant blunder of supposing that those who stand up for utility as the test of right and wrong use the term in that restricted and merely colloquial sense in which utility is opposed to pleasure. An apology is due to the philosophical opponents of utilitarianism, for even the momentary appearance of confounding them with anyone capable of so absurd a misconception; which is the more extraordinary, inasmuch as the contrary accusation, of referring everything to pleasure, and that, too, in its grossest form, is another of the common charges against utilitarianism: and, as has been pointedly remarked by an able writer,

Utilitarianism was published serially in *Fraser's Magazine* in 1861 and in book form, London, 1863.

the same sort of persons, and often the very same persons, denounce the theory "as impracticably dry when the word 'utility' precedes the word 'pleasure,' and as too practically voluptuous when the word 'pleasure' precedes the word 'utility'." Those who know anything about the matter are aware that every writer, from Epicurus to Bentham, who maintained the theory of utility, meant by it, not something to be contradistinguished from pleasure, but pleasure itself, together with exemption from pain; and instead of opposing the useful to the agreeable or the ornamental, have always declared that the useful means these, among other things. Yet the common herd, including the herd of writers, not only in newspapers and periodicals, but in books of weight and pretension, are perpetually falling into this shallow mistake. Having caught up the word "utilitarian," while knowing nothing whatever about it but its sound, they habitually express by it the rejection or the neglect of pleasure in some of its forms: of beauty, of ornament, or of amusement. Nor is the term thus ignorantly misapplied solely in disparagement, but occasionally in compliment, as though it implied superiority to frivolity and the mere pleasures of the moment. And this perverted use is the only one in which the word is popularly known, and the one from which the new generation are acquiring their sole notion of its meaning. Those who introduced the word, but who had for many years discontinued it as a distinctive appellation, may well feel themselves called upon to resume it if by doing so they can hope to contribute anything towards rescuing it from this utter degradation.

The creed which accepts as the foundation of morals "utility" or the "greatest happiness principle" holds that actions are right in proportion as they tend to promote happiness, wrong as they tend to produce the reverse of happiness. By happiness is intended pleasure, and the absence of pain; by unhappiness, pain, and the privation of pleasure. To give a clear view of the moral standard set up by the theory, much more requires to be said; in particular, what things it includes in the ideas of pain and pleasure; and to what extent this is left an open question. But these supplementary explanations do not affect the theory of life on which this theory of morality is grounded—namely, that pleasure and freedom from pain are the only things desirable as ends; and that all desirable things (which are as numerous in the utilitarian as in any other scheme) are desirable either for the pleasure inherent in themselves, or as means to the promotion of pleasure and the prevention of pain.

Now such a theory of life excites in many minds, and among them in some of the most estimable in feeling and purpose, inveterate dislike. To suppose that life has (as they express it) no higher end than pleasure—no better and nobler object of desire and pursuit —they designate as utterly mean and groveling; as a doctrine worthy only of swine, to whom the followers of Epicurus were, at a very early period, contemptuously likened; and modern holders of the doctrine are occasionally made the subject of equally polite comparisons by its German, French, and English assailants.

When thus attacked, the Epicureans have always answered that it is not they, but their accusers, who represent human nature in a degrading light, since the accusation supposes human beings to be capable of no pleasures except those of which swine are capable. If this supposition were true, the charge could not be gainsaid, but would then be no longer an imputation; for if the sources of pleasure were precisely the same to human beings and to swine, the rule of life which is good enough for the one would be good enough for the other. The comparison of the Epicurean life to that of beasts is felt as degrading, precisely because a beast's pleasures do not satisfy a human being's conceptions of happiness. Human beings have faculties more elevated than the animal appetites and, when once made conscious of them, do not regard anything as happiness which does not include their gratification. I do not, indeed, consider the Epicureans to have been by any means faultless in drawing out their scheme of consequences from the utilitarian principle. To do this in any sufficient manner, many Stoic, as well as Christian, elements require to be included. But there is no known Epicurean theory of life which does not assign to the pleasures of the intellect, of the feelings and imagination, and of the moral sentiments, a much higher value as pleasures than to those of mere sensation. It must be admitted, however, that utilitarian writers in general have placed the superiority of mental over bodily pleasures chiefly in the greater permanency, safety, uncostliness, etc., of the former—that is, in their circumstantial advantages rather than in their intrinsic nature. And on all these points utilitarians have fully proved their case; but they might have taken the other and, as it may be called, higher ground with entire consistency. It is quite compatible with the principle of utility to recognize the fact that some kinds of pleasure are more desirable and more valuable than others. It would be absurd that, while, in estimating all other things, quality is considered as well as quantity, the estimation of pleasures should be supposed to depend on quantity alone.

If I am asked what I mean by difference of quality in pleasures, or what makes one pleasure more valuable than another, merely as a pleasure, except its being greater in amount, there is but one possible answer. Of two pleasures, if there be one to which all or almost all who have experience of both give a decided preference, irrespective of any feeling of moral obligation to prefer it, that is the more desirable pleasure. If one of the two is, by those who are competently acquainted with both, placed so far above the other that they prefer it, even though knowing it to be attended with a greater amount of discontent, and would not resign it for any quantity of the other pleasure which their nature is capable of, we are justified in ascribing to the preferred enjoyment a superiority in quality so far outweighing quantity as to render it, in comparison, of small account.

Now it is an unquestionable fact that those who are equally acquainted with and equally capable of appreciating and enjoying both, do give a most marked preference to the manner of existence which employs their higher faculties. Few human creatures would consent to be changed into any of the lower animals for a promise of the fullest allowance of a beast's pleasures; no intelligent human being would consent to be a fool, no instructed person would be an ignoramus, no person of feeling and conscience would be selfish and base, even though they should be persuaded that the fool, the dunce, or the rascal is better satisfied with his lot than they are with theirs. They would not resign what they possess more than he for the most complete satisfaction of all the desires which they have in common with him. If they ever fancy they would, it is only in cases of unhappiness so extreme that to escape from it they would exchange their lot for almost any other, however undesirable in their own eyes. A being of higher faculties requires more to make him happy, is capable probably of more acute suffering, and certainly accessible to it at more points, than one of an inferior type; but in spite of these liabilities, he can never really wish to sink into what he feels to be a lower grade of existence. We may give what explanation we please of this unwillingness; we may attribute it to pride, a name which is given indiscriminately to some of the most and to some of the least estimable feelings of which mankind are capable: we may refer it to the love of liberty and personal independence, an appeal to which was with the Stoics one of the most effective means for the inculcation of it; to the love of power or to the love of excitement, both of which do really enter into and contribute to it; but its most appropriate appellation is a sense of dignity, which all human beings possess in one form or other, and in some, though by no means in exact, proportion to their higher faculties, and which is so essential a part of the happiness of those in whom it is strong that- nothing which conflicts with it could be otherwise than momentarily an object of desire to them. Whoever supposes that this preference takes place at a sacrifice of happiness—that the superior being, in anything like equal circumstances, is not happier than the inferior—confounds the two very different ideas of happiness and content. It is undisputable that the being whose capacities of enjoyment are low has the greatest chance of having them fully satisfied; and a highly endowed being will always feel that any happiness which he can look for, as the world is constituted, is imperfect. But he can learn to bear its imperfections, if they are at all bear-

able; and they will not make him envy the being who is indeed unconscious of the imperfections, but only because he feels not at all the good which those imperfections qualify. It is better to be a human being dissatisfied than a pig satisfied; better to be Socrates dissatisfied than a fool satisfied. And if the fool, or the pig, are of a different opinion, it is because they only know their own side of the question. The other party to the comparison knows both sides.

It may be objected that many who are capable of the higher pleasures occasionally, under the influence of temptation, postpone them to the lower. But this is quite compatible with a full appreciation of the intrinsic superiority of the higher. Men often, from infirmity of character, make their election for the nearer good, though they know it to be the less valuable; and this no less when the choice is between two bodily pleasures than when it is between bodily and mental. They pursue sensual indulgences to the injury of health, though perfectly aware that health is the greater good. It may be further objected that many who begin with youthful enthusiasm for everything noble, as they advance in years, sink into indolence and selfishness. But I do not believe that those who undergo this very common change voluntarily choose the lower description of pleasures in preference to the higher. I believe that, before they devote themselves exclusively to the one, they have already become incapable of the other. Capacity for the nobler feelings is in most natures a very tender plant, easily killed, not only by hostile influences, but by mere want of sustenance; and in the majority of young persons it speedily dies away if the occupations to which their position in life has devoted them, and the society into which it has thrown them, are not favorable to keeping that higher capacity in exercise. Men lose their high aspirations as they lose their intellectual tastes, because they have not time or opportunity for indulging them; and they addict themselves to inferior pleasures, not because they deliberately prefer them, but because they are either the only ones to which they have access, or the only ones which they are any longer capable of enjoying. It may be questioned whether any one who has remained equally susceptible to both classes of pleasures, ever knowingly and calmly preferred the lower, though many, in all ages, have broken down in an ineffectual attempt to combine both.

From this verdict of the only competent judges, I apprehend there can be no appeal. On a question which is the best worth having of two pleasures, or which of two modes of existence is the most grateful to the feelings, apart from its moral attributes and from its consequences, the judgment of those who are qualified by knowledge of both, or, if they differ, that of the majority of them, must be admitted as final. And there needs be the less hesitation to accept this judgment respecting the quality of pleasures, since there is no other tribunal to be referred to even on the question of quantity. What means are there of determining which is the acutest of two pains, or the intensest of two pleasurable sensations, except the general suffrage of those

who are familiar with both? Neither pains nor pleasures are homogeneous, and pain is always heterogeneous with pleasure. What is there to decide whether a particular pleasure is worth purchasing at the cost of a particular pain, except the feelings and judgment of the experienced? When, therefore, those feelings and judgment declare the pleasures derived from the higher faculties to be preferable *in kind,* apart from the question of intensity, to those of which the animal nature, disjointed from the higher faculties, is susceptible, they are entitled on this subject to the same regard.

I have dwelt on this point, as being a necessary part of a perfectly just conception of utility or happiness considered as the directive rule of human conduct. But it is by no means an indispensable condition to the acceptance of the utilitarian standard; for that standard is not the agent's own greatest happiness, but the greatest amount of happiness altogether; and if it may possibly be doubted whether a noble character is always the happier for its nobleness, there can be no doubt that it makes other people happier, and that the world in general is immensely a gainer by it. Utilitarianism, therefore, could only attain its end by the general cultivation of nobleness of character, even if each individual were only benefited by the nobleness of others, and his own, so far as happiness is concerned, were a sheer deduction from the benefit. But the bare enunciation of such an absurdity as this last renders refutation superfluous.

According to the greatest happiness principle, as above explained, the ultimate end, with reference to and for the sake of which all other things are desirable—whether we are considering our own good or that of other people —is an existence exempt as far as possible from pain, and as rich as possible in enjoyments, both in point of quantity and quality; the test of quality and the rule for measuring it against quantity being the preference felt by those who, in their opportunities of experience, to which must be added their habits of self-consciousness and self-observation, are best furnished with the means of comparison. This, being, according to the utilitarian opinion, the end of human action, is necessarily also the standard of morality, which may accordingly be defined "the rules and precepts for human conduct," by the observance of which an existence such as has been described might be, to the greatest extent possible, secured to all mankind; and not to them only, but, so far as the nature of things admits, to the whole sentient creation. . . .

[*The remainder of the chapter is devoted to Mill's answer to objections. Some of these objections, for example, that happiness is unobtainable, that utilitarianism is a "godless doctrine," that the doctrine is "worthy only of swine," would no longer be advanced by reputable philosophers, and can here be omitted. But a few of the objections and Mill's answers to them are worthy of attention. We shall begin with his reply to the objection that we should learn to do without happiness, since self-sacrifice is a duty.*]

 . . . The utilitarian morality does recognize in human beings the power of sacrificing their own greatest good for the good of others. It only refuses to admit that the sacrifice is itself a good. A sacrifice which does not increase or tend to increase the sum total of happiness, it considers as wasted. The only self-renunciation which it applauds is devotion to the happiness, or to some of the means of happiness, of others, either of mankind collectively or of individuals within the limits imposed by the collective interests of mankind.

I must again repeat what the assailants of utilitarianism seldom have the justice to acknowledge, that the happiness which forms the utilitarian standard of what is right in conduct is not the agent's own happiness but that of all concerned. As between his own happiness and that of others, utilitarianism requires him to be as strictly impartial as a disinterested and benevolent spectator. In the golden rule of Jesus of Nazareth, we read the complete spirit of the ethics of utility. "To do as you would be done by," and "to love your neighbor as yourself," constitute the ideal perfection of utilitarian morality. As the means of making the nearest approach to this ideal, utility would enjoin, first, that laws and social arrangements should place the happiness or (as, speaking practically, it may be called) the interest of every individual as nearly as possible in harmony with the interest of the whole; and, secondly, that education and opinion, which have so vast a power over human character, should so use that power as to establish in the mind of every individual an indissoluble association between his own happiness and the good of the whole, especially between his own happiness and the practice of such modes of conduct, negative and positive, as regard for the universal happiness prescribes; so that not only he may be unable to conceive the possibility of happiness to himself, consistently with conduct opposed to the general good, but also that a direct impulse to promote the general good may be in every individual one of the habitual motives of action, and the sentiments connected therewith may fill a large and prominent place in every human being's sentient existence. If the impugners of the utilitarian morality represented it to their own minds in this its true character, I know not what recommendation possessed by any other morality they could possibly affirm to be wanting to it; what more beautiful or more exalted developments of human nature any other ethical system can be supposed to foster, or what springs of action, not accessible to the utilitarian, such systems rely on for giving effect to their mandates.

The objectors to utilitarianism cannot always be charged with representing it in a discreditable light. On the contrary, those among them who entertain anything like a just idea of its disinterested character sometimes find fault with its standard as being too high for humanity. They say it is exacting too much to require that people shall always act from the inducement of promoting the general interests of society. But this is to mistake the very meaning of a standard of morals, and confound the rule of action with the motive of it. It is the business of ethics to tell us what are our duties, or by what test we may know them; but no system of ethics requires that the sole motive of all we do shall be a feeling of duty; on the contrary, ninety-nine hundredths of all our actions are done from other motives, and rightly so done if the rule of duty does not condemn them. It is the more unjust to utilitarianism that this particular misapprehension should be made a ground of objection to it, inasmuch as utilitarian moralists have gone beyond almost all others in affirming that the motive has nothing to do with the morality of the action, though much with the worth of the agent. He who saves a fellow creature from drowning does what is morally right, whether his motive be duty or the hope of being paid for his trouble; he who betrays the friend that trusts him is guilty of a crime, even if his object be to serve another friend to whom he is under greater obligations. But to speak only of actions done from the motive of duty, and in direct obedience to principle: it is a misapprehension to the utilitarian mode of thought to conceive it as implying that people should fix their minds upon so wide a generality as the world, or society at large. The great majority of good actions are intended not for the benefit of the world, but for that of individuals, of which the good of the world is made up; and the thoughts of the most virtuous man need not on these occasions travel beyond the particular persons concerned, except so far as is necessary to assure himself that in benefiting them he is not violating the rights, that is, the legitimate and authorized expectations, of any one else. The multiplication of happiness is, according to the utilitarian ethics, the object of virtue: the occasions on which any person (except one in a thousand) has it in his power to do this on an extended scale, in other words, to be a public benefactor, are but exceptional; and on these occasions alone is he called on to consider public utility; in every other case, private utility, the interest or happiness of some few persons, is all he has to attend to. Those alone the influence of whose actions extends to society in general need concern themselves habitually about so large an object. In the case of abstinences indeed—of things which people forbear to do from moral considerations, though the consequences in the particular case might be beneficial—it would be unworthy of an intelligent agent not to be consciously aware that the action is of a class which, if practiced generally, would be generally injurious, and that this is the ground of the obligation to abstain from it. The amount of regard for the public interest implied in this recognition is no greater than is demanded by every system of morals, for they all enjoin to abstain from whatever is manifestly pernicious to society.

The same considerations dispose of another reproach against the doctrine of utility, founded on a still grosser misconception of the purpose of a standard of morality, and of the very meaning of the words "right" and "wrong." It is often affirmed that utilitarianism renders men cold and unsympathizing; that it chills their moral feelings towards individuals; that it makes them regard only the dry and hard consideration of the consequences of actions, not taking into their moral estimate the

qualities from which those actions emanate. If the assertion means that they do not allow their judgment respecting the rightness or wrongness of an action to be influenced by their opinion of the qualities of the person who does it, this is a complaint not against utilitarianism, but against any standard of morality at all; for certainly no known ethical standard decides an action to be good or bad because it is done by a good or a bad man, still less because done by an amiable, a brave, or a benevolent man, or the contrary. These considerations are relevant, not to the estimation of actions, but of persons; and there is nothing in the utilitarian theory inconsistent with the fact that there are other things which interest us in persons besides the rightness and wrongness of their actions. The Stoics, indeed, with the paradoxical misuse of language which was part of their system, and by which they strove to raise themselves above all concern about anything but virtue, were fond of saying that he who has that has everything; that he, and only he, is rich, is beautiful, is a king. But no claim of this description is made for the virtuous man by the utilitarian doctrine. Utilitarians are quite aware that there are other desirable possessions and qualities besides virtue, and are perfectly willing to allow to all of them their full worth. They are also aware that a right action does not necessarily indicate a virtuous character, and that actions which are blamable often proceed from qualities entitled to praise. When this is apparent in any particular case, it modifies their estimation, not certainly of the act, but of the agent. . . .

Again, utility is often summarily stigmatized as an immoral doctrine by giving it the name of "expediency," and taking advantage of the popular use of that term to contrast it with principle. But the expedient, in the sense in which it is opposed to the right, generally means that which is expedient for the particular interest of the agent himself; as when a minister sacrifices the interests of his country to keep himself in place. When it means anything better than this, it means that which is expedient for some immediate object, some temporary purpose, but which violates a rule whose observance is expedient in a much higher degree. The expedient, in this sense, instead of being the same thing with the useful, is a branch of the hurtful. Thus it would often be expedient, for the purpose of getting over some momentary embarrassment, or attaining some object immediately useful to ourselves or others, to tell a lie. But inasmuch as the cultivation in ourselves of a sensitive feeling on the subject of veracity is one of the most useful, and the enfeeblement of that feeling one of the most hurtful, things to which our conduct can be instrumental; and inasmuch as any, even unintentional, deviation from truth does that much towards weakening the trustworthiness of human assertion, which is not only the principal support of all present social well-being, but the insufficiency of which does more than any one thing that can be named to keep back civilization, virtue, everything on which human happiness on the largest scale depends—we feel that the violation, for a present advantage, of a rule of such transcendent expediency is not expedient, and that he who, for the sake of convenience to himself or to some other individual, does what depends on him to deprive mankind of the good, and inflict upon them the evil, involved in the greater or less reliance which they can place in each other's word, acts the part of one of their worst enemies. Yet that even this rule, sacred as it is, admits of possible exceptions is acknowledged by all moralists; the chief of which is when the withholding of some fact (as of information from a malefactor, or of bad news from a person dangerously ill) would save an individual (especially an individual other than oneself) from great and unmerited evil, and when the withholding can only be effected by denial. But in order that the exception may not extend itself beyond the need, and may have the least possible effect in weakening reliance on veracity, it ought to be recognized and, if possible, its limits defined; and, if the principle of utility is good for anything, it must be good for weighing these conflicting utilities against one another, and marking out the region within which one or the other preponderates.

Again, defenders of utility often find themselves called upon to reply to such objections as this—that there is not time, previous to action, for calculating and weighing the effects of any line of conduct on the general happiness. This is exactly as if any one were to say that it is impossible to guide our conduct by Christianity because there is not time, on every occasion on which anything has to be done, to read through the Old and New Testaments. The answer to the objection is that there has been ample time, namely, the whole past duration of the human species. During all that time, mankind have been learning by experience the tendencies of actions; on which experience all the prudence, as well as all the morality, of life are dependent. People talk as if the commencement of this course of experience had hitherto been put off, and as if, at the moment when some man feels tempted to meddle with the property or life of another, he had to begin considering for the first time whether murder and theft are injurious to human happiness. Even then I do not think that he would find the question very puzzling; but, at all events, the matter is now done to his hand. It is truly a whimsical supposition that, if mankind were agreed in considering utility to be the test of morality, they would remain without any agreement as to what *is* useful, and would take no measures for having their notions on the subject taught to the young, and enforced by law and opinion. There is no difficulty in proving any ethical standard whatever to work ill if we suppose universal idiocy to be conjoined with it; but on any hypothesis short of that, mankind must by this time have acquired positive beliefs as to the effects of some actions on their happiness; and the beliefs which have thus come down are the rules of morality for the multitude, and for the philosopher until he has succeeded in finding better. That philosophers might easily do this, even now, on many subjects; that the received code of ethics is by no means of divine right;

and that mankind have still much to learn as to the effects of actions on the general happiness, I admit or rather earnestly maintain. The corollaries from the principle of utility, like the precepts of every practical art, admit of indefinite improvement, and, in a progressive state of the human mind, their improvement is perpetually going on. But to consider the rules of morality as improvable is one thing; to pass over the intermediate generalization entirely and endeavor to test each individual action directly by the first principle is another. It is a strange notion that the acknowledgment of a first principle is inconsistent with the admission of secondary ones. To inform a traveler respecting the place of his ultimate destination is not to forbid the use of landmarks and direction-posts on the way. The proposition that happiness is the end and aim of morality does not mean that no road ought to be laid down to that goal, or that persons going thither should not be advised to take one direction rather than another. Men really ought to leave off talking a kind of nonsense on this subject, which they would neither talk nor listen to on other matters of practical concernment. Nobody argues that the art of navigation is not founded on astronomy because sailors cannot wait to calculate the nautical almanac. Being rational creatures, they go to sea with it ready calculated; and all rational creatures go out upon the sea of life with their minds made up on the common questions of right and wrong, as well as on many of the far more difficult questions of wise and foolish. And this, as long as foresight is a human quality, it is to be presumed they will continue to do. Whatever we adopt as the fundamental principle of morality, we require subordinate principles to apply it by; the impossibility of doing without them, being common to all systems, can afford no argument against any one in particular; but gravely to argue as if no such secondary principles could be had, and as if mankind had remained till now, and always must remain, without drawing any general conclusions from the experience of human life, is as high a pitch, I think, as absurdity has ever reached in philosophical controversy. . . .

We are told that a utilitarian will be apt to make his own particular case an exception to moral rules, and, when under temptation, will see a utility in the breach of a rule, greater than he will see in its observance. But is utility the only creed which is able to furnish us with excuses for evil doing, and means of cheating our own conscience? They are afforded in abundance by all doctrines which recognize as a fact in morals the existence of conflicting considerations, which all doctrines do that have been believed by sane persons. It is not the fault of any creed, but of the complicated nature of human affairs, that rules of conduct cannot be so framed as to require no exceptions, and that hardly any kind of action can safely be laid down as either always obligatory or always condemnable. There is no ethical creed which does not temper the rigidity of its laws by giving a certain latitude, under the moral responsibility of the agent, for accommodation to peculiarities of circumstances; and under every creed, at the opening thus made, self-deception and dishonest casuistry get in. There exists no moral system under which there do not arise unequivocal cases of conflicting obligation. These are the real difficulties, the knotty points both in the theory of ethics and in the conscientious guidance of personal conduct. They are overcome practically, with greater or with less success, according to the intellect and virtue of the individual; but it can hardly be pretended that anyone will be the less qualified for dealing with them, from possessing an ultimate standard to which conflicting rights and duties can be referred. If utility is the ultimate source of moral obligations, utility may be invoked to decide between them when their demands are incompatible. Though the application of the standard may be difficult, it is better than none at all; while in other systems the moral laws all claiming independent authority, there is no common umpire entitled to interfere between them; their claims to precedence one over another rest on little better than sophistry, and, unless determined, as they generally are, by the unacknowledged influence of considerations of utility, afford a free scope for the action of personal desires and partialities. We must remember that only in these cases of conflict between secondary principles is it requisite that first principles should be appealed to. There is no case of moral obligation in which some secondary principle is not involved; and if only one, there can seldom be any real doubt which one it is, in the mind of any person by whom the principle itself is recognized.

Chapter IV

Of What Sort of Proof the Principle of Utility Is Susceptible

It has already been remarked that questions of ultimate ends do not admit of proof, in the ordinary acceptation of the term. To be incapable of proof by reasoning is common to all first principles, to the first premises of our knowledge, as well as to those of our conduct. But the former, being matters of fact, may be the subject of a direct appeal to the faculties which judge of fact—namely, our senses and our internal consciousness. Can an appeal be made to the same faculties on questions of practical ends? Or by what other faculty is cognizance taken of them?

Questions about ends are, in other words, questions what things are desirable. The utilitarian doctrine is that happiness is desirable, and the only thing desirable, as an end; all other things being only desirable as means to that end. What ought to be required of this doctrine, what conditions is it requisite that the doctrine should fulfill—to make good its claim to be believed?

The only proof capable of being given that an object is visible is that people actually see it. The only proof that a sound is audible is that people hear it; and so of the other sources of our experience. In like manner, I apprehend, the sole evidence it is possible to produce that anything is desirable is that people do actually desire it. If the end which the utilitarian doctrine proposes to itself were not, in theory and in practice, acknowledged to be an end, nothing could ever convince any person that it was so. No reason can be given why the general happiness is desirable, except that each person, so far as he believes it to be attainable, desires his own happiness. This, however, being a fact, we have not only all the proof which the case admits of, but all which it is possible to require, that happiness is a good; that each person's happiness is a good to that person, and the general happiness, therefore, a good to the aggregate of all persons. Happiness has made out its title as *one* of the ends of conduct, and consequently one of the criteria of morality.

But it has not, by this alone, proved itself to be the sole criterion. To do that, it would seem, by the same rule, necessary to show, not only that people desire happiness, but that they never desire anything else. Now it is palpable that they do desire things which, in common language, are decidedly distinguished from happiness. They desire, for example, virtue and the absence of vice, no less really than pleasure and the absence of pain. The desire of virtue is not as universal, but it is as authentic a fact as the desire of happiness. And hence the opponents of the utilitarian standard deem that they have a right to infer that there are other ends of human action besides happiness, and that happiness is not the standard of approbation and disapprobation.

But does the utilitarian doctrine deny that people desire virtue, or maintain that virtue is not a thing to be desired? The very reverse. It maintains not only that virtue is to be desired, but that it is to be desired disinterestedly, for itself.

Whatever may be the opinion of utilitarian moralists as to the original conditions by which virtue is made virtue, however they may believe (as they do) that actions and dispositions are only virtuous because they promote another end than virtue, yet this being granted, and it having been decided, from considerations of this description, what *is* virtuous, they not only place virtue at the very head of the things which are good as means to the ultimate end, but they also recognize as a psychological fact the possibility of its being, to the individual, a good in itself, without looking to any end beyond it; and hold that the mind is not in a right state, not in a state conformable to utility, not in the state most conducive to the general happiness, unless it does love virtue in this manner—as a thing desirable in itself, even although, in the individual instance, it should not produce those other desirable consequences which it tends to produce, and on account of which it is held to be virtue. This opinion is not, in the smallest degree, a departure from the happiness principle. The ingredients of happiness are very various, and each of them is desirable in itself, and not merely when considered as swelling an aggregate. The principle of utility does not mean that any given pleasure, as music, for instance, or any given exemption from pain, as for example health, is to be looked upon as means to a collective something termed happiness, and to be desired on that account. They are desired and desirable in and for themselves; besides being means, they are a part of the end. Virtue, according to the utilitarian doctrine, is not naturally and originally part of the end, but it is capable of becoming so; and in those who love it disinterestedly it has become so, and is desired and cherished, not as a means to happiness, but as a part of their happiness.

To illustrate this further, we may remember that virtue is not the only thing originally a means, and which if it were not a means to anything else would be and remain indifferent, but which by association with what it is a means to comes to be desired for itself, and that too with the utmost intensity. What, for example, shall we say of the love of money? There is nothing originally more desirable about money than about any heap of glittering pebbles. Its worth is solely that of the things which it will buy; the desires for other things than itself, which it is a means of gratifying. Yet the love of money is not only one of the strongest moving forces of human life, but money is, in many cases, desired in and for itself; the desire to possess it is often stronger than the desire to use it, and goes on increasing when all the desires which point to ends beyond it, to be compassed by it, are falling off. It may, then, be said truly that money is desired not for the sake of an end, but as part of the end. From being a means to happiness, it has come to be itself a principal ingredient of the individual's conception of happiness. The same may be said of the majority of the great objects of human life: power, for example, or fame, except that to each of these there is a certain amount of immediate pleasure annexed, which has at least the semblance of being naturally inherent in them—a thing which cannot be said of money. Still, however, the strongest nat-ural attraction, both of power and of fame, is the immense aid they give to the attainment of our other wishes; and it is the strong association thus gener-ated between them and all our objects of desire which gives to the direct desire of them the intensity it often assumes, so as in some characters to surpass in strength all other desires. In these cases the means have become a part of the end, and a more important part of it than any of the things which they are means to. What was once desired as an instrument for the attainment of hap-piness has come to be desired for its own sake. In being desired for its own sake it is, however, desired as *part* of happiness. The person is made, or thinks he would be made, happy by its mere possession; and is made unhappy by failure to obtain it. The desire of it is not a different thing from the desire of happiness any more than the love of music or the desire of health. They are included in happiness. They are some of the elements of which the desire of hap-piness is made up. Happiness is not an abstract idea but a concrete whole; and these are some of its parts. And the util-itarian standard sanctions and approves their being so. Life would be a poor thing, very ill provided with sources of happiness, if there were not this provi-sion of nature by which things origi-nally indifferent, but conducive to, or otherwise associated with, the satisfac-tion of our primitive desires, become in themselves sources of pleasure more valuable than the primitive pleasures, both in permanency, in the space of human existence that they are capable of covering, and even in intensity.

Virtue, according to the utilitarian conception, is a good of this description. There was no original desire of it, or motive to it, save its conduciveness to pleasure, and especially to protection from pain. But through the association thus formed it may be felt a good in itself, and desired as such with as great intensity as any other good; and with this difference between it and the love of money, of power, or of fame, that all of these may, and often do, render the individual noxious to the other mem-bers of the society to which he belongs, whereas there is nothing which makes him so much a blessing to them as the cultivation of the disinterested love of virtue. And consequently, the utilitarian standard, while it tolerates and approves those other acquired desires, up to the point beyond which they would be more injurious to the general happiness than promotive of it, enjoins and requires the cultivation of the love of virtue up to the greatest strength possible, as be-ing above all things important to the general happiness.

It results from the preceding consid-erations that there is in reality nothing desired except happiness. Whatever is desired otherwise than as a means to some end beyond itself, and ultimately to happiness, is desired as itself a part of happiness, and is not desired for it-self until it has become so. Those who desire virtue for its own sake desire it either because the consciousness of it is a pleasure, or because the consciousness of being without it is a pain, or for both reasons united; as in truth the pleasure and pain seldom exist separately, but almost always together—the same per-son feeling pleasure in the degree of virtue attained, and pain in not having attained more. If one of these gave him no pleasure, and the other no pain, he would not love or desire virtue, or would desire it only for the other benefits which it might produce to himself or to persons whom he cared for.

We have now, then, an answer to the question, of what sort of proof the principle of utility is susceptible. If the opinion which I have now stated is psychologically. true—if human nature is so constituted as to desire nothing which is not either a part of happiness or a means of happiness, we can have no other proof, and we require no other, that these are the only things desirable. If so, happiness is the sole end of human action, and the promotion of it the test by which to judge of all human conduct; from whence it necessarily follows that it must be the criterion of morality, since a part is included in the whole.

And now to decide whether this is really so, whether mankind do desire nothing for itself but that which is a pleasure to them, or of which the absence is a pain, we have evidently arrived at a question of fact and experience, dependent, like all similar questions, upon evidence. It can only be determined by practised self-consciousness and self-observation, assisted by observation of others. I believe that these sources of evidence, impartially consulted, will declare that desiring a thing and finding it pleasant, aversion to it and thinking of it as painful, are phenomena entirely inseparable or rather two parts of the same phenomenon; in strictness of language, two different modes of naming the same psycholog-

ical fact; that to think of an object as desirable (unless for the sake of its consequences) and to think of it as pleasant are one and the same thing; and that to desire anything except in proportion as the idea of it is pleasant, is a physical and metaphysical impossibility.

So obvious does this appear to me that I expect it will hardly be disputed; and the objection made will be, not that desire can possibly be directed to anything ultimately except pleasure and exemption from pain, but that the will is a different thing from desire; that a person of confirmed virtue or any other person whose purposes are fixed carries out his purposes without any thought of the pleasure he has in contemplating them or expects to derive from their fulfilment, and persists in acting on them, even though these pleasures are much diminished by changes in his character or decay of his passive sensibilities, or are outweighed by the pains which the pursuit of the purposes may bring upon him. All this I fully admit and have stated it elsewhere as positively and emphatically as anyone. Will, the active phenomenon, is a different thing from desire, the state of passive sensibility, and, though originally an offshoot from it, may in time take root and detach itself from the parent stock, so much so that in the case of an habitual purpose, instead of willing the thing because we desire it, we often desire it only because we will it. This, however, is but an instance of that familiar fact, the power of habit, and is nowise confined to the case of virtuous actions. Many indifferent things which men originally did from a motive of some sort, they continue to do from habit. Sometimes this is done unconsciously; the consciousness coming only after the action; at other times with conscious volition, but volition which has become habitual and is put in operation by the force of habit, in opposition perhaps to the deliberate preference, as often happens with those who have contracted habits of vicious or hurtful indulgence. Third and last comes the case in which the habitual act of will in the individual instance is not in contradiction to the general intention prevailing at other times, but in fulfilment of it; as in the case of the person of confirmed virtue and of all who pursue deliberately and consistently any determinate end. The distinction between will and desire thus understood is an authentic and highly important psychological fact; but the fact consists solely in this—that will, like all other parts of our constitution, is amenable to habit, and that we may will from habit what we no longer desire for itself, or desire only because we will it. It is not the less true that will, in the beginning, is entirely produced by desire; including in that term the repelling influence of pain as well as the attractive one of pleasure. Let us take into consideration no longer the person who has a confirmed will to do right, but him in whom that virtuous will is still feeble, conquerable by temptation, and not to be fully relied on; by what means can it be strengthened? How can the will to be virtuous, where it does not exist in sufficient force, be implanted or awakened? Only by making the person *desire* virtue—by making him think of it in a pleasurable light, or of its absence

in a painful one. It is by associating the doing right with pleasure, or the doing wrong with pain, or by eliciting and impressing and bringing home to the person's experience the pleasure naturally involved in the one or the pain in the other, that it is possible to call forth that will to be virtuous which, when confirmed, acts without any thought of either pleasure or pain. Will is the child of desire, and passes out of the dominion of its parent only to come under that of habit. That which is the result of habit affords no presumption of being intrinsically good; and there would be no reason for wishing that the purpose of virtue should become independent of pleasure and pain were it not that the influence of the pleasurable and painful associations which prompt to virtue is not sufficiently to be depended on for unerring constancy of action until it has acquired the support of habit. Both in feeling and in conduct, habit is the only thing which imparts certainty; and it is because of the importance to others of being able to rely absolutely on one's feelings and conduct, and to oneself of being able to rely on one's own, that the will to do right ought to be cultivated into this habitual independence. In other words, this state of the will is a means to good, not intrinsically a good; and does not contradict the doctrine that nothing is a good to human beings but in so far as it is either itself pleasurable or a means of attaining pleasure or averting pain.

But if this doctrine be true, the principle of utility is proved. Whether it is so or not, must now be left to the consideration of the thoughtful reader.

COMMENT

Bentham and Mill

"What good is happiness? It won't buy money." This witticism reverses the true relation between means and ends. Money is a means, and happiness is an end. Money is important because it contributes to happiness, and happiness is good for its own sake. It is illogical—and hence amusing—to speak as if money were the end and happiness only the means.

The ethical theory known as utilitarianism maintains that right action, like money, is valuable essentially as a means. Unlike Kant, the Utilitarians make *consequences* the test of right and wrong. An action is right if it brings about the best results.

But what are the *best results?* "The greatest happiness of the greatest number," declared Jeremy Bentham. By happiness he meant the surplus of pleasure over pain; and the proper end of moral action, he maintained, is to bring about this surplus in the lives of as many people as possible. Acts should be judged right in proportion as they tend to increase pleasure or decrease pain among the maximum number of people. The intrinsic value of the pleasure or disvalue of the pain is to be judged quantitatively, not qualitatively. What matters is that we get as much pleasure as possible, not that we get a certain kind. "Quantity of pleasure being equal," Bentham taught, "pushpin [a very simple game] is as good as poetry." The quantity has two dimensions—intensity and duration. The *more* intense and durable a pleasure is, and the *less* intense and durable a pain, the better—apart from future consequences. The pain of a toothache, for example, is worse the longer and more intense it is; the pleasure of a happy friendship is better the more intense and prolonged it is.

Bentham did not deny that there are, in a sense, *bad* pleasures and *good* pains. The pleasures of cruelty or intemperance produce, in the long run, an over-balance of pain—they are good in themselves but bad in their consequences, and their instrumental badness outweighs their intrinsic goodness. Similarly, there are pains with pleasant consequences. But nothing but pleasure is *intrinsically* good, and nothing but pain is *intrinsically* bad. The art of living well is to calculate the worth of actions in terms of all the plus values of pleasure and the minus values of pain, subtracting the latter from the former. Bentham exercised a great deal of ingenuity in working out the details of this "moral arithmetic."

So far he was expressing an *ethical* theory. In addition, he advanced the *psychological* doctrine that every man is naturally selfish and hence almost invariably seeks pleasure or the avoidance of pain for himself. This egoistic doctrine is inconsistent with the contention that everyone ought to seek "the greatest happiness of the greatest number." What sense is there in saying that man ought to aim at the greatest social good if his nature is inescapably selfish? Bentham tried to avoid contradiction by arguing that governments should establish a system of rewards and punishments which would induce individuals, on the very basis of their egoism, to further the maximum social happiness.

When Mill undertook the composition of *Utilitarianism*, he was trying to defend the ethical philosophy of his father and Bentham from the attacks made upon it, but he was too divided in mind to make a good defense. The conflict between his loyalty to Bentham and his deep independent convictions produced many strains and inconsistencies. His book is, nevertheless, worth very careful study, because even his confusions and errors are highly instructive.

Although Mill begins his discussion of Utilitarianism with remarks that appear to be in perfect agreement with Bentham's theory, he soon exhibits his independence. This divergence gives rise to some of the most fundamental issues in the whole field of ethics. Let us now consider some of these issues.

The Question of Qualities of Pleasure

In estimating the intrinsic value of pleasures, Mill subordinates Bentham's quantitative standards—intensity and duration—to a standard of quality. The pleasures of the cultivated life, he maintains, are superior in *kind* to the pleasures of the uncultivated. Hence the pleasures of a human being are qualitatively superior to the pleasures of a pig, and the pleasures of a Socrates are qualitatively superior to the pleasures of an uncultivated fool. This is a radical break with Bentham's quantitative hedonism, which maintains that the pleasure of a dolt is no better or worse intrinsically than the quantitatively equal pleasure of a highly developed person.

Is Mill correct in supposing that there are different kinds of pleasure? At first glance, the facts seem to bear out his view. The pleasure of reading a good philosophical book, for example, apparently differs qualitatively from the pleasure of playing a brisk game of handball. But is the qualitative difference in the *pleasures*, or is it in the differing *accompaniments* of the pleasures? If we consider pleasant *experiences*, and not bare pleasures, there *are* genuine qualitative differences; but these differences may be not in the pleasures but in the very different *contents* of experience that have the common property of pleasing. In the case of reading, the experience is quiet, meditative, and relaxed; in the case of playing handball, it is exciting, kinesthetic, and strenuous. Some psychologists, such as Edward Titchener, in his *Textbook on Psychology*, have maintained that the pleasures in such diverse experiences differ only in intensity and duration, and that the only qualitative differences are in such accompaniments as we have just pointed out. Mill inadvertently lends support to this interpretation, since he speaks of the "nobility," "dignity," "intellectuality," and so on, of the "pleasures" that he prefers. It would seem that he is talking not about bare pleasures, abstracted from any content, but, rather, about *experiences* which contain not only pleasure but various intellectual, moral, and esthetic qualities.

It is theoretically possible to maintain that there are qualitative differences in pure pleasures and that these differences are ethically important. Just as there are different kinds of colors—red, blue, green, and so on—so there might be different kinds of pleasures. And just as one might hold that warm colors, let us say, are qualitatively superior to cool colors, so one might contend that certain kinds of pleasures are qualitatively superior to others. One difficulty with this view is that we do not find such indisputable qualitative differences in pleasures. Even if we did, we might still be unable to tell whether some kinds of pleasure are really better than others.

This sort of qualitative hedonism, in any event, is not Mill's view. He *appears* to be advocating hedonism, but he is really maintaining, albeit unclearly and inconsistently, that the good is the pleasant *development* of the personality. This is a kind of synthesis of hedonism and self-realizationism rather than hedonism pure and simple.

The Question of Moral Arithmetic

Bentham maintained that the business of the legislator or moralist is to calculate the probable effects of alternative acts with a view to maximizing pleasure and minimizing pain. This entails the quantitative assessment of pleasures and pains. That there are great difficulties in comparing intensities with durations, adding up pleasures and pains, and subtracting pains from pleasures has often been pointed out. Bentham might reply that such calculation, although difficult, should be carried out as best we can, and that at least a rough estimation of the hedonic consequences of acts is indispensable to any rational direction of our lives.

By introducing questions of quality, Mill greatly restricts the applicability of Bentham's moral arithmetic. His qualitative test is *preference*—not the preference of the average man but that of the moral connoisseur. He tells us that wise persons, such as Socrates, are more competent than the unwise to compare pleasures, to judge which are qualitatively superior, and to decide whether, in a particular instance, considerations of quantity should be sacrificed to considerations of quality. "From this verdict of the only competent judges," he declares, "I apprehend there can be no appeal."

The difference between the approaches of Bentham and of Mill gives rise to a number of questions: To what extent does utilitarianism entail the measurement of pleasures and pains? Are intensities commensurable with durations, and pains with pleasures? Is the preference of the wise a better guide than quantitative assessment? Is the concept of a moral connoisseur sound?

The Question of the Social Distribution of Good

Bentham proposes that the morality of acts be determined by their contribution to "the greatest happiness of the greatest number"—and Mill, at times, employs the same phrase. But does this formula mean the greatest amount of happiness among men, or the greatest number of men who are happy? And, supposing that there is a conflict between greatest happiness and greatest number, should we sacrifice the greatest number to the greatest happiness, or the greatest happiness to the greatest number? The ambiguous formula of Bentham and Mill provides us with no answer.

There are indications, however, that Bentham is more democratic and equalitarian in his approach to the problem of distribution than Mill. Each person, he declared, should count for one, and no one for more than one. This tenet could be interpreted as meaning that the pleasure of any man is as intrinsically good as the quantitatively equal pleasure of any other man. But it could also be interpreted to mean that a smaller amount of pleasure *equally* distributed is morally preferable (at least on occasion) to a greater amount *unequally* distributed. If this was Bentham's real conviction, he was not a strict utilitarian and hedonist—for the principle of equality so interpreted is based upon a sense of distributive justice rather than upon the utilitrian principle of maximizing pleasure and minimizing pain.

Mill's position, in any event, is comparatively aristocratic. Although he verbally subscribes to Bentham's phrases, his emphasis upon quality, wisdom, and self-cultivation implies a very different standard than the greatest possible pleasure of the greatest possible number. The word "greatest" indicates a quantitative criterion—whether it be number of people or amount of pleasure. Mill's criterion, on the other hand, is qualitative. In effect, he favors an intellectual aristocracy—though it is worth noting that he does not identify the intellectually superior with the rich and powerful of the earth.

The differences between Bentham and Mill again serve to emphasize an important set of problems. What is the best distribution of good? Can it be reconciled with a quantitative hedonism? Should the controlling consideration be the number of people receiving the good, or the amount of the good? Or should both amount and number be subordinated, as in Mill, to considerations of quality?

The Question of Ultimate Principles

The ethical philosophy of Mill, like that of Bentham, falls into two main parts. The first part is a theory about the nature of right—the doctrine that the proper standard for judging right is best results. This theory is logically independent of hedonism, or of any other particular interpretation of goodness. It simply states that the right must be determined in the light of good consequences—whatever the good may be. The good might be pleasure, or satisfaction of desire, or actualization of potentialities—or almost anything else. Bentham and Mill speak as if the test of consequences is necessarily linked to one and only one end—namely, "happiness" as each conceives it. But this is manifestly not the case.

The question of the validity of utilitarianism—in the wide sense of the term—turns largely upon whether it can satisfactorily explain our many and varied duties. The nonutilitarian will argue that there are kinds of moral rectitude that cannot be interpreted as utilitarian rightness. He would say, for example, that having made a solemn promise, we have a duty to keep it *even if no more good is thereby to be achieved*. The utilitarian, in contrast, would maintain that there is no valid test of right and wrong except best results. Our duty is to help people and not to hurt them—and the more we help them and the less we hurt them the better. If it becomes clear that, in the long run, keeping a promise will have bad rather than good results, or results less good than some other alternative, our moral obligation is not to keep the promise but to choose whatever alternative yields the best results. This clash between the utilitarians and the nonutilitarians is one of the crucial issues in ethics—and the reader of this book should consider very carefully where the truth lies.

The second part of the ethical philosophy of Bentham and the two Mills is a theory about the nature of ultimate good and evil. Here again, as we have seen, there is disagreement between John Stuart Mill, who embraced a kind of hedonic self-realizationism, and Bentham, who clung to pure quantitative hedonism. The issue is extremely important, but it is not one that can be decided by any conclusive proof. Mill (not realizing the extent of his divergence from Bentham) undertook to "prove" that pleasure alone is ultimately good, but his so-called proof (he admits that *strict* or *conclusive* proof is impossible) contains some of the most widely advertised fallacies in the history of philosophy. We shall refrain from pointing out these fallacies, leaving to the reader the exercise of discovering them. Whether the fallacies are apparent only, being due to carelessness in the use of language, or whether they are *real* fallacies resulting from mental confusion, is a question of interpretation.

To decide the question what is ultimately good we must summon up whatever insight we can muster. If we imagine a world of men and a world of lower animals, *equal in the amount of pleasure they contain*, it might not follow that the two worlds are equal in ultimate goodness—because the men, in addition to experiencing pleasure, have insight into truth, love, imagination, excellence of character, enjoyment of beauty, and so forth. The reply of the hedonist, that all these things are good as means because they *give* pleasure, would not seem to the antihedonist an adequate answer. He would say that it is important not merely to feel pleasure, but to feel pleasure in certain ways, with certain accompaniments rather than others. *Real* happiness embraces the great goods of beauty and truth and nobility of character as having intrinsic and not merely instrumental value. To decide who is right, the hedonist or the antihedonist, is a very important question for the reader to answer.

Utilitarianism and Justice

A frequent criticism of utilitarianism is that it cannot be reconciled with our ideas of a just social order. According to the utilitarian standard, any distribution of goods and evils, however unjust, ought to be preferred to any other distribution, however just, if it would yield a greater surplus of happiness over unhappiness ("net good"). The sole aim of morals is to produce as much net-good as possible. To maintain such a view, the anti-utilitarian will argue, is shockingly to neglect the right of every man to fair treatment.

Take, for example, the matter of punishment. "If some kind of very cruel crime becomes common, and none of the criminals can be caught," remarks E. F. Carritt, "it might be highly expedient, as an example, to hang an innocent man, if a charge against him could be so framed that he were universally thought guilty."[1] Carritt concludes that a utilitarian would be logically bound in this instance to approve the hanging of an innocent person.

Or take the matter of the distribution of goods. Arguing on grounds that "each person possesses an inviolability founded on justice that even the welfare of society as a whole cannot override," John Rawls concludes that "all social primary goods —liberty and opportunity, income and wealth, and the bases of self-respect—are to be distributed equally unless an unequal distribution of any or all of these goods is to the advantage of the least favored."[2] How these "primary goods," which are instrumental to the chances of attaining all other goods, should be distributed raises the question of what distribution justice demands. Rawls believes that his standard of justice as fairness should take precedence over the utilitarian standard of net-good.

Consider Bentham's position. According to Bentham, any respect to be paid to justice is strictly derivative from the single end of attaining the greatest balance of pleasure over pain. Under certain conditions, slavery might yield the greatest balance, yet it would according to Rawls be unjust and immoral.

Bentham might reply as follows. We are never justified in imposing an evil that is not compensated by good results. Every person, being capable of enjoyment and suffering, is a locus of ultimate values, and is to be respected and treated as such. This means that every person is entitled to as much good and as little evil as possible, so long as this does not interfere with the greater net-good of others. Another important consideration is "the law of diminishing utility." This is the principle that, as men and women become more affluent, there is a diminishing return in happiness for every unit of money or resources expended. For example, if you give a half dollar to a poor and hungry man for a bowl of soup, you will contribute more to human satisfaction than if you give an equivalent sum to a wealthy man. This is a powerful reason for coming to the aid of the more destitute. It is also a reason for an equitable distribution of income, limiting the maximum as well as raising the minimum. With these principles in mind, Bentham could agree with his critics that it is wrong to dis-

---

[1] *Ethical and Political Thinking* (New York: Oxford University Press, 1947), p. 65.
[2] *A Theory of Justice* (Cambridge, Mass.: Harvard University Press), pp. 3, 302–303.

tribute goods arbitrarily or unfairly, but he would say that it is not arbitrary or unfair to be governed by best results.

This sort of defense is available to a quantitative utilitarian. Mill, with his theory of qualitative good, has an additional answer. In estimating best results, we should consider not only the quantity but the quality of the good-making property. States of experience that involve fairness may be qualitatively superior (other things being equal) to states that involve unfairness. The pleasures involving injustice are qualitatively inferior to the pleasures free from this taint. If so, it would be consistent with utilitarianism to prefer the pleasures of justice ("fairness") on the grounds of their qualitative superiority, and the conflict of justice with utility could be avoided.

The concept of "justice as fairness" is difficult to reduce to utilitarian criteria, unless we admit that fairness itself has intrinsic value and include it among the goods to be maximized. If we should nevertheless decide that justice cannot be wholly explained on utilitarian grounds, our principal duty may still be to promote the good, subject only to the constraint that justice should either not be violated or that the good in the particular instance is so great that it outweighs the violation. Rawls would not accept this compromise, because he believes that justice as a principle of right must have absolute priority over ultimate good, whether it be conceived as happiness, fulfillment of interest, or in any other manner. Here is a profound difference of philosophical conviction that the reader may well ponder.

Act-Utilitarianism and Rule-Utilitarianism

We can distinguish between "extreme" and "restricted" utilitarianism. The former is more often called "act-utilitarianism," and the latter "rule-utilitarianism." Extreme- or act-utilitarianism judges rightness in terms of the consequences of *individual* acts. According to this point of view, the right act is that which brings the best results in the particular circumstances. Since it may be inconvenient or difficult or impossible to estimate the consequences of individual acts, we are often forced to fall back upon "rules of thumb," but if breaking the rule *does* produce the best possible consequences, then the rule ought to be broken.

Restricted- or rule-utilitarianism maintains that acts are to be tested by rules and rules by consequences. The only exceptions are when rules conflict or when the particular act falls under no rules. Just as the rules of a game determine what is permissible, so the rules of moral practice determine what is *morally* permissible. When the umpire calls the batter out after three strikes, it would be absurd for him to plead with the umpire for another try. The batter has no choice but to abide by the rules. So likewise the rule-utilitarian insists upon obedience to the relevant moral rule, while justifying the rule by the consequences.

Note that the rule-utilitarian would have an answer to Carritt (see above) that the act-utilitarian would not have. Punishment is a practice, and in a civilized society this practice is highly institutionalized. For a judge or jury to condemn a man known to be innocent, even though there is some great advantage in doing so, is to violate the whole concept of punishment as a practice. The safeguards against such miscarriage of justice are built-in features of the institution of punishment. If the institution is justified on utilitarian grounds, so are these safeguards.

The choice between act-utilitarianism and rule-utilitarianism need not be exclusive. Both may be valid within limits, act-utilitarianism applying in the absence of institutionalized practice, and rule-utilitarianism applying when there is not only such practice but good utilitarian reasons for keeping the practice inviolate.

A number of philosophers have raised the interesting question whether Mill was an act-utilitarian or a rule-utilitarian. Here is a question of interpretation that the reader may wish to consider. He may also wish to ponder the question whether act-utilitarianism or rule-utilitarianism is the sounder theory, or whether and how it is best to combine them.

16

Power

FRIEDRICH NIETZSCHE (1844–1900)

Nietzsche was born in Rocken, near Leipzig. His father was the son and his mother the daughter of Lutheran ministers. The father died of softening of the brain when Nietzsche was four years old, and a younger brother died in infancy. In consequence, the boy was reared in a household of women—his mother, sister, grandmother, and two unmarried aunts. In 1858 he was sent for six years to a boarding school, where he studied Greek classics with great success and mathematics with no success at all. The medical records of the school contain the entry: ". . . short-sighted and often plagued by migraine headaches."

He disliked being called "the little minister" by his classmates, and when he attended the University of Bonn, he broke completely with the Christianity of his ancestors. Moving on to the University of Leipzig, he fell under the spell of Erwin Rohde, a great classical scholar, and became absorbed in the history of culture. He also became personally acquainted with Richard Wagner, and fell in love with Wagner's operas. After years of friendship, the two split when Nietzsche became convinced that Wagner was sacrificing his intellectual and artistic integrity to the glorification of Christianity and the German state.

After unfortunate experiences in military service in the Austro-German and Franco-Prussian wars, he finished his studies and became a university professor of classical philology in Basel, Switzerland, at the unheard-of age of twenty-four. His health was never good, and after a decade of teaching, he was forced to resign his professorship in 1879. Living on a small academic pension for the next ten years, he spent a very lonely life at health resorts in Switzerland, northern Italy, and the French Riviera. Although this was a period of great philosophical productivity, his emotional conflicts were unendurable, and in 1888 he became insane, never to recover. The tragic character of his life is epitomized in the words of one of his interpreters: "He was ill (often violently ill) more days than he was well. He was nearly blind at the age of thirty-five: he was lonely, unpopular,

598

unsuccessful, poor: no one understood him, and no one was interested in his work: he had every reason to believe that he had completely failed: finally he went mad."[1]

[1] A. H. J. Knight, *Some Aspects of the Life and Work of Nietzsche, and particularly of his connection with Greek Literature and Thought* (Cambridge at the University Press, 1933), p. 165.

Beyond Good and Evil

What Is Noble [1]

257

Every enhancement of the type "man" has so far been the work of an aristocratic society—and it will be so again and again—a society that believes in the long ladder of an order of rank[2] and differences in value between man and

From Friedrich Nietzsche, *Beyond Good and Evil: Prelude to a Philosophy of the Future.* Translated, with commentary, by Walter Kaufman. © Copyright, 1966, by Random House, Inc. Reprinted by permission of the publisher.

[1] *Vornehm.* [See Section 212 of *Beyond Good and Evil.*]

[2] *Stände: Stand* can mean—apart from position, state, condition—class, rank, profession, and *Stände* can mean the estates of the realm. Asked to indicate her *Stand* on a questionnaire, a German woman might write, even after World War II: *Strassenbahnschaffnerswitwe*, that is, "widow of a streetcar conductor."

man, and that needs slavery in some sense or other. Without that *pathos of distance* which grows out of the ingrained difference between strata—when the ruling caste constantly looks afar and looks down upon subjects and instruments and just as constantly practices obedience and command, keeping down and keeping at a distance—that other, more mysterious pathos could not have grown up either—the craving for an ever new widening of distances within the soul itself, the development of ever higher, rarer, more remote, further-stretching, more comprehensive states—in brief, simply the enhancement of the type "man," the continual "self-overcoming of man," to use a moral formula in a supra-moral sense.

To be sure, one should not yield to humanitarian illusions about the origins of an aristocratic society (and thus of the presupposition of this enhancement of the type "man"): truth is hard. Let us admit to ourselves, without trying to be considerate, how every higher culture on earth so far has *begun*. Human beings whose nature was still natural, barbarians in every terrible sense of the word, men of prey who were still in possession of unbroken strength of will and lust for power, hurled themselves upon weaker, more civilized, more peaceful races, perhaps traders or cattle raisers or, upon mellow old cultures whose last vitality was even then flaring up in splendid fireworks of spirit and corruption. In the beginning, the noble caste was always the barbarian caste: their predominance did not lie mainly in physical strength but in strength of the soul—they were more *whole* human beings (which also means, at every level, "more whole beasts").

258

Corruption as the expression of a threatening anarchy among the instincts and of the fact that the foundation of the affects, which is called "life," has been shaken: corruption is something totally different depending on the organism in which it appears. When, for example, an aristocracy, like that of France at the beginning of the Revolution, throws away its privileges with a sublime disgust and sacrifices itself to an extravagance of its own moral feelings, that is corruption; it was really only the last act of that centuries-old corruption which had led them to surrender, step by step, their governmental prerogatives, demoting themselves to a mere *function* of the monarchy (finally even to a mere ornament and showpiece). The essential characteristic of a good and healthy aristocracy, however, is that it experiences itself *not* as a function (whether of the monarchy or the commonwealth) but as their *meaning* and highest justification—that it therefore accepts with a good conscience the sacrifice of untold human beings who, *for its sake*, must be reduced and lowered to incomplete human beings, to slaves, to instruments. Their fundamental faith simply has to be that society must *not* exist for society's sake but only as the foundation and scaffolding on which a choice type of being is able to raise itself to its higher task and to a higher state of *being*[3]—comparable to those sun-seeking vines of Java—they are called *Sipo Matador*—that so long and so often enclasp an oak tree with their tendrils until eventually, high above it but supported by it, they can unfold their crowns in the open light and display their happiness.

259

Refraining mutually from injury, violence, and exploitation and placing one's will on a par with that of someone else —this may become, in a certain rough sense, good manners among individuals if the appropriate conditions are present (namely, if these men are actually similar in strength and value standards and belong together in *one* body). But as soon as this principle is extended, and possibly even accepted as the *fundamental principle of society*, it immediately proves to be what it really is— a will to the *denial* of life, a principle of disintegration and decay.

[3] Cf. the outlook of the heroes of the *Iliad*.

Here we must beware of superficiality and get to the bottom of the matter, resisting all sentimental weakness: life itself is *essentially* appropriation, injury, overpowering of what is alien and weaker; suppression, hardness, imposition of one's own forms, incorporation and at least, at its mildest, exploitation —but why should one always use those words in which a slanderous intent has been imprinted for ages?

Even the body within which individuals treat each other as equals, as suggested before—and this happens in every healthy aristocracy—if it is a living and not a dying body, has to do to other bodies what the individuals within it refrain from doing to each other: it will have to be an incarnate will to power, it will strive to grow, spread, seize, become predominant—not from any morality or immorality but because it is *living* and because life simply *is* will to power. But there is no point on which the ordinary consciousness of Europeans resists instruction as on this: everywhere people are now raving, even under scientific disguises, about coming conditions of society in which "the exploitative aspect" will be removed—which sounds to me as if they promised to invent a way of life that would dispense with all organic functions. "Exploitation" does not belong to a corrupt or imperfect and primitive society: it belongs to the *essence* of what lives, as a basic organic function; it is a consequence of the will to power, which is after all the will of life.

If this should be an innovation as a theory—as a reality it is the *primordial fact* of all history: people ought to be honest with themselves at least that far.

260

Wandering through the many subtler and coarser moralities which have so far been prevalent on earth, or still are prevalent, I found that certain features recurred regularly together and were closely associated—until I finally discovered two basic types and one basic difference.

There are *master morality* and *slave morality*[4]—I add immediately that in all the higher and more mixed cultures there also appear attempts at mediation between these two moralities, and yet more often the interpenetration and mutual misunderstanding of both, and at times they occur directly alongside each other—even in the same human being, within a *single* soul.[5] The moral discrimination of values has originated either among a ruling group whose consciousness of its difference from the ruled group was accompanied by delight —or among the ruled, the slaves and dependents of every degree.

In the first case, when the ruling group determines what is "good," the exalted, proud states of the soul are experienced as conferring distinction and determining the order of rank. The no-

[4] While the ideas developed here, and explicated at greater length a year later in the first part of the *Genealogy of Morals*, had been expressed by Nietzsche in 1878 in section 45 of *Human, All-Too-Human*, this is the passage in which his famous terms "master morality" and "slave morality" are introduced.

[5] These crucial qualifications, though added immediately, have often been overlooked. "Modern" moralities are clearly mixtures; hence their manifold tensions, hypocrisies, and contradictions.

ble human being separates from himself those in whom the opposite of such exalted, proud states finds expression: he depises them. It should be noted immediately that in this first type of morality the opposition of "good" and "*bad*" means approximately the same as "noble" and "contemptible." (The opposition of "good" and "*evil*" has a different origin.) One feels contempt for the cowardly, the anxious, the petty, those intent on narrow utility; also for the suspicious with their unfree glances, those who humble themselves, the doglike people who allow themselves to be maltreated, the begging flatterers, above all the liars: it is part of the fundamental faith of all aristocrats that the common people lie. "We truthful ones"— thus the nobility of ancient Greece referred to itself.

It is obvious that moral designations were everywhere first applied to *human beings* and only later, derivatively to actions. Therefore, it is a gross mistake when historians of morality start from such questions as: why was the compassionate act praised? The noble type of man experiences *itself* as determining values; it does not need approval; it judges, "what is harmful to me is harmful in itself"; it knows itself to be that which first accords honor to things; it is *value-creating*. Everything it knows as part of itself it honors: such a morality is self-glorification. In the foreground there is the feeling of fullness, of power that seeks to overflow, the happiness of high tension, the consciousness of wealth that would give and bestow: the noble human being, too, helps the unfortunate, but not, or almost not, from pity, but prompted more by an urge be-

gotten by excess of power. The noble human being honors himself as one who is powerful, also as one who has power over himself, who knows how to speak and be silent, who delights in being severe and hard with himself and respects all severity and hardness. "A hard heart Wotan put into my breast," says an old Scandinavian saga: a fitting poetic expression, seeing that it comes from the soul of a proud Viking. Such a type of man is actually proud of the fact that he is *not* made for pity, and the hero of the saga therefore adds as a warning: "If the heart is not hard in youth it will never harden." Noble and courageous human beings who think that way are furthest removed from that morality which finds the distinction of morality precisely in pity, or in acting for others, or in *désintéressement*; faith in oneself, pride in oneself, a fundamental hostility and irony against "selflessness" belong just as definitely to noble morality as does a slight disdain and caution regarding compassionate feelings and a "warm heart."

It is the powerful who *understand* how to honor; this is their art, their realm of invention. The profound reverence for age and tradition—all law rests on this double reverence—the faith and prejudice in favor of ancestors and disfavor of those yet to come are typical of the morality of the powerful; and when the men of "modern ideas," conversely, believe almost instinctively in "progress" and "the future" and more and more lack respect for age, this in itself would sufficiently betray the ignoble origin of these "ideas."

A morality of the ruling group, however, is most alien and embarrassing to the present taste in the severity of its principle that one has duties only to one's peers; that against beings of a lower rank, against everything alien, one may behave as one pleases or "as the heart desires," and in any case "beyond good and evil"—here pity and like feelings may find their place.[6] The capacity for, and the duty of, long gratitude and long revenge—both only among one's peers—refinement in repaying, the sophisticated concept of friendship, a certain necessity for having enemies (as it were, as drainage ditches for the affects of envy, quarrelsomeness, exuberance—at bottom, in order to be capable of being good *friends*): all these are typical characteristics of noble morality which, as suggested, is not the morality of "modern ideas" and therefore is hard to

empathize with today, also hard to dig up and uncover.[7]

It is different with the second type of morality, *slave morality*. Suppose the violated, oppressed, suffering, unfree, who are uncertain of themselves and weary, moralize: what will their moral valuations have in common? Probably, a pessimistic suspicion about the whole condition of man will find expression, perhaps a condemnation of man along with his condition. The slave's eye is not favorable to the virtues of the powerful: he is skeptical and suspicious, *subtly* suspicious, of all the "good" that is honored there—he would like to persuade himself that even their happiness is not genuine. Conversely, those qualities are brought out and flooded with light which serve to ease existence for those who suffer: here pity, the complaisant and obliging hand, the warm heart, patience, industry, humility, and friendliness are honored—for here these are the most useful qualities and almost the only means for enduring the pressure of existence. Slave morality is essentially a morality of utility.

Here is the place for the origin of that famous opposition of "good" and "evil": into evil one's feelings project power and dangerousness, a certain terribleness, subtlety, and strength that does not permit contempt to develop. According to slave morality, those who are "evil" thus inspire fear; according to

---

[6] The final clause that follows the dash, omitted in the Cowan translation, is crucial and qualifies the first part of the sentence: a noble person has no *duties* to animals but treats them in accordance with his feelings, which means, if he is noble, with pity.

The ruling masters, of course, are not always noble in this sense, and this is recognized by Nietzsche in *Twilight of the Idols*, in the chapter "The 'Improvers' of Mankind," in which he gives strong expression to his distaste for Manu's laws concerning outcastes (*Portable Nietzsche*, pp. 503–505); also in *The Will to Power* (ed. W. Kaufmann, New York, Random House, 1967), section 142. Indeed, in *The Antichrist*, section 57, Nietzsche contradicts outright his formulation above: "When the exceptional human being treats the mediocre more tenderly than himself and his peers, this is not mere courtesy of the heart—it is simply his *duty*."

More important: Nietzsche's obvious distaste for slave morality and the fact that he makes a point of liking master morality better does not imply that he endorses master morality. Cf. the text for note 5 above.

[7] Clearly, master morality cannot be discovered by introspection nor by the observation of individuals who are "masters" rather than "slaves." Both of these misunderstandings are widespread. What is called for is rather a rereading of, say, the *Iliad* and, to illustrate "slave morality," the New Testament.

master morality it is precisely those who are "good" that inspire, and wish to inspire, fear, while the "bad" are felt to be contemptible.

The opposition reaches its climax when, as a logical consequence of slave morality, a touch of disdain is associated also with the "good" of this morality—this may be slight and benevolent—because the good human being has to be *undangerous* in the slaves' way of thinking: he is good-natured, easy to deceive, a little stupid perhaps, *un bonhomme*.[8] Wherever slave morality becomes preponderant, language tends to bring the words "good" and "stupid" closer together.

One last fundamental difference: the longing for *freedom*, the instinct for happiness and the subtleties of the feeling of freedom belong just as necessarily to slave morality and morals as artful and enthusiastic reverence and devotion are the regular symptom of an aristocratic way of thinking and evaluating.

This makes plain why love *as passion*—which is our European specialty —simply must be of noble origin: as is well known, its invention must be credited to the Provençal knight-poets, those magnificent and inventive human beings of the *"gai saber"*[9] to whom Eu-

[8] Literally "a good human being," the term is used for precisely the type described here.

[9] "Gay science": in the early fourteenth century the term was used to designate the art of the troubadours, codified in *Leys d'amors*. Nietzsche subtitled his own *Fröhliche Wissenschaft* (1882), *"la gaya scienza,"* placed a quatrain on the title page, began the book with a fifteen-page "Prelude in German Rhymes," and in the second edition (1887) added, besides a Preface and Book V, an "Appendix" of further verses.

rope owes so many things and almost owes itself.—

261

Among the things that may be hardest to understand for a noble human being is vanity: he will be tempted to deny it, where another type of human being could not find it more palpable. The problem for him is to imagine people who seek to create a good opinion of themselves which they do not have of themselves—and thus also do not "deserve"—and who nevertheless end up *believing* this good opinion themselves. This strikes him half as such bad taste and lack of self-respect, and half as so baroquely irrational, that he would like to consider vanity as exceptional, and in most cases when it is spoken of he doubts it.

He will say, for example: "I may be mistaken about my value and nevertheless demand that my value, exactly as I define it, should be acknowledged by others as well—but this is no vanity (but conceit or, more frequently, what is called 'humility' or 'modesty')." Or: "For many reasons I may take pleasure in the good opinion of others: perhaps because I honor and love them and all their pleasures give me pleasure; perhaps also because their good opinion confirms and strengthens my faith in my own good opinion; perhaps because the good opinion of others, even in cases where I do not share it, is still useful to me or promises to become so—but all that is not vanity."

The noble human being must force himself, with the aid of history, to recognize that, since time immemorial, in all somehow dependent social strata the common man *was* only what he was *considered*: not at all used to positing values himself, he also attached no other value to himself than his masters attached to him (it is the characteristic *right of masters* to create values).

It may be understood as the consequence of an immense atavism that even now the ordinary man still always *waits* for an opinion about himself and then instinctively submits to that—but by no means only a "good" opinion; also a bad and unfair one (consider, for example, the great majority of the self-estimates and self-underestimates that believing women accept from their father-confessors, and believing Christians quite generally from their church).

In accordance with the slowly arising democratic order of things (and its cause, the intermarriage of masters and slaves), the originally noble and rare urge to ascribe value to oneself on one's own and to "think well" of oneself will actually be encouraged and spread more and more now; but it is always opposed by an older, ampler, and more deeply ingrained propensity—and in the phenomenon of "vanity" this older propensity masters the younger one. The vain person is delighted by *every* good opinion he hears of himself (quite apart from all considerations of its utility, and also apart from truth or falsehood), just as every bad opinion of him pains him: for he submits to both, he *feels* subjected to them in accordance with that oldest instinct of submission that breaks out in him.

It is "the slave" in the blood of the vain person, a residue of the slave's craftiness—and how much "slave" is still residual in woman, for example!—that seeks to *seduce* him to good opinions about himself; it is also the slave who afterwards immediately prostrates himself before these opinions as if he had not called them forth.

And to say it once more: vanity is an atavism.

262

A *species*[10] comes to be, a type becomes fixed and strong, through the long fight with essentially constant *unfavorable* conditions. Conversely, we know from the experience of breeders[11] that species accorded superabundant nourishment and quite generally extra protection and care soon tend most strongly toward variations of the type and become rich in marvels and monstrosities (including monstrous vices).

Now look for once at an aristocratic commonwealth—say, an ancient Greek *polis*,[12] or Venice—as an arrangement, whether voluntary or involuntary, for *breeding*:[13] human beings are together there who are dependent on themselves and want their species to prevail, most often because they *have to* prevail or run the terrible risk of being exterminated. Here that boon, that excess, and that protection which favor variations are lacking; the species needs itself as a species, as something that can prevail and make itself durable by virtue of its very hardness, uniformity, and sim-

---

[10] Throughout this section *Art* is rendered as species, and *Typus* as type. Elsewhere, *Art* is often translated as type.

[11] *Züchter*.

[12] City-state.

[13] *Züchtung*.

plicity of form, in a constant fight with its neighbors or with the oppressed who are rebellious or threaten rebellion. Manifold experience teaches them to which qualities above all they owe the fact that, despite all gods and men, they are still there, that they have always triumphed: these qualities they call virtues, these virtues alone they cultivate.[14] They do this with hardness, indeed they want hardness; every aristocratic morality is intolerant—in the education of youth, in their arrangements for women, in their marriage customs, in the relations of old and young, in their penal laws (which take into account deviants only)—they consider intolerance itself a virtue, calling it "justice."

In this way a type with few but very strong traits, a species of severe, warlike, prudently taciturn men, closemouthed and closely linked (and as such possessed of the subtlest feeling for the charms and *nuances* of association), is fixed beyond the changing generations; the continual fight against ever constant *unfavorable* conditions is, as mentioned previously, the cause that fixes and hardens a type.

Eventually, however, a day arrives when conditions become more fortunate and the tremendous tension decreases; perhaps there are no longer any enemies among one's neighbors, and the means of life, even for the enjoyment of life, are superabundant. At one stroke the bond and constraint of the old discipline[15] are torn: it no longer seems necessary, a condition of existence—if it persisted it would only be a form of

luxury, an archaizing *taste*. Variation, whether as deviation (to something higher, subtler, rarer) or as degeneration and monstrosity, suddenly appears on the scene in the greatest abundance and magnificence; the individual dares to be individual and different.

At these turning points of history we behold beside one another, and often mutually involved and entangled, a splendid, manifold, junglelike growth and upward striving, a kind of *tropical* tempo in the competition to grow, and a tremendous ruin and self-ruination, as the savage egoisms that have turned, almost exploded, against one another wrestle "for sun and light" and can no longer derive any limit, restraint, or consideration from their previous[16] morality. It was the morality itself that dammed up such enormous strength and bent the bow in such a threatening manner; now it is "outlived." The dangerous and uncanny point has been reached where the greater, more manifold, more comprehensive life transcends and *lives beyond* the old morality; the "individual" appears, obliged to give himself laws and to develop his own arts and wiles for self-preservation, self-enhancement, self-redemption.

All sorts of new what-fors and wherewithals; no shared formulas any longer; misunderstanding allied with disrespect; decay, corruption, and the highest desires gruesomely entangled; the genius of the race overflowing from all cornucopias of good and bad; a calamitous simultaneity of spring and fall, full of new charms and veils that char-

---

[14] *Züchtet sie gross.*
[15] *Zucht.*

[16] *Bisherigen:* elsewhere *bisher* has always been rendered as "so far"; see Preface, note 1.

acterize young, still unexhausted, still unwearied corruption. Again danger is there, the mother of morals, great danger, this time transposed into the individual, into the neighbor and friend, into the alley, into one's own child, into one's own heart, into the most personal and secret recesses of wish and will: what may the moral philosophers emerging in this age have to preach now?

These acute observers and loiterers discover that the end is approaching fast, that everything around them is corrupted and corrupts, that nothing will stand the day after tomorrow, except *one* type of man, the incurably *mediocre*. The mediocre alone have a chance of continuing their type and propogating—they are the men of the future, the only survivors: "Be like them! Become mediocre!" is now the only morality that still makes sense, that still gets a hearing.

But this morality of mediocrity is hard to preach: after all, it may never admit what it is and what it wants. It must speak of measure and dignity and duty and neighbor love—it will find it difficult *to conceal its irony.*—

263

There is an *instinct for rank* which, more than anything else, is a sign of a *high* rank; there is a delight in the nuances of reverence that allows us to infer noble origin and habits. The refinement, graciousness, and height of a soul is tested dangerously when something of the first rank passes by without being as yet protected by the shud-

ders of authority against obstrusive efforts and ineptitudes—something that goes its way unmarked, undiscovered, tempting, perhaps capriciously concealed and disguised, like a living touchstone. Anyone to whose task and practice it belongs to search out souls will employ this very art in many forms in order to determine the ultimate value of a soul and the unalterable, innate order of rank to which it belongs: he will test it for its *instinct of reverence.*

Différence engendre haine[17]: The baseness of some people suddenly spurts up like dirty water when some holy vessel, some precious thing from a locked shrine, some book with the marks of a great destiny, is carried past; and on the other hand there is a reflex of silence, a hesitation of the eye, a cessation of all gestures that express how a soul *feels* the proximity of the most venerable. The way in which reverence for the *Bible* has on the whole been maintained so far in Europe is perhaps the best bit of discipline and refinement of manners that Europe owes to Christianity: such books of profundity and ultimate significance require some external tyranny of authority for their protection in order to gain those millennia of *persistence* which are necessary to exhaust them and figure them out.

Much is gained once the feeling has finally been cultivated in the masses (among the shallow and in the high-speed intestines of every kind) that they are not to touch everything; that there are holy experiences before which they have to take off their shoes and keep away their unclean hands—this is al-

[17] Difference engenders hatred.

most their greatest advance toward humanity. Conversely, perhaps there is nothing about so-called educated people and believers in "modern ideas" that is as nauseous as their lack of modesty and the comfortable insolence of their eyes and hands with which they touch, lick, and finger everything; and it is possible that even among the common people, among the less educated, especially among peasants, one finds today more *relative* nobility of taste and tactful reverence than among the newspaper-reading *demi-monde* of the spirit, the educated.

264

One cannot erase from the soul of a human being what his ancestors liked most to do and did most constantly: whether they were, for example, assiduous savers and appurtenances of a desk and cash box, modest and bourgeois in their desires, modest also in their virutes; or whether they lived accustomed to commanding from dawn to dusk, fond of rough amusements and also perhaps of even rougher duties and responsibilities; or whether, finally, at some point they sacrificed ancient prerogatives of birth and possessions in order to live entirely for their faith—their "god"—as men of an inexorable and delicate conscience which blushes at every compromise. It is simply not possible that a human being should *not* have the qualities and preferences of his parents and ancestors in his body, whatever appearances may suggest to the contrary. This is the prob-

lem of race.[18]

If one knows something about the parents, an inference about the child is permissible: any disgusting incontinence, any sordid envy, a clumsy insistence that one is always right—these three things together have always constituted the characteristic type of the plebeian—that sort of thing must as surely be transferred to the child as corrupted blood; and with the aid of the best education one will at best *deceive* with regard to such a heredity.

And what else is the aim of education and "culture" today? In our very popularity-minded—that is, plebeian—age, "education" and "culture" *have* to be essentially the art of deceiving—about one's origins, the inherited plebs in one's body and soul. An educator who today preached truthfulness above all and constantly challenged his students, "be true! be natural! do not pretend!"—even such a virtuous and guileless ass would learn after a while to reach for that *furca* of Horace to *naturam expellere*: with what success? "Plebs" *usque recurret.*[19]—

[18] Here, as elsewhere, Nietzsche gives expression to his Lamarckian belief in the heredity of acquired characteristics, shared by Samuel Butler and Bernard Shaw but anathema to Nazi racists and almost universally rejected by geneticists. His Lamarckism is not just an odd fact about Nietzsche but symptomatic of his conception of body and spirit: he ridiculed belief in "pure" spirit but believed just as little in any "pure" body; he claimed that neither could be understood without the other. For a detailed discussion see Kaufmann, *Nietzsche*, Chapter 10.

[19] Horace's *Epistles*, I. 10, 24: "Try with a pitchfork to drive out nature, she always returns."

265

At the risk of displeasing innocent ears I propose: egoism belongs to the nature of a noble soul—I mean that unshakable faith that to a being such as "we are" other beings must be subordinate by nature and have to sacrifice themselves. The noble soul accepts this fact of its egoism without any question mark, also without any feeling that it might contain hardness, constraint, or caprice, rather as something that may be founded in the primordial law of things: if it sought a name for this fact it would say, "it is justice itself." Perhaps it admits under certain circumstances that at first make it hesitate that there are some who have rights equal to its own; as soon as this matter of rank is settled it moves among these equals with their equal privileges, showing the same sureness of modesty and delicate reverence that characterize its relations with itself—in accordance with an innate heavenly mechanism understood by all stars. It is merely another aspect of its egoism, this refinement and self-limitation in its relations with its equals —every star is such an egoist—it honors *itself* in them and in the rights it cedes to them; it does not doubt that the exchange of honors and rights is of the nature of all social relations and thus also belongs to the natural condition of things.

The noble soul gives as it takes, from that passionate and irritable instinct of repayment that lies in its depth. The concept "grace"[20] has no meaning or good odor *inter pares*;[21] there may be a sublime way of letting presents from above happen to one, as it were, and to drink them up thirstily like drops—but for this art and gesture the noble soul has no aptitude. Its egoism hinders it: quite generally it does not like to look "up"—but either *ahead*, horizontally and slowly, or down: *it knows itself to be at a height.*

COMMENT

The Will to Power

"Out of my will to be in good health, out of my will to live, I have made my philosophy," wrote Nietzsche. His approach to philosophy was intensely personal, like that of Pascal and Kierkegaard. However much they might differ in other respects, all three—Pascal, Kierkegaard, Nietzsche—can be considered existentialists. The problems which excited their concern were not separate and distinct from their lives; they were problems that arose out of the struggle and task of existing as a human being.

"The will to live" is the phrase used by Arthur Schopenhauer, the famous pessimist, to characterize the basic drive of all living things. While still in his early twenties, Nietzsche discovered Schopenhauer's book, *The World as Will and Idea*, in a secondhand bookstore. Although he was greatly influenced by Schopenhauer,

[20] *"Gnade."*   [21] Among equals.

he more often used the phrase "the will to power" than "the will to live." A living thing, he said, seeks above all to discharge its strength and master its environment. Evolution—a concept that was much discussed in Nietzsche's lifetime—seemed to him the triumph of strength over weakness. On the basis of an anti-Darwinian theory of evolution, Nietzsche extolled might and power. But by "power" he meant much more than physical dominance—he meant intellectual and spiritual mastery as well.

What does it mean to say that will is basic? In a general way, desire or will is the active element in consciousness. It shows itself in unrest and seeking, leading finally to action which brings the unrest to a close. We might define it as a drive or impulse toward a goal. If the drive succeeds, the result is a "state of satisfaction."

According to Nietzsche, it is impossible sharply to separate desire from feeling. The unrest of desire involves pain and the appeasement of desire involves joy or pleasure; these are phases of volition.

Schopenhauer believed that frustration and pain far outweigh satisfaction and pleasure. To a certain extent, Nietzsche agreed. The world, if unsubdued by the will to power, is a thoroughly nasty place. But Nietzsche's philosophy is a paradoxical combination of pessimism and optimism. By the triumph of the will to power an existence otherwise terrible becomes profoundly satisfying. As a creature of volition, man *must* will to change his world. The will to power makes possible "the transvaluation of values," and the emergence of higher types of life.

Nietzsche exalted, above all other types, the strong, proud, self-assertive, "great-souled" aristocrat. Fulfillment for the aristocrat is achieved through exploitation and subjugation of his inferiors. From this concept of the aristocrat Nietzsche derived his distinction between master and slave morality. The master morality is a discipine that the noble impose upon themselves in order to maintain their superiority. It is characterized by a reverence for the higher gradations of value, as set off against the baseness of the lower class. Even among the "slaves" (a term that Nietzsche uses to denote the masses of inferior people), the virtues of humility and meekness have mainly extrinsic worth; they are weapons of the weak in the struggle for power. The pity and charity of the slaves, no less than the pride and courage of the masters, are useful for survival. The weak, individually incapable of defense, can defend themselves against the masters only by banding together as a herd. Nietzsche detected attitudes of petty envy and resentment under the slaves' show of altruism. In modern life he saw a levelling tendency—a sheepish predisposition toward mediocrity and conformity. Defending the intrepid individual against mass-tyranny and vulgarity, he maintained that a new aristocratic morality is required to scale the heights.

Some Critical Questions

This interpretation of morality is at the opposite pole from Kant's categorical imperative. Nietzsche rejected the whole doctrine of the universalizability of the moral law. Power cannot be universalized—when some dominate, others must submit. Hence Nietzsche's ethics fails to meet Kant's formula of universal generalization. Who has the better moral creed, Kant or Nietzsche?

The Nietzschean ideal of aristocracy is just as sharply opposed to the democratic ideal. Whether Nietzsche is justified in this opposition depends in part on the meaning of democracy. Does it mean that whatever varies from the average should be crushed by the herd? If so, Nietzsche is justified in rejecting it. Does it mean that all men and women should have equal and abundant opportunity to develop their unequal abilities? If so, we wonder if Nietzsche was justified in his antidemocratic stand. Democracy in this latter sense, its defenders can argue, is fully compatible with aristocratic standards of excellence. The very fact of psychological inequality is all the more reason for equal opportunity, because without it, able men will often be handicapped by lack of opportunity, and the less gifted but fortunately situated will be preferred to their natural betters.

In both Schopenhauer and Nietzsche—though they differ greatly in other respects—we find an ethics based on the primacy of the will. Is this kind of ethics one-sided? Does it underplay the values of feeling and intellect? In contrast to Nietzsche, Bertrand Russell has asserted: "The good life is one motivated by love and guided by knowledge."[1] Is this a sounder interpretation than Nietzsche's?

Russell has also said:

> I dislike Nietzsche because he likes the contemplation of pain, because he erects conceit into a duty, because the men whom he most admires are conquerors, whose glory is cleverness in causing men to die. But I think the ultimate argument against his philosophy, as against any unpleasant but internally self-consistent ethic, lies not in an appeal to facts, but in an appeal to emotions.[2]

Is this a fair characterization of Nietzsche's ethics? Is Russell's "ultimate argument" an adequate alternative? His appeal is to emotion, Nietzsche's appeal is to will. But both reject ethical objectivism and deny the appeal to facts. In this respect they differ from John Dewey, who inveighs against the "dualism" of fact and value. They also differ from Aristotle, with his emphasis on reason, and from Cicero and Marcus Aurelius, with their emphasis on natural law. Here is an issue that goes to the foundation of ethics.

A comparison of Nietzsche and Marx is illuminating. Both were in revolt against the dominant values of their age, and both took their stand "beyond good and evil" as conceived by Christian and bourgeois. They looked to the future for their values: a future represented for Marx by the triumph of the proletariat, for Nietzsche by the emergence of the Overman. The contrast reaches its peak in

---

[1] *What I Believe* (New York: Dutton, 1925), p. 20.
[2] *A History of Western Philosophy* (New York: Simon & Schuster, 1945), pp. 772–773.

the clash between an egalitarian and an élitist morality. For Marx the ultimate reliance is on the solidarity of the many, for Nietzsche on the creativity of the few. Marx is concerned with the material needs of the downtrodden, Nietzsche with the artistic and cultural values of the "noble." The Marxian ideal is a classless humanism, the Nietzschean ideal is a power-élite. Who has the sounder ideals, Marx or Nietzsche?

17

Experiment

JOHN DEWEY (1859–1952)

John Dewey was born in the beautiful New England town of Burlington, Vermont. "All my forefathers," he has said, "earned an honest living as farmers, wheelwrights, coopers. I was absolutely the first one in seven generations to fall from grace."[1] But his father, a grocer, loved to recite from Shakespeare and Milton, and his parents gave their four sons the advantages of a college education and of a liberal moral and religious outlook. John took his undergraduate degree at the University of Vermont and his Doctor's degree in Philosophy at Johns Hopkins in 1884.

He taught at the University of Michigan from 1884 until 1894 (except for one year at the University of Minnesota), and then, for an additional ten-year period, at the University of Chicago. During these years, he gradually shifted from Hegelian idealism to his own version of pragmatism, or, as he preferred to call it, "instrumentalism." His ideas had begun to cause some controversy even before he went to Chicago, but this was mild compared with the storm that broke out when he began to apply his pragmatic ideals as director of the "Laboratory School" for children at the University of Chicago. Aided by his wife, for seven and a half years Dewey conducted a bold educational experiment based on the concepts of "learning by doing" and "education for democracy." Whereas traditional education had sought to instill obedience and receptivity, he sought to cultivate activity, initiative, diversity, and voluntary cooperation; and in so doing, he wrought a veritable revolution in educational theory and practice. The volume in which he explained what he was trying to do, *School and Society*, was first published in 1899 and has since been translated into a dozen European and Oriental languages and reprinted many times.

[1] Edwin E. Slosson, *Six Major Prophets* (Boston: Little, Brown, 1917), p. 268. (From a letter of Dewey to Slosson.)

Having achieved fame both as an educator and as a philosopher, Dewey in 1904 was called to Columbia University, where he remained until his retirement in 1929. With prodigious energy, he poured forth an immense volume of publications and engaged in many educational, political, and civic activities.

During the later years of his life, Dewey's interests continued to broaden, as indicated by the wide range of his writings—on education, religion, art, politics, ethics, logic, epistemology, and metaphysics. His many social and intellectual activities, however, did not prevent him from rearing a large family and forming many warm personal friendships. When he died at the age of ninety-two, he had had a more comprehensive and profound impact on the modern world than any other American philosopher.

Modest, unobstrusive, somewhat halting in speech, and ultra-democratic in manner, Dewey the human being has sometimes seemed to be quite different from Dewey the bold and independent thinker. This contrast has led many people to misinterpret and vulgarize his ideas and to underestimate his native radicalism. But if, as has been claimed, Dewey is more representative of democratic America than any other thinker, it is an intellectually adventurous and daring America that he represents.

Ethics

1. Reflection and Ends

The question of what ends a man should live for does not arise as a general problem in customary morality. It is forestalled by the habits and institutions which a person finds existing all about him. What others, especially elders, are doing provides the ends for which one should act. These ends are sanctioned by tradition; they are hallowed by the semidivine character of the ancestors who instituted the customs;

they are set forth by the wise elders, and are enforced by the rulers. Individuals trespass, deviating from these established purposes, but they do so with the conviction that thereby social condemnation, reënforced by supernatural penalties inflicted by divine beings, ensues. There are today multitudes of men and women who take their aims from what they observe to be going on around them. They accept the aims provided by religious teachers, by political authorities, by persons in the community who have prestige. Failure to adopt such a course would seem to many persons to be a kind of moral rebellion or anarchy. Many other persons find their ends practically forced upon them. Because of lack of education and because of economic stress they for the most part do just what they have to do. In the absence of the possibility of real choice, such a thing as reflection upon purposes and the attempt to frame a general theory of ends and of the good would seem to be idle luxuries.

There can, however, be no such thing as reflective morality except where men seriously ask by what purposes they should direct their conduct and why they should do so; what it is which makes their purposes good. This intellectual search for ends is bound to arise when customs fail to give required guidance. And this failure happens when old institutions break down; when invasions from without and inventions and innovations from within radically alter the course of life.

If habit fails, the sole alternative to caprice and random action is reflection. And reflection upon what one shall do is identical with formation of ends. Moreover, when social change is great, and a great variety of conflicting aims are suggested, reflection cannot be limited to the selection of one end out of a number which are suggested by conditions. Thinking has to operate creatively to form new ends.

Every habit introduces continuity into activity; it furnishes a permanent thread or axis. When custom breaks down, the only thing which can link together the succession of various acts is a common purpose running through separate acts. An end-in-view gives unity and continuity, whether it be the securing of an education, the carrying on of a military campaign, or the build-ing of a house. The more inclusive the aim in question the broader is the unification which is attained. Comprehensive ends may connect together acts performed during a long span of years. To the common soldier or even to the general in command, winning the campaign may be a sufficiently comprehensive aim to unify acts into conduct. But some one is bound to ask: What then? To what uses shall victory when achieved be put? At least that question is bound to be asked, provided men are intelligently interested in their behavior and are not governed by chance and the pressure of the passing moment. *The development of inclusive and enduring aims is the necessary condition of the application of reflection in conduct; indeed, they are two names for the same fact.* There can be no such thing as reflective morality where there is not solicitude for the ends to which action is directed.

Habit and impulse have consequences, just as every occurrence has effects. But merely as habit, impulse, and appetite they do not lead to foresight of what will happen as a consequence of their operation. An animal is moved by hunger and the outcome is satisfaction of appetite and the nourishment of the body. In the case of a human being, having mature experience upon which to fall back, obstacles in the way of satisfaction of hunger, difficulties encountered in the pursuit of food, will make a man aware of *what* he wants:—the outcome will be anticipated as an end-in-view, as something desired and striven for. Behavior has ends in the sense of results which *put an end* to that particular activity, while an *end-in-view* arises when a particular consequence is foreseen and being foreseen is consciously adopted by desire and deliberately made the directive purpose of action. A purpose or aim represents a craving, an urge, translated into the idea of an object, as blind hunger is transformed into a purpose through the thought of a food which is wanted, say flour, which then develops into the thought of grain to be sown and land to be cultivated:—a whole series of activities to be intelligently carried on.

An end-in-view thus differs on one side from a mere anticipation or prediction of an outcome, and on the other side from the propulsive force of mere habit and appetite. In distinction from the first, it involves a want, an impulsive urge and forward drive; in distinction from the second, it involves an intellectual factor, the thought of an object which gives meaning and direction to the urge. This connection between purpose and desire is the source of one whole class of moral problems. Attainment of learning, professional skill, wealth, power, would not be animating purposes unless the thought of some result were unified with some intense need of the self, for it takes *thought* to convert an impulse into a desire centered in an object. But on the other end, a strong craving tends to exclude thought. It is in haste for its own speedy realization. An intense appetite, say thirst, impels to immediate action without thought of its consequences, as a very thirsty man at sea tends to drink salt water without regard to objective results. Deliberation and inquiry, on the other hand, take time; they demand delay, the deferring of immediate action. Craving does not look beyond the moment, but it is of the very nature of thought to look toward a remote end.

2. Ends and the Good: the Union of Desire and Thought

There is accordingly a conflict brought about within the self. The impetus of reflection when it is aroused is to look ahead; to hunt out and to give weight to remoter consequences. But the force of craving, the impulsion of immediate need, call thought back to some near-by object in which want will find its immediate and direct satisfaction. The wavering and conflict which result are the ground for the theory which holds that there is an inherent warfare in the moral life between desire and reason; the theory that appetite and desire tend to delude us with deceptive goods, leading us away from the true end that reason holds up to view. In consequence, some moralists have gone so far as to hold that appetite and impulse are inherently evil, being expressions of the lust of the flesh, a power which pulls men away from the ends which reason approves. This view, however, is impossible. No idea or object could operate as an end and become a purpose unless it were connected with some need; otherwise it would be a mere idea without any moving and impelling power.

In short, while there is conflict, it is not between desire and reason, but between a desire which wants a near-by object and a desire which wants an object which is seen by thought to occur in consequence of an intervening series of conditions, or in the "long run"; it is a conflict between two objects presented in thought, one corresponding to a want or appetite just as it presents itself in isolation, the other corresponding to the want thought of in relation to other wants. Fear may suggest flight or lying to a man as ends to be sought; further thought may bring a man to a conviction that steadfastness and truthfulness will insure a much larger and more enduring good. There is an idea in each case; in the first case, an idea of personal safety; in the second instance, an idea of, say, the safety of others to be achieved by remaining at a post. In each case also there is desire; in the first instance a desire which lies close to natural impulse and instinct; in the second instance, a desire which would not be aroused were it not that *thought* brings into view remote consequences. *In one case, original impulse dictates the thought of the object; in the other case, this original impulse is transformed into a different desire because of objects which thought holds up to view.* But no matter how elaborate and how rational is the object of thought, it is impotent unless it arouses desire.

In other words, there is nothing intrinsically bad about raw impulse and desire. They *become* evil in contrast with another desire whose object includes more inclusive and more enduring consequences. What is morally dangerous in the desire as it first shows itself is its tendency to confine attention to its own immediate object and to shut out the thought of a larger whole of conduct. . . .

An understanding of the relationship between the propulsive, urging force of desire and the widening scope of thought enables us to understand what is meant by *will*, especially by the term a "strong will." Sometimes the latter is confused with mere stiff-necked obstinacy—a blind refusal to alter one's purpose no matter what new considerations thinking can produce. Sometimes it is confused with an intense although brief display of spasmodic external energy, even though the forceful manifestation is nothing better than a great ado about nothing. In reality "strength of will" (or, to speak more advisedly, of character) consists of an abiding identification of impulse with thought, in which impulse provides the drive while thought supplies consecutiveness, patience, and persistence, leading to a unified course of conduct. It is not the same as obstinacy because instead of insisting on repetition of the same act, it is observant of changes of conditions and is flexible in making new adjustments. It is *thinking* which is persisted in, even though special ends in view change, while the obstinate person insists upon the same act even when thinking would disclose a wiser course. . . .

From the peculiar union of desire and thought in voluntary action, it follows that every moral theory which tries to determine the *end* of conduct has a double aspect. In its relation to *desire*, it requires a theory of the *Good*: the Good is that which satisfies want, craving, which fulfills or makes complete the need which stirs to action. In its relation to *thought*, or as an *idea* of an object to be attained, it imposes upon those about to act the necessity for rational insight, or moral *wisdom*. For experience shows, as we have seen, that not every satisfaction of appetite and craving turns out to be a good; many ends *seem* good while we are under the influence of strong passion which in actual experience and in such thought as might have occurred in a cool moment are actually bad. The task of moral theory is thus to frame a theory of Good as the end or objective of desire, and also to frame a theory of the true, as distinct from the specious, good. In effect this latter need signifies the discovery of ends which will meet the demands of impartial and far-sighted thought as well as satisfy the urgencies of desire. . . .

3. Cultivation of Interests as the End

We have seen that the idea of Ends and the Good is the counterpart of the *intellectual* aspect of character and conduct. The difficulty in the way of attaining and maintaining practical wisdom is the urgency of immediate impulse and desire which swell and swell until they crowd out all thought of remote and comprehensive goods. The conflict is a real one and is at the heart of many of our serious moral struggles and lapses. In the main, solution is found in utilizing all possible occasions, when we are not in the presence of conflicting desires, to cultivate interest in those goods which we do approve in our calm moments of reflection. John Stuart Mill remarked that "the cultivated mind . . . finds sources of inexhaustible interest in all that surrounds it; in the objects of nature, the achievements of art, the imaginations of poetry, the incidents of

history, the ways of mankind, past, present and their prospects in the future." There are many times when the cultivation of these interests meets with no strong obstacle. The habits which are built up and reënforced under such conditions are the best bulwarks against weakness and surrender in the moments when the reflective or "true" good conflicts with that set up by temporary and intense desire. The proper course of action is, then, to multiply occasions for the enjoyment of these ends, to prolong and deepen the experiences connected with them. Morality then becomes positive instead of a struggle carried against the seductive force of lesser goods. This course of action gives no guarantee against occurrence of situations of conflict and of possible failure to maintain the greater good. But *reflective* attachment to the ends which reason presents is enormously increased when these ends have themselves been, on earlier occasions, *natural* goods enjoyed in the normal course of life. Ideal ends, those sustained by thought, do not lose their ideal character when they are directly appreciated; in the degree in which they become objects of positive interest their power to control and move conduct in times of stress is reenforced.

The truth hinted at in the hedonist view of moral wisdom, (that it consists in foresight and calculation of future enjoyments and sufferings) is that *present* enjoyment may accompany the thought of remote objects when they are held before the mind. Its error lies in supposing that in reflection our ideas go out to future pleasures instead of to future objects. A man in order to cultivate good health does not think of the pleasures it will bring to him: in thinking of the various objects and acts which will follow from good health he experiences a *present* enjoyment, and this enjoyment strengthens his effort to attain it. As Plato and Aristotle said over two thousand years ago, the aim of moral education is to develop a character which finds pleasure in right objects and pain in wrong ends.

Something similar is to be said of wisdom or prudence viewed as a judgment of ends which are expedient or that mark "good policy." As far as the maxim emphasizes means and conditions that are necessary to achievement, thus taking morals out of the region of sentimental vaporing and fantasies miscalled idealism, the principle is sound. Error lies in restriction of the domains of value in which achievement is desirable. It is folly rather than wisdom to include in the concept of success only tangible material goods and to exclude those of culture, art, science, sympathetic relations with others. Once a man has experienced certain kinds of good in a concrete and intimate way, he would rather fail in external achievement than forego striving for them. The zest of endeavor is itself an enjoyment to be fostered, and life is poor without it. As John Stuart Mill said, "some things called expedient are not useful but in reality are one branch of the harmful." To due reflection, things sometimes regarded as "practical" are in truth highly impolitic and shortsighted. But the way to eliminate preference for narrow and shortsighted expediences is not to condemn the practical as low and mercenary in comparison with spiritual ideals, but to cultivate all possible opportuni-

ties for the actual enjoyment of the reflective values and to engage in the activity, the practice, which extends their scope.

The morally wise, accordingly, appreciate the necessity of doing, of "exercise." They realize the importance of habit as a protection against beguilement by the goods proposed by immediate desire and urgent passion. But they also apprehend that abstinence for the sake of abstinence, mortification of the flesh for the sake of mortification, is not a rational end. The important ally to doing is sense of power, and this sense of power is the accompaniment of progress in actual achievement of a positive good. Next, if not equal in importance (in some temperaments, superior), is the esthetic factor. A golfer or tennis player may enjoy his exercises because he appreciates the value of "form." Emerson speaks of the *elegance* of abstinence. Moderation is the associate of proportion, and there is no art without measure. The restraint that ensues from a sense of the fitness of proportion is very different in quality from that which is exercised for its own sake. To find excess disgusting is more efficacious than finding it wrong although attractive.

Finally, the underlying truth of what is called Epicureanism contains an element upon which we have insisted: the importance of nurturing the *present* enjoyment of things worth while, instead of sacrificing present value to an unknown and uncertain future. If this course is popularly thought of as mere self-indulgence, as selfish and destructive of consecutive striving for remote ends, it is because emphasis is laid upon the bare fact of enjoyment instead of upon the *values* enjoyed. Here as with the other principles discussed, the conclusion is the need of fostering at every opportunity direct enjoyment of the kind of goods reflection approves. To deny direct satisfaction any place in morals is simply to weaken the moving force of the goods approved by thought.

Our discussion has centered on the goods which approve themselves to the thoughtful, or morally "wise," persons in their relation to the satisfaction which suggest themselves because of immediate and intense desire, impulse, and appetite. The office of reflection we have seen to be the formation of a judgment of value in which particular satisfactions are placed as integral parts of conduct as a consistent harmonious whole. If values did not get in one another's way, if, that is, the realization of one desire were not incompatible with that of another, there would be no need of reflection. We should grasp and enjoy each thing as it comes along. Wisdom, or as it is called on the ordinary plane, prudence, sound judgment, is the ability to foresee consequences in such a way that we form ends which grow into one another and reënforce one another. Moral folly is the surrender of the greater good for the lesser; it is snatching at one satisfaction in a way which prevents us from having others and which gets us subsequently into trouble and dissatisfaction.

Up to this point we have passed over the social conditions which affect the development of wise and prudent attitudes of mind. But it is clear that the education which one receives, not so much the formal schooling as the influ-ence of the traditions and institutions of the community in which one lives, and the habits of one's associates, are a profound influence. The simplest illustration is that of a spoiled child. The person who is encouraged to yield to every desire as it arises, the one who receives constantly the help of others in getting what he wants when he wants it, will have to possess extraordinary intellectual powers if he develops a habit of reflective valuation. What is true on this personal scale is true on a wide social scale. The general social order may be such as to put a premium upon the kind of satisfaction which is coarse, gross, "materialistic," and upon attitudes which are in impatient haste to grab any seeming near-by good. This state of affairs is characteristic of many phases of American life today. Love of power over others, of display and luxury, of pecuniary wealth, is fostered by our economic régime. Goods that are more ideal, esthetic, intellectual values, those of friendship which is more than a superficial comradeship, are forced into subordination. The need of fostering the reflective and contemplative attitudes of character is therefore the greater. Above all, there is the need to remake social conditions so that they will almost automatically support fuller and more enduring values and will reduce those social habits which favor the free play of impulse unordered by thought, or which make men satisfied to fall into mere routine and convention. . . .

In conclusion, we point out that the discussion enables us to give an empirically verifiable meaning to the conception of *ideal* values in contrast with *material* values. The distinction is one between goods which, when they present themselves to imagination, are approved by reflection after wide examination of their relations, and the goods which are such only because their wider connections are not looked into. We cannot draw up a catalogue and say that such and such goods are intrinsically and always ideal, and such and such other ones inherently base because material. There are circumstances under which enjoyment of a value called spiritual because it is associated with religion is mere indulgence; when its good, in other words, becomes one of mere sensuous emotion. There are occasions when attention to the material environment constitutes the ideal good because that is the act which thoroughgoing inquiry would approve. In a general way, of course, we can safely point out that certain goods are ideal in character: those of art, science, culture, interchange of knowledge and ideals, etc. But that is because past experience has shown that they are the *kind* of values which are likely to be approved upon searching reflection. Hence a *presumption* exists in their favor, but in concrete cases only a presumption. To suppose that the higher ideal value inheres in them *per se* would result in fostering the life of a dilettante and mere esthete, and would relegate all goods experienced in the natural course of life to a non-moral or anti-moral plane. There is in fact a place and time—that is, there are relationships—in which the satisfactions of the normal appetites, usually called physical and sensuous, have an ideal quality. Were it not so, some form of asceticism would be the only moral

course. The business of reflection in determining the true good cannot be done once for all, as, for instance, making out a table of values arranged in a hierarchical order of higher and lower. It needs to be done, and done over and over and over again, in terms of the conditions of concrete situations as they arise. In short, the need for reflection and insight is perpetually recurring.

4. Moral Judgments as Intuitive or Developed

That reflective morality, since it *is* reflective, involves thought, and knowledge is a truism. The truism raises, however, important problems of theory. What is the nature of knowledge in its moral sense? What is its function? How does it originate and operate? To these questions, writers upon morals have given different answers. Those, for example, who have dwelt upon approval and resentment as the fundamental ethical factor have emphasized its spontaneous and "instinctive" character—that is, its non-reflective nature—and have assigned a subordinate position to the intellectual factor in morals. Those who, like Kant, have made the authority of duty supreme, have marked off Moral Reason from thought and reasoning as they show themselves in ordinary life and in science. They have erected a unique faculty whose sole office is to make us aware of duty and of its imperatively rightful authority over conduct. The moralists who have insisted upon the identity of the Good with ends of desire have, on the contrary, made knowledge, in the sense of insight into the ends which bring enduring satisfaction, the supreme thing in conduct; ignorance, as Plato said, is the root of all evil. And yet, according to Plato, this assured insight into the true End and Good implies a kind of rationality which is radically different from that involved in the ordinary affairs of life. It can be directly attained only by the few who are gifted with those peculiar qualities which enable them to rise to metaphysical understanding of the ultimate constitution of the universe; others must take it on faith or as it is embodied, in a derived way, in laws and institutions. Without going into all the recondite problems associated with the conflict of views, we may say that two significant questions emerge. First, are thought and knowledge mere servants and attendants of emotion, or do they exercise a positive and transforming influence? Secondly, are the thought and judgment employed in connection with moral matters the same that are used in ordinary practical affairs, or are they something separate, having an *exclusively* moral significance? Putting the question in the form which it assumed in discussion during the nineteenth century: Is conscience a faculty of intuition independent of human experience, or is it a product and expression of experience?

The questions are stated in a theoretical form. They have, however, an important practical bearing. . . . Are praise and blame, esteem and condemnation, not only original and spontaneous tendencies, but are they also *ultimate*, incapable of being modified by the critical and constructive work of thought? Again, if conscience is a unique and separate faculty it is incapable of education and modification; it can only be directly appealed to. Most important of all, practically, is that some theories, like the Kantian, make a sharp separation between conduct that is moral and everyday conduct which is morally indifferent and neutral.

It would be difficult to find a question more significant for actual behavior than just this one: Is the moral region isolated from the rest of human activity? Does only one special class of human aims and relations have moral value? This conclusion is a necessary result of the view that our moral consciousness and knowledge is unique in kind. But if moral consciousness is not separate, then no hard and fast line can be drawn within conduct shutting off a moral realm from a non-moral. Now our whole previous discussion is bound up with the latter view. For it has found moral good and excellence in objects and activities which develop out of natural desires and normal social relations in family, neighborhood, and community. We shall accordingly now proceed to make explicit the bearing of this idea upon the nature of moral insight, comparing our conclusions with those arrived at by some other typical theories.

Moral judgments, whatever else they are, are a species of judgments of *value*. They characterize acts and traits of character as having *worth*, positive or negative. Judgments of value are not confined to matters which are explicitly moral in significance. Our estimates of poems, pictures, landscapes, from the standpoint of their esthetic quality, are value-judgments. Business men are rated with respect to their economic standing in giving of credit, etc. We do not content ourselves with a purely external statement about the weather as it is measured scientifically by the thermometer or barometer. We term it fine or nasty: epithets of value. Articles of furniture are judged useful, comfortable, or the reverse. Scientifically, the condition of the body and mind can be described in terms which neglect entirely the difference between health and disease, in terms, that is, of certain physical and chemical processes. When we pronounce the judgment, "well" or "ill" we estimate in value terms. When we judge the statements of others, whether made in casual conversation or in scientific discourse and pronounce them "true" or "false" we are making judgments of value. Indeed, the chief embarrassment in giving illustrations of value-judgments is that we are so constantly engaged in making them. In its popular sense, *all* judgment is estimation, appraisal, assigning value to something; a discrimination as to advantage, serviceability, fitness for a purpose, enjoyability, and so on.

There is a difference which must be noted between valuation as judgment (which involves thought in placing the thing judged in its relations and bearings) and valuing as a direct emotional and practical act. There is difference between esteem and estimation, between prizing and appraising. To esteem is to prize, hold dear, admire, approve; to estimate is to measure in intellectual fashion. One is direct, spontaneous; the other is reflex, reflective. We esteem before we estimate, and estimation comes in to consider whether and to what extent something is *worthy* of esteem. Is the object one which we

should admire? Should we really prize it? Does it have the qualities which *justify* our holding it dear? All growth in maturity is attended with this change from a spontaneous to a reflective and critical attitude. First, our affections go out to something in attraction or repulsion; we like and dislike. Then experience raises the question whether the object in question is what our esteem or disesteem took it to be, whether it is such as to justify our reaction to it.

The obvious difference between the two attitudes is that direct admiration and prizing are absorbed in the object, a person, act, natural scene, work of art or whatever, to the neglect of its place and effects, its connections with other things. That a lover does not see the beloved one as others do is notorious, and the principle is of universal application. For to think is to look at a thing in its *relations* with other things, and such judgment often modifies radically the original attitude of esteem and liking. A commonplace instance is the difference between natural liking for some object of food, and the recognition forced upon us by experience that it is not "good" for us, that it is not healthful. A child may like and prize candy inordinately; an adult tells him it is not good for him, that it will make him ill. "Good" to the child signifies that which tastes good; that which satisfies an immediate craving. "Good" from the standpoint of the more experienced person is that which serves certain ends, that which stands in certain connections with consequences. Judgment of value is the name of the act which searches for and takes into consideration these connections.

5. The Immediate Sense of Value and Its Limitations

The distinction between direct *valuing*, in the sense of prizing and being absorbed in an object or person, and *valuation* as reflective judgment, based upon consideration of a comprehensive scheme, has an important bearing upon the controversy as to the *intuitive* character of moral judgments. Our immediate responses of approval and reprobation may well be termed intuitive. They are not based upon any thought-out reason or ground. We just admire and resent, are attracted and repelled. This attitude is not only original and primitive but it persists in acquired dispositions. The reaction of an expert in any field is, relatively at least, intuitive rather than reflective. An expert in real estate will, for example, "size up" pecuniary values of land and property with a promptness and exactness which are far beyond the capacity of a layman. A scientifically trained person will see the meaning and possibilities of some line of investigation, where the untrained person might require years of study to make anything out of it. Some persons are happily gifted in their direct appreciation of personal relations; they are noted for tact, not in the sense of a superficial amiability but of real insight into human needs and affections. The results of prior experience, including previous conscious thinking, get taken up into direct habits, and express themselves in direct appraisals of value. Most of our moral judgments are intuitive, but this fact is not a proof of the existence of a separate faculty of moral insight, but is the result of past experience funded into direct outlook upon the scene of life. As Aristotle remarked in effect a long time ago, the immediate judgments of good and evil of a good man are more to be trusted than many of the elaborately reasoned out estimates of the inexperienced.

The immediate character of moral judgments is reënforced by the lessons of childhood and youth. Children are surrounded by adults who constantly pass judgments of value on conduct. And these comments are not coldly intellectual; they are made under conditions of a strongly emotional nature. Pains are taken to stamp them in by impregnating the childish response with elements of awe and mytsery, as well as ordinary reward and punishment. The attitudes remain when the circumstances of their origin are forgotten; they are made so much a part of the self that they seem to be inevitable and innate.

This fact, while it explains the intuitive character of reactions, also indicates a limitation of direct valuations. They are often the result of an education which was misdirected. If the conditions of their origin were intelligent, that is, if parents and friends who took part in their creation, were morally wise, they are likely to be intelligent. But arbitrary and irrelevant circumstances often enter in, and leave their impress as surely as do reasonable factors. The very fact of the early origin and now unconscious quality of the attendant intuitions is often distorting and limiting. It is almost impossible for later reflection to get at and correct that which has become unconsciously a part of the self. The warped and distorted will seem natural. Only the conventional and the fanatical are always immediately sure of right and wrong in conduct.

There is a permanent limit to the value of even the best of the intuitive appraisals of which we have been speaking. These are dependable in the degree in which conditions and objects of esteem are fairly uniform and recurrent. They do not work with equal sureness in the cases in which the new and unfamiliar enters in. "New occasions teach new duties." But they cannot teach them to those who suppose that they can trust without further reflection to estimates of the good and evil which are brought over from the past to the new occasion. Extreme intuitionalism and extreme conservatism often go together. Dislike to thoughtful consideration of the requirements of new situations is frequently a sign of fear that the result of examination will be a new insight which will entail the changing of settled habits and will compel departure from easy grooves in behavior —a process which is uncomfortable.

Taken in and of themselves, intuitions or immediate feelings of what is good and bad are of psychological rather than moral import. They are indications of formed habits rather than adequate evidence of what should be approved and disapproved. They afford at most, when habits already existing are of a good character, a *presumption* of correctness, and are guides, clews. But (a) nothing is more immediate and seemingly sure of itself than inveterate prejudice. The morals of a class, clique, or race when brought in contact with those of other races and peoples, are usually so sure of the rectitude of their own judgments of good and bad that they

are narrow and give rise to misunderstanding and hostility. (b) A judgment which is adequate under ordinary circumstance may go far astray under changed conditions. It goes without saying that false ideas about values have to be emended; it is not so readily seen that ideas of good and evil which were once true have to be modified as social conditions change. Men become attached to their judgments as they cling to other possessions which familiarity has made dear. Especially in times like the present, when industrial, political, and scientific transformations are rapidly in process, a revision of old appraisals is especially needed. (c) The tendency of undiluted intuitional theory is in the direction of an unquestioning dogmatism, what Bentham called *ipse dixitism*. Every intuition, even the best, is likely to become perfunctory and second-hand unless revitalized by consideration of its meaning—that is, of the consequences which will accrue from acting upon it. There is no necessary connection between a conviction of right and good in general and *what* is right and good in particular. A man may have a strong conviction of duty without enlightment as to just where his duty lies. When he assumes that because he is actuated by consciousness of duty in general, he can trust without reflective inquiry to his immediate ideas of the particular thing which is his duty, he is likely to become socially dangerous. If he is a person of strong will he will attempt to impose his judgments and standards upon others in a ruthless way, convinced that he is supported by the authority of Right and the Will of God.

6. The Nature and Office of Principles

It is clear that the various situations in which a person is called to deliberate and judge have common elements, and that values found in them resemble one another. It is also obvious that general ideas are a great aid in judging particular cases. If different situations were wholly unlike one another, nothing could be learned from one which would be of any avail in any other. But having like points, experience carries over from one to another, and experience is intellectually cumulative. Out of resembling experiences general ideas develop; through language, instruction, and tradition this gathering together of experiences of value into generalized points of view is extended to take in a whole people and a race. Through intercommunication the experience of the entire human race is to some extent pooled and crystallized in general ideas. These ideas constitute *principles*. We bring them with us to deliberation on particular situations.

These generalized points of view are of great use in surveying particular cases. But as they are transmitted from one generation to another, they tend to become fixed and rigid. Their origin in experience is forgotten and so is their proper use in further experience. They are thought of as if they existed in and of themselves and as if it were simply a question of bringing action under them in order to determine what is right and good. Instead of being treated as aids and instruments in judging values as the latter actually arise, they

are made superior to them. They become prescriptions, rules. Now a genuine principle differs from a rule in two ways: (a) A principle evolves in connection with the course of experience, being a generalized statement of what sort of consequences and values tend to be realized in certain kinds of situations; a rule is taken as something ready-made and fixed. (b) A principle is primarily intellectual, a method and scheme for judging, and is practical secondarily because of what it discloses; a rule is primarily practical.

Suppose that one is convinced that the rule of honesty is made known just in and of itself by a special faculty, and has absolutely nothing to do with recollection of past cases or forecast of possible future circumstances. How would such a rule apply itself to any particular case which needed to be judged? What bell would ring, what signal would be given, to indicate that *just* this case is the appropriate case for the application of the rule of honest dealing? And if by some miracle this question were answered, if we could know that here is a case for the rule of honesty, how should we know just what course in detail the rule calls for? For the rule, to be applicable to all cases, must omit the conditions which differentiate one case from another; it must contain only the very few similar elements which are to be found in all honest deeds. Reduced to this skeleton, not much would be left save the bare injunction to be honest whatever happens, leaving it to chance, the ordinary judgment of the individual, or to external authority to find out just *what* honesty specifically means in the given case.

This difficulty is so serious that all systems which have committed themselves to belief in a number of hard and fast rules having their origin in conscience, or in the word of God impressed upon the human soul or externally revealed, always have had to resort to a more and more complicated procedure to cover, if possible, all the cases. The moral life is finally reduced by them to an elaborate formalism and legalism.

Suppose, for example, we take the Ten Commandments as a starting-point. They are only ten, and naturally confine themselves to general ideas, and ideas stated mainly in negative form. Moreover, the same act may be brought under more than one rule. In order to resolve the practical perplexities and uncertainties which inevitably arise under such circumstances, *Casuistry* is built up (from the Latin *casus*, case). The attempt is made to foresee all the different cases of action which may conceivably occur, and provide in advance the exact rule for each case. For example, with reference to the rule "do not kill," a list will be made of all the different situations in which killing might occur:—accident, war, fulfillment of command of political superior (as by a hangman), self-defense (defense of one's own life, of others, of property), deliberate or premeditated killing with its different motives (jealousy, avarice, revenge, etc.), killing with slight premeditation, from sudden impulse, from different sorts and degrees of provocation. To each one of these possible cases is assigned its exact moral quality, its exact degree of turpitude and innocency. Nor can this process end with

overt acts; all the inner springs of action which affect regard for life must be similarly classified: envy, animosity, sudden rage, sullenness, cherishing of sense of injury, love of tyrannical power, hardness or hostility, callousness —all these must be specified into their different kinds and the exact moral worth of each determined. What is done for this one kind of case must be done for every part and phase of the entire moral life until it is all inventoried, catalogued, and distributed into pigeon-holes definitely labeled.

Dangers and evils attend this way of conceiving the moral life. (a) *It tends to magnify the letter of morality at the expense of its spirit*. It fixes attention not upon the positive good in an act, not upon the underlying agent's disposition which forms its spirit, nor upon the unique occasion and context which form its atmosphere, but upon its literal conformity with Rule A, Class I., Species 1, subhead (1), etc. The effect of this is inevitably to narrow the scope and lessen the depth of conduct. (i.) It tempts some to hunt for that classification of their act which will make it the most convenient or profitable for themselves. In popular speech, "casuistical" has come to mean a way of judging acts which splits hairs in the effort to find a way of acting that conduces to personal interest and profit, and which yet may be justified by some moral principle. (ii.) With others, this regard for the letter makes conduct formal and pedantic. It gives rise to a rigid and hard type of character conventionally attributed to the Pharisees of olden and the Puritans of modern time—the moral schemes of both classes being strongly impregnated with the notion of fixed moral rules.

(b) *This ethical system also tends in practice to a legal view of conduct.* Historically it always has sprung from carrying over legal ideas into morality. In the legal view liability to blame and to punishment inflicted from without by some superior authority, is necessarily prominent. Conduct is regulated through specific injunctions and prohibitions: Do this, Do not do that. Exactly the sort of analysis of which we have spoken above in the case of killing is necessary, so that there may be definite and regular methods of measuring guilt and assigning blame. Now liability, punishment, and reward are important factors in the conduct of life, but any scheme of morals is defective which puts the question of avoiding punishment in the foreground of attention, or which tends to create a pharisaical complacency in the mere fact of having conformed to command or rule.

(c) *Probably the worst evil of this moral system is that it tends to deprive moral life of freedom and spontaneity* and to reduce it (especially for the conscientious who take it seriously) to a more or less anxious and servile conformity to externally imposed rules. Obedience as loyalty to principle is a good, but this scheme practically makes it the only good and conceives it not as loyalty to ideals, but as conformity to commands. Moral rules exist just as independent deliverances on their own account, and the right thing is merely to follow them. This puts the center of moral gravity outside the concrete processes of living. All systems which emphasize the letter more than the spirit, legal consequences more than vital motives, put the individual under the weight of external authority. They lead to the kind of conduct described by St. Paul as under the law, not in the spirit, with its constant attendant weight of anxiety, uncertain struggle, and impending doom.

Many who strenuously object to all of these schemes of conduct, to everything which hardens it into forms by emphasizing external commands, authority, and punishments and rewards, fail to see that such evils are logically connected with any acceptance of the finality of fixed rules. They hold certain bodies of people, religious officers, political or legal authorities, responsible for what they object to in the scheme; while they still cling to the idea that morality is an effort to apply to particular deeds and projects a certain number of absolute unchanging moral rules. They fail to see that, if this were its nature, those who attempt to provide the machinery which would render it practically workable deserve praise rather than blame. In fact, the notion of absolute rules or precepts cannot be made workable except through certain superior authorities who declare and enforce them. Said Locke: "It is no small power it gives one man over another to be the dictator of principles and teacher of unquestionable truths."

There is another practically harmful consequence which follows from the identification of principles with rules. Take the case of, say, justice. There may be all but universal agreement in the notion that justice is the proper rule of conduct—so universal as to be admitted by all but criminals. But just what does justice demand in the concrete? The present state of such things as penology, prison reform, the tariff, sumptuary laws, trusts, the relation of capital and labor, collective bargaining, democratic government, private or public ownership of public utilities, communal versus private property, shows that persons of equally well-meaning dispositions find that justice means opposite things in practice, although all proclaim themselves devoted to justice as the rule of action. Taken as a principle, not as a rule, justice signifies the will to *examine* specific institutions and measures so as to find out how they operate with the view of introducing greater impartiality and equity into the consequences they produce.

This consideration brings us to the important fact regarding the nature of true moral principles. *Rules are practical; they are habitual ways of doing things. But principles are intellectual; they are the final methods used in judging suggested courses of action.* The fundamental error of the intuitionalist is that he is on the outlook for rules which will of themselves tell agents just what course of action to pursue; *whereas the object of moral principles is to supply standpoints and methods which will enable the individual to make for himself an analysis of the elements of good and evil in the particular situation in which he finds himself.* No genuine moral principle prescribes a specific course of action; rules,[1] like

[1] Of course, the word "rule" is often used to designate a principle—as in the case of the phrase "Golden Rule." We are speaking not of the words, but of their underlying ideas.

cooking recipes, may tell just what to do and how to do it. A moral principle, such as that of chastity, of justice, of the Golden Rule, gives the agent a basis for looking at and examining a particular question that comes up. It holds before him certain possible aspects of the act; it warms him against taking a short or partial view of the act. It economizes his thinking by supplying him with the main heads by reference to which to consider the bearings of his desires and purposes; it guides him in his thinking by suggesting to him the important considerations for which he should be on the lookout.

A moral principle, then, is not a command to act or forbear acting in a given way: *it is a tool for analyzing a special situation,* the right or wrong being determined by the situation in its entirety, and not by the rule as such. We sometimes hear it stated, for example, that the universal adoption of the Golden Rule would at once settle all industrial disputes and difficulties. But suppose that the principle were accepted in good faith by everybody; it would not at once tell everybody just what to do in all the complexities of his relations to others. When individuals are still uncertain of what their real goal may be, it does not finally decide matters to tell them to regard the good of others as they would their own. Nor does it mean that whatever in detail we want for ourselves we should strive to give to others. Because I am fond of classical music it does not follow that I should thrust as much of it as possible upon my neighbors. But the "Golden Rule" does furnish us a *point of view from which to consider acts;* it suggests the necessity of considering how our acts affect the interests of others as well as our own; it tends to prevent partiality of regard; it warns against setting an undue estimate upon a particular consequence of pain or pleasure, simply because it happens to affect us. In short, the Golden Rule does not issue special orders or commands; but it does clarify and illuminate the situations requiring intelligent deliberation. . . .

The important thing about knowledge in its moral aspect is not its actual extent so much as it is the *will* to know —the active desire to examine conduct in its bearing upon the general good. Actual information and insight are limited by conditions of birth, education, social environment. The notion of the intuitional theory that all persons possess a uniform and equal stock of moral judgments is contrary to fact. Yet there are common human affections and impulses which express themselves within every social environment;—there is no people the members of which do not have a belief in the value of human life, of care of offspring, of loyalty to tribal and community customs, etc., however restricted and one-sided they may be in the application of these beliefs. Beyond this point, there is always, on whatever level of culture, the possibility of being on the alert for opportunities to widen and deepen the meaning of existing moral ideas. The attitude of *seeking* for what is good may be cultivated under any conditions of race, class, and state of civilization. Persons who are ignorant in the conventional sense of education may display an interest in discovering and considering what is good which is absent in the highly literate and pol-

ished. From the standpoint of this interest, class divisions vanish. The moral quality of knowledge lies not in possession but in concern with increase. The essential evil of fixed standards and rules is that it tends to render men satisfied with the existing state of affairs and to take the ideas and judgments they already possess as adequate and final.

The need for constant revision and expansion of moral knowledge is one great reason why there is no gulf dividing non-moral knowledge from that which is truly moral. At any moment conceptions which once seemed to belong exclusively to the biological or physical realm may assume moral import. This will happen whenever they are discovered to have a bearing on the common good. When knowledge of bacteria and germs and their relation to the spread of disease was achieved, sanitation, public and private, took on a moral significance it did not have before. For they were seen to affect the health and well-being of the community. Psychiatrists and psychologists working within their own technical regions have brought to light facts and principles which profoundly affect old conceptions of, say, punishment and responsibility, especially in their place in the formation of disposition. It has been discovered, for example, that "problem children" are created by conditions which exist in families and in the reaction of parents to the young. In a rough way, it may be asserted that most of the morbid conditions of mind and character which develop later have their origin in emotional arrests and maladjustments of early life. These facts have not as yet made their way very far into popular understanding and action, but their ultimate moral import is incalculable. Knowledge once technically confined to physics and chemistry is applied in industry and has an effect on the lives and happiness of individuals beyond all estimate. The list of examples might be extended indefinitely. The important point is that any restriction of moral knowledge and judgments to a definite realm necessarily limits our perception of moral significance. A large part of the difference between those who are stagnant and reactionary and those who are genuinely progressive in social matters comes from the fact that the former think of morals as confined, boxed, within a round of duties and sphere of values which are fixed and final. Most of the serious moral problems of the present time are dependent for their solution upon a general realization that the contrary is the case. Probably the great need of the present time is that the traditional barriers between scientific and moral knowledge be broken down, so that there will be organized and consecutive endeavor to use all available scientific knowledge for human and social ends.

7. The Experimental Method

[To] assume the existence of final and unquestionable knowledge upon which we can fall back in order to settle automatically every moral problem . . . would involve the commitment to a dogmatic theory of morals. The alternative method may be called experimental.

It implies that reflective morality demands observation of particular situations, rather than fixed adherence to *a priori* principles; that free inquiry and freedom of publication and discussion must be encouraged and not merely grudgingly tolerated; that opportunity at different times and places must be given for trying different measures so that their effects may be capable of observation and of comparison with one another. It is, in short, the method of democracy, of a positive toleration which amounts to sympathetic regard for the intelligence and personality of others, even if they hold views opposed to ours, and of scientific inquiry into facts and testing of ideas.

The opposed method, even when we free it from the extreme traits of forcible suppression, censorship, and intolerant persecution which have often historically accompanied it, is the method of appeal to authority and to precedent. The will of divine beings, supernaturally revealed; of divinely ordained rulers; of so-called natural law, philosophically interpreted; of private conscience; of the commands of the state, or the constitution; of common consent; of a majority; of received conventions; of traditions coming from a hoary past; of the wisdom of ancestors; of precedents set up in the past, have at different times been the authority appealed to. The common feature of the appeal is that there is some voice so authoritative as to preclude the need of inquiry. The logic of the various positions is that while an open mind may be desirable in respect to physical truths, a completely settled and closed mind is needed in moral matters.

Adoption of the experimental method does not signify that there is no place for authority and precedent. On the contrary, precedent is . . . a valuable *instrumentality*. But precedents are to be *used* rather than to be implicitly followed; they are to be used as tools of analysis of present situations, suggesting points to be looked into and hypotheses to be tried. They are of much the same worth as are personal memories in individual crises; a storehouse to be drawn upon for suggestion. There is also a place for the use of authorities. Even in free scientific inquiry, present investigators rely upon the findings of investigators of the past. They employ theories and principles which are identified with scientific inquirers of the past. They do so, however, only as long *as no evidence is presented calling for a reëxamination of their findings and theories*. They never assume that these finding are so final that under no circumstances can they be questioned and modified. Because of partnership, love of certainty, and devotion to routine, accepted points of view gain a momentum which for long periods even in science may restrict observation and reflection. But this limitation is recognized to be a weakness of human nature and not a desirable use of the principle of authority.

In moral matters there is also a presumption in favor of principles that have had a long career in the past and that have been endorsed by men of insight; the presumption is especially strong when all that opposes them is the will of some individual for exemption because of an impulse or passion which is temporarily urgent. Such principles are no more to be lightly discarded than are scientific principles worked out in the past. But in one as in the other, newly discovered facts or newly instituted conditions may give rise to doubts and indicate the inapplicabley of accepted doctrines. In questions of social morality more fundamental than any particular principle held or decision reached is the attitude of *willingness to reëxamine and if necessary to revise current convictions, even if that course entails the effort to change by concerted effort existing institutions, and to direct existing tendencies to new ends.*

It is a caricature to suppose that emphasis upon the social character of morality leads to glorification of contemporary conditions just as they are. The position does insist that morals, to have vitality, must be related to these conditions or be up in the air. But there is nothing in the bare position which indicates whether the relation is to be one of favor or of opposition. A man walking in a bog must pay even more heed to his surroundings than a man walking on smooth pavement, but this fact does not mean that he is to surrender to these surroundings. The alternative is not between abdication and acquiescence on one side, and neglect and ignoring on the other; it is between a morals which is effective because related to what is, and a morality which is futile and empty because framed in disregard of actual conditions. Against the social consequences generated by existing conditions there always stands the idea of other and better social consequences which a change would bring into being.

COMMENT

Main Emphases in Dewey's Ethics

Dewey shifts the emphasis in ethical theory from *value* to *valuation*, being at least as much concerned with the process of appraisal as with the qualities appraised. Valuation, he maintains, should be in accordance with the methods of experimental logic. No one has insisted more strenuously than Dewey upon scientific study of the actual needs of human beings and the concrete, experimental means of satisfying these needs. "Not all who say Ideals, Ideals," he remarks, "shall enter into the kingdom of the ideal, but those who know and respect the roads that conduct to the kingdom."[1] His main contribution to ethical theory has been to explore the roads rather than to describe the destination. Indeed, he does not believe in a fixed destination but rather, in a never-ending and exploratory journey. Since conditions are constantly changing, rules cannot be made nor goals ascertained in advance. Living well is an experiment, and there should be flexible reappraisal and reorientation as the experiment progresses.

Valuation is stimulated by tension, conflict, unsatisfactoriness; and sucessful valuation points to ways of resolving the tensions and releasing the pent-up energies. In regard to ethics, as in pragmatist theory in general, inquiry is conceived to be instrumentalist—a tool for controlling experience. Values are not passively "given," without intelligent effort, but are actively constructed. There is a fundamental difference between what is merely "liked" and what is genuinely "likable," merely "desired" and really "desirable," merely "admired" and truly "admirable," merely "satisfying" and dependably "satisfactory." Only the latter are *values* in the sense that they have been *validated*. They can be achieved only if we know the conditions and consequences of our desires, affections, and enjoyments, and if we learn intelligently to coordinate and control them. The idea of a *good* should be treated as a hypothesis, to be tested like any other.

In the testing, we must see ends and means as "continuous"—the ends as means to future satisfactions, and the means as not merely instrumentally but intrinsically valuable or disvaluable. Kant, for example, was fundamentally mistaken in exalting virtue as an end apart from being a means, for the very qualities that make it good as end make it good as means also. Dewey believed that experience is most satisfactory when the instrumental and the consummatory are closely linked—when action and contemplation fructify each other. We should neither subordinate growth and spontaneity to static contemplation nor concentrate merely upon activity to the neglect of rational goals. Life should combine both repose and stimulation—the sense of achievement and the sense of adven-

[1] "The Pragmatic Acquiescence," *New Republic*, Vol. 49 (Jan. 5, 1927), p. 189.

ture. In thus insisting upon "the continuity of means and ends," Dewey is exhibiting the antidualistic tendency that pervades his entire philosophy. He protests strongly against the inveterate tendency to think in terms of hard-and-fast distinctions between, for example, facts and values, experience and nature, freedom and organization, learning and doing; and he seeks to resolve all such sharp dualisms by insisting upon the continuity and interpenetration of "opposites." Values are to be studied as natural facts, and facts are to be evaluated; experience is to be regarded as inseparable from nature, and nature is to be interpreted in terms of experience; freedom is to be secured by organization, and organization is to be liberalized by freedom; learning is to be achieved by doing, and doing is to be directed by learning. His whole philosophy can thus be regarded as a "revolt against dualism." In this respect he has much in common with Whitehead.

There is no sense, according to Dewey, in talking about *the* end of life—as if there were a single end or final consummation. Life is simply an ongoing process, with a plurality of ends which function also as means. His stress is upon the dynamic rather than the static, the specific rather than the general, the concrete and plural rather than the abstract and monistic. "Faith in the varied possibilities of diversified experience," he declares, "is attended with the joy of constant discovery and constant growing."[2]

The Cultivation of Interests

So far as Dewey is willing to fix upon a universal end-in-view it is the cultivation and fulfillment of interests. "Interest," as Dewey employs the term, implies an attitude of desire or striving, but it also includes an element of feeling and does not exclude thought. As cognitive-affective-volitional and implying an object, it is more inclusive and less subjective than "pleasure." Interests find expression in objects and are directed toward objects and are publicly describable in terms of their objective references and behavioral manifestations. To phrase the moral ideal in terms of interests is consistent with Dewey's emphasis upon the total organism in its environmental situation.

One of the central questions for an interest theory of values is whether "value" is to be construed in terms of unqualified or qualified interests. Ralph Barton Perry, in his famous *General Theory of Value*, argued for the first alternative, and Dewey for the second. To the question, What is value? Perry answered, "Any object of any interest." He added that moral principles define the adjustment of interest to interest for the sake of an inclusive and harmonious integration. But Dewey, more strenuously than Perry, insisted on the difference between prizing and appraising, between mere liking and finding something genuinely likable. He chose to confine the word "value" to those interests and objects that

---

[2] "What I Believe," *Forum* (March 1930), p. 179.

are reflectively approved after a searching examination of their qualities, relations, causes, and consequences, and he insisted that values had to be reconstructed and validated in the light of the experimental method of the sciences.

On the Distinction between Science, Technology, and Morals

According to some critics, Dewey's ethical philosophy is strong in method but weak in vision; strong in delineating the variety of experience but weak in revealing the unity of life; strong in its awareness of novelty but weak in its blindness to universal and enduring values; strong in opposing static absolutism but weak in yielding to mercurial relativism; strong in realizing the need for growth but weak in criticizing the direction of growth; strong in relating science, technology, and morals, weak in failing to distinguish them. Whether this estimate is justified we shall leave to the readers of this book to decide. The last point of criticism, however, calls for more detailed comment.

The heart of Dewey's ethical philosophy is the attempt to link science, technology, and morals, and it is therefore important to consider their interrelations. We can begin by noting three realms of discourse, as illustrated by the following sentences:

"That is a strong poison."

"You ought to use a strong poison" (said to a would-be murderer).

"You ought not to murder."

The first sentence is *descriptive*; it simply indicates a matter of fact, with no commendation or disparagement. The second sentence is *evaluative*, but in what Kant would call a *hypothetical* rather than a categorical sense. The "ought" here simply means that, *if* you want to murder this man, you ought to use a poison strong enough to accomplish your purpose. It does not express a *duty* to use a strong poison. The third sentence is also *evaluative*, but in what Kant would call a *categorical* rather than a hypothetical sense. It expresses a duty to refrain from murdering. Sentences of the first type are characteristic of pure science; sentences of the second type are characteristic of technology; and sentences of the third type are characteristic of morals. (To accept these distinctions, we would not have to agree with Kant's formulae for determining categorical imperatives. If we were utilitarians, for example, our formula might read: "So act that in every case there shall be no better results." If our duty is to achieve the best results possible, it is still our *duty*.)

The charge that can be made against Dewey is that he has failed to distinguish clearly among science, technology, and morals. In his laudable effort to relate them, he has obscured their differences. We shall not discuss whether he should have more definitely distinguished pure science and technology—this question is relevant to the issues presented in Chapter 3 and might well be debated in that connection. At present, we are concerned only with the relation between morals and science and between morals and technology.

1. Morals and Science. "Experience," Dewey notes, "actually presents esthetic and moral traits."[3] These stand on "the same level" as the redness of a rose or the absentmindedness of a professor—they are matters of fact which can be studied like any other. There is a valid point here that should not be denied. Human beings do exhibit esthetic and moral traits and experience satisfactions and enjoyments. These can be described like any other natural facts. Moral theories that try to exclude consideration of human nature and its environment are hopelessly unrealistic. If this is all that Dewey means, we need not disagree with him. But it is still the case that a psychologist bent upon *describing* human nature has a different task than the moralist bent upon *evaluating* moral alternatives. Such words as "good," "right," "ought," as used by the moralist, are nouns and adjectives of commendation, not of description. How can we make the leap from description to evaluation? How can we get, for example, from "desired" to *ethically* "desirable"? The latter does not mean *psychologically* desirable, in the sense that someone *can* desire it. It means *worth* desiring—desiring in the sense that it *ought* to be desired. A naturalistic theory of ethics, such as that of Dewey, seems to overlook the nondescriptive, purely ethical character of the moral *ought*.

Dewey could reply that "desirable" means that which one desires *after* one has seen all its conditions and consequences. But this does not solve the problem, because it is perfectly possible for a malevolent person to desire something that is morally evil after he has thoroughly understood its connections with other things. Dewey could also reply that the ethically desirable is that which is desired by a fair and impartial judge. But this definition is circular; it amounts to saying that something is ethically desirable (good or right) when it is approved by somebody who approves only what *is* ethically desirable. The only solution, Dewey's critics would say, is to admit a clear-cut distinction between facts and norms, morals and science—and this he fails to do. So runs the criticism that could be directed against Dewey. The reader should weigh this criticism carefully and decide whether it is valid.

2. Morals and Technology. Dewey often appears to be identifying morality with technology, or to be thinking of it as a kind of super-technology. There would seem to be much to support this point of view. The language of technological discourse, as we have already noted, is distinguished by normative terms, such as "ought" or "ought not," or by imperatives, such as "do this" or "do not do that." Such language is intended to direct choice among alternative possibilities. There are different kinds of norms and normative statements belonging to different levels of technological discourse. Many technological imperatives are mere counsels of skill, as when a carpenter says to his helper, "You ought to sharpen the teeth of that saw." He means, "*If* you want to use your saw effectively for the purpose at hand, you ought to sharpen its teeth." At a somewhat

[3] *Experience and Nature* (Chicago: Open Court, 1929), p. 2.

higher and more general level, the norms have a quasi-ethical or esthetic character, as in the case of the artistic norm of "beauty," the legal norm of "justice," the medical norm of "health," and the economic norm of "prosperity." Finally, there are highest level norms that pertain to a total economy of values. They are invoked when there is a conflict between lower-level oughts, and may be thought of as decidedly ethical. Morality will then be conceived as a technology of technologies, the function of which is to coordinate all the various techniques that a society has at its disposal.

This view of morality is by no means new. Aristotle had a similar conception of the art of arts, the technology of technologies. In the opening paragraphs of his *Ethics*, as we have seen, he pointed out that the arts are to be distinguished by the ends which they serve. Health is the aim of medicine, vessels of shipbuilding, victory of military strategy, and wealth of economics. The ends and the corresponding arts form a hierarchy, some being subservient to others. Bridle-making is subservient to horsemanship, horsemanship to strategy, and so on. Finally we arrive at some ultimate end and the art corresponding to it. This is the art of arts—the art whose function it is to harmonize and control all the other arts and whose end, therefore, is not this or that particular good but the good for man. Aristotle calls this highest art the art of politics, of which ethics, since it defines the ultimate good, is an integral part. Here the word "art" is being used in the same sense as we intend by "technology," and Aristotle's conception of politics as an "art of arts" is analogous to the conception of morality as a "technology of technologies."

Up to a point, this way of looking at morality seems sound, but it is important to recognize that morality, as a kind of supreme technology, is fundamentally different from ordinary technology—so different, indeed, that we should perhaps not call it a technology at all. An ordinary technological norm is an *instrument* of a decision-maker, not a *control* over him; and, therefore, to interpret moral norms as ordinary technological norms would imply that technology needs no control or is somehow self-regulating. Such a view is exceedingly mischievous, especially in this age of nuclear fission. Consequently, there must be norms controlling the decision-maker rather than norms which are merely his instruments. The right use of instrumental norms presupposes some noninstrumental criteria.

In the case of ordinary technology, in other words, it is not the right motivation of the agent that is in question but the skill to be used in carrying out a motivation that is taken for granted. In the case of morality, on the other hand, it is precisely the motivation that is most in question, and the problem of finding the right means is secondary. The norms of ordinary technology usually prescribe how to perform some action. The moral question, on the other hand, is not simply *how* to do something, but *what* to do.

Here, then, is a possible ground for criticism. Pragmatists such as Dewey, the critics might say, are prone to exaggerate the similarity between ordinary technology and morality. They are so intent upon the fluidity and instrumentality of norms that they neglect or even deny the question of *ultimate* motivation. They are inclined to take "the problematic situation" as it arises and to interpret right action as "problem-solving" within the context of this situation. The problem, as they see it, is "solved" when the diverse competing interests in the situation are brought into some kind of moving equilibrium, which leads to new "problematic situations" and thus to new and revised norms. So understood, morality is closely akin to ordinary technology. But morality cannot afford merely to implement and reconcile interests that are taken for granted. Its task is more radical. It criticizes interests in the light of ultimate norms; and, in exercising this sort of stubborn and very radical criticism, it differentiates itself from technology.

The question that we have posed is whether Dewey has sufficiently realized this fact, and whether he has also realized the clear-cut difference between morality (or ethics, as its theoretical basis) and natural science.

18

Language
and
Morals

LUDWIG WITTGENSTEIN (1889–1951)

Ludwig Wittgenstein, the youngest in a family of five boys and three girls, was born in Vienna to wealthy and cultivated parents. Although the family was of Jewish descent, Wittgenstein's grandfather was a convert to Protestantism and his mother was a Roman Catholic. Both she and her husband were highly musical, and Johannes Brahms was an intimate friend of the family. Inheriting the parental artistic bent, Wittgenstein could design a house, mold a statue, play a clarinet, conduct an orchestra, or write an imaginary dialogue.

He was taught at home until he was fourteen, and for three years thereafter went to school in Linz, Austria. Interested in physics and engineering, he then attended a technical school in Berlin-Charlottenburg. In 1908 he went to England, where he experimented with kites, registered as a research student in engineering at the University of Manchester, and constructed a jet reaction propeller for aircraft. He soon became absorbed in pure mathematics and the logic of Gottlob Frege and Bertrand Russell. During a period of great philosophical ferment at Cambridge University, where G. E. Moore, Russell, Whitehead, and Keynes were among the celebrities, he attended the university and studied the foundations of logic and the nature of language.

When World War I broke out, he returned to his native Austria, entered the army as a volunteer, and served on the Eastern front. He kept a notebook in his soldier's rucksack and snatched time to jot down the thoughts that later appeared in his *Tractatus-Logico Politicus* (published in 1922). After the death of his father, a leading industrialist, in 1912, he was in possession of a great fortune, but when the war was over he gave away all his money and thereafter lived with extreme frugality. From 1920 to 1926 he taught school in remote villages in Austria, and then occupied himself for two years in designing and building a mansion in Vienna for one of his sisters.

Returning to Cambridge in 1919, he presented the *Tractatus* as a thesis and received a Ph.D. degree. In the following year he was appointed a Fellow of Trinity College. Thereafter a radical transition in his thinking ensued and culminated in writing the *Philosophical Investigations* (published after his death in 1953). During the last two years of his life he suffered from cancer. When informed by his doctor that he had only a few days to live, he exclaimed "Good!" Before lapsing into unconsciousness he said, "Tell them I have had a wonderful life!"

A Lecture
on Ethics

Before I begin to speak about my subject proper let me make a few introductory remarks. I feel I shall have great difficulties in communicating my thoughts to you and I think some of them may be diminished by mentioning them to you beforehand. The first

From "A Lecture on Ethics," *Philosophical Review* (1965), pp. 3–12. This lecture was prepared by Wittgenstein for delivery in Cambridge sometime between September 1929 and December 1930. It was probably read to the society known as "The Heretics," to which Wittgenstein gave an address at that time. The manuscript bears no title. So far as is known, this was the only popular lecture ever composed or delivered by Wittgenstein. By permission of the estate of Wittgenstein and the *Philosophical Review*.

one, which almost I need not mention, is that English is not my native tongue and my expression therefore often lacks that precision and subtlety which would be desirable if one talks about a difficult subject. All I can do is to ask you to make my task easier by trying to get at my meaning in spite of the faults which I will constantly be committing against the English grammar. The second difficulty I will mention is this, that probably many of you come up to this lecture of mine with slightly wrong expectations. And to set you right in this point I will say a few words about the reason for choosing the subject I have chosen: When your former secretary honoured me by asking me to read a paper to your society, my first thought was that I would certainly do it and my second thought was that if I was to have the opportunity to speak to you I should speak about something which I am keen on communicating to you and that I should not misuse this opportunity to give you a lecture about, say, logic. I call this a misuse, for to explain a scientific matter to you it would need a course of lectures and not an hour's paper. Another alternative would have been to give you what's called a popular-scientific lecture, that is a lecture intended to make you believe that you understand a thing which actually you don't understand, and to gratify what I believe to be one of the lowest desires of modern people, namely the superficial curiosity about the latest discoveries of science. I rejected these alternatives and decided to talk to you about a subject which seems to me to be of general importance, hoping that it may help to clear up your thoughts about this subject (even if you should entirely disagree with what I will say about it). My third and last difficulty is one which, in fact, adheres to most lengthy philosophical lectures and it is this, that the hearer is incapable of seeing both the road he is led and the goal which it leads to. That is to say: he either thinks: "I understand all he says, but what on earth is he driving at" or else he thinks "I see what he's driving at, but how on earth is he going to get there." All I can do is again to ask you to be patient and to hope that in the end you may see both the way and where it leads to.

I will now begin. My subject, as you know, is Ethics and I will adopt the explanation of that term which Professor Moore has given in his book *Principia Ethica.* He says: "Ethics is the general enquiry into what is good." Now I am going to use the term Ethics in a slightly wider sense, in a sense in fact which includes what I believe to be the most essential part of what is generally called Aesthetics. And to make you see as clearly as possible what I take to be the subject matter of Ethics I will put before you a number of more or less synonymous expressions each of which could be substituted for the above definition, and by enumerating them I want to produce the same sort of effect which Galton produced when he took a number of photos of different faces on the same photographic plate in order to get the picture of the typical features they all had in common. And as by showing to you such a collective photo I could make you see what is the typical—say—Chinese face; so if you look through the row of synonyms which I will put before you, you will, I hope, be able to see the characteristic features they all have in common and these are the characteristic features of Ethics. Now instead of saying "Ethics is the enquiry into what is good" I could have said Ethics is the enquiry into what is valuable, or, into what is really important, or I could have said Ethics is the enquiry into the meaning of life; or into what makes life worth living, or into the right way of living. I believe if you look at all these phrases you will get a rough idea as to what it is that Ethics is concerned with. Now the first thing that strikes one about all these expressions is that each of them is actually used in two very different senses. I will call them the trivial or relative sense on the one hand and the ethical or absolute sense on the other. If for instance I say that this is a *good* chair this means that the chair serves a certain predetermined purpose and the word good here has only meaning so far as this purpose has been previously fixed upon. In fact the word good in the relative sense simply means coming up to a certain predetermined standard. Thus when we say that this man is a good pianist we mean that he can play pieces of a certain degree of difficulty with a certain degree of dexterity. And similarly if I say that it is *important* for me not to catch cold I mean that catching a cold produces certain describable disturbances in my life and if I say that this is the *right* road I mean that it's the right road relative to a certain goal. Used in this way these expressions don't present any difficult or deep problems. But this it not how Ethics uses them. Supposing that I could play tennis and one of you saw me playing and said "Well, you play pretty badly" and suppose I answered "I know, I'm playing badly but I don't want to play any better," all the other man could say would be "Ah then that's all right." But suppose I had told one of you a preposterous lie and he came up to me and said "You're behaving like a beast" and then I were to say "I know I behave badly, but then I don't want to behave any better," could he then say "Ah, then that's all right"? Certainly not; he would say "Well, you *ought* to want to behave better." Here you have an absolute judgment of value, whereas the first instance was one of a relative judgment. The essence of this difference

seems to be obviously this: Every judgment of relative value is a mere statement of facts and can therefore be put in such a form that it loses all the appearance of a judgment of value: Instead of saying "This is the right way to Granchester," I could equally well have said, "This is the right way you have to go if you want to get to Granchester in the shortest time"; "This man is a good runner" simply means that he runs a certain number of miles in a certain number of minutes, etc. Now what I wish to contend is that, although all judgments of relative value can be shown to be mere statements of facts, no statement of fact can ever be, or imply, a judgment of absolute value. Let me explain this: Suppose one of you were an omniscient person and therefore knew all the movements of all the bodies in the world dead or alive and that he also knew all the states of mind of all human beings that ever lived, and suppose this man wrote all he knew in a book, then this book would contain the whole description of the world; and what I want to say is, that this book would contain nothing that we would call an *ethical* judgment or anything that would logically imply such a judgment. It would of course contain all relative judgments of value and all true scientific propositions and in fact all true propositions that can be made. But all the facts described would, as it were, stand on the same level; and in the same way all propositions stand on the same level. There are no propositions which, in any absolute sense, are sublime, important, or trivial. Now perhaps some of you will agree to that and be reminded of Hamlet's words: "Nothing is either good or bad, but thinking makes it so." But this again could lead to a misunderstanding. What Hamlet says seems to imply that good and bad, though not qualities of the world outside us, are attributes to our states of mind. But what I mean is that a state of mind, so far as we mean by that a fact which we can describe, is in no ethical sense good or bad. If for instance in our world-book we read the description of a murder with all its details physical and psychological, the mere description of these facts will contain nothing which we could call an *ethical* proposition. The murder will be on exactly the same level as any other event, for instance the falling of a stone. Certainly the reading of this description might cause us pain or rage or any other emotion, or we might read about the pain or rage caused by this murder in other people when they heard of it, but there will simply be facts, facts, and facts but no Ethics. And now I must say that if I contemplate what Ethics really would have to be if there were such a science, this result seems to me quite obvious. It seems to me obvious that nothing we could ever think or say should be *the* thing. That we cannot write a scientific book, the subject matter of which could be intrinsically sublime and above all other subject matters. I can only describe my feeling by the metaphor, that, if a man could write a book on Ethics which really was a book on Ethics, this book would, with an explosion, destroy all the other books in the world. Our words used as we use them in science, are vessels capable only of containing and conveying meaning and sense, *natural* meaning and sense.

Ethics, if it is anything, is supernatural and our words will only express facts; as a teacup will only hold a teacup full of water and if I were to pour out a gallon over it. I said that so far as facts and propositions are concerned there is only relative value and relative good, right, etc. And let me, before I go on, illustrate this by a rather obvious example. The right road is the road which leads to an arbitrarily predetermined end and it is quite clear to us all that there is no sense in talking about the right road apart from such a predetermined goal. Now let us see what we could possibly mean by the expression, "*the* absolutely right road." I think it would be the road which *everybody* on seeing it would, *with logical necessity*, have to go, or be ashamed for not going. And similarly the *absolute good*, if it is a describable state of affairs, would be one which everybody, independent of his tastes and inclinations, would *necessarily* bring about or feel guilty for not bringing about. And I want to say that such a state of affairs is a chimera. No state of affairs has, in itself, what I would like to call the coercive power of an absolute judge. Then what have all of us who, like myself, are still tempted to use such expressions as "absolute good," "absolute value," etc., what have we in mind and what do we try to express? Now whenever I try to make this clear to myself it is natural that I should recall cases in which I would certainly use these expressions and I am then in the situation in which you would be if, for instance, I were to give you a lecture on the psychology of pleasure. What you would do then would be to try and recall some typical situation in which you always felt pleasure. For, bearing this situation in mind, all I should say to you would become concrete and, as it were, controllable. One man would perhaps choose as his stock example the sensation when taking a walk on a fine summer's day. Now in this situation I am, if I want to fix my mind on what I mean by absolute or ethical value. And there, in my case, it always happens that the idea of one particular experience presents itself to me which therefore is, in a sense, my experience *par excellence* and this is the reason why, in talking to you now, I will use this experience as my first and foremost example. (As I have said before, this is an entirely personal matter and others would find other examples more striking.) I will describe this experience in order, if possible, to make you recall the same or similar experiences, so that we may have a common ground for our investigation. I believe the best way of describing it is to say that when I have it *I wonder at the existence of the world*. And I am then inclined to use such phrases as "how extraordinary that anything should exist" or "how extraordinary that the world should exist." I will mention another experience straight away which I also know and which others of you might be acquainted with: it is, what one might call, the experience of feeling *absolutely* safe. I mean the state of mind in which one is inclined to say "I am safe, nothing can injure me whatever happens." Now let me consider these experiences, for, I believe, they exhibit the very characteristics we try to get clear about. And there the first thing I have to say is, that the verbal expression which we give to these experiences is nonsense! If I say "I wonder at the existence of the world" I am misusing language. Let me explain this: It has a perfectly good and clear sense to say that I wonder at something being the case; we all understand what it means to say that I wonder at the size of a dog which is bigger than any one I have ever seen before or at any thing which, in the common sense of the word, is extraordinary. In every such case I wonder at something being the case which I *could* conceive *not* to be the case. I wonder at the size of this dog because I could conceive of a dog of another, namely the ordinary size, at which I should not wonder. To say "I wonder at such and such being the case" has only sense if I can imagine it not to be the case. In this sense one can wonder at the existence of, say, a house when one sees it and has not visited it for a long time and has imagined that it had been pulled down in the meantime. But it is nonsense to say that I wonder at the existence of the world, because I cannot imagine it not existing. I could of course wonder at the world round me being as it is. If for instance I had this experience while looking into the blue sky, I could wonder at the sky being blue as opposed to the case when it's clouded. But that's not what I mean. I am wondering at the sky being *whatever it is*. One might be tempted to say that what I am wondering at is a tautology, namely at the sky being blue or not blue. But then it's just nonsense to say that one is wondering at a tautology. Now the same applies to the other experience which I have mentioned, the experience of absolute safety. We all know what it means in ordinary life to be safe. I am safe in my room, when I cannot be run over by an omnibus. I am safe if I have had whooping cough and cannot therefore get it again. To be safe essentially means that it is physically impossible that certain things should happen to me and therefore it's nonsense to say that I am safe *whatever* happens. Again this is a misuse of the word "safe" as the other example was of a misuse of the word "existence" or "wondering." Now I want to impress on you that a certain characteristic misuse of our language runs through *all* ethical and religious expressions. All these expressions *seem*, prima facie, to be just *similes*. Thus it seems that when we are using the word *right* in an ethical sense, although what we mean is not right in its trivial sense, it's something similar, and when we say "This is a good fellow," although the word good here doesn't mean what it means in the sentence "This is a good football player" there seems to be some similarity. And when we say "This man's life was valuable" we don't mean it in the same sense in which we would speak of some valuable jewelry but there seems to be some sort of analogy. Now all religious terms seem in this sense to be used as similes or allegorically. For when we speak of God and that he sees everything, and when we kneel and pray to him, all our terms and actions seem to be parts of a great and elaborate allegory which represents him as a human being of great power whose grace we try to win, etc., etc. But this allegory also describes the experience which I have just referred to. For the first of them is, I believe, exactly what

people were referring to when they said that God had created the world; and the experience of absolute safety has been described by saying that we feel safe in the hands of God. A third experience of the same kind is that of feeling guilty and again this was described by the phrase that God disapproves of our conduct. Thus in ethical and religious language we seem constantly to be using similes. But a simile must be the simile for *something*. And if I can describe a fact by means of a simile I must also be able to drop the simile and to describe the facts without it. Now in our case as soon as we try to drop the simile and simply to state the facts which stand behind it, we find that there are no such facts. And so, what at first appeared to be a simile now seems to be mere nonsense. Now the three experiences which I have mentioned to you (and I could have added others) seem to those who have experienced them, for instance to me, to have in some sense an intrinsic, absolute value. But when I say they are experiences, surely, they are facts; they have taken place then and there, lasted a certain definite time and consequently are describable. And so from what I have said some minutes ago I must admit it is nonsense to say that they have absolute value. And I will make my point still more acute by saying "It is the paradox that an experience, a fact, should seem to have supernatural value." Now there is a way in which I would be tempted to meet this paradox. Let me first consider, again, our first experience of wondering at the existence of the world and let me describe it in a slightly different way; we all know what in ordinary life would be called a miracle. It obviously is simply an event the like of which we have never yet seen. Now suppose such an event happened. Take the case that one of you suddenly grew a lion's head and began to roar. Certainly that would be as extraordinary a thing as I can imagine. Now whenever we should have recovered from our surprise, what I would suggest would be to fetch a doctor and have the case scientifically investigated and if it were not for hurting him I would have him vivisected. And where would the miracle have got to? For it is clear that when we look at it in this way everything miraculous has disappeared; unless what we mean by this term is merely that a fact has not yet been explained by science which again means that we have hitherto failed to group this fact with others in a scientific system. This shows that it is absurd to say "Science has proved that there are no miracles." The truth is that the scientific way of looking at a fact is not the way to look at it as a miracle. For imagine whatever fact you may; it is not in itself miraculous in the absolute sense of that term. For we see now that we have been using the word "miracle" in a relative and an absolute sense. And I will now describe the experience of wondering at the existence of the world by saying: it is the experience of seeing the world as a miracle. Now I am tempted to say that the right expression in language for the miracle of the existence of the world, though it is not any proposition *in* language, is the existence of language itself. But what then does it mean to be aware of this miracle at some times and not at other times? For all I have said by shifting the expression of the miraculous from an expression *by means of* language to the expression *by the existence* of language, all I have said is again that we cannot express what we want to express and that all we *say* about the absolute miraculous remains nonsense. Now the answer to all this will seem perfectly clear to many of you. You will say: Well, if certain experiences constantly tempt us to attribute a quality to them which we call absolute or ethical value and importance, this simply shows that by these words we *don't* mean nonsense, that after all what we mean by saying that an experience has absolute value *is just a fact like other facts* and that all it comes to is that we have not yet succeeded in finding the correct logical analysis of what we mean by our ethical and religious expressions. Now when this is urged against me I at once see clearly, as it were in a flash of light, not only that no decription that I can think of would do to describe what I mean by absolute value, but that I would reject every significant description that anybody could possibly suggest, *ab initio*, on the ground of its significance. That is to say: I see now that these nonsensical expressions were not nonsensical because I had not yet found the correct expressions, but that their nonsensicality was their very essence. For all I wanted to do with them was just *to go beyond* the world and that is to say beyond significant language. My whole tendency and I believe the tendency of all men who ever tried to write or talk Ethics or Religion was to run against the boundaries of language. This running against the walls of our cage is perfectly, absolutely hopeless. Ethics so far as it springs from the desire to say something about the ultimate meaning of life, the absolute good, the absolute valuable, can be no science. What it says does not add to our knowledge in any sense. But it is a document of a tendency in the human mind which I personally cannot help respecting deeply and I would not for my life ridicule it.

COMMENT

"A Lecture on Ethics" was delivered in 1929 or 1930. This was a period when Wittgenstein's thinking was in a transitional stage. He was moving away from the *Tractatus Logico-Philosophicus* toward the *Philosophical Investigations*. A brief examination of these two works may help us to understand the Lecture.

Sense versus Nonsense

The early Wittgenstein, as represented by the *Tractatus Logico-Philosophicus*, argued that to understand a sentence with factual import one must know to what each word refers. This might be called "the object-designation theory of meaning." A sentence is not only meaningful but true if (1) its words match up with the corresponding objects, and (2) the sentence is so constructed that it represents, by analogy of structure, the actual relationship of objects. If our pretended truth, when tested by observation or experiment, has no anchorage in fact, it is nothing but disguised gibberish. However, Wittgenstein did not agree with the "logical positivists," such as Rudolph Carnap and A. J. Ayer, that metaphysical statements are wholly nonsensical. "There is indeed the inexpressible," wrote Wittgenstein. "This *shows* itself; it is the mystical" (6.522). The thought seems to be that we may have "metaphysical insights that cannot be stated in language, but *if* they could be, they would be true insights and not mere muddles or expressions of feelings."[1] Nevertheless, the logical positivists regarded Wittgenstein as a valiant ally in dismissing most of the traditional problems of philosophy as nonsensical.

The late Wittgenstein, in the *Philosophical Investigations*, has a very different conception of meaning. He recognizes that there are many different kinds of meaning and many different ways of making sense. There are "countless different kinds of use of what we call 'symbols,' 'words,' 'sentences'" (Sec. 23). To understand the meaning is to be able to use the mode of expression in accordance with the customary social practice. He called such a customary practice a "language-game," and he contended that language-games vary fundamentally from one "form of life" to another. If the linguistic expression turns out to be an apt tool within

[1] Norman Malcolm, "Wittgenstein," *The Encyclopedia of Philosophy* (New York: The Macmillan Company and The Free Press, 1967), VIII, p. 334.

the context of its language-game, it is meaningful. This theory—that "the meaning is the use"—implies that useless discourse is gibberish.

Traditional philosophy, especially metaphysics, nearly always appears in the *Philosophical Investigations*, as a kind of false puzzlement which holds the philosopher "captive." "What *we* do," says Wittgenstein, "is to bring words back from their metaphysical to their *everyday* uses." The puzzlement can often be eliminated by a careful analysis of ordinary language as actually used in its appropriate "language-game."

Here, then, is a basic issue that applies to ethical as well as other discourse: Is it possible to talk good sense in areas that Wittgenstein (either for the reasons given in the early *Tractatus* or in the late *Investigations*) labels nonsense?

Ideal versus Ordinary Language

Throughout his career Wittgenstein was concerned with the adequacy of language. In the beginning he was searching, like the logical positivists, for a language that would be scientifically exact. In the *Investigations*, he maintained that "philosophy is a battle against the bewitchment of our intelligence by means of language" (Sec. 109), but he felt that there was little need for a highly refined and technical language. "Ordinary language is all right," he said (*Blue Book*, p. 28).

This contrast between his earlier and his later views has stirred up a great deal of controversy. Another famous analytical philosopher, J. L. Austin, defends the later view:

> . . . Our common stock of words embodies all the distinctions men have found worth drawing, and the connexions they have found worth making, in the lifetimes of many generations: these surely are likely to be more numerous, more sound, since they have stood up to the long test of the survival of the fittest, and more subtle, at least in all ordinary and reasonably practical matters, than any that you or I are likely to think up in our arm-chairs on an afternoon—the most favoured alternative method.[2]

Bertrand Russell, in sharp contrast, has written a witty and blistering attack on "the cult of ordinary language," declaring that he is "totally unable" to accept the view that " the language of daily life, with words used in their ordinary meanings, suffices for philosophy." He charges that this view "makes philosophy trivial" by encouraging endless dispute over "what silly people mean when they say silly things," that it excuses "ignorance of mathematics, physics, and neurology in those who have had only a classical education," and that "it makes almost inevitable the perpetuation among philosophers of the muddleheadedness they

---

[2] J. L. Austin, *Philosophical Papers* (Oxford: Clarendon Press, 1961), p. 129.

have taken over from common sense." "No one wants to alter the language of common sense," he writes, "any more than we wish to give up talking of the sun rising and setting. But astronomers find a different language better, and I contend that a different language is better in philosophy."[3] In this clash between the partizans of "ordinary language philosophy" and their opponents there is another issue that has agitated the philosophical world. This issue is applicable to ethics. Should the philosopher in wrestling with ethical questions seek a language of high precision that may include new and technical terms, or should he employ the language of ordinary men and women as they go about their daily affairs?

Two Other Points of Controversy

I shall barely mention two other points that have aroused a great deal of argument. First, there is the question of private versus public language. Wittgenstein, in the *Philosophical Investigations*, has a famous argument against the possibility of a purely private language (i.e., private to one person) which turns on the fact that such a language would have no publicly established rules for its use. Language, he argues, requires rules; following a rule is a social practice, and therefore one cannot follow a rule "privately" (Sec. 202). There is also an anti-introspectionist and behavioristic trend in his contention that language cannot be based upon "private" mental states. In opposition one can maintain that some language uses reach out into what is felt but not yet publicly articulated and capture it for the realm of the sayable. The highly creative individual, gifted with imagination, senses the possibilities of new modes of expression, and draws upon his private insights to break through the limits of the inexpressible.

Second, there is the question of "essences" versus "family resemblances." In a famous passage, Wittgenstein argues that we can find no mark or characteristic, no "essence," that is common to all games—nothing that would permit us to encompass all games in a formula or definition. We see only "a complicated network of similarities overlapping and criss-crossing," which he characterizes as "family resemblances." This doctrine applies to innumerable things besides games. Almost any word that we might try to define, such as "good" or "right," covers a great multiplicity of variations, and it therefore stands for no single essence and its meaning shifts as the contexts of life alter. In sharp contrast, the traditional theory, which stems from Socrates and Plato, is that whenever there is a class of things, such as right acts, there is a common essence or "universal" that is expressed in a sound definition.

We can imagine Plato arguing that games *do* have something in common. A game is an activity that can evoke an absorbing nonpractical interest in participant or spectator. If a so-called "game" wholly lacked this capacity it should

---

[3] Bertrand Russell, "The Cult of 'Common Usage,'" *Portraits from Memory* (London: George Allen and Unwin, 1956), pp. 154–159.

not be called a "game." (Perhaps the reader would prefer some other definition, but the point is that "game" *can* be defined.) Plato might add that some words can be defined very precisely—"circle," as a geometer defines it, would be an example. The fact that particular objects are more or less circular would not invalidate the definition. So likewise an ethical definition might constitute a standard that particular acts or states more or less approximate. The reader may wish to consider whether Plato or Wittgenstein has the sounder view.

Application to "A Lecture on Ethics"

In the *Tractatus* Wittgenstein contended that ethical terms and propositions, unless used in a merely descriptive way to characterize behavior, are meaningless:

> 6.41. . . . In the world everything is as it is and happens as it does happen. *In* it there is no value. . . .
> 6.42. Hence also there can be no ethical propositions.

About the time that he delivered his "Lecture on Ethics" he began to rebel against this limitation. "Man has the urge to thrust against the limits of language," he said, and ". . . the tendency, the thrust, *points* to something."[4] In the lecture Wittgenstein seems to be groping toward this "something." All of us try to express judgments of value, and we are unhappy if all such attempts are dismissed as nonsense.

Wittgenstein distinguishes between two different senses in which we use terms such as "right." We can use the word "right," for example, in a relative sense, as when we say that this is the *right* road to reach a certain destination. "Instead of saying 'This is the right way to Granchester,' I could equally well have said, 'This is the right way you have to go if you want to get to Granchester in the shortest time.'" This "if" usage of right is what Kant meant by a "hypothetical imperative." Wittgenstein then asks what could be meant by the expression, "*the* absolutely right road." He answers:

> I think it would be the road which *everybody* on seeing it would, *with logical necessity,* have to go, or be ashamed for not going. And similarly the *absolute good*, if it is a describable state of affairs, would be one which everybody, independent of his tastes and inclinations, would *necessarily* bring about or feel guilty for not bringing about.

This notion of a *moral* necessity (it should not be called logical) which we would be *guilty* not to heed is akin to Kant's concept of a categorical imperative.

[4] Friedrich Waismann, "Notes on Talks with Wittgenstein," *Philosophical Review*, Vol. 74 (1965), p. 12. Conversation with Moritz Schlick, Dec. 30, 1929.

Wittgenstein insists that no facts whatsoever can validate such an imperative. He calls it "supernatural," and compares it with an "absolute miracle." It is as puzzling and unanswerable as the question, "Why is there anything at all rather than nothing?" We may try to give a religious answer to this question, but the answer would be as "supernatural" and "nonsensical" as the attempt to justify the absolute moral imperative. What distinguishes Wittgenstein's position, at this transitional stage of his thinking, from that of the complete sceptic is his unwillingness to consign either ethics or religion to the scrap-heap. He concludes that ethics, in the attempt to deal with absolute values, "does not add to our knowledge in any sense," but that he respects it and would not for his life ridicule it.

Largely through the influence of the later Wittgenstein, analytic philosophy extended itself to include various uses of language, ranging from scientific language at one end of the spectrum to religious and moral language at the other. But common to all forms of analytic philosophy is the contention that philosophy is primarily concerned with clarification. It is not a criticism of life nor an addition to our stock of knowledge. Most of the philosophers we have reviewed in Part Three would regard this limited conception of philosophy as intolerable.

Part Four

SOCIAL PHILOSOPHY

SOCIAL PHILOSOPHY IS not a sharply distinct and separate field. The fundamental issues that divide social philosophers are ultimately metaphysical, epistemological, or ethical. Among the questions debated are the following: What is the basis of political obligation? What is the nature of a good social order? What is right social action? Is the state an organism? Are the actions of government to be justified by reference to the ends of the individual or of society? Does history have a pattern that can be known and predicted? All these questions involve metaphysical, epistemological, or ethical isues.

An example may help to make clear the nature of social philosophy. In his *Discourse on Political Economy,* Rousseau declares:

> The body politic . . . is also a moral being possessed of a will; and this general will, which tends always to the preservation and welfare of the whole and of every part, and is the source of the laws, constitutes for all the members of the State, in their relations to one another and to it, the rule of what is just or unjust.[1]

This sentence is replete with philosophical notions: that the body politic is a moral being; that is possesses a "general will" distinct from the individual wills of its members; that the general will is a *good* will; and that it defines, through the medium of law, what is just and what is unjust in the relations of citizens to one another and to the state. Philosophers, and not social scientists, are best fitted to clarify and criticize such ideas.

[1] *The Social Contract* (New York: Dutton, 1913), p. 253.

The philosophers presented in the following chapters discuss questions of great interest to all students of human affairs. Each represents a social ideal— in the case of Plato, intellectual aristocracy; of Marx, equality and fraternity (a "classless" communism); of Mill, freedom. We have been tempted to include other authors, such as Hobbes on peace and security, Rousseau on democracy, and Kropotkin on cooperative anarchism. Limitations of space have forced us to omit them.

Although we have included some contemporary writers, Kolakowski, Rogers, and Skinner, the reader may feel that we should have included more. It seemed preferable here as in other parts of the book to put the emphasis upon major philosophers even though they belong to the past. In the Comments, however, I have stressed their relation to contemporary issues.

19

Aristocracy

PLATO (428/7–348/7 B.C.)

As a member of one of the most distinguished families in Athens, Plato was in touch with political and social developments from his early childhood. He grew to manhood during the long, turbulent period of the Peloponnesian War, and his mind must have been deeply disturbed by war and revolution. Athens was finally defeated by Sparta when Plato was twenty-three, and he watched the ensuing oligarchical dictatorship, of which his uncle Charmides and his cousin Critias were leaders, with great hope. It soon turned to horror and anger, however, when his old friend Socrates was eventually tried and executed by the restored democratic faction. The shock of this event, occurring when he was just twenty-eight, was the decisive influence upon his entire career. He concluded that good government depends upon the rare union of power and wisdom, and resolved to emulate and so far as possible complete the work of Socrates. Retiring from Athens to Megara, he began to write his famous dialogues which lovingly portray his old master.

He is said to have spent the next ten years traveling in Greece, Italy, Egypt, and Asia Minor. For a time he lived at the court of Dionysius I, the tyrant of Syracuse, whose son-in-law, Dion, became Plato's friend and ardent admirer. At the age of forty he returned to Athens to found the Academy, a school for philosophers, mathematicians, and statesmen. This school was the main center of his interest for the remainder of his long life. In addition to teaching, he continued to write dialogues, which became more technical as he grew older. This quiet, academic life was interrupted in 367 B.C., when he was close on sixty. Dion, his old friend, persuaded him to return to Syracuse as tutor to Dionysius II, a young man of thirty, who had succeeded to the throne. The venture turned out badly. Dionysius and Dion eventually quarreled and Plato went back to Athens. Not easily dismayed, he returned to Syracuse six years later in the hope of remedying the situation—and once again met with broken promises and barely escaped with his life. Then he settled down in the Academy to spend the last years of his life teaching and writing. He died at the age of eighty or eighty-one and, according to Cicero, was hard at work at the very end. Generally considered the greatest of the Greek philosophers, he has exercised an immense influence on the thought and literature of the world ever since his death.

The Republic

Scene: The home of Cephalus, a retired manufacturer living at Piraeus, the harbor town about five miles from Athens.

Characters (in the following sections of the dialogue): Glaucon, Adeimantus, and Socrates, who narrates the entire conversation to an unspecified audience.

[*In the section of the* Republic *preceding our selections, Plato set forth some of the essential premises of his thought. He begins by a refutation of the Sophist theory that moral principles are purely relative; on the contrary, he maintains, they have a rational and absolute basis. Thrasymachus, a Sophist,*

Translated with introduction and notes by Francis MacDonald Cornford, Oxford University Press, London, 1941; New York, 1945. Reprinted by permission. Some of Cornford's footnotes have been omitted. The italicized glosses are his except for those supplied by the present editor and marked by the initials "M. R".

is introduced as a rather cynical advocate of the theory that "just or right means nothing but what is to the interest of the stronger party." This doctrine is similar to Karl Marx's declaration, in the Communist Manifesto, *that "the ruling ideas of every age are the ideas of the ruling class." But Marx looked forward to an all-human morality based upon the eventual achievement of a classless society, whereas Thrasymachus champions the doctrine that right means nothing but the interest of the dominant political force. Through the character of Socrates, Plato advances a number of objections to this theory. He argues that any statesman deserving of the name cares above all for the good of his subjects. The thirst for power results in uncontrolled competition; the wise ruler puts a limit to his personal ambitions. Unbridled power produces strife; true justice promotes harmony and concord. The human soul has its characteristic function, which is not the lust for power or sensual gratification but the subordination of impulse to rational principles of conduct. Plato thus maintains that there are objective principles of morality and justice.*

When Thrasymachus, worsted in the argument, sullenly withdraws, Glaucon and Adeimantus—Plato's elder brothers—step into the discussion. They ask Socrates to criticize a theory which they find both plausible and disturbing—that people prefer a just to an unjust life for reasons of mere expediency. A person, they are inclined to think, would be quite ready to commit injustice if he could escape the penalties. Socrates agrees to carry on the dialogue. M.R.]

The Ring of Gyges

Good, said Glaucon. Listen then, and I will begin with my first point: the nature and origin of justice.

What people say is that to do wrong is, in itself, a desirable thing; on the other hand, it is not at all desirable to suffer wrong, and the harm to the sufferer outweighs the advantage to the doer. Consequently, when men have had a taste of both, those who have not the power to seize the advantage and escape the harm decide that they would be better off if they made a compact neither to do wrong nor to suffer it. Hence they began to make laws and covenants with one another; and whatever the law prescribed they called lawful and right. That is what right or justice is and how it came into existence; it stands half-way between the best thing of all—to do wrong with impunity—and the worst, which is to suffer wrong without the power to retaliate. So justice is accepted as a compromise,

and valued, not as good in itself, but for lack of power to do wrong; no man worthy of the name, who had that power, would ever enter into such a compact with anyone; he would be mad if he did. That, Socrates, is the nature of justice according to this account, and such the circumstances in which it arose.

The next point is that men practise it against the grain, for lack of power to do wrong. How true that is, we shall best see if we imagine two men, one just, the other unjust, given full licence to do whatever they like, and then follow them to observe where each will be led by his desires. We shall catch the just man taking the same road as the unjust; he will be moved by self-interest, the end which it is natural to every creature to pursue as good, until forcibly turned aside by law and custom to respect the principle of equality.

Now, the easiest way to give them that complete liberty of action would be to imagine them possessed of the talisman found by Gyges, the ancestor of the famous Lydian. The story tells how he was a shepherd in the King's service. One day there was a great storm, and the ground where his flock was feeding was rent by an earthquake. Astonished at the sight, he went down into the chasm and saw, among other wonders of which the story tells, a brazen horse, hollow, with windows in its sides. Peering in, he saw a dead body, which seemed to be of more than human size. It was naked save for a gold ring, which he took from the finger and made his way out. When the shepherds met, as they did every month, to send an account to the King of the state of his flocks, Gyges came wearing the ring. As he was sitting with the others, he happened to turn the bezel of the ring inside his hand. At once he became invisible, and his companions, to his surprise, began to speak of him as if he had left them. Then, as he was fingering the ring, he turned the bezel outwards and became visible again. With that, he set about testing the ring to see if it really had this power, and always with the same result: according as he turned the bezel inside or out he vanished and reappeared. After this discovery he contrived to be one of the messengers sent to the court. There he seduced the Queen, and with her help murdered the King and seized the throne.

Now suppose there were two such magic rings, and one were given to the just man, the other to the unjust. No one, it is commonly believed, would have such iron strength of mind as to stand fast in doing right or keep his hands off other men's goods, when he could go to the market-place and fearlessly help himself to anything he wanted, enter houses and sleep with any woman he chose, set prisoners free and kill men at his pleasure, and in a word go about among men with the powers of a god. He would behave no better than the other; both would take the same course. Surely this would be strong proof that men do right only under compulsion; no individual thinks of it as good for him personally, since he does wrong whenever he finds he has the power. Every man believes that wrongdoing pays him personally much better, and, according to this theory, that is the truth. Granted full licence

to do as he liked, people would think him a miserable fool if they found him refusing to wrong his neighbours or to touch their belongings, though in public they would keep up a pretence of praising his conduct, for fear of being wronged themselves. So much for that.

Finally, if we are really to judge between the two lives, the only way is to contrast the extremes of justice and injustice. We can best do that by imagining our two men to be perfect types, and crediting both to the full with the qualities they need for their respective ways of life. To begin with the unjust man: he must be like any consummate master of a craft, a physician or a captain, who, knowing just what his art can do, never tries to do more, and can always retrieve a false step. The unjust man, if he is to reach perfection, must be equally discreet in his criminal attempts, and he must not be found out, or we shall think him a bungler; for the highest pitch of injustice is to seem just when you are not. So we must endow our man with the full complement of injustice; we must allow him to have secured a spotless reputation for virtue while committing the blackest crimes; he must be able to retrieve any mistake, to defend himself with convincing eloquence if his misdeeds are denounced, and, when force is required, to bear down all opposition by his courage and strength and by his command of friends and money.

Now set beside this paragon the just man in his simplicity and nobleness, one who, in Aeschylus' words, "would be, not seem, the best." There must, indeed, be no such seeming; for if his character were apparent, his reputation would bring him honours and rewards, and then we should not know whether it was for their sake that he was just or for justice's sake alone. He must be stripped of everything but justice, and denied every advantage the other enjoyed. Doing no wrong, he must have the worst reputation for wrong-doing, to test whether his virtue is proof against all that comes of having a bad name; and under this lifelong imputation of wickedness, let him hold on his course of justice unwavering to the point of death. And so, when the two men have carried their justice and injustice to the last extreme, we may judge which is the happier.

My dear Glaucon, I exclaimed, how vigorously you scour these two characters clean for inspection, as if you were burnishing a couple of statues![1]

I am doing my best, he answered. Well, given two such characters, it is not hard, I fancy, to describe the sort of life that each of them may expect; and if the description sounds rather coarse, take it as coming from those who cry up the merits of injustice rather than from me. They will tell you that our just man will be thrown into prison, scourged and racked, will have his eyes burnt out, and, after every kind of torment, be impaled. That will teach him how much better it is to seem virtuous than to be so. In fact those lines of Aeschylus I quoted are more fitly applied to the unjust man, who, they say, is a realist and does not live for appearances: "he would be, not seem" unjust,

. . . reaping the harvest sown
In those deep furrows of the thoughtful heart
Whence wisdom springs.

With his reputation for virtue, he will hold offices of state, ally himself by marriage to any family he may choose, become a partner in any business, and, having no scruples about being dishonest, turn all these advantages to profit. If he is involved in a lawsuit, public or private, he will get the better of his opponents, grow rich on the proceeds, and be able to help his friends and harm his enemies. Finally, he can make sacrifices to the gods and dedicate offerings with due magnificence, and, being in a much better position than the just man to serve the gods as well as his chosen friends, he may reasonably hope to stand higher in the favour of heaven. So much better, they say, Socrates, is the life prepared for the unjust by gods and men. [*Socrates sees no way of immediately refuting the theory advanced by Glaucon and suggests that an answer can best be found if the argument is projected from the level of the individual to that of the community. He proposes to study the origin and nature of the state, in the hope of thereby discovering the nature of justice and other virtues. —M.R.*]

The Virtues in the State

[*Plato's original aim in constructing an ideal state was to find in it justice*

---

[1] At Elis and Athens officials called *phaidryntai,* 'burnishers,' had the duty of cleaning cult statues (A. B. Cook, *Zeus,* iii. 967). At 612 c, where this passage is recalled, it is admitted to be an extravagant supposition, that the just and unjust should exchange reputations.

exemplified on a larger scale than in the individual. Assuming that four cardinal qualities make up the whole of virtue, he now asks wherein consist the wisdom, courage, temperance, and justice of the state, or, in other words, of the individuals composing the state in their public capacity as citizens.

Wisdom in the conduct of state affairs will be the practical prudence or good counsel of the deliberative body. Only the philosophic Rulers will possess the necessary insight into what is good for the community as a whole. They will have "right belief" grounded on immediate knowledge of the meaning of goodness in all its forms. The Auxiliaries will have only a right belief accepted on the authority of the Rulers. Their functions will be executive, not deliberative.

The Courage of the state will obviously be manifested in the fighting force. Socrates had defined courage as knowledge of what really is, or is not, to be feared, and he had regarded it as an inseparable part of all virtue, which consists in knowing what things are really good or evil. If the only real evil is moral evil, then poverty, suffering, and all the so-called evils that others can inflict on us, including death itself, are not to be feared, since, if they are met in the right spirit, they cannot make us worse men. This knowledge only the philosophic Rulers will possess to the full. The courage of the Auxiliaries will consist in the power of holding fast to the conviction implanted by their education.

Temperance is not, as we might expect, the peculiar virtue of the lowest order in the state. As self-mastery, it

means the subordination of the lower elements to the higher; but government must be with the willing consent of the governed, and temperance will include the unanimous agreement of all classes as to who should rule and who obey.[2] It is consequently like a harmony pervading and uniting all parts of the whole, a principle of solidarity. In the Laws, *which stresses the harmonious union of different and complementary elements, this virtue overshadows even* Justice.

Justice is the complementary principle of differentiation, keeping the parts distinct. It has been before us all through the construction of the state since it first appeared on the economic level as the division of labor based on natural aptitudes. "Doing one's own work" now has the larger sense of a concentration on one's peculiar duty or function in the community. This conception of "doing and possessing what properly belongs to one" is wide enough to cover the justice of the law-courts, assuring to each man his due rights. Injustice will mean invasion and encroachment upon the rights and duties of others.

The virtue described in this chapter is what Plato calls "civic" or "popular" virtue. Except in the Rulers, it is not directly based on that ultimate knowledge of good and evil which is wisdom, to be attained only at the end of the higher education of the philosopher.]

So now at last, son of Ariston, said I, your commonwealth is established. The

---

[2] At *Statesman* 276 E the true king is distinguished from the despot by the voluntary submission of his subjects to his rule.

next thing is to bring to bear upon it all the light you can get from any quarter, with the help of your brother and Polemarchus and all the rest, in the hope that we may see where justice is to be found in it and where injustice, how they differ, and which of the two will bring happiness to its possessor, no matter whether gods and men see that he has it or not.

Nonsense, said Glaucon; you promised to conduct the search yourself, because it would be a sin not to uphold justice by every means in your power.

That is true; I must do as you say, but you must all help.

We will.

I suspect, then, we may find what we are looking for in this way. I take it that our state, having been founded and built up on the right lines, is good in the complete sense of the word.

It must be.

Obviously, then, it is wise, brave, temperate, and just.

Obviously.

Then if we find some of these qualities in it, the remainder will be the one we have not found. It is as if we were looking somewhere for one of any four things: if we detected that one immediately, we should be satisfied; whereas if we recognized the other three first, that would be enough to indicate the thing we wanted; it could only be the remaining one. So here we have four qualities. Had we not better follow that method in looking for the one we want?

Surely.

To begin then: the first quality to come into view in our state seems to be its wisdom; and there appears to be something odd about this quality.[3]

What is there odd about it?

I think the state we have described really has wisdom; for it will be prudent in counsel, won't it?

Yes.

And prudence in counsel is clearly a form of knowledge; good counsel cannot be due to ignorance and stupidity.

Clearly.

But there are many and various kinds of knowledge in our commonwealth. There is the knowledge possessed by the carpenters or the smiths, and the knowledge how to raise crops. Are we to call the state wise and prudent on the strength of these forms of skill?

No; they would only make it good at furniture-making or working in copper or agriculture.

Well then, is there any form of knowledge, possessed by some among the citizens of our new-founded commonwealth, which will enable it to take thought, not for some particular interest, but for the best possible conduct of the state as a whole in its internal and external relations?

Yes, there is.

What is it, and where does it reside?

It is precisely that art of guardianship which resides in those Rulers whom we just now called Guardians in the full sense.

And what would you call the state on the strength of that knowledge?

Prudent and truly wise.

And do you think there will be more

---

[3] Because the wisdom of the whole resides in the smallest part, as explained below.

or fewer of these genuine Guardians in our state than there will be smiths?

Far fewer.

Fewer, in fact, than any of those other groups who are called after the kind of skill they possess?

Much fewer.

So, if a state is constituted on natural principles, the wisdom it possesses as a whole will be due to the knowledge residing in the smallest part, the one which takes the lead and governs the rest. Such knowledge is the only kind that deserves the name of wisdom, and it appears to be ordained by nature that the class privileged to possess it should be the smallest of all.

Quite true.

Here then we have more or less made out one of our four qualities and its seat in the structure of the commonwealth.

To my satisfaction, at any rate.

Next there is courage. It is not hard to discern that quality or the part of the community in which it resides so as to entitle the whole to be called brave.

Why do you say so?

Because anyone who speaks of a state as either brave or cowardly can only be thinking of that part of it which takes the field and fights in its defence; the reason being, I imagine, that the character of the state is not determined by the bravery or cowardice of the other parts.

No.

Courage, then, is another quality which a community owes to a certain part of itself. And its being brave will mean that, in this part, it possesses the power of preserving, in all circum-

stances, a conviction about the sort of things that it is right to be afraid of—the conviction implanted by the education which the law-giver has established. Is not that what you mean by courage?

I do not quite understand. Will you say it again?

I am saying that courage means preserving something.

Yes, but what?

The conviction, inculcated by lawfully established education, about the sort of things which may rightly be feared. When I added "in all circumstances," I meant preserving it always and never abandoning it, whether under the influence of pain or of pleasure, of desire or of fear. If you like, I will give an illustration.

Please do.

You know how dyers who want wool to take a purple dye, first select the white wool from among all the other colors, next treat it very carefully to make it take the dye in its full brilliance, and only then dip it in the vat. Dyed in that way, wool gets a fast color, which no washing, even with soap, will rob of its brilliance; whereas if they choose wool of any color but white, or if they neglect to prepare it, you know what happens.

Yes, it looks washed-out and ridiculous.

That illustrates the result we were doing our best to achieve when we were choosing our fighting men and training their minds and bodies. Our only purpose was to contrive influences whereby they might take the color of our institutions like a dye, so that, in virtue of having both the right temperament and the right education, their convictions about what ought to be feared and on all other subjects might be indelibly fixed, never to be washed out by pleasure and pain, desire and fear, solvents more terribly effective than all the soap and fuller's earth in the world. Such a power of constantly preserving, in accordance with our institutions, the right conviction about the things which ought, or ought not, to be feared, is what I call courage. That is my position, unless you have some objection to make.

None at all, he replied; if the belief were such as might be found in a slave or an animal—correct, but not produced by education—you would hardly describe it as in accordance with our institutions, and you would give it some other name than courage.

Quite true.

Then I accept your account of courage.

You will do well to accept it, at any rate as applying to the courage of the ordinary citizen;[4] if you like we will go into it more fully some other time. At present we are in search of justice, rather than of courage; and for that purpose we have said enough.

I quite agree.

Two qualities, I went on, still remain to be made out in our state, temperance and the object of our whole inquiry, justice. Can we discover justice without troubling ourselves further about temperance?

I do not know, and I would rather not have justice come to light first, if

that means that we should not go on to consider temperance. So if you want to please me, take temperance first.

Of course I have every wish to please you.

Do go on then.

I will. At first sight, temperance seems more like some sort of concord or harmony than the other qualities did.

How so?

Temperance surely means a kind of orderliness, a control of certain pleasures and appetites. People use the expression, "master of oneself," whatever that means, and various other phrases that point the same way.

Quite true.

Is not "master of oneself" an absurd expression? A man who was master of himself would presumably be also subject to himself, and the subject would be master; for all these terms apply to the same person.

No doubt.

I think, however, the phrase means that within the man himself, in his soul, there is a better part and a worse; and that he is his own master when the part which is better by nature has the worse under its control. It is certainly a term of praise; whereas it is considered a disgrace, when, through bad breeding or bad company, the better part is overwhelmed by the worse, like a small force outnumbered by a multitude. A man in that condition is called a slave to himself and intemperate.

Probably that is what is meant.

Then now look at our newly founded state and you will find one of these two conditions realized there. You will agree that it deserves to be called mas-

---

[4] As distinct from the perfect courage of the philosophic Ruler, based on immediate knowledge of values.

ter of itself, if temperance and self-mastery exist where the better part rules the worse.

Yes, I can see that is true.

It is also true that the great mass of multifarious appetites and pleasures and pains will be found to occur chiefly in children and women and slaves, and, among free men so called, in the inferior multitude; whereas the simple and moderate desires which, with the aid of reason and right belief, are guided by reflection, you will find only in a few, and those with the best inborn dispositions and the best educated.

Yes, certainly.

Do you see that this state of things will exist in your commonwealth, where the desires of the inferior multitude will be controlled by the desires and wisdom of the superior few? Hence, if any society can be called master of itself and in control of pleasures and desires, it will be ours.

Quite so.

On all these grounds, then, we may describe it as temperate. Furthermore, in our state, if anywhere, the governors and the governed will share the same conviction on the question who ought to rule.[5] Don't you think so?

I am quite sure of it.

Then, if that is their state of mind, in which of the two classes of citizens will temperance reside—in the governors or in the governed?

In both, I suppose.

So we were not wrong in divining a

resemblance between temperance and some kind of harmony. Temperance is not like courage and wisdom, which made the state wise and brave by residing each in one particular part. Temperance works in a different way; it extends throughout the whole gamut of the state, producing a consonance of all its elements from the weakest to the strongest as measured by any standard you like to take—wisdom, bodily strength, numbers, or wealth. So we are entirely justified in identifying with temperance this unanimity or harmonious agreement between the naturally superior and inferior elements on the question which of the two should govern, whether in the state or in the individual.

I fully agree.

Good, said I. We have discovered in our commonwealth three out of our four qualities, to the best of our present judgment. What is the remaining one, required to make up its full complement of goodness? For clearly this will be justice.

Clearly.

Now is the moment, then, Glaucon, for us to keep the closest watch, like huntsmen standing round a covert, to make sure that justice does not slip through and vanish undetected. It must certainly be somewhere hereabouts; so keep your eyes open for a view of the quarry, and if you see it first, give me the alert.

I wish I could, he answered; but you will do better to give me a lead and not count on me for more than eyes to see what you show me.

Pray for luck, then, and follow me.

[5] This principle of freedom—government with consent of the governed—is thus recognized. The "democratic" freedom to "do whatever you like" is condemned in later chapters.

The thicket looks rather impenetrable, said I; too dark for it to be easy to start up the game. However, we must push on.

Of course we must.

Here I gave the view halloo. Glaucon, I exclaimed, I believe we are on the track and the quarry is not going to escape us altogether.

That is good news.

Really, I said, we have been extremely stupid. All this time the thing has been under our very noses from the start, and we never saw it. We have been as absurd as a person who hunts for something he has all the time got in his hand. Instead of looking at the thing, we have been staring into the distance. No doubt that is why it escaped us.

What do you mean?

I believe we have been talking about the thing all this while without ever understanding that we were giving some sort of account of it.

Do come to the point. I am all ears.

Listen, then, and judge whether I am right. You remember how, when we first began to establish our commonwealth and several times since, we have laid down, as a universal principle, that everyone ought to perform the one function in the community for which his nature best suited him. Well, I believe that that principle, or some form of it, is justice.

We certainly laid that down.

Yes, and surely we have often heard people say that justice means minding one's own business and not meddling with other men's concerns; and we have often said so ourselves.

We have.

Well, my friend, it may be that this minding of one's own business, when it takes a certain form, is actually the same thing as justice. Do you know what makes me think so?

No, tell me.

I think that this quality which makes it possible for the three we have already considered, wisdom, courage, and temperance, to take their place in the commonwealth, and so long as it remains present secures their continuance, must be the remaining one. And we said that, when three of the four were found, the one left over would be justice.

It must be so.

Well now, if we had to decide which of these qualities will contribute most to the excellence of our commonwealth, it would be hard to say whether it was the unanimity of rules and subjects, or the soldier's fidelity to the established conviction about what is, or is not, to be feared, or the watchful intelligence of the Rulers; or whether its excellence were not above all due to the observance by everyone, child or woman, slave or freeman or artisan, ruler or ruled, of this principle that one should do his own proper work without interfering with others.

It would be hard to decide, no doubt.

It seems, then, that this principle can at any rate claim to rival wisdom, temperance, and courage as conducing to the excellence of a state. And would you not say that the only possible competitor of these qualities must be justice?

Yes, undoubtedly.

Here is another thing which points to the same conclusion. The judging of law-suits is a duty that you will lay upon your Rulers, isn't it?

Of course.

And the chief aim of their decisions will be that neither party shall have what belongs to another or be deprived of what is his own.

Yes.

Because that is just?

Yes.

So here again justice admittedly means that a man should possess and concern himself with what properly belongs to him.[6]

True.

Again, do you agree with me that no great harm would be done to the community by a general interchange of most forms of work, the carpenter and the cobbler exchanging their positions and their tools and taking on each other's jobs, or even the same man undertaking both?

Yes, there would not be much harm in that.

But I think you will also agree that another kind of interchange would be disastrous. Suppose, for instance, someone whom nature designed to be an artisan or tradesman should be emboldened by some advantage, such as wealth or command of votes or bodily strength, to try to enter the order of fighting men; or some member of that order should aspire, beyond his merits, to a seat in the council-chamber of the Guardians. Such interference and exchange of social positions and tools, or the attempt to combine all these forms of work in the same person, would be fatal to the commonwealth.

Most certainly.

[6] Here the legal conception of justice is connected with its moral significance.

Where there are three orders, then, any plurality of functions or shifting from one order to another is not merely utterly harmful to the community, but one might fairly call it the extreme of wrongdoing. And you will agree that to do the greatest of wrongs to one's own community is injustice.

Surely.

This, then, is injustice. And, conversely, let us repeat that when each order—tradesman, Auxiliary, Guardian—keeps to its own proper business in the commonwealth and does its own work, that is justice and what makes a just society.

I entirely agree.

The Three Parts of the Soul

[*It has been shown that justice in the state means that the three chief social functions—deliberative and governing, executive, and productive—are kept distinct and rightly performed. Since the qualities of a community are those of the component individuals, we may expect to find three corresponding elements in the individual soul. All three will be present in every soul; but the structure of society is based on the fact that they are developed to different degrees in different types of character.*

The existence of three elements or "parts" of the soul is established by an analysis of the conflict of motives. A simple case is the thirsty man's appetite for drink, held in check by the rational reflection that to drink will be bad for him. That two distinct elements must be at work here follows from the general principle that the same thing cannot act or be affected in two opposite ways at the same time. By "thirst" is meant simply the bare craving for drink; it must not be confused with a desire for some good (e.g., health or pleasure) expected as a consequence of drinking. This simple craving says, "Drink"; Reason says, "Do not drink": the contradiction shows that two elements are at work.

A third factor is the "spirited" element, akin to our "sense of honor," manifested in indignation, which takes the side of reason against appetite, but cannot be identified with reason, since it is found in children and animals and it may be rebuked by reason.

This analysis is not intended as a complete outline of psychology; that could be reached only by following "a longer road." It is concerned with the factors involved in moral behavior. . . .]

The Virtues in the Individual

[*The virtues in the state were the qualities of the citizen, as such, considered as playing the special part in society for which he was qualified by the predominance in his nature of the philosophic, the pugnacious, or the commercial spirit. But all three elements exist in every individual, who is thus a replica of society in miniature. In the perfect man reason will rule, with the spirited element as its auxiliary, over the bodily appetites. Self-control or temperance will be a condition of internal harmony, all the parts being content with their legitimate satisfactions. Justice finally appears, no longer only as a matter of external behavior toward others, but as an internal order of the soul, from which right behavior will* necessarily follow. Injustice is the opposite state of internal discord and faction. To ask whether justice or injustice pays the better is now seen to be as absurd as to ask whether health is preferable to disease.]

And so, after a stormy passage, we have reached the land. We are fairly agreed that the same three elements exist alike in the state and in the individual soul.

That is so.

Does it not follow at once that state and individual will be wise or brave by virtue of the same element in each and in the same way? Both will possess in the same manner any quality that makes for excellence.

That must be true.

Then it applies to justice: we shall conclude that a man is just in the same way that a state was just. And we have surely not forgotten that justice in the state meant that each of the three orders in it was doing its own proper work. So we may henceforth bear in mind that each one of us likewise will be a just person, fulfilling his proper function, only if the several parts of our nature fulfill theirs.

Certainly.

And it will be the business of reason to rule with wisdom and forethought on behalf of the entire soul; while the spirited element ought to act as its subordinate and ally. The two will be brought into accord, as we said earlier, by that combination of mental and bodily training which will tune up one string of the instrument and relax the other, nourishing the reasoning part on the study of noble literature and allaying the other's wildness by harmony and rhythm. When both have been thus nurtured and trained to know their own true functions, they must be set in command over the appetites, which form the greater part of each man's soul and are by nature insatiably covetous. They must keep watch lest this part, by battening on the pleasures that are called bodily, should grow so great and powerful that it will no longer keep to its own work, but will try to enslave the others and usurp a dominion to which it has no right, thus turning the whole of life upside down. At the same time, those two together will be the best of guardians for the entire soul and for the body against all enemies from without: the one will take counsel, while the other will do battle, following its ruler's commands and by its own bravery giving effect to the ruler's designs.

Yes, that is all true.

And so we call an individual brave in virtue of this spirited part of his nature, when, in spite of pain or pleasure, it holds fast to the injunctions of reason about what he ought or ought not to be afraid of.

True.

And wise in virtue of that small part which rules and issues these injunctions, possessing as it does the knowledge of what is good for each of the three elements and for all of them in common.

Certainly.

And, again, temperate by reason of the unanimity and concord of all three, when there is no internal conflict between the ruling element and its two subjects, but all are agreed that reason should be ruler.

Yes, that is an exact account of temperance, whether in the state or in the individual.

Finally, a man will be just by observing the principle we have so often stated.

Necessarily.

Now is there any indistinctness in our vision of justice, that might make it seem somehow different from what we found it to be in the state?

I don't think so.

Because, if we have any lingering doubt, we might make sure by comparing it with some commonplace notions. Suppose, for instance, that a sum of money were entrusted to our state or to an individual of corresponding character and training, would anyone imagine that such a person would be specially likely to embezzle it?

No.

And would he not be incapable of sacrilege and theft, or of treachery to friend or country; never false to an oath or any other compact; the last to be guilty of adultery or of neglecting parents or the due service of the gods?

Yes.

And the reason for all this is that each part of his nature is exercising its proper function, of ruling or of being ruled.

Yes, exactly.

Are you satisfied, then, that justice is the power which produces states or individuals of whom that is true, or must we look further?

There is no need; I am quite satisfied.

And so our dream has come true—I mean the inkling we had that, by some happy chance, we had lighted upon a rudimentary form of justice from the very moment when we set about founding our commonwealth. Our principle that the born shoemaker or carpenter had better stick to his trade turns out to have been an adumbration of justice; and that is why it has helped us. But in reality justice, though evidently analogous to this principle, is not a matter of external behavior, but of the inward self and of attending to all that is, in the fullest sense, a man's proper concern. The just man does not allow the several elements in his soul to usurp one another's functions; he is indeed one who sets his house in order, by self-mastery and discipline coming to be at peace with himself, and bringing into tune those three parts, like the terms in the proportion of a musical scale, the highest and lowest notes and the mean between them, with all the intermediate intervals. Only when he has linked these parts together in well-tempered harmony and has made himself one man instead of many, will he be ready to go about whatever he may have to do, whether it be making money and satisfying bodily wants, or business transactions, or the affairs of state. In all these fields when he speaks of just and honorable conduct, he will mean the behavior that helps to produce and to preserve this habit of mind; and by wisdom he will mean the knowledge which presides over such conduct. Any action which tends to break down this habit will be for him unjust; and the notions governing it he will call ignorance and folly.

That is perfectly true, Socrates.

Good, said I. I believe we should not be thought altogether mistaken, if we claimed to have discovered the just man and the just state, and wherein their justice consists.

Indeed we should not.

Shall we make that claim, then?

Yes, we will.

So be it, said I. Next, I suppose, we have to consider injustice.

Evidently.

This must surely be a sort of civil strife among the three elements, whereby they usurp and encroach upon one another's functions and some one part of the soul rises up in rebellion against the whole, claiming a supremacy to which it has no right because its nature fits it only to be the servant of the ruling principle. Such turmoil and aberration we shall, I think, identify with injustice, intemperance, cowardice, ignorance, and in a word with all wickedness.

Exactly.

And now that we know the nature of justice and injustice, we can be equally clear about what is meant by acting justly and again by unjust action and wrong-doing.

How do you mean?

Plainly, they are exactly analogous to those wholesome and unwholesome activities which respectively produce a healthy or unhealthy condition in the body; in the same way just and unjust conduct produce a just or unjust character. Justice is produced in the soul, like health in the body, by establishing the elements concerned in their natural relations of control and subordination, whereas injustice is like disease and means that this natural order is inverted.

Quite so.

It appears, then, that virtue is as it were the health and comeliness and well-being of the soul, as wickedness is disease, deformity, and weakness.

True.

And also that virtue and wickedness are brought about by one's way of life, honorable or disgraceful.

That follows.

So now it only remains to consider which is the more profitable course: to do right and live honorably and be just, whether or not anyone knows what manner of man you are, or to do wrong and be unjust, provided that you can escape the chastisement which might make you a better man.

But really, Socrates, it seems to me ridiculous to ask that question now that the nature of justice and injustice has been brought to light. People think that all the luxury and wealth and power in the world cannot make life worth living when the bodily constitution is going to rack and ruin; and are we to believe that, when the very principle whereby we live is deranged and corrupted, life will be worth living so long as a man can do as he will, and wills to do anything rather than to free himself from vice and wrongdoing and to win justice and virtue?

Yes, I replied, it is a ridiculous question. . . .

The Paradox: Philosophers Must Be Kings

[*Challenged to show that the ideal state can exist, Socrates first claims that an ideal is none the worse for not being realizable on earth. The assertion that theory comes closer than practice to truth or reality is characteristically Platonic. The ideal state or man is the* true *state or man; for if men, who are in fact always imperfect, could reach perfection, they would only be realizing all that their nature aims at being and might conceivably be. Further, the realm of ideals is the* real *world, unchanging and eternal, which can be known by thought. The visible and tangible things commonly called real are only a realm of fleeting appearance, where the ideal is imperfectly manifested in various degrees of approximation. . . .*

An ideal has an indispensable value for practice, in that thought thereby gives to action its right aim. So, instead of proving that the ideal state or man can exist here, it is enough to discover the least change, within the bounds of possibility, that would bring the actual state nearest to the ideal. This change would be the union, in the same persons, of political power and the love of wisdom, so as to close the gulf, which had been growing wider since the age of Pericles, between the men of thought and the men of action. The corresponding change in the individual is the supremacy of the reason, the divine element in man, over the rest of our nature.]

But really, Socrates, Glaucon continued, if you are allowed to go on like this, I am afraid you will forget all about the question you thrust aside some time ago: whether a society so constituted can ever come into existence, and if so, how. No doubt, if it did exist, all manner of good things would come about. I can even add some that you have passed over. Men who acknowledged one another as fathers, sons, or brothers and always used those names among themselves would never desert one another; so they would fight with unequalled bravery. And if their womenfolk went out with them to war, either in the ranks or drawn up in the rear to intimidate the enemy and act as a reserve in case of need, I am sure all this would make them invincible. At home, too, I can see many advantages you have not mentioned. But, since I admit that our commonwealth would have all these merits and any number more, if once it came into existence, you need not describe it in further detail. All we have now to do is to convince ourselves that it can be brought into being and how.

This is a very sudden onslaught, said I; you have no mercy on my shilly-shallying. Perhaps you do not realize that, after I have barely escaped the first two waves,[7] the third, which you are now bringing down upon me, is the most formidable of all. When you have seen what it is like and heard my reply, you will be ready to excuse the very natural fears which made me shrink from putting forward such a paradox for discussion.

The more you talk like that, he said, the less we shall be willing to let you off from telling us how this constitution can come into existence; so you had better waste no more time.

Well, said I, let me begin by reminding you that what brought us to this point was our inquiry into the nature of justice and injustice.

True; but what of that?

Merely this: suppose we do find out what justice is,[8] are we going to demand that a man who is just shall have a character which exactly corresponds in every respect to the ideal of justice? Or shall we be satisfied if he comes as near to the ideal as possible and has in him a larger measure of that quality than the rest of the world?

That will satisfy me.

If so, when we set out to discover the essential nature of justice and injustice and what a perfectly just and a perfectly unjust man would be like, supposing them to exist, our purpose was to use them as ideal patterns: we were to observe the degree of happiness or unhappiness that each exhibited, and to draw the necessary inference that our own destiny would be like that of the one we most resembled. We did not set out to show that these ideals could exist in fact.

That is true.

Then suppose a painter had drawn an ideally beautiful figure complete to the last touch, would you think any the worse of him, if he could not show that a person as beautiful as that could exist?

No, I should not.

Well, we have been constructing in discourse the pattern of an ideal state. Is our theory any the worse, if we cannot prove it possible that a state so organized should be actually founded?

Surely not.

That, then, is the truth of the matter. But if, for your satisfaction, I am to do my best to show under what conditions our ideal would have the best chance of

[7] The equality of women and the abolition of the family. [These concepts have been spoken of as waves, and the wave metaphor is now continued.]

[8] Justice, as a "civic" virtue, has been defined . . . ; but the wise man's virtue, based on knowledge, has still to be described.

being realized, I must ask you once more to admit that the same principle applies here. Can theory ever be fully realized in practice? Is it not in the nature of things that action should come less close to truth than thought? People may not think so; but do you agree or not?

I do.

Then you must not insist upon my showing that this construction we have traced in thought could be reproduced in fact down to the last detail. You must admit that we shall have found a way to meet your demand for realization, if we can discover how a state might be constituted in the closest accordance with our description. Will not that content you? It would be enough for me.

And for me too.

Then our next attempt, it seems, must be to point out what defect in the working of existing states prevents them from being so organized, and what is the least change that would effect a transformation into this type of government—a single change if possible, or perhaps two; at any rate let us make the changes as few and insignificant as may be.

By all means.

Well, there is one change which, as I believe we can show, would bring about this revolution—not a small change, certainly, nor an easy one, but possible.

What is it?

I have now to confront what we called the third and greatest wave. But I must state my paradox, even though the wave should break in laughter over my head and drown me in ignominy. Now mark what I am going to say.

Go on.

Unless either philosophers become kings in their countries or those who are now called kings and rulers come to be sufficiently inspired with a genuine desire for wisdom; unless, that is to say, political power and philosophy meet together, while the many natures who now go their several ways in the one or the other direction are forcibly debarred from doing so, there can be no rest from troubles, my dear Glaucon, for states, nor yet, as I believe, for all mankind; nor can this commonwealth which we have imagined ever till then see the light of day and grow to its full stature. This it was that I have so long hung back from saying; I knew what a paradox it would be, because it is hard to see that there is no other way of happiness either for the state or for the individual. . . .

Definition of the Philosopher: The Two Worlds

[*The word "philosophy" originally meant curiosity, the desire for fresh experience, such as led Solon to travel and see the world* (Herod. i. 30), *or the pursuit of intellectual culture, as in Pericles' speech: "We cultivate the mind* (φιλοσοφοῦμεν) *without loss of manliness"* (Thuc. ii. 40). *This sense has to be excluded: the Rulers are not to be dilettanti or mere amateurs of the arts. They are to desire knowledge of the whole of truth and reality, and hence of the world of essential Forms, in contrast with the world of appearances.*

The doctrine of Forms is here more explicitly invoked. Corresponding to the two worlds, the mind has two faculties: Knowledge of the real and Belief in appearances (doxa). Faculties can be distinguished only by (1) *the states of mind they produce*, and (2) *their fields of objects*. By both tests Knowledge and Belief differ. (1) Knowledge is infallible (there is no false knowledge); Belief may be true or false. (2) Knowledge, by definition, is of unique, unchanging objects. Just in this respect the Forms resemble the laws of nature sought by modern natural science: a law is an unseen intelligible principle, a unity underlying an unlimited multiplicity of similar phenomena, and supposed to be unalterable. The Forms, however, are not laws of the sequence or coexistence of phenomena, but ideals or patterns, which have a real existence independent of our minds[9] and of which the many individual things called by their names in the world of appearances are like images or reflections. If we are disposed, with Aristotle, to deny that Platonic Forms or ideals exist apart from individual things in the visible world, we should remember that the essence of the doctrine is the conviction that the differences beween good and evil, right and wrong, true and false, beautiful and ugly, are absolute, not 'relative' to the customs or tastes or desires of individual men or social groups. We can know them or (as is commonly the case) not know them;

they cannot change or vary from place to place or from time to time. This conviction has been, and is, held by many who cannot accept, at its face value, Plato's mode of expressing it.

A Form, such as Beauty itself, excludes its opposite, Ugliness: it can never be or become ugly. But any particular beautiful thing may be also ugly in some aspects or situations: it may cease to be beautiful and become ugly; it may seem beautiful to me, ugly to you; and it must begin and cease to exist in time. Such things cannot be objects of knowledge. Our apprehension of these many changing things is here called doxa and compared to dream experience, which is neither wholly real nor utterly non-existent. Doxa is usually rendered by "Opinion." Here 'Belief' is preferred as having a corresponding verb which, unlike 'opine,' is in common use. But both terms are inadequate. Doxa and its cognates denote our apprehension of anything that 'seems': (1) *what seems to exist*, sensible appearances, phenomena; (2) *what seems* true, opinions, beliefs, whether really true or false; (3) *what seems* right, legal and deliberative decisions, and the "many conventional notions" of current morality (479 D), which vary from place to place and from time to time. The amateur of the arts and the politician live in the twilight realm of these fluctuating beliefs.]

Now, I continued, if we are to elude those assailants you have described, we must, I think, define for them whom we mean by these lovers of wisdom who, we have dared to assert, ought

---

[9] Hence most modern critics avoid the term 'Idea,' though this is Plato's word, because it now suggests a thought existing only 'in our minds.'

to be our rulers. Once we have a clear view of their character, we shall be able to defend our position by pointing to some who are naturally fitted to combine philosophic study with political leadership, while the rest of the world should accept their guidance and let philosophy alone.

Yes, this is the moment for a definition.

Here, then, is a line of thought which may lead to a satisfactory explanation. Need I remind you that a man will deserve to be called a lover of this or that, only if it is clear that he loves that thing as a whole, not merely in parts?

You must remind me, it seems; for I do not see what you mean.

That answer would have come better from someone less susceptible to love than yourself, Glaucon. You ought not to have forgotten that any boy in the bloom of youth will arouse some sting of passion in a man of your amorous temperament and seem worthy of his attentions. Is not this your way with your favourites? You will praise a snub nose as piquant and a hooked one as giving a regal air, while you call a straight nose perfectly proportioned; the swarthy, you say, have a manly look, the fair are children of the gods; and what do you think is that word 'honey-pale,' if not the euphemism of some lover who had no fault to find with sallowness on the cheek of youth? In a word, you will carry pretence and extravagance to any length sooner than reject a single one that is in the flower of his prime.

If you insist on taking me as an example of how lovers behave, I will agree for the sake of argument.

Again, do you not see the same behaviour in people with a passion for wine? They are glad of any excuse to drink wine of any sort. And there are the men who covet honour, who, if they cannot lead an army, will command a company, and if they cannot win the respect of important people, are glad to be looked up to by nobodies, because they must have someone to esteem them.

Quite true.

Do you agree, then, that when we speak of a man as having a passion for a certain kind of thing, we mean that he has an appetite for everything of that kind without discrimination?

Yes.

So the philosopher, with his passion for wisdom, will be one who desires all wisdom, not only some part of it. If a student is particular about his studies, especially while he is too young to know which are useful and which are not, we shall say he is no lover of learning or of wisdom; just as, if he were dainty about his food, we should say he was not hungry or fond of eating, but had a poor appetite. Only the man who has a taste for every sort of knowledge and throws himself into acquiring it with an insatiable curiosity will deserve to be called a philosopher. Am I not right?

That description, Glaucon replied, would include a large and ill-assorted company. It is curiosity, I suppose, and a delight in fresh experience that gives some people a passion for all that is to be seen and heard at theatrical and musical performances. But they are a queer set to reckon among philosophers, considering that they would never go near anything like a philosophical discussion, though they run round at all the Dionysiac festivals in town or country as if they were under contract to listen to every company of performers without fail. Will curiosity entitle all these enthusiasts, not to mention amateurs of the minor arts, to be called philosophers?

Certainly not; though they have a certain counterfeit resemblance?

And whom do you mean by the genuine philosophers?

Those whose passion it is to see the truth.

That must be so; but will you explain?

It would not be easy to explain to everyone; but you, I believe, will grant my premiss.

Which is—?

That since beauty and ugliness are opposite, they are two things; and consequently each of them is one. The same holds of justice and injustice, good and bad, and all the essential Forms: each in itself is one; but they manifest themselves in a great variety of combinations, with actions, with material things, and with one another, and so each seems to be many.[10]

That is true.

On the strength of this premiss, then, I can distinguish your amateurs of the arts and men of action from the phi-

[10] At 523 A ff., it is explained how confused impressions of opposite qualities in sense-perception provoke reflection to isolate and define the corresponding universals or Forms.

losophers we are concerned with, who are alone worthy of the name.

What is your distinction?

Your lovers of sights and sounds delight in beautiful tones and colours and shapes and in all the works of art into which these enter; but they have not the power of thought to behold and to take delight in the nature of Beauty itself. That power to approach Beauty and behold it as it is in itself, is rare indeed.

Quite true.

Now if a man believes in the existence of beautiful things, but not of Beauty itself, and cannot follow a guide who would lead him to a knowledge of it, is he not living in a dream? Consider: does not dreaming, whether one is awake or asleep, consist in mistaking a semblance for the reality it resembles?

I should certainly call that dreaming.

Contrast with him the man who holds that there is such a thing as Beauty itself and can discern that essence as well as the things that partake of its character, without ever confusing the one with the other—is he a dreamer or living in a waking state?

He is very much awake.

So may we say that he knows, while the other has only a belief in appearances; and might we call their states of mind knowledge and belief?

Certainly.

But this person who, we say, has only belief without knowledge may be aggrieved and challenge our statement. Is there any means of soothing his resentment and converting him gently, without telling him plainly that he is not in his right mind?

We surely ought to try.

Come then, consider what we are to say to him. Or shall we ask him a question, assuring him that, far from grudging him any knowledge he may have, we shall be only too glad to find that there is something he knows? But, we shall say, tell us this: When a man knows, must there not be something that he knows? Will you answer for him, Glaucon?

My answer will be, that there must.

Something real or unreal?

Something real; how could a thing that is unreal ever be known?

Are we satisfied, then, on this point, from however many points of view we might examine it: that the perfectly real is perfectly knowable, and the utterly unreal is entirely unknowable?

Quite satisfied.

Good. Now if there is something so constituted that it both *is* and *is not,* will it not lie between the purely real and the utterly unreal?

It will.

Well then, as knowledge corresponds to the real, and absence of knowledge necessarily to the unreal, so, to correspond to this intermediate thing, we must look for something between ignorance and knowledge, if such a thing there be.

Certainly.

Is there not a thing we call belief?

Surely.

A different power from knowledge, or the same?

Different.

Knowledge and belief, then, must have different objects, answering to their respective powers.

Yes.

And knowledge has for its natural object the real—to know the truth about reality. However, before going further, I think we need a definition. Shall we distinguish under the general name of "faculties"[11] those powers which enable us—or anything else—to do what we can do? Sight and hearing, for instance, are what I call faculties, if that will help you to see the class of things I have in mind.

Yes, I understand.

Then let me tell you what view I take of them. In a faculty I cannot find any of those qualities, such as colour or shape, which, in the case of many other things, enable me to distinguish one thing from another. I can only look to its field of objects and the state of mind it produces, and regard these as sufficient to identify it and to distinguish it from faculties which have different fields and produce different states. Is that how you would go to work?

Yes.

Let us go back, then, to knowledge. Would you class that as a faculty?

Yes; and I should call it the most powerful of all.

And is belief also a faculty?

It can be nothing else, since it is what gives us the power of believing.

But a little while ago you agreed that knowledge and belief are not the same thing.

Yes; there could be no sense in identifying the infallible with the fallible.[12]

[11] The Greek here uses only the common word for "power" (*dynamis*), but Plato is defining the special sense we express by "faculty."

[12] This marks one distinction between the

Good. So we are quite clear that knowledge and belief are different things?

They are.

If so, each of them, having a different power, must have a different field of objects.

Necessarily.

The field of knowledge being the real; and its power, the power of knowing the real as it is.

Yes.

Whereas belief, we say, is the power of believing. Is its object the same as that which knowledge knows? Can the same things be possible objects of knowledge and of belief?[13]

Not if we hold to the principles we agreed upon. If it is of the nature of a different faculty to have a different field, and if both knowledge and belief are faculties and, as we assert, different ones, it follows that the same things cannot be possible objects of both.

So if the real is the object of knowledge, the object of belief must be something other than the real.

Yes.

Can it be the unreal? Or is that an impossible object even for belief? Consider: if a man has a belief, there must

be something before his mind; he cannot be believing nothing, can he?

No.

He is believing something, then; whereas the unreal could only be called nothing at all.

Certainly.

Now we said that ignorance must correspond to the unreal, knowledge to the real. So what he is believing cannot be real nor yet unreal.

True.

Belief, then, cannot be either ignorance or knowledge.

It appears not.

Then does it lie outside and beyond these two? Is it either more clear and certain than knowledge or less clear and certain than ignorance?

No, it is neither.

It rather seems to you to be something more obscure than knowledge, but not so dark as ignorance, and so to lie between the two extremes?

Quite so.

Well, we said earlier that if some object could be found such that it both *is* and at the same time *is not,* that object would lie between the perfectly real and the utterly unreal; and that the corresponding faculty would be neither knowledge nor ignorance, but a faculty to be found situated between the two.

Yes.

And now what we have found between the two is the faculty we call belief.

True.

It seems, then, that what remains to be discovered is that object which can be said both to be and not to be and cannot properly be called either purely

---

two states of mind. Further, even if true, belief, unlike knowledge, is (1) produced by persuasion, not by instruction; (2) cannot "give an account" of itself; and (3) can be shaken by persuasion (*Timaeus* 51 E).

[13] If "belief" bore its common meaning, we might answer, yes. But in this context it is essentially belief in *appearances.* It includes perception by the senses, and these can never perceive objects of thought, such as Beauty itself.

real or purely unreal. If that can be found, we may justly call it the object of belief, and so give the intermediate faculty the intermediate object, while the two extreme objects will fall to the extreme faculties.

Yes.

On these assumptions, then, I shall call for an answer from our friend who denies the existence of Beauty itself or of anything that can be called an essential Form of Beauty remaining unchangeably in the same state for ever, though he does recognize the existence of beautiful things as a plurality—that lover of things seen who will not listen to anyone who says that Beauty is one, Justice is one, and so on. I shall say to him, Be so good as to tell us: of all these many beautiful things is there one which will not appear ugly? Or of these many just or righteous actions, is there one that will not appear unjust or unrighteous?

No, replied Glaucon, they must inevitably appear to be in some way both beautiful and ugly; and so with all the other terms your question refers to.

And again the many things which are doubles are just as much halves as they are doubles. And the things we call large or heavy have just as much right to be called small or light.

Yes; any such thing will always have a claim to both opposite designations.

Then, whatever any one of these many things may be said to be, can you say that it absolutely *is* that, any more than that it *is not* that?

They remind me of those punning riddles people ask at dinner parties, or the child's puzzle about what the eunuch threw at the bat and what the

bat was perched on.[14] These things have the same ambiguous character, and one cannot form any stable conception of them either as being or as not being, or as both being and not being, or as neither.

Can you think of any better way of disposing of them than by placing them between reality and unreality? For I suppose they will not appear more obscure and so less real than unreality, or clearer and so more real than reality.

Quite true.

It seems, then, we have discovered that the many conventional notions of the mass of mankind about what is beautiful or honourable or just and so on are adrift in a sort of twilight between pure reality and pure unreality.

We have.

And we agreed earlier that, if any such object were discovered, it should be called the object of belief and not of knowledge. Fluctuating in that half-way region, it would be seized upon by the intermediate faculty.

Yes.

So when people have an eye for the multitude of beautiful things or of just actions or whatever it may be, but can neither behold Beauty or Justice itself nor follow a guide who would lead them to it, we shall say that all they have is beliefs, without any real knowledge of the objects of their belief.

---

[14] A man who was not a man (eunuch), seeing and not seeing (seeing imperfectly) a bird that was not a bird (bat) perched on a bough that was not a bough (a reed), pelted and did not pelt it (aimed at it and missed) with a stone that was not a stone (pumice-stone).

That follows.

But what of those who contemplate the realities themselves as they are for ever in the same unchangeable state? Shall we not say that they have, not mere belief, but knowledge?

That too follows.

And, further, that their affection goes out to the objects of knowledge, whereas the others set their affections on the objects of belief; for it was they, you remember, who had a passion for the spectacle of beautiful colours and sounds, but would not hear of Beauty itself being a real thing.

I remember.

So we may fairly call them lovers of belief rather than of wisdom—not philosophical, in fact, but philodoxical. Will they be seriously annoyed by that description?

Not if they will listen to my advice. No one ought to take offence at the truth.

The name of philosopher, then, will be reserved for those whose affections are set, in every case, on the reality.

By all means.

The Philosopher's Fitness to Rule

[*The above definition of the philosopher might suggest an unpractical head-in-air, unfit to control life in the state. But the qualities most valuable in a ruler will follow naturally from the master passion for truth in a nature of the type described earlier, when it is perfected by time and education.*]

So at last, Glaucon, after this long and weary way, we have come to see who are the philosophers and who are not.

I doubt if the way could have been shortened.

Apparently not. I think, however, that we might have gained a still clearer view if this had been the only topic to be discussed; but there are so many others awaiting us, if we mean to discover in what ways the just life is better than the unjust.

Which are we to take up now?

Surely the one that follows next in order. Since the philosophers are those who can apprehend the eternal and unchanging, while those who cannot do so, but are lost in the mazes of multiplicity and change, are not philosophers, which of the two ought to be in control of a state?

I wonder what would be a reasonable solution.

To establish as Guardians whichever of the two appear competent to guard the laws and ways of life in society.

True.

Well, there can be no question whether a guardian who is to keep watch over anything needs to be keen-sighted or blind. And is not blindness precisely the condition of men who are entirely cut off from knowledge of any reality, and have in their soul no clear pattern of perfect truth, which they might study in every detail and constantly refer to, as a painter looks at his model, before they proceed to embody notions of justice, honour, and goodness in earthly institutions or, in their character of Guardians, to preserve such institutions as already exist?

Certainly such a condition is very like blindness.

Shall we, then, make such as these our Guardians in preference to men who, besides their knowledge of realities, are in no way inferior to them in experience and in every excellence of character?

It would be absurd not to choose the philosophers, whose knowledge is perhaps their greatest point of superiority, provided they do not lack those other qualifications.

What we have to explain, then, is how those qualifications can be combined in the same persons with philosophy.

Certainly.

The first thing, as we said at the outset, is to get a clear view of their inborn disposition.[15] When we are satisfied on that head, I think we shall agree that such a combination of qualities is possible and that we need look no further for men fit to be in control of a commonwealth. One trait of the philosophic nature we may take as already granted: a constant passion for any knowledge that will reveal to them something of that reality which endures for ever and is not always passing into and out of existence. And, we may add, their desire is to know the whole of that reality; they will not willingly renounce any part of it as relatively small and insignificant, as we said before when we compared them to the lover and to the man who covets honour.

True.

Is there not another trait which the nature we are seeking cannot fail to possess—truthfulness, a love of truth and a hatred of falsehood that will not tolerate untruth in any form?

Yes, it is natural to expect that.

It is not merely natural, but entirely necessary that an instinctive passion for any object should extend to all that is closely akin to it; and there is nothing more closely akin to wisdom than truth. So the same nature cannot love wisdom and falsehood; the genuine lover of knowledge cannot fail, from his youth up, to strive after the whole of truth.

I perfectly agree.

Now we surely know that when a man's desires set strongly in one direction, in every other channel they flow more feebly, like a stream diverted into another bed. So when the current has set towards knowledge and all that goes with it, desire will abandon those pleasures of which the body is the instrument and be concerned only with the pleasure which the soul enjoys independently—if, that is to say, the love of wisdom is more than a mere pretence. Accordingly, such a one will be temperate and no lover of money; for he will be the last person to care about the things for the sake of which money is eagerly sought and lavishly spent.

That is true.

Again, in seeking to distinguish the philosophic nature, you must not overlook the least touch of meanness. Nothing could be more contrary than pettiness to a mind constantly bent on grasping the whole of things, both divine and human.

Quite true.

And do you suppose that one who is so high-minded and whose thought

---

[15] The subject of the present chapter. The next will explain why the other qualifications, of experience and character, are too often lacking.

can contemplate all time and all existence will count this life of man a matter of much concern?

No, he could not.

So for such a man death will have no terrors.

None.

A mean and cowardly nature, then, can have no part in the genuine pursuit of wisdom.

I think not.

And if a man is temperate and free from the love of money, meanness, pretentiousness, and cowardice, he will not be hard to deal with or dishonest. So, as another indication of the philosophic temper, you will observe whether, from youth up, he is fairminded, gentle, and sociable.

Certainly.

Also you will not fail to notice whether he is quick or slow to learn. No one can be expected to take a reasonable delight in a task in which much painful effort makes little headway. And if he cannot retain what he learns, his forgetfulness will leave no room in his head for knowledge; and so, having all his toil for nothing, he can only end by hating himself as well as his fruitless occupation. We must not, then, count a forgetful mind as competent to pursue wisdom; we must require a good memory.

By all means.

Further, there is in some natures a crudity and awkwardness that can only tend to a lack of measure and proportion; and there is a close affinity between proportion and truth. Hence, besides our other requirements, we shall look for a mind endowed with measure and grace, which will be instinctively drawn to see every reality in its true light.

Yes.

Well then, now that we have enumerated the qualities of a mind destined to take its full part in the apprehension of reality, have you any doubt about their being indispensable and all necessarily going together?

None whatever.

Then have you any fault to find with a pursuit which none can worthily follow who is not by nature quick to learn and to remember, magnanimous and gracious, the friend and kinsman of truth, justice, courage, temperance?

No; Momus[16] himself could find no flaw in it.

Well then, when time and education have brought such characters as these to maturity, would you entrust the care of your commonwealth to anyone else? . . .

Four Stages of Cognition: The Line

[Socrates has contrasted the realm of sensible appearances and shifting beliefs with the realm of eternal and unchanging Forms, dominated (as we now know) by the Good. The philosopher was he whose affections were set on knowledge of that real world. The Guardians' primary education in literature and art was mainly confined to the world of appearance and belief, though it culminated in the perception of "images" of the moral ideals, the beauty of which would excite love for the individual person in whose soul

[16] The spirit of faultfinding, one of the children of Night in Hesiod's *Theogony*.

they dwelt (402). *The higher intellectual training now to be described is to detach the mind from appearances and individuals and to carrry it across the boundary between the two worlds and all the way beyond to the vision of the Good. It thus corresponds to the "greater mysteries" of which Diotima speaks in the* Symposium *(210), where Eros, detached from its individual object, advances to the vision of Beauty itself (the Good considered as the object of desire). The next chapter will give an allegorical picture of this progress.*

The allegory is here prefaced by a diagram. A line is divided into two parts, whose inequality symbolizes that the visible world has a lower degree of reality and truth than the intelligible. Each part is then subdivided in the same proportion as the whole line, (thus $A + B : C + D = A : B = C :$

D). The four sections correspond to four states of mind or modes of cognition, each clearer and more certain than the one below.

The lower part $(A + B)$ *is at first called "the Visible," but elsewhere the field of* doxa *in the wide sense explained above* (p. 689); *and so it includes the "many conventional notions of the multitude" about morality* (479 D). *It is the physical and moral world as apprehended by those "lovers of appearance" who do not recognize the absolute ideals which Plato calls real.*

(A) The lowest form of cognition is called eikasia. *The word defies translation, being one of those current terms to which Plato gives a peculiar sense, to be inferred from the context. It is etymologically connected with* eikon = *image, likeness, and with* eikos = *likely, and it can mean either likeness*

Objects	States of Mind
The Good	
	Intelligence (*noesis*) or
Forms	D Knowledge (*episteme*)
Intelligible World	
Mathematical objects	C Thinking (*dianoia*)
Visible Things	B Belief (*pistis*)
World of Appearances	
Images	A Imagining (*eikasia*)

(representation) or likening (comparison) or estimation of likelihood (conjecture). Perhaps "imagining" is the least unsatisfactory rendering. It seems to be the wholly unenlightened state of mind which takes sensible appearances and current moral notions at their face value—the condition of the unreleased prisoners in the Cave allegory below, who see only images of images.

(B) The higher section stands for common-sense belief (pistis) in the reality of the visible and tangible things commonly called substantial. In the moral sphere it would include "correct beliefs without knowledge" (506 c), such as the young Guardians were taught to hold. True beliefs are sufficient guides for action, but are insecure until based on knowledge of the reasons for them (Meno 97).

Higher education is to effect an escape from the prison of appearances by training the intellect, first in mathematics, and then in moral philosophy. (C) The lower section of the intelligible contains the subject-matter of the mathematical sciences (511 B).[17] Two characteristics of mathematical procedure are mentioned: (a) the use of visible diagrams and models as imperfect illustrations of the objects and truths of pure thought. Here is a sort of bridge carrying the mind across from the visible thing to the intelligible reality, which it must learn to distinguish. (b) Each branch of mathematics starts from unquestioned assumptions (postulates, axioms, definitions)

[17] The interpretation of the higher part of the Line is the subject of a long controversy which cannot be pursued here.

and reasons from them deductively. The premises may be true and the conclusions may follow, but the whole structure hangs in the air until the assumptions themselves shall have been shown to depend on an unconditional principle. (This may be conjectured to be Unity itself, an aspect of the Good.) Meanwhile the state of mind is dianoia, the ordinary word for "thought" or "thinking," here implying a degree of understanding which falls short of perfect knowledge (533 D). Dianoia suggests discursive thinking or reasoning from premiss to conclusion, whereas noesis is constantly compared to the immediate act of vision and suggests rather the direct intuition or apprehension of its object.

(D) The higher method is called Dialectic, a word which since Hegel has acquired misleading associations. In the Republic it simply means the technique of philosophic conversation (dialogue) carried on by question and answer and seeking to render, or to receive from a respondent, an "account" (logos) of some Form, usually a moral Form such as Justice in this dialogue. At this stage visible illustrations are no longer available, and the movement at first is not downward, deducing conclusions from premises, but upward, examining the premises themselves and seeking the ultimate principle on which they all depend. It is suggested that, if the mind could ever rise to grasp the supreme Form, it might then descend by a deduction confirming the whole structure of moral and mathematical knowledge. The state of mind is called intelligence or rational intuition (noesis) and *knowledge* (episteme, 533 E) *in the full sense. . . .*]

CONCEIVE, then, that there are these two powers I speak of, the Good reigning over the domain of all that is intelligible, the Sun over the visible world—or the heaven as I might call it; only you would think I was showing off my skill in etymology.[18] At any rate you have these two orders of things clearly before your mind: the visible and the intelligible?

I have.

Now take a line divided into two unequal parts, one to represent the visible order, the other the intelligible; and divide each part again in the same proportion, symbolizing degrees of comparative clearness or obscurity. Then (A) one of the two sections in the visible world will stand for images. By images I mean first shadows, and then reflections in water or in close-grained, polished surfaces, and everything of that kind, if you understand.

Yes, I understand.

Let the second section (B) stand for the actual things of which the first are likenesses, the living creatures about us and all the works of nature or of human hands.

So be it.

Will you also take the proportion in which the visible world has been divided as corresponding to degrees of reality and truth, so that the likeness shall stand to the original in the same ratio as the sphere of appearances and belief to the sphere of knowledge?

[18] Some connected the word for heaven (οὐρανός) with ὁρᾶν 'to see' (*Cratylus*, 396 B). It is sometimes used for the whole of the visible universe.

Certainly.

Now consider how we are to divide the part which stands for the intelligible world. There are two sections. In the first (C) the mind uses as images those actual things which themselves had images in the visible world; and it is compelled to pursue its inquiry by starting from assumptions and travelling, not up to a principle, but down to a conclusion. In the second (D) the mind moves in the other direction, from an assumption up towards a principle which is not hypothetical; and it makes no use of the images employed in the other section, but only of Forms, and conducts its inquiry solely by their means.

I don't quite understand what you mean.

Then we will try again; what I have just said will help you to understand. (C) You know, of course, how students of subjects like geometry and arithmetic begin by postulating odd and even numbers, or the various figures and the three kinds of angle, and other such data in each subject. These data they take as known; and, having adopted them as assumptions, they do not feel called upon to give any account of them to themselves or to anyone else, but treat them as self-evident. Then, starting from these assumptions, they go on until they arrive, by a series of consistent steps, at all the conclusions they set out to investigate.

Yes, I know that.

You also know how they make use of visible figures and discourse about them, though what they really have in mind is the originals of which these figures are images: they are not reasoning, for instance, about this particular square and diagonal which they have drawn, but about *the* Square and *the* Diagonal; and so in all cases. The diagrams they draw and the models they make are actual things, which may have their shadows or images in water; but now they serve in their turn as images, while the student is seeking to behold those realities which only thought can apprehend.[19]

True.

This, then, is the class of things that I spoke of as intelligible, but with two qualifications: first, that the mind, in studying them, is compelled to employ assumptions, and, because it cannot rise above these, does not travel upwards to a first principle; and second, that it uses as images those actual things which have images of their own in the section below them and which, in comparison with those shadows and reflections, are reputed to be more palpable and valued accordingly.

I understand: you mean the subject-matter of geometry and of the kindred arts.

(D) Then by the second section of the intelligible world you may understand me to mean all that unaided reasoning apprehends by the power of dialectic, when it treats its assumptions, not as first principles, but as *hypotheses* in the literal sense, things 'laid

down' like a flight of steps up which it may mount all the way to something that is not hypothetical, the first principle of all; and having grasped this, may turn back and, holding on to the consequences which depend upon it, descend at last to a conclusion, never making use of any sensible object, but only of Forms, moving through Forms from one to another, and ending with Forms.

I understand, he said, though not perfectly; for the procedure you describe sounds like an enormous undertaking. But I see that you mean to distinguish the field of intelligible reality studied by dialectic as having a greater certainty and truth than the subject-matter of the 'arts,' as they are called, which treat their assumptions as first principles. The students of these arts are, it is true, compelled to exercise thought in contemplating objects which the senses cannot perceive; but because they start from assumptions without going back to a first principle, you do not regard them as gaining true understanding about those objects, although the objects themselves, when connected with a first principle, are intelligible. And I think you would call the state of mind of the students of geometry and other such arts, not intelligence, but thinking, as being something between intelligence and mere acceptance of appearances.

You have understood me quite well enough, I replied. And now you may take, as corresponding to the four sections, these four states of mind: *intelligence* for the highest, *thinking* for the second, *belief* for the third, and for the

[19] Conversely, the fact that the mathematician can use visible objects as illustrations indicates that the realities and truths of mathematics are embodied, though imperfectly, in the world of visible and tangible things; whereas the counterparts of the moral Forms can only be beheld by thought.

last *imagining*.[20] These you may arrange as the terms in a proportion, assigning to each a degree of clearness and certainty corresponding to the measure in which their objects possess truth and reality.

I understand and agree with you. I will arrange them as you say.

The Allegory of the Cave

[*The progress of the mind from the lowest state of unenlightenment to knowledge of the Good is now illustrated by the famous parable comparing the world of appearance to an underground Cave. In Empedocles' religious poem the powers which conduct the soul to its incarnation say, "We have come under this cavern's roof." The image was probably taken from mysteries held in caves or dark chambers representing the underworld, through which the candidates for initiation were led to the revelation of sacred objects in a blaze of light. The idea that the body is a prison-house, to which the soul is condemned for past misdeeds, is attributed by Plato to the Orphics.*

One moral of the allegory is drawn from the distress caused by a too sudden passage from darkness to light. The earlier warning against plunging untrained minds into the discussion of moral problems (498 A), as the Sophists and Socrates himself had done, is reinforced by the picture of the dazed prisoner dragged out into the sunlight. Plato's ten years' course of pure mathematics is to habituate the intellect to

abstract reasoning before moral ideas are called in question (537 E, ff.).]

Next, said I, here is a parable to illustrate the degrees in which our nature may be enlightened or unenlightened. Imagine the condition of men living in a sort of cavernous chamber underground, with an entrance open to the light and a long passage all down the cave.[21] Here they have been from childhood, chained by the leg and also by the neck, so that they cannot move and can see only what is in front of them, because the chains will not let them turn their heads. At some distance higher up is the light of a fire burning behind them; and between the prisoners and the fire is a track[22] with a parapet built along it, like the screen at a puppet-show, which hides the performers while they show their puppets over the top.

I see, said he.

Now behind this parapet imagine persons carrying along various artificial objects, including figures of men and animals in wood or stone or other materials, which project above the parapet. Naturally, some of these persons will be talking, others silent.[23]

[20] Plato never uses hard and fast technical terms. The four here proposed are not defined or strictly employed in the sequel.

[21] The *length* of the "way in" (*eisodos*) to the chamber where the prisoners sit is an essential feature, explaining why no daylight reaches them.

[22] The track crosses the passage into the cave at right angles, and is *above* the parapet built along it.

[23] A modern Plato would compare his Cave to an underground cinema, where the audience watch the play of shadows thrown by the film passing before a light at their backs. The film itself is only an image of "real" things and events in the world outside

It is a strange picture, he said, and a strange sort of prisoners.

Like ourselves, I replied; for in the first place prisoners so confined would have seen nothing of themselves or of one another, except the shadows thrown by the fire-light on the wall of the Cave facing them, would they?

Not if all their lives they had been prevented from moving their heads.

And they would have seen as little of the objects carried past.

Of course.

Now, if they could talk to one another, would they not suppose that their words referred only to those passing shadows which they saw?[24]

Necessarily.

And suppose their prison had an echo from the wall facing them? When one of the people crossing behind them spoke, they could only suppose that the sound came from the shadow passing before their eyes.

No doubt.

In every way, then, such prisoners would recognize as reality nothing but the shadows of those artificial objects.[25]

Inevitably.

Now consider what would happen if their release from the chains and the healing of their unwisdom should come about in this way. Suppose one of them set free and forced suddenly to stand up, turn his head, and walk with eyes lifted to the light; all these movements would be painful, and he would be too dazzled to make out the objects whose shadows he had been used to see. What do you think he would say, if someone told him that what he had formerly seen was meaningless illusion, but now, being somewhat nearer to reality and turned towards more real objects, he was getting a truer view? Suppose further that he were shown the various objects being carried by and were made to say, in reply to questions, what each of them was. Would he not be perplexed and believe the objects now shown him to be not so real as what he formerly saw?[26]

Yes, not nearly so real.

And if he were forced to look at the fire-light itself, would not his eyes ache, so that he would try to escape and turn back to the things which he could see distinctly, convinced that they really were clearer than these other objects now being shown to him?

Yes.

And suppose someone were to drag him away forcibly up the steep and rugged ascent and not let him go until he had hauled him out into the sunlight, would he not suffer pain and vexation at such treatment, and, when he had come out into the light, find his eyes so full of its radiance that he could

---

the cinema. For the film Plato has to substitute the clumsier apparatus of a procession of artificial objects carried on their heads by persons who are merely part of the machinery, providing for the movement of the objects and the sounds whose echo the prisoners hear. The parapet prevents these persons' shadows from being cast on the wall of the Cave.

[24] Adam's text and interpretation. The prisoners, having seen nothing but shadows, cannot think their words refer to the objects carried past behind their backs. For them shadows (images) are the only realities.

[25] The state of mind called *eikasia* in the previous chapter.

[26] The first effect of Socratic questioning is perplexity.

not see a single one of the things that he was now told were real?

Certainly he would not see them all at once.

He would need, then, to grow accustomed before he could see things in that upper world.[27] At first it would be easiest to make out shadows, and then the images of men and things reflected in water, and later on the things themselves. After that, it would be easier to watch the heavenly bodies and the sky itself by night, looking at the light of the moon and stars rather than the Sun and the Sun's light in the day-time.

Yes, surely.

Last of all, he would be able to look at the Sun and contemplate its nature, not as it appears when reflected in water or any alien medium, but as it is in itself in its own domain.

No doubt.

And now he would begin to draw the conclusion that it is the Sun that produces the seasons and the course of the year and controls everything in the visible world, and moreover is in a way the cause of all that he and his companions used to see.

Clearly he would come at last to that conclusion.

Then if he called to mind his fellow prisoners and what passed for wisdom in his former dwelling-place, he would surely think himself happy in the change and be sorry for them. They may have had a practice of honouring and commending one another, with prizes for the man who had the keenest eye for the passing shadows and the best memory for the order in which they followed or accompanied one another, so that he could make a good guess as to which was going to come next.[28] Would our released prisoner be likely to covet those prizes or to envy the men exalted to honour and power in the Cave? Would he not feel like Homer's Achilles, that he would far sooner "be on earth as a hired servant in the house of a landless man"[29] or endure anything rather than go back to his old beliefs and live in the old way?

Yes, he would prefer any fate to such a life.

Now imagine what would happen if he went down again to take his former seat in the Cave. Coming suddenly out of the sunlight, his eyes would be filled with darkness. He might be required once more to deliver his opinion on those shadows, in competition with the prisoners who had never been released, while his eyesight was still dim and unsteady; and it might take some time to become used to the darkness. They would laugh at him and say that he had gone up only to come back with his sight ruined; it was worth no one's while even to attempt the ascent. If they could lay hands on the man who was trying to set them free and lead them up, they would kill him.[30]

[27] Here is the moral—the need of habituation by mathematical study before discussing moral ideas and ascending through them to the Form of the Good.

[28] The empirical politician, with no philosophic insight, but only a "knack of remembering what usually happens" (*Gorg.* 501 A). He has *eikasia* = conjecture as to what is likely (*eikos*).

[29] This verse (already quoted at 386 c), being spoken by the ghost of Achilles, suggests that the Cave is comparable with Hades.

[30] An allusion to the fate of Socrates.

Yes, they would.

Every feature in this parable, my dear Glaucon, is meant to fit our earlier analysis. The prison dwelling corresponds to the region revealed to us through the sense of sight, and the fire-light within it to the power of the Sun. The ascent to see the things in the upper world you may take as standing for the upward journey of the soul into the region of the intelligible; then you will be in possession of what I surmise, since that is what you wish to be told. Heaven knows whether it is true; but this, at any rate, is how it appears to me. In the world of knowledge, the last thing to be perceived and only with great difficulty is the essential Form of Goodness. Once it is perceived, the conclusion must follow that, for all things, this is the cause of whatever is right and good; in the visible world it gives birth to light and to the lord of light, while it is itself sovereign in the intelligible world and the parent of intelligence and truth. Without having had a vision of this Form no one can act with wisdom, either in his own life or in matters of state.

So far as I can understand, I share your belief.

Then you may also agree that it is no wonder if those who have reached this height are reluctant to manage the affairs of men. Their souls long to spend all their time in that upper world—naturally enough, if here once more our parable holds true. Nor, again, is it at all strange that one who comes from the contemplation of divine things to the miseries of human life should appear awkward and ridiculous when, with eyes still dazed and not yet accustomed to the darkness, he is compelled, in a law-court or elsewhere, to dispute about the shadows of justice or the images that cast those shadows, and to wrangle over the notions of what is right in the minds of men who have never beheld Justice itself.[31]

It is not at all strange.

No; a sensible man will remember that the eyes may be confused in two ways—by a change from light to darkness or from darkness to light; and he will recognize that the same thing happens to the soul. When he sees it troubled and unable to discern anything clearly, instead of laughing thoughtlessly, he will ask whether, coming from a brighter existence, its unaccustomed vision is obscured by the darkness, in which case he will think its condition enviable and its life a happy one; or whether, emerging from the depths of ignorance, it is dazzled by excess of light. If so, he will rather feel sorry for it; or, if he were inclined to laugh, that would be less ridiculous than to laugh at the soul which has come down from the light.

That is a fair statement.

If this is true, then, we must conclude that education is not what it is said to be by some, who profess to put knowledge into a soul which does not possess it, as if they could put sight into blind eyes. On the contrary, our own account signifies that the soul of every man does possess the power of learning the truth and the organ to see it with; and that, just as one might have to turn the

[31] In the *Gorgias* 486 A, Callicles, forecasting the trial of Socrates, taunts him with the philosopher's inability to defend himself in a court.

whole body round in order that the eye should see light instead of darkness, so the entire soul must be turned away from this changing world, until its eye can bear to contemplate reality and that supreme splendour which we have called the Good. Hence there may well be an art whose aim would be to effect this very thing, the conversion of the soul, in the readiest way; not to put the power of sight into the soul's eye, which already has it, but to ensure that, instead of looking in the wrong direction, it is turned the way it ought to be.

Yes, it may well be so.

It looks, then, as though wisdom were different from those ordinary virtues, as they are called, which are not far removed from bodily qualities, in that they can be produced by habituation and exercise in a soul which has not possessed them from the first. Wisdom, it seems, is certainly the virtue of some diviner faculty, which never loses its power, though its use for good or harm depends on the direction towards which it is turned. You must have noticed in dishonest men with a reputation for sagacity the shrewd glance of a narrow intelligence piercing the objects to which it is directed. There is nothing wrong with their power of vision, but it has been forced into the service of evil, so that the keener its sight, the more harm it works.

Quite true.

And yet if the growth of a nature like this had been pruned from earliest childhood, cleared of those clinging overgrowths which come of gluttony and all luxurious pleasure and, like leaden weights charged with affinity to this mortal world, hang upon the soul, bending its vision downwards; if, freed from these, the soul were turned round towards true reality, then this same power in these very men would see the truth as keenly as the objects it is turned to now.

Yes, very likely.

Is it not also likely, or indeed certain after what has been said, that a state can never be properly governed either by the uneducated who know nothing of truth or by men who are allowed to spend all their days in the pursuit of culture? The ignorant have no single mark before their eyes at which they must aim in all the conduct of their own lives and of affairs of state; and the others will not engage in action if they can help it, dreaming that, while still alive, they have been translated to the Islands of the Blest.

Quite true.

It is for us, then, as founders of a commonwealth, to bring compulsion to bear on the noblest natures. They must be made to climb the ascent to the vision of Goodness, which we called the highest object of knowledge; and, when they have looked upon it long enough, they must not be allowed, as they now are, to remain on the heights, refusing to come down again to the prisoners or to take any part in their labours and rewards, however much or little these may be worth.

Shall we not be doing them an injustice, if we force on them a worse life than they might have?

You have forgotten again, my friend, that the law is not concerned to make any one class specially happy, but to ensure the welfare of the commonwealth as a whole. By persuasion or constraint it will unite the citizens in harmony, making them share whatever benefits each class can contribute to the common good; and its purpose in forming men of that spirit was not that each should be left to go his own way, but that they should be instrumental in binding the community into one.

You will see, then, Glaucon, that there will be no real injustice in compelling our philosophers to watch over and care for the other citizens. We can fairly tell them that their compeers in other states may quite reasonably refuse to collaborate: there they have sprung up, like a self-sown plant, in despite of their country's institutions; no one has fostered their growth, and they cannot be expected to show gratitude for a care they have never received. "But," we shall say, "it is not so with you. We have brought you into existence for your country's sake as well as for your own, to be like leaders and king-bees in a hive; you have been better and more thoroughly educated than those others and hence you are more capable of playing your part both as men of thought and as men of action. You must go down, then, each in his turn, to live with the rest and let your eyes grow accustomed to the darkness. You will then see a thousand times better than those who live there always; you will recognize every image for what it is and know what it represents, because you have seen justice, beauty, and goodness in their reality; and so you and we shall find life in our commonwealth no mere dream, as it is in most existing states, where men live fighting one another about shadows and quarrelling for power, as if that were a great prize;

whereas in truth government can be at its best and free from dissension only where the destined rulers are least desirous of holding office."

Quite true.

Then will our pupils refuse to listen and to take their turns at sharing in the work of the community, though they may live together for most of their time in a purer air?

No; it is a fair demand, and they are fair-minded men. No doubt, unlike any ruler of the present day, they will think of holding power as an unavoidable necessity.

Yes, my friend; for the truth is that you can have a well-governed society only if you can discover for your future rulers a better way of life than being in office; then only will power be in the hands of men who are rich, not in gold, but in the wealth that brings happiness, a good and wise life. All goes wrong when, starved for lack of anything good in their lives, men turn to public affairs hoping to snatch from thence the happiness they hunger for. They set about fighting for power, and this internecine conflict ruins them and their country. The life of true philosophy is the only one that looks down upon offices of state; and access to power must be confined to men who are not in love with it; otherwise rivals will start fighting. So whom else can you compel to undertake the guardianship of the commonwealth, if not those who, besides understanding best the principles of government, enjoy a nobler life than the politician's and look for rewards of a different kind?

There is indeed no other choice.

COMMENT

The Means of Achieving the Ideal

Since the foregoing excerpts from the *Republic* state Plato's ideal as well as his philosophical premises, I need add, to complete the exposition, only a few remarks about the way in which he believed the ideal could be implemented.

If the Guardians are to be wise, they must be very carefully bred, selected, reared, and educated. The biological fitness of the ruling class should be guaranteed by a comprehensive program of eugenics; the most select parents should be induced to have the greatest number of children. Even more important is education, which Plato regards as the main foundation of the state.

He conceives education as a journey of the mind from the concrete practicalities of sensory experience to the eternal and abstract realities of the intellect. It begins with the arts and gymnastics and mounts upward through mathematics, astronomy, and harmonics (the mathematical theory of musical form), to philosophy. The preliminary education continues until about the age of eighteen; then follows two years of military training, for males and females alike. The Guardians are then provisionally selected by "ordeals of toil and pain," and only those who manifest the proper character and intelligence will receive the highest training. The program of mathematical and scientific training will occupy the prospective Guardians from the age of twenty to thirty, and they will then have intensive training in philosophy ("dialectics") for five additional years, or until they have "grasped by pure intelligence the very nature of Goodness itself." The students who have distinguished themselves throughout this long and arduous training will serve a political apprenticeship for about fifteen years, discharging the subordinate functions "suitable to the young." Finally, those who have fully proved their mettle, both men and women, will be selected at the age of fifty to fulfill the high function of philosopher-kings. Others, fit to be soldiers but incapable of the highest intellectual flights, remain Auxiliaries; and the great mass of the people, as members of the producing class, receive the lesser education appropriate to their station.

Every precaution should be taken to ward off temptations and keep the Guardians and Auxiliaries faithful to the state. The chief temptations arise from private interests. The competitive struggle for property, Plato believes, is incompatible with full devotion to the social good. Hence he proposes that the Guardians and Auxiliaries should have no private possessions or acquisitive occupations and that they should receive their maintenance from the state. This proposal is not the same as modern communism, since it applies only to the Auxiliaries and Guardians and not to the producers who constitute the bulk of the population.

Plato also believes that normal marriage and family life are incompatible with a wholehearted devotion to the state, since there is always a temptation to prefer family interests to community welfare. Hence he proposes to abolish private homes and monogamous marriage among the Guardians and Auxiliaries. They should live and share their meals together, realizing the principle that "friends have all things in common." Sexual intercourse should be strictly controlled in the interests of the eugenics program.

Such is the pattern of the aristocratic state. But even the "best" of states may decay, and Plato imaginatively sketches, in a section here omitted, the decline of the state through successive stages of timocracy—the rule of the military class; oligarchy—the rule of the wealthy; democracy—the rule of the many; and tyranny—the rule of the irresponsible dictator. Finally, he discusses art and rewards and punishments after death, but these topics do not now concern us.

Some Main Issues

No one will agree with all the details of Plato's argument, but even when we least agree we can find his ideas challenging. Among the principal issues that he presents are the following:

1. FORCE VERSUS MORALITY. In Books I and II of the *Republic,* Plato raises one of the basic issues in political philosophy—the question as to whether force or morality is the foundation of the state. Against Thrasymachus, Socrates (as a character in the dialogue) argues that the authority of the ruler is morally based on right rather than might. In reply to Glaucon and Adeimantus, he maintains that social obligation is based on duty rather than selfish expediency. The policies of the state, he insists, should conform to the pattern of the Good, which wise men, long disciplined by education, can alone discern. He distinguishes between *opinion* and *knowledge* about goodness, and maintains that genuine knowledge requires an intellectual grasp of *"forms."* The form is the universal essence that is somehow exemplified in particular instances. All beautiful things, for example, exemplify the form of beauty, and all just acts and institutions exemplify the form of justice.

According to Plato, these forms or universals are real, but they exist in their full and essential reality apart from particular things. The perfection, unity, and eternality of the forms separates them from the imperfection, multiplicity, and impermanence of particular things. The sensible nature of the thing declares itself as relative and contingent and points to the imperishable essence which is connected with it and yet independent of it—a form free from limitation, change, defilement. The nature of this super-reality is hard to define—Plato appears to have struggled with the problem throughout his whole philosophical career. In the *Phaedo,* the particulars are said to "participate" in the forms, or the forms are said to be "present" in the particulars. Elsewhere in Plato's dialogues the individual things are said to "imitate" the forms, or to be related as an imperfect "copy" to a pattern or archetype. But all such language is metaphorical, and the essential truth is that the universal somehow transcends the particulars. In the *Republic,* this is taken to mean that the pattern of the ideal state is eternal and hence exempt from the relativities of power politics and shifting expediency.

Whether Plato's theory—or any doctrine of eternal and objective universals—is sound has been one of the principal questions of philosophy from his day until the present. It is possible to agree with him that universals are real, and yet to differ from him in holding that they are immanent in particulars rather than separate and transcendent. "Justice" really exists, but in particular instances—not in "a heaven above the heavens" or as a separate, eternal essence. The "form," in this sense, is simply the characteristic common to all members of the class of things (in this case, the class of just things). The human mind has the power to notice resemblances and to abstract (that is, mentally to extricate) the common characteristics. Thus, universals can be said to consist, on the one hand, of common properties in things, and on the other hand, of concepts which represent these properties. This theory of real but immanent universals is the doctrine of Aristotle, and it serves as well as Plato's theory as an alternative to moral relativism. What is required is that moral concepts must conform to real objective distinctions, and on this point Plato and Aristotle agree.

2. THE "CLOSED" VERSUS THE "OPEN" SOCIETY. With his vision fixed upon eternal forms, Plato wishes, after a fundamental revolution in human affairs, to arrest history and preserve the ideal state in its static perfection. As means to this end, he proposes rigorous censorship of the arts and religion, the use of myths and "noble lies" to reconcile the lower classes to their subordinate status, and the regulation of all details of social life, including marriage and the ownership of property, among the Guardians and Auxiliaries. In effect, he insists upon a tight, "closed" unity of the body politic.

This emphasis upon a static unity is related to his organic theory of the state. Plato maintains that the state is the human soul writ large, just as the soul is the state writ small. There is some question as to how literally we should understand this doctrine, but it seems to imply that the state, like the individual personality, is an organism—that is, a living being with a life and worth of its own. Individuals appear mainly to derive their character and value from their relation to this organic whole. This sort of ethical organicism receives its most express and elaborate expression in the social philosophy of Hegel, but it is foreshadowed in the *Republic*.

The contrasting ideal of an "open" society—in which the freedom and intrinsic value of the individual are primarily emphasized—was eloquently formulated by John Stuart Mill in *On Liberty* (see Chap. 25). Both Mill and Plato, in a sense, maintain an ethics of self-realization, but Plato contends that the private interest of the individual is at one with the interest of the state, whereas Mill is distrustful of the state and believes that self-realization lies in the cultivation of individuality.

We can roughly divide political philosophers into two schools of thought corresponding to their positions on this issue. In one camp are the organic theorists—Plato, Rousseau, Hegel, and Marx—who stress the importance of the general will and the value and significance of collective processes. In the other group are the individualistic theorists—Hume, Bentham, Mill, and Jefferson—who disbelieve in the organic nature of society and regard social institutions as means to the happiness of individuals. The dispute between these two schools of thought is perhaps the most important conflict in the whole of political philosophy.

3. ARISTOCRACY VERSUS DEMOCRACY. The basic tenet of Plato's social philosophy, as we have seen, is that philosopher-kings should rule. This conviction is consistent with his general attitude toward life: he habitually prefers the choice goods to the common goods. Hence he ranks democracy, whose slogan is "equality," as fourth in his classification of five types of government, superior only to tyranny and inferior to aristocracy, timocracy, and oligarchy. The typical democrat seems to him an ill-educated and superficial fellow who wishes to drag all excellent things down to the mediocre level of the average.

The democrat might reply that philosopher-kings are difficult to find or to produce and that a government *of* the few is almost certain to be a government *for* the few. No one can be trusted with irresponsible power, not even the so-called wise. It is the wearer of the shoe who knows where it pinches, and consequently he cannot allow the few aristocrats to choose his shoes for him. If the state exacts duties of its citizens, moreover, it should grant them rights—for responsibility implies freedom. It is only by living as free men—by participating in government and exercising self-rule—that we cease to be mere imitators and become fully developed human beings. With such arguments, the democrat might answer Plato.

If we democrats and liberals are sensible, however, we will not indiscriminately reject the whole of Plato's social philosophy. We need experts in our government and wisdom in our lives. We should adapt to our own ends Plato's great ideal of a state based upon education, and we should seek to reconcile the aristocratic ideal of excellence with the democratic ideal of sharing. Our goal should be a culture both high in attainment and broad in terms of democratic participation.

20

History
and
Freedom

GEORG WILHELM FRIEDRICH HEGEL (1770–1831)

Hegel was born at Stuttgart, where his father held a minor governmental position. Trained in theology at a seminary in Tübingen, he was a rather indifferent student and was often reprimanded for cutting classes. He joined his student-friend Friedrich von Schelling in founding a radical club devoted to discussing the ideas of the French Revolution. His chief interest, however, lay in classical literature, especially in the tragedies of Sophocles. After receiving his doctoral degree, he spent the next six years as a private tutor, first at Berne, and then at Frankfurt. In 1801 he was appointed an instructor at the University of Jena, where he collaborated with Schelling in editing a philosophical journal. The years 1801–1806 were the period of his philosophical awakening, culminating in the publication of his *Philosophy of Mind*. Threatened by the victorious advance of Napoleon's army, he rushed the manuscript to the printer just before the battle of Jena in 1806.

Forced to flee, he settled down for the next eight years as headmaster of a boy's school in Nuremberg. There he married and his two sons were born. In 1816 he accepted a professorship at Heidelberg, and two years later he moved on to the University of Berlin where he became the acknowledged leader of philosophic thought in Germany. Nevertheless, his intellectual independence aroused the hostility of the conservative elements at the Prussian court, and in the last year of his life he ran into trouble with the Prussian censorship. In the autumn of 1831 he was suddenly taken ill with cholera, and a day later—November 14, 1831—he was dead.

Logic
and
the Philosophy
of History

1. [Dialectic and Change]

It is of the highest importance to ascertain and understand rightly the nature of Dialectic. Wherever there is movement, wherever there is life, wherever anything is carried into effect in the actual world, there Dialectic is at work. It is also the soul of all knowledge which is truly scientific. In the popular way of looking at things, the refusal to be bound by the abstract deliverances of understanding appears as fairness, which, according to the proverb Live and let live, demands that each should have its turn; we admit the one, but we admit the other also. But when we look more closely, we find that the limitations of the finite do not merely come from without; that its own nature is the cause of its abrogation, and

Section 1 is from *The Logic of Hegel*, translated from *The Encyclopedia of the Philosophical Sciences* by William Wallace (Oxford: Clarendon Press, 1892). The other sections are from the Introduction to *The Philosophy of History*, translated by J. Sibree (London, 1857).

that by its own act it passes into its counterpart. We say, for instance, that man is mortal, and seem to think that the ground of his death is in external circumstances only; so that if this way of looking were correct, man would have two special properties, vitality and —also—mortality. But the true view of the matter is that life, as life, involves the germ of death, and that the finite, being radically self-contradictory, involves its own self-suppression.

Nor, again, is Dialectic to be confounded with mere Sophistry. The essence of Sophistry lies in giving authority to a partial and abtract principle, in its isolation, as may suit the interest and particular situation of the individual at the time. For example, a regard to my existence, and my having the means of existence, is a vital motive of conduct, but if I exclusively emphasise this consideration or motive of my welfare, and draw the conclusion that I may steal or betray my country, we have a case of Sophistry. Similarly, it is a vital principle in conduct that I should be subjectively free, that is to say, that I should

697

have an insight into what I am doing, and a conviction that it is right. But if my pleading insists on this principle alone I fall into Sophistry, such as would overthrow all the principles of morality. From this sort of party-pleading Dialectic is wholly different; its purpose is to study things in their own being and movement and thus to demonstrate the finitude of the partial categories of understanding.

Dialectic, it may be added, is no novelty in philosophy. Among the ancients Plato is termed the inventor of Dialectic; and his right to the name rests on the fact, that the Platonic philosophy first gave the free scientific, and thus at the same time the objective, form to Dialectic. Socrates, as we should expect from the general character of his philosophising, has the dialectic element in a predominantly subjective shape, that of Irony. He used to turn his Dialectic, first against ordinary consciousness, and then especially against the Sophists. In his conversations he used to simulate the wish for some clearer knowledge about the subject under discussion, and after putting all sorts of questions with that intent, he drew on those with whom he conversed to the opposite of what their first impressions had pronounced correct. If, for instance, the Sophists claimed to be teachers, Socrates by a series of questions forced the Sophist Protagoras to confess that all learning is only recollection. In his more strictly scientific dialogues Plato employs the dialectical method to show the finitude of all hard and fast terms of understanding. Thus in the Parmenides he deduces the many from the one, and shows nevertheless that the many

cannot but define itself as the one. In this grand style did Plato treat Dialectic. In modern times it was, more than any other, Kant who resuscitated the name of Dialectic, and restored it to its post of honour. He did it . . . by working out the Antinomies of the reason. The problem of these Antinomies is no mere subjective piece of work oscillating between one set of grounds and another; it really serves to show that every abstract proposition of understanding, taken precisely as it is given, naturally veers round into its opposite.

However reluctant Understanding may be to admit the action of Dialectic, we must not suppose that the recognition of its existence is peculiarly confined to the philosopher. It would be truer to say that Dialectic gives expression to a law which is felt in all other grades of consciousness, and in general experience. Everything that surrounds us may be viewed as an instance of Dialectic. We are aware that everything finite, instead of being stable and ultimate, is rather changeable and transient; and this is exactly what we mean by that Dialectic of the finite, by which the finite, as implicitly other than what it is, is forced beyond its own immediate or natural being to turn suddenly into its opposite. We have before this identified Understanding with what is implied in the popular idea of the goodness of God; we may now remark of Dialectic, in the same objective signification, that its principle answers to the idea of his power. All things, we say,— that is, the finite world as such,—are doomed; and in saying so, we have a vision of Dialectic as the universal and irresistible power before which nothing can stay, however secure and stable it may deem itself. The category of power does not, it is true, exhaust the depth of the divine nature or the notion of God; but it certainly forms a vital element in all religious consciousness.

Apart from this general objectivity of Dialectic, we find traces of its presence in each of the particular provinces and phases of the natural and the spiritual world. Take as an illustration the motion of the heavenly bodies. At this moment the planet stands in this spot, but implicitly it is the possibility of being in another spot; and that possibility of being otherwise the planet brings into existence by moving. Similarly the 'physical' elements prove to be Dialectical. The process of meteorological action is the exhibition of their Dialectic. It is the same dynamic that lies at the root of every other natural process, and, as it were, forces nature out of itself. To illustrate the presence of Dialectic in the spiritual world, especially in the provinces of law and morality, we have only to recollect how general experience shows us the extreme of one state or action suddenly shifting into its opposite: a Dialectic which is recognised in many ways in common proverbs. Thus *summum jus summa injuria*: which means, that to drive an abstract right to its extremity is to do a wrong. In political life, as every one knows, extreme anarchy and extreme despotism naturally lead to one another. The perception of Dialectic in the province of individual Ethics is seen in the well-known adages, Pride comes before a fall: Too much wit outwits itself. Even feeling, bodily as well as mental, has its Dialectic. Every one knows how the extremes of pain and pleasure pass into each other: the heart overflowing with joy seeks relief in tears, and the deepest melancholy will at times betray its presence by a smile. . . .

Positive and negative are supposed to express an absolute difference. The two however are at bottom the same: the name of either might be transferred to the other. Thus, for example, debts and assets are not two particular, self-subsisting species of property. What is negative to the debtor, is positive to the creditor. A way to the east is also a way to the west. Positive and negative are therefore intrinsically conditioned by one another, and are only in relation to each other. The north pole of the magnet cannot be without the south pole, and *vice versa*. If we cut a magnet in two, we have not a north pole in one piece, and a south pole in the other. Similarly, in electricity, the positive and the negative are not two diverse and independent fluids. In opposition, the different is not confronted by any other, but by *its* other. Usually we regard different things as unaffected by each other. Thus we say: I am a human being, and around me are air, water, animals, and all sorts of things. Everything is thus put outside of every other. But the aim of philosophy is to banish indifference, and to ascertain the necessity of things. By that means the other is seen to stand over against *its* other. Thus, for example, inorganic nature is not to be considered merely something else than organic nature, but the necessary antithesis of it. Both are in essential relation to one another; and the one of the two is, only in so far as it excludes the other from it, and thus relates itself thereto. Nature in like manner is not without mind, nor mind without nature. An important step has been taken, when we cease in thinking to use phrases like: Of course something else is also possible. While we so speak, we are still tainted with contingency: and all true thinking, we have already said, is a thinking of necessity.

In modern physical science the opposition, first observed to exist in magnetism as polarity, has come to be regarded as a universal law pervading the whole of nature. This would be a real scientific advance, if care were at the same time taken not to let mere variety revert without explanation, as a valid category, side by side with opposition. Thus at one time the colours are regarded as in polar opposition to one another, and called complementary colours: at another time they are looked at in their indifferent and merely quantitative difference of red, yellow, green, &c.

Instead of speaking by the maxim of Excluded Middle (which is the maxim of abstract understanding) we should rather say: Everything is opposite. Neither in heaven nor in earth, neither in the world of mind nor of nature, is there anywhere such an abstract 'Either —or' as the understanding maintains. Whatever exists is concrete, with difference and opposition in itself. The finitude of things will then lie in the want of correspondence between their immediate being, and what they essentially are. Thus, in inorganic nature, the acid is implictly at the same time the base: in other words, its only being consists in its relation to its other. Hence also the acid is not something that persists

quietly in the contrast: it is always in effort to realise what it potentially is. Contradiction is the very moving principle of the world: and it is ridiculous to say that contradiction is unthinkable. The only thing correct in that statement is that contradiction is not the end of the matter, but cancels itself. But contradiction, when cancelled, does not leave abstract identity; for that is itself only one side of the contrariety. The proximate result of opposition (when realised as contradiction) is the Ground, which contains identity as well as difference superseded and deposed to elements in the completer notion.[1]

2. [History as a Rational Pattern]

The only Thought which Philosophy brings with it to the contemplation of History, is the simple conception of *Reason*; that Reason is the Sovereign of the World; that the history of the world, therefore, presents us with a rational process. This conviction and intuition is a hypothesis in the domain of history as such. In that of Philosophy it is no hypothesis. It is there proved by speculative cognition, that Reason—and this term may here suffice us, without investigating the relation sustained by the Universe to the Divine Being—is *Substance*, as well as *Infinite Power*; its

[1] Hegel's concept of the Ground involves the interdependence of opposites. Because the negative depends on the positive, the positive is the ground of the negative. Similarly the negative is the ground of the positive. In Hegel's example, the north pole of the magnet cannot exist without the south pole, and *vice versa*. Each is equally the ground, and in this sense, the ground is the synthesis, or identity, of difference.—M.R.

own *Infinite Material* underlying all the natural and spiritual life which it originates, as also the *Infinite Form*—that which sets this Material in motion. On the one hand, Reason is the *substance* of the Universe; viz. that by which and in which all reality has its being and subsistence. On the other hand, it is the *Infinite Energy* of the Universe; since Reason is not so powerless as to be incapable of producing anything but a mere ideal, a mere intention—having its place outside reality, nobody knows where; something separate and abstract, in the heads of certain human beings. It is *the infinite complex of things*, their entire Essence and Truth. It is its own material which it commits to its own Active Energy to work up; not needing, as finite action does, the conditions of an external material of given means from which it may obtain its support, and the objects of its activity. It supplies its own nourishment, and is the object of its own operations. While it is exclusively its own basis of existence, and absolute final aim, it is also the energizing power realizing this aim; developing it not only in the phenomena of the Natural, but also of the Spiritual Universe—the History of the World. That this "Idea" or "Reason" is the *True*, the *Eternal*, the absolutely *powerful* essence; that it reveals itself in the World, and that in that World nothing else is revealed but this and its honor and glory—is the thesis which, as we have said, has been proved in Philosophy, and is here regarded as demonstrated.

In those of my hearers who are not acquainted with Philosophy, I may fairly presume, at least, the existence of a *belief* in Reason, a desire, a thirst for acquaintance with it, in entering upon this course of Lectures. It is, in fact, the wish for rational insight, not the ambition to amass a mere heap of requirements, that should be presupposed in every case as possessing the mind of the learner in the study of science. If the clear idea of Reason is not already developed in our minds, in beginning the study of Universal History, we should at least have the firm, unconquerable faith that Reason *does* exist there; and that the World of intelligence and conscious volition is not abandoned to chance, but must show itself in the light of the self-cognizant Idea. Yet I am not obliged to make any such preliminary demand upon your faith. What I have said thus provisionally, and what I shall have further to say, is, even in reference to *our* branch of science, not to be regarded as hypothetical, but as a summary view of the whole; the *result of the investigation* we are about to pursue; a result which happens to be known to *me*, because I have traversed the entire field. It is only an inference from the history of the World, that its development has been a rational process; that the history in question has constituted the rational necessary course of the World-Spirit—that Spirit whose nature is always one and the same, but which unfolds this its one nature in the phenomena of the World's existence. This must, as before stated, present itself as the ultimate *result* of History. But we have to take the latter as it is. We must proceed historically—empirically. . . .

We might then announce it as the first condition to be observed, that we should faithfully adopt all that is historical. But in such general expressions themselves, as "faithfully" and "adopt," lies the ambiguity. Even the ordinary, the "impartial" historiographer, who believes and professes that he maintains a simply receptive attitude; surrendering himself only to the data supplied him—is by no means passive as regards the exercise of his thinking powers. He brings his categories with him, and sees the phenomena presented to his mental vision, exclusively through these media. And, especially in all that pretends to the name of science, it is indispensable that Reason should not sleep—that reflection should be in full play. To him who looks upon the world rationally, the world in its turn presents a rational aspect. The relation is mutual. . . .

The inquiry into the *essential destiny* of Reason—as far as it is considered in reference to the World—is identical with the question, *what is the ultimate design of the world?* And the expression implies that that design is destined to be realized. Two points of consideration suggest themselves: first, the *import* of this design—its abstract definition; and secondly, its *realization*.

It must be observed at the outset, that the phenomenon we investigate—Universal History—belongs to the realm of *Spirit*. The term "*World*," includes both physical and psychical Nature. Physical Nature also plays its part in the World's History, and attention will have to be paid to the fundamental natural relations thus involved. But Spirit, and the course of its development, is our sub-stantial object. Our task does not require us to contemplate Nature as a Rational System in itself—though in its own proper domain it proves itself such—but simply in its relation to *Spirit*. On the stage on which we are observing it—Universal History—Spirit displays itself in its most concrete reality. Notwithstanding this (or rather for the very purpose of comprehending the *general* principles which this, its form of *concrete reality*, embodies) we must premise some abstract characteristics of the *nature of Spirit*. Such an explanation, however, cannot be given here under any other form than that of bare assertion. The present is not the occasion for unfolding the idea of Spirit speculatively; for whatever has a place in an Introduction, must, as already observed, be taken as simply historical; something assumed as having been explained and proved elsewhere; or whose demonstration awaits the sequel of the Science of History itself.

We have therefore to mention here:

1. The abstract characteristics of the nature of Spirit.

2. What means Spirit uses in order to realize its Idea.

3. Lastly, we must consider the shape which the perfect embodiment of Spirit assumes—the State.

3. [Freedom as the Essence of Spirit]

1. The nature of Spirit may be understood by a glance at its direct opposite—*Matter*. As the essence of Matter is Gravity, so, on the other hand, we may affirm that the substance, the essence of Spirit is Freedom. All will readily as-

sent to the doctrine that Spirit, among other properties, is also endowed with Freedom; but philosophy teaches that all the qualities of Spirit exist only through Freedom; that all are but means for attaining freedom; that all seek and produce this and this alone. It is a result of speculative Philosophy, that Freedom is the sole truth of Spirit.

The destiny of the spiritual World, and—since this is the *substantial World*, while the physical remains subordinate to it, or, in the language of speculation, has no truth *as against* the spiritual—the *final cause of the World at large*, we allege to be the consciousness of its own freedom on the part of Spirit, and *ipso facto*, the *reality* of that freedom. But that this term "Freedom," without further qualification, is an indefinite, and incalculable ambiguous term; and that while that which it represents is the *ne plus ultra* of attainment, it is liable to an infinity of misunderstandings, confusions and errors, and to become the occasion for all imaginable excesses—has never been more clearly known and felt than in modern times. Yet, for the present, we must content ourselves with the term itself without further definition. Attention was also directed to the importance of the infinite difference between a principle in the abstract, and its realization in the concrete. In the process before us, the essential nature of freedom—which involves in it absolute necessity—is to be displayed as coming to a consciousness of itself (for it is in its very nature self-consciousness) and thereby realizing its existence. Itself is its own object of attainment, and the sole aim of Spirit. This result it is, at which the process of

the World's History has been continually aiming; and to which the sacrifices that have ever and anon been laid on the vast altar of the earth, through the long lapse of ages, have been offered. This is the only aim that sees itself realized and fulfilled; the only pole of repose amid the ceaseless change of events and conditions, and the sole efficient principle that pervades them. This final aim is God's purpose with the world; but God is the absolutely perfect Being, and can, therefore, will nothing other than himself—his own Will. The Nature of His Will—that is, His Nature itself—is what we here call the Idea of Freedom; translating the language of Religion into that of Thought. The question, then, which we may next put, is: What means does this principle of Freedom use for its realization? This is the second point we have to consider.

4. [The Means by which Freedom Is Realized]

2. The question of the *means* by which Freedom develops itself to a World, conducts us to the phenomenon of History itself. Although Freedom is, primarily, an undeveloped idea, the means it uses are external and phenomenal; presenting themselves in History to our sensuous vision. The first glance at History convinces us that the actions of men proceed from their needs, their passions, their characters and talents; and impresses us with the belief that such needs, passions and interests are the sole springs of action—the efficient agents in this scene of activity. Among these may, perhaps, be found aims of a liberal or universal kind—benevolence

it may be, or noble patriotism; but such virtues and general views are but insignificant as compared with the World and its doings. We may perhaps see the Ideal of Reason actualized in those who adopt such aims, and within the sphere of their influence; but they bear only a trifling proportion to the mass of the human race; and the extent of that influence is limited accordingly. Passions, private aims, and the satisfaction of selfish desires, are, on the other hand, most effective springs of action. Their power lies in the fact that they respect none of the limitations which justice and morality would impose on them; and that these natural impulses have a more direct influence over man than the artificial and tedious discipline that tends to order and self-restraint, law and morality. When we look at this display of passions, and the consequences of their violence; the Unreason which is associated not only with them, but even (rather we might say *especially*) with *good* designs and righteous aims; when we see the evil, the vice, the ruin that has befallen the most flourishing kingdoms which the mind of man ever created; we can scarce avoid being filled with sorrow at this universal taint of corruption; and, since this decay is not the work of mere Nature, but of the Human Will—a moral imbitterment—a revolt of the Good Spirit (if it have a place within us) may well be the result of our reflections. Without rhetorical exaggeration, a simply truthful combination of the miseries that have overwhelmed the noblest of nations and polities, and the finest exemplars of private virtue—forms a picture of most fearful aspect, and excites emotions of the profoundest and most hopeless sadness, counterbalanced by no consolatory result. We endure in beholding it a mental torture, allowing no defence or escape but the consideration that what has happened could not be otherwise; that it is a fatality which no intervention could alter. And at last we draw back from the intolerable disgust with which these sorrowful reflections threaten us into the more agreeable environment of our individual life—the Present formed by our private aims and interests. In short we retreat into the selfishness that stands on the quiet shore, and thence enjoys in safety the distant spectacle of "wrecks confusedly hurled." But even regarding History as the slaughter-bench at which the happiness of peoples, the wisdom of States, and the virtue of individuals have been victimized—the question involuntarily arises—to what principle, to what final aim these enormous sacrifices have been offered. . . .

The *first* remark we have to make, and which—though already presented more than once—cannot be too often repeated when the occasion seems to call for it—is that what we call *principle*, *aim*, *destiny*, or the nature and idea of Spirit, is something merely general and abstract. Principle—Plan of Existence—Law—is a hidden, undeveloped essence, which *as such*—however true in itself—is not completely real. Aims, principles, etc., have a place in our thoughts, in our subjective design only; but not yet in the sphere of reality. That which exists for itself only, is a possibility, a potentiality; but has not yet emerged into Existence. A *second* element must be introduced in order to produce actuality

—viz. actuation, realization; and whose motive power is the Will—the activity of man in the widest sense. It is only by this activity that that Idea as well as abstract characteristics generally, are realized, actualized; for of themselves they are powerless. The motive power that puts them in operation, and gives them determinate existence, is the need, instinct, inclination, and passion of man. . . .

We assert then that nothing has been accomplished without interest on the part of the actors; and—if interest be called passion, inasmuch as the whole individuality, to the neglect of all other actual or possible interests and claims, is devoted to an object with every fibre of volition, concentrating all its desires and powers upon it—we may affirm absolutely that *nothing great in the World* has been accomplished without *passion*. Two elements, therefore, enter into the object of our investigation; the first the Idea, the second the complex of human passions; the one the warp, the other the woof of the vast arras-web of Universal History. . . .

From this comment on the second essential element in the historical embodiment of an aim, we infer—glancing at the institution of the State in passing—that a State is then well constituted and internally powerful, when the private interest of its citizens is one with the common interest of the State; when the one finds its gratification and realization in the other—a proposition in itself very important. But in a State many institutions must be adopted, much political machinery invented, accompanied by appropriate political arrangements—necessitating long struggles of the un-

derstanding before what is really appropriate can be discovered—involving, moreover, contentions with private interest and passions, and a tedious discipline of these latter, in order to bring about the desired harmony. The epoch, when a State attains this harmonious condition, marks the period of its bloom, its virtue, its vigor, and its prosperity. But the history of mankind does not begin with a *conscious* aim of any kind, as it is the case with the particular circles into which men form themselves of set purpose. The mere social instinct implies a conscious purpose of security for life and property; and when society has been constituted, this purpose becomes more comprehensive. The History of the World begins with its general aim—the realization of the Idea of Spirit—only in an *implicit* form (*an sich*) that is, as Nature; a hidden, most profoundly hidden, unconscious instinct; and the whole process of History (as already observed) is directed to rendering this unconscious impulse a conscious one. Thus appearing in the form of merely natural existence, natural will—that which has been called the subjective side—physical craving, instinct, passion, private interest, as also opinion and subjective conception—spontaneously present themselves at the very commencement. This vast congeries of volitions, interests and activities constitute the instruments and means of the World-Spirit for attaining its object; bringing it to consciousness, and realizing it. And this aim is none other than finding itself—coming to itself—and contemplating itself in concrete actuality. But that those manifestations of vitality on the part of individuals and peoples, in which they seek and satisfy their own purposes, are, at the same time, the means and instruments of a higher and broader purpose of which they know nothing—which they realize unconsciously—might be made a matter of question; rather has been questioned, and in every variety of form negatived, decried and condemned as mere dreaming and "Philosophy." But on this point I announced my view at the very outset, and asserted our hypothesis—which, however, will appear in the sequel, in the form of a legitimate inference—and our belief, that Reason governs the world, and has consequently governed its history. In relation to this independently universal and substantial existence—all else is subordinate, subservient to it, and the means for its development. . . .

5. [Great Men and the Cunning of Reason]

He is happy who finds his condition suited to his special character, will, and fancy, and so enjoys himself in that condition. The History of the World is not the theatre of happiness. Periods of happiness are blank pages in it, for they are period of harmony—periods when the antithesis is in abeyance. Reflection on self—the Freedom above described—is abstractly defined as the formal element of the activity of the absolute Idea. The realizing *activity* of which we have spoken is the middle term of the Syllogism, one of whose extremes is the Universal essence, the *Idea*, which reposes in the penetralia of Spirit; and the other, the complex of external things—objective matter. That

activity is the medium by which the universal latent principle is translated into the domain of objectivity.

I will endeavor to make what has been said more vivid and clear by examples.

The building of a house is, in the first instance, a subjective aim and design. On the other hand we have, as means, the several substances required for the work—Iron, Wood, Stones. The elements are made use of in working up this material: fire to melt the iron, wind to blow the fire, water to set wheels in motion, in order to cut the wood, etc. The result is, that the wind, which has helped to build the house; is shut out by the house; so also are the violence of rains and floods, and the destructive powers of fire, so far as the house is made fireproof. The stones and beams obey the law of gravity—press downward—and so high walls are carried up. Thus the elements are made use of in accordance with their nature, and yet to co-operate for a product, by which their operation is limited. Thus the passions of men are gratified; they develop themselves and their aims in accordance with their natural tendencies, and build up the edifice of human society; thus fortifying a position for Right and Order *against themselves*.

The connection of events above indicated involves also the fact, that in history an additional result is commonly produced by human actions beyond that which they aim at and obtain—that which they immediately recognize and desire. They gratify their own interest; but something further is thereby accomplished, latent in the actions in question, though not present to their consciousness, and not included in their design. An analogous example is offered in the case of a man who, from a feeling of revenge—perhaps not an unjust one, but produced by injury on the other's part—burns that other man's house. A connection is immediately established between the deed itself and a train of circumstances not directly included in it, taken abstractedly. In itself it consisted in merely presenting a small flame to a small portion of a beam. Events not involved in that simple act follow of themselves. The part of the beam which was set fire to is connected with its remote portions; the beam itself is united with the woodwork of the house generally, and this with other houses; so that a wide conflagration ensues, which destroys the goods and chattels of many other persons besides his against whom the act of revenge was first directed; perhaps even costs not a few men their lives. This lay neither in the deed abstractedly, nor in the design of the man who committed it. But the action has a further general bearing. In the design of the doer it was only revenge executed against an individual in the destruction of his property, but it is moreover a crime, and that involves punishment also. This may not have been present to the mind of the perpetrator, still less in his intention; but his deed itself, the general principles it calls into play, its substantial content entails it. By this example I wish only to impress on you the consideration that in a simple act, something further may be implicated than lies in the intention and consciousness of the agent. The example before us involves, however, this additional consideration, that the sub-

stance of the act, consequently we may say the act itself, recoils upon the perpetrator—reacts upon him with destructive tendency. This union of the two extremes—the embodiment of a general idea in the form of direct reality, and the elevation of a speciality into connection with universal truth—is brought to pass, at first sight, under the conditions of an utter diversity of nature between the two, and an indifference of the one extreme toward the other. The aims which the agents set before them are limited and special; but it must be remarked that the agents themselves are intelligent thinking beings. The purport of their desires is interwoven with *general, essential* considerations of justice, good, duty, etc.; for mere desire—volition in its rough and savage forms—falls not within the scene and sphere of Universal History. Those general considerations, which form at the same time a norm for directing aims and actions, have a determinate purport; for such an abstraction as "good for its own sake," has no place in living reality. If men are to act, they must not only intend the Good, but must have decided for themselves whether this or that particular thing is a Good. What special course of action, however, is good or not, is determined, as regards the ordinary contingencies of private life, by the laws and customs of a State; and here no great difficulty is presented. Each individual has his position; he knows on the whole what a just, honorable course of conduct is. As to ordinary, private relations, the assertion that it is difficult to choose the right and good—the regarding it as the mark of an exalted morality to find difficulties and raise scruples on that score—may be set down to an evil or perverse will, which seeks to evade duties not in themselves of a perplexing nature; or, at any rate, to an idly reflective habit of mind—where a feeble will affords no sufficient exercise to the faculties—leaving them therefore to find occupation within themselves, and to expend themselves on moral self-adulation.

It is quite otherwise with the comprehensive relations that History has to do with. In this sphere are presented those momentous collisions between existing, acknowledged duties, laws, and rights, and those contingencies which are adverse to this fixed system; which assail and even destroy its foundations and existence; whose tenor may nevertheless seem good—on the large scale advantageous—yes, even indispensable and necessary. These contingencies realize themselves in History: they involve a general principle of a different order from that on which depends the *permanence* of a people or a State. This principle is an essential phase in the development of the *creating* Idea, of Truth, striving and urging toward [consciousness of] itself. Historical men—*World-Historical Individuals*—are those in whose aim such a general principle lies.

Caesar, in danger of losing a position, not perhaps at that time of superiority, yet at least of equality with the others who were at the head of the State, and of succumbing to those who were just on the point of becoming his enemies—belongs essentially to this category. These enemies—who were at the same time pursuing *their* personal aims—had the form of the constitution, and

the power conferred by an appearance of justice, on their side. Caesar was contending for the maintenance of his position, honor, and safety; and, since the power of his opponents included the sovereignty over the provinces of the Roman Empire, his victory secured for him the conquest of that entire Empire; and he thus became (though leaving the form of the constitution) the Autocrat of the State. That which secured for him the execution of a design, which in the first instance was of negative import—the Autocracy of Rome—was, however, at the same time an independently necessary feature in the history of Rome and of the world. It was not then his private gain merely, but an unconscious impulse that occasioned the accomplishment of that for which the time was ripe. Such are all great historical men—whose own particular aims involve those large issues which are the will of the World-Spirit. They may be called Heroes, inasmuch as they have derived their purposes and their vocation, not from the calm, regular course of things, sanctioned by the existing order; but from a concealed fount—one which has not attained to phenomenal, present existence—from that inner Spirit, still hidden beneath the surface, which, impinging on the outer world as on a shell, bursts it in pieces, because it is another kernel than that which belonged to the shell in question. They are men, therefore, who appear to draw the impulse of their life from themselves; and whose deeds have produced a condition of things and a complex of historical relations which appear to be only *their* interest, and *their* work.

Such individuals had no conscious-

ness of the general Idea they were unfolding, while prosecuting those aims
of theirs; on the contrary, they were
practical, political men. But at the same
time they were thinking men, who had
an insight into the requirements of the
time—*what was ripe for development.*
This was the very Truth for their age,
for their world; the species next in
order, so to speak, and which was already formed in the womb of time. It
was theirs to know this nascent principle; the necessary, directly sequent
step in progress, which their world was
to take; to make this their aim, and to
expend their energy in promoting it.
World-historical men—the Heroes of an
epoch—must, therefore, be recognized
as its clear-sighted ones; *their* deeds,
their words are the best of that time.
Great men have formed purposes to
satisfy themselves, not others. Whatever prudent designs and counsels they
might have learned from others, would
be the more limited and inconsistent
features in their career; for it was they
who best understood affairs; from
whom *others* learned, and approved, or
at least acquiesced in—their policy. For
that Spirit which had taken this fresh
step in history is the inmost soul of all
individuals; but in a state of unconsciousness which the great men in question aroused. Their fellows, therefore,
follow these soul-leaders; for they feel
the irresistible power of their own inner
Spirit thus embodied. If we go on to
cast a look at the fate of these World-
Historical persons, whose vocation it
was to be the agents of the World-
Spirit—we shall find it to have been no
happy one. They attained no calm enjoyment; their whole life was labor and
trouble; their whole nature was naught
else but their master-passion. When
their object is attained they fall off like
empty hulls from the kernel. They die
early, like Alexander; they are murdered, like Caesar; transported to St.
Helena, like Napoleon. This fearful
consolation—that historical men have
not enjoyed what is called happiness,
and of which only private life (and this
may be passed under very various external circumstances) is capable—this
consolation those may draw from history, who stand in need of it; and it is
craved by Envy—vexed at what is great
and transcendent—striving, therefore, to
depreciate it, and to find some flaw in it.
Thus in modern times it has been demonstarted *ad nauseam* that princes are
generally unhappy on their thrones; in
consideration of which the possession
of a throne is tolerated, and men acquiesce in the fact that not themselves
but the personages in question are its
occupants. The Free Man, we may observe, is not envious, but gladly recognizes what is great and exalted, and re-
joices that it exists.

It is in the light of those common
elements which constitute the interest
and therefore the passions of individuals, that these historical men are to be
regarded. They are *great* men, because
they willed and accomplished something great; not a mere fancy, a mere
intention, but that which met the case
and fell in with the needs of the age.
This mode of considering them also
excludes the so-called "psychological"
view, which—serving the purpose of
envy most effectually—contrives so to
refer all actions to the heart—to bring
them under such a subjective aspect—

as that their authors appear to have done everything under the impulse of some passion, mean or grand—some *morbid craving*—and on account of these passions and cravings to have been not moral men. Alexander of Macedon partly subdued Greece, and then Asia; therefore he was possessed by a *morbid craving* for conquest. He is alleged to have acted from a craving for fame, for conquest; and the proof that these were the impelling motives is that he did that which resulted in fame. What pedagogue has not demonstrated of Alexander the Great—of Julius Caesar—that they were instigated by such passions, and were consequently immoral men?—whence the conclusion immediately follows that he, the pedagogue, is a better man than they, because he has not such passions; a proof of which lies in the fact that he does not conquer Asia—vanquish Darius and Porus—but while he enjoys life himself, lets others enjoy it too. These psychologists are particularly fond of contemplating those peculiarities of great historical figures which appertain to them as private persons. Man must eat and drink; he sustains relations to friends and acquaintances; he has passing impulses and ebullitions of temper. "No man is a hero to his valet-de-chambre," is a well-known proverb; I have added—and Goethe repeated it ten years later—"but not because the former is no hero, but because the latter is a valet." He takes off the hero's boots, assists him to bed, knows that he prefers champagne, etc. Historical personnages waited upon in historical literature by such psychological valets, come poorly off; they are brought down by these their attendants to a level with

—or rather a few degrees below the level of—the morality of such exquisite discerners of spirits. The Thersites of Homer who abuses the kings is a standing figure for all times. Blows—that is, beating with a solid cudgel—he does not get in every age, as in the Homeric one; but his envy, his egotism, is the thorn which he has to carry in his flesh; and the undying worm that gnaws him is the tormenting consideration that his excellent views and vituperations remain absolutely without result in the world. But our satisfaction at the fate of Thersitism also, may have its sinister side.

A World-historical individual is not so unwise as to indulge a variety of wishes to divide his regards. He is devoted to the One Aim, regardless of all else. It is even possible that such men may treat other great, even sacred interests, inconsiderately; conduct which is indeed obnoxious to moral reprehension. But so mighty a form must trample down many an innocent flower—crush to pieces many an object in its path.

The special interest of passion is thus inseparable from the active development of a general principle: for it is from the special and determinate and from its negation that the Universal results. Particularity contends with its like, and some loss is involved in the issue. *It* is not the general idea that is implicated in opposition and combat, and that is exposed to danger. It remains in the background, untouched and uninjured. This may be called the *cunning of reason*—that it sets the passions to work for itself, while that which develops its existence through such impulsion pays the penalty, and suffers loss. For it is *phenomenal* being that is so treated, and of this, part is of no value, part is positive and real. The particular is for the most part of too trifling value as compared with the general: individuals are sacrificed and abandoned. The Idea pays the penalty of determinate existence and of corruptibility, not from itself, but from the passions of individuals. . . .

6. [The State as the Embodiment of Freedom]

The third point to be analyzed is, therefore—what is the object to be realized by these means; *i.e.* what is the form it assumes in the realm of reality. We have spoken of *means*; but in the carrying out of a subjective, limited aim, we have also to take into consideration the element of a *material*, either already present or which has to be procured. Thus the question would arise: What is the material in which the Ideal of Reason is wrought out? The primary answer would be—Personality itself— human desires—Subjectivity generally. In human knowledge and volition, as its material element, Reason attains positive existence. We have considered subjective volition where it has an object which is the truth and essence of a reality; viz. where it constitutes a great world-historical passion. As a subjective will, occupied with limited passions, it is dependent, and can gratify its desires only within the limits of this dependence. But the subjective will has also a substantial life—a reality—in which it moves in the region of *essen-*

tial being, and has the essential itself as the object of its existence. This essential being is the union of the *subjective* with the *rational* Will: it is the moral Whole, the *State*, which is that form of reality in which the individual has and enjoys his freedom; but on the condition of his recognizing, believing in and willing that which is common to the Whole. And this must not be understood as if the subjective will of the social unit attained its gratification and enjoyment through that common Will; as if this were a means provided for its benefit; as if the individual, in his relations to other individuals, thus limited his freedom, in order that this universal limitation—the mutual constraint of all— might secure a small space of liberty for each. Rather, we affirm, are Law, Morality, Government, and they alone, the positive reality and completion of Freedom. Freedom of a low and limited order is mere caprice, which finds its exercise in the sphere of particular and limited desires.

Subjective volition—Passion—is that which sets men in activity, that which effects "practical" realization. The Idea is the inner spring of action; the State is the actually existing, realized moral life. For it is the Unity of the universal, essential Will, with that of the individual; and this is "Morality." The Individual living in this unity has a moral life; possesses a value that consists in this substantiality alone. Sophocles in his Antigone, says, "The divine commands are not of yesterday, nor of today; no, they have an infinite existence, and no one could say whence they came." The laws of morality are not accidental, but are the essentially Rational. It is the very object of the State that what is essential in the practical activity of men, and in their dispositions, should be duly recognized; that it should have a manifest existence, and maintain its position. It is the absolute interest of Reason that this moral Whole should exist: and herein lies the justification and merit of heroes who have founded states—however rude these may have been. In the history of the World, only those peoples can come under our notice which form a state. For it must be understood that this latter is the realization of Freedom, *i.e.* of the absolute final aim, and that it exists for its own sake. It must further be understood that all the worth which the human being possesses—all spiritual reality, he possesses only through the State. For his spiritual reality consists in this, that his own essence—Reason— is objectively present to him, that it possesses objective immediate existence for him. Thus only is he fully conscious; thus only is he a partaker of morality— of a just and moral social and political life. For Truth is the Unity of the universal and subjective Will; and the Universal is to be found in the State, in its laws, its universal and rational arrangements. The State is the Divine Idea as it exists on Earth. We have in it, therefore, the object of History in a more definite shape than before; that in which Freedom obtains objectivity, and lives in the enjoyment of this objectivity. For Law is the objectivity of Spirit; volition in its true form. Only that will which obeys law, is free; for it obeys itself—it is independent and so free. When the State or our country constitutes a community of existence; when the subjective will of man submits to laws—the contradiction between Liberty and Necessity vanishes. The Rational has necessary existence, as being the reality and substance of things, and we are free in recognizing it as law, and following it as the substance of our own being. The objective and the subjective will are then reconciled, and present one identical homogeneous whole.

COMMENT

The Basis of Hegel's Social Philosophy

Hegel's philosophy is called "idealism," but he was not an idealist in the ordinary philosophical sense of the term. He did not maintain with Berkeley that the whole of reality consists of minds and their ideas, nor with Royce that a single Infinite Mind contains us and all our experiences and all things besides.[1] Rather he was an "idealist" in holding that "ideas" provide a pattern, a kind of conceptual blueprint, for interpreting human life and the natural world. All things are developing in accordance with a logical scheme. The processes of nature and the stages

[1] See J. N. Findlay, *Hegel* (London: George Allen and Unwin Ltd., 1958) especially Chapter One. Hegel is often misinterpreted.

of history are the acting out, the making explicit, of a latent rationality. Every spirit, and every thing, is part of a single vast web of logically interrelated entities —nothing is really separate, like a hard impenetrable atom or an enclosed self-subsistent mind.

Since things are essentially related to one another, they cannot be understood truly apart from such relationships. The truth is a whole, each integral part of which is mutilated when considered in isolation. To see things together, therefore, is to enrich vision, to see things apart is to impoverish it. No proposition taken in isolation is wholly true because no thing taken in isolation is wholly real.

This point of view is basic in Hegel's social philosophy. He believes that individualism is false because separate individuals are unreal. Apart from their social relations, human beings are as artificial and insubstantial as the personifications in an allegory. They are shaped and constituted by the social forces penetrating into them—by the customs, traditions, institutions, and cultural life of the society.

A social group is more than a mere aggregate, an arithmetical sum total of its parts. The mark of an aggregate is that its parts can be joined or separated without essential change in their internal characteristics. No genuine social group is such an aggregate—its members are too interdependent; they are sustained in their activity by one another and by the whole. The group has a total character impressed on every member—a concrete and ineluctable unity of its own, with an organized social structure and distinctive social functions. The common interests of a group regarded as a single individual, therefore, cannot be identified with the several interests of its members. A mob, acting as no individual would act, is simply the more pathological embodiment of a basic and universal fact: that every coherent group has an *esprit de corps*, a common interest, a collective will, a kind of group mind. All of us have experienced such group feeling and group thought, the experience of being merged in something greater than ourselves, the experience of being dominated by the group spirit.

Hegel's sense of interrelatedness was reinforced by his theory of a new kind of logic, which would take account of the continuities and gradations of reality. He had noticed that there is a characteristic pattern of thought in the give-and-take of fruitful argument. The first stage tends to be that of unqualified assertion (the thesis), an idea being advanced as unqualifiedly true and intelligible in and of itself. The second stage is a sceptical rejoinder (the antithesis); the original idea, opposed by a counter notion, is shown to be false and incomplete when taken in its initial and unqualified form. As the argument proceeds each person is made to see the strength in the opposing position, and the disputants, if the outcome is fruitful, finally reach an agreement involving a more inclusive organization of thought (the synthesis). Thus a larger truth emerges from the strife of partisan views.

Hegel believed that this concrete movement of thought differs from the abstract character of formal logic. The traditional logic, following the theory of Aristotle, conceived opposition as the contradiction of a positive and a negative: "X is Y" being opposed by "X is not Y." From this opposition no new synthesis can spring. Thinking of the characteristic way in which arguments develop, Hegel conceived of opposition, not as the juxtaposition of a positive and a negative, but as the opposition of two *positive* terms, the thesis and antithesis, which implicate and yet in a sense negate each other, their mutuality and opposition forcing us to reconcile them in a wider thought-construct (the synthesis). In turn, the synthesis tends to become a new thesis, and the process begins anew. Thus each new idea, not being the whole truth, is inevitably tainted with falsehood, and must be gathered up and transformed in a more comprehensive whole.

Contradiction and its resolution in the realm of thought are paralleled by a similar movement in the field of human affairs. Here, too, there are antithetical tendencies, each bent upon destroying its opposite, and producing a kind of crisis by its inordinate one-sidedness. The clash of these tendencies exposes the logical ridiculousness of each factor taken in isolation, and thus releases corrective forces which restore the balance. In this way the whole process leads on to more coherent and comprehensive states of equilibrium.

It must not be supposed that all development can be fitted into a neat, triadic pattern. The terms "thesis," "antithesis," and "synthesis" have been used much more frequently by expositors of Hegel than by Hegel himself. In his preface to *The Phenomenology of the Spirit*, he warns against a violent forcing of any and every sort of material into the triadic pattern. His own philosophical thinking, although predominantly "dialectical," is too rich and various to reduce to any simple scheme.

Applied to problems of ethics and social philosophy, the dialectical approach implies that the good life is "a unity of the multiform and an accord of the discordant." The proper reconciliation of conflicts is to be found, not in exalting one set of ideas or values at the expense of another, but in the creative interpenetration and reconciliation of "opposites." So it is with the great antinomies that plague and yet enrich men's experience: growth and order, impulse and rationality, breadth and specialization, practicality and idealism. In dealing with each of these polarities, we should seek no one-sided or fragmentary solution but a happy union of the apparently incompatible. So it is with the antinomy between the individual and the community. Only folly and disaster can result from denying either of these antithetical modes. Individuality, if pitted against community, is a dangerous half-truth, while community, if considered total and absolute, is no less delusory. The only happy solution is to recognize that the full development of individuality requires identification with the community, just as the rich unfolding of community requires the cultivation of individuality.

From these premises, Hegel derives a doctrine of freedom. He rejects the view that freedom could be anything merely negative, such as an absence of restraint. We cannot find freedom in detachment from all connections that make demands upon us. Such freedom is illusory, because the detached individual is lonely, empty, unreal. Nor can we find freedom in self-assertion. A man is as big as his interests;

if he asserts only his own worth, he shrinks to the vanishing point. Nor can we find freedom in capricious interests, because then we garner no coherent happiness. Freedom requires organization and discipline, a coherence of personality that expresses itself in coherent action and striving. The only real freedom is to be found in social participation. The way for a man to become free is to achieve a deep and comprehensive self through many sympathetic relations to other things, other people, and the institutions which embody their collective life.

History as the Development of Freedom

History develops in determinate stages, each stage being an outgrowth of the preceding one. The "inward guiding soul" of this process is the dialectical development of ideas, above all, the idea of freedom. In the earlier stages the idea is fragmentary, unsatisfactory, not quite real. The ancient Oriental peoples were not free because they did not grasp the meaning of freedom. They thought that "*one* is free." For them the tyrant-ruler alone is free because they had no understanding that the human spirit—man in his essential though unrealized nature—is free. The Greeks and Romans, with their system of slavery, "knew only that *some* are free." Freedom, of a limited kind, was realized for the citizen, but at the cost of servitude for the noncitizen. Not until modern times did the "Germanic world," under the influence of Christianity, realize that "man, as man, is free: that it is the *freedom* of Spirit which constitutes its essence."[2] After centuries of historical development, mankind begins to be conscious of freedom as a birthright. Thus man is free by nature in the sense that his destiny is to be free, but he realizes this destiny only by historical stages amid incalculable waste and suffering. It is impossible to skip over the stages of development and to realize an idea before its time has come. Thought will fall on barren soil if it is premature; it will take root and become fertile only if it corresponds to the spirit of the age.

Society, in this process of transformation, is a unified whole—a gestalt or configuration. Its various aspects—economic, political, and cultural—combine to form a characteristic pattern that evolves from stage to stage. If an historian tries to study one part, such as art or law or religion, in abstraction from the pattern as a whole, he is bound to deal with it unrealistically and therefore falsely. The characteristics of a social order are unique and inseparable from that order, just as the characteristics of a period are unique and specific to that period. Pattern and periodicity belong together and must be kept in mind if history is to be interpreted aright.

History is teleological, but in a peculiar way. The laws of historical development

[2] The freedom thus attributed to the "Germanic world" is not to be understood narrowly. As Avineri points out: ". . . This term is coeval with Western Christendom—with the states which were established by the descendants of the Germanic peoples on the ruins of the Western Roman Empire: the 'Germanic world' thus encompasses not only Germany and the Nordic nations, but France, Italy, Spain and England as well." Shlomo Avineri, *Hegel's Theory of the Modern State* (Cambridge University Press, 1972), p. 228.

operate behind the backs and over the heads of individuals in the form of irresistible anonymous power. What happens in history is rarely what any individual wills, but the distress and defeat of individuals are the very means by which freedom and progress prevail. "This may be called the *cunning of reason*—that it sets the passions to work for itself, while that which develops its existence through such impulsion pays the penalty, and suffers loss." Great men, as the movers and shakers of history, might seem to be an exception to this tragic fate—they play the role of historical midwife, helping a new age come to birth. But they are not necessarily happy and free themselves. To a great extent, they embody the tragic and destructive forces necessary to negate the old and thus to release the new. As with lesser human beings, the ends they achieve are usually unintended.

The ideal culmination of history is the reconciliation of self and society. The well-integrated person finds his fulfillment in a well-integrated society: the duality of subject and object is overcome. The principal means to bring about this end is the participation of the individual in the state. It is here that the culmination of freedom is reached, because the state, in providing the widest and deepest integration of interests, supplies the individual with the richest form of social participation. Hence its claim upon the individual is higher than that of any lesser organization, such as the family or the business association. In the ideal state, "the private interests of its citizens is one with the common interest of the state," and "the one finds its gratification and realization in the other." Although the ideal has not been attained, history is moving in that direction.

Hegel extolled the state in rhapsodic language, but he did not seek to abolish individual distinctions. Unlike a fascist, he believed that freedom requires differentiation in all its fullness. He even reserved to the individual a sphere of private conscience "which as such does not come within the sphere of the state." In the Hegelian philosophical system the state belongs to the realm of "the Objective Spirit," and this realm is transcended by art, religion, and philosophy—the three forms of the Absolute Spirit. These spheres of culture have an independent meaning and value, and do not exist for the enhancement and glorification of the state. But all cultural spheres, according to Hegel, will flourish best in a well-integrated state.

Some Critical Questions

At his best, Hegel expressed a valid insight: that freedom and organization should not be pitted against one another as opposites but should be reconciled and synthesized in a free and organized community. But there are critical questions that can be asked:

1. THE CONCEPT OF UNCONSCIOUS TELEOLOGY. Hegel denies that there is a God outside of history, manipulating it according to plan. For him God *is* the his-

torical and evolutionary process. Hegel also denies that individuals can direct history toward consciously envisioned goals. Passion and unreason, not foresight, are the instruments through which objective reason comes to historical fruition. History is a teleology without a mind, a purposeful development without a governing purpose. It is like Adam Smith's "invisible hand" guiding men's selfish economic acts to a favorable social end. Smith's notion has been much criticized. Likewise Aristotle's notion of unconscious teleology has often been attacked as self-contradictory. How sound is Hegel's concept of "the cunning of reason"?

2. THE THEORY OF HISTORICAL PROGRESS. Hegel advances a theory of progress according to which the world is rational. When evil appears it is the negative element (the antithesis) in a dialectical process. Evil though it be, it is necessary for historical development. "Spirit . . . makes war upon itself—consumes its own existence; but in this very destruction it works up that existence into a new form, and each successive phase becomes in turn a material, working on which it exalts itself to a new grade." This entire theory, that history has an overall discoverable pattern and that this pattern is dialectical and progressive, has been subjected to severe criticism. Can Hegel's theory stand the test of critical examination? If some of his ideas of historical development have to be rejected, can others be salvaged?

3. THE CONCEPT OF SOCIAL CONFIGURATION. The term *gestalt* or *configuration* is used to designate a unity in which the parts are essentially related to one another and to the whole. A national culture, according to Hegel, is such a configuration. It is a unique pattern of religion, art, language, morality, ideology, political and economic activity, embodied in customs, traditions, institutions, and such artifacts as books, laws, tools, and works of art. Impressed upon individuals, it pervasively molds their mentality and behaviour; but it endures and develops from stage to stage even though individuals come and go. This is a powerful concept that has had a profound influence on social ideals and historical interpretations. To what extent is it valid?

4. THE THEORY OF THE STATE. For Hegel the state is the great agency of integration and synthesis, and as such it is the means to and embodiment of freedom. Very different is the interpretation of Marx, who defines the state as the supreme coercive agency within the society. The police and the military are at the very foundation of the state. The state, as the organ of class-domination, is not an agency of integration but an agency of repression. Which interpretation, Hegel's or Marx's, is more nearly correct?

5. LAW AND FREEDOM. Closely related to the state is the rule of law. For liberal individualists such as Thoreau, freedom is a condition in which there is as little law as possible. Law curbs and restricts freedom. The duty of the indi-

vidual is to follow his own conscience even at the cost of civil disobedience. This is an anti-Hegelian notion. Freedom, according to Hegel, is achieved when law is internalized and made part of one's conscience. An antisocial "freedom" is mere caprice. The reader might ask himself to what extent Socrates in the *Crito* agrees with Thoreau, and to what extent with Hegel? Who is right?

6. THE IDEALISTIC INTERPRETATION OF HISTORY. Basic to Hegel's philosophy of history is his idealistic approach. History, he contends, is a rational pattern in which ideas and passions are the dynamic forces of change and development. Opposed to this approach is Marx's "materialistic interpretation of history." We shall postpone the question of the idealistic *versus* the materialistic interpretation until we have examined the Marxian theory.

21

Communism

KARL MARX (1818–1883)

Born in Treves in the German Rhineland, Marx was the son of well-to-do Jewish parents who had been converted to Christianity. He studied law, history, and philosophy at the Universities of Bonn, Berlin, and Jena, imbibing the doctrines of Hegel, then at the height of his fame. His Doctor's thesis was on the materialism of Democritus and Epicurus. In 1842–1843 he edited a newspaper at Cologne, which was suppressed by the Prussian government because of its advanced ideas. After marrying Jennie von Westphalen, a beautiful young woman of aristocratic lineage, he went to Paris, where he studied the socialist movement. There he met Friedrich Engels, a young German who worked in the family business of Ermen and Engels, cotton spinners in Manchester, first as clerk, eventually as manager and part owner. On the basis of the socialist convictions which they shared, the two young men formed a friendship that endured throughout their lives.

In 1845, the Prussian government, incensed by Marx's continued attacks, persuaded the French authorities to deport him. He then went with Engels to live in Brussels, where he continued his political and journalistic activities. During this period he wrote, singly or in collaboration with Engels, a number of socialist works, the most famous of which was the *Communist Manifesto*, published on the eve of the revolutionary disturbances of 1848. Expelled in turn from Belgium, Marx returned to Cologne, where he founded a radical newspaper and participated in the revolutionary uprisings of 1848–1849. The ensuing political reaction compelled him to seek refuge in England.

With his family, he spent the remainder of his life in London. There he worked for years in the British Museum, accumulating the research materials for his indictment of capitalist society. Having only a small income as a correspondent for the *New York Tribune*, he lived with his wife and children in a squalid attic, often without sufficient food, decent clothing, or other basic necessities. His later years were saddened by ill health and the death of three of his children, but nothing could divert him from unremitting service to his ideals. In 1864, he helped to organize the First International, a radical political organization which continued under his direction until 1872. His major work was *Capital*, a detailed historical and economic analysis of capitalist society, which he referred to as "the task to which I have sacrificed my health, my happiness in life, and my family." Volume One was published in 1867 and the two remaining volumes after his death.

Communism
and History

I. The Materialist Conception of History

I was led by my studies to the conclusion that legal relations as well as forms of state could neither be under-

All passages except the Speech at the Anniversary of the *People's Paper* and the selection from the *Communist Manifesto* are taken from *Karl Marx: Selected Writings in Sociology and Social Philosophy*, edited by T. B. Bottomore and M. Rubel (London: C. A. Watts & Co. Ltd., 1956), or *Karl Marx: Early Writings*, edited by T. B. Bottomore (London: C. A. Watts & Co. Ltd., 1963). Translations are by Bottomore. Reprinted by permission of the publisher. Each passage is followed by a reference to its original source.

stood by themselves, nor explained by the so-called general progress of the human mind, but that they are rooted in the material conditions of life, which are summed up by Hegel after the fashion of the English and French writers of the eighteenth century under the name *civil society*, and the anatomy of civil society is to be sought in political economy. The study of the latter which I had begun in Paris, I continued in Brussels where I had emigrated on account of an expulsion order issued by M. Guizot. The general conclusion at which I arrived and which, once reached, continued to serve as the guiding thread in my studies, may be formulated briefly as follows: In the social production which men carry on they enter into definite relations that are indispensable and independent of their will; these relations of production correspond to a definite stage of development of their material powers of production. The totality of these relations of production constitutes the economic structure of society—the real foundation, on which legal and political superstructures arise and to which definite forms of social consciousness correspond. The mode of production of material life determines the general character of the social, political and spiritual processes of life. It is not the consciousness of men that determines their being, but, on the contrary, their social being determines their consciousness. At a certain stage of their development, the material forces of production in society come in conflict with the existing relations of production, or— what is but a legal expression for the same thing—with the property relations within which they had been at work before. From forms of development of the forces of production these relations turn into their fetters. Then occurs a period of social revolution. With the change of the economic foundation the entire immense superstructure is more or less rapidly transformed. In considering such transformations the distinction should always be made between the material transformation of the economic conditions of production which can be determined with the precision of natural science, and the legal, political, religious, aesthetic or philosophical —in short ideological, forms in which men become conscious of this conflict and fight it out. Just as our opinion of an individual is not based on what he thinks of himself, so can we not judge of such a period of transformation by its own consciousness; on the contrary, this consciousness must rather be explained from the contradictions of material life, from the existing conflict between the social forces of production and the relations of production. No social order ever disappears before all the productive forces for which there is room in it have been developed; and new, higher relations of production never appear before the material conditions of their existence have matured in the womb of the old society. Therefore, mankind always sets itself only such problems as it can solve; since, on closer examination, it will always be found that the problem itself arises only when the material conditions necessary for its solution already exist or are at least in the process of formation. In broad outline we can designate the Asiatic, the ancient, the feudal, and the modern bourgeois modes of production as progressive epochs in the economic formation of society. The bourgeois relations of production are the last antagonistic form of the social process of production; not in the sense of individual antagonisms, but of conflict arising from conditions surrounding the life of individuals in society. At the same time the productive forces developing in the womb of bourgeois society create the material conditions for the solution of that antagonism. With this social formation, therefore, the prehistory of human society comes to an end.

Preface to *A Contribution to the Critique of Political Economy* (1859)

The premises from which we begin are not arbitrary ones, not dogmas, but real premises from which abstraction can be made only in the imagination. They are the real individuals, their activity and their material conditions of life, including those which they find already in existence and those produced by their activity. These premises can thus be established in a purely empirical way.

The first premise of all human history is, of course, the existence of living human individuals. The first fact to be established, therefore, is the physical constitution of these individuals and their consequent relation to the rest of Nature. Of course we cannot here investigate the actual physical nature of man or the natural conditions in which man finds himself—geological, orohydrographical, climatic and so on. All historiography must begin from these natural bases and their modification in the course of history by men's activity.

Men can be distinguished from animals by consciousness, by religion, or by anything one likes. They themselves begin to distinguish themselves from animals as soon as they begin to *produce* their means of subsistence, a step which is determined by their physical constitution. In producing their means of subsistence men indirectly produce their actual material life.

The way in which men produce their means of subsistence depends in the first place on the nature of the existing means which they have to reproduce. This mode of production should not be regarded simply as the reproduction of the physical existence of individuals. It is already a definite form of activity of these individuals, a definite way of expressing their life, a definite *mode of life*. As individuals express their life, so they are. What they are, therefore, coincides with their production, with *what* they produce and with *how* they produce it. What individuals are, therefore, depends on the material conditions of their production. . . .

This conception of history, therefore, rests on the exposition of the real process of production, starting out from the simple material production of life, and on the comprehension of the form or intercourse connected with and created by this mode of production, i.e. of civil society in its various stages as the basis of all history, and also in its action as the State. From this starting point, it explains all the different theoretical productions and forms of consciousness, religion, philosophy, ethics, etc., and traces their origins and growth, by which means the matter can of course be displayed as a whole (and consequently, also the reciprocal action of these various sides on one another). Unlike the idealist view of history, it . . . remains constantly on the real ground of history; it does not explain practice from the idea but explains the formation of ideas from material practice, and accordingly comes to the conclusion that all the forms of and products of consciousness can be dissolved, not by intellectual criticism, . . . but only by the practical overthrow of the actual social relations . . . ; that not criticism but revolution is the driving force of history, as well as of religion, philosophy, and all other types of theory. It shows that history does not end by being resolved into "self-consciousness," as "spirit of the spirit," but that at each stage of history there is found a material result, a sum of productive forces, a historically created relation of individuals to Nature and to one another, which is handed down to each generation from its predecessors, a mass of productive forces, capital, and circumstances, which is indeed modified by the new generation but which also prescribes for it its conditions of life and gives it a definite development, a special character. It shows that circumstances make men just as much as men make circumstances. . . .

The fact is, therefore, that determinate individuals, who are productively active in a definite way, enter into these determinate social and political relations. Empirical observation must, in each particular case, show empirically, and without any mystification or speculation, the connection of the social and political structure with production. The social structure and the State are continually evolving out of the life-process of determinate individuals, of individuals not as they may appear in their own or other people's imagination, but as they really are: i.e. as they act, produce their material life, and are occupied within determinate material limits, presuppositions and conditions, which are independent of their will.

The production of ideas, conceptions and consciousness is at first directly interwoven with the material activity and the material intercourse of men, the language of real life. Representation and thought, the mental intercourse of men, still appear at this stage as the direct emanation of their material behaviour. The same applies to mental production as it is expressed in the political, legal, moral, religious and metaphysical language of a people. Men are the producers of their conceptions, ideas, etc.,—real, active men, as they are conditioned by a determinate development of their productive forces, and of the intercourse which corresponds to these, up to its most extensive forms. Consciousness can never be anything else than conscious existence, and the existence of men is their actual life process. If in all ideology men and their circumstances appear upside down as in a *camera obscura*, this phenomenon arises from their historical life process just as the inversion of objects on the retina does from their physical life-process.

In direct contrast to German philosophy, which descends from heaven to earth, here we ascend from earth to heaven. That is to say, we do not set out from what men say, imagine, or conceive, nor from what has been said, thought, imagined, or conceived of men, in order to arrive at men in the flesh. We begin with real, active men, and from their real life-process show the development of the ideological reflexes and echoes of this life-process. The phantoms of the human brain also are necessary sublimates of men's material life-process, which can be empirically established and which is bound to material preconditions. Morality, religion, metaphysics, and other ideologies, and their corresponding forms of consciousness, no longer retain therefore their appearance of autonomous existence. They have no history, no development; it is men, who, in developing their material production and their material intercourse, change, along with this their real existence, their thinking and the products of their thinking. Life is not determined by consciousness, but consciousness by life. Those who adopt the first method of approach begin with consciousness, regarded as the living individual; those who adopt the second, which corresponds with real life, begin with the real living individuals themselves, and consider consciousness only as *their* consciousness. . . .

The ideas of the ruling class are, in every age, the ruling ideas: i.e. the class which is the dominant *material* force in society is at the same time its dominant *intellectual* force. The class which has the means of material production at its disposal, has control at the same time over the means of mental production, so that in consequence the ideas of those who lack the means of mental production are, in general, subject to it. The dominant ideas are nothing more than the ideal expression of the dominant material realationships, the dominant material relationships grasped as ideas, and thus of the relationships which make one class the ruling one; they are consequently the ideas of its dominance. The individuals composing the ruling class possess among other things consciousness, and therefore think. In so far, therefore, as they rule as a class and determine the whole extent of an epoch, it is self-evident that they do this in their whole range and thus, among other things, rule also as thinkers, as producers of ideas, and regulate the production and distribution of the ideas of their age. Consequently their ideas are the ruling ideas of the age. For instance, in an age and in a country

where royal power, aristocracy and the bourgeoisie are contending for domination and where, therefore, domination is shared, the doctrine of the separation of powers appears as the dominant idea and is enunciated as an "eternal law." The division of labour, which we saw earlier as one of the principal forces of history up to the present time, manifests itself also in the ruling class, as the division of mental and material labour, so that within this class one part appears as the thinkers of the class (its active conceptualizing ideologies, who make it their chief source of livelihood to develop and perfect the illusions of the class about itself), while the others have a more passive and receptive attitude to these ideas and illusions, because they are in reality the active members of this class and have less time to make up ideas and illusions about themselves. This cleavage within the ruling class may even develop into a certain opposition and hostility between the two parts, but in the event of a practical collision in which the class itself is endangered, it disappears of its own accord and with it also the illusion that the ruling ideas were not the ideas of the ruling class and had a power distinct from the power of this class. The existence of revolutionary ideas in a particular age presupposes the existence of a revolutionary class. . . .

If, in considering the course of history, we detach the ideas of the ruling class from the ruling class itself and attribute to them an independent existence, if we confine ourselves to saying that in a particular age these or those ideas were dominant, without paying attention to the conditions of production and the world conditions which are the source of the ideas, it is possible to say, for instance, that during the time that the aristocracy was dominant the concepts honour, loyalty, etc., were dominant; during the dominance of the bourgeoisie the concepts freedom, equality, etc. The ruling class itself in general imagines this to be the case. This conception of history which is common to all historians, particularly since the eighteenth century, will necessarily come up against the phenomenon that increasingly abstract ideas hold sway, i.e. ideas which increasingly take on the form of universality. For each new class which puts itself in the place of the one ruling before it, is compelled, simply in order to achieve its aims, to represent its interest as the common interest of all members of society, i.e. employing an ideal formula, to give its ideas the form of universality and to represent them as the only rational and universally valid ones. The class which makes a revolution appears from the beginning not as a class but as the representative of the whole of society, simply because it is opposed to a *class*. It appears as the whole mass of society confronting the single ruling class. It can do this because at the beginning its interest really is more closely connected with the common interest of all other non-ruling classes and has been unable under the constraint of the previously existing conditions to develop as the particular interest of a particular class. Its victory, therefore, also benefits many individuals of the other classes which are not achieving a dominant position, but only in so far as it now puts these individuals in a position to raise them-

selves into the ruling class. When the French bourgeoisie overthrew the rule of the aristocracy it thereby made it possible for many proletarians to raise themselves above the proletariat, but only in so far as they became bourgeois. Every new class, therefore, achieves its domination only on a broader basis than that of the previous ruling class. On the other hand, the opposition of the non-ruling class to the new ruling class later develops all the more sharply and profoundly. These two characteristics entail that the struggle to be waged against this new ruling class has as its object a more decisive and radical negation of the previous conditions of society than could have been accomplished by all previous classes which aspired to rule.

The German Ideology (with Engels, 1845–1846)

II. The Class Struggle

The history of all hitherto existing society[1] is the history of class struggles.

[1] That is, all *written* history. In 1847, the prehistory of society, the social organization existing previous to recorded history, was all but unknown. Since then, Haxthausen discovered common ownership of land in Russia, Maurer proved it to be the social foundation from which all Teutonic races started in history, and by and by village communities were found to be, or to have been, the primitive form of society everywhere from India to Ireland. The inner organization of this primitive Communistic society was laid bare, in its typical form, by Morgan's crowning discovery of the true nature of the *gens* and its relation to the *tribe*. With the dissolution of these primeval communities society begins to be differentiated into separate and finally antagonistic classes. I have attempted to retrace this process of dissolution in: *Der Ursprung*

Freeman and slave, patrician and plebeian, lord and serf, guild-master[2] and journeyman, in a word, oppressor and oppressed, stood in constant opposition to one another, carried on an uninterrupted, now hidden, now open fight, a fight that each time ended either in a revolutionary reconstitution of society at large or in the common ruin of the contending classes.

In the earlier epochs of history we find almost everywhere a complicated arrangement of society into various orders, a manifold gradation of social rank. In ancient Rome we have patricians, knights, plebeians, slaves; in the Middle Ages, feudal lords, vassals, guild-masters, journeymen, apprentices, serfs; in almost all of these classes, again, subordinate gradations.

The modern bourgeois society that has sprouted from the ruins of feudal society has not done away with class antagonisms. It has but established new classes, new conditions of oppression, new forms of struggle in place of the old ones.

Our epoch, the epoch of the bourgeoisie, possesses, however, this distinctive feature: it has simplified the class antagonisms. Society as a whole is splitting up more and more into two great hostile camps, into two great classes directly facing each other: Bourgeoisie and Proletariat.[3]

From the serfs of the Middle Ages sprang the chartered burghers of the earliest towns. From these burgesses the first elements of the bourgeoisie were developed.

The discovery of America, the rounding of the Cape, opened up fresh ground for the rising bourgeoisie. The East Indian and Chinese markets, the colonization of America, trade with the colonies, the increase in the means of exchange and in commodities generally, gave to commerce, to navigation, to industry, an impulse never before known, and thereby, to the revolutionary element in the tottering feudal society, a rapid development.

The feudal system of industry, under which industrial production was monopolized by closed guilds, now no longer sufficed for the growing wants of the new markets. The manufacturing system took its place. The guild-masters were pushed on one side by the manufacturing middle class; division of labor between the different corporate guilds vanished in the face of division of labor in each single workshop.

Meantime the markets kept ever growing, the demand ever rising. Even manufacture no longer sufficed. Thereupon, steam and machinery revolutionized industrial production. The place of manufacture was taken by the giant, Modern Industry, the place of the industrial middle class by industrial millionaires—the leaders of whole industrial armies, the modern bourgeois.

---

der Familie, des Privateigenthus und des Staats, 2nd edition, Stuttgart, 1886. [*1888*] (Footnotes by Engels.)

[2] Guild-master, that is, a full member of a guild, a master within, not a head of a guild. [*1888*]

[3] By bourgeoisie is meant the class of modern Capitalists, owners of the means of social production and employers of wage labor. By proletariat, the class of modern wage-laborers who, having no means of production of their own, are reduced to selling their labor power in order to live. [*1888*]

Modern industry has established the world market, for which the discovery of America paved the way. This market has given an immense development to commerce, to navigation, to communication by land. This development has, in its turn, reacted on the extension of industry; and in proportion as industry, commerce, navigation, railways extended, in the same proportion the bourgeoisie developed, increased its capital, and pushed into the background every class handed down from the Middle Ages.

We see, therefore, how the modern bourgeoisie is itself the product of a long course of development, of a series of revolutions in the modes of production and of exchange.

Each step in the development of the bourgeoisie was accompanied by a corresponding political advance of that class. An oppressed class under the sway of the feudal nobility, an armed and self-governing association in the medieval commune;[4] here independent urban republic (as in Italy and Germany), there taxable "third estate" of the monarchy (as in France), afterward, in the period of manufacture proper, serving

[4] "Commune" was the name taken in France by the nascent towns even before they had conquered from their feudal lords and masters local self-government and political rights as the "Third Estate." Generally speaking, for the economic development of the bourgeoisie, England is here taken as the typical country; for its political development, France. [*1888*]

This was the name given their urban communities by the townsmen of Italy and France, after they had purchased or wrested their initial rights of self-government from their feudal lords. [*1890*]

either the semi-feudal or the absolute monarchy as a counterpoise against the nobility, and, in fact, cornerstone of the great monarchies in general, the bourgeoisie has at last, since the establishment of Modern Industry and of the world market, conquered for itself, in the modern representative State, exclusive political sway. The executive of the modern State is but a committee for managing the common affairs of the whole bourgeoisie.

The bourgeoisie, historically, has played a most revolutionary part.

The bourgeoisie, wherever it has got the upper hand, has put an end to all feudal, patriarchal, idyllic relations. It has pitilessly torn asunder the motley feudal ties that bound man to his "natural superiors," and has left remaining no other nexus between man and man than naked self-interest, than callous "cash payment." It has drowned the most heavenly ecstasies of religious fervor, of chilvalrous enthusiasm, of philistine sentimentalism, in the icy water of egotistical calculation. It has resolved personal worth into exchange value, and in place of the numberless indefeasible chartered freedoms has set up that single, unconscionable freedom—Free Trade. In one word, for exploitation, veiled by religious and political illusions, it has substituted naked, shameless, direct, brutal exploitation.

The bourgeoisie has stripped of its halo every occupation hitherto honored and looked up to with reverent awe. It has converted the physician, the lawyer, the priest, the poet, the man of science, into its paid wage-laborers.

The bourgeoisie has torn away from the family its sentimental veil, and has reduced the family relation to a mere money relation.

The bourgeoisie has disclosed how it came to pass that the brutal display of vigor in the Middle Ages, which Reactionists so much admire, found its fitting complement in the most slothful indolence. It has been the first to show what man's activity can bring about. It has accomplished wonders far surpassing Egyptian pyramids, Roman aqueducts and Gothic cathedrals; it has conducted expeditions that put in the shade all former Exoduses of nations and crusades.

The bourgeoisie cannot exist without constantly revolutionizing the instruments of production, and thereby the relations of production, and with them the whole relations of society. Conservation of the old modes of production in unaltered form was, on the contrary, the first condition of existence for all earlier industrial classes. Constant revolutionizing of production, uninterrupted disturbance of all social conditions, everlasting uncertainty and agitation distinguish the bourgeois epoch from all earlier ones. All fixed, fast-frozen relations, with their train of ancient and venerable prejudices and opinions, are swept away, all new-formed ones become antiquated before they can ossify. All that is solid melts into air, all that is holy is profaned, and man is at last compelled to face with sober senses his real conditions of life and his relations with his kind.

The need of a constantly expanding market for its products chases the bourgeoisie over the whole surface of the globe. It must nestle everywhere, settle everywhere, establish connections everywhere.

The bourgeoisie has through its exploitation of the world market given a cosmopolitan character to production and consumption in every country. To the great chagrin of Reactionists, it has drawn from under the feet of industry the national ground on which it stood. All old-established national industries have been destroyed or are daily being destroyed. They are dislodged by new industries, whose introduction becomes a life and death question for all civilized nations, by industries that no longer work up indigenous raw material but raw material drawn from the remotest zones; industries whose products are consumed, not only at home, but in every quarter of the globe. In place of the old wants, satisfied by the production of the country, we find new wants, requiring for their satisfaction the products of distant lands and climes. In place of the old local and natial seclusion and self-sufficiency, we have intercourse in every direction, universal interdependence of nations. And as in material, so also in intellectual production. The intellectual creations of individual nations become common property. National one-sidedness and narrow-mindedness become more and more impossible, and from the numerous national and local literatures there arises a world literature.

The bourgeoisie, by the rapid improvement of all instruments of production, by the immensely facilitated means of communication, draws all, even the most barbarian, nations into civilization. The cheap prices of its commodities are the heavy artillery with which it batters down all Chinese walls, with which it forces the barbarians' intensely obstinate hatred of foreigners to capitulate. It compels all nations, on pain of extinction, to adopt the bourgeois mode of production; it compels them to introduce what it calls civilization into their midst, i.e., to become bourgeois themselves. In a word, it creates a world after its own image.

The bourgeoisie has subjected the country to the rule of the towns. It has created enormous cities, has greatly increased the urban population as compared with the rural, and has thus rescued a considerable part of the population from the idiocy of rural life. Just as it has made the country dependent on the towns, so it has made barbarian and semi-barbarian countries dependent on the civilized ones, nations of peasants on nations of bourgeois, the East on the West.

The bourgeoisie keeps doing away more and more with the scattered state of the population, of the means of production, and of property. It has agglomerated population, centralized means of production, and has concentrated property in a few hands. The necessary consequence of this was political centralization. Independent or but loosely connected provinces with separate interests, laws, governments and systems of taxation became lumped together into one nation, with one government, one code of laws, one national class interest, one frontier and one customs tariff.

The bourgeoisie during its rule of scarce one hundred years has created more massive and more colossal productive forces than have all preceding generations together. Subjection of nature's forces to man, machinery, application of chemistry to industry and agriculture, steam navigation, railways, electric telegraphs, clearing of whole continents for cultivation, canalization of rivers, whole populations conjured out of the ground—what earlier century had even a presentiment that such productive forces slumbered in the lap of social labor?

We see then: the means of production and of exchange, on the foundation of which the bourgeoisie built itself up, were generated in feudal society. At a certain stage in the development of these means of production and of exchange, the conditions under which feudal society produced and exchanged, the feudal organization of agriculture and manufacturing industry, in a word, the feudal relations of property became no longer compatible with the already developed productive forces; they became so many fetters. They had to be burst asunder; they were burst asunder.

Into their place stepped free competition, accompanied by a social and political constitution adapted to it and by the economic and political sway of the bourgeois class.

A similar movement is going on before our own eyes. Modern bourgeois society with its relations of production, of exchange and of property, a society that has conjured up such gigantic means of production and of exchange, is like the sorcerer who is no longer able to control the powers of the nether world whom he has called up by his spells. For many a decade past the history of industry and commerce is but the history of the revolt of modern productive forces against modern conditions of production, against the property relations that are the conditions for the existence of the bourgeoisie and of its rule. It is enough to mention the commercial crises that by their periodical return put on trial, each time more threateningly, the existence of the entire bourgeois society. In these crises a great part not only of the existing products, but also of the previously created productive forces, are periodically destroyed. In these crises there breaks out an epidemic that in all earlier epochs would have seemed an absurdity—the epidemic of over-production. Society suddenly finds itself put back into a state of momentary barbarism; it appears as if a famine, a universal war of devastation had cut off the supply of every means of subsistence; industry and commerce seem to be destroyed; and why? Because there is too much civilization, too much means of subsistence, too much industry, too much commerce. The productive forces at the disposal of society no longer tend to further the development of the conditions of bourgeois property; on the contrary, they have become too powerful for these conditions, by which they are fettered, and as soon as they overcome these fetters, they bring disorder into the whole of bourgeois society, endanger the existence of bourgeois property. The conditions of bourgeois society are too narrow to comprise the wealth created by them. And how does the bourgeoisie get over these crises? On the one hand by enforced destruction of a mass of productive forces, on the other, by the conquest of new markets and by the more thorough exploitation of the old ones. That is to say, by paving the way for more extensive and more destructive crises and by diminishing the means whereby crises are prevented.

The weapons with which the bourgeoisie felled feudalism to the ground are now turned against the bourgeoisie itself.

But not only has the bourgeoisie forged the weapons that bring death to itself; it has also called into existence the men who are to wield those weapons—the modern working class, the proletarians.

In proportion as the bourgeoisie, i.e., capital, is developed, in the same proportion is the proletariat, the modern working class, developed—a class of laborers who live only as long as they find work, and who find work only as long as their labor increases capital. These laborers, who must sell themselves piecemeal, are a commodity like every other article of commerce, and are consequently exposed to all the vicissitudes of competition, to all the fluctuations of the market.

Owing to the extensive use of machinery and to division of labor, the work of the proletarians has lost all individual character and, consequently, all charm for the workman. He becomes an appendage of the machine, and it is only the most simple, most monotonous, and most easily acquired knack that is required of him. Hence, the cost of production of a workman is restricted almost entirely to the means of subsistence that he requires for his maintenance and for the propagation of his race. But the price of a commodity, and therefore also of labor, is equal to its cost of production. In proportion, therefore, as the repulsiveness of the work increases, the wage decreases. Nay more, in proportion as the use of machinery and division of labor increase, in the same proportion the burden of toil also increases, whether by prolongation of the working hours, by increase of the work exacted in a given time or by increased speed of the machinery, etc.

Modern industry has converted the little workshop of the patriarchal master into the great factory of the industrial capitalist. Masses of laborers, crowded into the factory, are organized like soldiers. As privates of the industrial army they are placed under the command of a perfect hierarchy of officers and sergeants. Not only are they slaves of the bourgeois class and of the bourgeois State; they are daily and hourly enslaved by the machine, by the overseer and, above all, by the individual bourgeois manufacturer himself. The more openly this despotism proclaims gain to be its end and aim, the more petty, the more hateful and the more embittering it is.

The less the skill and exertion of strength implied in manual labor, in other words, the more modern industry becomes developed, the more is the labor of men superseded by that of women. Differences of age and sex no longer have any distinctive social validity for the working class. All are instruments of labor, more or less expensive to use, according to their age and sex.

No sooner is the exploitation of the laborer by the manufacturer so far at an end that he receives his wages in cash, than he is set upon by the other portions of the bourgeoisie, the landlord, the shopkeeper, the pawnbroker, etc.

The lower strata of the middle class—the small tradespeople, shopkeepers and retired tradesmen generally, the handicraftsmen and peasants—all these sink gradually into the proletariat, partly because their diminutive capital does not suffice for the scale on which Modern Industry is carried on and is swamped in the competition with the large capitalists, partly because their specialized skill is rendered worthless by new methods of production. Thus the proletariat is recruited from all classes of the population.

The proletariat goes through various stages of development. With its birth begins its struggle with the bourgeoisie. At first the contest is carried on by individual laborers, then by the work people of the factory, then by the operatives of one trade in one locality against the individual bourgeois who directly exploits them. They direct their attacks not against the bourgeois conditions of production, but against the instruments of production themselves; they destroy imported wares that compete with their labor, they smash machinery to pieces, they set factories ablaze, they seek to restore by force the vanished status of the workman of the Middle Ages.

At this stage the laborers still form an incoherent mass scattered over the whole country and broken up by their mutual competition. If anywhere they unite to form more compact bodies, this is not yet the consequence of their own active union but of the union of the bourgeoisie, which class, in order to attain its own political ends, is compelled to set the whole proletariat in motion and, moreover is, for a time, yet able to do so. At this stage, therefore, the proletarians do not fight their enemies, but the enemies of their enemies, the remnants of absolute monarchy, the landowners, the non-industrial bourgeois, the petty bourgeoisie. Thus the whole historical movement is concentrated in the hands of the bourgeoisie; every victory so obtained is a victory for the bourgeoisie.

But with the development of industry the proletariat not only increases in number; it becomes concentrated in greater masses, its strength grows, and it feels that strength more. The various interests and conditions of life within the ranks of the proletariat are more and more equalized in proportion as machinery obliterates all distinctions of labor and nearly everywhere reduces wages to the same low level. The growing competition among the bourgeois, and the resulting commercial crises, make the wages of the workers ever more fluctuating. The unceasing improvement of machinery, ever more rapidly developing, makes their livelihood more and more precarious; the collisions between individual workmen and individual bourgeois take more and more the character of collisions between two classes. Thereupon the workers begin to form combinations (Trades' Unions) against the bourgeois; they club together in order to keep up the rate of wages; they found permanent associations in order to make provision beforehand for these occasional revolts. Here and there the contest breaks out into riots.

Now and then the workers are victorious, but only for a time. The real fruit of their battles lies, not in the immediate result, but in the ever expanding union of the workers. This union is helped on by the improved means of communication that are created by modern industry and that place the workers of different localities in contact with one another. It was just this contact that was needed to centralize the numerous local struggles, all of the same character, into one national struggle between classes. But every class struggle is a political struggle. And that union, to attain which the burghers of the Middle Ages with their miserable highways required centuries, the modern proletarians, thanks to railways, achieve in a few years.

This organization of the proletarians into a class and consequently into a political party is continually being upset again by the competition between the workers themselves. But it ever rises up again, stronger, firmer, mightier. It compels legislative recognition of particular interests of the workers, by taking advantage of the divisions among the bourgeoisie itself. Thus the ten-hours' bill in England was carried.

Altogether, collisions between the classes of the old society in many ways further the course of development of the proletariat. The bourgeoisie finds itself involved in a constant battle. At first with the aristocracy; later on, with those portions of the bourgeoisie itself whose interests have become antagonistic to the progress of industry; at all times with the bourgeoisie of foreign countries. In all these battles it sees itself compelled to appeal to the proletariat, to ask for its help, and thus to drag it into the political arena. The bourgeoisie itself, therefore, supplies the proletariat with its own elements of political and general education; in other words, it furnishes the proletariat with weapons for fighting the bourgeoisie.

Further, as we have already seen, entire sections of the ruling classes are precipitated into the proletariat by the advance of industry, or are at least threatened in their conditions of existence. These also supply the proletariat with fresh elements of enlightenment and progress.

Finally, in times when the class struggle nears the decisive hour, the process of dissolution going on within the ruling class, in fact within the whole range of old society, assumes such a violent, glaring character that a small section of the ruling class cuts itself adrift and joins the revolutionary class, the class that holds the future in its hands. Therefore, just as, at an earlier period a section of the nobility went over to the bourgeoisie, so now a portion of the bourgeoisie goes over to the proletariat, and in particular a portion of the bourgeois ideologists who have raised themselves to the level of comprehending theoretically the historical movement as a whole.

Of all the classes that stand face to face with the bourgeoisie today, the proletariat alone is a really revolutionary class. The other classes decay and finally disappear in the face of modern industry; the proletariat is its special and essential product.

The lower middle class, the small manufacturer, the shopkeeper, the artisan, the peasant, all these fight against the bourgeoisie to save from extinction their existence as fractions of the middle class. They are therefore not revolutionary, but conservative. Nay more, they are reactionary, for they try to roll back the wheel of history. If by chance they are revolutionary, they are so only in view of their impending transfer into the proletariat; they thus defend not their present, but their future interests; they desert their own standpoint to place themselves at that of the proletariat.

The "dangerous class," the social scum, that passively rotting mass thrown off by the lowest layers of the old society may here and there be swept into the movement by a proletariat revolution; its conditions of life, however, prepare it far more for the part of a bribed tool of reactionary intrigue.

In the conditions of the proletariat, those of the old society at large are already virtually swamped. The proletarian is without property; his relation to his wife and children has no longer anything in common with the bourgeois family relations; modern industrial labor, modern subjection to capital, the same in England as in France, in America as in Germany, has stripped him of every trace of national character. Law, morality, religion are to him so many bourgeois prejudices behind which lurk in ambush just as many bourgeois interests.

All the preceding classes that got the upper hand sought to fortify their already acquired status by subjecting society at large to their conditions of appropriation. The proletarians cannot become masters of the productive forces of society except by abolishing their own previous mode of appropriation, and thereby also every other previous mode of appropriation. They have nothing of their own to secure and to fortify; their mission is to destroy all previous securities for, and insurances of, individual property.

All previous historical movements were movements of minorities or in the interest of minorities. The proletarian movement is the self-conscious, independent movement of the immense majority in the interest of the immense majority. The proletariat, the lowest stratum of our present society, cannot stir, cannot raise itself up, without the whole superincumbent strata of official society being sprung into the air.

Though not in substance, yet in form, the struggle of the proletariat with the bourgeoisie is at first a national struggle. The proletariat of each country must, of course, first of all settle matters with its own bourgeoisie.

In depicting the most general phases of the development of the proletariat, we traced the more or less veiled civil war raging within existing society up to the point where that war breaks out into open revolution, and where the violent overthrow of the bourgeoisie lays the foundation for the sway of the proletariat.

Hitherto, every form of society has been based, as we have already seen, on the antagonism of oppressing and oppressed classes. But in order to oppress a class certain conditions must be assured to it under which it can, at least, continue its slavish existence. The serf, in the period of serfdom, raised himself to membership in the commune, just as the petty bourgeois, under the yoke of feudal absolutism, managed to develop into a bourgeois. The modern laborer, on the contrary, instead of rising with the progress of industry sinks deeper and deeper below the conditions of existence of his own class. He becomes a pauper, and pauperism develops more rapidly than population and wealth. And here it becomes evident that the bourgeoisie is unfit any longer to be the ruling class in society and to impose its conditions of existence upon society as an over-riding law. It is unfit to rule because it is incompetent to assure an existence to its slave within his slavery, because it cannot help letting him sink into such a state that it has to feed him instead of being fed by him. Society can no longer live under this bourgeoisie, in other words, its existence is no longer compatible with society.

The essential condition for the existence and for the sway of the bourgeois class is the formation and augmentation of capital; the condition for capital is wage labor. Wage labor rests exclusively on competition between the laborers. The advance of industry, whose involuntary promoter is the bourgeoisie, replaces the isolation of the laborers, due to competition, by their revolutionary combination due to association. The development of Modern Industry therefore cuts from under its feet the very foundation on which the bourgeois produces and appropriates products. What the bourgeoisie therefore produces, above all, are its own grave-diggers. Its fall and the victory of the proletariat are equally inevitable.

Communist Manifesto (with Engels, 1848), translated by Samuel Moore for the English edition of 1888.

III. Alienation

We shall begin from a *contemporary* economic fact. The worker becomes poorer the more wealth he produces and the more his production increases in power and extent. The worker becomes an ever cheaper commodity the more goods he creates. The *devaluation* of the human world increases in direct relation with the *increase in value* of the world of things. Labor does not only create goods; it also produces itself and the worker as a *commodity*, and indeed in the same proportion as it produces goods.

This fact simply implies that the object produced by labor, its product, now stands opposed to it as an *alien being*, as a *power independent* of the producer. The product of labor is labor which has been embodied in an object and turned into a physical thing; this product is an *objectification* of labor. The performance of work is at the same time its objectification. The performance of work appears in the sphere of political economy as a *vitiation* of the worker, objectification as a *loss* and as *servitude to the object*, and appropriation as *alienation*.

So much does the performance of work appear as vitiation that the worker is vitiated to the point of starvation. So much does objectification appear as loss of the object that the worker is deprived of the most essential things not only of life but also of work. Labor itself becomes an object which he can acquire only by the greatest effort and with unpredictable interruptions. So much does the appropriation of the object appear as alienation that the

more objects the worker produces the fewer he can possess and the more he falls under the domination of his product, of capital.

All these consequences follow from the fact that the worker is related to the *product of his labor* as to an *alien* object. For it is clear on this presupposition that the more the worker expends himself in work the more powerful becomes the world of objects which he creates in face of himself, the poorer he becomes in his inner life, and the less he belongs to himself. It is just the same as in religion. The more of himself man attributes to God the less he has left in himself. The worker puts his life into the object, and his life then belongs no longer to himself but to the object. The greater his activity, therefore, the less he possesses. What is embodied in the product of his labor is no longer his own. The greater this product is, therefore, the more he is diminished. The *alienation* of the worker in his product means not only that his labor becomes an object, assumes an external existence, but that it exists independently, *outside himself*, and alien to him, and that it stands opposed to him as an autonomous power. The life which he has given to the object sets itself against him as an alien and hostile force.

Let us now examine more closely the phenomenon of *objectification*, the worker's production and the *alienation* and *loss* of the object it produces, which is involved in it. The worker can create nothing without *nature*, without the *sensuous external world*. The latter is the material in which his labor is realized, in which it is active, out of which and through which it produces things.

But just as nature affords the *means of existence* of labor in the sense that labor cannot *live* without objects upon which it can be exercised, so also it provides the *means of existence* in a narrower sense; namely the means of physical existence for the *worker* himself. Thus, the more the worker *appropriates* the external world of sensuous nature by his labor the more he deprives himself of *means of existence*, in two repects: first, that the sensuous external world becomes progressively less an object belonging to his labor or a means of existence of his labor, and secondly, that it becomes progressively less a means of existence in the direct sense, a means for the physical subsistence of the worker.

In both respects, therefore, the worker becomes a slave of the object; first, in that he receives an *object of work*, i.e., receives *work*, and secondly that he receives *means of subsistence*. Thus the object enables him to exist, first as a *worker* and secondly, as a *physical subject*. The culmination of this enslavement is that he can only maintain himself as a *physical subject* so far as he is worker, and that it is only as a *physical subject* that he is a worker.

(The alienation of the worker in his object is expressed as follows in the laws of political economy: the more the worker produces the less he has to consume; the more value he creates the more worthless he becomes; the more refined his product the more crude and misshapen the worker; the more civilized the product the more barbarous the worker; the more powerful the work the more feeble the worker; the more the work manifests intelligence the more the worker declines in intelligence and becomes a slave of nature.)

Political economy conceals the alienation in the nature of labor insofar as it does not examine the direct relationship between the worker (work) and production. Labor certainly produces marvels for the rich but it produces privation for the worker. It produces palaces, but hovels for the worker. It produces beauty, but deformity for the worker. It replaces labor by machinery, but it casts some of the workers back into a barbarous kind of work and turns the others into machines. It produces intelligence, but also stupidity and cretinism for the workers.

The direct relationship of labor to its products is the relationship of the worker to the objects of his production. The relationship of property owners to the objects of production and to production itself is merely a *consequence* of this first relationship and confirms it. We shall consider this second aspect later.

Thus, when we ask what is the important relationship of labor, we are concerned with the relationship of the *worker* to production.

So far we have considered the alienation of the worker only from one aspect; namely, *his relationship with the products of his labor*. However, alienation appears not only in the result, but also in the *process*, of *production*, within *productive activity* itself. How could the worker stand in an alien relationship to the product of his activity if he did not alienate himself in the act of production itself? The product is indeed only the *résumé* of activity, of production. Consequently, if the product of labor is alienation, production itself must be active alienation—the alienation of activity and the activity of alienation. The alienation of the object of labor merely summarizes the alienation in the work activity itself.

What constitutes the alienation of labor? First, that the work is *external* to the worker, that it is not part of his nature; and that, consequently, he does not fulfill himself in his work but denies himself, has a feeling of misery rather than well being, does not develop freely his mental and physical energies but is physically exhausted and mentally debased. The worker therefore feels himself at home only during his leisure time, whereas at work he feels homeless. His work is not voluntary but imposed, *forced labor*. It is not the satisfaction of a need, but only a *means* for satisfying other needs. Its alien character is clearly shown by the fact that as soon as there is no physical or other compulsion it is avoided like the plague. External labor, labor in which man alienates himself, is a labor of self-sacrifice, of mortification. Finally, the external character of work for the worker is shown by the fact that it is not his own work but work for someone else, that in work he does not belong to himself but to another person.

Just as in religion the spontaneous activity of human fantasy, of the human brain and heart, reacts independently as an alien activity of gods or devils upon the individual, so the activity of the worker is not his own spontaneous activity. It is another's activity and a loss of his own spontaneity.

We arrive at the result that man (the worker) feels himself to be freely active only in his animal functions—eating, drinking and procreating, or at most also in his dwelling and in personal adornment—while in his human functions he is reduced to an animal. The animal becomes human and the human becomes animal.

Eating, drinking and procreating are of course also genuine human functions. But abstractly considered, apart from the environment of other human activities, and turned into final and sole ends, they are animal functions.

We have now considered the act of alienation of practical human activity, labor, from two aspects: (1) the relationship of the worker to the *product of labor* as an alien object which dominates him. This relationship is at the same time the relationship to the sensuous external world, to natural objects, as an alien and hostile world, (2) the relationship of labor to the *act of production* within *labor*. This is the relationship of the worker to his own activity as something alien and not belonging to him, activity as suffering (passivity), strength as powerlessness, creation as emasculation, the *personal* physical and mental energy of the worker, his personal life (for what is life but activity?) as an activity which is directed against himself, independent of him and not belonging to him. This is *self-alienation* as against the above-mentioned alienation of the *thing*.

We have now to infer a third characteristic of *alienated labor* from the two we have considered.

Man is a species-being[5] not only in the sense that he makes the community (his own as well as those of other things) his objects both practically and theoretically, but also (and this is simply another expression for the same thing) in the sense that he treats himself as the present, living species, as a *universal* and consequently free being.

Species-life, for man as for animals, has its physical basis in the fact that man (like animals) lives from inorganic nature, and since man is more universal than an animal so the range of inorganic nature from which he lives is more universal. Plants, animals, minerals, air, light, etc. constitute, from the theoretical aspect, a part of human consciousness as objects of natural science and art; they are man's spiritual inorganic nature, his intellectual means of life, which he must first prepare for enjoyment and perpetuation. So also, from the practical aspect they form a part of human life and activity. In practice man lives only from these natural products, whether in the form of food, heating, clothing, housing, etc. The universality of man appears in practice in the universality which makes the whole of nature into his inorganic body: (1) as a direct means of life; and equally (2) as the material object and instrument of his life activity. Nature is the *inorganic body* of man;

[5] The term "species-being" is taken from Feuerbach's *Das Wesen des Christentums* (The Essence of Christianity). Feuerbach used the notion in making a distinction between consciousness in man and in animals. Man is conscious not merely of himself as an individual but of the human species or "human essence."—*Tr. Note*

that is to say, nature excluding the human body itself. To say that man *lives* from nature means that nature is his *body* with which he must remain in a continuous interchange in order not to die. The statement that the physical and mental life of man, and nature, are interdependent means simply that nature is interdependent with itself, for man is a part of nature.

Since alienated labor: (1) alienates nature from man; and (2) alienates man from himself, from his own active function, his life activity; so it alienates him from the species. It makes *species-life* into a means of individual life. In the first place it alienates species-life and individual life, and secondly, it turns the latter, as an abstraction, into the purpose of the former, also in its abstract and alienated form.

For labor, *life activity, productive life*, now appear to man only as *means* for the satisfaction of a need, the need to maintain his physical existence. Productive life is, however, species-life. It is life creating life. In this type of life activity resides the whole character of a species, its species-character; and free, conscious activity is the species-character of human beings. Life itself appears only as a *means of life*.

The animal is one with its life activity. It does not distinguish the activity from itself. It is *its activity*. But man makes his life activity itself an object of his will and consciousness. He has a conscious life activity. It is not a determination with which he is completely identified. Conscious life activity distinguishes man from the life activity of animals. Only for this reason is he a species-being. Or rather, he is only a self-conscious being, i.e. his own life is an object for him, because he is a species-being. Only for this reason is his activity free activity. Alienated labor reverses the relationship, in that man because he is a self-conscious being makes his life activity, his *being*, only a means for his *existence*.

The practical construction of an *objective world*, the *manipulation* of inorganic nature, is the confirmation of man as a conscious species-being, i.e. a being who treats the species as his own being or himself as a species-being. Of course, animals also produce. They construct nests, dwellings, as in the case of bees, beavers, ants, etc. But they only produce what is strictly necessary for themselves or their young. They produce only in a single direction, while man produces universally. They produce only under the compulsion of direct physical need, while man produces when he is free from physical need and only truly produces in freedom from such need. Animals produce only themselves, while man reproduces the whole of nature. The products of animal production belong directly to their physical bodies, while man is free in face of his product. Animals construct only in accordance with the standards and needs of the species to which they belong, while man knows how to produce in accordance with the standards of every species and knows how to apply the appropriate standard to the object. Thus man constructs also in accordance with the laws of beauty.

It is just in his work upon the objective world that man really proves himself as a *species-being*. This production is his active species life. By means of it nature appears as *his* work and his reality. The object of labor is, therefore, the *objectification of man's species life*; for he no longer reproduces himself merely intellectually, as in consciousness, but actively and in a real sense, and he sees his own reflection in a world which he has constructed. While, therefore, alienated labor takes away the object of production from man, it also takes away his *species life*, his real objectivity as a species-being, and changes his advantage over animals into a disadvantage in so far as his inorganic body, nature, is taken from him.

Just as alienated labor transforms free and self-directed activity into a means, so it transforms the species life of man into a means of physical existence.

Consciousness, which man has from his species, is transformed through alienation so that species life becomes only a means for him.

(3) Thus alienated labor turns the *species life of man*, and also nature as his mental species-property, into an *alien* being and into a *means* for his *individual existence*. It alienates from man his own body, external nature, his mental life and his *human* life.

(4) A direct consequence of the alienation of man from the product of his activity and from his species life is that *man* is *alienated* from other *men*. When man confronts himself he also confronts *other* men. What is true of man's relationship to his work, to the product of his work and to himself, is also true of his relationship to other

men, to their labor and to the objects of their labor.

In general, the statement that man is alienated from his species life means that each man is alienated from others, and that each of the others is likewise alienated from human life.

Human alienation, and above all the relation of man to himself, is first realized and expressed in the relationship between each man and other men. Thus in the relationship of alienated labor every man regards other men according to the standards and relationships in which he finds himself placed as a worker.

We began with an economic fact, the alienation of the worker and his production. We have expressed this fact in conceptual terms as *alienated labor*, and in analyzing the concept we have merely analyzed an economic fact.

Let us now examine further how this concept of alienated labor must express and reveal itself in reality. If the product of labor is alien to me and confronts me as an alien power, to whom does it belong? If my own activity does not belong to me but is an alien, forced activity, to whom does it belong? To a being *other* than myself. And who is this being? The *gods*? It is apparent in the earliest stages of advanced production, e.g., temple building, etc. in Egypt, India, Mexico, and in the service rendered to gods, that the product belonged to the gods. But the gods alone were never the lords of labor. And no more was *nature*. What a contradiction it would be if the more man subjugates nature by his labor, and the more the marvels of the gods are

rendered superfluous by the marvels of industry, he should abstain from his joy in producing and his enjoyment of the product for love of these powers.

The *alien* being to whom labor and the product of labor belong, to whose service labor is devoted, and to whose enjoyment the product of labor goes, can only be *man* himself. If the product of labor does not belong to the worker, but confronts him as an alien power, this can only be because it belongs to *a man other than the worker*. If his activity is a torment to him it must be a source of enjoyment and pleasure to another. Not the gods, nor nature, but only man himself can be this alien power over men.

Economic and Philosophical Manuscripts (1844)

The so-called Revolutions of 1848 were but poor incidents—small fractures and fissures in the dry crust of European society. However, they denounced the abyss. Beneath the apparently solid surface, they betrayed oceans of liquid matter, only needing expansion to rend into fragments continents of hard rock. Noisedly and confusedly they proclaimed the emancipation of the proletarian, *i.e.*, the secret of the nineteenth century, and of the revolution of that century. That social revolution, it is true, was no novelty invented in 1848. Steam, electricity, and the self-acting mule were revolutionists of a rather more dangerous character than even citizens Barbès, Raspail and Blanqui. But, although the atmosphere in which we live weighs upon everyone with a

20,000 pound force, do you feel it? No more than European society before 1848 felt the revolutionary atmosphere enveloping and pressing it from all sides.

There is one great fact, characteristic of this, our nineteenth century, a fact which no party dares deny. On the one hand, there have started into life industrial and scientific forces, which no epoch of the former human history had ever suspected. On the other hand, there exist symptoms of decay, far surpassing the horrors recorded of the latter times of the Roman empire. In our days everything seems pregnant with its contrary; machinery gifted with the wonderful power of shortening and fructifying human labor, we behold starving and overworking it. The new-fangled sources of wealth, by some strange weird spell, are turned into sources of want. The victories of art seem bought by the loss of character. At the same pace that mankind masters nature, man seems to become enslaved to other men or to his own infamy. Even the pure light of science seems unable to shine but on the dark background of ignorance. All our inventions and progress seem to result in endowing material forces with intellectual life, and in stultifying human life into a material force. This antagonism between modern industry and science on the one hand, modern misery and dissolution on the other hand; this antagonism between the productive powers and the social relations of our epoch, is a fact, palpable, overwhelming, and not to be controverted. Some parties may wail over it; others may wish to get rid of modern arts in order to get rid of modern conflicts. Or they may imagine that so signal a progress in industry wants to be completed by as signal a regress in politics.

On our part, we do not mistake the shape of the shrewd spirit that continues to mark all these contradictions. We know that to work well the new-fangled forces of society, they only want to be mastered by new-fangled men—and such are the working men. They are as much the invention of modern times as machinery itself. In the signs that bewilder the middle class, the aristocracy and the poor prophets of regression, we do recognize our brave friend, Robin Goodfellow, the old mole that can work in the earth so fast, that worthy pioneer—the revolution. The English working men are the first born sons of modern industry. They will then, certainly, not be the last in aiding the social revolution produced by that industry, a revolution, which means the emancipation of their own class all over the world, which is as universal as capital-rule and wages-slavery. I know the heroic struggles the English working class have gone through since the middle of the last century—struggles less glorious because they are shrouded in obscurity and buried by the middle class historians. To revenge the misdeeds of the ruling class there existed in the middle ages in Germany a secret tribunal, called the "Vehmgericht." If a red cross was seen marked on a house people knew that its owner was doomed by the "Vehm." All the houses of Europe are now marked with the mysterious red cross.

History is the judge—its executioner, the proletarian.

Speech by Marx at the anniversary celebration of the *People's Paper*, a Chartist publication, in April 1856.

IV. Communist Revolution and Future Society

(1) In the development of the productive forces a stage is reached where productive forces and means of intercourse are called into being which, under the existing relations, can only work mischief, and which are, therefore, no longer productive, but destructive, forces (machinery and money). Associated with this is the emergence of a class which has to bear all the burdens of society without enjoying its advantages, which is excluded from society and is forced into the most resolute opposition to all other classes; a class which comprises the majority of the members of society and in which there develops a consciousness of the need for a fundamental revolution, the communist consciousness. This consciousness can, of course, also arise in other classes from the observation of the situation of this class.

(2) The conditions under which determinate productive forces can be used are also the conditions for the dominance of a determinate social class, whose social power, derived from its property ownership, invariably finds its *practical* and ideal expression in a particular form of the State. Consequently, every revolutionary struggle is directed against the class which has so far been dominant.

(3) In all former revolutions the form of activity was always left unaltered and it was only a question of redistributing this activity among different people, of introducing a new division of labour. The communist revolution, however, is directed against the former *mode* of activity, does away with *labour*, and abolishes all class rule along with the classes themselves, because it is effected by the class which no longer counts as a class in society, which is not recognized as a class, and which is the expression of the dissolution of all classes, nationalities, etc., within contemporary society.

(4) For the creation on a mass scale of this communist consciousness, as well as for the success of the cause itself, it is necessary for men themselves to be changed on a large scale, and this change can only occur in a practical movement, in a *revolution*. Revolution is necessary not only because the *ruling* class cannot be overthrown in any other way, but also because only in a revolution can *the class which overthrows it* rid itself of the accumulated rubbish of the past and become capable of reconstructing society. . . .

The transformation of personal powers (relationships) into material powers through the division of labour cannot be undone again merely by dismissing the idea of it from one's mind, but only by the action of individuals who reestablish their control over these material powers and abolish the division of labour. This is not possible without a community. Only in association with others has each individual the means of cultivating his talents in all directions. Only in a community therefore is personal freedom possible. In the previous substitutes for community, in the State, etc., personal freedom existed only for those individuals who grew up in the ruling class and only in so far as they were members of this class. The illusory community in which, up to the present, individuals have combined, always acquired an independent existence apart from them, and since it was a union of one class against another it represented for the dominated class not only a completely illusory community but also a new shackle. In a genuine community individuals gain their freedom in and through their association.

The German Ideology (1845–1846)

The possessing class and the proletarian class express the same human alienation. But the former is satisfied with its situation, feels itself well established in it, recognizes this self-alienation as *its own* power, and thus has the appearance of a human existence. The latter feels itself crushed by this self-alienation, sees in it its own impotence and the reality of an inhuman situation. It is, to use an expression of Hegel's, "in the midst of degradation the *revolt* against degradation," a revolt to which it is forced by the contradiction between its *humanity* and its situation, which is an open, clear and absolute negation of its humanity.

Within the framework of alienation, therefore, the property owners are the *conservative* and the proletarians the *destructive* party.

It is true that, in its economic development, private property advances towards its own dissolution; but it only does this through a development which is independent of itself, unconscious and achieved against its will—solely because it produces the proletariat *as* proletariat, poverty conscious of its moral and physical poverty, degradation conscious of its degradation, and for this reason trying to abolish itself. The proletariat carries out the sentence which private property, by creating the proletariat, passes upon itself, just as it carries out the sentence which wage-labour, by creating wealth for others and poverty for itself, passes upon itself. If the proletariat triumphs this does not mean that it becomes the absolute form of society, for it is only victorious by abolishing itself as well as its opposite. Thus the proletariat disappears along with the opposite which conditions it, private property.

If socialist writers attribute this world-historical role to the proletariat this is not at all . . . because they regard the proletarians as *gods*. On the contrary, in the fully developed proletariat, everything human is taken away, even the *appearance* of humanity. In the conditions of existence of the proletariat are condensed, in their most inhuman form, all the conditions of existence of present-day society. Man has lost himself, but he has not only acquired, at the same time, a theoretical consciousness of his loss, he has been forced, by an ineluctable and imperious *distress*—by practical *necessity*—to revolt against this inhumanity. It is for these reasons that the proletariat can and must emancipate itself. But it can only emancipate itself by destroying its own conditions of existence. It can only destroy its own conditions of existence by destroying *all* the inhuman conditions of existence of present-day society, conditions which are epitomized in its situation. It is not in vain that it passes through the rough but stimulating school of *labour*. It is not a matter of knowing what this or that proletarian, or even the proletariat as a whole, *conceives* as its aims at any particular moment. It is a question of knowing *what* the proletariat *is*, and what it must historically accomplish in accordance with its *nature*. Its aim and its historical activity are ordained for it, in a tangible and irrevocable way, by its own situation as well as by the whole organization of present-day civil society. It is unnecessary to show here that a large part of the English and French proletariat has already become *aware* of its historic mission, and works incessantly to clarify this awareness.

The Holy Family (with Engels, 1845)

The realm of freedom only begins, in fact, where that labour which is determined by need and external purposes, ceases; it is therefore, by its very nature, outside the sphere of material production proper. Just as the savage must wrestle with Nature in order to satisfy his wants, to maintain and reproduce his life, so also must civilized man, and he must do it in all forms of society and under any possible mode of production. With his development the realm of natural necessity expands, because his wants increase, but at the same time the forces of production, by which these wants are satisfied, also increase. Freedom in this field cannot consist of anything else but the fact that socialized mankind, the associated

producers, regulate their interchange with Nature rationally, bring it under their common control, instead of being ruled by it as by some blind power, and accomplish their task with the least expenditure of energy and under such conditions as are proper and worthy for human beings. Nevertheless, this always remains a realm of necessity. Beyond it begins that development of human potentiality for its own sake, the true realm of freedom, which however can only flourish upon that realm of necessity as its basis. The shortening of the working day is its fundamental prerequisite.

Capital, Vol. III (published posthumously)

What we have to deal with here is a communist society, not as it has *developed* on its own foundation, but, on the contrary, just as it *emerges* from capitalist society; and which is thus in every respect, economically, morally and intellectually, still stamped with the birth-marks of the old society from whose womb it emerges. Accordingly, the individual producer receives back from society—after the deductions have been made—exactly what he contributes to it. What he has contributed to it is his individual quantum of labour. For example, the social working day consists of the sum of the individual hours of work; the individual labour-time of the individual producer is the part of the social working day contributed by him, his share in it. He receives a certificate from society that he has furnished such and such an amount of labour (after deducting his labour for the common funds), and with this certificate he draws from the social stock of means of consumption as much as costs the same amount of labour. The same amount of labour which he has given to society in one form he receives back in another.

Here obviously the same principle prevails as that which regulates the exchange of commodities, as far as this is exchange of equal values. Content and form are changed, because under the altered conditions no one can give anything except his labour, and because on the other hand, nothing can pass into the ownership of individuals except individual means of consumption. But, as far as the distribution of the latter among the individual producers is concerned, the same principle prevails as in the exchange of commodity-equivalents: a given amount of labour in another form.

Hence, *equal right* here is still in principle—*bourgeois right*, although principle and practice are no longer at loggerheads, whereas the exchange of equivalents in commodity exchange only exists *on the average* and not in the individual case.

In spite of this advance, *equal right* is still burdened with bourgeois limitations. The right of the producers is *proportional* to the labour they supply; the equality consists in the fact that measurement is made with an *equal standard, labour.*

But one man is superior to another physically or mentally and so supplies more labour in the same time, or can labour for a longer time; and labour, to serve as a measure, must be defined by its duration or intensity, otherwise it ceases to be a standard of measure-

ment. The *equal* right is an unequal right for unequal labour. It recognizes no class differences, because everyone is only a worker like everyone else; but it tacitly recognizes unequal individual endowment, and thus natural privileges in respect of productive capacity. *It is, therefore, in its content, a right of inequality, like every right.* Right by its very nature can consist only in the application of an equal standard; but unequal individuals (and they would not be different individuals if they were not unequal) can only be assessed by an equal standard in so far as they are regarded from a single aspect, from one particular side only, as for instance, in the present case, they are regarded *only as workers*, and nothing more is seen in them, everything else being ignored. Further, one worker is married, another not; one has more children than another, and so on. Thus, with an equal performance of labour, and hence an equal share in the social consumption fund, one individual will in fact receive more than another, one will be richer than another, and so on. To avoid all these defects, right instead of being equal would have to be unequal.

But these defects are inevitable in the first phase of communist society as it is when it has just emerged after prolonged birth-pangs from capitalist society. Right can never be higher than the economic structure of society and the cultural development conditioned by it.

In a higher phase of communist society, when the enslaving subordination of the individual to the division of labour, and with it the antithesis between mental and physical labour, has vanished; when labour is no longer merely a means of life but has become life's principal need; when the productive forces have also increased with the all-round development of the individual, and all the springs of co-operative wealth flow more abundantly—only then will it be possible completely to transcend the narrow outlook of bourgeois right and only then will society be able to inscribe on its banners: From each according to his ability, to each according to his needs!

Critique of the Gotha Program (1875)

LESZEK KOLAKOWSKI (1927–   )

Kolakowski served a lengthy period as a member of the Polish Communist Party until he was expelled in 1966. He rose to the position of professor of philosophy at the University of Warsaw and editor of Poland's leading philosophical journal. In 1968 he lost his position at the university because of his uncompromising support of student protest. Subsequently he travelled, lectured, and taught in Canada, the United States, and England. A playwright and essayist as well as a philosopher, he is best known in the West for such striking essays as "The Priest and the Jester" and "Responsibility and History," but he has written longer works including *The Alienation of Reason: A History of Positivist Thought* (New York: Doubleday, 1968). The following pungent article, "What Is Socialism?", was written in 1956 for a Polish student journal but was never printed in Poland. It circulated in manuscript and finally reached the hands of Richard C. Hottelet, the American journalist, and thereafter publication in the United States.

What
Is
Socialism?

We will tell you what socialism is. But first we must tell you what socialism is not. It is a matter about which we once had a quite different opinion than we have today.

Well, then, socialism is not:

A society in which a person who has commited no crime sits at home waiting for the police.

From *The New Leader*, February 18, 1957. Reprinted by permission.

A society in which is it a crime to be the brother, sister, son, or wife of a criminal.

A society in which one person is unhappy because he says what he thinks, and another happy because he does not say what is in his mind.

A society in which a person lives better because he does not think at all.

A society in which a person is unhappy because he is a Jew, and another feels better for not being a Jew.

A state which utilizes nationalistic slogans.

A state whose government believes that nothing is more important than its power.

A state which makes a pact with crime, and then adapts its ideology to this pact.

A state which would like to see its foreign ministry determine the political opinion of all mankind.

A state which finds it difficult to distinguish between enslavement and liberation.

A state in which racist agitators enjoy full freedom.

A state in which there is private ownership of the means of production.

A state which considers itself solidly socialist because it has liquidated private ownership of the means of production.

A state which has difficulty differentiating between social revolution and armed assault.

A state which does not believe that people must be happier under socialism than elsewhere.

A society which is very melancholy.

A caste system.

A state which always knows the will of the people before it asks them.

A state which can mistreat the people with impunity.

A state in which a view of history is important.

A state in which the philosophers and writers always say the same as the generals and ministers, but always after them.

A state in which street maps of cities are state secrets.

A state in which the returns of parliamentary elections are always predictable.

A state in which there is slave labor.

A state in which feudal fetters exist.

A state which has a world monopoly on scientific progress.

A state in which an entire people, through no desire of its own, is moved to a new location.

A state in which the workers have no influence on the government.

A state which believes that it alone can redeem humanity.

A state which considers itself to be always in the right.

A state in which history is a servant of policy.

A state whose soldiers move into the the territory of another country first.

A state where anyone who praises the national leaders is better off.

A state in which one can be condemned without trial.

A society whose leaders appoint themselves to their posts.

A society in which ten people live in one room.

A society which has illiterates and smallpox epidemics.

A state which does not permit travel abroad.

A state which has more spies than nurses, and more people in prison than in hospitals.

A state in which the number of officials increases faster than that of workers.

A state in which one is forced to resort to lies.

A state in which one is compelled to be a thief.

A state in which one is forced to resort to crime.

A state which possesses colonies.

A state whose neighbors curse geography.

A state which produces excellent jet planes and bad shoes.

A state in which cowards live better than the valiant.

A state in which lawyers in most cases agree with the state prosecutor.

Empire, tyranny, oligarchy, bureaucracy.

A state in which the majority of people seek God in order to find solace in their misery.

A state which awards prizes to pseudo-authors and knows more about painting than the painters.

A nation which oppresses other nations.

A nation which is oppressed by another nation.

A state which wants all its citizens to have the same opinions in philosophy, foreign policy, economics, literature, and ethics.

A state whose government defines its citizens' rights, but whose citizens do not define the government's rights.

A state in which one is responsible for one's ancestors.

A state in which one part of the population receives salaries forty times higher than those of the remainder.

Any system of government toward which most of the governed are hostile.

A single, isolated state.

A group of backward countries.

A state whose citizens may not read the greatest works of contemporary literature, not see the greatest works of contemporary painting, and not hear the greatest works of modern music.

A state which is always well pleased with itself.

A state which asserts that the world is very complicated, but actually believes it to be extremely simple.

A state in which one must suffer long before one can get a doctor.

A society that has beggars.

A state which believes everyone to be enamored of it, whereas in truth it is the opposite.

A state which is convinced that nobody in the world can conceive anything better.

A state which does not mind being hated as long as it is feared.

A state which determines who may criticize it and how.

A state in which one must each day refute what one affirmed the day before and always believe it to be the same.

A state which does not like to see its citizens read back numbers of newspapers.

A state in which many ignoramuses rank as scholars.

That was the first part. But now listen attentively, we will tell you what socialism it: Well, then, socialism is a good thing.

Warsaw, 1956.

COMMENT

In this chapter we are dealing with an extremely complex thinker whose ideas were not only ambiguous but subject to change and development. Marx once even remarked, "One thing I know and that is that I am not a Marxist."[1] He was aware of the common tendency among "Marxists" to reduce and distort his ideas, being perhaps as misinterpreted by friend as by foe.

Despite some unguarded statements, his theory was not a simple-minded economic determinism. An example of the ambiguity and complexity of his doctrine is the passage that we have quoted from his Preface to *A Contribution to the Critique of Political Economy*. One interpretation is that the economic system is the "base" that "determines" the political and cultural "superstructure." According to this view, the various strata in the social order—the economy, the state with its laws, and the cultural spheres of art, science, philosophy, religion, and morality—are all distinct and externally related factors, in which the "higher," the political and cultural, are determined by the "lower," the economic. This interpretation becomes less convincing when we ask certain questions. When Marx repeatedly uses the word "material," does he mean simply "economic," or does he mean to include the biological constitution of the human being and the interaction between man and external nature? Does Marx believe that thought processes are no more than epiphenomena or echoes of economic factors? Or is he saying that a certain form of thought—ideology—is an echo, but that there are other forms of thought that are relatively independent? Can we characterize the base without introducing something from the superstructure, such as science, law, or art? If not, is the base-superstructure metaphor awkward and misleading?

We should be on our guard against interpreting the Marxian theory as a pure economic determinism. Marx refers in many passages to the influence of political and cultural factors on the economic system. The following statement is an example:

> All circumstances . . . which affect man . . . have a greater or lesser influence upon all his functions and activities, including his functions and activities as the creator of material wealth, or commodities. In this sense, it can truly be asserted that all human relations and functions, however and wherever they manifest themselves, influence material production and have a more or less determining effect upon it.[2]

Marx thus maintained that all sorts of forces enter into the very complex interaction of causal factors. It is an interaction of unequal forces of which the economic, in the long run, are by far the most powerful.

Contrary to the usual interpretation of his doctrine, he did not suppose that all history can be arranged in a definite series of stages, beginning with primi-

[1] Karl Marx and Friedrich Engels, *Selected Correspondence* (New York: International Publishers, 1936), p. 472.
[2] *Theories of Surplus Value*, in Marx, *Selected Writings in Sociology and Social Philosophy*, edited by T. B. Bottomore and M. Rubel (C. A. Watts & Co. Ltd., 1956), p. 100.

tive communism and going on to slavery, feudalism, capitalism, socialism, and finally advanced communism. In his Preface to *Capital*, we must admit, he seems to be espousing a rigid scheme of historical development." "The natural laws of capitalist production," he said, are "working with iron necessity toward inevitable results. The country that is more developed industrially only shows, to the less developed, the image of its own future." But commenting on this statement in a letter to a Russian sympathizer, Vera Zasulich, he explained that he meant to restrict "the historical inevitability of this line of development to the countries of Western Europe." Elsewhere he pointed out that the historical development in India, China, and Russia deviated greatly from the pattern in Western Europe. In his *Economic and Philosophical Manuscripts* (1844), he distinguished between democratic and autocratic forms of communism, and in his famous speech at the Hague in 1872 he declared that the "emancipation of the workers" may be achieved peacefully in the more democratic countries. Thus he advocated a complex multilinear theory of history rather than the simple unilinear theory that is usually attributed to him.

In a passage in the *Manuscripts* referring to some radical theories then extant, he condemned raw and repressive forms of communism. "This entirely crude and unreflective communism," he declared, "would negate the personality of man in every sphere. . . . It would be a system in which universal envy sets itself up as a power, and . . . in this form of envy, it would reduce everything to a common level." "Crude communism," he went on to say, "is only the culmination of such envy and levelling down to a preconceived minimum." He spoke of it as "the negation of the whole world of culture and civilization.[3]

These remarks were made in 1844, but in his later works, Marx occasionally recognized the dangers of collectivism and bureaucracy. In the 1850s he wrote articles for the New York *Daily Tribune* in which he characterized "Oriental despotism," the state managerialism of the old Asiatic societies, as dooming the masses to a kind of "general [state] slavery."[4] In his comments of 1871 on the Paris Commune, he emphasized the need for popular control of the revolutionary government, warning against bureaucracy and militarism. His ultimate ideal was to abolish the coercive state and to organize society on a decentralized basis. His works contain an impassioned protest against the dehumanizing process of mass industry, with its tendency toward the depersonalization of life. Although expressed most fully in the early *Economic and Philosophical Manuscripts*, his theory of "alienation" remains basic in the later works, but more often implicit than explicit. For example, Marx's speech at the anniversary celebration of the *People's Paper* (1856), mentions two basic sides of the process of alienation: first, material forces taking on "life" and dominating human beings, and second,

---

[3] *Economic and Philosophical Manuscripts*, in T. B. Bottomore, *Karl Marx: Early Writings* (London: C. A. Watts & Co., 1963), pp. 153–154.

[4] See Karl Wittfogel, *Oriental Despotism* (New Haven, Conn.: Yale University Press, 1959).

life being stultified into a material force. Marx seldom used the *word* "alienation" in his later publications, but in his unpublished manuscript *Grundrisse der Kritik der politischen Ökonomie* (1857–1858) the word occurs frequently. In these later works, he still thought of man as estranged from other men, from his work, from his products, from his society, from nature. He also clung to the ideal of dealienation, demanding that human beings be treated as human beings, and things as things. A nonalienated man would be truly a man, free, creative, well-rounded, no longer the victim of impersonal forces.

Hegel and Marx

A comparison of Marx and Hegel on the philosophy of history will throw light on both men. I shall first summarize the ideas that they share. History is visualized in terms of historical stages. The dynamism of historical change is the conflict of opposites: in Hegel, the battle of great ideas or cultural forces; in Marx, the conflict between static class-structure and dynamic technology, and between the bourgeoisie and the proletariat, or between other historical classes. Each stage is at first an advance, but contradictions develop: the old fetters the new, the traditions fetter the innovations. A social crisis results from this state of conflict and disequilibrium: legitimate wants are frustrated, resources are unused or misused, potentialities are fettered by the disproportionate development of societal factors, and dissenters arise to challenge and overthrow the existing order. Mankind thus evolves from stage to stage through conflict and alienation. Human beings become more or less conscious of their alienation, and they move through it and out of it into a new measure of freedom. The conflicts in history, the sufferings and the alienations, are necessary for human progress. The ideal— "the transition from the kingdom of necessity to the kingdom of freedom"— comes only at the end of the process. So much for the similarities.

The differences are sharp and profound. Marx's emphasis upon economic forces and material needs is very different from Hegel's emphasis on human reason and spirituality. The Marxian vision of history as culminating in the abolition of economic classes and "the withering away of the state" has no counterpart in Hegel. The final stages in Hegel's scenario are the strong national state and the hierarchical class-structure in a world of competing states and classes. So far as there is reconciliation it is within and through the state. All this is contrary to Marx.

Criticism

History has not altogether turned out as Marx expected. The prediction of the necessary pauperization of the industrial workers and their consequent radicalization is inaccurate. Where socialist revolution initially occurred, it has been in the more backward countries such as Czarist Russia and nonindustrialized China, not as Marx expected in the advanced industrial countries. Evils of the old order, such as massive repression, have lingered on and in some cases have been intensified.

All over the world, even within the socialist nations, a New Left has emerged intent upon achieving "socialism with a human face." As an example I have reproduced Kolakowski's "What Is Socialism?" It is a witty and scathing comment on the totalitarian element in "socialist" states such as Stalin's Russia. Since the death of Stalin there has been a "thaw," but deep frost remains. This is not to deny that there have been very substantial advances in the level of productivity both in the Soviet Union and Red China. Despite these and other gains the conflict between the libertarian and the authoritarian left is acute.

In various respects we can question and debate the validity of Marx's ideas in comparison with the ideas of Hegel and in terms of their intrinsic worth. I shall leave this task to the readers of this book. If, in conclusion, I should venture some opinions of my own, I would say this: We need to be sensitive, as Marx was sensitive, to the enormous burden of human suffering. His humanitarian concern does honor to him as a man. If we were as sincerely concerned it would be very much to our credit. But even though his ideas are far from the caricature that is so often presented, Marx was too sure about the way history would go, too one-sided in his emphasis upon economic forces, and too ready to accept dictatorship in his eagerness for revolutionary change. With our different tradition of civil liberties and human rights, we need to cherish the free, humane values of our civilization—and so we have to revise and supplement Marx.

22

Liberal Democracy

JOHN STUART MILL

(For biographical note see pages 573-574.)

On Liberty

Chapter I

Introductory

. . . The object of this Essay is to asssert one very simple principle, as entitled to govern absolutely the dealings of society with the individual in the way of compulsion and control, whether the means used be physical force in the form of legal penalties, or the moral coercion of public opinion. That principle is, that the sole end for which mankind are warranted, in-

On Liberty was first published in London in 1859.

dividually or collectively, in interfering with the liberty of action of any of their number, is self-protection. That the only purpose for which power can be rightfully exercised over any member of a civilized community, against his will, is to prevent harm to others. His own good, either physical or moral, is not a sufficient warrant. He cannot rightfully be compelled to do or forbear because it will be better for him to do so, because it will make him happier, because, in the opinions of others, to do so would be wise, or even right. These are good reasons for remonstrating with him, or reasoning with him, or persuading him, or entreating him, but not for compelling him, or visiting him with any evil in case he do otherwise. To justify that, the conduct from which it is desired to deter him must be calculated to produce evil to some one else. The only part of the conduct of anyone, for which he is amenable to society, is that which concerns others. In the part which merely concerns himself, his independence is, of right, absolute. Over himself, over his own body and mind, the individual is sovereign.

It is perhaps hardly necessary to say that this doctrine is meant to apply only to human beings in the maturity of their faculties. We are not speaking of children, or of young persons below the age which the law may fix as that of manhood or womanhood. Those who are still in a state to require being taken care of by others, must be protected against their own actions as well as against external injury. For the same reason, we may leave out of consideration those backward states of society in which the race itself may be considered as in its nonage. The early difficulties in the way of spontaneous progress are so great, and there is seldom any choice of means for overcoming them; and a ruler full of the spirit of improvement is warranted in the use of any expedients that will attain an end, perhaps otherwise unattainable. Despotism is a legitimate mode of government in dealing with barbarians, provided the end be their improvement, and the means justified by actually effecting that end. Liberty, as a principle, has no application to any state of things anterior to the time

when mankind have become capable of being improved by free and equal discussion. Until then, there is nothing for them but implicit obedience to an Akbar or a Charlemagne, if they are so fortunate as to find one. But as soon as mankind have attained the capacity of being guided to their own improvement by conviction or persuasion (a period long since reached in all nations with whom we need here concern ourselves), compulsion, either in the direct form or in that of pains and penalties for noncompliance, is no longer admissible as a means to their own good, and justifiable only for the security of others.

It is proper to state that I forego any advantage which could be derived to my argument from the idea of abstract right, as a thing independent of utility. I regard utility as the ultimate appeal on all ethical questions; but it must be utility in the largest sense, grounded on the permanent interests of a man as a progressive being. Those interests, I contend, authorized the subjection of individual spontaneity to external control, only in respect to those actions of each which concern the interest of other people. If anyone does an act hurtful to others, there is a *prima facie* case for punishing him, by law, or, where legal penalties are not safely applicable, by general disapprobation. There are also many positive acts for the benefit of others, which he may rightfully be compelled to perform: such as to give evidence in a court of justice; to bear his fair share in the common defense, or in any other joint work necessary to the interest of the society of which he enjoys the protection; and to perform certain acts of individual beneficence, such as saving a fellow-creature's life, or interposing to protect the defenseless against ill-usage, things which wherever it is obviously a man's duty to do, he may rightfully be made responsible to society for not doing. A person may cause evil to others not only by his actions but by his inaction, and in either case he is justly accountable to them for the injury. The latter case, it is true, requires a much more cautious exercise of compulsion than the former. To make anyone answerable for doing evil to others is the rule; to make him answerable for not preventing evil is, comparatively speaking, the exception. Yet there are many cases clear enough and grave enough to justify that exception. In all things which regard the external relations of the individual, he is *de jure* amenable to those whose interests are concerned, and, if need be, to society as their protector. There are often good reasons for not holding him to the responsibility; but these reasons must arise from the special expediencies of the case: either because it is a kind of case in which he is on the whole likely to act better, when left to his own discretion, than when controlled in any way in which society have it in their power to control him; or because the attempt to exercise control would produce other evils, greater than those which it would prevent. When such reasons as these preclude the enforcement of responsibility, the conscience of the agent himself should step into the vacant judgment seat, and protect those interests of others which have no external protection; judging himself all the more rigidly, because the case does not admit of his being made accountable to the judgment of his fellow-creatures.

But there is a sphere of action in which society, as distinguished from the individual, has, if any, only an indirect interest; comprehending all that portion of a person's life and conduct which affects only himself, or if it also affects others, only with their free, voluntary, and undeceived consent and participation. When I say only himself, I mean directly, and in the first instance; for whatever affects himself, may affect others through himself; and the objection which may be grounded on this contingency, will receive consideration in the sequel. This, then, is the appropriate region of human liberty. It comprises, *first,* the inward domain of consciousness; demanding liberty of conscience in the most comprehensive sense; liberty of thought and feeling; absolute freedom of opinion and sentiment on all subjects, practical or speculative, scientific, moral or theological. The liberty of expressing and publishing opinions may seem to fall under a different principle, since it belongs to that part of the conduct of an individual which concerns other people; but, being almost of as much importance as the liberty of thought itself, and resting in great part on the same reasons, is practically inseparable from it. *Secondly,* the principle requires liberty of tastes and pursuits; of framing the plan of our life to suit our own character; of doing as we like, subject to such consequences as may follow: without impediment from our fellow-creatures, so long as what we do does not harm them, even though they should think our conduct foolish, perverse, or wrong. *Thirdly,* from this liberty of each individual, follows the liberty, within the same limits, of combination among individuals; freedom to unite, for any purpose not involving harm to others: the persons combining being supposed to be of full age, and not forced or deceived.

No society in which these liberties are not, on the whole, respected, is free, whatever may be its form of government; and none is completely free in which they do not exist absolute and unqualified. The only freedom which deserves the name, is that of pursuing our own good in our own way, so long as we do not attempt to deprive others of theirs, or impede their efforts to obtain it. Each is the proper guardian of his own health, whether bodily, or mental and spiritual. Mankind are greater gainers by suffering each other to live as seems good to themselves, than by compelling each to live as seems good to the rest.

Though this doctrine is anything but new, and, to some persons, may have the air of a truism, there is no doctrine which stands more directly opposed to the general tendency of existing opinion and practice. . . . There is . . . an inclination to stretch unduly the powers of society over the individual, both by the force of opinion and even by that of legislation; and as the tendency of all the changes taking place in the world is to strengthen society, and diminish the power of the individual, this encroachment is not one of the evils which tend spontaneously to disappear, but, on the contrary, to grow more and more formidable. The disposition of mankind, whether as rulers or as fellow-citizens, to impose their own opinions and inclinations as a rule of conduct on others, is so energetically supported by some of the best and by some of the worst feelings incident to human nature, that it is hardly ever kept under restraint by anything but want of power; and as the power is not declining, but growing, unless a strong barrier of moral conviction can be raised against the mischief, we must expect, in the present circumstances of the world, to see it increase. . . .

Chapter II

Of the Liberty of Thought and Discussion

The time, it is to be hoped, is gone by, when any defence would be necessary of the "liberty of the press" as one of the securities against corrupt or tyrannical government. . . . Speaking generally, it is not, in constitutional countries, to be apprehended that the government, whether completely responsible to the people or not, will often attempt to control the expression of opinion, except when in doing so it makes itself the organ of the general intolerance of the public. Let us suppose, therefore, that the government is entirely at one with the people, and never thinks of exerting any power of coercion unless in agreement with what it conceives to be their voice. But I deny the right of the people to exercise such coercion, either by themselves or by their government. The power itself is illegitimate. The best government has no more title to it than the worst. It is as noxious, or more noxious, when exerted in accordance with public opinion, than when in opposition to it. If all mankind minus one were of one opinion, and only one person were of the contrary opinion, mankind would be no more justified in silencing that one person, than he, if he had the power, would be justified in silencing mankind. Were an opinion a personal possession of no value except to the owner; if to be obstructed in the enjoyment of it were simply a private injury, it would make some difference whether the injury was inflicted only on a few persons or on many. But the peculiar evil of silencing the expression of an opinion is, that it is robbing the human race: posterity as well as the existing generation; those who dissent from the opinion, still more than those who hold it. If the opinion is right, they are deprived of the opportunity of exchanging error for truth; if wrong, they lose, what is almost as great a benefit, the clearer perception and livelier impression of truth, produced by its collision with error.

It is necessary to consider separately these two hypotheses, each of which has a distinct branch of the argument corresponding to it. We can never be sure that the opinion we are endeavoring to stifle is a false opinion; and if we were sure, stifling it would be an evil still.

First: the opinion which it is attempted to suppress by authority may possibly be true. Those who desire to suppress it, of course deny its truth; but they are not infallible. They have no authority to decide the question for all mankind, and exclude every other person from the means of judging. To refuse a hearing to an opinion, because they are sure that it is false, is to assume that *their* certainty is the same thing as *absolute* certainty. All silencing of discussion is an assumption of infallibility. Its condemnation may be allowed to rest on this common argument, not the worse for being common.

Unfortunately for the good sense of mankind, the fact of their fallibility is far from carrying the weight in their practical judgment which is always allowed to it in theory; for while everyone well knows himself to be fallible, few think it necessary to take any precautions against their own fallibility, or admit the supposition that any opinion of which they feel very certain, may be one of the examples of the error to which they acknowledge themselves to be liable. Absolute princes, or others who are accustomed to unlimited deference, usually feel this complete confidence in their own opinions on nearly all subjects. People more happily situated, who sometimes hear their opinons disputed, and are not wholly unused to be set right when they are wrong, place the same unbounded reliance only on such of their opinions as are shared by all who surround them, or to whom they habitually defer; for in proportion to a man's want of confidence in his own solitary judgment, does he usually repose, with implicit trust, on the infallibility of "the world" in general. And the world, to each individual, means the part of it with which he comes in contact—his party, his sect, his church, his class of society; the man may be called, by comparison, almost liberal and large-minded to whom it means anything so comprehensive as his own country or his own age. Nor is his faith in this collective authority at all shaken by his being aware that other ages, countries, sects, churches, classes, and parties have thought, and even now think, the exact reverse. He devolves upon his own world the responsibility of being in the right against the dissentient worlds of other people; and it never troubles him that mere accident has decided which of these numerous worlds is the object of his reliance, and that the same causes which make him a Churchman in London, would have made him a Buddhist or a Confucian in Peking. Yet it is as evident in itself as any amount of argument can make it, that ages are no more infallible than individuals; every age having held many opinions which subsequent ages have deemed not only false but absurd; and it is as certain that many opinions now general will be rejected by future ages, as it is that many, once general, are rejected by the present.

The objection likely to be made to this argument would probably take some such form as the following. There is no greater assumption of infallibility in forbidding the propagation of error, than in any other thing which is done by public authority on its own judgment and responsibility. Judgment is given to men that they may use it. Because it may be used erroneously, are men to be told that they ought not to use it at all? To prohibit what they think pernicious, is not claiming exemption from error, but fulfilling the duty incumbent on them, although fallible, of acting on their conscientious conviction. If we were never to act on our opinions, because those opinions may be wrong, we should leave all our interests uncared for, and all our duties un-

performed. An objection which applies to all conduct can be no valid objection to any conduct in particular. It is the duty of governments, and of individuals, to form the truest opinions they can; to form them carefully, and never impose them upon others unless they are quite sure of being right. But when they are sure (such reasoners may say), it is not conscientiousness but cowardice to shrink from acting on their opinions, and allow doctrines which they honestly think dangerous to the welfare of mankind, either in this life or in another, to be scattered abroad without restraint, because other people, in less enlightened times, have persecuted opinions now believed to be true. Let us take care, it may be said, not to make the same mistake; but governments and nations have made mistakes in other things, which are not denied to be fit subjects for the exercise of authority: they have laid on bad taxes, made unjust wars. Ought we therefore to lay on no taxes, and, under whatever provocation, make no wars? Men, and governments, must act to the best of their ability. There is no such thing as absolute certainty, but there is assurance sufficient for the purposes of human life. We may, and must, assume our opinion to be true for the guidance of our own conduct: and it is assuming no more when we forbid bad men to pervert society by the propagation of opinions which we regard as false and pernicious.

I answer that it is assuming very much more. There is the greatest difference between presuming an opinion to be true because, with every opportunity for contesting it, it has not been refuted, and assuming its truth for the purpose of not permitting its refutation. Complete liberty of contradicting and disproving our opinion is the very condition which justifies us in assuming its truth for purposes of action; and on no other terms can a being with human faculties have any rational assurance of being right.

When we consider either the history of opinion, or the ordinary conduct of human life, to what is it to be ascribed that the one and the other are no worse than they are? Not certainly to the inherent force of the human understanding; for, on any matter not self-evident, there are ninety-nine persons totally incapable of judging of it for one who is capable; and the capacity of the hundredth person is only comparative: for the majority of the eminent men of every past generation held many opinions now known to be erroneous, and did or approved numerous things which no one will now justify. Why is it, then, that there is on the whole a preponderance among mankind of rational opinions and rational conduct? If there really is this preponderance—which there must be unless human affairs are, and have always been, in an almost desperate state—it is owing to a quality of the human mind, the source of everything respectable in man either as an intellectual or as a moral being, namely, that his errors are corrigible. He is capable of rectifying his mistakes, by discussion and experience. Not by experience alone. There must be discussion, to show how experience is to be interpreted. Wrong opinions and practices gradually yield to fact and argument; but facts and arguments, to produce any effect on the mind, must be brought before it. Very

few facts are able to tell their own story, without comments to bring out their meaning. The whole strength and value, then, of human judgment, depending on the one property, that it can be set right when it is wrong, reliance can be placed on it only when the means of setting it right are kept constantly at hand. In the case of any person whose judgment is really deserving of confidence, how has it become so? Because he has kept his mind open to criticism of his opinions and conduct. Because it has been his practice to listen to all that could be said against him; to profit by as much of it as was just, and expound to himself, and upon occasion to others, the fallacy of what was fallacious. Because he has felt that the only way in which a human being can make some approach to knowing the whole of a subject, is by hearing what can be said about it by persons of every variety of opinion, and studying all modes in which it can be looked at by every character of mind. No wise man ever acquired his wisdom in any mode but this; nor is it in the nature of human intellect to become wise in any other manner. The steady habit of correcting and completing his own opinion by collating it with those of others, so far from causing doubt and hesitation in carrying it into practice, is the only stable foundation for a just reliance on it: for, being cognizant of all that can, at least obviously, be said against him, and having taken up his position against all gainsayers—knowing that he has sought for objections and difficulties, instead of avoiding them, and has shut out no light which can be thrown upon the subject from any quarter—he has a right to think his judgment better than that of any person, or any multitude, who have not gone through a similar process.

It is not too much to require that what the wisest of mankind, those who are best entitled to trust their own judgment, find necessary to warrant their relying on it, should be submitted to by that miscellaneous collection of a few wise and many foolish individuals, called the public. The most intolerant of churches, the Roman Catholic Church, even at the canonization of a saint, admits, and listens patiently to, a "devil's advocate." The holiest of men, it appears, cannot be admitted to posthumous honors, until all that the devil could say against him is known and weighed. If even the Newtonian philosophy were not permitted to be questioned, mankind could not feel as complete assurance of its truth as they now do. The beliefs which we have most warrant for, have no safeguard to rest on but a standing invitation to the whole world to prove them unfounded. If the challenge is not accepted, or is accepted and the attempt fails, we are far enough from certainty still; but we have done the best that the existing state of human reason admits of; we have neglected nothing that could give the truth a chance of reaching us: if the lists are kept open, we may hope that if there be a better truth, it will be found when the human mind is capable of receiving it; and in the meantime we may rely on having attained such approach to truth as is possible in our own day. This is the amount of certainty attainable by a fallible being, and this the sole way of attaining it.

Strange it is that men should admit the validity of the arguments for free discussion, but object to their being "pushed to an extreme"; not seeing that unless the reasons are good for an extreme case, they are not good for any case. Strange that they should imagine that they are not assuming infallibility, when they acknowledge that there should be free discussion on all subjects which can possibly be *doubtful,* but think that some particular principle or doctrine should be forbidden to be questioned because it is so *certain,* that is, because *they are certain* that it is certain. To call any proposition certain while there is anyone who would deny its certainty if permitted, but who is not permitted, is to assume that we ourselves, and those who agree with us, are the judges of certainty, and judges without hearing the other side.

In the present age—which has been described as "destitute of faith, but terrified at scepticism"—in which people feel sure, not so much that their opinions are true, as that they should not know what to do without them—the claims of an opinion to be protected from public attack are rested not so much on its truth, as on its importance to society. There are, it is alleged, certain beliefs so useful, not to say indispensable, to well-being that it is as much the duty of governments to uphold those beliefs, as to protect any other of the interests of society. In a case of such necessity, and so directly in the line of their duty, something less than infallibility may, it is maintained, warrant, and even bind, governments to act on their own opinion, confirmed by the general opinion of mankind. It is also often argued, and still oftener thought, that none but bad men would desire to weaken these salutary beliefs; and there can be nothing wrong, it is thought, in restraining bad men, and prohibiting what only such men would wish to practice. This mode of thinking makes the justification of restraints on discussion not a question of the truth of doctrines, but of their usefulness; and flatters itself by that means to escape the responsibility of claiming to be an infallible judge of opinions. But those who thus satisfy themselves, do not perceive that the assumption of infallibility is merely shifted from one point to another. The usefulness of an opinion is itself matter of opinion: as disputable, as open to discussion, and requiring discussion as much as the opinion itself. There is the same need of an infallible judge of opinions to decide an opinion to be noxious, as to decide it to be false, unless the opinion condemned has full opportunity of defending itself. And it will not do to say that the heretic may be allowed to maintain the utility or harmlessness of his opinion, though forbidden to maintain its truth. The truth of an opinion is part of its utility. If we would know whether or not it is desirable that a proposition should be believed, is it possible to exclude the consideration of whether or not it is true? In the opinion, not of bad men, but of the best men, no belief which is contrary to truth can be really useful; and can you prevent such men from urging that plea, when they are charged with culpability for denying some doctrine which they are told is useful, but which they believe to be false? Those who are on the side of received opinions never fail to take all

possible advantages of this plea: you do not find *them* handling the question of utility as if it could be completely abstracted from that of truth; on the contrary, it is, above all, because their doctrine is "the truth," that the knowledge or the belief of it is held to be so indispensable. There can be no fair discussion of the question of usefulness when an argument so vital may be employed on one side, but not on the other. And in point of fact, when law or public feeling do not permit the truth of an opinion to be disputed, they are just as little tolerant of a denial of its usefulness. The utmost they allow is an extenuation of its absolute necessity, or of the positive guilt of rejecting it.

In order more fully to illustrate the mischief of denying a hearing to opinions because we, in our own judgment, have condemned them, it will be desirable to fix down the discussion to a concrete case; and I choose, by preference, the cases which are least favorable to me—in which the argument against freedom of opinion, both on the score of truth and on that of utility, is considered the strongest. Let the opinions impugned be the belief in a God and in a future state, or any of the commonly received doctrines of morality. To fight the battle on such ground gives a great advantage to an unfair antagonist; since he will be sure to say (and many who have no desire to be unfair will say it internally), "Are these the doctrines which you do not deem sufficiently certain to be taken under the protection of laws? Is the belief in a God one of the opinions to feel sure of which you hold to be assuming infallibility?" But I must be permitted to observe that it is not the feeling sure of a doctrine (be it what it may) which I call an assumption of infallibility. It is the undertaking to decide that question *for others,* without allowing them to hear what can be said on the contrary side. And I denounce and reprobate this pretension not the less if put forth on the side of my most solemn convictions. However positive anyone's persuasion may be, not only of the falsity but of the pernicious consequences—not only of the pernicious consequences, but (to adopt expressions which I altogether condemn) the immorality and impiety of an opinion; yet if, in pursuance of that private judgment, though backed by the public judgment of his country or his contemporaries, he prevents the opinion from being heard in its defense, he assumes infallibility. And so far from the assumption being less objectionable or less dangerous because the opinion is called immoral or impious, this is the case of all others in which it is most fatal. These are exactly the occasions on which the men of one generation commit those dreadful mistakes which excite the astonishment and horror of posterity. It is among such that we find the instances memorable in history, when the arm of the law has been employed to root out the best men and the noblest doctrines; with deplorable success as to the men, though some of the doctrines have survived to be (as if in mockery) invoked in defense of similar conduct toward those who dissent from *them,* or from their received interpretation.

Mankind can hardly be too often reminded, that there was once a man named Socrates, between whom and the legal authorities and public opinion of his time there took place a memorable collision. Born in an age and country abounding in individual greatness, this man has been handed down to us by those who best knew both him and the age, as the most virtuous man in it; while *we* know him as the head and prototype of all subsequent teachers of virtue, the source equally of the lofty inspiration of Plato and the judicious utilitarianism of Aristotle, . . . the two head-springs of ethical as of all other philosophy. This acknowledged master of all the eminent thinkers who have since lived—whose fame, still growing after more than two thousand years, all but outweighs the whole remainder of the names which make his native city illustrious—was put to death by his countrymen, after a judicial conviction, for impiety and immorality. Impiety, in denying the gods recognized by the State; indeed his accuser asserted (see the *Apologia*) that he believed in no gods at all. Immorality, in being, by his doctrines and instructions, a "corruptor of youth." Of these charges the tribunal, there is every ground for believing, honestly found him guilty, and condemned the man who probably of all then born had deserved best of mankind to be put to death as a criminal.

To pass from this to the only other instance of judicial iniquity, the mention of which, after the condemnation of Socrates, would not be an anticlimax: the event which took place on Calvary rather more than eighteen hundred years ago. The man who left on the memory of those who witnessed his life and conversation such an impression of his moral grandeur that eighteen subsequent centuries have done homage to him as the Almighty in person, was ignominiously put to death, as what? As a blasphemer. Men did not merely mistake their benefactor; they mistook him for the exact contrary of what he was, and treated him as that prodigy of impiety which they themselves are now held to be for their treatment of him. The feelings with which mankind now regard these lamentable transactions, especially the later of the two, render them extremely unjust in their judgment of the unhappy actors. These were, to all appearance, not bad men—not worse than men commonly are, but rather the contrary; men who possessed in a full, or somewhat more than a full measure, the religious, moral, and patriotic feelings of their time and people: the very kind of men who, in all times, our own included, have every chance of passing through life blameless and respected. The high-priest who rent his garments when the words were pronounced which, according to all the ideas of his country, constituted the blackest guilt, was in all probability quite as sincere in his horror and indignation as the generality of respectable and pious men now are in the religious and moral sentiments they profess; and most of those who now shudder at his conduct, if they had lived in his time, and been born Jews, would have acted precisely as he did. Orthodox Christians who are tempted to think that those who stoned to death the first martyrs must have been worse

men than they themselves are, ought to remember that one of those persecutors was Saint Paul.

Let us add one more example, the most striking of all, if the impressiveness of an error is measured by the wisdom and virtue of him who falls into it. If ever anyone possessed of power had grounds for thinking himself the best and most enlightened among his contemporaries, it was the Emperor Marcus Aurelius. Absolute monarch of the whole civilized world, he preserved through life not only the most unblemished justice, but what was less to be expected from his Stoical breeding, the tenderest heart. The few failings which are attributed to him were all on the side of indulgence; while his writings, the highest ethical product of the ancient mind, differ scarcely perceptibly, if they differ at all, from the most characteristic teachings of Christ. This man, a better Christian in all but the dogmatic sense of the word than almost any of the ostensibly Christian sovereigns who have since reigned, persecuted Christianity. Placed at the summit of all the previous attainments of humanity, with an open, unfettered intellect, and a character which led him of himself to embody in his moral writings the Christian ideal, he yet failed to see that Christianity was to be a good and not an evil to the world, with his duties to which he was so deeply penetrated. Existing society he knew to be in a deplorable state. But such as it was, he saw, or thought he saw, that it was held together, and prevented from being worse, by belief and reverence of the received divinities. As a ruler of mankind, he deemed it his duty not to suffer society to fall in pieces; and saw not how, if its existing ties were removed, any others could be formed which could again knit it together. The new religion openly aimed at dissolving these ties: unless, therefore, it was his duty to adopt that religion, it seemed to be his duty to put it down. Inasmuch then as the theology of Christianity did not appear to him true or of divine origin; inasmuch as this strange history of a crucified God was not credible to him, and a system which purported to rest entirely upon a foundation to him so wholly unbelievable, could not be foreseen by him to be that renovating agency which, after all abatements, it has in fact proved to be; the gentlest and most amiable of philosophers and rulers, under a solemn sense of duty, authorized the persecution of Christianity. To my mind this is one of the most tragical facts in all history. It is a bitter thought, how different a thing the Christianity of the world might have been, if the Christian faith had been adopted as the religion of the empire under the auspices of Marcus Aurelius instead of those of Constantine. But it would be equally unjust to him and false to truth to deny that no one plea which can be urged for punishing anti-Christian teaching was wanting to Marcus Aurelius for punishing as he did the propagation of Christianity. No Christian more firmly believes that atheism is false, and tends to the dissolution of society, than Marcus Aurelius believed the same things of Christianity; he who, of all men then living, might have been thought the most capable of appreciating it. Unless anyone who ap-

proves of punishment for the promulgation of opinions, flatters himself that he is a wiser and better man than Marcus Aurelius—more deeply versed in the wisdom of his time, more elevated in his intellect above it—more earnest in his search for truth, or more single-minded in his devotion to it when found; let him abstain from that assumption of the joint infallibility of himself and the multitude, which the great Antoninus made with so unfortunate a result.

Aware of the impossibility of defending the use of punishment for restraining irreligious opinions by any argument which will not justify Marcus Antoninus, the enemies of religious freedom, when hard pressed, occasionally accept this consequence, and say, with Dr. Johnson, that the persecutors of Christianity were in the right; that persecution is an ordeal through which truth ought to pass, and always passes successfully, legal penalties being, in the end, powerless against truth, though sometimes beneficially effective against mischievous errors. This is a form of the argument for religious intolerance sufficiently remarkable not to be passed without notice.

A theory which maintains that truth may justifiably be persecuted because persecution cannot possibly do it any harm, cannot be charged with being intentionally hostile to the reception of new truths; but we cannot commend the generosity of its dealing with the persons to whom mankind are indebted for them. To discover to the world something which deeply concerns it, and of which it was previously ignorant; to prove to it that it had been mistaken on some vital point of temporal or spiritual interest, is as important a service as a human being can render to his fellow-creatures, and in certain cases, as in those of the early Christians and of the Reformers, those who think with Dr. Johnson believe it to have been the most precious gift which could be bestowed on mankind. That the authors of such splendid benefits should be requited by martyrdom, that their reward should be to be dealt with as the vilest of criminals, is not, upon this theory, a deplorable error and misfortune, for which humanity should mourn in sackcloth and ashes, but the normal and justifiable state of things. The propounder of a new truth, according to this doctrine, should stand, as stood, in the legislation of the Locrians, the proposer of a new law, with a halter round his neck to be instantly tightened if the public assembly did not, on hearing his reasons, then and there adopt his proposition. People who defend this mode of treating benefactors cannot be supposed to set much value on the benefit; and I believe this view of the subject is mostly confined to the sort of persons who think that new truths may have been desirable once, but that we have had enough of them now.

But, indeed, the dictum that truth always triumphs over persecution is one of those pleasant falsehoods which men repeat after one another till they pass into commonplaces, but which all experience refutes. History teems with instances of truth put down by persecution. If not suppressed forever, it may be thrown back for centuries. To speak only of religious opinions: the Refor-

mation broke out at least twenty times before Luther, and was put down. Arnold of Brescia was put down. Fra Dolcino was put down. Savonarola was put down. The Albigeois were put down. The Vaudois were put down. The Lollards were put down. The Hussites were put down. Even after the era of Luther, wherever persecution was persisted in, it was successful. In Spain, Italy, Flanders, the Austrian Empire, Protestantism was rooted out; and, most likely, would have been so in England, had Queen Mary lived, or Queen Elizabeth died. Persecution has always succeeded, save where the heretics were too strong a party to be effectually persecuted. No reasonable person can doubt that Christianity might have been extirpated in the Roman Empire. It spread, and became predominant, because the persecutions were only occasional, lasting but a short time, and separated by long intervals of almost undisturbed propagandism. It is a piece of idle sentimentality that truth, merely as truth, has any inherent power denied to error of prevailing against the dungeon and the stake. Men are not more zealous for truth than they often are for error, and a sufficient application of legal or even of social penalties will generally succeed in stopping the propagation of either. The real advantage which truth has, consists in this, that when an opinion is true, it may be extinguished once, twice, or many times, but in the course of ages there will generally be found persons to rediscover it, until some one of its reappearances falls on a time when from favorable circumstances it escapes persecution until it has made such head as to withstand all subsequent attempts to suppress it.

It will be said that we do not now put to death the introducers of new opinions: we are not like our fathers who slew the prophets, we even build sepulchres to them. It is true we no longer put heretics to death; and the amount of penal infliction which modern feeling would probably tolerate, even against the most obnoxious opinions, is not sufficient to extirpate them. . . . But though we do not now inflict so much evil on those who think differently from us as it was formerly our custom to do, it may be that we do ourselves as much evil as ever by our treatment of them. Socrates was put to death, but the Socratic philosophy rose like the sun in heaven, and spread its illumination over the whole intellectual firmament. Christians were cast to the lions, but the Christian church grew up a stately and spreading tree, overtopping the older and less vigorous growths, and stifling them by its shade. Our merely social intolerance kills no one, roots out no opinions, but induces men to disguise them, or to abstain from any active effort for their diffusion. With us, heretical opinions do not perceptibly gain, or even lose, ground in each decade or generation; they never blaze out far and wide, but continue to smolder in the narrow circles of thinking and studious persons among whom they originate, without ever lighting up the general affairs of mankind with either a true or a deceptive light. And thus is kept up a state of things very satisfactory to some minds, because, without the unpleasant process of fining or imprisoning any-body, it maintains all prevailing opinions outwardly undisturbed, while it does not absolutely interdict the exercise of reason by dissentients afflicted with the malady of thought. A convenient plan for having peace in the intellectual world, and keeping all things going on therein very much as they do already! But the price paid for this sort of intellectual pacification is the sacrifice of the entire moral courage of the human mind. A state of things in which a large portion of the most active and inquiring intellects find it advisable to keep the general principles and grounds of their convictions within their own breasts, and attempt, in what they address to the public, to fit as much as they can of their own conclusions to premises which they have internally renounced, cannot send forth the open, fearless characters, and logical, consistent intellects who once adorned the thinking world. The sort of men who can be looked for under it, are either mere conformers to commonplace, or time-servers for truth, whose arguments on all great subjects are meant for their hearers, and are not those which have convinced themselves. Those who avoid this alternative, do so by narrowing their thoughts and interest to things which can be spoken of without venturing within the region of principles—that is, to small practical matters which would come right of themselves if but the minds of mankind were strengthened and enlarged, and which will never be made effectually right until then; while that which would strengthen and enlarge men's minds, free and daring speculation on the highest subjects, is abandoned.

Those in whose eyes this reticence on the part of heretics is no evil should consider, in the first place, that in consequence of it there is never any fair and thorough discussion of heretical opinions; and that such of them as could not stand such a discussion, though they may be prevented from spreading, do not disappear. But it is not the minds of heretics that are deteriorated most by the ban placed on all inquiry which does not end in the orthodox conclusions. The greatest harm done is to those who are not heretics, and whose whole mental development is cramped, and their reason cowed, by the fear of heresy. Who can compute what the world loses in the multitude of promising intellects combined with timid characters, who dare not follow out any bold, vigorous, independent train of thought, lest it should land them in something which would admit of being considered irreligous or immoral? Among them we may occasionally see some man of deep conscientousness, and subtle and refined understanding, who spends a life in sophisticating with an intellect which he cannot silence, and exhausts the resources of ingenuity in attempting to reconcile the promptings of his conscience and reason with orthodoxy, which he does not, perhaps, to the end succeed in doing. No one can be a great thinker who does not recognize that as a thinker it is his first duty to follow his intellect to whatever conclusions it may lead. Truth gains more even by the errors of one who, with due study and preparation, thinks for himself, than by the true opinions of those who only hold them because they do not suffer themselves to think. Not that it is solely, or chiefly, to form great thinkers, that freedom of thinking is required. On the contrary, it is as much and even more indispensable to enable average human beings to attain the mental stature which they are capable of. There have been, and may again be, great individual thinkers in a general atmosphere of mental slavery. But there never has been, nor ever will be, in that atmosphere an intellectually active people. Where any people has made a temporary approach to such a character, it has been because the dread of heterodox speculation was for a time suspended. Where there is a tacit convention that principles are not to be disputed; where the discussion of the greatest questions which can occupy humanity is considered to be closed, we cannot hope to find that generally high scale of mental activity which has made some periods of history so remarkable. Never when controversy avoided the subjects which are large and important enough to kindle enthusiasm, was the mind of a people stirred up from its foundations, and the impulse given which raised even persons of the most ordinary intellect to something of the dignity of thinking beings. Of such we have had an example in the condition of Europe during the times immediately following the Reformation; another, though limited to the Continent and to a more cultivated class, in the speculative movement of the latter half of the eighteenth century; and a third, of still briefer duration, in the intellectual fermentation of Germany during the Goethean and Fichtean period. These periods differed widely in the particular opinions which they developed; but were alike in this, that during all three the yoke of authority was broken. In each, an old mental despotism had been thrown off, and no new one had yet taken its place. The impulse given at these three periods has made Europe what it now is. Every single improvement which has taken place either in the human mind or in institutions, may be traced distinctly to one or other of them. Appearances have for some time indicated that all three impulses are well nigh spent; and we can expect no fresh start until we again assert our mental freedom.

Let us now pass to the second division of the argument, and dismissing the supposition that any of the received opinions may be false, let us assume them to be true, and examine into the worth of the manner in which they are likely to be held, when their truth is not freely and openly canvassed. However unwilling a person who has a strong opinion may admit the possibility that his opinion may be false, he ought to be moved by the consideration that, however true it may be, if it is not fully, frequently, and fearlessly discussed, it will be held as a dead dogma, not a living truth.

There is a class of persons (happily not quite so numerous as formerly) who think it enough if a person assents undoubtingly to what they think true,· though he has no knowledge whatever of the grounds of the opinion, and could not make a tenable defense of it

against the most superficial objections. Such persons, if they can once get their creed taught from authority, naturally think that no good, and some harm, comes of its being allowed to be questioned. Where their influence prevails, they make it nearly impossible for the received opinion to be rejected wisely and considerately, though it may still be rejected rashly and ignorantly; for to shut out discussion entirely is seldom possible, and when it once gets in, beliefs not grounded on conviction are apt to give way before the slightest semblance of an argument. Waiving, however, this possibility—assuming that the true opinion abides in the mind, but abides as a prejudice, a belief independent of, and proof against, argument—this is not the way in which truth ought to be held by a rational being. This is not knowing the truth. Truth, thus held, is but one superstition the more, accidentally clinging to the words which enunciate a truth.

If the intellect and judgment of mankind ought to be cultivated, a thing which Protestants at least do not deny, on what can these faculties be more appropriately exercised by anyone, than on the things which concern him so much that it is considered necessary for him to hold opinions on them? If the cultivation of the understanding consists in one thing more than in another, it is surely in learning the grounds of one's own opinions. Whatever people believe, on subjects on which it is of the first importance to believe rightly, they ought to be able to defend against at least the common objections. But, some one may say, "Let them be *taught* the grounds of their opinions. It does not follow that opinions must be merely parroted because they are never heard controverted. Persons who learn geometry do not simply commit the theorems to memory, but understand and learn likewise the demonstrations; and it would be absurd to say that they remain ignorant of the grounds of geometrical truths, because they never hear any one deny, and attempt to disprove them." Undoubtedly: and such teaching suffices on a subject like mathematics, where there is nothing at all to be said on the wrong side of the question. The peculiarity of the evidence of mathematical truths is that all the argument is on one side. There are no objections, and no answers to objections. But on every subject on which difference of opinion is possible, the truth depends on a balance to be struck between two sets of conflicting reasons. Even in natural philosophy, there is always some other explanation possible of the same facts—some geocentric theory instead of heliocentric, some phlogiston instead of oxygen—and it has to be shown why that other theory cannot be the true one; and until this is shown, and until we know how it is shown, we do not understand the grounds of our opinion. But when we turn to subjects infinitely more complicated, to morals, religion, politics, social relations, and the business of life, three-fourths of the arguments for every disputed opinion consist in dispelling the appearances which favor some opinion different from it. The greatest orator, save one, of antiquity, has left it on record that he always studied his adversary's case with as great, if not still greater, in-

tensity than even his own. What Cicero practiced as the means of forensic success requires to be imitated by all who study any subject in order to arrive at the truth. He who knows only his own side of the case, knows little of that. His reasons may be good, and no one may have been able to refute them. But if he is equally unable to refute the reasons on the opposite side; if he does not so much as know what they are, he has no ground for preferring either opinion. The rational position for him would be suspension of judgment, and unless he contents himself with that, he is either led by authority, or adopts, like the generality of the world, the side to which he feels most inclination. Nor is it enough that he should hear the arguments of adversaries from his own teachers, presented as they state them, and accompanied by what they offer as refutations. That is not the way to do justice to the arguments, or bring them into real contact with his own mind. He must be able to hear them from persons who actually believe them; who defend them in earnest, and do their very utmost for them. He must know them in their most plausible and persuasive form; he must feel the whole force of the difficulty which the true view of the subject has to encounter and dispose of; else he will never really possess himself of the portion of truth which meets and removes that difficulty. Ninety-nine in a hundred of what are called educated men are in this condition; even of those who can argue fluently for their opinions. Their conclusion may be true, but it might be false for anything they know: they have never thrown themselves into the mental position of those who think differently from them, and considered what such persons may have to say; and consequently they do not, in any proper sense of the word, know the doctrine which they themselves profess. They do not know those parts of it which explain and justify the remainder; the considerations which show that a fact which seemingly conflicts with another is reconcilable with it, or that, of two apparently strong reasons, one and not the other ought to be preferred. All that part of the truth which turns the scale, and decides the judgment of a completely informed mind, they are strangers to; nor is it ever really known but to those who have attended equally and impartially to both sides, and endeavored to see the reasons of both in the strongest light. So essential is this discipline to a real understanding of moral and human subjects, that if opponents of all important truths do not exist, it is indispensable to imagine them, and supply them with the strongest arguments which the most skilful devil's advocate can conjure up. . . .

If, however, the mischievous operation of the absence of free discussion, when the received opinions are true, were confined to leaving men ignorant of the grounds of those opinions, it might be thought that this, if an intellectual, is no moral evil, and does not affect the worth of the opinions, regarded in their influence on the character. The fact, however, is that not only the grounds of the opinion are forgotten in the absence of discussion, but too often the meaning of the opinion itself. The words which convey it

cease to suggest ideas, or suggest only a small portion of those they were originally employed to communicate. Instead of a vivid conception and a living belief, there remain only a few phrases retained by rote; or, if any part, the shell and husk only of the meaning is retained, the finer essence being lost. The great chapter in human history which this fact occupies and fills, cannot be too earnestly studied and meditated on.

It is illustrated in the experience of almost all ethical doctrines and religious creeds. They are full of meaning and vitality to those who originate them, and to the direct disciples of the originators. Their meaning continues to be felt in undiminished strength, and is perhaps brought out into even fuller consciousness, so long as the struggle lasts to give the doctrine or creed an ascendancy over other creeds. At last it either prevails, and becomes the general opinion, or its progress stops; it keeps possession of the ground it has gained, but ceases to spread further. When either of these results has become apparent, controversy on the subject flags, and gradually dies away. The doctrine has taken its place, if not as a received opinion, as one of the admitted sects or divisions of opinion: those who hold it have generally inherited, not adopted it; and conversion from one of these doctrines to another, being now an exceptional fact, occupies little place in the thoughts of their professors. Instead of being, as at first, constantly on the alert either to defend themselves against the world, or to bring the world over to them, they have subsided into acquiescence, and neither listen, when they can help it, to arguments against their creed, nor trouble dissentients (if there be such) with arguments in its favor. From this time may usually be dated the decline in the living power of the doctrine. We often hear the teachers of all creeds lamenting the difficulty of keeping up in the minds of believers a lively apprehension of the truth which they nominally recognize, so that it may penetrate the feelings, and acquire a real mastery over the conduct. No such difficulty is complained of while the creed is still fighting for its existence: even the weaker combatants then know and feel what they are fighting for, and the difference between it and other doctrines; and in that period of every creed's existence, not a few persons may be found, who have realized its fundamental principles in all the forms of thought, have weighed and considered them in all their important bearings, and have experienced the full effect on the character which belief in that creed ought to produce in a mind thoroughly imbued with it. But when it has come to be an hereditary creed, and to be received passively, not actively; when the mind is no longer compelled, in the same degree as at first, to exercise its vital powers on the questions which its belief presents to it: there is a progressive tendency to forget all of the belief except the formularies, or to give it a dull and torpid assent, as if accepting it on trust dispensed with the necessity of realizing it in consciousness, or testing it by personal experience, until it almost ceases to connect itself at all with the inner life of the human being. Then are seen

the cases, so frequent in this age of the world as almost to form the majority, in which the creed remains as it were outside the mind, incrusting and petrifying it against all other influences addressed to the higher parts of our nature; manifesting its power by not suffering any fresh and living conviction to get in, but itself doing nothing for the mind or heart, except standing sentinel over them to keep them vacant.

To what an extent doctrines intrinsically fitted to make the deepest impression upon the mind may remain in it as dead beliefs, without being ever realized in the imagination, the feelings, or the understanding, is exemplified by the manner in which the majority of believers hold the doctrines of Christianity. By Christianity I here mean what is accounted such by all churches and sects—the maxims and precepts contained in the New Testament. These are considered sacred, and accepted as laws, by all professing Christians. Yet it is scarcely too much to say that not one Christian in a thousand guides or tests his individual conduct by reference to those laws. The standard to which he does refer it, is the custom of his nation, his class, or his religious profession. He has thus, on the one hand, a collection of ethical maxims, which he believes to have been vouchsafed to him by infallible wisdom as rules for his government; and on the other a set of every-day judgments and practices, which go a certain length with some of those maxims, not so great a length with others, stand in direct opposition to some, and are, on the whole, a compromise between the Christian creed and the interests and suggestions of worldly life. To the first of these standards he gives his homage; to the other his real allegiance. . . .

The same thing holds true, generally speaking, of all traditional doctrines—those of prudence and knowledge of life, as well as of morals or religion. All languages and literatures are full of general observations on life, both as to what it is, and how to conduct oneself in it; observations which everybody knows, which everybody repeats, or hears with acquiescence, which are received as truisms, yet of which most people first truly learn the meaning when experience, generally of a painful kind, has made it a reality to them. How often, when smarting under some unforeseen misfortune or disappointment, does a person call to mind some proverb or common saying, familiar to him all his life, the meaning of which, if he had ever before felt it as he does now, would have saved him from the calamity. There are indeed reasons for this, other than the absence of discussion; there are many truths of which the full meaning *cannot* be realized until personal experience has brought it home. But much more of the meaning even of these would have been understood, and what was understood would have been far more deeply impressed on the mind, if the man had been accustomed to hear it argued *pro* and *con* by people who did understand it. The fatal tendency of mankind to leave off thinking about a thing when it is no longer doubtful, is the cause of half their errors. A contemporary author has well spoken of "the deep slumber of a decided opinion."

But what! (it may be asked) Is the absence of unanimity an indispensable condition of true knowledge? Is it necessary that some part of mankind should persist in error to enable any to realize the truth? Does a belief cease to be real and vital as soon as it is generally received; and is a proposition never thoroughly understood and felt unless some doubt of it remains? As soon as mankind have unanimously accepted a truth, does the truth perish within them? The highest aim and best result of improved intelligence, it has hitherto been thought, is to unite mankind more and more in the acknowledgment of all important truths; and does the intelligence only last as long as it has not achieved its object? Do the fruits of conquest perish by the very completeness of the victory?

I affirm no such thing. As mankind improve, the number of doctrines which are no longer disputed or doubted will be constantly on the increase: and the well-being of mankind may almost be measured by the number and gravity of the truths which have reached the point of being uncontested. The cessation, on one question after another, of serious controversy, is one of the necessary incidents of the consolidation of opinion; a consolidation as salutary in the case of true opinions, as it is dangerous and noxious when the opinions are erroneous. But though this gradual narrowing of the bounds of diversity of opinion is necessary in both senses of the term, being at once inevitable and indispensable, we are not therefore obliged to conclude that all its consequences must be beneficial. The loss of so important an aid to the intelligent and living apprehension of a truth, as is afforded by the necessity of explaining it to, or defending it against, opponents, though not sufficient to outweigh, is no trifling drawback from, the benefit of its universal recognition. Where this advantage can no longer be had, I confess I should like to see the teachers of mankind endeavoring to provide a substitute for it; some contrivance for making the difficulties of the question as present to the learner's consciousness, as if they were pressed upon him by a dissentient champion, eager for his conversion. . . .

It is the fashion of the present time to disparage negative logic—that which points out weaknesses in theory or errors in practice, without establishing positive truths. Such negative criticism would indeed be poor enough as an ultimate result; but as a means to attaining any positive knowledge or conviction worthy the name, it cannot be valued too highly; and until people are again systematically trained to it, there will be few great thinkers, and a low general average of intellect, in any but the mathematical and physical departments of speculation. On any other subject no one's opinions deserve the name of knowledge, except so far as he has either had forced upon him by others, or gone through of himself, the same mental process which would have been required of him in carrying on an active controversy with opponents. That, therefore, which when absent, it is so indispensable, but so difficult, to create, how worse than absurd it is to forego, when spontaneously offering itself! If there are any persons who contest a received opinion, or who will do so if law or opinion will let them, let us

thank them for it, open our minds to listen to them, and rejoice that there is some one to do for us what we otherwise ought, if we have any regard for either the certainty or the vitality of our convictions, to do with much greater labor for ourselves.

It still remains to speak of one of the principal causes which make diversity of opinion advantageous, and will continue to do so until mankind shall have entered a stage of intellectual advancement which at present seems at an incalculable distance. We have hitherto considered only two possibilities: that the received opinion may be false, and some other opinion consequently true; or that, the received opinion being true, a conflict with the opposite error is essential to a clear apprehension and deep feeling of its truth. But there is a commoner case than either of these: when the conflicting doctrines, instead of being one true and the other false, share the truth between them; and the nonconforming opinion is needed to supply the remainder of the truth, of which the received doctrine embodies only a part. Popular opinions, on subjects not palpable to sense, are often true, but seldom or never the whole truth. They are a part of the truth; sometimes a greater, sometimes a smaller part, but exaggerated, distorted, and disjointed from the truths by which they ought to be accompanied and limited. Heretical opinions, on the other hand, are generally some of these suppressed and neglected truths, bursting the bonds which kept them down, and neither seeking reconciliation with the truth contained in the common opinion, or fronting it as enemies, and setting themselves up, with similar exclusiveness, as the whole truth. The latter case is hitherto the most frequent, as, in the human mind, one-sidedness has always been the rule, and many-sidedness the exception. Hence, even in revolutions of opinion, one part of the truth usually sets while another rises. Even progress, which ought to superadd, for the most part only substitutes, one partial and incomplete truth for another; improvement consisting chiefly in this, that the new fragment of truth is more wanted, more adapted to the needs of the time, than that which it displaces. Such being the partial character of prevailing opinions, even when resting on a true foundation, every opinion which embodies somewhat of the portion of truth which the common opinion omits, ought to be considered precious, with whatever amount of error and confusion that truth may be blended. No sober judge of human affairs will feel bound to be indignant because those who force on our notice truths which we should otherwise have overlooked, overlook some of those which we see. Rather, he will think that so long as popular truth is one-sided, it is more desirable than otherwise that unpopular truth should have one-sided assertors too; such being usually the most energetic, and the most likely to compel reluctant attention to the fragment of wisdom which they proclaim as if it were the whole.

Thus, in the eighteenth century, when nearly all the instructed, and all those of the uninstructed who were led by them, were lost in admiration of what is called civilization, and of the marvels of modern science, literature, and philosophy, and while greatly overrating the amount of unlikeness between the men of modern and those of ancient times, indulged the belief that the whole of the difference was in their own favor; with what a salutary shock did the paradoxes of Rousseau explode like bombshells in the midst, dislocating the compact mass of one-sided opinion, and forcing its elements to recombine in a better form and with additional ingredients. Not that the current opinions were on the whole farther from the truth than Rousseau's were: on the contrary, they were nearer to it: they contained more of positive truth, and very much less of error. Nevertheless there lay in Rousseau's doctrine, and has floated down the stream of opinion along with it, a considerable amount of exactly those truths which the popular opinion wanted; and these are the deposit which was left behind when the flood subsided. The superior worth of simplicity of life, the enervating and demoralizing effect of the trammels and hypocrisies of artificial society, are ideas which have never been entirely absent from cultivated minds since Rousseau wrote; and they will in time produce their due effect, though at present needing to be asserted as much as ever, and to be asserted by deeds, for words, on this subject, have nearly exhausted their power.

In politics, again, it is almost a commonplace, that a party of order or stability, and a party of progress or reform, are both necessary elements of a healthy state of political life; until the one or the other shall have so enlarged its mental grasp as to be a party equally of order and of progress, knowing and distinguishing what is fit to be preserved from what ought to be swept away. Each of these modes of thinking derives its utility from the deficiencies of the other; but it is in a great measure the opposition of the other that keeps each within the limits of reason and sanity. Unless opinions favorable to democracy and to aristocracy, to property and to equality, to coöperation and to competition, to luxury and to abstinence, to sociality and individuality, to liberty and discipline, and all the other standing antagonisms of practical life, are expressed with equal freedom, and enforced and defended with equal talent and energy, there is no chance of both elements obtaining their due: one scale is sure to go up, and the other down. Truth, in the great practical concerns of life, is so much a question of the reconciling and combining of opposites, that very few have minds sufficiently capacious and impartial to make the adjustment with an approach to correctness, and it has to be made by the rough process of a struggle between combatants fighting under hostile banners. On any of the great open questions just enumerated, if either of the two opinions has a better claim than the other, not merely to be tolerated, but to be encouraged and countenanced, it is the one which happens at the particular time and place to be in a minority. That is the opinion which, for the time being, represents the neglected interests, the side of human well-being which is in danger of obtaining less than its share. I am aware that there is not, in this country, any intolerance of differences of opinion on most of these topics. They are adduced to show, by admitted and multiplied examples, the universality of the fact that only through diversity of opinion is there, in the existing state of human intellect, a chance of fair play to all sides of the truth. When there are persons to be found who form an exception to the apparent unanimity of the world on any subject, even if the world is in the right, it is always probable that dissentients have something worth hearing to say for themselves, and that truth would lose something by their silence. . . .

We have now recognized the necessity to the mental well-being of mankind (on which all their other well-being depends) of freedom of opinion, and freedom of the expression of opinion, on four distinct grounds; which we will now briefly recapitulate.

First, if any opinion is compelled to silence, that opinion may, for aught we can certainly know, be true. To deny this is to assume our own infallibility.

Secondly, though the silenced opinion be an error, it may, and very commonly does, contain a portion of truth; and since the general or prevailing opinion on any subject is rarely or never the whole truth, it is only by the collision of adverse opinions that the remainder of the truth has any chance of being supplied.

Thirdly, even if the received opinion be not only true, but the whole truth; unless it is suffered to be, and actually is, vigorously and earnestly contested, it will, by most of those who receive it, be held in the manner of a prejudice, with little comprehension or feeling of its rational grounds. And not only this, but, fourthly, the meaning of the doctrine itself will be in danger of being lost, or enfeebled, and deprived of its vital effect on the character and conduct: the dogma becoming a mere formal procession, inefficacious for good, but cumbering the ground, and preventing the growth of any real and heartfelt conviction, from reason or personal experience. . . .

Chapter III

Of Individuality, As One of the Elements of Well-being

Such being the reasons which make it imperative that human beings should be free to form opinions, and to express their opinions without reserve; and such the baneful consequences to the intellectual, and through that to the moral nature of man, unless this liberty is either conceded, or asserted in spite of prohibition; let us next examine whether the same reasons do not require that men should be free to act upon their opinions—to carry these out in their lives, without hindrance, either physical or moral, from their fellow-men, so long as it is at their own risk and peril. This last proviso is of course indispensable. No one pretends that actions should be as free as opinions. On the contrary, even opinions lose their immunity when the circumstances in which they are expressed are such as to constitute their expression a positive instigation to some mischievous act. An opinion that corn-dealers are starvers of the poor, or that private property is robbery, ought to be unmolested when simply circulated

through the press, but may justly incur punishment when delivered orally to an excited mob assembled before the house of a corn-dealer, or when handed about among the same mob in the form of a placard. Acts, of whatever kind, which without justifiable cause do harm to others, may be, and in the more important cases absolutely require to be, controlled by the unfavorable sentiments, and, when needful, by the active interference of mankind. The liberty of the individual must be thus far limited; he must not make himself a nuisance to other people. But if he refrains from molesting others in what concerns them, and merely acts according to his own inclination and judgment in things which concern himself, the same reasons which show that opinion should be free, prove also that he should be allowed, without molestation, to carry his opinions into practice at his own cost. That mankind are not infallible; that their truths, for the most part, are only half-truths; that unity of opinion, unless resulting from the fullest and freest comparison of opposite opinions, is not desirable, and diversity not an evil, but a good, until mankind are much more capable than at present of recognizing all sides of the truth, are principles applicable to men's modes of action, not less than to their opinions. As it is useful that while mankind are imperfect there should be different opinions, so it is that there should be different experiments of living; that free scope should be given to varieties of character, short of injury to others; and that the worth of different modes of life should be proved practically, when any one thinks fit to try them. It is desirable, in short, that in things which do not primarily concern others, individuality should assert itself. Where not the person's own character, but the traditions or customs of other people are the rule of conduct, there is wanting one of the principal ingredients of human happiness, and quite the chief ingredient of individual and social progress.

In maintaining this principle, the greatest difficulty to be encountered does not lie in the appreciation of means toward an acknowledged end, but in the indifference of persons in general to the end in itself. If it were felt that the free development of individuality is one of the leading essentials of well-being; that it is not only a coördinate element with all that is designated by the terms civilization, instruction, education, culture, but is itself a necessary part and condition of all those things; there would be no danger that liberty should be undervalued, and the adjustment of the boundaries between it and social control would present no extraordinary difficulty. But the evil is, that individual spontaneity is hardly recognized by the common modes of thinking as having any intrinsic worth, or deserving any regard on its own account. The majority, being satisfied with the ways of mankind as they now are (for it is they who make them what they are), cannot comprehend why those ways should not be good enough for everybody; and what is more, spontaneity forms no part of the ideal of the majority of moral and social reformers, but is rather looked on with jealousy, as a troublesome and perhaps rebellious obstruction to the general acceptance of what these reformers, in their own judgment, think

would be best for mankind. Few persons, out of Germany, even comprehend the meaning of the doctrine which Wilhelm von Humboldt, so eminent both as a *savant* and as a politician, made the text of a treatise—that "the end of man, or that which is prescribed by the eternal or immutable dictates of reason, and not suggested by vague and transient desires, is the highest and most harmonious development of his powers to a complete and consistent whole"; that, therefore, the object "towards which every human being must ceaselessly direct his efforts, and on which especially those who design to influence their fellow-men must ever keep their eyes, is the individuality of power and development"; that for this there are two requisites, "freedom, and variety of situations"; and that from the union of these arise "individual vigor and manifold diversity," which combine themselves in "originality."[1]

Little, however, as people are accustomed to a doctrine like that of Von Humboldt, and surprising as it may be to them to find so high a value attached to individuality, the question, one must nevertheless think, can only be one of degree. No one's idea of excellence in conduct is that people should do absolutely nothing but copy one another. No one would assert that people ought not to put into their mode of life, and into the conduct of their concerns, any impress whatever of their own judgment, or of their own individual character. On the other hand, it would be absurd to pretend that people ought to

[1] *The Sphere and Duties of Government,* from the German of Baron Wilhelm von Humboldt, pp. 11–13.

live as if nothing whatever had been known in the world before they came into it; as if experience had as yet done nothing toward showing that one mode of existence, or of conduct, is preferable to another. Nobody denies that people should be so taught and trained in youth as to know and benefit by the ascertained results of human experience. But it is the privilege and proper condition of a human being, arrived at the maturity of his faculties, to use and interpret experience in his own way. It is for him to find out what part of recorded experience is properly applicable to his own circumstances and character. The traditions and customs of other people are to a certain extent, evidence of what their experience has taught *them*: presumptive evidence, and as such, have a claim to his deference. But in the first place, their experience may be too narrow, or they may not have interpreted it rightly. Secondly, their interpretation of experience may be correct, but unsuitable to him. Customs are made for customary circumstances and customary characters, and his circumstances or his character may be uncustomary. Thirdly, though the customs be both good as customs, and suitable to him, yet to conform to custom, merely *as* custom, does not educate or develop in him any of the qualities which are the distinctive endowment of a human being. The human faculties of perception, judgment, discriminative feeling, mental activity, and even moral preference, are exercised only in making a choice. He who does anything because it is the custom makes no choice. He gains no practice either in discerning or in desiring what is best. The

mental and moral, like the muscular powers, are improved only by being used. The faculties are called into no exercise by doing a thing merely because others do it, no more than by believing a thing only because others believe it. If the grounds of an opinion are not conclusive to the person's own reason, his reason cannot be strengthened, but is likely to be weakened, by his adopting it; and if the inducements to an act are not such as are consentaneous to his own feelings and character (where affection, or the rights of others, are not concerned) it is so much done toward rendering his feelings and character inert and torpid, instead of active and energetic.

He who lets the world, or his own portion of it, choose his plan of life for him, has no need of any other faculty than the ape-like one of imitation. He who chooses his plan for himself, employs all his faculties. He must use observation to see, reasoning and judgment to foresee, activity to gather materials for decision, discrimination to decide, and when he has decided, firmness and self-control to hold to his deliberate decision. And these qualities he requires and exercises exactly in proportion as the part of his conduct which he determines according to his own judgment and feelings is a large one. It is possible that he might be guided in some good path, and kept out of harm's way, without any of these things. But what will be his comparative worth as a human being? It really is of importance, not only what men do, but also what manner of men they are that do it. Among the works of man which human life is rightly employed in perfecting and beautifying, the first in importance surely is man himself. Supposing it were possible to get houses built, corn grown, battles fought, causes tried, and even churches erected and prayers said, by machinery—by automatons in human form—it would be a considerable loss to exchange for these automatons even the men and women who at present inhabit the more civilized parts of the world, and who assuredly are but starved specimens of what nature can and will produce. Human nature is not a machine to be built after a model, and set to do exactly the work prescribed for it, but a tree, which requires to grow and develop itself on all sides, according to the tendency of the inward forces which make it a living thing.

It will probably be conceded that it is desirable people shall exercise their understandings, and that an intelligent following of custom, or even occasionally an intelligent deviation from custom, is better than a blind and simply mechanical adhesion to it. To a certain extent it is admitted that our understanding should be our own: but there is not the same willingness to admit that our desires and impulses should be our own likewise; or that to possess impulses of our own, and of any strength, is anything but a peril and a snare. Yet desires and impulses are as much a part of a perfect human being as beliefs and restraints; and strong impulses are only perilous when not properly balanced—when one set of aims and inclinations is developed into strength, while others, which ought to coexist with them, remain weak and inactive. It is not because men's desires are strong that they act ill; it is because their consciences are weak. There is no natural connection between strong impulses and a weak conscience. The natural connection is the other way. To say that one person's desires and feelings are stronger and more various than those of another, is merely to say that he has more of the raw material of human nature, and is therefore capable, perhaps of more evil, but certainly of more good. Strong impulses are but another name for energy. Energy may be turned to bad uses; but more good may always be made of an energetic nature than of an indolent and impassive one. Those who have most natural feeling are always those whose cultivated feelings may be made the strongest. The same strong susceptibilities which make the personal impulses vivid and powerful, are also the source from whence are generated the most passionate love of virtue, and the sternest self-control. It is through the cultivation of these that society both does its duty and protects its interests; not by rejecting the stuff of which heroes are made because it knows not how to make them. A person whose desires and impulses are his own—are the expression of his own nature, as it has been developed and modified by his own culture—is said to have a character. One whose desires and impulses are not his own, has no character, no more than a steam-engine has a character. If, in addition to being his own, his impulses are strong, and are under the government of a strong will, he has an energetic character. Whoever thinks that individuality of desires and impulses should not be encouraged to unfold itself, must maintain that society has no need of strong natures—is not the better for containing many persons who have much character—and that a high general average of energy is not desirable. . . .

It is not by wearing down into uniformity all that is individual in themselves, but by cultivating it, and calling it forth, within the limits imposed by the rights and interests of others, that human beings become a noble and beautiful object of contemplation; and as the works partake the character of those who do them, by the same process human life also becomes rich, diversified, and animating, furnishing more abundant aliment to high thoughts and elevating feelings, and strengthening the tie which binds every individual to the race, by making the race infinitely better worth belonging to. In proportion to the development of his individuality, each person becomes more valuable to himself, and is therefore capable of being more valuable to others. There is a greater fullness of life about his own existence, and when there is more life in the units there is more in the mass which is composed of them. As much compression as is necessary to prevent the stronger specimens of human nature from encroaching on the rights of others cannot be dispensed with; but for this there is ample compensation even in the point of view of human development. The means of development which the individual loses by being prevented from gratifying his inclinations to the injury of others, are chiefly obtained at the expense of the development of other people. And even to himself there is a full equivalent in the better development of the social part of his nature, rendered possible by the restraint put upon the selfish part. To be held to rigid rules of justice for the sake of others, develops the feelings and capacities which have the good of others for their object. But to be restrained in things not affecting their good, by their mere displeasure, develops nothing valuable, except such force of character as may unfold itself in resisting the restraint. If acquiesced in, it dulls and blunts the whole nature. To give any fair play to the nature of each, it is essential that different persons should be allowed to lead different lives. In proportion as this latitude has been exercised in any age, has that age been noteworthy to posterity. Even despotism does not produce its worst effects, so long as individuality exists under it; and whatever crushes individuality is despotism, by whatever name it may be called, and whether it professes to be enforcing the will of God or the injunctions of men.

Having said that the individuality is the same thing with development, and that it is only the cultivation of individuality which produces, or can produce, well-developed human beings, I might here close the argument: for what more or better can be said of any condition of human affairs than that it brings human beings themselves nearer to the best thing they can be? or what worse can be said of any obstruction to good than that it prevents this? Doubtless, however, these considerations will not suffice to convince those who most need convincing; and it is necessary further to show that these developed human beings are of some use to the undeveloped—to point out to those who do not desire liberty, and would not avail themselves of it, that they may be in some intelligible manner rewarded for allowing other people to make use of it without hindrance.

In the first place, then, I would suggest that they might possibly learn something from them. It will not be denied by anybody that originality is a valuable element in human affairs. There is always need of persons not only to discover new truths, and point out when what were once truths are true no longer, but also to commence new practices, and set the example of more enlightened conduct, and better taste and sense in human life. This cannot well be gainsaid by anybody who does not believe that the world has already attained perfection in all its ways and practices. It is true that this benefit is not capable of being rendered by everybody alike: there are but few persons, in comparison with the whole of mankind, whose experiments, if adopted by others, would be likely to be any improvement on established practice. But these few are the salt of the earth; without them, human life would become a stagnant pool. Not only is it they who introduce good things which did not before exist; it is they who keep the life in those which already exist. If there were nothing new to be done, would human intellect cease to be necessary? Would it be a reason why those who do the old things should forget why they are done, and do them like cattle, not like human beings? There is only too great a tendency in the best beliefs and practices to degenerate into the mechanical; and unless there were a succession of persons whose over-recurring originality prevents the grounds of those beliefs and practices from becoming merely traditional, such dead matter would not resist the smallest shock from anything really alive, and there would be no reason why civilization should not die out, as in the Byzantine Empire. Persons of genius, it is true, are, and are always likely to be, a small minority; but in order to have them, it is necessary to preserve the soil in which they grow. Genius can only breathe freely in an *atmosphere* of freedom. Persons of genius are, *ex vi termini* [by the force of the phraseology], more individual than any other people—less capable, consequently, of fitting themselves, without hurtful compression, into any of the small number of molds which society provides in order to save its members the trouble of forming their own character. If from timidity they consent to be forced into one of these molds, and to let all that part of themselves which cannot expand under the pressure remain unexpanded, society will be little the better for their genius. If they are of a strong character, and break their fetters, they become a mark for the society which has not succeeded in reducing them to commonplace, to point out with solemn warning as "wild," "erratic," and the like; much as if one should complain of the Niagara river for not flowing smoothly between its banks like a Dutch canal.

I insist thus emphatically on the importance of genius, and the necessity of allowing it to unfold itself freely both in thought and in practice, being well aware that no one will deny the position in theory, but knowing also that almost everyone, in reality, is totally indifferent to it. People think genius a fine thing if it enables a man to write an exciting poem, or paint a picture. But in its true sense, that of originality in thought and action, though no one says that it is not a thing to be admired, nearly all, at heart, think that they can do very well without it. Unhappily this is too natural to be wondered at. Originality is the one thing which unoriginal minds cannot feel the use of. They cannot see what it is to do for them: how should they? If they could see what it would do for them, it would not be originality. The first service which originality has to render them, is that of opening their eyes: which being once fully done, they would have a chance of being themselves original. Meanwhile, recollecting that nothing was ever yet done which someone was not the first to do, and that all good things which exist are the fruits of originality, let them be modest enough to believe that there is something still left for it to accomplish, and assure themselves that they are more in need of originality, the less they are conscious of the want.

In sober truth, whatever homage may be professed, or even paid, to real or supposed mental superiority, the general tendency of things throughout the world is to render mediocrity the ascendant power among mankind. In ancient history, in the Middle Ages, and in a diminishing degree through the long transition from feudality to the present time, the individual was a power in himself; and if he had either great talents or a high social position, he was a considerable power. At present individuals are lost in the crowd. In politics it is almost a triviality to say that public

opinion now rules the world. The only power deserving the name is that of masses, and of governments while they make themselves the organ of the tendencies and instincts of masses. This is as true in the moral and social relations of private life as in public transactions. Those whose opinions go by the name of public opinion are not always the same sort of public: in America they are the whole white population; in England, chiefly the middle class. But they are always a mass, that is to say, collective mediocrity. And what is a still greater novelty, the mass do not now take their opinions from dignitaries in Church or State, from ostensible leaders, or from books. Their thinking is done for them by men much like themselves, addressing them or speaking in their name, on the spur of the moment, through the newspapers. I am not complaining of all this. I do not assert that anything better is compatible, as a general rule, with the present low state of the human mind. But that does not hinder the government of mediocrity from being mediocre government. No government by a democracy or a numerous aristocracy, either in its political acts or in the opinions, qualities, and tone of mind which it fosters, ever did or could rise above mediocrity, except in so far as the sovereign Many have let themselves be guided (which in their best times they always have done) by the counsels and influence of a more highly gifted and instructed One or Few. The initiation of all wise or noble things comes and must come from individuals; generally at first from some one individual. The honor and glory of the average man is that he is capable of following that initiative; that he can respond internally to wise and noble things, and be led to them with his eyes open. I am not countenancing the sort of "hero-worship" which applauds the strong man of genius for forcibly seizing on the government of the world and making it do his bidding in spite of itself. All he can claim is, freedom to point out the way. The power of compelling others into it is not only inconsistent with the freedom and development of all the rest, but corrupting to the strong man himself. It does seem, however, that when the opinions of masses of merely average men are everywhere become or becoming the dominant power, the counterpoise and corrective to that tendency would be the more and more pronounced individuality of those who stand on the higher eminences of thought. It is in these circumstances most especially, that exceptional individuals, instead of being deterred, should be encouraged in acting differently from the mass. In other times there was no advantage in their doing so, unless they acted not only differently but better. In this age, the mere example of nonconformity, the mere refusal to bend the knee to custom, is itself a service. Precisely because the tyranny of opinion is such as to make eccentricity a reproach, it is desirable, in order to break through that tyranny, that people should be eccentric. Eccentricity has always abounded when and where strength of character has abounded; and the amount of eccentricity in a society has generally been proportional to the amount of genius, mental vigor, and moral courage it contained. That so few now dare to be eccentric marks the chief danger of the time.

I have said that it is important to give the freest scope possible to uncustomary things, in order that it may in time appear which of these are fit to be converted into customs. But independence of action, and disregard of custom, are not solely deserving of encouragement for the chance they afford that better modes of action, and customs more worthy of general adoption, may be struck out; nor is it only persons of decided mental superiority who have a just claim to carry on their lives in their own way. There is no reason that all human existence should be constructed on some one or some small number of patterns. If a person possesses any tolerable amount of common sense and experience, his own mode of laying out his existence is the best, not because it is the best in itself, but because it is his own mode. Human beings are not like sheep; and even sheep are not undistinguishably alike. A man cannot get a coat or a pair of boots to fit him unless they are either made to his measure, or he has a whole warehouseful to choose from: and is it easier to fit him with a life than with a coat, or are human beings more like one another in their whole physical and spiritual conformation than in the shape of their feet? If it were only that people have diversities of taste, that is reason enough for not attempting to shape them all after one model. But different persons also require different conditions for their spiritual development; and can no more exist healthily in the same moral, than all the variety of plants can in the same physical, atmosphere and climate. The same things which are helps to one person towards the cultivation of his higher nature are hindrances to another. The same mode of life is a healthy excitement to one, keeping all his faculties of action and enjoyment in their best order, while to another it is a distracting burthen, which suspends or crushes all internal life. Such are the differences among human beings in their sources of pleasure, their susceptibilities of pain, and the operation on them of different physical and moral agencies, that unless there is a corresponding diversity in their modes of life, they neither obtain their fair share of happiness, nor grow up to the mental, moral, and æsthetic stature of which their nature is capable. . . .

There is one characteristic of the present direction of public opinion peculiarly calculated to make it intolerant of any marked demonstration of individuality. The general average of mankind are not only moderate in intellect, but also moderate in inclinations: they have no tastes or wishes strong enough to incline them to do anything unusual, and they consequently do not understand those who have, and class all such with the wild and intemperate whom they are accustomed to look down upon. Now, in addition to this fact which is general, we have only to suppose that a strong movement has set in towards the improvement of morals, and it is evident what we have to expect. In these days such a movement has set in; much has actually been effected in the way of increased regularity of conduct and discouragement of excesses; and there is a philanthropic spirit abroad, for the exercise of which there is no

more inviting field than the moral and prudential improvement of our fellow-creatures. These tendencies of the times cause the public to be more disposed than at most former periods to prescribe general rules of conduct, and endeavor to make every one conform to the approved standard. And that standard, express or tacit, is to desire nothing strongly. Its ideal of character is to be without any marked character; to maim by compression, like a Chinese lady's foot, every part of human nature which stands out prominently, and tends to make the person markedly dissimilar in outline to commonplace humanity.

As is usually the case with ideals which exclude one-half of what is desirable, the present standard of approbation produces only an inferior imitation of the other half. Instead of great energies guided by vigorous reason, and strong feelings strongly controlled by a conscientious will, its result is weak feelings, and weak energies, which therefore can be kept in outward conformity to rule without any strength either of will or of reason. Already energetic characters on any large scale are becoming merely traditional. There is now scarcely any outlet for energy in this country except business. The energy expended in this may still be regarded as considerable. What little is left from that employment is expended on some hobby; which may be a useful, even a philanthropic hobby, but is always some one thing, and generally a thing of small dimensions. The greatness of England is now all collective; individually small, we only appear capable of anything great by our habit of combining; and with this our moral and religious philanthropists are perfectly contented. But it was men of another stamp than this that made England what it has been; and men of another stamp will be needed to prevent its decline.

The despotism of custom is everywhere the standing hindrance to human advancement, being in unceasing antagonism to that disposition to aim at something better than customary, which is called, according to circumstances, the spirit of liberty, or that of progress or improvement. The spirit of improvement is not always a spirit of liberty, for it may aim at forcing improvements on an unwilling people; and the spirit of liberty, in so far as it resists such attempts, may ally itself locally and temporarily with the opponents of improvement; but the only unfailing and permanent source of improvement is liberty, since by it there are as many possible independent centers of improvement as there are individuals. The progressive principle, however, in either shape, whether as the love of liberty or of improvement, is antagonistic to the sway of custom, involving at least emancipation from that yoke; and the contest between the two constitutes the chief interest of the history of mankind. . . .

What has made the European family of nations an improving, instead of a stationary portion of mankind? Not any superior excellence in them, which, when it exists, exists as the effect not as the cause; but their remarkable diversity of character and culture. Individuals, classes, nations, have been extremely unlike one another: they have struck out a great variety of paths, each leading to something valuable; and

although at every period those who traveled in different paths have been intolerant of one another, and each would have thought it an excellent thing if all the rest could have been compelled to travel his road, their attempts to thwart each other's development have rarely had any permanent success, and each has in time endured to receive the good which the others have offered. Europe is, in my judgment, wholly indebted to this plurality of paths for its progressive and many-sided development. But it already begins to possess this benefit in a considerably less degree. M. de Tocqueville, in his last important work, remarks how much more the Frenchmen of the present day resemble one another than did those even of the last generation. The same remark might be made of Englishmen in a far greater degree. In a passage already quoted from Wilhelm von Humboldt, he points out two things as necessary conditions of human development, because necessary to render people unlike one another: namely, freedom, and variety of situations. The second of these two conditions is in this country every day diminishing. The circumstances which surround different classes and individuals, and shape their characters, are daily becoming more assimilated. Formerly, different ranks, different neighborhoods, different trades and professions, lived in what might be called different worlds; at present to a great degree in the same. Comparatively speaking, they now read the same things, listen to the same things, see the same things, go to the same places, have their hopes and fears directed to the same objects, have the same rights and liberties, and the same means of asserting them. Great as are the differences of position which remain, they are nothing to those which have ceased. And the assimilation is still proceeding. All the political changes of the age promote it, since they all tend to raise the low and to lower the high. Every extension of education promotes it, because education brings people under common influences, and gives them access to the general stock of facts and sentiments. Improvement in the means of communication promotes it, by bringing the inhabitants of distant places into personal contact, and keeping up a rapid flow of changes of residence between one place and another. The increase of commerce and manufactures promotes it, by diffusing more widely the advantages of easy circumstances, and opening all objects of ambition, even the highest, to general competition, whereby the desire of rising becomes no longer the character of a particular class, but of all classes. A more powerful agency than even all these, in bringing about a general similarity among mankind, is the complete establishment, in this and other free countries, of the ascendancy of public opinion in the State. As the various social eminences which enabled persons entrenched on them to disregard the opinion of the multitude gradually become leveled; as the very idea of resisting the will of the public, when it is positively known that they have a will, disappears more and more from the minds of practical politicians: there ceases to be any social support for nonconformity—any substantive power in society which, itself opposed to the ascendancy of numbers, is interested in taking under its protection opinions and tendencies at variance with those of the public.

The combination of all these causes forms so great a mass of influences hostile to individuality, that it is not easy to see how it can stand its ground. It will do so with increasing difficulty, unless the intelligent part of the public can be made to feel its value—to see that it is good there should be differences, even though not for the better, even though, as it may appear to them, some should be for the worse. If the claims of individuality are ever to be asserted, the time is now, while much is still wanting to complete the enforced assimilation. It is only in the earlier stages that any stand can be successfully made against the encroachment. The demand that all other people shall resemble ourselves grows by what it feeds on. If resistance waits till life is reduced *nearly* to one uniform type, all deviations from that type will come to be considered impious, immoral, even monstrous and contrary to nature. Mankind speedily become unable to conceive diversity, when they have been for some time unaccustomed to see it.

Of the
Stationary
State

1. [Stationary State of Wealth and Population Is Dreaded and Deprecated by Writers]

The preceding chapters comprise the general theory of the economical progress of society, in the sense in which those terms are commonly understood; the progress of capital, of population, and of the productive arts. But in contemplating any progressive movement, not in its nature unlimited, the mind is not satisfied with merely tracing the laws of the movement; it cannot but ask the further question, to what goal? Towards what ultimate point is society tending by its industrial progress? When the progress ceases, in what condition are we to expect that it will leave mankind?

It must always have been seen, more or less distinctly, by political economists, that the increase of wealth is not boundless: that at the end of what they term the progressive state lies the stationary state, that all progress in wealth is but a postponement of this, and that each

From John Stuart Mill, *Principles of Political Economy with Some of Their Applications to Social Philosophy*, 7th edition, 1871. Volume II, Book IV, Chapter VI.

step in advance is an approach to it. We have now been led to recognise that this ultimate goal is at all times near enough to be fully in view; that we are always on the verge of it, and that if we have not reached it long ago, it is because the goal itself flies before us. The richest and most prosperous countries would very soon attain the stationary state, if no further improvements were made in the productive arts, and if there were a suspension of the overflow of capital from those countries into the uncultivated or ill-cultivated regions of the earth.

This impossibility of ultimately avoiding the stationary state—this irresistible necessity that the stream of human industry should finally spread itself out into an apparently stagnant sea—must have been, to the political economists of the last two generations, an unpleasing and discouraging prospect; for the tone and tendency of their speculations goes completely to identify all that is economically desirable with the progressive state, and with that alone. With Mr. McCulloch, for example, prosperity does not mean a large production and a good distribution of wealth, but a rapid increase of it; his test of prosperity is high profits; and as the tendency of that very increase of wealth, which he calls prosperity, is towards low profits, economical progress, according to him, must tend to the extinction of prosperity. Adam Smith always assumes that the condition of the mass of the people, though it may not be positively distressed, must be pinched and stinted in a stationary condition of wealth, and can only be satisfactory in a progressive state. The doctrine that, to however distant a time incessant struggling may put off our doom, the progress of society must "end in shallows and in miseries," far from being, as many people still believe, a wicked invention of Mr. Malthus, was either expressly or tacitly affirmed by his most distinguished predecessors, and can only be successfully combated on his principles. Before attention had been directed to the principle of population as the active force in determining the remuneration of labour, the increase of mankind was virtually treated as a constant quantity; it was, at all events, assumed that in the natural and normal state of human affairs population must constantly increase, from which it followed that a constant increase of the means of support was essential to the physical comfort of the mass of mankind. The publication of Mr. Malthus' Essay is the era from which better views of this subject must be dated; and notwithstanding the acknowledged errors of his first edition, few writers have done more than himself, in the subsequent editions, to promote these juster and more hopeful anticipations.

Even in a progressive state of capital, in old countries, a conscientious or prudential restraint on population is indispensable, to prevent the increase of numbers from outstripping the increase of capital, and the condition of the classes who are at the bottom of society from being deteriorated. Where there is not, in the people, or in some very large proportion of them, a resolute resistance to this deterioration—a determination to preserve an established standard of comfort—the condition of the poorest class sinks, even in a progressive state, to the lowest point which they will consent to endure. The same determination would be equally effectual to keep up their condition in the stationary state, and would be quite as likely to exist. Indeed, even now, the countries in which the greatest prudence is manifested in the regulating of population, are often those in which capital increases least rapidly. Where there is an indefinite prospect of employment for increased numbers, there is apt to appear less necessity for prudential restraint. If it were evident that a new hand could not obtain employment but by displacing, or succeeding to, one already employed, the combined influences of prudence and public opinion might in some measure be relied on for restricting the coming generation within the numbers necessary for replacing the present.

2. [But the Stationary State Is Not in Itself Undesirable]

I cannot, therefore, regard the stationary state of capital and wealth with the unaffected aversion so generally manifested towards it by political economists of the old school. I am inclined to believe that it would be, on the whole, a very considerable improvement on our present condition. I confess I am not charmed with the ideal of life held out by those who think that the normal state of human beings is that of struggling to get on; that the trampling, crushing, elbowing, and treading on each other's heels, which form the existing type of social life, are the most desirable lot of human kind, or anything but the disagreeable symptoms of one of the phases of industrial progress. It may be a necessary stage in the progress of civilization, and those European nations which have hitherto been so fortunate as to be preserved from it, may have it yet to undergo.[1] It is an incident of growth, not a mark of decline, for it is not necessarily destructive of the higher aspirations and the heroic virtues; as America, in her great civil war, has proved to the world, both by her conduct as a people and by numerous splendid individual examples, and as England, it is to be hoped, would also prove, on an equally trying and exciting occasion. But it is not a kind of social perfection which philanthropists to come will feel any very eager desire to assist in realizing. Most fitting, indeed, is it, that while riches are power, and to grow as rich as possible the universal object of ambition, the path to its attainment should be open to all, without favour or partiality. But the best state for human nature is that in which, while no one is poor, no one desires to be richer, nor has any reason to fear being thrust back, by the efforts of others to push themselves forward.

That the energies of mankind should be kept in employment by the struggle for riches, as they were formerly by the struggle of war, until the better minds succeed in educating the others into better things, is undoubtedly more desirable than that they should rust and stagnate. While minds are coarse they require coarse stimuli, and let them have them. In the meantime, those who do not accept the present very early stage of human improvement as its ultimate type, may be excused for being comparatively indifferent to the kind of economical progress which excites the congratulations of ordinary politicians; the mere increase of production and accumulation. For the safety of national independence it is essential that a country should not fall much behind its neighbours in these things. But in themselves they are of little importance, so long as either the increase of population or anything else prevents the mass of the people from reaping any part of the benefit of them. I know not why it should be matter of congratulation that persons who are already richer than any one needs to be, should have doubled their means of consuming things which give little or no pleasure except as representative of wealth; or that numbers of individuals should pass over, every

---

[1] The northern and middle states of America are a specimen of this stage of civilization in very favourable circumstances; having, apparently, got rid of all social injustices and inequalities that affect persons of Caucasian race and of the male sex, while the proportion of population to capital and land is such as to ensure abundance to every able-bodied member of the community who does not forfeit it by misconduct. They have the six points of Chartism, and they have no poverty: and all that these advantages do for them is that the life of the whole of one sex is devoted to dollar-hunting, and of the other to breeding dollar-hunters.

year, from the middle classes into a richer class, or from the class of the occupied rich to that of the unoccupied. It is only in the backward countries of the world that increased production is still an important object: in those most advanced, what is economically needed is a better distribution, of which one indispensable means is a stricter restraint on population. Levelling institutions, either of a just or of an unjust kind, cannot alone accomplish it; they may lower the heights of society, but they cannot, of themselves, permanently raise the depths.

On the other hand, we may suppose this better distribution of property attained, by the joint effect of the prudence and frugality of individuals, and of a system of legislation favouring equality of fortunes, so far as is consistent with the just claim of the individual to the fruits, whether great or small, of his or her own industry. We may suppose, for instance, a limitation of the sum which any one person may acquire by gift or inheritance, to the amount sufficient to constitute a moderate independence. Under this twofold influence, society would exhibit these leading features: a well-paid and affluent body of labourers; no enormous fortunes, except what were earned and accumulated during a single lifetime; but a much larger body of persons than at present, not only exempt from the coarser toils, but with sufficient leisure, both physical and mental, from mechanical details, to cultivate freely the graces of life, and afford examples of them to the classes less favourably circumstanced for their growth. This condition of society, so greatly preferable to the pres-

ent, is not only perfectly compatible with the stationary state, but, it would seem, more naturally allied with that state than with any other.

There is room in the world, no doubt, and even in old countries, for a great increase of population, supposing the arts of life to go on improving, and capital to increase. But even if innocuous, I confess I see very little reason for desiring it. The density of population necessary to enable mankind to obtain, in the greatest degree, all the advantages both of cooperation and of social intercourse, has, in all the most populous countries, been attained. A population may be too crowded, though all be amply supplied with food and raiment. It is not good for man to be kept perforce at all times in the presence of his species. A world from which solitude is extirpated, is a very poor ideal. Solitude, in the sense of being often alone, is essential to any depth of meditation or of character; and solitude in the presence of natural beauty and grandeur, is the cradle of thoughts and aspirations which are not only good for the individual, but which society could ill do without. Nor is there much satisfaction in contemplating the world with nothing left to the spontaneous activity of nature; with every rood of land brought into cultivation, which is capable of growing food for human beings; every flowery waste or natural pasture ploughed up, all quadrupeds or birds which are not domesticated for man's use exterminated as his rivals for food, every hedgerow or superfluous tree rooted out, and scarcely a place left where a wild shrub or flower could grow without being eradicated as a weed in the name of improved agriculture. If the earth must lose that great portion of its pleasantness which it owes to things that the unlimited increase of wealth and population would extirpate from it, for the mere purpose of enabling it to support a larger, but not a better or a happier population, I sincerely hope, for the sake of posterity, that they will be content to be stationary, long before necessity compels them to it.

It is scarcely necessary to remark that a stationary condition of capital and population implies no stationary state of human improvement. There would be as much scope as ever for all kinds of mental culture, and moral and social progress; as much room for improving the Art of Living, and much more likelihood of its being improved, when minds ceased to be engrossed by the art of getting on. Even the industrial arts might be as earnestly and as successfully cultivated, with this sole difference, that instead of serving no purpose but the increase of wealth, industrial improvements would produce their legitimate effect, that of abridging labour. Hitherto it is questionable if all the mechanical inventions yet made have lightened the day's toil of any human being. They have enabled a greater population to live the same life of drudgery and imprisonment, and an increased number of manufacturers and others to make fortunes. They have increased the comforts of the middle classes. But they have not yet begun to effect those great changes in human destiny, which it is in their nature and in their futurity to accomplish. Only when, in addition to just institutions, the increase of mankind shall be under the deliberate guidance of judicious foresight, can the conquest made from the powers of nature by the intellect and energy of scientific discoverers, become the common property of the species, and the means of improving and elevating the universal lot.

COMMENT

The Basis of Mill's Argument

The older liberals, especially Locke and Jefferson, espoused liberty as an inalienable natural right. Mill, in contrast, avowedly based his argument upon "utility, in the largest sense." Progress, he maintained, is desirable for human welfare, and free thought and action are necessary for that end. The ultimate standard for judging social institutions is their contribution to happiness. Mill thus began by running up the banner of utilitarianism.

The real premise of his argument, however, is not the calculation of pleasure and pain but the inner value of character and unhampered individuality. In Chapter III of *On Liberty*, he mentions with approval the doctrine of "self-realization" advocated by Wilhelm von Humboldt. "The end of man," according to this German writer, "is the highest and most harmonious development of his powers to a complete and consistent whole," and for this there are two requisites, "freedom and variety of situations." This theory of self-realization is the focus of Mill's teaching. It underlies his decided preference for highly developed individuals rather than "ape-like imitators." Liberty enables a man to be a man—to attain the full use and development of his powers. To live freely is to unfold one's individual human capacities; to live servilely—by custom, imitation, social pressure, or repressive political rule—is to be less than a man. Liberty is the acknowledgment of the peculiar dignity of man as man—and of *each* man in his matchless individuality. There is slight trace in this essay of the earlier teaching of the Utilitarians that it does not matter what men are like provided that they have as much pleasure and as little pain as possible.

Mill had become convinced that the modern enemy of liberty is the tyranny of the majority. No longer is the problem that of overthrowing a tyrannical king or the oligarchy of a few. It is the much more difficult problem of freeing dissident individuals and minorities from the pressure of a mass-society. Mill had been shocked by Alexis de Tocqueville's classic study, *Democracy in America* (1835–1840), which maintained that the ultimate triumph of democracy is inevitable and that its tendency is to reduce all men to a level of equal mediocrity. Sharing de Tocqueville's alarm, Mill believed that a truly liberal society must be created as a safeguard against mass illiberalism. Such a society would be deeply respectful of human freedom. His argument, therefore, is primarily a defense of individuality against the conventionalities of society, the despotism of social custom, and the overweening powers of government.

Freedom of association is not discussed at length in *On Liberty* but receives greater attention in Mill's other works, *Representative Government* and *Principles of Political Economy*. Most of his argument in *On Liberty* is devoted to "liberty of thought and expression" and "liberty of action." Since his plea speaks eloquently for itself, there is no need to summarize it here.

Of the Stationary State

No ideas in this book are more relevant to contemporary issues than Mill's discussion of "the stationary state" in his *Principles of Political Economy*. The ecological crisis that he foresaw has now become a severe problem all over the world. An explosive increase in population has been combined with dwindling natural resources. Technological escalation is rapidly diminishing the fossil fuels and minerals necessary for industrial survival. Equally distressing are the pollution of air and water, the destruction of forests and grasslands, the extinction of plant and animal species, the increase in human starvation, and the threat of nuclear holocaust. Thoughtful writers, such as Paul Ehrlich and Robert Heilbroner, have warned that the human race, if it continues on its headlong reckless course, will break its silly neck.

Back in the Victorian age, one of the few challenges to the middle-class faith in human progress was Malthus' formula that population tends to increase in geometrical progression (1, 2, 4, 8, 16, 32 . . .) while subsistence tends to increase only in arithmetical progression (1, 2, 3, 4, 5, 6 . . .). Although the liberals discounted Malthus' formula and the socialists denounced it, Mill believed that the disproportion between rapidly expanding population and slowly increasing subsistence would become a very serious problem. Before reaching the age of twenty, he was arrested for distributing birth control literature and sentenced by the Lord Mayor of London to imprisonment for fourteen days. Although he served part of his sentence, jail did not change his convictions. In the years that have intervened between his age and ours, the use of contraceptive devices, the development of scientific methods of agriculture, and the increase in individual efficiency, have delayed but not prevented the ecological crisis.

In *Principles of Political Economy*, Mill not only anticipated the crisis but understood the transvaluation that should accompany it. He recognized that democratic theory—the theory by which we justify and sustain our democratic societies—must no longer be tied to the idea of continual growth in population and production. He rejected the whole ideology of possessive individualism, with its notion that happiness lies in the indefinite increase in material goods. Far from bemoaning the necessary limits of growth, he welcomed "the stationary state" as the basis for a reorientation of human aspirations. Qualitative enrichment must take priority over quantitative expansion. The harmony of man with nature and the internal culture of the individual must become the prime objectives.

Individual and Social Standards of Human Fulfillment

The traditional theory of democracy is the doctrine of natural rights which we reviewed in Chapter 15. The language of the American Declaration of Independence and the French Declaration of the Rights of Man, for example, is largely derived from this tradition. Mill believed that his doctrine of the supreme importance of individuality contradicts the natural rights tradition, but his standard of self-realization is not so far removed from that of natural rights as might be supposed at first glance. What distinguishes his doctrine from most theories of natural right is the strong emphasis upon the diversity of human nature. To live freely is to unfold one's *individual* human capacities. His theory in this sense is complementary rather than contradictory to the natural rights theory. It calls attention to the individual, and not merely the generic, elements in human nature.

More than the older natural rights theorists, such as Locke and Rousseau, Mill was aware that society must adapt itself to changing historical circumstances. Similarly Dewey, in his version of democratic liberalism, was keenly aware of the tides of historical change and their relevance to democratic ideals. This is also the characteristic approach of Marxists who insist that "democracy," "socialism," and "communism" are historical concepts with changing meaning and content. Typical is Marx's remark in *The Critique of the Gotha Program* that "right can never be higher than the economic structure of the society and the cultural development conditioned by it." But Mill, more than either Marx or Dewey, insisted on the autonomy and self-fulfillment of the individual.

Dewey was more deeply imbued with a social concept of human life. The conception of the individual as preformed he regarded as radically false. For a human being—one with language and institutions and capacity to learn—there is no original "human nature" that can be isolated and understood apart from its social and cultural situation. Armed with a social concept of man, Dewey maintained that freedom implies not the *absence* of external restraints—the negative condition of freedom that the older liberals emphasized—but the *presence* of opportunity and adequate resources. Fundamental to Dewey's whole concept of democracy is his ideal of shared experience. He wished to abolish fixities, boundaries, and monopolies, to enhance communication and strengthen neighborliness, to develop social intelligence by an unfettered educational process, and thus to create "a freer and more humane experience in which all share and to which all contribute." The readings from Dewey in this book are illustrative of this ideal.

The contrast between the more individualistic emphasis of Mill and the more social emphasis of Dewey should incite lively discussion. While thinking about these differences, however, we should not overlook the similarities. Mill became increasingly convinced as he grew older that real freedom requires the resources and opportunities that enable a person to fulfill his potentialities and effectuate his choices. In his essay on Coleridge, he contended that "a State ought to be considered a great benefit society, or mutual insurance company, for helping (under the necessary regulations for preventing abuse) that large proportion of its members who cannot help themselves." He was inclined to favor cooperative ownership and management of industry by the workers instead of either capitalistic or state-socialistic operation. "There can be little doubt," he said in *Principles of Political Economy*, "that the relation of masters and workpeople will be gradually superseded by partnership in one of two forms: in some cases, association of the labourers with the capitalist; in others, and perhaps finally in all, association of labourers among themselves." In his *Autobiography*, he declared that "the social problem of the future" is "how to unite the greatest individual liberty of action with a common ownership of the raw materials of the globe, and an equal participation of all in the benefits of combined labour." He was nevertheless opposed to state intervention "to chain up the free agency of individuals."

Conclusion

In Part Four we have examined the ideas of three major figures in social philosophy—Plato, Marx, and Mill. They differ in many respects, and not least in their attitudes toward democracy. Plato believed in the cultivation of excellence by the rule of wise men—he rejected democracy because its leaders are neither wise nor devoted to excellence. Marx regarded democracy in a capitalist society as a facade for the rule of wealth and privilege, and he predicted that it would be superseded by a socialist state. Socialism, in turn, will develop into a cooperative anarchism, and the state, as a coercive organization, will "wither away." Mill regarded representative democracy as the best form of government for a modern civilized society, but he warned against the tyranny of the majority and he defended the liberties of the dissident individual. If we add to these characterizations other relevant ideas, such as the concept of natural rights, we have a wide and rich gamut of theories.

Even so we have scarcely plumbed the meaning of democracy. It would be well to ponder the words of Walt Whitman in *Democratic Vistas*:

> We have frequently printed the word Democracy. Yet I cannot too often repeat that it is a word the real gist of which sleeps, quite unawakened, nothwithstanding the resonance and the many angry tempests out of which its syllables have come, from pen and tongue. It is a great word, whose history, I suppose, remains unwritten, because that history has yet to be enacted.

Its history is unenacted because its meaning is still latent, and because it calls for a transformation more profound that the world has ever seen.

23

The Control
of Human Behavior

We conclude with a symposium in which two famous psychologists, B. F. Skinner and Carl Rogers, debate the philosophical issues involved in the educational and political moulding of human beings. In a discussion highly pertinent to our scientific and technological age, some of the most crucial issues that have been raised in preceding chapters are brought to a sharp focus. Faced by "the spectre of predictable man," we are forced to reconsider our most basic concepts and ideals.

BURRHUS FREDERIC SKINNER (1904–   )

and CARL RANSOM ROGERS (1902–   )

B. F. Skinner studied English and Greek classics at Hamilton College in Clinton, New York. Turning from literature to psychology, he received his Master's degree in 1930 and Doctor's degree in 1931 at Harvard, where he has taught since 1947. During World War II he worked for the Office of Scientific Research and Development, training pigeons to pilot bombs and torpedoes through a guidance system activated by the birds' pecking in response to radar. His other remarkable exploits include teaching pigeons how to play ping-pong, and the invention of mechanical baby-tenders and teaching machines. The machines, combined with his theory of "programmed instruction," could revolutionize teaching methods. His novel, *Walden Two* (1948), depicts a Utopian community run on the prin-

797

ciples of behavioral psychology. In other widely read books, *Science and Human Behavior* (1953), *Cumulative Record* (revised, 1961), and *Beyond Freedom and Dignity* (1971), he applies his theory to the full range of human phenomena.

Carl Rogers received his M.A. in 1928 and Ph.D. in 1931 from Teachers' College, Columbia University. He has worked as a clinical psychologist in Rochester, New York, and at the Universities of Ohio and Chicago. In 1957 he became Professor of Psychology and Psychiatry at the University of Wisconsin, and since 1964 he has been a resident fellow at the Western Behavioral Sciences Institute at La Jolla, California. He is best known for his "client-centered" theory of psychotherapy, which prescribes a person-to-person relationship between therapist and patient and encourages the patient, within wide limits, to control the course, pace, and length of his treatment. Rogers and his wife Helen love isolated spots in Mexico and the Carribean, where they paint, take colored photographs, swim and lie on the beach. In these spots, he has said, his most important ideas have come to him. Like Skinner, he is deeply interested in the philosophical implications of psychology.

Some Issues Concerning the Control of Human Behavior: A Symposium

I [Skinner]

Science is steadily increasing our power to influence, change, mold—in a word, control—human behavior. It has extended our "understanding" (whatever that may be) so that we deal more successfully with people in nonscientific ways, but it has also identified conditions or variables which can be used to predict and control behavior in a new,

and increasingly rigorous, technology. The broad disciplines of government and economics offer examples of this, but there is special cogency in those contributions of anthropology, sociology, and psychology which deal with individual behavior. Carl Rogers has listed some of the achievements to date in a recent paper.[1] Those of his examples which show or imply the control of the single organism are primarily due, as we should expect, to psychology. It is the experimental study of behavior

[1] Carl Rogers, *Teachers College Record,* Vol. 57 (1956), p. 316.

which carries us beyond awkward or inaccessible "principles," "factors," and so on, to variables which can be directly manipulated.

It is also, and for more or less the same reasons, the conception of human behavior emerging from an experimental analysis which most directly challenges traditional views. Psychologists themselves often do not seem to be aware of how far they have moved in this direction. But the change is not passing unnoticed by others. Until only recently it was customary to deny the possibility of a rigorous science of human behavior by arguing, either that a lawful science was impossible because man was a free agent, or that merely statistical predictions would always leave room for personal freedom. But those who used to take this line have become most vociferous in expressing their alarm at the way these obstacles are being surmounted.

Now, the control of human behavior has always been unpopular. Any undisguised effort to control usually arouses emotional reactions. We hesitate to admit, even to ourselves, that we are engaged in control, and we may refuse to control, even when this would be helpful, for fear of criticism. Those who have explicitly avowed an interest in control have been roughly treated by history. Machiavelli is the great prototype. As Macaulay said of him, "Out of his surname they coined an epithet for a knave and out of his Christian name a synonym for the devil." There were obvious reasons. The control that Machiavelli analyzed and recommended, like most political control, used techniques that were aversive to the con-

trollee. The threats and punishments of the bully, like those of the government operating on the same plan, are not designed—whatever their success—to endear themselves to those who are controlled. Even when the techniques themselves are not aversive, control is usually exercised for the selfish purposes of the controller and, hence, has indirectly punishing effects upon others.

Man's natural inclination to revolt against selfish control has been exploited to good purpose in what we call the philosophy and literature of democracy. The doctrine of the rights of man has been effective in arousing individuals to concerted action against governmental and religious tyranny. The literature which has had this effect has greatly extended the number of terms in our language which express reactions to the control of men. But the ubiquity and ease of expression of this attitude spells trouble for any science which may give birth to a powerful technology of behavior. Intelligent men and women, dominated by the humanistic philosophy of the past two centuries, cannot view with equanimity what Andrew Hacker has called "the specter of predictable man."[2] Even the statistical or actuarial prediction of human events, such as the number of fatalities to be expected on a holiday weekend, strikes many people as uncanny and evil, while the prediction and control of individual behavior is regarded as little less than the work of the devil. I am not so much concerned here with the political or economic consequences for psychology,

[2] Andrew Hacker, *Antioch Review*, Vol. 14 (1954), p. 195.

although research following certain channels may well suffer harmful effects. We ourselves, as intelligent men and women, and as exponents of Western thought, share these attitudes. They have already interfered with the free exercise of a scientific analysis, and their influence threatens to assume more serious proportions. . . .

Education

The techniques of education were once frankly aversive. The teacher was usually older and stronger than his pupils and was able to "make them learn." This meant that they were not actually taught but were surrounded by a threatening world from which they could escape only by learning. Usually they were left to their own resources in discovering how to do so. Claude Coleman has published a grimly amusing reminder of these older practices. He tells of a schoolteacher who published a careful account of his services during 51 years of teaching, during which he administered: ". . . 911,527 blows with a cane; 124,010 with a rod; 20,989 with a ruler; 136,715 with the hand; 10,295 over the mouth; 7,905 boxes on the ear; [and] 1,115,800 slaps on the head. . . ."[3]

Progressive education was a humanitarian effort to substitute positive reinforcement for such aversive measures, but in the search for useful human values in the classroom it has never fully replaced the variables it abandoned. Viewed as a branch of behavioral technology, education remains relatively in-

[3] Claude Coleman, *Bulletin of the American Association of University Professors*, Vol. 39 (1953), p. 457.

efficient. We supplement it, and rationalize it, by admiring the pupil who learns *for himself*; and we often attribute the learning process, or knowledge itself, to something *inside* the individual. We admire behavior which seems to have inner sources. Thus we admire one who *recites* a poem more than one who simply *reads* it. We admire one who *knows* the answer more than one who *knows where to look it up*. We admire the *writer* rather than the reader. We admire the arithmetician who can do a problem in his head rather than with a slide rule or calculating machine, or in "original" ways rather than by a strict application of rules. In general we feel that any aid or "crutch"—except those aids to which we are now thoroughly accustomed—reduces the credit due. In Plato's *Phædrus,* Thamus, the king, attacks the invention of the alphabet on similar grounds! He is afraid "it will produce forgetfulness in the minds of those who learn to use it, because they will not practice their memories. . . ." In other words, he holds it more admirable to remember than to use a memorandum. He also objects that pupils "will read many things without instruction. . . [and] will therefore seem to know many things when they are for the most part ignorant." In the same vein we are today sometimes contemptuous of book learning, but, as educators, we can scarcely afford to adopt this view without reservation.

By admiring the student for knowledge and blaming him for ignorance, we escape some of the responsibility of teaching him. We resist any analysis of the educational process which threatens the notion of inner wisdom or questions the contention that the fault of ignorance lies with the student. More powerful techniques which bring about the same changes in behavior by manipulating *external* variables are decried as brainwashing or thought control. We are quite unprepared to judge *effective* educational measures. As long as only a few pupils learn much of what is taught, we do not worry about uniformity or regimentation. We do not fear the feeble technique; but we should view with dismay a system under which every student learned everything listed in a syllabus—although such a condition is far from unthinkable. Similarly, we do not fear a system which is so defective that the student must *work* for an education; but we are loath to give credit for anything learned without effort—although this could well be taken as an ideal result—and we flatly refuse to give credit if the student already knows what a school teaches.

A world in which people are wise and good without trying, without "having to be," without "choosing to be," could conceivably be a far better world for everyone. In such a world we should not have to "give anyone credit"—we should not need to admire anyone—for being wise and good. From our present point of view we cannot believe that such a world would be admirable. We do not even permit ourselves to imagine what it would be like.

Government

Government has always been the special field of aversive control. The state is frequently defined in terms of the power to punish, and jurisprudence

leans heavily upon the associated notion of personal responsibility. Yet it is becoming increasingly difficult to reconcile current practice and theory with these earlier views. In criminology, for example, there is a strong tendency to drop the notion of responsibility in favor of some such alternative as capacity or controllability. But no matter how strongly the facts, or even practical expedience, support such a change, it is difficult to make the change in a legal system designed on a different plan. When governments resort to other techniques (for example, positive reinforcement), the concept of responsibility is no longer relevant and the theory of government is no longer applicable.

The conflict is illustrated by two decisions of the Supreme Court in the 1930's which dealt with, and disagreed on, the definition of control or coercion.[4] The Agricultural Adjustment Act proposed that the Secretary of Agriculture make "rental or benefit payments" to those farmers who agreed to reduce production. The government agreed that the Act would be unconstitutional if the farmer had been *compelled* to reduce production but was not, since he was merely *invited* to do so. Justice Roberts expressed the contrary majority view of the court that "The power to confer or withhold unlimited benefits is the power to coerce or destroy." This recognition of positive reinforcement was withdrawn a few years later in another case in which Justice Cardozo wrote "To hold that motive or temptation is equiv-

[4] P. A. Freund and others, *Constitutional Law: Cases and Other Problems* (Boston: Little, Brown, 1954), p. 233.

alent to coercion is to plunge the law in endless difficulties."[5] We may agree with him, without implying that the proposition is therefore wrong. Sooner or later the law must be prepared to deal with all possible techniques of governmental control.

The uneasiness with which we view government (in the broadest possible sense) when it does not use punishment is shown by the reception of my utopian novel, *Walden Two*. This was essentially a proposal to apply a behavioral technology to the construction of a workable, effective, and productive pattern of government. It was greeted with wrathful violence. *Life* magazine called it "a travesty on the good life," and "a menace . . . a triumph of mortmain or the dead hand not envisaged since the days of Sparta . . . a slur upon a name, a corruption of an impulse." Joseph Wood Krutch devoted a substantial part of his book, *The Measure of Man,* to attacking my views and those of the protagonist, Frazier, in the same vein, and Morris Viteles has recently criticized the book is a similar manner in *Science*.[6] Perhaps the reaction is best expressed in a quotation from *The Quest for Utopia* by Negley and Patrick:

"Halfway through this contemporary utopia, the reader may feel sure, as we did, that this is a beautifully ironic satire on what has been called 'behavioral engineering.' The longer one stays in this better world of the psychologist, however, the plainer it becomes that the inspiration is not satiric, but messianic. This is indeed the behaviorally engi-

neered society, and while it was to be expected that sooner or later the principle of psychological conditioning would be made the basis of a serious construction of utopia—Brown anticipated it in *Limanora*—yet not even the effective satire of Huxley is adequate preparation for the shocking horror of the idea when positively presented. Of all the dictatorships espoused by utopists, this is the most profound, and incipient dictators might well find in this utopia a guidebook of political practice."[7]

One would scarcely guess that the authors are talking about a world in which there is food, clothing, and shelter for all, where everyone chooses his own work and works on the average only 4 hours a day, where music and the arts flourish, where personal relationships develop under the most favorable circumstances, where education prepares every child for the social and intellectual life which lies before him, where—in short—people are truly happy, secure, productive, creative, and forward-looking. What is wrong with it? Only one thing: someone "planned it that way." If these critics had come upon a society in some remote corner of the world which boasted similar advantages, they would undoubtedly have hailed it as providing a pattern we all might well follow—provided that it was clearly the result of a natural process of cultural evolution. Any evidence that intelligence had been used in arriving at this version of the good life would, in their eyes, be a serious flaw. No mat-

[5] Freund: *Constitutional Law,* p. 244.
[6] M. Viteles, *Science,* Vol. 122 (1955), p. 1167.

[7] Glenn Negley and J. M. Patrick, *The Quest for Utopia* (New York: Schuman, 1952).

ter if the planner of *Walden Two* diverts none of the proceeds of the community to his own use, no matter if he has no current control or is, indeed, unknown to most of the other members of the community (he planned that, too), somewhere back of it all he occupies the position of prime mover. And this, to the child of the democratic tradition, spoils it all.

The dangers inherent in the control of human behavior are very real. The possibility of the misuse of scientific knowledge must always be faced. We cannot escape by denying the power of a science of behavior or arresting its development. It is no help to cling to familiar philosophies of human behavior simply because they are more reassuring. As I have pointed out elsewhere,[8] the new techniques emerging from a science of behavior must be subject to the explicit countercontrol which has already been applied to earlier and cruder forms. Brute force and deception, for example, are now fairly generally suppressed by ethical practices and by explicit governmental and religious agencies. A similar countercontrol of scientific knowledge in the interests of the group is a feasible and promising possibility. Although we cannot say how devious the course of its evolution may be, a cultural pattern of control and countercontrol will presumably emerge which will be most widely supported because it is most widely reinforcing.

If we cannot foresee all the details of this (as we obviously cannot), it is important to remember that this is true of

[8] B. F. Skinner, *Transactions of the New York Academy of Sciences,* Vol. 17 (1955), p. 547.

the critics of science as well. The dire consequences of new techniques of control, the hidden menace in original cultural designs—these need some proof. It is only another example of my present point that the need for proof is so often overlooked. Man has got himself into some pretty fixes, and it is easy to believe that he will do so again. But there is a more optimistic possibility. The slow growth of the methods of science, now for the first time being applied to human affairs, *may* mean a new and exciting phase of human life to which historical analogies will not apply and in which earlier political slogans will not be appropriate. If we are to use the knowledge that a science of behavior is now making available with any hope of success, we must look at human nature as it is brought into focus through the methods of science rather than as it has been presented to us in a series of historical accidents.

If the advent of a powerful science of behavior causes trouble, it will not be because science itself is inimical to human welfare but because older conceptions have not yielded easily or gracefully. We expect resistance to new techniques of control from those who have heavy investments in the old, but we have no reason to help them preserve a series of principles that are not ends in themselves but rather outmoded means to an end. What is needed is a new conception of human behavior which is compatible with the implications of a scientific analysis. All men control and are controlled. The question of government in the broadest possible sense is not how freedom is to be preserved but what kinds of control are to be used and to what ends. Control must be analyzed and considered in its proper proportions. No one, I am sure, wishes to develop new master-slave relationships to bend the will of the people to despotic rulers in new ways. These are patterns of control appropriate to a world without science. They may well be the first to go when the experimental analysis of behavior comes into its own in the design of cultural practices.

II [Rogers]

There are, I believe, a number of matters in connection with this important topic on which the authors of this article, and probably a large majority of psychologists, are in agreement. These matters then are not issues as far as we are concerned, and I should like to mention them briefly in order to put them to one side.

Points of agreement

I am sure we agree that men—as individuals and as societies—have always endeavored to understand, predict, influence, and control human behavior— their own behavior and that of others.

I believe we agree that the behavioral sciences are making and will continue to make increasingly rapid progress in the understanding of behavior, and that as a consequence the capacity to predict and to control behavior is developing with equal rapidity.

I believe we agree that to deny these advances, or to claim that man's behavior cannot be a field of science, is unrealistic. Even though this is not an issue for us, we should recognize that many intelligent men still hold strongly to the view that the actions of men are free in some sense such that scientific knowledge of man's behavior is impossible. Thus Reinhold Niebuhr, the noted theologian, heaps scorn on the concept of psychology as a science of man's behavior and even says, "In any event, no scientific investigation of past behavior can become the basis of predictions of future behavior."[9] So, while this is not an issue for psychologists, we should at least notice in passing that it is an issue for many people.

I believe we are in agreement that the tremendous potential power of a science which permits the prediction and control of behavior may be misused, and that the possibility of such misuse constitutes a serious threat.

Consequently Skinner and I are in agreement that the whole question of the scientific control of human behavior is a matter with which psychologists and the general public should concern themselves. As Robert Oppenheimer told the American Psychological Association last year[10] the problems that psychologists will pose for society by their growing ability to control behavior will be much more grave than the problems posed by the ability of physicists to control the reactions of matter. I am not sure whether psychologists generally recognize this. My impression is that by and large they hold a laissez-faire attitude. Obviously Skinner and I do not hold this laissez-faire view, or we would not have written this article.

[9] Reinhold Niebuhr, *The Self and the Dramas of History* (New York: Scribner's, 1955), p. 47.

[10] Robert Oppenheimer, *American Psychologist*, Vol. 11 (1956), p. 127.

Points at issue

With these several points of basic and important agreement, are there then any issues that remain on which there are differences? I believe there are. They can be stated very briefly: Who will be controlled? Who will exercise control? What type of control will be exercised? Most important of all, toward what end or what purpose, or in the pursuit of what value, will control be exercised?

It is on questions of this sort that there exist ambiguities, misunderstandings, and probably deep differences. These differences exist among psychologists, among members of the general public in this country, and among various world cultures. Without any hope of achieving a final resolution of these questions, we can, I believe, put these issues in clearer form.

Some meanings

To avoid ambiguity and faulty communication, I would like to clarify the meanings of some of the terms we are using.

Behavioral science is a term that might be defined from several angles but in the context of this discussion it refers primarily to knowledge that the existence of certain describable conditions in the human being and/or in his environment is followed by certain describable consequences in his actions.

Prediction means the prior identification of behaviors which then occur. Because it is important in some things I wish to say later, I would point out that one may predict a highly specific behavior, such as an eye blink, or one may predict a class of behaviors. One might correctly predict "avoidant behavior," for example, without being able to specify whether the individual will run away or simply close his eyes.

The word *control* is a very slippery one, which can be used with any one of several meanings. I would like to specify three that seem most important for our present purposes. *Control* may mean: (i) The setting of conditions by *B* for *A*, *A* having no voice in the matter, such that certain predictable behaviors then occur in *A*. I refer to this as external control. (ii) The setting of conditions by *B* for *A*, *A* giving some degree of consent to these conditions, such that certain predictable behaviors then occur in *A*. I refer to this as the influence of *B* on *A*. (iii) The setting of conditions by *A* such that certain predictable behaviors then occur in himself. I refer to this as internal control. It will be noted that Skinner lumps together the first two meanings, external control and influence, under the concept of control. I find this confusing.

Usual concept of control of human behavior

With the underbrush thus cleared away (I hope), let us review very briefly the various elements that are involved in the usual concept of the control of human behavior as mediated by the behavioral sciences. I am drawing here on the previous writings of Skinner, on his present statements, on the writings of others who have considered in either friendly or antagonistic fashion the meanings that would be involved in such control. I have not excluded the science fiction writers, as reported recently by Vandenburg,[11] since they often show an awareness of the issues involved, even though the methods described are as yet fictional. These then are the elements that seem common to these different concepts of the application of science to human behavior.

1) There must first be some sort of decision about goals. Usually desirable goals are assumed, but sometimes, as in George Orwell's book *1984*, the goal that is selected is an aggrandizement of individual power with which most of us would disagree. In a recent paper Skinner suggests that one possible set of goals to be assigned to the behavioral technology is this: "Let men be happy, informed, skillful, well-behaved and productive."[12] In the first draft of his part of this article, which he was kind enough to show me, he did not mention such definite goals as these, but desired "improved" education practices, "wiser" use of knowledge in government, and the like. In the final version of his article he avoids even these value-laden terms, and his implicit goal is the very general one that scientific control of behavior is desirable, because it would perhaps bring "a far better world for everyone."

Thus the first step in thinking about the control of human behavior is the choice of goals, whether specific or general. It is necessary to come to terms in some way with the issue, "For what purpose?"

2) A second element is that, whether the end selected is highly specific or is a very general one such as wanting "a

better world," we proceed by the methods of science to discover the means to these ends. We continue through further experimentation and investigation to discover more effective means. The method of science is self-correcting in thus arriving at increasingly effective ways of achieving the purpose we have in mind.

3) The third aspect of such control is that as the conditions or methods are discovered by which to reach the goals, some person or some group establishes these conditions and uses these methods, having in one way or another obtained the power to do so.

4) The fourth element is the exposure of individuals to the prescribed conditions, and this leads, with a high degree of probability, to behavior which is in line with the goals desired. Individuals are now happy, if that has been the goal, or well-behaved, or submissive, or whatever it has been decided to make them.

5) The fifth element is that if the process I have described is put in motion then there is a continuing social organization which will continue to produce the types of behavior that have been valued.

Some flaws

Are there any flaws in this way of viewing the control of human behavior? I believe there are. In fact the only element in this description with which I find myself in agrement is the second. It seems to me quite incontrovertibly true that the scientific method is an excellent way to discover the means by which to achieve our goals. Beyond that,

---

[11] S. G. Vandenberg, *American Psychologist*, Vol. 11 (1956), p. 339.

[12] B. F. Skinner, *American Scholar*, Vol. 25 (1955–1956), p. 47.

I feel many sharp differences, which I will try to spell out.

I believe that in Skinner's presentation here and in his previous writings, there is a serious underestimation of the problem of power. To hope that the power which is being made available by the behavioral sciences will be exercised by the scientists, or by a benevolent group, seems to me a hope little supported by either recent or distant history. It seems far more likely that behavioral scientists, holding their present attitudes, will be in the position of the German rocket scientists specializing in guided missiles. First they worked devotedly for Hitler to destroy the U.S.S.R. and the United States. Now, depending on who captured them, they work devotedly for the U.S.S.R. in the interest of detroying the United States, or devotedly for the United States in the interest of detroying the U.S.S.R. If behavioral scientists are concerned solely with advancing their science, it seems most probable that they will serve the purposes of whatever individual or group has the power.

But the major flaw I see in this review of what is involved in the scientific control of human behavior is the denial, misunderstanding, or gross underestimation of the place of ends, goals or values in their relationship to science. This error (as it seems to me) has so many implications that I would like to devote some space to it.

Ends and values in relation to science

In sharp contradiction to some views that have been advanced, I would like to propose a two-pronged thesis: (i) In any scientific endeavor—whether "pure" or applied science—there is a prior subjective choice of the purpose or value which that scientific work is perceived as serving. (ii) This subjective value choice which brings the scientific endeavor into being must always lie outside of that endeavor and can never become a part of the science involved in that endeavor.

Let me illustrate the first point from Skinner himself. It is clear that in his earlier writing it is recognized that a prior value choice is necessary, and it is specified as the goal that men are to become happy, well-behaved, productive, and so on. I am pleased that Skinner has retreated from the goals he then chose, because to me they seem to be stultifying values. I can only feel that he was choosing these goals for others, not for himself. I would hate to see Skinner become "well-behaved," as that term would be defined for him by behavioral scientists. His recent article in the *American Psychologist*[13] shows that he certainly does not want to be "productive" as that value is defined by most psychologists. And the most awful fate I can imagine for him would be to have him constantly "happy." It is the fact that he is very unhappy about many things which makes me prize him.

In the first draft of his part of this article, he also included such prior value choices, saying for example, "We must decide how we are to use the knowledge which a science of human behavior is now making available." Now he

13 B. F. Skinner, *American Psychologist,* Vol. 11 (1956), p. 221.

has dropped all mention of such choices, and if I understand him correctly, he believes that science can proceed without them. He has suggested this view in another recent paper, stating that "We must continue to experiment in cultural design . . . testing the consequences as we go. Eventually the practices which make for the greatest biological and psychological strength of the group will presumably survive."[14]

I would point out, however, that to choose to experiment is a value choice. Even to move in the direction of perfectly random experimentation is a value choice. To test the consequences of an experiment is possible only if we have first made a subjective choice of a criterion value. And implicit in his statement is a valuing of biological and psychological strength. So even when trying to avoid such choice, it seems inescapable that a prior subjective value choice is necessary for any scientific endeavor, or for any application of scientific knowledge. . . :

Is the situation hopeless?

The thoughtful reader may recognize that, although my remarks up to this point have introduced some modifications in the conception of the processes by which human behavior will be controlled, these remarks may have made such control seem, if anything, even more inevitable. We might sum it up this way: Behavioral science is clearly moving forward; the increasing power

[14] B. F. Skinner, *Transactions of the New York Academy of Sciences,* Vol. 17 (1955), p. 549.

for control which it gives will be held by someone or some group; such an individual or group will surely choose the values or goals to be achieved; and most of us will then be increasingly controlled by means so subtle that we will not even be aware of them as controls. Thus, whether a council of wise psychologists (if this is not a contradiction in terms), or a Stalin, or a Big Brother has the power, and whether the goal is happiness, or productivity, or resolution of the Oedipus complex, or submission, or love of Big Brother, we will inevitably find ourselves moving toward the chosen goal and probably thinking that we ourselves desire it. Thus, if this line of reasoning is correct, it appears that some form of *Walden Two* or of *1984* (and at a deep philosophic level they seem indistinguishable) is coming. The fact that it would surely arrive piecemeal, rather than all at once, does not greatly change the fundamental issues. In any event, as Skinner has indicated in his writings, we would then look back upon the concepts of human freedom, the capacity for choice, the responsibility for choice, and the worth of the human individual as historical curiosities which once existed by cultural accident as values in a prescientific civilization.

I believe that any person observant of trends must regard something like the foregoing sequence as a real possibility. It is not simply a fantasy. Something of that sort may even be the most likely future. But is it an inevitable future? I want to devote the remainder of my remarks to an alternative possibility.

Alternative set of values

Suppose we start with a set of ends, values, purposes, quite different from the type of goals we have been considering. Suppose we do this quite openly, setting them forth as a possible value choice to be accepted or rejected. Suppose we select a set of values that focuses on fluid elements of process rather than static attributes. We might then value: man as a process of becoming, as a process of achieving worth and dignity through the development of his potentialities; the individual human being as a self-actualizing process, moving on to more challenging and enriching experiences; the process by which the individual creatively adapts to an ever-new and changing world; the process by which knowledge transcends itself, as, for example, the theory of relativity transcended Newtonian physics, itself to be transcended in some future day by a new perception.

If we select values such as these we turn to our science and technology of behavior with a very different set of questions. We will want to know such things as these: Can science aid in the discovery of new modes of richly rewarding living? more meaningful and satisfying modes of interpersonal relationships? Can science inform us on how the human race can become a more intelligent participant in its own evolution—its physical, psychological and social evolution? Can science inform us on ways of releasing the creative capacity of individuals, which seem so necessary if we are to survive in this fantastically expanding atomic age? Oppenheimer has pointed out[15] that knowledge, which used to double in millenia or centuries, now doubles in a generation or a decade. It appears that we must discover the utmost in release of creativity if we are to be able to adapt effectively. In short, can science discover the methods by which man can most readily become a continually developing and self-transcending process, in his behavior, his thinking, his knowledge? Can science predict and release an essentially "unpredictable" freedom?

It is one of the virtues of science as a method that it is as able to advance and implement goals and purposes of this sort as it is to serve static values, such as states of being well-informed, happy, obedient. Indeed we have some evidence of this. . . .

Possible concept of the control of human behavior

It is quite clear that the point of view I am expressing is in sharp contrast to the usual conception of the relationship of the behavioral sciences to the control of human behavior. In order to make this contrast even more blunt, I will state this possibility in paragraphs parallel to those used before.

1) It is possible for us to choose to value man as a self-actualizing process of becoming; to value creativity, and the process by which knowledge becomes self-transcending.

[15] Robert Oppenheimer, *Roosevelt University Occasional Papers*, Vol. 2 (1956).

2) We can proceed, by the methods of science, to discover the conditions which necessarily precede these processes and, through continuing experimentation, to discover better means of achieving these purposes.

3) It is possible for individuals or groups to set these conditions, with a minimum of power or control. According to present knowledge, the only authority necessary is the authority to establish certain qualities of interpersonal relationships.

4) Exposed to these conditions, present knowledge suggests that individuals become more self-responsible, make progress in self-actualization, become more flexible, and become more creatively adaptive.

5) Thus such an initial choice would inaugurate the beginnings of a social system or subsystem in which values, knowledge, adaptive skills, and even the concept of science would be continually changing and self-transcending. The emphasis would be upon man as a process of becoming.

I believe it is clear that such a view as I have been describing does not lead to any definable utopia. It would be impossible to predict its final outcome. It involves a step-by-step development, based on a continuing subjective choice of purposes, which are implemented by the behavioral sciences. It is in the direction of the "open society," as that term has been defined by Popper,[16] where individuals carry responsibility for personal decisions. It is at the opposite pole from his concept of the closed

[16] Karl R. Popper, *The Open Society and Its Enemies* (London: Routledge and Kegan Paul, 1945).

society, of which *Walden Two* would be an example.

I trust it is also evident that the whole emphasis is on process, not on end-states of being. I am suggesting that it is by choosing to value certain qualitative elements of the process of becoming that we can find a pathway toward the open society.

The choice

It is my hope that we have helped to clarify the range of choice which will lie before us and our children in regard to the behavioral sciences. We can choose to use our growing knowledge to enslave people in ways never dreamed of before, depersonalizing them, controlling them by means so carefully selected that they will perhaps never be aware of their loss of personhood. We can choose to utilize our scientific knowledge to make men happy, well-behaved, and productive, as Skinner earlier suggested. Or we can insure that each person learns all the syllabus which we select and set before him, as Skinner now suggests. Or at the other end of the spectrum of choice we can choose to use the behavioral sciences in ways which will free, not control; which will bring about constructive variability, not conformity; which will develop creativity, not contentment; which will facilitate each person in his self-directed process of becoming; which will aid individuals, groups, and even the concept of science to become self-transcending in freshly adaptive ways of meeting life and its problems. The choice is up to us, and, the human race being what it is, we are likely to stumble about, making at times some nearly disastrous value choices and at other times highly constructive ones.

I am aware that to some, this setting forth of a choice is unrealistic, because a choice of values is regarded as not possible. Skinner has stated: "Man's vaunted creative powers . . . his capacity to choose and our right to hold him responsible for his choice—none of these is conspicuous in this new self-portrait (provided by science). Man, we once believed, was free to express himself in art, music, and literature, to inquire into nature, to seek salvation in his own way. He could initiate action and make spontaneous and capricious changes of course. . . . But science insists that action is initiated by forces impinging upon the individual, and that caprice is only another name for behavior for which we have not yet found a cause."[17]

I can understand this point of view, but I believe that it avoids looking at the great paradox of behavioral science. Behavior, when it is examined scientifically, is surely best understood as determined by prior causation. This is one great fact of science. But responsible personal choice, which is the most essential element in being a person, which is the core experience in psychotherapy, which exists prior to any scientific endeavor, is an equally prominent fact in our lives. To deny the experience of responsible choice is, to me, as restricted a view as to deny the possibility of a behavioral science. That these two important elements of our experience appear to be in contradiction has perhaps the same significance as the contradiction between the wave theory and the corpuscular theory of light, both of which can be shown to be true, even though incompatible. We cannot profitably deny our subjective life, any more than we can deny the objective description of that life.

In conclusion then, it is my contention that science cannot come into being without a personal choice of the values we wish to achieve. And these values we choose to implement will forever lie outside of the science which implements them; the goals we select, the purposes we wish to follow, must always be outside of the science which achieves them. To me this has the encouraging meaning that the human person, with his capacity of subjective choice, can and will always exist, separate from and prior to any of his scientific undertakings. Unless as individuals and groups we choose to relinquish our capacity of subjective choice, we will always remain persons, not simply pawns of a self-created science.

III [Skinner]

. . . The values I have occasionally recommended (and Rogers has not led me to recant) are transitional. Other things being equal, I am betting on the group whose practices make for healthy, happy, secure, productive, and creative people. And I insist that the values recommended by Rogers are transitional, too, for I can ask him the same kind of question. Man as a process of becoming—*what?* Self-actualization—

[17] B. F. Skinner, *American Scholar,* Vol. 25 (1955–1956), p. 47.

for what? Inner control is no more a goal than external.

What Rogers seems to me to be proposing, both here and elsewhere, is this: Let us use our increasing power of control to create individuals who will not need and perhaps will no longer respond to control. Let us solve the problem of our power by renouncing it. At first blush this seems as implausible as a benevolent despot. Yet power has occasionally been foresworn. A nation has burned its Reichstag, rich men have given away their wealth, beautiful women have become ugly hermits in the desert, and psychotherapists have become nondirective. When this happens, I look to other possible reinforcements for a plausible explanation. A people relinquish democratic power when a tyrant promises them the earth. Rich men give away wealth to escape the accusing finger of their fellowmen. A woman destroys her beauty in the hope of salvation. And a psychotherapist relinquishes control because he can thus help his client more effectively.

The solution that Rogers is suggesting is thus understandable. But is he correctly interpreting the result? What evidence is there that a client ever becomes truly *self*-directing? What evidence is there that he ever makes a truly *inner* choice of ideal or goal? Even though the therapist does not do the choosing, even though he encourages "self-actualization"—he is not out of control as long as he holds himself ready to step in when occasion demands —when, for example, the client chooses the goal of becoming a more accomplished liar or murdering his boss. But supposing the therapist does withdraw

completely or is no longer necessary— what about all the other forces acting upon the client? Is the self-chosen goal independent of his early ethical and religious training? of the folk-wisdom of his group? of the opinions and attitudes of others who are important to him? Surely not. The therapeutic situation is only a small part of the world of the client. From the therapist's point of view it may appear to be possible to relinquish control. But the control passes, not to a "self," but to forces in other parts of the client's world. The solution of the therapist's problem of power cannot be *our* solution, for we must consider *all* the forces acting upon the individual.

The child who must be prodded and nagged is something less than a fully developed human being. We want to see him hurrying to his appointment, not because each step is taken in response to verbal reminders from his mother, but because certain temporal contigencies, in which dawdling has been punished and hurrying reinforced, have worked a change in his behavior. Call this a state of better organization, a greater sensitivity to reality, or what you will. The plain fact is that the child passes from a temporary verbal control exercised by his parents to control by certain inexorable features of the environment. I should suppose that something of the same sort happens in successful psychotherapy. Rogers seems to me to be saying this: Let us put an end, as quickly as possible, to any pattern of master-and-slave, to any direct obedience to command, to the submissive following of suggestions. Let the individual be free to adjust himself to more rewarding features of the world about him. In the end, let his teachers and counselors "wither away," like the Marxist state. I not only agree with this as a useful ideal, I have constructed a fanciful world to demonstrate its advantages. It saddens me to hear Rogers say that "at a deep philosophic level" *Walden Two* and George Orwell's *1984* "seem indistinguishable." They could scarcely be more unlike—at any level. The book *1984* is a picture of immediate aversive control for vicious selfish purposes. The founder of *Walden Two*, on the other hand, has built a community in which neither he nor any other person exerts any *current* control. His achievement lay in his original *plan*, and when he boasts of this ("It is enough to satisfy the thirstiest tyrant") we do not fear him but only pity him for his weakness.

Another critic of *Walden Two*, Andrew Hacker,[18] has discussed this point in considering the bearing of mass conditioning upon the liberal notion of autonomous man. In drawing certain parallels between the Grand Inquisition passage in Dostoevsky's *Brothers Karamazov*, Huxley's *Brave New World*, and *Walden Two*, he attempts to set up a distinction to be drawn in any society between conditioners and conditioned. He assumes that "the conditioner can be said to be autonomous in the traditional liberal sense." But

[18] Andrew Hacker, *Journal of Politics*, Vol. 17 (1955), p. 17.

then he notes: "Of course the conditioner has been conditioned. But he has not been conditioned by the conscious manipulation of another *person*." But how does this affect the resulting behavior? Can we not soon forget the origins of the "artificial" diamond which is identical with the real thing? Whether it is an "accidental" cultural pattern, such as is said to have produced the founder of *Walden Two*, or the engineered environment which is about to produce his successors, we are dealing with sets of conditions generating human behavior which will ultimately be measured by their contribution to the strength of the group. We look to the future, not the past, for the test of "goodness" or acceptability.

If we are worthy of our democratic heritage we shall, of course, be ready to resist any tyrannical use of science for immediate or selfish purposes. But if we value the achievements and goals of democracy we must not refuse to apply science to the design and construction of cultural patterns, even though we may then find ourselves in some sense in the position of controllers. Fear of control, generalized beyond any warrant, has led to a misinterpretation of valid practices and the blind rejection of intelligent planning for a better way of life. In terms which I trust Rogers will approve, in conquering this fear we shall become more mature and better organized and shall, thus, more fully actualize ourselves as human beings.

COMMENT

The discussion between Skinner and Rogers is a fitting conclusion to this book. It surveys "the enduring questions" from a fresh and contemporary perspective. Among these questions are the following:

1. WHAT IS THE CORRECT METHOD OF INQUIRY? Skinner, as a brilliant experimentalist, operates in the tradition of empiricists such as Locke, Hume, and Peirce. He rejects the introspective method and traces knowledge back to experience rather than to innate mental factors. Scientific method as he interprets it is based upon sensory and, therefore, public observation. The study of human activities, he insists, should concentrate upon the forms of external behavior, exhibited with various regularities and probabilities. He thinks that there is no great difference in method between animal and human psychology.

Rogers, as a clinical psychologist and psychotherapist, seeks to understand the unfolding development of inner needs and purposes. Although he could not be called a rationalist, he agrees with Descartes in recognizing an innate structure to the mind and in distinguishing rather sharply between the human and animal levels of behavior. For him, man is to be studied at his own level and each man is to be understood in his own terms. Like the existentialists, Kierkegaard and Buber, he seeks to penetrate behind all masks and false fronts to "that self which one truly is." Using language identical with Buber's, he has said that the deepest and most satisfying interpersonal contact is "a real I-Thou relationship, not an I-It relationship."[1]

2. WHAT IS THE RELATION BETWEEN MIND AND BODY? Skinner opposes Cartesian dualism. Although he is too sophisticated to deny that there are thoughts and feelings, he declares that a scientific psychology must wholly abandon the conception of psychic causes. He has defined such mental factors as "intentions" in terms of observable relations that refer exclusively to antecedent stimulus conditions and motions of bodies. Everything that a psychologist legitimately wants to say about mental events, he believes, can be said in purely behavioral terms.

Although Rogers does not accept so sharp a dualism as that of Descartes, he insists that the inner life is causally important and nonreducible. Man is a psychophysiological organism, and it is a mistake to slight or disregard the mental side of his nature.

---

[1] For Rogers' sympathy with Kierkegaard, see Clark E. Moustakes (ed.), *The Self* (New York: Harper & Row, 1956), pp. 197–198; and for his relation to Buber, see Maurice S. Friedman, *Martin Buber: The Life of Dialogue* (New York: Harper & Row, 1960), pp. 191–195. Also see the dialogue between Buber and Rogers in Martin Buber, *The Knowledge of Man* (New York: Harper & Row, 1965), pp. 166–184.

3. Do Men Have Free Will? Skinner agrees with Spinoza in rejecting the possibility of undetermined choices and final causes. He has said that a scientific theory of human behavior "must abolish the conception of the individual as a doer, as an originator of action."[2] Explaining behavior in terms of stimuli impinging upon the individual, he is sceptical that a person "ever becomes truly *self*-directing," or "that he ever makes a truly *inner* choice of ideal or goal." Although, like Hume, he speaks of freedom of action, it is within the context of a deterministic theory.

Rogers aligns himself with free-will advocates such as Kant. He is as insistent upon the importance and reality of "subjective value choice" as Skinner is on "conditioning." His aim as a therapist is to liberate the individual from both inner and outer blocks so as to permit more freedom and self-direction. Granted that there are limits to our environmental opportunities and our given and potential nature, we are free within these limits to guide our growth by reflective goals.

4. What Is the Natural Basis of Ethics? Skinner tends toward an "evolutionary ethics" based upon the principle of "the survival of the fittest." When pressed for justification of his ethical preferences, he falls back upon the criterion of "the strength of the group" and "the survival of mankind." He is much more inclined than Rogers to think that science can supply the norms for the control of human behavior.

Rogers believes that human beings, by nature, are loaded and cocked to develop in certain ways, and that it is good to realize this potential. The ethical goal is fulfillment of what is deepest in a man's nature. He thus approximates the humanism of the natural-law tradition that stems from Aristotle and Cicero, but he differs in putting greater emphasis upon the freedom and uniqueness of the individual person. "Basic human nature," he has said, "is something that is really to be *trusted*. . . . It's been very much my experience in therapy that one does not need to supply motivation toward the positive or toward the constructive. That exists in the individual. . . . If we can release what is most basic in the individual . . . it will be constructive."[3] To pursue this goal calls for a "subjective value choice" that lies outside the scope of science.

5. How Should Human Behavior Be Controlled? In view of the contrasting answers of Skinner and Rogers to the foregoing questions, we should not be surprised that they differ radically in their educational and political ideals.

Skinner approaches education as a technological problem, believing that the art of teaching should be based upon the science of learning. He puts great stress upon "what are called contingencies of reinforcement—the relations which prevail between behavior on the one hand and the consequences of that behavior

[2] B. F. Skinner, *Cumulative Record* (New York: Appleton-Century-Crofts, 1959), p. 236.
[3] Martin Buber, *The Knowledge of Man*, pp. 179–180.

on the other."[4] These consequences he proposes to manipulate by rewards ("positive reinforcement") more than punishments ("aversive control" or "negative reinforcement"). He advocates "programmed instruction" with the aid of ingenious teaching machines. The sad thing, he declares, is that we are not making use of a tenth of the knowledge about learning that we have at our disposal.

In sketching his Utopia in *Walden Two,* he applies the same basic principle as in his educational theory—namely, control over positive and negative reinforcements (the carrot and stick approach, with emphasis upon the carrot). His proposal for social reconstruction resembles Plato's in the *Republic,* except that psychological-engineers replace philosopher-kings. Having found that he can do amazing things with rats and pigeons, he believes that equally amazing results can be achieved by the scientific and technological reshaping of human beings within an "engineered environment." For him, the viable choice is not between freedom and control but between scientific control, on the one hand, and caprice and unscientific control, on the other. He is convinced that we gain freedom *through* control and not otherwise. Although he recognizes that authoritarian figures may shape people the wrong way, he thinks that counter-controls can be devised that will minimize this danger.

For Rogers the idea of manipulating human beings, whether in school or in society, is highly distasteful. He draws a sharper distinction than does Skinner between the training of animals and the education of human beings. For the latter he advocates something like the "Socratic method" when liberally interpreted. This method was described by Ralph Cudworth, the seventeenth-century Platonist, as based upon the belief that "knowledge was not to be poured into the soul like liquor, but rather to be invited and gently drawn forth from it; nor the mind so much to be filled therewith from without, like a vessel, as to be kindled and awaked."[5] Rogers, I think, would put more emphasis than Cudworth upon environmental factors in the teaching process, but he too wishes to release inner potentialities and to awaken and kindle the mind.

Because he dislikes the manipulation of human beings even by "positive reinforcement," he sees a deeper affinity between *Walden Two* and Orwell's *1984* than Skinner is willing to admit. He is convinced that the freedom of persons ought categorically to be respected, and that the goal of happiness by contrived reinforcement should not override the demands of freedom. In the tradition of Mill and Dewey he proposes a liberal set of values to guide us politically as well as educationally. "We can choose the behavioral sciences," he says, "in ways which will free, not control." He warns against the danger that science will be used, as in Hitler's Germany or Stalin's Russia, for vicious or totalitarian ends.

[4] B. F. Skinner, *The Technology of Teaching* (New York: Appleton-Century-Crofts, 1968), p. 9.

[5] Ralph Cudworth, *Treatise Concerning Eternal and Immutable Morality,* American ed. of *Works,* ed. T. Birch, 1838, p. 427. I am indebted to Noam Chomsky, *Cartesian Linguistics,* for this reference.

There is nothing in science itself, in the absence of "subjective value choice," that can prevent such abuse.

In this clash of opinion between Rogers and Skinner there are exciting grounds for debate and discussion.

Selected Bibliography

INTRODUCTION: THE NATURE OF PHILOSOPHY

*Blanshard, Brand, *On Philosophical Style*. Bloomington: Indiana University Press, 1967.

Cohen, Morris R., *The Faith of a Liberal*. New York: Holt, Rinehart and Winston, 1946, chs. 42–46.

Collingwood, R. G., *Speculum Mentis*. Oxford: Clarendon Press, 1924.

*Danto, Arthur C., *What Philosophy Is*. New York: Harper & Row, 1968.

Ducasse, C. J., *Philosophy as a Science*. New York: Piest, 1941.

Edwards, Paul (ed.), *The Encyclopedia of Philosophy*, 8 vols. New York: Macmillan and Free Press, 1967. An invaluable reference work with extensive bibliographies.

James, William, *Some Problems of Philosophy*. New York: Longmans, Green, 1911, Ch. 1.

Jaspers, Karl, *The Perennial Scope of Philosophy*. New York: Philosophical Library, 1949.

Körner, Stephen, *What Is Philosophy?* London: Allen Lane, 1969.

Merleau-Ponty, M., *In Praise of Philosophy*. Evanston, Ill.: Northwestern University Press, 1963.

Montague, William P., *Great Visions of Philosophy*. La Salle, Ill.: Open Court, 1950. Prologue.

Newell, R. W., *The Concept of Philosophy*. London: Methuen, 1967.

Perry, Ralph Barton, *A Defence of Philosophy*. Cambridge, Mass.: Harvard University Press, 1931.

*Russell, Bertrand, *The Problems of Philosophy*. London: Oxford University Press, 1912, Ch. 15.

*Schlick, Moritz, "The Turning Point in Philosophy," in A. J. Ayer (ed.), *Logical Positivism*. New York: Free Press, 1959.

Wisdom, J. O., *Philosophy and Its Place in Our Culture*. London: Gordon and Breach, 1975.

CHAPTER 1. THE SOCRATIC QUEST

Cornford, F. M., *Before and After Socrates*. Cambridge University Press, 1932.

Ferguson, John (ed.), *Socrates: A Source Book*. London: Macmillan, 1970.

Field, G. C., *Plato and His Contemporaries*. London: Methuen, 1930.

*Guardini, Romano, *The Death of Socrates*. New York: Sheed and Ward, 1948. (Meridian paperbound.)

Gulley, Norman, *The Philosophy of Socrates*. New York: St. Martin's Press, 1968.

Guthrie, W. K. C., *Socrates*. London: Cambridge University Press, 1971.

*Jaeger, Werner, *Paideia: The Idea of Greek Culture*. Oxford: Blackwell, 1947.

*Taylor, A. E., *Socrates*. New York: Appleton, 1933. (Anchor pb.)

*Vlastos, Gregory (ed.), *The Philosophy of Socrates*. New York: Doubleday, 1971.

CHAPTER 2. TELEOLOGY

Aristotle

Allan, D. J., *The Philosophy of Aristotle*. New York: Oxford University Press, 1970.

Farrington, Benjamin, *Aristotle*. New York: Praeger, 1969.

* Titles marked by an asterisk are available paperbound.

*Jaeger, W., *Aristotle: Fundamentals of the History of His Development.* Oxford: Clarendon Press, 1934. (Oxford pb.)

*Mure, G. R. G., *Aristotle.* London: Benn, 1932. (Oxford pb.)

*Randall, John H., *Aristotle.* New York: Columbia University Press, 1960.

*Ross, W. D., *Aristotle,* 2nd ed. London: Methuen, 1930. (Barnes and Noble pb.)

Solmsen, Friedrich, *Aristotle's System of the Physical World.* Ithaca, N.Y.: Cornell University Press, 1961.

Stocks, J. L., *Aristotelianism.* New York: Longmans, Green, 1922.

*Taylor, A. E., *Aristotle.* London: Nelson, 1943.

Woodbridge, F. J. E., *Aristotle's Vision of Nature.* New York: Columbia University Press, 1965.

Teleology

Braithwaite, R. B., *Scientific Explanation.* Cambridge University Press, 1953.

Canfield, John V. (ed.), *Purpose in Nature.* Englewood Cliffs, N.J.: Prentice-Hall, 1966.

*Collins, James, *Interpreting Modern Philosophy.* Princeton University Press, 1972.

Hobhouse, L. T., *Development and Purpose.* London: Macmillan, 1913.

*Langer, Susanne K., *Mind: An Essay on Human Feeling.* Baltimore: Johns Hopkins University Press, 1967, 1972, and forthcoming. Especially Vol. II.

Nagel, Ernest, "Teleological Explanation and Teleological Systems" in *The Structure of Science.* New York: Harcourt Brace Jovanovich, 1961.

Russell, E. S., *The Directiveness of Organic Activities.* Cambridge University Press, 1945.

Sinnott, Edmund, *Cell and Psyche.* Chapel Hill: University of North Carolina Press, 1950.

Smith, F. V., *Purpose in Animal Behavior.* London: Hutchinson, 1971.

*Teilhard de Chardin, Pierre, *The Phenomenon of Man.* New York: Harper & Row, 1959.

Tolman, E. C., *Purposive Behavior in Animals and Men.* New York: Century, 1932.

CHAPTER 3. MATERIALISM

*Anderson, Alan Ross (ed.), *Minds and Machines.* Englewood Cliffs, N.J.: Prentice-Hall, 1964.

Eliot, Hugh, *Modern Science and Materialism.* London: Longmans, Green, 1919.

*Hook, Sidney (ed.), *Dimensions of Mind.* New York: Macmillan, 1961.

Lange, F. A., *The History of Materialism.* New York: Harcourt Brace Jovanovich, 1925.

Laslett, P. (ed.), *The Physical Basis of Mind.* Oxford: Blackwell, 1951.

McDougall, William, *Modern Materialism and Emergent Evolution.* New York: Nostrand, 1929.

O'Connor, John M. (ed.), *Modern Materialism.* New York: Harcourt Brace Jovanovich, 1969.

*Rosenthal, David M. (ed.), *Materialism and the Mind-Body Problem.* Englewood Cliffs, N.J.: Prentice-Hall, 1971.

Smart, J. J. C., *Philosophy and Scientific Realism.* London: Routledge and K. Paul, 1963.

Winspear, Alban D., *Lucretius and Scientific Thought.* Montreal: Harvest House, 1963.

See also the works of the older materialists Epicurus, Hobbes, Diderot, Holbach, and La Mettrie.

CHAPTER 4. DUALISM AND THE QUEST FOR CERTAINTY

Descartes

Balz, A. G. A., *Descartes and the Modern Mind.* New Haven, Conn.: Yale University Press, 1952.

Beck, Leslie J., *The Method of Descartes.* Oxford: Clarendon Press, 1952.

———, *The Metaphysics of Descartes.* Oxford: Clarendon Press, 1965.

Caton, Hiram, *The Origin of Subjectivity: An Essay on Descartes.* New Haven: Yale University Press, 1973.

*Doney, Willis (ed.), *Descartes.* New York: Doubleday, 1968.

Joachim, H. H., *Descartes' Rules for the Direction of the Mind.* London: Allen and Unwin, 1957.

*Keeling, Stanley V., *Descartes*, 2nd ed. New York: Oxford University Press, 1968.

*Kenny, Anthony, *Descartes.* New York: Random House, 1968.

*Malcolm, Norman, *Problems of Mind: Descartes to Wittgenstein.* New York: Harper & Row, 1971.

Roth, L., *Descartes' Discourse on Method.* Oxford: Clarendon Press, 1937.

*Sesonske, Alexander and Noel Fleming (eds.), *Meta-Meditations.* Belmont, Cal.: Wadsworth, 1965.

Smith, Norman Kemp, *New Studies in the Philosophy of Descartes.* London: Macmillan, 1952.

Vrooman, Jack Rochford, *René Descartes: A Biography.* New York: Putnam, 1970.

Dualism and the Mind-Body Problem

*Broad, C. D., *The Mind and Its Place in Nature.* New York: Harcourt Brace Jovanovich, 1925. Ch. 3. (Littlefield pb.)

*Campbell, Keith, *Body and Mind.* New York: Doubleday, 1970.

Ducasse, C. D., *Nature, Mind, and Death.* La Salle, Ill.: Open Court, 1951.

*Flew, Anthony (ed.), *Body, Mind, and Death.* New York: Macmillan, 1964.

*Hampshire, Stuart (ed.), *Philosophy of Mind.* New York: Harper & Row, 1966.

*Hook, Sidney (ed.), *Dimensions of Mind.* New York: New York University Press, 1960.

Laird, John, *Our Minds and Their Bodies.* London: Oxford University Press, 1925.

Lewis, H. D., *The Elusive Mind.* New York: Humanities Press, 1969.

Peursen, C. A. van, *Body, Soul, Spirit.* London: Oxford University Press, 1966.

Pratt, J. B., *Matter and Spirit.* New York: Macmillan, 1926.

*Ryle, Gilbert, *The Concept of Mind.* New York: Barnes & Noble, 1949.

*Sherrington, Charles, *Man on His Nature.* Cambridge University Press, 1940.

*Spicker, Stuart F. (ed.), *The Philosophy of the Body: Rejections of Cartesian Dualism.* Chicago: Quadrangle, 1970.

Strawson, P. F., *Individuals.* London: Methuen, 1959. Ch. 3. (Anchor pb.)

Strong, Charles Augustus, *Why the Mind Has a Body.* New York: Macmillan, 1903.

Vesey, G. N. A. (ed.), *Body and Mind.* London: Allen and Unwin, 1964.

*Wisdom, John, *Problems of Mind and Matter.* Cambridge University Press, 1934.

The Quest for Certainty

*Ayer, A. J., *The Problem of Knowledge.* Harmondsworth: Penguin, 1965. Ch. 2.

Malcolm, Norman, *Dreaming.* London: Routledge and K. Paul, 1962.

———, *Knowledge and Certainty.* Englewood Cliffs, N.J.: Prentice-Hall, 1963.

Moore, G. E., "Certainty" "A Defense of Common Sense" and "Proof of an External World," in *Philosophical Papers.* London: Macmillan, 1959.

Popkin, Richard H., "Skepticism" in Paul Edwards (ed.), *The Encyclopedia of Philosophy.* New York: Macmillan and Free Press, 1967. Bibliography.

Rollins, C. D., "Certainty" in Paul Edwards (ed.), *The Encyclopedia of Philosophy.* New York: Macmillan and Free Press, 1967. Bibliography.

Santayana, George, *Scepticism and Animal Faith.* New York: Scribner's, 1923.

*Wittgenstein, Ludwig, *On Certainty.* Oxford: Blackwell, 1969. (Harper pb.)

CHAPTER 5. MONISM

Freeman, Eugene and Maurice Mandelbaum (eds.), *Spinoza: Essays in Interpretation.* La Salle, Ill.: Open Court, 1975.

Hall, Roland, "Monism and Pluralism" in Paul Edwards (ed.), *The Encyclopedia of Philosophy.* New York: Macmillan and Free Press, 1967. Bibliography.

Hallett, H. F., *Benedict de Spinoza: The Elements of His Philosophy.* London: Athlone, 1957.

*Hampshire, Stuart, *Spinoza.* Harmondsworth: Penguin, 1951. Recommended.

James, William, *A Pluralistic Universe.* London: Longmans, Green, 1909.

*Jaspers, Karl, *Spinoza.* New York: Harcourt Brace Jovanovich, 1974.

Oko, Adolph S., *The Spinoza Bibliography.* Boston: G. K. Hall, 1964.

Quinton, A. M., "Pluralism and Monism" in *Encyclopedia Brittanica,* 1971. Vol. 18, pp. 66–68.

Wolfson, H. A., *The Philosophy of Spinoza,* 2 vols. Cambridge, Mass.: Harvard University Press, 1954.

Wrightman, W. P. D., *Science and Monism.* London: G. Allen and Unwin, 1934.

CHAPTER 6. EMPIRICISM

Locke

Aaron, R. I., *John Locke,* 3rd ed. Oxford: Clarendon Press, 1971. Recommended.

Clapp, James Gordon, "John Locke," in Paul Edwards (ed.), *The Encyclopedia of Philosophy.* New York: Macmillan and Free Press, 1967. Bibliography.

Gibson, James, *Locke's Theory of Knowledge.* Cambridge University Press, 1917. Recommended.

Mabbott, J. D., *John Locke.* London: Macmillan, 1973.

*O'Connor, D. J., John Locke. Harmondsworth: Penguin, 1952.

Smith, Norman Kemp, *John Locke.* Manchester University Press, 1933.

Woolhouse, R. S., *Locke's Philosophy of Science and Knowledge.* New York: Barnes & Noble, 1971.

Yolton, John W., *Locke and the Compass of Human Understanding.* Cambridge University Press, 1970.

———, *Locke and the Way of Ideas.* Oxford: Clarendon Press, 1956.

Peirce

Ayer, A. J., *The Origins of Pragmatism.* London: Macmillan, 1974.

Buchler, Justus, *Charles Peirce's Empiricism.* New York: Harcourt Brace Jovanovich, 1939.

——— (ed.), *The Philosophy of Peirce: Selected Writings.* New York: Harcourt Brace Jovanovich, 1940.

*Gallie, W. B., *Peirce and Pragmatism.* Harmondsworth: Penguin, 1952.

Goudge, Thomas A., *The Thought of C. S. Peirce.* University of Toronto Press, 1950.

Murphey, Murray G., *The Development of Peirce's Philosophy.* Cambridge, Mass.: Harvard University Press, 1961.

Reilly, Francis E., *Charles Peirce's Theory of Scientific Method.* New York: Fordham University Press, 1970.

Scheffler, Israel, *Four Pragmatists: A Critical Introduction to Peirce, James, Mead, and Dewey.* New York: Humanities Press, 1974.

Thompson, Manley, *The Pragmatic Philosophy of C. S. Peirce.* University of Chicago Press, 1953.

Wiener, Philip P. and Frederick H. Young (eds.), *Studies in the Philosophy of Charles Sanders Peirce*. Cambridge, Mass.: Harvard University Press, 1952.

Scientific Method

*Beveridge, W. I. B., *The Art of Scientific Investigation*. New York: Random House, 1961.
Blake, R. M., Ducasse, C. J., and Madden, E. H., *Theories of Scientific Method*. Seattle: University of Washington Press, 1960.
Bronowski, Jacob, *The Ascent of Man*. Boston: Little, Brown and Company, 1974.
Burks, Arthur W., *Cause, Chance, Reason: An Inquiry into the Nature of Scientific Evidence*. University of Chicago Press, 1975.
Cohen, Morris R., *Reason and Nature*, 2nd ed. Glencoe, Ill.: Free Press, 1953.
Columbia Associates, *Introduction to Reflective Thinking*. Boston: Houghton Mifflin, 1923.
Feigl, Herbert and May Brodbeck (eds.), *Readings in the Philosophy of Science*. New York: Appleton-Century-Crofts, 1953.
Gingerich, Owen, *Nature of Scientific Discovery*. Washington: Smithsonian Institution, 1945.
Harre, R., *An Introduction to the Logic of the Sciences*. London: Macmillan, 1960.
Madden, Edward H. (ed.), *The Structure of Scientific Thought*. Boston: Houghton Mifflin, 1960.
Nagel, Ernest, *The Structure of Science*. New York: Harcourt Brace Jovanovich, 1961.

CHAPTER 7. IDEALISM

Adams, George P., *Idealism and the Modern Age*. New Haven, Conn.: Yale University Press, 1919.
Blanshard, Brand, *The Nature of Thought*, 2 vols. New York: Macmillan, 1940.
Bradley, F. H., *Appearance and Reality*. Oxford: Clarendon Press, 1930.
Ewing, A. C., *Idealism: A Critical Survey*. London: Methuen, 1934.
——— (ed.), *The Idealist Tradition from Berkeley to Blanshard*. New York: Free Press, 1957.
Hoernle, R. F. A., *Idealism as a Philosophy*. New York: Doran, 1927.
Ritchie, A. D., *George Berkeley: A Reappraisal*. Manchester University Press, 1967.
*Royce, Josiah, *The Spirit of Modern Philosophy*. New York: Tudor, 1955.
Steinkraus, Warren E. (ed.), *New Studies in Berkeley's Philosophy*. New York: Holt, Rinehart and Winston, 1966.
Tipton, I. C., *Berkeley*. London: Methuen, 1974.
*Warnock, G. J., *Berkeley*. Harmondsworth: Penguin, 1953.

CHAPTER 8. CAUSATION, FREE WILL, AND THE LIMITS OF KNOWLEDGE

Hume

*Basson, Anthony H., *David Hume*. Harmondsworth: Penguin, 1958.
*Bennett, Jonathan, *Locke, Berkeley, Hume*. Oxford: Clarendon Press, 1971.
Church, R. W., *Hume's Theory of the Understanding*. Ithaca, N.Y.: Cornell University Press, 1935.
Flew, Anthony, *Hume's Philosophy of Belief*. New York: Humanities Press, 1961.
Hendel, C. W., *Studies in the Philosophy of David Hume*, rev. ed. Indianapolis: Bobbs-Merrill, 1963.

Laing, B. M., *David Hume*. London: Oxford University Press, 1932.
Laird, John, *Hume's Philosophy of Human Nature*. London: Methuen, 1932.
Macnabb, D. G. C., *David Hume*. London: Hutchinson, 1951.
Noxon, James H., *Hume's Philosophical Development*. Oxford: Clarendon Press, 1973.
Price, H. H., *Hume's Theory of the External World*. Oxford: Clarendon Press, 1940.
*Smith, Norman Kemp, *The Philosophy of David Hume*. London: Macmillan, 1941. (St. Martin's pb.)
Stove, David C., *Probability and Hume's Inductive Scepticism*. Oxford: Clarendon Press, 1973.

Kant

Bennett, Jonathan, *Kant's Dialectic*. New York: Cambridge University Press, 1974.
*Ewing, A. C., *A Short Commentary on Kant's Critique of Pure Reason*. London: Methuen, 1938. (Phoenix pb.)
Goldmann, Lucien, *Immanuel Kant*. London: NLB, 1971.
*Körner, S., *Kant*. Harmondsworth: Penguin, 1955.
Paton, H. J., Kant's Metaphysic of Experience, 2 Vols. London: Macmillan, 1936. Difficult.
Smith, Norman Kemp, *A Commentary to Kant's Critique of Pure Reason*, 2nd ed. New York: Macmillan, 1962. Difficult.
Strawson, P. F., *The Bounds of Sense*. London: Methuen, 1966.
Weldon, T. D., *Kant's Critique of Pure Reason*. London: Oxford University Press, 1958.
*Wolff, Robert Paul (ed.), *Kant*. New York: Doubleday, 1967.
———, *Kant's Theory of Mental Activity*. Cambridge, Mass.: Harvard University Press, 1963.

Causation

*Ayer, A. J., *Foundations of Empirical Knowledge*. London: Macmillan, 1951. Ch. 4. (St. Martin's pb.)
Braithwaite, R. B., *Scientific Explanation*. New York: Cambridge University Press, 1953. Chs. 9, 10.
Carnap, Rudolf, *Logical Foundations of Probability*, 2nd ed. University of Chicago Press, 1962.
Bunge, Mario, *Causality*. Cambridge, Mass.: Harvard University Press, 1959.
Ducasse, C. J., *Nature, Mind and Death*. La Salle, Ill.: Open Court, 1951. Part II.
Russell, Bertrand, *Mysticism and Logic*. London: Allen and Unwin, 1917. Ch. 9.
Taylor, Richard, "Causation," in Paul Edwards (ed.), *The Encyclopedia of Philosophy*. New York: Macmillan and Free Press, 1967. Bibliography.
Wright, G. H. von, *Causality and Determinism*. New York: Columbia University Press, 1974.

Free Will

*Austin, J. L., "Ifs and Cans" in *Philosophical Papers*. New York: Oxford University Press, 1961.
*Berofsky, Bernard (ed.), *Free Will and Determinism*. New York: Harper & Row, 1966.
*Bradley, F. H., *Ethical Studies*. Oxford: Clarendon Press, 1927. First Essay.
*Bergson, Henri, *Time and Free Will*. New York: Macmillan, 1921. (Harper pb.)
Campbell, C. A., *In Defence of Free Will*. New York: Humanities Press, 1968.
Davis, William H., *The Freewill Question*. The Hague: Nijhoff, 1971.
*Dworkin, Gerald (ed.), *Determinism, Free Will and Moral Responsibility*. Englewood Cliffs, N.J.: Prentice-Hall, 1970.
Farrer, Austin, *The Freedom of the Will*. New York: Scribner's, 1960.
Hampshire, Stuart, *Freedom of the Individual*. New York: Harper & Row, 1965.

*Hook, Sidney (ed.), *Determinism and Freedom in the Age of Science*. New York: Collier, 1961.

Lucas, J. R., *The Freedom of the Will*. Oxford: Clarendon Press, 1970.

*O'Connor, D. J., *Free Will*. New York: Doubleday, 1971.

Schlick, Moritz, *Problems of Ethics*. Englewood Cliffs, N.J.: Prentice-Hall, 1939. Ch. 7. Defence of Hume's view of free will.

A detailed and annotated bibliography of works on determinism and free will can be found in Paul Edwards and Arthur Pap (eds.), *A Modern Introduction to Philosophy*, 3rd ed. New York: Free Press, 1973, pp. 99–114.

The Limits of Knowledge

*A. J. Ayer, *The Problem of Knowledge*. Harmondsworth: Penguin, 1956.

Hintikka, Jaakko, *Knowledge and Belief*. Ithaca, N.Y.: Cornell University Press, 1962.

*Russell, Bertrand, *Human Knowledge*. New York: Simon & Schuster, 1948.

Vaihinger, Hans, *The Philosophy of "As If."* New York: Harcourt Brace Jovanovich, 1935.

See bibliography for Chapter 4, "Dualism and the Quest for Certainty."

CHAPTER 9. INDIVIDUALITY AND CREATIVE PROCESS

Kierkegaard and Existentialism

*Barrett, William, Irrational Man. New York: Doubleday, 1958.

*Bretall, Robert (ed.), *A Kierkegaard Anthology*. Princeton University Press, 1946. (Reprinted by Modern Library.)

*Camus, Albert, *The Myth of Sisyphus*. New York: Random House, 1955.

Gill, Richard, *The Fabric of Existentialism*. Englewood Cliffs, N.J.: Prentice-Hall, 1973.

*Grene, Marjorie, *Introduction to Existentialism*. University of Chicago Press, 1959.

Harper, Ralph, *The Existential Experience*. Baltimore: Johns Hopkins University Press, 1972.

*Heidegger, Martin, *Existence and Being*. Chicago: Regnery, 1949. Difficult.

*Jaspers, Karl, *Reason and Existenz*. London: Routledge and K. Paul, 1956. (Noonday pb.)

*Kaufmann, Walter (ed.), *Existentialism from Dostoevsky to Sartre*. New York: World, 1956.

Malantschuk, Gregor, *Kierkegaard's Thought*. Princeton University Press, 1971.

Murphy, Arthur E., "On Kierkegaard's Claim that Truth is Subjectivity" in *Reason and the Common Good*. Englewood Cliffs, N.J.: Prentice-Hall, 1963.

*Sartre, Jean-Paul, *Being and Nothingness*. New York: Philosophical Library, 1956.

———, *Existentialism and Humanism*. London: Methuen, 1948. Recommended.

Thompson, Josiah, *Kierkegaard*. New York: Knopf, 1973.

*Tillich, Paul, *The Courage to Be*. New Haven, Conn.: Yale University Press, 1952.

Zaner, Richard M., *Phenomenology and Existentialism*. New York: Putnam, 1973.

Bergson

Bergson, Henri, *Creative Evolution*. New York: Holt, Rinehart and Winston, 1911.

———, *The Creative Mind*. New York: Philosophical Library, 1946.

*———, *An Introduction to Metaphysics*. New York: Putnam's, 1912. (Library of Liberal Arts pb.)

*———, *Two Sources of Morality and Religion*. New York: Holt, Rinehart and Winston, 1935. (Doubleday pb.)

Gunter, P. A. Y., *Henri Bergson: A Bibliography*. Bowling Green, Ohio: Bowling Green University, 1974.

Hanna, Thomas (ed.), *The Bergsonian Heritage*. New York: Columbia University Press, 1962.

Lindsay, A. D., *The Philosophy of Bergson*. London: Dent, 1911.

Luce, A. A., *Bergson's Doctrine of Intuition*. London: Society for Promoting Christian Knowledge, 1922.

Whitehead

Christian, William A., *An Interpretation of Whitehead's Metaphysics*. New Haven: Yale University Press, 1959.

Emmet, Dorothy M., *Whitehead's Philosophy of Organism*. London: Macmillan, 1932.

Hall, David L., *The Civilization of Experience: A Whiteheadean Theory of Culture*. New York: Fordham University Press, 1973.

Hartshorne, Charles, *Whitehead's Philosophy*. Lincoln: University of Nebraska Press, 1972.

Johnson, A. H., *Experiential Realism*. New York: Humanities Press, 1973.

———, *Whitehead's Theory of Reality*. New York: Dover, 1962.

*Lowe, Victor, *Understanding Whitehead*. Baltimore: Johns Hopkins University Press, 1962.

Northrop, F. C. S. and Mason W. Gross (eds.), *Alfred North Whitehead: An Anthology*. New York: Macmillan, 1953.

Schilpp, P. A. (ed.), *The Philosophy of Alfred North Whitehead*, 2nd ed. New York: Tudor, 1951. Bibliography.

Sherburne, Donald W., *A Whiteheadean Aesthetic*. New Haven: Yale University Press, 1961.

Art, Reality, and Human Values

*Dewey, John, *Art as Experience*. New York: Putnam's, 1958.

*Gombrich, E. H., *Art and Illusion*, 2nd ed. New York: Pantheon, 1957.

*Langer, Susanne K., *Feeling and Form*. New York: Scribner's, 1953.

Mandelbaum, Maurice (ed.), *Art, Perception, and Reality*. Baltimore: Johns Hopkins University Press, 1972.

Nahm, Milton C. (ed.), *Readings in the Philosophy of Art and Aesthetics*. Englewood Cliffs, N.J.: Prentice Hall, 1975.

Rader, Melvin and Bertram Jessup, *Art and Human Values*. Englewood Cliffs, N.J.: Prentice-Hall, 1976.

*Read, Herbert, *Education Through Art*, 3rd ed. New York: Pantheon, 1958.

*———, *Icon and Idea: The Function of Art in the Development of Human Consciousness*. Cambridge, Mass.: Harvard University Press, 1965.

Reid, Louis Arnaud, *Meaning in the Arts*. New York: Humanities Press, 1969.

———, *A Study in Aesthetics*. New York: Macmillan, 1931.

CHAPTER 10. THE BASIS OF RELIGIOUS BELIEF

Faith and Reason

Blanshard, Brand, *Reason and Belief*. New Haven: Yale University Press, 1975.

Farrer, Austin, *Faith and Speculation*. New York: New York University Press, 1967.

Hick, J. H., *Faith and Knowledge*. Ithaca, N.Y.: Cornell University Press, 1957.

McTaggart, J. M. E., *Some Dogmas of Religion*. New York: McKay, 1930.

Mitchell, Basil (ed.), *Faith and Logic*. London: George Allen and Unwin, 1957.

Popkin, Richard H., "Blaise Pascal" in Paul Edwards (ed.), *The Encyclopedia of Philosophy*. New York: Macmillan and Free Press, 1967. Bibliography.
*Smith, John E., *Reason and God*. New Haven: Yale University Press, 1961.
*Tillich, Paul, *Dynamics of Faith*. New York: Harper & Row, 1958.

Mystical and Other Religious Experience

*Bergson, Henri, *Two Sources of Morality and Religion*. New York: Holt, Rinehart and Winston, 1935. (Doubleday pb.)
Hügel, F. von, *The Mystical Element in Religion*. London: Dent, 1923.
Mourant, John A., *Readings in the Philosophy of Religion*. New York: Crowell, 1954. Contains selections from the mystics.
Passmore, John, *The Perfectibility of Man*. London: Duckworth, 1970.
*Smart, Ninian, *The Religious Experience of Mankind*. New York: Scribner's, 1969.
Stace, Walter T., *Mysticism and Philosophy*. Philadelphia: Lippincott, 1960.
*———, *The Teachings of the Mystics*. New York: New American Library, 1960.
———, *Time and Eternity*. Princeton University Press, 1960.
*Underhill, Evelyn, *Mysticism*. New York: Dutton, 1914.

CHAPTER 11. GOD AND MAN

Theism

Alexander, Samuel, *Space, Time and Deity*. New York: Macmillan, 1920. Vol. 2.
Barnes, Jonathan, *The Ontological Argument*. New York: St. Martin's Press, 1972.
*Copleston, F. C., *Aquinas*. Harmondsworth: Penguin, 1955. Ch. 3.
Edwards, Paul and Arthur Pap (eds.), *A Modern Introduction to Philosophy*, 3rd ed. New York: Free Press, 1973. Part V. Bibliography.
Ewing, A. C., *Value and Reality: The Philosophical Case for Theism*. New York: Humanities Press, 1973.
Flew, Anthony, *Hume's Philosophy of Belief*. New York: Humanities Press, 1961.
Garrigou-Lagrange, R., *God, His Existence and His Nature*, 2 Vols. St. Louis: Herter, 1934, 1936.
Gibson, A. Boyce, *Theism and Empiricism*. New York: Schocken Books, 1970.
Gilson, Etienne, *The Philosophy of St. Thomas Aquinas*. Cambridge: Heffner, 1929.
Hartshorne, Charles, *The Logic of Perfection*. La Salle, Ill.: Open Court, 1962. On the Ontological Argument.
Hick, John, *Evil and the God of Love*. London: Macmillan, 1966.
———, *God and the Universe of Faiths*. New York: St. Martin's Press, 1973.
Hicks, G. Dawes, *The Philosophical Bases of Theism*. London: Allen and Unwin, 1937.
Hume, David, *Dialogues Concerning Natural Religion*, ed. by Norman Kemp Smith. New York: Nelson, 1947. Contains detailed analysis of Hume's arguments and background material.
Kenny, Anthony, *The Five Ways: St. Thomas Aquinas' Proofs of God's Existence*. New York: Schocken Books, 1969.
Malcolm, Norman, "Anselm's Ontological Arguments," *Philosophical Review* Vol. 69 (1960).
Matson, Wallace, *The Existence of God*. Ithaca, N.Y.: Cornell University Press, 1965.
McPherson, Thomas, *The Argument from Design*. New York: St. Martin's Press, 1972.
Mill, John Stuart, *Three Essays on Religion*. London: Longmans, Green, 1885.
*Plantinga, Alvin (ed.), *The Ontological Argument: From Anselm to Contemporary Philosophers*. New York: Doubleday, 1967.

Rowe, William L., *The Cosmological Argument*. Princeton University Press, 1975.
Tennant, F. R., *Philosophical Theology*, 2 Vols. Cambridge University Press, 1928, 1930.
*Whitehead, Alfred North, *Religion in the Making*. New York: Macmillan, 1926. (New American Library pb.)

Humanism

*Baier, Kurt, "The Meaning of Life" in Morris Weitz (ed.), *Twentieth Century Philosophy: The Analytic Tradition*. New York: Free Press, 1966.
*Dewey, John, *A Common Faith*. New Haven: Yale University Press, 1934.
*Egner, Robert E. and Lester E. Denonn (eds.), *The Basic Writings of Bertrand Russell*. New York: Simon & Schuster, 1967. Part XV.
*Freud, Sigmund, *The Future of an Illusion*. New York: Doubleday, 1957.
*Kaufman, Walter, *Critique of Religion and Philosophy*. New York: Harper & Row, 1958. (Doubleday pb.)
*———, *The Faith of a Heretic*. New York: Doubleday, 1961.
Kurtz, P. W. (ed.), *The Humanist Alternative*. London: Pemberton Books, 1973.
Lubac, Henri de, *The Drama of Atheist Humanism*. New York: Meridian, 1950.
Nielsen, Kai, *Skepticism*. New York: St. Martin's Press, 1973.
Robinson, Richard, *An Atheist's Values*. Oxford: Clarendon Press, 1964.
Santayana, George, *Reason in Religion*. New York: Scribner's, 1948.
Stace, W. T., *Man Against Darkness and Other Essays*. University of Pittsburgh Press, 1967.

CHAPTER 12. REASON

Blanshard, Brand, *Reason and Goodness*. London: Allen and Unwin, 1961.
Hardie, W. F. R., *Aristotle's Ethical Theory*. Oxford: Clarendon Press, 1968.
*Mure, G. R. G., *Aristotle*. New York: Oxford University Press, 1939. Ch. 7.
Oates, Whitney J., *Aristotle and the Problem of Value*. Princeton University Press, 1961.
Ross, W. D., *Aristotle,* 2nd ed. London: Methuen, 1930. Ch. 7.
Santayana, George, *Reason in Science*. New York: Scribner's, 1928. Chs. 8–10.
*Toulmin, Stephen, *The Place of Reason in Ethics*. Cambridge University Press, 1950.
*Veatch, Henry Babcock, *Rational Man: A Modern Interpretation of Aristotelian Ethics*. Bloomington: Indiana University Press, 1962.
*Walsh, J. J. and H. L. Shapiro (eds.), *Aristotle's Ethics*. Belmont, Cal.: Wadsworth, 1967.
Wild, John, *Introduction to Realistic Philosophy*. New York: Harper & Row, 1948. Part I.
Wilson, J., *Reason and Morals*. Cambridge University Press, 1961.

CHAPTER 13. NATURE

Barry, Brian, *The Liberal Theory of Justice*. Oxford: Clarendon Press, 1973. A criticism of Rawls' theory of justice.
Entreves, A. P. d', *Natural Law*. London: Hutchinson, 1951.
Gierke, Otto, *Natural Law and the Theory of Society*. London: Cambridge University Press, 1934.
Huxley, Thomas Henry and Julian, *Touchstone for Ethics*. New York: Harper & Row, 1947.
Maritain, Jacques, *The Rights of Man and Natural Law*. New York: Scribner's, 1945.
*Mill, John Stuart, "Nature" in *Three Essays on Religion*. London: Longmans, Green, 1885. (Liberal Arts pb.)

Needham, Joseph, *Human Law and the Laws of Nature in China and the West*. New York: Oxford University Press, 1951.

Oates, Whitney J. (ed.), *The Stoic and Epicurean Philosophers*. New York: Random House, 1940. Includes complete extant writings of Epictetus and Marcus Aurelius.

*Rawls, John, *A Theory of Justice*. Cambridge: Harvard University Press, 1971. A modern theory in the tradition of the social contract and natural law.

Ritchie, David G., *Natural Rights*. London: *Allen*, 1916.

Sandbach, F. H., *The Stoics*. New York: Norton, 1975.

Simon, Yves, *The Tradition of Natural Law*. New York: Fordham University Press, 1964.

Wild, John, *Plato's Modern Enemies and the Theory of Natural Law*. University of Chicago Press, 1953.

CHAPTER 14. DUTY

Acton, H. B., *Kant's Moral Philosophy*. New York: St. Martin's Press, 1970.

*Beck, L. W., *Commentary on Kant's Critique of Practical Reason*. University of Chicago Press, 1960.

Ewing, A. C., "What Would Happen If Everybody Acted Like Me?" *Philosophy,* Vol. 28 (1953).

Hare, R. M., "Universalizability," *Proceedings of the Aristotelian Society* (1954–1955)

*Murphy, Jefferie G., *Kant: The Philosophy of Right*. New York: St. Martin's Press, 1970.

Nell, Onara, *Acting on Principle: An Essay on Kantian Ethics*. New York: Columbia University Press, 1975.

*Paton, H. J., *The Categorical Imperative*. London: Hutchinson, 1947. (Harper pb.)

Prichard, H. A., *Duty and Interest*. New York: Oxford University Press, 1928.

———, *Moral Obligation*. New York: Oxford University Press, 1950.

Rose, W. D., *Foundations of Ethics*. New York: Oxford University Press, 1939.

———, *Kant's Ethical Theory*. New York: Oxford University Press, 1954.

———, *The Right and the Good*. New York: Oxford University Press, 1930.

Singer, Marcus G., *Generalization in Ethics*. New York: Knopf, 1961.

Teale, Alfred E., *Kantian Ethics*. New York: Oxford University Press, 1951.

Ward, Keith, *The Development of Kant's View of Ethics*. Oxford: Blackwell, 1972.

Williams, T. C., *The Concept of the Categorical Imperative*. Oxford: Clarendon Press, 1968.

Wolff, Robert Paul, *The Autonomy of Morals: A Commentary on Kant's Groundwork of the Metaphysics of Morals*. New York: Harper & Row, 1973.

*———, (ed.), *Kant*. New York: Doubleday, 1967. Part Two.

CHAPTER 15. UTILITY

Anschutz, Richard P., *The Philosophy of John Stuart Mill*. Oxford: Clarendon Press, 1953.

Baumgardt, R. B., *Bentham and the Ethics of Today*. Princeton University Press, 1952.

*Britton, Karl, *John Stuart Mill*. Harmondsworth: Penguin, 1953.

Hodgson, D. H., *Consequences of Utilitarianism*. Oxford: Clarendon Press, 1967.

Lyons, D., *Forms and Limits of Utilitarianism*. Oxford: Clarendon Press, 1965.

McCloskey, H. J., *John Stuart Mill*. London: Macmillan, 1971.

*Moore, G. E., *Ethica Principia*. Cambridge University Press, 1903. Ideal utilitarianism.

Narveson, Jan, *Morality and Utility*. Baltimore: Johns Hopkins University Press, 1966.

Plamenatz, John, *The English Utilitarians*. Oxford: Blackwell, 1958.

Rawls, John, "Two Concepts of Rules," *Philosophical Review*, Vol. 64 (1955).

Rescher, Nicholas, *Distributive Justice: A Constructive Critique of the Utilitarian Theory of Distribution.* Indianapolis: Bobbs-Merrill, 1966.
Ryan, Alan, *John Stuart Mill.* New York: Pantheon Books, 1970.
Schlick, Moritz, *The Problems of Ethics.* Englewood Cliffs, N.J.: Prentice-Hall, 1938.
*Sidgwick, Henry, *The Methods of Ethics.* London: Macmillan, 1922. (Dover pb.)
Smart, J. J. C. and Bernard Williams, *Utilitarianism: For and Against.* Cambridge University Press, 1973.
*Smith, James M. and Ernest Sosa (eds.), *Mill's Utilitarianism.* Belmont, Cal.: Wadsworth, 1969.

CHAPTER 16. POWER

*Brinton, Crane, Nietzsche. New York: Harper & Row, 1965.
Copleston, Frederick, *Friedrich Nietzsche: Philosopher of Culture.* New York: Barnes & Noble, 1975.
Danto, Arthur, *Nietzsche as Philosopher.* New York: Macmillan, 1965.
Hollingdale, R. G., *Nietzsche: The Man and His Philosophy.* Baton Rouge: Louisiana State University Press, 1965.
Jaspers, Karl, *Nietzsche.* Tucson: University of Arizona Press, 1965.
*Kaufmann, Walter, *Nietzsche.* Princeton University Press, 1950. (Vintage pb.)
Knight, A. H. J., *Some Aspects of the Life and Works of Nietzsche.* Cambridge University Press, 1933.
Lavrin, Janko, *Nietzsche: A Biographical Introduction.* New York: Scribner's, 1971.
Lea, Frank Alfred, *The Tragic Philosopher.* London: Methuen, 1957.
Morgan, George Allen. *What Nietzsche Means.* Cambridge. Mass.: Harvard University Press, 1941.
*Russell, Bertrand. *Power: A New Social Analysis.* New York: Norton, 1938.
*Solomon, Robert C. (ed.), *Nietzsche.* New York: Doubleday, 1973.
Wilcox, Crane, *Truth and Value in Nietzsche.* New York: Harper & Row, 1965.

CHAPTER 17. EXPERIMENT

Bernstein, Richard J., *John Dewey.* New York: Washington Square Press, 1966.
Boydston, Jo Ann, *Checklist of Writings About John Dewey.* Carbondale, Ill.: Southern Illinois University Press, 1974.
——, *Guide to the Works of John Dewey.* Carbondale, Ill.: University of Southern Illinois Press, 1967.
*Dewey, John, *Experience and Nature,* rev. ed. La Salle, Ill.: Open Court, 1929.
——, *Human Nature and Conduct.* New York: Holt, Rinehart and Winston, 1922.
*——, *The Quest for Certainty.* New York: Minton Balch, 1929. (Putnam pb.)
*——, *Reconstruction in Philosophy,* enlarged ed. Boston: Beacon Press, 1948.
Geiger, George R., *John Dewey in Perspective.* New York: Oxford University Press, 1958.
Gouinlock, James, *John Dewey's Philosophy of Value.* New York: Humanities Press, 1972.
Hook, Sidney, *John Dewey: An Intellectual Portrait.* Westport, Conn.: Greenwood Press, 1971.
Schilpp, P. A. (ed.), *The Philosophy of John Dewey,* 3rd ed. La Salle, Ill.: Open Court, 1975.
*Smith, John E., *The Spirit of American Philosophy.* New York: Oxford University Press, 1966.

CHAPTER 18. LANGUAGE AND MORALS

Binkley, Timothy, *Wittgenstein's Language*. New York: Humanities Press, 1975.
*Hare, R. M., *The Language of Morals*. Oxford: Clarendon Press, 1952.
*Hartnack, Justus, *Wittgenstein and Modern Philosophy*. New York: Doubleday, 1962.
Kerner, George C., *The Revolution in Ethical Theory*. New York: Oxford University Press, 1966.
*Malcolm, Norman, *Ludwig Wittgenstein: A Memoir*. London: Oxford University Press, 1958. With a Biographical Sketch by Georg Henrik Von Wright.
Pitcher, George, *The Philosophy of Wittgenstein*. Englewood Cliffs, N.J.: Prentice-Hall, 1964.
*Stevenson, Charles L., *Ethics and Language*. New Haven, Conn.: Yale University Press, 1945.
Waismann, Friedrich, *The Principles of Linguistic Philosophy*. London: Macmillan, 1965.
*Wittgenstein, Ludwig, *The Blue and Brown Books*. Oxford: Blackwell, 1958. (Harper pb.)
*———, *Philosophical Investigations*. New York: Macmillan, 1953.

CHAPTER 19. ARISTOCRACY

*Barker, Ernest, *Greek Political Thought: Plato and His Predecessors*. London: Methuen, 1918. (Barnes & Noble pb.)
Brumbaugh, R. S., *Plato for the Modern Age*. New York: Crowell-Collier and Macmillan, 1962.
Cross, R. C. and A. D. Woozley, *Plato's Republic*. New York: St. Martin's Press, 1964.
Field, G. C., *The Philosophy of Plato*, 2nd ed. London: Oxford University Press, 1969.
Gosling, J. C. B., *Plato*. London: Routledge and Kegan Paul, 1973.
Gould, John, *The Development of Plato's Ethics*. New York: Columbia University Press, 1955.
*Grube, G. M. A., *Plato's Thought*. Boston: Beacon Press, 1935.
Jaeger, Werner, *Paidea*, Vol. II. Oxford: Blackwell, 1947.
*Koyre, Alexander, *Discovering Plato*. New York: Columbia University Press, 1945.
Levinson, Ronald, *In Defense of Plato*. Cambridge, Mass.: Harvard University Press, 1953.
Murphy, N. R., *The Interpretation of Plato's Republic*. Oxford: Clarendon Press, 1951.
*Popper, Karl R., *The Open Society and Its Enemies*. Princeton University Press, 1950. (Harper pb.)
Strauss, Leo, *The City and Man*. University of Chicago Press, 1964.
*Thorson, T. L. (ed.), *Plato: Totalitarian or Democrat*. Englewood Cliffs, N.J.: Prentice-Hall, 1963.
*Vlastos, Gregory (ed.), *Plato*, Vol. 2. New York: Doubleday, 1971.
———, *Plato's Universe*. Seattle, University of Washington Press, 1975.
Wild, John, *Plato's Theory of Man*. Cambridge, Mass.: Harvard University Press, 1946.

CHAPTER 20. HISTORY AND FREEDOM

*Avineri, Shlomo, *Hegel's Theory of the Modern State*. Cambridge University Press, 1972.
Findlay, J. N., *Hegel: A Re-Examination*. New York: Macmillan, 1958.
Hegel, G. W. F., *Lectures on the Philosophy of World History*, ed. by D. Forbes and H. B. Nisbet. Cambridge University Press, 1975. New translation.
*Kaufmann, Walter, *Hegel: A Reinterpretation*. New York: Doubleday, 1966.
Kelly, George A., *Idealism, Politics and History: Sources of Hegelian Thought*. Cambridge University Press, 1969.
Lauer, J. Q., *Hegel's Idea of Philosophy*. New York: Fordham University Press, 1974.

Loewenberg, J., *Hegel's Phenomenology*. La Salle, Ill.: Open Court, 1965.
*Löwith, Karl, *From Hegel to Nietzsche*. New York: Holt, Rinehart and Winston, 1964. (Anchor pb.)
*Marcuse, Herbert, *Reason and Revolution: Hegel and the Rise of Social Theory*, 2nd ed. New York: Humanities Press, 1954. (Beacon pb.)
*MacIntyre, Alisdair (ed.), *Hegel*. New York: Doubleday, 1972.
Rosen, Stanley, *G. W. F. Hegel*. New Haven: Yale University Press, 1974.
Steinkraus, Warren E. (ed.), *New Studies in Hegel's Philosophy*. New York: Holt, Rinehart and Winston, 1971.
Taylor, G., *Hegel*. Cambridge University Press, 1975.
Wilkins, B. F., *Hegel's Philosophy of History*. Ithaca, N.Y.: Cornell University Press, 1974.

CHAPTER 21. COMMUNISM

*Avineri, Shlomo, *The Social and Political Thought of Karl Marx*. London: Cambridge University Press, 1969.
*Buber, Martin, *Paths in Utopia*. Boston: Beacon Press, 1958.
Evans, Michael, *Karl Marx*. Bloomington: Indiana University Press, 1975.
*Fromm, Erich, *Marx's Concept of Man*. New York: Ungar, 1961.
Gregor, A. James, *A Survey of Marxism*. New York: Random House, 1965.
Heiss, Robert, *Hegel, Kierkegaard, Marx*. New York: Delacorte Press, 1975.
Hook, Sidney, *From Hegel to Marx*. New York: Reynal and Hitchcock, 1963.
Kamenka, Eugene, *The Ethical Foundations of Marxism*. London: Routledge and K. Paul, 1962.
*Lefebrvre, Henri, *The Sociology of Marx*. New York: Random House, 1969.
*Lichtheim, George, *Marxism*. New York: Praeger, 1961.
*Marcuse, Herbert, *Reason and Revolution*, 2nd ed. New York: Humanities Press, 1954. (Beacon pb.)
*McLellan, David, *Karl Marx: His Life and Thought*. New York: Harper & Row, 1973.
*———, *The Thought of Karl Marx*. New York: Harper & Row, 1971.
Ollman, Bertell, *Alienation: Marx's Conception of Man in Capitalist Society*. Cambridge University Press, 1971.
*Plamenatz, John, *German Marxism and Russian Communism*. New York: Harper & Row, 1965.
*Popper, Karl R., *The Open Society and Its Enemies*, 5th rev. ed. Princeton University Press, 1950.
*———, *The Poverty of Historicism*. Boston: Beacon Press, 1957.
Sartre, Jean-Paul, *Between Existentialism and Marxism*. New York: Pantheon Press, 1975.
*Venable, Vernon, *Human Nature: The Marxian View*. New York: Knopf, 1945. (Meridian pb.)

Reinterpretation and Revision of Marxism

*Bender, Frederic L. (ed.), *The Betrayal of Marx*. New York: Harper & Row, 1975.
*Fromm, Erich (ed.), *Socialist Humanism*. New York: Doubleday, 1967.
Howard, Dick and Karl E. Klare (eds.), *The Unknown Dimension: European Marxism Since Leninism*. New York: Basic Books, 1972.
Kline, George L., "Leszek Kolakowski and the Revision of Marxism," *European Philosophy Today*. Chicago: Quadrangle Books, 1965.
*Kolakowski, Leszek, *Toward a Marxist Humanism*. New York: Grove Press, 1968.

————, *Marxism and Beyond*. London: Pall Mall Press, 1968.
———— and Stuart Hampshire (eds.), *The Socialist Idea: A Reappraisal*. London: Weidenfeld and Nicolson, 1974.
*Lukacs, Georg, *History and Class Consciousness*. Boston: Massachusetts Institute of Technology Press, 1971. First published in 1923. Anticipates later "humanist" revisionism.
*Labedz, Leopold (ed.), *Revisionism*. New York: Praeger, 1962.
*Mezaros, Istvan, *Marx's Theory of Alienation*. London: Merlin Press, 1970.
*Petrovic, Gajo, *Marx in the Mid-Twentieth Century*. New York: Doubleday, 1967.
*Tucker, Robert C., *Philosophy and Myth in Karl Marx*. Cambridge University Press, 1961.

CHAPTER 22. LIBERAL DEMOCRACY

Anschutz, R. P., *The Philosophy of J. S. Mill*. Oxford: Clarendon Press, 1953.
*Bay, Christian, *The Structure of Freedom*. Palo Alto, Cal.: Stanford University Press, 1958.
*Berlin, Isaiah, *Four Essays on Liberty*. London: Oxford University Press, 1969.
————, *Two Concepts of Liberty*. London: Oxford University Press, 1958.
*Britton, Karl, *John Stuart Mill*. Baltimore: Penguin, 1953.
Cowling, Maurice, *Mill and Liberalism*. Cambridge University Press, 1963.
*Dewey, John, *Freedom and Culture*. New York: Minton, Balch, 1939. (Putnam pb.)
*————, *Individualism Old and New*. New York: Minton, Balch, 1930. (Putnam pb.)
*————, *Liberalism and Social Action*. New York: Putnam's, 1935.
*Green, Thomas Hill, *Lectures on the Principles of Political Obligation* (1882). New York: McKay, 1942. (University of Michigan Press pb.)
Hampshire, Stuart, *Freedom of the Individual*. Princeton University Press, 1975.
Laski, Harold, *The Rise of Liberalism*. New York: Harper & Row, 1936.
MacPherson, C. B., *The Political Theory of Possessive Individualism*. Oxford: Clarendon Press, 1962.
Meiklejohn, Alexander, *Free Speech and Its Relation to Self-Government*. New York: Harper & Row, 1948.
Nozick, Robert, *Anarchy, State, and Utopia*. New York: Basic Books, 1974. Difficult.
Packe, Michael St. John, *The Life of John Stuart Mill*. New York: Macmillan, 1954.
*Plamenatz, J. P., *Consent, Freedom and Political Obligation*. London: Oxford University Press, 1968.
*Radcliff, Peter (ed.), *Limits of Liberty: Studies of Mill's On Liberty*. Belmont, Cal.: Wadsworth, 1966.
Robson, John M., *The Improvement of Mankind: The Social and Political Thought of John Stuart Mill*. London: Routledge and K. Paul, 1968.
Russell, Bertrand, *Authority and the Individual*. New York: Simon & Schuster, 1949.
*————, *Freedom and Organization, 1814–1914*. New York: Norton, 1914.

CHAPTER 23. THE CONTROL OF HUMAN BEHAVIOR

*Allport, Gordon, *Personality and Social Encounter*. Boston: Beacon Press, 1960.
Bertocci, Peter A. and Richard M. Millard, *Personality and the Good*. New York: David McKay, 1963.
Carpenter, Finley, *The Skinner Primer: Behind Freedom and Dignity*. New York: Free Press, 1974.
*Chomsky, Noam, *Language and Mind*, 2nd ed. New York: Harcourt Brace Jovanovich, 1972.

*Freud, Sigmund, *Civilization and Its Discontents*. New York: Norton, 1962.

*Hook, Sidney (ed.), *Dimensions of Mind*. New York: Collier, 1961.

Karen, R. L., *An Introduction to Behavior Theory and Its Applications*. New York: Harper & Row, 1974.

Machan, T. R., *The Pseudo-Science of B. F. Skinner*. New York: Arlington House, 1974.

*Marcuse, Herbert, *One Dimensional Man*. Boston: Beacon Press, 1964.

Puligandla, R., *Fact and Fiction in B. F. Skinner's Science and Utopia*. St. Louis: W. H. Green, 1974.

*Rogers, Carl R., *Client-Centered Therapy*. Boston: Houghton Mifflin, 1951.

———, *On Becoming a Person*. Boston: Houghton Mifflin, 1961.

Rothblatt, R. (ed.), *Changing Perspectives on Man*. University of Chicago Press, 1968.

*Skinner, B. F., *Beyond Freedom and Dignity*. New York: Knopf, 1971.

*———, *Science and Human Behavior*. New York: Macmillan, 1953.

*———, *Walden Two*. New York: Macmillan, 1948.

*Wann, T. W. (ed.), *Behaviorism and Phenomenology*. University of Chicago Press, 1964. See especially the essays by B. F. Skinner and Norman Malcolm.

Index*

A

A priori knowledge, 133–134, 200–202, 303–307, 321–322

A priori moral principles, 539–541, 560–561

Absolute, the, 163

Actuality and potentiality, 58–59

Aesthetic education, 351–355, 364

Aesthetic unity, 158

Agnosticism, concerning external world, 123–124, 295–297, 319–320

concerning God, 316, 451–452, 471–472

see also Scepticism, Phenomena and noumena

Alienation, 735–741, 743–744, 751–752

Amiel, Henri Frederic, quoted, 406

Analytic and synthetic judgments, 305–307

Anselm, Saint, biographical note, 430

ontological proof of God, 430–431, 465–467

quoted, 430–431

Anytus, accuser of Socrates, 11, 17, 18, 22, 23, 25, 27

Aquinas, Saint Thomas, biographical note, 432

proofs of God's existence, 432–435, 465, 466, 467–469, 471

quoted, 432–435

Aristocracy, as rule by best men, 33, 35

as rule by the powerful, 599–600

as rule by wise men, 670–672, 679–681, 689–691, 692–695, 816

Aristotle, basic concepts, 57–59

biographical note, 45–46

ends in morals and politics, 475–477

Aristotle *(cont.)*

ethical concepts questioned, 496–498

chance and luck, 49–52, 55–56, 61

change, 46–49

four causes, 48–49, 59

friendship and self-love, 491–494

happiness, 475–483

intellectual goodness, 494–496

moral goodness, 483–491

necessity, 56–57

quoted, 46–57, 475–496

substance, 57–58, 164

teleology (final cause), 48–49, 53–57, 60–61

universals, 694

Art, depicts individuality, 338–346

in education and human development, 351–355, 364

vivid values in, 351–352

Atheism, 19–21, 27, 458–460, 471–472

Atomic theory, 70–83, 86–92

see also Physics

Austin, J. L., quoted, 648

Avineri, Shlomo, quoted, 715

Ayer, A. J., 647

B

Bacon, Francis, 192, 226–227

Belief, and doubt, 195–197, 207–209

fixation of, 195–203, 207–209

right to religious, 389–402, 423–425

see also Faith

*Names and topics mentioned only casually have been omitted.

Bentham, Jeremy, biographical note, 566
  compared with Mill, 573, 590–591, 593–594
  intuition, 625
  pleasure and pain, 567
    measurement of, 571–573, 590, 591, 592
    as motivating actions, 567, 590–591
    value of, 571–573, 590–595
  questions pertaining to his theory, 592–596
  quoted, 567–573, 590
  utility, utilitarianism, 567–570, 590, 593–596
Bergson, Henri, art, 338–346
  biographical note, 338
  comedy, 343–346
  generality or type, 341–346, 362–363
  individuality, 340–343, 344, 362–363
  intuition, 338–341, 362–363
  quoted, 338–346
  tragedy, 342–345
Berkeley, George, abstract ideas, 255–256,
    271–272
  biographical note, 238–239
  correspondence between ideas and things,
    247–254, 262–265, 277
  egocentric predicament, 260–261, 275
  esse est percipi, 242–243, 256–257, 260–261,
    274–275
  God, 268–269
  qualities, painful and pleasant, 243–247
    primary and secondary, 251–256, 260, 276
  quoted, 239–269, 271
  relativity of perception, 245–250, 252–255,
    261–262, 264, 275–276
  substance or substratum, 240, 248–249, 258–
    260, 271–272
Blake, Ralph, biographical note, 516
  natural laws, 517–520, 521, 525
  natural rights, 516–522
  relation between fact and value, 517–518,
    525–526
  quoted, 516–522
  values, 520–521, 525–526
Blake, William, quoted, 360, 426–427
Body and mind, *see* Mind and body
Buber, Martin, I-Thou and I-It, 563–564
  quoted, 563, 564

C

Campbell, C. A., quoted, 323
Carritt, E. F., 596, quoted, 594–595
Categorical imperative, *see* Imperatives
Categories, Kantian, 304, 309–315, 321
Cause, Aristotle on, 48–49, 59, 60–62
  final, 48–49, 53–57, 59, 60–63, 140–143,
    165, 509
  Hume on, 284–287, 302–303, 318–320
  Kant on, 302–303, 316, 321–322, 333
Certainty, 95–100, 109, 115–117, 132–135,
    186–187, 196, 233–234
Chance and luck, 49–52, 55–56, 61
Change, Aristotelian analysis of, 46–49
  and dialectic, 697–700, 752
  and permanence, 68–70, 74–77, 86–87, 352–
    353
  universality of, 506, 509–510
Charity, 380–381
Christ, Christianity, 381, 422, 471, 598, 605,
    607, 763–767, 772–773
Cicero, Marcus Tullius, biographical note,
    499–500
  morality based on natural law, 496, 500–
    504, 523–524, 560, 611, 815
  quoted, 500–504, 524
Class struggle, 725–734
Clearness of ideas, and distinctness, 115, 135,
    204–207
  how to attain, 210–216, 231–232, 234
Clifford, William Kingdon, 394, 395, 397,
    quoted, 392–393
Cogito, 109, 114, 134–135, 232
Cognition, stages of, 681–689
Cohen, Morris and Ernest Nagel, biographical
    note, 216–217
  facts and evidence, 217–218, 219
  hypotheses, 218–219
  quoted, 217–226, 229
  scientific method, 217–221, 223–226, 229,
    236–237
  scientific theories, 221–223
Coleman, Claude, quoted, 800
Comedy, 343–346
Common sense, 219, 233

Communism, 742–746, 751
  see also Marx, Socialism
Composition theory, 227–228
Concatenism, 159–160, 162, 163–164, 166–167
Configuration (*gestalt*), 717
Constant, Benjamin, 562
Contradiction, 713–714
Copernicus, 192
Correspondence, *see* Ideas
Creative process, Creativity, 351–354, 355, 365
  see also Art, Individuality
Criticism, philosophy as, 1, 2, 4–5
Cudworth, Ralph, quoted, 816

D

Darwin, Charles, 62, 89
Death, 22–24, 29–31, 42–44, 83–86, 462–464
Deduction, 96–102, 133–134, 166
  see also Knowledge, demonstrative
Democracy, aristocracy *versus*, 695
  human fulfillment in, 794–795
  natural rights in, 525, 526–527
  and stationary society, 789–792, 794
  see also Liberalism, Liberty
Democritus, 87–88, quoted, 87
Descartes, René, biographical note, 93–94
  certainty, 95–99, 102, 132–135
  cogito, 109, 114, 134–135, 232
  criticism of, 205–206, 229–234
  deduction, 98–99, 132–133
  doubt, 95–97, 104–108, 115–116, 117–121, 134–135, 230–231
  intuition, 98, 132–133, 362
  method, 95–103, 132–135, 205, 227
  mind and body, 108–114, 120–121, 135–137, 348, 814
  proofs of God, 116–117
  quoted, 5, 47–121, 132, 133, 135
Design, as argument for God, 435, 438–452, 454–456, 469–470
Determinism, 140, 145, 146–148, 150–152, 165, 166, 815
  see also Fatalism, Free will

Dewey, John, biographical note, 613–614
  compared with Mill, 795
  cultivation of interests as end, 618–621
  democracy, 527, 794–795, 796
  ends and means, 633–634, 636–637
  experimental method in ethics, 631–632
  moral intuition, defect of, 621–625
  moral principles, 626–631
  pragmatic method, pragmatism, 235–236, 560, 611
  quoted, 614–632, 633, 634, 636
  reflection in ethics, 614–616
  science, technology, and morals, 635–638
  thoughtless valuing and thoughtful valuation, 623–625, 633
Dialectic, 10, 201–202, 408, 685, 697–700, 713–714
Diogenes Laertius, quoted, 11
Dionysius the Areopagite, 408
Doubt, 95–97, 104–108, 115–116, 117–121, 134–135, 195–196, 207–209, 230–231
  see also Scepticism
Dreaming, 105–106, 108, 136, 188, and reality, 128–129
Dualism, alternatives to, 136–137, 138
  Cartesian, 108–114, 120–121, 122–123
  criticism of, 136–137
  defense of, 122–132, 137–138
  revolt against, 122–124, 347–349, 363–364
  see also Mind and body
Duration, 347, 352–353, art as revealing, 338–341, 362–363
Duty, as basis of morality, 528–559, 560–564
  to the state, 22, 24, 34–41, 502–504, 524
  see also Imperatives, categorical

E

Eckhart, Master, quoted, 359
Eddington, Arthur, quoted, 123
Education, 18, 22, 25, 349–352, 681–691
Emergence, doctrine of, 90–91, 363
Empedocles, 10, 50, 54, 55
Empiricism, 226–227
  see also Locke, Lovejoy, Method, Peirce

Ends, cultivation of interests as end, 618–621
and the good, 616–618
and means, 475–477, 633–634, 636–638, 807–808
in morals and politics, 475–477
and reflection, 614–616, 620–621
see also Good
Engels, Friedrich, 719
quoted (in collaboration with Marx), 722–734, 743–744
Epicurus, Epicureans, 65, 67, 85, 519, 574, 575–576
Ethics, *a priori*, 539–541, 560
deontological *versus* utilitarian, 559–560
experimental method in, 631–632
relation to politics, 475–477
types of, 473–474
Euripides, quoted, 493
Evil, problem of, 444, 453–454, 458–464, 470, 471–472
Evolution, 62, 89, 608, 610
Existentialism, diversity of, 359
Kierkegaard as illustrating, 327–337, 358–362
as philosophy of crisis, 358
External objects, knowledge of, 117–121, 124–130, 187–188, 247–254, 262–265, 277, 295–297, 314–315, 319

F

Facts and ideals, 460–461, 496, 517–518, 523–524, 526, 635
see also Natural law, Natural rights
Faith, moral basis of, 315–316, 322
religious wager in justification of, 381–388, 391–392, 397, 421–423
will to believe, 389–402, 423–425
Family resemblance *versus* essence, 649–650
Fatalism, fate, 211–212, 214
Feuerbach, Ludwig, 721, 738
Force, gospel of, 357, 459–460
Form and matter, *see* Matter
Forms, *see* Universals

Freedom, political, 744, 753, 792–793, 816–817
see also Liberalism, Liberty
Free will *versus* determinism, 77–78, 91–92, 140, 146–148, 150–152, 163, 165, 211–212, 287–292, 315–316, 322–324, 362, 554–557, 558–559, 564, 815
Freud, Sigmund, 464–465
Friendship, 493–494

G

Galileo, 192
Gaunilo, 465–466
God, argument for a finite God, 452–456, 470
Cartesian arguments for, 116–117
cosmological or first-cause argument for, 436–438, 467–469
"death" of, 471–472
teleological or design argument for, 435, 438–452, 469–470
see also Pantheism
Goethe, J. W., quoted, 710
Golden Rule, 629–630
Goldmann, Lucien, 421
Good, Aristotelian theory of questioned, 496–497
conceptions of, 473–474
intellectual, 494–496
moral, 483–491
problem of explaining, 454–456
see also Happiness, Right, Morality
Good will, 528–531, 534–536, 542–543, 558–559, 560–561

H

Hacker, Andrew, quoted, 799, 813
Happiness, as fulfillment of interest, 520–521, 618–621
as life of reason, 479–480, 494–496, 497
as pleasure, 520, 567, 571–573, 575–579, 590–596
Hartshorne, Charles, 467

Hedonism, 497, 593, 594
  see also Pleasure, Utilitarianism
Hegel, Georg Wilhelm Friedrich, biographical note, 696
  compared with Marx, 717, 718, 752
  critical questions, 716–718
  cunning of reason, 710–711
  dialectic, 697–700, 713–714
  essential relatedness, 713
  great men, 708–710
  history as rational, 700–702, 710–712
    as development of freedom, 702–706, 711–712, 714
  quoted, 697–712
  state as embodiment of freedom, 705, 711–712, 716, 717–718
Heisenberg, Werner, 91
History, *see* Hegel, Marx
Hobbes, Thomas, 86, 519
Holmes, Edmond, quoted, 425–426
Holmes, Oliver Wendell, Jr., 190, 234
Horace, quoted, 608
Human behavior, control of, 797, 815–817
  science of, 798–800, 803–805, 814, 816–817
Humanism without theism, 458–464, 471–472
Humboldt, Wilhelm von, 786
  quoted, 778, 792–793
Hume, David, biographical note, 278–279
  cause and effect, 283–287, 318
  forms of reasoning, 282–284, 299–300
  impressions and ideas, 279–282, 317
  influence on Kant, 302–303, 310–311, 321–322
  knowledge of external objects, 295–297, 319
    of the future, 292–295, 318–319
    of the self, 297–299, 320
  liberty (free will) and necessity, 287–292, 323, 324
  on proofs of existence of God, 436–452, 465, 468–470
  quoted, 279–300, 319–320, 436–452, 468
  scepticism, 318–321

Huxley, Thomas Henry, 394
  quoted, 392
Hypothetical imperatives, *see* Imperatives

I

I and Thou, 563–564
Idealism, of Berkeley, 239–277
  of Hegel, 712–713
Ideas, abstract, 255–256
  clarification of, 204–216, 234
  complex, 180–184, 228
  how related to external objects, 122–125, 179–180, 185–186, 187–188, 228–229, 247–254, 262–265, 277
  origin of, 171–173, 310–311
  of reflection, 171, 172–173, 175–177
  relation to impressions, 279–282, 317
  of sensation, 171, 172–173, 175–180
  simple, 173–180
Imagination, as deceptive, 373–375
  poetic, 344–345
  role in human life, 415–416
  see also Aesthetic education, Art, Poetry
Immortality, 315–316, 322
Imperatives, categorical and hypothetical, 542–548
  formulas of categorical, 548–558
  moral and technological, 636–638
Individual, individuality, and the crowd, 327–332, 359–360
  and truth, 327–332, 338–345, 359–360
  and type, 338–343, 344, 362–363
  value of, 351–352, 357, 497–498, 777–787, 794–795, 809–810
Infinity, 369–372, 381, 384–385
Inquiry, 233–234, 235, 814
  limits of, 299–300, 314–315, 321–322
  see also Method
Intrinsic and instrumental values, *see* Ends, and means
Intuition, Bergson on, 338–340, 362–363
  definition of, 98, 362
  Descartes on, 98–99, 132–133, 233
  Kant on, as sensory awareness, 307–309
  Locke on, 186, 187, 188–189

J

James, William, biographical note, 152–153
concatenism, 155–156, 159–160, 162–164, 166–167
faith, 389–402, 423–425
free will, 323, 815
God as finite, 470
kinds of oneness (monism), 154–163, 166
mysticism, 402–412, 427
pragmatism, 163–164, 234–235, 236
quoted, 153–164, 389–412, 428
Jeans, James, quoted, 123
Jefferson, Thomas, 525
Johnson, Samuel, 765–766
Justice, 501–504, 526–527, 594–596, 597

K

Kant, Immanuel, analytic and synthetic judgments, 305–307
a priori and *a posteriori* knowledge, 303–307
a priori moral principles, 539–541, 560–561
biographical note, 300–301
categorical and hypothetical imperatives, 542–548, 610–611, 633
categories, 309–314
dialectic, 698
duty, 531–534, 559, 621, 633
formulas of categorical imperative, 548–558
free will (autonomy), 315–316, 323, 324, 555–557, 559, 564
God, 315–316, 322, 466, 470
immortality, 315–316, 322
intuition, pure forms of, 307–309
phenomena and noumena, 314–315, 321–322, 323
practical reason, 234, 322, 541–542
quoted, 302–316, 321, 528–559
Kepler, Johannes, 192, 200
Kierkegaard, Sören, biographical note, 325
as existentialist, 359–362, 609, 814
individuality and truth, 327–332, 359–360
need to make things difficult, 332–333, 360–361

Kierkegaard, Sören (*cont.*)
quoted, 327–337, 360, 361
truth as subjectivity, 333–337, 361
Kingsley, Charles, 405
Knight, A. H. J., quoted, 598–599
Knowledge, *a priori,* 133–134, 200–201, 303–307, 560
demonstrative, 186–187, 301
extent of, 123–132, 170, 188–189, 314–315
of external objects, 123–132, 187–188, 295–297
of future events, 292–295, 318–319
kinds of, 184–186
of the self, 109, 114, 134–135, 232, 297–299, 320
see also Cognition, Perception
Kolakowski, Leszek, biographical note, 747
quoted, 747–749
representative of New Left, 753
what socialism is, 749
what socialism is not, 747–749

L

Lamarck, Jean-Baptiste, 608
La Mettrie, Julien, 86
Langer, Susanne, quoted, 63
Language, in ethical discourse, 642–648, 651–652
nonsensical, 648–649
ordinary, 649–650
private, 650
see also Meaning
Law, civil, 37–41, 503–504, 801–802
moral, 533–536, 547–548, 551–552, 554–559
natural, 378, 500–504, 507–508, 516–522, 523–524, 525–526
physical (scientific), 519–520, 523
see also Imperatives
Liberalism, 694–695, 754–787, 792–793, 794–796, 808–811
as open society, 694–695, 810
see also Democracy, Individual, Liberty
Liberty, 754–787, 808–811
of action, 756–757, 777–787, 792–793

Liberty (*cont.*)
  of association, 757, 793
  of thought and discussion, 756, 757–777, 792–793
Locke, John, assumptions of, 227–228
  and Berkeley, 269–272
  biographical note, 168
  ideas, 170–171
    complex, 180–184, 228
    origin of, 171–173, 310–311
    of reflection, 171, 172–173, 175–177
    of sensation, 171, 172–173, 175–180
    simple, 173–180
  knowledge, 132, 169–170, 184–189
    extent of, 170, 188–189
  natural rights, 794
  primary and secondary qualities, 177–180, 228, 269–271
  quoted, 124, 169–189, 628
  on representative perception, 122–123, 187–188, 228–229
  substances, 124, 181, 182–184, 229
Lovejoy, Arthur O., biographical note, 122
  defense of dualism, 122–132, 137–138, 364
  on direct ("naive") realism, 125, 138–139
  on .implications of physics, 126–128, 131–132
  quoted, 122–132
  on representative realism, 122–123, 126–132
Luck, *see* Chance and luck
Lucretius, 4
  biographical note, 65
  characteristics of mind and spirit, 80–84, 91–92
  death, 83–86, 91
  empty space, 71–74
  free will, 77–78, 91–92, 324
  properties of matter, 70–83
  quoted, 65–86, 87
  secondary qualities, 88
Luther, Martin, quoted, 404

M

Macaulay, Thomas Babbington, quoted, 354
Malcolm, Norman, 467, quoted, 647

Malthus, Thomas, 789, 794
Marcus Aurelius, biographical note, 505
  death and flux, 506, 508, 509–510, 512, 515
  harmony with nature, 505, 508, 509–510, 512, 515
  man's social nature, 507–508, 509, 511–512, 514, 515–516
  pantheism, 505, 508, 510–511, 515
  quoted, 505–516
  unity of nature, 511, 512–513, 514
Marx, Karl, alienation, 735–741, 743–744, 751–752
  biographical note, 719–720
  class struggle, 725–734
  communism (socialism), 527, 694, 742–746, 751
  comparison with Hegel, 717, 718, 752
  comparison with Nietzsche, 611–612
  materialist interpretation of history, 718, 720–734, 740–742, 750–751, 752, 753
  quoted, 720–746, 750, 751
  revolution, 721, 724–725, 728–734, 741–746, 752–753
  state and ruling class, 717, 724–725, 727, 750, 752
Materialism, 68–84, 86–92
  see also Lucretius
Materialist interpretation of history, 718, 720–734, 740–742, 750–751, 752, 753
Matter, and form, 58, 307
  properties of, 68–83, 86, 135–136
  see also Materialism
McTaggart, J. M. E., quoted, 367
Mead, George Herbert, 236
Mean between extremes, 485–491, 498
Meaning, clarification of, 204–216, 231–232, 234
  philosophy as elucidation of, 2–3, 647–649
  pragmatic theory of, 234–236
Meletus, accuser of Socrates, 11, 17–21, 23, 24, 25–26, 27
Metaphysics and epistemology, 7
Method, Cartesian, 93–103, 132–135, 229–234
  dialectical, 10, 201–202, 408, 697–700, 713–714
  experimental, in ethics, 631–632

Method, Cartesian (*cont.*)
  Peirce's scientific-pragmatic, 196–216, 228–234
  pragmatic, 234–236
  scientific, 200–203, 214–216, 217–226, 236–237
  Socratic, 2–3, 5, 10, 14–17
Mill, John Stuart, biographical note, 573–574
  compared with Bentham, 573, 590–591, 593–594
  compared with Dewey, 794–795
  individuality, 694, 777–787
  liberalism, 694–695, 792–793, 794–796
  liberty, 754–787
    of action, 765–757, 777–787, 792–793
    of association, 757, 793
    of thought and discussion, 756, 757–777, 792–793
  meaning of utilitarianism, 574–584
  proof of utilitarianism, 585–589, 594
  qualities of pleasure, 576–577, 591–592
  questions concerning his ethical theory, 591–596
  quoted, 574–589, 618, 619, 754–791
  stationary state of civilization, 788–791, 793–794
Mind and body, 80–84, 90–92, 108–114, 120–121, 122, 135–137
  see also Dualism
Monism, of God-Nature, 140, 143–145, 164–166
  kinds of, 154–163, 166
Montague, William Pepperell, biographical note, 452
  God as finite, 452–456, 470
  problem of evil, 453–454
  problem of good, 454–456
  quoted, 452–456
Moore, G. E., quoted, 641
Morals, Morality, deontological theory of, 539–558, 559–560
  force *versus*, 693–694
  master and slave, 601–604, 605, 610
  moral goodness (Aristotelian), 483–491
  moral judgments, 621–625
  moral principles, 626–631

Morals, Morality (*cont.*)
  nature as basis of, 500–527
  reflective, 618–621, 631–632
  and religious faith, 315–316, 322
  science and, 633–634, 635–636
  technology and, 635, 636–638
  utilitarian, 567–597
  see also Duty, Right
Morgan, Lewis Henry, 725
Motion, 59, 72–73, 130–131
Mysticism, 402–451, 470

N

Nagel, Ernest, *see* Cohen
Natural law, *see* Law
Natural rights, 516–522, 524, 526–527
Natural selection, 62, 89, 450–451, 470
Nature, good as fulfillment of man's, 479–480, 482–484, 495–496, 497, 509, 511, 516, 525
  good as harmony with, 500–504, 505, 508–509
  man's disproportion to, 369–373
  man's place in, 738–739
Necessity, consistent with free will, 287–292, 323
  of God's nature, 140, 145–148, 150, 165, 431, 434, 436–437, 465–466, 467–469, 515, 524–525
  in human life, 463–464, 472
  in nature, 56–57, 462–463
Negley, Glenn, quoted, 802
Newton, Isaac, 469
Nietzsche, Friedrich, aristocracy of power, 599–601, 605–606, 609–610, 611
  beyond good and evil, 602–604, 606
  biographical note, 598–599
  critical questions concerning, 610–612
  death of God, 471
  master and slave morality, 600–603, 604–605, 609, 612
  nobility of soul, 602–603, 604–605, 609, 612
  quoted, 471, 599–609
  will to power, 600–601, 609–610
Noumena, *see* Phenomena and noumena

O

Obligation, *see* Duty, Imperatives
One and Many, *see* Concatenism, Monism, Pluralism
Organicism, Organism, 89–90, 347, 353, 363–364, 365
Ought, as imperative, 542–543, 561, 635
  implies "can," 323
  and "is," 523–524, 526
  moral distinguished from technological, 636–637

P

Pantheism, 140, 160–161, 164–165, 505, 508, 510–511, 515, 523, 524–525
  see also Monism, Mysticism
Pascal, Blaise, biographical note, 368
  error, sources of, 373–376, 421
  as existentialist, 359, 609
  faith, 387–388, 397, 421–423
  heart has its reasons, 224, 387
  justice, 375, 378–379
  man's disproportion to nature, 369–373
  man's greatness, 379–381, 422
  man's misery, 369–373, 380–381, 423
  quoted, 369–388, 397, 423
  scepticism, 369–376, 382–383
  self-love, 376–378
  wager, 381–387, 391–392, 422–424, 428
Patrick, J. M. quoted, 802
Peirce, Charles Sanders, biographical note, 190–191
  clarification of ideas, 204–216, 231–232, 234
  criticism of Descartes, 205–206, 229–234
  fixation of belief, 196–203, 207–209
  pragmatism, 234–235
  quoted, 191–216, 230, 231, 232, 233
  scientific method, 192–193, 200–207, 214–216, 231–234
Perception, *esse est percipi*, 242–243, 256–257, 260–261, 265, 274–275
  relativity of, 245–250, 252–255, 261–262, 264, 275–276

Perception (*cont.*)
  representative, 87–89, 117–120, 122–125, 127–132, 135–136, 137–138, 177–179, 187–188, 228–229
  see also Ideas, Qualities
Perry, Ralph Barton, 275, quoted, 234–235
Personal identity, *see* Self
Phenomena and noumena, 314–315, 321–322
Philosopher, definition of, 672–679
  as ruler, 670–672, 679–681, 689–691, 695, 816
  Socrates as, 9–44
Philosophy, analytical, 2–3, 647
  critical, 1, 2, 4–5
  linguistic, 648–649
  as cultivation of wisdom, 3–5, 9, 14–17, 22
  defined, 1–5
  social, 653–654
  speculative, 1, 3
Physics, Physicists, contemporary, 123–128, 131–132, 138
  epistemological implications, 126–128, 131–132
  method in, 133–134
  near-agnosticism among, 123–124
Plato, aristocracy (rule by wise), 527, 670–672, 679–681, 689–691, 692–695, 796
  biographical note, 655–656
  "closed" society, 694–695
  cognition, stages of, 681–690
  dialectic, 685
  education, 619, 681–691, 692
  forms (universals), 649–650, 672–679, 681–690, 693–694
  harmony, 420, 656
  justice, 656–659, 660, 664–666
  moral relativism versus absolutism, 656–657, 693–694
  parts of the soul, 666–667
    of the state, 660
  quoted, 12–44, 656–691
  teleological argument for God, 469
  virtues in the individual, 667–670
    in the state, 659–666
  see also Socrates

Pleasure, measurement of, 571–573, 590–591, 592
  as motivating actions, 567, 587–589, 590–591
  qualities of, 576–578, 591–592
  value of, 481, 484–485, 496, 497, 571–573, 575–579, 590–595
Pluralism, 155–156, 163, 164, 166
  see also Concatenism
Poetry, comic and tragic, 341–346
  discloses individual's emotion, 340–341
  kinship with religion, 413, 419–421, 427–429
  see also Art
Poincaré, Henri, quoted, 223
Politics, relation to ethics, 475–477
  see also State
Pope, Alexander, quoted, 422
Potentiality, *see* Actuality and potentiality
Power, aristocracy of, 599–601, 605–606, 609–610, 612
  and happiness, 586–587
  religious attitude toward, 459–461, 471
  will to, 609–610
Pragmatism, 163–164, 167, 234–236
Primary qualities, *see* Qualities

Q

Qualities, painful and pleasant, 243–247
  of pleasure, 576–577, 591–592
  primary, 73–78, 87–89, 112–113, 135–136, 138, 177–178, 179–180, 228, 251–256, 260, 269–271, 276, 297
  secondary, 78–80, 88–89, 135, 137–138, 228, 251–252, 256, 260, 270–271, 276, 297

R

Rankine, W. J. M., quoted, 222
Rationalism, 132–134
Rawls, John, 526, quoted, 595

Realism, direct ("naive"), 125, 137–138
  representative, 122–123, 126–132
Reality, 7, 212–216
  art as revealing, 338–346, 351–352
  see also Knowledge, Truth
Reason, happiness as life of, 479–480, 494–496, 497
  intellectual good as actualization of, 494–496
  moral good as guidance by, 483–487
  as part of soul, 479–480, 666–667
  wisdom as virtue of, 667–668
Reasoning, *a priori* and *a posteriori*, 303–307
  analytic and synthetic, 305–307
  forms of, 282–284, 293–294, 299–300
  pure and practical, 322, 541–542
Relations, degrees of intensity of, 166–167
  essential (internal), 713–714
  see also Concatenism, Monism
Relativism, in master and slave morality, 601–604, 605, 610
  universals ("forms") opposed to, 693–694
Relativity, theory of, 123, 126, 131–132
Religion, *see* God, Faith, Mysticism, Theism
Representative perception, *see* Perception
Revolution, 524, 721, 724–725, 727–728, 733–734, 740–746, 753
Right, deontological interpretation of, 528–564
  in distribution of goods, 744–746
  utilitarian interpretation of, 568–570, 575, 579–589, 593–597
Rights, correlative with duties, 516–517
  legal, 516–517
  natural, 516–522, 524, 526–527
Rousseau, Jean Jacques, 526, 794
Royce, Josiah, 157, 159, 712
Rules, for direction of reasoning, 95–103
  moral, 583–584
  and utilitarianism, 596–597
  see also Law
Russell, Bertrand, biographical note, 456–457
  free man's worship, 462–464, 472
  opposition of fact and ideal, 460–461, 464, 471
  on ordinary language, 648–649

Russell, Bertrand (*cont.*)
  quoted, 458–464, 471, 472, 611, 648–649
  renunciation, 461–462
  worship of force and power, 459–460

S

Santayana, George, biographical note, 412
  comparison with James, 427–429
  kinship of poetry and religion, 413, 419–421, 427–429
  moral import of religion, 413, 415–419, 420–421
  quoted, 224, 412, 413–421, 428–429
  religion as imaginative, 413–418
Scepticism, 240–241, 292–300, 314–315, 318–321, 321–322, 369–376, 382–383, 398
  see also Doubt
Schiller, F. C. S., 236
Schlick, Moritz, quoted, 2, 3
Schopenhauer, Arthur, 609, 611
Science, and aesthetic needs, 354–355
  and adventure, 357–358
  behavioral, 798–800, 803, 817
  and education, 349–352
  method of, 192–193, 200–203, 214–216, 217–226, 233–234, 236–237
  and morals, 631–632, 635–638
  and philosophy, 346–349, 363–364
Secondary qualities, *see* Qualities
Self, knowledge of, 109, 114, 134–135, 232, 297–299
Self-love, 376–378, 491–492, 604–605
Shakespeare, William, 344, quoted, 642
Skinner, B. F., biographical note, 797–798
  on education, 800–801
  governmental control of behavior, 801–804
  issues in discussion with Rogers, 804–805, 814–817
  quoted, 798–804, 811–813, 815, 815–816
  science and control of behavior, 798–804, 812–813, 815–816
Smith, Adam, 717, 789

Socialism, 747–749, 753
  see also Communism, Marx
Socrates, on death, 42–44
  his defense, 12–31
  duty to state, 32–41
  life and character, 9–11
  method, 2–3, 5, 10, 14–17
  quoted as character in Plato's dialogues, 12–44, 656–691
  his trial, 10–11, 12–31
Soul, parts of, 482–483, 666–667
Space, as *a priori* form, 307–309
  empty, 71–73
Spencer, Herbert, 2
Spinoza, Baruch, biographical note, 139
  determinism, 140, 145, 146–148, 150–152, 165, 166, 324, 815
  on final causes, 140–143, 165
  God-Universe, 140–145, 147–149, 150, 152, 165, 467
  good and evil, 140, 143–145
  monism, 140, 145–147, 164–166
  pantheism, 140, 160–161, 164–165
  quoted, 140–152, 164, 165
State, as authoritarian, 198–199, 202
  duty to, 22, 24, 34–41, 503–504, 524
  as embodiment of freedom, 705, 711–712, 716, 717–718
  laws of, 502–504, 524
  Marx's interpretation of, 717, 721, 724–725, 734
  totalitarian, 748–749, 753
Stationary society, 788–791, 793–794
Stoicism, 523–525
  see also Marcus Aurelius
Stephen, Fitz-James, 389, quoted, 402
Stout, G. F., quoted, 91
Substance (substratum), Aristotle on, 47–48, 57–58
  Berkeley on, 240, 248–249, 258–260, 271–272
  Hume on self as, 297–299, 320
  Locke on, 181, 182–184, 229
  Spinoza on, 164–165
Synthetic judgments, *see* Analytic and synthetic judgments

T

Technology, behavioral, 798–800, 803–813, 815–817
　distinguished from science and morals, 635
　and morals, 636–638
　in the stationary state, 788–792, 793–794
Teleology, as explanatory, 48–49, 53–57, 60–63
　opposition to, 140–143, 165
　see also Cause, final
Theism, and humanism, 471–472
　see also God
Thompson, J. Arthur, quoted, 62
Thoreau, David, 9, 717–718
Time, as *a priori* form, 309
Titchener, Edward, 591
Tocqueville, Alexis de, 786, 793
Tragedy, 342–345, 462–463
Truth, as contextual and public, 231–232
　crowd opposed to, 327–332
　pragmatic conception of, 234–236
　religious, 387–388, 396–401
　subjective, 333–337, 361

U

Universals, and family resemblance, 649–650
　Platonic forms as, 649–650, 672–679, 681–690, 693–694
Utilitarianism, act versus rule, 596–597
　hedonistic, 567–597
　non-hedonistic, 593
　see also Bentham, Mill

V

Value, values, and art, 349, 351–355
　and science, 348, 354

Value (*cont.*)
　and valuation, 623–625, 633
Virtue, virtues, in the individual, 667–670
　intellectual, 482, 494–496
　moral, 483–491
　in the state, 659–666
　see also Duty, Right
Vivekananda, Swami, quoted, 160–161

W

Whitehead, Alfred North, art and aesthetic education, 351–355, 364
　biographical note, 346
　education, 349–352
　on fundamental assumptions, 227, 228
　on human purposiveness, 62
　organicism, 347, 353, 356, 363–364, 365
　revolt against dualism, 138, 363–365
　science and civilization, 346–349, 356–358, 363
　quoted, 346–358, 364
Whitman, Walt, on democracy, 796
　on mysticism, 410, 427
　quoted, 427, 796
Wittgenstein, Ludwig, absolute and relative judgments of value, 642–647, 650–651
　biographical note, 639–640
　ethical and religious language as non-factual, 641–647
　family resemblance *versus* essence, 359, 649–650
　ordinary *versus* ideal language, 648–649
　private language impossible, 649
　quoted, 640–647, 648, 650
Wordsworth, William, quoted, 426
Wrong-doing, intentional or unintentional? 19, 36